Health, United States, 2006

With Chartbook on Trends in the Health of Americans

U.S. DEPARTMENT OF HEALTH AND HUMAN SERVICES
Centers for Disease Control and Prevention
National Center for Health Statistics

November 2006
DHHS Publication No. 2006-1232

Preface

Health, United States, 2006 is the 30th report on the health status of the Nation and is submitted by the Secretary of the Department of Health and Human Services to the President and Congress of the United States in compliance with Section 308 of the Public Health Service Act. This report was compiled by the National Center for Health Statistics (NCHS), Centers for Disease Control and Prevention (CDC). The National Committee on Vital and Health Statistics served in a review capacity.

The *Health, United States* series presents national trends in health statistics. Each report includes an executive summary, highlights, a chartbook, trend tables, extensive appendixes, and an index.

Chartbook

The *Chartbook on Trends in the Health of Americans* updates and expands information from previous chartbooks and introduces this year's special feature on pain. Pain affects physical and mental functioning, affects quality of life, reduces productivity, and is a major reason for health care utilization. The chartbook assesses the Nation's health by presenting trends and current information on selected determinants and measures of health status and utilization of health care. Many measures are shown separately for persons of different ages because of the strong effect of age on health. Selected figures also highlight differences in determinants and measures of health status and utilization of health care by such characteristics as sex, race, Hispanic origin, education, and poverty status.

Trend Tables

The chartbook section is followed by 147 trend tables organized around four major subject areas: health status and determinants, health care utilization, health care resources, and health care expenditures. A major criterion used in selecting the trend tables is availability of comparable national data over a period of several years. The tables present data for selected years to highlight major trends in health statistics. Earlier editions of *Health, United States* may present data for additional years that are not included in the current printed report. Where possible, these additional years of data are available in Excel spreadsheet files on the *Health, United States* website. Tables with additional data years are listed in Appendix III.

Racial and Ethnic Data

Many tables in *Health, United States* present data according to race and Hispanic origin consistent with Department-wide emphasis on expanding racial and ethnic detail when presenting health data. Trend data on race and ethnicity are presented in the greatest detail possible after taking into account the quality of data, the amount of missing data, and the number of observations. Standards for classification of federal data on race and ethnicity are described in Appendix II, Race.

Education and Income Data

Many tables in *Health, United States* present data according to socioeconomic status, using education and poverty level as proxy measures. Education and income data are generally obtained directly from survey respondents, and are not generally available from records-based data collection systems including the National Health Care Survey (see Appendix I). State vital statistics systems currently report mother's education on the birth certificate and, based on information from an informant, decedent's education on the death certificate. See Appendix II, Education; Family income; Poverty.

Disability Data

Disability is a complex concept and can include presence of physical or mental impairments that limit a person's ability to perform an important activity, and use of or need for accommodations or interventions required to improve functioning. Information on disability in the U.S. population is critical to health planning and policy. Although some information is currently available from federal data collection systems, the information is limited by a lack of standard definitions and survey questions on disability. Several current initiatives are underway to coordinate and standardize measurement of disability across federal data systems. Until such standardized information is available, *Health, United States* includes the following disability-related information for the civilian noninstitutionalized population: prevalence of limitations of activity due to chronic conditions (Table 58), vision and hearing limitations for adults (Table 59), and limitations in Activities of Daily Living (ADL) and Instrumental Activities of Daily Living (IADL) for the population age 65 and over (Table 58). In addition, disability-related information is provided for the nursing home population (Table 102), Medicare enrollees (Table 139), Medicaid recipients (Table 140), and veterans with service-connected disabilities (Table 142).

Changes in This Edition

Each volume of *Health, United States* is prepared to maximize its usefulness as a standard reference source while maintaining its continuing relevance. Comparability is fostered by including similar trend tables in each volume. Timeliness is maintained by (1) adding new tables each year to reflect emerging topics in public health and (2) improving the content of ongoing tables. *Health, United States, 2006* includes five new trend tables on: the population in federal and state prisons and local jails (Table 2), based on data from the Bureau of Justice Statistics; joint pain (Table 57) and access to care problems due to cost (Table 78), based on the National Health Interview Survey; physician practice characteristics (Table 117), based on the National Ambulatory Medical Care Survey; and health professionals' wages (Table 108), based on data from the Bureau of Labor Statistics.

The *Health, United States, 2006* Chartbook section includes new charts on the population in group quarters (Figure 2), length of time without health insurance (Figure 7), binge drinking and marijuana use among high school students (Figure 11), untreated dental caries among children (Figure 14), percentage of the adult population with three or more chronic conditions (Figure 15), dental visits among children (Figure 19), influenza vaccination among adults (Figure 20), emergency department visits for falls (Figure 21), and hospitalizations with bariatric procedures (Figure 23). The Special Feature includes 10 new charts on pain prevalence and associated health care treatment and costs (Figures 28–37).

Appendixes

Appendix I describes each data source used in the report and provides references for further information about the sources. Data sources are listed alphabetically within two broad categories: (1) Government Sources and (2) Private and Global Sources.

Appendix II is an alphabetical listing of terms used in the report. It also presents standard populations used for age adjustment (Tables I, II, and III); ICD codes for causes of death shown in *Health, United States* from the Sixth through Tenth Revisions and the years when the Revisions were in effect (Tables IV and V); comparability ratios between ICD–9 and ICD–10 for selected causes (Table VI); ICD–9–CM codes for external cause-of-injury, diagnostic, and procedure categories (Tables VII, X, and XI); effects of adding probe questions for Medicare and Medicaid on health insurance rates in the National Health Interview Survey (Table VIII); industry codes according to the 2002 North American Industry Classification System (Table IX); National Drug Code (NDC) Therapeutic Class recodes of generic analgesic drugs (Table XII); and sample tabulations of NHIS data comparing the 1977 and 1997 Standards for the Classification of Federal Data on Race and Ethnicity (Tables XIII and XIV).

Appendix III lists tables for which additional years of trend data are available electronically in Excel spreadsheet files on the *Health, United States* website and CD-ROM, described below under Electronic Access.

Index

The Index to Trend Tables and Chartbook Figures is a useful tool for locating data by topic. Tables are cross-referenced by such topics as Child and adolescent health; Elderly population age 65 years and over; Women's health; Men's health; state data; American Indian, Asian, Black, and Hispanic origin populations; Education; Injury; Disability; and Metropolitan and nonmetropolitan data.

Electronic Access

Health, United States may be accessed in its entirety on the World Wide Web at www.cdc.gov/nchs/hus.htm. From the *Health, United States* website, one may also register for the *Health, United States* electronic mailing list to receive announcements about release dates and notices of updates to tables.

Health, United States, 2006, the chartbook, and each of the trend tables are available as Acrobat PDF files on the website. Chartbook figures are available as downloadable

PowerPoint® slides. Trend tables and chartbook data tables are available as downloadable Excel spreadsheet files. Trend tables listed in Appendix III include additional years of data not shown in the printed report or .pdf files. Both PDF and spreadsheet files for selected tables will be updated on the website if more current data become available near the time when the printed report is released. Readers who register with the electronic mailing list will be notified of these table updates. Previous editions of *Health, United States* and chartbooks, starting with the 1993 edition, also may be accessed from the *Health, United States* website.

Health, United States is also available on CD-ROM, where it can be viewed, searched, printed, and saved using Adobe Acrobat software on the CD-ROM.

Copies of the Report

Copies of *Health, United States, 2006*, and the CD-ROM can be purchased from the Government Printing Office (GPO) through links to GPO on the National Center for Health Statistics website, Publications and Information Products page.

Questions?

For answers to questions about this report, contact:

Office of Information Services
Information Dissemination Staff
National Center for Health Statistics
Centers for Disease Control and Prevention
3311 Toledo Road, Fifth Floor
Hyattsville, MD 20782
Phone: 301-458-INFO or toll free 866-441-NCHS
E-mail: nchsquery@cdc.gov
Internet: www.cdc.gov/nchs

Acknowledgments

Overall responsibility for planning and coordinating the content of this volume rested with the Office of Analysis and Epidemiology, National Center for Health Statistics (NCHS), under the direction of Amy B. Bernstein, Diane M. Makuc, and Linda T. Bilheimer.

Production of *Health, United States, 2006*, highlights, trend tables, and appendixes was managed by Amy B. Bernstein, Sheila Franco, and Virginia M. Freid. Trend tables were prepared by Amy B. Bernstein, Alan J. Cohen, Margaret A. Cooke, La-Tonya D. Curl, Catherine R. Duran, Sheila Franco, Virginia M. Freid, Ji-Eun Lee, Andrea P. MacKay, Livia Navon, Patricia N. Pastor, Mitchell B. Pierre, Jr., Rebecca A. Placek, Laura A. Pratt, Cynthia A. Reuben, and Henry Xia, with assistance from Zahiyah J. Hines, Anita L. Powell, and Ilene B. Rosen. Appendix II tables and the index were assembled by Anita L. Powell. Production planning and coordination of trend tables were managed by Rebecca A. Placek. Administrative and word processing assistance were provided by Lillie C. Featherstone, Lamont Henderson, and Rhonda Robinson.

Production of the *Chartbook on Trends in the Health of Americans* was managed by Virginia M. Freid. Data and analysis for specific charts were provided by Amy B. Bernstein, Margaret A. Cooke, Sheila Franco, Virginia M. Freid, Deborah D. Ingram, Ji-Eun Lee, Rebecca L. Middendorf, Patricia N. Pastor, and Cynthia A. Reuben. Graphs were drafted by La-Tonya D. Curl and data tables were prepared by Rebecca A. Placek. Technical assistance and programming were provided by Alan J. Cohen, Catherine R. Duran, Livia Navon, Mitchell B. Pierre, Jr., and Henry Xia.

Publications management and editorial review were provided by Demarius V. Miller, Office of Information Services, Information Design and Publishing Staff. Oversight review for publications and electronic products was provided by Margot A. Palmer, Acting Director, Office of Information Services. The designer was Sarah Hinkle, CDC/CoCHIS/ NCHM/Division of Creative Services; production was done by Jacqueline M. Davis and Zung T. Le, CDC/CoCHIS/NCHM/ Division of Creative Services; and printing was managed by Patricia L. Wilson, CDC/OCOO/MASO.

Electronic access through the NCHS Internet site and CD-ROM was provided by Christine J. Brown, Jacqueline M. Davis, Zung T. Le, Demarius V. Miller, Sharon L. Ramirez, and Patricia L. Wilson.

Data and technical assistance were provided by staff of the following NCHS organizations: *Division of Health Care Statistics*: Catharine W. Burt, Carol J. DeFrances, Marni J. Hall, Esther Hing, Lola Jean Kozak, Karen L. Lipkind, Eric Nawar, Maria F. Owings, William Pearson, Michelle Podgornik, Robert Pokras, Robin E. Remsburg, Susan M. Schappert, and Genevieve W. Strahan; *Division of Health Examination Statistics*: Lisa Broitman, Margaret D. Carroll, Bruce Dye, Rosemarie Hirsch, Clifford L. Johnson, Ryne Paulose, and Susan E. Schober; *Division of Health Interview Statistics*: Patricia F. Adams, Veronica E. Benson, Barbara Bloom, Viona I. Brown, Margaret Lethbridge-Cejku, Pei-Lu Chiu, Robin A. Cohen, Richard H. Coles, Marcie Cynamon, Achintya Dey, Cathy C. Hao, Kristina Kotulak-Hays, Susan S. Jack, Jane B. Page, Eve Powell-Griner, Jeannine Schiller, Charlotte A. Schoenborn, Mira L. Shanks, and Luong Tonthat; *Division of Vital Statistics*: Robert N. Anderson, Elizabeth Arias, Thomas D. Dunn, Donna L. Hoyert, Joyce A. Martin, Kenneth D. Kochanek, T.J. Mathews, Arialdi M. Minino, Sherry L. Murphy, and Stephanie J. Ventura; *Office of Analysis and Epidemiology*: Lois Fingerhut, Richard F. Gillum, Deborah D. Ingram, Patricia A. Knapp, and Rashmi Tandon; *Office of International Statistics*: Juan Rafael Albertorio-Diaz and Francis C. Notzon; *Office of the Director*: Donna Pickett; and *Office of Research and Methodology*: Meena Khare.

Additional data and technical assistance were also provided by the following organizations of the Centers for Disease Control and Prevention: *Epidemiology Program Office*: Samuel L. Groseclose and Patsy A. Hall; *National Center for Chronic Disease Prevention and Health Promotion*: Laura Kann, Steve Kinchen, Shari L. Shanklin, and Lilo Strauss; *National Center for HIV, STD, and TB Prevention*: Chandra M. Pendergraft; *National Immunization Program*: Natalie J. Darling; by the following organizations within the Department of Health and Human Services: *Agency for Healthcare Research and Quality*: David Kashihara, Steven Machlin, and Marc W. Zodet; *Centers for Medicare & Medicaid Services*: Cathy A. Cowan, Cherron A. Cox, Frank Eppig, Denise F. Franz, David A. Gibson, Deborah W. Kidd, and Anna Long; *National Institutes of Health*: Catherine C. Cowie, Lynn A. G. Ries, and Douglas Rugh; *Substance Abuse and Mental Health Services Administration*: Daniel Foley; and by the following governmental and nongovernmental organizations: *U.S.*

Census Bureau: Bernadette D. Proctor; *Bureau of Justice Statistics*: Allen Beck; *Bureau of Labor Statistics*: Stella Cromartie, Kay Ford, Daniel Ginsburg, John Stinson, and Peggy Suarez; *Department of Veterans Affairs*: William Kloiber, Dat Tran, and Henry Caplan; *American Association of Colleges of Pharmacy*: Jennifer M. Patton; *American Association of Colleges of Podiatric Medicine*: Moraith G. North; *American Dental Education Association*: Richard Weaver; *Association of Schools of Public Health*: Mah-Sere K. Sow; *Cowles Research Group*: C. McKeen Cowles; and *InterStudy*: Tracy Coats.

Contents

Contents

Executive Summary and Highlights

Chartbook on Trends in the Health of Americans

Trend Tables

Appendixes

List of Chartbook Figures

Population

Health Insurance and Expenditures

Health Risk Factors

Morbidity and Activity Limitation

Health Care Utilization

Mortality

Special Feature: Pain

List of Trend Tables

Health Status and Determinants

Population

Fertility and Natality

Mortality

Inpatient Care

Health Care Resources

Personnel

Facilities

Health Care Expenditures and Payors

National Health Expenditures

Executive Summary and Highlights

Executive Summary

Health, United States, 2006, is the 30th annual report on the health status of the Nation prepared by the Secretary of the Department of Health and Human Services for the President and Congress. In a chartbook and 147 detailed tables, it provides an annual picture of health for the entire Nation. Trends are presented on health status and health care utilization, resources, and expenditures.

For those entrusted with safeguarding the Nation's health, monitoring the health of the American people is an essential step in making sound health policy and setting priorities for research and programs. Measures of the population's health provide essential information for assessing how the Nation's resources should be directed to improve the health of the population. Examination of emerging trends identifies diseases, conditions, and risk factors that warrant study and intervention. *Health, United States* presents trends and current information on measures and determinants of the Nation's health. It also identifies differences in health and health care among people of differing races and ethnicities, genders, education and income levels, and geographic locations, and it shows whether these differences are narrowing or increasing. Given the increasing diversity of the Nation and the continuing changes in the health care infrastructure, this is a challenging task, but it is a critically important undertaking.

Overall Health of the Nation

The health of the Nation continues to improve overall in many respects, in part because of the significant resources devoted to public health programs, research, health care, and health education. Life expectancy in the United States continues a long-term upward trend, although the most dramatic increases were in the early part of the 20th century. Over the past century, many diseases have been controlled or their morbidity and mortality substantially reduced. Notable achievements in public health have included the control of infectious diseases such as typhoid and cholera through decontamination of water; implementation of widespread vaccination programs to contain polio, diphtheria, pertussis, and measles; fluoridation of water to drastically reduce the prevalence of dental caries; and improvements in motor vehicle safety through vehicle redesign and efforts to increase usage of seatbelts and motorcycle helmets (1). A sharp

decline in deaths from cardiovascular disease is a major public health achievement that resulted in large part from public education campaigns emphasizing a healthy lifestyle and increased use of cholesterol and hypertension-lowering medications (2). Advances in medical technology, including diagnostic imaging technologies, procedures, and new prescription drugs have extended and improved the quality of countless lives.

Yet, even as progress is made in improving life expectancy, increased longevity is accompanied by increased prevalence of chronic conditions and their associated pain and disability. In recent years, progress in some arenas—declines in infant and cause-specific mortality, morbidity from chronic conditions, reduction in prevalence of risk factors including smoking and lack of exercise—has not been as rapid as in earlier years or trends have been moving in the wrong direction. Moreover, improvements have not been equally distributed by income, race, ethnicity, education, and geography.

Health Status and Its Determinants

In 2003, American men could expect to live 3 years longer, and women more than 1 year longer, than they did in 1990 (Table 27 and Figure 24). Mortality from heart disease, stroke, and cancer continued to decline in recent years (Table 29 and Figure 27). With longer life expectancy, however, comes increasing prevalence of chronic diseases and conditions that are associated with aging. Some diseases, including diabetes and hypertension, produce cumulative damage if not properly treated, while others, such as emphysema and some types of cancer, develop slowly or after long periods of environmental exposure. In 2001–2004, 10% of persons 20 years of age and over and more than one-fifth of adults 60 years and over had diabetes, including those with diabetes previously diagnosed by a physician and those with undiagnosed diabetes determined by results of a fasting blood sugar test (Table 55). About 30% of adults age 20 and over had elevated blood pressure or reported they were taking medications for high blood pressure in 2001–2004, and 17% had high serum cholesterol (Tables 69 and 70). The percentage of the population reporting fair or poor health status, or a limitation of their usual activity due to any chronic condition, increases sharply with age (Tables 58 and 60). In 2004, 32% of those 75 years of age and over reported fair or poor health compared with 22% of people age 65–74 and 6% of young adults age 25–44 years.

Of particular concern in recent years has been the increase in overweight and obesity, which are risk factors for many chronic diseases and disabilities including heart disease, hypertension, and back pain. The rising number of children and adults who are overweight, and the large percentage of Americans who are not physically active (Figures 12, 13, and Tables 72–74) raise additional concerns about Americans' future health (3).

Decreased cigarette smoking among adults is a prime example of a trend that has contributed to overall declines in mortality. However, the rapid drop in cigarette smoking in the two decades following the first Surgeon General's Report in 1964 has slowed in recent years. About one-quarter of men and one-fifth of women were current smokers in 2004 (Figure 10 and Table 63). The percentage of the population with high serum cholesterol has also been decreasing, in part due to the increased use of new cholesterol-lowering medications (Table 70) (4).

Prevalence of some risky behaviors among children and young adults remains at unacceptable levels. In 2005, 30% of high school students in grades 11–12 reported binge drinking, and 22% had used marijuana in the past 30 days. Marijuana use increased from 12% to 20% between 1991 and 2003 among students in grades 9–10 (Figure 11). The percentage of high school students who seriously considered suicide has declined since 1991, but the percentage who attempted suicide has remained stable (7%–9%) (Table 62).

Health Care Utilization and Resources

People use health care services for many reasons: to treat illnesses, injuries, and health conditions; to prevent or delay future health care problems; to reduce pain and increase quality of life; and to obtain information about their health status and prognoses. The study of trends in health care utilization provides important information on these phenomena and spotlights areas that warrant further study. Utilization trends may also be used to project future health care needs and expenditures, as well as training and supply needs.

Americans are increasingly using many types of preventive or early-detection health services. In 2004, 83% of children 19–35 months of age had received a combined vaccination series protecting them against several childhood infectious diseases, and the percentage of children receiving varicella (chickenpox) vaccine has increased sharply since it was first

recommended in 1996 (Table 81). The percentage of women receiving Pap smears and mammograms has increased since 1987 but has leveled off in recent years (Tables 84 and 85).

Rates of ambulatory care visits to office-based physicians and hospital outpatient departments have remained steady since the mid-1990s at 3 to 4 visits per person (data table for Figure 22 and Table 89). Admissions to hospitals and length of stay declined substantially in the 1980s and 1990s, but these declines appear to have leveled off (Tables 96–98). Hospital inpatient care is becoming more intensive and complex, with more procedures such as insertion of coronary artery stents, and hip and knee replacements being performed, particularly on older persons (Table 99). Hospitalizations for procedures that can be performed on an outpatient basis, such as hernia repairs and knee arthroscopies have declined sharply in inpatient settings, and imaging procedures such as diagnostic ultrasound and computerized axial tomography are increasingly performed on an outpatient basis.

The numbers of hospitals and hospital beds continue to decrease. Occupancy rates declined from 1975 to 1990 and have been stable since then (Table 112). The number of physicians in the United States has been increasing along with the overall population, but physicians are not distributed equally across the Nation (Table 104). New and different types of health practitioners and healthcare support occupations continue to evolve. The numbers of dental hygienists and dental assistants, pharmacy technicians, diagnostic medical sonographers, massage therapists, medical assistants, and medical equipment preparers have increased, on average, by 5% or more per year since 1999, while the numbers of audiologists, respiratory therapy technicians, recreational therapists, and occupational therapist aides have all declined, on average, by 5% or more per year (Table 108). Projections indicate that there may be an increasing shortage of nurses and pharmacists, as well as other health professionals, needed to care for our aging population (5,6).

Expenditures and Health Insurance

The United States spends more on health per capita than any other country, and health spending continues to increase rapidly. Much of this spending is for care that controls or reduces the impact of chronic diseases and conditions affecting an aging population. In 2004, national health care expenditures in the United States totaled $1.9 trillion, a 7.9%

increase from 2003 (Table 120). Hospital spending, which accounts for 30% of total national health expenditures, increased by 8.6% in 2004 (Table 123). Spending for prescription drugs increased 8.2% in 2004, compared with an average annual growth of 13% from 2000 to 2003. Spending for prescription drugs accounted for 10% of national health expenditures in 2004.

Overall, private health insurance paid for 36% of total personal health care expenditures in 2004, the federal government 34%, state and local government 11%, and out-of-pocket payments paid for 15% (Figure 9). The percentage of the population under 65 years of age with no health insurance coverage at the time they were interviewed fluctuated around 16%–18% between 1994 and 2004 (Figure 6 and Table 135).

Many people under age 65, particularly those with low incomes, do not have health insurance coverage consistently throughout the year. In 2004, about 20% of people under age 65 reported that they had been uninsured for at least part of the 12 months prior to their interview (Figure 7). In 2004, only 2% of people under age 65 who were insured continuously for all 12 months before their interview reported that they did not receive needed medical care due to cost, compared with about 20% of people who were uninsured for at least part of the 12 months before their interview (Table 78).

Disparities in Risk Factors, Access, and Utilization

Efforts to improve Americans' health in the 21st century will be shaped by important changes in demographics. Ours is a Nation that is growing older and becoming more racially and ethnically diverse. In 2005, nearly one-third of adults and about two-fifths of children were identified as black, Hispanic, Asian, American Indian or Alaska Native. In 2005, 14% of Americans identified themselves as Hispanic, 12% as black, and 4% as Asian (Figure 3).

Residents of institutions such as nursing homes, military barracks, and prisons have specialized health care needs and these populations are not generally included in many of the surveys that assess our Nation's health. Among men age 20–34 years, 11%–13% of non-Hispanic black men, 3%–4% of Hispanic men, and about 2% of white non-Hispanic men resided in local jails or state or federal prisons on June 30, 2004 (Table 2).

Health, United States, 2006, identifies major disparities in health and health care by socioeconomic status, race, ethnicity, and insurance status. Persons living in poverty are considerably more likely to be in fair or poor health and to have disabling conditions, and less likely to have used many types of health care than those with incomes of 200% of the poverty line or higher (Tables 58, 60, and 78–80). In 2004, adults living in poverty were almost twice as likely to report having trouble seeing—even with eyeglasses or contact lenses—as higher income persons (Table 59). Adults 45–64 years of age living below the federal poverty line were two to three times as likely to have three or more chronic conditions as those with incomes of 200% of the poverty line or higher (Figure 15).

Significant racial and ethnic disparities remain across a wide range of health measures. The gap in life expectancy between the black and white populations has narrowed, but persists (Table 27). Disparities in risk factors, access to health care, and morbidity also remain. Hispanic and American Indian persons under 65 years are more likely to be uninsured than those in other racial and ethnic groups (Table 135). Obesity, a major risk factor for many chronic diseases, varies by race and ethnicity—51% of black non-Hispanic women age 20 and over were obese in 2001–2004, compared with 39% of women of Mexican origin and 31% of non-Hispanic white women (Table 73, age adjusted). In 2003–2004, about two-thirds of non-Hispanic white older adults and about one-half of Hispanic and non-Hispanic black older adults received influenza vaccinations in the past year (Figure 20). In 1999–2002, Mexican-origin children 6–17 years of age were almost twice as likely to have untreated caries as were non-Hispanic white school-age children (Figure 14 and Table 75).

Many aspects of the health of the Nation have improved, but the health of some racial and ethnic groups has improved less than others. The large differences in health status by race and Hispanic origin documented in this report may be explained by factors including socioeconomic status, health practices, psychosocial stress and resources, environmental exposures, discrimination, and access to health care (7). Socioeconomic and cultural differences among racial and ethnic groups in the United States will likely continue to influence future patterns of disease, disability, and health care use.

Special Feature: Pain

Pain is a major determinant of quality of life, and affects physical and mental functioning. In addition to the direct costs of treating pain—including health care for diagnosis and treatment, drugs, therapies, and other medical costs—it results in lost work time and reduced productivity and concentration at work, or while conducting other activities (8,9). Although pain serves the important function of identifying tissue damage or inflammation, when the damage has healed and the pain remains, identifying either the cause of the remaining pain, or how to treat it, can be frustrating, time-consuming, and expensive.

In 1999–2002, more than one-quarter of Americans (26%) age 20 and over reported that they had a problem with pain—of any sort—that persisted for more than 24 hours in duration at some time during the month preceding their interview (Figure 28). Almost 60% of adults 65 years of age and over who reported pain indicated that it lasted for 1 year or more, compared with 37% of younger adults age 20–44 years who reported pain (Figure 29). In general, women reported pain more than men, and non-Hispanic white adults reported pain more than people of other races and ethnicities. Lower-income adults also reported pain more than higher-income adults (Figures 28, 31, and 32). Prevalence of joint pain increased with age with about one-fifth of adults age 18–44 years, and one-half of people age 65 and over, reporting any joint pain in the last 30 days (Figure 32). Severe headaches or migraines were twice as common among adult women as men (21% compared with 10%), and are most common among women in their reproductive years (Table 56).

A considerable amount of health care resources is devoted to treating pain, and the amount has been increasing. For example, rates of hospitalizations with procedures to replace painful hips and knees have increased substantially in the last decade (Figure 35). In 2002–2003, ambulatory medical care or prescribed medicine expenses for headaches averaged $566 per person for headache-related care among noninstitutionalized adults who reported a headache expense, representing more than $4 billion in total expenses—not including self-treatment, over-the-counter drugs, and inpatient hospital expenses for this condition (Figure 36). The percentage of people using prescription narcotic drugs in the past month increased by 30% between 1988–1994 and 1999–2002, largely due to increased use among non-Hispanic white women and women age 45 years and over (Figure 34 and data table for Figure 34). Yet, even with greater use of pain relieving medications, surgical interventions, and other treatments, in 1999–2002 more than 10% of Americans age 20 and over reported pain that had lasted for more than 1 year (data tables for Figures 28 and 29).

To improve the health of all Americans and to enable policymakers to chart future trends, target resources most effectively, and set program and policy priorities, it is critical that the Nation keep collecting and disseminating reliable and accurate information about all components of health, including current health status, the determinants of health, resources, and outcomes. The following highlights from *Health, United States, 2006 With Chartbook on Trends in the Health of Americans* summarize the latest findings gathered from across the public and private health care sectors to help the Department of Health and Human Services, the President, and the Congress in carrying out this essential mission.

References

1. Centers for Disease Control and Prevention. Ten great public health achievements—United States, 1900–1999. MMWR 1999;48(12):241–3. Available from: www.cdc.gov/mmwr/preview/mmwrhtml/00056796.htm.

2. Centers for Disease Control and Prevention. Achievements in Public Health, 1900–1999: Decline in deaths from heart disease and stroke—United States, 1900–1999. MMWR 1999;48(30):649–56. Available from: www.cdc.gov/mmwr/preview/mmwrhtml/mm4830a1.htm.

3. Ogden CL, Carroll MD, Curtin LR, McDowell MA, Tabak CJ, Flegal KM. Prevalence of overweight and obesity in the United States, 1999–2004. JAMA 2006;295(13):1549–55.

4. Carroll MD, Lacher DA, Sorlie PD, Cleeman JI, Gordon DJ, Wolz M, Grundy SM, Johnson CL. Trends in serum lipids and lipoproteins of adults, 1960–2002. JAMA 2005;294(14):1773–81.

5. Kenreigh CA, Wagner LT. The pharmacist shortage: where do we stand? Medscape Pharmacists 2006;7(1) Medscape posted 01/13/2006. Available from: www.medscape.com/viewarticle/521115.

6. Buerhaus PI, Staiger DO, Auerbach DI. New signs of a strengthening U.S. nurse labor market? Health Aff 2004;23(6):w526–w533.

7. Williams DR, Rucker TD. Understanding and addressing racial disparities in health care. Health Care Finan Rev 2000;21(4):75–90.

8. McCool WF, Smith T, Aberg C. Pain in women's health: A multi-faceted approach toward understanding. J Midwifery Womens Health 2004;49(6):473–81.

9. Luo X, Pietrobon R, Sun SX, Liu GG, Hey L. Estimates and patterns of direct health care expenditures among individuals with back pain in the United States. Spine 2004;29(1):79–86.

Highlights

Health, United States, 2006, is the 30th report on the health status of the Nation. In a chartbook and 147 trend tables, it presents current and historic information on the health of the U.S. population. The trend tables are organized around four major subject areas: health status and determinants, health care utilization, health care resources, and health care expenditures and payors. The 2006 Chartbook on Trends in the Health of Americans focuses on selected determinants and measures of health and includes a special feature on pain, which affects quality of life for virtually all Americans at some point in their lives.

Life Expectancy and Mortality

Life expectancy and infant mortality rates are often used to gauge the overall health of a population. Life expectancy shows a long-term upward trend and infant mortality shows a long-term downward trend. As overall death rates have declined, racial and ethnic disparities in mortality persist, but the gap in life expectancy between the black and white populations has narrowed.

In 2004, **life expectancy** at birth for the total population reached a record high of 77.9 years (preliminary data), up from 75.4 years in 1990 (Table 27).

Between 1990 and 2004, **life expectancy at birth** increased 3.4 years for **males** and 1.6 years for **females** (preliminary data). The gap in life expectancy between males and females narrowed from 7.0 years in 1990 to 5.2 years in 2004 (Figure 24 and Table 27).

Between 1990 and 2004 (preliminary data), **life expectancy at birth** increased more for the **black** than for the **white population**, thereby narrowing the gap in life expectancy between these two racial groups. In 1990, life expectancy at birth for the white population was 7.0 years longer than for the black population. By 2004, the difference had narrowed to 5.0 years (Table 27).

Overall mortality was 29% higher for **black Americans** than for white Americans in 2004 (preliminary data) compared with 37% higher in 1990. In 2004, age-adjusted death rates for the black population exceeded those for the white population by 44% for **stroke**, 30% for **heart disease**, 23% for **cancer**, and 774% for **HIV disease** (preliminary data and Table 29).

In 2004, the **infant mortality** rate decreased to 6.8 infant deaths per 1,000 live births (preliminary data). In 2002, the infant mortality rate had increased for the first time in more than 40 years (Figure 25 and Table 22).

Large disparities in **infant mortality** rates among **racial and ethnic groups** continue to exist. In 2003, infant mortality rates were highest for infants of non-Hispanic black mothers (13.6 deaths per 1,000 live births), American Indian mothers (8.7 per 1,000), and Puerto Rican mothers (8.2 per 1,000); and lowest for infants of Cuban mothers (4.6 per 1,000 live births) and Asian or Pacific Islander mothers (4.8 per 1,000) (Table 19).

The **leading cause of death** differs by age group. In 2004, the leading cause of death was congenital malformations for infants; unintentional injuries for children, adolescents, and young adults (age 1–44 years); cancer for middle-aged adults age 45–64 years; and heart disease for older adults age 65 years and over (preliminary data and Table 32).

Age-adjusted mortality from **heart disease**, the leading cause of death overall, declined 16% between 2000 and 2004 (preliminary data), continuing a long-term downward trend (Figure 27 and Table 36).

Age-adjusted mortality from **cancer**, the second leading cause of death overall, decreased 8% between 2000 and 2004 (preliminary data), continuing the decline that began in 1990 (Figure 27 and Table 38).

The age-adjusted death rate for **motor-vehicle injuries** has remained stable between 2000 and 2004 (preliminary data) after declining steadily between 1970 and 2000. Death rates for motor vehicle injuries are higher at age 15–24 years and 75 years and over than at other ages (Table 44).

The age-adjusted death rate for **HIV disease** has declined slowly between 1999 and 2004 (preliminary data), after a sharp decrease between 1995 and 1999. The death rate for HIV disease is higher at age 35–54 years than at other ages (Table 42).

In 2004, **homicide** continued to be the leading cause of death for young **black males 15–24 years of age**. The homicide rate for young black males declined by 12% from 2003 to 2004 (preliminary data and Table 45).

In 2003, young **American Indian males 15–24 years of age** continued to have substantially higher death rates for motor vehicle-related injuries and for suicide than young males in other race/ethnicity groups. Death rates for the American Indian population are known to be underestimated (Tables 44 and 46).

The **suicide rate for non-Hispanic white men 65 years of age and over** is higher than in other groups. In 2003, the suicide rate for older non-Hispanic white men was 2–4 times the rate for older men in other race/ethnicity groups and about 8 times the rate for older non-Hispanic white women (Table 46).

Health Behaviors

Health behaviors have a significant effect on health status. Pregnant teenagers are less likely to receive early prenatal care and more likely to drop out of school and to live in poverty, than are other parents. Heavy and chronic use of alcohol and use of illicit drugs increase the risk of disease and injuries. Cigarette smoking increases the risk of lung cancer, heart disease, emphysema, and other diseases. Regular physical activity lessens the risk of disease and enhances mental and physical functioning.

The **birth rate for teenagers** declined in 2004 for the 13th consecutive year, to 41.1 births per 1,000 women age 15–19 years, 1% lower than in 2003. Rates declined for teenagers age 15–17 years and 18–19 years, but increased for teenagers age 10–14 years (Table 4).

In 2004, the **birth rate for unmarried women** reached a record high of 46.1 births per 1,000 unmarried women age 15–44 years, up 3% from 2003. In 2004, 36% of all births were to unmarried women and the percentages generally increased for all age, race, and Hispanic origin subgroups (Table 10).

Between 2003 and 2005, the percentage of **high school students who reported smoking cigarettes** in the past month remained stable at 22%–23% after declining from 36% in 1997 (Figure 10).

In 2005, 30% of **students in grades 11–12** reported **binge drinking** five or more alcoholic drinks in a row and 22% reported **marijuana use** in the past month (Figure 11).

Between 1993 and 2005, the percentage of **high school students** who reported attempting suicide (8%–9%) and whose **suicide attempts** required medical attention (2%–3%) remained fairly constant. Girls were more likely than boys to consider or attempt suicide. However in 2003 adolescent boys

(15–19 years of age) were more than 4 times as likely to die from suicide as were adolescent girls, in part reflecting their choice of more lethal methods, such as firearms (Tables 46 and 62).

The percentage of adults who reported consuming **five or more alcoholic drinks in one day** declines with age. In 2004, among current drinkers, 56% of adults 18–24 years of age compared with 9% of adults 65 years of age and over reported this level of alcohol consumption in the past year (Table 68).

In 2004, 23% of men and 19% of women 18 years of age and over were **current smokers**. This is a sharp decline from 1965, when more than one-half of adult men and one-third of adult women smoked, but declines have slowed since 1990 (Table 63).

In 2004, almost one-third of **adults 18 years of age and over engaged in regular leisure-time physical activity**. Adults in families with incomes above twice the poverty level were more likely to engage in regular leisure-time physical activity (34%) than adults in lower-income families (20%–21%) (age adjusted) (Table 72).

More than one-half of adults **65 years of age and over** were inactive in their leisure-time, one-quarter had some level of leisure-time activity with an additional 22% reporting regular **leisure-time activity** in 2004 (Table 72).

Health Status and Risk Factors

Measures of morbidity presented in this report include the incidence and prevalence of specific diseases and conditions. Other measures of health status include limitation of activity and limitations in activities of daily living caused by chronic conditions, and respondent-assessed health status.

Low birthweight is associated with elevated risk of death and disability in infants. In 2004, the low birthweight rate (less than 2,500 grams, or 5.5 pounds, at birth) increased to 8.1%, up from 7.0% in 1990 (Table 13).

Between 1976–1980 and 2003–2004, the prevalence of **overweight among children** 6–11 years of age more than doubled from 7% to 19% and the prevalence of overweight among **adolescents** 12–19 years of age more than tripled from 5% to 17% (Figure 13 and Table 74).

Among adults 20–74 years of age, **overweight and obesity** rates have increased since 1960–1962. These increases are driven largely by increases in the percentage of adults who are obese. From 1960–1962 through 2003–2004, the percentage of adults who are overweight but not obese has remained steady at 32%–34% (age adjusted). During that time period, the percentage of obese adults has increased from 13% to 34% (age adjusted) (Figure 13 and Table 73).

The prevalence of **hypertension**, defined as elevated blood pressure or taking antihypertensive medication, increases with age. In 2001–2004, 30% of men and 33% of women age 45–54 years had hypertension, compared with 69% of men and 82% of women age 75 years and over (Table 69).

Between 1988–1994 and 2001–2004, the percentage of adults with **elevated serum cholesterol levels** greater than 240 mg/dL declined substantially for older adults. However, older women were more likely to have high serum cholesterol than men. In 2001–2004, 26% of women age 65–74 years had high serum cholesterol, compared with 11% of men age 65–74 years (Table 70).

In 2001–2004, the prevalence of **diabetes** (including diagnosed and undiagnosed) increased with age from 11% among adults 40–59 years of age to 23% among adults 60 years of age and over. The percentage of adults with undiagnosed diabetes was 3% among those 40–59 years of age and 6% among those 60 years of age and over (Table 55).

In 2004, approximately 2.2 million **workplace injuries and illnesses** in the private sector involved days away from work, job transfer, or restricted duties at work for a rate of 2.5 cases per 100 full-time workers. Transportation and warehousing reported the highest injury and illness rate, 4.9 cases per 100. The next highest rates were reported by the agriculture, forestry, fishing and hunting (3.7 per 100), and manufacturing industries (3.6 per 100) (Table 50).

Poor and near poor **children** are more likely to have **untreated dental caries** than children in families with incomes above twice the poverty level. In 1999–2002, 32% of poor children 6–17 years of age had untreated dental caries, compared with 13% of children in families with incomes at least twice the poverty level (Table 75).

Between 1988–1994 and 1999–2002, approximately one-quarter (24%–28%) of **adults 18–64** years of age had

untreated dental caries, down from nearly one-half (48%) in 1971–1974 (Table 75).

In 2004, 17% of persons 65 years of age and over had any **trouble seeing** even with glasses and 11% were deaf or had a lot of **trouble hearing** (Table 59).

In 2004, **limitation of activity** due to chronic health conditions was reported for 7% of **children** under the age of 18 years. Among school-age children (5–17 years of age), learning disabilities and Attention Deficit/Hyperactivity Disorder (ADHD or ADD) were frequently reported as a cause of activity limitation (Figure 16 and Table 58).

Arthritis and other musculoskeletal conditions were the leading **cause of activity limitation** among working-age **adults 18–64 years** of age in 2003–2004. Mental illness was the second most frequently mentioned condition causing activity limitation among adults 18–44 years of age and the third most frequently mentioned among adults 45–54 years of age (Figure 17).

Among persons **age 65 years of age and over**, arthritis and heart disease or other circulatory conditions were the two most frequently reported causes of **activity limitation** in 2003–2004 (Figure 18).

Health Care Access and Utilization

People use health care services for many reasons: to treat illnesses, injuries, and health conditions; to prevent or delay future health care problems; to reduce pain and increase quality of life; and to obtain information about their health status and prognoses. The health care delivery system offers a wide variety of services, ranging from preventive and primary care, to new and better medicines, to use of sophisticated and increasingly technological and complex procedures and interventions.

In 2003–2004, 6% of children under 6 years of age and 15% of children 6–17 years of age had **no health care visit** to a doctor or clinic within the past 12 months (Table 79).

Adults 18–64 years of age were the most likely to report **not receiving needed medical care or delaying their care due to cost**. In 2004, 7% of adults 18–64 years of age reported that they did not get needed care during the past 12 months, 10% delayed care, and 9% did not get prescription drugs due to the cost (Table 78).

In 2004, 20%–21% of people under age 65 years who were uninsured for all or part of the preceding year **did not receive needed health care** in the past 12 months **due to cost**, compared with 2% of people with health insurance for the full year (Table 78).

Almost all adults 65 years of age and over have Medicare coverage. Despite having this health insurance, among those with incomes below or near the poverty level, in 2004, 4%–6% **did not get needed medical care** during the past 12 months, 6%–9% **delayed their care,** and 8%–12% **did not get the prescription drugs** they needed due to the cost. Medicare coverage for prescription drugs began in 2006 (Table 78).

In 2003–2004, **visit rates to physician offices and hospital outpatient departments** among persons 18–44 years of age were more than twice as high for women as for men, largely due to medical care associated with female reproduction (Figure 22).

The percentage of mothers receiving **prenatal care** in the first trimester of pregnancy remained unchanged at 84% for the 43-state reporting areas for which comparable trend data were available in 2004. In 2004 the percentage of mothers with early prenatal care varied substantially by race and ethnicity, from 70% for American Indian mothers to 89% for non-Hispanic white mothers (Table 7).

In 2004, 83% of children 19–35 months of age received the **combined vaccination** series of four doses of DTaP (diphtheria-tetanus-acellular pertussis) vaccine, three doses of polio vaccine, one dose of MMR (measles-mumps-rubella vaccine), and three doses of Hib (Haemophilus influenzae type b) vaccine. Children living below the poverty threshold were less likely to have received the combined vaccination series than were children living at or above poverty (78% compared with 85%) (Table 81).

In 2004, 65% of noninstitutionalized adults **65 years of age and over** reported an **influenza vaccination** within the past year, more than double the percentage in 1989. In 2004, the percentage of older adults ever having received a pneumococcal vaccine was 57%, up sharply from 14% in 1989 (Table 83).

In 2004, 54% of **children** 2–5 years of age and 84% of children 6–17 years of age had a **dental visit** in the past year. Children with family income below or near the poverty

level were less likely than children with higher family income to have had a visit (Figure 19 and Table 91).

Use of **prescription medications** among adults increases with age. In 1999–2002, the percentage of adults who reported using prescription medications in the prior month rose from 36% of those 18–44 years of age to 64% at 45–64 years of age and 85% at 65 years of age and over. In each age group women were more likely than men to use prescription drugs (Table 93).

In 1999–2002, more than one-half of adults 65 years of age and over took **three or more prescription drugs** in the past month (Table 93).

In 2004, adults 75 years of age and over had a higher **rate of visits to the hospital emergency department** than other age groups (58 visits per 100 persons compared with 29–45 per 100 persons in other age groups) (Table 89).

Children under 6 years of age were more likely than children 6–17 years of age to have had an **emergency department (ED) visit** within the past 12 months in 2004 (26% compared with 18%) (Table 86).

In 2003–2004, **falls** accounted for 34% of **hospital emergency department injury visits** for men 65 years of age and over and 48% for women in that age group. Falls also accounted for 22%–24% of children's injury-related visits to emergency departments (Table 88).

Heart disease and injuries were among the most common reasons for **inpatient hospitalization** among adults 45–64 years of age in 2004. Among this age group, the **discharge rate** for heart disease was 80% higher for men than for women and the discharge rate for injuries was 18% higher for men than women (Table 97).

Between 1993–1994 and 2003–2004, the hospital discharge rate for **cardiac catheterization** among adults 75 years of age and over increased 42%, while the rate among adults 65–74 years of age remained stable. By 2003–2004, the cardiac catheterization rate for adults 75 years of age and over had risen to a level similar to that for adults 65–74 years of age (Table 99).

The number of **gastric bypass and other inpatient bariatric procedures** performed on obese adults 18–44 years of age more than tripled between 1999–2001 and 2002–2004 (data table for Figure 23). Bariatric procedures were more common among women than men (Figure 23).

Between 1992–1993 and 2003–2004, the hospital discharge rate for **knee replacement surgery**, which is typically performed for osteoarthritis, nearly doubled among **adults 65 years of age and over** (Figure 35).

Health Care System Influences, Resources, and Personnel

Major changes continue to occur in the delivery of health care in the United States, driven in part by changes in payment policies intended to rein in rising costs and by advances in technology that have allowed more complex treatments to be performed on an outpatient basis. Hospital inpatient utilization has been stable in recent years. The number of physicians continues to increase, but supply is not equally distributed across the country, and some office-based physicians are not accepting new patients. The supply of other practitioners, including pharmacists and nurses, may not be increasing as rapidly as needed to keep in pace with our aging population.

In 2004, 43% of **doctor visits** were to specialty care physicians, up from 34% in 1980. During this period, the proportion of office-based doctor visits to general and family practice physicians decreased from 34% to 23% (Table 90).

In 2004, 63% of **surgeries** were performed on an **outpatient** basis, compared with 51% in 1990 and 16% in 1980 (Table 100).

The age-adjusted average **length of inpatient hospital** stays has remained stable at 4.8 to 4.9 days during the period 2000–2004, after declining from 7.5 days in 1980 (Table 96).

Between 1990 and 2004, the number of **community hospital beds** declined from about 927,000 to 808,000. Since 1990, the community hospital occupancy rate has remained steady at 62%–67% (Table 112).

Between 1990 and 2002, the overall number of **inpatient mental health beds** in the United States declined by 22%. In Veterans Affairs medical centers the number of mental health beds declined by 55%, in state and county mental hospitals and private psychiatric hospitals the decline was 42%, and in psychiatric units of non-federal general hospitals the decline was 25% (Table 113).

In 2004, there were over 7,500 Medicare-certified **home health agencies**, up from about 6,900 in 2003, but below the high of 10,800 in 1997. The number of Medicare-certified

hospices increased to over 2,600 after remaining stable at about 2,300 from 1997 to 2003 (Table 118).

In 2004, there were nearly 1.8 million **nursing home beds** in about 16,000 facilities certified for use by Medicare and Medicaid beneficiaries. Between 1995 and 2004, nursing home bed occupancy was relatively stable, estimated at 83% in 2004. **Occupancy rates** were 90% or higher in 11 states and the District of Columbia in 2004 (Table 116).

Between 1999 and 2004, the **number** of dental hygienists and assistants, diagnostic medical sonographers, pharmacy technicians, message therapists, and medical equipment preparers increased by 6%–12% annually. The **hourly wages** of pharmacists, radiation therapists, physician assistants, and nuclear medicine technologists rose 6%–8% annually (Table 108).

In 2003–2004, 27% of **physicians** reported they were not accepting new Medicaid patients and 41% were not accepting new capitated privately insured patients, compared with 12%–14% not accepting new Medicare and non-capitated privately-insured patients. Two-fifths of physician offices perform some lab tests in the office. Practices with 10 or more physicians were more likely to perform lab tests in the office (62%) than offices with one physician (27%) (Table 117).

Health Insurance Coverage and Payors

Major payors for health care include public programs such as Medicare and Medicaid, and private health insurers. Medicaid is jointly funded by the federal and state governments to provide health care for certain groups of low-income persons. Medicare is funded through the federal government and covers the health care of most persons 65 years of age and over and disabled persons. Almost 70% of the population under 65 years of age has private health insurance, most of which is obtained through the workplace.

Uninsured Population

Between 1995 and 2004, the percentage of the **population under 65 years of age with no health insurance coverage** (public or private) at a point in time ranged between 16.1% and 17.5%. Among the under 65 population, the poor and near poor (those with family incomes less than 200% of poverty) were much more likely than the nonpoor to be uninsured (Figure 6 and Table 135).

In 2004, 9% of children under 18 years of age had **no health insurance coverage** at a point in time. Between 2000 and 2004, among children in families with income just above the poverty level (100%–150% of poverty), the percentage uninsured dropped from 25% to 16%. However, children in low-income families remained substantially more likely than children in higher-income families to lack coverage (Table 135).

In 2004, 30% of **young adults** 18–24 years of age were uninsured at a point in time. This age group was more than twice as likely to be uninsured as those 45–64 years of age (Table 135).

In 2004, persons of **Hispanic origin and American Indians** under 65 years of age were more likely to have **no health insurance coverage** at a point in time than were those in other racial and ethnic groups. Non-Hispanic white persons were the least likely to lack coverage (Table 135).

Many people under 65 years of age, particularly those with a low family income, do not have health insurance coverage consistently throughout the year. In 2004, one-fifth of people under 65 years of age **were uninsured for at least part of the 12 months prior to interview**. Two-fifths of people of Mexican origin were similarly uninsured for at least part of the 12 months prior to interview (data table for Figure 7).

The likelihood of being **uninsured** varies substantially among the **states**. In 2002–2004, the average percentage of the population with no health insurance coverage ranged from 8.5% in Minnesota to 25% in Texas (Table 147).

Private Health Insurance

During 2002 to 2004, 69% of the population under 65 years of age had **private health insurance**. Between 1995 and 2001 the proportion had fluctuated between 71%–73% after declining from 77% in 1984 (Figure 6 and Table 133).

Between 2001 and 2004, the proportion of the population under 65 years of age with **private health insurance obtained through the workplace** (a current or former employer or union) declined from 67% to 64% (Table 133).

Federal and State Health Insurance Programs

In 2005, the **Medicare** program had about 43 million **enrollees and expenditures** of $336 billion (preliminary data Table 137).

Of the 36 million **Medicare enrollees in the fee-for-service program** in 2003, 11% were 85 years of age and over and 16% were disability beneficiaries under 65 years of age (Table 138).

In 2004, among children under 18 years of age, 26% were covered by **Medicaid or the State Children's Health Insurance Program**, a 7 percentage point increase since 2000 (Table 134).

In 2003, children under 21 years of age accounted for 48% of **Medicaid recipients** but only 17% of expenditures. Aged, blind, and disabled persons accounted for 23% of recipients and 67% of expenditures (Table 140).

Health Care Expenditures

The United States spends more on health per capita than any other country, and health spending continues to increase rapidly. Spending increases are due to increased intensity and cost of services, and a higher volume of services needed to treat an aging population.

The United States spends a larger **share of the gross domestic product (GDP) on health** than does any other major industrialized country. In 2003, the United States devoted 15% of its GDP to health, compared with over 11% in Switzerland and Germany, and more than 10% in Iceland, France, and Norway, the countries with the next highest shares (Table 119).

In 2004, **national health care expenditures** in the United States totaled $1.9 trillion, a 7.9% increase compared with an 8.6% per year increase from 2000–2003. In the 1990s, annual growth had slowed to 6.6% following an average annual growth rate of 11% during the 1980s (Table 120).

In 2004, national health expenditures in the United States grew 7.9%, compared with 7.0% growth in the GDP. **Health expenditures as a percentage of the GDP** was 16% in 2004 (Figure 8 and Table 120).

Prescription drug expenditures increased 8.2% in 2004, compared with 10.2% in 2003 and 14.3% in 2002. Prescription drugs posted annual increases of 3%–5% in the Consumer Price Index in 2000 to 2005 (Tables 121 and 123).

Expenditures for hospital care accounted for 30% of all national health expenditures in 2004. Physician services accounted for 21% of the total in 2004, prescription drugs for 10%, and nursing home care for 6% (Table 123).

In 2003, 96% of persons 65 years of age and over in the civilian noninstitutionalized population reported **medical expenses** that averaged about $8,210 per person with expense. Nineteen percent of expenses were paid out-of-pocket, 16% by private insurance, and 63% by public programs (primarily Medicare and Medicaid) (Tables 125 and 126).

The burden of **out-of-pocket expenses** for health care varies considerably by age. In 2003, over two-fifths of those 65 years of age and over with health care expenses paid $1,000 or more out-of-pocket, compared with 29% of those 45–64 years of age, and 12% of adults 18–44 years of age (Table 127).

In 2004, 34% of **personal health care expenditures** were paid by the federal government and 11% by state and local government; private health insurance paid 36% and consumers paid 15% out-of-pocket (Figure 9 and Table 124).

Special Feature: Pain

Pain affects physical and mental functioning, and can profoundly affect quality of life. In addition to the direct costs of treating pain—including visits for diagnosis and treatment, drugs, therapies, and other medical costs—it can cause loss of productivity and concentration. Patterns of self-reported pain vary considerably by age, sex, race and ethnicity, and poverty.

In 1999–2002, more than one-quarter of Americans (26%) 20 years of age and over reported that they had a problem with **pain in the past 30 days** that persisted for more than 24 hours (Figure 28).

Nearly 60% of adults 65 years of age and over who reported pain lasting more than 24 hours stated that it **lasted for one year or more** compared with 37% of young adults 20–44 years of age who reported pain in 1999–2002 (Figure 29).

In 2004, more than one-quarter of adults 18 years of age and over reported experiencing **low back pain** in the past 3 months (Figure 30 and Table 56).

In 2004, 15% of adults 18 years of age and over reported experiencing **migraine or severe headache** in the past 3 months. The percentage of young adults 18–44 years of age who reported migraine or severe headache was almost three times the percentage for adults 65 years of age and over (Figure 30 and Table 56).

In 2004, almost one-third of adults 18 years of age and over and one-half of older adults 65 years of age and over reported **joint pain**, aching, or stiffness (excluding the back or neck) during the 30 days prior to interview. The knee was the site of joint pain most commonly reported in all age groups (Table 57).

In 2003, the percentage of adults 18 years of age and over who reported **severe joint pain** increased with age. Women were more likely to report severe joint pain than men (10% compared with 7%) (Figure 32).

In 2003–2004, 50% of **ED visits** for persons with a severe pain recorded had **narcotic analgesic drugs** prescribed, or provided during the visit. Among visits with severe pain recorded, those made by children under 18 years of age and adults 65 years of age and over were less likely than visits by persons in other age groups to have a narcotic drug provided in the ED (Figure 33).

The percentage of adults who reported using a **narcotic drug in the past month** increased from 3.2% in 1988–1994 to 4.2% in 1999–2002 (age adjusted). This increase has been driven largely by an increase in narcotic drug use among white non-Hispanic women and women 45 years of age and over (Figure 34).

Between 1992–1993 and 2003–2004, the hospital discharge rate for **knee replacement** among adults 65 years of age and over increased by nearly 90%, from 39 to 73 discharges per 10,000 persons. Knee replacement was more common among older women than older men (Figure 35).

Between 1992–1993 and 2003–2004, the hospital discharge rate for **hip replacement** among adults 65 years of age and over (excluding those performed for fractured hips) increased almost 60% from 25 to 40 discharges per 10,000 population. Nonfracture hip replacement rates were similar among older men and women (Figure 35).

In 2002–2003, 3.5% of adults 18 years of age and over had ambulatory care visits or prescribed medicine purchases to treat **migraines or other types of headache** during the year. Their **average annual expenditure** for these treatments was $566 (in 2003 dollars) (data table for Figure 36).

In 2004, 28% of adults 18 years of age and over **with low back pain** in the past 3 months said they had a **limitation of activity** caused by a chronic condition, compared with 10% of adults who did not report recent low back pain. People with recent low back pain were almost five times as likely to have **serious psychological distress** as people without recent low back pain (Figure 37).

Chartbook on Trends in the Health of Americans

Population

Age

The population age 65 and over is increasing at a faster rate than the total population.

From 1950 to 2005, the total resident population of the United States increased from 151 million to 296 million, representing an average annual growth rate of 1.2% (Figure 1). During the same period, the population 65 years of age and over grew on average 2.0% per year, increasing from 12 to 37 million persons. The population 75 years of age and over grew the fastest (on average, 2.8% per year), increasing from 4 to 18 million persons.

Projections indicate that the rate of growth for the total population from now to 2050 will be slower, but older age groups will continue to grow more rapidly than the total population (1). By 2029, all of the baby boomers (those born in the post World War II period 1946–1964) will be age 65 years and over. As a result, the population age 65–74 years will increase from 6% to 10% of the total population between 2005 and 2030 (data table for Figure 1). As the baby boomers age, the population 75 years and over will also rise from 6% to 9% of the population by 2030 and continue to grow to 12% in 2050. By 2040 the population age 75 years and over will exceed the population 65–74 years of age.

Reference

1. Day JC. National population projections. U.S. Census Bureau. Available from: www.census.gov/population/www/pop-profile/natproj.html.

Figure 1. Total population and older population: United States, 1950-2050

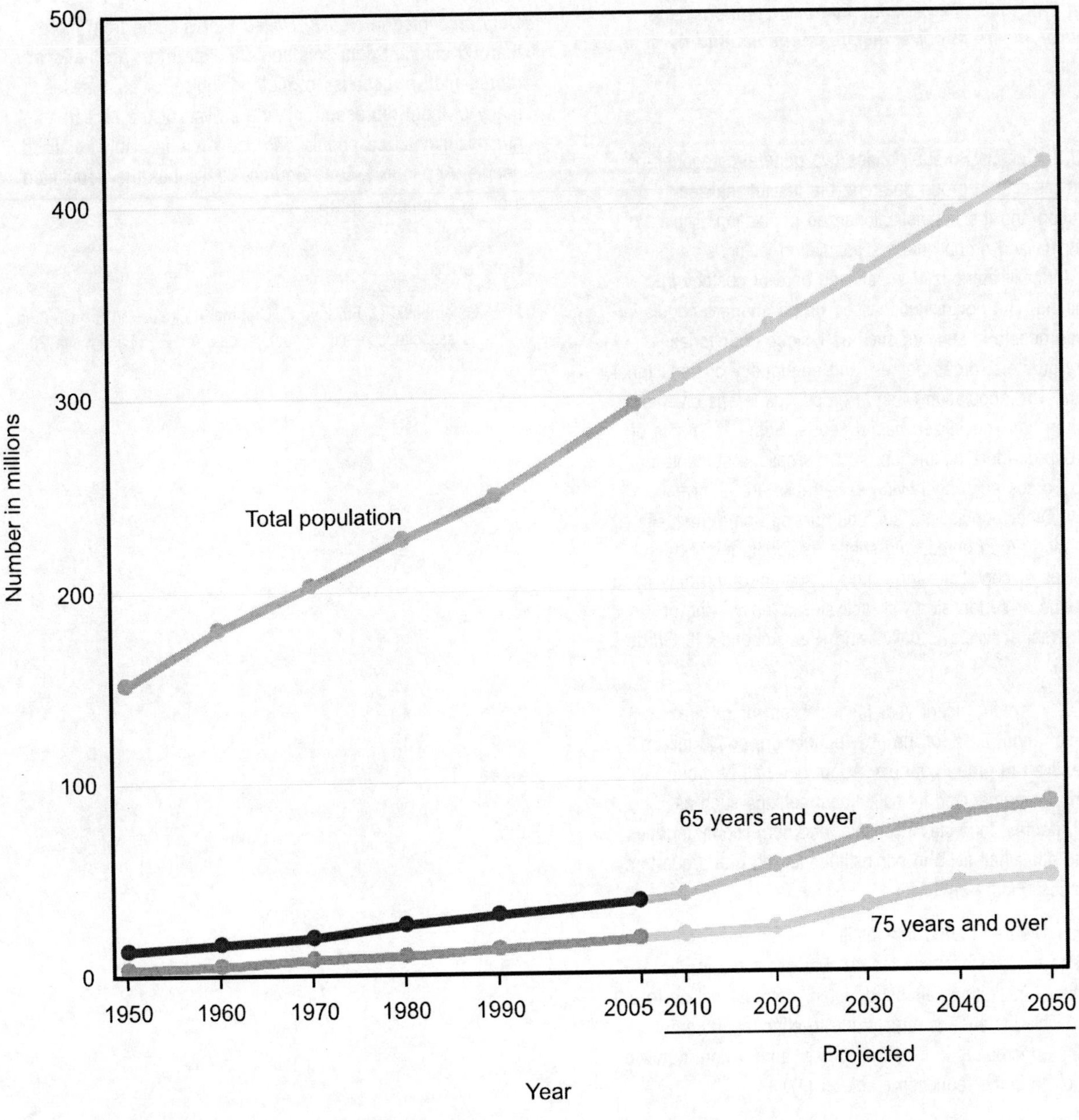

NOTE: See data table for data points graphed and additional notes.

SOURCE: U.S. Census Bureau.

Population in Group Quarters

About four million Americans live in institutions—the largest numbers in correctional institutions and nursing homes.

The U.S. Census Bureau defines two general categories of people residing in group quarters: the institutionalized population and the noninstitutionalized population. The institutionalized group quarters population includes people under formally authorized supervised care or custody in institutions. The noninstitutionalized group quarters population includes people in settings such as college dormitories, military quarters, group homes, and emergency or transitional shelters. The population living in group quarters is diverse and often has specialized health needs. Some segments of the group quarters population, such as college students or Armed Forces personnel living in barracks are relatively healthy. Other populations such as nursing home, mentally ill or disabled group home, and shelter residents might have disabilities or conditions requiring medical care and may need assistance or supervision with activities of daily living or instrumental activities of daily living (See Appendix II, Group quarters).

In 2000, the most recent year for which estimates are available, about 2.8% of the U.S. population, or 7.8 million people, lived in group quarters. About one-half of group quarters residents lived in institutional settings such as nursing homes, long-stay hospitals, and correctional facilities and the other half lived in noninstitutionalized group quarters residences (Figure 2).

Between 1990 and 2000, the institutionalized population increased by 22% because the number of people in correctional institutions almost doubled (from 1.1 million to 2.0 million). This increase is largely due to changes in sentencing guidelines, increases in illegal drug use, and a more punitive approach to crime reduction (Table 2) (1).

During the same period, the noninstitutionalized group quarters population grew by 11%. This increase was fueled by the population residing in group homes, which more than doubled between 1990 and 2000. Group homes include community-based homes for the mentally ill, mentally retarded, physically handicapped, and drug/alcohol halfway houses not operated for correctional purposes. They also include some assisted living facilities and group homes for dementia patients.

Data presented in *Health, United States* come from more than 60 different data sets and although most are nationally representative, because of methodological or cost issues many of them represent only the civilian or the civilian noninstitutionalized populations and exclude institutionalized people. Appendix I, Data Sources, describes the population that each data set represents.

Reference

1. Golembeski C, Fullilove R. Criminal (In)justice in the city and its associated health consequences. Am J Public Health 2005; 95:1701–6.

Figure 2. Population in group quarters, by type of setting: United States, 1990 and 2000

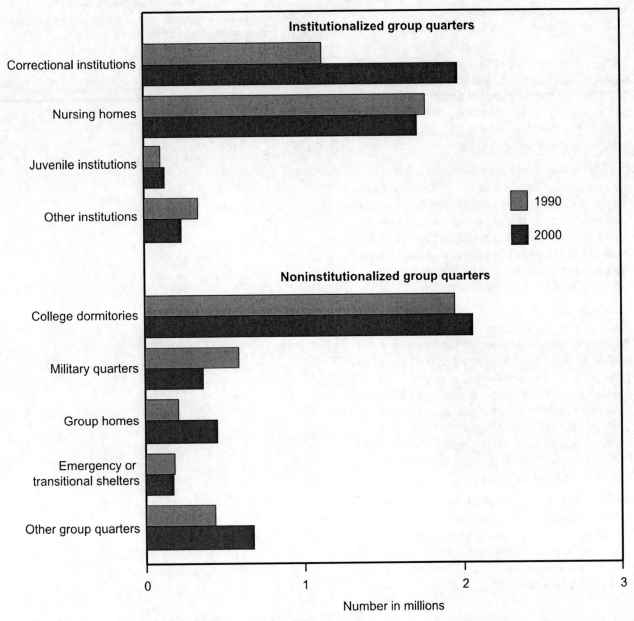

NOTES: Other institutions include hospital or wards, hospices, and schools for the handicapped. See data table for data points graphed and additional notes.

SOURCE: U.S. Census Bureau.

Race and Ethnicity

The percentage of Americans who identify themselves as Hispanic or Asian continues to increase.

Changes in the racial and ethnic composition of the population have important consequences for the Nation's health because many measures of disease and disability differ significantly by race and ethnicity. One of the overarching goals of U.S. public health policy is elimination of racial and ethnic disparities in health.

Diversity has long been a characteristic of the U.S. population, but the racial and ethnic composition of the Nation has changed over time. In recent decades, the percentage of the population that is of Hispanic origin or Asian has more than doubled (data table for Figure 3). In 2005, nearly 30% of adults and almost 40% of children identified themselves as Hispanic, black, Asian, American Indian or Alaska Native, or Native Hawaiian or Other Pacific Islander.

In the 1980 and 1990 decennial censuses, Americans could choose only one racial category to describe their race (1). Beginning with the 2000 census, the question on race was modified to allow the choice of more than one racial category. Although overall, a small percentage of persons of non-Hispanic origin selected two or more races in 2005, the percentage of children described as being of more than one race was more than twice as high as the percentage of adults (Figure 3). The number of American adults identifying themselves or their children as multiracial is expected to increase in the future (2).

The percentage of persons reporting two or more races varies considerably among racial groups. For example, the percentage of persons reporting a specified race in combination with one or more additional racial groups was 1.6% for white persons and 35.7% for American Indian or Alaska Native persons in 2005 (3).

References

1. Grieco EM, Cassidy RC. Overview of race and Hispanic origin. Census 2000 brief. U.S. Census Bureau. March 2001.

2. Waters MC. Immigration, intermarriage, and the challenges of measuring racial/ethnic identities. Am J Public Health 2000; 90(11):1735–7.

3. U.S. Census Bureau. Monthly postcensal resident population, by single year of age, sex, race, and Hispanic origin. Available from: www.census.gov/popest/national/asrh/2004_nat_res.html [data for July 1, 2005].

Figure 3. Population in selected race and Hispanic origin groups, by age: United States, 1980-2005

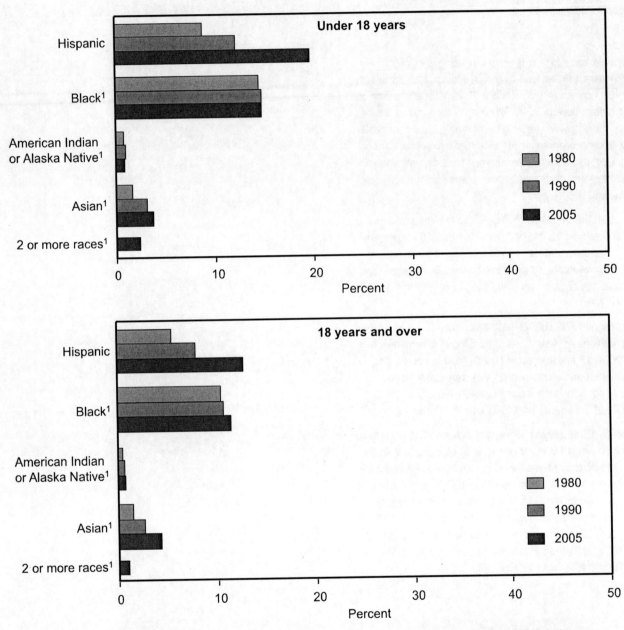

¹Not Hispanic.

NOTES: Persons of Hispanic origin may be of any race. Race data for 2005 are not directly comparable with data for 1980 and 1990. Individuals could report only one race in 1980 and 1990, and more than one race in 2005. Persons who selected only one race in 2005 are included in single-race categories; persons who selected more than one race in 2005 are shown as having 2 or more races and are not included in single-race categories. In 1980 and 1990 the Asian category includes Asian and Native Hawaiian or Other Pacific Islander; in 2005, this category includes only Asian. See data table for data points graphed and data for Native Hawaiian or Other Pacific Islander.

SOURCE: U.S. Census Bureau.

Poverty

The poverty rate has increased in recent years among people under age 65.

Children and adults in families with incomes below or near the federal poverty level have worse health than those with higher incomes (see Appendix II, Poverty for a definition of the federal poverty level). Although, in some cases, illness can lead to poverty, more often poverty causes poor health by its connection with inadequate nutrition, substandard housing, exposure to environmental hazards, unhealthy lifestyles, and decreased access to and use of health care services (1).

In 2004, the overall percentage of the U.S. population living in poverty was 12.7%, up from 11.3% in 2000 (2). Poverty rates for children under 18 years of age and working-age adults have increased since 2000, whereas the percentage of people age 65 years and over living in poverty has declined since 2002.

Starting in 1974, children have been more likely than either working-age or older adults to be living in poverty (Figure 4). In 2004, 13 million children (17.8%) lived in poverty and another 16 million children (21.4%) were classified as near-poor with family income between 100% and less than 200% of the poverty level (data table for Figure 5).

Prior to 1974, persons 65 years of age and over were more likely to live in poverty than people of other ages. With the availability of inflation-adjusted government social insurance programs such as Social Security and Supplemental Security Income, the poverty rate of older adults declined rapidly until 1974 and continued to decline gradually to 9.7% in 1999 (3). In 2004, 3.5 million persons age 65 years and over or 9.8% of older adults lived in poverty. An additional 10 million were near-poor (data table for Figure 5).

Figure 4. Poverty by age: United States, 1966-2004

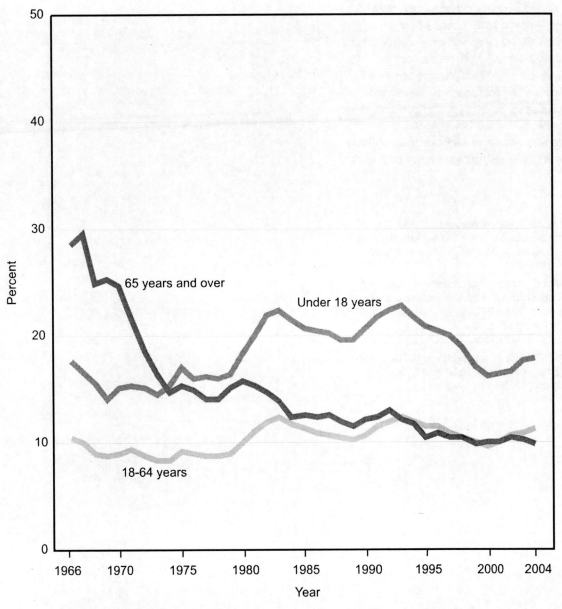

NOTES: Data shown are the percentage of persons with family income below the poverty level. See data table for data points graphed and additional notes.

SOURCE: U.S. Census Bureau, Current Population Survey.

Poverty *(Continued)*

At all ages, a higher percentage of Hispanic and black persons than non-Hispanic white persons were poor (Figure 5). In 2004, 29%–34% of Hispanic and black children were poor compared with 10%–11% of Asian and non-Hispanic white children. Similarly, among persons 65 years of age and over, almost one-fifth of Hispanic and one-quarter of black persons were poor, compared with 8% of non-Hispanic white persons and 14% of Asians. In 2002–2004, nearly one-quarter of American Indian or Alaska Native persons lived in poverty (estimate based on 3 years of data) (2).

References

1. Pamuk E, Makuc D, Heck K, Reuben C, Lochner K. Socioeconomic Status and Health Chartbook. Health, United States, 1998. Hyattsville, MD: National Center for Health Statistics. 1998.

2. DeNavas-Walt C, Proctor B, Hill LC. Income, poverty, and health insurance coverage in the United States: 2004. Current population reports, series P-60 no 229. Washington, DC: U.S. Government Printing Office. 2005. Available from: www.census.gov/prod/2005pubs/p60-229.pdf.

3. Hungerford T, Rassette M, Iams H, Koenig M. Trends in the economic status of the elderly. Social Security Bulletin 2001–2002; 64(3):12–22.

Figure 5. Low income by age, race, and Hispanic origin: United States, 2004

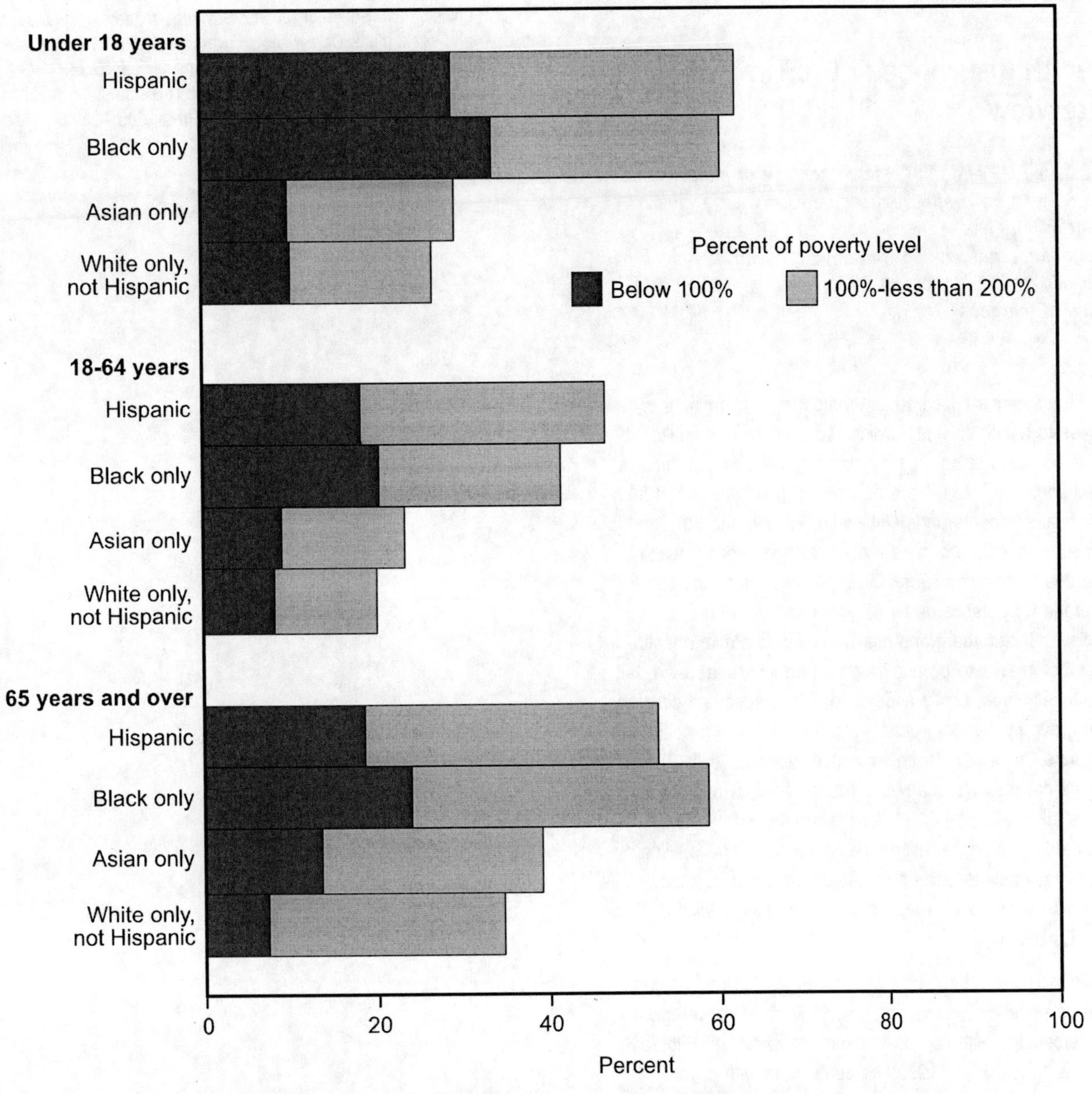

NOTES: Percent of poverty level is based on family income and family size and composition using U.S. Census Bureau poverty thresholds. Persons of Hispanic origin may be of any race. Black and Asian races include persons of Hispanic and non-Hispanic origin. See data table for data points graphed and additional notes.

SOURCE: U.S. Census Bureau, Current Population Survey.

Health Insurance and Expenditures

Health Insurance at the Time of Interview

Between 1999 and 2004, the percentage of people under age 65 with no health insurance coverage at a given point in time has remained between 16% and 17%, whereas the percentage with private health insurance has declined and public programs have expanded to fill in some of the gaps.

Health insurance coverage is an important determinant of access to health care (1). Uninsured children and adults under 65 years of age are substantially less likely to have a usual source of health care or a recent health care visit than their insured counterparts (Tables 76, 77, 79, and 80). Uninsured people are more likely to forego needed health care due to cost concerns (Table 78). The major source of coverage for persons under 65 years of age is private employer-sponsored group health insurance. Private health insurance may also be purchased on an individual basis, but is generally more costly and provides less adequate coverage than group insurance. Public programs such as Medicaid and the State Children's Health Insurance Program (SCHIP) provide coverage for many low-income children and adults. Almost all adults age 65 and over are covered by the Medicare program, resulting in very few older adults without health insurance. Medicare enrollees may have additional private or public coverage to supplement their Medicare benefit package.

Between 1984 and 1994, private coverage declined among persons under 65 years of age, while Medicaid coverage and the percentage with no health insurance increased (Figure 6). After rising to 73% in 1999, the percentage with private health insurance decreased reaching 69% between 2002 and 2004. This decrease was offset by an increase in the percentage with Medicaid, resulting in little change in the percentage uninsured.

Reference

1. Institute of Medicine. Committee on the consequences of uninsurance. Series of reports: Coverage matters: Insurance and health care; Care without coverage; Health insurance is a family matter; A shared destiny: Community effects of uninsurance; Hidden costs, value lost: Uninsurance in America. Washington, DC: National Academy Press. 2001–2003.

Figure 6. Health insurance coverage at the time of interview among persons under 65 years of age: United States, 1984-2004

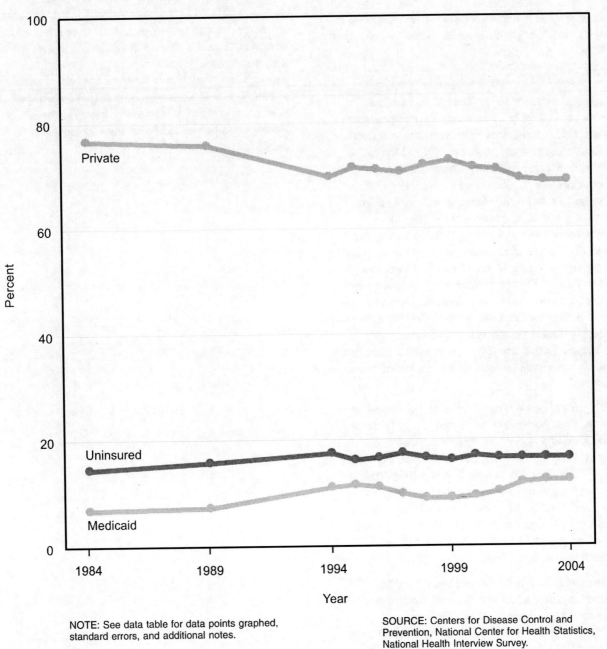

NOTE: See data table for data points graphed, standard errors, and additional notes.

SOURCE: Centers for Disease Control and Prevention, National Center for Health Statistics, National Health Interview Survey.

Length of Time Without Health Insurance

Persons of Mexican origin were more likely than those in other race/ethnicity groups to be uninsured for more than 12 months.

Many people under age 65, particularly those with low incomes, do not have health insurance coverage consistently throughout the year. Reasons for discontinuities in coverage may include loss or change of employment and financial reverses, divorce, births and other changes in life circumstances, and migration between states. Respondents to the National Health Interview Survey (NHIS) were asked whether they had health insurance at the time of their interview and the type of coverage. Those covered by health insurance at the time of interview were asked whether there was any time during the 12 months prior to the interview when they did not have health insurance. People who were uninsured at the time of interview were asked how long it had been since they last had health coverage. These questions provide estimates of the percentage of persons without coverage at a point in time (Figure 6), as well as estimates of the percentage without coverage for different lengths of time (Figure 7).

In 2004, 20% of people under 65 years of age reported being uninsured for at least part of the 12 months prior to interview. Among those who reported any time without insurance coverage during the 12 months prior to interview, the majority reported being uninsured for more than 12 months. About 11% of persons under 65 years reported being uninsured for more than 12 months, 8% reported being uninsured for any period up to 12 months, and 1% reported being uninsured and had missing data for the length of time they were uninsured (data table for Figure 7).

Children under 18 years of age were less likely to be uninsured than were adults, because low-income children are eligible for public programs such as SCHIP, designed specifically for them. The percentage of adults under 65 years of age without health insurance coverage decreased with age (Figure 7). In 2004, adults 18–24 years of age were more likely than adults age 55–64 years to lack coverage for at least part of the 12 months prior to interview (36% compared with 13%). About 20% of persons 18–24 years of age lacked coverage for more than 12 months.

People with family income below or near the poverty level were almost three times as likely to have no health insurance coverage for at least part of the 12 months prior to interview as those with family income twice the poverty level or higher, and were more than three times as likely to be uninsured for more than 12 months. Persons of Mexican origin were more likely than those in any other race/ethnicity group to be uninsured for at least part of the 12 months prior to interview. In 2004, 41% of Mexican-origin persons lacked coverage for at least part of the 12 months prior to interview with 32% of Mexican-origin persons lacking coverage for more than 12 months.

Figure 7. Uninsured for at least part of the 12 months prior to interview among persons under 65 years of age, by length of time uninsured and selected characteristics: United States, 2004

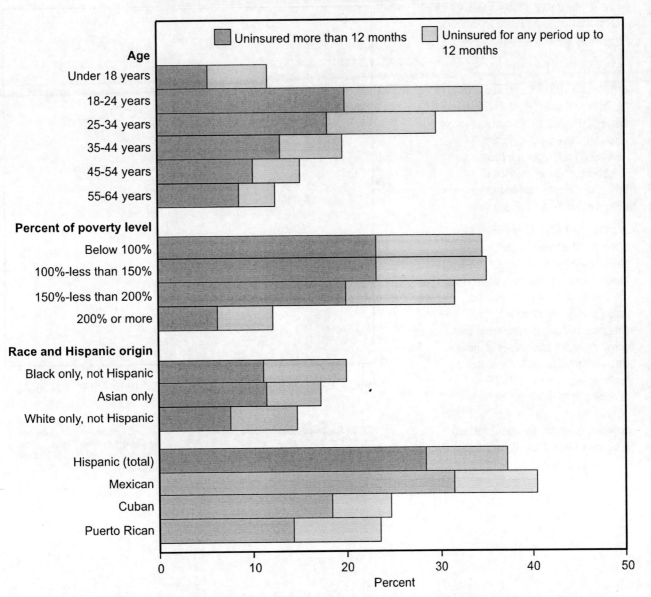

NOTES: Persons of Hispanic origin may be of any race. Asian and American Indian or Alaska Native races include persons of Hispanic and non-Hispanic origin. Percent of poverty level is based on family income and family size and composition using U.S. Census Bureau poverty thresholds. See data table for data points graphed, standard errors, and additional notes.

SOURCE: Centers for Disease Control and Prevention, National Center for Health Statistics, National Health Interview Survey.

Health Care Expenditures

In 2004, the United States spent $1.9 trillion on health care, comprising 16% of its Gross Domestic Product.

In 2004, the United States spent 16% (up from 14% in 2000) of its Gross Domestic Product (GDP) on health care, a greater share than any other developed country for which data are collected by the Organisation of Economic Co-operation and Development (Figure 8 and Tables 119 and 120).

In 2004, the United States spent $1.9 trillion on health care, an average of $6,280 per person (Table 120). Personal health care expenditures, a component of national health expenditures that includes spending for hospital care, physician services, nursing home care, dental care, and other types of medical care accounted for 83% of national health expenditures in 2004. The remaining 17% was spent on administration, government public health activities, research, and structures and equipment (Table 123) (1).

Figure 8. National health expenditures as a percentage of Gross Domestic Product: United States, 1960-2004

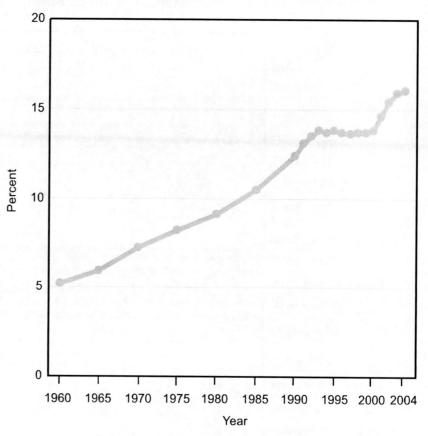

NOTE: See data table for data points graphed and additional notes.

SOURCE: Centers for Medicare & Medicaid Services, Office of the Actuary, National Health Statistics Group, National Health Accounts.

Health Care Expenditures *(Continued)*

Overall, private health insurance paid for 36% of total personal health expenditures in 2004, the federal government 34%, state and local government 11%, and out-of-pocket payments accounted for 15% (Figure 9). Since 1980, the share of total expenditures paid out-of-pocket declined by 12 percentage points (Table 124). This decline resulted from an expansion of benefits in both private health insurance plans and in government programs. Despite the decline in the share of health care expenditures paid out-of-pocket, the inflation in health care costs over recent years means that consumers may still have significant out-of-pocket expenditures for their health care.

In 2004, 37% of personal health care expenditures were for hospital care, 26% for physician care, 12% for prescription drugs, 7% for nursing home care, and the remaining 18% for other personal health care, including visits to nonphysician medical providers, medical supplies, and other health services (Figure 9). Since 1980, the share of total personal health care expenditures devoted to hospital care has declined by 9 percentage points and the prescription drug expenditure share has doubled, reflecting the shift in health care from inpatient to ambulatory care settings and the increasing contribution of prescription drugs to health care services and spending (Table 123).

Reference

1. Smith C, Cowan C, Heffler S, Catlin A. National health spending in 2004: recent slowdown led by prescription drug spending. Health Aff 2006;25(1):186–96.

Figure 9. Personal health care expenditures, by source of funds and type of expenditures: United States, 2004

Expenditures $1.6 trillion

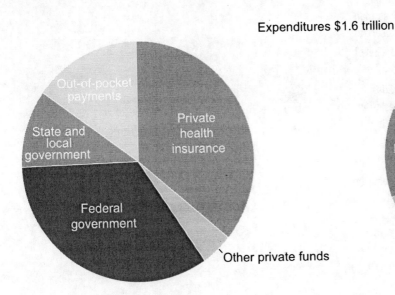

Source of funds

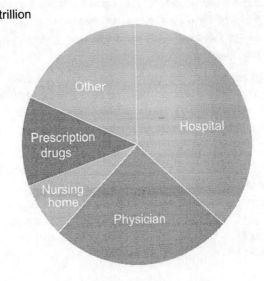

Type of expenditures

NOTE: See data table for data points graphed and additional notes.

SOURCE: Centers for Medicare & Medicaid Services, Office of the Actuary, National Health Statistics Group, National Health Accounts.

Health Risk Factors

Cigarette Smoking

Fewer Americans are smoking, but nearly one-fifth of women and one-quarter of men and high school students still are current smokers, as are 10% of pregnant women.

Smoking is associated with a significantly increased risk of heart disease, stroke, lung and other types of cancer, and chronic lung diseases (1). Decreasing cigarette smoking among adolescents and adults is a major public health objective for the Nation. Preventing smoking among teenagers and young adults is critical because smoking usually begins in adolescence (2). Smoking during pregnancy contributes to elevated risk of miscarriage, premature delivery, and having a low birthweight infant (3).

Following the first Surgeon General's Report on smoking in 1964, cigarette smoking declined sharply for men and at a slower pace for women (Figure 10). Since 1990, the percentage of men and women who smoke has declined more slowly. By 2004, 23% of men and 19% of women were smokers. Cigarette smoking by adults continues to be strongly associated with educational attainment. Adults with less than a high school education were almost three times as likely to smoke as those with a bachelor's degree or more education (Table 64).

Cigarette smoking among high school students in grades 9–12 decreased between 1997 and 2005 after increasing in the early 1990s. In 2005, 8% of high school students had used smokeless tobacco, 14% had smoked cigars, and 9% had smoked frequently in the past 30 days (4).

Among mothers with a live birth, the percentage reporting on the birth certificate that they smoked cigarettes during pregnancy declined between 1989 and 2004 from 20% to 10%. Maternal smoking has declined for all racial and ethnic groups, but differences among these groups persist (Table 12).

References

1. U.S. Department of Health and Human Services. The health consequences of smoking: A report of the Surgeon General. Atlanta, GA: Centers for Disease Control and Prevention; 2004. Available from: www.cdc.gov/tobacco/sgr/sgr_2004/index.htm.

2. U.S. Department of Health and Human Services. Preventing tobacco use among young people: A report of the Surgeon General. Atlanta, GA: Centers for Disease Control and Prevention; 1994. Available from: www.cdc.gov/tobacco/sgr/sgr_1994/.

3. Mathews TJ. Smoking during pregnancy in the 1990s. National vital statistics reports 2001;49(7). Hyattsville, MD: National Center for Health Statistics. 2001. Available from: www.cdc.gov/nchs/data/nvsr/nvsr49/nvsr49_07.pdf.

4. Centers for Disease Control and Prevention. Youth Risk Behavior Surveillance—United States, 2005. MMWR 2006;55(SS-5):1–33.

Figure 10. Cigarette smoking among men, women, high school students, and mothers during pregnancy: United States, 1965-2005

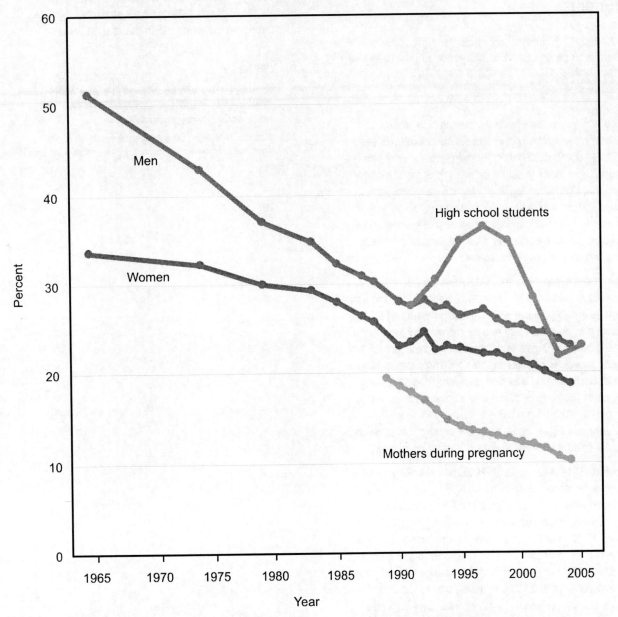

NOTES: Estimates for men and women are age adjusted. Cigarette smoking is defined as: (for men and women 18 years of age and over) at least 100 cigarettes in lifetime and now smoke every day or some days; (for students in grades 9–12) 1 or more cigarettes in the 30 days preceding the survey; and (for mothers with a live birth) during pregnancy. See data table for data points graphed, standard errors, and additional notes.

SOURCES: Centers for Disease Control and Prevention, National Center for Health Statistics, National Health Interview Survey (data for men and women); National Vital Statistics System (data for mothers during pregnancy); National Center for Chronic Disease Prevention and Health Promotion, Youth Risk Behavior Survey (data for high school students).

Binge Drinking and Current Marijuana Use Among High School Students

In 2005, 30% of high school students in grades 11–12 reported binge drinking and 22% reported marijuana use in the past 30 days.

Binge drinking and marijuana use among high school students have serious consequences. Alcohol use has been related to academic difficulties, social problems, risky sexual behavior, and motor vehicle accidents (1). Some studies have found that high school students who use marijuana get lower grades and are less likely to graduate than students who do not use marijuana (2). Tracking changes in binge drinking and marijuana use is important for evaluating efforts to prevent these behaviors among adolescents.

Estimates from the 1991 and 2003 Youth Risk Behavior Surveys are presented for students in grades 9–10, and from the 1993 and 2005 surveys for students in grades 11–12. Presentation of these years of data shows changes in binge drinking and marijuana use as students progress through high school, as well as changes in these behaviors over a 12-year period. Binge drinking was measured by asking students if they drank five or more drinks of alcohol in a row on one or more of the 30 days preceding the survey and current marijuana use by asking students if they used marijuana one or more times during the 30 days preceding the survey.

Between 1991–1993 and 2003–2005, binge drinking by male students decreased, while binge drinking by female students remained relatively stable (Figure 11). Among male students, binge drinking increased markedly between grades 9–10 and grades 11–12 in both time periods. Among female students, binge drinking increased between grades 9–10 and grades 11–12 in 1991–1993, but showed little change by grade level in 2003–2005. In 2005, 33% of male students and 27% of female students in grades 11–12 reported binge drinking in the past 30 days.

Between 1991–1993 and 2003–2005, current marijuana use increased among students in grades 9–10, but marijuana use remained unchanged among students in grades 11–12 (data table for Figure 11). Marijuana use increased markedly among both male and female students between grades 9–10 and grades 11–12 in 1991–1993, but showed little change by

grade level in 2003–2005 (Figure 11). Marijuana use by students in grades 9–10 in 2003 was similar to marijuana use by students in grades 11–12 ten years earlier. In 2005, 25% of male students and 19% of female students in grades 11–12 reported marijuana use in the past 30 days.

References

1. Substance Abuse and Mental Health Services Administration. Consequences of underage alcohol use. Available from: ncadi.samhsa.gov/govpubs/rpo992/.

2. National Institute on Drug Abuse. InfoFacts: Marijuana. Available from: www.drugabuse.gov/Infofacts/marijuana.html/.

Figure 11. Binge drinking and current marijuana use among high school students, by sex, grade level, and year: United States, 1991, 1993, 2003, and 2005

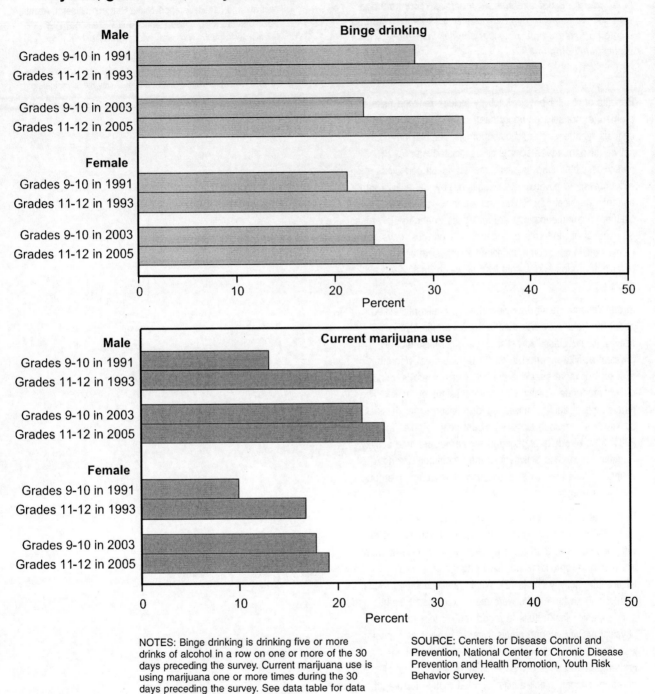

NOTES: Binge drinking is drinking five or more drinks of alcohol in a row on one or more of the 30 days preceding the survey. Current marijuana use is using marijuana one or more times during the 30 days preceding the survey. See data table for data points graphed and standard errors.

SOURCE: Centers for Disease Control and Prevention, National Center for Chronic Disease Prevention and Health Promotion, Youth Risk Behavior Survey.

Physical Activity

Most adults do not exercise as much as recommended, with people living in or near poverty less likely to engage in regular leisure-time physical activity than those with higher family income.

Benefits of regular physical activity include reduced risks of premature mortality, coronary heart disease, diabetes, colon cancer, hypertension, and osteoporosis. Regular physical activity also improves symptoms associated with musculoskeletal conditions and mental health conditions such as depression and anxiety. In addition, physical activity can enhance physical functioning and aid in weight control (1). National recommendations are for adults to engage in at least 30 minutes of moderate physical activity on most days of the week. Additional recommendations for physical activity target older age groups and weight loss or weight maintenance goals (2).

In the National Health Interview Survey, adults are asked about the frequency and duration of leisure-time physical activity. Adults classified as having regular leisure-time physical activity reported at least 20 minutes of vigorous activity 3 or more sessions per week or at least 30 minutes of light/moderate activity 5 or more sessions per week. The percentage of adults who engaged in leisure-time physical activity has remained stable in recent years (Table 72). In 2004, 30% of adults engaged in regular leisure-time activity. Regular leisure-time activity was more common among younger adults than older adults and more common among men than women.

Regular leisure-time physical activity levels vary by poverty and race and ethnicity (Figure 12). Adults living in families with income more than twice poverty were about 60% more likely than lower-income adults to engage in regular leisure-time activity (Table 72). Within family income groups, non-Hispanic white adults were more likely than Hispanic and non-Hispanic black adults to report regular leisure-time physical activity. Among adults living in families with income less than twice the poverty level, 24% to 25% of non-Hispanic white adults compared with 16% to 18% of Hispanic and non-Hispanic black adults reported regular leisure-time physical activity (percents are age adjusted).

References

1.   U.S. Department of Health and Human Services. Physical activity and health: A report of the Surgeon General. Atlanta, GA: Centers for Disease Control and Prevention. 1996. Available from: www.cdc.gov/nccdphp/sgr/sgr.htm.

2.   U.S. Department of Health and Human Services and U.S. Department of Agriculture. Dietary Guidelines for Americans, 2005. Available from: www.healthierus.gov/dietaryguidelines/.

Figure 12. Regular leisure-time physical activity among adults 18 years of age and over, by percent of poverty level, race and Hispanic origin: United States, 2004

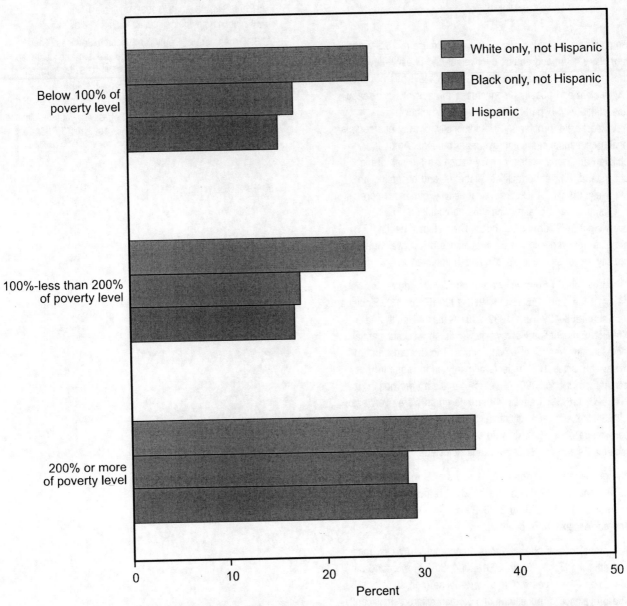

NOTES: Data are for the civilian noninstitutionalized population and are age adjusted. Adults classified with regular leisure-time physical activity reported 3 or more sessions per week of vigorous activity of at least 20 minutes duration or 5 or more sessions per week of light/moderate activity lasting at least 30 minutes in duration. Percent of poverty level is based on family income and family size and composition using U.S. Census Bureau poverty thresholds. See data table for data points graphed, standard errors, and additional notes.

SOURCE: Centers for Disease Control and Prevention, National Center for Health Statistics, National Health Interview Survey.

Overweight and Obesity

Two-thirds of American adults are overweight and one-third are obese.

Surplus body weight is associated with excess morbidity and mortality (1). Among adults, overweight and obesity elevate the risk of heart disease, diabetes, and some types of cancer. Overweight and obesity also increase the severity of disease associated with hypertension, arthritis, and other musculoskeletal problems (2). Additionally, obesity has serious health consequences among younger persons. Among children and adolescents, obesity increases the risk of high cholesterol, liver abnormalities, diabetes, and becoming an overweight adult (3). Diet, physical activity, genetic factors, environment, and health conditions all contribute to overweight in children and adults. The potential health benefits from reduction in the prevalence of overweight and obesity are of significant public health importance.

The prevalence of overweight and obesity changed little between the early 1960s and 1976–1980 (Figure 13). Findings from the 1988–1994 and 1999–2004 National Health and Nutrition Examination Surveys, however, showed substantial increases in overweight among adults. The upward trend in overweight since 1980 reflects primarily an increase in the percentage of adults 20–74 years of age who are obese. In 2003–2004, 67% of adults in that age group were overweight with 34% obese (age adjusted). Since 1960–1962, the percentage of adults who were overweight but not obese has remained steady at 32%–34% (age adjusted).

The percentage of children (6–11 years of age) and adolescents (12–19 years of age) who are overweight has risen since 1976–1980. In 2003–2004, 17%–19% of children and adolescents were overweight.

The prevalence of obesity varies among adults by sex, race, and ethnicity (Table 73). In 2001–2004, 30% of men and 34% of women 20–74 years of age were obese (age adjusted). The prevalence of obesity among women differed significantly by racial and ethnic group. In 2001–2004, one-half of non-Hispanic black women were obese compared with nearly one-third of non-Hispanic white women. In contrast, the prevalence of obesity among men was similar by race and ethnicity.

References

1. National Institutes of Health. Clinical guidelines on the identification, evaluation, and treatment of overweight and obesity in adults: The evidence report. NIH Pub. No. 98–4083. 1998. Available from: www.nhlbi.nih.gov/guidelines/obesity/ob_gdlns.htm.

2. U.S. Department of Health and Human Services. The Surgeon General's call to action to prevent and decrease overweight and obesity. Rockville, MD: U.S. Department of Health and Human Services; 2001. Available from: www.surgeongeneral.gov/topics/obesity/.

3. Dietz WH. Health consequences of obesity in youth: Childhood predictors of adult disease. Pediatrics 1998;101(3 Pt 2): 518–25.

Figure 13. Overweight and obesity, by age: United States, 1960-2004

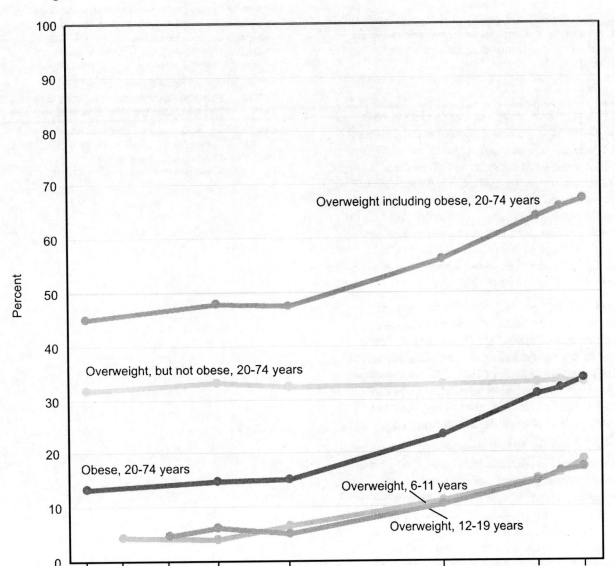

NOTES: Estimates for adults are age adjusted. For adults: overweight including obese is defined as a body mass index (BMI) greater than or equal to 25, overweight but not obese as a BMI greater than or equal to 25 but less than 30, and obese as a BMI greater than or equal to 30. For children: overweight is defined as a BMI at or above the sex- and age-specific 95th percentile BMI cut points from the 2000 CDC Growth Charts: United States. Obese is not defined for children. See data table for data points graphed, standard errors, and additional notes.

SOURCES: Centers for Disease Control and Prevention, National Center for Health Statistics, National Health Examination Survey and National Health and Nutrition Examination Survey.

Untreated Dental Caries

Throughout the period 1971–1974 to 1999–2002, children of Mexican origin and non-Hispanic black children had a higher prevalence of untreated dental caries than non-Hispanic white children.

Dental caries, or tooth decay, is caused by bacteria and is one of the most common chronic diseases in young children. If left untreated, it can cause pain, infection, and even loss of teeth (1). Good oral hygiene, including tooth brushing, flossing, regular professional cleaning, and the application of dental sealants can help prevent damage caused by dental caries. The progression of caries can be stopped by treatment. Once destroyed, tooth structure does not regenerate. Although primary or baby teeth are eventually replaced by permanent teeth, early childhood caries is a major predictor of caries in later years (2).

Between 1971–1974 and 1988–1994, the percentage of children with untreated dental caries declined, especially among children 6–17 years of age. This decline was largely due to fluoridation of the water supply and to topically applied fluoride treatments (1,2,3). Since 1988–1994, the percentage of children with untreated dental caries has not significantly changed, except for a decrease among non-Hispanic black children 6–17 years of age (data table for Figure 14).

Throughout the period 1971–1974 to 1999–2002, children of Mexican origin and non-Hispanic black children had a higher prevalence of untreated caries than non-Hispanic white children (Figure 14). In 1999–2002, Mexican children 6–17 years of age had untreated dental caries almost twice as frequently as non-Hispanic white children of the same age. Non-Hispanic black school-age children were 58% more likely to have untreated dental caries than non-Hispanic white children.

References

1. Centers for Disease Control and Prevention. Surveillance for dental caries, dental sealants, tooth retention, edentulism, and enamel fluorosis—United States, 1988–1994 and 1999–2002. MMWR 54(SS-3):1–44. 2005. Available from: www.cdc.gov/mmwr/preview/mmwrhtml/ss5403a1.htm.

2. National Institutes of Health Consensus Development Conference Statement. Diagnosis and management of dental caries throughout life. J Dent Educ 2001;65(10):1162–8.

3. Centers for Disease Control and Prevention. Ten great public health achievements—United States, 1900–1999. MMWR 48(12):241–3. 1999. Available from: www.cdc.gov/mmwr/preview/mmwrhtml/00056796.htm.

Figure 14. Untreated dental caries among children, by age, race and Hispanic origin: United States, 1971-2002

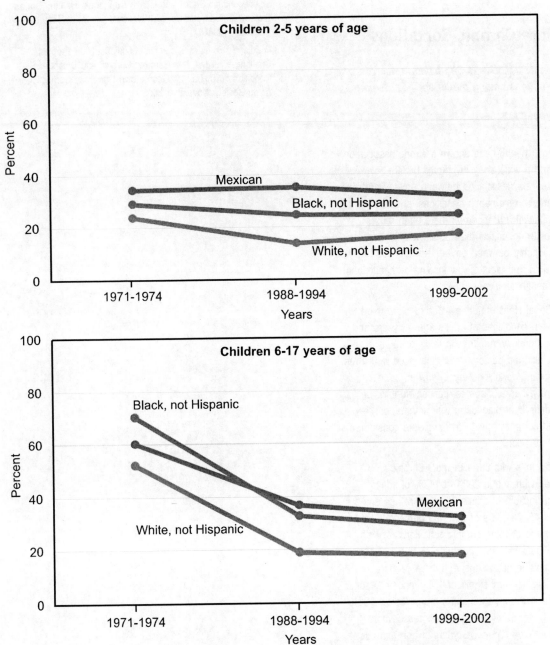

NOTES: Persons of Mexican origin may be of any race. See data table for data points graphed, standard errors, and additional notes.

SOURCE: Centers for Disease Control and Prevention, National Center for Health Statistics, National Health and Nutrition Examination Survey.

Morbidity and Limitation of Activity

Three or More Chronic Conditions

Poverty was strongly associated with having three or more chronic conditions among adults age 45–74 years in 2004.

Many studies of adult health have shown a strong association between poverty and a wide array of chronic health conditions (1). Given the association between poverty and the risk factors for many chronic health conditions, it is not surprising that adults with low incomes more often report multiple serious health conditions than adults with higher incomes. The relationship between poverty and serious health problems reflects both the effect of low income on health and the effect of poor health on income (1,2).

Data from the National Health Interview Survey were used to assess chronic health conditions of adults age 45 years and over living in the community. Adults with three or more chronic conditions included persons ever diagnosed with three or more of the following conditions: hypertension, heart disease, stroke, emphysema, diabetes, cancer, arthritis, or asthma. Among adults ever diagnosed with asthma, only those who reported currently having asthma were considered to have a chronic condition.

The percentage of adults with three or more chronic conditions increased with age in 2004 from 7% of adults 45–54 years of age to 36% of adults 75 years of age and over. Among adults 45–74 years of age, the percentage of persons reporting three or more chronic conditions rose as income declined (Figure 15). Among adults 75 years of age and over, the percentage of persons with three or more chronic conditions did not vary significantly by income. Adults 55–64 years of age in the lowest income group (below 100% of the poverty level) were as likely to have three or more chronic conditions as older adults 75 years of age and over in the highest income group (400% or more of the poverty level).

References

1. Pamuk E, Makuc D, Heck K, Reuben C, Lochner K. Socioeconomic Status and Health Chartbook. Health, United States, 1998. Hyattsville, MD: National Center for Health Statistics. 1998.

2. Freidland RB. Multiple chronic conditions. Data Profiles, Challenges for the 21st Century: Chronic and Disabling Conditions: Number 12. Georgetown University Center on an Aging Society. November 2003.

Figure 15. Three or more chronic conditions among adults 45 years of age and over, by age and percent of poverty level: United States, 2004

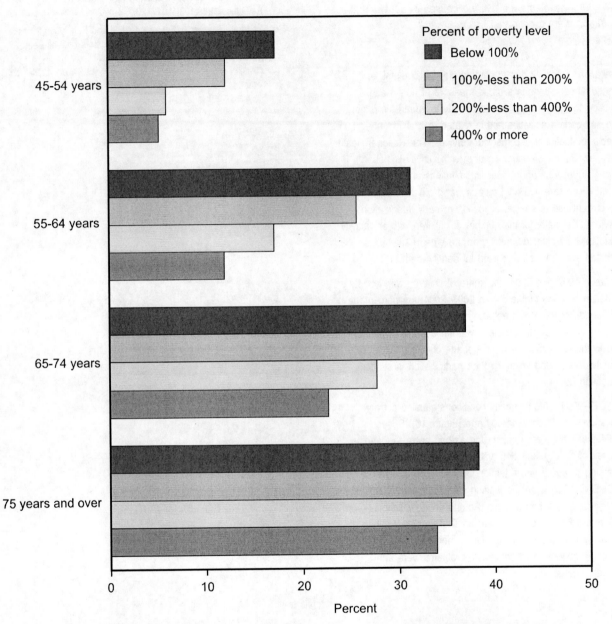

NOTES: Adults who had ever been told by a physician they had 3 or more of the following conditions: hypertension, heart disease, stroke, emphysema, diabetes, cancer, arthritis and related diseases, or current asthma. Percent of poverty level is based on family income and family size and composition using U.S. Census Bureau poverty thresholds. See data table for data points graphed, standard errors, and additional notes.

SOURCE: Centers for Disease Control and Prevention, National Center for Health Statistics, National Health Interview Survey.

Limitation of Activity: Children

Conditions associated with learning, emotional, and behavioral problems are leading causes of activity limitation among children.

Limitation of activity due to chronic physical, mental, or emotional conditions is a broad measure of health and functioning that gauges a child's ability to engage in major age-appropriate activities and is related to a child's need for special educational and medical services. The National Health Interview Survey identifies children with activity limitation through questions about specific limitations in activities such as play, self-care, walking, memory, and other activities, and the current use of special education or early intervention services. Estimates of the number of children with an activity limitation may differ depending on the type of limitations included and the methods used to identify them (1).

Between 1997 and 2004, the share of children with activity limitation was 7% (Table 58). In 2003–2004, the percentage of school-age children with activity limitation (8%) was double the percentage of preschoolers with limitation (4%) primarily due to the large number of school-age children who were identified as limited solely by their participation in special education (2).

In 2003–2004, chronic health conditions causing activity limitation in children varied by age (Figure 16). Speech problems, mental retardation, and asthma were the leading causes of activity limitation among preschool children. Learning disability and Attention Deficit/Hyperactivity Disorder (ADHD or ADD) were the leading causes of activity limitation among all school-age children. Among younger school-age children, speech problems were another important cause of activity limitation and among older school-age children, other mental, emotional, and behavioral problems were an important cause.

References

1. Newacheck PW, Strickland B, Shonkoff JP, et al. An epidemiologic profile of children with special health care needs. Pediatrics 1998;102(1):117–23.

2. Federal Interagency Forum on Child and Family Statistics. America's Children: Key National Indicators of Well-Being, 2005. Washington, D.C. 2005.

Figure 16. Selected chronic health conditions causing limitation of activity among children, by age: United States, 2003-2004

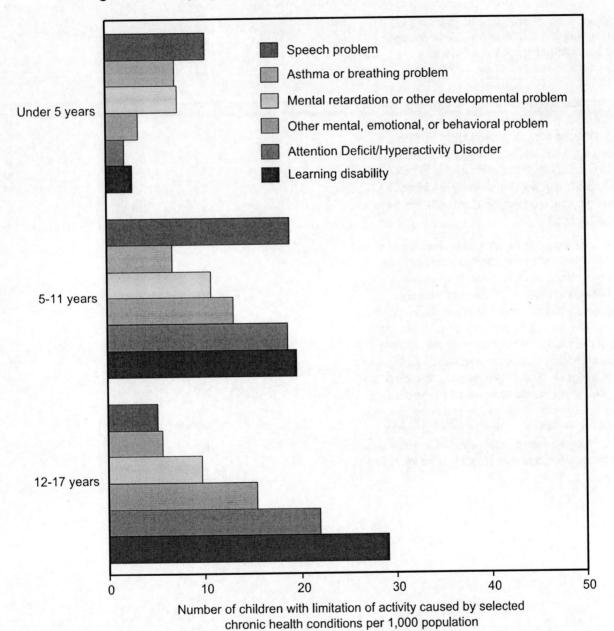

NOTES: Children with more than one chronic health condition causing activity limitation are counted in each category. See data table for data points graphed, standard errors, and additional notes.

SOURCE: Centers for Disease Control and Prevention, National Center for Health Statistics, National Health Interview Survey.

Limitation of Activity: Working-Age and Older Adults

Arthritis and other musculoskeletal conditions are the most frequently reported cause of activity limitation among both working-age and older adults.

Chronic physical, mental, and emotional conditions can limit the ability of adults to carry out important activities such as working and doing everyday household chores. With advancing age, an increasing percentage of adults experience limitation of activity. Estimates of the number of working-age and older adults with limitation of activity are important for determining current and future types of health care needs and associated costs (1).

Between 1997 and 2004, the percentage of working-age adults 18–64 years of age reporting an activity limitation caused by a chronic health condition remained relatively stable (Table 58). In 2003–2004, the percentage of working-age adults who reported limitations ranged from 6% at age 18–44 years to 21% at age 55–64 years (2). Arthritis and other musculoskeletal conditions were the most frequently mentioned conditions causing limitation among working-age adults of all ages in 2003–2004 (Figure 17). Among adults 18–44 years of age, mental illness was the second leading cause of activity limitation followed by fractures or joint injury. Among adults 45–64 years of age, heart and circulatory conditions were the second leading cause of limitation. Other frequently mentioned conditions included mental illness and diabetes.

Figure 17. Selected chronic health conditions causing limitation of activity among working-age adults, by age: United States, 2003-2004

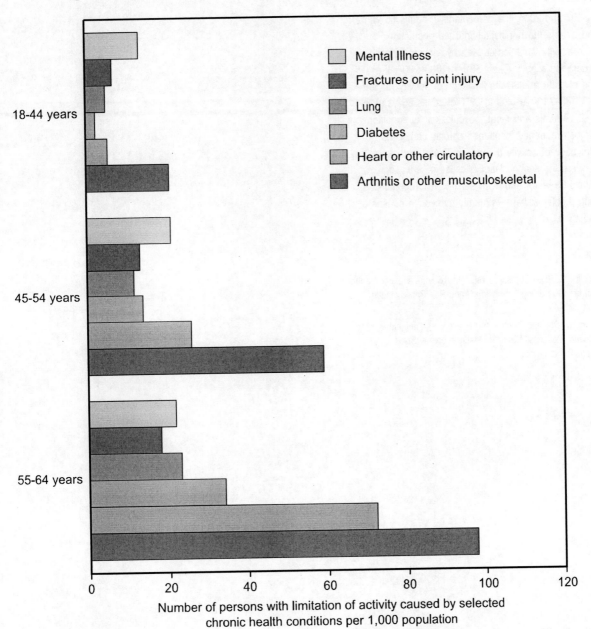

Number of persons with limitation of activity caused by selected chronic health conditions per 1,000 population

Legend:
- Mental Illness
- Fractures or joint injury
- Lung
- Diabetes
- Heart or other circulatory
- Arthritis or other musculoskeletal

NOTES: Data are for the civilian noninstitutionalized population. Persons may report more than one chronic health condition as the cause of their activity limitation. See data table for data points graphed, standard errors, and additional notes.

SOURCE: Centers for Disease Control and Prevention, National Center for Health Statistics, National Health Interview Survey.

Limitation of Activity: Working-Age and Older Adults *(Continued)*

Between 1997 and 2004, the percentage of adults 65 years of age and over in the noninstitutionalized population reporting an activity limitation caused by a chronic health condition declined slightly (Table 58). In 2003–2004, the percentage of older adults with limitation of activity ranged from 26% of 65–74 year olds to 62% of adults 85 years old and over (2). Arthritis and other musculoskeletal conditions were the most frequently mentioned chronic conditions causing limitation of activity (Figure 18). Heart and circulatory conditions were the second leading cause of limitations. Among adults 85 years and over, senility, vision conditions, and hearing problems were frequently mentioned causes of activity limitation.

References

1. Guralnik JM, Fried LP, Salive ME. Disability as a public health outcome in the aging population. Annu Rev Public Health 1996;17:25–46.

2. Centers for Disease Control and Prevention, National Center for Health Statistics, National Health Interview Survey, unpublished analysis.

Figure 18. Selected chronic health conditions causing limitation of activity among older adults, by age: United States, 2003-2004

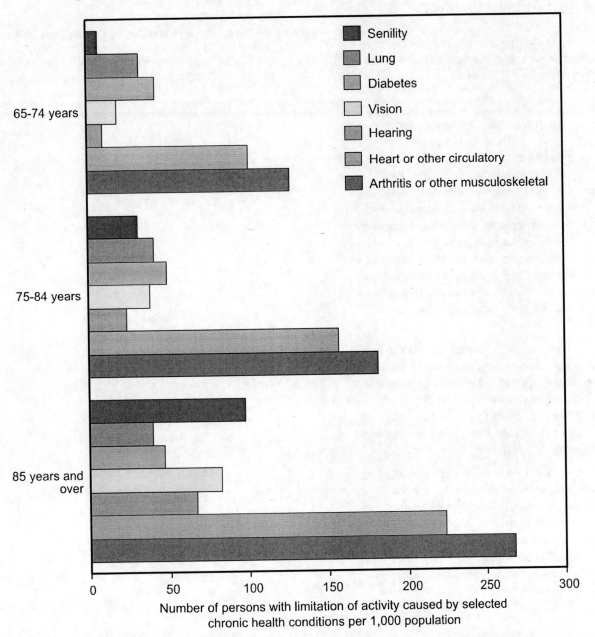

Number of persons with limitation of activity caused by selected chronic health conditions per 1,000 population

NOTES: Data are for the civilian noninstitutionalized population. Persons may report more than one chronic health condition as the cause of their activity limitation. See data table for data points graphed, standard errors, and additional notes.

SOURCE: Centers for Disease Control and Prevention, National Center for Health Statistics, National Health Interview Survey.

Health Care Utilization

Dental Visit Among Children

Hispanic children 6–17 years of age are less likely to have a recent dental visit than children in other racial and ethnic groups.

The American Dental Association recommends that children see a dentist for the first time within 6 months of the appearance of the first tooth and no later than the child's first birthday (1). The American Academy of Pediatric Dentistry also recommends that all children should visit a dentist in their first year of life and every 6 months thereafter, or as indicated by the individual child's risk status or susceptibility to disease (2). Attitudes and habits established at an early age are critical in maintaining good oral health throughout life. Benefits of early dental intervention include assessment of risk status, analysis of fluoride exposure and feeding practices, such as excessive sugar consumption, and oral hygiene counseling.

Preschool children 2–5 years of age are less likely to have a recent dental visit than school-age children 6–17 years of age (Figure 19). On average, 54% of preschool-age children had a dental visit in the past year compared with 84% of school-age children in 2004 (data table for Figure 19). No difference in the recent use of dental visits among preschool-age children was noted by race and ethnicity.

In contrast to younger children, the proportion of school-age children with a recent dental visit varies by race and ethnicity (Figure 19). Among school-age children 6–17 years of age, Hispanic children had lower levels of recent dental visits than children in other racial and ethnic groups. Non-Hispanic black and Mexican-origin children were more likely to have untreated dental caries than non-Hispanic white children (Figure 14 and Table 75).

References:

1. American Dental Association. ADA statement on early childhood caries. 2000. Available from: www.ada.org/prof/resources/positions/statements/caries.asp.

2. American Academy of Pediatric Dentistry. Guideline on periodicity of examination, preventive dental services, anticipatory guidance, and oral treatment for children. Available from: www.aapd.org/media/Policies_Guidelines/G_Periodicity.pdf.

1135466

Figure 19. Dental visit in the past year among children, by age, race and Hispanic origin: United States, 2004

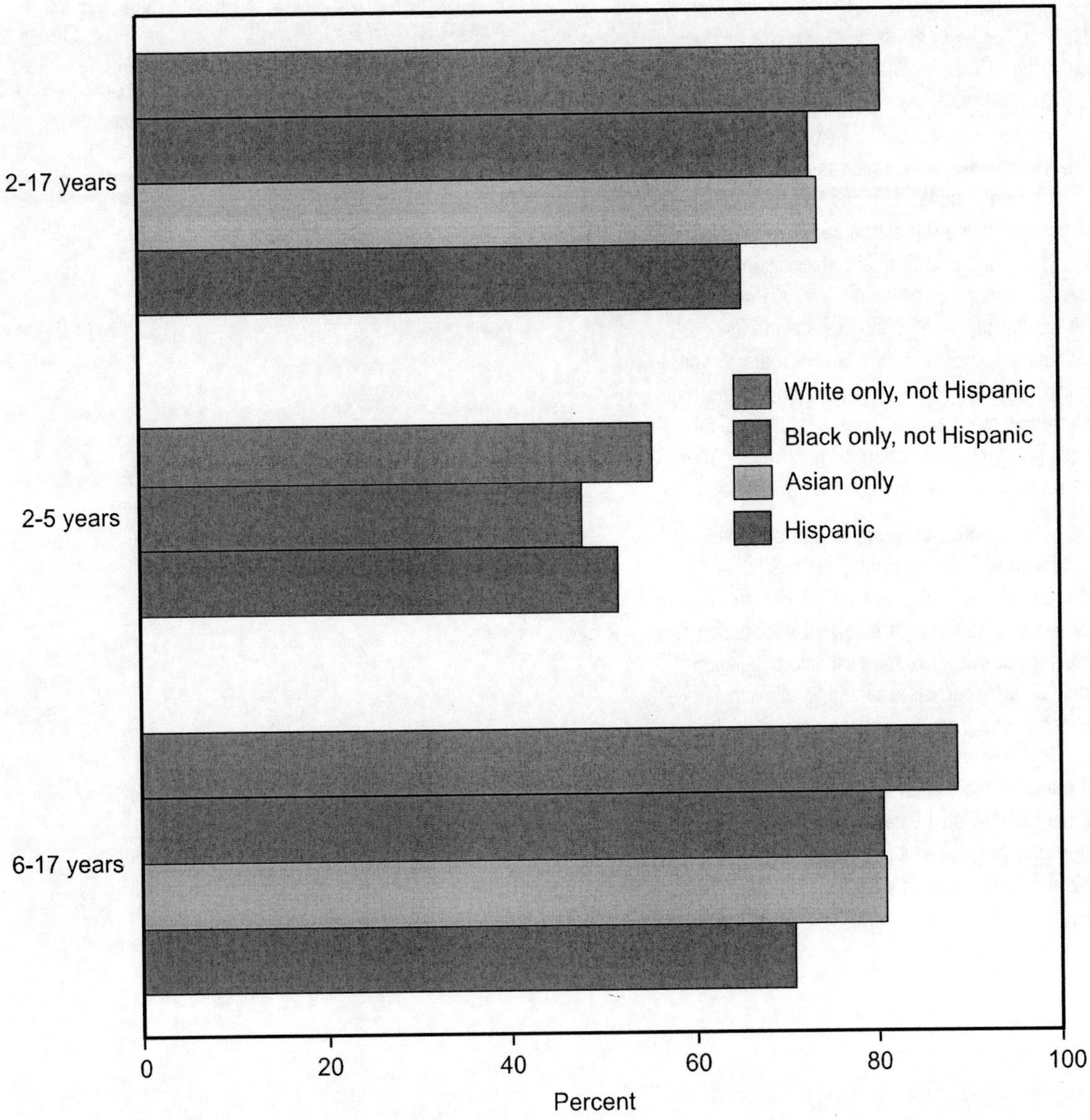
2-17 years
2-5 years
6-17 years
White only, not Hispanic
Black only, not Hispanic
Asian only
Hispanic
0
20
40
60
80
100
Percent

NOTES: Asian race includes children of Hispanic and non-Hispanic origin. Data for Asian children 2–5 years of age are not shown because they are not reliable. See data table for data points graphed, standard errors, and additional notes.

SOURCE: Centers for Disease Control and Prevention, National Center for Health Statistics, National Health Interview Survey.

Influenza Vaccination: Adults 50 Years of Age and Over

Non-Hispanic black and Hispanic adults age 50 and over were less likely to receive influenza vaccinations than non-Hispanic white adults in 2003–2004.

Annual influenza vaccination can lessen the risk of hospitalization and death among persons 65 years of age and over and also prevent influenza-related complications for persons 18–64 years of age with medical conditions (1). In 2000, the Advisory Committee on Immunization Practices (ACIP) broadened the universal recommendations for influenza vaccination to include adults 50–64 years of age, in addition to adults 65 years of age and over, due to the high prevalence of chronic medical conditions in adults 50–64 years of age (2). In 2003–2004, about 64% of adults 50–64 years of age had one or more chronic medical conditions (3).

In 2003–2004, 65% of adults 65 years of age and over reported an influenza vaccination during the preceding 12 months, compared with 36% of adults 50–64 years of age (data table for Figure 20). Although influenza vaccination rates have increased for non-Hispanic and Hispanic population groups, substantial gaps persist by race and ethnicity (Table 83). Influenza vaccination coverage among adults 50–64 years of age was about 30% lower for non-Hispanic blacks and Hispanic persons than non-Hispanic white persons (Figure 20). Similarly, influenza vaccination rates among adults 65 years of age and over were about 30% lower for non-Hispanic blacks and Hispanic persons than for non-Hispanic whites.

References

1. Hak E, Buskens E, van Essen GA, et al. Clinical effectiveness of influenza vaccination in persons younger than 65 years with high-risk medical conditions: the PRISMA study. Arch Intern Med 2005;165:274–80.

2. Centers for Disease Control and Prevention. Prevention and Control of Influenza. Recommendations of the Advisory Committee on Immunization Practices (ACIP). MMWR 2000;49(RR03):1–38.

3. Centers for Disease Control and Prevention. National Center for Health Statistics, National Health Interview Survey, unpublished analysis.

Figure 20. Influenza vaccination during the past year among adults 50 years of age and over, by race and Hispanic origin: United States, 2003-2004

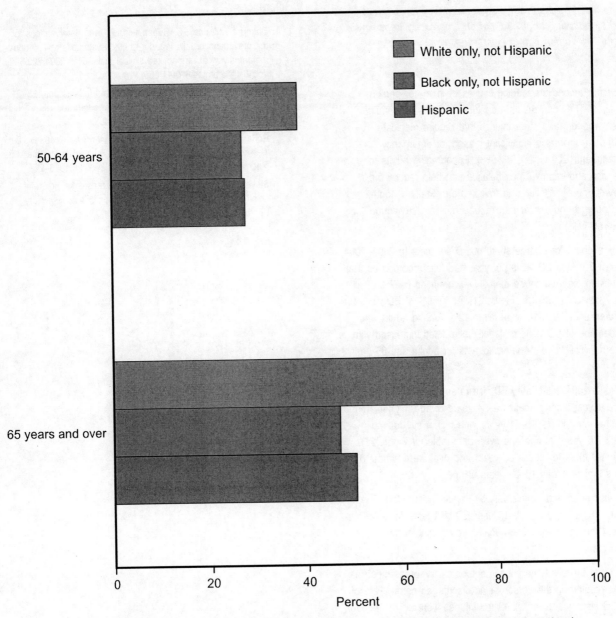

NOTES: Data are for the civilian noninstitutionalized population. Persons of Hispanic origin may be of any race. See data table for data points graphed, standard errors, and additional notes.

SOURCE: Centers for Disease Control and Prevention, National Center for Health Statistics, National Health Interview Survey.

Emergency Department Visits for Falls

Falls are the reason for many emergency department visits, including about 20% of all emergency department visits for women age 85 years and over.

Falls are among the leading causes of injury for persons of all ages. They can result in fractures, sprains and strains, open wounds, and other injuries that require medical treatment and are a significant reason for emergency department (ED) visits (Table 88). Encouraging adults to exercise and improve their balance can help reduce the prevalence of falls among frail seniors. Making homes and playgrounds safer can reduce falls among young children (1,2).

Falls account for a large share of ED services. In 2002–2004, almost 8 million ED visits per year had falls recorded as their first-listed external cause of injury—accounting for 7% of all ED visits (data table for Figure 21). About 8% of ED visits for children under age 18 were fall-related. Among adults, the percentage of ED visits that were fall-related increased with age from 5% at 18–44 years to 18% for adults age 85 years and over.

In 2002–2004, fall-related ED visit rates per 10,000 population were lowest among adults 18–64 years of age, higher among children and adults 65–74 years, and higher still among adults 75 years of age and over (data table for Figure 21). Fall visit rates for adults 85 years and over were almost 8 times that of adults 18–64 years of age.

ED visit rates due to falls vary by gender (Figure 21). Boys under 18 years of age had higher ED visit rates for falls than girls. Starting at age 45–64 years, women had higher rates than men.

ED visits for falls have varying outcomes. Whereas most fall visits resulted in the person being discharged home, 12% of all ED visits made for fall-related injuries were severe enough to result in hospitalization, transfer to another hospital or health care facility, or death in the ED. Among men and women age 85 and over, ED visits for falls were more likely to have a severe outcome than visits for younger persons. Fracture of the hip and other lower extremities are among the most common types of fall-related injuries that resulted in hospitalization among older adults (3). Loss of bone mass

that occurs disproportionately in post-menopausal women may explain, in part, women's greater rate of hip fracture (4).

References

1. Chang JT, Morton SC, Rubenstein LZ, et al. Interventions for the prevention of falls in older adults: Systematic review and meta-analysis of randomized clinical trials. BMJ 2004;328:680, doi:10.1136/bmj.328.7441.680.

2. McDonald E, Girasek D, Gielen A. Home Injuries pp. 123–61 in K. Liller (Ed), Injury Prevention for Children and Adolescents. APHA: Washington, DC. 2006.

3. Roudsari BS, Ebel BE, Corso PS, Molinari NM, Koepsell TD. The acute medical costs of fall-related injuries among the U.S. older adults. Injury, Int. J Care Injured 2005;26:1316–22.

4. Stevens JA, Sogolow ED. Gender differences for non-fatal unintentional fall-related injuries among older adults. Injury Prevention 2005;11:115–9.

Figure 21. Emergency department visits for falls, by sex and age: United States, 2002-2004

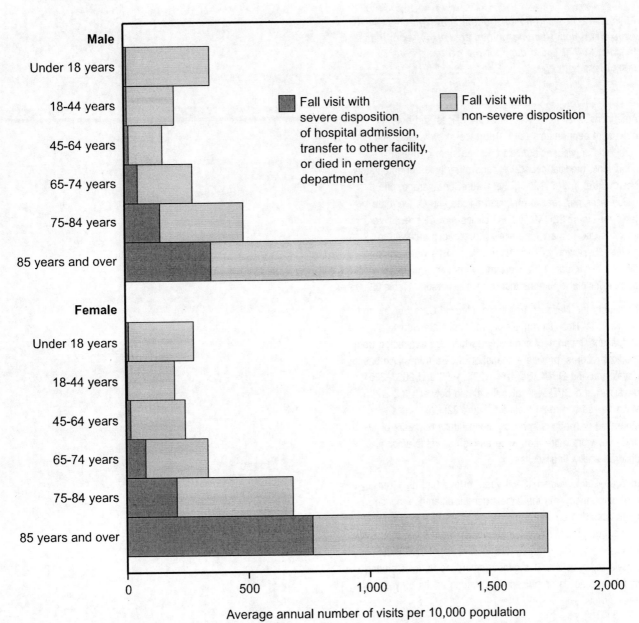

NOTES: Visits with a severe disposition for males 65–74 years and females 44 years or younger have a relative standard error of 20%–30%. See data table for data points graphed, standard errors, and additional notes.

SOURCE: Centers for Disease Control and Prevention, National Center for Health Statistics, National Hospital Ambulatory Medical Care Survey.

Visits to Physician Offices and Hospital Outpatient Departments

Physician office and hospital outpatient department visit rates were higher among women age 18–44 years than for men in that age group, but the gender difference disappears with age.

Americans of all ages visit physician offices and hospital outpatient departments (OPDs) to receive preventive and screening services, diagnosis and treatment of health conditions, medical counseling, and other types of ambulatory health care. In 2003–2004, there were, on average, one billion visits per year to physician offices and OPDs (data table for Figure 22). Many OPD clinics provide preventive services and primary care similar to services received in private physicians' offices. About 8% of visits were made in OPDs overall, but OPDs were more frequently used as sites of care for black persons than for white persons (Table 89).

Data from the National Ambulatory Medical Care Survey and the National Hospital Ambulatory Medical Care Survey Outpatient Department component, which are abstracted from medical records, provide a snapshot of care from office-based physicians and OPDs. Between 1997–1998 and 2003–2004, physician and OPD visit rates fluctuated between 3.2 and 3.7 visits per person (data table for Figure 22). Visit rates increased with age with rates among adults 65 years of age and over were more than twice as high as rates among children and young adults.

In 2003–2004, women 18–64 years of age had higher visit rates than men, with the largest gender difference in visit rates occurring among adults 18–44 years of age (Figure 22). In this age group, visit rates for women were more than twice as high as for men, largely due to care associated with female reproduction. This gender difference narrows among middle-age adults and disappears among adults 65 years of age and over.

Figure 22. Visits to physician offices and hospital outpatient departments, by sex and age: United States, 1997-2004

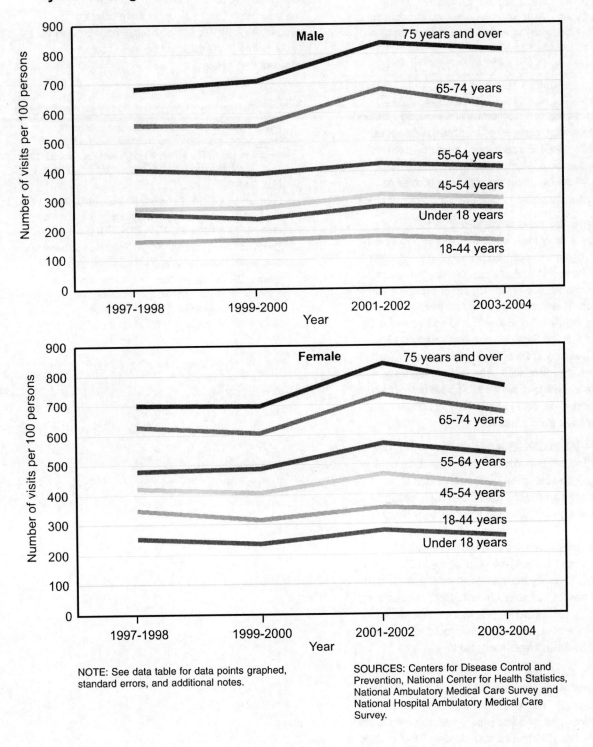

NOTE: See data table for data points graphed, standard errors, and additional notes.

SOURCES: Centers for Disease Control and Prevention, National Center for Health Statistics, National Ambulatory Medical Care Survey and National Hospital Ambulatory Medical Care Survey.

Bariatric Procedures

The number of inpatient bariatric procedures among obese adults age 18–64 years has increased substantially since 1996–1998, with more than four-fifths of these procedures performed on women.

Almost one-third of American adults are obese (Table 73). Obesity has serious health consequences, including increased risk for hypertension, diabetes, osteoarthritis, sleep apnea, and heart disease (1). Because losing weight by dieting is often ineffective for long-term weight loss (2), bariatric procedures—including gastric bypass—have become an increasingly popular option for those who are morbidly obese.

Bariatric procedures are recommended for those who are morbidly obese (body mass index 40 or higher or body mass index 35 or higher with comorbid conditions (see Appendix II, Body Mass Index (BMI)). Bariatric procedures to treat obesity involve reducing the size of the stomach or bypassing part of the intestines. These approaches promote weight loss by reducing the body's ability to absorb food and increasing the sensation of fullness. Bariatric procedures usually result in substantial weight loss. On average, patients lose more than half of their body weight after the procedures (2). Many patients see a reversal or substantial improvement in many of the comorbidities associated with obesity, including diabetes, hypertension, and sleep apnea (2).

From 1996–1998 to 2002–2004, the average annual number of inpatient bariatric procedures among obese patients 18–64 years of age increased more than nine-fold, from about 10,000 to more than 100,000 (data table for Figure 23). In 2002–2004, there were about five times as many bariatric surgeries among women as men age 18–64 years (Figure 23). There were more than 60,000 bariatric procedures among adults 18–44 years of age in 2002–2004 and over 40,000 among those 45–64 years of age. Bariatric procedures may be performed on an inpatient or outpatient basis. These estimates include only inpatient procedures. Therefore, the total number of bariatric procedures performed is greater than the estimates presented here.

Bariatric procedures have many serious side effects and a reported mortality of approximately 1% in the year following the procedures (3). Between 1998 and 2003, 10% of hospitalizations in which gastric bypass was performed had a complication during the hospital stay (4). One-fifth of patients are hospitalized in the first year following their procedures and some patients experience serious complications including wound infection, bowel obstruction, and hernia (3). The long-term health consequences of the procedures are unknown. As more Americans undergo these procedures, a clearer picture of the risks and benefits of bariatric procedures will emerge.

References

1. National Institutes of Health. Clinical guidelines on the identification, evaluation, and treatment of overweight and obesity in adults: The evidence report. NIH Pub. No. 98–4083. 1998. Available from: www.nhlbi.nih.gov/guidelines/obesity/ob_gdlns.htm.

2. Buchwald H, Avidor Y, Braunwald E, Jensen MD, Pories W, Fahrbach K, Schoelles K. Bariatric surgery: A systematic review and meta-analysis. JAMA 2004;292(14):1724–37.

3. Zingmond DS, McGory ML, Ko CY. Hospitalization before and after gastric bypass surgery. JAMA 2005;294(15):1918–24.

4. Shinogle JA, Owings MF, Kozak LJ. Gastric bypass as treatment for obesity: Trends, characteristics, and complications. Obes Res 2005;13(12):2202–9.

Figure 23. Average annual hospital inpatient gastric bypass and other bariatric procedures among adults 18-64 years of age with obesity, by sex and age: United States, 1999-2004

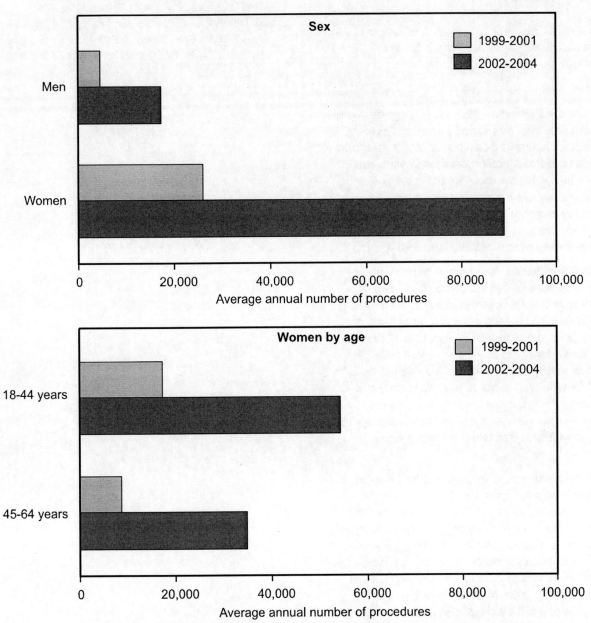

NOTES: Up to four procedures were coded for each hospital stay. Bariatric procedures were any-listed procedures. See data table for data points graphed, procedure codes, and additional notes.

SOURCE: Centers for Disease Control and Prevention, National Center for Health Statistics, National Hospital Discharge Survey.

Mortality

Life Expectancy

Life expectancy continues to increase, and the gap in life expectancy between males and females has been narrowing.

Life expectancy is a measure often used to gauge the overall health of a population. As a summary measure of mortality, life expectancy represents the average number of years of life that could be expected if current death rates were to remain constant. Shifts in life expectancy are often used to describe trends in mortality. Life expectancy at birth is strongly influenced by infant and child mortality. Life expectancy later in life reflects death rates at or above a given age and is independent of the effect of mortality at younger ages (1).

From 1900 through 2003, life expectancy at birth increased from 48 to 75 years for men and from 51 to 80 years for women (Figure 24). Life expectancy at age 65 has also increased since the beginning of the 20th century. Among men, life expectancy at age 65 rose from 12 to 17 years and among women from 12 to 20 years. In contrast to life expectancy at birth, which increased sharply early in the 20th century, life expectancy at age 65 improved primarily after mid-century. Improved access to health care, advances in medicine, healthier lifestyles, and better health before age 65 are factors underlying decreased death rates among older Americans (2).

Athough the overall trend in life expectancy for the United States was upward throughout the 20th century, the gain in years of life expectancy for women generally exceeded that for men until the 1970s, widening the gap in life expectancy between men and women. After the 1970s, the gain in life expectancy for men exceeded that for women and the gender gap in life expectancy began to narrow. Between 1990 and 2003, the total gain in life expectancy for women was 1.3 years compared with 3.0 years for men, reflecting proportionately greater decreases in heart disease and cancer mortality for men than for women and proportionately larger increases in chronic lower respiratory diseases mortality among women (3).

References

1. Arriaga EE. Measuring and explaining the change in life expectancies. Demography 1984;21(1):83–96.

2. Fried LP. Epidemiology of aging. Epidemiol Rev 2000; 22(1):95–106.

3. Arias E. United States life tables, 2003. National vital statistics reports. Hyattsville, MD: National Center for Health Statistics. 2006.

Figure 24. Life expectancy at birth and at 65 years of age, by sex: United States, 1900-2003

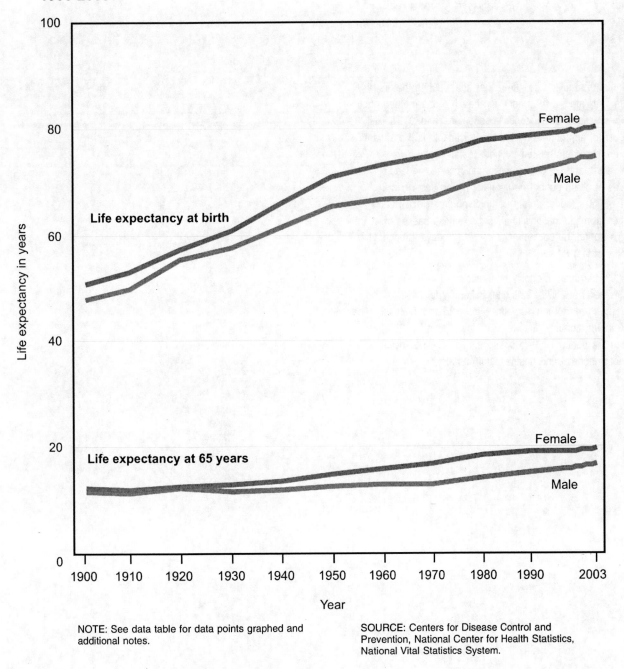

NOTE: See data table for data points graphed and additional notes.

SOURCE: Centers for Disease Control and Prevention, National Center for Health Statistics, National Vital Statistics System.

Infant Mortality

Infant mortality rates have decreased for most racial and ethnic groups, but large disparities between the groups persist.

The infant mortality rate, the risk of death during the first year of life, is related to the underlying health of the mother, public health practices, socioeconomic conditions, and availability and use of appropriate health care for infants and pregnant women. Disorders related to short gestation and low birthweight, and congenital malformations are the leading causes of death during the neonatal period (less than 28 days of life). Sudden Infant Death Syndrome (SIDS) and congenital malformations rank as the leading causes of infant deaths during the postneonatal period (28 days through 11 months of life) (1).

In 2003, the infant mortality rate decreased to 6.9 infant deaths per 1,000 live births after increasing in 2002 for the first time in more than 40 years (Figure 25 and Table 22). The 2003 infant mortality rate was 76% lower than in 1950. During the period 1950–2003, substantial declines occurred for both neonatal and postneonatal mortality.

Figure 25. Infant, neonatal, and postneonatal mortality rates: United States, 1950-2003

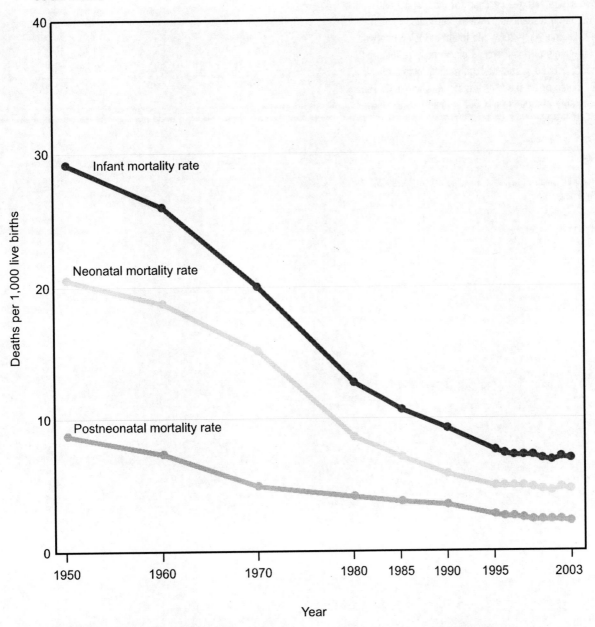

NOTES: Infant is defined as under 1 year of age, neonatal as under 28 days of age, and postneonatal as between 28 days and 1 year of age. See data table for data points graphed and additional notes.

SOURCE: Centers for Disease Control and Prevention, National Center for Health Statistics, National Vital Statistics System.

Infant Mortality *(Continued)*

Infant mortality rates have declined for most racial and ethnic groups, but large disparities between the groups remain (Table 19). During 2001–2003, the infant mortality rate was highest for infants of non-Hispanic black mothers (Figure 26). Infant mortality rates were also high among infants of American Indian or Alaska Native mothers and Puerto Rican mothers. Infants of mothers of Cuban origin had the lowest infant mortality rates.

Reference

1. Heron MP, Smith BL. Deaths: Leading causes for 2003, forthcoming.

Figure 26. Infant mortality rates, by detailed race and Hispanic origin of mother: United States, 2001-2003

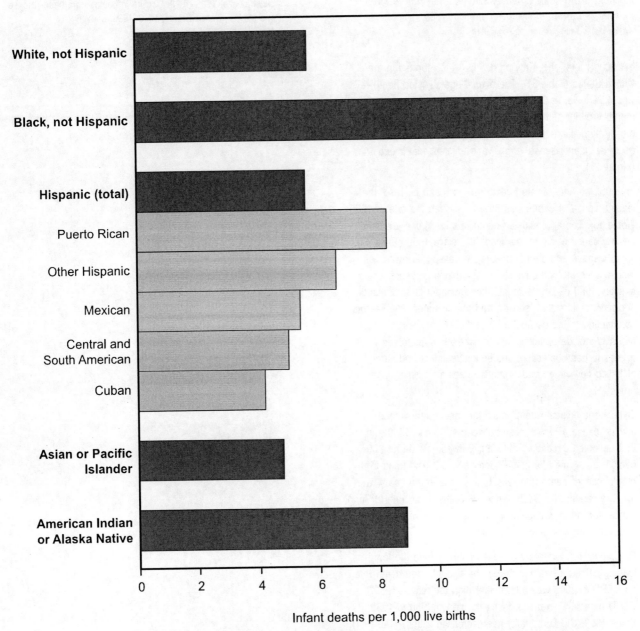

Infant deaths per 1,000 live births

NOTES: Infant is defined as under 1 year of age. Persons of Hispanic origin may be of any race. Asian or Pacific Islander and American Indian or Alaska Native races include persons of Hispanic and non-Hispanic origin. See data table for data points graphed and additional notes.

SOURCE: Centers for Disease Control and Prevention, National Center for Health Statistics, National Vital Statistics System, National Linked Birth/Infant Death Data Sets.

Leading Causes of Death for All Ages

Mortality from heart disease, stroke, and unintentional injuries is substantially lower than in 1950.

In 2003, a total of 2.4 million deaths were reported in the United States (Table 31). The overall age-adjusted death rate was 42% lower in 2003 than in 1950. The reduction in overall mortality during the last half of the 20th century was driven mostly by declines in mortality for such leading causes of death as heart disease, stroke, and unintentional injuries (Figure 27).

In 2003, the age-adjusted death rate for heart disease, the leading cause of death, was 60% lower than the rate in 1950 (Table 36). The age-adjusted death rate for stroke, the third leading cause of death, declined 70% since 1950 (Table 37). Heart disease and stroke mortality are associated with risk factors such as high cholesterol, high blood pressure, smoking, and dietary factors. Other important factors include socioeconomic status, obesity, and physical inactivity. Factors contributing to the decline in heart disease and stroke mortality include better control of risk factors, improved access to early detection, and better treatment and care, including new drugs and expanded uses for existing drugs (1).

Overall age-adjusted death rates for cancer, the second leading cause of death, rose between 1960 and 1990 and then reversed direction (Table 38). Between 1990 and 2003 overall death rates for cancer declined 12%. The trend in the overall cancer death rate reflects the trend in the death rate for lung cancer (Table 39). Since 1970, the death rate for lung cancer for the total population has been higher than the death rate for any other cancer site.

Chronic lower respiratory diseases (CLRD) were the fourth leading cause of death in 2003. The age-adjusted death rate for CLRD in 2003 was 53% higher than the rate in 1980. CLRD mortality increased during the period 1980 to 1999. Since 1999, CLRD mortality has decreased slightly (Table 41).

The fifth leading cause of death in 2003 was unintentional injuries. Age-adjusted death rates for unintentional injuries declined during the period 1950–1992 (Table 29). Since 1992, the unintentional injury mortality rate has gradually increased. Despite recent increases, the death rate for unintentional injuries in 2003 was still 52% lower than the rate in 1950.

Reference

1. Centers for Disease Control and Prevention. Achievements in public health, 1990–1999: Decline in deaths from heart disease and stroke—United States, 1990–1999. MMWR 1999;48(30):649–56.

Figure 27. Death rates for leading causes of death for all ages: United States, 1950-2003

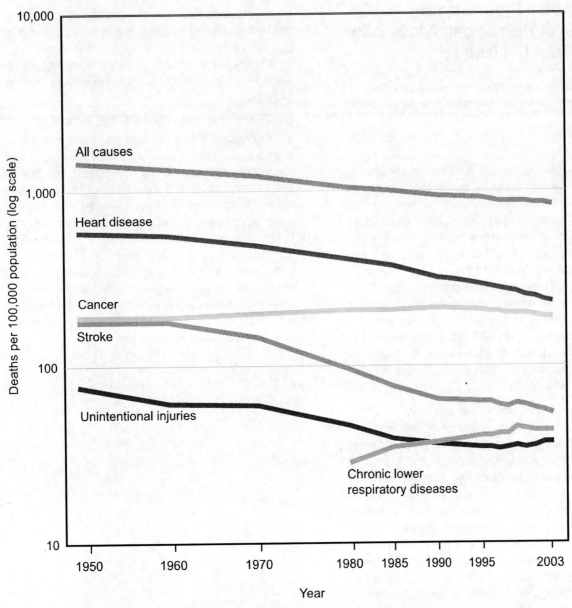

NOTES: Estimates are age adjusted. Causes of death shown are the five leading causes of death for all ages in 2003. CLRD is chronic lower respiratory diseases. Starting with 1999 data, causes of death were coded according to ICD-10. See data table for data points graphed and additional notes.

SOURCE: Centers for Disease Control and Prevention, National Center for Health Statistics, National Vital Statistics System.

Special Feature: Pain

Introduction: Prevalence and Duration of Pain among Adults in the Month Prior to Interview

More than one-quarter of American adults experienced pain that lasted a day or more during the month prior to interview.

Pain hurts—physically, mentally, emotionally, and at times financially. All persons experience pain at some time during their lives. It affects physical and mental functioning, and can profoundly affect quality of life. Treating it is often expensive, time-consuming, and sometimes extremely frustrating. In addition to the direct costs of treating pain—including medical practitioner and hospital visits for diagnosis and treatment, drugs, therapies, and other medical costs—it causes work-loss time, and loss of productivity and concentration at work or while conducting other activities (1,2). Because of these and other factors, the 106th U.S. Congress passed Title VI, Sec. 1603, of H.R. 3244, which declared the 10-year period beginning January 1, 2001, as the "Decade of Pain Control and Research."

The International Association for the Study of Pain (IASP) defines pain as "an unpleasant sensory and emotional experience associated with actual or potential tissue damage, or described in terms of such damage" (3). Pain is a symptom produced when inflammation or changes to the nervous system due to illness or injury are transmitted to the brain, producing a physical sensation that alerts the brain that damage has occurred. Generally, as the inflammation subsides or the wound heals the pain lessens and eventually goes away, although in some cases it does not. Pain can be constant or episodic, last for a minute or most of a lifetime, and can be dull or sharp, throbbing or piercing, localized or widespread, severe or less severe, and ultimately, tolerable or intolerable. Pain can have an undetectable or a nonphysical cause, making it hard to treat.

Pain is always subjective. Although it is a physical sensation, perceptions of pain are influenced by social, cultural, and psychological factors, producing different sensations in different people. Pain in older adults has been shown to be underreported, possibly because of a reluctance to report pain, resignation to the presence of pain, and skepticism about the beneficial effects of potential treatments (4). Perceptions of pain differ by the context in which it occurs; expectations about how much pain one "should" feel; anxiety and feelings about a loss of control that can increase pain; past pain experiences; coexisting physical and mental conditions; and many other factors (5). Research has shown that distracting patients in severe pain can lessen it, and that focusing on pain can make it worse.

Data from the 1999–2002 National Health and Nutrition Examination Survey show that more than one-quarter of Americans (26%) age 20 years and over reported that they had a problem with pain—of any sort—that persisted for more than 24 hours in duration in the month prior to interview (Figure 28). Adults age 45–64 years were the most likely to report pain lasting more than 24 hours (30%). Twenty-five percent of young adults age 20–44 reported pain, and adults age 65 years and over were the least likely to report pain (21%). Women reported pain more often than men, and non-Hispanic white adults reported pain more often than adults of other races and ethnicities. Adults living in families with income less than twice the poverty level reported pain more often than higher income adults.

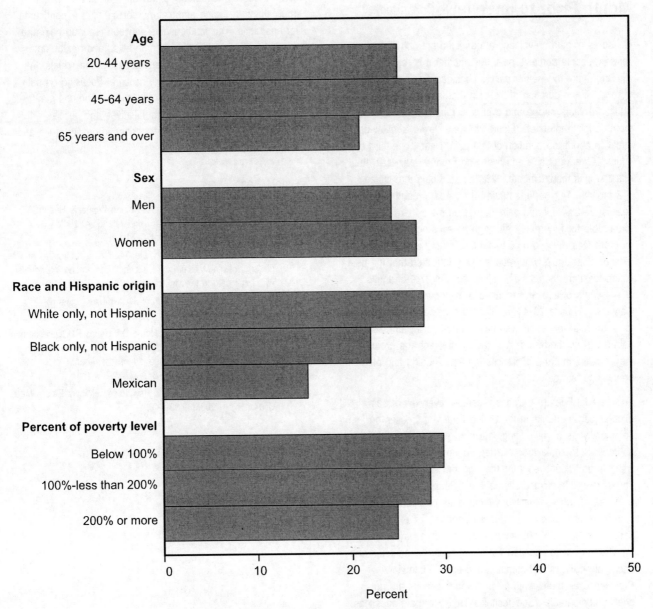

Figure 28. Adults 20 years of age and over reporting pain in the month prior to interview, by selected characteristics: United States, 1999-2002

Percent

NOTES: Respondents were asked to report pain that lasted more than 24 hours. Percent of poverty level is based on family income and family size and composition using U.S. Census Bureau poverty thresholds. See data table for data points graphed, standard errors, and additional notes.

SOURCE: Centers for Disease Control and Prevention, National Center for Health Statistics, National Health and Nutrition Examination Survey.

Introduction: Prevalence and Duration of Pain among Adults in the Month Prior to Interview (Continued)

Measures of pain prevalence are affected not only by how different people perceive pain, but whether it is reported at all. One factor in whether pain is considered salient enough to report is the duration of the pain that is experienced. Adults 20 years of age and over who reported pain in the month prior to interview (Figure 28) were asked a follow-up question about the duration of that pain. Nearly one-third of adults 20 years of age and over who reported pain said that it lasted less than 1 month, 12% reported pain that lasted 1–3 months, 14% reported pain that lasted 3 months to 1 year, and 42% reported pain that lasted more than 1 year (data table for Figure 29). Although persons age 65 years and over are less likely to report pain lasting 24 hours or more, 57% of older adults who reported pain indicated that the pain lasted for more than 1 year compared with 37% of adults 20–44 years of age who reported pain (Figure 29). Conversely, adults 20–44 years were considerably more likely to report relatively short-lived pain. Therefore the duration of pain (long- or short-lived) reported by different age groups may explain, in part, differences in pain reporting and pain prevalence by age.

This Special Feature provides a general overview of pain experienced by adults in the United States. It focuses on common types of pain using data from several national data sources. Some data are collected during in-person interviews with the participant reporting the location, extent, duration, and severity of selected sites of pain. Because some types of pain persist, while other types recur more or less frequently, pain questions have different recall periods. For example, people are asked about any pain that lasted a day or more in the month prior to interview but about severe headaches and back pain during the 3-month period prior to interview. Prevalence estimates with different recall periods are not directly comparable. (See Technical Notes for pain questions and recall periods.)

Another way to gather information on pain is to ask respondents about use of medications to control severe pain, such as prescription narcotic drugs. Pain in individuals can be indirectly inferred from measures of health care utilization, for example, use of hospital procedures for pain reduction such as hip and knee replacement.

The Special Feature presents data on the prevalence and possible effects of pain in terms of health status and health care utilization measures, as well as some economic implications including ambulatory medical care expenditures for headache. The relationships between reported pain and race/ethnicity, gender, age, income level, and health status are complex and raise important issues for individuals, the health care system, and society at large. Focusing on pain prevalence and its effects for population subgroups may provide insight for public health initiatives and policies with the ultimate goal of reducing disparities in quality of life and level of functioning.

References

1. McCool WF, Smith T, Aberg C. Pain in Women's Health: A multi-faceted approach toward understanding. J Midwivery Womens Health 2004;49(6):473–81.

2. Luo X, Pietrobon R, Sun SX, Liu GG, Hey L. Estimates and patterns of direct health care expenditures among individuals with back pain in the United States. Spine 2004;29:79–86.

3. IASP website. Available from: www.iasp-pain.org/terms-p.html#Pain.

4. Yong HH, Gibson SJ, de L Horne DJ, Helms RD. Development of a pain attitudes questionnaire to assess stoicism and cautiousness for possible age differences. Journal of Gerontology 2001;56B:279–84.

5. Hansen GR, Streltzer J. The Psychology of Pain. Emerg Med Clin of N Am 2005;23:339–48.

Figure 29. Duration of pain among adults reporting pain, by age: United States, 1999-2002

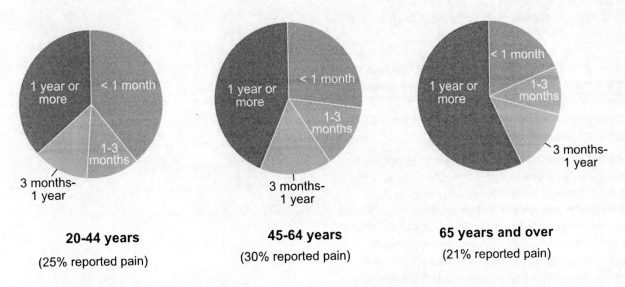

20-44 years

(25% reported pain)

45-64 years

(30% reported pain)

65 years and over

(21% reported pain)

NOTES: Respondents who reported pain lasting more than 24 hours in duration in the month prior to interview (Figure 28) were asked a follow-up question about the duration of that pain. See data table for data points graphed, standard errors, and additional notes.

SOURCE: Centers for Disease Control and Prevention, National Center for Health Statistics, National Health and Nutrition Examination Survey.

Low Back, Migraine/Severe Headache, Neck, and Face Pain

The prevalence of low back pain, migraine/severe headache, neck, and face pain varies significantly by age.

Pain occurs in many different parts of the body, each with its own prevalence and presentation patterns. Low back pain and severe headache are two of the most common sources of pain that interfere with an individual's ability to enjoy social activities and negatively affect quality of life (1).

In the National Health Interview Survey, adults 18 years of age and over were asked a series of questions about whether they have had four types of pain during the 3 months prior to interview (low back, migraine/severe headache, neck, and facial ache in the jaw or joint in front of the ear). Respondents were instructed to report pain that lasted a whole day or more and not to include minor aches or pains. Respondents could report more than one type of pain and were included in each reported category. Trends in the percentage of Americans reporting each of these types of pain have been stable in recent years (Table 56).

Low back pain was the most commonly reported of the four types of pain overall and in each age group (Figure 30). In 2004, more than one-quarter of adults reported low back pain in the past 3 months (data table for Figure 30). Low back pain was most commonly reported among adults 45 years of age and over.

In 2004, 15% of adults reported migraine/severe headache and 15% also reported neck pain. Adults 18–44 years of age reported migraine/severe headache pain almost three times as frequently as adults 65 years and over. Migraine/severe headache is particularly prevalent among women in their reproductive years (Table 56). In contrast to the pattern for migraine/severe headache, prevalence of neck pain varied less by age and was higher among adults 45–64 years of age than among those in other age groups.

Facial ache or pain in the joint in front of the ear was reported by 4% of adults in 2004. It was more common among younger and middle-age adults than among older adults 65 years of age and over.

Reference

1. National Institute of Neurological Disorders and Stroke. Low back pain fact sheet. Available from: www.ninds.nih.gov/health_and_medical/pubs/back_pain.htm.

Figure 30. Adults reporting low back pain, migraine, neck, and face pain in the 3 months prior to interview, by age: United States, 2004

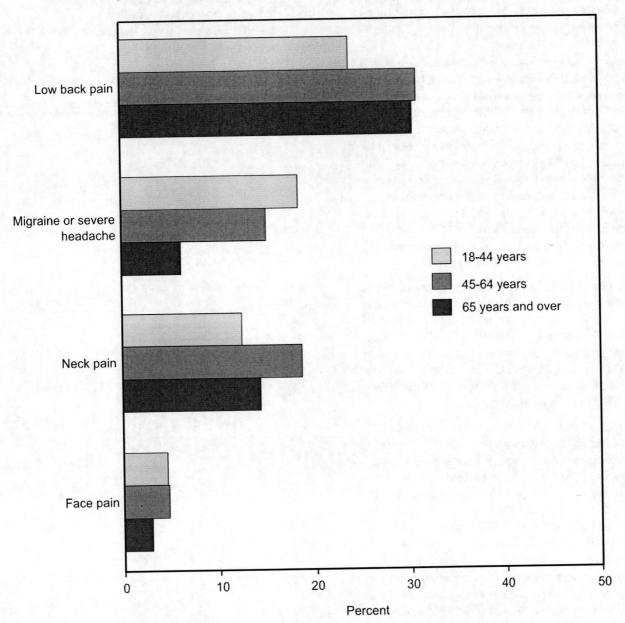

Percent

NOTES: Respondents were asked to report pain that lasted a whole day or more. Respondents reporting more than one type of pain were included in each category. See data table for data points graphed, standard errors, and additional notes.

SOURCE: Centers for Disease Control and Prevention, National Center for Health Statistics, National Health Interview Survey.

Low Back Pain

Women of all ages, race and ethnicity groups, and income levels report low back pain more often than men.

Low back pain is the second most common neurological ailment in the United States—only headache (when all types and severity levels are considered) is more common (1). Obesity, smoking, weight gain during pregnancy, stress, poor physical condition, posture inappropriate for the activity being performed, and poor sleeping position can contribute to low back pain. Low back pain places considerable stress on the health care system in terms of visits and procedures for diagnosis, treatment, and medication management. In addition, there are substantial indirect costs associated with reduced productivity. Low back pain is the most common cause of job-related disability and a leading contributor to missed work, and reduced productivity at work (1,2).

In the National Health Interview Survey, the presence of pain is measured by asking adult respondents 18 years of age and over about low back pain and other selected types of pain during the 3 months prior to interview. Respondents were instructed to report low back pain that lasted a whole day or more and not to include minor aches or pains. Trends in the percentage of adults reporting low back pain have remained stable in recent years (Table 56).

Women reported low back pain more often than men (29% compared with 25%) (data table for Figure 31). Gender differences persist within age, race and ethnicity (except among Asian adults), and income subgroups (Figure 31). Older women reported low back pain more often than older men (33% compared with 27%). Non-Hispanic black women reported low back pain about 30% more often, and Hispanic women reported it 40% more often than their male counterparts. Non-Hispanic white women and men had a higher prevalence of low back pain than other race and Hispanic origin groups, and they had a smaller male/female difference in prevalence than other racial and ethnic groups. Women of each income level reported low back pain more often than men at the same income level. Poor women were more likely to report low back pain than higher income women. Conversely, about one-quarter of men at all income levels reported low back pain.

References

1. National Institute of Neurological Disorders and Stroke. Low back pain fact sheet. Available from: www.ninds.nih.gov/health_and_medical/pubs/back_pain.htm.

2. Hemp P. Presenteeism: at work—but out of it. Harv Bus Rev 2004;82(10):49–58.

Figure 31. Adults 18 years of age and over reporting low back pain in the 3 months prior to interview, by selected characteristics: United States, 2004

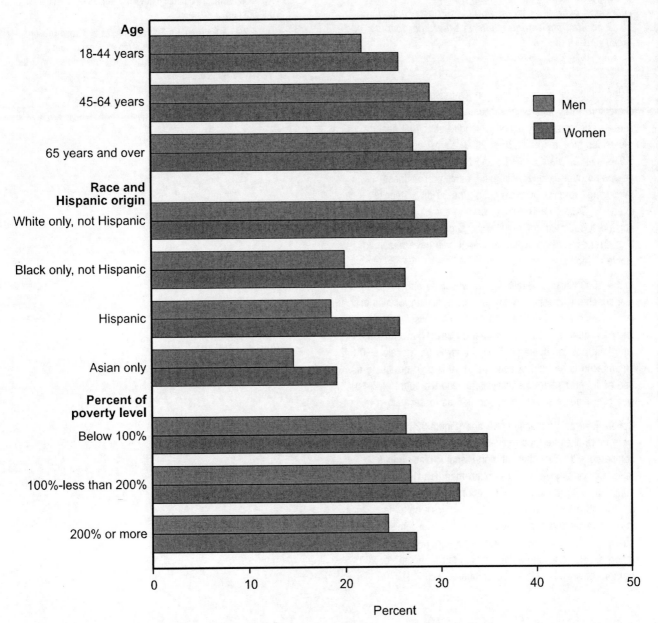

NOTES: Asian race includes persons of Hispanic and non-Hispanic origin. Persons of Hispanic origin may be of any race. Percent of poverty level is based on family income and family size and composition using U.S. Census Bureau poverty thresholds. See data table for data points graphed and additional notes.

SOURCE: Centers for Disease Control and Prevention, National Center for Health Statistics, National Health Interview Survey.

Joint Pain

Severe joint pain is more common among adults age 65 years and over, low-income adults, and non-Hispanic black adults than among adults in other age, income, and racial and ethnic groups.

Osteoarthritis is the most common joint disorder and is characterized by joint pain, stiffness, and swelling. Joint pain can also be caused by injury, prolonged abnormal posture, or repetitious movements (1,2). In 2003, almost one-third of adults age 18 years and over and one-half of adults age 65 years and over reported joint pain, aching, or stiffness (excluding the back or neck) during the 30 days prior to interview (Table 57). The knee was the site of joint pain most commonly reported, followed by the shoulder, fingers, and hips. Trends in the prevalence of joint pain have remained stable in recent years.

In the 2003 National Health Interview Survey only, respondents who reported any joint pain, aching, or stiffness in or around a joint during the past 30 days were asked a follow-up question "During the past 30 days, how bad was your joint pain on average? Please answer on a scale of 0 to 10 where 0 is no pain or aching and 10 is pain or aching as bad as it can be." In this analysis, a reported score of 7–10 was classified as severe pain and 0–6 as lesser pain.

Severe joint pain increased with age (Figure 32). Women were more likely to report severe joint pain than men (10% compared with 7%). Although non-Hispanic black adults reported overall joint pain less often than non-Hispanic white adults, they were more likely to report severe joint pain. Asian adults had a lower percentage of severe joint pain than adults in other racial and ethnic groups. Persons with family income below 200% of the poverty line were nearly twice as likely to report severe joint pain as adults with family income of 200% or more of poverty (12%–13% compared with 7%).

References

1. Medline Plus, National Library of Medicine: Osteoarthritis. Available from: www.nlm.nih.gov/medlineplus/ency/article/000423.htm.

2. Latko WA, Armstrong TJ, Franzblau A, et al. Cross-sectional study of the relationship between repetitive work and the prevalence of upper limb musculoskeletal disorders. Am J Ind Med 1999 Aug;36:248–59.

Figure 32. Adults 18 years of age and over reporting joint pain in the 30 days prior to interview, by severity level and selected characteristics: United States, 2003

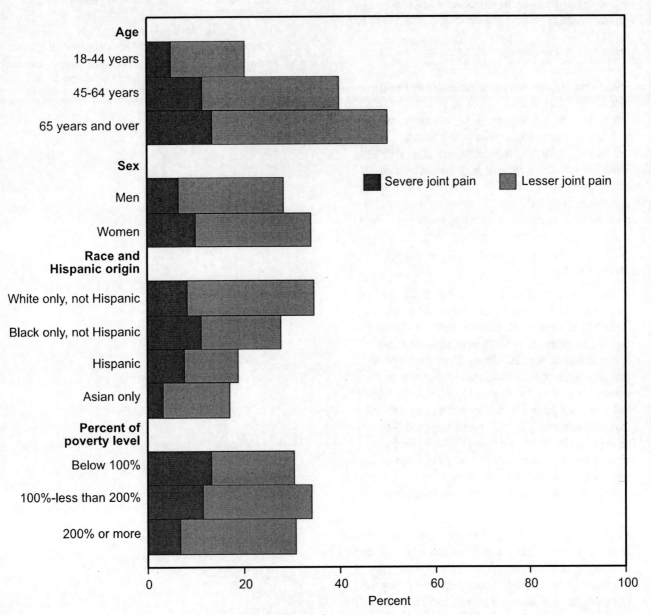

NOTES: Adults who reported joint pain, aching, or stiffness during the past 30 days were asked to report on average the severity of the pain on a scale of 0–10 where 0 is no pain and 10 is pain or aching as bad as it can be. In this analysis, lesser pain is defined as 0–6 and severe pain as a response of 7–10. Percent of poverty level is based on family income and family size and composition using U.S. Census Bureau poverty thresholds. See data table for data points graphed, standard errors, and additional notes.

SOURCE: Centers for Disease Control and Prevention, National Center for Health Statistics, National Health Interview Survey.

Narcotic Analgesic Drug Visits in Emergency Departments

In one-half of emergency department visits with severe pain recorded, a narcotic analgesic drug was prescribed or received.

The presence of pain can be discerned directly by asking people about the presence, type, location, and duration of specific types of pain (Figures 28–32). In addition, pain can be examined by investigating health care utilization involving pain treatments, such as emergency department (ED) visits during which narcotic analgesic drugs were prescribed. Narcotic analgesic drugs are used primarily to treat severe pain (Appendix II, Table XII). Physicians' decisions to prescribe narcotic analgesics are highly variable (1). Some studies conclude that narcotic analgesic drugs are underused in EDs, particularly among children, older adults, and minority populations (2).

In 2003–2004, 23% of all ED visits had a narcotic analgesic drug prescribed or provided during the visit (data table for Figure 33). In the National Hospital Ambulatory Medical Care Survey Emergency Room Component, presenting level of pain is abstracted from ED records. The presenting level of pain is recorded as none, mild, moderate, severe, or unknown or missing. About 16% of all ED visits in 2003–2004 had a recorded presenting pain level of no pain, 16% mild pain, 21% moderate pain, 14% severe pain, and 33% were unknown or missing on pain level (3). Children under 11 years of age were more likely to have an unknown or missing presenting pain level, but no difference in the percentage of unknown or missing pain level was noted by gender or by race.

Among ED visits with severe pain recorded, 50% had narcotic analgesic drugs prescribed or provided during the visit (data table for Figure 33). Males and females had similar rates of narcotic drugs for severe pain during ED visits (Figure 33). Children under age 18 were less likely than adults to receive a narcotic drug in the ED, regardless of presenting level of pain. Adults 65 years of age and over with severe pain were less likely to receive a narcotic drug than other adults with severe pain. Black people were less likely than white people to receive narcotic drugs for severe pain in the ED (40% compared with 53%).

References

1. Tamayo-Sarver JH, Dawson NV, Cydulka RK, Wigton RS, Baker DW. Variability in emergency physician decisionmaking about prescribing opioid analgesics. Ann Emerg Med. 2004 Apr;43(4):483–93.

2. Rupp T, Delaney KA. Inadequate analgesia in emergency medicine. Ann Emerg Med. 2004 Apr;43(4):494–503.

3. Centers for Disease Control and Prevention, National Center for Health Statistics, National Hospital Ambulatory Medical Care Survey, unpublished analysis.

Figure 33. Narcotic analgesic drug visits to the emergency department among visits with a severe pain level recorded, by age, sex, and race: United States, 2003-2004

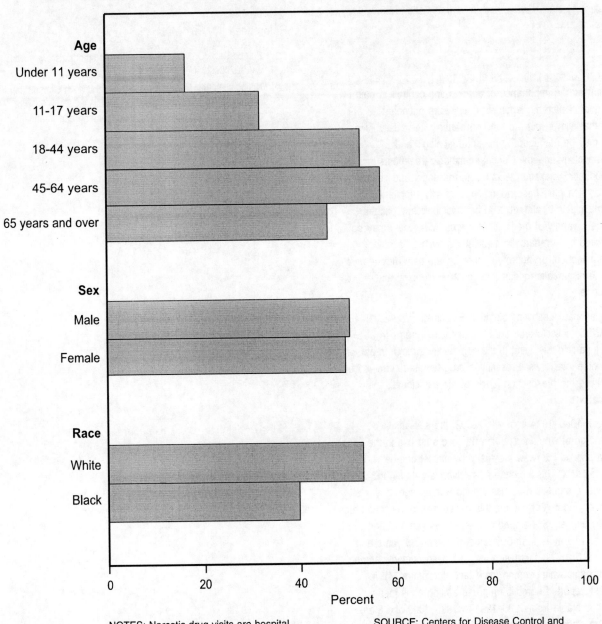

NOTES: Narcotic drug visits are hospital emergency department visits with narcotic drugs prescribed or provided during the visit. See data table for data points graphed, standard errors, and additional notes.

SOURCE: Centers for Disease Control and Prevention, National Center for Health Statistics, National Hospital Ambulatory Medical Care Survey, Emergency Department Component.

Prescription Narcotic Drug Use

The use of narcotic drugs among women has increased from 1988–1994 to 1999–2002, largely due to increased use among non-Hispanic white women and women age 45 years and over.

In recent decades, the medical community has increasingly recognized the importance of treating and controlling pain (1). The goal of pain management is to return patients to a pain level that allows them to function better in their daily lives. Pain may be managed by nonpharmacologic and pharmacologic means. Nonpharmacologic treatments include biofeedback, relaxation techniques, massage, and heat or cold application. These approaches usually supplement pharmacologic treatment (2). Pharmacologic approaches include a variety of medication options. Minor pain may be controlled by non-narcotic medications such as aspirin, acetaminophen, or ibuprofen. More severe pain may require the use of narcotic medications, such as codeine and oxycodone.

The National Health and Nutrition Examination Survey (NHANES) collects data on the prescription drug use of survey participants living in the community through in-person household interviews. Prescription drug use is determined by examining the prescription labels of the participant's medications.

Between 1988–1994 and 1999–2002, the age-adjusted percentage of women reporting narcotic drug use in the month prior to interview increased by almost one-half from 3.6% to 5.3%. This increase was driven largely by an increase in narcotic drug use among women age 45 years and over (Figure 34). During this period, use of narcotic drugs rose by almost 75% among women 45–64 years of age to 5.7% and by more than 50% among women 65 years and over to 6.8%. This increased use has been primarily among non-Hispanic white women (data table for Figure 34). In contrast, reported narcotic drug use among adult men remained stable from 1988–1994 to 1999–2002 and there were no significant differences in use for men by race or ethnicity.

In 1999–2002, women of all ages reported more narcotic drug use than men (Figure 34). Non-Hispanic white women were almost twice as likely to report narcotic use as women of Mexican origin (5.9% compared with 3.2%).

References

1. Phillips DM. JCAHO pain management standards are unveiled. JAMA 2000;284(4):428–9.

2. National Pharmaceutical Council, Inc. and Joint Commission on Accreditation of Healthcare Organizations. Pain: Current understanding of assessment, management, and treatments. Reston, VA: NPC; 2001.

Figure 34. Adults 18 years of age and over reporting narcotic drug use in the month prior to interview, by sex and age: United States, 1988-1994 and 1999-2002

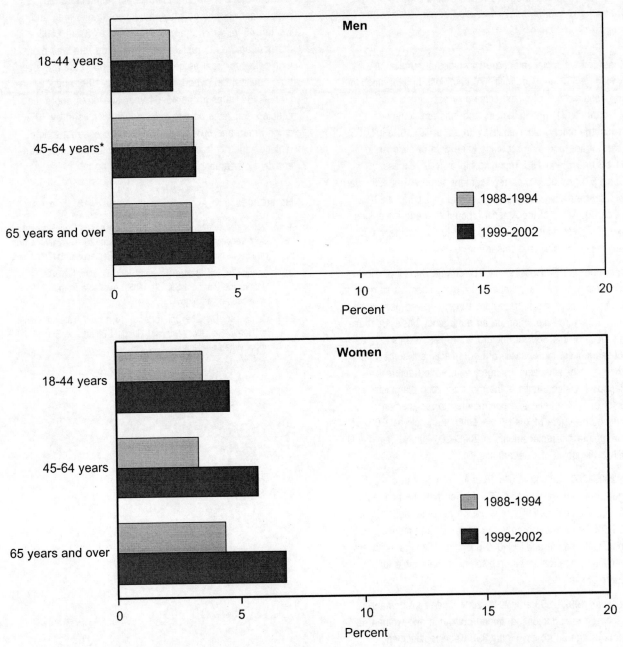

NOTES: *1999–2002 data have a relative standard error of 20%–30%. See data table for data points graphed, standard errors, and additional notes.

SOURCE: Centers for Disease Control and Prevention, National Center for Health Statistics, National Health and Nutrition Examination Survey.

Knee and Nonfracture Hip Replacements

Rates of hospitalizations to replace painful hips and knees have substantially increased since 1992–1993.

Knee and hip replacement are two types of surgical procedures for treating significant pain, loss of joint function, and impaired mobility most commonly associated with osteoarthritis (1). Painful knees and hips are common symptoms among older adults, with about 30% of adults 65 years of age and over reporting knee pain or stiffness in the past 30 days and 15% reporting hip pain or stiffness (Table 57). In 2003, knee replacement surgery was estimated to cost the Nation $11.9 billion and hip replacement $12.2 billion (2). Aging of the American population and increasing trends in overweight and obesity may further increase the prevalence of joint problems in the future.

Data from the National Hospital Discharge Survey provide information on trends in knee and hip replacement surgery. In addition to pain, hip replacement surgery is also performed to treat a fractured hip, often on an emergency basis. Because the focus of this Special Feature is on pain and its consequences, the analysis of hip replacement surgery excludes hip replacement surgery with a hip fracture diagnosis. Osteoarthritis is the most common diagnosis associated with knee and nonfracture hip replacement procedures—97% of knee replacements and almost 70% of nonfracture hip replacements in 2003–2004 were for patients with a diagnosis of osteoarthritis (3).

In 2003–2004 among adults 18 years of age and over, the knee replacement rate was 52% higher than the nonfracture hip replacement rate. There were, on average, approximately 428,000 hospital discharges per year with any mention of a knee replacement and 282,000 hospital discharges with any mention of nonfracture hip replacement (data table for Figure 35).

Between 1992–1993 and 2003–2004, knee replacement discharge rates increased among both men and women 45 years of age and over (Figure 35). Knee replacement discharges were more common among adults 65 years of age and over than among those age 45–64 years. During this time period, rates nearly tripled among adults 45–64 years of age and nearly doubled among adults 65 years and over. In

both 1992–1993 and 2003–2004, hospital discharges with knee replacement surgery were more common among women than men.

Between 1992–1993 and 2003–2004, nonfracture hip replacement discharge rates increased among men and women 45 years of age and over (Figure 35). In 2003–2004, the nonfracture hip replacement discharge rate was more than twice as great among older adults 65 years and over than adults 45–64 years. Between 1992–1993 and 2003–2004, rates in the 45–64 year age group more than doubled and rates among older adults increased by 70% among men and 50% among women. In contrast to knee replacement, nonfracture hip replacement discharges were equally likely among men and women.

References

1. National Institutes of Health. NIH Consensus Development Conference on Total Knee Replacement. 2003. Available from: consensus.nih.gov/2003/2003TotalKneeReplacement117html.htm.

2. Agency for Healthcare Research and Quality. HCUP Nationwide Inpatient Sample (NIS). Available from: www.hcup-us.ahrq.gov/.

3. Centers for Disease Control and Prevention, National Center for Health Statistics, National Hospital Discharge Survey, unpublished analysis.

Figure 35. Hospital discharges for knee and nonfracture hip replacement surgery among adults 45 years of age and over, by sex and age: United States, 1992-1993 and 2003-2004

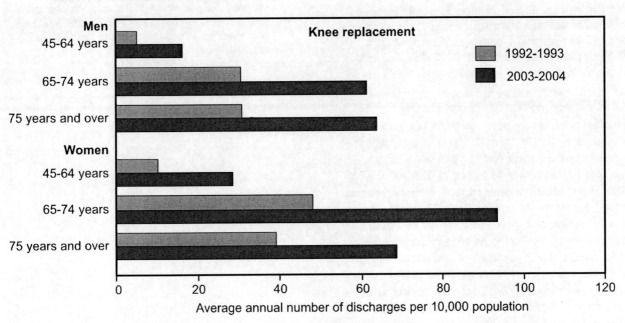

Average annual number of discharges per 10,000 population

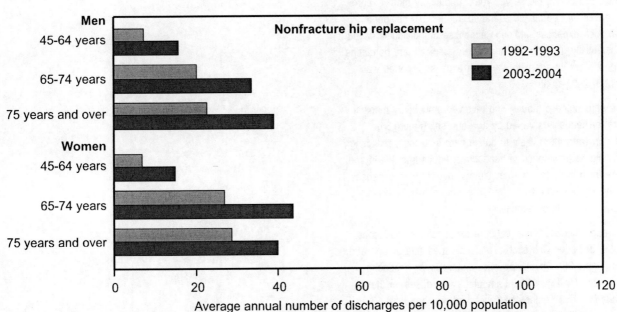

Average annual number of discharges per 10,000 population

NOTES: Up to four inpatient hospital procedures were coded for each stay. Hip replacement excludes procedures for hip fracture. See data table for data points graphed, standard errors, and additional notes.

SOURCE: Centers for Disease Control and Prevention, National Center for Health Statistics, National Hospital Discharge Survey.

Ambulatory Medical Care Expenses Associated with Headaches

Ambulatory medical care expenses for adults suffering from headaches and who sought ambulatory medical care or purchased prescribed medications averaged about $570 per person per year in 2002–2003.

Recent statistics on headaches suggest that only a small proportion of adults who experience headaches receive professional medical treatment for their condition, indicating that many people manage their pain themselves using painkillers purchased over the counter, or other self-care. In 2003, 15% of adults reported a migraine or severe headache in the 3 months prior to interview (Table 56). However, data from the Medical Expenditure Panel Surveys for 2002 and 2003 indicate only 3.5% of adults had ambulatory visits and/or prescribed drug purchases for treatment of headaches over a one-year period (1). Ambulatory medical care includes care obtained in doctors' offices, hospital outpatient clinics, and emergency rooms, as well as prescribed medicines purchased during the survey year. Ambulatory medical care expenses for headaches averaged about $570 per person with such expenses, although expenses of individuals varied substantially. The median ambulatory medical care headache expense per person with any such expense reported was $212 in 2002–2003.

The percentage of adults who received ambulatory medical care for headaches varied by age and sex (Figure 36). Women were more likely to obtain care than men, reflecting their higher prevalence of headaches. Adults age 45–64 years were most likely to have ambulatory medical care expenses for headaches and those age 65 years or over were least likely to have these expenses.

Average ambulatory medical care expenses for headaches ($566) per adult with such expenses varied little by age and sex (Figure 36). Ambulatory care expenses for headache accounted for 15% of total ambulatory expenses for these adults (1). This percentage decreased with age from 18% among adults age 18–44 years to 10.5% among those 65 years or over. The smaller share of ambulatory care expenses for headaches among adults 65 years and over compared with younger adults resulted in large part from increasing expenses for other medical conditions among older adults.

Reference

1. Machlin SR, Miller GE. Health service use and expenses for migraines and other headaches, 2002–03 (average annual estimates). Statistical Brief #115. February 2006. Agency for Healthcare Research and Quality, Rockville, MD. Available from: www.meps.ahrq.gov/mepsweb/data_files/publications/st115/stat115.pdf.

Figure 36. Adults reporting ambulatory medical care use for headaches and associated ambulatory medical care expenses, by age and sex: United States, 2002-2003

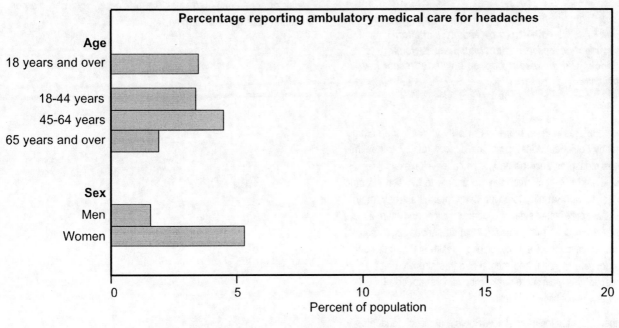

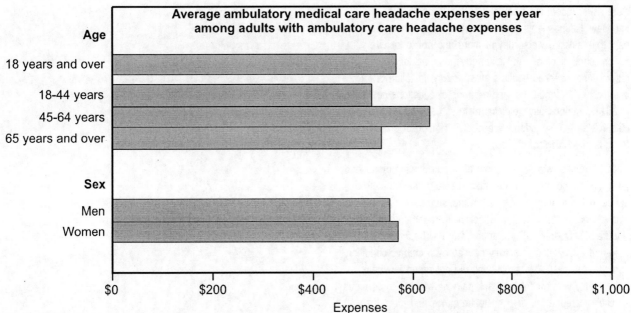

NOTES: Estimates are for adults age 18 and over who had ambulatory medical care (office-based, hospital outpatient, and emergency room settings) and/or prescribed medicine expenses for headaches. See data table for data points graphed, standard errors, and additional notes.

SOURCE: Agency for Heathcare Research and Quality, Center for Financing, Access, and Cost Trends, Household Component, Medical Expenditure Panel Survey.

Health Status Measures among Adults with and without Low Back Pain

People with recent low back pain have worse overall health status as measured by activity limitation, respondent-assessed health status, and serious psychological distress than people without recent low back pain.

Pain interferes with an individual's ability to work and engage in many social activities. It may be directly related to health status measures such as activity limitation—for example, people with low back pain may be unable to function in some jobs or to work at all. Moreover, even intermittent pain may affect people's assessments of their physical and mental health. Pain does not necessarily cause serious psychological distress, limitation of activity, or poor health status, but may interact with physical and mental health status to affect perceptions of pain, care-seeking behaviors, speed of recovery, and ability to function.

In the National Health Interview Survey, adult respondents were asked about low back pain in the 3 months prior to interview. Respondents were instructed to report low back pain that lasted a whole day or more and not to include minor aches or pains. Additional questions included respondent-assessed health status, activity limitation due to chronic health conditions, and a series of questions designed to assess serious psychological distress (See Appendix II, Health status, respondent-assessed; Limitation of activity; Serious psychological distress).

In 2004, adults who reported low back pain lasting more than 24 hours during the past 3 months reported worse health status, using a number of different measures, than people who did not report recent low back pain, regardless of age (Figure 37). Overall, 28% of adults with low back pain said they had a limitation of activity caused by a chronic condition, compared with 10% of adults who did not report low back pain. Adults with recent low back pain were about three times as likely to report fair or poor health status and more than four times as likely to experience serious psychological distress as people without low back pain.

Within each age group, adults with low back pain reported worse health status than those without low back pain. For

example, among adults 65 years and over more than one-half who reported recent low back pain had a limitation in their usual activity compared with 27% without recent low back pain, and 40% with recent low back pain rated their health as fair or poor, compared with 19% of older people who did not report recent low back pain.

Figure 37. Health status measures among adults 18 years of age and over with and without low back pain, by age: United States, 2004

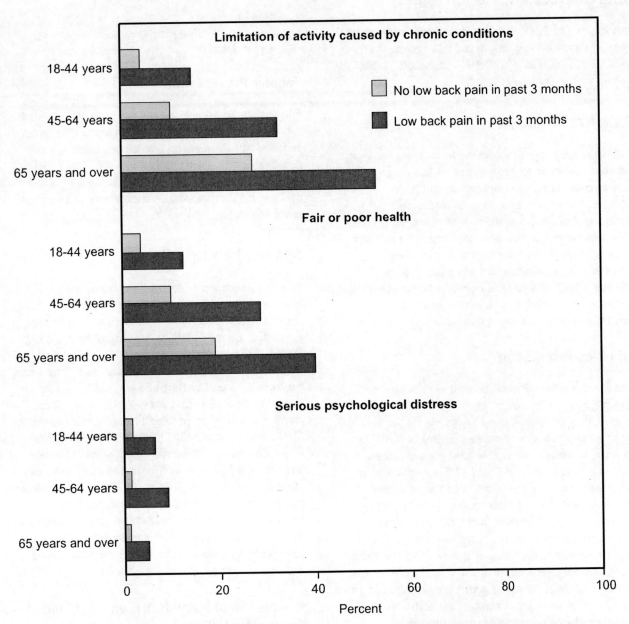

NOTES: Respondents were asked to report low back pain that lasted a whole day or more. See data table for data points graphed, standard errors, and additional notes.

SOURCE: Centers for Disease Control and Prevention, National Center for Health Statistics, National Health Interview Survey.

Technical Notes

Data Sources and Comparability

Data for *The Chartbook on Trends in the Health of Americans* come from many different surveys and data systems and cover a broad range of years. Detailed descriptions of data sources are contained in Appendix I.

Data Presentation

Many measures in *The Chartbook on Trends in the Health of Americans* are shown for people in specific age groups because of the strong effect age has on most health outcomes. Some estimates are age adjusted using the age distribution of the 2000 standard population, and this is noted in the data tables that accompany each figure (see Appendix II, Age adjustment). For some figures, data years are combined to increase sample size and reliability of the estimates. Time trends for some measures are not presented because of the relatively short amount of time that comparable national estimates are available.

Graphic Presentation

Most line charts, for which only selected years of data are displayed, have dot markers on the data years. Line charts for which data are displayed for every year in the trend are shown without the use of dot markers. Figures 24 and 27 do not show dot markers, although selected years of data are graphed for years prior to 1997 and 1995 respectively. Most trends are shown on a linear scale to emphasize absolute differences over time. The linear scale is the scale most frequently used and recognized, and it emphasizes the absolute changes between data points over time (1). The time trend for overall mortality measures is shown on a logarithmic (or log) scale to emphasize the rate of change and to enable measures with large differences in magnitude to be shown on the same chart. Log scales emphasize the relative or percentage change between data points. Readers are cautioned that one potential disadvantage to log scale is that the absolute magnitude of changes may appear smaller than the untransformed statistics would indicate (2). When interpreting data on a log scale, the following points should be kept in mind:

1. A sloping straight line indicates a constant rate (not amount) of increase or decrease in the values,
2. A horizontal line indicates no change,
3. The slope of the line indicates the rate of increase or decrease,
4. Parallel lines, regardless of their magnitude, depict similar rates of change (1).

Tabular Presentation

Following the Technical Notes are data tables that present the data points graphed in each figure. Some data tables contain additional data that were not graphed because of space considerations. Standard errors for data points are provided for many measures. Additional information clarifying and qualifying the data are included in table notes and Appendix I and II references.

Special Feature: Pain

Data on pain prevalence, location, and characteristics presented in the Special Feature on Pain come from a variety of data sources, including the National Health and Nutrition Examination Survey (NHANES), the National Health Interview Survey (NHIS), the National Hospital Ambulatory Medical Care Survey (NHAMCS) Emergency Department Component, the National Hospital Discharge Survey (NHDS), and the Medical Expenditure Panel Survey (MEPS). Data on pain prevalence is self-reported using a survey questionnaire in the NHANES and the NHIS. The NHANES also contains data on prescription drug use in the past month, which is collected from the participant by viewing medication containers (when available). Data from the NHDS and NHAMCS are abstracted from medical records. Exact wording of the questions, including reference periods for which the pain occurred, vary by survey. Detailed descriptions of these data sources are contained in Appendix I and information about the specific questions used in the Special Feature are below.

National Health and Nutrition Examination Survey (NHANES)

NHANES self-reported questions on pain: The 1999–2002 NHANES contained a series of questions for respondents concerning pain they experienced during the past month. Figures 28 and 29 use data based on the following questions:

"DURING THE PAST MONTH, (have you/has sampled adult) had a problem with pain that lasted more than 24 hours?"

For people who responded "yes" to this question, a follow-up question was asked:

"For how long (have you/has sample adult) experienced this pain? Would you say . . .

    1 = Less than a month,

    2 = At least 1 month but less than 3 months,

    3 = At least 3 months but less than 1 year, or

    4 = Greater than 1 year?

    7 = Refused

    9 = Don't know"

NHANES prescription drug data: The questionnaire administered to all participants also included a question on whether they had taken a prescription drug in the past month. Those who answered "yes" were asked to show the interviewer the medication containers for all the prescriptions. For each drug reported, the interviewer entered the product's complete name from the container. If no container was available, the interviewer asked the participant to verbally report the name of the drug. Additionally, participants were asked how long they had been taking the drug and the main reason for use. All reported medication names were converted to their standard generic ingredient name. For multi-ingredient products, the ingredients were listed in alphabetical order (i.e., Tylenol #3 would be listed as Acetaminophen; Codeine). No trade or proprietary names were provided on the data file. More information on prescription drug data collection and coding in the NHANES is available from: www.cdc.gov/nchs/data/nhanes/frequency/rxq_rxdoc.pdf. More information on NHANES III prescription drug data collection and coding is available from: www.cdc.gov/nchs/data/nhanes/nhanes3/PUPREMED-acc.pdf. Also see Appendix I, National Health and Nutrition Examination Survey.

National Health Interview Survey (NHIS)

NHIS self-reported questions on pain: Sample adults and knowledgable proxy respondents (1% of sample adult respondents) were asked a series of questions about pain. The recall period varies by the type of pain mentioned. For back pain, severe headache or migraine, neck pain, and face pain, respondents were asked about pain that occurred at any time in the past 3 months. Respondents were also asked about joint pain they experienced in the past 30 days. The exact questions used were:

"The following questions are about pain you may have experienced in the PAST 3 MONTHS. Please refer to pain that LASTED A WHOLE DAY OR MORE. Do not report aches and pains that are fleeting or minor.

DURING THE PAST 3 MONTHS, did [you/sample adult] have severe headaches or migraines?"

This identical question was asked for several types of pain, substituting the following types of pain for "severe headaches or migraines": neck pain; low back pain; and facial ache or pain in the jaw muscles or the joint in front of the ear.

Additionally, respondents were also asked:

"DURING THE PAST 30 DAYS, have you had any symptoms of pain, aching, or stiffness in or around a joint?"

In 2003 only, respondents who reported joint symptoms were asked a follow-up question:

"DURING THE PAST 30 DAYS, how bad was your joint pain on average?" Respondents were instructed to answer on a scale of 0–10 where 0 is no pain or aching and 10 is pain or aching as bad as it can be. In the Figure 32 analysis, lesser joint pain was defined as 0–6 and severe pain was defined as a response of 7–10. This analysis excludes a small number of adults who did not provide information on both joint pain questions.

National Hospital Ambulatory Medical Care Survey (NHAMCS) Emergency Department Component

For each hospital emergency department (ED) visit sampled in the NHAMCS, the presenting level of pain as recorded on the medical record is abstracted to the patient record form, using the following categories: Unknown, None, Mild, Moderate, and Severe. In 2003–2004, presenting level of pain was unknown or missing in 33% of ED visits. This could be due to unconsciousness, poor communication with the patient (or young child), or failure to record the pain level on the medical record for some other reason. Narcotic drugs were prescribed or provided in 16% of ED visits with unknown or missing pain level (see data table for Figure 33).

NHAMCS drug data: Data collection in the NHAMCS-ED component is from the medical record rather than from individuals. Medications that were prescribed or provided during the ED visit are recorded on the patient record form. Generic as well as brand name drugs are included, as are nonprescription and prescription drugs. Up to eight medications per visit could be listed in 2003–2004.

For more information on drugs collected by the NAMCS/NHAMCS, see the Ambulatory Care Drug Database, available from: www2.cdc.gov/drugs/, or ftp://ftp.cdc.gov/pub/Health_Statistics/NCHS/Dataset_Documentation/NAMCS/doc01.pdf, or ftp://ftp.cdc.gov/pub/Health_Statistics/NCHS/Dataset_Documentation/NHAMCS/doc01.pdf. Also see Appendix I, National Ambulatory Care Medical Survey and National Hospital Ambulatory Medical Care Survey, and Appendix II, Drugs; National Drug Code Directory (NDC).

National Hospital Discharge Survey (NHDS)

The National Hospital Discharge Survey collects data on hospital stays in non-federal short-stay hospitals in the United States, including diagnoses, procedures performed, age, sex, and race. Up to four procedures are coded for each hospital stay. Procedure codes are based on the *International Classification of Diseases, Ninth Revision, Clinical Modification* (ICD–9–CM). In Figure 35, ICD–9–CM codes used for knee replacement are 81.54 and for hip replacement 81.51–52, excluding hip fracture codes 820 and 733.14). In 2003–2004, 28% of hip replacements were for hip fracture. Data in Figure 35 show any-listed procedures; if more than one procedure with the same ICD code (e.g., hip replacement) is performed during the hospitalization it is counted only once.

Medical Expenditure Panel Survey (MEPS)

The Medical Expenditure Panel Survey produces nationally representative estimates of health care use, expenditures, source of payment, and insurance coverage for the United States civilian noninstitutionalized population. For each medical care visit or prescription drug during a 1-year period, the respondent reports the condition for which the visit was made, which is then coded using the ICD–9–CM system. Expenses associated with each visit or prescription drug are recorded. In Figure 36, headache is classified using

ICD–9–CM codes 346, 784.0, and 307.81. See Appendix I: Medical Expenditure Panel Survey.

References

1. Page RM, Cole GE, Timmreck TC. Basic epidemiological methods and biostatistics: A practical guidebook. Sudbury, MA: Jones and Bartlett Publishers, 1995.

2. Jekel JF, Elmore JG, Katz DL. Epidemiology biostatistics and preventive medicine. Philadelphia, PA: W.B. Saunders Company, 1996.

Data Tables for Figures 1–37

Data table for Figure 1. Total population and older population: United States, 1950–2050

Year	All ages	65 years and over	65–74 years	75 years and over
		Number		
1950	150,697,361	12,194,612	8,339,960	3,854,652
1960	179,323,175	16,559,580	10,996,842	5,562,738
1970	203,211,926	20,065,502	12,435,456	7,630,046
1980	226,545,805	25,549,427	15,580,605	9,968,822
1990	248,709,873	31,078,895	18,045,495	13,033,400
2000	281,421,906	34,991,753	18,390,986	16,600,767
2004	293,655,404	36,293,985	18,463,472	17,830,513
2005	296,496,649	36,681,501	18,615,309	18,066,192
2010	308,935,581	40,243,713	21,269,509	18,974,204
2020	335,804,546	54,631,891	31,779,159	22,852,732
2030	363,584,435	71,453,471	37,947,933	33,505,538
2040	391,945,658	80,049,634	35,469,908	44,579,726
2050	419,853,587	86,705,637	37,942,437	48,763,200
		Percent		
1950	100.0	8.1	5.5	2.6
1960	100.0	9.2	6.1	3.1
1970	100.0	9.9	6.1	3.8
1980	100.0	11.3	6.9	4.4
1990	100.0	12.5	7.3	5.2
2000	100.0	12.4	6.5	5.9
2004	100.0	12.4	6.3	6.1
2005	100.0	12.4	6.3	6.1
2010	100.0	13.0	6.9	6.1
2020	100.0	16.3	9.5	6.8
2030	100.0	19.7	10.4	9.2
2040	100.0	20.4	9.0	11.4
2050	100.0	20.7	9.0	11.6

NOTES: Data are for the resident population. Data for 1950 exclude Alaska and Hawaii. Data for 2010–2050 are projected. See Appendix II, Population.

SOURCES: U.S. Census Bureau: 1950 Nonwhite population by race. Special Report P-E, No.3B. Washington, DC. U.S. Government Printing Office, 1951 [data for 1950]; U.S. Census of Population: 1960, Number of inhabitants, PC(1)-A1, United States Summary, 1964 [data for 1960]; Number of inhabitants, final report PC(1)-A1, United States Summary, 1971 [data for 1970]; U.S. Census Bureau, 1980 Census of Population, General population characteristics, United States Summary (PC80–1-B1) [data for 1980]; 1990 Census of Population, General population characteristics, United States Summary (CP-1-1) [data for 1990]; Table 1. Annual estimates of the population by sex and five-year age groups for the United States: April 1, 2000 to July 1, 2004 (NC-EST2004-01) available from: www.census.gov/popest/national/asrh/NC-EST2004/NC-EST2004-01.xls [data for Census 2000]; U.S. Census Bureau: Monthly postcensal resident populations, from April 1, 2000 to July 1, 2005 by age, sex, race, and Hispanic origin available from: www.census.gov/popest/national/asrh/2004_nat_res.html [data for 2004 and 2005]; U.S. interim projections by age, sex, race, and Hispanic origin detail file. Available from: www.census.gov/ipc/www/usinterimproj/ [data for projections].

Data table for Figure 2. Population in group quarters, by type of setting: United States, 1990 and 2000

Population and setting	1990		2000	
	Number	Percent	Number	Percent
Total U.S. population	248,709,870	100.00	281,421,910	100.00
Total in group quarters	6,697,740	2.69	7,778,630	2.76
Institutionalized group quarters	3,334,020	1.34	4,059,040	1.44
Correctional institutions	1,115,110	0.45	1,976,020	0.70
Nursing homes	1,772,030	0.71	1,720,500	0.61
Juvenile institutions	104,200	0.04	128,280	0.05
Other institutions	342,680	0.14	234,240	0.08
Noninstitutionalized group quarters	3,363,730	1.35	3,719,590	1.32
College dormitories	1,953,560	0.79	2,064,130	0.73
Military quarters	589,700	0.24	355,160	0.13
Group homes	211,680	0.09	454,060	0.16
Emergency and transitional shelters	178,640	0.07	170,710	0.06
Other noninstitutional group quarters	430,160	0.17	675,550	0.24

NOTES: Numbers are rounded to the nearest 10. Other institutions include hospitals or wards, hospices, and schools for the handicapped. Other noninstitutional group quarters include shelters for abused women, soup kitchens, crews of maritime vessels, agriculture workers' dormitories, and religious group quarters. See Appendix II, Group quarters; Population.

SOURCE: U.S. Census Bureau, Census 2000 Summary File 1, Matrix PCT16; 1990 Summary tape file 1 (STF 1)-100-Percent data.

Data table for Figure 3. Population in selected race and Hispanic origin groups, by age: United States, 1980–2005

Race and Hispanic origin	All ages				Under 18 years				18 years and over			
	1980	1990	2000	2005	1980	1990	2000	2005	1980	1990	2000	2005
Total	100.0	100.0	100.0	100.0	100.0	100.0	100.0	100.0	100.0	100.0	100.0	100.0
Hispanic or Latino	6.4	9.0	12.5	14.4	8.8	12.2	17.1	19.7	5.5	7.9	11.0	12.7
Not Hispanic or Latino:												
White	79.9	75.7	69.5	66.9	74.2	68.9	61.3	58.3	82.1	78.1	72.3	69.7
Black or African American	11.5	11.8	12.2	12.3	14.5	14.7	14.9	14.7	10.4	10.7	11.3	11.4
American Indian or Alaska Native	0.6	0.7	0.7	0.8	0.8	1.0	1.0	0.9	0.5	0.6	0.7	0.7
Asian	1.6	2.8	3.7	4.2	1.7	3.1	3.5	3.8	1.5	2.7	3.8	4.3
Native Hawaiian or Other Pacific Islander	...	...	0.1	0.1	...	...	0.2	0.2	...	...	0.1	0.1
2 or more races	...	...	1.2	1.3	...	...	2.2	2.4	...	...	0.9	1.0

... Category not applicable.

NOTES: Data are for the resident population. Persons of Hispanic origin may be of any race. Race data for 2000 and beyond are not directly comparable with data for 1980 and 1990. Individuals could report only one race in 1980 and 1990, and more than one race beginning in 2000. Persons who selected only one race in 2000 and beyond are shown in single-race categories; persons who selected more than one race in 2000 and beyond are shown as having 2 or more races and are not included in the single-race categories. In 1980 and 1990, the Asian category included Asian and Native Hawaiian or Other Pacific Islander; in 2000 and beyond this category includes only Asian. See Appendix II, Hispanic origin; Race.

SOURCES: U.S. Census Bureau: U.S. population estimates, by age, sex, race, and Hispanic origin: 1980 to 1991. Current population reports, series P-25, no 1095. Washington, DC. U.S. Government Printing Office, February 1993 [data for April 1, 1980 and April 1, 1990]; U.S. Census Bureau: Monthly postcensal resident populations, from July 1, 2000 to July 1, 2004 by age, sex, race, and Hispanic origin, available from: www.census.gov/popest/national/asrh/2004_nat_res.html [data for April 1, 2000 and July 1, 2005].

Data table for Figure 4. Poverty by age: United States, 1966–2004

Year	All ages	Under 18 years	18–64 years	65 years and over
		Percent of persons with family income below the poverty level		
1966	14.7	17.6	10.5	28.5
1967	14.2	16.6	10.0	29.5
1968	12.8	15.6	9.0	25.0
1969	12.1	14.0	8.7	25.3
1970	12.6	15.1	9.0	24.6
1971	12.5	15.3	9.3	21.6
1972	11.9	15.1	8.8	18.6
1973	11.1	14.4	8.3	16.3
1974	11.2	15.4	8.3	14.6
1975	12.3	17.1	9.2	15.3
1976	11.8	16.0	9.0	15.0
1977	11.6	16.2	8.8	14.1
1978	11.4	15.9	8.7	14.0
1979	11.7	16.4	8.9	15.2
1980	13.0	18.3	10.1	15.7
1981	14.0	20.0	11.1	15.3
1982	15.0	21.9	12.0	14.6
1983	15.2	22.3	12.4	13.8
1984	14.4	21.5	11.7	12.4
1985	14.0	20.7	11.3	12.6
1986	13.6	20.5	10.8	12.4
1987	13.4	20.3	10.6	12.5
1988	13.0	19.5	10.5	12.0
1989	12.8	19.6	10.2	11.4
1990	13.5	20.6	10.7	12.2
1991	14.2	21.8	11.4	12.4
1992	14.8	22.3	11.9	12.9
1993	15.1	22.7	12.4	12.2
1994	14.5	21.8	11.9	11.7
1995	13.8	20.8	11.4	10.5
1996	13.7	20.5	11.4	10.8
1997	13.3	19.9	10.9	10.5
1998	12.7	18.9	10.5	10.5
1999	11.9	17.1	10.1	9.7
2000	11.3	16.2	9.6	9.9
2001	11.7	16.3	10.1	10.1
2002	12.1	16.7	10.6	10.4
2003	12.5	17.6	10.8	10.2
2004	12.7	17.8	11.3	9.8

NOTES: Data are for the civilian noninstitutionalized population. Poverty level is based on family income and family size and composition using U.S. Census Bureau poverty thresholds. See Appendix II, Poverty. See related Table 3.

SOURCES: U.S. Census Bureau, Current Population Survey, March 1967–2005. U.S. Census Bureau. DeNavas-Walt C, Proctor B, Hill LC. Income, poverty, and health insurance coverage in the United States: 2004. Current population reports, series P-60, no 229. Washington, DC: U.S. Government Printing Office. 2005.

Data table for Figure 5. Low income by age, race, and Hispanic origin: United States, 2004

Characteristic	Percent of poverty level			
	Below 100%	100%–less than 200%	Below 100%	100%–less than 200%
	Percent		Number in millions	
All ages				
All races and origins	12.7	18.5	37.0	53.8
Hispanic or Latino	21.9	30.3	9.1	12.6
Black or African American only.	24.7	24.0	9.0	8.7
Asian only	9.8	16.3	1.2	2.0
White only, not Hispanic or Latino	8.6	15.1	16.9	29.4
Under 18 years				
All races and origins	17.8	21.4	13.0	15.7
Hispanic or Latino	28.9	33.3	4.1	4.7
Black or African American only.	33.6	26.9	3.8	3.0
Asian only	10.0	19.4	0.3	0.6
White only, not Hispanic or Latino	10.5	16.2	4.5	7.0
18–64 years				
All races and origins	11.3	15.5	20.5	28.2
Hispanic or Latino	18.3	28.3	4.6	7.2
Black or African American only.	20.3	21.1	4.5	4.7
Asian only	9.3	14.0	0.8	1.2
White only, not Hispanic or Latino	8.3	11.9	10.2	14.7
65 years and over				
All races and origins	9.8	28.1	3.5	9.9
Hispanic or Latino	18.7	34.0	0.4	0.7
Black or African American only.	23.9	34.7	0.7	1.0
Asian only	13.6	25.5	0.1	0.3
White only, not Hispanic or Latino	7.5	27.1	2.2	7.8

NOTES: Data are for the civilian noninstitutionalized population. Persons of Hispanic origin may be of any race. Black and Asian races include persons of both Hispanic and non-Hispanic origin. Percent of poverty level is based on family income and family size and composition using U.S. Census Bureau poverty thresholds. See related Table 3. See Appendix II, Hispanic origin; Poverty; Race.

SOURCES: DeNavas-Walt C, Proctor B, Hill LC. Income, poverty, and health insurance coverage in the United States: 2004. Current population reports, series P-60 no 229. Washington, DC: U.S. Government Printing Office. 2005; Age and sex of all people, family members, and unrelated individuals iterated by income-to-poverty ratio and race: 2004, available from: pubdb3.census.gov/macro/032005/pov/new01_000.htm.

Data table for Figure 6. Health insurance coverage at the time of interview among persons under 65 years of age: United States, 1984–2004

| | Health insurance coverage at the time of interview | | | | | |
| | Private | | Medicaid | | Uninsured | |
Year	Percent	SE	Percent	SE	Percent	SE
1984	76.8	0.6	6.8	0.3	14.5	0.4
1989	75.9	0.4	7.2	0.2	15.6	0.3
1994	69.9	0.4	11.2	0.3	17.5	0.3
1995	71.3	0.4	11.5	0.2	16.1	0.2
1996	71.2	0.5	11.1	0.3	16.6	0.3
1997	70.7	0.4	9.7	0.2	17.5	0.2
1998	72.1	0.4	8.9	0.2	16.6	0.2
1999	72.8	0.3	9.1	0.2	16.1	0.2
2000	71.5	0.4	9.5	0.2	17.0	0.3
2001	71.2	0.4	10.4	0.2	16.4	0.3
2002	69.4	0.4	11.8	0.2	16.8	0.2
2003	68.9	0.4	12.3	0.2	16.5	0.3
2004	68.8	0.4	12.5	0.2	16.4	0.2

SE is standard error.

NOTES: Data are for the civilian noninstitutionalized population. Medicaid includes other public assistance through 1996; includes state-sponsored health plans starting in 1997; and includes State Children's Health Insurance Program (SCHIP) starting in 1999. Uninsured persons are not covered by private insurance, Medicaid, SCHIP, public assistance (through 1996), state-sponsored or other government-sponsored health plans (starting in 1997), Medicare, or military plans. Persons with Indian Health Service only are considered uninsured. Percents do not add to 100 because the percentage of persons with Medicare, military plans, and other government-sponsored plans is not shown and because persons with both private insurance and Medicaid appear in both categories. Starting with third-quarter 2004 data, persons under 65 years of age with no reported coverage were asked explicitly about Medicaid coverage. Estimates for Medicaid coverage shown in this table include the additional information. See Appendix II, Health insurance coverage. See related Tables 133–135.

SOURCE: Centers for Disease Control and Prevention, National Center for Health Statistics, National Health Interview Survey.

Data table for Figure 7. Health insurance status prior to interview among persons under 65 years of age, by selected characteristics: United States, 2004

| Characteristic | Length of time uninsured prior to interview | | | | | |
| | Total uninsured prior to interview | | More than 12 months | | Any period up to 12 months | |
	Percent	SE	Percent	SE	Percent	SE
Age						
Under 65 years	20.1	0.3	11.4	0.2	7.6	0.2
Under 18 years	12.5	0.3	5.4	0.2	6.3	0.2
18–24 years.	36.1	0.7	19.9	0.6	14.8	0.5
25–34 years.	31.1	0.6	18.1	0.4	11.7	0.4
35–44 years.	20.9	0.4	13.0	0.4	6.7	0.2
45–54 years.	16.2	0.4	10.1	0.3	5.0	0.2
55–64 years.	13.4	0.4	8.7	0.3	3.7	0.2
Percent of poverty level						
Below 100%	35.8	0.7	23.2	0.7	11.4	0.5
100%–less than 150%	36.3	0.8	23.2	0.8	11.8	0.6
150%–less than 200%	32.7	1.1	19.9	0.9	11.7	0.6
200% or more	13.1	0.3	6.3	0.2	5.8	0.2
Race and Hispanic origin						
Black or African American only, not Hispanic or Latino	21.3	0.6	11.1	0.4	8.8	0.4
Asian only.	18.7	1.3	11.4	1.0	5.7	0.7
White only, not Hispanic or Latino	15.6	0.3	7.6	0.2	7.1	0.2
Hispanic or Latino (total)	38.2	0.7	28.4	0.6	8.9	0.3
Mexican.	41.2	0.8	31.5	0.8	8.9	0.4
Cuban.	24.9	2.1	18.3	2.0	6.3	1.2
Puerto Rican	24.2	1.8	14.2	1.5	9.2	1.2

SE is standard error.

NOTES: Data are for the civilian noninstitutionalized population. Total uninsured prior to interview includes 1.1% of people with unknown length of time uninsured. Persons of Hispanic origin may be of any race. Total for Hispanic includes groups not shown separately. Asian only race includes persons of Hispanic and non-Hispanic origin. Uninsured persons are not covered by private insurance, Medicaid, State Children's Health Insurance Program (SCHIP), state-sponsored or other government-sponsored health plans, Medicare, or military plans. Persons with Indian Health Service only are considered uninsured. Percent of poverty level is based on family income and family size and composition using U.S. Census Bureau poverty thresholds. Missing family income data were imputed for 32% of persons under 65 years of age in 2004. See Appendix II, Family income; Health insurance coverage, length of time uninsured; Hispanic origin; Poverty; Race.

SOURCE: Centers for Disease Control and Prevention, National Center for Health Statistics, National Health Interview Survey.

Data table for Figure 8. National health expenditures as a percentage of Gross Domestic Product: United States, 1960–2004

Year	Percent
1960	5.2
1965	5.9
1970	7.2
1975	8.2
1980	9.1
1985	10.5
1990	12.4
1991	13.1
1992	13.5
1993	13.8
1994	13.7
1995	13.8
1996	13.7
1997	13.6
1998	13.7
1999	13.7
2000	13.8
2001	14.6
2002	15.4
2003	15.9
2004	16.0

NOTES: See related Table 120. See Appendix I, National Health Accounts.

SOURCE: Centers for Medicare & Medicaid Services, Office of the Actuary, National Health Statistics Group, National Health Accounts.

Data table for Figure 9. Personal health care expenditures, by source of funds and type of expenditures: United States, 2004

Personal health care expenditures and source of funds	Total	Type of expenditures				
		Hospital care	Physician services	Nursing home	Prescription drugs	Other
		Amount in billions				
All personal health care expenditures	$1,560.2	$570.8	$399.9	$115.2	$188.5	$285.9
		Percent distribution				
All personal health care expenditures	100.0	36.6	25.6	7.4	12.1	18.3
Source of funds		Percent distribution				
All sources of funds	100.0	100.0	100.0	100.0	100.0	100.0
Out-of-pocket payments	15.1	3.3	10.0	27.7	24.9	34.4
Private health insurance	36.1	35.6	48.5	7.8	47.6	23.5
Other private funds	4.4	4.9	6.9	3.6	0.0	3.2
Government	44.4	56.3	34.6	60.8	27.5	38.9
Medicaid	17.5	17.3	6.9	44.3	19.3	20.1
Medicare	19.2	28.6	20.5	13.9	1.8	12.2
Other government	7.7	10.4	7.2	2.6	6.4	6.3
Federal	33.9	45.3	28.5	42.0	16.9	26.9
State and local	10.5	10.9	6.1	18.8	10.6	12.0

NOTES: Other expenditures include dental services, other professional services, home health care, nonprescription drugs and other medical nondurables, vision products and other medical durables, and other personal health care, not shown separately. See related Tables 123–124. See Appendix I, National Health Accounts.

SOURCE: Centers for Medicare & Medicaid Services, Office of the Actuary, National Health Statistics Group, National Health Accounts.

Data table for Figure 10. Cigarette smoking among men, women, high school students, and mothers during pregnancy: United States, 1965–2005

Year	Men		Women		High school students		Mothers during pregnancy
	Percent	SE	Percent	SE	Percent	SE	Percent
1965	51.2	0.3	33.7	0.3	- - -	- - -	- - -
1974	42.8	0.5	32.2	0.4	- - -	- - -	- - -
1979	37.0	0.5	30.1	0.5	- - -	- - -	- - -
1983	34.8	0.6	29.4	0.4	- - -	- - -	- - -
1985	32.2	0.5	27.9	0.4	- - -	- - -	- - -
1987	30.9	0.4	26.5	0.4	- - -	- - -	- - -
1988	30.3	0.4	25.7	0.3	- - -	- - -	- - -
1989	- - -	- - -	- - -	- - -	- - -	- - -	19.5
1990	28.0	0.4	22.9	0.3	- - -	- - -	18.4
1991	27.6	0.4	23.5	0.3	27.5	1.4	17.8
1992	28.1	0.5	24.6	0.5	- - -	- - -	16.9
1993	27.3	0.6	22.6	0.4	30.5	1.0	15.8
1994	27.6	0.5	23.1	0.5	- - -	- - -	14.6
1995	26.5	0.6	22.7	0.5	34.8	1.2	13.9
1996	- - -	- - -	- - -	- - -	- - -	- - -	13.6
1997	27.1	0.4	22.2	0.4	36.4	1.1	13.2
1998	25.9	0.4	22.1	0.4	- - -	- - -	12.9
1999	25.2	0.5	21.6	0.4	34.8	1.3	12.6
2000	25.2	0.4	21.1	0.4	- - -	- - -	12.2
2001	24.6	0.4	20.7	0.4	28.5	1.0	12.0
2002	24.6	0.4	20.0	0.4	- - -	- - -	11.4
2003	23.7	0.4	19.4	0.4	21.9	1.1	10.7
2004	23.0	0.4	18.7	0.4	- - -	- - -	10.2
2005	- - -	- - -	- - -	- - -	23.0	1.2	- - -

SE is standard error.

- - - Data not available.

NOTES: Data for men and women are for the civilian noninstitutionalized population. Estimates for men and women are age adjusted to the 2000 standard population using five age groups: 18–24 years, 25–34 years, 35–44 years, 45–64 years, and 65 years and over. Age-adjusted estimates in this table may differ from other age-adjusted estimates based on the same data and presented elsewhere if different age groups are used in the adjustment procedure. Cigarette smoking is defined as follows: among men and women 18 years and over, those who ever smoked 100 cigarettes in their lifetime and now smoke every day or some days; among high school students in grades 9–12, those who smoked cigarettes on 1 or more of the 30 days preceding the survey; and among mothers with a live birth, those who smoked during pregnancy. Data for mothers who smoked during pregnancy are based on the 1989 Revision of the U.S. Certificate of Live Birth. Some states did not require the reporting of mother's tobacco use during pregnancy on the birth certificate and are not included in this analysis. Reporting of tobacco use during pregnancy increased from 43 states and the District of Columbia (DC) in 1989 to 49 states and DC in 2000–2002. Starting with 2003 data, some reporting areas adopted the 2003 Revision of the U.S. Standard Certificate of Live Birth and 1 state continued to not report data. Tobacco use during pregnancy data based on the 2003 Revision are not comparable with data based on the 1989 Revision of the U.S. Standard Certificate of Live Birth and are excluded from this analysis. See Appendix II, Age adjustment; Cigarette smoking; Tobacco use. See related Tables 12 and 63.

SOURCES: Centers for Disease Control and Prevention, National Center for Health Statistics, National Health Interview Survey (data for men and women); National Vital Statistics System (data for mothers during pregnancy); National Center for Chronic Disease Prevention and Health Promotion, Youth Risk Behavior Survey (data for high school students).

Data table for Figure 11. Binge drinking and current marijuana use among high school students, by sex, grade level, and year: United States, 1991, 1993, 2003, and 2005

Sex, grade level, and year	Binge drinking		Current marijuana use	
	Percent	SE	Percent	SE
Both sexes				
Attended grades 9–10 in 1991	24.8	1.6	11.5	1.1
Attended grades 11–12 in 1993.	35.4	1.4	20.3	1.3
Attended grades 9–10 in 2003	23.4	1.2	20.1	1.4
Attended grades 11–12 in 2005.	30.1	1.5	21.9	1.0
Male				
Attended grades 9–10 in 1991	28.2	2.0	13.0	1.3
Attended grades 11–12 in 1993.	41.2	1.8	23.6	1.8
Attended grades 9–10 in 2003	22.9	1.3	22.5	1.6
Attended grades 11–12 in 2005.	33.2	1.7	24.7	1.1
Female				
Attended grades 9–10 in 1991	21.3	1.6	9.9	1.1
Attended grades 11–12 in 1993.	29.2	1.3	16.7	1.3
Attended grades 9–10 in 2003	23.9	1.4	17.7	1.3
Attended grades 11–12 in 2005.	27.0	1.6	19.0	1.4

SE is standard error.

NOTES: Binge drinking is drinking five or more drinks of alcohol in a row on one or more of the 30 days preceding the survey. Current marijuana use is using marijuana one or more times during the 30 days preceding the survey.

SOURCE: Centers for Disease Control and Prevention, National Center for Chronic Disease Prevention and Health Promotion, National Youth Risk Behavior Survey.

Data table for Figure 12. Regular leisure-time physical activity among adults 18 years of age and over, by percent of poverty level, race and Hispanic origin: United States, 2004

Characteristic	Percent	SE
Below 100% of poverty level		
Not Hispanic or Latino:		
White only	24.8	1.3
Black or African American only.	17.1	1.6
Hispanic	15.5	1.3
100%–less than 200% of poverty level		
Not Hispanic or Latino:		
White only	24.3	1.1
Black or African American only.	17.6	1.7
Hispanic	17.0	1.2
200% or more of poverty level		
Not Hispanic or Latino:		
White only	35.5	0.5
Black or African American only.	28.4	1.3
Hispanic	29.3	1.3

SE is standard error.

NOTES: Data are for the civilian noninstitutionalized population. Data are age adjusted to the 2000 standard population using five age groups: 18–44 years, 45–54 years, 55–64 years, 65–74 years, and 75 years and over. Adults were asked about the frequency and duration of vigorous and light/moderate physical activity during leisure time. Adults classified with regular leisure-time physical activity reported 3 or more sessions per week of vigorous activity of at least 20 minutes duration or 5 or more sessions per week of light/moderate activity lasting at least 30 minutes in duration. Percent of poverty level is based on family income and family size and composition using U.S. Census Bureau poverty thresholds. Missing family income data were imputed for 35% of adults in 2004. See Appendix II, Age adjustment; Family income; Physical activity, leisure-time; Poverty. See related Table 72.

SOURCE: Centers for Disease Control and Prevention, National Center for Health Statistics, National Health Interview Survey.

Data table for Figure 13. Overweight and obesity, by age: United States, 1960–2004

| | Children 6–11 years | | Adolescents 12–19 years | | Adults 20–74 years | | | | | |
| | Overweight | | Overweight | | Overweight including obese | | Overweight but not obese | | Obese | |
Year	Percent	SE	Percent	SE	Percent	SE	Percent	SE	Percent	SE
1960–1962.	- - -	- - -	- - -	- - -	44.8	1.0	31.5	0.5	13.3	0.6
1963–1965.	4.2	0.4	- - -	- - -	- - -	- - -	- - -	- - -	- - -	- - -
1966–1970.	- - -	- - -	4.6	0.3	- - -	- - -	- - -	- - -	- - -	- - -
1971–1974.	4.0	0.5	6.1	0.6	47.7	0.7	33.1	0.6	14.6	0.5
1976–1980.	6.5	0.6	5.0	0.5	47.4	0.8	32.3	0.6	15.1	0.5
1988–1994.	11.3	1.0	10.5	0.9	56.0	0.9	32.7	0.6	23.3	0.7
1999–2000.	15.1	1.4	14.8	0.9	64.1	1.9	33.1	1.1	31.0	1.5
2001–2002.	16.3	1.6	16.7	1.1	65.7	0.9	33.6	1.1	32.1	1.2
2003–2004.	18.8	1.3	17.4	1.7	67.1	1.3	33.2	1.1	33.9	1.3

SE is standard error.
- - - Data not available.

NOTES: Data are for the civilian noninstitutionalized population. Estimates for adults are age adjusted to the 2000 standard population using five age groups: 20–34 years, 35–44 years, 45–54 years, 55–64 years, and 65–74 years. Age-adjusted estimates in this table may differ from other age-adjusted estimates based on the same data and presented elsewhere if different age groups are used in the adjustment procedure. For children and adolescents: overweight is defined as a body mass index (BMI) at or above the sex- and age-specific 95th percentile BMI cut points from the 2000 CDC Growth Charts: United States (See www.cdc.gov/growthcharts/); obese is not defined for children. For adults: overweight including obese is defined as a BMI greater than or equal to 25; overweight but not obese as a BMI greater than or equal to 25 but less than 30; and obese as a BMI greater than or equal to 30. Data for 1966–1970 are for adolescents 12–17 years, not 12–19 years. Pregnant adolescents were excluded beginning in 1971–1974. Pregnant women 20 years of age and over were excluded in all years. See Appendix II, Age adjustment; Body mass index (BMI). See related Tables 73 and 74.

SOURCES: Centers for Disease Control and Prevention, National Center for Health Statistics. National Health Examination Survey and National Health and Nutrition Examination Survey.

Data table for Figure 14. Untreated dental caries among children, by age, race and Hispanic origin: United States, 1971–2002

Characteristic	1971–1974		1988–1994		1999–2002	
	Percent	SE	Percent	SE	Percent	SE
	Children 2–17 years					
Total	48.3	1.5	22.4	0.9	21.0	1.0
Race and Hispanic origin						
Not Hispanic or Latino:						
White	45.7	1.5	17.6	1.0	17.4	1.8
Black or African American	61.0	2.6	30.6	1.4	26.9	1.3
Mexican	53.7	4.2	36.1	1.6	31.9	1.4
	Children 2–5 years					
Total	25.0	1.7	19.1	1.2	19.3	1.6
Race and Hispanic origin						
Not Hispanic or Latino:						
White	23.7	1.8	13.8	1.6	16.9	2.1
Black or African American	29.0	3.2	24.7	1.9	24.1	2.6
Mexican	34.1	6.5	34.9	1.7	31.4	1.8
	Children 6–17 years					
Total	54.8	1.6	23.6	1.2	21.5	1.1
Race and Hispanic origin						
Not Hispanic or Latino:						
White	51.9	1.6	18.9	1.2	17.5	2.0
Black or African American	70.1	3.3	32.8	1.5	27.7	1.2
Mexican	60.2	7.7	36.6	2.1	32.0	1.5

SE is standard error.

NOTES: Untreated dental caries refers to untreated coronal caries, that is, caries on the crown or enamel surface of the tooth. Root caries are not included. For children 2–5 years of age, only dental caries in primary teeth was evaluated. Caries in both permanent and primary teeth was evaluated for children 6–11 years of age. For children 12–17 years of age, only dental caries in permanent teeth was evaluated. Total includes children of all other races and Hispanic origins not shown separately. Persons of Mexican origin may be of any race. Starting with 1999 data, race-specific estimates are tabulated according to the 1997 Revisions to the Standards for the Classification of Federal Data on Race and Ethnicity and are not strictly comparable with estimates for earlier years. See Appendix II, Dental caries; Hispanic origin; Race. See related Table 75.

SOURCE: Centers for Disease Control and Prevention, National Center for Health Statistics, National Health and Nutrition Examination Survey.

Data table for Figure 15. Three or more chronic conditions among adults 45 years of age and over, by age and percent of poverty level: United States, 2004

Percent of poverty level	45–54 years		55–64 years		65–74 years		75 years and over	
	Percent	SE	Percent	SE	Percent	SE	Percent	SE
Total	7.3	0.4	17.2	0.7	28.2	1.0	35.9	1.1
Below 100%...................	17.3	1.7	31.3	2.5	37.0	3.0	38.2	3.1
100%–less than 200%.............	12.2	1.6	25.7	2.1	32.9	2.1	36.7	1.8
200%–less than 400%.............	6.0	0.7	17.1	1.3	27.7	1.7	35.4	1.8
400% or more..................	5.2	0.5	12.0	0.9	22.6	1.7	33.9	2.8

SE is standard error.

NOTES: Chronic health conditions, except for asthma, were determined by asking if a doctor or health professional ever told the respondent that he or she had a specified condition. Current asthma was determined by asking if a doctor or health professional ever told the respondent he or she had asthma and whether the respondent still had asthma. The health measure, three or more chronic conditions, includes three or more of the following conditions: hypertension, heart disease, stroke, emphysema, diabetes, cancer, arthritis and related diseases, or current asthma. Heart disease includes coronary heart disease, angina or angina pectoris, heart attack or myocardial infarction, and any other kind of heart condition or heart disease. Diabetes includes all types with the exception of diabetic conditions related to pregnancy. Cancer includes all types with the exception of non-melanoma skin cancer. Arthritis includes arthritis, rheumatoid arthritis, gout, lupus, or fibromyalgia. Percent of poverty level is based on family income and family size and composition using U.S. Census Bureau poverty thresholds. Missing family income data were imputed for 37% of adults 45 years of age and over in 2004. See Appendix II, Condition; Family income; Poverty.

SOURCE: Centers for Disease Control and Prevention, National Center for Health Statistics, National Health Interview Survey.

Data table for Figure 16. Selected chronic health conditions causing limitation of activity among children, by age: United States, 2003–2004

Type of chronic health condition	Under 5 years		5–11 years		12–17 years	
	Rate	SE	Rate	SE	Rate	SE
	Number of children with limitation of activity caused by selected chronic health conditions per 1,000 population					
Speech problem	10.4	1.0	19.0	1.2	5.2	0.6
Asthma or breathing problem	7.2	0.8	6.8	0.7	5.7	0.6
Mental retardation or other developmental problem	7.5	0.9	10.8	0.9	9.8	0.9
Other mental, emotional, or behavioral problem	3.4	0.6	13.1	1.1	15.4	1.2
Attention Deficit/Hyperactivity Disorder	*1.9	0.5	18.7	1.2	21.9	1.3
Learning disability	2.7	0.5	19.6	1.2	29.1	1.5

SE is standard error.
* Estimates are considered unreliable. Data preceded by an asterisk have a relative standard error (RSE) of 20% to 30%.

NOTES: Data are for noninstitutionalized children. Children with limitation of activity caused by chronic health conditions were either identified by enrollment in special programs (special education or early intervention services) or by a limitation in their ability to perform activities usual for their age group because of a physical, mental, or emotional problem. Conditions refer to response categories in the National Health Interview Survey. Children who were reported to have more than one chronic health condition as the cause of their activity limitation were counted in each reported category. Starting in 2001, the condition list for children was expanded to include categories for Attention Deficit/Hyperactivity Disorder (ADHD or ADD) and learning disability. Thus, comparable data for this figure are not available prior to 2001. See Appendix II, Condition; Limitation of activity. See related Table 58.

SOURCE: Centers for Disease Control and Prevention, National Center for Health Statistics, National Health Interview Survey.

Data table for Figure 17. Selected chronic health conditions causing limitation of activity among working-age adults, by age: United States, 2003–2004

Type of chronic health condition	18–44 years		45–54 years		55–64 years	
	Rate	SE	Rate	SE	Rate	SE
	Number of persons with limitation of activity caused by selected chronic health conditions per 1,000 population					
Mental illness	13.3	0.5	20.9	1.0	21.7	1.3
Fractures or joint injury.	6.6	0.4	13.1	0.8	18.2	1.1
Lung	5.0	0.3	11.6	0.8	23.0	1.3
Diabetes.	2.4	0.2	13.9	0.8	34.1	1.5
Heart or other circulatory	5.4	0.3	26.0	1.1	72.1	2.3
Arthritis or other musculoskeletal.	20.8	0.7	59.1	1.6	97.7	2.7

SE is standard error.

NOTES: Data are for the civilian noninstitutionalized population. Conditions refer to response categories in the National Health Interview Survey; some conditions include several response categories. Mental illness includes depression, anxiety or emotional problem, and other mental conditions. Heart or other circulatory includes heart problem, stroke problem, hypertension or high blood pressure, and other circulatory system conditions. Arthritis or other musculoskeletal includes arthritis or rheumatism, back or neck problem, and other musculoskeletal system conditions. Persons may report more than one chronic health condition as the cause of their activity limitation. See related Table 58. See Appendix II, Condition; Limitation of activity.

SOURCE: Centers for Disease Control and Prevention, National Center for Health Statistics, National Health Interview Survey.

Data table for Figure 18. Selected chronic health conditions causing limitation of activity among older adults, by age: United States, 2003–2004

Type of chronic health condition	65–74 years		75–84 years		85 years and over	
	Rate	SE	Rate	SE	Rate	SE
	Number of persons with limitation of activity caused by selected chronic health conditions per 1,000 population					
Senility.	7.1	0.8	31.6	2.2	97.8	7.0
Lung	32.9	2.0	41.2	2.5	39.7	4.6
Diabetes.	42.6	1.9	49.1	2.7	47.2	5.2
Vision.	19.0	1.5	38.7	2.5	82.8	6.6
Hearing	9.9	1.0	24.1	1.9	66.7	5.7
Heart or other circulatory	100.9	3.3	156.7	5.0	223.7	9.9
Arthritis or other musculoskeletal.	127.1	3.7	181.1	5.1	268.3	10.2

SE is standard error.

NOTES: Data are for the civilian noninstitutionalized population. Conditions refer to response categories in the National Health Interview Survey; some conditions include several response categories. Vision includes vision conditions or problems seeing and hearing includes hearing problems. Heart or other circulatory includes heart problem, stroke problem, hypertension or high blood pressure, and other circulatory system conditions. Arthritis or other musculoskeletal includes arthritis or rheumatism, back or neck problem, and other musculoskeletal system conditions. Senility is the term offered to respondents on a flashcard, but this category may include Alzheimer's disease or other types of dementia reported by the respondent. Persons may report more than one chronic health condition as the cause of their activity limitation. See related Table 58. See Appendix II, Condition; Limitation of activity.

SOURCE: Centers for Disease Control and Prevention, National Center for Health Statistics, National Health Interview Survey.

Data table for Figure 19. Dental visit in the past year among children, by age, race and Hispanic origin: United States, 2004

Characteristic	2004	
	Percent	SE
Children 2–17 years		
Total.	76.4	0.5
Race and Hispanic origin		
Not Hispanic or Latino:		
White only.	80.9	0.6
Black or African American only.	72.9	1.4
Hispanic	65.3	1.1
Asian only.	73.8	2.7
Children 2–5 years		
Total.	53.7	1.1
Race and Hispanic origin		
Not Hispanic or Latino:		
White only.	55.6	1.6
Black or African American only.	47.8	3.4
Hispanic	51.8	2.1
Asian only.	*	*
Children 6–17 years		
Total.	83.8	0.5
Race and Hispanic origin		
Not Hispanic or Latino:		
White only.	88.7	0.6
Black or African American only.	80.4	1.4
Hispanic	70.7	1.3
Asian only.	80.9	2.8

SE is standard error.
* Estimates are considered unreliable. Relative standard error greater than 30%.

NOTES: Total includes children of all races not shown separately. Persons of Hispanic origin may be of any race. Asian race includes children of Hispanic and non-Hispanic origin. See Appendix II, Dental visit; Hispanic origin; Race. See related Tables 75, 91, and Figure 14.

SOURCE: Centers for Disease Control and Prevention, National Center for Health Statistics, National Health Interview Survey.

Data table for Figure 20. Influenza vaccination during the past year among adults 50 years of age and over, by race and Hispanic origin: United States, 2003–2004

Race and Hispanic origin	Influenza vaccination during the past 12 months			
	50–64 years		65 years and over	
	Percent	SE	Percent	SE
Total	36.4	0.5	65.1	0.5
Hispanic or Latino	27.5	1.3	50.1	1.9
Not Hispanic or Latino:				
White only	38.5	0.6	68.0	0.6
Black or African American only.	27.0	1.2	46.7	1.7

SE is standard error.

NOTES: Data are for the civilian noninstitutionalized population. Excludes Flu Mist. Persons of Hispanic origin may be of any race. See Appendix II, Hispanic origin; Race. See related Table 83.

SOURCE: Centers for Disease Control and Prevention, National Center for Health Statistics, National Health Interview Survey.

Data table for Figure 21. Emergency department visits for falls, by sex and age: United States, 2002–2004

| | Emergency department visits for falls | | | | | | | | |
| | Both sexes | | | Male | | | Female | | |
Age and disposition for fall visits	Average annual in thousands	Number per 10,000 population	SE	Average annual in thousands	Number per 10,000 population	SE	Average annual in thousands	Number per 10,000 population	SE
All ages:									
All visits for falls	7,857	275.0	8.0	3,607	258.6	8.5	4,249	290.7	10.0
Fall visits with severe visit disposition	919	32.2	1.6	346	24.8	1.6	574	39.3	2.4
Under 18 years:									
All visits for falls	2,314	317.4	13.8	1,311	351.7	17.3	1,003	281.5	15.2
Fall visits with severe visit disposition	85	11.6	1.9	49	13.1	2.4	36	*10.1	2.7
18–44 years:									
All visits for falls	2,247	203.8	7.1	1,141	208.9	9.5	1,106	198.8	9.5
Fall visits with severe visit disposition	97	8.8	1.2	61	11.2	1.9	36	*6.5	1.4
45–64 years:									
All visits for falls	1,377	201.9	8.2	526	158.9	9.3	852	242.4	12.2
Fall visits with severe visit disposition	140	20.6	2.0	68	20.6	2.9	72	20.6	2.7
65–74 years:									
All visits for falls	564	311.6	17.9	234	283.5	27.7	331	335.1	22.7
Fall visits with severe visit disposition	127	69.9	8.2	47	*57.4	11.9	79	80.4	11.3
75–84 years:									
All visits for falls	743	606.5	31.6	243	488.4	36.5	501	687.1	46.1
Fall visits with severe visit disposition	224	182.6	16.4	74	149.7	22.4	149	205.1	20.9
85 years and over:									
All visits for falls	611	1,554.3	93.8	153	1,178.1	124.9	458	1,740.1	123.1
Fall visits with severe visit disposition	247	627.8	53.8	46	355.2	48.0	201	762.3	78.9

See footnotes at end of table.

Data table for Figure 21. Emergency department visits for falls, by sex and age: United States, 2002–2004—Con.

Age and disposition for fall visits	Both sexes		Male		Female	
	Fall visits as a percent of all emergency department visits	SE	Fall visits as a percent of all emergency department visits	SE	Fall visits as a percent of all emergency department visits	SE
All ages:						
All visits for falls	7.1	0.1	7.0	0.2	7.1	0.2
Fall visits with severe visit disposition	0.8	0.0	0.7	0.0	1.0	0.1
Under 18 years:						
All visits for falls	8.3	0.3	8.9	0.4	7.6	0.3
Fall visits with severe visit disposition	0.3	0.0	0.3	0.1	*0.3	0.1
18–44 years:						
All visits for falls	4.9	0.1	5.7	0.2	4.3	0.2
Fall visits with severe visit disposition	0.2	0.0	0.3	0.1	*0.1	0.0
45–64 years:						
All visits for falls	6.6	0.2	5.4	0.3	7.6	0.3
Fall visits with severe visit disposition	0.7	0.1	0.7	0.1	0.6	0.1
65–74 years:						
All visits for falls	8.4	0.4	7.6	0.6	9.1	0.6
Fall visits with severe visit disposition	1.9	0.2	*1.5	0.3	2.2	0.3
75–84 years:						
All visits for falls	11.4	0.5	9.1	0.6	12.9	0.7
Fall visits with severe visit disposition	3.4	0.3	2.8	0.4	3.8	0.4
85 years and over:						
All visits for falls	18.3	0.8	13.9	1.3	20.5	1.1
Fall visits with severe visit disposition	7.4	0.5	4.2	0.5	9.0	0.8

SE is standard error.

* Estimates are considered unreliable. Data preceded by an asterisk have a relative standard error (RSE) of 20% to 30%.

0.0 Quantity more than zero but less than 0.05.

NOTES: Visits for falls had a first-listed external cause of injury code of E880–886, E888, E957, E968.1, and E987. Severe visit disposition is an emergency department visit resulting in a hospital admission, transfer to another facility, or the person died in the emergency department. In 2002–2004, 85% of visits with a severe disposition outcome were hospitalized, 15% were transferred to another facility, and less than 1% died in the emergency department.

SOURCE: Centers for Disease Control and Prevention, National Center for Health Statistics, National Hospital Ambulatory Medical Care Survey.

Data table for Figure 22. Visits to physician offices and hospital outpatient departments, by sex and age: United States, 1997–2004

Sex and age	1997–1998	1999–2000	2001–2002	2003–2004
Both sexes	Average annual visits in thousands			
Total.	884,528	874,094	1,041,286	998,226
Under 18 years	183,286	170,960	202,661	194,133
18–44 years	279,065	263,239	293,581	276,862
45–54 years	118,642	125,585	155,717	149,219
55–64 years	97,214	104,594	129,279	134,179
65–74 years	107,784	104,786	127,813	117,042
75 years and over	98,538	104,930	132,235	126,791
Male				
Total.	352,838	356,872	420,251	407,032
Under 18 years	95,027	88,472	103,545	101,578
18–44 years	87,262	88,808	96,590	86,681
45–54 years	45,426	49,325	61,611	60,670
55–64 years	42,356	44,327	52,493	55,975
65–74 years	45,399	45,106	55,434	50,878
75 years and over	37,368	40,834	50,578	51,250
Female				
Total.	531,691	517,222	621,035	591,194
Under 18 years	88,260	82,488	99,115	92,555
18–44 years	191,804	174,431	196,991	190,182
45–54 years	73,216	76,260	94,106	88,549
55–64 years	54,858	60,266	76,787	78,204
65–74 years	62,385	59,681	72,379	66,164
75 years and over	61,169	64,096	81,657	75,541

See footnotes at end of table.

Data table for Figure 22. Visits to physician offices and hospital outpatient departments, by sex and age: United States, 1997–2004—Con.

Sex and age	Rate	SE	Rate	SE	Rate	SE	Rate	SE
Both sexes				Number of visits per 100 persons				
Total	330.0	9.5	318.6	10.8	369.8	9.4	347.9	10.1
Under 18 years	255.8	9.0	236.9	11.4	279.2	9.9	265.9	12.6
18–44 years	257.5	8.8	241.7	9.9	266.8	8.6	251.1	9.4
45–54 years	349.8	11.4	342.6	12.9	396.0	12.6	365.1	12.9
55–64 years	443.7	15.6	442.0	16.4	501.1	15.9	473.6	17.5
65–74 years	598.1	22.8	583.4	23.0	707.9	25.4	644.6	26.1
75 years and over	694.3	30.4	700.3	28.1	837.8	33.0	777.4	34.0
Male								
Total	269.9	8.3	267.0	9.2	306.1	8.3	290.3	9.1
Under 18 years	259.2	9.9	239.6	11.8	278.9	10.1	272.2	13.8
18–44 years	163.1	6.2	165.4	7.5	177.7	7.3	158.5	6.1
45–54 years	274.5	10.6	275.9	11.7	321.1	12.3	303.8	12.9
55–64 years	405.5	16.4	392.1	16.7	424.5	15.4	411.4	18.4
65–74 years	560.6	25.2	555.9	23.7	676.9	26.4	614.8	25.6
75 years and over	682.5	32.8	707.6	30.3	834.2	34.5	809.4	38.2
Female								
Total	387.1	11.5	367.7	12.9	430.5	11.5	402.9	12.0
Under 18 years	252.3	9.0	234.1	11.6	279.5	10.8	259.4	12.2
18–44 years	349.4	13.2	315.9	13.8	353.9	12.4	342.2	14.6
45–54 years	421.6	15.0	406.2	16.3	467.4	15.9	423.5	15.6
55–64 years	478.6	17.6	487.8	19.0	571.5	20.1	531.1	19.8
65–74 years	628.8	25.1	606.0	26.4	733.7	29.7	669.7	30.8
75 years and over	701.7	32.3	695.7	29.5	840.1	37.4	757.1	35.2

SE is standard error.

NOTES: For 1997–1999 data, population estimates are 1990-based postcensal estimates as of July 1 and are adjusted for net underenumeration using the 1990 National Population Adjustment Matrix from the U.S. Census Bureau. Starting with 2000 data, population estimates are based on the 2000 census. See Appendix I, Population Census and Population Estimates. See related Table 89. Starting with *Health, United States, 2005,* data from 2001 and onwards use a revised weighting scheme. See Appendix I, National Ambulatory Medical Care Survey.

SOURCES: Centers for Disease Control and Prevention, National Center for Health Statistics, National Ambulatory Medical Care Survey, and National Hospital Ambulatory Medical Care Survey.

Data table for Figure 23. Average annual hospital inpatient gastric bypass and other bariatric procedures among adults 18–64 years of age with obesity, by sex and age: United States, 1996–2004

Sex and age	1996–1998	1999–2001	2002–2004
	Number	Number	Number
	Average annual		
Both sexes			
18–64 years	*11,111	30,475	106,242
18–44 years.	*6,927	19,067	63,602
45–64 years.	*4,184	11,409	42,640
Men			
18–64 years	*1,789	4,570	17,134
18–44 years.	*	*1,871	9,246
45–64 years.	*	*2,699	7,888
Women			
18–64 years	*9,322	25,905	89,108
18–44 years.	*6,083	17,196	54,356
45–64 years.	*3,239	8,709	34,751

*Estimates are considered unreliable. Data preceded by an asterisk have a relative standard error (RSE) of 20% to 30%. Data not shown have an RSE of greater than 30%.

NOTES: Obesity is defined as diagnosis codes 278.00 or 278.01 on the discharge record. Up to four procedures were coded for each non-federal hospital stay. Data in this table are for any listed procedure; if more than one bariatric procedure is performed during the same hospital stay, it is counted only once. Procedures codes 44.31, 44.39, 44.69 define bariatric surgery. Starting with 2003 data, procedure codes 43.7, 43.89, 45.51, and 45.91 are also included. In addition to these seven codes, the 2004 data define bariatric surgery using procedures codes 44.68, 44.95, 44.96, 44.97, and 44.98. Procedure groupings and code numbers are based on the International *Classification of Diseases, 9th Revision, Clinical Modification* (ICD–9–CM). Data on adults age 65 and over are considered unreliable because of the small number of procedures performed and therefore are not presented. See Appendix II, *International Classification of Diseases, 9th Revision,Clinical Modification* (ICD–9–CM).

SOURCE: Centers for Disease Control and Prevention, National Center for Health Statistics, National Hospital Discharge Survey.

Data table for Figure 24. Life expectancy at birth and at 65 years of age, by sex: United States, 1900–2003

Year	At birth		At 65 years	
	Male	Female	Male	Female
	Life expectancy in years			
1900–1902	47.9	50.7	11.5	12.2
1909–1911	49.9	53.2	11.2	12.0
1919–1921	55.5	57.4	12.2	12.7
1929–1931	57.7	60.9	11.7	12.8
1939–1941	61.6	65.9	12.1	13.6
1949–1951	65.5	71.0	12.7	15.0
1959–1961	66.8	73.2	13.0	15.8
1969–1971	67.0	74.6	13.0	16.8
1979–1981	70.1	77.6	14.2	18.4
1989–1991	71.8	78.8	15.1	19.0
1997	73.6	79.4	15.9	19.2
1998	73.8	79.5	16.0	19.2
1999	73.9	79.4	16.1	19.1
2000	74.3	79.7	16.2	19.3
2001	74.4	79.8	16.4	19.4
2002	74.5	79.9	16.6	19.5
2003	74.8	80.1	16.8	19.8

NOTES: Death rates used to calculate life expectancies for 1997–1999 are based on postcensal 1990-based population estimates; life expectancies for 2000 and beyond are calculated with death rates based on census 2000. See Appendix I, Population Census and Population Estimates. Life expectancies prior to 1997 are from decennial life tables based on census data and deaths for a 3-year period around the census year. The middle year in each 3-year period is plotted in Figure 24. Beginning in 1997, the annual life tables are complete life tables based on a methodology similar to that used for decennial life tables. Alaska and Hawaii were included beginning in 1959. For decennial periods prior to 1929–31, data are limited to death registration states: 1900–1902 and 1909–1911, 10 states and the District of Columbia; 1919- 1921, 34 states and the District of Columbia. Deaths to nonresidents were excluded beginning in 1970. See Appendix II, Life expectancy. See related Table 27.

SOURCE: Arias, E. United States life tables, 2003. National vital statistics reports; vol 54 no 14. Hyattsville, MD: National Center for Health Statistics. 2006.

Data table for Figure 25. Infant, neonatal, and postneonatal mortality rates: United States, 1950–2003

Year	Infant	Neonatal	Postneonatal
	Deaths per 1,000 live births		
1950	29.2	20.5	8.7
1960	26.0	18.7	7.3
1970	20.0	15.1	4.9
1980	12.6	8.5	4.1
1985	10.6	7.0	3.7
1990	9.2	5.8	3.4
1995	7.6	4.9	2.7
1996	7.3	4.8	2.5
1997	7.2	4.8	2.5
1998	7.2	4.8	2.4
1999	7.1	4.7	2.3
2000	6.9	4.6	2.3
2001	6.8	4.5	2.3
2002	7.0	4.7	2.3
2003	6.9	4.6	2.2

NOTES: Infant is defined as under 1 year of age, neonatal as under 28 days of age, and postneonatal as between 28 days and 1 year of age. See related Table 22.

SOURCE: Centers for Disease Control and Prevention, National Center for Health Statistics, National Vital Statistics System.

Data table for Figure 26. Infant mortality rates, by detailed race and Hispanic origin of mother: United States, 2001–2003

Race and Hispanic origin of mother	Infant deaths per 1,000 live births
White, not Hispanic or Latino	5.7
Black or African American, not Hispanic or Latino	13.6
Hispanic or Latino	5.6
Puerto Rican	8.3
Other and unknown Hispanic or Latino	6.6
Mexican	5.4
Central and South American	5.0
Cuban	4.2
Asian or Pacific Islander	4.8
American Indian or Alaska Native	8.9

NOTES: Infant is defined as under 1 year of age. Persons of Hispanic origin may be of any race. Asian or Pacific Islander and American Indian or Alaska Native races include persons of Hispanic and non-Hispanic origin. Starting in 2003, some states reported multiple-race data. The multiple-race data for these states were bridged to the single race categories of the 1977 Office of Management and Budget standards for comparability with other states. Estimates are not shown for Asian or Pacific Islander subgroups during the transition from single race to multiple race reporting. See Appendix II, Hispanic origin; Race. See related Table 19.

SOURCE: Centers for Disease Control and Prevention, National Center for Health Statistics, National Vital Statistics System, National Linked Birth/Infant Death Data Sets.

Data table for Figure 27. Death rates for leading causes of death for all ages: United States, 1950–2003

Year	All causes	Heart disease	Cancer	Stroke	Chronic lower respiratory diseases	Unintentional injuries
			Deaths per 100,000 population			
1950	1,446.0	586.8	193.9	180.7	- - -	78.0
1960	1,339.2	559.0	193.9	177.9	- - -	62.3
1970	1,222.6	492.7	198.6	147.7	- - -	60.1
1980	1,039.1	412.1	207.9	96.2	28.3	46.4
1985	988.1	375.0	211.3	76.4	34.5	38.5
1990	938.7	321.8	216.0	65.3	37.2	36.3
1995	909.8	293.4	209.9	63.1	40.1	34.4
1996	894.1	285.7	206.7	62.5	40.6	34.5
1997	878.1	277.7	203.4	61.1	41.1	34.2
1998	870.6	271.3	200.7	59.3	41.8	34.5
1998 (Comparability-modified)	870.6	267.4	202.1	62.8	43.8	35.6
1999	875.6	266.5	200.8	61.6	45.4	35.3
2000	869.0	257.6	199.6	60.9	44.2	34.9
2001	854.5	247.8	196.0	57.9	43.7	35.7
2002	845.3	240.8	193.5	56.2	43.5	36.9
2003	832.7	232.3	190.1	53.5	43.3	37.3

- - - Data not available.

NOTES: Estimates are age adjusted to the year 2000 standard population using age groups from under 1 year, 1–4 years, 10-year age groups from 5–14 through 75–84 years, and 85 years and over. Causes of death shown are the five leading causes of death for all ages in 2003. The 1950 death rates are based on the 6th revision of the International Classification of Disease (ICD-6), 1960 death rates on the ICD-7, 1970 death rates on the ICDA-8, and 1980–1998 death rates on the ICD-9. The 1998 (comparability-modified) death rates use comparability ratios to adjust the rate to be comparable to records classified according to ICD-10. Starting with 1999 data, death rates are based on ICD-10. Comparability ratios across revisions for selected causes are available from: www.cdc.gov/nchs/data/statab/comp2.pdf. Death rates for chronic lower respiratory diseases are available from 1980 when a category that included bronchitis, emphysema, asthma, and other chronic lung diseases was introduced in ICD-9. Cancer refers to malignant neoplasms; stroke to cerebrovascular diseases; and unintentional injuries is preferred to the term, accidents, in the public health community. Rates for 1991–1999 were computed using intercensal population estimates based on the 2000 census. Rates for 2000 were computed using 2000 census counts. Rates for 2001 and beyond were computed using postcensal estimates based on the 2000 census. See Appendix I, Population Census and Population Estimates. See Appendix II, Age adjustment; Cause of death; Comparability ratio. See related Tables 29, 31, 35, 36, 37, 38, 39, and 41.

SOURCE: Centers for Disease Control and Prevention, National Center for Health Statistics, National Vital Statistics System.

Data table for Figure 28. Adults 20 years of age and over reporting pain in the month prior to interview, by selected characteristics: United States, 1999–2002

Characteristic	Percent	SE
Age		
20 years and over	25.8	0.7
20–44 years.	25.1	0.9
45–64 years.	29.6	1.4
65 years and over	21.0	0.9
Sex		
Men	24.4	0.8
Women.	27.1	0.9
Race and Hispanic origin		
Not Hispanic or Latino:		
White only	27.8	0.8
Black only	22.1	1.4
Mexican	15.3	1.1
Percent of poverty level		
Below 100%	29.8	1.7
100%–less than 200%	28.3	1.3
200% or more	24.8	0.8

SE is standard error.

NOTES: Data are for the civilian noninstitutionalized population. Respondents were asked to report pain that lasted more than 24 hours in duration during the month prior to interview. Persons of Mexican origin may be of any race. Percent of poverty level is based on family income and family size and composition using U.S. Census Bureau poverty thresholds. See Appendix II, Family income; Hispanic origin; Poverty; Race.

SOURCE: Centers for Disease Control and Prevention, National Center for Health Statistics, National Health and Nutrition Examination Survey.

Data table for Figure 29. Duration of pain among adults reporting pain, by age: United States, 1999–2002

Age	Less than 1 month		1 month to less than 3 months		3 months to less than 1 year		1 year or more	
	Percent	SE	Percent	SE	Percent	SE	Percent	SE
20 years and over	32.0	1.2	12.3	0.9	13.7	0.9	42.0	1.0
20–44 years.	39.1	1.9	11.9	1.6	12.5	1.6	36.5	1.8
45–64 years.	27.2	1.9	13.6	1.1	15.5	1.6	43.7	1.7
65 years and over	18.9	2.2	10.4	1.4	13.4	2.2	57.3	1.6

SE is standard error.

NOTES: Data are for the civilian noninstitutionalized population. Respondents who reported pain lasting more than 24 hours in duration in the month prior to interview (see Figure 28), were asked a question about the duration of that pain. Percentages shown are among adults who reported pain.

SOURCE: Centers for Disease Control and Prevention, National Center for Health Statistics, National Health and Nutrition Examination Survey.

Data table for Figure 30. Adults reporting low back pain, migraine, neck, and face pain in the 3 months prior to interview, by age: United States, 2004

Age	Low back pain		Severe headache or migraine		Neck pain		Face pain	
	Percent	SE	Percent	SE	Percent	SE	Percent	SE
18 years and over	27.2	0.3	15.3	0.3	14.8	0.3	4.3	0.1
18–44 years.	23.9	0.5	18.4	0.4	12.4	0.3	4.5	0.2
45–64 years.	30.8	0.5	15.0	0.4	18.7	0.5	4.7	0.2
65 years and over	30.4	0.7	6.2	0.3	14.4	0.5	2.9	0.2

SE is standard error.

NOTES: Data are for the civilian noninstitutionalized population. Respondents were asked: "During the past 3 months, did you have neck pain? Or low back pain? Or facial ache or pain in the jaw muscles or the joint in front of the ear? Or severe headache or migraine?" Respondents were asked to report pain that lasted a whole day or more and to not report aches or pains that are fleeting or minor. Respondents reporting more than one type of pain were included in each category. See related Table 56.

SOURCE: Centers for Disease Control and Prevention, National Center for Health Statistics, National Health Interview Survey.

Data table for Figure 31. Adults 18 years of age and over reporting low back pain in the 3 months prior to interview, by selected characteristics: United States, 2004

Characteristic	Total		Men		Women	
	Percent	SE	Percent	SE	Percent	SE
Age						
18 years and over	27.2	0.3	25.0	0.5	29.2	0.4
18–44 years.	23.9	0.5	22.0	0.6	25.8	0.6
45–64 years.	30.8	0.5	28.9	0.8	32.5	0.7
65 years and over	30.4	0.7	27.2	1.1	32.8	0.9
Race and Hispanic origin						
Hispanic	22.1	0.7	18.5	0.9	25.8	1.0
Not Hispanic or Latino:						
White only	29.1	0.4	27.4	0.6	30.7	0.5
Black or African American only.	23.5	0.8	20.1	1.2	26.3	1.1
Asian only.	16.9	1.3	14.6	1.8	19.2	2.0
Percent of poverty level						
Below 100%	31.3	1.0	26.3	1.4	34.8	1.1
100%–less than 200%	29.5	0.8	26.7	1.2	31.8	0.9
200% or more	25.9	0.4	24.4	0.5	27.3	0.5

SE is standard error.

NOTES: Data are for the civilian noninstitutionalized population. Respondents were asked: "During the past 3 months, did you have low back pain?" Respondents were asked to report pain that lasted a whole day or more and to not report aches or pains that were fleeting or minor. Persons of Hispanic origin may be of any race. Asian only race includes persons of Hispanic and non-Hispanic origin. Percent of poverty level is based on family income and family size and composition using U.S. Census Bureau poverty thresholds. Missing family income data were imputed for 35% of persons 18 years of age and over in 2004. See Appendix II, Family income; Hispanic origin; Poverty; Race. See related Table 56.

SOURCE: Centers for Disease Control and Prevention, National Center for Health Statistics, National Health Interview Survey.

Data table for Figure 32. Adults 18 years of age and over reporting joint pain in the 30 days prior to interview, by severity level and selected characteristics: United States, 2003

Characteristic	Any joint pain		Severe joint pain		Lesser joint pain	
	Percent	SE	Percent	SE	Percent	SE
Age						
18 years and over	31.4	0.4	8.4	0.2	23.0	0.3
18–44 years.	20.5	0.4	4.9	0.2	15.6	0.4
45–64 years.	39.9	0.6	11.5	0.4	28.5	0.6
65 years and over	49.9	0.8	13.6	0.5	36.3	0.8
Sex						
Men	28.5	0.5	6.5	0.2	21.9	0.4
Women.	34.1	0.5	10.1	0.3	24.0	0.4
Race and Hispanic origin						
Hispanic	18.9	0.7	7.8	0.4	11.1	0.5
Not Hispanic or Latino:						
White only	34.7	0.4	8.2	0.2	26.5	0.4
Black only	27.8	0.9	11.2	0.6	16.6	0.7
Asian only	17.2	1.5	3.3	0.7	13.9	1.4
Percent of poverty level						
Below 100%	30.6	0.9	13.4	0.6	17.2	0.7
100%–less than 200%	34.0	0.8	11.5	0.5	22.6	0.7
200% or more	30.9	0.4	6.7	0.2	24.2	0.4

SE is standard error.

NOTES: Data are for the civilian noninstitutionalized population. Respondents were asked "During the past 30 days, have you had any symptoms of pain, aching, or stiffness in or around a joint?" Respondents, who reported joint symptoms, were asked "During the past 30 days, how bad was your joint pain on average?" Respondents were instructed to answer on a scale of 0–10 where 0 is no pain or aching and 10 is pain or aching as bad as it can be. In this analysis, lesser joint pain was defined as 0–6 and severe pain was defined as a response of 7–10. This analysis excludes a small number of adults who did not provide information on both joint pain questions. Persons of Hispanic origin may be of any race. Asian only race includes persons of Hispanic and non-Hispanic origin. Percent of poverty level is based on family income and family size and composition using U.S. Census Bureau poverty thresholds. Missing family income data were imputed for 36% of persons 18 years of age and over in 2003. See Appendix II, Family income; Hispanic origin; Poverty; Race. See related Table 57.

SOURCE: Centers for Disease Control and Prevention, National Center for Health Statistics, National Health Interview Survey.

Data table for Figure 33. Narcotic analgesic drug visits to the emergency department, by pain level, age, sex, and race: United States, average annual 2003–2004

Age, sex, and race	Emergency department visit with narcotic analgesic drugs		Narcotic analgesic drug visit by level of pain									
			No pain		Mild pain		Moderate pain		Severe pain		Unknown/ missing pain level	
	Percent	SE	Percent	SE	Percent	SE	Percent	SE	Percent	SE	Percent	SE
Total...................	22.9	0.5	5.1	0.3	18.5	0.7	33.1	0.9	49.8	1.0	15.6	0.5
Age												
Under 11 years............	4.1	0.3	*1.4	0.3	4.4	0.7	9.1	1.1	16.7	2.3	2.9	0.3
11–17 years	14.8	0.8	*2.1	0.5	11.8	1.5	20.5	1.6	32.1	2.6	10.8	1.0
18–44 years	30.2	0.7	6.7	0.6	23.0	0.9	37.8	1.1	52.8	1.3	22.7	0.9
45–64 years	30.0	0.7	7.8	1.0	24.7	1.2	39.0	1.3	56.9	1.5	21.1	0.9
65 years and over	19.7	0.6	5.6	0.5	19.8	1.3	32.9	1.6	46.0	1.8	15.1	0.8
Sex												
Male....................	21.6	0.5	5.1	0.5	18.1	0.9	32.6	1.0	50.3	1.3	14.3	0.5
Female..................	24.0	0.6	5.1	0.4	18.9	0.9	33.6	1.0	49.5	1.1	16.7	0.6
Race												
White....................	24.4	0.5	5.3	0.4	19.9	0.8	35.3	0.9	53.0	1.1	16.6	0.5
Black	18.2	0.6	4.3	0.6	14.2	1.0	26.3	1.5	39.5	1.8	12.3	0.8

SE is standard error.

* Data are considered unreliable. Data preceded by an asterisk have a relative standard error of 20% to 30%.

NOTES: The race groups include persons of Hispanic and non-Hispanic origin. Visits are classified as narcotic analgesic drug visits if at least one narcotic analgesic drug was prescribed or provided during the visit. For listing of narcotic analgesic drugs, see Appendix II, National Drug Code (NDC) Directory therapeutic class; Table XII. Estimates for race in this table are for visits where only one race was recorded. Estimates for visits where multiple races were checked are unreliable and not presented.

SOURCES: Centers for Disease Control and Prevention, National Center for Health Statistics, National Hospital Ambulatory Medical Care Survey, Emergency Department Component.

Data table for Figure 34. Adults 18 years of age and over reporting narcotic drug use in the month prior to interview, by sex, age, race and ethnicity: United States, 1988–1994 and 1999–2002

Characteristic	1988–1994		1999–2002	
	Percent	SE	Percent	SE
Both sexes				
Total, age adjusted	3.2	0.2	4.2	0.3
Total, crude	3.2	0.2	4.2	0.3
18–44 years	2.9	0.3	3.6	0.4
45–64 years	3.3	0.4	4.6	0.7
65 years and over	3.9	0.4	5.7	0.5
Not Hispanic or Latino:				
White only	3.4	0.3	4.6	0.4
Black or African American only	3.4	0.2	3.8	0.7
Mexican	3.3	0.3	2.9	0.4
Men				
Total, age adjusted	2.8	0.3	3.0	0.3
Total, crude	2.7	0.3	3.0	0.3
18–44 years	2.4	0.4	2.5	0.4
45–64 years	3.3	0.6	*3.4	0.7
65 years and over	3.2	0.5	4.1	0.6
Not Hispanic or Latino:				
White only	2.9	0.4	3.3	0.4
Black or African American only	2.8	0.4	*2.9	0.7
Mexican	3.3	0.5	*2.7	0.6
Women				
Total, age adjusted	3.6	0.2	5.3	0.4
Total, crude	3.6	0.2	5.4	0.4
18–44 years	3.5	0.3	4.6	0.6
45–64 years	3.3	0.5	5.7	0.8
65 years and over	4.4	0.5	6.8	0.9
Not Hispanic or Latino:				
White only	3.8	0.3	5.9	0.5
Black or African American only	3.8	0.5	4.5	0.8
Mexican	3.3	0.4	3.2	0.5

SE is standard error.

* Estimates are considered unreliable. Data preceded by an asterisk have a relative standard error (RSE) of 20% to 30%.

NOTES: Data are for the civilian noninstitutionalized population. Narcotic drugs are defined as drugs in NDC class 1721. Estimates for 2000 and later years use weights derived from the 2000 census. Total and race-ethnicity estimates are age adjusted to the 2000 standard population using three age groups: 18–44 years, 45–64 years, and 65 years and over. Persons of Mexican origin may be of any race. Starting with data year 1999, race-specific estimates are tabulated according to the 1997 Revisions to the Standards for the Classification of Federal Data on Race and Ethnicity. See Appendix II, Age adjustment; Drugs; National Drug Code (NDC) Directory therapeutic class; Hispanic origin; Race.

SOURCE: Centers for Disease Control and Prevention, National Center for Health Statistics, National Health and Nutrition Examination Survey.

Data table for Figure 35. Hospital discharges for knee and nonfracture hip replacement surgery among adults 18 years of age and over, by sex and age: United States, 1992–1993 and 2003–2004

	Knee replacement					
	1992–1993	1992–1993		2003–2004	2003–2004	
Sex and age	Average annual number of hospital discharges with procedure performed in thousands	Hospital discharges with procedure performed per 10,000 population	SE	Average annual number of hospital discharges with procedure performed in thousands	Hospital discharges with procedure performed per 10,000 population	SE
Both sexes						
18 years and over	166	8.7	0.6	428	19.7	1.4
18–44 years	3	0.3	0.1	7	0.7	0.1
45–64 years	38	7.8	0.7	158	22.7	1.8
65 years and over	124	38.6	3.0	263	72.9	5.4
65–74 years	74	40.4	3.5	145	78.7	6.0
75 years and over	50	36.1	3.1	118	66.9	5.2
Men						
18 years and over	54	6.0	0.5	152	14.4	1.4
18–44 years	2	0.3	0.1	3	0.5	0.1
45–64 years	12	5.2	0.6	56	16.4	1.9
65 years and over	40	30.7	2.5	94	62.3	6.9
65–74 years	25	30.7	3.0	51	61.2	7.2
75 years and over	15	30.8	3.3	42	63.7	7.4
Women						
18 years and over	111	11.2	0.9	276	24.5	1.6
18–44 years	2	0.3	0.1	5	0.8	0.2
45–64 years	26	10.2	1.2	102	28.6	2.4
65 years and over	84	43.9	3.8	169	80.5	5.2
65–74 years	49	48.1	5.0	93	93.4	6.4
75 years and over	35	39.1	3.6	76	68.7	5.2

See footnotes at end of table.

Data table for Figure 35. Hospital discharges for knee and nonfracture hip replacement surgery among adults 18 years of age and over, by sex and age: United States, 1992–1993 and 2003–2004—Con.

Sex and age	Nonfracture hip replacement					
	1992–1993	1992–1993		2003–2004	2003–2004	
	Average annual number of hospital stays with procedure performed in thousands	Hospital stays with procedure performed per 10,000 population	SE	Average annual number of hopital stays with procedure performed in thousands	Hospital stays with procedure performed per 10,000 population	SE
Both sexes						
18 years and over	126	6.6	0.5	282	13.0	1.1
18–44 years	10	0.9	0.1	33	3.0	0.4
45–64 years	35	7.1	0.7	107	15.3	1.5
65 years and over	81	25.2	1.9	142	39.5	3.3
65–74 years	44	24.0	1.9	72	39.2	3.8
75 years and over	37	26.7	2.5	70	39.7	3.4
Men						
18 years and over	51	5.6	0.4	125	11.9	1.1
18–44 years	6	1.0	0.2	17	3.1	0.4
45–64 years	17	7.3	0.8	53	15.8	1.6
65 years and over	28	21.2	1.8	54	36.2	3.5
65–74 years	16	20.3	2.3	28	33.8	4.1
75 years and over	11	22.8	2.7	26	39.2	4.2
Women						
18 years and over	75	7.6	0.7	157	14.0	1.2
18–44 years	4	0.8	0.1	16	2.9	0.4
45–64 years	17	6.9	0.9	53	14.9	1.6
65 years and over	53	27.9	2.4	88	41.8	3.7
65–74 years	28	27.0	2.5	44	43.7	4.4
75 years and over	26	28.9	3.1	44	40.0	4.1

SE is standard error.

NOTES: Up to four inpatient hospital procedures were coded for each stay. Procedure codes are based on the *International Classification of Diseases, Ninth Revision, Clinical Modification* (knee replacement 81.54 and hip replacement 81.51–52, excluding hip fracture codes 820 and 733.14). In 2003–2004, 28% of hip replacements were for hip fracture. This table shows any-listed procedures; if more than one procedure with the same ICD code (e.g., hip replacement) is performed during the hospitalization it is counted only once. Rates are based on the civilian population as of July 1.

SOURCE: Centers for Disease Control and Prevention, National Center for Health Statistics, National Hospital Discharge Survey.

Data table for Figure 36. Adults reporting ambulatory medical care use for headaches and associated ambulatory medical care expenses, by age and sex: United States 2002–2003

Age and sex	Percent with ambulatory medical care for headaches	SE	Headache expenses per person with headache expense in dollars	SE
Age				
18 years and over	3.5	0.12	$566	$31
18–44 years.	3.4	0.16	516	46
45–64 years.	4.5	0.22	633	43
65 years and over	1.9	0.21	536	92
Sex				
Men	1.6	0.12	552	66
Women.	5.3	0.19	570	34

SE is standard error.

NOTES: Data are for the civilian noninstitutionalized population. Estimates for 2002 have been adjusted to 2003 dollars using the Consumer Price Index (All Urban Consumers: U.S. City Average: All items). Ambulatory medical care is defined as having one or more visits to a medical provider (office-based, hospital outpatient and emergency department settings) and/or at least one prescribed medicine purchase during the year. ICD–9–CM codes 346, 784.0, and 307.81 were used to identify migraines and headaches.

SOURCE: Agency for Healthcare Research and Quality, Financing, Access, and Cost Trends, Household Component, Medical Expenditure Panel Survey.

Data table for Figure 37. Health status measures among adults 18 years of age and over with and without low back pain, by age: United States, 2004

Health status measure and age	Low back pain in the 3 months prior to interview		No low back pain in the 3 months prior to interview	
	Percent	SE	Percent	SE
Limitation of activity caused by chronic conditions				
18 years and over	28.1	0.6	9.6	0.2
18–44 years	14.8	0.7	4.1	0.2
45–64 years	32.4	1.0	10.5	0.4
65 years and over	52.9	1.4	27.1	0.8
Fair or poor health, respondent-assessed				
18 years and over	23.5	0.5	8.1	0.2
18–44 years	12.6	0.6	3.7	0.2
45–64 years	28.8	0.9	10.1	0.4
65 years and over	39.8	1.4	19.3	0.7
Serious psychological distress				
18 years and over	7.2	0.3	1.5	0.1
18–44 years	6.4	0.5	1.7	0.1
45–64 years	9.3	0.6	1.4	0.1
65 years and over	5.0	0.6	1.1	0.2

SE is standard error.

NOTES: Data are for the civilian noninstitutionalized population. Respondents were asked: "During the past 3 months, did you have low back pain?" Respondents were instructed to report pain that lasted a whole day or more and to not report aches or pains that were fleeting or minor. See related Tables 56 and 58. Serious psychological distress is measured by a six-question scale that asks respondents how often they experience six symptoms. See Appendix II, Health status, respondent-assessed; Limitation of activity; Serious psychological distress.

SOURCE: Centers for Disease Control and Prevention, National Center for Health Statistics, National Health Interview Survey.

Trend Tables

Table 1 (page 1 of 3). **Resident population, by age, sex, race, and Hispanic origin: United States, selected years 1950–2004**

[Data are based on decennial census updated with data from multiple sources]

Sex, race, Hispanic origin, and year	Total resident population	Under 1 year	1–4 years	5–14 years	15–24 years	25–34 years	35–44 years	45–54 years	55–64 years	65–74 years	75–84 years	85 years and over
All persons						Number in thousands						
1950	150,697	3,147	13,017	24,319	22,098	23,759	21,450	17,343	13,370	8,340	3,278	577
1960	179,323	4,112	16,209	35,465	24,020	22,818	24,081	20,485	15,572	10,997	4,633	929
1970	203,212	3,485	13,669	40,746	35,441	24,907	23,088	23,220	18,590	12,435	6,119	1,511
1980	226,546	3,534	12,815	34,942	42,487	37,082	25,635	22,800	21,703	15,581	7,729	2,240
1990	248,710	3,946	14,812	35,095	37,013	43,161	37,435	25,057	21,113	18,045	10,012	3,021
2000	281,422	3,806	15,370	41,078	39,184	39,892	45,149	37,678	24,275	18,391	12,361	4,240
2002	288,369	4,034	15,575	41,037	40,590	39,928	44,917	40,084	26,602	18,274	12,735	4,593
2003	290,811	4,004	15,766	40,969	41,206	39,873	44,371	40,805	27,900	18,337	12,869	4,713
2004	293,655	4,077	15,994	40,751	41,701	40,032	44,109	41,619	29,079	18,463	12,971	4,860
Male												
1950	74,833	1,602	6,634	12,375	10,918	11,597	10,588	8,655	6,697	4,024	1,507	237
1960	88,331	2,090	8,240	18,029	11,906	11,179	11,755	10,093	7,537	5,116	2,025	362
1970	98,912	1,778	6,968	20,759	17,551	12,217	11,231	11,199	8,793	5,437	2,436	542
1980	110,053	1,806	6,556	17,855	21,419	18,382	12,570	11,009	10,152	6,757	2,867	682
1990	121,239	2,018	7,581	17,971	18,915	21,564	18,510	12,232	9,955	8,303	3,745	841
2000	138,054	1,949	7,862	21,043	20,079	20,121	22,448	18,497	11,645	8,303	4,879	1,227
2002	141,661	2,064	7,962	21,013	20,821	20,203	22,367	19,676	12,784	8,301	5,081	1,390
2003	143,037	2,046	8,060	20,977	21,183	20,222	22,134	20,044	13,424	8,349	5,154	1,445
2004	144,537	2,085	8,178	20,860	21,438	20,336	22,034	20,453	13,999	8,428	5,218	1,508
Female												
1950	75,864	1,545	6,383	11,944	11,181	12,162	10,863	8,688	6,672	4,316	1,771	340
1960	90,992	2,022	7,969	17,437	12,114	11,639	12,326	10,393	8,036	5,881	2,609	567
1970	104,300	1,707	6,701	19,986	17,890	12,690	11,857	12,021	9,797	6,998	3,683	969
1980	116,493	1,727	6,259	17,087	21,068	18,700	13,065	11,791	11,551	8,824	4,862	1,559
1990	127,471	1,928	7,231	17,124	18,098	21,596	18,925	12,824	11,158	10,139	6,267	2,180
2000	143,368	1,857	7,508	20,034	19,105	19,771	22,701	19,181	12,629	10,088	7,482	3,013
2002	146,708	1,970	7,614	20,025	19,769	19,726	22,550	20,408	13,817	9,973	7,654	3,203
2003	147,773	1,958	7,706	19,992	20,024	19,650	22,237	20,761	14,475	9,988	7,714	3,269
2004	149,118	1,992	7,817	19,890	20,263	19,696	22,075	21,166	15,079	10,036	7,753	3,352
White male												
1950	67,129	1,400	5,845	10,860	9,689	10,430	9,529	7,836	6,180	3,736	1,406	218
1960	78,367	1,784	7,065	15,659	10,483	9,940	10,564	9,114	6,850	4,702	1,875	331
1970	86,721	1,501	5,873	17,667	15,232	10,775	9,979	10,090	7,958	4,916	2,243	487
1980	94,976	1,487	5,402	14,773	18,123	15,940	11,010	9,774	9,151	6,096	2,600	621
1990	102,143	1,604	6,071	14,467	15,389	18,071	15,819	10,624	8,813	7,127	3,397	760
2000	113,445	1,524	6,143	16,428	15,942	16,232	18,568	15,670	10,067	7,343	4,419	1,109
2002	115,966	1,603	6,212	16,363	16,482	16,214	18,368	16,553	11,045	7,288	4,580	1,257
2003	116,875	1,594	6,296	16,322	16,726	16,159	18,129	16,807	11,590	7,308	4,638	1,307
2004	117,916	1,625	6,381	16,229	16,896	16,205	17,994	17,116	12,062	7,358	4,688	1,361
White female												
1950	67,813	1,341	5,599	10,431	9,821	10,851	9,719	7,868	6,168	4,031	1,669	314
1960	80,465	1,714	6,795	15,068	10,596	10,204	11,000	9,364	7,327	5,428	2,441	527
1970	91,028	1,434	5,615	16,912	15,420	11,004	10,349	10,756	8,853	6,366	3,429	890
1980	99,835	1,412	5,127	14,057	17,653	15,896	11,232	10,285	10,325	7,951	4,457	1,440
1990	106,561	1,524	5,762	13,706	14,599	17,757	15,834	10,946	9,698	9,048	5,687	2,001
2000	116,641	1,447	5,839	15,576	14,966	15,574	18,386	15,921	10,731	8,757	6,715	2,729
2002	118,780	1,528	5,915	15,519	15,471	15,412	18,115	16,794	11,716	8,590	6,825	2,895
2003	119,474	1,525	5,999	15,488	15,658	15,310	17,813	17,034	12,263	8,576	6,859	2,950
2004	120,353	1,551	6,081	15,405	15,831	15,302	17,625	17,329	12,741	8,595	6,874	3,020
Black or African American male						Number in thousands						
1950	7,300	- - -	[1]944	1,442	1,162	1,105	1,003	772	459	299	[2]113	- - -
1960	9,114	281	1,082	2,185	1,305	1,120	1,086	891	617	382	137	29
1970	10,748	245	975	2,784	2,041	1,226	1,084	979	739	461	169	46
1980	12,585	269	967	2,614	2,807	1,967	1,235	1,024	854	567	228	53
1990	14,420	322	1,164	2,700	2,669	2,592	1,962	1,175	878	614	277	66
2000	17,407	313	1,271	3,454	2,932	2,586	2,705	1,957	1,090	683	330	87
2002	17,979	344	1,290	3,454	3,107	2,589	2,726	2,149	1,177	701	349	93
2003	18,190	336	1,301	3,444	3,180	2,613	2,705	2,218	1,232	711	355	96
2004	18,417	337	1,320	3,414	3,248	2,650	2,695	2,278	1,293	722	359	101

See footnotes at end of table.

Table 1 (page 2 of 3). Resident population, by age, sex, race, and Hispanic origin: United States, selected years 1950–2004

[Data are based on decennial census updated with data from multiple sources]

Sex, race, Hispanic origin, and year	Total resident population	Under 1 year	1–4 years	5–14 years	15–24 years	25–34 years	35–44 years	45–54 years	55–64 years	65–74 years	75–84 years	85 years and over
Black or African American female						Number in thousands						
1950	7,745	- - -	[1]941	1,446	1,300	1,260	1,112	796	443	322	[2]125	- - -
1960	9,758	283	1,085	2,191	1,404	1,300	1,229	974	663	430	160	38
1970	11,832	243	970	2,773	2,196	1,456	1,309	1,134	868	582	230	71
1980	14,046	266	951	2,578	2,937	2,267	1,488	1,258	1,059	776	360	106
1990	16,063	316	1,137	2,641	2,700	2,905	2,279	1,416	1,135	884	495	156
2000	19,187	302	1,228	3,348	2,971	2,866	3,055	2,274	1,353	971	587	233
2002	19,769	330	1,249	3,351	3,091	2,855	3,079	2,503	1,464	987	616	243
2003	19,958	323	1,260	3,337	3,140	2,862	3,052	2,579	1,531	999	627	247
2004	20,184	324	1,279	3,306	3,193	2,886	3,037	2,651	1,607	1,011	636	254
American Indian or Alaska Native male												
1980	702	17	59	153	161	114	75	53	37	22	9	2
1990	1,024	24	88	206	192	183	140	86	55	32	13	3
2000	1,488	28	109	301	271	229	229	165	88	45	18	5
2002	1,535	21	101	295	287	237	233	181	101	51	22	6
2003	1,553	21	96	293	294	240	232	187	107	53	24	6
2004	1,572	22	90	290	300	244	233	192	114	56	25	7
American Indian or Alaska Native female												
1980	718	16	57	149	158	118	79	57	41	27	12	4
1990	1,041	24	85	200	178	186	148	92	61	41	21	6
2000	1,496	26	106	293	254	219	236	174	95	54	28	10
2002	1,541	20	98	287	271	223	238	192	109	60	32	12
2003	1,558	21	93	286	278	224	235	198	115	62	33	13
2004	1,576	21	88	282	285	227	233	204	122	65	35	14
Asian or Pacific Islander male												
1980	1,814	35	130	321	334	366	252	159	110	72	30	6
1990	3,652	68	258	598	665	718	588	347	208	133	57	12
2000	5,713	84	339	861	934	1,073	947	705	399	231	112	27
2002	6,180	95	358	900	946	1,163	1,040	793	461	261	130	33
2003	6,419	94	367	917	983	1,211	1,068	832	496	277	138	36
2004	6,633	101	387	927	994	1,238	1,112	866	531	292	146	39
Asian or Pacific Islander female												
1980	1,915	34	127	307	325	423	269	192	126	71	33	9
1990	3,805	65	247	578	621	749	664	371	264	166	65	17
2000	6,044	81	336	817	914	1,112	1,024	812	451	305	152	41
2002	6,618	91	352	868	936	1,235	1,118	919	529	337	181	53
2003	6,783	89	354	882	947	1,254	1,137	950	565	351	196	59
2004	7,005	96	368	898	954	1,281	1,179	983	609	365	208	64
Hispanic or Latino male												
1980	7,280	187	661	1,530	1,646	1,256	761	570	364	200	86	19
1990	11,388	279	980	2,128	2,376	2,310	1,471	818	551	312	131	32
2000	18,162	395	1,506	3,469	3,564	3,494	2,653	1,551	804	474	203	50
2002	19,991	426	1,598	3,721	3,656	3,978	3,027	1,823	935	523	244	60
2003	20,599	442	1,682	3,832	3,759	4,016	3,101	1,910	991	542	261	65
2004	21,347	463	1,769	3,919	3,794	4,163	3,242	2,023	1,058	566	280	71
Hispanic or Latino female												
1980	7,329	181	634	1,482	1,546	1,249	805	615	411	257	117	30
1990	10,966	268	939	2,039	2,028	2,073	1,448	868	632	403	209	59
2000	17,144	376	1,441	3,318	3,017	3,016	2,476	1,585	907	603	303	101
2002	18,770	408	1,530	3,545	3,147	3,354	2,782	1,832	1,040	658	356	121
2003	19,300	424	1,611	3,659	3,235	3,363	2,815	1,908	1,097	680	380	128
2004	19,975	443	1,694	3,744	3,303	3,454	2,919	2,006	1,164	705	405	139

See footnotes at end of table.

Table 1 (page 3 of 3). Resident population, by age, sex, race, and Hispanic origin: United States, selected years 1950–2004

[Data are based on decennial census updated with data from multiple sources]

Sex, race, Hispanic origin, and year	Total resident population	Under 1 year	1–4 years	5–14 years	15–24 years	25–34 years	35–44 years	45–54 years	55–64 years	65–74 years	75–84 years	85 years and over
White, not Hispanic or Latino male					Number in thousands							
1980	88,035	1,308	4,772	13,317	16,554	14,739	10,284	9,229	8,803	5,906	2,519	603
1990	91,743	1,351	5,181	12,525	13,219	15,967	14,481	9,875	8,303	6,837	3,275	729
2000	96,551	1,163	4,761	13,238	12,628	12,958	16,088	14,223	9,312	6,894	4,225	1,062
2002	97,329	1,198	4,729	12,941	13,086	12,480	15,534	14,851	10,168	6,793	4,348	1,201
2003	97,660	1,173	4,718	12,797	13,237	12,393	15,225	15,025	10,660	6,796	4,390	1,245
2004	97,986	1,184	4,706	12,623	13,376	12,301	14,957	15,228	11,071	6,824	4,422	1,294
White, not Hispanic or Latino female												
1980	92,872	1,240	4,522	12,647	16,185	14,711	10,468	9,700	9,935	7,707	4,345	1,411
1990	96,557	1,280	4,909	11,846	12,749	15,872	14,520	10,153	9,116	8,674	5,491	1,945
2000	100,774	1,102	4,517	12,529	12,183	12,778	16,089	14,446	9,879	8,188	6,429	2,633
2002	101,363	1,140	4,496	12,263	12,567	12,296	15,531	15,091	10,740	7,970	6,489	2,780
2003	101,555	1,121	4,488	12,125	12,673	12,188	15,201	15,261	11,236	7,935	6,499	2,829
2004	101,789	1,128	4,477	11,964	12,783	12,095	14,916	15,466	11,652	7,932	6,491	2,888

- - - Data not available.

[1]Population for age group under 5 years.

[2]Population for age group 75 years and over.

NOTES: The race groups, white, black, American Indian or Alaska Native, and Asian or Pacific Islander, include persons of Hispanic and non-Hispanic origin. Persons of Hispanic origin may be of any race. Starting with *Health, United States, 2003*, intercensal population estimates for the 1990s and 2000 are based on the 2000 census. Population estimates for 2001 and later years are 2000-based postcensal estimates. Population figures are census counts as of April 1 for 1950, 1960, 1970, 1980, 1990, and 2000; estimates as of July 1 for other years. See Appendix I, Population Census and Population Estimates. Populations for age groups may not sum to the total due to rounding. Although population figures are shown rounded to the nearest 1,000, calculations of birth rates and death rates shown in this volume are based on unrounded population figures for decennial years and for all years starting with 1991. See Appendix II, Rate. Unrounded population figures are available in the spreadsheet version of this table. Available from: www.cdc.gov/nchs/hus.htm. Data for additional years are available. See Appendix III.

SOURCES: U.S. Census Bureau: 1950 Nonwhite Population by Race. Special Report P-E, No. 3B. Washington, DC: U.S. Government Printing Office, 1951; U.S. Census of Population: 1960, Number of Inhabitants, PC(1)-A1, United States Summary, 1964; 1970, Number of Inhabitants, Final Report PC(1)-A1, United States Summary, 1971; U.S. population estimates, by age, sex, race, and Hispanic origin: 1980 to 1991. Current population reports, series P–25, no 1095. Washington, DC: U.S. Government Printing Office, Feb. 1993; National Center for Health Statistics. Estimates of the July 1, 1991–July 1, 1999, April 1, 2000, and July 1, 2001–July 1, 2004 United States resident population by age, sex, race, and Hispanic origin, prepared under a collaborative arrangement with the U.S. Census Bureau, Population Estimates Program. Available from: www.cdc.gov/nchs/about/major/dvs/popbridge/popbridge.htm. 2004.

Table 2 (page 1 of 2). Inmates in state or federal prisons and local jails, by sex, race, Hispanic origin, and age: United States, selected years 1999–2004

[Data are based on reporting by a census of departments of correction and the Federal Bureau of Prisons and a sample of jails]

Sex, race, Hispanic origin, and age	1999	2000	2003	2004	1999	2000	2003	2004
	Number of inmates in thousands [1]				Inmates per 100,000 population [2]			
Total [3,4]	1,861	1,932	2,079	2,131	- - -	686	716	726
Male [3,4]	1,711	1,776	1,902	1,948	1,261	1,297	1,331	1,348
Female [3,4]	149	156	176	183	106	110	119	123
White, not Hispanic: [4]								
Male	610	664	665	696	630	683	681	717
Female	54	64	76	82	53	63	75	81
Black, not Hispanic: [4]								
Male	757	792	832	843	4,617	4,777	4,834	4,919
Female	68	70	67	68	375	380	352	359
Hispanic: [4]								
Male	296	291	364	367	1,802	1,715	1,778	1,717
Female	23	20	28	29	142	117	148	143
Male								
18–19	79	81	72	73	1,868	1,917	1,709	1,727
20–24	299	310	346	352	3,130	3,177	3,316	3,255
25–29	317	330	332	340	3,363	3,580	3,417	3,390
30–34	321	334	314	316	3,193	3,362	2,944	3,060
35–39	282	294	292	292	2,474	2,613	2,641	2,755
40–44	190	198	241	250	1,699	1,747	2,096	2,187
45–54	157	165	224	238	896	903	1,129	1,162
55 and over	49	51	66	72	193	199	238	247
Female								
18–19	4	4	4	5	92	96	109	112
20–24	19	20	25	27	205	210	255	264
25–29	29	30	26	27	303	324	277	283
30–34	37	39	33	34	370	391	316	330
35–39	29	31	36	36	257	272	322	346
40–44	16	17	27	29	144	149	232	247
45–54	12	12	20	22	63	64	97	101
55 and over	3	3	4	4	8	8	11	11
White, not Hispanic male								
18–19	24	26	24	24	885	942	882	911
20–24	91	100	103	107	1,462	1,560	1,610	1,641
25–29	96	105	93	98	1,535	1,732	1,607	1,666
30–34	114	125	104	107	1,674	1,861	1,545	1,691
35–39	106	116	109	111	1,302	1,460	1,467	1,607
40–44	74	81	99	105	897	972	1,206	1,314
45–54	71	78	94	101	522	553	626	664
55 and over	27	30	37	40	129	139	162	170
Black, not Hispanic male								
18–19	35	37	33	33	5,787	6,027	5,365	5,473
20–24	136	143	161	162	10,407	10,593	11,329	11,054
25–29	152	160	154	156	12,334	13,118	12,809	12,603
30–34	142	150	135	135	11,225	11,892	10,627	10,979
35–39	130	136	127	125	9,548	10,054	9,570	10,036
40–44	79	83	102	105	6,224	6,399	7,639	7,993
45–54	59	62	93	99	3,399	3,409	4,425	4,546
55 and over	13	13	19	21	611	635	842	898

See footnotes at end of table.

Table 2 (page 2 of 2). Inmates in state or federal prisons and local jails, by sex, race, Hispanic origin, and age: United States, selected years 1999–2004

[Data are based on reporting by a census of departments of correction and the Federal Bureau of Prisons and a sample of jails]

Sex, race, Hispanic origin, and age	1999	2000	2003	2004	1999	2000	2003	2004
Hispanic male	Number of inmates in thousands [1]				Inmates per 100,000 population [2]			
18–19....................	16	16	13	14	2,524	2,419	1,888	1,957
20–24....................	62	60	74	75	4,141	3,885	3,620	3,577
25–29....................	60	58	78	79	4,220	4,084	3,719	3,606
30–34....................	56	55	68	69	3,844	3,756	3,451	3,438
35–39....................	40	40	51	50	2,898	2,781	2,975	2,866
40–44....................	31	31	36	36	2,746	2,621	2,537	2,403
45–54....................	22	22	33	34	1,521	1,426	1,761	1,652
55 and over	7	8	9	9	460	468	501	473
White, not Hispanic female								
18–19....................	2	2	2	2	63	71	68	71
20–24....................	7	8	11	12	121	137	178	191
25–29....................	10	11	11	12	154	187	191	203
30–34....................	13	15	14	15	185	224	211	237
35–39....................	10	13	16	16	128	159	211	238
40–44....................	6	7	12	13	73	87	143	162
45–54....................	5	6	9	10	33	39	58	63
55 and over	1	2	2	2	5	7	8	8
Black, not Hispanic female								
18–19....................	1	1	2	2	224	231	254	262
20–24....................	7	7	9	9	524	525	607	625
25–29....................	13	14	10	10	956	993	744	746
30–34....................	19	19	13	12	1,362	1,409	891	905
35–39....................	14	14	14	14	940	962	926	993
40–44....................	7	8	11	11	512	513	732	764
45–54....................	4	5	8	8	214	209	318	327
55 and over	1	1	1	1	27	28	28	29
Hispanic female								
18–19....................	1	1	1	1	94	87	166	162
20–24....................	4	4	5	5	284	246	295	304
25–29....................	5	4	5	5	357	296	268	268
30–34....................	5	4	5	5	372	301	319	313
35–39....................	4	3	5	5	308	247	333	331
40–44....................	2	2	4	4	203	168	276	271
45–54....................	2	2	3	3	133	106	149	136
55 and over	0	0	1	1	11	9	29	25

- - - Data not available.
0 is greater than 0 but less than 500.
[1]Estimates as of June 30 of year shown.
[2]Inmate estimates as of June 30 of year shown. Population is U.S. resident population for July 1 of year shown.
[3]Includes all other races not shown separately. See Appendix II, Hispanic origin; Race.
[4]Includes all other ages not shown separately. A small number of inmates are under age 18.

NOTES: Data are for inmates in custody. See Appendix I, The Annual Survey and Census of Jails; National Prisoner Statistics. Starting with 2004 data, inmates reporting more than one race are excluded.

SOURCES: Harrison PM, Beck AJ. Prison and Jail Inmates at Midyear 2004. Bureau of Justice Statistics Bulletin. Washington, DC: U.S. Department of Justice, 2005. Reports for earlier years are available from: www.ojp.usdoj.gov/bjs/prisons.htm.

Table 3 (page 1 of 2). Persons and families below poverty level, by selected characteristics, race, and Hispanic origin: United States, selected years 1973–2004

[Data are based on household interviews of the civilian noninstitutionalized population]

Selected characteristics, race, and Hispanic origin[1]	1973	1980	1985	1990	1995	2000[2]	2002	2003	2004
All persons				*Percent below poverty*					
All races	11.1	13.0	14.0	13.5	13.8	11.3	12.1	12.5	12.7
White only.	8.4	10.2	11.4	10.7	11.2	9.5	10.2	10.5	10.8
Black or African American only	31.4	32.5	31.3	31.9	29.3	22.5	24.1	24.4	24.7
Asian only	- - -	- - -	- - -	12.2	14.6	9.9	10.1	11.8	9.8
Hispanic or Latino	21.9	25.7	29.0	28.1	30.3	21.5	21.8	22.5	21.9
Mexican.	- - -	- - -	28.8	28.1	31.2	22.9	- - -	- - -	- - -
Puerto Rican	- - -	- - -	43.3	40.6	38.1	25.6	- - -	- - -	- - -
White only, not Hispanic or Latino	7.5	9.1	9.7	8.8	8.5	7.4	8.0	8.2	8.6
Related children under 18 years of age in families									
All races	14.2	17.9	20.1	19.9	20.2	15.6	16.3	17.2	17.3
White only.	9.7	13.4	15.6	15.1	15.5	12.4	13.1	13.9	14.2
Black or African American only	40.6	42.1	43.1	44.2	41.5	30.9	32.1	33.6	33.3
Asian only.	- - -	- - -	- - -	17.0	18.6	12.5	11.4	12.1	9.5
Hispanic or Latino	27.8	33.0	39.6	37.7	39.3	27.6	28.2	29.5	28.6
Mexican.	- - -	- - -	37.4	35.5	39.3	29.5	- - -	- - -	- - -
Puerto Rican	- - -	- - -	58.6	56.7	53.2	32.1	- - -	- - -	- - -
White only, not Hispanic or Latino	- - -	11.3	12.3	11.6	10.6	8.5	8.9	9.3	9.9
Related children under 18 years of age in families with female householder and no spouse present									
All races	- - -	50.8	53.6	53.4	50.3	40.1	39.6	41.8	41.9
White only.	- - -	41.6	45.2	45.9	42.5	33.9	34.7	37.0	38.2
Black or African American only	- - -	64.8	66.9	64.7	61.6	49.3	47.5	49.8	49.2
Asian only.	- - -	- - -	- - -	32.2	42.4	38.0	29.8	37.4	18.8
Hispanic or Latino	- - -	65.0	72.4	68.4	65.7	49.8	47.9	50.6	51.9
Mexican.	- - -	- - -	64.4	62.4	65.9	51.4	- - -	- - -	- - -
Puerto Rican	- - -	- - -	85.4	82.7	79.6	55.3	- - -	- - -	- - -
White only, not Hispanic or Latino	- - -	- - -	- - -	39.6	33.5	28.0	29.2	30.7	31.5
All persons				*Number below poverty in thousands*					
All races	22,973	29,272	33,064	33,585	36,425	31,581	34,570	35,861	36,997
White only.	15,142	19,699	22,860	22,326	24,423	21,645	23,466	24,272	25,301
Black or African American only	7,388	8,579	8,926	9,837	9,872	7,982	8,602	8,781	9,000
Asian only.	- - -	- - -	- - -	858	1,411	1,258	1,161	1,401	1,209
Hispanic or Latino	2,366	3,491	5,236	6,006	8,574	7,747	8,555	9,051	9,132
Mexican.	- - -	- - -	3,220	3,764	5,608	5,460	- - -	- - -	- - -
Puerto Rican	- - -	- - -	1,011	966	1,183	814	- - -	- - -	- - -
White only, not Hispanic or Latino	12,864	16,365	17,839	16,622	16,267	14,366	15,567	15,902	16,870
Related children under 18 years of age in families									
All races	9,453	11,114	12,483	12,715	13,999	11,005	11,646	12,340	12,460
White only.	5,462	6,817	7,838	7,696	8,474	6,834	7,203	7,624	7,868
Black or African American only	3,822	3,906	4,057	4,412	4,644	3,495	3,570	3,750	3,694
Asian only.	- - -	- - -	- - -	356	532	407	302	331	269
Hispanic or Latino	1,364	1,718	2,512	2,750	3,938	3,342	3,653	3,982	3,989
Mexican.	- - -	- - -	1,589	1,733	2,655	2,537	- - -	- - -	- - -
Puerto Rican	- - -	- - -	535	490	610	329	- - -	- - -	- - -
White only, not Hispanic or Latino	- - -	5,174	5,421	5,106	4,745	3,715	3,848	3,957	4,179

See footnotes at end of table.

Table 3 (page 2 of 2). Persons and families below poverty level, by selected characteristics, race, and Hispanic origin: United States, selected years 1973–2004

[Data are based on household interviews of the civilian noninstitutionalized population]

Selected characteristics, race, and Hispanic origin[1]	1973	1980	1985	1990	1995	2000[2]	2002	2003	2004
Related children under 18 years of age in families with female householder and no spouse present				Number below poverty in thousands					
All races	---	5,866	6,716	7,363	8,364	6,300	6,564	7,085	7,132
White only	---	2,813	3,372	3,597	4,051	3,090	3,271	3,580	3,774
Black or African American only	---	2,944	3,181	3,543	3,954	2,908	2,855	3,026	2,952
Asian only	---	---	---	80	145	162	85	119	55
Hispanic or Latino	---	809	1,247	1,314	1,872	1,407	1,501	1,727	1,837
Mexican	---	---	553	615	1,056	938	---	---	---
Puerto Rican	---	---	449	382	459	242	---	---	---
White only, not Hispanic or Latino	---	---	---	2,411	2,299	1,832	1,949	2,033	2,109

- - - Data not available.

[1]The race groups, white, black, and Asian, include persons of Hispanic and non-Hispanic origin. Persons of Hispanic origin may be of any race. Starting with 2002 data, race-specific estimates are tabulated according to the 1997 Revisions to the Standards for the Classification of Federal Data on Race and Ethnicity and are not strictly comparable with estimates for earlier years. The three single race categories shown in the table conform to the 1997 Standards. For 2002 and later years, race-specific estimates are for persons who reported only one racial group. Prior to data year 2002, data were tabulated according to the 1977 Standards in which the Asian only category included Native Hawaiian and Other Pacific Islander. Estimates for single race categories prior to 2002 are based on answers to the Current Population Survey questionnaire which asked respondents to choose only a single race. See Appendix II, Hispanic origin; Race.
[2]Estimates are consistent with 2001 data through implementation of the 2000 census-based population controls and a 28,000 household sample expansion.

NOTES: Estimates of poverty for 1991–1998 are based on 1990 postcensal population estimates. Estimates for 1999 and later years are based on 2000 census population controls. Poverty level is based on family income and family size using U.S. Census Bureau poverty thresholds. See Appendix II, Poverty. The Current Population Survey is not large enough to produce reliable annual estimates for American Indian or Alaska Native persons, or for Native Hawaiians. The 2002–2004 average poverty rate for American Indian or Alaskan Native only was 24.3%, representing 554,000 persons. Data for additional years are available. See Appendix III.

SOURCES: U.S. Census Bureau, Current Population Survey 2000–2005 Annual Social and Economic Supplements; DeNavas-Walt C, Proctor BD, Lee CH. Income, Poverty and Health Insurance Coverage in the United States: 2004. Current population reports, series P–60, no 229. Washington, DC: U.S. Government Printing Office. 2005.

Table 4 (page 1 of 3). Crude birth rates, fertility rates, and birth rates by age, race, and Hispanic origin of mother: United States, selected years 1950–2004

[Data are based on birth certificates]

Race, Hispanic origin, and year	Crude birth rate[1]	Fertility rate[2]	10–14 years	15–19 years Total	15–17 years	18–19 years	20–24 years	25–29 years	30–34 years	35–39 years	40–44 years	45–54 years[3]
All races						Live births per 1,000 women						
1950	24.1	106.2	1.0	81.6	40.7	132.7	196.6	166.1	103.7	52.9	15.1	1.2
1960	23.7	118.0	0.8	89.1	43.9	166.7	258.1	197.4	112.7	56.2	15.5	0.9
1970	18.4	87.9	1.2	68.3	38.8	114.7	167.8	145.1	73.3	31.7	8.1	0.5
1980	15.9	68.4	1.1	53.0	32.5	82.1	115.1	112.9	61.9	19.8	3.9	0.2
1985	15.8	66.3	1.2	51.0	31.0	79.6	108.3	111.0	69.1	24.0	4.0	0.2
1990	16.7	70.9	1.4	59.9	37.5	88.6	116.5	120.2	80.8	31.7	5.5	0.2
1995	14.6	64.6	1.3	56.0	35.5	87.7	107.5	108.8	81.1	34.0	6.6	0.3
2000	14.4	65.9	0.9	47.7	26.9	78.1	109.7	113.5	91.2	39.7	8.0	0.5
2002	13.9	64.8	0.7	43.0	23.2	72.8	103.6	113.6	91.5	41.4	8.3	0.5
2003	14.1	66.1	0.6	41.6	22.4	70.7	102.6	115.6	95.1	43.8	8.7	0.5
2004	14.0	66.3	0.7	41.1	22.1	70.0	101.7	115.5	95.3	45.4	8.9	0.5
Race of child:[4] White												
1950	23.0	102.3	0.4	70.0	31.3	120.5	190.4	165.1	102.6	51.4	14.5	1.0
1960	22.7	113.2	0.4	79.4	35.5	154.6	252.8	194.9	109.6	54.0	14.7	0.8
1970	17.4	84.1	0.5	57.4	29.2	101.5	163.4	145.9	71.9	30.0	7.5	0.4
1980	14.9	64.7	0.6	44.7	25.2	72.1	109.5	112.4	60.4	18.5	3.4	0.2
Race of mother:[5] White												
1980	15.1	65.6	0.6	45.4	25.5	73.2	111.1	113.8	61.2	18.8	3.5	0.2
1985	15.0	64.1	0.6	43.3	24.4	70.4	104.1	112.3	69.9	23.3	3.7	0.2
1990	15.8	68.3	0.7	50.8	29.5	78.0	109.8	120.7	81.7	31.5	5.2	0.2
1995	14.1	63.6	0.8	49.5	29.6	80.2	104.7	111.7	83.3	34.2	6.4	0.3
2000	13.9	65.3	0.6	43.2	23.3	72.3	106.6	116.7	94.6	40.2	7.9	0.4
2002	13.5	64.8	0.5	39.4	20.5	68.0	101.6	117.4	95.5	42.4	8.2	0.5
2003	13.6	66.1	0.5	38.3	19.8	66.2	100.6	119.5	99.3	44.8	8.7	0.5
2004	13.5	66.1	0.5	37.7	19.5	65.0	99.2	118.6	99.1	46.4	8.9	0.5
Race of child:[4] Black or African American												
1960	31.9	153.5	4.3	156.1	- - -	- - -	295.4	218.6	137.1	73.9	21.9	1.1
1970	25.3	115.4	5.2	140.7	101.4	204.9	202.7	136.3	79.6	41.9	12.5	1.0
1980	22.1	88.1	4.3	100.0	73.6	138.8	146.3	109.1	62.9	24.5	5.8	0.3
Race of mother:[5] Black or African American												
1980	21.3	84.9	4.3	97.8	72.5	135.1	140.0	103.9	59.9	23.5	5.6	0.3
1985	20.4	78.8	4.5	95.4	69.3	132.4	135.0	100.2	57.9	23.9	4.6	0.3
1990	22.4	86.8	4.9	112.8	82.3	152.9	160.2	115.5	68.7	28.1	5.5	0.3
1995	17.8	71.0	4.1	94.4	68.5	135.0	133.7	95.6	63.0	28.4	6.0	0.3
2000	17.0	70.0	2.3	77.4	49.0	118.8	141.3	100.3	65.4	31.5	7.2	0.4
2002	15.7	65.8	1.8	66.6	40.0	107.6	127.1	99.0	64.4	31.5	7.4	0.4
2003	15.7	66.3	1.6	63.8	38.2	103.7	126.1	100.4	66.5	33.2	7.7	0.5
2004	16.0	67.6	1.6	63.3	37.2	104.4	127.7	103.6	67.9	34.0	7.9	0.5
American Indian or Alaska Native mothers[5]												
1980	20.7	82.7	1.9	82.2	51.5	129.5	143.7	106.6	61.8	28.1	8.2	*
1985	19.8	78.6	1.7	79.2	47.7	124.1	139.1	109.6	62.6	27.4	6.0	*
1990	18.9	76.2	1.6	81.1	48.5	129.3	148.7	110.3	61.5	27.5	5.9	*
1995	15.3	63.0	1.6	72.9	44.6	122.2	123.1	91.6	56.5	24.3	5.5	*
2000	14.0	58.7	1.1	58.3	34.1	97.1	117.2	91.8	55.5	24.6	5.7	0.3
2002	13.8	58.0	0.9	53.8	30.7	89.2	112.6	91.8	56.4	25.4	5.8	0.3
2003	13.8	58.4	1.0	53.1	30.6	87.3	110.0	93.5	57.4	25.4	5.5	0.4
2004	14.0	58.9	0.9	52.5	30.0	87.0	109.7	92.8	58.0	26.8	6.0	0.2

See footnotes at end of table.

[Data are based on birth certificates]

Race, Hispanic origin, and year	Crude birth rate[1]	Fertility rate[2]	Age of mother									
			10–14 years	15–19 years			20–24 years	25–29 years	30–34 years	35–39 years	40–44 years	45–54 years[3]
				Total	15–17 years	18–19 years						
Asian or Pacific Islander mothers[5]			Live births per 1,000 women									
1980	19.9	73.2	0.3	26.2	12.0	46.2	93.3	127.4	96.0	38.3	8.5	0.7
1985	18.7	68.4	0.4	23.8	12.5	40.8	83.6	123.0	93.6	42.7	8.7	1.2
1990	19.0	69.6	0.7	26.4	16.0	40.2	79.2	126.3	106.5	49.6	10.7	1.1
1995	16.7	62.6	0.7	25.5	15.6	40.1	64.2	103.7	102.3	50.1	11.8	0.8
2000	17.1	65.8	0.3	20.5	11.6	32.6	60.3	108.4	116.5	59.0	12.6	0.8
2002	16.5	64.1	0.3	18.3	9.0	31.5	60.4	105.4	109.6	56.5	12.5	0.9
2003	16.8	66.3	0.2	17.4	8.8	29.8	59.6	108.5	114.6	59.9	13.5	0.9
2004	16.8	67.1	0.2	17.3	8.9	29.6	59.8	108.6	116.9	62.1	13.6	1.0
Hispanic or Latino mothers[5,6]												
1980	23.5	95.4	1.7	82.2	52.1	126.9	156.4	132.1	83.2	39.9	10.6	0.7
1990	26.7	107.7	2.4	100.3	65.9	147.7	181.0	153.0	98.3	45.3	10.9	0.7
1995	24.1	98.8	2.6	99.3	68.3	145.4	171.9	140.4	90.5	43.7	10.7	0.6
2000	23.1	95.9	1.7	87.3	55.5	132.6	161.3	139.9	97.1	46.6	11.5	0.6
2002	22.6	94.4	1.4	83.4	50.7	133.0	164.3	139.4	95.1	47.8	11.5	0.7
2003	22.9	96.9	1.3	82.3	49.7	132.0	163.4	144.4	102.0	50.8	12.2	0.7
2004	22.9	97.8	1.3	82.6	49.7	133.5	165.3	145.6	104.1	52.9	12.4	0.7
White, not Hispanic or Latino mothers[5,6]												
1980	14.2	62.4	0.4	41.2	22.4	67.7	105.5	110.6	59.9	17.7	3.0	0.1
1990	14.4	62.8	0.5	42.5	23.2	66.6	97.5	115.3	79.4	30.0	4.7	0.2
1995	12.5	57.5	0.4	39.3	22.0	66.2	90.2	105.1	81.5	32.8	5.9	0.3
2000	12.2	58.5	0.3	32.6	15.8	57.5	91.2	109.4	93.2	38.8	7.3	0.4
2002	11.7	57.4	0.2	28.5	13.1	51.9	84.3	109.3	94.4	40.9	7.6	0.5
2003	11.8	58.5	0.2	27.4	12.4	50.0	83.5	110.8	97.6	43.2	8.1	0.5
2004	11.6	58.4	0.2	26.7	12.0	48.7	81.9	110.0	97.1	44.8	8.2	0.5
Black or African American, not Hispanic or Latino mothers[5,6]												
1980	22.9	90.7	4.6	105.1	77.2	146.5	152.2	111.7	65.2	25.8	5.8	0.3
1990	23.0	89.0	5.0	116.2	84.9	157.5	165.1	118.4	70.2	28.7	5.6	0.3
1995	18.2	72.8	4.2	97.2	70.4	139.2	137.8	98.5	64.4	28.8	6.1	0.3
2000	17.3	71.4	2.4	79.2	50.1	121.9	145.4	102.8	66.5	31.8	7.2	0.4
2002	16.1	67.4	1.9	68.3	41.0	110.3	131.0	102.1	66.1	32.1	7.5	0.4
2003	15.9	67.1	1.6	64.7	38.7	105.3	128.1	102.1	67.4	33.4	7.7	0.5
2004	15.8	67.0	1.6	63.1	37.1	103.9	126.9	103.0	67.4	33.7	7.8	0.5

See footnotes at end of table.

Table 4 (page 3 of 3). Crude birth rates, fertility rates, and birth rates by age, race, and Hispanic origin of mother: United States, selected years 1950–2004

[Data are based on birth certificates]

- - - Data not available.

* Rates based on fewer than 20 births are considered unreliable and are not shown.

[1]Live births per 1,000 population.

[2]Total number of live births regardless of age of mother per 1,000 women 15–44 years of age.

[3]Prior to 1997, data are for live births to mothers 45–49 years of age per 1,000 women 45–49 years of age. Starting with 1997 data, rates are for live births to mothers 45–54 years of age per 1,000 women 45–49 years of age. See Appendix II, Age.

[4]Live births are tabulated by race of child. See Appendix II, Race, Birth File.

[5]Live births are tabulated by race and/or Hispanic origin of mother. See Appendix II, Race, Birth File.

[6]Prior to 1993, data from states lacking an Hispanic-origin item on the birth certificate were excluded. See Appendix II, Hispanic origin. Rates in 1985 were not calculated because estimates for the Hispanic and non-Hispanic populations were not available.

NOTES: Data are based on births adjusted for underregistration for 1950 and on registered births for all other years. Starting with 1970 data, births to persons who were not residents of the 50 states and the District of Columbia are excluded. Starting with *Health, United States, 2003*, rates for 1991–1999 were revised using intercensal population estimates based on the 2000 census. Rates for 2000 were computed using the 2000 census counts and starting in 2001 rates were computed using 2000-based postcensal estimates. See Appendix I, Population Census and Population Estimates. The race groups, white, black, American Indian or Alaska Native, and Asian or Pacific Islander, include persons of Hispanic and non-Hispanic origin. Persons of Hispanic origin may be of any race. Starting with 2003 data, some states reported multiple-race data. The multiple-race data for these states were bridged to the single race categories of the 1977 Office of Management and Budget standards for comparability with other states. See Appendix II, Race. Interpretation of trend data should take into consideration expansion of reporting areas and immigration. Data for additional years are available. See Appendix III.

SOURCES: Centers for Disease Control and Prevention, National Center for Health Statistics, National Vital Statistics System, Birth File. Martin JA, Hamilton BE, Sutton PD, Ventura SJ, Menacker F, Kirmeyer S. Births: Final Data for 2004. National vital statistics reports. vol 55 no 1. Hyattsville, MD: National Center for Health Statistics. 2006; Hamilton BE, Sutton PD, Ventura SJ. Revised birth and fertility rates for the 1990s and new rates for Hispanic populations, 2000 and 2001: United States. National vital statistics reports. vol 51 no 12. Hyattsville, MD: National Center for Health Statistics. 2003; Ventura SJ. Births of Hispanic parentage, 1980 and 1985. Monthly vital statistics report. vol 32 no 6 and vol 36 no 11, suppl. Public Health Service. Hyattsville, MD. 1983 and 1988; Internet release of *Vital statistics of the United States, 2000, vol 1, natality*, tables 1–1 and 1–7 available from: www.cdc.gov/nchs/datawh/statab/unpubd/natality/natab2000.htm.

Table 5 (page 1 of 2). Live births, by plurality, and detailed race and Hispanic origin of mother: United States, selected years 1970–2004

[Data are based on birth certificates]

Plurality of birth and race and Hispanic origin of mother	1970	1971	1975	1980	1985	1990	1995	2000	2003	2004
All births					Number of live births					
All races	3,731,386	3,555,970	3,144,198	3,612,258	3,760,561	4,158,212	3,899,589	4,058,814	4,089,950	4,112,052
White	3,109,956	2,939,568	2,576,818	2,936,351	3,037,913	3,290,273	3,098,885	3,194,005	3,225,848	3,222,928
Black or African American	561,992	553,750	496,829	568,080	581,824	684,336	603,139	622,598	599,847	616,074
American Indian or Alaska Native	22,264	23,254	22,690	29,389	34,037	39,051	37,278	41,668	43,052	43,927
Asian or Pacific Islander[1]	- - -	27,004	28,884	74,355	104,606	141,635	160,287	200,543	221,203	229,123
Chinese	7,044	7,222	7,778	11,671	16,405	22,737	27,380	34,271	- - -	- - -
Japanese	7,744	7,846	6,725	7,482	8,035	8,674	8,901	8,969	- - -	- - -
Filipino	8,066	7,946	10,359	13,968	20,058	25,770	30,551	32,107	- - -	- - -
Hawaiian	- - -	3,718	3,711	4,669	4,938	6,099	5,787	6,608	- - -	- - -
Other Asian or Pacific Islander	- - -	272	311	36,565	55,170	78,355	87,668	118,588	- - -	- - -
Hispanic or Latino[2]	- - -	- - -	- - -	307,163	372,814	595,073	679,768	815,868	912,329	946,349
Mexican	- - -	- - -	- - -	215,439	242,976	385,640	469,615	581,915	654,504	677,621
Puerto Rican	- - -	- - -	- - -	33,671	35,147	58,807	54,824	58,124	58,400	61,221
Cuban	- - -	- - -	- - -	7,163	10,024	11,311	12,473	13,429	14,867	14,943
Central and South American	- - -	- - -	- - -	21,268	40,985	83,008	94,996	113,344	135,586	143,520
Other and unknown Hispanic or Latino	- - -	- - -	- - -	29,622	43,682	56,307	47,860	49,056	48,972	49,044
Not Hispanic or Latino:[2]										
White	- - -	- - -	- - -	1,256,777	1,407,460	2,626,500	2,382,638	2,362,968	2,321,904	2,296,683
Black or African American	- - -	- - -	- - -	300,480	337,448	661,701	587,781	604,346	576,033	578,772
Twin births										
All races	- - -	63,298	59,192	68,339	77,102	93,865	96,736	118,916	128,665	132,219
White	- - -	49,972	46,715	53,104	60,351	72,617	76,196	93,235	101,297	103,438
Black or African American	- - -	12,452	11,375	13,638	14,646	18,164	17,000	20,626	20,633	21,618
American Indian or Alaska Native	- - -	362	348	491	537	699	769	900	1,047	1,086
Asian or Pacific Islander[1]	- - -	320	505	1,045	1,536	2,320	2,771	4,155	5,688	6,077
Chinese	- - -	80	120	135	232	368	507	748	- - -	- - -
Japanese	- - -	98	115	103	131	161	217	218	- - -	- - -
Filipino	- - -	92	176	173	247	388	542	612	- - -	- - -
Hawaiian	- - -	46	92	69	74	101	98	109	- - -	- - -
Other Asian or Pacific Islander	- - -	4	2	565	852	1,302	1,407	2,468	- - -	- - -
Hispanic or Latino[2]	- - -	- - -	- - -	5,154	6,550	10,713	12,685	16,470	19,472	20,351
Mexican	- - -	- - -	- - -	3,599	4,292	6,701	8,341	11,130	12,954	13,485
Puerto Rican	- - -	- - -	- - -	631	705	1,226	1,248	1,461	1,666	1,759
Cuban	- - -	- - -	- - -	102	201	228	312	371	465	562
Central and South American	- - -	- - -	- - -	371	665	1,463	1,769	2,361	3,141	3,393
Other and unknown Hispanic or Latino	- - -	- - -	- - -	451	687	1,095	1,015	1,147	1,246	1,152
Not Hispanic or Latino:[2]										
White	- - -	- - -	- - -	23,004	28,402	60,210	62,370	76,018	81,691	83,346
Black or African American	- - -	- - -	- - -	7,278	8,400	17,646	16,622	20,173	20,010	20,605
Triplet and higher order multiple births										
All races	- - -	1,034	1,066	1,337	1,925	3,028	4,973	7,325	7,663	7,275
White	- - -	834	909	1,104	1,648	2,639	4,505	6,551	6,733	6,326
Black or African American	- - -	196	151	211	240	321	352	521	650	605
American Indian or Alaska Native	- - -	0	2	9	13	4	20	18	33	22
Asian or Pacific Islander[1]	- - -	0	4	9	23	61	96	235	247	322
Chinese	- - -	0	0	3	2	13	21	29	- - -	- - -
Japanese	- - -	0	4	6	0	0	3	8	- - -	- - -
Filipino	- - -	0	0	0	4	15	15	57	- - -	- - -
Hawaiian	- - -	0	0	0	0	3	3	6	- - -	- - -
Other Asian or Pacific Islander	- - -	0	0	0	17	30	54	135	- - -	- - -
Hispanic or Latino[2]	- - -	- - -	- - -	78	106	235	355	659	784	723
Mexican	- - -	- - -	- - -	43	82	121	202	391	480	483
Puerto Rican	- - -	- - -	- - -	12	14	28	35	73	88	103
Cuban	- - -	- - -	- - -	0	3	9	24	15	28	*
Central and South American	- - -	- - -	- - -	8	4	59	59	122	140	95
Other and unknown Hispanic or Latino	- - -	- - -	- - -	15	3	18	35	58	48	24
Not Hispanic or Latino:[2]										
White	- - -	- - -	- - -	490	779	2,358	4,050	5,821	5,922	5,590
Black or African American	- - -	- - -	- - -	128	132	306	340	506	631	577

See footnotes at end of table.

Table 5 (page 2 of 2). Live births, by plurality, and detailed race and Hispanic origin of mother: United States, selected years 1970–2004

[Data are based on birth certificates]

- - - Data not available.

[1]Starting with 2003 data, estimates are not shown for Asian or Pacific Islander subgroups during the transition from single race to multiple race reporting. See Appendix II, Race, Birth File.

[2]Prior to 1993, data from states lacking an Hispanic-origin item on the birth certificate were excluded. See Appendix II, Hispanic origin. Data for non-Hispanic white and non-Hispanic black women for years prior to 1989 are not nationally representative and are provided for comparison with Hispanic data.

NOTES: The race groups, white, black, American Indian or Alaska Native, and Asian or Pacific Islander, include persons of Hispanic and non-Hispanic origin. Persons of Hispanic origin may be of any race. Starting with 2003 data, some states reported multiple-race data. The multiple-race data for these states were bridged to the single race categories of the 1977 Office of Management and Budget standards for comparability with other states. See Appendix II, Race. Interpretation of trend data should take into consideration expansion of reporting areas and immigration. Data for additional years are available. See Appendix III.

SOURCES: Centers for Disease Control and Prevention, National Center for Health Statistics, National Vital Statistics System, Birth File. Martin JA, Hamilton BE, Sutton PD, Ventura SJ, Kirmeyer S. Births: Final Data for 2004. National vital statistics reports. vol 55 no 1. Hyattsville, MD: National Center for Health Statistics. 2006; Births: Final data for each data year 1997–2003. National vital statistics reports. Hyattsville, MD; Final natality statistics for each data year 1970–1996. Monthly vital statistics report. Hyattsville, MD.

Table 6. Twin and higher order multiple births, by race, Hispanic origin, and age of mother: United States, selected years 1971–2004

[Data are based on birth certificates]

Plurality of birth and race, Hispanic origin, and age of mother	1971	1975	1980	1985	1990	1995	1997	2000	2002	2003	2004
Twin births					Number per 1,000 live births						
All races	17.8	18.8	18.9	20.5	22.6	24.8	26.8	29.3	31.1	31.5	32.2
White	17.0	18.1	18.1	19.9	22.1	24.6	26.7	29.2	31.0	31.4	32.1
Black or African American	22.5	22.9	24.0	25.2	26.5	28.2	30.0	33.1	34.4	34.4	35.1
American Indian or Alaska Native. . .	15.6	15.3	16.7	15.8	17.9	20.6	20.6	21.6	23.2	24.3	24.7
Asian or Pacific Islander [1]	11.9	17.5	14.1	14.7	16.4	17.3	19.2	20.7	25.7	25.7	26.5
Chinese	11.1	15.4	11.6	14.1	16.2	18.5	19.8	21.8	27.6	- - -	- - -
Japanese	12.5	17.1	13.8	16.3	18.6	24.4	22.7	24.3	34.2	- - -	- - -
Filipino	11.6	17.0	12.4	12.3	15.1	17.7	17.5	19.1	22.9	- - -	- - -
Hawaiian	*12.4	24.8	14.8	15.0	16.6	16.9	16.7	16.5	23.2	- - -	- - -
Other Asian or Pacific Islander . . .	*	*	15.5	15.4	16.6	16.0	19.4	20.8	25.5	- - -	- - -
Hispanic or Latino [2]	- - -	- - -	16.8	17.6	18.0	18.7	19.5	20.2	20.7	21.3	21.5
Mexican	- - -	- - -	16.7	17.7	17.4	17.8	18.5	19.1	19.2	19.8	19.9
Puerto Rican	- - -	- - -	18.7	20.1	20.8	22.8	23.0	25.1	28.8	28.5	28.7
Cuban	- - -	- - -	14.2	20.1	20.2	25.0	28.6	27.6	28.7	31.3	37.6
Central and South American	- - -	- - -	17.4	16.2	17.6	18.6	20.6	20.8	22.1	23.2	23.6
Other and unknown Hispanic or Latino	- - -	- - -	15.2	15.7	19.4	21.2	21.1	23.4	23.8	25.4	23.5
Not Hispanic or Latino: [2]											
White	- - -	- - -	18.3	20.2	22.9	26.2	28.8	32.2	34.8	35.2	36.3
Black or African American	- - -	- - -	24.2	24.9	26.7	28.3	30.0	33.4	34.7	34.7	35.6
Age of mother:											
Under 20 years	11.6	12.7	12.8	13.0	14.3	14.2	15.0	15.8	15.8	15.3	15.7
20–24 years	16.2	17.6	17.4	18.3	19.2	19.9	20.4	22.0	22.4	22.4	22.8
25–29 years	19.8	20.9	20.5	21.6	23.5	24.8	26.3	28.2	29.0	29.6	30.2
30–34 years	23.7	24.5	23.5	25.5	27.6	30.6	33.7	36.5	38.9	39.2	40.1
35–39 years	27.3	25.8	25.3	26.3	30.2	35.7	39.3	43.5	47.7	47.8	48.5
40–44 years	22.3	23.3	23.0	20.5	24.7	32.3	38.6	45.2	52.5	51.3	53.7
45–49 years	*18.1	*	*	*18.9	*23.8	101.9	133.2	153.1	189.7	189.2	195.4
50–54 years	- - -	- - -	- - -	- - -	- - -	- - -	347.2	313.7	384.0	374.6	379.7
Triplet and higher order multiple births					Number per 100,000 live births						
All races	29.1	33.9	37.0	51.2	72.8	127.5	173.6	180.5	184.0	187.4	176.9
White	28.4	35.3	37.6	54.2	80.2	145.4	195.9	205.1	206.0	208.7	196.3
Black or African American	35.4	30.4	37.1	41.2	46.9	58.4	88.3	83.7	102.6	108.4	98.2
American Indian or Alaska Native. . .	*	*	*	*	*	*53.7	*	*	*54.3	*76.7	*50.1
Asian or Pacific Islander	*	*	*	*22.0	43.1	59.9	103.1	117.2	108.1	111.7	140.5
Hispanic or Latino [2]	- - -	- - -	25.4	28.4	39.5	52.2	72.7	80.8	84.1	85.9	76.4
Not Hispanic or Latino: [2]											
White	- - -	- - -	39.0	55.3	89.8	170.0	230.8	246.3	250.4	255.0	243.4
Black or African American	- - -	- - -	42.6	39.1	46.2	57.8	90.0	83.7	102.2	109.5	99.7
Age of mother:											
Under 20 years	9.1	10.9	14.8	13.8	15.9	17.6	20.7	23.2	21.5	12.8	20.6
20–24 years	25.4	28.1	31.4	35.0	32.4	35.3	46.8	44.2	50.0	48.4	41.7
25–29 years	43.7	45.4	42.8	66.3	73.9	118.3	151.0	163.3	153.5	158.9	158.7
30–34 years	36.4	53.5	58.3	71.2	126.3	217.2	293.6	307.3	297.7	309.1	285.0
35–39 years	35.7	45.1	47.6	70.0	156.8	285.3	403.2	368.5	406.0	409.5	375.3
40–44 years	*	*	*	*	*57.6	273.6	315.4	415.5	393.6	330.7	364.6
45–49 years	*	*	*	*	*	*1,466.8	2,100.2	*1,586.6	2,010.0	1,919.6	1,235.2
50–54 years	- - -	- - -	- - -	- - -	- - -	- - -	*	*9,019.6	*	*	*

- - - Data not available.

* Rates preceded by an asterisk are based on fewer than 50 births. Rates based on fewer than 20 births are considered unreliable and are not shown.

[1] Starting with 2003 data, estimates are not shown for Asian or Pacific Islander subgroups during the transition from single race to multiple race reporting. See Appendix II, Race, Birth File.

[2] Prior to 1993, data from states lacking an Hispanic-origin item on the birth certificate were excluded. See Appendix II, Hispanic origin. Data for non-Hispanic white and non-Hispanic black women for years prior to 1989 are not nationally representative and are provided for comparison with Hispanic data.

NOTES: The race groups, white, black, American Indian or Alaska Native, and Asian or Pacific Islander, include persons of Hispanic and non-Hispanic origin. Persons of Hispanic origin may be of any race. Starting with 2003 data, some states reported multiple-race data. The multiple-race data for these states were bridged to the single race categories of the 1977 Office of Management and Budget standards for comparability with other states. See Appendix II, Race. Interpretation of trend data should take into consideration expansion of reporting areas and immigration. Data for additional years are available. See Appendix III.

SOURCES: Centers for Disease Control and Prevention, National Center for Health Statistics, National Vital Statistics System, Birth File; Martin JA, Park MM. Trends in Twin and Triplet Births: 1980–97. National vital statistics reports. Vol 47 no 24. Hyattsville, MD: National Center for Health Statistics. 1999.

Table 7. Prenatal care for live births, by detailed race and Hispanic origin of mother: United States, selected years 1970–2004

[Data are based on birth certificates]

Prenatal care, race, and Hispanic origin of mother	1970	1975	1980	1985	1990	1995	2000	2002	2003[1]	43 reporting areas 2003[2]	43 reporting areas 2004[1]
Prenatal care began during 1st trimester					Percent of live births[3]						
All races	68.0	72.4	76.3	76.2	75.8	81.3	83.2	83.7	84.1	84.0	83.9
White	72.3	75.8	79.2	79.3	79.2	83.6	85.0	85.4	85.7	85.5	85.4
Black or African American	44.2	55.5	62.4	61.5	60.6	70.4	74.3	75.2	75.9	76.1	76.4
American Indian or Alaska Native	38.2	45.4	55.8	57.5	57.9	66.7	69.3	69.8	70.8	70.6	69.9
Asian or Pacific Islander[4]	- - -	- - -	73.7	74.1	75.1	79.9	84.0	84.8	85.4	85.4	85.6
Chinese	71.8	76.7	82.6	82.0	81.3	85.7	87.6	87.2	- - -	- - -	- - -
Japanese	78.1	82.7	86.1	84.7	87.0	89.7	91.0	90.5	- - -	- - -	- - -
Filipino	60.6	70.6	77.3	76.5	77.1	80.9	84.9	85.4	- - -	- - -	- - -
Hawaiian	- - -	- - -	68.8	67.7	65.8	75.9	79.9	78.1	- - -	- - -	- - -
Other Asian or Pacific Islander	- - -	- - -	67.4	69.9	71.9	77.0	82.5	83.9	- - -	- - -	- - -
Hispanic or Latino[5]	- - -	- - -	60.2	61.2	60.2	70.8	74.4	76.7	77.5	77.3	77.5
Mexican	- - -	- - -	59.6	60.0	57.8	69.1	72.9	75.7	76.5	76.9	77.2
Puerto Rican	- - -	- - -	55.1	58.3	63.5	74.0	78.5	79.9	81.2	80.3	79.9
Cuban	- - -	- - -	82.7	82.5	84.8	89.2	91.7	92.0	92.1	86.5	86.6
Central and South American	- - -	- - -	58.8	60.6	61.5	73.2	77.6	78.7	79.2	78.1	77.6
Other and unknown Hispanic or Latino	- - -	- - -	66.4	65.8	66.4	74.3	75.8	76.7	77.0	77.5	78.1
Not Hispanic or Latino:[5]											
White	- - -	- - -	81.2	81.4	83.3	87.1	88.5	88.6	89.0	89.1	88.9
Black or African American	- - -	- - -	60.8	60.2	60.7	70.4	74.3	75.2	75.9	76.2	76.5
Prenatal care began during 3rd trimester or no prenatal care											
All races	7.9	6.0	5.1	5.7	6.1	4.2	3.9	3.6	3.5	3.6	3.6
White	6.3	5.0	4.3	4.8	4.9	3.5	3.3	3.1	3.0	3.1	3.2
Black or African American	16.6	10.5	8.9	10.2	11.3	7.6	6.7	6.2	6.0	5.9	5.7
American Indian or Alaska Native	28.9	22.4	15.2	12.9	12.9	9.5	8.6	8.0	7.6	7.7	7.9
Asian or Pacific Islander[4]	- - -	- - -	6.5	6.5	5.8	4.3	3.3	3.1	3.1	3.1	3.0
Chinese	6.5	4.4	3.7	4.4	3.4	3.0	2.2	2.1	- - -	- - -	- - -
Japanese	4.1	2.7	2.1	3.1	2.9	2.3	1.8	2.1	- - -	- - -	- - -
Filipino	7.2	4.1	4.0	4.8	4.5	4.1	3.0	2.8	- - -	- - -	- - -
Hawaiian	- - -	- - -	6.7	7.4	8.7	5.1	4.2	4.7	- - -	- - -	- - -
Other Asian or Pacific Islander	- - -	- - -	9.3	8.2	7.1	5.0	3.8	3.5	- - -	- - -	- - -
Hispanic or Latino[5]	- - -	- - -	12.0	12.4	12.0	7.4	6.3	5.5	5.3	5.3	5.4
Mexican	- - -	- - -	11.8	12.9	13.2	8.1	6.9	5.8	5.6	5.5	5.5
Puerto Rican	- - -	- - -	16.2	15.5	10.6	5.5	4.5	4.1	3.7	3.9	3.9
Cuban	- - -	- - -	3.9	3.7	2.8	2.1	1.4	1.3	1.3	2.9	2.9
Central and South American	- - -	- - -	13.1	12.5	10.9	6.1	5.4	4.9	4.7	4.9	5.1
Other and unknown Hispanic or Latino	- - -	- - -	9.2	9.4	8.5	6.0	5.9	5.3	5.4	5.6	5.5
Not Hispanic or Latino:[5]											
White	- - -	- - -	3.5	4.0	3.4	2.5	2.3	2.2	2.1	2.1	2.2
Black or African American	- - -	- - -	9.7	10.9	11.2	7.6	6.7	6.2	6.0	5.9	5.7

- - - Data not available.

[1]Reporting areas that have adopted the 2003 revision of the U.S. Standard Certificate of Live Birth are excluded because prenatal care data based on the 2003 revision are not comparable with data based on the 1989 and earlier revisions of the U.S. Standard Certificate of Live Birth. In 2003, Pennsylvania and Washington adopted the 2003 revision; in 2004, Florida, Idaho, Kentucky, New Hampshire, New York State (excluding New York City), South Carolina, and Tennessee adopted the 2003 Revision. See Appendix II, Prenatal care.

[2]Data for 2003 are limited to the 43 reporting areas using the 1989 revision of the U.S. Standard Certificate of Live Birth in 2004 and are provided for comparison with 2004.

[3]Excludes live births where trimester when prenatal care began is unknown.

[4]Starting with 2003 data, estimates are not shown for Asian or Pacific Islander subgroups during the transition from single race to multiple race reporting. See Appendix II, Race; Birth File.

[5]Prior to 1993, data from states lacking an Hispanic-origin item on the birth certificate were excluded. See Appendix II, Hispanic origin. Data for non-Hispanic white and non-Hispanic black women for years prior to 1989 are not nationally representative and are provided for comparison with Hispanic data.

NOTES: Data are based on the 1989 and earlier revisions of the U.S. Standard Certificate of Live Birth. Data for 1970 and 1975 exclude births that occurred in states not reporting prenatal care. The race groups, white, black, American Indian or Alaska Native, and Asian or Pacific Islander, include persons of Hispanic and non-Hispanic origin. Persons of Hispanic origin may be of any race. Starting with 2003 data, some states reported multiple-race data. The multiple-race data for these states were bridged to the single race categories of the 1977 Office of Management and Budget standards for comparability with other states. See Appendix II, Race. Interpretation of trend data should take into consideration changes in reporting areas and immigration. Data for additional years are available. See Appendix III.

SOURCES: Centers for Disease Control and Prevention, National Center for Health Statistics, National Vital Statistics System, Birth File. Martin JA, Hamilton BE, Sutton PD, Ventura SJ, Menacker F, Kirmeyer S. Births: Final Data for 2004. National vital statistics reports. vol 55 no 1. Hyattsville, MD: National Center for Health Statistics. 2006; Births: Final data for each data year 1997–2003. National vital statistics reports. Hyattsville, MD; Final natality statistics for each data year 1970–1996. Monthly vital statistics report. Hyattsville, MD.

Table 8 (page 1 of 3). Early prenatal care by race and Hispanic origin of mother, geographic division, and state: United States, average annual 1996–1998, 1999–2001, and 2002–2004

[Data are based on birth certificates]

Geographic division and state	All races			Not Hispanic or Latino White			Not Hispanic or Latino Black or African American		
	1996–1998	1999–2001	2002–2004	1996–1998	1999–2001	2002–2004	1996–1998	1999–2001	2002–2004
	Percent of live births with early prenatal care (beginning in the 1st trimester)								
United States [1]	82.4	83.2	83.8	87.7	88.5	88.9	72.4	74.3	76.1
New England [1]	88.1	89.5	89.2	90.6	92.0	91.9	77.8	80.7	80.1
Connecticut	88.4	89.1	88.1	91.9	92.9	92.4	79.4	82.1	80.3
Maine	89.3	88.7	87.9	89.7	89.0	88.4	84.3	80.1	76.4
Massachusetts	87.4	89.5	89.8	90.4	92.4	92.4	76.3	79.3	80.0
New Hampshire [1]	89.5	90.8	- - -	89.9	91.6	- - -	77.2	75.7	- - -
Rhode Island	89.6	91.1	90.2	92.0	93.5	92.8	80.0	84.7	81.2
Vermont	87.6	88.5	89.8	87.8	88.8	90.2	*73.6	78.3	72.1
Middle Atlantic [1]	81.7	82.0	- - -	88.2	88.4	- - -	68.3	69.7	- - -
New Jersey	81.6	80.6	79.8	89.5	89.3	88.9	64.5	63.8	63.5
New York [1]	85.4	85.0	- - -	89.1	88.9	- - -	70.5	70.6	- - -
New York City	73.5	75.5	79.2	83.1	85.2	88.0	69.4	71.0	73.5
Pennsylvania [1]	84.3	85.3	- - -	87.9	88.4	- - -	68.7	72.4	- - -
East North Central	83.4	84.0	85.4	87.5	88.2	89.0	70.1	71.7	74.2
Illinois	82.2	82.9	85.3	89.3	89.9	90.9	69.5	71.4	74.2
Indiana	80.1	80.6	81.2	82.6	83.6	84.5	65.4	68.2	69.2
Michigan	84.2	84.2	85.9	88.3	88.8	89.7	71.0	69.7	71.9
Ohio	85.3	86.8	87.8	87.8	89.0	89.8	72.7	76.3	78.8
Wisconsin	84.3	84.0	84.9	88.0	87.8	88.5	67.5	69.5	74.0
West North Central	85.2	86.0	86.6	88.0	89.0	89.5	72.4	75.3	77.5
Iowa	87.3	88.1	88.7	88.7	89.5	90.3	74.1	77.2	77.1
Kansas	85.6	86.5	87.0	89.1	90.0	90.1	76.0	78.5	79.3
Minnesota	84.0	84.6	86.1	87.4	88.7	90.2	65.0	66.7	72.2
Missouri	85.9	87.5	88.2	88.4	89.7	90.1	73.4	78.0	80.3
Nebraska	84.1	83.6	83.2	87.0	87.0	86.7	72.0	69.9	71.9
North Dakota	85.0	86.2	86.4	87.1	88.9	89.2	76.8	76.9	82.6
South Dakota	82.2	80.1	78.0	86.0	84.3	83.1	70.5	67.6	63.5
South Atlantic [1]	84.3	84.6	84.3	89.5	89.9	90.3	74.3	76.0	77.3
Delaware	83.2	85.4	85.6	88.2	89.9	89.9	73.0	78.2	81.2
District of Columbia	67.6	73.9	76.8	89.4	90.7	90.8	62.7	68.6	71.5
Florida [1]	83.6	83.9	- - -	88.6	89.1	- - -	72.6	74.0	- - -
Georgia	85.8	86.8	84.2	91.0	91.7	90.4	78.6	80.8	79.1
Maryland	88.3	85.7	83.4	92.9	91.4	90.7	79.8	77.4	75.5
North Carolina	84.0	84.7	84.3	90.0	91.0	90.7	73.4	75.9	76.3
South Carolina [1]	80.4	79.7	- - -	87.5	86.4	- - -	69.0	70.4	- - -
Virginia	84.9	85.2	85.4	90.0	90.3	90.5	73.4	75.7	77.6
West Virginia	82.6	85.8	85.9	83.2	86.5	86.4	67.1	72.5	75.0
East South Central [1]	83.0	83.7	- - -	87.9	88.5	- - -	70.7	73.1	- - -
Alabama	82.1	82.8	83.7	88.7	89.7	90.0	69.7	71.7	75.5
Kentucky [1]	85.6	86.7	- - -	86.8	87.9	- - -	75.9	78.7	- - -
Mississippi	79.8	81.8	84.4	89.0	89.4	90.8	69.3	73.3	77.2
Tennessee [1]	83.7	83.4	- - -	87.7	87.7	- - -	72.0	73.0	- - -
West South Central	78.9	79.9	81.2	85.8	86.9	87.2	72.1	74.5	76.1
Arkansas	76.1	79.5	81.1	80.7	83.6	84.6	63.8	69.5	73.3
Louisiana	81.5	83.1	84.5	89.1	90.4	90.8	71.2	73.4	75.9
Oklahoma	78.6	78.9	77.6	81.9	82.7	81.7	68.0	71.0	70.4
Texas	78.6	79.5	81.1	86.8	87.6	88.1	74.8	76.7	77.4
Mountain [1]	78.1	77.7	77.5	84.8	85.2	85.3	71.3	71.8	72.6
Arizona	74.7	76.4	76.5	84.4	86.9	87.5	71.5	74.6	78.2
Colorado	82.2	80.7	79.5	87.5	87.8	86.2	76.4	74.3	71.2
Idaho [1]	78.7	81.1	- - -	81.6	83.5	- - -	72.2	75.9	- - -
Montana	82.5	83.2	83.8	84.9	86.1	86.7	75.9	86.5	85.2
Nevada	76.1	75.1	75.6	83.3	84.5	84.6	66.8	67.6	70.0
New Mexico	69.2	68.1	69.1	77.8	75.7	76.8	62.3	64.6	68.2
Utah	83.2	79.7	79.9	86.4	83.7	83.7	67.2	60.0	60.3
Wyoming	81.9	82.9	85.5	83.8	84.4	87.0	69.7	78.3	86.1
Pacific [1]	81.7	84.0	86.3	86.8	88.1	89.4	79.0	81.4	83.4
Alaska	80.9	80.0	80.2	83.4	83.6	84.0	82.3	83.1	83.7
California	81.6	84.5	87.0	87.7	89.7	90.6	79.0	81.8	83.5
Hawaii	84.3	85.1	82.7	90.1	90.3	86.7	89.5	91.2	90.3
Oregon	80.4	81.2	81.1	83.1	84.2	84.4	78.4	76.4	75.6
Washington [1]	83.2	82.9	- - -	86.0	86.0	- - -	77.0	75.8	- - -

See footnotes at end of table.

Table 8 (page 2 of 3). Early prenatal care by race and Hispanic origin of mother, geographic division, and state: United States, average annual 1996–1998, 1999–2001, and 2002–2004

[Data are based on birth certificates]

Geographic division and state	Hispanic or Latino[2]			American Indian or Alaska Native[3]			Asian or Pacific Islander[3]		
	1996–1998	1999–2001	2002–2004	1996–1998	1999–2001	2002–2004	1996–1998	1999–2001	2002–2004
	Percent of live births with early prenatal care (beginning in the 1st trimester)								
United States[1]	73.4	74.9	77.1	68.2	69.4	69.9	82.2	83.9	85.3
New England[1]	77.4	80.4	81.1	75.8	81.0	84.1	82.2	85.4	86.1
Connecticut	78.2	78.8	76.9	75.2	82.1	85.4	85.9	87.5	87.7
Maine	80.2	80.6	80.5	72.9	76.2	78.0	81.5	86.8	82.1
Massachusetts	75.9	80.2	83.0	71.1	82.3	88.5	81.0	84.7	86.1
New Hampshire[1]	77.3	80.4	- - -	86.2	81.9	- - -	84.6	85.3	- - -
Rhode Island	82.6	86.7	86.8	81.5	81.9	80.9	81.5	83.8	81.8
Vermont	82.8	82.2	79.4	*79.3	*82.4	*85.7	75.7	85.6	86.9
Middle Atlantic[1]	70.7	71.6	- - -	74.2	77.1	- - -	77.8	78.5	- - -
New Jersey	71.0	68.6	67.9	71.8	73.8	67.9	83.2	83.3	84.8
New York[1]	73.9	73.3	- - -	72.5	74.8	- - -	81.9	82.7	- - -
New York City	69.3	72.4	77.0	77.5	77.5	84.7	72.9	73.2	77.0
Pennsylvania[1]	71.5	73.5	- - -	78.2	82.4	- - -	78.5	81.1	- - -
East North Central	72.4	72.6	77.0	72.6	75.2	75.7	82.1	83.4	86.0
Illinois	72.6	74.0	79.6	75.1	77.8	81.4	85.2	85.0	88.1
Indiana	65.9	63.1	64.5	68.1	74.2	70.9	81.8	81.0	83.5
Michigan	73.2	71.6	77.9	73.9	75.6	79.4	85.6	87.0	88.2
Ohio	76.8	76.7	78.7	79.4	80.4	80.9	86.0	88.7	90.3
Wisconsin	71.3	69.6	70.7	69.3	72.7	71.2	62.3	65.8	70.0
West North Central	67.8	69.7	73.4	66.9	66.3	65.8	73.2	78.2	81.2
Iowa	71.0	73.3	75.5	69.9	74.7	75.9	82.0	83.7	87.6
Kansas	65.9	69.4	74.1	77.7	80.4	82.0	82.5	85.4	86.2
Minnesota	61.7	63.2	69.6	62.1	62.2	64.0	61.2	69.5	74.5
Missouri	76.8	78.2	79.7	76.9	77.3	80.4	84.2	87.8	88.4
Nebraska	67.6	68.1	70.0	67.5	68.3	68.5	82.1	80.7	83.7
North Dakota	73.8	77.5	80.5	70.1	66.8	66.9	78.4	86.3	87.2
South Dakota	72.2	68.5	63.9	64.3	61.8	57.7	74.8	80.1	72.3
South Atlantic[1]	78.1	77.3	70.4	73.9	73.7	80.6	85.4	86.6	86.1
Delaware	68.7	72.3	72.0	*76.2	78.1	87.1	84.0	89.2	90.1
District of Columbia	64.1	70.8	70.5	*83.3	*61.9	*	73.2	77.9	81.7
Florida[1]	81.4	81.4	- - -	69.4	64.2	- - -	87.1	87.8	- - -
Georgia	76.0	77.9	71.0	82.9	81.7	83.5	87.3	90.2	88.6
Maryland	81.4	77.3	68.1	84.0	82.6	78.7	89.5	87.0	84.9
North Carolina	68.5	69.1	69.9	72.5	76.5	80.2	81.9	83.5	85.0
South Carolina[1]	65.9	61.7	- - -	76.1	77.4	- - -	76.0	79.5	- - -
Virginia	72.8	71.6	71.1	81.0	80.2	82.1	83.7	85.7	85.5
West Virginia	76.5	67.4	74.2	*84.2	*74.4	*69.2	82.2	80.4	86.1
East South Central[1]	66.7	60.8	- - -	75.7	78.6	- - -	83.4	84.6	- - -
Alabama	62.5	55.7	53.1	80.0	79.4	81.4	83.4	86.7	87.4
Kentucky[1]	74.0	68.6	- - -	79.4	85.2	- - -	84.6	87.2	- - -
Mississippi	77.1	73.4	77.0	72.8	75.8	72.2	80.1	83.0	85.9
Tennessee[1]	64.5	58.5	- - -	73.8	78.2	- - -	84.0	83.1	- - -
West South Central	71.3	72.5	75.6	70.4	70.9	72.5	85.6	87.3	88.1
Arkansas	59.8	66.2	70.6	68.4	74.0	75.4	73.4	78.6	82.4
Louisiana	83.8	85.0	83.7	78.0	80.7	84.4	83.7	85.7	88.3
Oklahoma	68.6	66.7	64.6	69.3	69.4	70.2	81.7	80.7	80.3
Texas	71.4	72.6	76.0	74.1	74.6	79.4	86.6	88.4	89.0
Mountain[1]	65.3	65.0	66.6	60.9	63.8	64.9	78.0	78.9	79.1
Arizona	64.1	65.7	66.8	61.0	65.9	68.0	82.4	84.5	84.2
Colorado	68.3	65.5	67.6	71.9	68.3	67.6	80.0	82.6	80.8
Idaho[1]	61.2	66.9	- - -	59.3	67.5	- - -	78.2	80.4	- - -
Montana	76.7	79.3	80.1	66.4	65.6	66.1	79.7	80.4	83.7
Nevada	64.0	61.8	64.1	70.3	67.4	68.6	78.5	79.2	80.2
New Mexico	66.2	65.5	66.7	55.6	58.8	59.2	74.3	75.0	76.1
Utah	64.5	61.3	64.1	59.0	55.3	56.7	69.8	64.7	65.7
Wyoming	71.1	73.5	79.6	65.1	71.8	70.9	84.4	82.2	84.7
Pacific[1]	76.6	80.3	84.3	72.7	72.5	73.0	83.5	85.5	87.1
Alaska	78.1	80.8	78.2	75.7	71.3	70.3	75.2	76.4	75.1
California	77.0	81.0	84.8	71.8	73.9	76.0	84.2	86.5	88.5
Hawaii	83.0	83.7	81.1	82.9	83.4	81.2	82.3	83.4	81.2
Oregon	66.6	69.2	70.2	66.2	68.7	68.9	80.2	81.8	81.7
Washington[1]	70.8	71.8	- - -	72.1	72.0	- - -	80.5	81.6	- - -

See footnotes at end of table.

Table 8 (page 3 of 3). Early prenatal care by race and Hispanic origin of mother, geographic division, and state: United States, average annual 1996–1998, 1999–2001, and 2002–2004

[Data are based on birth certificates]

---

* Percents preceded by an asterisk are based on fewer than 50 births. Percents not shown are based on fewer than 20 births.
[1]Reporting areas that have adopted the 2003 revision of the U.S. Standard Certificate of Live Birth are excluded because prenatal care data based on the 2003 revision are not comparable with data based on the 1989 revision of the U.S. Standard Certificate of Live Birth. In 2003, Pennsylvania and Washington adopted the 2003 revision; in 2004, Florida, Idaho, Kentucky, New Hampshire, New York State (excluding New York City), South Carolina, and Tennessee adopted the 2003 revision. See Appendix II, Prenatal Care.
[2]Persons of Hispanic origin may be of any race. See Appendix II, Hispanic origin.
[3]Includes persons of Hispanic and non-Hispanic origin.

NOTES: Data are based on the 1989 revision of the U.S. Standard Certificate of Live Birth. Starting with 2003 data, some states reported multiple-race data. The multiple-race data for these states were bridged to the single race categories of the 1977 Office of Management and Budget standards for comparability with other states. See Appendix II, Race.

SOURCE: Centers for Disease Control and Prevention, National Center for Health Statistics, National Vital Statistics System, Birth File.

Table 9. Teenage childbearing, by detailed race and Hispanic origin of mother: United States, selected years 1970–2004

[Data are based on birth certificates]

Maternal age, race, and Hispanic origin of mother	1970	1975	1980	1985	1990	1995	2000	2001	2002	2003	2004
Age of mother under 18 years					Percent of live births						
All races	6.3	7.6	5.8	4.7	4.7	5.3	4.1	3.8	3.6	3.4	3.4
White	4.8	6.0	4.5	3.7	3.6	4.3	3.5	3.3	3.1	3.0	3.0
Black or African American	14.8	16.3	12.5	10.6	10.1	10.8	7.8	7.3	6.9	6.6	6.4
American Indian or Alaska Native	7.5	11.2	9.4	7.6	7.2	8.7	7.3	6.8	6.6	6.6	6.4
Asian or Pacific Islander[1]	- - -	- - -	1.5	1.6	2.1	2.2	1.5	1.3	1.1	1.1	1.1
Chinese	1.1	0.4	0.3	0.3	0.4	0.3	0.2	0.2	0.2	- - -	- - -
Japanese	2.0	1.7	1.0	0.9	0.8	0.8	0.6	0.5	0.6	- - -	- - -
Filipino	3.7	2.4	1.6	1.6	2.0	2.2	1.6	1.5	1.2	- - -	- - -
Hawaiian	- - -	- - -	6.6	5.7	6.5	7.6	5.7	4.9	4.5	- - -	- - -
Other Asian or Pacific Islander	- - -	- - -	1.2	1.8	2.4	2.5	1.7	1.5	1.3	- - -	- - -
Hispanic or Latino[2]	- - -	- - -	7.4	6.4	6.6	7.6	6.3	5.8	5.6	5.4	5.4
Mexican	- - -	- - -	7.7	6.9	6.9	8.0	6.6	6.2	6.0	5.8	5.8
Puerto Rican	- - -	- - -	10.0	8.5	9.1	10.8	7.8	7.4	6.9	6.9	6.8
Cuban	- - -	- - -	3.8	2.2	2.7	2.8	3.1	2.7	2.7	2.4	2.4
Central and South American	- - -	- - -	2.4	2.4	3.2	4.1	3.3	3.1	2.8	2.8	2.8
Other and unknown Hispanic or Latino	- - -	- - -	6.5	7.0	8.0	9.0	7.6	6.8	6.5	6.3	6.3
Not Hispanic or Latino:[2]											
White	- - -	- - -	4.0	3.2	3.0	3.4	2.6	2.3	2.2	2.1	2.0
Black or African American	- - -	- - -	12.7	10.7	10.2	10.8	7.8	7.3	6.9	6.6	6.5
Age of mother 18–19 years											
All races	11.3	11.3	9.8	8.0	8.1	7.9	7.7	7.5	7.1	6.9	6.8
White	10.4	10.3	9.0	7.1	7.3	7.2	7.1	6.9	6.6	6.4	6.4
Black or African American	16.6	16.9	14.5	12.9	13.0	12.4	11.9	11.5	11.1	10.7	10.7
American Indian or Alaska Native	12.8	15.2	14.6	12.4	12.3	12.7	12.4	12.5	11.9	11.6	11.5
Asian or Pacific Islander[1]	- - -	- - -	3.9	3.4	3.7	3.5	3.0	3.0	2.7	2.4	2.3
Chinese	3.9	1.7	1.0	0.6	0.8	0.6	0.7	0.8	0.7	- - -	- - -
Japanese	4.1	3.3	2.3	1.9	2.0	1.7	1.4	1.2	1.1	- - -	- - -
Filipino	7.1	5.0	4.0	3.7	4.1	4.1	3.7	3.6	3.3	- - -	- - -
Hawaiian	- - -	- - -	13.3	12.3	11.9	11.5	11.7	11.3	10.2	- - -	- - -
Other Asian or Pacific Islander	- - -	- - -	3.8	3.5	3.9	3.8	3.2	3.1	2.8	- - -	- - -
Hispanic or Latino[2]	- - -	- - -	11.6	10.1	10.2	10.3	9.9	9.7	9.3	8.9	8.9
Mexican	- - -	- - -	12.0	10.6	10.7	10.8	10.4	10.3	9.8	9.5	9.4
Puerto Rican	- - -	- - -	13.3	12.4	12.6	12.7	12.2	11.8	10.9	11.0	10.8
Cuban	- - -	- - -	9.2	4.9	5.0	4.9	4.4	4.8	5.5	5.5	5.4
Central and South American	- - -	- - -	6.0	5.8	5.9	6.5	6.5	6.3	5.7	5.6	5.6
Other and unknown Hispanic or Latino	- - -	- - -	10.8	10.5	11.1	11.1	11.3	10.5	10.2	9.6	9.9
Not Hispanic or Latino:[2]											
White	- - -	- - -	8.5	6.5	6.6	6.4	6.1	5.9	5.6	5.4	5.4
Black or African American	- - -	- - -	14.7	12.9	13.0	12.4	12.0	11.6	11.1	10.8	10.8

- - - Data not available.

[1]Starting with 2003 data, estimates are not shown for Asian or Pacific Islander subgroups during the transition from single race to multiple race reporting. See Appendix II, Race, Birth File.

[2]Prior to 1993, data from states lacking an Hispanic-origin item on the birth certificate were excluded. See Appendix II, Hispanic origin. Data for non-Hispanic white and non-Hispanic black women for years prior to 1989 are not nationally representative and are provided for comparison with Hispanic data.

NOTES: The race groups, white, black, American Indian or Alaska Native, and Asian or Pacific Islander, include persons of Hispanic and non-Hispanic origin. Persons of Hispanic origin may be of any race. Starting with 2003 data, some states reported multiple-race data. The multiple-race data for these states were bridged to the single race categories of the 1977 Office of Management and Budget standards for comparability with other states. See Appendix II, Race. Interpretation of trend data should take into consideration expansion of reporting areas and immigration. Data for additional years are available. See Appendix III.

SOURCES: Centers for Disease Control and Prevention, National Center for Health Statistics, National Vital Statistics System, Birth File.

Table 10. Nonmarital childbearing by detailed race and Hispanic origin of mother, and maternal age: United States, selected years 1970–2004

[Data are based on birth certificates]

Race, Hispanic origin of mother, and maternal age	1970	1975	1980	1985	1990	1995	2000	2001	2002	2003	2004
	Live births per 1,000 unmarried women 15–44 years of age[1]										
All races and origins	26.4	24.5	29.4	32.8	43.8	44.3	44.0	43.8	43.7	44.9	46.1
White[2]	13.9	12.4	18.1	22.5	32.9	37.0	38.2	38.5	38.9	40.4	41.6
Black or African American[2]	95.5	84.2	81.1	77.0	90.5	74.5	70.5	68.2	66.2	66.3	67.2
Asian or Pacific Islander	- - -	- - -	- - -	- - -	- - -	- - -	20.9	21.2	21.3	22.2	23.6
Hispanic or Latino[3]	- - -	- - -	- - -	- - -	89.6	88.7	87.2	87.8	87.9	92.2	95.7
White, not Hispanic or Latino	- - -	- - -	- - -	- - -	24.4	28.1	28.0	27.8	27.8	28.6	29.4
	Percent of live births to unmarried mothers										
All races and origins	10.7	14.3	18.4	22.0	28.0	32.2	33.2	33.5	34.0	34.6	35.8
White	5.5	7.1	11.2	14.7	20.4	25.3	27.1	27.7	28.5	29.4	30.5
Black or African American	37.5	49.5	56.1	61.2	66.5	69.9	68.5	68.4	68.2	68.2	68.8
American Indian or Alaska Native	22.4	32.7	39.2	46.8	53.6	57.2	58.4	59.7	59.7	61.3	62.3
Asian or Pacific Islander[4]	- - -	- - -	7.3	9.5	13.2	16.3	14.8	14.9	14.9	15.0	15.5
Chinese	3.0	1.6	2.7	3.0	5.0	7.9	7.6	8.4	9.0	- - -	- - -
Japanese	4.6	4.6	5.2	7.9	9.6	10.8	9.5	9.2	10.3	- - -	- - -
Filipino	9.1	6.9	8.6	11.4	15.9	19.5	20.3	20.4	20.0	- - -	- - -
Hawaiian	- - -	- - -	32.9	37.3	45.0	49.0	50.0	50.6	50.4	- - -	- - -
Other Asian or Pacific Islander	- - -	- - -	5.4	8.5	12.6	16.2	13.8	13.7	13.5	- - -	- - -
Hispanic or Latino[3]	- - -	- - -	23.6	29.5	36.7	40.8	42.7	42.5	43.5	45.0	46.4
Mexican	- - -	- - -	20.3	25.7	33.3	38.1	40.7	40.8	42.1	43.7	45.2
Puerto Rican	- - -	- - -	46.3	51.1	55.9	60.0	59.6	58.9	59.1	59.8	61.0
Cuban	- - -	- - -	10.0	16.1	18.2	23.8	27.3	27.2	29.8	31.4	33.2
Central and South American	- - -	- - -	27.1	34.9	41.2	44.1	44.7	44.3	44.8	46.0	47.6
Other and unknown Hispanic or Latino	- - -	- - -	22.4	31.1	37.2	44.0	46.2	44.2	44.4	46.7	46.6
Not Hispanic or Latino:[3]											
White	- - -	- - -	9.5	12.4	16.9	21.2	22.1	22.5	23.0	23.6	24.5
Black or African American	- - -	- - -	57.2	62.0	66.7	70.0	68.7	68.6	68.4	68.5	69.3
	Number of live births, in thousands										
Live births to unmarried mothers	399	448	666	828	1,165	1,254	1,347	1,349	1,366	1,416	1,470
Maternal age	Percent distribution of live births to unmarried mothers										
Under 20 years	50.1	52.1	40.8	33.8	30.9	30.9	28.0	26.6	25.4	24.3	23.7
20–24 years	31.8	29.9	35.6	36.3	34.7	34.5	37.4	38.2	38.6	38.8	38.5
25 years and over	18.1	18.0	23.5	29.9	34.4	34.7	34.6	35.2	35.9	36.9	37.8

- - - Data not available.

[1]Rates computed by relating births to unmarried mothers, regardless of age of mother, to unmarried women 15–44 years of age. Population data for unmarried American Indian or Alaska Native women are not available for rate calculations. Prior to 2000, population data for unmarried Asian or Pacific Islander women were not available for rate calculations.

[2]For 1970 and 1975, birth rates are by race of child.

[3]Prior to 1993, data from states lacking an Hispanic-origin item on the birth certificate were excluded. See Appendix II, Hispanic origin. Data for non-Hispanic white and non-Hispanic black women for years prior to 1989 are not nationally representative and are provided for comparison with Hispanic data.

[4]Starting with 2003 data, estimates are not shown for Asian or Pacific Islander subgroups during the transition from single race to multiple race reporting. See Appendix II, Race, Birth File.

NOTES: National estimates for 1970 and 1975 for unmarried mothers are based on births occurring in states reporting marital status of mother. Changes in reporting procedures for marital status occurred in some states during the 1990s. Interpretation of trend data should also take into consideration expansion of reporting areas and immigration. See Appendix II, Marital status. The race groups, white, black, American Indian or Alaska Native, and Asian or Pacific Islander, include persons of Hispanic and non-Hispanic origin. Persons of Hispanic origin may be of any race. Starting with 2003 data, some states reported multiple-race data. The multiple-race data for these states were bridged to the single race categories of the 1977 Office of Management and Budget standards for comparability with other states. See Appendix II, Race. Starting with Health, United States, 2003, rates for 1991–1999 were revised using intercensal population estimates based on the 2000 census. Rates for 2000 were computed using the 2000 census counts and starting with 2001, rates were computed using 2000-based postcensal estimates. Data for additional years are available. See Appendix III.

SOURCES: Centers for Disease Control and Prevention, National Center for Health Statistics, National Vital Statistics System, Birth File. Martin JA, Hamilton BE, Sutton PD, Ventura SJ, Menacker F, Kirmeyer S. Births: Final Data for 2004. National vital statistics reports. vol 55 no 1. Hyattsville, MD: National Center for Health Statistics. 2006; Hamilton BE, Sutton PD, Ventura SJ. Revised birth and fertility rates for the 1990s and new rates for Hispanic populations, 2000 and 2001: United States. National vital statistics reports. vol 51 no 12. Hyattsville, MD: National Center for Health Statistics. 2003; Births: Final data for each data year 1997–2003. National vital statistics reports. Hyattsville, MD; Final natality statistics for each data year 1993–1996. Monthly vital statistics report. Hyattsville, MD; Ventura SJ. Births to unmarried mothers: United States, 1980–1992. Vital Health Stat 21(53). 1995.

Table 11. Maternal education for live births, by detailed race and Hispanic origin of mother: United States, selected years 1970–2004

[Data are based on birth certificates]

Education, race, and Hispanic origin of mother	1970	1975	1980	1985	1990	1995	2000	2002	2003[1]	43 reporting areas 2003[2]	2004[1]
Less than 12 years of education						Percent of live births[3]					
All races	30.8	28.6	23.7	20.6	23.8	22.6	21.7	21.5	21.6	22.1	22.2
White	27.1	25.1	20.8	17.8	22.4	21.6	21.4	21.6	21.8	22.5	22.7
Black or African American	51.2	45.3	36.4	32.6	30.2	28.7	25.5	24.4	24.0	23.9	23.8
American Indian or Alaska Native	60.5	52.7	44.2	39.0	36.4	33.0	30.8	30.5	30.5	30.2	30.1
Asian or Pacific Islander[4]	- - -	- - -	21.0	19.4	20.0	16.1	11.6	10.3	9.9	10.0	9.3
Chinese	23.0	16.5	15.2	15.5	15.8	12.9	11.7	11.3	- - -	- - -	- - -
Japanese	11.8	9.1	5.0	4.8	3.5	2.6	2.1	2.2	- - -	- - -	- - -
Filipino	26.4	22.3	16.4	13.9	10.3	8.0	6.2	5.3	- - -	- - -	- - -
Hawaiian	- - -	- - -	20.7	18.7	19.3	17.6	16.7	14.3	- - -	- - -	- - -
Other Asian or Pacific Islander	- - -	- - -	27.6	24.3	26.8	21.2	13.5	11.6	- - -	- - -	- - -
Hispanic or Latino[5]	- - -	- - -	51.1	44.5	53.9	52.1	48.9	48.1	47.5	48.7	48.4
Mexican	- - -	- - -	62.8	59.0	61.4	58.6	55.0	54.2	53.6	53.1	52.5
Puerto Rican	- - -	- - -	55.3	46.6	42.7	38.6	33.4	31.5	29.9	31.7	31.6
Cuban	- - -	- - -	24.1	21.1	17.8	14.4	11.9	11.8	11.5	13.4	13.0
Central and South American	- - -	- - -	41.2	37.0	44.2	41.7	37.2	35.8	35.3	38.0	39.1
Other and unknown Hispanic or Latino	- - -	- - -	40.1	36.5	33.3	33.8	31.4	31.7	30.1	28.3	29.4
Not Hispanic or Latino:[5]											
White	- - -	- - -	18.1	15.7	15.2	13.3	12.2	11.7	11.5	11.0	11.0
Black or African American	- - -	- - -	37.3	33.4	30.0	28.6	25.3	24.3	23.8	23.5	23.4
16 years or more of education											
All races	8.6	11.4	14.0	16.7	17.5	21.4	24.7	25.9	26.6	26.7	26.9
White	9.6	12.7	15.5	18.6	19.3	23.1	26.3	27.3	27.9	27.8	28.0
Black or African American	2.8	4.3	6.2	7.0	7.2	9.5	11.7	12.7	13.4	13.8	13.7
American Indian or Alaska Native	2.7	2.2	3.5	3.7	4.4	6.2	7.8	8.7	8.5	8.3	8.6
Asian or Pacific Islander[4]	- - -	- - -	30.8	30.3	31.0	35.0	42.8	45.7	47.1	46.8	48.6
Chinese	34.0	37.8	41.5	35.2	40.3	49.0	55.6	57.3	- - -	- - -	- - -
Japanese	20.7	30.6	36.8	38.1	44.1	46.2	51.1	53.5	- - -	- - -	- - -
Filipino	28.1	36.6	37.1	35.2	34.5	36.7	40.5	43.3	- - -	- - -	- - -
Hawaiian	- - -	- - -	7.9	6.5	6.8	9.7	13.5	14.6	- - -	- - -	- - -
Other Asian or Pacific Islander	- - -	- - -	29.2	30.2	27.3	30.5	40.7	44.4	- - -	- - -	- - -
Hispanic or Latino[5]	- - -	- - -	4.2	6.0	5.1	6.1	7.6	8.3	8.7	7.8	8.0
Mexican	- - -	- - -	2.2	3.0	3.3	4.0	5.1	5.5	5.9	5.9	6.1
Puerto Rican	- - -	- - -	3.0	4.6	6.5	8.7	10.4	11.8	12.9	11.7	12.0
Cuban	- - -	- - -	11.6	15.0	20.4	26.5	31.0	30.5	31.3	34.5	35.4
Central and South American	- - -	- - -	6.1	8.1	8.6	10.3	14.1	15.5	16.0	14.1	14.2
Other and unknown Hispanic or Latino	- - -	- - -	5.5	7.2	8.5	10.5	12.5	13.2	14.4	14.5	14.0
Not Hispanic or Latino:[5]											
White	- - -	- - -	16.6	19.4	22.6	27.7	32.5	34.3	35.5	36.4	37.0
Black or African American	- - -	- - -	5.8	6.7	7.3	9.5	11.7	12.7	13.4	13.9	13.8

- - - Data not available.

[1]Reporting areas that have adopted the 2003 revision of the U.S. Standard Certificate of Live Birth are excluded because maternal education data based on the 2003 revision are not comparable with data based on the 1989 and earlier revisions of the U.S. Standard Certificate of Live Birth. In 2003, Pennsylvania and Washington adopted the 2003 revision; in 2004, Florida, Idaho, Kentucky, New Hampshire, New York State (excluding New York City), South Carolina, and Tennessee adopted the 2003 revision. See Appendix II, Education.

[2]Data for 2003 are limited to the 43 reporting areas using the 1989 revision of the U.S. Standard Certificate of Live Birth in 2004 and are provided for comparison with 2004.

[3]Excludes live births for whom education of mother is unknown.

[4]Starting with 2003 data, estimates are not shown for Asian or Pacific Islander subgroups during the transition from single race to multiple race reporting. See Appendix II, Race, Birth File.

[5]Prior to 1993, data are shown only for states with an Hispanic-origin item and education of mother item on the birth certificate. See Appendix II, Education; Hispanic origin. Data for non-Hispanic white and non-Hispanic black women for years prior to 1989 are not nationally representative and are provided for comparison with Hispanic data.

NOTES: Data are based on the 1989 and earlier revisions of the U.S. Standard Certificate of Live Birth. Maternal education groups shown in this table generally represent the group at highest risk for unfavorable birth outcomes (less than 12 years of education) and the group at lowest risk (16 years or more of education). In 1992–2002, education of mother was reported on the birth certificate by all 50 states and the District of Columbia. See Appendix II, Education. Prior to 1992, data from states lacking an education of mother item were excluded. The race groups, white, black, American Indian or Alaska Native, and Asian or Pacific Islander, include persons of Hispanic and non-Hispanic origin. Persons of Hispanic origin may be of any race. Starting with 2003 data, some states reported multiple-race data. The multiple-race data for these states were bridged to the single race categories of the 1977 Office of Management and Budget standards for comparability with other states. See Appendix II, Race. Interpretation of trend data should take into consideration changes in reporting areas and immigration. Data for additional years are available. See Appendix III.

SOURCE: Centers for Disease Control and Prevention, National Center for Health Statistics, National Vital Statistics System, Birth File.

Table 12. Mothers who smoked cigarettes during pregnancy, by detailed race, Hispanic origin, age, and education of mother: United States, selected years, 1989–2004

[Data are based on birth certificates]

Characteristic of mother	1989	1990	1995	2000	2002	2003[1]	42 reporting areas	
							2003[2]	2004[1]
Race of mother	Percent of mothers who smoked[3,4]							
All races	19.5	18.4	13.9	12.2	11.4	10.7	10.4	10.2
White	20.4	19.4	15.0	13.2	12.3	11.6	11.1	11.0
Black or African American	17.1	15.9	10.6	9.1	8.7	8.1	8.3	8.2
American Indian or Alaska Native	23.0	22.4	20.9	20.0	19.7	18.1	18.2	18.2
Asian or Pacific Islander[5]	5.7	5.5	3.4	2.8	2.5	2.2	2.2	2.2
Chinese	2.7	2.0	0.8	0.6	0.5	- - -	- - -	- - -
Japanese	8.2	8.0	5.2	4.2	4.0	- - -	- - -	- - -
Filipino	5.1	5.3	3.4	3.2	2.9	- - -	- - -	- - -
Hawaiian	19.3	21.0	15.9	14.4	13.7	- - -	- - -	- - -
Other Asian or Pacific Islander	4.2	3.8	2.7	2.3	2.1	- - -	- - -	- - -
Hispanic origin and race of mother[6]								
Hispanic or Latino	8.0	6.7	4.3	3.5	3.0	2.7	2.7	2.6
Mexican	6.3	5.3	3.1	2.4	2.2	2.0	2.1	2.0
Puerto Rican	14.5	13.6	10.4	10.3	9.0	7.9	8.5	8.5
Cuban	6.9	6.4	4.1	3.3	2.8	2.4	5.8	6.4
Central and South American	3.6	3.0	1.8	1.5	1.3	1.1	1.1	1.2
Other and unknown Hispanic or Latino . .	12.1	10.8	8.2	7.4	6.5	6.6	6.9	6.4
Not Hispanic or Latino:								
White	21.7	21.0	17.1	15.6	15.0	14.3	13.8	13.8
Black or African American	17.2	15.9	10.6	9.2	8.8	8.3	8.4	8.4
Age of mother[3]								
Under 15 years	7.7	7.5	7.3	7.1	5.8	5.3	5.1	4.1
15–19 years	22.2	20.8	16.8	17.8	16.7	15.4	14.9	14.2
15–17 years	19.0	17.6	14.6	15.0	13.4	11.9	11.5	10.5
18–19 years	23.9	22.5	18.1	19.2	18.2	17.1	16.5	16.0
20–24 years	23.5	22.1	17.1	16.8	16.7	16.1	15.5	15.5
25–29 years	19.0	18.0	12.8	10.5	9.9	9.4	9.0	9.2
30–34 years	15.7	15.3	11.4	8.0	7.1	6.5	6.2	6.1
35–39 years	13.6	13.3	12.0	9.1	7.8	6.8	6.7	6.3
40–54 years[7]	13.2	12.3	10.1	9.5	8.4	8.0	7.8	7.2
Education of mother[8]	Percent of mothers 20 years of age and over who smoked[3,4]							
0–8 years	18.9	17.5	11.0	7.9	6.8	6.2	5.7	5.5
9–11 years	42.2	40.5	32.0	28.2	26.8	25.5	24.2	23.7
12 years	22.8	21.9	18.3	16.6	16.0	15.2	14.9	14.9
13–15 years	13.7	12.8	10.6	9.1	8.8	8.5	8.3	8.4
16 years or more	5.0	4.5	2.7	2.0	1.7	1.6	1.5	1.5

- - - Data not available.

[1]Reporting areas that have adopted the 2003 revision of the U.S. Standard Certificate of Live Birth are excluded because maternal tobacco use and education data based on the 2003 revision are not comparable with data based on the 1989 and earlier revisions of the U.S. Standard Certificate of Live Birth. In 2003, Pennsylvania and Washington adopted the 2003 revision; in 2004 Florida, Idaho, Kentucky, New Hampshire, New York State (excluding New York City), South Carolina, and Tennessee adopted the 2003 revision. In addition, California did not require reporting of tobacco use during pregnancy. See Appendix II, Cigarette smoking.

[2]Data for 2003 are limited to the 42 reporting areas using the 1989 revision of the U.S. Standard Certificate of Live Birth in 2004 and are provided for comparison with 2004.

[3]Data from states that did not require the reporting of mother's tobacco use during pregnancy on the birth certificate are not included. Reporting area for tobacco use increased from 43 states and the District of Columbia (DC) in 1989 to 49 states and DC in 2000–2002. See Appendix II, Cigarette smoking.

[4]Excludes live births for whom smoking status of mother is unknown.

[5]Maternal tobacco use during pregnancy was not reported on the birth certificates of California, which in 2004 accounted for 30% of the births to Asian or Pacific Islander mothers. Starting with 2003 data, estimates are not shown for Asian or Pacific Islander subgroups during the transition from single race to multiple race reporting. See Appendix II, Race, Birth File.

[6]Data from states that did not require the reporting of Hispanic origin of mother on the birth certificate are not included. Reporting of Hispanic origin increased from 47 states in 1989 to include all 50 states and DC by 1993. See Appendix II, Hispanic origin.

[7]Prior to 1997, data are for live births to mothers 45–49 years of age.

[8]Data from states that did not require the reporting of mother's education on the birth certificate are not included. See Appendix II, Education.

NOTES: Data are based on the 1989 revision of the U.S. Standard Certificate of Live Birth. The race groups, white, black, American Indian or Alaska Native, and Asian or Pacific Islander, include persons of Hispanic and non-Hispanic origin. Persons of Hispanic origin may be of any race. Starting with 2003 data, some states reported multiple-race data. The multiple-race data for these states were bridged to the single race categories of the 1977 Office of Management and Budget standards for comparability with other states. See Appendix II, Race. Interpretation of trend data should take into consideration changes in reporting areas and immigration. Data for additional years are available. See Appendix III.

SOURCES: Centers for Disease Control and Prevention, National Center for Health Statistics, National Vital Statistics System, Birth File.

Table 13. Low-birthweight live births, by detailed race, Hispanic origin, and smoking status of mother: United States, selected years 1970–2004

[Data are based on birth certificates]

Birthweight, race and Hispanic origin of mother, and smoking status of mother	1970	1975	1980	1985	1990	1995	1999	2000	2002	2003	2004
Low birthweight (less than 2,500 grams)					Percent of live births[1]						
All races	7.93	7.38	6.84	6.75	6.97	7.32	7.62	7.57	7.82	7.93	8.08
White	6.85	6.27	5.72	5.65	5.70	6.22	6.57	6.55	6.80	6.94	7.07
Black or African American	13.90	13.19	12.69	12.65	13.25	13.13	13.11	12.99	13.29	13.37	13.44
American Indian or Alaska Native	7.97	6.41	6.44	5.86	6.11	6.61	7.15	6.76	7.23	7.37	7.45
Asian or Pacific Islander[2]	- - -	- - -	6.68	6.16	6.45	6.90	7.45	7.31	7.78	7.78	7.89
Chinese	6.67	5.29	5.21	4.98	4.69	5.29	5.19	5.10	5.52	- - -	- - -
Japanese	9.03	7.47	6.60	6.21	6.16	7.26	7.95	7.14	7.57	- - -	- - -
Filipino	10.02	8.08	7.40	6.95	7.30	7.83	8.30	8.46	8.61	- - -	- - -
Hawaiian	- - -	- - -	7.23	6.49	7.24	6.84	7.69	6.76	8.14	- - -	- - -
Other Asian or Pacific Islander	- - -	- - -	6.83	6.19	6.65	7.05	7.76	7.67	8.16	- - -	- - -
Hispanic or Latino[3]	- - -	- - -	6.12	6.16	6.06	6.29	6.38	6.41	6.55	6.69	6.79
Mexican	- - -	- - -	5.62	5.77	5.55	5.81	5.94	6.01	6.16	6.28	6.44
Puerto Rican	- - -	- - -	8.95	8.69	8.99	9.41	9.30	9.30	9.68	10.01	9.82
Cuban	- - -	- - -	5.62	6.02	5.67	6.50	6.80	6.49	6.50	7.04	7.72
Central and South American	- - -	- - -	5.76	5.68	5.84	6.20	6.38	6.34	6.53	6.70	6.70
Other and unknown Hispanic or Latino	- - -	- - -	6.96	6.83	6.87	7.55	7.63	7.84	7.87	8.01	7.78
Not Hispanic or Latino:[3]											
White	- - -	- - -	5.69	5.61	5.61	6.20	6.64	6.60	6.91	7.04	7.20
Black or African American	- - -	- - -	12.71	12.62	13.32	13.21	13.23	13.13	13.39	13.55	13.74
Cigarette smoker[4]	- - -	- - -	- - -	- - -	11.25	12.18	12.06	11.88	12.15	12.40	12.54
Nonsmoker[4]	- - -	- - -	- - -	- - -	6.14	6.79	7.21	7.19	7.48	7.66	7.79
Very low birthweight (less than 1,500 grams)											
All races	1.17	1.16	1.15	1.21	1.27	1.35	1.45	1.43	1.46	1.45	1.48
White	0.95	0.92	0.90	0.94	0.95	1.06	1.15	1.14	1.17	1.17	1.20
Black or African American	2.40	2.40	2.48	2.71	2.92	2.97	3.14	3.07	3.13	3.07	3.07
American Indian or Alaska Native	0.98	0.95	0.92	1.01	1.01	1.10	1.26	1.16	1.28	1.30	1.28
Asian or Pacific Islander[2]	- - -	- - -	0.92	0.85	0.87	0.91	1.08	1.05	1.12	1.09	1.14
Chinese	0.80	0.52	0.66	0.57	0.51	0.67	0.68	0.77	0.74	- - -	- - -
Japanese	1.48	0.89	0.94	0.84	0.73	0.87	0.86	0.75	0.97	- - -	- - -
Filipino	1.08	0.93	0.99	0.86	1.05	1.13	1.41	1.38	1.31	- - -	- - -
Hawaiian	- - -	- - -	1.05	1.03	0.97	0.94	1.41	1.39	1.55	- - -	- - -
Other Asian or Pacific Islander	- - -	- - -	0.96	0.91	0.92	0.91	1.09	1.04	1.17	- - -	- - -
Hispanic or Latino[3]	- - -	- - -	0.98	1.01	1.03	1.11	1.14	1.14	1.17	1.16	1.20
Mexican	- - -	- - -	0.92	0.97	0.92	1.01	1.04	1.03	1.06	1.06	1.13
Puerto Rican	- - -	- - -	1.29	1.30	1.62	1.79	1.86	1.93	1.96	2.01	1.96
Cuban	- - -	- - -	1.02	1.18	1.20	1.19	1.49	1.21	1.15	1.37	1.30
Central and South American	- - -	- - -	0.99	1.01	1.05	1.13	1.15	1.20	1.20	1.17	1.19
Other and unknown Hispanic or Latino	- - -	- - -	1.01	0.96	1.09	1.28	1.32	1.42	1.44	1.28	1.27
Not Hispanic or Latino:[3]											
White	- - -	- - -	0.87	0.91	0.93	1.04	1.15	1.14	1.17	1.18	1.20
Black or African American	- - -	- - -	2.47	2.67	2.93	2.98	3.18	3.10	3.15	3.12	3.15
Cigarette smoker[4]	- - -	- - -	- - -	- - -	1.73	1.85	1.91	1.91	1.88	1.92	1.88
Nonsmoker[4]	- - -	- - -	- - -	- - -	1.18	1.31	1.43	1.40	1.45	1.44	1.47

- - - Data not available.

[1]Excludes live births with unknown birthweight. Percent based on live births with known birthweight.

[2]Starting with 2003 data, estimates are not shown for Asian or Pacific Islander subgroups during the transition from single race to multiple race reporting. See Appendix II, Race, Birth File.

[3]Prior to 1993, data from states lacking an Hispanic-origin item on the birth certificate were excluded. See Appendix II, Hispanic origin. Data for non-Hispanic white and non-Hispanic black women for years prior to 1989 are not nationally representative and are provided for comparison with Hispanic data.

[4]Percent based on live births with known smoking status of mother and known birthweight. Data from states that did not require the reporting of mother's tobacco use during pregnancy on the birth certificate are not included. Reporting area for tobacco use increased from 43 states and the District of Columbia (DC) in 1989 to 49 states and DC in 2000–2002. Data for 2003 and 2004 exclude states that implemented the 2003 revision of the U.S. Standard Certificate of Live Birth: Pennsylvania and Washington (in 2003), Florida, Idaho, Kentucky, New Hampshire, New York State (excluding New York City), Pennsylvania, South Carolina, Tennessee, and Washington (in 2004). Tobacco use data based on the 2003 revision are not comparable with data based on the 1989 revision of the U.S. Standard Certificate of Live Birth. California has never required reporting of tobacco use during pregnancy. See Appendix II, Cigarette smoking.

NOTES: The race groups, white, black, American Indian or Alaska Native, and Asian or Pacific Islander, include persons of Hispanic and non-Hispanic origin. Persons of Hispanic origin may be of any race. Starting with 2003 data, some states reported multiple-race data. The multiple-race data for these states were bridged to the single race categories of the 1977 Office of Management and Budget standards for comparability with other states. See Appendix II, Race. Interpretation of trend data should take into consideration expansion of reporting areas and immigration. Data for additional years are available. See Appendix III.

SOURCES: Centers for Disease Control and Prevention, National Center for Health Statistics, National Vital Statistics System, Birth File.

Table 14 (page 1 of 2). Low-birthweight live births among mothers 20 years of age and over, by detailed race, Hispanic origin, and education of mother: United States, selected years 1989–2004

[Data are based on birth certificates]

Education, race, and Hispanic origin of mother	1989	1990	1995	2000	2002	2003[1]	43 reporting areas 2003[2]	43 reporting areas 2004[1]
Less than 12 years of education	Percent of live births weighing less than 2,500 grams[3]							
All races	9.0	8.6	8.4	8.2	8.2	8.4	8.2	8.3
White	7.3	7.0	7.1	7.1	7.1	7.3	7.1	7.2
Black or African American	17.0	16.5	16.0	14.8	15.0	15.2	15.3	15.3
American Indian or Alaska Native	7.3	7.4	8.0	7.2	8.4	8.0	8.0	8.7
Asian or Pacific Islander[4]	6.6	6.4	6.7	7.2	7.4	7.5	7.6	7.7
Chinese	5.4	5.2	5.3	5.3	4.4	- - -	- - -	- - -
Japanese	4.0	10.6	11.0	6.8	4.7	- - -	- - -	- - -
Filipino	6.9	7.2	7.5	8.6	9.0	- - -	- - -	- - -
Hawaiian	11.0	10.7	9.8	9.4	7.8	- - -	- - -	- - -
Other Asian or Pacific Islander	6.8	6.4	6.7	7.5	8.1	- - -	- - -	- - -
Hispanic or Latino[5]	6.0	5.7	5.8	6.0	6.0	6.2	6.2	6.2
Mexican	5.3	5.2	5.4	5.6	5.7	5.9	5.9	6.0
Puerto Rican	11.3	10.3	10.5	10.9	10.4	11.2	11.0	10.5
Cuban	9.4	7.9	9.2	8.4	7.5	7.9	9.7	12.1
Central and South American	5.8	5.8	6.2	6.2	6.2	6.4	6.5	6.4
Other and unknown Hispanic or Latino	8.2	8.0	7.7	8.6	7.8	8.1	8.9	7.7
Not Hispanic or Latino:[5]								
White	8.4	8.3	8.9	9.0	9.3	9.5	9.4	9.6
Black or African American	17.6	16.7	16.2	15.2	15.3	15.7	15.9	16.1
12 years of education								
All races	7.1	7.1	7.6	7.9	8.2	8.4	8.3	8.4
White	5.7	5.8	6.4	6.8	7.0	7.2	7.2	7.3
Black or African American	13.4	13.1	13.3	13.0	13.4	13.5	13.5	13.7
American Indian or Alaska Native	5.6	6.1	6.5	6.7	7.1	7.2	7.2	7.2
Asian or Pacific Islander[4]	6.4	6.5	7.0	7.4	7.9	7.8	7.8	7.7
Chinese	5.1	4.9	5.7	5.6	5.2	- - -	- - -	- - -
Japanese	7.4	6.2	7.4	7.2	7.1	- - -	- - -	- - -
Filipino	6.8	7.6	7.7	8.1	8.7	- - -	- - -	- - -
Hawaiian	7.0	6.7	6.6	6.8	8.3	- - -	- - -	- - -
Other Asian or Pacific Islander	6.5	6.7	7.1	7.7	8.2	- - -	- - -	- - -
Hispanic or Latino[5]	5.9	6.0	6.1	6.2	6.5	6.5	6.5	6.7
Mexican	5.2	5.5	5.6	5.8	6.1	6.1	6.1	6.4
Puerto Rican	8.8	8.3	8.7	8.8	9.3	9.8	10.1	9.8
Cuban	5.3	5.2	6.7	6.5	6.0	6.4	7.2	8.3
Central and South American	5.7	5.8	5.9	6.0	6.4	6.6	6.6	6.8
Other and unknown Hispanic or Latino	6.1	6.6	7.1	7.3	7.7	7.4	7.8	7.7
Not Hispanic or Latino:[5]								
White	5.7	5.7	6.5	6.9	7.3	7.5	7.5	7.6
Black or African American	13.6	13.2	13.4	13.1	13.5	13.7	13.7	13.9
13 years or more of education								
All races	5.5	5.4	6.0	6.6	7.0	7.1	7.1	7.2
White	4.6	4.6	5.3	5.8	6.2	6.4	6.4	6.5
Black or African American	11.2	11.1	11.4	11.6	12.0	12.0	12.0	12.2
American Indian or Alaska Native	5.6	4.7	5.7	6.5	7.0	7.3	7.4	6.5
Asian or Pacific Islander[4]	6.1	6.0	6.6	7.0	7.6	7.6	7.6	7.8
Chinese	4.5	4.4	5.1	4.8	5.7	- - -	- - -	- - -
Japanese	6.6	6.0	7.1	7.0	7.7	- - -	- - -	- - -
Filipino	7.2	7.0	7.6	8.3	8.4	- - -	- - -	- - -
Hawaiian	6.3	4.7	5.0	4.5	7.2	- - -	- - -	- - -
Other Asian or Pacific Islander	6.1	6.2	6.7	7.4	7.9	- - -	- - -	- - -
Hispanic or Latino[5]	5.5	5.5	5.9	6.2	6.6	6.8	6.8	6.8
Mexican	5.1	5.2	5.6	5.8	6.2	6.3	6.3	6.6
Puerto Rican	7.4	7.4	7.9	7.9	8.9	9.1	9.3	8.9
Cuban	4.9	5.0	5.6	5.9	6.4	6.9	7.5	8.1
Central and South American	5.2	5.6	5.8	6.3	6.5	6.8	6.8	6.7
Other and unknown Hispanic or Latino	5.4	5.2	6.1	6.6	7.0	7.6	7.8	6.9
Not Hispanic or Latino:[5]								
White	4.6	4.5	5.2	5.8	6.2	6.4	6.3	6.5
Black or African American	11.2	11.1	11.5	11.7	12.1	12.1	12.1	12.3

See footnotes at end of table.

Table 14 (page 2 of 2). Low-birthweight live births among mothers 20 years of age and over, by detailed race, Hispanic origin, and education of mother: United States, selected years 1989–2004

[Data are based on birth certificates]

[1]Reporting areas that have adopted the 2003 revision of the U.S. Standard Certificate of Live Birth are excluded because maternal education data based on the 2003 revision are not comparable with data based on the 1989 or earlier revisions to the U.S. Standard Certificate of Live Birth. In 2003, Pennsylvania and Washington adopted the 2003 revision; in 2004, Florida, Idaho, Kentucky, New Hampshire, New York State (excluding New York City), South Carolina, and Tennessee adopted the 2003 revision. See Appendix II, Education.

[2]Data for 2003 are limited to the 43 reporting areas using the 1989 revision of the U.S. Standard Certificate of Live Birth in 2004, and are provided for comparison with 2004.

[3]Excludes live births with unknown birthweight. Percent based on live births with known birthweight.

[4]Starting with 2003 data, estimates are not shown for Asian or Pacific Islander subgroups during the transition from single race to multiple race reporting. See Appendix II, Race, Birth File.

[5]Prior to 1993, data shown only for states with an Hispanic-origin item and education of mother item on the birth certificate. See Appendix II, Education; Hispanic origin.

NOTES: Data are based on the 1989 or earlier revisions of the U.S. Standard Certificate of Live Birth. In 1992–2002, education of mother was reported on the birth certificate by all 50 states and the District of Columbia. Prior to 1992, data from states lacking an education of mother item were excluded. Starting with 2003 data, states adopting the 2003 revision of the U. S. Standard Certificate of Live Birth are excluded. See Appendix II, Education. The race groups, white, black, American Indian or Alaska Native, and Asian or Pacific Islander, include persons of Hispanic and non-Hispanic origin. Persons of Hispanic origin may be of any race. Starting with 2003 data, some states reported multiple-race data. The multiple-race data for these states were bridged to the single race categories of the 1977 Office of Management and Budget standards for comparability with other states. See Appendix II, Race. Interpretation of trend data should take into consideration changes in reporting areas and immigration. Data for additional years are available. See Appendix III.

SOURCE: Centers for Disease Control and Prevention, National Center for Health Statistics, National Vital Statistics System, Birth File.

Table 15 (page 1 of 3). **Low-birthweight live births, by race and Hispanic origin of mother, geographic division, and state: United States, average annual 1996–1998, 1999–2001, and 2002–2004**

[Data are based on birth certificates]

	All races			Not Hispanic or Latino					
				White			Black or African American		
Geographic division and state	1996–1998	1999–2001	2002–2004	1996–1998	1999–2001	2002–2004	1996–1998	1999–2001	2002–2004
	Percent of live births weighing less than 2,500 grams[1]								
United States	7.49	7.62	7.94	6.46	6.67	7.05	13.13	13.14	13.56
New England	6.78	7.02	7.45	6.06	6.30	6.80	11.79	11.93	12.03
Connecticut	7.43	7.47	7.68	6.16	6.33	6.60	12.82	12.53	12.60
Maine	5.88	6.03	6.42	5.95	6.06	6.41	*13.27	*9.97	*8.57
Massachusetts.	6.77	7.11	7.64	6.13	6.43	6.98	11.12	11.44	11.86
New Hampshire	5.44	6.36	6.44	5.31	6.04	6.51	*	11.88	10.19
Rhode Island	7.28	7.27	8.17	6.46	6.52	7.50	11.35	12.55	11.52
Vermont	6.32	5.90	6.63	6.22	5.79	6.67	*	*	*
Middle Atlantic.	7.73	7.82	8.06	6.27	6.56	6.86	13.02	12.73	13.02
New Jersey	7.84	7.94	8.13	6.26	6.54	7.03	13.86	13.45	13.42
New York.	7.77	7.75	7.98	6.19	6.47	6.68	12.32	11.97	12.50
Pennsylvania	7.57	7.84	8.14	6.36	6.68	6.97	13.86	13.87	13.86
East North Central	7.64	7.76	8.05	6.47	6.63	7.03	13.73	13.81	14.06
Illinois	7.96	7.99	8.28	6.44	6.59	7.13	14.22	14.03	14.45
Indiana	7.76	7.62	7.86	7.06	7.04	7.29	13.68	12.85	13.33
Michigan	7.72	7.95	8.17	6.35	6.43	6.90	13.51	14.47	14.21
Ohio	7.66	7.93	8.38	6.64	6.95	7.36	13.34	13.36	13.83
Wisconsin	6.40	6.59	6.80	5.58	5.82	6.06	13.21	13.28	13.49
West North Central	6.69	6.78	7.12	6.20	6.27	6.63	12.91	12.47	12.62
Iowa	6.38	6.23	6.74	6.11	5.97	6.57	12.66	12.58	11.50
Kansas	6.96	6.99	7.22	6.49	6.66	6.92	13.20	12.36	12.95
Minnesota	5.84	6.17	6.34	5.61	5.79	5.86	11.42	10.61	10.51
Missouri.	7.68	7.64	8.10	6.65	6.68	7.18	13.48	13.22	13.76
Nebraska.	6.60	6.73	7.04	6.32	6.37	6.86	11.58	12.81	12.32
North Dakota	6.15	6.26	6.46	6.17	6.23	6.26	*11.69	*	*10.25
South Dakota.	5.73	6.15	6.90	5.72	6.02	6.74	*10.36	*11.42	*8.08
South Atlantic	8.45	8.57	8.87	6.75	7.00	7.38	13.09	13.07	13.51
Delaware.	8.54	8.84	9.45	6.50	7.28	7.85	14.41	13.71	14.36
District of Columbia	13.60	12.37	11.19	6.15	6.56	5.91	16.28	15.17	14.09
Florida.	7.98	8.10	8.49	6.77	6.92	7.29	12.30	12.42	13.02
Georgia.	8.62	8.72	9.08	6.58	6.85	7.29	12.83	12.82	13.42
Maryland	8.68	8.88	9.13	6.39	6.70	7.14	13.37	13.12	13.16
North Carolina	8.80	8.87	9.00	7.08	7.39	7.64	13.82	13.72	14.16
South Carolina	9.30	9.69	10.08	6.99	7.30	7.77	13.60	14.29	15.01
Virginia	7.77	7.85	8.13	6.28	6.52	6.80	12.49	12.39	12.82
West Virginia	8.10	8.28	8.96	7.95	8.11	8.80	12.94	13.20	13.52
East South Central	8.98	9.32	9.71	7.42	7.77	8.21	13.48	13.97	14.71
Alabama	9.26	9.56	10.09	7.33	7.58	8.18	13.34	13.87	14.63
Kentucky	7.94	8.26	8.69	7.49	7.73	8.25	12.73	13.69	13.82
Mississippi.	10.03	10.55	11.40	7.34	7.72	8.50	13.31	14.03	15.31
Tennessee.	8.89	9.21	9.23	7.46	7.96	8.08	14.07	14.12	14.37
West South Central	7.77	7.90	8.30	6.73	6.95	7.43	13.29	13.42	14.04
Arkansas.	8.57	8.66	8.92	7.31	7.48	7.78	13.41	13.60	14.54
Louisiana.	10.05	10.25	10.69	6.98	7.36	7.76	14.49	14.40	14.91
Oklahoma	7.27	7.55	7.92	6.80	7.23	7.63	12.63	12.93	13.48
Texas	7.30	7.43	7.88	6.54	6.68	7.23	12.51	12.76	13.45
Mountain	7.34	7.34	7.56	7.08	7.08	7.32	13.70	13.37	13.68
Arizona.	6.80	6.95	7.00	6.63	6.73	6.94	12.88	13.19	12.09
Colorado	8.75	8.43	8.94	8.34	8.02	8.71	14.48	14.39	14.98
Idaho	6.02	6.43	6.48	5.84	6.31	6.39	*	*	*8.87
Montana	6.56	6.65	7.10	6.28	6.69	6.94	*	*	*15.63
Nevada.	7.57	7.45	7.86	7.28	7.38	7.51	13.78	12.69	13.87
New Mexico.	7.63	7.87	8.21	7.68	7.85	8.01	13.46	13.37	14.99
Utah	6.65	6.60	6.55	6.44	6.43	6.32	15.06	12.49	13.76
Wyoming	8.76	8.32	8.67	8.69	8.15	8.57	*15.82	*14.29	*
Pacific	6.07	6.13	6.50	5.47	5.59	5.98	11.73	11.56	11.96
Alaska.	5.78	5.70	5.93	5.30	5.03	4.98	12.00	10.64	9.52
California.	6.15	6.20	6.56	5.61	5.72	6.13	11.90	11.73	12.14
Hawaii.	7.34	7.74	8.26	5.35	5.60	6.47	9.79	10.77	11.47
Oregon	5.39	5.52	5.99	5.14	5.32	5.92	10.71	10.64	10.67
Washington	5.63	5.74	6.04	5.25	5.40	5.61	10.32	10.30	10.83

See footnotes at end of table.

Table 15 (page 2 of 3). Low-birthweight live births, by race and Hispanic origin of mother, geographic division, and state: United States, average annual 1996–1998, 1999–2001, and 2002–2004

[Data are based on birth certificates]

Geographic division and state	Hispanic or Latino[2]			American Indian or Alaska Native[3]			Asian or Pacific Islander[3]		
	1996–1998	1999–2001	2002–2004	1996–1998	1999–2001	2002–2004	1996–1998	1999–2001	2002–2004
	Percent of live births weighing less than 2,500 grams[1]								
United States	6.38	6.42	6.68	6.69	7.08	7.35	7.24	7.42	7.82
New England	8.28	8.17	8.31	8.17	7.54	8.18	7.19	7.39	7.83
Connecticut	8.94	8.60	8.41	*10.94	*8.09	8.97	7.73	7.59	7.96
Maine	*5.74	*4.91	*5.46	*	*	*	*5.03	*5.42	7.85
Massachusetts	8.03	8.28	8.46	*6.37	*6.84	*6.13	6.95	7.38	7.66
New Hampshire	*6.48	5.89	5.35	*	*	*	*8.30	5.83	6.08
Rhode Island	7.68	7.07	8.24	*10.49	*10.67	12.37	8.30	8.78	10.83
Vermont	*	*	*	*	*	*	*	*	*6.52
Middle Atlantic	7.71	7.49	7.59	8.21	8.96	8.60	7.32	7.38	7.85
New Jersey	7.30	7.19	7.22	12.20	10.04	10.67	7.52	7.67	7.86
New York	7.65	7.41	7.48	7.40	8.44	6.84	7.24	7.24	7.84
Pennsylvania	9.34	8.95	9.11	7.31	9.41	11.03	7.26	7.38	7.91
East North Central	6.33	6.40	6.42	6.51	7.04	7.24	7.52	7.85	8.17
Illinois	6.11	6.38	6.41	7.70	9.05	8.63	8.02	8.37	8.23
Indiana	7.00	6.10	6.19	*10.98	*6.89	*9.54	6.50	7.42	7.59
Michigan	6.48	6.37	6.41	6.12	7.24	6.50	7.25	7.72	8.22
Ohio	7.38	7.23	7.18	7.20	8.39	10.04	7.43	7.36	8.67
Wisconsin	6.56	6.29	6.10	5.71	5.97	6.29	6.81	7.02	7.45
West North Central	6.09	6.06	6.12	6.12	6.65	7.17	7.04	7.42	7.51
Iowa	6.21	5.83	6.16	8.48	*7.36	8.72	7.63	7.72	7.11
Kansas	5.95	6.00	6.14	6.40	6.36	7.08	7.49	7.34	7.15
Minnesota	6.13	5.98	5.85	6.21	6.92	7.18	6.66	7.48	7.41
Missouri	6.24	5.98	6.39	7.87	8.95	6.53	7.18	6.89	7.83
Nebraska	6.08	6.49	6.05	6.36	6.32	7.11	7.94	7.91	7.70
North Dakota	*5.88	*6.89	*6.42	5.66	6.21	7.15	*	*	*6.56
South Dakota	*6.14	*6.07	7.12	5.58	6.25	7.14	*	*9.37	*12.89
South Atlantic	6.37	6.30	6.61	9.00	9.22	9.86	7.54	7.75	8.16
Delaware	7.76	6.62	7.06	*	*	*	8.04	8.98	9.61
District of Columbia	6.73	6.99	8.20	*	*	*	*8.43	*8.79	7.36
Florida	6.55	6.49	6.90	7.35	7.08	7.68	7.98	8.51	8.57
Georgia	5.36	5.66	5.94	*7.21	9.79	8.48	7.51	7.67	8.40
Maryland	6.29	6.80	7.09	*8.48	9.95	11.07	7.15	7.37	7.67
North Carolina	6.14	6.21	6.22	10.22	10.33	11.16	7.61	8.05	7.79
South Carolina	5.99	6.57	6.46	*9.40	10.20	*9.11	7.56	7.10	8.97
Virginia	6.68	5.96	6.31	*6.94	*9.23	*10.13	7.30	7.15	7.95
West Virginia	*	*	*8.26	*	*	*	*6.58	*7.94	*8.24
East South Central	6.53	6.73	6.51	7.73	7.61	8.12	7.60	7.84	7.99
Alabama	6.51	6.68	6.93	*7.60	*8.25	11.50	7.94	7.59	8.52
Kentucky	7.14	7.18	7.13	*10.38	*	*9.93	6.78	7.68	7.35
Mississippi	5.26	6.92	6.79	*6.59	8.42	6.00	6.00	7.75	7.58
Tennessee	6.56	6.57	5.97	*7.88	*7.13	*7.43	8.40	8.03	8.22
West South Central	6.61	6.73	7.05	6.20	6.57	6.96	7.50	7.75	8.09
Arkansas	6.34	5.92	5.96	*5.97	7.95	8.41	7.40	8.80	6.78
Louisiana	6.04	6.70	7.25	8.02	8.41	10.31	8.37	7.92	8.55
Oklahoma	6.13	6.03	6.55	6.07	6.34	6.53	7.02	7.19	7.13
Texas	6.63	6.76	7.08	6.34	6.76	7.54	7.45	7.74	8.19
Mountain	7.22	7.21	7.35	6.72	7.14	7.28	8.57	8.33	8.87
Arizona	6.52	6.67	6.67	6.57	7.12	6.84	7.54	7.69	8.20
Colorado	8.71	8.23	8.46	8.16	8.60	9.82	9.92	10.10	10.14
Idaho	6.95	6.78	6.73	7.07	7.82	7.07	*5.97	7.62	6.51
Montana	7.69	7.02	8.11	7.43	6.77	7.71	*8.97	*6.42	*8.76
Nevada	6.26	6.21	6.61	6.23	7.80	6.73	9.17	7.88	9.41
New Mexico	7.69	7.93	8.38	6.27	6.88	7.18	9.26	8.28	7.62
Utah	7.55	7.33	7.06	7.44	6.58	7.64	7.50	7.18	7.94
Wyoming	8.33	7.86	8.60	7.51	8.93	10.62	*	*17.06	*
Pacific	5.55	5.59	5.94	6.10	6.38	6.59	6.95	7.10	7.49
Alaska	6.48	6.09	5.62	5.73	5.83	6.08	6.43	7.05	6.79
California	5.53	5.59	5.95	5.85	6.27	6.54	6.84	6.98	7.33
Hawaii	7.08	7.63	8.41	*7.37	*6.11	*	7.95	8.29	8.79
Oregon	5.72	5.51	5.28	5.72	6.79	7.35	6.45	6.08	7.12
Washington	5.53	5.31	5.67	7.09	7.14	7.03	6.12	6.41	6.88

See footnotes at end of table.

Table 15 (page 3 of 3). Low-birthweight live births, by race and Hispanic origin of mother, geographic division, and state: United States, average annual 1996–1998, 1999–2001, and 2002–2004

[Data are based on birth certificates]

* Percents preceded by an asterisk are based on fewer than 50 births. Percents not shown are based on fewer than 20 births.
[1]Excludes live births with unknown birthweight.
[2]Persons of Hispanic origin may be of any race. See Appendix II, Hispanic origin.
[3]Includes persons of Hispanic and non-Hispanic origin.

NOTES: For information on very low birthweight live births, see Table 36 in Martin JA, Hamilton BE, Sutton PD, Ventura SJ, Menacker F, Kirmeyer S. Births: Final Data for 2004. National vital statistics reports. Hyattsville, MD: National Center for Health Statistics. 2006. Starting with 2003 data, some states reported multiple-race data. The multiple-race data for these states were bridged to the single race categories of the 1977 Office of Management and Budget standards for comparability with other states. See Appendix II, Race.

SOURCE: Centers for Disease Control and Prevention, National Center for Health Statistics, National Vital Statistics System, Birth File.

Table 16. Legal abortions and legal abortion ratios, by selected patient characteristics: United States, selected years 1973–2002

[Data are based on reporting by State health departments and by hospitals and other medical facilities]

Characteristic	1973	1975	1980	1985	1990	1995	1998[1]	1999[1]	2000[2]	2001[2]	2002[2]
	Number of legal abortions reported in thousands										
Centers for Disease Control and Prevention	616	855	1,298	1,329	1,429	1,211	884	862	857	853	854
Alan Guttmacher Institute[3]	745	1,034	1,554	1,589	1,609	1,359	1,319	1,315	1,313	1,303	1,293
	Abortions per 100 live births[4]										
Total	19.6	27.2	35.9	35.4	34.4	31.1	26.4	25.6	24.5	24.6	24.6
Age											
Under 15 years	123.7	119.3	139.7	137.6	81.8	66.4	75.0	70.9	70.8	74.4	75.3
15–19 years	53.9	54.2	71.4	68.8	51.1	39.9	39.1	37.5	36.1	36.6	36.8
20–24 years	29.4	28.9	39.5	38.6	37.8	34.8	32.9	31.6	30.0	30.4	30.3
25–29 years	20.7	19.2	23.7	21.7	21.8	22.0	21.6	20.8	19.8	20.0	20.0
30–34 years	28.0	25.0	23.7	19.9	19.0	16.4	15.7	15.2	14.5	14.7	14.8
35–39 years	45.1	42.2	41.0	33.6	27.3	22.3	20.0	19.3	18.1	18.0	18.0
40 years and over	68.4	66.8	80.7	62.3	50.6	38.5	33.8	32.9	30.1	30.4	31.0
Race											
White[5]	32.6	27.7	33.2	27.7	25.8	20.3	18.9	17.7	16.7	16.5	16.4
Black or African American[6]	42.0	47.6	54.3	47.2	53.7	53.1	51.2	52.9	50.3	49.1	49.5
Hispanic origin[7]											
Hispanic or Latino	- - -	- - -	- - -	- - -	- - -	27.1	27.3	26.1	22.5	23.0	23.3
Not Hispanic or Latino	- - -	- - -	- - -	- - -	- - -	27.9	27.1	25.2	23.3	23.2	23.7
Marital status											
Married	7.6	9.6	10.5	8.0	8.7	7.6	7.1	7.0	6.5	6.5	6.5
Unmarried	139.8	161.0	147.6	117.4	86.3	64.5	62.7	60.4	57.0	57.2	57.0
Previous live births[8]											
0	43.7	38.4	45.7	45.1	36.0	28.6	25.5	24.3	22.6	26.4	23.3
1	23.5	22.0	20.2	21.6	22.7	22.0	21.4	20.6	19.4	18.0	19.4
2	36.8	36.8	29.5	29.9	31.5	30.6	30.0	29.0	27.4	25.5	27.9
3	46.9	47.7	29.8	18.2	30.1	30.7	30.5	29.8	28.5	26.4	29.1
4 or more[9]	44.7	43.5	24.3	21.5	26.6	23.7	24.3	24.2	23.7	21.9	23.6
	Percent distribution[10]										
Total	100.0	100.0	100.0	100.0	100.0	100.0	100.0	100.0	100.0	100.0	100.0
Period of gestation											
Under 9 weeks	36.1	44.6	51.7	50.3	51.6	54.0	55.7	57.6	58.1	59.1	60.5
9–10 weeks	29.4	28.4	26.2	26.6	25.3	23.1	21.5	20.2	19.8	19.0	18.4
11–12 weeks	17.9	14.9	12.2	12.5	11.7	10.9	10.9	10.2	10.2	10.0	9.6
13–15 weeks	6.9	5.0	5.1	5.9	6.4	6.3	6.4	6.2	6.2	6.2	6.0
16–20 weeks	8.0	6.1	3.9	3.9	4.0	4.3	4.1	4.3	4.3	4.3	4.1
21 weeks and over	1.7	1.0	0.9	0.8	1.0	1.4	1.4	1.5	1.4	1.4	1.4
Previous induced abortions											
0	- - -	81.9	67.6	60.1	57.1	55.1	53.8	53.7	54.7	55.5	55.3
1	- - -	14.9	23.5	25.7	26.9	26.9	27.0	27.1	26.4	25.8	25.8
2	- - -	2.5	6.6	9.8	10.1	10.9	11.4	11.5	11.3	11.0	11.3
3 or more	- - -	0.7	2.3	4.4	5.9	7.1	7.8	7.7	7.6	7.7	7.6

- - - Data not available.

[1]In 1998 and 1999, Alaska, California, New Hampshire, and Oklahoma did not report abortion data to CDC. For comparison, in 1997, the 48 corresponding reporting areas reported about 900,000 legal abortions.   [2]In 2000, 2001, and 2002, Alaska, California, and New Hampshire did not report abortion data to CDC.
[3]No surveys were conducted in 1983, 1986, 1989, 1990, 1993, 1994, 1997, 1998, 2001, or 2002. Data for these years were estimated by interpolation.
[4]For calculation of ratios by each characteristic, abortions with characteristic unknown were distributed in proportion to abortions with characteristic known.
[5]For 1989 and later years, white race includes women of Hispanic ethnicity.   [6]Before 1989, black race includes races other than white.
[7]Reporting area increased from 20–22 states, the District of Columbia (DC), and New York City (NYC) in 1991–1995 to 31 states and NYC in 2002. California, Florida, Illinois, and Arizona, states with large Hispanic populations, do not report Hispanic ethnicity.   [8]For 1973–1975, data indicate number of living children.
[9]For 1975, data refer to four previous live births, not four or more. For five or more previous live births, the ratio is 47.3.
[10]For calculation of percent distribution by each characteristic, abortions with characteristic unknown were excluded.

NOTES: The number of areas reporting adequate data (less than or equal to 15% missing) for each characteristic varies from year to year. See Appendix I, Abortion Surveillance. For methodological differences between these two data sources, see Appendix I, Abortion Surveillance and Alan Guttmacher Institute Abortion Provider Survey. Data for additional years are available. See Appendix III.

SOURCES: Centers for Disease Control and Prevention, National Center for Chronic Disease Prevention and Health Promotion: Abortion Surveillance, 1973, 1975, 1979–1980. Atlanta, GA: Public Health Service, 1975, 1977, 1983; CDC MMWR Surveillance Summaries. Abortion Surveillance, United States, 1984 and 1985, Vol. 38, No. SS–2, 1989; 1990, Vol. 42, No. SS–6, 1993; 1995, Vol. 47, No. SS–2, 1998; 1997, Vol. 49, No. SS–11, 2000; 1998, Vol. 51, No. SS–3, 2002; 1999, Vol. 51, No. SS–9, 2002; 2000, Vol. 52, No. SS–12, 2003; 2001, Vol. 53, No. SS–9, 2004; 2002, Vol. 54, No. SS–7, 2005. Alan Guttmacher Institute Abortion Provider Survey. Finer LB, Henshaw SK. Abortion incidence and services in the United States in 2000. Perspect Sex Reprod Health 2003;35(1)6–15. Finer LB, Henshaw SK. Estimates of U.S. abortion incidence in 2001 and 2002. The Alan Guttmacher Institute. May 2005, available from: www.guttmacher.org/pubs/2005/05/18/ab_incidence.pdf.

This table will be updated on the Web. Go to www.cdc.gov/nchs/hus.htm.

Table 17 (page 1 of 4). Contraceptive use among women 15–44 years of age, by age, race, Hispanic origin, and method of contraception: United States, selected years 1982–2002

[Data are based on household interviews of samples of women of childbearing age]

Race, Hispanic origin, and year[1]	Age in years				
	15–44	15–19	20–24	25–34	35–44
	Number of women in population in thousands				
All women:[2]					
1982	54,099	9,521	10,629	19,644	14,305
1988	57,900	9,179	9,413	21,726	17,582
1995	60,201	8,961	9,041	20,758	21,440
2002	61,561	9,834	9,840	19,522	22,365
Not Hispanic or Latino:					
White only:					
1982	41,279	7,010	8,081	14,945	11,243
1988	42,575	6,531	6,630	15,929	13,486
1995	42,154	5,865	6,020	14,471	15,798
2002	39,498	6,069	5,938	12,073	15,418
Black or African American only:					
1982	6,825	1,383	1,456	2,392	1,593
1988	7,408	1,362	1,322	2,760	1,965
1995	8,060	1,334	1,305	2,780	2,641
2002	8,250	1,409	1,396	2,587	2,857
Hispanic or Latino:[3]					
1982	4,393	886	811	1,677	1,018
1988	5,557	999	1,003	2,104	1,451
1995	6,702	1,150	1,163	2,450	1,940
2002	9,107	1,521	1,632	3,249	2,705
	Percent of women in population using contraception				
All women:[2]					
1982	55.7	24.2	55.8	66.7	61.6
1988	60.3	32.1	59.0	66.3	68.3
1995	64.2	29.8	63.5	71.1	72.3
2002	61.9	31.5	60.7	68.6	69.9
Not Hispanic or Latino:					
White only:					
1982	57.3	23.6	58.7	67.8	63.5
1988	63.0	34.0	62.6	67.7	71.5
1995	66.2	30.5	65.4	72.9	73.6
2002	64.6	35.0	66.3	69.9	71.4
Black or African American only:					
1982	51.6	29.8	52.3	63.5	52.0
1988	56.8	35.7	61.8	63.5	58.7
1995	62.3	36.1	67.6	66.8	68.3
2002	57.6	32.9	50.8	67.9	63.8
Hispanic or Latino:[3]					
1982	50.6	*	*36.8	67.2	59.0
1988	50.4	*18.3	40.8	67.4	54.3
1995	59.0	26.1	50.6	69.2	70.8
2002	59.0	20.4	57.4	66.2	72.9

See footnotes at end of table.

Table 17 (page 2 of 4). Contraceptive use among women 15–44 years of age, by age, race, Hispanic origin, and method of contraception: United States, selected years 1982–2002

[Data are based on household interviews of samples of women of childbearing age]

Method of contraception and year	Age in years				
	15–44	15–19	20–24	25–34	35–44
Female sterilization	Percent of contracepting women				
1982	23.2	–	*4.5	22.1	43.5
1988	27.6	*	*4.6	25.0	47.6
1995	27.8	*	4.0	23.8	45.0
2002	27.0	–	3.6	21.7	45.8
Male sterilization					
1982	10.9	*	*3.6	10.1	19.9
1988	11.7	*	*	10.2	20.8
1995	10.9	–	*	7.8	19.5
2002	10.2	–	*	7.2	18.2
Implant[4]					
1982	. . .	. . .	. . .	. . .	. . .
1988	. . .	. . .	. . .	. . .	. . .
1995	1.3	*	3.7	*1.3	*
2002	1.2	*	*	*1.9	*
Injectable[4]					
1982	. . .	. . .	. . .	. . .	. . .
1988	. . .	. . .	. . .	. . .	. . .
1995	3.0	9.7	6.1	2.9	*0.8
2002	5.4	13.9	10.2	5.3	*1.8
Birth control pill					
1982	28.0	63.9	55.1	25.7	*3.7
1988	30.8	58.8	68.2	32.6	4.3
1995	27.0	43.8	52.1	33.4	8.7
2002	31.0	53.8	52.5	34.8	15.0
Intrauterine device					
1982	7.1	*	*4.2	9.7	6.9
1988	2.0	–	*	2.1	3.1
1995	0.8	–	*	*0.8	1.1
2002	2.2	*	1.8	3.7	*
Diaphragm					
1982	8.1	*6.0	10.2	10.3	4.0
1988	5.7	*	*3.7	7.3	6.0
1995	1.9	*	*	1.7	2.8
2002	0.6	–	*	*	*
Condom					
1982	12.0	20.8	10.7	11.4	11.3
1988	14.6	32.8	14.5	13.7	11.2
1995	23.4	45.8	33.7	23.7	15.3
2002	23.8	44.6	36.0	23.1	15.6
Periodic abstinence-calendar rhythm					
1982	3.3	2.0	3.1	3.3	3.7
1988	1.7	*	1.1	1.8	2.0
1995	3.3	*	*1.5	3.7	3.9
2002	2.0	*	*2.3	*1.7	*2.4
Periodic abstinence-natural family planning					
1982	0.6	–	*	0.9	*
1988	0.6	–	*	0.7	0.7
1995	*0.5	–	*	*0.7	*
2002	*0.4	–	-	*	*
Withdrawal					
1982	2.0	2.9	3.0	1.8	1.3
1988	2.2	3.0	3.4	2.8	0.8
1995	6.1	13.2	7.1	6.0	4.5
2002	8.8	15.0	11.9	10.7	4.7
Other methods[5]					
1982	4.9	2.6	5.4	4.8	5.3
1988	3.2	*	1.8	3.8	3.5
1995	3.2	*	3.2	3.1	3.4
2002	1.7	*	*	*1.5	*1.8

See footnotes at end of table.

Table 17 (page 3 of 4). **Contraceptive use among women 15–44 years of age, by age, race, Hispanic origin, and method of contraception: United States, selected years 1982–2002**

[Data are based on household interviews of samples of women of childbearing age]

Method of contraception and year	Not Hispanic or Latino[1]		Hispanic or Latino[3]
	White only	Black or African American only	
	Percent of contracepting women		
Female sterilization			
1982	22.0	30.0	23.0
1988	25.6	37.8	31.7
1995	24.5	39.9	36.6
2002	23.9	39.2	33.8
Male sterilization			
1982	13.0	*1.5	*
1988	14.3	*0.9	*
1995	13.7	*1.8	*4.0
2002	12.9	*	4.7
Implant[4]			
1982	. . .	. . .	. . .
1988	. . .	. . .	. . .
1995	*1.0	*2.4	*2.0
2002	*0.8	*	*3.1
Injectable[4]			
1982	. . .	. . .	. . .
1988	. . .	. . .	. . .
1995	2.4	5.4	4.7
2002	4.2	9.4	7.3
Birth control pill			
1982	26.4	37.9	30.2
1988	29.5	38.2	33.4
1995	28.7	23.7	23.0
2002	34.9	23.1	22.1
Intrauterine device			
1982	5.8	9.3	19.2
1988	1.5	3.2	*5.0
1995	0.7	*	*
2002	1.7	*	5.3
Diaphragm			
1982	9.2	*3.2	*
1988	6.6	*2.0	*
1995	2.3	*	*
2002	*	*	–
Condom			
1982	13.1	6.3	*6.9
1988	15.2	10.1	13.7
1995	22.5	24.9	21.2
2002	21.7	29.6	24.1
Periodic abstinence-calendar rhythm			
1982	3.2	2.9	3.9
1988	1.6	1.9	*
1995	3.3	*1.7	3.2
2002	2.3	*	*
Periodic abstinence-natural family planning			
1982	0.7	0.3	–
1988	0.7	*	*
1995	0.7	*	*
2002	*	*	*
Withdrawal			
1982	2.1	1.3	2.6
1988	2.0	1.4	4.5
1995	6.4	3.3	5.7
2002	9.5	4.9	6.3
Other methods[5]			
1982	4.6	7.3	5.0
1988	3.0	4.4	2.6
1995	3.3	3.8	*2.2
2002	*1.7	*1.9	*1.2

See footnotes at end of table.

Table 17 (page 4 of 4). Contraceptive use among women 15–44 years of age, by age, race, Hispanic origin, and method of contraception: United States, selected years 1982–2002

[Data are based on household interviews of samples of women of childbearing age]

– Quantity zero.

- - - Data not available.

. . . Data not applicable.

* Estimates are considered unreliable. Data preceded by an asterisk have a relative standard error of 20%–30%.

[1]Starting with 1995 data, race-specific estimates are tabulated according to 1997 Revisions to the Standards for Classification of Federal Data on Race and Ethnicity and are not strictly comparable with estimates for earlier years. Starting with 1995 data, race-specific estimates are for persons who reported only one racial group. Prior to data year 1995, data were tabulated according to the 1977 Standards. Estimates for single race categories prior to 1995 included persons who reported one race or, if they reported more than one race, identified one race as best representing their race. See Appendix II, Race.

[2]Includes women of other or unknown race not shown separately.

[3]Persons of Hispanic origin may be of any race. See Appendix II, Hispanic origin.

[4]Data collected starting with the 1995 survey.

[5]In 2002, includes female condom, foam, cervical cap, Today Sponge®, suppository or insert, jelly or cream, and other methods. See Appendix II, Contraception, for the list of other methods reported in previous surveys.

NOTES: Survey collects up to four methods of contraception used in the month of interview. Percents may not add to the total because more than one method could have been used in the month of interview. These data replace estimates of most effective method used and may differ from previous editions of *Health, United States.* Standard errors for selected years are available in the spreadsheet version of this table. Available from: www.cdc.gov/nchs/hus.htm.

SOURCE: Centers for Disease Control and Prevention, National Center for Health Statistics, National Survey of Family Growth.

Table 18. Breastfeeding among mothers 15–44 years of age, by year of baby's birth, and selected characteristics of mother: United States, average annual 1986–1988 through 1999–2001

[Data are based on household interviews of samples of women of childbearing age]

Selected characteristics of mother	1986–1988	1989–1991	1992–1994	1995–1998	1999–2001
			Percent of babies breastfed		
Total	54.1	53.3	57.6	64.4	66.5
Age at baby's birth					
Under 20 years	28.4	34.7	41.0	49.5	47.3
20–24 years	48.2	44.3	50.0	55.9	59.3
25–29 years	58.2	56.4	57.4	68.1	63.5
30–44 years	68.6	66.0	70.2	72.8	80.0
Race and Hispanic origin[1]					
Not Hispanic or Latino:					
White	59.1	58.4	61.7	66.5	68.7
Black or African American	22.3	22.4	26.1	47.9	45.3
Hispanic or Latino	55.6	57.0	63.8	71.2	76.0
Education[2]					
No high school diploma or GED	31.8	36.5	44.6	50.6	46.6
High school diploma or GED	47.4	45.5	51.1	55.9	61.6
Some college, no bachelor's degree	62.2	61.4	64.3	70.1	75.6
Bachelor's degree or higher	78.4	80.6	82.5	82.0	81.3
Geographic region[3]					
Northeast	51.3	53.5	56.5	61.6	66.9
Midwest	52.3	49.6	51.7	61.7	61.9
South	44.6	43.6	48.6	58.1	60.9
West	71.4	69.5	77.3	78.1	78.9
		Percent of babies who were breastfed 3 months or more			
Total	34.6	31.8	33.6	45.8	48.4
Age at baby's birth					
Under 20 years	18.5	*10.5	*11.7	30.0	30.0
20–24 years	26.1	24.1	25.1	36.6	41.8
25–29 years	36.9	32.3	35.6	46.3	43.7
30–44 years	50.1	46.8	46.7	57.5	62.4
Race and Hispanic origin[1]					
Not Hispanic or Latino:					
White	37.7	35.2	36.6	47.8	49.7
Black or African American	11.6	11.5	13.3	29.6	33.7
Hispanic or Latino	38.2	33.9	35.0	49.7	54.3
Education[2]					
No high school diploma or GED	21.8	17.6	25.2	33.9	37.0
High school diploma or GED	28.2	28.0	27.4	36.9	43.1
Some college, no bachelor's degree	38.7	33.1	38.7	49.6	52.8
Bachelor's degree or higher	55.0	56.1	59.3	64.5	64.1
Geographic region[3]					
Northeast	29.9	37.2	36.4	48.2	48.8
Midwest	30.3	31.5	30.1	42.0	42.8
South	27.7	20.1	26.2	38.9	44.4
West	52.4	42.9	45.3	58.2	59.2

* Estimates are considered unreliable. Data preceded by an asterisk have a relative standard error of 20%–30%.

[1]Persons of Hispanic origin may be of any race. All race-specific estimates are tabulated according to 1997 Revisions to the Standards for Classification of Federal Data on Race and Ethnicity and are for persons who reported only one racial group. See Appendix II, Race.

[2]Educational attainment is presented only for women 22–44 years of age. Education is as of year of interview. GED stands for General Educational Development high school equivalency diploma. See Appendix II, Education.

[3]See Appendix II, Geographic region and division.

NOTES: Data are based on single births to mothers 15–44 years of age at interview, including those births that occurred when the mothers were younger than 15 years of age. Data on breastfeeding during 1986–1994 are based on responses to questions in the National Survey of Family Growth (NSFG) Cycle 5, conducted in 1995. Data for 1995–2001 are based on the NSFG Cycle 6 conducted in 2002. See Appendix I, National Survey of Family Growth. Standard errors are available in the spreadsheet version of this table. Available from: www.cdc.gov/nchs/hus.htm.

SOURCE: Centers for Disease Control and Prevention, National Center for Health Statistics, National Survey of Family Growth, Cycle 5 (1995), Cycle 6 (2002).

Table 19 (page 1 of 3). Infant, neonatal, and postneonatal mortality rates, by detailed race and Hispanic origin of mother: United States, selected years 1983–2003

[Data are based on linked birth and death certificates for infants]

Race and Hispanic origin of mother	1983[1]	1985[1]	1990[1]	1995[2]	1999[2]	2000[2]	2001[2]	2002[2]	2003[2]
	Infant[3] deaths per 1,000 live births								
All mothers	10.9	10.4	8.9	7.6	7.0	6.9	6.8	7.0	6.8
White	9.3	8.9	7.3	6.3	5.8	5.7	5.7	5.8	5.7
Black or African American	19.2	18.6	16.9	14.6	14.0	13.5	13.3	13.8	13.5
American Indian or Alaska Native	15.2	13.1	13.1	9.0	9.3	8.3	9.7	8.6	8.7
Asian or Pacific Islander[4]	8.3	7.8	6.6	5.3	4.8	4.9	4.7	4.8	4.8
Chinese	9.5	5.8	4.3	3.8	2.9	3.5	3.2	3.0	- - -
Japanese	*5.6	*6.0	*5.5	*5.3	*3.5	*4.5	*4.0	*4.9	- - -
Filipino	8.4	7.7	6.0	5.6	5.8	5.7	5.5	5.7	- - -
Hawaiian	11.2	*9.9	*8.0	*6.5	*7.0	9.0	*7.3	9.6	- - -
Other Asian or Pacific Islander	8.1	8.5	7.4	5.5	5.1	4.8	4.8	4.7	- - -
Hispanic or Latino[5,6]	9.5	8.8	7.5	6.3	5.7	5.6	5.4	5.6	5.6
Mexican	9.1	8.5	7.2	6.0	5.5	5.4	5.2	5.4	5.5
Puerto Rican	12.9	11.2	9.9	8.9	8.3	8.2	8.5	8.2	8.2
Cuban	7.5	8.5	7.2	5.3	4.6	4.6	4.2	3.7	4.6
Central and South American	8.5	8.0	6.8	5.5	4.7	4.6	5.0	5.1	5.0
Other and unknown Hispanic or Latino . .	10.6	9.5	8.0	7.4	7.2	6.9	6.0	7.1	6.7
Not Hispanic or Latino:									
White[6]	9.2	8.6	7.2	6.3	5.8	5.7	5.7	5.8	5.7
Black or African American[6]	19.1	18.3	16.9	14.7	14.1	13.6	13.5	13.9	13.6
	Neonatal[3] deaths per 1,000 live births								
All mothers	7.1	6.8	5.7	4.9	4.7	4.6	4.5	4.7	4.6
White	6.1	5.8	4.6	4.1	3.9	3.8	3.8	3.9	3.9
Black or African American	12.5	12.3	11.1	9.6	9.5	9.1	8.9	9.3	9.2
American Indian or Alaska Native	7.5	6.1	6.1	4.0	5.0	4.4	4.2	4.6	4.5
Asian or Pacific Islander[4]	5.2	4.8	3.9	3.4	3.2	3.4	3.1	3.4	3.4
Chinese	5.5	3.3	2.3	2.3	1.8	2.5	1.9	2.4	- - -
Japanese	*3.7	*3.1	*3.5	*3.3	*2.8	*2.6	*2.5	*3.7	- - -
Filipino	5.6	5.1	3.5	3.4	3.9	4.1	4.0	4.1	- - -
Hawaiian	*7.0	*5.7	*4.3	*4.0	*4.9	*6.2	*3.6	*5.6	- - -
Other Asian or Pacific Islander	5.0	5.4	4.4	3.7	3.3	3.4	3.2	3.3	- - -
Hispanic or Latino[5,6]	6.2	5.7	4.8	4.1	3.9	3.8	3.6	3.8	3.9
Mexican	5.9	5.4	4.5	3.9	3.7	3.6	3.5	3.6	3.8
Puerto Rican	8.7	7.6	6.9	6.1	5.9	5.8	6.0	5.8	5.7
Cuban	*5.0	6.2	5.3	*3.6	*3.5	*3.2	*2.5	*3.2	3.4
Central and South American	5.8	5.6	4.4	3.7	3.3	3.3	3.4	3.5	3.6
Other and unknown Hispanic or Latino . .	6.4	5.6	5.0	4.8	4.8	4.6	3.9	5.1	4.7
Not Hispanic or Latino:									
White[6]	5.9	5.6	4.5	4.0	3.8	3.8	3.8	3.9	3.8
Black or African American[6]	12.0	11.9	11.0	9.6	9.6	9.2	9.0	9.3	9.3
	Postneonatal[3] deaths per 1,000 live births								
All mothers	3.8	3.6	3.2	2.6	2.3	2.3	2.3	2.3	2.2
White	3.2	3.1	2.7	2.2	1.9	1.9	1.9	1.9	1.9
Black or African American	6.7	6.3	5.9	5.0	4.5	4.3	4.4	4.5	4.3
American Indian or Alaska Native	7.7	7.0	7.0	5.1	4.3	3.9	5.4	4.0	4.2
Asian or Pacific Islander[4]	3.1	2.9	2.7	1.9	1.7	1.4	1.6	1.4	1.4
Chinese	4.0	*2.5	*2.0	*1.5	*1.2	*1.0	*1.3	*0.7	- - -
Japanese	*	*2.9	*	*	*	*	*	*	- - -
Filipino	*2.8	2.7	2.5	2.2	1.9	1.6	*1.5	1.7	- - -
Hawaiian	*4.2	*4.3	*3.8	*	*	*	*3.7	*4.0	- - -
Other Asian or Pacific Islander	3.0	3.0	3.0	1.9	1.8	1.4	1.6	1.4	- - -
Hispanic or Latino[5,6]	3.3	3.2	2.7	2.1	1.8	1.8	1.8	1.8	1.7
Mexican	3.2	3.2	2.7	2.1	1.8	1.8	1.7	1.8	1.7
Puerto Rican	4.2	3.5	3.0	2.8	2.4	2.4	2.5	2.4	2.5
Cuban	*2.5	*2.3	*1.9	*1.7	*	*	*1.7	*	*
Central and South American	2.6	2.4	2.4	1.9	1.4	1.4	1.6	1.6	1.4
Other and unknown Hispanic or Latino . .	4.2	3.9	3.0	2.6	2.5	2.3	2.1	2.0	1.9
Not Hispanic or Latino:									
White[6]	3.2	3.0	2.7	2.2	1.9	1.9	1.9	1.9	1.9
Black or African American[6]	7.0	6.4	5.9	5.0	4.6	4.4	4.5	4.6	4.3

See footnotes at end of table.

[Data are based on linked birth and death certificates for infants]

Race and Hispanic origin of mother	1983–1985[1,7]	1986–1988[1,7]	1989–1991[1,7]	1995–1997[2,7]	1998–2000[2,7]	2001–2003[2,7]
	Infant[3] deaths per 1,000 live births					
All mothers	10.6	9.8	9.0	7.4	7.0	6.9
White	9.0	8.2	7.4	6.1	5.8	5.7
Black or African American	18.7	17.9	17.1	14.1	13.8	13.5
American Indian or Alaska Native	13.9	13.2	12.6	9.2	9.0	9.0
Asian or Pacific Islander[4]	8.3	7.3	6.6	5.1	5.1	4.8
Chinese	7.4	5.8	5.1	3.3	3.5	- - -
Japanese	6.0	6.9	5.3	4.9	3.8	- - -
Filipino	8.2	6.9	6.4	5.7	5.9	- - -
Hawaiian	11.3	11.1	9.0	7.0	8.7	- - -
Other Asian or Pacific Islander	8.6	7.6	7.0	5.4	5.2	- - -
Hispanic or Latino[5,6]	9.2	8.3	7.5	6.1	5.7	5.6
Mexican	8.8	7.9	7.2	5.9	5.5	5.4
Puerto Rican	12.3	11.1	10.4	8.5	8.1	8.3
Cuban	8.0	7.3	6.2	5.3	4.3	4.2
Central and South American	8.2	7.5	6.6	5.3	4.9	5.0
Other and unknown Hispanic or Latino	9.8	9.0	8.2	7.1	6.9	6.6
Not Hispanic or Latino:						
White[6]	8.8	8.1	7.3	6.1	5.8	5.7
Black or African American[6]	18.5	17.9	17.2	14.2	13.9	13.6
	Neonatal[3] deaths per 1,000 live births					
All mothers	6.9	6.3	5.7	4.8	4.7	4.6
White	5.9	5.2	4.7	4.0	3.9	3.9
Black or African American	12.2	11.7	11.1	9.4	9.3	9.1
American Indian or Alaska Native	6.7	5.9	5.9	4.4	4.8	4.5
Asian or Pacific Islander[4]	5.2	4.5	3.9	3.3	3.5	3.3
Chinese	4.3	3.3	2.7	2.1	2.4	- - -
Japanese	3.4	4.4	3.0	2.8	2.6	- - -
Filipino	5.3	4.5	4.0	3.7	4.2	- - -
Hawaiian	7.4	7.1	4.8	4.5	6.1	- - -
Other Asian or Pacific Islander	5.5	4.7	4.2	3.5	3.5	- - -
Hispanic or Latino[5,6]	6.0	5.3	4.8	4.0	3.8	3.8
Mexican	5.7	5.0	4.5	3.8	3.7	3.6
Puerto Rican	8.3	7.2	7.0	5.7	5.6	5.8
Cuban	5.9	5.3	4.6	3.7	3.1	3.1
Central and South American	5.7	4.9	4.4	3.7	3.4	3.5
Other and unknown Hispanic or Latino	6.1	5.8	5.2	4.6	4.6	4.6
Not Hispanic or Latino:						
White[6]	5.7	5.1	4.6	4.0	3.8	3.8
Black or African American[6]	11.8	11.4	11.1	9.4	9.4	9.2
	Postneonatal[3] deaths per 1,000 live births					
All mothers	3.7	3.5	3.3	2.5	2.3	2.3
White	3.1	3.0	2.7	2.1	1.9	1.9
Black or African American	6.4	6.2	6.0	4.7	4.4	4.4
American Indian or Alaska Native	7.2	7.3	6.7	4.8	4.2	4.5
Asian or Pacific Islander[4]	3.1	2.8	2.6	1.8	1.6	1.5
Chinese	3.1	2.5	2.4	1.2	1.1	- - -
Japanese	2.6	2.5	2.2	2.1	*1.2	- - -
Filipino	2.9	2.4	2.3	2.1	1.7	- - -
Hawaiian	3.9	4.0	4.1	*2.5	*2.6	- - -
Other Asian or Pacific Islander	3.1	2.9	2.8	1.9	1.7	- - -
Hispanic or Latino[5,6]	3.2	3.0	2.7	2.1	1.8	1.8
Mexican	3.2	2.9	2.7	2.1	1.8	1.7
Puerto Rican	4.0	3.9	3.4	2.8	2.5	2.5
Cuban	2.2	2.0	1.6	1.5	*1.1	*1.1
Central and South American	2.5	2.6	2.2	1.7	1.5	1.5
Other and unknown Hispanic or Latino	3.7	3.2	3.0	2.5	2.3	2.0
Not Hispanic or Latino:						
White[6]	3.1	3.0	2.7	2.2	2.0	1.9
Black or African American[6]	6.7	6.5	6.1	4.8	4.5	4.5

See footnotes at end of table.

Table 19 (page 3 of 3). Infant, neonatal, and postneonatal mortality rates, by detailed race and Hispanic origin of mother: United States, selected years 1983–2003

[Data are based on linked birth and death certificates for infants]

* Estimates are considered unreliable. Rates preceded by an asterisk are based on fewer than 50 deaths in the numerator. Rates not shown are based on fewer than 20 deaths in the numerator.

[1] Rates based on unweighted birth cohort data.

[2] Rates based on a period file using weighted data. See Appendix I, National Vital Statistics System, Linked Birth/Infant Death Data Set.

[3] Infant (under 1 year of age), neonatal (under 28 days), and postneonatal (28 days–11 months).

[4] Starting with 2003 data, estimates are not shown for Asian or Pacific Islander subgroups during the transition from single race to multiple race reporting. See Appendix II, Race, Birth file.

[5] Persons of Hispanic origin may be of any race.

[6] Prior to 1995, data shown only for states with an Hispanic-origin item on their birth certificates. See Appendix II, Hispanic origin.

[7] Average annual mortality rate.

NOTES: The race groups white, black, American Indian or Alaska Native, and Asian or Pacific Islander include persons of Hispanic and non-Hispanic origin. Starting with 2003 data, some states reported multiple-race data. The multiple-race data for these states were bridged to the single race categories of the 1977 Office of Management and Budget standards for comparability with other states. See Appendix II, Race. National linked files do not exist for 1992–1994. Data for additional years are available. See Appendix III.

SOURCE: Centers for Disease Control and Prevention, National Center for Health Statistics, National Vital Statistics System, Linked Birth/Infant Death Data Set.

Table 20 (page 1 of 2). Infant mortality rates among mothers 20 years of age and over, by education, detailed race, and Hispanic origin of mother: United States, selected years 1983–2003

[Data are based on linked birth and death certificates for infants]

Education, race, and Hispanic origin of mother	1983[1]	1985[1]	1990[1]	1995[2]	1999[2]	2000[2]	2001[2]	2002[2]	2003[2,3]
Less than 12 years of education				Infant deaths per 1,000 live births					
All mothers	15.0	14.3	10.8	8.9	8.0	7.9	7.6	7.9	7.9
White	12.5	12.2	9.0	7.6	6.9	6.8	6.5	6.7	6.8
Black or African American	23.4	21.5	19.5	17.0	14.8	14.7	14.0	15.6	14.8
American Indian or Alaska Native	14.5	17.3	14.3	12.7	11.0	10.1	12.9	8.6	8.7
Asian or Pacific Islander[4]	9.7	8.0	6.6	5.7	5.4	5.9	5.5	4.5	6.3
Hispanic or Latino[5,6]	10.9	10.4	7.3	6.0	5.6	5.4	5.1	5.3	5.5
Mexican	8.7	10.0	7.0	5.8	5.5	5.2	4.9	5.0	5.4
Puerto Rican	15.3	11.8	10.1	10.6	9.4	9.6	7.8	10.1	9.2
Cuban	*14.5	*	*	*	*	*	*	*	*
Central and South American	9.8	8.7	7.0	5.1	4.4	4.9	5.0	5.7	5.4
Other and unknown Hispanic or Latino	9.2	11.2	9.9	7.3	7.0	7.6	5.8	6.0	6.1
Not Hispanic or Latino:[6]									
White	12.8	12.5	10.9	9.9	8.9	9.2	9.0	9.4	9.2
Black or African American	24.7	21.6	19.7	17.3	15.1	15.0	14.3	15.9	15.3
12 years of education									
All mothers	10.2	9.9	8.8	7.8	7.4	7.3	7.3	7.6	7.5
White	8.7	8.5	7.1	6.4	6.0	6.0	6.0	6.3	6.1
Black or African American	17.8	17.6	16.0	14.7	14.0	13.3	12.9	13.6	13.5
American Indian or Alaska Native	15.5	10.9	13.4	7.9	9.0	7.8	9.6	8.8	9.4
Asian or Pacific Islander[4]	10.0	8.0	7.5	5.5	5.6	5.0	5.9	5.3	5.9
Hispanic or Latino[5,6]	8.4	9.1	7.0	5.9	5.3	5.0	5.1	5.4	5.5
Mexican	6.9	9.3	6.8	5.7	5.0	4.9	4.7	5.2	5.3
Puerto Rican	9.5	11.1	8.5	6.5	8.0	7.2	9.2	8.1	7.5
Cuban	*6.9	*9.2	*8.0	*	*	*	*	*	*4.6
Central and South American	8.7	7.5	6.5	6.1	4.8	4.2	4.8	4.6	5.4
Other and unknown Hispanic or Latino	8.8	8.3	7.4	6.5	6.7	5.8	5.6	7.2	5.3
Not Hispanic or Latino:[6]									
White	8.7	8.2	7.1	6.5	6.2	6.3	6.2	6.7	6.4
Black or African American	17.8	18.3	16.1	14.8	14.1	13.5	13.1	13.7	13.6
13 years or more of education									
All mothers	8.1	7.7	6.4	5.4	5.1	5.0	5.1	5.0	5.1
White	7.2	6.6	5.4	4.7	4.3	4.2	4.3	4.2	4.3
Black or African American	15.3	15.8	13.7	11.9	11.4	11.4	11.7	11.1	11.3
American Indian or Alaska Native	12.5	*8.5	6.8	5.9	7.4	6.7	6.7	7.3	7.1
Asian or Pacific Islander[4]	6.6	6.2	5.1	4.4	4.0	3.9	3.7	4.0	3.8
Hispanic or Latino[5,6]	9.0	6.4	5.7	5.0	4.7	4.5	4.6	4.5	4.8
Mexican	*8.3	*5.8	5.5	5.2	4.8	4.5	4.7	4.7	4.8
Puerto Rican	10.9	*7.1	7.3	6.3	6.3	6.5	5.9	5.4	6.4
Cuban	*	*6.3	*5.3	*5.3	*4.5	*4.9	*4.0	*3.0	*4.6
Central and South American	*7.1	*6.6	5.6	3.7	3.9	3.7	4.1	4.2	3.9
Other and unknown Hispanic or Latino	11.6	*6.2	5.4	5.2	4.5	4.2	3.8	3.9	5.4
Not Hispanic or Latino:[6]									
White	7.0	6.6	5.4	4.6	4.2	4.2	4.3	4.2	4.3
Black or African American	14.8	15.1	13.7	12.0	11.5	11.5	11.8	11.2	11.3

See footnotes at end of table.

Table 20 (page 2 of 2). Infant mortality rates among mothers 20 years of age and over, by education, detailed race, and Hispanic origin of mother: United States, selected years 1983–2003

[Data are based on linked birth and death certificates for infants]

Education, race, and Hispanic origin of mother	Average annual mortality rate					
	1983–1985[1]	1986–1988[1]	1989–1991[1]	1995–1997[2]	1998–2000[2]	2001–2003[2,3]
Less than 12 years of education	Infant deaths per 1,000 live births					
All mothers	14.6	13.8	11.1	8.6	8.0	7.7
White	12.4	11.4	9.2	7.3	6.9	6.6
Black or African American	21.8	21.1	20.3	16.0	14.8	14.8
American Indian or Alaska Native	15.2	16.8	13.8	11.4	10.2	10.7
Asian or Pacific Islander[4]	9.5	8.2	6.9	5.8	5.7	5.0
Hispanic or Latino[5,6]	10.6	9.9	7.5	5.8	5.5	5.2
Mexican	9.5	8.3	7.1	5.6	5.3	5.0
Puerto Rican	14.1	12.8	11.7	9.5	8.9	8.9
Cuban	*10.5	*9.4	*8.2	*6.7	*	*
Central and South American	8.6	9.2	6.8	5.4	5.0	5.4
Other and unknown Hispanic or Latino . .	10.1	10.6	10.0	7.0	7.4	5.9
Not Hispanic or Latino:[6]						
White	12.6	11.8	11.0	9.6	9.1	9.2
Black or African American	22.6	21.6	20.6	16.3	15.1	15.1
12 years of education						
All mothers	10.0	9.6	8.9	7.6	7.4	7.4
White	8.5	8.0	7.2	6.3	6.0	6.1
Black or African American	17.7	17.1	16.4	14.1	13.9	13.2
American Indian or Alaska Native	13.4	11.6	12.3	8.5	8.7	9.2
Asian or Pacific Islander[4]	9.3	7.9	7.5	5.6	5.5	5.6
Hispanic or Latino[5,6]	9.1	8.3	6.8	5.8	5.2	5.3
Mexican	7.8	8.2	6.5	5.6	5.0	5.0
Puerto Rican	10.8	10.1	8.6	7.6	7.5	8.6
Cuban	8.6	6.6	7.6	5.4	*3.7	*3.9
Central and South American	8.7	7.4	6.3	5.5	4.8	4.7
Other and unknown Hispanic or Latino . .	8.8	7.7	7.0	6.6	6.1	6.4
Not Hispanic or Latino:[6]						
White	8.3	7.9	7.3	6.4	6.3	6.5
Black or African American	17.9	17.4	16.5	14.2	14.0	13.4
13 years or more of education						
All mothers	7.8	7.2	6.4	5.3	5.1	5.0
White	6.9	6.2	5.5	4.5	4.4	4.2
Black or African American	15.3	14.9	13.7	11.6	11.3	11.4
American Indian or Alaska Native	10.4	8.4	8.1	6.6	7.0	7.0
Asian or Pacific Islander[4]	6.7	5.9	5.1	4.1	4.1	3.9
Hispanic or Latino[5,6]	7.4	7.0	5.8	5.0	4.6	4.6
Mexican	7.6	6.4	5.7	5.1	4.7	4.7
Puerto Rican	8.1	6.9	7.8	6.4	6.2	5.6
Cuban	5.5	5.9	4.2	4.3	4.2	3.5
Central and South American	7.2	7.6	5.4	4.0	3.9	4.2
Other and unknown Hispanic or Latino . .	7.9	7.5	5.6	5.3	4.1	3.8
Not Hispanic or Latino:[6]						
White	6.8	6.1	5.4	4.5	4.3	4.2
Black or African American	14.7	14.9	13.8	11.7	11.4	11.5

* Estimates are considered unreliable. Rates preceded by an asterisk are based on fewer than 50 deaths in the numerator. Rates not shown are based on fewer than 20 deaths in the numerator.

[1] Rates based on unweighted birth cohort data.

[2] Rates based on a period file using weighted data. See Appendix I, National Vital Statistics System, Linked Birth/Infant Death Data Set.

[3] Data for 2003 and 2001–2003 exclude Pennsylvania and Washington, which implemented the 2003 revision of the U.S. Standard Certificate of Live Birth. Maternal education data based on the 2003 revision are not comparable with data based on the 1989 and earlier revisions of the U.S. Standard Certificate of Live Birth.

[4] Asian or Pacific Islander births occurred disproportionately in the states not reporting maternal education on the birth certificate prior to 1992. Starting with 1992 data, maternal education was reported by all 50 states and the District of Columbia. See Appendix II, Education.

[5] Persons of Hispanic origin may be of any race.

[6] Prior to 1995, data shown only for states with an Hispanic-origin item and education of mother on their birth certificates. See Appendix II, Education; Hispanic origin.

NOTES: Prior to 1995, data are shown only for states reporting education of mother on their birth certificates. See Appendix II, Education. The race groups white, black, American Indian or Alaska Native, and Asian or Pacific Islander include persons of Hispanic and non-Hispanic origin. Starting with 2003 data, some states reported multiple-race data. The multiple-race data for these states were bridged to the single race categories of the 1977 Office of Management and Budget standards for comparability with other states. See Appendix II, Race. National linked files do not exist for 1992–1994. Data for additional years are available. See Appendix III.

SOURCE: Centers for Disease Control and Prevention, National Center for Health Statistics, National Vital Statistics System, Linked Birth/Infant Death Data Set.

Table 21. Infant mortality rates by birthweight: United States, selected years 1983–2003

[Data are based on linked birth and death certificates for infants]

Birthweight	1983[1]	1985[1]	1990[1]	1995[2]	2000[2]	2001[2]	2002[2]	2003[2]
	Infant deaths per 1,000 live births[3]							
All birthweights	10.9	10.4	8.9	7.6	6.9	6.8	7.0	6.8
Less than 2,500 grams..............	95.9	93.9	78.1	65.3	60.2	59.4	60.3	59.4
Less than 1,500 grams	400.6	387.7	317.6	270.7	246.9	246.9	253.2	253.1
Less than 500 grams............	890.3	895.9	898.2	904.9	847.9	856.8	863.6	866.2
500–999 grams................	584.2	559.2	440.1	351.0	313.8	313.0	321.5	319.0
1,000–1,499 grams	162.3	145.4	97.9	69.6	60.9	59.4	57.7	56.9
1,500–1,999 grams.............	58.4	54.0	43.8	33.5	28.7	27.6	26.9	28.0
2,000–2,499 grams.............	22.5	20.9	17.8	13.7	11.9	11.4	11.7	11.0
2,500 grams or more	4.7	4.3	3.7	3.0	2.5	2.5	2.4	2.3
2,500–2,999 grams................	8.8	7.9	6.7	5.5	4.6	4.5	4.5	4.1
3,000–3,499 grams................	4.4	4.3	3.7	2.9	2.4	2.3	2.3	2.2
3,500–3,999 grams...............	3.2	3.0	2.6	2.0	1.7	1.7	1.6	1.6
4,000 grams or more..............	3.3	3.2	2.4	2.0	1.6	1.6	1.5	1.6
4,000–4,499 grams	2.9	2.9	2.2	1.8	1.5	1.5	1.4	1.3
4,500–4,999 grams	3.9	3.8	2.5	2.2	2.1	2.0	2.0	2.4
5,000 grams or more[4]	14.4	14.7	9.8	8.5	*6.1	*6.5	*5.1	*6.4

* Estimates are considered unreliable. Rates preceded by an asterisk are based on fewer than 50 deaths in the numerator.
[1] Rates based on unweighted birth cohort data.
[2] Rates based on a period file using weighted data; unknown birthweight imputed when period of gestation is known and proportionately distributed when period of gestation is unknown. See Appendix I, National Vital Statistics System, Linked Birth/Infant Death Data Set.
[3] For calculation of birthweight-specific infant mortality rates, unknown birthweight has been distributed in proportion to known birthweight separately for live births (denominator) and infant deaths (numerator).
[4] In 1989, a birthweight-gestational age consistency check instituted for the natality file resulted in a decrease in the number of deaths to infants coded with birthweights of 5,000 grams or more and a discontinuity in the mortality trend for infants weighing 5,000 grams or more at birth. Starting with 1989 data, the rates are believed to be more accurate.

NOTES: National linked files do not exist for 1992–1994. Data for additional years are available. See Appendix III.

SOURCE: Centers for Disease Control and Prevention, National Center for Health Statistics, National Vital Statistics System, Linked Birth/Infant Death Data Set.

Table 22. Infant mortality rates, fetal mortality rates, and perinatal mortality rates, by race: United States, selected years 1950–2003

[Data are based on death certificates, fetal death records, and birth certificates]

Race and year	Infant[1]	Neonatal[1] Under 28 days	Neonatal[1] Under 7 days	Postneonatal[1]	Fetal mortality rate[2]	Late fetal mortality rate[3]	Perinatal mortality rate[4]
All races		Deaths per 1,000 live births					
1950[5]	29.2	20.5	17.8	8.7	18.4	14.9	32.5
1960[5]	26.0	18.7	16.7	7.3	15.8	12.1	28.6
1970	20.0	15.1	13.6	4.9	14.0	9.5	23.0
1980	12.6	8.5	7.1	4.1	9.1	6.2	13.2
1990	9.2	5.8	4.8	3.4	7.5	4.3	9.1
1995	7.6	4.9	4.0	2.7	7.0	3.6	7.6
1997	7.2	4.8	3.8	2.5	6.8	3.5	7.3
1998	7.2	4.8	3.8	2.4	6.7	3.4	7.2
1999	7.1	4.7	3.8	2.3	6.7	3.4	7.1
2000	6.9	4.6	3.7	2.3	6.6	3.3	7.0
2001	6.8	4.5	3.6	2.3	6.5	3.3	6.9
2002	7.0	4.7	3.7	2.3	6.4	3.2	6.9
2003	6.9	4.6	3.7	2.2	6.2	3.0	6.7
Race of child:[6] White							
1950[5]	26.8	19.4	17.1	7.4	16.6	13.3	30.1
1960[5]	22.9	17.2	15.6	5.7	13.9	10.8	26.2
1970	17.8	13.8	12.5	4.0	12.3	8.6	21.0
1980	11.0	7.5	6.2	3.5	8.1	5.7	11.9
Race of mother:[7] White							
1980	10.9	7.4	6.1	3.5	8.1	5.7	11.8
1990	7.6	4.8	3.9	2.8	6.4	3.8	7.7
1995	6.3	4.1	3.3	2.2	5.9	3.3	6.5
1997	6.0	4.0	3.2	2.0	5.8	3.2	6.3
1998	6.0	4.0	3.1	2.0	5.7	3.1	6.2
1999	5.8	3.9	3.1	1.9	5.7	3.0	6.1
2000	5.7	3.8	3.0	1.9	5.6	2.9	5.9
2001	5.7	3.8	3.0	1.9	5.5	2.9	5.9
2002	5.8	3.9	3.1	1.9	5.5	2.8	5.9
2003	5.7	3.9	3.1	1.8	5.2	2.7	5.8
Race of child:[6] Black or African American							
1950[5]	43.9	27.8	23.0	16.1	32.1	- - -	- - -
1960[5]	44.3	27.8	23.7	16.5	- - -	- - -	- - -
1970	32.6	22.8	20.3	9.9	23.2	- - -	34.5
1980	21.4	14.1	11.9	7.3	14.4	8.9	20.7
Race of mother:[7] Black or African American							
1980	22.2	14.6	12.3	7.6	14.7	9.1	21.3
1990	18.0	11.6	9.7	6.4	13.3	6.7	16.4
1995	15.1	9.8	8.2	5.3	12.7	5.7	13.8
1997	14.2	9.4	7.8	4.8	12.5	5.5	13.2
1998	14.3	9.5	7.8	4.8	12.3	5.3	13.1
1999	14.6	9.8	7.9	4.8	12.6	5.4	13.2
2000	14.1	9.4	7.6	4.7	12.4	5.4	13.0
2001	14.0	9.2	7.6	4.8	12.1	5.3	12.8
2002	14.4	9.5	7.8	4.8	11.9	5.2	12.8
2003	14.0	9.4	7.5	4.6	12.0	5.1	12.4

- - - Data not available.

[1]Infant (under 1 year of age), neonatal (under 28 days), early neonatal (under 7 days), and postneonatal (28 days–11 months).
[2]Number of fetal deaths of 20 weeks or more gestation per 1,000 live births plus fetal deaths.
[3]Number of fetal deaths of 28 weeks or more gestation (late fetal deaths) per 1,000 live births plus late fetal deaths.
[4]Number of late fetal deaths plus infant deaths within 7 days of birth per 1,000 live births plus late fetal deaths.
[5]Includes births and deaths of persons who were not residents of the 50 states and the District of Columbia.
[6]Infant deaths, live births, and fetal deaths are tabulated by race of child. See Appendix II, Race.
[7]Infant deaths are tabulated by race of decedent; fetal deaths and live births are tabulated by race of mother. See Appendix II, Race.

NOTES: Infant mortality rates in this table are based on infant deaths from the mortality file (numerator) and live births from the natality file (denominator). Inconsistencies in reporting race for the same infant between the birth and death certificate can result in underestimated infant mortality rates for races other than white or black. Infant mortality rates for minority population groups are available from the Linked Birth/Infant Death Data Set and are presented in Tables 19–20 and 23–24. Data for additional years are available. See Appendix III.

SOURCE: Centers for Disease Control and Prevention, National Center for Health Statistics, National Vital Statistics System: Hoyert DL, Heron MP, Murphy SL, Kung HC. Deaths: Final data for 2003. National vital statistics reports. Vol 54 no 13. Hyattsville, MD: National Center for Health Statistics. 2006; and unpublished numbers.

This table will be updated on the Web. Go to www.cdc.gov/nchs/hus.htm.

Table 23 (page 1 of 3). Infant mortality rates, by race and Hispanic origin of mother, geographic division, and state: United States, average annual 1989–1991, 1998–2000, and 2001–2003

[Data are based on linked birth and death certificates for infants]

Geographic division and state	All races 1989–1991[1]	All races 1998–2000[2]	All races 2001–2003[2]	Not Hispanic or Latino / White 1989–1991[1]	Not Hispanic or Latino / White 1998–2000[2]	Not Hispanic or Latino / White 2001–2003[2]	Not Hispanic or Latino / Black or African American 1989–1991[1]	Not Hispanic or Latino / Black or African American 1998–2000[2]	Not Hispanic or Latino / Black or African American 2001–2003[2]
				Infant[3] deaths per 1,000 live births					
United States	9.0	7.0	6.9	7.3	5.8	5.7	17.2	13.9	13.6
New England[4]	7.3	5.6	5.3	6.2	4.6	4.4	15.1	12.2	11.5
Connecticut	7.9	6.5	6.0	5.9	4.7	4.6	17.0	13.5	13.6
Maine	6.6	5.4	5.2	6.2	5.4	5.1	*	*	*
Massachusetts	7.0	5.0	4.9	5.9	4.2	4.0	14.2	11.2	10.2
New Hampshire[4]	7.1	5.4	4.3	7.2	4.7	4.2	*	*	*
Rhode Island	8.7	6.4	6.9	7.5	4.9	5.3	*13.6	*13.5	*11.8
Vermont	6.6	6.3	5.1	6.3	6.2	5.0	*	*	*
Middle Atlantic	9.2	6.6	6.4	6.6	5.0	5.0	18.5	13.1	12.3
New Jersey	8.4	6.4	5.9	6.1	4.4	3.9	17.8	13.8	13.1
New York	9.5	6.3	6.0	6.3	4.7	4.6	18.4	11.8	11.2
Pennsylvania	9.2	7.2	7.4	7.2	5.6	6.0	19.1	15.4	14.1
East North Central	9.8	8.0	7.7	7.7	6.3	6.2	19.1	16.1	15.7
Illinois	10.7	8.5	7.6	7.6	6.2	5.9	20.5	17.1	15.5
Indiana	9.4	7.8	7.7	8.4	6.9	7.0	17.3	15.4	13.8
Michigan	10.5	8.1	8.2	7.7	6.0	6.3	20.7	16.4	16.7
Ohio	9.0	7.9	7.8	7.7	6.7	6.3	16.2	14.4	15.4
Wisconsin	8.4	6.9	6.8	7.4	5.7	5.5	17.0	16.6	17.5
West North Central	8.5	6.8	6.5	7.4	6.0	5.7	17.5	14.7	13.8
Iowa	8.2	6.2	5.6	7.8	5.8	5.3	15.8	17.3	*12.3
Kansas	8.5	7.0	7.1	7.8	7.1	6.3	15.4	10.5	15.8
Minnesota	7.3	5.9	5.1	6.4	5.2	4.5	18.5	13.0	8.4
Missouri	9.7	7.5	7.9	8.0	6.1	6.5	18.0	16.0	15.7
Nebraska	8.1	7.0	6.4	7.2	6.2	5.6	18.3	16.2	15.2
North Dakota	8.0	8.0	7.5	7.3	7.0	6.8	*	*	*
South Dakota	9.5	7.8	6.9	7.5	6.7	5.7	*	*	*
South Atlantic	10.4	8.1	8.1	7.6	6.0	6.1	17.2	13.9	13.9
Delaware	11.2	8.8	9.5	8.2	6.5	7.6	20.1	15.8	16.4
District of Columbia	20.3	13.5	10.9	*8.2	*	*3.8	23.9	16.8	14.8
Florida	9.4	7.2	7.4	7.2	5.8	5.9	16.2	12.6	13.3
Georgia	11.9	8.3	8.7	8.4	5.9	6.3	17.9	13.5	13.5
Maryland	9.1	8.1	8.0	6.3	5.2	5.4	15.0	13.9	13.2
North Carolina	10.7	9.0	8.3	8.0	6.7	6.2	16.9	15.7	15.1
South Carolina	11.8	9.5	8.9	8.4	6.3	6.1	17.2	15.5	14.5
Virginia	9.9	7.2	7.5	7.4	5.6	5.7	18.0	12.8	14.2
West Virginia	9.1	7.6	7.9	8.8	7.6	7.7	*15.7	*9.8	*12.5
East South Central	10.4	8.8	8.8	8.1	6.7	6.8	16.5	15.0	14.7
Alabama	11.4	9.8	9.0	8.6	7.1	6.7	16.8	15.4	14.1
Kentucky	8.7	7.4	6.6	8.1	6.9	6.3	14.4	12.7	10.1
Mississippi	11.5	10.3	10.5	7.9	6.6	7.1	15.2	14.7	14.7
Tennessee	10.2	8.4	9.1	7.8	6.4	7.1	18.2	15.6	16.9
West South Central[4]	8.4	6.9	7.0	7.2	6.2	6.3	14.2	12.2	12.8
Arkansas	9.8	8.4	8.5	8.1	7.4	7.6	15.2	12.6	13.1
Louisiana[4]	10.2	9.1	9.8	7.5	6.2	7.0	14.3	13.5	13.9
Oklahoma[4]	8.0	8.5	7.8	7.3	8.2	7.2	12.7	13.5	14.3
Texas	7.9	6.0	6.2	6.9	5.5	5.7	14.1	11.0	11.9
Mountain	8.4	6.6	6.1	7.9	6.1	5.5	16.9	13.7	13.2
Arizona	8.8	7.0	6.6	8.2	6.6	6.1	17.3	15.0	13.8
Colorado	8.7	6.5	6.0	8.0	5.9	5.2	16.7	14.8	14.2
Idaho	8.9	7.2	6.2	8.9	6.8	6.0	*	*	*
Montana	9.0	6.8	7.3	8.0	6.0	6.9	*	*	*
Nevada	8.6	6.7	5.8	7.8	6.1	5.4	16.9	12.1	12.8
New Mexico	8.4	6.9	6.1	8.1	7.0	6.1	*17.2	*	*
Utah	7.0	5.3	5.2	6.8	5.2	4.8	*	*	*
Wyoming	8.4	7.0	6.0	8.0	6.8	5.6	*	*	*
Pacific	7.7	5.6	5.4	7.0	4.9	4.9	15.4	11.7	10.9
Alaska	9.2	6.3	6.8	7.2	5.0	5.1	*	*	*
California	7.6	5.5	5.3	6.9	4.8	4.7	15.4	12.0	11.1
Hawaii	7.0	7.4	7.0	5.5	6.4	5.3	*13.6	*	*
Oregon	8.0	5.6	5.6	7.4	5.3	5.6	21.3	*8.5	*9.3
Washington	8.0	5.3	5.7	7.4	4.8	5.3	15.1	10.1	9.4

See footnotes at end of table.

Table 23 (page 2 of 3). **Infant mortality rates, by race and Hispanic origin of mother, geographic division, and state: United States, average annual 1989–1991, 1998–2000, and 2001–2003**

[Data are based on linked birth and death certificates for infants]

Geographic division and state	Hispanic or Latino[5]			American Indian or Alaska Native[6]			Asian or Pacific Islander[6]		
	1989–1991[1]	1998–2000[2]	2001–2003[2]	1989–1991[1]	1998–2000[2]	2001–2003[2]	1989–1991[1]	1998–2000[2]	2001–2003[2]
	Infant[3] deaths per 1,000 live births								
United States.........	7.5	5.7	5.6	12.6	9.0	9.0	6.6	5.1	4.8
New England[7].........	8.1	6.9	6.5	*	*	*	5.8	3.9	3.8
Connecticut.........	7.9	8.6	6.3	*	*	*	*	*	*
Maine.............	*	*	*	*	*	*	*	*	*
Massachusetts.......	8.3	5.5	6.3	*	*	*	5.7	3.9	3.4
New Hampshire[7].....	- - -	*	*	*	*	*	*	*	*
Rhode Island........	*7.2	*6.4	8.8	*	*	*	*	*	*
Vermont...........	*	*	*	*	*	*	*	*	*
Middle Atlantic.........	9.1	6.2	5.9	*11.6	*	*10.9	6.4	4.2	3.6
New Jersey.........	7.5	6.2	6.1	*	*	*	5.6	4.6	3.7
New York..........	9.4	5.9	5.5	*15.2	*	*11.9	6.4	4.0	3.4
Pennsylvania.........	10.9	8.5	8.0	*	*	*	7.8	*3.8	4.0
East North Central......	8.7	7.2	6.3	11.6	8.5	9.6	6.1	6.2	5.4
Illinois.............	9.2	7.2	5.9	*	*	*	6.0	6.7	5.4
Indiana............	*7.2	6.8	6.4	*	*	*	*	*6.6	*
Michigan...........	7.9	6.6	7.3	*10.7	*	*	*6.1	6.7	5.2
Ohio..............	8.0	8.7	8.2	*	*	*	*4.8	*4.3	*5.1
Wisconsin..........	*7.3	7.4	6.9	*11.9	*8.3	*12.7	*6.7	*5.8	*6.6
West North Central......	9.3	6.4	6.5	17.1	11.4	11.1	7.4	6.0	5.2
Iowa.............	*11.9	*6.1	*6.5	*	*	*	*	*	*
Kansas............	8.7	5.2	7.3	*	*	*	*	*	*
Minnesota..........	*8.4	6.9	5.7	17.3	*10.4	*9.8	*5.1	6.8	5.5
Missouri...........	*9.1	*6.5	7.0	*	*	*	*9.1	*	*6.2
Nebraska...........	*8.8	7.8	6.2	*18.2	*15.4	*	*	*	*
North Dakota........	*	*	*	*13.8	*15.1	*11.4	*	*	*
South Dakota........	*	*	*	19.9	13.3	12.6	*	*	*
South Atlantic.........	7.4	5.2	5.6	12.7	8.6	9.0	6.8	5.2	5.2
Delaware...........	*	*	*6.9	*	*	*	*	*	*
District of Columbia....	*8.8	*9.1	*7.2	*	*	*	*	*	*
Florida............	7.1	4.9	5.3	*	*	*7.4	*6.2	5.2	5.1
Georgia...........	9.0	5.1	6.4	*	*	*	*8.2	*4.5	6.5
Maryland..........	7.2	5.8	6.0	*	*	*	7.5	*4.8	4.3
North Carolina.......	*7.5	6.2	6.1	12.2	11.7	11.0	*6.3	*6.2	*4.8
South Carolina.......	*	*5.9	5.3	*	*	*	*	*	*7.9
Virginia...........	7.6	4.7	4.9	*	*	*	6.0	5.4	5.0
West Virginia........	*	*	*	*	*	*	*	*	*
East South Central......	*5.9	6.1	6.5	*	*	*11.3	*7.7	*5.9	6.5
Alabama...........	*	*7.3	7.0	*	*	*	*	*	*
Kentucky...........	*	*	*4.9	*	*	*	*	*	*
Mississippi.........	*	*	*	*	*	*	*	*	*
Tennessee..........	*	*5.4	6.6	*	*	*	*	*5.9	*6.4
West South Central[7]....	7.0	5.2	5.4	8.4	7.9	7.4	6.7	4.3	4.9
Arkansas..........	*	*5.7	*5.3	*	*	*	*	*	*
Louisiana[7]..........	- - -	*4.9	*4.5	*	*	*	*	*	*9.9
Oklahoma[7].........	- - -	5.4	5.6	7.8	8.2	7.4	*	*	*
Texas.............	7.0	5.2	5.4	*	*	*	6.8	4.2	4.4
Mountain.............	7.9	6.6	6.0	11.6	8.8	8.7	8.1	5.5	6.1
Arizona...........	8.0	6.7	6.2	11.4	8.7	9.7	*8.5	*5.1	*6.2
Colorado...........	8.5	6.5	6.3	*16.5	*	*	*7.8	*4.9	*6.7
Idaho.............	*7.2	8.7	7.0	*	*	*	*	*	*
Montana...........	*	*	*	16.7	*11.3	*9.4	*	*	*
Nevada...........	7.0	6.0	4.4	*	*	*	*	*6.0	*4.3
New Mexico.........	7.8	6.6	5.9	9.8	7.6	6.0	*	*	*
Utah.............	*7.0	5.7	6.4	*10.0	*	*	*10.7	*6.2	*7.9
Wyoming..........	*	*	*	*	*	*	*	*	*
Pacific..............	7.1	5.2	5.1	14.6	9.4	9.2	6.5	5.2	4.8
Alaska.............	*	*	*	15.7	9.7	10.6	*	*	*
California..........	7.0	5.2	5.1	11.0	9.3	7.3	6.4	4.8	4.3
Hawaii.............	10.7	7.5	*6.8	*	*	*	7.1	7.6	7.3
Oregon............	8.5	6.4	4.7	*15.7	*10.6	*8.9	*8.4	*4.2	*4.7
Washington.........	7.6	5.0	5.2	19.6	9.2	10.6	6.2	5.3	4.7

See footnotes at end of table.

Table 23 (page 3 of 3). Infant mortality rates, by race and Hispanic origin of mother, geographic division, and state: United States, average annual 1989–1991, 1998–2000, and 2001–2003

[Data are based on linked birth and death certificates for infants]

---

* Estimates are considered unreliable. Rates preceded by an asterisk are based on fewer than 50 deaths in the numerator. Rates not shown are based on fewer than 20 deaths in the numerator.
- - - Data not available.
[1]Rates based on unweighted birth cohort data.
[2]Rates based on period file using weighted data. See Appendix I, National Vital Statistics System, Linked Birth/Infant Death Data Set.
[3]Under 1 year of age.
[4]Rates for white and black are substituted for non-Hispanic white and non-Hispanic black for Louisiana 1989, Oklahoma 1989–1990, and New Hampshire 1989–1991.
[5]Persons of Hispanic origin may be of any race. See Appendix II, Hispanic origin.
[6]Includes persons of Hispanic origin.
[7]Rates for Hispanic origin exclude data from states not reporting Hispanic origin on the birth certificate for 1 or more years in a 3-year period.

NOTES: Starting with 2003 data, some states reported multiple-race data. The multiple-race data for these states were bridged to the single race categories of the 1977 Office of Management and Budget standards for comparability with other states. See Appendix II, Race. National linked files do not exist for 1992–1994.

SOURCE: Centers for Disease Control and Prevention, National Center for Health Statistics, National Vital Statistics System, Linked Birth/Infant Death Data Set.

Table 24 (page 1 of 3). **Neonatal mortality rates, by race and Hispanic origin of mother, geographic division, and state: United States, average annual 1989–1991, 1998–2000, and 2001–2003**

[Data are based on linked birth and death certificates for infants]

Geographic division and state	All races			Not Hispanic or Latino					
				White			Black or African American		
	1989–1991[1]	1998–2000[2]	2001–2003[2]	1989–1991[1]	1998–2000[2]	2001–2003[2]	1989–1991[1]	1998–2000[2]	2001–2003[2]
	Neonatal[3] deaths per 1,000 live births								
United States.	5.7	4.7	4.6	4.6	3.8	3.8	11.1	9.4	9.2
New England[4]	5.1	4.2	3.9	4.2	3.5	3.3	11.0	9.1	8.4
Connecticut	5.7	4.9	4.4	4.2	3.6	3.5	12.5	9.7	9.2
Maine	4.5	3.9	4.0	4.2	3.9	3.9	*	*	*
Massachusetts	4.9	3.9	3.7	4.1	3.3	3.0	10.4	8.8	7.8
New Hampshire[4]	4.3	3.9	3.0	4.4	3.4	2.9	*	*	*
Rhode Island	6.4	4.8	5.1	5.3	3.8	3.7	*9.8	*9.3	*9.6
Vermont	4.1	4.3	3.7	3.9	4.4	3.8	*	*	*
Middle Atlantic	6.3	4.7	4.5	4.6	3.5	3.6	12.3	9.1	8.5
New Jersey	5.8	4.6	4.2	4.5	3.2	2.8	11.4	9.5	8.9
New York	6.5	4.5	4.2	4.3	3.3	3.3	12.6	8.4	7.7
Pennsylvania	6.2	5.0	5.4	4.9	4.0	4.4	12.5	10.3	9.8
East North Central	6.3	5.4	5.2	4.9	4.3	4.3	12.1	10.7	10.3
Illinois	7.0	5.8	5.2	5.1	4.3	4.3	12.7	11.1	9.9
Indiana	6.0	5.2	5.0	5.2	4.6	4.6	11.5	10.1	9.0
Michigan	6.9	5.5	5.7	4.9	4.0	4.4	14.0	11.4	11.2
Ohio	5.5	5.4	5.3	4.8	4.6	4.3	9.8	9.8	10.4
Wisconsin	5.1	4.6	4.7	4.6	3.8	3.8	9.1	10.8	11.2
West North Central.	5.0	4.5	4.3	4.5	3.9	3.8	10.2	9.9	9.4
Iowa	4.8	4.0	3.5	4.5	3.7	3.2	*10.5	*10.5	*9.1
Kansas	4.9	4.7	4.7	4.6	4.7	4.0	8.3	7.5	11.2
Minnesota	4.3	3.9	3.4	3.9	3.5	3.1	10.7	8.8	4.5
Missouri	6.0	4.9	5.4	5.0	3.9	4.4	10.6	10.8	11.1
Nebraska	4.5	4.7	4.4	4.2	4.1	4.0	*9.8	*10.7	*11.2
North Dakota	5.0	5.0	5.2	4.7	4.7	4.8	*	*	*
South Dakota	5.1	4.3	3.4	4.5	4.1	3.0	*	*	*
South Atlantic	6.9	5.6	5.5	4.9	4.0	4.0	11.7	9.8	9.7
Delaware	7.5	6.3	7.0	5.8	4.2	5.7	12.4	12.6	12.2
District of Columbia. . . .	14.1	9.4	7.7	*5.2	*	*	16.7	11.9	10.3
Florida	6.2	4.7	4.9	4.7	3.8	3.7	10.5	8.2	8.9
Georgia	7.9	5.7	5.8	5.5	3.8	4.1	12.0	9.4	9.2
Maryland	5.9	5.9	5.8	3.9	3.6	4.0	10.2	10.3	9.5
North Carolina	7.3	6.5	5.8	5.3	4.8	4.1	11.9	11.5	10.9
South Carolina	7.7	6.7	6.1	5.4	4.1	3.9	11.3	11.4	10.5
Virginia	6.8	5.1	5.1	4.8	3.8	3.7	13.0	9.3	10.1
West Virginia	5.8	4.6	5.1	5.6	4.6	4.8	*9.7	*	*9.6
East South Central	6.6	5.7	5.5	5.0	4.2	4.1	10.6	9.9	9.6
Alabama	7.5	6.2	5.7	5.7	4.3	4.1	11.1	10.3	9.0
Kentucky	5.0	4.8	4.0	4.6	4.5	3.9	8.9	8.0	5.7
Mississippi	7.1	6.3	6.4	4.9	3.8	4.1	9.5	9.3	9.2
Tennessee	6.5	5.5	5.8	4.9	4.1	4.2	11.8	10.6	11.9
West South Central[4]	5.0	4.2	4.4	4.2	3.8	3.9	8.4	7.6	8.1
Arkansas	5.4	4.9	5.1	4.5	4.3	4.5	8.5	7.7	8.3
Louisiana[4]	6.3	5.9	6.2	4.8	4.0	4.3	8.5	8.8	9.0
Oklahoma[4]	4.4	5.2	4.6	4.1	5.2	4.2	6.3	8.1	8.6
Texas	4.7	3.7	4.0	4.1	3.3	3.5	8.5	6.8	7.5
Mountain.	4.8	4.2	4.0	4.4	3.8	3.6	10.1	9.0	9.0
Arizona	5.3	4.5	4.3	4.9	4.2	4.0	11.0	9.7	9.5
Colorado	5.0	4.3	4.3	4.7	3.8	3.5	10.9	11.1	11.0
Idaho.	5.3	4.8	3.9	5.2	4.5	3.8	*	*	*
Montana	4.6	3.7	4.4	4.2	3.2	4.4	*	*	*
Nevada	4.3	3.8	3.4	3.8	3.2	3.0	*8.3	*6.1	7.3
New Mexico	5.0	4.0	3.9	4.8	4.3	3.8	*	*	*
Utah	3.7	3.5	3.5	3.6	3.4	3.3	*	*	*
Wyoming	3.9	4.4	3.8	3.8	4.1	3.7	*	*	*
Pacific.	4.6	3.7	3.6	4.0	3.2	3.2	9.2	7.2	7.0
Alaska	4.1	3.2	3.0	3.7	2.8	*2.8	*	*	*
California	4.6	3.7	3.6	4.1	3.2	3.1	9.2	7.4	7.2
Hawaii	4.3	5.4	4.8	3.5	*4.7	*4.3	*	*	*
Oregon	4.4	3.6	3.7	4.0	3.4	3.7	*11.6	*	*
Washington	4.3	3.3	3.7	3.8	2.9	3.5	9.7	6.4	6.1

See footnotes at end of table.

Table 24 (page 2 of 3). Neonatal mortality rates, by race and Hispanic origin of mother, geographic division, and state: United States, average annual 1989–1991, 1998–2000, and 2001–2003

[Data are based on linked birth and death certificates for infants]

Geographic division and state	Hispanic or Latino[5]			American Indian or Alaska Native[6]			Asian or Pacific Islander[6]		
	1989–1991[1]	1998–2000[2]	2001–2003[2]	1989–1991[1]	1998–2000[2]	2001–2003[2]	1989–1991[1]	1998–2000[2]	2001–2003[2]
	Neonatal[3] deaths per 1,000 live births								
United States.	4.8	3.8	3.8	5.9	4.8	4.5	3.9	3.5	3.3
New England[7].	5.5	5.2	4.9	*	*	*	4.4	2.7	3.0
Connecticut	5.3	6.5	4.9	*	*	*	*	*	*
Maine	*	*	*	*	*	*	*	*	*
Massachusetts	5.8	4.4	4.7	*	*	*	*3.9	*2.6	*2.6
New Hampshire[7]	- - -	*	*	*	*	*	*	*	*
Rhode Island	*4.9	*4.1	*6.4	*	*	*	*	*	*
Vermont.	*	*	*	*	*	*	*	*	*
Middle Atlantic.	6.2	4.3	4.2	*	*	*5.6	4.1	3.0	2.6
New Jersey	5.1	4.3	4.2	*	*	*	*3.4	3.3	2.7
New York.	6.4	4.1	3.9	*	*	*	4.1	2.9	2.4
Pennsylvania	7.3	5.7	5.4	*	*	*	*5.2	*2.7	*3.2
East North Central	5.9	5.1	4.5	*6.2	*4.5	*5.4	3.6	4.4	4.0
Illinois	6.4	5.0	4.1	*	*	*	3.9	4.9	3.9
Indiana	*4.7	5.0	4.3	*	*	*	*	*	*
Michigan	5.2	4.2	5.1	*	*	*	*	*4.3	3.9
Ohio	*5.4	6.6	6.1	*	*	*	*	*2.6	*4.2
Wisconsin	*3.9	5.5	5.0	*	*	*6.5	*	*4.4	*4.9
West North Central.	5.3	4.6	4.5	6.1	5.0	5.5	4.6	4.3	3.5
Iowa	*	*4.6	*4.6	*	*	*	*	*	*
Kansas	*5.4	*3.5	4.9	*	*	*	*	*	*
Minnesota	*	*4.8	3.9	*4.9	*	*	*3.2	*5.0	*3.4
Missouri	*	*4.7	5.1	*	*	*	*	*	*4.5
Nebraska.	*	*5.8	*3.9	*	*	*	*	*	*
North Dakota	*	*	*	*	*	*	*	*	*
South Dakota	*	*	*	*8.2	*5.1	*5.5	*	*	*
South Atlantic	5.2	3.7	3.9	7.4	6.3	6.1	4.6	3.8	3.9
Delaware.	*	*	*	*	*	*	*	*	*
District of Columbia. . . .									
Florida.	5.1	3.5	3.6	*	*	*	*4.4	3.8	3.7
Georgia.	*5.7	3.5	4.3	*	*	*	*5.3	*3.3	5.3
Maryland	*4.7	4.8	4.2	*	*	*	*4.5	*3.7	*3.5
North Carolina	*5.5	4.5	4.1	*7.7	*9.1	*8.0	*	*4.0	*3.4
South Carolina	*	*4.4	*3.8	*	*	*	*	*4.0	*
Virginia	*4.8	3.5	3.6	*	*	*	*4.1	4.1	3.6
West Virginia	*	*	*	*	*	*	*	*	*
East South Central.	*	3.7	4.1	*	*	*	*	*4.3	*4.3
Alabama	*	*4.1	*4.3	*	*	*	*	*	*
Kentucky.	*	*	*	*	*	*	*	*	*
Mississippi	*	*	*	*	*	*	*	*	*
Tennessee	*	*3.8	4.4	*	*	*	*	*	*
West South Central[7]	4.2	3.3	3.5	4.3	4.2	3.8	4.1	2.8	3.1
Arkansas.	*	*4.2	*3.5	*	*	*	*	*	*
Louisiana[7]	- - -	*	*	*	*	*	*	*	*7.6
Oklahoma[7]	- - -	*3.3	3.3	*3.7	4.3	3.8	*	*	*
Texas	4.2	3.3	3.5	*	*	*	4.0	2.8	2.8
Mountain.	4.7	4.3	4.2	5.8	4.8	4.0	4.6	3.4	3.8
Arizona	5.0	4.5	4.3	5.4	5.0	4.3	*	*	*3.2
Colorado	4.4	4.6	4.8	*	*	*	*	*	*4.7
Idaho.	*	*5.7	*5.1	*	*	*	*	*	*
Montana	*	*	*	*7.6	*6.4	*	*	*	*
Nevada	*4.1	3.9	2.7	*	*	*	*	*4.0	*
New Mexico	4.9	3.8	3.9	4.9	*3.4	*3.4	*	*	*
Utah	*3.6	3.7	4.3	*	*	*	*	*	*5.1
Wyoming	*	*	*	*	*	*	*	*	*
Pacific.	4.5	3.6	3.5	6.5	4.7	4.0	3.7	3.5	3.2
Alaska.	*	*	*	*5.7	*4.2	*3.2	*	*	*
California	4.4	3.5	3.5	6.3	*5.0	*3.7	3.6	3.1	2.9
Hawaii	*6.6	*5.3	*4.4	*	*	*	4.2	5.4	4.7
Oregon	6.5	4.6	3.3	*	*	*	*5.3	*3.1	*3.1
Washington	4.9	3.3	3.5	*8.5	*4.8	*5.0	*2.7	3.6	3.1

See footnotes at end of table.

Table 24 (page 3 of 3). Neonatal mortality rates, by race and Hispanic origin of mother, geographic division, and state: United States, average annual 1989–1991, 1998–2000, and 2001–2003

[Data are based on linked birth and death certificates for infants]

* Estimates are considered unreliable. Rates preceded by an asterisk are based on fewer than 50 deaths in the numerator. Rates not shown are based on fewer than 20 deaths in the numerator.
- - - Data not available.
[1]Rates based on unweighted birth cohort data.
[2]Rates based on period file using weighted data. See Appendix I, National Vital Statistics System, Linked Birth/Infant Death Data Set.
[3]Infants under 28 days of age.
[4]Rates for white and black are substituted for non-Hispanic white and non-Hispanic black for Louisiana 1989, Oklahoma 1989–1990, and New Hampshire 1989–1991.
[5]Persons of Hispanic origin may be of any race. See Appendix II, Hispanic origin.
[6]Includes persons of Hispanic origin.
[7]Rates for Hispanic origin exclude data from states not reporting Hispanic origin on the birth certificate for 1 or more years in a 3-year period.

NOTES: Starting with 2003 data, some states reported multiple-race data. The multiple-race data for these states were bridged to the single race categories of the 1977 Office of Management and Budget standards for comparability with other states. See Appendix II, Race. National linked files do not exist for 1992–1994.

SOURCE: Centers for Disease Control and Prevention, National Center for Health Statistics, National Vital Statistics System, Linked Birth/Infant Death Data Set.

Table 25. Infant mortality rates and international rankings: Selected countries and territories, selected years 1960–2003

[Data are based on reporting by countries]

Country[2]	1960	1970	1980	1990	2000	2001	2002	2003	International rankings[1] 1960	International rankings[1] 2003
	Infant[3] deaths per 1,000 live births									
Australia	20.2	17.9	10.7	8.2	5.2	5.3	5.0	4.8	5	17
Austria	37.5	25.9	14.3	7.8	4.8	4.8	4.1	4.5	24	16
Belgium	23.9	21.1	12.1	8.0	4.8	4.5	4.4	4.3	11	12
Bulgaria	45.1	27.3	20.2	14.8	13.3	14.4	13.3	12.0	30	35
Canada	27.3	18.8	10.4	6.8	5.3	5.2	5.4	5.3	15	25
Chile	120.3	82.2	33.0	16.0	11.7	8.3	7.8	7.8	36	31
Costa Rica	67.8	65.4	20.3	15.3	10.2	10.8	11.2	10.1	33	34
Cuba	37.3	38.7	19.6	10.7	7.2	6.2	6.5	6.3	23	27
Czech Republic	20.0	20.2	16.9	10.8	4.1	4.0	4.2	3.9	4	7
Denmark	21.5	14.2	8.4	7.5	5.3	4.9	4.4	4.4	8	15
England and Wales	22.4	18.5	12.0	7.9	5.6	5.4	5.2	5.3	9	25
Finland	21.0	13.2	7.6	5.6	3.8	3.2	3.0	3.1	6	4
France	27.5	18.2	10.0	7.3	4.4	4.5	4.1	3.9	16	7
Germany[4]	35.0	22.5	12.4	7.0	4.4	4.3	4.2	4.2	22	11
Greece	40.1	29.6	17.9	9.7	5.9	5.1	5.1	4.8	25	17
Hong Kong	41.5	19.2	11.2	5.9	2.9	2.7	2.4	2.3	26	1
Hungary	47.6	35.9	23.2	14.8	9.2	8.1	7.2	7.3	31	30
Ireland	29.3	19.5	11.1	8.2	6.2	5.7	5.0	5.1	18	21
Israel[5]	31.0	18.9	15.6	9.9	5.4	5.1	5.4	4.9	20	20
Italy	43.9	29.6	14.6	8.2	4.5	4.7	4.5	4.3	29	12
Japan	30.7	13.1	7.5	4.6	3.2	3.1	3.0	3.0	19	3
Netherlands	17.9	12.7	8.6	7.1	5.1	5.4	5.0	4.8	2	17
New Zealand	22.6	16.7	13.0	8.4	6.3	5.6	6.2	5.2	10	23
Northern Ireland	27.2	22.9	13.4	7.5	5.1	6.1	4.7	5.2	14	23
Norway	18.9	12.7	8.1	7.0	3.8	3.9	3.5	3.4	3	6
Poland	54.8	36.7	25.5	19.3	8.1	7.7	7.5	7.0	32	29
Portugal	77.5	55.5	24.3	11.0	5.5	5.0	5.0	4.1	35	9
Puerto Rico	43.3	27.9	18.5	13.4	9.9	9.2	9.8	9.8	27	33
Romania	75.7	49.4	29.3	26.9	18.6	18.4	17.3	16.7	34	37
Russian Federation[6]	- - -	- - -	22.0	17.6	15.2	14.6	13.2	12.4	- - -	36
Scotland	26.4	19.6	12.1	7.7	5.7	5.5	5.3	5.1	13	21
Singapore	34.8	21.4	11.7	6.7	2.5	2.2	2.9	2.5	21	2
Slovakia	28.6	25.7	20.9	12.0	8.6	6.2	7.6	7.9	17	32
Spain	43.7	28.1	12.3	7.6	3.9	4.4	4.1	4.1	28	9
Sweden	16.6	11.0	6.9	6.0	3.4	3.7	3.3	3.1	1	4
Switzerland	21.1	15.1	9.1	6.8	4.9	5.0	4.5	4.3	7	12
United States	26.0	20.0	12.6	9.2	6.9	6.8	7.0	6.9	12	28

- - - Data not available.

[1]Rankings are from lowest to highest infant mortality rates (IMR). Countries with the same IMR receive the same rank. The country with the next highest IMR is assigned the rank it would have received had the lower-ranked countries not been tied, i.e., skip a rank. Some of the variation in IMRs is due to differences among countries in distinguishing between fetal and infant deaths.

[2]Refers to countries, territories, cities, or geographic areas with at least 1 million population and with complete counts of live births and infant deaths according to the United Nations Demographic Yearbook.

[3]Under 1 year of age.

[4]Rates for 1990 and earlier years were calculated by combining information from the Federal Republic of Germany and the German Democratic Republic.

[5]Includes data for East Jerusalem and Israeli residents in certain other territories under occupation by Israeli military forces since June 1967.

[6]Excludes infants born alive after less than 28 weeks gestation, of less than 1,000 grams in weight and 35 centimeters in length, who die within 7 days of birth.

NOTE: Some rates for selected countries and selected years were revised and differ from previous editions of Health, United States.

SOURCES: Organisation for Economic Cooperation and Development (OECD): OECD Health Data 2005, A Comparative Analysis of 30 Countries, www.oecd.org/els/health/; United Nations: 2000 Demographic Yearbook, United Nations Publication, Sales No. E/F.02.XIII.1, New York, 2002; World Health Organization Statistical Information System (WHOSIS), www3.who.int/whosis/; United States and Puerto Rico: Centers for Disease Control and Prevention, National Center for Health Statistics. Vital Statistics of the United States, vol. II, mortality part A (selected years). Public Health Service. Washington, DC; Sweden: Statistics Sweden; Costa Rica: Dirección General de Estadísticas y Censos. Elaboracón y estimación, Centro Centroamericano de Población, Universidad de Costa Rica, http://ccp.ucr.ac.cr/observa/index1.htm; Russian Federation: Goskomstat, www.gks.ru/eng/; Israel: Central Bureau Statistics of Israel, www.cbs.gov.il/engindex.htm.

Table 26 (page 1 of 2). Life expectancy at birth and at 65 years of age, by sex: Selected countries and territories, selected years 1980–2002

[Data are based on reporting by countries]

Country	Male							Female						
	1980	1990	1995	2000	2001	2002	2002	1980	1990	1995	2000	2001	2002	2002
At birth	Life expectancy in years						Rank	Life expectancy in years						Rank
Australia	71.0	73.9	75.0	76.6	77.0	77.4	6	78.1	80.1	80.8	82.0	82.4	82.6	7
Austria	69.0	72.2	73.3	75.1	75.6	75.8	15	76.1	78.8	79.9	81.1	81.5	81.7	10
Belgium	70.0	72.7	73.4	74.6	74.9	75.1	22	76.8	79.4	80.2	80.8	81.1	81.1	15
Bulgaria	68.5	68.3	67.4	68.5	68.6	68.9	34	73.9	75.0	74.9	75.1	75.4	75.6	35
Canada	71.7	74.4	75.1	76.7	77.0	77.2	7	78.9	80.8	81.1	81.9	82.1	82.1	8
Chile	- - -	71.1	71.8	72.6	72.7	72.9	29	- - -	76.9	77.8	78.6	78.7	78.9	29
Costa Rica	71.9	74.7	74.0	75.4	75.6	76.2	12	77.0	79.1	78.6	80.2	79.9	81.0	18
Cuba	72.2	74.6	75.4	74.7	74.7	74.7	25	- - -	76.9	77.7	79.0	79.2	79.2	28
Czech Republic[1]	66.8	67.6	69.7	71.7	72.1	72.1	30	73.9	75.4	76.6	78.4	78.5	78.7	32
Denmark	71.2	72.0	72.7	74.5	74.7	74.8	24	77.3	77.7	77.8	79.3	79.3	79.5	27
England and Wales	70.8	73.1	74.3	75.6	76.0	76.2	12	76.8	78.6	79.5	80.3	80.6	80.7	19
Finland	69.2	70.9	72.8	74.2	74.6	74.9	23	77.6	78.9	80.2	81.0	81.5	81.5	11
France	70.2	72.8	73.9	75.3	75.5	75.8	15	78.4	80.9	81.8	82.7	82.9	83.0	4
Germany[2]	69.6	72.0	73.3	75.0	75.6	75.4	19	76.1	78.4	79.7	81.0	81.3	81.2	14
Greece	72.2	74.6	75.0	75.5	75.4	75.4	19	76.8	79.5	80.3	80.6	80.7	80.7	19
Hong Kong	71.6	74.6	76.0	78.0	78.4	78.6	1	77.9	80.3	81.5	83.9	84.6	84.5	2
Hungary	65.5	65.1	65.3	67.4	68.1	68.4	35	72.7	73.7	74.5	75.9	76.4	76.7	34
Ireland	70.1	72.1	72.9	73.4	74.7	75.2	21	75.6	77.6	78.4	79.1	79.7	80.3	25
Israel	72.2	75.1	75.5	76.7	77.1	77.5	5	75.8	78.5	79.5	81.1	81.6	81.4	13
Italy	70.6	73.6	74.9	76.6	76.7	76.8	8	77.4	80.1	81.3	82.5	82.8	82.9	6
Japan	73.4	75.9	76.4	77.7	78.1	78.3	2	78.8	81.9	82.9	84.6	84.9	85.2	1
Netherlands	72.5	73.8	74.6	75.5	75.8	76.0	14	79.2	80.9	80.4	80.5	80.7	80.7	19
New Zealand	70.0	72.4	74.4	76.3	76.3	76.3	11	76.3	78.3	79.7	81.1	81.1	81.1	15
Northern Ireland	68.3	72.1	73.5	74.8	75.2	75.6	18	75.0	78.0	78.9	79.8	80.1	80.4	24
Norway	72.3	73.4	74.8	76.0	76.2	76.4	10	79.2	79.8	80.8	81.4	81.5	81.5	11
Poland	66.0	66.7	67.6	69.7	70.2	70.4	32	74.4	76.3	76.4	77.9	78.3	78.8	31
Portugal	67.7	70.4	71.6	73.2	73.5	73.8	27	75.2	77.4	78.7	80.0	80.3	80.5	22
Puerto Rico	70.8	69.1	69.6	71.1	71.4	71.6	31	76.9	77.2	78.9	80.1	80.3	80.5	22
Romania	66.6	66.6	65.5	67.8	67.7	67.4	36	71.9	73.1	73.5	74.8	75.0	74.8	36
Russian Federation	61.4	63.8	58.3	59.2	59.1	58.9	37	73.0	74.4	71.7	72.4	72.3	72.0	37
Scotland	69.0	71.1	72.1	73.1	73.3	73.5	28	75.2	76.7	77.7	78.6	78.8	78.9	29
Singapore	69.8	73.1	74.2	76.1	76.4	76.5	9	74.7	77.6	78.6	80.1	80.3	81.1	15
Slovakia[1]	66.8	66.6	68.4	69.2	69.6	69.9	33	74.3	75.4	76.3	77.4	77.7	77.8	33
Spain	72.5	73.3	74.3	75.7	75.6	75.8	15	78.6	80.3	81.5	82.5	82.9	83.5	3
Sweden	72.8	74.8	76.2	77.4	77.6	77.7	4	78.8	80.4	81.4	82.0	82.1	82.1	8
Switzerland	72.8	74.0	75.3	76.9	77.4	77.8	3	79.6	80.7	81.7	82.6	83.0	83.0	4
United States	70.0	71.8	72.5	74.1	74.4	74.5	26	77.4	78.8	78.9	79.5	79.8	79.9	26

See footnotes at end of table.

[Data are based on reporting by countries]

	Male							Female						
Country	1980	1990	1995	2000	2001	2002	2002	1980	1990	1995	2000	2001	2002	2002
At 65 years	Life expectancy in years						Rank	Life expectancy in years						Rank
Australia	13.7	15.2	15.7	16.9	17.2	17.4	4	17.9	19.0	19.5	20.4	20.7	20.8	5
Austria	12.9	14.3	14.9	16.0	16.3	16.3	16	16.3	17.8	18.6	19.4	19.8	19.7	12
Belgium	13.0	14.3	14.8	15.5	15.8	15.8	22	16.9	18.5	19.1	19.5	19.7	19.7	12
Bulgaria	12.7	12.9	12.8	12.8	13.1	13.1	33	14.7	15.4	15.4	15.4	15.8	15.8	34
Canada	14.5	15.7	16.0	16.8	17.1	17.2	7	18.9	19.9	20.0	20.4	20.6	20.6	6
Chile	- - -	14.6	14.9	15.3	15.4	15.4	25	- - -	17.6	18.1	18.6	18.7	18.8	25
Costa Rica	16.1	17.1	16.7	17.2	17.1	17.8	2	18.1	19.3	18.6	19.6	19.4	20.5	8
Cuba	- - -	- - -	- - -	16.7	16.8	16.8	10	- - -	- - -	- - -	19.0	19.3	19.3	19
Czech Republic[1]	11.2	11.6	12.7	13.7	14.0	14.0	30	14.3	15.2	16.0	17.1	17.2	17.4	31
Denmark	13.6	14.0	14.1	15.2	15.2	15.4	25	17.6	17.8	17.5	18.3	18.4	18.3	28
England and Wales	12.9	14.1	14.8	15.8	16.1	16.3	16	16.9	17.9	18.3	19.0	19.2	19.2	21
Finland	12.5	13.7	14.5	15.5	15.7	15.8	22	16.5	17.7	18.6	19.3	19.6	19.6	17
France	13.6	15.5	16.1	16.7	16.9	17.0	8	18.2	19.8	20.6	21.2	21.3	21.3	3
Germany[2]	13.0	14.0	14.7	15.7	16.0	16.2	18	16.7	17.6	18.5	19.4	19.6	19.7	12
Greece	14.6	15.7	16.1	16.2	16.6	16.7	11	16.8	18.0	18.4	18.3	18.7	18.8	25
Hong Kong	13.9	15.3	16.2	17.3	17.7	17.8	2	13.9	18.8	19.5	21.5	22.1	22.0	2
Hungary	11.6	12.0	12.1	12.7	13.0	13.1	33	14.6	15.3	15.8	16.4	16.7	17.0	32
Ireland	12.6	13.3	13.6	14.6	15.0	15.3	27	15.7	16.9	17.3	17.8	18.3	18.6	27
Israel	14.4	15.9	16.0	16.9	17.2	17.3	6	15.8	17.8	18.0	19.3	19.8	19.7	12
Italy	13.3	15.1	15.8	16.5	16.5	16.6	13	17.1	18.8	19.6	20.4	20.4	20.6	6
Japan	14.6	16.2	16.5	17.5	17.8	18.0	1	17.7	20.0	20.9	22.4	22.7	23.0	1
Netherlands	13.7	14.4	14.7	15.3	15.5	15.6	24	18.0	18.9	19.0	19.2	19.3	19.3	19
New Zealand	13.2	14.7	15.6	16.7	16.7	16.7	11	17.0	18.3	19.1	20.0	20.0	20.0	10
Northern Ireland	11.9	13.7	14.4	15.3	15.7	15.9	21	15.8	17.5	18.0	18.5	18.7	18.9	24
Norway	14.3	14.6	15.1	16.0	16.1	16.2	18	18.0	18.5	19.1	19.7	19.8	19.7	12
Poland	12.0	12.7	12.9	13.6	13.9	14.0	30	15.5	16.2	16.6	17.3	17.6	17.9	30
Portugal	12.9	13.9	14.6	15.3	15.6	15.0	29	16.5	17.0	17.8	18.7	18.9	19.0	23
Puerto Rico	- - -	- - -	- - -	- - -	- - -	- - -		- - -	- - -	- - -	- - -	- - -	- - -	
Romania	12.6	13.3	12.9	13.5	13.5	13.0	35	14.2	15.3	15.4	15.9	16.1	15.8	34
Russian Federation	11.6	12.1	10.9	11.1	11.1	10.9	36	15.6	15.9	15.1	15.2	15.3	15.1	36
Scotland	12.3	13.1	13.8	14.7	14.9	15.1	28	16.2	16.7	17.3	17.8	18.0	18.1	29
Singapore	12.6	14.5	14.6	15.8	16.0	16.0	20	15.4	16.9	17.3	19.0	19.2	19.2	21
Slovakia[1]	12.3	12.2	12.7	12.9	13.0	13.3	32	15.4	15.7	16.1	16.5	16.8	17.0	32
Spain	14.8	15.4	16.0	16.5	16.5	16.5	15	17.9	19.0	19.8	20.4	20.4	20.5	8
Sweden	14.3	15.3	16.0	16.7	16.9	16.9	9	17.9	19.0	19.6	20.0	20.1	20.0	10
Switzerland	14.4	15.3	16.1	16.9	17.2	17.4	4	17.9	19.4	20.2	20.7	21.0	21.0	4
United States	14.1	15.1	15.6	16.3	16.4	16.6	13	18.3	18.9	18.9	19.2	19.4	19.5	18

- - - Data not available.

[1]In 1993, Czechoslovakia was divided into two nations, the Czech Republic and Slovakia. Data for years prior to 1993 are from the Czech and Slovak regions of Czechoslovakia.

[2]Until 1990, estimates refer to the Federal Republic of Germany; from 1995 onwards, data refer to Germany after reunification.

NOTES: Rankings are from highest to lowest life expectancy (LE) for the most recent year available. Since calculation of LE estimates varies among countries, comparisons among them and their interpretation should be made with caution. See Appendix II, Life expectancy. Countries with the same LE receive the same rank. The country with the next lower LE is assigned the rank it would have received had the higher-ranked countries not been tied, i.e., skip a rank. Some estimates for selected countries and selected years were revised and differ from the previous editions of Health, United States. Data for additional years are available. See Appendix III.

SOURCES: Organisation for Economic Cooperation and Development (OECD) Health Data 2005, A Comparative Analysis of 30 Countries, www.oecd.org/els/health/; European health for all database, World Health Organization Regional Office for Europe, www.who.dk/hfadb; Centers for Disease Control and Prevention, National Center for Health Statistics. Vital statistics of the United States (selected years). Public Health Service. Washington, DC. www.cdc.gov/nchs/fastats/lifexpec.htm; Puerto Rico: Commonwealth of Puerto Rico, Department of Health, Auxiliary Secretariat for Planning, Evaluation, Statistics, and Information Systems: Unpublished data; Singapore: Singapore Department of Statistics, Population Statistics Section, www.singstat.gov.sg/stats/singstat/internet.html; England and Wales, Northern Ireland, and Scotland: Government Actuary's Department, London www.gad.gov.uk; Hong Kong: Government of Hong Kong, Special Administrative Region, Department of Health, http://info.gov.hk/dh/index.htm; Costa Rica: Instituto Nacional de Estadística y Censos (INEC) y Centro Centroamericano de Población (CCP) http://ccp.ucr.ac.cr/observa/series/serie3.htm; Chile: Instituto Nacional de Estadísticas, Departamento de Demografía. Gobierno de Chile. Ministerio de Salud Departamento de Estadísticas e Información de Salud; Puerto Rico (1999–2001): Pan American Health Organization, Special Program for Health Analysis. Regional Initiative for Health Basic Data, Technical Information Health System, Washington, DC 2005. Cuba and Singapore (2000–2001): WHO Statistical Information System (WHOSIS) www3.who.int/whosis/core/core_select.cfm.

Table 27. Life expectancy at birth, at 65 years of age, and at 75 years of age, by race and sex: United States, selected years 1900–2003

[Data are based on death certificates]

Specified age and year	All races Both sexes	All races Male	All races Female	White Both sexes	White Male	White Female	Black or African American[1] Both sexes	Black or African American[1] Male	Black or African American[1] Female
At birth				Remaining life expectancy in years					
1900[2,3]	47.3	46.3	48.3	47.6	46.6	48.7	33.0	32.5	33.5
1950[3]	68.2	65.6	71.1	69.1	66.5	72.2	60.8	59.1	62.9
1960[3]	69.7	66.6	73.1	70.6	67.4	74.1	63.6	61.1	66.3
1970	70.8	67.1	74.7	71.7	68.0	75.6	64.1	60.0	68.3
1980	73.7	70.0	77.4	74.4	70.7	78.1	68.1	63.8	72.5
1990	75.4	71.8	78.8	76.1	72.7	79.4	69.1	64.5	73.6
1995	75.8	72.5	78.9	76.5	73.4	79.6	69.6	65.2	73.9
1996	76.1	73.1	79.1	76.8	73.9	79.7	70.2	66.1	74.2
1997	76.5	73.6	79.4	77.1	74.3	79.9	71.1	67.2	74.7
1998	76.7	73.8	79.5	77.3	74.5	80.0	71.3	67.6	74.8
1999	76.7	73.9	79.4	77.3	74.6	79.9	71.4	67.8	74.7
2000	77.0	74.3	79.7	77.6	74.9	80.1	71.9	68.3	75.2
2001	77.2	74.4	79.8	77.7	75.0	80.2	72.2	68.6	75.5
2002	77.3	74.5	79.9	77.7	75.1	80.3	72.3	68.8	75.6
2003	77.5	74.8	80.1	78.0	75.3	80.5	72.7	69.0	76.1
At 65 years									
1950[3]	13.9	12.8	15.0	- - -	12.8	15.1	13.9	12.9	14.9
1960[3]	14.3	12.8	15.8	14.4	12.9	15.9	13.9	12.7	15.1
1970	15.2	13.1	17.0	15.2	13.1	17.1	14.2	12.5	15.7
1980	16.4	14.1	18.3	16.5	14.2	18.4	15.1	13.0	16.8
1990	17.2	15.1	18.9	17.3	15.2	19.1	15.4	13.2	17.2
1995	17.4	15.6	18.9	17.6	15.7	19.1	15.6	13.6	17.1
1996	17.5	15.7	19.0	17.6	15.8	19.1	15.8	13.9	17.2
1997	17.7	15.9	19.2	17.8	16.0	19.3	16.1	14.2	17.6
1998	17.8	16.0	19.2	17.8	16.1	19.3	16.1	14.3	17.4
1999	17.7	16.1	19.1	17.8	16.1	19.2	16.0	14.3	17.3
2000	18.0	16.2	19.3	18.0	16.3	19.4	16.2	14.2	17.7
2001	18.1	16.4	19.4	18.2	16.5	19.5	16.4	14.4	17.9
2002	18.2	16.6	19.5	18.2	16.6	19.5	16.6	14.6	18.0
2003	18.4	16.8	19.8	18.5	16.9	19.8	17.0	14.9	18.5
At 75 years									
1980	10.4	8.8	11.5	10.4	8.8	11.5	9.7	8.3	10.7
1990	10.9	9.4	12.0	11.0	9.4	12.0	10.2	8.6	11.2
1995	11.0	9.7	11.9	11.1	9.7	12.0	10.2	8.8	11.1
1996	11.1	9.8	12.0	11.1	9.8	12.0	10.3	9.0	11.2
1997	11.2	9.9	12.1	11.2	9.9	12.1	10.7	9.3	11.5
1998	11.3	10.0	12.2	11.3	10.0	12.2	10.5	9.2	11.3
1999	11.2	10.0	12.1	11.2	10.0	12.1	10.4	9.2	11.1
2000	11.4	10.1	12.3	11.4	10.1	12.3	10.7	9.2	11.6
2001	11.5	10.2	12.4	11.5	10.2	12.3	10.8	9.3	11.7
2002	11.5	10.3	12.4	11.5	10.3	12.3	10.9	9.5	11.7
2003	11.8	10.5	12.6	11.7	10.5	12.6	11.4	9.8	12.4

- - - Data not available.

[1]Data shown for 1900–1960 are for the nonwhite population.

[2]Death registration area only. The death registration area increased from 10 states and the District of Columbia in 1900 to the coterminous United States in 1933. See Appendix II, Registration area.

[3]Includes deaths of persons who were not residents of the 50 states and the District of Columbia.

NOTES: Populations for computing life expectancy for 1991–1999 are 1990-based postcensal estimates of U.S. resident population. See Appendix I, Population Census and Population Estimates. In 1997, life table methodology was revised to construct complete life tables by single years of age that extend to age 100 (Anderson RN. Method for constructing complete annual U.S. life tables. National Center for Health Statistics. Vital Health Stat 2(129). 1999). Previously, abridged life tables were constructed for 5-year age groups ending with 85 years and over. Life table values for 2000 and later years were computed using a slight modification of the new life table method due to a change in the age detail of populations received from the U.S. Census Bureau. Starting with 2003 data, California, Hawaii, Idaho, Maine, Montana, New York, and Wisconsin reported multiple-race data. The multiple-race data for these states were bridged to the single race categories of the 1977 Office of Management and Budget standards for comparability with other states. Data for additional years are available. See Appendix III.

SOURCES: Centers for Disease Control and Prevention, National Center for Health Statistics, National Vital Statistics System; Grove RD, Hetzel AM. Vital statistics rates in the United States, 1940–1960. Washington, DC: U.S. Government Printing Office, 1968; life expectancy trend data available from: www.cdc.gov/nchs/deaths.htm; Hoyert DL, Heron M, Murphy SL, Kung HC. Deaths: Final data for 2003. National vital statistics reports. Vol 54 no 13. Hyattsville, MD: National Center for Health Statistics. 2006.

This table will be updated on the Web. Go to www.cdc.gov/nchs/hus.htm.

Table 28 (page 1 of 2). Age-adjusted death rates, by race, Hispanic origin, geographic division, and state: United States, average annual 1979–1981, 1989–1991, and 2001–2003

[Data are based on death certificates]

Geographic division and state	All persons			White	Black or African American	American Indian or Alaska Native	Asian or Pacific Islander	Hispanic or Latino[1]	White, not Hispanic or Latino
	1979–1981	1989–1991	2001–2003	2001–2003	2001–2003	2001–2003	2001–2003	2001–2003	2001–2003
	Age-adjusted death rate per 100,000 population[2]								
United States	1,022.8	942.2	842.7	826.1	1,081.6	683.0	475.6	631.4	834.5
New England	979.9	882.4	784.3	784.9	874.5	*	373.3	542.0	782.7
Connecticut	961.5	857.5	756.1	749.0	879.6	*	312.3	575.5	744.4
Maine	1,002.9	918.7	836.7	836.1	837.2	*	493.6	*	834.8
Massachusetts	982.6	884.8	788.5	792.1	874.1	*	379.3	560.2	791.3
New Hampshire	982.3	891.7	776.7	779.6	731.3	*	336.9	394.3	768.0
Rhode Island	990.8	889.6	798.8	799.3	899.4	*	499.7	456.5	800.6
Vermont	990.2	908.6	784.1	787.6	*	*	*	*	789.5
Middle Atlantic	1,059.1	967.8	813.8	805.6	952.2	*	385.8	596.2	806.0
New Jersey	1,047.5	956.0	810.3	792.3	1,055.1	*	367.2	544.7	803.5
New York	1,051.8	973.7	781.6	785.1	841.5	*	394.8	603.9	779.2
Pennsylvania	1,076.4	963.4	859.9	838.5	1,142.0	*	372.5	704.0	837.2
East North Central	1,048.0	957.9	867.2	842.1	1,136.8	*	389.9	535.1	844.1
Illinois	1,063.7	973.8	849.3	815.6	1,148.1	*	393.4	508.2	824.4
Indiana	1,048.3	962.0	901.6	886.8	1,154.3	*	311.6	522.1	890.7
Michigan	1,050.2	966.0	868.1	833.7	1,134.9	*	377.7	651.0	827.8
Ohio	1,070.6	967.4	901.6	882.0	1,124.9	*	366.1	622.5	880.7
Wisconsin	956.4	879.1	793.2	780.7	1,075.4	*	493.9	381.8	783.9
West North Central	951.6	876.6	815.0	800.7	1,124.7	*	442.8	592.6	797.1
Iowa	919.9	848.2	774.4	772.3	1,066.4	*	418.9	590.5	772.7
Kansas	940.1	867.2	834.9	824.2	1,152.0	*	332.4	577.1	818.6
Minnesota	892.9	825.2	736.7	730.4	925.0	1,189.9	516.1	515.5	722.6
Missouri	1,033.7	952.4	909.4	888.0	1,162.9	*	421.2	719.2	888.1
Nebraska	930.6	867.9	799.9	790.1	1,105.7	1,176.4	417.9	583.0	787.9
North Dakota	922.4	818.4	765.1	747.0	*	1,480.5	*	*	724.6
South Dakota	941.9	846.4	782.1	745.3	*	1,494.8	*	337.6	746.6
South Atlantic	1,033.1	951.3	859.2	819.9	1,089.5	*	375.7	584.2	833.5
Delaware	1,069.7	1,001.9	856.7	826.3	1,065.1	*	358.8	673.9	826.6
District of Columbia	1,243.1	1,255.3	1,011.2	630.0	1,246.2	*	438.8	147.1	674.1
Florida	960.8	870.9	787.0	766.1	1,024.5	*	330.9	620.7	789.0
Georgia	1,094.3	1,037.4	949.0	903.8	1,130.4	*	373.9	360.5	911.1
Maryland	1,063.3	985.2	866.9	813.8	1,084.5	*	377.0	299.0	824.2
North Carolina	1,050.4	986.0	907.3	865.6	1,106.6	929.1	358.4	289.9	870.6
South Carolina	1,104.6	1,030.0	939.3	886.7	1,111.6	*	389.9	358.2	889.8
Virginia	1,054.0	963.1	857.2	824.3	1,076.5	*	437.7	481.9	827.3
West Virginia	1,100.3	1,031.5	994.0	994.0	1,157.3	*	*	327.1	996.7
East South Central	1,079.3	1,031.6	991.3	959.2	1,181.8	*	401.6	386.3	962.1
Alabama	1,091.2	1,037.9	997.2	957.7	1,162.4	*	329.5	323.5	962.1
Kentucky	1,088.9	1,024.5	983.5	977.0	1,157.5	*	419.7	763.2	977.0
Mississippi	1,108.7	1,071.4	1,024.8	961.3	1,186.1	*	461.0	224.9	965.1
Tennessee	1,045.5	1,011.8	977.1	946.8	1,215.4	*	413.6	305.2	950.5
West South Central	1,036.8	974.9	904.9	880.9	1,159.0	*	418.9	712.1	905.8
Arkansas	1,017.0	996.3	949.5	924.5	1,172.5	*	568.0	191.0	933.8
Louisiana	1,132.6	1,074.6	1,004.5	935.9	1,207.0	*	481.7	510.7	943.5
Oklahoma	1,025.6	961.4	967.9	966.3	1,161.1	*	424.3	699.9	970.1
Texas	1,014.9	947.6	863.6	847.5	1,129.6	*	406.9	721.1	875.0
Mountain	961.8	878.2	808.1	803.1	990.8	933.5	515.0	741.5	804.3
Arizona	951.5	873.5	788.0	778.9	977.3	966.5	452.5	747.5	778.7
Colorado	941.1	856.1	784.5	785.9	928.0	514.4	458.1	770.9	781.0
Idaho	936.7	856.6	800.4	799.0	1,024.9	1,057.0	532.0	599.8	801.6
Montana	1,013.6	890.2	841.3	822.9	900.0	1,288.3	446.5	708.4	821.2
Nevada	1,077.4	1,017.4	920.1	921.2	1,125.1	764.4	603.3	518.3	952.7
New Mexico	967.1	891.9	820.1	814.1	877.0	900.6	432.4	801.5	805.7
Utah	924.9	823.2	778.2	778.0	987.4	866.3	617.7	618.8	781.4
Wyoming	1,016.1	897.4	852.9	845.8	767.9	1,358.2	*	768.9	847.1

See footnotes at end of table.

This table will be updated on the Web. Go to www.cdc.gov/nchs/hus.htm.

Table 28 (page 2 of 2). Age-adjusted death rates, by race, Hispanic origin, geographic division, and state: United States, average annual 1979–1981, 1989–1991, and 2001–2003

[Data are based on death certificates]

Geographic division and state	All persons			White	Black or African American	American Indian or Alaska Native	Asian or Pacific Islander	Hispanic or Latino[1]	White, not Hispanic or Latino
	1979–1981	1989–1991	2001–2003	2001–2003	2001–2003	2001–2003	2001–2003	2001–2003	2001–2003
Age-adjusted death rate per 100,000 population[2]									
Pacific	966.5	900.1	767.9	784.1	1,035.3	*	528.7	606.1	806.6
Alaska	1,087.4	944.6	812.5	762.9	742.4	1,161.7	555.0	656.8	764.4
California	975.5	911.0	762.3	778.8	1,049.0	*	496.2	605.9	808.5
Hawaii	801.2	752.2	655.0	682.1	372.3	*	647.9	1,163.8	677.0
Oregon	953.9	893.0	823.7	827.5	1,004.4	*	498.9	459.2	834.9
Washington	947.7	869.4	785.2	788.9	965.9	960.0	540.0	540.9	792.4

* Data for states with population under 10,000 in the middle year of a 3-year period or fewer than 50 deaths for the 3-year period are considered unreliable and are not shown. Data for American Indian or Alaska Native category in states with more than 10% misclassification of American Indian or Alaska Native deaths on death certificates or without information on misclassification are also not shown (Support Services International, Inc. Methodology for adjusting IHS mortality data for miscoding race-ethnicity of American Indian or Alaska Native on state death certificates. Report submitted to Indian Health Service. 1996). Division death rates for American Indians or Alaska Natives are not shown when any state within the division does not meet reliability criteria.

[1]Caution should be used when comparing death rates by Hispanic origin and race among states. Estimates of death rates may be affected by several factors including possible misreporting of race and Hispanic origin on the death certificate, migration patterns between United States and country of origin for persons who were born outside the United States, and possible biases in population estimates. See Appendix I, National Vital Statistics System, Mortality File and Appendix II, Hispanic origin; Race.

[2]Average annual death rates, age adjusted using the year 2000 standard population. Prior to 2001, age-adjusted rates were calculated using standard million proportions based on rounded population numbers. Starting with 2001 data, unrounded population numbers are used to calculate age-adjusted rates. See Appendix II, Age adjustment. Denominators for rates are resident population estimates for the middle year of each 3-year period, multiplied by 3. See Appendix I, Population Census and Population Estimates.

NOTES: The race groups, white, black, American Indian or Alaska Native, and Asian or Pacific Islander, include persons of Hispanic and non-Hispanic origin. Persons of Hispanic origin may be of any race. Death rates for the American Indian or Alaska Native and Asian or Pacific Islander populations are known to be underestimated. See Appendix II, Race, for a discussion of sources of bias in death rates by race and Hispanic origin. Starting with 2003 data, California, Hawaii, Idaho, Maine, Montana, New York, and Wisconsin reported multiple-race data. The multiple-race data for these states were bridged to the single race categories of the 1977 Office of Management and Budget standards for comparability with other states.

SOURCES: Centers for Disease Control and Prevention, National Center for Health Statistics, National Vital Statistics System; numerator data from annual mortality files; denominator data from state population estimates prepared by the U.S. Census Bureau 1980 from April 1, 1980 MARS Census File; 1990 from April 1, 1990 MARS Census File; 2002 from National Center for Health Statistics. Estimates of the July 1, 2002, resident populations of the United States by state and county, race, age, sex, and Hispanic origin, prepared under a collaborative arrangement with the U.S. Census Bureau. Available from: www.cdc.gov/nchs/about/major/dvs/popbridge/popbridge.htm. 2005.

This table will be updated on the Web. Go to www.cdc.gov/nchs/hus.htm.

Table 29 (page 1 of 4). Age-adjusted death rates for selected causes of death, by sex, race, and Hispanic origin: United States, selected years 1950–2003

[Data are based on death certificates]

Sex, race, Hispanic origin, and cause of death[1]	1950[2,3]	1960[2,3]	1970[3]	1980[3]	1990	2000[4]	2001	2002	2003
All persons	\multicolumn{9}{c}{Age-adjusted death rate per 100,000 population[5]}								
All causes	1,446.0	1,339.2	1,222.6	1,039.1	938.7	869.0	854.5	845.3	832.7
Diseases of heart	586.8	559.0	492.7	412.1	321.8	257.6	247.8	240.8	232.3
Ischemic heart disease	- - -	- - -	- - -	345.2	249.6	186.8	177.8	170.8	162.9
Cerebrovascular diseases	180.7	177.9	147.7	96.2	65.3	60.9	57.9	56.2	53.5
Malignant neoplasms	193.9	193.9	198.6	207.9	216.0	199.6	196.0	193.5	190.1
Trachea, bronchus, and lung	15.0	24.1	37.1	49.9	59.3	56.1	55.3	54.9	54.1
Colon, rectum, and anus	- - -	30.3	28.9	27.4	24.5	20.8	20.1	19.7	19.1
Prostate[6]	28.6	28.7	28.8	32.8	38.4	30.4	29.1	27.9	26.5
Breast[7]	31.9	31.7	32.1	31.9	33.3	26.8	26.0	25.6	25.3
Chronic lower respiratory diseases	- - -	- - -	- - -	28.3	37.2	44.2	43.7	43.5	43.3
Influenza and pneumonia	48.1	53.7	41.7	31.4	36.8	23.7	22.0	22.6	22.0
Chronic liver disease and cirrhosis	11.3	13.3	17.8	15.1	11.1	9.5	9.5	9.4	9.3
Diabetes mellitus	23.1	22.5	24.3	18.1	20.7	25.0	25.3	25.4	25.3
Human immunodeficiency virus (HIV) disease	- - -	- - -	- - -	- - -	10.2	5.2	5.0	4.9	4.7
Unintentional injuries	78.0	62.3	60.1	46.4	36.3	34.9	35.7	36.9	37.3
Motor vehicle-related injuries	24.6	23.1	27.6	22.3	18.5	15.4	15.3	15.7	15.3
Suicide[8]	13.2	12.5	13.1	12.2	12.5	10.4	10.7	10.9	10.8
Homicide[8]	5.1	5.0	8.8	10.4	9.4	5.9	7.1	6.1	6.0
Male									
All causes	1,674.2	1,609.0	1,542.1	1,348.1	1,202.8	1,053.8	1,029.1	1,013.7	994.3
Diseases of heart	697.0	687.6	634.0	538.9	412.4	320.0	305.4	297.4	286.6
Ischemic heart disease	- - -	- - -	- - -	459.7	328.2	241.4	228.5	220.4	209.9
Cerebrovascular diseases	186.4	186.1	157.4	102.2	68.5	62.4	59.0	56.5	54.1
Malignant neoplasms	208.1	225.1	247.6	271.2	280.4	248.9	243.7	238.9	233.3
Trachea, bronchus, and lung	24.6	43.6	67.5	85.2	91.1	76.7	75.2	73.2	71.7
Colon, rectum, and anus	- - -	31.8	32.3	32.8	30.4	25.1	24.2	23.7	22.9
Prostate	28.6	28.7	28.8	32.8	38.4	30.4	29.1	27.9	26.5
Chronic lower respiratory diseases	- - -	- - -	- - -	49.9	55.4	55.8	54.0	53.5	52.3
Influenza and pneumonia	55.0	65.8	54.0	42.1	47.8	28.9	26.6	27.0	26.1
Chronic liver disease and cirrhosis	15.0	18.5	24.8	21.3	15.9	13.4	13.2	12.9	13.0
Diabetes mellitus	18.8	19.9	23.0	18.1	21.7	27.8	28.1	28.6	28.9
Human immunodeficiency virus (HIV) disease	- - -	- - -	- - -	- - -	18.5	7.9	7.5	7.4	7.1
Unintentional injuries	101.8	85.5	87.4	69.0	52.9	49.3	50.2	51.5	51.8
Motor vehicle-related injuries	38.5	35.4	41.5	33.6	26.5	21.7	21.8	22.1	21.6
Suicide[8]	21.2	20.0	19.8	19.9	21.5	17.7	18.2	18.4	18.0
Homicide[8]	7.9	7.5	14.3	16.6	14.8	9.0	10.8	9.4	9.4
Female									
All causes	1,236.0	1,105.3	971.4	817.9	750.9	731.4	721.8	715.2	706.2
Diseases of heart	484.7	447.0	381.6	320.8	257.0	210.9	203.9	197.2	190.3
Ischemic heart disease	- - -	- - -	- - -	263.1	193.9	146.5	139.9	133.6	127.2
Cerebrovascular diseases	175.8	170.7	140.0	91.7	62.6	59.1	56.4	55.2	52.3
Malignant neoplasms	182.3	168.7	163.2	166.7	175.7	167.6	164.7	163.1	160.9
Trachea, bronchus, and lung	5.8	7.5	13.1	24.4	37.1	41.3	41.0	41.6	41.3
Colon, rectum, and anus	- - -	29.1	26.5	23.8	20.6	17.7	17.2	16.7	16.2
Breast	31.9	31.7	32.1	31.9	33.3	26.8	26.0	25.6	25.3
Chronic lower respiratory diseases	- - -	- - -	- - -	14.9	26.6	37.4	37.6	37.4	37.8
Influenza and pneumonia	41.9	43.8	32.7	25.1	30.5	20.7	19.2	19.9	19.4
Chronic liver disease and cirrhosis	7.8	8.7	11.9	9.9	7.1	6.2	6.2	6.3	6.0
Diabetes mellitus	27.0	24.7	25.1	18.0	19.9	23.0	23.1	23.0	22.5
Human immunodeficiency virus (HIV) disease	- - -	- - -	- - -	- - -	2.2	2.5	2.5	2.5	2.4
Unintentional injuries	54.0	40.0	35.1	26.1	21.5	22.0	22.5	23.5	24.1
Motor vehicle-related injuries	11.5	11.7	14.9	11.8	11.0	9.5	9.3	9.6	9.3
Suicide[8]	5.6	5.6	7.4	5.7	4.8	4.0	4.0	4.2	4.2
Homicide[8]	2.4	2.6	3.7	4.4	4.0	2.8	3.3	2.8	2.6

See footnotes at end of table.

This table will be updated on the Web. Go to www.cdc.gov/nchs/hus.htm.

Table 29 (page 2 of 4). Age-adjusted death rates for selected causes of death, by sex, race, and Hispanic origin: United States, selected years 1950–2003

[Data are based on death certificates]

Sex, race, Hispanic origin, and cause of death[1]	1950[2,3]	1960[2,3]	1970[3]	1980[3]	1990	2000[4]	2001	2002	2003
White[9]			Age-adjusted death rate per 100,000 population[5]						
All causes	1,410.8	1,311.3	1,193.3	1,012.7	909.8	849.8	836.5	829.0	817.0
Diseases of heart	584.8	559.0	492.2	409.4	317.0	253.4	243.5	236.7	228.2
Ischemic heart disease	- - -	- - -	- - -	347.6	249.7	185.6	176.5	169.8	161.7
Cerebrovascular diseases	175.5	172.7	143.5	93.2	62.8	58.8	55.8	54.2	51.4
Malignant neoplasms	194.6	193.1	196.7	204.2	211.6	197.2	193.9	191.7	188.5
Trachea, bronchus, and lung	15.2	24.0	36.7	49.2	58.6	56.2	55.6	55.3	54.5
Colon, rectum, and anus	- - -	30.9	29.2	27.4	24.1	20.3	19.6	19.2	18.6
Prostate[6]	28.4	27.7	27.4	30.5	35.5	27.8	26.6	25.7	24.4
Breast[7]	32.4	32.0	32.5	32.1	33.2	26.3	25.5	25.0	24.7
Chronic lower respiratory diseases	- - -	- - -	- - -	29.3	38.3	46.0	45.6	45.4	45.4
Influenza and pneumonia	44.8	50.4	39.8	30.9	36.4	23.5	21.7	22.6	21.9
Chronic liver disease and cirrhosis	11.5	13.2	16.6	13.9	10.5	9.6	9.6	9.6	9.5
Diabetes mellitus	22.9	21.7	22.9	16.7	18.8	22.8	23.0	23.1	23.0
Human immunodeficiency virus (HIV) disease	- - -	- - -	- - -	- - -	8.3	2.8	2.6	2.6	2.5
Unintentional injuries	77.0	60.4	57.8	45.3	35.5	35.1	36.0	37.5	38.2
Motor vehicle-related injuries	24.4	22.9	27.1	22.6	18.5	15.6	15.6	16.0	15.7
Suicide[8]	13.9	13.1	13.8	13.0	13.4	11.3	11.7	12.0	11.8
Homicide[8]	2.6	2.7	4.7	6.7	5.5	3.6	4.9	3.7	3.7
Black or African American[9]									
All causes	1,722.1	1,577.5	1,518.1	1,314.8	1,250.3	1,121.4	1,101.2	1,083.3	1,065.9
Diseases of heart	586.7	548.3	512.0	455.3	391.5	324.8	316.9	308.4	300.2
Ischemic heart disease	- - -	- - -	- - -	334.5	267.0	218.3	211.6	203.0	195.0
Cerebrovascular diseases	233.6	235.2	197.1	129.1	91.6	81.9	78.8	76.3	74.3
Malignant neoplasms	176.4	199.1	225.3	256.4	279.5	248.5	243.1	238.8	233.3
Trachea, bronchus, and lung	11.1	23.7	41.3	59.7	72.4	64.0	62.5	61.9	60.8
Colon, rectum, and anus	- - -	22.8	26.1	28.3	30.6	28.2	27.6	26.8	26.4
Prostate[6]	30.9	41.2	48.5	61.1	77.0	68.1	66.1	62.0	57.4
Breast[7]	25.3	27.9	28.9	31.7	38.1	34.5	34.4	34.0	34.0
Chronic lower respiratory diseases	- - -	- - -	- - -	19.2	28.1	31.6	30.9	31.2	30.1
Influenza and pneumonia	76.7	81.1	57.2	34.4	39.4	25.6	24.1	24.0	23.3
Chronic liver disease and cirrhosis	9.0	13.6	28.1	25.0	16.5	9.4	9.3	8.5	8.4
Diabetes mellitus	23.5	30.9	38.8	32.7	40.5	49.5	49.2	49.5	49.2
Human immunodeficiency virus (HIV) disease	- - -	- - -	- - -	- - -	26.7	23.3	22.8	22.5	21.3
Unintentional injuries	79.9	74.0	78.3	57.6	43.8	37.7	37.6	36.9	36.1
Motor vehicle-related injuries	26.0	24.2	31.1	20.2	18.8	15.7	15.4	15.0	14.9
Suicide[8]	4.5	5.0	6.2	6.5	7.1	5.5	5.5	5.3	5.2
Homicide[8]	28.3	26.0	44.0	39.0	36.3	20.5	21.2	21.0	21.0
American Indian or Alaska Native[9]									
All causes	- - -	- - -	- - -	867.0	716.3	709.3	686.7	677.4	685.0
Diseases of heart	- - -	- - -	- - -	240.6	200.6	178.2	159.6	157.4	160.2
Ischemic heart disease	- - -	- - -	- - -	173.6	139.1	129.1	114.0	114.0	114.1
Cerebrovascular diseases	- - -	- - -	- - -	57.8	40.7	45.0	41.3	37.5	34.6
Malignant neoplasms	- - -	- - -	- - -	113.7	121.8	127.8	131.0	125.4	119.3
Trachea, bronchus, and lung	- - -	- - -	- - -	20.7	30.9	32.3	34.2	33.1	31.3
Colon, rectum, and anus	- - -	- - -	- - -	9.5	12.0	13.4	12.0	14.2	11.8
Prostate[6]	- - -	- - -	- - -	20.7	17.8	19.6	19.0	15.2	17.8
Breast[7]	- - -	- - -	- - -	10.8	13.7	13.6	11.8	13.8	14.0
Chronic lower respiratory diseases	- - -	- - -	- - -	14.2	25.4	32.8	30.0	30.1	31.7
Influenza and pneumonia	- - -	- - -	- - -	44.4	36.1	22.3	22.5	20.4	24.1
Chronic liver disease and cirrhosis	- - -	- - -	- - -	45.3	24.1	24.3	22.6	22.8	22.6
Diabetes mellitus	- - -	- - -	- - -	29.6	34.1	41.5	40.4	43.2	43.7
Human immunodeficiency virus (HIV) disease	- - -	- - -	- - -	- - -	1.8	2.2	2.7	2.2	2.5
Unintentional injuries	- - -	- - -	- - -	99.0	62.6	51.3	51.3	53.8	56.4
Motor vehicle-related injuries	- - -	- - -	- - -	54.5	32.5	27.3	25.9	28.8	28.1
Suicide[8]	- - -	- - -	- - -	11.9	11.7	9.8	10.5	10.2	10.0
Homicide[8]	- - -	- - -	- - -	15.5	10.4	6.8	6.8	8.4	7.3

See footnotes at end of table.

This table will be updated on the Web. Go to www.cdc.gov/nchs/hus.htm.

Table 29 (page 3 of 4).
Table 29 (page 3 of 4). Age-adjusted death rates for selected causes of death, by sex, race, and Hispanic origin: United States, selected years 1950–2003

[Data are based on death certificates]

Sex, race, Hispanic origin, and cause of death[1]	1950[2,3]	1960[2,3]	1970[3]	1980[3]	1990	2000[4]	2001	2002	2003
Asian or Pacific Islander[9]				Age-adjusted death rate per 100,000 population[5]					
All causes.................................	- - -	- - -	- - -	589.9	582.0	506.4	492.1	474.4	465.7
Diseases of heart.......................	- - -	- - -	- - -	202.1	181.7	146.0	137.6	134.6	127.6
Ischemic heart disease....................	- - -	- - -	- - -	168.2	139.6	109.6	103.0	98.6	92.8
Cerebrovascular diseases	- - -	- - -	- - -	66.1	56.9	52.9	51.2	47.7	45.2
Malignant neoplasms......................	- - -	- - -	- - -	126.1	134.2	121.9	119.5	113.6	113.5
Trachea, bronchus, and lung.............	- - -	- - -	- - -	28.4	30.2	28.1	28.2	25.6	26.9
Colon, rectum, and anus..................	- - -	- - -	- - -	16.4	14.4	12.7	13.2	12.5	12.1
Prostate[6].............................	- - -	- - -	- - -	10.2	16.8	12.5	11.6	10.2	10.9
Breast[7]................................	- - -	- - -	- - -	11.9	13.7	12.3	12.9	12.8	12.6
Chronic lower respiratory diseases	- - -	- - -	- - -	12.9	19.4	18.6	17.7	15.8	16.2
Influenza and pneumonia....................	- - -	- - -	- - -	24.0	31.4	19.7	19.0	17.5	17.3
Chronic liver disease and cirrhosis	- - -	- - -	- - -	6.1	5.2	3.5	3.5	3.2	3.0
Diabetes mellitus..........................	- - -	- - -	- - -	12.6	14.6	16.4	16.9	17.4	17.3
Human immunodeficiency virus (HIV) disease	- - -	- - -	- - -	- - -	2.2	0.6	0.7	0.8	0.7
Unintentional injuries......................	- - -	- - -	- - -	27.0	23.9	17.9	17.4	17.9	18.0
Motor vehicle-related injuries.............	- - -	- - -	- - -	13.9	14.0	8.6	8.1	8.4	8.4
Suicide[8]................................	- - -	- - -	- - -	7.8	6.7	5.5	5.4	5.4	5.6
Homicide[8]...............................	- - -	- - -	- - -	5.9	5.0	3.0	4.2	2.9	2.9
Hispanic or Latino[9,10]									
All causes.................................	- - -	- - -	- - -	- - -	692.0	665.7	658.7	629.3	621.2
Diseases of heart.......................	- - -	- - -	- - -	- - -	217.1	196.0	192.2	180.5	173.2
Ischemic heart disease....................	- - -	- - -	- - -	- - -	173.3	153.2	149.9	138.3	130.0
Cerebrovascular diseases	- - -	- - -	- - -	- - -	45.2	46.4	44.9	41.3	40.5
Malignant neoplasms......................	- - -	- - -	- - -	- - -	136.8	134.9	132.3	128.4	126.6
Trachea, bronchus, and lung.............	- - -	- - -	- - -	- - -	26.5	24.8	23.8	23.7	23.2
Colon, rectum, and anus..................	- - -	- - -	- - -	- - -	14.7	14.1	14.1	13.7	13.4
Prostate[6].............................	- - -	- - -	- - -	- - -	23.3	21.6	23.5	21.6	20.2
Breast[7]................................	- - -	- - -	- - -	- - -	19.5	16.9	16.3	15.5	16.1
Chronic lower respiratory diseases	- - -	- - -	- - -	- - -	19.3	21.1	20.7	20.6	20.2
Influenza and pneumonia....................	- - -	- - -	- - -	- - -	29.7	20.6	20.5	19.2	18.4
Chronic liver disease and cirrhosis	- - -	- - -	- - -	- - -	18.3	16.5	15.8	15.4	14.7
Diabetes mellitus..........................	- - -	- - -	- - -	- - -	28.2	36.9	36.7	35.6	35.0
Human immunodeficiency virus (HIV) disease ...	- - -	- - -	- - -	- - -	16.3	6.7	6.2	5.8	5.9
Unintentional injuries......................	- - -	- - -	- - -	- - -	34.6	30.1	30.7	30.7	30.6
Motor vehicle-related injuries.............	- - -	- - -	- - -	- - -	19.5	14.7	15.0	15.2	15.1
Suicide[8]................................	- - -	- - -	- - -	- - -	7.8	5.9	5.7	5.7	5.6
Homicide[8]...............................	- - -	- - -	- - -	- - -	16.2	7.5	8.3	7.3	7.7

See footnotes at end of table.

This table will be updated on the Web. Go to www.cdc.gov/nchs/hus.htm.

Table 29 (page 4 of 4). Age-adjusted death rates for selected causes of death, by sex, race, and Hispanic origin: United States, selected years 1950–2003

[Data are based on death certificates]

Sex, race, Hispanic origin, and cause of death[1]	1950[2,3]	1960[2,3]	1970[3]	1980[3]	1990	2000[4]	2001	2002	2003
White, not Hispanic or Latino[10]				Age-adjusted death rate per 100,000 population[5]					
All causes............................	- - -	- - -	- - -	- - -	914.5	855.5	842.9	837.5	826.1
Diseases of heart	- - -	- - -	- - -	- - -	319.7	255.5	245.6	239.2	230.9
Ischemic heart disease	- - -	- - -	- - -	- - -	251.9	186.6	177.5	171.0	163.3
Cerebrovascular diseases	- - -	- - -	- - -	- - -	63.5	59.0	56.0	54.6	51.7
Malignant neoplasms	- - -	- - -	- - -	- - -	215.4	200.6	197.4	195.6	192.4
Trachea, bronchus, and lung	- - -	- - -	- - -	- - -	60.3	58.2	57.7	57.5	56.7
Colon, rectum, and anus.................	- - -	- - -	- - -	- - -	24.6	20.5	19.9	19.5	18.8
Prostate[6]...........................	- - -	- - -	- - -	- - -	36.1	28.0	26.7	25.8	24.6
Breast[7]...........................	- - -	- - -	- - -	- - -	33.9	26.8	26.0	25.6	25.2
Chronic lower respiratory diseases	- - -	- - -	- - -	- - -	39.2	47.2	47.0	46.9	47.0
Influenza and pneumonia.................	- - -	- - -	- - -	- - -	36.5	23.5	21.7	22.6	22.0
Chronic liver disease and cirrhosis	- - -	- - -	- - -	- - -	9.9	9.0	9.0	9.0	9.0
Diabetes mellitus......................	- - -	- - -	- - -	- - -	18.3	21.8	22.1	22.2	22.1
Human immunodeficiency virus (HIV) disease ...	- - -	- - -	- - -	- - -	7.4	2.2	2.1	2.1	2.0
Unintentional injuries	- - -	- - -	- - -	- - -	35.0	35.3	36.2	38.0	38.8
Motor vehicle-related injuries	- - -	- - -	- - -	- - -	18.2	15.6	15.5	16.0	15.5
Suicide[8]...........................	- - -	- - -	- - -	- - -	13.8	12.0	12.5	12.9	12.7
Homicide[8]...........................	- - -	- - -	- - -	- - -	4.0	2.8	4.0	2.8	2.7

- - - Data not available.

[1]Underlying cause of death code numbers are based on the applicable revision of the *International Classification of Diseases* (ICD) for data years shown. For the period 1980–1998, causes were coded using ICD–9 codes that are most nearly comparable with the 113 cause list for ICD–10. See Appendix II, Cause of death; tables IV and V.

[2]Includes deaths of persons who were not residents of the 50 states and the District of Columbia.

[3]Underlying cause of death was coded according to the Sixth Revision of the International Classification of Diseases (ICD) in 1950, Seventh Revision in 1960, Eighth Revision in 1970, and Ninth Revision in 1980–1998. See Appendix II, Cause of death; tables IV and V.

[4]Starting with 1999 data, cause of death is coded according to ICD–10. See Appendix II, Cause of death; Comparability ratio; tables V and VI.

[5]Age-adjusted rates are calculated using the year 2000 standard population. Prior to 2003, age-adjusted rates were calculated using standard million proportions based on rounded population numbers. Starting with 2003 data, unrounded population numbers are used to calculate age-adjusted rates. See Appendix II, Age adjustment.

[6]Rate for male population only.

[7]Rate for female population only.

[8]Figures for 2001 include September 11-related deaths for which death certificates were filed as of October 24, 2002. See Appendix II, Cause of death; table V for terrorism-related ICD–10 codes.

[9]The race groups, white, black, Asian or Pacific Islander, and American Indian or Alaska Native, include persons of Hispanic and non-Hispanic origin. Persons of Hispanic origin may be of any race. Death rates for the American Indian or Alaska Native and Asian or Pacific Islander populations are known to be underestimated. See Appendix II, Race, for a discussion of sources of bias in death rates by race and Hispanic origin.

[10]Prior to 1997, excludes data from states lacking an Hispanic-origin item on the death certificate. See Appendix II, Hispanic origin.

NOTES: Starting with *Health, United States, 2003*, rates for 1991–1999 were revised using intercensal population estimates based on the 2000 census. Rates for 2000 were revised based on 2000 census counts. Rates for 2001 and later years were computed using 2000-based postcensal estimates. See Appendix I, Population Census and Population Estimates. Starting with 2003 data, California, Hawaii, Idaho, Maine, Montana, New York, and Wisconsin reported multiple-race data. The multiple-race data for these states were bridged to the single race categories of the 1977 Office of Management and Budget standards for comparability with other states. Data for additional years are available. See Appendix III.

SOURCES: Centers for Disease Control and Prevention, National Center for Health Statistics, National Vital Statistics System; Grove RD, Hetzel AM. Vital statistics rates in the United States, 1940–1960. Washington, DC: U.S. Government Printing Office. 1968; numerator data from National Vital Statistics System, annual mortality files; denominator data from national population estimates for race groups from Table 1 and unpublished Hispanic population estimates for 1985–1996 prepared by the Housing and Household Economic Statistics Division, U.S. Census Bureau; additional mortality tables are available from: www.cdc.gov/nchs/datawh/statab/unpubd/mortabs.htm; Hoyert DL, Heron M, Murphy SL, Kung HC. Deaths: Final data for 2003. National vital statistics reports. Vol 54 no 13. Hyattsville, MD: National Center for Health Statistics. 2006.

This table will be updated on the Web. Go to www.cdc.gov/nchs/hus.htm.

Table 30 (page 1 of 4). Years of potential life lost before age 75 for selected causes of death, by sex, race, and Hispanic origin: United States, selected years 1980–2003

[Data are based on death certificates]

Sex, race, Hispanic origin, and cause of death[2]	Crude	Age adjusted[1]					
	2003	1980	1990	2000[3]	2001	2002	2003
All persons	Years lost before age 75 per 100,000 population under 75 years of age						
All causes	7,562.0	10,448.4	9,085.5	7,578.1	7,531.2	7,499.6	7,466.9
Diseases of heart	1,214.1	2,238.7	1,617.7	1,253.0	1,221.1	1,212.7	1,187.9
Ischemic heart disease	785.1	1,729.3	1,153.6	841.8	809.7	792.0	765.1
Cerebrovascular diseases	207.0	357.5	259.6	223.3	211.9	208.1	203.6
Malignant neoplasms.	1,628.0	2,108.8	2,003.8	1,674.1	1,651.7	1,622.7	1,586.9
Trachea, bronchus, and lung.	425.9	548.5	561.4	443.1	431.2	423.4	412.2
Colorectal	137.4	190.0	164.7	141.9	142.4	141.0	133.8
Prostate[4]	56.5	84.9	96.8	63.6	61.8	60.1	58.6
Breast[5]	328.2	463.2	451.6	332.6	328.1	316.8	313.7
Chronic lower respiratory diseases	187.8	169.1	187.4	188.1	185.8	184.5	183.9
Influenza and pneumonia.	91.6	160.2	141.5	87.1	82.3	82.7	90.8
Chronic liver disease and cirrhosis	162.6	300.3	196.9	164.1	164.7	160.5	159.6
Diabetes mellitus.	189.1	134.4	155.9	178.4	180.5	184.3	184.6
Human immunodeficiency virus (HIV) disease	151.5	- - -	383.8	174.6	167.8	161.8	153.3
Unintentional injuries	1,085.8	1,543.5	1,162.1	1,026.5	1,036.8	1,079.2	1,084.6
Motor vehicle-related injuries.	572.1	912.9	716.4	574.3	572.5	585.8	569.6
Suicide[6]	344.3	392.0	393.1	334.5	342.6	346.7	343.3
Homicide[6]	275.4	425.5	417.4	266.5	311.0	274.4	274.3
Male							
All causes	9,418.1	13,777.2	11,973.5	9,572.2	9,507.1	9,470.0	9,416.4
Diseases of heart	1,652.4	3,352.1	2,356.0	1,766.0	1,708.3	1,706.9	1,664.2
Ischemic heart disease	1,130.0	2,715.1	1,766.3	1,255.4	1,201.8	1,179.6	1,138.8
Cerebrovascular diseases	222.8	396.7	286.6	244.6	233.5	227.6	225.9
Malignant neoplasms.	1,700.8	2,360.8	2,214.6	1,810.8	1,782.4	1,754.2	1,711.4
Trachea, bronchus, and lung.	500.0	821.1	764.8	554.9	535.9	520.5	504.6
Colorectal	156.4	214.9	194.3	167.3	166.6	168.2	157.7
Prostate	56.5	84.9	96.8	63.6	61.8	60.1	58.6
Chronic lower respiratory diseases	194.7	235.1	224.8	206.0	200.7	200.7	199.5
Influenza and pneumonia.	105.4	202.5	180.0	102.8	96.9	97.3	106.4
Chronic liver disease and cirrhosis	229.5	415.0	283.9	236.9	233.6	226.6	229.4
Diabetes mellitus.	216.6	140.4	170.4	203.8	209.6	217.2	218.2
Human immunodeficiency virus (HIV) disease	220.1	- - -	686.2	258.9	247.7	237.0	223.7
Unintentional injuries	1,554.0	2,342.7	1,715.1	1,475.6	1,490.1	1,542.2	1,537.7
Motor vehicle-related injuries.	809.0	1,359.7	1,018.4	796.4	803.5	817.2	795.0
Suicide[6]	552.6	605.6	634.8	539.1	552.3	555.7	548.2
Homicide[6]	440.1	675.0	658.0	410.5	480.5	425.0	430.5
Female							
All causes	5,710.7	7,350.3	6,333.1	5,644.6	5,609.2	5,580.0	5,560.5
Diseases of heart	776.9	1,246.0	948.5	774.6	765.4	748.8	739.5
Ischemic heart disease	441.0	852.1	600.3	457.6	444.3	430.2	415.0
Cerebrovascular diseases	191.3	324.0	235.9	203.9	192.1	190.3	183.0
Malignant neoplasms.	1,555.4	1,896.8	1,826.6	1,555.3	1,538.4	1,507.7	1,477.3
Trachea, bronchus, and lung.	352.0	310.4	382.2	342.1	336.6	335.4	328.1
Colorectal	118.5	168.7	138.7	118.7	120.4	115.9	111.9
Breast.	328.2	463.2	451.6	332.6	328.1	316.8	313.7
Chronic lower respiratory diseases	180.9	114.0	155.9	172.3	172.8	170.0	169.9
Influenza and pneumonia.	77.8	122.0	106.2	72.3	68.7	69.1	76.0
Chronic liver disease and cirrhosis	95.9	194.5	115.1	94.5	98.8	97.4	92.6
Diabetes mellitus.	161.6	128.5	142.3	154.4	153.0	153.1	152.9
Human immunodeficiency virus (HIV) disease	83.0	- - -	87.8	92.0	89.4	88.1	84.1
Unintentional injuries	618.9	755.3	607.4	573.2	578.3	610.3	624.6
Motor vehicle-related injuries.	335.8	470.4	411.6	348.5	337.2	349.8	339.2
Suicide[6]	136.6	184.2	153.3	129.1	131.9	136.6	136.6
Homicide[6]	111.1	181.3	174.3	118.9	137.4	119.6	112.9

See footnotes at end of table.

This table will be updated on the Web. Go to www.cdc.gov/nchs/hus.htm.

Table 30 (page 2 of 4). **Years of potential life lost before age 75 for selected causes of death, by sex, race, and Hispanic origin: United States, selected years 1980–2003**

[Data are based on death certificates]

Sex, race, Hispanic origin, and cause of death[2]	Crude	Age adjusted[1]					
	2003	1980	1990	2000[3]	2001	2002	2003
White[7]	Years lost before age 75 per 100,000 population under 75 years of age						
All causes	7,123.2	9,554.1	8,159.5	6,949.5	6,941.6	6,936.6	6,910.6
Diseases of heart	1,147.5	2,100.8	1,490.3	1,149.4	1,115.0	1,111.8	1,081.3
Ischemic heart disease	782.6	1,682.7	1,113.4	805.3	773.0	759.5	731.5
Cerebrovascular diseases	175.7	300.7	213.1	187.1	175.6	173.5	166.7
Malignant neoplasms	1,647.4	2,035.9	1,929.3	1,627.8	1,610.2	1,582.8	1,546.5
Trachea, bronchus, and lung	442.1	529.9	544.2	436.3	427.5	418.5	407.9
Colorectal	134.3	186.8	157.8	134.1	135.0	134.0	125.5
Prostate[4]	51.6	74.8	86.6	54.3	53.1	51.3	50.5
Breast[5]	318.7	460.2	441.7	315.6	309.6	297.5	295.0
Chronic lower respiratory diseases	197.8	165.4	182.3	185.3	184.7	183.5	184.2
Influenza and pneumonia	84.6	130.8	116.9	77.7	72.7	75.1	82.2
Chronic liver disease and cirrhosis	170.1	257.3	175.8	162.7	164.4	162.9	162.3
Diabetes mellitus	170.4	115.7	133.7	155.6	156.2	160.3	160.3
Human immunodeficiency virus (HIV) disease	81.6	- - -	309.0	94.7	88.4	84.7	82.1
Unintentional injuries	1,109.6	1,520.4	1,139.7	1,031.8	1,049.0	1,101.6	1,117.7
Motor vehicle-related injuries	583.7	939.9	726.7	586.1	585.1	604.0	588.5
Suicide[6]	375.5	414.5	417.7	362.0	373.5	380.1	375.0
Homicide[6]	157.3	271.7	234.9	156.6	204.0	159.7	159.3
Black or African American[7]							
All causes	11,575.2	17,873.4	16,593.0	12,897.1	12,579.7	12,401.0	12,304.0
Diseases of heart	1,891.0	3,619.9	2,891.8	2,275.2	2,248.9	2,212.8	2,205.7
Ischemic heart disease	980.6	2,305.1	1,676.1	1,300.1	1,260.6	1,218.7	1,182.6
Cerebrovascular diseases	410.3	883.2	656.4	507.0	491.3	474.1	479.6
Malignant neoplasms	1,835.4	2,946.1	2,894.8	2,294.7	2,228.4	2,196.6	2,163.9
Trachea, bronchus, and lung	444.1	776.0	811.3	593.0	557.5	561.9	542.1
Colorectal	179.0	232.3	241.8	222.4	219.6	213.7	214.4
Prostate[4]	106.0	200.3	223.5	171.0	164.1	160.3	154.3
Breast[5]	446.0	524.2	592.9	500.0	501.7	495.9	490.6
Chronic lower respiratory diseases	184.5	203.7	240.6	232.7	220.5	222.8	212.3
Influenza and pneumonia	144.9	384.9	330.8	161.2	152.1	146.7	157.5
Chronic liver disease and cirrhosis	138.9	644.0	371.8	185.6	181.5	161.3	158.9
Diabetes mellitus	334.3	305.3	361.5	383.4	392.6	396.7	396.0
Human immunodeficiency virus (HIV) disease	620.8	- - -	1,014.7	763.3	743.5	720.6	670.1
Unintentional injuries	1,100.1	1,751.5	1,392.7	1,152.8	1,133.4	1,129.3	1,082.1
Motor vehicle-related injuries	554.6	750.2	699.5	580.8	571.7	558.5	536.2
Suicide[6]	204.0	238.0	261.4	208.7	201.5	196.5	199.5
Homicide[6]	1,028.1	1,580.8	1,612.9	941.6	963.6	962.2	965.0
American Indian or Alaska Native[7]							
All causes	7,865.7	13,390.9	9,506.2	7,758.2	7,991.8	8,278.0	8,541.6
Diseases of heart	896.6	1,819.9	1,391.0	1,030.1	1,027.7	959.9	1,099.3
Ischemic heart disease	559.3	1,208.2	901.8	709.3	695.2	648.4	708.1
Cerebrovascular diseases	154.9	269.3	223.3	198.1	193.5	201.7	190.7
Malignant neoplasms	815.1	1,101.3	1,141.1	995.7	1,099.5	1,066.0	997.2
Trachea, bronchus, and lung	168.0	181.1	268.1	227.8	238.7	226.3	223.9
Colorectal	67.7	78.8	82.4	93.8	87.9	115.7	85.5
Prostate[4]	22.2	66.7	42.0	44.5	35.2	36.3	34.7
Breast[5]	126.0	205.5	213.4	174.1	175.2	187.1	146.8
Chronic lower respiratory diseases	126.7	89.3	129.0	151.8	139.3	137.0	163.6
Influenza and pneumonia	152.7	307.9	206.3	124.0	141.3	100.9	171.8
Chronic liver disease and cirrhosis	441.3	1,190.3	535.1	519.4	506.0	495.8	504.6
Diabetes mellitus	283.8	305.5	292.3	305.6	297.3	344.7	355.2
Human immunodeficiency virus (HIV) disease	73.1	- - -	70.1	68.4	88.1	79.9	80.7
Unintentional injuries	1,894.4	3,541.0	2,183.9	1,700.1	1,632.0	1,764.6	1,818.4
Motor vehicle-related injuries	1,169.2	2,102.4	1,301.5	1,032.2	989.4	1,089.3	1,081.8
Suicide[6]	451.9	515.0	495.9	403.1	420.6	420.8	418.2
Homicide[6]	349.3	628.9	434.2	278.5	287.0	366.5	323.1

See footnotes at end of table.

This table will be updated on the Web. Go to www.cdc.gov/nchs/hus.htm.

Table 30 (page 3 of 4). Years of potential life lost before age 75 for selected causes of death, by sex, race, and Hispanic origin: United States, selected years 1980–2003

[Data are based on death certificates]

Sex, race, Hispanic origin, and cause of death[2]	Crude	Age adjusted[1]					
	2003	1980	1990	2000[3]	2001	2002	2003
Asian or Pacific Islander[7]	Years lost before age 75 per 100,000 population under 75 years of age						
All causes	3,498.2	5,378.4	4,705.2	3,811.1	3,798.7	3,635.5	3,657.5
Diseases of heart	488.4	952.8	702.2	567.9	547.1	539.4	534.3
Ischemic heart disease.	317.5	697.7	486.6	381.1	369.4	352.0	354.7
Cerebrovascular diseases	175.1	266.9	233.5	199.4	198.8	186.5	192.9
Malignant neoplasms.	889.1	1,218.6	1,166.4	1,033.8	1,029.6	990.3	959.1
Trachea, bronchus, and lung.	154.3	238.2	204.7	185.8	180.8	173.8	173.9
Colorectal	88.0	115.9	105.1	91.6	97.2	92.8	94.4
Prostate[4]	10.8	17.0	32.4	18.8	13.3	20.8	14.6
Breast[5].	189.2	222.2	216.5	200.8	205.0	188.4	192.3
Chronic lower respiratory diseases	39.4	56.4	72.8	56.5	52.1	44.8	45.1
Influenza and pneumonia	43.6	79.3	74.0	48.6	45.4	38.0	47.7
Chronic liver disease and cirrhosis	34.8	85.6	72.4	44.8	44.5	40.0	36.8
Diabetes mellitus.	70.2	83.1	74.0	77.0	83.8	76.4	79.9
Human immunodeficiency virus (HIV) disease	23.1	- - -	77.0	19.9	21.6	24.8	22.3
Unintentional injuries	442.4	742.7	636.6	425.7	431.4	431.1	429.6
Motor vehicle-related injuries.	280.1	472.6	445.5	263.4	275.9	269.7	269.6
Suicide[6].	185.0	217.1	200.6	168.6	166.4	162.7	172.1
Homicide[6]	126.7	201.1	205.8	113.1	165.1	127.5	120.6
Hispanic or Latino[7,8]							
All causes	5,346.5	- - -	7,963.3	6,037.6	5,982.2	5,865.9	5,910.0
Diseases of heart	514.4	- - -	1,082.0	821.3	791.6	796.9	767.7
Ischemic heart disease.	307.3	- - -	756.6	564.6	539.1	540.1	501.3
Cerebrovascular diseases	128.9	- - -	238.0	207.8	201.4	193.4	187.3
Malignant neoplasms.	744.2	- - -	1,232.2	1,098.2	1,099.1	1,052.9	1,056.5
Trachea, bronchus, and lung.	86.5	- - -	193.7	152.1	154.9	150.5	144.9
Colorectal	65.1	- - -	100.2	101.4	95.8	96.7	100.1
Prostate[4]	20.3	- - -	47.7	42.9	49.4	44.1	43.4
Breast[5].	161.3	- - -	299.3	230.7	233.6	205.1	218.4
Chronic lower respiratory diseases	45.8	- - -	78.8	68.5	67.6	69.0	67.1
Influenza and pneumonia	65.7	- - -	130.1	76.0	66.1	65.5	76.4
Chronic liver disease and cirrhosis	155.9	- - -	329.1	252.1	247.7	237.9	221.8
Diabetes mellitus.	134.6	- - -	177.8	215.6	212.1	207.1	214.0
Human immunodeficiency virus (HIV) disease	148.0	- - -	600.1	209.4	190.3	179.1	175.4
Unintentional injuries	1,028.5	- - -	1,190.6	920.1	945.8	958.1	961.5
Motor vehicle-related injuries.	623.0	- - -	740.8	540.2	554.0	569.6	563.6
Suicide[6].	196.7	- - -	256.2	188.5	185.1	185.6	188.3
Homicide[6]	395.9	- - -	720.8	335.1	365.2	330.2	345.0

See footnotes at end of table.

This table will be updated on the Web. Go to www.cdc.gov/nchs/hus.htm.

Table 30 (page 4 of 4). Years of potential life lost before age 75 for selected causes of death, by sex, race, and Hispanic origin: United States, selected years 1980–2003

[Data are based on death certificates]

Sex, race, Hispanic origin, and cause of death[2]	Crude 2003	Age adjusted[1] 1980	1990	2000[3]	2001	2002	2003
White, not Hispanic or Latino[8]		Years lost before age 75 per 100,000 population under 75 years of age					
All causes	7,394.8	- - -	8,022.5	6,960.5	6,970.9	6,997.9	6,961.6
Diseases of heart	1,263.6	- - -	1,504.0	1,175.1	1,144.4	1,143.8	1,114.7
Ischemic heart disease.	870.2	- - -	1,127.2	824.7	794.7	781.3	755.8
Cerebrovascular diseases	183.1	- - -	210.1	183.0	170.6	169.4	162.8
Malignant neoplasms.	1,814.0	- - -	1,974.1	1,668.4	1,652.3	1,629.7	1,590.6
Trachea, bronchus, and lung.	510.4	- - -	566.8	460.3	451.9	443.7	433.5
Colorectal	147.0	- - -	162.1	136.2	138.5	137.6	127.7
Prostate[4]	57.7	- - -	89.2	54.9	53.2	51.7	51.0
Breast[5]	346.3	- - -	451.5	322.3	315.9	305.9	301.8
Chronic lower respiratory diseases	226.5	- - -	188.1	193.8	194.3	193.3	194.2
Influenza and pneumonia.	87.4	- - -	112.3	76.4	72.9	75.8	82.1
Chronic liver disease and cirrhosis	170.4	- - -	162.4	150.9	153.0	152.1	153.2
Diabetes mellitus.	175.4	- - -	131.2	150.2	151.0	155.8	154.9
Human immunodeficiency virus (HIV) disease	66.3	- - -	271.2	76.0	71.0	67.8	65.4
Unintentional injuries	1,110.3	- - -	1,114.7	1,041.4	1,057.2	1,117.4	1,135.8
Motor vehicle-related injuries.	567.5	- - -	715.7	588.8	584.1	603.3	585.3
Suicide[6].	407.5	- - -	433.0	389.2	405.3	413.9	408.1
Homicide[6]	105.5	- - -	162.0	113.2	160.1	114.8	109.6

- - - Data not available.

* Rate based on fewer than 20 deaths is considered unreliable and is not shown.

[1]Age-adjusted rates are calculated using the year 2000 standard population. Prior to 2003, age-adjusted rates were calculated using standard million proportions based on rounded population numbers. Starting with 2003 data, unrounded population numbers are used to calculate age-adjusted rates. See Appendix II, Age adjustment.

[2]Underlying cause of death code numbers are based on the applicable revision of the *International Classification of Diseases* (ICD) for data years shown. For the period 1980–1998, causes were coded using ICD–9 codes that are most nearly comparable with the 113 cause list for ICD–10. See Appendix II, Cause of death; tables IV and V.

[3]Starting with 1999 data, cause of death is coded according to ICD–10. See Appendix II, Cause of death; Comparability ratio; tables V and VI.

[4]Rate for male population only.

[5]Rate for female population only.

[6]Figures for 2001 include September 11-related deaths for which death certificates were filed as of October 24, 2002. See Appendix II, Cause of death; table V for terrorism-related ICD–10 codes.

[7]The race groups, white, black, Asian or Pacific Islander, and American Indian or Alaska Native, include persons of Hispanic and non-Hispanic origin. Persons of Hispanic origin may be of any race. Death rates for the American Indian or Alaska Native and Asian or Pacific Islander populations are known to be underestimated. See Appendix II, Race, for a discussion of sources of bias in death rates by race and Hispanic origin.

[8]Prior to 1997, excludes data from states lacking an Hispanic-origin item on the death certificate. See Appendix II, Hispanic origin.

NOTES: Starting with *Health, United States, 2003*, rates for 1991–1999 were revised using intercensal population estimates based on the 2000 census. Rates for 2000 were revised based on 2000 census counts. Rates for 2001 and later years were computed using 2000-based postcensal estimates. See Appendix I, Population Census and Population Estimates. See Appendix II, Years of potential life lost (YPLL) for definition and method of calculation. Starting with 2003 data, California, Hawaii, Idaho, Maine, Montana, New York, and Wisconsin reported multiple-race data. The multiple-race data for these states were bridged to the single race categories of the 1977 Office of Management and Budget standards for comparability with other states. Data for additional years are available. See Appendix III.

SOURCES: Centers for Disease Control and Prevention, National Center for Health Statistics, National vital statistics system; numerator data from annual mortality files; denominator data from national population estimates for race groups from Table 1 and unpublished Hispanic population estimates for 1990–1996 prepared by the Housing and Household Economic Statistics Division, U.S. Census Bureau.

This table will be updated on the Web. Go to www.cdc.gov/nchs/hus.htm.

Table 31 (page 1 of 4). Leading causes of death and numbers of deaths, by sex, race, and Hispanic origin: United States, 1980 and 2003

[Data are based on death certificates]

Sex, race, Hispanic origin, and rank order	1980 Cause of death	Deaths	2003 Cause of death	Deaths
All persons				
. . .	All causes	1,989,841	All causes	2,448,288
1.	Diseases of heart	761,085	Diseases of heart	685,089
2.	Malignant neoplasms	416,509	Malignant neoplasms	556,902
3.	Cerebrovascular diseases	170,225	Cerebrovascular diseases	157,689
4.	Unintentional injuries	105,718	Chronic lower respiratory diseases	126,382
5.	Chronic obstructive pulmonary diseases	56,050	Unintentional injuries	109,277
6.	Pneumonia and influenza	54,619	Diabetes mellitus	74,219
7.	Diabetes mellitus	34,851	Influenza and pneumonia	65,163
8.	Chronic liver disease and cirrhosis	30,583	Alzheimer's disease	63,457
9.	Atherosclerosis	29,449	Nephritis, nephrotic syndrome and nephrosis	42,453
10.	Suicide	26,869	Septicemia	34,069
Male				
. . .	All causes	1,075,078	All causes	1,201,964
1.	Diseases of heart	405,661	Diseases of heart	336,095
2.	Malignant neoplasms	225,948	Malignant neoplasms	287,990
3.	Unintentional injuries	74,180	Unintentional injuries	70,532
4.	Cerebrovascular diseases	69,973	Cerebrovascular diseases	61,426
5.	Chronic obstructive pulmonary diseases	38,625	Chronic lower respiratory diseases	60,714
6.	Pneumonia and influenza	27,574	Diabetes mellitus	35,438
7.	Suicide	20,505	Influenza and pneumonia	28,778
8.	Chronic liver disease and cirrhosis	19,768	Suicide	25,203
9.	Homicide	18,779	Nephritis, nephrotic syndrome and nephrosis	20,481
10.	Diabetes mellitus	14,325	Alzheimer's disease	18,335
Female				
. . .	All causes	914,763	All causes	1,246,324
1.	Diseases of heart	355,424	Diseases of heart	348,994
2.	Malignant neoplasms	190,561	Malignant neoplasms	268,912
3.	Cerebrovascular diseases	100,252	Cerebrovascular diseases	96,263
4.	Unintentional injuries	31,538	Chronic lower respiratory diseases	65,668
5.	Pneumonia and influenza	27,045	Alzheimer's disease	45,122
6.	Diabetes mellitus	20,526	Diabetes mellitus	38,781
7.	Atherosclerosis	17,848	Unintentional injuries	38,745
8.	Chronic obstructive pulmonary diseases	17,425	Influenza and pneumonia	36,385
9.	Chronic liver disease and cirrhosis	10,815	Nephritis, nephrotic syndrome and nephrosis	21,972
10.	Certain conditions originating in the perinatal period	9,815	Septicemia	19,082
White				
. . .	All causes	1,738,607	All causes	2,103,714
1.	Diseases of heart	683,347	Diseases of heart	594,842
2.	Malignant neoplasms	368,162	Malignant neoplasms	481,556
3.	Cerebrovascular diseases	148,734	Cerebrovascular diseases	134,705
4.	Unintentional injuries	90,122	Chronic lower respiratory diseases	116,917
5.	Chronic obstructive pulmonary diseases	52,375	Unintentional injuries	93,381
6.	Pneumonia and influenza	48,369	Alzheimer's disease	59,184
7.	Diabetes mellitus	28,868	Diabetes mellitus	59,099
8.	Atherosclerosis	27,069	Influenza and pneumonia	57,645
9.	Chronic liver disease and cirrhosis	25,240	Nephritis, nephrotic syndrome and nephrosis	33,707
10.	Suicide	24,829	Suicide	28,485
Black or African American				
. . .	All causes	233,135	All causes	291,300
1.	Diseases of heart	72,956	Diseases of heart	77,372
2.	Malignant neoplasms	45,037	Malignant neoplasms	62,660
3.	Cerebrovascular diseases	20,135	Cerebrovascular diseases	18,806
4.	Unintentional injuries	13,480	Diabetes mellitus	12,892
5.	Homicide	10,172	Unintentional injuries	12,351
6.	Certain conditions originating in the perinatal period	6,961	Homicide	8,392
7.	Pneumonia and influenza	5,648	Nephritis, nephrotic syndrome and nephrosis	7,855
8.	Diabetes mellitus	5,544	Chronic lower respiratory diseases	7,709
9.	Chronic liver disease and cirrhosis	4,790	Human immunodeficiency virus (HIV) disease	7,479
10.	Nephritis, nephrotic syndrome, and nephrosis	3,416	Septicemia	6,206

See footnotes at end of table.

This table will be updated on the Web. Go to www.cdc.gov/nchs/hus.htm.

[Data are based on death certificates]

Sex, race, Hispanic origin, and rank order	1980		2003	
	Cause of death	Deaths	Cause of death	Deaths
American Indian or Alaska Native				
. . .	All causes	6,923	All causes	13,147
1.	Diseases of heart	1,494	Diseases of heart	2,712
2.	Unintentional injuries	1,290	Malignant neoplasms	2,154
3.	Malignant neoplasms	770	Unintentional injuries	1,573
4.	Chronic liver disease and cirrhosis	410	Diabetes mellitus	783
5.	Cerebrovascular diseases	322	Chronic liver disease and cirrhosis	570
6.	Pneumonia and influenza	257	Cerebrovascular diseases	552
7.	Homicide	217	Chronic lower respiratory diseases	512
8.	Diabetes mellitus	210	Influenza and pneumonia	390
9.	Certain conditions originating in the perinatal period	199	Suicide	322
10.	Suicide	181	Nephritis, nephrotic syndrome and nephrosis	255
Asian or Pacific Islander				
. . .	All causes	11,071	All causes	40,127
1.	Diseases of heart	3,265	Malignant neoplasms	10,532
2.	Malignant neoplasms	2,522	Diseases of heart	10,163
3.	Cerebrovascular diseases	1,028	Cerebrovascular diseases	3,626
4.	Unintentional injuries	810	Unintentional injuries	1,972
5.	Pneumonia and influenza	342	Diabetes mellitus	1,445
6.	Suicide	249	Influenza and pneumonia	1,256
7.	Certain conditions originating in the perinatal period	246	Chronic lower respiratory diseases	1,244
8.	Diabetes mellitus	227	Suicide	722
9.	Homicide	211	Nephritis, nephrotic syndrome and nephrosis	636
10.	Chronic obstructive pulmonary diseases	207	Septicemia	456
Hispanic or Latino				
. . .	- - -	- - -	All causes	122,026
1.	- - -	- - -	Diseases of heart	28,298
2.	- - -	- - -	Malignant neoplasms	24,070
3.	- - -	- - -	Unintentional injuries	10,418
4.	- - -	- - -	Cerebrovascular diseases	6,658
5.	- - -	- - -	Diabetes mellitus	6,179
6.	- - -	- - -	Chronic liver disease and cirrhosis	3,382
7.	- - -	- - -	Homicide	3,355
8.	- - -	- - -	Chronic lower respiratory diseases	3,174
9.	- - -	- - -	Influenza and pneumonia	2,948
10.	- - -	- - -	Certain conditions originating in the perinatal period	2,628
White male				
. . .	All causes	933,878	All causes	1,025,650
1.	Diseases of heart	364,679	Diseases of heart	291,560
2.	Malignant neoplasms	198,188	Malignant neoplasms	249,053
3.	Unintentional injuries	62,963	Unintentional injuries	59,912
4.	Cerebrovascular diseases	60,095	Chronic lower respiratory diseases	55,397
5.	Chronic obstructive pulmonary diseases	35,977	Cerebrovascular diseases	51,646
6.	Pneumonia and influenza	23,810	Diabetes mellitus	28,939
7.	Suicide	18,901	Influenza and pneumonia	25,009
8.	Chronic liver disease and cirrhosis	16,407	Suicide	22,830
9.	Diabetes mellitus	12,125	Alzheimer's disease	17,086
10.	Atherosclerosis	10,543	Nephritis, nephrotic syndrome and nephrosis	16,408
Black or African American male				
. . .	All causes	130,138	All causes	148,022
1.	Diseases of heart	37,877	Diseases of heart	37,466
2.	Malignant neoplasms	25,861	Malignant neoplasms	32,442
3.	Unintentional injuries	9,701	Unintentional injuries	8,385
4.	Cerebrovascular diseases	9,194	Cerebrovascular diseases	7,866
5.	Homicide	8,274	Homicide	7,083
6.	Certain conditions originating in the perinatal period	3,869	Diabetes mellitus	5,425
7.	Pneumonia and influenza	3,386	Human immunodeficiency virus (HIV) disease	5,033
8.	Chronic liver disease and cirrhosis	3,020	Chronic lower respiratory diseases	4,247
9.	Chronic obstructive pulmonary diseases	2,429	Nephritis, nephrotic syndrome and nephrosis	3,642
10.	Diabetes mellitus	2,010	Influenza and pneumonia	2,906

See footnotes at end of table.

This table will be updated on the Web. Go to www.cdc.gov/nchs/hus.htm.

Table 31 (page 3 of 4). Leading causes of death and numbers of deaths, by sex, race, and Hispanic origin: United States, 1980 and 2003

[Data are based on death certificates]

Sex, race, Hispanic origin, and rank order	1980 Cause of death	Deaths	2003 Cause of death	Deaths
American Indian or Alaska Native male				
. . .	All causes	4,193	All causes	7,106
1	Unintentional injuries	946	Diseases of heart	1,529
2	Diseases of heart	917	Malignant neoplasms	1,092
3	Malignant neoplasms	408	Unintentional injuries	1,043
4	Chronic liver disease and cirrhosis	239	Diabetes mellitus	367
5	Cerebrovascular diseases	163	Chronic liver disease and cirrhosis	317
6	Homicide	162	Chronic lower respiratory diseases	269
7	Pneumonia and influenza	148	Suicide	265
8	Suicide	147	Cerebrovascular diseases	242
9	Certain conditions originating in the perinatal period	107	Influenza and pneumonia	184
10	Diabetes mellitus	86	Homicide	175
Asian or Pacific Islander male				
. . .	All causes	6,809	All causes	21,186
1	Diseases of heart	2,174	Diseases of heart	5,540
2	Malignant neoplasms	1,485	Malignant neoplasms	5,403
3	Unintentional injuries	556	Cerebrovascular diseases	1,672
4	Cerebrovascular diseases	521	Unintentional injuries	1,192
5	Pneumonia and influenza	227	Chronic lower respiratory diseases	801
6	Suicide	159	Diabetes mellitus	707
7	Chronic obstructive pulmonary diseases	158	Influenza and pneumonia	679
8	Homicide	151	Suicide	511
9	Certain conditions originating in the perinatal period	128	Nephritis, nephrotic syndrome and nephrosis	304
10	Diabetes mellitus	103	Homicide	287
Hispanic or Latino male				
. . .	- - -	- - -	All causes	68,119
1	- - -	- - -	Diseases of heart	14,867
2	- - -	- - -	Malignant neoplasms	12,671
3	- - -	- - -	Unintentional injuries	7,899
4	- - -	- - -	Cerebrovascular diseases	3,070
5	- - -	- - -	Diabetes mellitus	2,976
6	- - -	- - -	Homicide	2,809
7	- - -	- - -	Chronic liver disease and cirrhosis	2,387
8	- - -	- - -	Suicide	1,711
9	- - -	- - -	Chronic lower respiratory diseases	1,697
10	- - -	- - -	Human immunodeficiency virus (HIV) disease	1,465
White female				
. . .	All causes	804,729	All causes	1,078,064
1	Diseases of heart	318,668	Diseases of heart	303,282
2	Malignant neoplasms	169,974	Malignant neoplasms	232,503
3	Cerebrovascular diseases	88,639	Cerebrovascular diseases	83,059
4	Unintentional injuries	27,159	Chronic lower respiratory diseases	61,520
5	Pneumonia and influenza	24,559	Alzheimer's disease	42,098
6	Diabetes mellitus	16,743	Unintentional injuries	33,469
7	Atherosclerosis	16,526	Influenza and pneumonia	32,636
8	Chronic obstructive pulmonary diseases	16,398	Diabetes mellitus	30,160
9	Chronic liver disease and cirrhosis	8,833	Nephritis, nephrotic syndrome and nephrosis	17,299
10	Certain conditions originating in the perinatal period	6,512	Septicemia	15,271
Black or African American female				
. . .	All causes	102,997	All causes	143,278
1	Diseases of heart	35,079	Diseases of heart	39,906
2	Malignant neoplasms	19,176	Malignant neoplasms	30,218
3	Cerebrovascular diseases	10,941	Cerebrovascular diseases	10,940
4	Unintentional injuries	3,779	Diabetes mellitus	7,467
5	Diabetes mellitus	3,534	Nephritis, nephrotic syndrome and nephrosis	4,213
6	Certain conditions originating in the perinatal period	3,092	Unintentional injuries	3,966
7	Pneumonia and influenza	2,262	Chronic lower respiratory diseases	3,462
8	Homicide	1,898	Septicemia	3,431
9	Chronic liver disease and cirrhosis	1,770	Influenza and pneumonia	2,966
10	Nephritis, nephrotic syndrome, and nephrosis	1,722	Alzheimer's disease	2,631

See footnotes at end of table.

This table will be updated on the Web. Go to www.cdc.gov/nchs/hus.htm.

Table 31 (page 4 of 4). Leading causes of death and numbers of deaths, by sex, race, and Hispanic origin: United States, 1980 and 2003

[Data are based on death certificates]

Sex, race, Hispanic origin, and rank order	1980 Cause of death	1980 Deaths	2003 Cause of death	2003 Deaths
American Indian or Alaska Native female				
. . .	All causes	2,730	All causes	6,041
1.	Diseases of heart	577	Diseases of heart	1,183
2.	Malignant neoplasms	362	Malignant neoplasms	1,062
3.	Unintentional injuries	344	Unintentional injuries	530
4.	Chronic liver disease and cirrhosis	171	Diabetes mellitus	416
5.	Cerebrovascular diseases	159	Cerebrovascular diseases	310
6.	Diabetes mellitus	124	Chronic liver disease and cirrhosis	253
7.	Pneumonia and influenza	109	Chronic lower respiratory diseases	243
8.	Certain conditions originating in the perinatal period	92	Influenza and pneumonia	206
9.	Nephritis, nephrotic syndrome, and nephrosis	56	Septicemia	138
10.	Homicide	55	Nephritis, nephrotic syndrome and nephrosis	128
Asian or Pacific Islander female				
. . .	All causes	4,262	All causes	18,941
1.	Diseases of heart	1,091	Malignant neoplasms	5,129
2.	Malignant neoplasms	1,037	Diseases of heart	4,623
3.	Cerebrovascular diseases	507	Cerebrovascular diseases	1,954
4.	Unintentional injuries	254	Unintentional injuries	780
5.	Diabetes mellitus	124	Diabetes mellitus	738
6.	Certain conditions originating in the perinatal period	118	Influenza and pneumonia	577
7.	Pneumonia and influenza	115	Chronic lower respiratory diseases	443
8.	Congenital anomalies	104	Nephritis, nephrotic syndrome and nephrosis	332
9.	Suicide	90	Alzheimer's disease	293
10.	Homicide	60	Essential (primary) hypertension and hypertensive renal disease	265
Hispanic or Latino female				
. . .	- - -	- - -	All causes	53,907
1.	- - -	- - -	Diseases of heart	13,431
2.	- - -	- - -	Malignant neoplasms	11,399
3.	- - -	- - -	Cerebrovascular diseases	3,588
4.	- - -	- - -	Diabetes mellitus	3,203
5.	- - -	- - -	Unintentional injuries	2,519
6.	- - -	- - -	Influenza and pneumonia	1,519
7.	- - -	- - -	Chronic lower respiratory diseases	1,477
8.	- - -	- - -	Alzheimer's disease	1,202
9.	- - -	- - -	Certain conditions originating in the perinatal period	1,169
10.	- - -	- - -	Nephritis, nephrotic syndrome and nephrosis	1,101

. . . Category not applicable.
- - - Data not available.

NOTES: For cause of death codes based on the *International Classification of Diseases, 9th Revision* (ICD–9) in 1980 and ICD–10 in 2002, see Appendix II, Cause of death; tables IV and V. Starting with 2003 data, California, Hawaii, Idaho, Maine, Montana, New York, and Wisconsin reported multiple-race data. The multiple-race data for these states were bridged to the single race categories of the 1977 Office of Management and Budget standards for comparability with other states.

SOURCES: Centers for Disease Control and Prevention, National Center for Health Statistics, National Vital Statistics System; *Vital statistics of the United States, Vol II, mortality, part A*, 1980. Washington, DC: Public Health Service. 1985; 2003 annual mortality file.

This table will be updated on the Web. Go to www.cdc.gov/nchs/hus.htm.

Table 32 (page 1 of 2). Leading causes of death and numbers of deaths, by age: United States, 1980 and 2003

[Data are based on death certificates]

Age and rank order	1980		2003	
	Cause of death	Deaths	Cause of death	Deaths
Under 1 year				
. . .	All causes	45,526	All causes	28,025
1.	Congenital anomalies	9,220	Congenital malformations, deformations and chromosomal abnormalities	5,621
2.	Sudden infant death syndrome	5,510	Disorders related to short gestation and low birth weight, not elsewhere classified	4,849
3.	Respiratory distress syndrome	4,989	Sudden infant death syndrome	2,162
4.	Disorders relating to short gestation and unspecified low birthweight	3,648	Newborn affected by maternal complications of pregnancy	1,710
5.	Newborn affected by maternal complications of pregnancy	1,572	Newborn affected by complications of placenta, cord and membranes	1,099
6.	Intrauterine hypoxia and birth asphyxia	1,497	nintentional injuries	945
7.	Unintentional injuries	1,166	Respiratory distress of newborn	831
8.	Birth trauma	1,058	Bacterial sepsis of newborn	772
9.	Pneumonia and influenza	1,012	Neonatal hemorrhage	649
10.	Newborn affected by complications of placenta, cord, and membranes	985	Diseases of circulatory system	591
1–4 years				
. . .	All causes	8,187	All causes	4,965
1.	Unintentional injuries	3,313	Unintentional injuries	1,717
2.	Congenital anomalies	1,026	Congenital malformations, deformations and chromosomal abnormalities	541
3.	Malignant neoplasms	573	Malignant neoplasms	392
4.	Diseases of heart	338	Homicide	376
5.	Homicide	319	Diseases of heart	186
6.	Pneumonia and influenza	267	Influenza and pneumonia	163
7.	Meningitis	223	Septicemia	85
8.	Meningococcal infection	110	Certain conditions originating in the perinatal period	79
9.	Certain conditions originating in the perinatal period	84	Chronic lower respiratory diseases	55
10.	Septicemia	71	In situ neoplasms, benign neoplasms and neoplasms of uncertain or unknown behavior	51
5–14 years				
. . .	All causes	10,689	All causes	6,954
1.	Unintentional injuries	5,224	Unintentional injuries	2,618
2.	Malignant neoplasms	1,497	Malignant neoplasms	1,076
3.	Congenital anomalies	561	Congenital malformations, deformations and chromosomal abnormalities	386
4.	Homicide	415	Homicide	324
5.	Diseases of heart	330	Diseases of heart	264
6.	Pneumonia and influenza	194	Suicide	250
7.	Suicide	142	Influenza and pneumonia	147
8.	Benign neoplasms	104	Chronic lower respiratory diseases	118
9.	Cerebrovascular diseases	95	In situ neoplasms, benign neoplasms and neoplasms of uncertain or unknown behavior	79
10.	Chronic obstructive pulmonary diseases	85	Septicemia	77
15–24 years				
. . .	All causes	49,027	All causes	33,568
1.	Unintentional injuries	26,206	Unintentional injuries	15,272
2.	Homicide	6,537	Homicide	5,368
3.	Suicide	5,239	Suicide	3,988
4.	Malignant neoplasms	2,683	Malignant neoplasms	1,651
5.	Diseases of heart	1,223	Diseases of heart	1,133
6.	Congenital anomalies	600	Congenital malformations, deformations and chromosomal abnormalities	451
7.	Cerebrovascular diseases	418	Influenza and pneumonia	224
8.	Pneumonia and influenza	348	Cerebrovascular diseases	221
9.	Chronic obstructive pulmonary diseases	141	Chronic lower respiratory diseases	191
10.	Anemias	133	Human immunodeficiency virus (HIV) disease	178

See footnotes at end of table.

This table will be updated on the Web. Go to www.cdc.gov/nchs/hus.htm.

Table 32 (page 2 of 2). Leading causes of death and numbers of deaths, by age: United States, 1980 and 2003

[Data are based on death certificates]

Age and rank order	1980		2003	
	Cause of death	Deaths	Cause of death	Deaths
25–44 years				
. . .	All causes	108,658	All causes	130,761
1.	Unintentional injuries	26,722	Unintentional injuries	29,307
2.	Malignant neoplasms	17,551	Malignant neoplasms	19,250
3.	Diseases of heart	14,513	Diseases of heart	16,850
4.	Homicide	10,983	Suicide	11,667
5.	Suicide	9,855	Homicide	7,626
6.	Chronic liver disease and cirrhosis	4,782	Human immunodeficiency virus (HIV) disease	6,928
7.	Cerebrovascular diseases	3,154	Chronic liver disease and cirrhosis	3,378
8.	Diabetes mellitus	1,472	Cerebrovascular diseases	3,043
9.	Pneumonia and influenza	1,467	Diabetes mellitus	2,706
10.	Congenital anomalies	817	Influenza and pneumonia	1,365
45–64 years				
. . .	All causes	425,338	All causes	439,300
1.	Diseases of heart	148,322	Malignant neoplasms	145,535
2.	Malignant neoplasms	135,675	Diseases of heart	102,792
3.	Cerebrovascular diseases	19,909	Unintentional injuries	25,007
4.	Unintentional injuries	18,140	Diabetes mellitus	16,389
5.	Chronic liver disease and cirrhosis	16,089	Cerebrovascular diseases	16,073
6.	Chronic obstructive pulmonary diseases	11,514	Chronic lower respiratory diseases	15,614
7.	Diabetes mellitus	7,977	Chronic liver disease and cirrhosis	13,894
8.	Suicide	7,079	Suicide	10,324
9.	Pneumonia and influenza	5,804	Human immunodeficiency virus (HIV) disease	5,959
10.	Homicide	4,019	Septicemia	5,808
65 years and over				
. . .	All causes	1,341,848	All causes	1,804,373
1.	Diseases of heart	595,406	Diseases of heart	563,390
2.	Malignant neoplasms	258,389	Malignant neoplasms	388,911
3.	Cerebrovascular diseases	146,417	Cerebrovascular diseases	138,134
4.	Pneumonia and influenza	45,512	Chronic lower respiratory diseases	109,139
5.	Chronic obstructive pulmonary diseases	43,587	Alzheimer's disease	62,814
6.	Atherosclerosis	28,081	Influenza and pneumonia	57,670
7.	Diabetes mellitus	25,216	Diabetes mellitus	54,919
8.	Unintentional injuries	24,844	Nephritis, nephrotic syndrome and nephrosis	35,254
9.	Nephritis, nephrotic syndrome, and nephrosis	12,968	Unintentional injuries	34,335
10.	Chronic liver disease and cirrhosis	9,519	Septicemia	26,445

. . . Category not applicable.

NOTES: For cause of death codes based on the *International Classification of Diseases, 9th Revision* (ICD–9) in 1980 and ICD–10 in 2002, see Appendix II, Cause of death; tables IV and V.

SOURCES: Centers for Disease Control and Prevention, National Center for Health Statistics, National Vital Statistics System; *Vital statistics of the United States, Vol II, mortality, part A*, 1980. Washington, DC: Public Health Service. 1985; 2003 annual mortality file.

This table will be updated on the Web. Go to www.cdc.gov/nchs/hus.htm.

Table 33 (page 1 of 3). Age-adjusted death rates, by race, sex, region, and urbanization level: United States, average annual 1995–1997, 1998–2000, and 2001–2003

[Data are based on the National Vital Statistics System]

Sex, region, and urbanization level[1]	All races			White			Black or African American		
	1995–1997	1998–2000	2001–2003	1995–1997	1998–2000	2001–2003	1995–1997	1998–2000	2001–2003
Both sexes	Age-adjusted death rate per 100,000 standard population[2]								
All regions:									
Metropolitan counties:									
Large	886.3	854.1	821.3	857.1	831.0	802.2	1,167.8	1,106.1	1,063.8
Medium.	872.6	857.4	835.8	852.6	839.8	821.2	1,171.4	1,139.1	1,097.7
Small	896.8	886.8	868.7	875.5	866.7	850.7	1,190.9	1,170.2	1,140.9
Nonmetropolitan counties:									
Micropolitan.	920.6	907.9	892.4	899.4	888.3	875.6	1,225.6	1,188.8	1,154.2
Nonmicropolitan.	940.1	926.6	910.9	916.9	903.0	890.9	1,198.8	1,186.7	1,144.0
Northeast:									
Metropolitan counties:									
Large	888.4	837.5	800.0	864.4	822.7	790.4	1,089.3	994.5	941.4
Medium.	862.2	838.6	808.7	851.3	830.6	802.7	1,111.4	1,047.6	982.9
Small	864.2	849.4	826.1	859.0	845.7	822.6	1,157.9	1,060.4	1,061.6
Nonmetropolitan counties:									
Micropolitan.	888.3	858.3	834.3	887.6	858.2	835.8	*	*	*
Nonmicropolitan.	898.4	884.1	851.3	897.3	881.1	850.8	*	*	*
Midwest:									
Metropolitan counties:									
Large	919.6	900.1	863.2	873.2	857.3	824.4	1,225.6	1,189.2	1,142.4
Medium.	885.2	878.4	851.7	864.9	860.1	835.9	1,190.3	1,162.8	1,107.2
Small	865.6	857.4	832.2	852.5	845.5	820.9	1,194.3	1,157.5	1,141.8
Nonmetropolitan counties:									
Micropolitan.	876.8	870.0	842.6	872.2	865.6	840.5	1,216.5	1,205.3	1,076.4
Nonmicropolitan.	877.0	857.8	838.4	867.6	848.7	831.1	1,343.2	1,347.3	1,088.5
South:									
Metropolitan counties:									
Large	903.4	881.3	858.3	851.6	836.9	818.0	1,202.1	1,145.7	1,113.2
Medium.	897.0	886.3	868.7	854.9	847.0	833.7	1,187.5	1,161.8	1,127.9
Small	954.9	949.5	936.1	919.9	916.4	907.5	1,199.5	1,183.6	1,152.4
Nonmetropolitan counties:									
Micropolitan.	981.2	970.0	965.1	939.2	932.4	934.0	1,237.1	1,199.0	1,173.4
Nonmicropolitan.	1,010.3	1,004.2	992.9	981.1	975.3	970.2	1,196.8	1,184.4	1,151.2
West:									
Metropolitan counties:									
Large	831.9	797.9	762.5	839.2	808.9	776.1	1,125.0	1,074.9	1,038.9
Medium.	823.3	802.0	788.3	834.1	815.8	805.6	1,069.3	1,017.8	974.3
Small	830.8	811.4	798.8	830.1	811.0	799.8	1,020.3	1,014.2	954.0
Nonmetropolitan counties:									
Micropolitan.	867.1	852.7	842.7	867.5	853.0	842.6	*	*	*
Nonmicropolitan.	875.6	851.1	841.1	855.3	829.2	822.3	*	*	*

See footnotes at end of table.

This table will be updated on the Web. Go to www.cdc.gov/nchs/hus.htm.

Table 33 (page 2 of 3). Age-adjusted death rates, by race, sex, region, and urbanization level: United States, average annual 1995–1997, 1998–2000, and 2001–2003

[Data are based on the National Vital Statistics System]

Sex, region, and urbanization level[1]	All races			White			Black or African American		
	1995–1997	1998–2000	2001–2003	1995–1997	1998–2000	2001–2003	1995–1997	1998–2000	2001–2003
Male	Age-adjusted death rate per 100,000 standard population[2]								
All regions:									
Metropolitan counties:									
Large	1,101.1	1,036.5	981.0	1,061.8	1,006.1	956.2	1,514.0	1,395.7	1,319.0
Medium	1,085.9	1,041.7	999.4	1,059.9	1,019.8	980.3	1,504.6	1,418.1	1,354.4
Small	1,123.2	1,084.7	1,044.7	1,096.2	1,059.8	1,022.9	1,528.3	1,463.0	1,410.3
Nonmetropolitan counties:									
Micropolitan	1,156.9	1,116.6	1,077.3	1,130.0	1,091.9	1,056.6	1,583.6	1,506.3	1,438.9
Nonmicropolitan	1,190.5	1,144.8	1,104.1	1,161.7	1,115.1	1,080.2	1,549.8	1,511.2	1,419.3
Northeast:									
Metropolitan counties:									
Large	1,111.7	1,025.7	963.0	1,078.5	1,006.2	950.0	1,431.2	1,265.4	1,176.9
Medium	1,079.7	1,028.2	974.2	1,066.4	1,018.9	967.5	1,397.0	1,288.1	1,190.8
Small	1,080.7	1,042.4	993.3	1,075.0	1,038.3	991.5	1,449.6	1,338.9	1,206.8
Nonmetropolitan counties:									
Micropolitan	1,110.1	1,055.0	1,006.9	1,109.3	1,056.4	1,010.0	*	*	*
Nonmicropolitan	1,115.5	1,067.2	1,020.9	1,114.8	1,064.0	1,021.8	*	*	*
Midwest:									
Metropolitan counties:									
Large	1,148.9	1,100.0	1,034.9	1,088.4	1,045.5	985.8	1,581.6	1,499.7	1,421.1
Medium	1,107.3	1,075.1	1,019.7	1,082.2	1,053.8	1,002.0	1,500.9	1,420.7	1,329.7
Small	1,088.5	1,056.9	1,011.3	1,072.7	1,042.5	998.6	1,490.5	1,429.6	1,377.1
Nonmetropolitan counties:									
Micropolitan	1,110.9	1,073.2	1,027.2	1,105.5	1,068.4	1,026.1	1,552.4	1,458.4	1,253.2
Nonmicropolitan	1,113.3	1,061.9	1,023.3	1,101.9	1,051.2	1,015.2	1,659.2	1,697.6	1,319.5
South:									
Metropolitan counties:									
Large	1,125.6	1,068.8	1,023.7	1,056.1	1,010.5	972.8	1,563.7	1,450.2	1,378.9
Medium	1,123.2	1,078.6	1,040.4	1,065.8	1,027.9	994.6	1,550.3	1,467.3	1,414.8
Small	1,210.6	1,169.0	1,132.1	1,165.3	1,126.5	1,095.1	1,557.4	1,493.9	1,442.8
Nonmetropolitan counties:									
Micropolitan	1,245.2	1,204.9	1,170.0	1,190.0	1,155.4	1,128.3	1,613.8	1,538.4	1,481.6
Nonmicropolitan	1,293.5	1,254.6	1,209.4	1,257.3	1,217.4	1,181.4	1,554.9	1,513.7	1,435.3
West:									
Metropolitan counties:									
Large	1,017.9	955.3	903.5	1,025.8	966.5	917.8	1,409.4	1,313.1	1,257.3
Medium	1,003.5	957.8	933.3	1,017.4	973.3	949.4	1,278.3	1,192.7	1,146.2
Small	1,011.7	971.1	938.8	1,010.9	971.0	940.0	1,210.2	1,110.4	1,117.2
Nonmetropolitan counties:									
Micropolitan	1,050.0	1,018.9	990.3	1,049.8	1,016.6	987.6	*	*	*
Nonmicropolitan	1,066.5	1,017.0	991.4	1,042.5	989.0	965.3	*	*	*

See footnotes at end of table.

This table will be updated on the Web. Go to www.cdc.gov/nchs/hus.htm.

Table 33 (page 3 of 3). Age-adjusted death rates, by race, sex, region, and urbanization level: United States, average annual 1995–1997, 1998–2000, and 2001–2003

[Data are based on the National Vital Statistics System]

Sex, region, and urbanization level[1]	All races			White			Black or African American		
	1995–1997	1998–2000	2001–2003	1995–1997	1998–2000	2001–2003	1995–1997	1998–2000	2001–2003
Female	Age-adjusted death rate per 100,000 standard population[2]								
All regions:									
Metropolitan counties:									
Large	731.0	720.2	699.5	709.0	701.7	683.7	931.7	909.9	885.5
Medium.	717.8	720.5	708.9	702.6	705.8	697.2	938.3	943.9	912.9
Small	733.9	741.1	733.1	716.4	723.9	717.4	959.3	969.2	949.8
Nonmetropolitan counties:									
Micropolitan.	747.5	751.6	747.5	730.6	735.3	733.1	978.2	973.6	954.6
Nonmicropolitan.	750.8	757.1	754.8	731.9	737.8	737.1	948.7	957.8	946.7
Northeast:									
Metropolitan counties:									
Large	733.2	705.4	680.4	715.4	692.9	672.2	868.4	820.4	785.1
Medium.	713.9	705.8	686.9	705.4	698.9	681.9	903.7	875.9	825.5
Small	714.5	712.3	701.3	710.0	708.7	697.3	960.0	889.0	947.2
Nonmetropolitan counties:									
Micropolitan.	731.2	715.0	705.0	731.1	714.2	705.7	*	*	*
Nonmicropolitan.	738.2	743.0	714.4	736.9	740.4	713.0	*	*	*
Midwest:									
Metropolitan counties:									
Large	761.4	759.5	736.4	727.0	726.1	705.8	977.7	973.3	943.0
Medium.	732.7	740.4	726.7	716.5	724.6	713.2	968.6	975.8	934.8
Small	711.8	716.0	700.3	701.3	706.3	690.4	972.4	951.7	958.9
Nonmetropolitan counties:									
Micropolitan.	712.6	723.3	704.3	708.8	719.1	701.8	969.8	1,042.4	932.3
Nonmicropolitan.	699.7	700.7	691.3	692.2	693.1	684.8	1,128.5	1,139.8	931.5
South:									
Metropolitan counties:									
Large	739.9	740.7	730.1	700.2	704.7	695.8	955.7	940.4	929.4
Medium.	728.4	739.1	731.6	696.1	706.2	702.6	940.7	954.5	930.0
Small	773.4	789.7	785.7	744.4	761.2	761.1	960.9	977.2	954.0
Nonmetropolitan counties:									
Micropolitan.	788.8	796.0	804.7	754.9	764.3	778.5	981.8	972.8	962.5
Nonmicropolitan.	801.0	814.7	820.9	776.4	790.3	799.9	943.6	953.2	948.9
West:									
Metropolitan counties:									
Large	688.7	675.8	650.0	694.8	685.6	662.0	913.9	899.8	871.1
Medium.	684.1	680.1	672.0	694.3	693.4	689.8	895.5	871.2	828.5
Small	686.7	683.6	682.3	686.1	683.3	683.1	851.8	910.5	794.1
Nonmetropolitan counties:									
Micropolitan.	714.1	712.7	712.2	715.9	715.2	714.1	*	*	*
Nonmicropolitan.	711.2	705.2	706.3	695.5	689.5	693.7	*	*	*

* Estimates of death rates for the black population in nonmetropolitan counties in the Northeast and West may be unreliable, possibly due to anomalies in population estimates for the black population in nonmetropolitan counties in these regions.

[1] Urbanization levels are for county of residence of decedent. See Appendix II, Urbanization for definition of urbanization levels.

[2] Average annual death rates, age-adjusted using the year 2000 standard population. In earlier editions of *Health, United States*, age-adjusted rates were calculated using standard million proportions based on rounded population numbers. Starting with *Health, United States 2006*, unrounded population numbers are used to calculate age-adjusted rates. See Appendix II, Age adjustment. Denominators for rates are population estimates for the middle year of each 3-year period multiplied by 3. The 1996 and 1999 population estimates used to compute rates for 1995–1997 and 1998–2000 are intercensal population estimates based on the 2000 census. See Appendix I, Population Census and Population Estimates.

NOTE: The race groups, white and black, include persons of Hispanic and non-Hispanic origin. Data have been revised and differ from previous editions of *Health, United States*.

SOURCE: Centers for Disease Control and Prevention, National Center for Health Statistics, National Vital Statistics System, Compressed Mortality File.

This table will be updated on the Web. Go to www.cdc.gov/nchs/hus.htm.

Table 34 (page 1 of 2). Age-adjusted death rates among persons 25–64 years of age for selected causes of death, by sex and educational attainment: Selected states, 1994–2003

[Data are based on death certificates]

Cause of death[2] and year	Both sexes Years of educational attainment[1]			Male Years of educational attainment[1]			Female Years of educational attainment[1]		
	Less than 12	12	13 or more	Less than 12	12	13 or more	Less than 12	12	13 or more
All causes	Age-adjusted death rate per 100,000 population[3]								
1994	594.6	506.4	254.8	793.6	707.1	323.5	397.3	342.9	182.1
1995	604.7	512.5	251.9	801.1	713.2	316.8	408.6	348.1	183.5
1996	579.6	492.5	241.8	763.9	669.6	300.7	396.6	344.2	180.3
1997	554.1	473.4	232.7	719.7	634.4	283.4	387.2	337.5	180.2
1998	561.6	465.8	223.9	727.6	627.1	271.9	395.6	330.9	174.3
1999	585.3	474.5	219.1	763.7	636.7	264.2	409.9	337.3	172.6
2000	591.0	484.5	216.7	780.2	641.8	260.8	409.0	347.7	171.9
2001	576.6	480.9	214.6	745.8	631.2	257.3	407.1	348.6	171.5
2002	575.1	490.9	211.3	726.1	650.2	253.5	416.6	350.7	168.8
2003[4]	669.9	490.9	211.7	826.8	650.9	252.5	496.8	349.4	171.0
Chronic and noncommunicable diseases									
1994	440.5	380.7	193.7	561.9	504.4	228.4	325.0	286.8	155.5
1995	445.1	384.0	192.1	563.4	507.3	224.4	332.1	290.0	156.3
1996	432.7	375.3	189.0	550.6	486.9	222.1	321.2	287.7	153.4
1997	419.0	368.8	187.4	527.0	474.1	219.0	316.0	284.6	153.8
1998	425.2	362.9	180.9	534.4	470.2	211.3	321.3	277.9	148.6
1998 comparability-modified[5]	429.5	366.5	182.7	539.7	474.9	213.4	324.5	280.7	150.1
1999[6]	447.0	369.8	177.2	563.0	477.6	205.5	337.2	283.6	147.4
2000	446.2	377.6	175.7	567.2	481.5	202.9	334.3	292.3	147.2
2001	436.5	370.7	171.1	545.1	468.2	195.7	331.7	290.3	145.5
2002	432.0	374.4	168.6	528.9	478.2	193.9	334.9	288.5	142.6
2003[4]	502.7	373.4	167.6	603.6	478.5	191.8	396.7	286.4	142.7
Injuries									
1994	95.8	73.4	31.9	149.4	119.2	45.7	38.9	31.7	17.9
1995	96.6	74.3	31.6	149.4	120.3	45.3	40.0	32.1	17.8
1996	92.3	73.0	32.0	139.8	116.2	45.7	40.6	32.7	18.4
1997	92.7	73.5	31.9	138.8	116.4	45.5	41.1	33.4	18.4
1998	93.9	73.8	31.2	139.4	116.6	44.4	43.8	33.7	18.3
1998 comparability-modified[5]	95.4	75.0	31.7	141.6	118.4	45.1	44.5	34.2	18.6
1999[6]	95.5	75.5	30.6	145.1	118.9	43.3	42.6	34.4	18.1
2000	100.4	76.7	30.3	155.1	119.2	43.1	43.7	35.3	17.9
2001[7]	97.9	80.7	33.2	147.0	122.7	47.6	44.8	38.6	19.3
2002	99.6	85.2	32.2	143.3	129.6	45.5	49.2	41.0	19.2
2003[4]	116.6	88.3	33.5	162.9	133.7	46.8	60.5	42.6	20.6
Communicable diseases									
1994	57.5	51.6	28.9	81.5	82.8	49.1	32.5	23.7	8.4
1995	62.1	53.4	27.9	87.3	84.7	46.7	35.8	25.2	8.9
1996	53.7	43.3	20.2	72.5	65.6	32.6	33.8	23.0	8.0
1997	41.6	30.1	12.9	53.1	42.9	18.4	29.3	18.7	7.6
1998	41.5	28.2	11.4	52.8	39.4	15.7	29.6	18.4	7.0
1998 comparability-modified[5]	35.6	24.2	9.8	45.3	33.8	13.5	25.4	15.8	6.0
1999[6]	42.1	28.5	10.8	54.8	39.5	15.1	29.4	18.8	6.6
2000	43.5	29.4	10.3	56.9	40.4	14.3	30.3	19.5	6.4
2001	41.4	28.7	9.9	52.9	39.4	13.6	29.7	19.0	6.3
2002	42.7	30.5	10.2	53.0	41.6	13.8	31.8	20.4	6.7
2003[4]	49.6	28.3	10.2	59.3	37.8	13.5	38.7	19.8	7.2
HIV disease:									
1994	36.2	36.5	21.4	54.7	63.0	39.7	16.8	12.3	2.9
1995	39.7	38.0	20.6	59.0	64.4	37.8	19.0	13.7	3.5
1996	31.9	27.7	13.1	45.4	45.4	23.8	17.2	11.2	2.4
1997	19.4	14.3	5.8	26.3	23.0	10.1	11.8	6.2	1.6
1998	17.3	11.7	4.3	23.4	18.3	7.5	10.6	5.6	1.1
1998 comparability-modified[5]	18.7	12.7	4.7	25.3	19.8	8.1	11.5	6.1	1.2
1999[6]	19.0	13.1	4.6	26.1	20.1	7.9	11.7	6.6	1.4
2000	19.8	13.2	4.1	26.9	19.8	7.1	12.6	7.1	1.2
2001	18.4	12.5	3.8	25.0	18.6	6.4	11.6	6.8	1.2
2002	18.2	12.6	3.8	23.4	18.6	6.3	12.6	6.9	1.3
2003[4]	19.6	10.6	3.4	23.9	15.5	5.8	14.5	5.8	1.2

See footnotes at end of table.

This table will be updated on the Web. Go to www.cdc.gov/nchs/hus.htm.

Table 34 (page 2 of 2). **Age-adjusted death rates among persons 25–64 years of age for selected causes of death, by sex and educational attainment: Selected states, 1994–2003**

[Data are based on death certificates]

Cause of death[2] and year	Both sexes			Male			Female		
	Years of educational attainment[1]			Years of educational attainment[1]			Years of educational attainment[1]		
	Less than 12	12	13 or more	Less than 12	12	13 or more	Less than 12	12	13 or more
Other communicable diseases:	Age-adjusted death rate per 100,000 population[3]								
1994	21.2	15.1	7.5	26.8	19.7	9.4	15.7	11.4	5.5
1995	22.4	15.5	7.2	28.2	20.3	8.8	16.8	11.5	5.5
1996	21.8	15.7	7.2	27.2	20.2	8.8	16.7	11.9	5.6
1997	22.2	15.9	7.1	26.8	19.9	8.2	17.6	12.5	6.0
1998	24.2	16.5	7.1	29.4	21.1	8.2	19.0	12.8	5.9
1998 comparability-modified[5]	19.4	13.2	5.7	23.5	16.9	6.6	15.2	10.2	4.7
1999[6]	23.1	15.4	6.2	28.8	19.4	7.2	17.6	12.2	5.3
2000	23.7	16.2	6.2	30.0	20.6	7.2	17.7	12.4	5.1
2001	22.9	16.2	6.1	27.9	20.8	7.1	18.1	12.2	5.1
2002	24.5	17.9	6.4	29.6	23.0	7.5	19.1	13.5	5.4
2003[4]	30.1	17.8	6.8	35.4	22.3	7.7	24.2	13.9	6.0

[1]Educational attainment for the numerator is based on the death certificate item highest grade completed. Educational attainment for the denominator is based on answers to the Current Population Survey question, What is the highest level of school completed or highest degree received? (Kominski R, Adams A. Educational Attainment in the United States: March 1993 and 1992, U.S. Bureau of the Census, Current Population Reports, P20–476, Washington, DC. 1994.)

[2]Underlying cause of death was coded according to the Ninth Revision of the *International Classification of Diseases* (ICD) in 1994–1998 and the Tenth Revision starting in 1999. See Appendix II, Cause of death; tables IV and V.

[3]Age-adjusted to the 2000 standard population using four age groups: 25–34, 35–44, 45–54, and 55–64 years. Prior to 2003, age-adjusted rates were calculated using standard million proportions based on rounded population numbers. Starting with 2003 data, unrounded population numbers are used to calculate age-adjusted rates. See Appendix II, Age adjustment; table I. Death records that are missing information about decedent's education are not included. Percent with no stated education averages 2–9% for causes of death in this table. Age-adjusted death rates for 1994–2000 were calculated using 1990-based postcensal population estimates in the denominator. Starting with 2001 data, rates were computed using 2000-based postcensal estimates. See Appendix I, Population Census and Population Estimates.

[4]Starting with 2003 data, data from California, Idaho, Montana, and New York are excluded. These states implemented the 2003 revision of the U.S. Standard Certificate of Death. Educational attainment data from the revised death certificate are not comparable with educational attainment data collected using the 1989 revision of the U.S. Standard Certificate of Death. Because of different education profiles of the four excluded states compared with the remaining states and the District of Columbia, 2003 data are not directly comparable to earlier years. See Appendix II, Education.

[5]Calculated by multiplying the 1998 rate by its comparability ratio to adjust for differences between ICD–9 and ICD–10. Comparability-modified 1998 rates were revised in *Health, United States, 2005* and may differ from previous editions. See Appendix II, Cause of death; Comparability ratio; table VI.

[6]Starting with 1999 data, cause of death is coded according to ICD–10. To estimate change between 1998 and 1999, compare the 1999 rate with the comparability-modified rate for 1998. See Appendix II, Cause of death; Comparability ratio; tables V and VI.

[7]Figures include September 11, 2001-related deaths for which death certificates were filed as of October 24, 2002. See Appendix II, Cause of death; table V for terrorism-related ICD–10 codes.

NOTES: Based on data from 43–47 states and the District of Columbia. Death rates for age groups 65 years and over are not shown because reporting quality of educational attainment on the death certificate is poorer among older decedents. See Appendix II, Education, for information about reporting states and sources of bias in death rates by educational attainment. Injury data for 1999–2003 were revised and may differ from previous editions of *Health, United States*.

SOURCES: Centers for Disease Control and Prevention, National Center for Health Statistics, National Vital Statistics System; numerator data from annual mortality files; denominator data from unpublished population estimates prepared by the Housing and Household Economic Statistics Division, U.S. Census Bureau.

This table will be updated on the Web. Go to www.cdc.gov/nchs/hus.htm.

Table 35 (page 1 of 4). Death rates for all causes, by sex, race, Hispanic origin, and age: United States, selected years 1950–2003

[Data are based on death certificates]

Sex, race, Hispanic origin, and age	1950[1]	1960[1]	1970	1980	1990	2000	2002	2003
All persons			Deaths per 100,000 resident population					
All ages, age adjusted[2]	1,446.0	1,339.2	1,222.6	1,039.1	938.7	869.0	845.3	832.7
All ages, crude	963.8	954.7	945.3	878.3	863.8	854.0	847.3	841.9
Under 1 year	3,299.2	2,696.4	2,142.4	1,288.3	971.9	736.7	695.0	700.0
1–4 years	139.4	109.1	84.5	63.9	46.8	32.4	31.2	31.5
5–14 years	60.1	46.6	41.3	30.6	24.0	18.0	17.4	17.0
15–24 years	128.1	106.3	127.7	115.4	99.2	79.9	81.4	81.5
25–34 years	178.7	146.4	157.4	135.5	139.2	101.4	103.6	103.6
35–44 years	358.7	299.4	314.5	227.9	223.2	198.9	202.9	201.6
45–54 years	853.9	756.0	730.0	584.0	473.4	425.6	430.1	433.2
55–64 years	1,901.0	1,735.1	1,658.8	1,346.3	1,196.9	992.2	952.4	940.9
65–74 years	4,104.3	3,822.1	3,582.7	2,994.9	2,648.6	2,399.1	2,314.7	2,255.0
75–84 years	9,331.1	8,745.2	8,004.4	6,692.6	6,007.2	5,666.5	5,556.9	5,463.1
85 years and over	20,196.9	19,857.5	16,344.9	15,980.3	15,327.4	15,524.4	14,828.3	14,593.3
Male								
All ages, age adjusted[2]	1,674.2	1,609.0	1,542.1	1,348.1	1,202.8	1,053.8	1,013.7	994.3
All ages, crude	1,106.1	1,104.5	1,090.3	976.9	918.4	853.0	846.6	840.3
Under 1 year	3,728.0	3,059.3	2,410.0	1,428.5	1,082.8	806.5	761.5	777.4
1–4 years	151.7	119.5	93.2	72.6	52.4	35.9	35.2	35.1
5–14 years	70.9	55.7	50.5	36.7	28.5	20.9	20.0	19.8
15–24 years	167.9	152.1	188.5	172.3	147.4	114.9	117.3	116.5
25–34 years	216.5	187.9	215.3	196.1	204.3	138.6	142.2	141.4
35–44 years	428.8	372.8	402.6	299.2	310.4	255.2	257.5	255.0
45–54 years	1,067.1	992.2	958.5	767.3	610.3	542.8	547.5	552.2
55–64 years	2,395.3	2,309.5	2,282.7	1,815.1	1,553.4	1,230.7	1,184.0	1,165.5
65–74 years	4,931.4	4,914.4	4,873.8	4,105.2	3,491.5	2,979.6	2,855.3	2,771.7
75–84 years	10,426.0	10,178.4	10,010.2	8,816.7	7,888.6	6,972.6	6,760.5	6,641.8
85 years and over	21,636.0	21,186.3	17,821.5	18,801.1	18,056.6	17,501.4	16,254.5	15,794.0
Female								
All ages, age adjusted[2]	1,236.0	1,105.3	971.4	817.9	750.9	731.4	715.2	706.2
All ages, crude	823.5	809.2	807.8	785.3	812.0	855.0	848.0	843.4
Under 1 year	2,854.6	2,321.3	1,863.7	1,141.7	855.7	663.4	625.3	619.1
1–4 years	126.7	98.4	75.4	54.7	41.0	28.7	27.0	27.8
5–14 years	48.9	37.3	31.8	24.2	19.3	15.0	14.7	14.0
15–24 years	89.1	61.3	68.1	57.5	49.0	43.1	43.7	44.4
25–34 years	142.7	106.6	101.6	75.9	74.2	63.5	64.0	64.6
35–44 years	290.3	229.4	231.1	159.3	137.9	143.2	148.8	148.5
45–54 years	641.5	526.7	517.2	412.9	342.7	312.5	316.9	318.4
55–64 years	1,404.8	1,196.4	1,098.9	934.3	878.8	772.2	738.0	732.7
65–74 years	3,333.2	2,871.8	2,579.7	2,144.7	1,991.2	1,921.2	1,864.7	1,823.0
75–84 years	8,399.6	7,633.1	6,677.6	5,440.1	4,883.1	4,814.7	4,757.9	4,675.5
85 years and over	19,194.7	19,008.4	15,518.0	14,746.9	14,274.3	14,719.2	14,209.6	14,062.5
White male[3]								
All ages, age adjusted[2]	1,642.5	1,586.0	1,513.7	1,317.6	1,165.9	1,029.4	992.9	973.9
All ages, crude	1,089.5	1,098.5	1,086.7	983.3	930.9	887.8	884.0	877.6
Under 1 year	3,400.5	2,694.1	2,113.2	1,230.3	896.1	667.6	650.9	658.7
1–4 years	135.5	104.9	83.6	66.1	45.9	32.6	31.5	31.5
5–14 years	67.2	52.7	48.0	35.0	26.4	19.8	18.4	18.4
15–24 years	152.4	143.7	170.8	167.0	131.3	105.8	109.7	108.9
25–34 years	185.3	163.2	176.6	171.3	176.1	124.1	128.3	128.8
35–44 years	380.9	332.6	343.5	257.4	268.2	233.6	239.3	237.6
45–54 years	984.5	932.2	882.9	698.9	548.7	496.9	505.4	509.2
55–64 years	2,304.4	2,225.2	2,202.6	1,728.5	1,467.2	1,163.3	1,118.6	1,102.3
65–74 years	4,864.9	4,848.4	4,810.1	4,035.7	3,397.7	2,905.7	2,795.4	2,707.3
75–84 years	10,526.3	10,299.6	10,098.8	8,829.8	7,844.9	6,933.1	6,738.8	6,620.6
85 years and over	22,116.3	21,750.0	18,551.7	19,097.3	18,268.3	17,716.4	16,473.2	16,037.9

See footnotes at end of table.

This table will be updated on the Web. Go to www.cdc.gov/nchs/hus.htm.

Table 35 (page 2 of 4). Death rates for all causes, by sex, race, Hispanic origin, and age: United States, selected years 1950–2003

[Data are based on death certificates]

Sex, race, Hispanic origin, and age	1950[1]	1960[1]	1970	1980	1990	2000	2002	2003
Black or African American male[3]				Deaths per 100,000 resident population				
All ages, age adjusted[2]	1,909.1	1,811.1	1,873.9	1,697.8	1,644.5	1,403.5	1,341.4	1,319.1
All ages, crude	1,257.7	1,181.7	1,186.6	1,034.1	1,008.0	834.1	816.7	813.7
Under 1 year	- - -	5,306.8	4,298.9	2,586.7	2,112.4	1,567.6	1,351.5	1,410.0
1–4 years[4]	1,412.6	208.5	150.5	110.5	85.8	54.5	54.4	53.7
5–14 years	95.1	75.1	67.1	47.4	41.2	28.2	28.9	26.8
15–24 years	289.7	212.0	320.6	209.1	252.2	181.4	172.6	171.3
25–34 years	503.5	402.5	559.5	407.3	430.8	261.0	264.5	256.2
35–44 years	878.1	762.0	956.6	689.8	699.6	453.0	434.7	426.7
45–54 years	1,905.0	1,624.8	1,777.5	1,479.9	1,261.0	1,017.7	983.0	991.4
55–64 years	3,773.2	3,316.4	3,256.9	2,873.0	2,618.4	2,080.1	2,039.2	2,011.2
65–74 years	5,310.3	5,798.7	5,803.2	5,131.1	4,946.1	4,253.5	4,024.5	3,981.3
75–84 years[5]	10,101.9	8,605.1	9,454.9	9,231.6	9,129.5	8,486.0	8,169.6	8,067.0
85 years and over	- - -	14,844.8	12,222.3	16,098.8	16,954.9	16,791.0	15,635.5	14,903.4
American Indian or Alaska Native male[3]								
All ages, age adjusted[2]	- - -	- - -	- - -	1,111.5	916.2	841.5	794.2	797.0
All ages, crude	- - -	- - -	- - -	597.1	476.4	415.6	439.6	457.6
Under 1 year	- - -	- - -	- - -	1,598.1	1,056.6	700.2	896.8	911.5
1–4 years	- - -	- - -	- - -	82.7	77.4	44.9	48.3	57.3
5–14 years	- - -	- - -	- - -	43.7	33.4	20.2	22.0	29.3
15–24 years	- - -	- - -	- - -	311.1	219.8	136.2	145.1	153.1
25–34 years	- - -	- - -	- - -	360.6	256.1	179.1	193.1	185.3
35–44 years	- - -	- - -	- - -	556.8	365.4	295.2	321.5	338.1
45–54 years	- - -	- - -	- - -	871.3	619.9	520.0	539.4	583.6
55–64 years	- - -	- - -	- - -	1,547.5	1,211.3	1,090.4	1,059.2	1,058.3
65–74 years	- - -	- - -	- - -	2,968.4	2,461.7	2,478.3	2,366.5	2,237.3
75–84 years	- - -	- - -	- - -	5,607.0	5,389.2	5,351.2	4,748.3	4,644.0
85 years and over	- - -	- - -	- - -	12,635.2	11,243.9	10,725.8	9,219.2	9,583.8
Asian or Pacific Islander male[3]								
All ages, age adjusted[2]	- - -	- - -	- - -	786.5	716.4	624.2	578.4	562.7
All ages, crude	- - -	- - -	- - -	375.3	334.3	332.9	331.4	330.0
Under 1 year	- - -	- - -	- - -	816.5	605.3	529.4	461.9	496.9
1–4 years	- - -	- - -	- - -	50.9	45.0	23.3	27.1	24.8
5–14 years	- - -	- - -	- - -	23.4	20.7	12.9	14.4	14.6
15–24 years	- - -	- - -	- - -	80.8	76.0	55.2	58.6	56.3
25–34 years	- - -	- - -	- - -	83.5	79.6	55.0	54.5	53.8
35–44 years	- - -	- - -	- - -	128.3	130.8	104.9	100.0	95.9
45–54 years	- - -	- - -	- - -	342.3	287.1	249.7	248.4	242.6
55–64 years	- - -	- - -	- - -	881.1	789.1	642.4	594.5	565.5
65–74 years	- - -	- - -	- - -	2,236.1	2,041.4	1,661.0	1,487.1	1,472.8
75–84 years	- - -	- - -	- - -	5,389.5	5,008.6	4,328.2	4,090.8	4,041.0
85 years and over	- - -	- - -	- - -	13,753.6	12,446.3	12,125.3	10,938.5	10,391.7
Hispanic or Latino male[3,6]								
All ages, age adjusted[2]	- - -	- - -	- - -	- - -	886.4	818.1	766.7	748.1
All ages, crude	- - -	- - -	- - -	- - -	411.6	331.3	328.7	330.7
Under 1 year	- - -	- - -	- - -	- - -	921.8	637.1	644.0	665.5
1–4 years	- - -	- - -	- - -	- - -	53.8	31.5	34.2	33.8
5–14 years	- - -	- - -	- - -	- - -	26.0	17.9	17.4	18.4
15–24 years	- - -	- - -	- - -	- - -	159.3	107.7	114.4	112.9
25–34 years	- - -	- - -	- - -	- - -	234.0	120.2	112.5	118.1
35–44 years	- - -	- - -	- - -	- - -	341.8	211.0	192.5	189.8
45–54 years	- - -	- - -	- - -	- - -	533.9	439.0	423.4	436.4
55–64 years	- - -	- - -	- - -	- - -	1,123.7	965.7	937.4	920.8
65–74 years	- - -	- - -	- - -	- - -	2,368.2	2,287.9	2,193.4	2,115.7
75–84 years	- - -	- - -	- - -	- - -	5,369.1	5,395.3	5,043.5	4,948.5
85 years and over	- - -	- - -	- - -	- - -	12,272.1	13,086.2	11,674.1	11,029.2

See footnotes at end of table.

This table will be updated on the Web. Go to www.cdc.gov/nchs/hus.htm.

Table 35 (page 3 of 4). Death rates for all causes, by sex, race, Hispanic origin, and age: United States, selected years 1950–2003

[Data are based on death certificates]

Sex, race, Hispanic origin, and age	1950[1]	1960[1]	1970	1980	1990	2000	2002	2003
White, not Hispanic or Latino male[6]				Deaths per 100,000 resident population				
All ages, age adjusted[2]	---	---	---	---	1,170.9	1,035.4	1,002.2	984.0
All ages, crude	---	---	---	---	985.9	978.5	983.9	979.1
Under 1 year	---	---	---	---	865.4	658.7	643.5	647.2
1–4 years	---	---	---	---	43.8	32.4	30.3	30.2
5–14 years	---	---	---	---	25.7	20.0	18.3	18.1
15–24 years	---	---	---	---	123.4	103.5	106.7	105.9
25–34 years	---	---	---	---	165.3	123.0	130.9	129.9
35–44 years	---	---	---	---	257.1	233.9	244.9	243.8
45–54 years	---	---	---	---	544.5	497.7	509.9	513.2
55–64 years	---	---	---	---	1,479.7	1,170.9	1,126.5	1,110.5
65–74 years	---	---	---	---	3,434.5	2,930.5	2,824.1	2,738.5
75–84 years	---	---	---	---	7,920.4	6,977.8	6,801.7	6,692.2
85 years and over	---	---	---	---	18,505.4	17,853.2	16,641.9	16,234.4
White female[3]								
All ages, age adjusted[2]	1,198.0	1,074.4	944.0	796.1	728.8	715.3	701.3	693.1
All ages, crude	803.3	800.9	812.6	806.1	846.9	912.3	907.0	902.3
Under 1 year	2,566.8	2,007.7	1,614.6	962.5	690.0	550.5	519.4	520.7
1–4 years	112.2	85.2	66.1	49.3	36.1	25.5	24.5	25.5
5–14 years	45.1	34.7	29.9	22.9	17.9	14.1	13.7	13.1
15–24 years	71.5	54.9	61.6	55.5	45.9	41.1	42.4	43.2
25–34 years	112.8	85.0	84.1	65.4	61.5	55.1	56.9	58.0
35–44 years	235.8	191.1	193.3	138.2	117.4	125.7	133.2	132.9
45–54 years	546.4	458.8	462.9	372.7	309.3	281.4	286.8	287.2
55–64 years	1,293.8	1,078.9	1,014.9	876.2	822.7	730.9	698.7	693.7
65–74 years	3,242.8	2,779.3	2,470.7	2,066.6	1,923.5	1,868.3	1,819.7	1,780.6
75–84 years	8,481.5	7,696.6	6,698.7	5,401.7	4,839.1	4,785.3	4,742.5	4,671.6
85 years and over	19,679.5	19,477.7	15,980.2	14,979.6	14,400.6	14,890.7	14,382.8	14,240.6
Black or African American female[3]								
All ages, age adjusted[2]	1,545.5	1,369.7	1,228.7	1,033.3	975.1	927.6	901.8	885.6
All ages, crude	1,002.0	905.0	829.2	733.3	747.9	733.0	724.4	717.9
Under 1 year	---	4,162.2	3,368.8	2,123.7	1,735.5	1,279.8	1,172.0	1,132.2
1–4 years[4]	1,139.3	173.3	129.4	84.4	67.6	45.3	39.5	39.7
5–14 years	72.8	53.8	43.8	30.5	27.5	20.0	19.9	18.9
15–24 years	213.1	107.5	111.9	70.5	68.7	58.3	54.4	54.0
25–34 years	393.3	273.2	231.0	150.0	159.5	121.8	116.4	113.5
35–44 years	758.1	568.5	533.0	323.9	298.6	271.9	272.3	270.0
45–54 years	1,576.4	1,177.0	1,043.9	768.2	639.4	588.3	579.4	582.3
55–64 years	3,089.4	2,510.9	1,986.2	1,561.0	1,452.6	1,227.2	1,184.2	1,178.8
65–74 years	4,000.2	4,064.2	3,860.9	3,057.4	2,865.7	2,689.6	2,545.0	2,487.2
75–84 years[5]	8,347.0	6,730.0	6,691.5	6,212.1	5,688.3	5,696.5	5,584.4	5,385.5
85 years and over	---	13,052.6	10,706.6	12,367.2	13,309.5	13,941.3	13,734.2	13,616.7
American Indian or Alaska Native female[3]								
All ages, age adjusted[2]	---	---	---	662.4	561.8	604.5	581.1	592.1
All ages, crude	---	---	---	380.1	330.4	346.1	367.7	387.7
Under 1 year	---	---	---	1,352.6	688.7	492.2	744.1	676.2
1–4 years	---	---	---	87.5	37.8	39.8	42.0	43.0
5–14 years	---	---	---	33.5	25.5	17.7	21.2	17.9
15–24 years	---	---	---	90.3	69.0	58.9	61.7	61.5
25–34 years	---	---	---	178.5	102.3	84.8	87.5	88.7
35–44 years	---	---	---	286.0	156.4	171.9	176.8	196.0
45–54 years	---	---	---	491.4	380.9	284.9	324.7	364.4
55–64 years	---	---	---	837.1	805.9	772.1	747.5	785.0
65–74 years	---	---	---	1,765.5	1,679.4	1,899.8	1,828.9	1,710.7
75–84 years	---	---	---	3,612.9	3,073.2	3,850.0	3,667.4	3,834.3
85 years and over	---	---	---	8,567.4	8,201.1	9,118.2	7,866.4	7,920.2

See footnotes at end of table.

This table will be updated on the Web. Go to www.cdc.gov/nchs/hus.htm.

Table 35 (page 4 of 4). **Death rates for all causes, by sex, race, Hispanic origin, and age: United States, selected years 1950–2003**

[Data are based on death certificates]

Sex, race, Hispanic origin, and age	1950[1]	1960[1]	1970	1980	1990	2000	2002	2003
Asian or Pacific Islander female[3]				Deaths per 100,000 resident population				
All ages, age adjusted[2]	- - -	- - -	- - -	425.9	469.3	416.8	395.9	392.7
All ages, crude	- - -	- - -	- - -	222.5	234.3	262.3	269.7	279.2
Under 1 year	- - -	- - -	- - -	755.8	518.2	434.3	391.4	427.5
1–4 years	- - -	- - -	- - -	35.4	32.0	20.0	19.6	20.1
5–14 years	- - -	- - -	- - -	21.5	13.0	11.7	10.4	11.5
15–24 years	- - -	- - -	- - -	32.3	28.8	22.4	23.8	28.8
25–34 years	- - -	- - -	- - -	45.4	37.5	27.6	26.6	29.9
35–44 years	- - -	- - -	- - -	89.7	69.9	65.6	53.9	58.2
45–54 years	- - -	- - -	- - -	214.1	182.7	155.5	149.5	150.8
55–64 years	- - -	- - -	- - -	440.8	483.4	390.9	372.0	359.2
65–74 years	- - -	- - -	- - -	1,027.7	1,089.2	996.4	1,024.7	989.9
75–84 years	- - -	- - -	- - -	2,833.6	3,127.9	2,882.4	2,713.6	2,681.8
85 years and over	- - -	- - -	- - -	7,923.3	10,254.0	9,052.2	8,400.6	8,329.2
Hispanic or Latino female[3,6]								
All ages, age adjusted[2]	- - -	- - -	- - -	- - -	537.1	546.0	518.3	515.8
All ages, crude	- - -	- - -	- - -	- - -	285.4	274.6	274.0	279.3
Under 1 year	- - -	- - -	- - -	- - -	746.6	553.6	539.1	552.4
1–4 years	- - -	- - -	- - -	- - -	42.1	27.5	25.3	26.3
5–14 years	- - -	- - -	- - -	- - -	17.3	13.4	13.5	12.8
15–24 years	- - -	- - -	- - -	- - -	40.6	31.7	34.1	35.5
25–34 years	- - -	- - -	- - -	- - -	62.9	43.4	40.0	43.0
35–44 years	- - -	- - -	- - -	- - -	109.3	100.5	94.9	95.5
45–54 years	- - -	- - -	- - -	- - -	253.3	223.8	219.8	219.1
55–64 years	- - -	- - -	- - -	- - -	607.5	548.4	524.3	527.9
65–74 years	- - -	- - -	- - -	- - -	1,453.8	1,423.2	1,368.7	1,342.9
75–84 years	- - -	- - -	- - -	- - -	3,351.3	3,624.5	3,526.4	3,506.4
85 years and over	- - -	- - -	- - -	- - -	10,098.7	11,202.8	10,186.0	10,128.1
White, not Hispanic or Latino female[6]								
All ages, age adjusted[2]	- - -	- - -	- - -	- - -	734.6	721.5	709.9	702.1
All ages, crude	- - -	- - -	- - -	- - -	903.6	1,007.3	1,010.6	1,007.6
Under 1 year	- - -	- - -	- - -	- - -	655.3	530.9	504.8	502.5
1–4 years	- - -	- - -	- - -	- - -	34.0	24.4	23.8	24.9
5–14 years	- - -	- - -	- - -	- - -	17.6	13.9	13.6	12.9
15–24 years	- - -	- - -	- - -	- - -	46.0	42.6	43.8	44.3
25–34 years	- - -	- - -	- - -	- - -	60.6	56.8	60.3	61.2
35–44 years	- - -	- - -	- - -	- - -	116.8	128.1	138.3	138.0
45–54 years	- - -	- - -	- - -	- - -	312.1	285.0	292.1	293.1
55–64 years	- - -	- - -	- - -	- - -	834.5	742.1	710.5	705.0
65–74 years	- - -	- - -	- - -	- - -	1,940.2	1,891.0	1,846.0	1,807.9
75–84 years	- - -	- - -	- - -	- - -	4,887.3	4,819.3	4,787.9	4,720.5
85 years and over	- - -	- - -	- - -	- - -	14,533.1	14,971.7	14,504.3	14,377.2

- - - Data not available.

[1] Includes deaths of persons who were not residents of the 50 states and the District of Columbia.
[2] Age-adjusted rates are calculated using the year 2000 standard population. Prior to 2003, age-adjusted rates were calculated using standard million proportions based on rounded population numbers. Starting with 2003 data, unrounded population numbers are used to calculate age-adjusted rates. See Appendix II, Age adjustment.
[3] The race groups, white, black, Asian or Pacific Islander, and American Indian or Alaska Native, include persons of Hispanic and non-Hispanic origin. Persons of Hispanic origin may be of any race. Death rates for the American Indian or Alaska Native and Asian or Pacific Islander populations are known to be underestimated. See Appendix II, Race, for a discussion of sources of bias in death rates by race and Hispanic origin.
[4] In 1950, rate is for the age group under 5 years.
[5] In 1950, rate is for the age group 75 years and over.
[6] Prior to 1997, excludes data from states lacking an Hispanic-origin item on the death certificate. See Appendix II, Hispanic origin.

NOTES: Starting with *Health, United States, 2003*, rates for 1991–1999 were revised using intercensal population estimates based on the 2000 census. Rates for 2000 were revised based on 2000 census counts. Rates for 2001 and later years were computed using 2000-based postcensal estimates. See Appendix I, Population Census and Population Estimates. Starting with 2003 data, California, Hawaii, Idaho, Maine, Montana, New York, and Wisconsin reported multiple-race data. The multiple-race data for these states were bridged to the single race categories of the 1977 Office of Management and Budget standards for comparability with other states. Data for additional years are available. See Appendix III.

SOURCES: Centers for Disease Control and Prevention, National Center for Health Statistics, National Vital Statistics System; Grove RD, Hetzel AM. Vital statistics rates in the United States, 1940–1960. Washington, DC: U.S. Government Printing Office, 1968; numerator data from National Vital Statistics System, annual mortality files; denominator data from national population estimates for race groups from Table 1 and unpublished Hispanic population estimates for 1985–1996 prepared by the Housing and Household Economic Statistics Division, U.S. Census Bureau; additional mortality tables are available from: www.cdc.gov/nchs/datawh/statab/unpubd/mortabs.htm; Hoyert DL, Heron M, Murphy SL, Kung HC. Deaths: Final data for 2003. National vital statistics reports. Vol 54 no 13. Hyattsville, MD: National Center for Health Statistics. 2006.

This table will be updated on the Web. Go to www.cdc.gov/nchs/hus.htm.

Table 36 (page 1 of 3). Death rates for diseases of heart, by sex, race, Hispanic origin, and age: United States, selected years 1950–2003

[Data are based on death certificates]

Sex, race, Hispanic origin, and age	1950[1,2]	1960[1,2]	1970[2]	1980[2]	1990	2000[3]	2002	2003
All persons			Deaths per 100,000 resident population					
All ages, age adjusted[4]	586.8	559.0	492.7	412.1	321.8	257.6	240.8	232.3
All ages, crude	355.5	369.0	362.0	336.0	289.5	252.6	241.7	235.6
Under 1 year	3.5	6.6	13.1	22.8	20.1	13.0	12.4	11.0
1–4 years	1.3	1.3	1.7	2.6	1.9	1.2	1.1	1.2
5–14 years	2.1	1.3	0.8	0.9	0.9	0.7	0.6	0.6
15–24 years	6.8	4.0	3.0	2.9	2.5	2.6	2.5	2.7
25–34 years	19.4	15.6	11.4	8.3	7.6	7.4	7.9	8.2
35–44 years	86.4	74.6	66.7	44.6	31.4	29.2	30.5	30.7
45–54 years	308.6	271.8	238.4	180.2	120.5	94.2	93.7	92.5
55–64 years	808.1	737.9	652.3	494.1	367.3	261.2	241.5	233.2
65–74 years	1,839.8	1,740.5	1,558.2	1,218.6	894.3	665.6	615.9	585.0
75–84 years	4,310.1	4,089.4	3,683.8	2,993.1	2,295.7	1,780.3	1,677.2	1,611.1
85 years and over	9,150.6	9,317.8	7,891.3	7,777.1	6,739.9	5,926.1	5,446.8	5,278.4
Male								
All ages, age adjusted[4]	697.0	687.6	634.0	538.9	412.4	320.0	297.4	286.6
All ages, crude	423.4	439.5	422.5	368.6	297.6	249.8	240.7	235.0
Under 1 year	4.0	7.8	15.1	25.5	21.9	13.3	12.9	12.1
1–4 years	1.4	1.4	1.9	2.8	1.9	1.4	1.1	1.1
5–14 years	2.0	1.4	0.9	1.0	0.9	0.8	0.7	0.7
15–24 years	6.8	4.2	3.7	3.7	3.1	3.2	3.3	3.4
25–34 years	22.9	20.1	15.2	11.4	10.3	9.6	10.5	10.5
35–44 years	118.4	112.7	103.2	68.7	48.1	41.4	43.1	42.8
45–54 years	440.5	420.4	376.4	282.6	183.0	140.2	138.4	136.2
55–64 years	1,104.5	1,066.9	987.2	746.8	537.3	371.7	343.4	331.7
65–74 years	2,292.3	2,291.3	2,170.3	1,728.0	1,250.0	898.3	827.1	785.3
75–84 years	4,825.0	4,742.4	4,534.8	3,834.3	2,968.2	2,248.1	2,110.1	2,030.3
85 years and over	9,659.8	9,788.9	8,426.2	8,752.7	7,418.4	6,430.0	5,823.5	5,621.5
Female								
All ages, age adjusted[4]	484.7	447.0	381.6	320.8	257.0	210.9	197.2	190.3
All ages, crude	288.4	300.6	304.5	305.1	281.8	255.3	242.7	236.2
Under 1 year	2.9	5.4	10.9	20.0	18.3	12.5	11.8	9.8
1–4 years	1.2	1.1	1.6	2.5	1.9	1.0	1.0	1.3
5–14 years	2.2	1.2	0.8	0.9	0.8	0.5	0.6	0.5
15–24 years	6.7	3.7	2.3	2.1	1.8	2.1	1.7	2.1
25–34 years	16.2	11.3	7.7	5.3	5.0	5.2	5.2	5.7
35–44 years	55.1	38.2	32.2	21.4	15.1	17.2	18.0	18.6
45–54 years	177.2	127.5	109.9	84.5	61.0	49.8	50.6	50.2
55–64 years	510.0	429.4	351.6	272.1	215.7	159.3	147.2	141.9
65–74 years	1,419.3	1,261.3	1,082.7	828.6	616.8	474.0	440.1	417.5
75–84 years	3,872.0	3,582.7	3,120.8	2,497.0	1,893.8	1,475.1	1,389.7	1,331.1
85 years and over	8,796.1	9,016.8	7,591.8	7,350.5	6,478.1	5,720.9	5,283.3	5,126.7
White male[5]								
All ages, age adjusted[4]	700.2	694.5	640.2	539.6	409.2	316.7	294.1	282.9
All ages, crude	433.0	454.6	438.3	384.0	312.7	265.8	256.0	249.5
45–54 years	423.6	413.2	365.7	269.8	170.6	130.7	128.6	125.3
55–64 years	1,081.7	1,056.0	979.3	730.6	516.7	351.8	324.0	313.2
65–74 years	2,308.3	2,297.9	2,177.2	1,729.7	1,230.5	877.8	807.8	761.1
75–84 years	4,907.3	4,839.9	4,617.6	3,883.2	2,983.4	2,247.0	2,112.0	2,030.1
85 years and over	9,950.5	10,135.8	8,818.0	8,958.0	7,558.7	6,560.8	5,939.8	5,747.2
Black or African American male[5]								
All ages, age adjusted[4]	639.4	615.2	607.3	561.4	485.4	392.5	371.0	364.3
All ages, crude	346.2	330.6	330.3	301.0	256.8	211.1	206.3	206.0
45–54 years	622.5	514.0	512.8	433.4	328.9	247.2	246.0	248.1
55–64 years	1,433.1	1,236.8	1,135.4	987.2	824.0	631.2	605.3	580.9
65–74 years	2,139.1	2,281.4	2,237.8	1,847.2	1,632.9	1,268.8	1,192.7	1,195.5
75–84 years[6]	4,106.1	3,533.6	3,783.4	3,578.8	3,107.1	2,597.6	2,449.6	2,426.6
85 years and over	- - -	6,037.9	5,367.6	6,819.5	6,479.6	5,633.5	5,125.7	4,850.3

See footnotes at end of table.

This table will be updated on the Web. Go to www.cdc.gov/nchs/hus.htm.

Table 36 (page 2 of 3). Death rates for diseases of heart, by sex, race, Hispanic origin, and age: United States, selected years 1950–2003

[Data are based on death certificates]

Sex, race, Hispanic origin, and age	1950[1,2]	1960[1,2]	1970[2]	1980[2]	1990	2000[3]	2002	2003
American Indian or Alaska Native male[5]				Deaths per 100,000 resident population				
All ages, age adjusted[4]	- - -	- - -	- - -	320.5	264.1	222.2	201.2	203.2
All ages, crude	- - -	- - -	- - -	130.6	108.0	90.1	92.0	98.5
45–54 years	- - -	- - -	- - -	238.1	173.8	108.5	104.2	116.7
55–64 years	- - -	- - -	- - -	496.3	411.0	285.0	273.2	293.5
65–74 years	- - -	- - -	- - -	1,009.4	839.1	748.2	638.4	655.6
75–84 years	- - -	- - -	- - -	2,062.2	1,788.8	1,655.7	1,422.7	1,309.9
85 years and over	- - -	- - -	- - -	4,413.7	3,860.3	3,318.3	3,162.4	3,266.5
Asian or Pacific Islander male[5]								
All ages, age adjusted[4]	- - -	- - -	- - -	286.9	220.7	185.5	169.8	158.3
All ages, crude	- - -	- - -	- - -	119.8	88.7	90.6	89.4	86.3
45–54 years	- - -	- - -	- - -	112.0	70.4	61.1	60.6	62.7
55–64 years	- - -	- - -	- - -	306.7	226.1	182.6	154.2	152.9
65–74 years	- - -	- - -	- - -	852.4	623.5	482.5	422.4	398.3
75–84 years	- - -	- - -	- - -	2,010.9	1,642.2	1,354.7	1,252.4	1,145.1
85 years and over	- - -	- - -	- - -	5,923.0	4,617.8	4,154.2	3,841.3	3,524.6
Hispanic or Latino male[5,7]								
All ages, age adjusted[4]	- - -	- - -	- - -	- - -	270.0	238.2	219.8	206.8
All ages, crude	- - -	- - -	- - -	- - -	91.0	74.7	74.0	72.2
45–54 years	- - -	- - -	- - -	- - -	116.4	84.3	80.5	79.6
55–64 years	- - -	- - -	- - -	- - -	363.0	264.8	256.0	235.6
65–74 years	- - -	- - -	- - -	- - -	829.9	684.8	657.7	625.0
75–84 years	- - -	- - -	- - -	- - -	1,971.3	1,733.2	1,599.5	1,543.5
85 years and over	- - -	- - -	- - -	- - -	4,711.9	4,897.5	4,301.8	3,874.5
White, not Hispanic or Latino male[7]								
All ages, age adjusted[4]	- - -	- - -	- - -	- - -	413.6	319.9	297.7	286.9
All ages, crude	- - -	- - -	- - -	- - -	336.5	297.5	289.2	282.9
45–54 years	- - -	- - -	- - -	- - -	172.8	134.3	133.1	129.8
55–64 years	- - -	- - -	- - -	- - -	521.3	356.3	327.6	317.7
65–74 years	- - -	- - -	- - -	- - -	1,243.4	885.1	813.5	767.3
75–84 years	- - -	- - -	- - -	- - -	3,007.7	2,261.9	2,129.9	2,049.9
85 years and over	- - -	- - -	- - -	- - -	7,663.4	6,606.6	5,994.1	5,821.0
White female[5]								
All ages, age adjusted[4]	478.0	441.7	376.7	315.9	250.9	205.6	192.1	185.4
All ages, crude	289.4	306.5	313.8	319.2	298.4	274.5	261.0	253.8
45–54 years	141.9	103.4	91.4	71.2	50.2	40.9	41.7	41.1
55–64 years	460.2	383.0	317.7	248.1	192.4	141.3	130.6	125.2
65–74 years	1,400.9	1,229.8	1,044.0	796.7	583.6	445.2	414.7	392.0
75–84 years	3,925.2	3,629.7	3,143.5	2,493.6	1,874.3	1,452.4	1,368.2	1,315.2
85 years and over	9,084.7	9,280.8	7,839.9	7,501.6	6,563.4	5,801.4	5,350.6	5,193.6
Black or African American female[5]								
All ages, age adjusted[4]	536.9	488.9	435.6	378.6	327.5	277.6	263.2	253.8
All ages, crude	287.6	268.5	261.0	249.7	237.0	212.6	205.0	200.0
45–54 years	525.3	360.7	290.9	202.4	155.3	125.0	124.9	124.1
55–64 years	1,210.2	952.3	710.5	530.1	442.0	332.8	312.3	304.7
65–74 years	1,659.4	1,680.5	1,553.2	1,210.3	1,017.5	815.2	734.0	712.0
75–84 years[6]	3,499.3	2,926.9	2,964.1	2,707.2	2,250.9	1,913.1	1,821.9	1,699.6
85 years and over	- - -	5,650.0	5,003.8	5,796.5	5,766.1	5,298.7	5,111.2	4,976.5

See footnotes at end of table.

This table will be updated on the Web. Go to www.cdc.gov/nchs/hus.htm.

Table 36 (page 3 of 3). Death rates for diseases of heart, by sex, race, Hispanic origin, and age: United States, selected years 1950–2003

[Data are based on death certificates]

Sex, race, Hispanic origin, and age	1950[1,2]	1960[1,2]	1970[2]	1980[2]	1990	2000[3]	2002	2003
American Indian or Alaska Native female[5]				Deaths per 100,000 resident population				
All ages, age adjusted[4]	- - -	- - -	- - -	175.4	153.1	143.6	123.6	127.5
All ages, crude	- - -	- - -	- - -	80.3	77.5	71.9	68.5	75.9
45–54 years	- - -	- - -	- - -	65.2	62.0	40.2	29.7	45.4
55–64 years	- - -	- - -	- - -	193.5	197.0	149.4	124.3	153.4
65–74 years	- - -	- - -	- - -	577.2	492.8	391.8	365.8	390.3
75–84 years	- - -	- - -	- - -	1,364.3	1,050.3	1,044.1	1,002.5	950.3
85 years and over	- - -	- - -	- - -	2,893.3	2,868.7	3,146.3	2,372.5	2,284.1
Asian or Pacific Islander female[5]								
All ages, age adjusted[4]	- - -	- - -	- - -	132.3	149.2	115.7	108.1	104.2
All ages, crude	- - -	- - -	- - -	57.0	62.0	65.0	67.4	68.2
45–54 years	- - -	- - -	- - -	28.6	17.5	15.9	16.4	14.8
55–64 years	- - -	- - -	- - -	92.9	99.0	68.8	61.8	60.3
65–74 years	- - -	- - -	- - -	313.3	323.9	229.6	239.9	207.2
75–84 years	- - -	- - -	- - -	1,053.2	1,130.9	866.2	796.9	769.7
85 years and over	- - -	- - -	- - -	3,211.0	4,161.2	3,367.2	3,067.4	3,020.0
Hispanic or Latino female[5,7]								
All ages, age adjusted[4]	- - -	- - -	- - -	- - -	177.2	163.7	149.7	145.8
All ages, crude	- - -	- - -	- - -	- - -	79.4	71.5	69.7	69.6
45–54 years	- - -	- - -	- - -	- - -	43.5	28.2	30.2	27.0
55–64 years	- - -	- - -	- - -	- - -	153.2	111.2	105.7	102.1
65–74 years	- - -	- - -	- - -	- - -	460.4	366.3	346.4	330.6
75–84 years	- - -	- - -	- - -	- - -	1,259.7	1,169.4	1,090.8	1,067.0
85 years and over	- - -	- - -	- - -	- - -	4,440.3	4,605.8	4,032.8	3,962.5
White, not Hispanic or Latino female[7]								
All ages, age adjusted[4]	- - -	- - -	- - -	- - -	252.6	206.8	193.7	187.1
All ages, crude	- - -	- - -	- - -	- - -	320.0	304.9	292.3	285.1
45–54 years	- - -	- - -	- - -	- - -	50.2	41.9	42.6	42.4
55–64 years	- - -	- - -	- - -	- - -	193.6	142.9	132.0	126.6
65–74 years	- - -	- - -	- - -	- - -	584.7	448.5	417.4	394.8
75–84 years	- - -	- - -	- - -	- - -	1,890.2	1,458.9	1,377.2	1,324.0
85 years and over	- - -	- - -	- - -	- - -	6,615.2	5,822.7	5,384.5	5,232.2

- - - Data not available.

[1]Includes deaths of persons who were not residents of the 50 states and the District of Columbia.

[2]Underlying cause of death was coded according to the Sixth Revision of the International Classification of Diseases (ICD) in 1950, Seventh Revision in 1960, Eighth Revision in 1970, and Ninth Revision in 1980–1998. See Appendix II, Cause of death; tables IV and V.

[3]Starting with 1999 data, cause of death is coded according to ICD–10. See Appendix II, Cause of death; Comparability ratio; tables V and VI.

[4]Age-adjusted rates are calculated using the year 2000 standard population. Prior to 2003, age-adjusted rates were calculated using standard million proportions based on rounded population numbers. Starting with 2003 data, unrounded population numbers are used to calculate age-adjusted rates. See Appendix II, Age adjustment.

[5]The race groups, white, black, Asian or Pacific Islander, and American Indian or Alaska Native, include persons of Hispanic and non-Hispanic origin. Persons of Hispanic origin may be of any race. Death rates for the American Indian or Alaska Native and Asian or Pacific Islander populations are known to be underestimated. See Appendix II, Race, for a discussion of sources of bias in death rates by race and Hispanic origin.

[6]In 1950, rate is for the age group 75 years and over.

[7]Prior to 1997, excludes data from states lacking an Hispanic-origin item on the death certificate. See Appendix II, Hispanic origin.

NOTES: Starting with *Health, United States, 2003*, rates for 1991–1999 were revised using intercensal population estimates based on the 2000 census. Rates for 2000 were revised based on 2000 census counts. Rates for 2001 and later years were computed using 2000-based postcensal estimates. See Appendix I, Population Census and Population Estimates. For the period 1980–1998, diseases of heart was coded using ICD–9 codes that are most nearly comparable with diseases of heart codes in the 113 cause list for ICD–10. See Appendix II, Cause of death; table V. Age groups were selected to minimize the presentation of unstable age-specific death rates based on small numbers of deaths and for consistency among comparison groups. Starting with 2003 data, California, Hawaii, Idaho, Maine, Montana, New York, and Wisconsin reported multiple-race data. The multiple-race data for these states were bridged to the single race categories of the 1977 Office of Management and Budget standards for comparability with other states. Data for additional years are available. See Appendix III.

SOURCES: Centers for Disease Control and Prevention, National Center for Health Statistics, National Vital Statistics System; numerator data from annual mortality files; denominator data from national population estimates for race groups from Table 1 and unpublished Hispanic population estimates for 1985–1996 prepared by the Housing and Household Economic Statistics Division, U.S. Census Bureau; additional mortality tables are available from: www.cdc.gov/nchs/datawh/statab/unpubd/mortabs.htm; Hoyert DL, Heron M, Murphy SL, Kung HC. Deaths: Final data for 2003. National vital statistics reports. Vol 54 no 13. Hyattsville, MD: National Center for Health Statistics. 2006.

This table will be updated on the Web. Go to www.cdc.gov/nchs/hus.htm.

Table 37 (page 1 of 3). Death rates for cerebrovascular diseases, by sex, race, Hispanic origin, and age: United States, selected years 1950–2003

[Data are based on death certificates]

Sex, race, Hispanic origin, and age	1950[1,2]	1960[1,2]	1970[2]	1980[2]	1990	2000[3]	2002	2003
All persons				Deaths per 100,000 resident population				
All ages, age adjusted[4]	180.7	177.9	147.7	96.2	65.3	60.9	56.2	53.5
All ages, crude	104.0	108.0	101.9	75.0	57.8	59.6	56.4	54.2
Under 1 year	5.1	4.1	5.0	4.4	3.8	3.3	2.9	2.5
1–4 years	0.9	0.8	1.0	0.5	0.3	0.3	0.3	0.3
5–14 years	0.5	0.7	0.7	0.3	0.2	0.2	0.2	0.2
15–24 years	1.6	1.8	1.6	1.0	0.6	0.5	0.4	0.5
25–34 years	4.2	4.7	4.5	2.6	2.2	1.5	1.4	1.5
35–44 years	18.7	14.7	15.6	8.5	6.4	5.8	5.4	5.5
45–54 years	70.4	49.2	41.6	25.2	18.7	16.0	15.1	15.0
55–64 years	194.2	147.3	115.8	65.1	47.9	41.0	37.2	35.6
65–74 years	554.7	469.2	384.1	219.0	144.2	128.6	120.3	112.9
75–84 years	1,499.6	1,491.3	1,254.2	786.9	498.0	461.3	431.0	410.7
85 years and over	2,990.1	3,680.5	3,014.3	2,283.7	1,628.9	1,589.2	1,445.9	1,370.1
Male								
All ages, age adjusted[4]	186.4	186.1	157.4	102.2	68.5	62.4	56.5	54.1
All ages, crude	102.5	104.5	94.5	63.4	46.7	46.9	44.2	42.9
Under 1 year	6.4	5.0	5.8	5.0	4.4	3.8	3.2	2.8
1–4 years	1.1	0.9	1.2	0.4	0.3	*	0.4	0.3
5–14 years	0.5	0.7	0.8	0.3	0.2	0.2	0.2	0.2
15–24 years	1.8	1.9	1.8	1.1	0.7	0.5	0.5	0.5
25–34 years	4.2	4.5	4.4	2.6	2.1	1.5	1.4	1.6
35–44 years	17.5	14.6	15.7	8.7	6.8	5.8	5.3	5.8
45–54 years	67.9	52.2	44.4	27.2	20.5	17.5	16.7	16.7
55–64 years	205.2	163.8	138.7	74.6	54.3	47.2	42.7	40.8
65–74 years	589.6	530.7	449.5	258.6	166.6	145.0	135.0	127.8
75–84 years	1,543.6	1,555.9	1,361.6	866.3	551.1	490.8	445.9	431.4
85 years and over	3,048.6	3,643.1	2,895.2	2,193.6	1,528.5	1,484.3	1,317.9	1,236.0
Female								
All ages, age adjusted[4]	175.8	170.7	140.0	91.7	62.6	59.1	55.2	52.3
All ages, crude	105.6	111.4	109.0	85.9	68.4	71.8	68.2	65.1
Under 1 year	3.7	3.2	4.0	3.8	3.1	2.7	2.5	2.2
1–4 years	0.7	0.7	0.7	0.5	0.3	0.4	0.3	0.3
5–14 years	0.4	0.6	0.6	0.3	0.2	0.2	0.2	0.1
15–24 years	1.5	1.6	1.4	0.8	0.6	0.5	0.3	0.5
25–34 years	4.3	4.9	4.7	2.6	2.2	1.5	1.4	1.4
35–44 years	19.9	14.8	15.6	8.4	6.1	5.7	5.5	5.3
45–54 years	72.9	46.3	39.0	23.3	17.0	14.5	13.6	13.4
55–64 years	183.1	131.8	95.3	56.8	42.2	35.3	32.1	30.9
65–74 years	522.1	415.7	333.3	188.7	126.7	115.1	108.1	100.5
75–84 years	1,462.2	1,441.1	1,183.1	740.1	466.2	442.1	421.2	396.8
85 years and over	2,949.4	3,704.4	3,081.0	2,323.1	1,667.6	1,632.0	1,501.5	1,429.4
White male[5]								
All ages, age adjusted[4]	182.1	181.6	153.7	98.7	65.5	59.8	54.2	51.7
All ages, crude	100.5	102.7	93.5	63.1	46.9	48.4	45.7	44.2
45–54 years	53.7	40.9	35.6	21.7	15.4	13.6	12.9	12.9
55–64 years	182.2	139.0	119.9	64.0	45.7	39.7	35.6	33.3
65–74 years	569.7	501.0	420.0	239.8	152.9	133.8	123.8	117.3
75–84 years	1,556.3	1,564.8	1,361.6	852.7	539.2	480.0	437.5	422.4
85 years and over	3,127.1	3,734.8	3,018.1	2,230.8	1,545.4	1,490.7	1,327.4	1,247.0
Black or African American male[5]								
All ages, age adjusted[4]	228.8	238.5	206.4	142.0	102.2	89.6	81.7	79.5
All ages, crude	122.0	122.9	108.8	73.0	53.0	46.1	43.5	43.2
45–54 years	211.9	166.1	136.1	82.1	68.4	49.5	46.5	46.9
55–64 years	522.8	439.9	343.4	189.7	141.7	115.4	110.3	112.1
65–74 years	783.6	899.2	780.1	472.3	326.9	268.5	262.9	237.4
75–84 years[6]	1,504.9	1,475.2	1,445.7	1,066.3	721.5	659.2	587.8	588.9
85 years and over	- - -	2,700.0	1,963.1	1,873.2	1,421.5	1,458.8	1,252.2	1,180.3

See footnotes at end of table.

This table will be updated on the Web. Go to www.cdc.gov/nchs/hus.htm.

Table 37 (page 2 of 3). **Death rates for cerebrovascular diseases, by sex, race, Hispanic origin, and age: United States, selected years 1950–2003**

[Data are based on death certificates]

Sex, race, Hispanic origin, and age	1950[1,2]	1960[1,2]	1970[2]	1980[2]	1990	2000[3]	2002	2003
American Indian or Alaska Native male[5]				Deaths per 100,000 resident population				
All ages, age adjusted[4]	- - -	- - -	- - -	66.4	44.3	46.1	37.1	34.9
All ages, crude	- - -	- - -	- - -	23.1	16.0	16.8	15.4	15.6
45–54 years	- - -	- - -	- - -	*	*	13.3	15.4	15.5
55–64 years	- - -	- - -	- - -	72.0	39.8	48.6	34.5	30.7
65–74 years	- - -	- - -	- - -	170.5	120.3	144.7	96.6	101.4
75–84 years	- - -	- - -	- - -	523.9	325.9	373.3	276.4	280.7
85 years and over	- - -	- - -	- - -	1,384.7	949.8	834.9	768.3	596.9
Asian or Pacific Islander male[5]								
All ages, age adjusted[4]	- - -	- - -	- - -	71.4	59.1	58.0	50.8	48.5
All ages, crude	- - -	- - -	- - -	28.7	23.3	27.2	25.9	26.0
45–54 years	- - -	- - -	- - -	17.0	15.6	15.0	14.9	14.7
55–64 years	- - -	- - -	- - -	59.9	51.8	49.3	40.4	42.2
65–74 years	- - -	- - -	- - -	197.9	167.9	135.6	112.9	128.3
75–84 years	- - -	- - -	- - -	619.5	483.9	438.7	390.3	355.7
85 years and over	- - -	- - -	- - -	1,399.0	1,196.6	1,415.6	1,233.6	1,093.0
Hispanic or Latino male[5,7]								
All ages, age adjusted[4]	- - -	- - -	- - -	- - -	46.5	50.5	44.3	43.0
All ages, crude	- - -	- - -	- - -	- - -	15.6	15.8	15.0	14.9
45–54 years	- - -	- - -	- - -	- - -	20.0	18.1	18.6	18.1
55–64 years	- - -	- - -	- - -	- - -	49.2	48.8	45.0	43.5
65–74 years	- - -	- - -	- - -	- - -	126.4	136.1	124.6	113.9
75–84 years	- - -	- - -	- - -	- - -	356.6	392.9	338.5	337.1
85 years and over	- - -	- - -	- - -	- - -	866.3	1,029.9	856.7	837.4
White, not Hispanic or Latino male[7]								
All ages, age adjusted[4]	- - -	- - -	- - -	- - -	66.3	59.9	54.4	51.9
All ages, crude	- - -	- - -	- - -	- - -	50.6	53.9	51.3	49.7
45–54 years	- - -	- - -	- - -	- - -	14.9	13.0	12.1	12.1
55–64 years	- - -	- - -	- - -	- - -	45.1	38.7	34.5	32.1
65–74 years	- - -	- - -	- - -	- - -	154.5	133.1	123.2	116.9
75–84 years	- - -	- - -	- - -	- - -	547.3	482.3	441.1	426.0
85 years and over	- - -	- - -	- - -	- - -	1,578.7	1,505.9	1,345.9	1,264.2
White female[5]								
All ages, age adjusted[4]	169.7	165.0	135.5	89.0	60.3	57.3	53.4	50.5
All ages, crude	103.3	110.1	109.8	88.6	71.6	76.9	73.0	69.5
45–54 years	55.0	33.8	30.5	18.6	13.5	11.2	10.4	10.0
55–64 years	156.9	103.0	78.1	48.6	35.8	30.2	27.4	25.8
65–74 years	498.1	383.3	303.2	172.5	116.1	107.3	99.5	92.1
75–84 years	1,471.3	1,444.7	1,176.8	728.8	456.5	434.2	414.1	389.9
85 years and over	3,017.9	3,795.7	3,167.6	2,362.7	1,685.9	1,646.7	1,516.9	1,442.1
Black or African American female[5]								
All ages, age adjusted[4]	238.4	232.5	189.3	119.6	84.0	76.2	71.8	69.8
All ages, crude	128.3	127.7	112.2	77.8	60.7	58.3	55.8	54.8
45–54 years	248.9	166.2	119.4	61.8	44.1	38.1	35.7	36.0
55–64 years	567.7	452.0	272.4	138.4	96.9	76.4	70.1	71.8
65–74 years	754.4	830.5	673.5	361.7	236.7	190.9	181.2	175.3
75–84 years[6]	1,496.7	1,413.1	1,338.3	917.5	595.0	549.2	532.2	498.3
85 years and over	- - -	2,578.9	2,210.5	1,891.6	1,495.2	1,556.5	1,434.3	1,414.2

See footnotes at end of table.

This table will be updated on the Web. Go to www.cdc.gov/nchs/hus.htm.

Table 37 (page 3 of 3). **Death rates for cerebrovascular diseases, by sex, race, Hispanic origin, and age: United States, selected years 1950–2003**

[Data are based on death certificates]

Sex, race, Hispanic origin, and age	1950[1,2]	1960[1,2]	1970[2]	1980[2]	1990	2000[3]	2002	2003
American Indian or Alaska Native female[5]				Deaths per 100,000 resident population				
All ages, age adjusted[4]	- - -	- - -	- - -	51.2	38.4	43.7	38.0	34.2
All ages, crude	- - -	- - -	- - -	22.0	19.3	21.5	21.5	19.9
45–54 years	- - -	- - -	- - -	*	*	14.4	13.5	14.6
55–64 years	- - -	- - -	- - -	*	40.7	37.9	33.1	26.0
65–74 years	- - -	- - -	- - -	128.3	100.5	79.5	112.4	94.8
75–84 years	- - -	- - -	- - -	404.2	282.0	391.1	304.8	304.7
85 years and over	- - -	- - -	- - -	1,095.5	776.2	931.5	689.9	569.1
Asian or Pacific Islander female[5]								
All ages, age adjusted[4]	- - -	- - -	- - -	60.8	54.9	49.1	45.4	42.6
All ages, crude	- - -	- - -	- - -	26.4	24.3	28.7	29.2	28.8
45–54 years	- - -	- - -	- - -	20.3	19.7	13.3	12.6	12.6
55–64 years	- - -	- - -	- - -	43.7	42.1	33.3	32.1	30.8
65–74 years	- - -	- - -	- - -	136.1	124.0	102.8	112.5	95.6
75–84 years	- - -	- - -	- - -	446.6	396.6	386.0	331.7	330.2
85 years and over	- - -	- - -	- - -	1,545.2	1,395.0	1,246.6	1,149.8	1,042.4
Hispanic or Latino female[5,7]								
All ages, age adjusted[4]	- - -	- - -	- - -	- - -	43.7	43.0	38.6	38.1
All ages, crude	- - -	- - -	- - -	- - -	20.1	19.4	18.4	18.6
45–54 years	- - -	- - -	- - -	- - -	15.2	12.4	12.0	11.7
55–64 years	- - -	- - -	- - -	- - -	38.5	31.9	27.6	27.8
65–74 years	- - -	- - -	- - -	- - -	102.6	95.2	85.6	86.0
75–84 years	- - -	- - -	- - -	- - -	308.5	311.3	307.2	302.8
85 years and over	- - -	- - -	- - -	- - -	1,055.3	1,108.9	918.5	902.3
White, not Hispanic or Latino female[7]								
All ages, age adjusted[4]	- - -	- - -	- - -	- - -	61.0	57.6	53.9	50.8
All ages, crude	- - -	- - -	- - -	- - -	77.2	85.5	82.1	78.2
45–54 years	- - -	- - -	- - -	- - -	13.2	10.9	10.1	9.7
55–64 years	- - -	- - -	- - -	- - -	35.7	29.9	27.2	25.5
65–74 years	- - -	- - -	- - -	- - -	116.9	107.6	100.2	92.1
75–84 years	- - -	- - -	- - -	- - -	461.9	438.3	418.4	393.6
85 years and over	- - -	- - -	- - -	- - -	1,714.7	1,661.6	1,536.7	1,461.3

- - - Data not available.

* Rates based on fewer than 20 deaths are considered unreliable and are not shown.

[1]Includes deaths of persons who were not residents of the 50 states and the District of Columbia.

[2]Underlying cause of death was coded according to the Sixth Revision of the International Classification of Diseases (ICD) in 1950, Seventh Revision in 1960, Eighth Revision in 1970, and Ninth Revision in 1980–1998. See Appendix II, Cause of death; tables IV and V.

[3]Starting with 1999 data, cause of death is coded according to ICD–10. See Appendix II, Cause of death; Comparability ratio; tables V and VI.

[4]Age-adjusted rates are calculated using the year 2000 standard population. Prior to 2003, age-adjusted rates were calculated using standard million proportions based on rounded population numbers. Starting with 2003 data, unrounded population numbers are used to calculate age-adjusted rates. See Appendix II, Age adjustment.

[5]The race groups, white, black, Asian or Pacific Islander, and American Indian or Alaska Native, include persons of Hispanic and non-Hispanic origin. Persons of Hispanic origin may be of any race. Death rates for the American Indian or Alaska Native and Asian or Pacific Islander populations are known to be underestimated. See Appendix II, Race, for a discussion of sources of bias in death rates by race and Hispanic origin.

[6]In 1950, rate is for the age group 75 years and over.

[7]Prior to 1997, excludes data from states lacking an Hispanic-origin item on the death certificate. See Appendix II, Hispanic origin.

NOTES: Starting with *Health, United States, 2003*, rates for 1991–1999 were revised using intercensal population estimates based on the 2000 census. Rates for 2000 were revised based on 2000 census counts. Rates for 2001 and later years were computed using 2000-based postcensal estimates. See Appendix I, Population Census and Population Estimates. For the period 1980–1998, cerebrovascular diseases was coded using ICD–9 codes that are most nearly comparable with cerebrovascular diseases codes in the 113 cause list for ICD–10. See Appendix II, Cause of death; table V. Age groups were selected to minimize the presentation of unstable age-specific death rates based on small numbers of deaths and for consistency among comparison groups. Starting with 2003 data, California, Hawaii, Idaho, Maine, Montana, New York, and Wisconsin reported multiple-race data. The multiple-race data for these states were bridged to the single race categories of the 1977 Office of Management and Budget standards for comparability with other states. Data for additional years are available. See Appendix III.

SOURCES: Centers for Disease Control and Prevention, National Center for Health Statistics, National Vital Statistics System; Grove RD, Hetzel AM. Vital statistics rates in the United States, 1940–1960. Washington, DC: U.S. Government Printing Office. 1968; numerator data from National Vital Statistics System, annual mortality files; denominator data from national population estimates for race groups from Table 1 and unpublished Hispanic population estimates for 1985–1996 prepared by the Housing and Household Economic Statistics Division, U.S. Census Bureau; additional mortality tables are available from: www.cdc.gov/nchs/datawh/statab/unpubd/mortabs.htm; Hoyert DL, Heron M, Murphy SL, Kung HC. Deaths: Final data for 2003. National vital statistics reports. Vol 54 no 13. Hyattsville, MD: National Center for Health Statistics. 2006.

This table will be updated on the Web. Go to www.cdc.gov/nchs/hus.htm.

Table 38 (page 1 of 4). Death rates for malignant neoplasms, by sex, race, Hispanic origin, and age: United States, selected years 1950–2003

[Data are based on death certificates]

Sex, race, Hispanic origin, and age	1950[1,2]	1960[1,2]	1970[2]	1980[2]	1990	2000[3]	2002	2003
All persons	\multicolumn{8}{c}{Deaths per 100,000 resident population}							
All ages, age adjusted[4]	193.9	193.9	198.6	207.9	216.0	199.6	193.5	190.1
All ages, crude	139.8	149.2	162.8	183.9	203.2	196.5	193.2	191.5
Under 1 year	8.7	7.2	4.7	3.2	2.3	2.4	1.8	1.9
1–4 years	11.7	10.9	7.5	4.5	3.5	2.7	2.6	2.5
5–14 years	6.7	6.8	6.0	4.3	3.1	2.5	2.6	2.6
15–24 years	8.6	8.3	8.3	6.3	4.9	4.4	4.3	4.0
25–34 years	20.0	19.5	16.5	13.7	12.6	9.8	9.7	9.4
35–44 years	62.7	59.7	59.5	48.6	43.3	36.6	35.8	35.0
45–54 years	175.1	177.0	182.5	180.0	158.9	127.5	123.8	122.2
55–64 years	390.7	396.8	423.0	436.1	449.6	366.7	351.1	343.0
65–74 years	698.8	713.9	754.2	817.9	872.3	816.3	792.1	770.3
75–84 years	1,153.3	1,127.4	1,169.2	1,232.3	1,348.5	1,335.6	1,311.9	1,302.5
85 years and over	1,451.0	1,450.0	1,320.7	1,594.6	1,752.9	1,819.4	1,723.9	1,698.2
Male								
All ages, age adjusted[4]	208.1	225.1	247.6	271.2	280.4	248.9	238.9	233.3
All ages, crude	142.9	162.5	182.1	205.3	221.3	207.2	203.8	201.3
Under 1 year	9.7	7.7	4.4	3.7	2.4	2.6	2.0	1.7
1–4 years	12.5	12.4	8.3	5.2	3.7	3.0	2.7	2.8
5–14 years	7.4	7.6	6.7	4.9	3.5	2.7	2.9	2.8
15–24 years	9.7	10.2	10.4	7.8	5.7	5.1	4.9	4.6
25–34 years	17.7	18.8	16.3	13.4	12.6	9.2	9.2	8.9
35–44 years	45.6	48.9	53.0	44.0	38.5	32.7	31.5	30.8
45–54 years	156.2	170.8	183.5	188.7	162.5	130.9	128.0	127.4
55–64 years	413.1	459.9	511.8	520.8	532.9	415.8	399.8	386.8
65–74 years	791.5	890.5	1,006.8	1,093.2	1,122.2	1,001.9	964.8	931.7
75–84 years	1,332.6	1,389.4	1,588.3	1,790.5	1,914.4	1,760.6	1,711.3	1,695.4
85 years and over	1,668.3	1,741.2	1,720.8	2,369.5	2,739.9	2,710.7	2,491.1	2,413.8
Female								
All ages, age adjusted[4]	182.3	168.7	163.2	166.7	175.7	167.6	163.1	160.9
All ages, crude	136.8	136.4	144.4	163.6	186.0	186.2	183.0	182.0
Under 1 year	7.6	6.8	5.0	2.7	2.2	2.3	1.6	2.1
1–4 years	10.8	9.3	6.7	3.7	3.2	2.5	2.4	2.1
5–14 years	6.0	6.0	5.2	3.6	2.8	2.2	2.4	2.4
15–24 years	7.6	6.5	6.2	4.8	4.1	3.6	3.6	3.4
25–34 years	22.2	20.1	16.7	14.0	12.6	10.4	10.2	9.9
35–44 years	79.3	70.0	65.6	53.1	48.1	40.4	40.0	39.1
45–54 years	194.0	183.0	181.5	171.8	155.5	124.2	119.8	117.1
55–64 years	368.2	337.7	343.2	361.7	375.2	321.3	306.0	302.3
65–74 years	612.3	560.2	557.9	607.1	677.4	663.6	648.5	635.3
75–84 years	1,000.7	924.1	891.9	903.1	1,010.3	1,058.5	1,046.7	1,040.1
85 years and over	1,299.7	1,263.9	1,096.7	1,255.7	1,372.1	1,456.4	1,391.1	1,381.9
White male[5]								
All ages, age adjusted[4]	210.0	224.7	244.8	265.1	272.2	243.9	235.2	230.1
All ages, crude	147.2	166.1	185.1	208.7	227.7	218.1	215.5	213.1
25–34 years	17.7	18.8	16.2	13.6	12.3	9.2	9.1	8.9
35–44 years	44.5	46.3	50.1	41.1	35.8	30.9	30.5	29.9
45–54 years	150.8	164.1	172.0	175.4	149.9	123.5	121.8	119.9
55–64 years	409.4	450.9	498.1	497.4	508.2	401.9	386.0	375.6
65–74 years	798.7	887.3	997.0	1,070.7	1,090.7	984.3	954.8	922.7
75–84 years	1,367.6	1,413.7	1,592.7	1,779.7	1,883.2	1,736.0	1,695.3	1,683.6
85 years and over	1,732.7	1,791.4	1,772.2	2,375.6	2,715.1	2,693.7	2,486.8	2,412.1
Black or African American male[5]								
All ages, age adjusted[4]	178.9	227.6	291.9	353.4	397.9	340.3	319.6	308.8
All ages, crude	106.6	136.7	171.6	205.5	221.9	188.5	181.5	178.3
25–34 years	18.0	18.4	18.8	14.1	15.7	10.1	11.2	10.3
35–44 years	55.7	72.9	81.3	73.8	64.3	48.4	43.0	41.7
45–54 years	211.7	244.7	311.2	333.0	302.6	214.2	197.3	207.0
55–64 years	490.8	579.7	689.2	812.5	859.2	626.4	610.3	583.8
65–74 years	636.5	938.5	1,168.9	1,417.2	1,613.9	1,363.8	1,274.7	1,221.5
75–84 years[6]	853.5	1,053.3	1,624.8	2,029.6	2,478.3	2,351.8	2,223.0	2,144.2
85 years and over	- - -	1,155.2	1,387.0	2,393.9	3,238.3	3,264.8	2,976.1	2,825.5

See footnotes at end of table.

This table will be updated on the Web. Go to www.cdc.gov/nchs/hus.htm.

Table 38 (page 2 of 4). Death rates for malignant neoplasms, by sex, race, Hispanic origin, and age: United States, selected years 1950–2003

[Data are based on death certificates]

Sex, race, Hispanic origin, and age	1950[1,2]	1960[1,2]	1970[2]	1980[2]	1990	2000[3]	2002	2003
American Indian or Alaska Native male[5]				Deaths per 100,000 resident population				
All ages, age adjusted[4]	---	---	---	140.5	145.8	155.8	141.9	139.9
All ages, crude	---	---	---	58.1	61.4	67.0	70.4	70.3
25–34 years	---	---	---	*	*	*	*	*
35–44 years	---	---	---	*	22.8	21.4	18.9	19.0
45–54 years	---	---	---	86.9	86.9	70.3	76.1	81.9
55–64 years	---	---	---	213.4	246.2	255.6	261.4	222.7
65–74 years	---	---	---	613.0	530.6	648.0	604.9	565.4
75–84 years	---	---	---	936.4	1,038.4	1,152.5	1,069.3	995.2
85 years and over	---	---	---	1,471.2	1,654.4	1,584.2	1,036.3	1,459.1
Asian or Pacific Islander male[5]								
All ages, age adjusted[4]	---	---	---	165.2	172.5	150.8	137.9	137.2
All ages, crude	---	---	---	81.9	82.7	85.2	84.0	84.2
25–34 years	---	---	---	6.3	9.2	7.4	7.9	7.6
35–44 years	---	---	---	29.4	27.7	26.1	22.7	21.7
45–54 years	---	---	---	108.2	92.6	78.5	82.8	77.0
55–64 years	---	---	---	298.5	274.6	229.2	224.7	196.1
65–74 years	---	---	---	581.2	687.2	559.4	481.7	498.1
75–84 years	---	---	---	1,147.6	1,229.9	1,086.1	1,012.7	1,056.9
85 years and over	---	---	---	1,798.7	1,837.0	1,823.2	1,544.3	1,545.6
Hispanic or Latino male[5,7]								
All ages, age adjusted[4]	---	---	---	---	174.7	171.7	161.4	156.5
All ages, crude	---	---	---	---	65.5	61.3	61.2	61.5
25–34 years	---	---	---	---	8.0	6.9	6.3	6.8
35–44 years	---	---	---	---	22.5	20.1	18.4	18.2
45–54 years	---	---	---	---	96.6	79.4	78.4	81.1
55–64 years	---	---	---	---	294.0	253.1	254.3	246.5
65–74 years	---	---	---	---	655.5	651.2	622.3	617.6
75–84 years	---	---	---	---	1,233.4	1,306.4	1,190.8	1,163.9
85 years and over	---	---	---	---	2,019.4	2,049.7	1,869.0	1,668.6
White, not Hispanic or Latino male[7]								
All ages, age adjusted[4]	---	---	---	---	276.7	247.7	239.6	234.6
All ages, crude	---	---	---	---	246.2	244.4	243.8	241.8
25–34 years	---	---	---	---	12.8	9.7	9.8	9.4
35–44 years	---	---	---	---	36.8	32.3	32.5	31.9
45–54 years	---	---	---	---	153.9	127.2	125.9	123.8
55–64 years	---	---	---	---	520.6	412.0	395.5	384.8
65–74 years	---	---	---	---	1,109.0	1,002.1	975.3	942.0
75–84 years	---	---	---	---	1,906.6	1,750.2	1,716.5	1,707.8
85 years and over	---	---	---	---	2,744.4	2,714.1	2,507.7	2,441.7
White female[5]								
All ages, age adjusted[4]	182.0	167.7	162.5	165.2	174.0	166.9	162.4	160.2
All ages, crude	139.9	139.8	149.4	170.3	196.1	199.4	195.8	194.6
25–34 years	20.9	18.8	16.3	13.5	11.9	10.1	9.9	9.4
35–44 years	74.5	66.6	62.4	50.9	46.2	38.2	38.5	37.3
45–54 years	185.8	175.7	177.3	166.4	150.9	120.1	115.3	112.1
55–64 years	362.5	329.0	338.6	355.5	368.5	319.7	303.1	299.8
65–74 years	616.5	562.1	554.7	605.2	675.1	665.6	650.4	638.9
75–84 years	1,026.6	939.3	903.5	905.4	1,011.8	1,063.4	1,053.1	1,046.3
85 years and over	1,348.3	1,304.9	1,126.6	1,266.8	1,372.3	1,459.1	1,395.1	1,386.5

See footnotes at end of table.

This table will be updated on the Web. Go to www.cdc.gov/nchs/hus.htm.

Table 38 (page 3 of 4). Death rates for malignant neoplasms, by sex, race, Hispanic origin, and age: United States, selected years 1950–2003

[Data are based on death certificates]

Sex, race, Hispanic origin, and age	1950[1,2]	1960[1,2]	1970[2]	1980[2]	1990	2000[3]	2002	2003
Black or African American female[5]				Deaths per 100,000 resident population				
All ages, age adjusted[4]	174.1	174.3	173.4	189.5	205.9	193.8	190.3	187.7
All ages, crude	111.8	113.8	117.3	136.5	156.1	151.8	151.7	151.4
25–34 years	34.3	31.0	20.9	18.3	18.7	13.5	13.3	13.9
35–44 years	119.8	102.4	94.6	73.5	67.4	58.9	56.2	55.4
45–54 years	277.0	254.8	228.6	230.2	209.9	173.9	168.2	167.2
55–64 years	484.6	442.7	404.8	450.4	482.4	391.0	385.4	380.4
65–74 years	477.3	541.6	615.8	662.4	773.2	753.1	741.1	714.6
75–84 years[6]	605.3	696.3	763.3	923.9	1,059.9	1,124.0	1,123.1	1,116.9
85 years and over	- - -	728.9	791.5	1,159.9	1,431.3	1,527.7	1,468.0	1,475.3
American Indian or Alaska Native female[5]								
All ages, age adjusted[4]	- - -	- - -	- - -	94.0	106.9	108.3	112.9	105.6
All ages, crude	- - -	- - -	- - -	50.4	62.1	61.3	71.0	68.2
25–34 years	- - -	- - -	- - -	*	*	*	9.4	*
35–44 years	- - -	- - -	- - -	36.9	31.0	23.7	23.6	24.3
45–54 years	- - -	- - -	- - -	96.9	104.5	59.7	80.6	75.7
55–64 years	- - -	- - -	- - -	198.4	213.3	200.9	202.5	195.8
65–74 years	- - -	- - -	- - -	350.8	438.9	458.3	473.2	411.2
75–84 years	- - -	- - -	- - -	446.4	554.3	714.0	703.9	784.4
85 years and over	- - -	- - -	- - -	786.5	843.7	983.2	1,001.2	686.0
Asian or Pacific Islander female[5]								
All ages, age adjusted[4]	- - -	- - -	- - -	93.0	103.0	100.7	95.9	96.7
All ages, crude	- - -	- - -	- - -	54.1	60.5	72.1	72.6	75.6
25–34 years	- - -	- - -	- - -	9.5	7.3	8.1	6.4	7.2
35–44 years	- - -	- - -	- - -	38.7	29.8	28.9	23.6	25.8
45–54 years	- - -	- - -	- - -	99.8	93.9	78.2	78.5	77.6
55–64 years	- - -	- - -	- - -	174.7	196.2	176.5	171.2	166.7
65–74 years	- - -	- - -	- - -	301.9	346.2	357.4	358.1	361.5
75–84 years	- - -	- - -	- - -	522.1	641.4	650.1	606.4	616.9
85 years and over	- - -	- - -	- - -	800.0	971.7	988.5	910.1	907.9
Hispanic or Latino female[5,7]								
All ages, age adjusted[4]	- - -	- - -	- - -	- - -	111.9	110.8	106.1	105.9
All ages, crude	- - -	- - -	- - -	- - -	60.7	58.5	58.1	59.1
25–34 years	- - -	- - -	- - -	- - -	9.7	7.8	7.5	7.4
35–44 years	- - -	- - -	- - -	- - -	34.8	30.7	28.4	28.0
45–54 years	- - -	- - -	- - -	- - -	100.5	84.7	78.0	80.2
55–64 years	- - -	- - -	- - -	- - -	205.4	192.5	179.8	185.9
65–74 years	- - -	- - -	- - -	- - -	404.8	410.0	395.6	379.7
75–84 years	- - -	- - -	- - -	- - -	663.0	716.5	692.2	702.1
85 years and over	- - -	- - -	- - -	- - -	1,022.7	1,056.5	1,031.2	1,014.8

See footnotes at end of table.

This table will be updated on the Web. Go to www.cdc.gov/nchs/hus.htm.

Table 38 (page 4 of 4). Death rates for malignant neoplasms, by sex, race, Hispanic origin, and age: United States, selected years 1950–2003

[Data are based on death certificates]

Sex, race, Hispanic origin, and age	1950[1,2]	1960[1,2]	1970[2]	1980[2]	1990	2000[3]	2002	2003
White, not Hispanic or Latino female[7]				Deaths per 100,000 resident population				
All ages, age adjusted[4]	- - -	- - -	- - -	- - -	177.5	170.0	165.9	163.8
All ages, crude	- - -	- - -	- - -	- - -	210.6	220.6	218.5	217.6
25–34 years	- - -	- - -	- - -	- - -	11.9	10.5	10.3	9.8
35–44 years	- - -	- - -	- - -	- - -	47.0	38.9	39.9	38.6
45–54 years	- - -	- - -	- - -	- - -	154.9	123.0	118.7	115.1
55–64 years	- - -	- - -	- - -	- - -	379.5	328.9	312.8	308.9
65–74 years	- - -	- - -	- - -	- - -	688.5	681.0	667.7	657.6
75–84 years	- - -	- - -	- - -	- - -	1,027.2	1,075.3	1,068.3	1,062.4
85 years and over	- - -	- - -	- - -	- - -	1,385.7	1,468.7	1,405.4	1,399.1

- - - Data not available.
* Rates based on fewer than 20 deaths are considered unreliable and are not shown.
[1]Includes deaths of persons who were not residents of the 50 states and the District of Columbia.
[2]Underlying cause of death was coded according to the Sixth Revision of the International Classification of Diseases (ICD) in 1950, Seventh Revision in 1960, Eighth Revision in 1970, and Ninth Revision in 1980–1998. See Appendix II, Cause of death; tables IV and V.
[3]Starting with 1999 data, cause of death is coded according to ICD–10. See Appendix II, Cause of death; Comparability ratio; tables V and VI.
[4]Age-adjusted rates are calculated using the year 2000 standard population. Prior to 2003, age-adjusted rates were calculated using standard million proportions based on rounded population numbers. Starting with 2003 data, unrounded population numbers are used to calculate age-adjusted rates. See Appendix II, Age adjustment.
[5]The race groups, white, black, Asian or Pacific Islander, and American Indian or Alaska Native, include persons of Hispanic and non-Hispanic origin. Persons of Hispanic origin may be of any race. Death rates for the American Indian or Alaska Native and Asian or Pacific Islander populations are known to be underestimated. See Appendix II, Race, for a discussion of sources of bias in death rates by race and Hispanic origin.
[6]In 1950, rate is for the age group 75 years and over.
[7]Prior to 1997, excludes data from states lacking an Hispanic-origin item on the death certificate. See Appendix II, Hispanic origin.

NOTES: Starting with *Health, United States, 2003*, rates for 1991–1999 were revised using intercensal population estimates based on the 2000 census. Rates for 2000 were revised based on 2000 census counts. Rates for 2001 and later years were computed using 2000-based postcensal estimates. See Appendix I, Population Census and Population Estimates. See Appendix II, Cause of death; tables IV and V. Age groups were selected to minimize the presentation of unstable age-specific death rates based on small numbers of deaths and for consistency among comparison groups. Starting with 2003 data, California, Hawaii, Idaho, Maine, Montana, New York, and Wisconsin reported multiple-race data. The multiple-race data for these states were bridged to the single race categories of the 1977 Office of Management and Budget standards for comparability with other states. Data for additional years are available. See Appendix III.

SOURCES: Centers for Disease Control and Prevention, National Center for Health Statistics, National Vital Statistics System; Grove RD, Hetzel AM. Vital statistics rates in the United States, 1940–1960. Washington, DC: U.S. Government Printing Office. 1968; numerator data from National Vital Statistics System, annual mortality files; denominator data from national population estimates for race groups from Table 1 and unpublished Hispanic population estimates for 1985–1996 prepared by the Housing and Household Economic Statistics Division, U.S. Census Bureau; additional mortality tables are available from: www.cdc.gov/nchs/datawh/statab/unpubd/mortabs.htm; Hoyert DL, Heron M, Murphy SL, Kung HC. Deaths: Final data for 2003. National vital statistics reports. Vol 54 no 13. Hyattsville, MD: National Center for Health Statistics. 2006.

This table will be updated on the Web. Go to www.cdc.gov/nchs/hus.htm.

Table 39 (page 1 of 3). Death rates for malignant neoplasms of trachea, bronchus, and lung, by sex, race, Hispanic origin, and age: United States, selected years 1950–2003

[Data are based on death certificates]

Sex, race, Hispanic origin, and age	1950[1,2]	1960[1,2]	1970[2]	1980[2]	1990	2000[3]	2002	2003
All persons			Deaths per 100,000 resident population					
All ages, age adjusted[4]	15.0	24.1	37.1	49.9	59.3	56.1	54.9	54.1
All ages, crude	12.2	20.3	32.1	45.8	56.8	55.3	54.7	54.4
Under 25 years	0.1	0.0	0.1	0.0	0.0	0.0	0.0	0.0
25–34 years	0.8	1.0	0.9	0.6	0.7	0.5	0.4	0.4
35–44 years	4.5	6.8	11.0	9.2	6.8	6.1	6.0	5.6
45–54 years	20.4	29.6	43.4	54.1	46.8	31.6	30.3	30.3
55–64 years	48.7	75.3	109.1	138.2	160.6	122.4	115.3	111.0
65–74 years	59.7	108.1	164.5	233.3	288.4	284.2	275.0	269.3
75–84 years	55.8	91.5	163.2	240.5	333.3	370.8	377.6	377.8
85 years and over	42.3	65.6	101.7	176.0	242.5	302.1	297.2	298.9
Male								
All ages, age adjusted[4]	24.6	43.6	67.5	85.2	91.1	76.7	73.2	71.7
All ages, crude	19.9	35.4	53.4	68.6	75.1	65.5	63.7	62.9
Under 25 years	0.0	0.0	0.1	0.1	0.0	*	0.0	*
25–34 years	1.1	1.4	1.3	0.8	0.9	0.5	0.4	0.4
35–44 years	7.1	10.5	16.1	11.9	8.5	6.9	6.2	6.1
45–54 years	35.0	50.6	67.5	76.0	59.7	38.5	36.6	36.5
55–64 years	83.8	139.3	189.7	213.6	222.9	154.0	144.0	136.7
65–74 years	98.7	204.3	320.8	403.9	430.4	377.9	355.9	346.6
75–84 years	82.6	167.1	330.8	488.8	572.9	532.2	527.9	525.1
85 years and over	62.5	107.7	194.0	368.1	513.2	521.2	482.2	475.1
Female								
All ages, age adjusted[4]	5.8	7.5	13.1	24.4	37.1	41.3	41.6	41.3
All ages, crude	4.5	6.4	11.9	24.3	39.4	45.4	46.0	46.1
Under 25 years	0.1	0.0	0.0	*	*	*	*	*
25–34 years	0.5	0.5	0.5	0.5	0.5	0.5	0.4	0.4
35–44 years	1.9	3.2	6.1	6.5	5.2	5.3	5.8	5.1
45–54 years	5.8	9.2	21.0	33.7	34.5	25.0	24.3	24.4
55–64 years	13.6	15.4	36.8	72.0	105.0	93.3	88.8	87.1
65–74 years	23.3	24.4	43.1	102.7	177.6	206.9	207.7	204.8
75–84 years	32.9	32.8	52.4	94.1	190.1	265.6	277.8	279.4
85 years and over	28.2	38.8	50.0	91.9	138.1	212.8	217.0	221.0
White male[5]								
All ages, age adjusted[4]	25.1	43.6	67.1	83.8	89.0	75.7	72.5	71.1
All ages, crude	20.8	36.4	54.6	70.2	77.8	69.4	67.7	66.9
45–54 years	35.1	49.2	63.3	70.9	55.2	35.7	34.2	34.1
55–64 years	85.4	139.2	186.8	205.6	213.7	150.8	139.3	133.1
65–74 years	101.5	207.5	325.0	401.0	422.1	374.9	356.4	347.1
75–84 years	85.5	170.4	336.7	493.5	572.2	529.9	527.8	524.6
85 years and over	67.4	109.4	199.6	374.1	516.3	522.4	486.6	478.5
Black or African American male[5]								
All ages, age adjusted[4]	17.8	42.6	75.4	107.6	125.4	101.1	95.0	92.4
All ages, crude	12.1	28.1	47.7	66.6	73.7	58.3	56.0	54.9
45–54 years	34.4	68.4	115.4	133.8	114.9	70.7	64.6	63.6
55–64 years	68.3	146.8	234.3	321.1	358.6	223.5	223.6	210.0
65–74 years	53.8	168.3	300.5	472.3	585.4	488.8	444.6	427.1
75–84 years[6]	36.2	107.3	271.6	472.9	645.4	642.5	626.2	622.2
85 years and over	- - -	82.8	137.0	311.3	499.5	562.8	484.6	502.5
American Indian or Alaska Native male[5]								
All ages, age adjusted[4]	- - -	- - -	- - -	31.7	47.5	42.9	41.3	37.6
All ages, crude	- - -	- - -	- - -	14.2	20.0	18.1	19.8	19.4
45–54 years	- - -	- - -	- - -	*	26.6	14.5	14.9	17.1
55–64 years	- - -	- - -	- - -	72.0	97.8	86.0	92.7	79.2
65–74 years	- - -	- - -	- - -	202.8	194.3	184.8	185.2	186.0
75–84 years	- - -	- - -	- - -	*	356.2	367.9	326.2	284.9
85 years and over	- - -	- - -	- - -	*	*	*	*	*

See footnotes at end of table.

This table will be updated on the Web. Go to www.cdc.gov/nchs/hus.htm.

Table 39 (page 2 of 3). **Death rates for malignant neoplasms of trachea, bronchus, and lung, by sex, race, Hispanic origin, and age: United States, selected years 1950–2003**

[Data are based on death certificates]

Sex, race, Hispanic origin, and age	1950[1,2]	1960[1,2]	1970[2]	1980[2]	1990	2000[3]	2002	2003
Asian or Pacific Islander male[5]				Deaths per 100,000 resident population				
All ages, age adjusted[4]	- - -	- - -	- - -	43.3	44.2	40.9	36.3	37.9
All ages, crude	- - -	- - -	- - -	22.1	20.7	22.7	21.5	22.7
45–54 years	- - -	- - -	- - -	33.3	18.8	17.2	15.6	17.5
55–64 years	- - -	- - -	- - -	94.4	74.4	61.4	64.9	50.4
65–74 years	- - -	- - -	- - -	174.3	215.8	183.2	137.7	157.5
75–84 years	- - -	- - -	- - -	301.3	307.5	323.2	301.2	333.3
85 years and over	- - -	- - -	- - -	*	421.3	378.0	346.5	328.4
Hispanic or Latino male[5,7]								
All ages, age adjusted[4]	- - -	- - -	- - -	- - -	44.1	39.0	36.2	34.5
All ages, crude	- - -	- - -	- - -	- - -	16.2	13.3	13.1	12.8
45–54 years	- - -	- - -	- - -	- - -	21.5	14.8	12.6	12.6
55–64 years	- - -	- - -	- - -	- - -	80.7	58.6	60.7	55.4
65–74 years	- - -	- - -	- - -	- - -	195.5	167.3	161.7	161.8
75–84 years	- - -	- - -	- - -	- - -	313.4	327.5	299.1	277.3
85 years and over	- - -	- - -	- - -	- - -	420.7	368.8	307.9	290.9
White, not Hispanic or Latino male[7]								
All ages, age adjusted[4]	- - -	- - -	- - -	- - -	91.1	77.9	75.0	73.6
All ages, crude	- - -	- - -	- - -	- - -	84.7	78.9	77.8	77.3
45–54 years	- - -	- - -	- - -	- - -	57.8	37.7	36.5	36.5
55–64 years	- - -	- - -	- - -	- - -	221.0	157.7	145.7	139.4
65–74 years	- - -	- - -	- - -	- - -	431.4	387.3	369.5	359.6
75–84 years	- - -	- - -	- - -	- - -	580.4	537.7	538.3	537.0
85 years and over	- - -	- - -	- - -	- - -	520.9	527.3	493.3	486.8
White female[5]								
All ages, age adjusted[4]	5.9	6.8	13.1	24.5	37.6	42.3	42.6	42.3
All ages, crude	4.7	5.9	12.3	25.6	42.4	49.9	50.7	50.7
45–54 years	5.7	9.0	20.9	33.0	34.6	24.8	24.2	23.8
55–64 years	13.7	15.1	37.2	71.9	105.7	96.1	91.0	89.8
65–74 years	23.7	24.8	42.9	104.6	181.3	213.2	215.1	212.2
75–84 years	34.0	32.7	52.6	95.2	194.6	272.7	285.8	286.6
85 years and over	29.3	39.1	50.6	92.4	138.3	215.9	220.2	224.4
Black or African American female[5]								
All ages, age adjusted[4]	4.5	6.8	13.7	24.8	36.8	39.8	40.1	40.2
All ages, crude	2.8	4.3	9.4	18.3	28.1	30.8	31.6	32.0
45–54 years	7.5	11.3	23.9	43.4	41.3	32.9	31.7	33.4
55–64 years	12.9	17.9	33.5	79.9	117.9	95.3	95.3	91.0
65–74 years	14.0	18.1	46.1	88.0	164.3	194.1	189.3	190.0
75–84 years[6]	*	31.3	49.1	79.4	148.1	224.3	242.6	248.0
85 years and over	- - -	34.2	44.8	85.8	134.9	185.9	191.0	194.8
American Indian or Alaska Native female[5]								
All ages, age adjusted[4]	- - -	- - -	- - -	11.7	19.3	24.8	27.1	26.4
All ages, crude	- - -	- - -	- - -	6.0	11.2	14.0	16.4	16.4
45–54 years	- - -	- - -	- - -	*	22.9	12.1	11.4	15.1
55–64 years	- - -	- - -	- - -	*	53.7	52.6	52.5	42.5
65–74 years	- - -	- - -	- - -	*	78.5	151.5	162.8	147.8
75–84 years	- - -	- - -	- - -	*	111.8	136.3	163.4	190.1
85 years and over	- - -	- - -	- - -	*	*	*	168.3	*

See footnotes at end of table.

This table will be updated on the Web. Go to www.cdc.gov/nchs/hus.htm.

Table 39 (page 3 of 3). Death rates for malignant neoplasms of trachea, bronchus, and lung, by sex, race, Hispanic origin, and age: United States, selected years 1950–2003

[Data are based on death certificates]

Sex, race, Hispanic origin, and age	1950[1,2]	1960[1,2]	1970[2]	1980[2]	1990	2000[3]	2002	2003
Asian or Pacific Islander female[5]				Deaths per 100,000 resident population				
All ages, age adjusted[4]	- - -	- - -	- - -	15.4	18.9	18.4	17.5	18.7
All ages, crude	- - -	- - -	- - -	8.4	10.5	12.6	12.9	14.1
45–54 years	- - -	- - -	- - -	13.5	11.3	9.9	9.0	11.4
55–64 years	- - -	- - -	- - -	24.6	38.3	30.4	28.9	28.0
65–74 years	- - -	- - -	- - -	62.4	71.6	77.0	79.9	76.3
75–84 years	- - -	- - -	- - -	117.7	137.9	135.0	116.8	142.6
85 years and over	- - -	- - -	- - -	*	172.9	175.3	170.4	180.6
Hispanic or Latino female[5,7]								
All ages, age adjusted[4]	- - -	- - -	- - -	- - -	14.1	14.7	14.6	14.8
All ages, crude	- - -	- - -	- - -	- - -	7.2	7.2	7.6	7.8
45–54 years	- - -	- - -	- - -	- - -	8.7	7.1	7.3	7.9
55–64 years	- - -	- - -	- - -	- - -	25.1	22.2	23.2	22.4
65–74 years	- - -	- - -	- - -	- - -	66.8	66.0	69.5	61.2
75–84 years	- - -	- - -	- - -	- - -	94.3	112.3	104.6	119.6
85 years and over	- - -	- - -	- - -	- - -	118.2	137.5	130.1	137.5
White, not Hispanic or Latino female[7]								
All ages, age adjusted[4]	- - -	- - -	- - -	- - -	39.0	44.1	44.6	44.3
All ages, crude	- - -	- - -	- - -	- - -	46.2	56.4	57.9	58.1
45–54 years	- - -	- - -	- - -	- - -	36.6	26.4	26.0	25.6
55–64 years	- - -	- - -	- - -	- - -	111.3	102.2	96.8	95.7
65–74 years	- - -	- - -	- - -	- - -	186.4	222.9	225.9	223.9
75–84 years	- - -	- - -	- - -	- - -	199.1	279.2	294.3	295.1
85 years and over	- - -	- - -	- - -	- - -	139.0	218.0	223.4	227.4

0.0 Quantity more than zero but less than 0.05.

* Rates based on fewer than 20 deaths are considered unreliable and are not shown.

- - - Data not available.

[1]Includes deaths of persons who were not residents of the 50 states and the District of Columbia.

[2]Underlying cause of death was coded according to the Sixth Revision of the International Classification of Diseases (ICD) in 1950, Seventh Revision in 1960, Eighth Revision in 1970, and Ninth Revision in 1980–1998. See Appendix II, Cause of death; tables IV and V.

[3]Starting with 1999 data, cause of death is coded according to ICD–10. See Appendix II, Cause of death; Comparability ratio; tables V and VI.

[4]Age-adjusted rates are calculated using the year 2000 standard population. Prior to 2003, age-adjusted rates were calculated using standard million proportions based on rounded population numbers. Starting with 2003 data, unrounded population numbers are used to calculate age-adjusted rates. See Appendix II, Age adjustment.

[5]The race groups, white, black, Asian or Pacific Islander, and American Indian or Alaska Native, include persons of Hispanic and non-Hispanic origin. Persons of Hispanic origin may be of any race. Death rates for the American Indian or Alaska Native and Asian or Pacific Islander populations are known to be underestimated. See Appendix II, Race, for a discussion of sources of bias in death rates by race and Hispanic origin.

[6]In 1950, rate is for the age group 75 years and over.

[7]Prior to 1997, excludes data from states lacking an Hispanic-origin item on the death certificate. See Appendix II, Hispanic origin.

NOTES: Starting with *Health, United States, 2003*, rates for 1991–1999 were revised using intercensal population estimates based on the 2000 census. Rates for 2000 were revised based on 2000 census counts. Rates for 2001 and later years were computed using 2000-based postcensal estimates. See Appendix I, Population Census and Population Estimates. For the period 1980–1998, lung cancer was coded using ICD–9 codes that are most comparable with lung cancer codes in the 113 cause list for ICD–10. See Appendix II, Cause of death; table V. Age groups were selected to minimize the presentation of unstable age-specific death rates based on small numbers of deaths and for consistency among comparison groups. Starting with 2003 data, California, Hawaii, Idaho, Maine, Montana, New York, and Wisconsin reported multiple-race data. The multiple-race data for these states were bridged to the single race categories of the 1977 Office of Management and Budget standards for comparability with other states. Data for additional years are available. See Appendix III.

SOURCES: Centers for Disease Control and Prevention, National Center for Health Statistics, National Vital Statistics System; Grove RD, Hetzel AM. Vital statistics rates in the United States, 1940–1960. Washington, DC: U.S. Government Printing Office. 1968; numerator data from National Vital Statistics System, annual mortality files; denominator data from national population estimates for race groups from Table 1 and unpublished Hispanic population estimates for 1985–1996 prepared by the Housing and Household Economic Statistics Division, U.S. Census Bureau; additional mortality tables are available from: www.cdc.gov/nchs/datawh/statab/unpubd/mortabs.htm; Hoyert DL, Heron M, Murphy SL, Kung HC. Deaths: Final data for 2003. National vital statistics reports. Vol 54 no 13. Hyattsville, MD: National Center for Health Statistics. 2006.

This table will be updated on the Web. Go to www.cdc.gov/nchs/hus.htm.

Table 40 (page 1 of 2). Death rates for malignant neoplasm of breast among females, by race, Hispanic origin, and age: United States, selected years 1950–2003

[Data are based on death certificates]

Race, Hispanic origin, and age	1950[1,2]	1960[1,2]	1970[2]	1980[2]	1990	2000[3]	2002	2003
All females				Deaths per 100,000 resident population				
All ages, age adjusted[4]	31.9	31.7	32.1	31.9	33.3	26.8	25.6	25.3
All ages, crude	24.7	26.1	28.4	30.6	34.0	29.2	28.3	28.2
Under 25 years	*	*	*	*	*	*	*	*
25–34 years	3.8	3.8	3.9	3.3	2.9	2.3	2.1	2.1
35–44 years	20.8	20.2	20.4	17.9	17.8	12.4	12.0	12.2
45–54 years	46.9	51.4	52.6	48.1	45.4	33.0	31.4	30.4
55–64 years	69.9	70.8	77.6	80.5	78.6	59.3	56.2	56.6
65–74 years	95.0	90.0	93.8	101.1	111.7	88.3	84.4	82.6
75–84 years	139.8	129.9	127.4	126.4	146.3	128.9	125.9	123.7
85 years and over	195.5	191.9	157.1	169.3	196.8	205.7	191.5	189.4
White[5]								
All ages, age adjusted[4]	32.4	32.0	32.5	32.1	33.2	26.3	25.0	24.7
All ages, crude	25.7	27.2	29.9	32.3	35.9	30.7	29.5	29.3
35–44 years	20.8	19.7	20.2	17.3	17.1	11.3	10.7	11.1
45–54 years	47.1	51.2	53.0	48.1	44.3	31.2	29.4	28.4
55–64 years	70.9	71.8	79.3	81.3	78.5	57.9	55.0	54.9
65–74 years	96.3	91.6	95.9	103.7	113.3	89.3	84.6	82.6
75–84 years	143.6	132.8	129.6	128.4	148.2	130.2	126.5	124.6
85 years and over	204.2	199.7	161.9	171.7	198.0	205.5	192.6	189.4
Black or African American[5]								
All ages, age adjusted[4]	25.3	27.9	28.9	31.7	38.1	34.5	34.0	34.0
All ages, crude	16.4	18.7	19.7	22.9	29.0	27.9	28.2	28.5
35–44 years	21.0	24.8	24.4	24.1	25.8	20.9	22.0	20.8
45–54 years	46.5	54.4	52.0	52.7	60.5	51.5	49.8	48.9
55–64 years	64.3	63.2	64.7	79.9	93.1	80.9	76.6	81.1
65–74 years	67.0	72.3	77.3	84.3	112.2	98.6	101.1	100.1
75–84 years[6]	81.0	87.5	101.8	114.1	140.5	139.8	145.0	141.0
85 years and over	- - -	92.1	112.1	149.9	201.5	238.7	209.1	222.4
American Indian or Alaska Native[5]								
All ages, age adjusted[4]	- - -	- - -	- - -	10.8	13.7	13.6	13.8	14.0
All ages, crude	- - -	- - -	- - -	6.1	8.6	8.7	9.6	9.4
35–44 years	- - -	- - -	- - -	*	*	*	*	*
45–54 years	- - -	- - -	- - -	*	23.9	14.4	18.7	14.1
55–64 years	- - -	- - -	- - -	*	*	40.0	28.5	31.2
65–74 years	- - -	- - -	- - -	*	*	42.5	48.7	38.5
75–84 years	- - -	- - -	- - -	*	*	71.8	*	96.5
85 years and over	- - -	- - -	- - -	*	*	*	*	*
Asian or Pacific Islander[5]								
All ages, age adjusted[4]	- - -	- - -	- - -	11.9	13.7	12.3	12.8	12.6
All ages, crude	- - -	- - -	- - -	8.2	9.3	10.2	10.8	11.0
35–44 years	- - -	- - -	- - -	10.4	8.4	8.1	6.8	7.6
45–54 years	- - -	- - -	- - -	23.4	26.4	22.3	21.3	20.1
55–64 years	- - -	- - -	- - -	35.7	33.8	31.3	33.1	33.8
65–74 years	- - -	- - -	- - -	*	38.5	34.7	38.3	40.7
75–84 years	- - -	- - -	- - -	*	48.0	37.5	48.7	41.4
85 years and over	- - -	- - -	- - -	*	*	68.2	69.3	64.7
Hispanic or Latino[5,7]								
All ages, age adjusted[4]	- - -	- - -	- - -	- - -	19.5	16.9	15.5	16.1
All ages, crude	- - -	- - -	- - -	- - -	11.5	9.7	9.2	9.8
35–44 years	- - -	- - -	- - -	- - -	11.7	8.7	7.8	9.1
45–54 years	- - -	- - -	- - -	- - -	32.8	23.9	21.6	21.0
55–64 years	- - -	- - -	- - -	- - -	45.8	39.1	33.5	38.8
65–74 years	- - -	- - -	- - -	- - -	64.8	54.9	48.7	48.4
75–84 years	- - -	- - -	- - -	- - -	67.2	74.9	73.1	70.8
85 years and over	- - -	- - -	- - -	- - -	102.8	105.8	105.3	114.8

See footnotes at end of table.

This table will be updated on the Web. Go to www.cdc.gov/nchs/hus.htm.

Table 40 (page 2 of 2). Death rates for malignant neoplasm of breast among females, by race, Hispanic origin, and age: United States, selected years 1950–2003

[Data are based on death certificates]

Race, Hispanic origin, and age	1950[1,2]	1960[1,2]	1970[2]	1980[2]	1990	2000[3]	2002	2003
White, not Hispanic or Latino[7]				Deaths per 100,000 resident population				
All ages, age adjusted[4]	- - -	- - -	- - -	- - -	33.9	26.8	25.6	25.2
All ages, crude	- - -	- - -	- - -	- - -	38.5	33.8	32.9	32.6
35–44 years	- - -	- - -	- - -	- - -	17.5	11.6	11.1	11.3
45–54 years	- - -	- - -	- - -	- - -	45.2	31.7	30.0	29.1
55–64 years	- - -	- - -	- - -	- - -	80.6	59.2	56.7	56.0
65–74 years	- - -	- - -	- - -	- - -	115.7	91.4	87.0	85.1
75–84 years	- - -	- - -	- - -	- - -	151.4	132.2	128.9	127.1
85 years and over	- - -	- - -	- - -	- - -	201.5	208.3	195.8	192.3

* Rates based on fewer than 20 deaths are considered unreliable and are not shown.

0.0 Quantity more than zero but less than 0.05.

- - - Data not available.

[1]Includes deaths of persons who were not residents of the 50 states and the District of Columbia.

[2]Underlying cause of death was coded according to the Sixth Revision of the International Classification of Diseases (ICD) in 1950, Seventh Revision in 1960, Eighth Revision in 1970, and Ninth Revision in 1980–1998. See Appendix II, Cause of death; tables IV and V.

[3]Starting with 1999 data, cause of death is coded according to ICD–10. See Appendix II, Cause of death; Comparability ratio; tables V and VI.

[4]Age-adjusted rates are calculated using the year 2000 standard population. Prior to 2003, age-adjusted rates were calculated using standard million proportions based on rounded population numbers. Starting with 2003 data, unrounded population numbers are used to calculate age-adjusted rates. See Appendix II, Age adjustment.

[5]The race groups, white, black, Asian or Pacific Islander, and American Indian or Alaska Native, include persons of Hispanic and non-Hispanic origin. Persons of Hispanic origin may be of any race. Death rates for the American Indian or Alaska Native and Asian or Pacific Islander populations are known to be underestimated. See Appendix II, Race, for a discussion of sources of bias in death rates by race and Hispanic origin.

[6]In 1950, rate is for the age group 75 years and over.

[7]Prior to 1997, excludes data from states lacking an Hispanic-origin item on the death certificate. See Appendix II, Hispanic origin.

NOTES: Starting with *Health, United States, 2003*, rates for 1991–1999 were revised using intercensal population estimates based on the 2000 census. Rates for 2000 were revised based on 2000 census counts. Rates for 2001 and 2002 were computed using 2000-based postcensal estimates. See Appendix I, Population Census and Population Estimates. Age groups were selected to minimize the presentation of unstable age-specific death rates based on small numbers of deaths and for consistency among comparison groups. Starting with 2003 data, California, Hawaii, Idaho, Maine, Montana, New York, and Wisconsin reported multiple-race data. The multiple-race data for these states were bridged to the single race categories of the 1977 Office of Management and Budget standards for comparability with other states. Data for additional years are available. See Appendix III.

SOURCES: Centers for Disease Control and Prevention, National Center for Health Statistics, National Vital Statistics System; numerator data from annual mortality files; denominator data from national population estimates for race groups from Table 1 and unpublished Hispanic population estimates for 1985–1996 prepared by the Housing and Household Economic Statistics Division, U.S. Census Bureau; additional mortality tables are available from: www.cdc.gov/nchs/datawh/statab/unpubd/mortabs.htm; Hoyert DL, Heron M, Murphy SL, Kung HC. Deaths: Final data for 2003. National vital statistics reports. Vol 54 no 13. Hyattsville, MD: National Center for Health Statistics. 2006.

This table will be updated on the Web. Go to www.cdc.gov/nchs/hus.htm.

Table 41 (page 1 of 3). Death rates for chronic lower respiratory diseases, by sex, race, Hispanic origin, and age: United States, selected years 1980–2003

[Data are based on death certificates]

Sex, race, Hispanic origin, and age	1980[1]	1990	1995	2000[2]	2001	2002	2003
All persons			Deaths per 100,000 resident population				
All ages, age adjusted[3]	28.3	37.2	40.1	44.2	43.7	43.5	43.3
All ages, crude	24.7	34.9	38.6	43.4	43.2	43.3	43.5
Under 1 year	1.6	1.4	1.1	0.9	1.0	1.0	0.8
1–4 years	0.4	0.4	0.2	0.3	0.3	0.4	0.3
5–14 years	0.2	0.3	0.4	0.3	0.3	0.3	0.3
15–24 years	0.3	0.5	0.7	0.5	0.4	0.5	0.5
25–34 years	0.5	0.7	0.9	0.7	0.7	0.8	0.7
35–44 years	1.6	1.6	1.9	2.1	2.2	2.2	2.1
45–54 years	9.8	9.1	8.7	8.6	8.5	8.7	8.7
55–64 years	42.7	48.9	46.8	44.2	44.1	42.4	43.3
65–74 years	129.1	152.5	159.6	169.4	167.9	163.0	163.2
75–84 years	224.4	321.1	349.3	386.1	379.8	386.7	383.0
85 years and over	274.0	433.3	520.1	648.6	644.7	637.6	635.1
Male							
All ages, age adjusted[3]	49.9	55.5	54.8	55.8	54.0	53.5	52.3
All ages, crude	35.1	40.8	41.4	43.5	42.7	42.9	42.4
Under 1 year	1.9	1.6	1.4	1.2	1.1	1.1	1.1
1–4 years	0.5	0.5	0.2	0.4	0.4	0.6	0.5
5–14 years	0.2	0.4	0.5	0.4	0.3	0.4	0.4
15–24 years	0.4	0.5	0.7	0.6	0.5	0.6	0.5
25–34 years	0.6	0.7	0.9	0.8	0.7	0.8	0.8
35–44 years	1.7	1.7	1.7	1.9	2.0	2.2	1.9
45–54 years	12.1	9.4	8.8	9.0	8.8	9.1	9.1
55–64 years	59.9	58.6	52.3	47.8	46.9	45.2	46.5
65–74 years	210.0	204.0	195.6	195.2	191.3	184.8	183.6
75–84 years	437.4	500.0	483.8	488.5	475.1	480.8	464.9
85 years and over	583.4	815.1	889.8	967.9	916.9	894.8	865.9
Female							
All ages, age adjusted[3]	14.9	26.6	31.8	37.4	37.6	37.4	37.8
All ages, crude	15.0	29.2	36.0	43.2	43.7	43.7	44.4
Under 1 year	1.3	1.2	*	*	*	*	*
1–4 years	*	*	*	0.3	*	0.3	*
5–14 years	0.3	0.3	0.2	0.3	0.2	0.3	0.2
15–24 years	0.3	0.5	0.6	0.4	0.4	0.4	0.4
25–34 years	0.5	0.7	0.9	0.7	0.7	0.7	0.6
35–44 years	1.5	1.5	2.2	2.2	2.3	2.3	2.3
45–54 years	7.7	8.8	8.7	8.3	8.1	8.2	8.2
55–64 years	27.6	40.3	41.9	41.0	41.5	39.8	40.3
65–74 years	67.1	112.3	130.8	148.2	148.5	144.9	146.0
75–84 years	98.7	214.2	265.3	319.2	317.3	324.1	328.3
85 years and over	138.7	286.0	377.7	518.5	530.8	526.0	533.0
White male[4]							
All ages, age adjusted[3]	51.6	56.6	55.9	57.2	55.5	54.9	53.8
All ages, crude	37.9	44.3	45.5	48.3	47.6	47.8	47.4
35–44 years	1.2	1.3	1.4	1.6	1.7	1.8	1.7
45–54 years	11.4	8.6	8.1	8.4	8.6	8.8	8.9
55–64 years	60.0	58.7	52.7	48.6	48.0	46.0	47.6
65–74 years	218.4	208.1	200.0	201.4	198.3	192.3	191.6
75–84 years	459.8	513.5	497.9	503.6	489.4	495.2	478.5
85 years and over	611.2	847.0	918.3	997.4	943.6	923.4	894.4
Black or African American male[4]							
All ages, age adjusted[3]	34.0	47.6	47.4	47.5	46.3	46.3	44.4
All ages, crude	19.3	25.2	24.4	24.3	23.6	24.1	23.3
35–44 years	5.8	5.3	4.3	4.8	4.7	5.7	4.0
45–54 years	19.7	18.8	16.9	15.0	13.3	14.4	13.3
55–64 years	66.6	67.4	60.5	54.6	49.8	52.3	50.5
65–74 years	142.0	184.5	178.7	176.9	168.0	158.0	155.1
75–84 years	229.8	390.9	370.0	370.3	380.8	392.2	382.2
85 years and over	271.6	498.0	624.1	693.1	671.7	645.4	601.6

See footnotes at end of table.

This table will be updated on the Web. Go to www.cdc.gov/nchs/hus.htm.

[Data are based on death certificates]

Sex, race, Hispanic origin, and age	1980[1]	1990	1995	2000[2]	2001	2002	2003
American Indian or Alaska Native male[4]			Deaths per 100,000 resident population				
All ages, age adjusted[3]	23.0	38.3	35.6	43.7	35.0	35.9	40.3
All ages, crude	8.4	13.8	12.3	15.3	13.1	14.3	17.3
35–44 years	*	*	*	*	*	*	*
45–54 years	*	*	*	*	*	*	*
55–64 years	*	*	36.5	46.4	35.7	34.5	43.8
65–74 years	*	135.7	132.1	111.3	115.1	126.1	125.9
75–84 years	*	363.8	307.3	416.6	306.0	348.9	387.0
85 years and over	*	*	*	770.7	614.8	500.3	563.8
Asian or Pacific Islander male[4]							
All ages, age adjusted[3]	21.5	29.8	28.9	28.3	27.0	25.0	25.2
All ages, crude	8.7	11.3	11.8	12.6	12.7	12.0	12.5
35–44 years	*	*	*	*	*	*	*
45–54 years	*	*	*	4.8	3.6	2.6	*
55–64 years	*	22.1	15.7	8.8	14.4	11.5	12.7
65–74 years	70.6	91.4	87.9	71.3	65.5	58.5	58.4
75–84 years	155.7	258.6	240.6	254.3	239.3	235.9	234.9
85 years and over	472.4	615.2	650.4	670.7	640.4	582.5	590.7
Hispanic or Latino male[4,5]							
All ages, age adjusted[3]	- - -	28.6	31.8	28.8	27.6	27.2	27.1
All ages, crude	- - -	8.4	8.9	8.0	7.8	8.1	8.2
35–44 years	- - -	*	1.1	0.9	0.7	1.0	1.0
45–54 years	- - -	4.1	3.9	3.4	3.2	3.8	3.2
55–64 years	- - -	17.2	19.1	18.2	16.1	17.5	16.6
65–74 years	- - -	81.0	82.4	72.4	75.5	69.2	68.1
75–84 years	- - -	252.4	292.0	250.3	224.0	243.3	231.2
85 years and over	- - -	613.9	689.0	671.1	676.1	602.4	646.5
White, not Hispanic or Latino male[5]							
All ages, age adjusted[3]	- - -	57.9	56.6	58.5	56.9	56.5	55.4
All ages, crude	- - -	48.5	50.2	55.1	54.6	55.1	54.9
35–44 years	- - -	1.4	1.4	1.7	1.9	2.0	1.8
45–54 years	- - -	9.0	8.4	8.9	9.1	9.3	9.5
55–64 years	- - -	61.3	54.6	50.8	50.5	48.3	50.0
65–74 years	- - -	213.4	204.3	208.8	206.1	200.4	200.2
75–84 years	- - -	523.7	501.7	513.6	500.9	506.7	491.0
85 years and over	- - -	860.6	922.6	1,008.6	951.5	935.4	903.6
White female[4]							
All ages, age adjusted[3]	15.5	27.8	33.3	39.5	39.8	39.7	40.3
All ages, crude	16.4	32.8	40.8	49.7	50.3	50.5	51.5
35–44 years	1.3	1.2	1.7	1.8	1.9	2.0	2.1
45–54 years	7.6	8.3	8.4	7.9	8.0	8.1	8.1
55–64 years	28.7	41.9	44.0	43.2	44.1	42.4	42.9
65–74 years	71.0	118.8	139.0	159.6	160.4	157.0	158.6
75–84 years	104.0	226.3	279.5	339.1	338.3	345.4	352.0
85 years and over	144.2	298.4	395.5	544.8	557.9	554.5	562.8
Black or African American female[4]							
All ages, age adjusted[3]	9.1	16.6	20.2	22.7	22.4	22.6	22.0
All ages, crude	6.8	12.6	15.5	17.6	17.5	17.7	17.3
35–44 years	3.4	3.8	5.4	4.7	4.9	4.6	4.6
45–54 years	9.3	14.0	12.8	13.4	11.7	11.6	11.9
55–64 years	20.8	33.4	34.7	35.3	33.3	31.5	32.4
65–74 years	32.7	64.7	78.7	82.9	84.3	82.0	83.3
75–84 years	41.1	96.0	132.7	158.4	151.7	167.4	153.2
85 years and over	63.2	133.0	185.8	255.0	266.1	262.0	256.4

See footnotes at end of table.

This table will be updated on the Web. Go to www.cdc.gov/nchs/hus.htm.

Table 41 (page 3 of 3). Death rates for chronic lower respiratory diseases, by sex, race, Hispanic origin, and age: United States, selected years 1980–2003

[Data are based on death certificates]

Sex, race, Hispanic origin, and age	1980[1]	1990	1995	2000[2]	2001	2002	2003
American Indian or Alaska Native female[4]			Deaths per 100,000 resident population				
All ages, age adjusted[3]	7.7	16.8	22.8	26.2	27.3	26.4	26.1
All ages, crude	3.8	8.7	11.5	13.4	14.8	15.1	15.6
35–44 years	*	*	*	*	*	*	*
45–54 years	*	*	*	*	*	*	*
55–64 years	*	*	38.8	31.6	37.3	34.1	39.0
65–74 years	*	56.4	79.5	136.8	114.2	119.1	101.2
75–84 years	*	116.7	191.3	175.8	217.9	194.8	217.2
85 years and over	*	*	*	362.2	345.3	353.4	296.2
Asian or Pacific Islander female[4]							
All ages, age adjusted[3]	5.8	11.0	12.1	11.7	11.1	9.3	9.9
All ages, crude	2.6	5.2	6.3	6.8	6.8	6.0	6.5
35–44 years	*	*	*	*	*	*	*
45–54 years	*	*	3.6	*	*	*	*
55–64 years	*	15.2	9.6	6.2	7.0	4.9	6.0
65–74 years	*	26.5	29.2	29.2	30.2	24.6	24.8
75–84 years	*	80.6	113.2	88.9	79.4	77.0	77.2
85 years and over	*	232.5	227.8	299.5	288.5	219.1	253.8
Hispanic or Latino female[4,5]							
All ages, age adjusted[3]	- - -	13.4	16.9	16.3	16.5	16.2	15.8
All ages, crude	- - -	6.3	7.7	7.2	7.5	7.6	7.7
35–44 years	- - -	*	1.4	1.3	1.2	1.4	1.0
45–54 years	- - -	4.9	4.6	3.3	4.1	3.1	3.8
55–64 years	- - -	14.4	12.9	10.8	12.1	10.6	9.3
65–74 years	- - -	36.6	43.1	38.0	40.3	41.5	41.5
75–84 years	- - -	101.1	125.0	136.0	132.7	129.8	129.6
85 years and over	- - -	269.0	402.6	387.8	384.4	385.5	365.6
White, not Hispanic or Latino female[5]							
All ages, age adjusted[3]	- - -	28.5	34.0	40.7	41.1	41.2	41.8
All ages, crude	- - -	35.7	44.7	56.2	57.2	57.7	59.0
35–44 years	- - -	1.2	1.7	1.9	2.0	2.1	2.2
45–54 years	- - -	8.5	8.5	8.3	8.3	8.6	8.5
55–64 years	- - -	43.7	46.2	45.8	46.8	45.1	45.7
65–74 years	- - -	122.8	143.0	167.6	168.8	165.5	167.6
75–84 years	- - -	231.9	284.5	347.2	347.3	355.7	363.5
85 years and over	- - -	302.1	393.7	548.7	562.7	559.8	569.5

* Rates based on fewer than 20 deaths are considered unreliable and are not shown.

- - - Data not available.

[1]For the period 1980–1998, underlying cause of death was coded according to the Ninth Revision of the International Classification of Diseases (ICD), using ICD–9 codes for chronic lower respiratory diseases (CLRD) that are most nearly comparable with CLRD codes in the 113 cause list for ICD–10. See Appendix II, Cause of death; tables IV and V.

[2]Starting with 1999 data, cause of death is coded according to ICD–10. See Appendix II, Cause of death; Comparability ratio; tables V and VI.

[3]Age-adjusted rates are calculated using the year 2000 standard population. Prior to 2003, age-adjusted rates were calculated using standard million proportions based on rounded population numbers. Starting with 2003 data, unrounded population numbers are used to calculate age-adjusted rates. See Appendix II, Age adjustment.

[4]The race groups, white, black, Asian or Pacific Islander, and American Indian or Alaska Native, include persons of Hispanic and non-Hispanic origin. Persons of Hispanic origin may be of any race. Death rates for the American Indian or Alaska Native and Asian or Pacific Islander populations are known to be underestimated. See Appendix II, Race, for a discussion of sources of bias in death rates by race and Hispanic origin.

[5]Prior to 1997, excludes data from states lacking an Hispanic-origin item on the death certificate. See Appendix II, Hispanic origin.

NOTES: Starting with *Health, United States, 2003*, rates for 1991–1999 were revised using intercensal population estimates based on the 2000 census. Rates for 2000 were revised based on 2000 census counts. Rates for 2001 and later years were computed using 2000-based postcensal estimates. See Appendix I, Population Census and Population Estimates. Age groups were selected to minimize the presentation of unstable age-specific death rates based on small numbers of deaths and for consistency among comparison groups. Starting with 2003 data, California, Hawaii, Idaho, Maine, Montana, New York, and Wisconsin reported multiple-race data. The multiple-race data for these states were bridged to the single race categories of the 1977 Office of Management and Budget standards for comparability with other states. Data for additional years are available. See Appendix III.

SOURCES: Centers for Disease Control and Prevention, National Center for Health Statistics, National Vital Statistics System; numerator data from annual mortality files; denominator data from national population estimates for race groups from Table 1 and unpublished Hispanic population estimates for 1985–1996 prepared by the Housing and Household Economic Statistics Division, U.S. Census Bureau; additional mortality tables are available from: www.cdc.gov/nchs/datawh/statab/unpubd/mortabs.htm; Hoyert DL, Heron M, Murphy SL, Kung HC. Deaths: Final data for 2003. National vital statistics reports. Vol 54 no 13. Hyattsville, MD: National Center for Health Statistics. 2006.

This table will be updated on the Web. Go to www.cdc.gov/nchs/hus.htm.

Table 42 (page 1 of 2). Death rates for human immunodeficiency virus (HIV) disease, by sex, race, Hispanic origin, and age: United States, selected years 1987–2003

[Data are based on death certificates]

Sex, race, Hispanic origin, and age[1]	1987[2]	1990	1995	2000[3]	2001	2002	2003
All persons			Deaths per 100,000 resident population				
All ages, age adjusted[4]	5.6	10.2	16.2	5.2	5.0	4.9	4.7
All ages, crude	5.6	10.1	16.2	5.1	5.0	4.9	4.7
Under 1 year	2.3	2.7	1.5	*	*	*	*
1–4 years	0.7	0.8	1.3	*	*	*	*
5–14 years	0.1	0.2	0.5	0.1	0.1	0.1	0.1
15–24 years	1.3	1.5	1.7	0.5	0.6	0.4	0.4
25–34 years	11.7	19.7	28.3	6.1	5.3	4.6	4.0
35–44 years	14.0	27.4	44.2	13.1	13.0	12.7	12.0
45–54 years	8.0	15.2	26.0	11.0	10.5	11.2	10.9
55–64 years	3.5	6.2	10.9	5.1	5.2	5.1	5.4
65–74 years	1.3	2.0	3.6	2.2	2.1	2.2	2.4
75–84 years	0.8	0.7	0.7	0.7	0.7	0.8	0.7
85 years and over	*	*	*	*	*	*	*
Male							
All ages, age adjusted[4]	10.4	18.5	27.3	7.9	7.5	7.4	7.1
All ages, crude	10.2	18.5	27.6	7.9	7.6	7.4	7.1
Under 1 year	2.2	2.4	1.7	*	*	*	*
1–4 years	0.7	0.8	1.2	*	*	*	*
5–14 years	0.2	0.3	0.5	0.1	0.1	*	*
15–24 years	2.2	2.2	2.0	0.5	0.5	0.4	0.4
25–34 years	20.7	34.5	45.5	8.0	7.1	5.9	5.1
35–44 years	26.3	50.2	75.5	19.8	19.5	18.8	17.5
45–54 years	15.5	29.1	46.2	17.8	16.8	17.7	17.2
55–64 years	6.8	12.0	19.7	8.7	8.6	8.5	9.1
65–74 years	2.4	3.7	6.4	3.8	3.5	3.9	4.0
75–84 years	1.2	1.1	1.3	1.3	1.5	1.4	1.5
85 years and over	*	*	*	*	*	*	*
Female							
All ages, age adjusted[4]	1.1	2.2	5.3	2.5	2.5	2.5	2.4
All ages, crude	1.1	2.2	5.3	2.5	2.5	2.5	2.4
Under 1 year	2.5	3.0	1.2	*	*	*	*
1–4 years	0.7	0.8	1.5	*	*	*	*
5–14 years	*	0.2	0.5	0.1	*	*	*
15–24 years	0.3	0.7	1.4	0.4	0.6	0.4	0.4
25–34 years	2.8	4.9	10.9	4.2	3.5	3.3	2.8
35–44 years	2.1	5.2	13.3	6.5	6.7	6.7	6.5
45–54 years	0.8	1.9	6.6	4.4	4.4	4.8	4.8
55–64 years	0.5	1.1	2.8	1.8	2.0	1.9	2.1
65–74 years	0.5	0.8	1.4	0.8	0.9	0.8	1.0
75–84 years	0.5	0.4	0.3	0.3	*	0.3	0.3
85 years and over	*	*	*	*	*	*	*
All ages, age adjusted[4]							
White male	8.7	15.7	20.4	4.6	4.4	4.3	4.2
Black or African American male	26.2	46.3	89.0	35.1	33.8	33.3	31.3
American Indian or Alaska Native male	*	3.3	10.5	3.5	4.2	3.4	3.5
Asian or Pacific Islander male	2.5	4.3	6.0	1.2	1.2	1.5	1.1
Hispanic or Latino male[5]	18.8	28.8	40.8	10.6	9.7	9.1	9.2
White, not Hispanic or Latino male[5]	10.7	14.1	17.9	3.8	3.6	3.5	3.4
White female	0.6	1.1	2.5	1.0	0.9	0.9	0.9
Black or African American female	4.6	10.1	24.4	13.2	13.4	13.4	12.8
American Indian or Alaska Native female	*	*	2.5	1.0	*	*	1.5
Asian or Pacific Islander female	*	*	0.6	0.2	*	*	*
Hispanic or Latino female[5]	2.1	3.8	8.8	2.9	2.7	2.6	2.7
White, not Hispanic or Latino female[5]	0.5	0.7	1.7	0.7	0.6	0.6	0.6

See footnotes at end of table.

This table will be updated on the Web. Go to www.cdc.gov/nchs/hus.htm.

Table 42 (page 2 of 2). Death rates for human immunodeficiency virus (HIV) disease, by sex, race, Hispanic origin, and age: United States, selected years 1987–2003

[Data are based on death certificates]

Sex, race, Hispanic origin, and age[1]	1987[2]	1990	1995	2000[3]	2001	2002	2003
Age 25–44 years	Deaths per 100,000 resident population						
All persons	12.7	23.2	36.3	9.8	9.4	8.9	8.2
White male	19.2	35.0	46.1	8.8	8.3	7.7	7.2
Black or African American male	60.2	102.0	179.4	55.4	53.5	49.9	44.8
American Indian or Alaska Native male	*	7.7	28.5	5.5	7.3	8.3	6.4
Asian or Pacific Islander male	4.1	8.1	12.1	1.9	2.1	1.8	1.9
Hispanic or Latino male[5]	36.8	59.3	73.9	14.3	12.4	11.5	10.3
White, not Hispanic or Latino male[5]	23.3	31.6	41.2	7.4	7.2	6.6	6.2
White female	1.2	2.3	5.9	2.1	1.9	1.8	1.8
Black or African American female	11.6	23.6	53.6	26.7	26.0	25.9	23.6
American Indian or Alaska Native female	*	*	*	*	*	*	*
Asian or Pacific Islander female	*	*	1.2	*	*	*	*
Hispanic or Latino female[5]	4.9	8.9	17.2	4.6	4.3	3.8	3.8
White, not Hispanic or Latino female[5]	1.0	1.5	4.2	1.6	1.3	1.3	1.3
Age 45–64 years							
All persons	5.8	11.1	19.9	8.7	8.4	8.7	8.7
White male	9.9	18.6	26.0	8.1	7.7	7.8	7.9
Black or African American male	27.3	53.0	133.2	71.6	68.8	70.7	68.1
American Indian or Alaska Native male	*	*	*	*	7.8	*	*
Asian or Pacific Islander male	*	6.5	9.1	2.1	1.9	3.4	2.1
Hispanic or Latino male[5]	25.8	37.9	67.1	23.3	21.5	20.3	22.5
White, not Hispanic or Latino male[5]	12.6	16.9	22.4	6.5	6.1	6.4	6.2
White female	0.5	0.9	2.4	1.3	1.2	1.4	1.4
Black or African American female	2.6	7.5	27.0	19.6	20.8	21.4	21.8
American Indian or Alaska Native female	*	*	*	*	*	*	*
Asian or Pacific Islander female	*	*	*	*	*	*	*
Hispanic or Latino female[5]	*	3.1	12.6	5.8	5.4	5.7	5.3
White, not Hispanic or Latino female[5]	0.5	0.7	1.5	0.9	0.8	0.9	0.9

* Rates based on fewer than 20 deaths are considered unreliable and are not shown.

[1]The race groups, white, black, Asian or Pacific Islander, and American Indian or Alaska Native, include persons of Hispanic and non-Hispanic origin. Persons of Hispanic origin may be of any race. Death rates for the American Indian or Alaska Native and Asian or Pacific Islander populations are known to be underestimated. See Appendix II, Race, for a discussion of sources of bias in death rates by race and Hispanic origin.

[2]Categories for the coding and classification of human immunodeficiency virus (HIV) disease were introduced in the United States in 1987. For the period 1987–1998, underlying cause of death was coded according to the Ninth Revision of the International Classification of Diseases (ICD). See Appendix II, Cause of death; Human immunodeficiency virus (HIV) disease; tables IV and V.

[3]Starting with 1999 data, cause of death is coded according to ICD–10. To estimate change between 1998 and 1999, compare the 1999 rate with the comparability-modified rate for 1998. See Appendix II, Cause of death; Comparability ratio; tables V and VI.

[4]Age-adjusted rates are calculated using the year 2000 standard population. Prior to 2003, age-adjusted rates were calculated using standard million proportions based on rounded population numbers. Starting with 2003 data, unrounded population numbers are used to calculate age-adjusted rates. See Appendix II, Age adjustment.

[5]Prior to 1997, excludes data from states lacking an Hispanic-origin item on the death certificate. See Appendix II, Hispanic origin.

NOTES: Starting with *Health, United States, 2003*, rates for 1991–1999 were revised using intercensal population estimates based on the 2000 census. Rates for 2000 were revised based on 2000 census counts. Rates for 2001 and 2002 were computed using 2000-based postcensal estimates. See Appendix I, Population Census and Population Estimates. Starting with 2003 data, California, Hawaii, Idaho, Maine, Montana, New York, and Wisconsin reported multiple-race data. The multiple-race data for these states were bridged to the single race categories of the 1977 Office of Management and Budget standards for comparability with other states. Data for additional years are available. See Appendix III.

SOURCES: Centers for Disease Control and Prevention, National Center for Health Statistics, National Vital Statistics System; numerator data from annual mortality files; denominator data from national population estimates for race groups from Table 1 and unpublished Hispanic population estimates for 1987–1996 prepared by the Housing and Household Economic Statistics Division, U.S. Census Bureau; additional mortality tables are available from: www.cdc.gov/nchs/datawh/statab/unpubd/mortabs.htm; Hoyert DL, Heron M, Murphy SL, Kung HC. Deaths: Final data for 2003. National vital statistics reports. Vol 54 no 13. Hyattsville, MD: National Center for Health Statistics. 2006.

This table will be updated on the Web. Go to www.cdc.gov/nchs/hus.htm.

Table 43. Maternal mortality for complications of pregnancy, childbirth, and the puerperium, by race, Hispanic origin, and age: United States, selected years 1950–2003

[Data are based on death certificates]

Race, Hispanic origin, and age	1950[1,2]	1960[1,2]	1970[2]	1980[2]	1990[2]	2000[3]	2001	2002	2003[4]
	Number of deaths								
All persons	2,960	1,579	803	334	343	396	399	357	495
White	1,873	936	445	193	177	240	228	190	280
Black or African American	1,041	624	342	127	153	137	150	148	183
American Indian or Alaska Native	- - -	- - -	- - -	3	4	6	5	–	7
Asian or Pacific Islander	- - -	- - -	- - -	11	9	13	16	19	25
Hispanic or Latino[5]	- - -	- - -	- - -	- - -	47	81	81	62	92
White, not Hispanic or Latino[5]	- - -	- - -	- - -	- - -	125	160	151	128	188
All persons	Deaths per 100,000 live births								
All ages, age adjusted[6]	73.7	32.1	21.5	9.4	7.6	8.2	8.8	7.6	9.7
All ages, crude	83.3	37.1	21.5	9.2	8.2	9.8	9.9	8.9	12.1
Under 20 years	70.7	22.7	18.9	7.6	7.5	*	8.8	6.7	6.2
20–24 years	47.6	20.7	13.0	5.8	6.1	7.4	6.9	5.8	7.7
25–29 years	63.5	29.8	17.0	7.7	6.0	7.9	8.5	7.5	8.7
30–34 years	107.7	50.3	31.6	13.6	9.5	10.0	10.1	9.3	10.9
35 years and over[7]	222.0	104.3	81.9	36.3	20.7	22.7	18.9	18.4	33.1
White									
All ages, age adjusted[6]	53.1	22.4	14.4	6.7	5.1	6.2	6.5	4.8	6.9
All ages, crude	61.1	26.0	14.3	6.6	5.4	7.5	7.2	6.0	8.7
Under 20 years	44.9	14.8	13.8	5.8	*	*	7.4	*	*
20–24 years	35.7	15.3	8.4	4.2	3.9	5.6	5.3	3.4	5.3
25–29 years	45.0	20.3	11.1	5.4	4.8	5.9	5.8	4.6	6.9
30–34 years	75.9	34.3	18.7	9.3	5.0	7.1	8.1	6.7	6.8
35 years and over[7]	174.1	73.9	59.3	25.5	12.6	18.0	11.4	13.3	23.8
Black or African American									
All ages, age adjusted[6]	- - -	92.0	65.5	24.9	21.7	20.1	22.4	22.9	25.5
All ages, crude	- - -	103.6	60.9	22.4	22.4	22.0	24.7	24.9	30.5
Under 20 years	- - -	54.8	32.3	13.1	*	*	*	*	*
20–24 years	- - -	56.9	41.9	13.9	14.7	15.3	14.6	14.9	15.8
25–29 years	- - -	92.8	65.2	22.4	14.9	21.8	24.7	27.1	20.7
30–34 years	- - -	150.6	117.8	44.0	44.2	34.8	30.6	28.4	46.1
35 years and over[7]	- - -	299.5	207.5	100.6	79.7	62.8	71.0	62.9	104.1
Hispanic or Latino[5,8]									
All ages, age adjusted[6]	- - -	- - -	- - -	- - -	7.4	9.0	8.8	6.0	8.6
All ages, crude	- - -	- - -	- - -	- - -	7.9	9.9	9.5	7.1	10.1
White, not Hispanic or Latino[5]									
All ages, age adjusted[6]	- - -	- - -	- - -	- - -	4.4	5.5	5.8	4.4	6.3
All ages, crude	- - -	- - -	- - -	- - -	4.8	6.8	6.5	5.6	8.1

- - - Data not available.
– Quantity zero.
* Rates based on fewer than 20 deaths are considered unreliable and are not shown.
[1]Includes deaths of persons who were not residents of the 50 states and the District of Columbia.
[2]Underlying cause of death was coded according to the Sixth Revision of the International Classification of Diseases (ICD) in 1950, Seventh Revision in 1960, Eighth Revision in 1970, and Ninth Revision in 1980–1998. See Appendix II, Cause of death; tables IV and V.
[3]Starting with 1999 data, cause of death is coded according to ICD–10. Major changes in the classification and coding of maternal deaths account for an increase in the number of maternal deaths under ICD–10. See Appendix II, Cause of death; tables V and VI; Comparability ratio; International Classification of Diseases (ICD); Maternal death.
[4]Increases are due to methodological changes in reporting and data processing. See Appendix II, Maternal death.
[5]Prior to 1997, excludes data from states lacking an Hispanic-origin item on the death certificate. See Appendix II, Hispanic origin.
[6]Rates are age adjusted to the 1970 distribution of live births by mother's age in the United States. See Appendix II, Age adjustment.
[7]Rates computed by relating deaths of women 35 years and over to live births to women 35–49 years. See Appendix II, Rate: Death and related rates.
[8]Age-specific maternal mortality rates are not calculated because rates based on fewer than 20 deaths are considered unreliable.

NOTES: The race groups, white, black, Asian or Pacific Islander, and American Indian or Alaska Native, include persons of Hispanic and non-Hispanic origin. Persons of Hispanic origin may be of any race. For 1950 and 1960, rates were based on live births by race of child; for all other years, rates are based on live births by race of mother. See Appendix II, Race. Rates are not calculated for American Indian or Alaska Native and Asian or Pacific Islander mothers because rates based on fewer than 20 deaths are considered unreliable. Data for additional years are available. See Appendix III.

SOURCES: Centers for Disease Control and Prevention, National Center for Health Statistics, National Vital Statistics System; numerator data from annual mortality files; denominator data from annual natality files; Hoyert DL, Heron M, Murphy SL, Kung HC. Deaths: Final data for 2003. National vital statistics reports. Vol 54 no 13. Hyattsville, MD: National Center for Health Statistics. 2006.

This table will be updated on the Web. Go to www.cdc.gov/nchs/hus.htm.

Table 44 (page 1 of 4). Death rates for motor vehicle-related injuries, by sex, race, Hispanic origin, and age: United States, selected years 1950–2003

[Data are based on death certificates]

Sex, race, Hispanic origin, and age	1950[1,2]	1960[1,2]	1970[2]	1980[2]	1990	2000[3]	2002	2003
All persons	Deaths per 100,000 resident population							
All ages, age adjusted[4]	24.6	23.1	27.6	22.3	18.5	15.4	15.7	15.3
All ages, crude	23.1	21.3	26.9	23.5	18.8	15.4	15.7	15.4
Under 1 year	8.4	8.1	9.8	7.0	4.9	4.4	3.0	3.6
1–14 years	9.8	8.6	10.5	8.2	6.0	4.3	3.9	4.0
1–4 years	11.5	10.0	11.5	9.2	6.3	4.2	3.9	3.9
5–14 years	8.8	7.9	10.2	7.9	5.9	4.3	3.9	4.0
15–24 years	34.4	38.0	47.2	44.8	34.1	26.9	28.2	26.6
15–19 years	29.6	33.9	43.6	43.0	33.1	26.0	27.6	25.7
20–24 years	38.8	42.9	51.3	46.6	35.0	28.0	28.8	27.5
25–34 years	24.6	24.3	30.9	29.1	23.6	17.3	17.8	17.1
35–44 years	20.3	19.3	24.9	20.9	16.9	15.3	15.8	15.7
45–64 years	25.2	23.0	26.5	18.0	15.7	14.3	14.5	14.6
45–54 years	22.2	21.4	25.5	18.6	15.6	14.2	14.8	14.9
55–64 years	29.0	25.1	27.9	17.4	15.9	14.4	14.1	14.2
65 years and over	43.1	34.7	36.2	22.5	23.1	21.4	21.5	21.0
65–74 years	39.1	31.4	32.8	19.2	18.6	16.5	17.0	16.2
75–84 years	52.7	41.8	43.5	28.1	29.1	25.7	25.7	24.9
85 years and over	45.1	37.9	34.2	27.6	31.2	30.4	28.0	28.8
Male								
All ages, age adjusted[4]	38.5	35.4	41.5	33.6	26.5	21.7	22.1	21.6
All ages, crude	35.4	31.8	39.7	35.3	26.7	21.3	21.9	21.4
Under 1 year	9.1	8.6	9.3	7.3	5.0	4.6	3.3	3.9
1–14 years	12.3	10.7	13.0	10.0	7.0	4.9	4.6	4.7
1–4 years	13.0	11.5	12.9	10.2	6.9	4.7	4.5	4.4
5–14 years	11.9	10.4	13.1	9.9	7.0	5.0	4.6	4.8
15–24 years	56.7	61.2	73.2	68.4	49.5	37.4	39.3	36.9
15–19 years	46.3	51.7	64.1	62.6	45.5	33.9	36.0	33.3
20–24 years	66.7	73.2	84.4	74.3	53.3	41.2	42.6	40.4
25–34 years	40.8	40.1	49.4	46.3	35.7	25.5	26.5	25.5
35–44 years	32.5	29.9	37.7	31.7	24.7	22.0	22.3	22.5
45–64 years	37.7	33.3	38.9	26.5	21.9	20.2	20.7	20.9
45–54 years	33.6	31.6	37.2	27.6	22.0	20.4	21.3	21.5
55–64 years	43.1	35.6	40.9	25.4	21.7	19.8	19.9	20.0
65 years and over	66.6	52.1	54.4	33.9	32.1	29.5	29.8	28.5
65–74 years	59.1	45.8	47.3	27.3	24.2	21.7	22.7	21.3
75–84 years	85.0	66.0	68.2	44.3	41.2	35.6	35.3	34.3
85 years and over	78.1	62.7	63.1	56.1	64.5	57.5	51.7	50.0
Female								
All ages, age adjusted[4]	11.5	11.7	14.9	11.8	11.0	9.5	9.6	9.3
All ages, crude	10.9	11.0	14.7	12.3	11.3	9.7	9.8	9.5
Under 1 year	7.6	7.5	10.4	6.7	4.9	4.2	2.8	3.3
1–14 years	7.2	6.3	7.9	6.3	4.9	3.7	3.3	3.3
1–4 years	10.0	8.4	10.0	8.1	5.6	3.8	3.3	3.5
5–14 years	5.7	5.4	7.2	5.7	4.7	3.6	3.3	3.2
15–24 years	12.6	15.1	21.6	20.8	17.9	15.9	16.6	15.8
15–19 years	12.9	16.0	22.7	22.8	20.0	17.5	18.9	17.8
20–24 years	12.2	14.0	20.4	18.9	16.0	14.2	14.3	13.9
25–34 years	9.3	9.2	13.0	12.2	11.5	8.8	8.8	8.5
35–44 years	8.5	9.1	12.9	10.4	9.2	8.8	9.3	8.9
45–64 years	12.6	13.1	15.3	10.3	10.1	8.7	8.7	8.6
45–54 years	10.9	11.6	14.5	10.2	9.6	8.2	8.6	8.5
55–64 years	14.9	15.2	16.2	10.5	10.8	9.5	8.9	8.8
65 years and over	21.9	20.3	23.1	15.0	17.2	15.8	15.7	15.6
65–74 years	20.6	19.0	21.6	13.0	14.1	12.3	12.3	11.9
75–84 years	25.2	23.0	27.2	18.5	21.9	19.2	19.3	18.7
85 years and over	22.1	22.0	18.0	15.2	18.3	19.3	17.7	19.5
White male[5]								
All ages, age adjusted[4]	37.9	34.8	40.4	33.8	26.3	21.8	22.4	21.9
All ages, crude	35.1	31.5	39.1	35.9	26.7	21.6	22.4	22.0
Under 1 year	9.1	8.8	9.1	7.0	4.8	4.2	2.9	3.9
1–14 years	12.4	10.6	12.5	9.8	6.6	4.8	4.5	4.7
15–24 years	58.3	62.7	75.2	73.8	52.5	39.6	41.9	39.2
25–34 years	39.1	38.6	47.0	46.6	35.4	25.1	26.6	25.9
35–44 years	30.9	28.4	35.2	30.7	23.7	21.8	22.3	22.6
45–64 years	36.2	31.7	36.5	25.2	20.6	19.7	20.6	20.6
65 years and over	67.1	52.1	54.2	32.7	31.4	29.4	29.8	28.8

See footnotes at end of table.

This table will be updated on the Web. Go to www.cdc.gov/nchs/hus.htm.

Table 44 (page 2 of 4). Death rates for motor vehicle-related injuries, by sex, race, Hispanic origin, and age: United States, selected years 1950–2003

[Data are based on death certificates]

Sex, race, Hispanic origin, and age	1950[1,2]	1960[1,2]	1970[2]	1980[2]	1990	2000[3]	2002	2003
Black or African American male[5]				Deaths per 100,000 resident population				
All ages, age adjusted[4]	34.8	39.6	51.0	34.2	29.9	24.4	23.2	22.7
All ages, crude	37.2	33.1	44.3	31.1	28.1	22.5	21.5	21.1
Under 1 year	- - -	*	10.6	7.8	*	6.7	*	*
1–14 years[6]	10.4	11.2	16.3	11.4	8.9	5.5	5.3	4.8
15–24 years	42.5	46.4	58.1	34.9	36.1	30.2	29.6	27.9
25–34 years	54.4	51.0	70.4	44.9	39.5	32.6	31.7	29.0
35–44 years	46.7	43.6	59.5	41.2	33.5	27.2	25.3	26.4
45–64 years	54.6	47.8	61.7	39.5	33.3	27.1	24.8	26.1
65 years and over	52.6	48.2	53.4	42.4	36.3	32.1	30.4	28.9
American Indian or Alaska Native male[5]								
All ages, age adjusted[4]	- - -	- - -	- - -	78.9	48.3	35.8	39.0	35.2
All ages, crude	- - -	- - -	- - -	74.6	47.6	33.6	37.3	35.9
1–14 years	- - -	- - -	- - -	15.1	11.6	7.8	7.1	9.8
15–24 years	- - -	- - -	- - -	126.1	75.2	56.8	57.2	60.2
25–34 years	- - -	- - -	- - -	107.0	78.2	49.8	49.9	45.5
35–44 years	- - -	- - -	- - -	82.8	57.0	36.3	47.2	43.6
45–64 years	- - -	- - -	- - -	77.4	45.9	32.0	40.7	36.0
65 years and over	- - -	- - -	- - -	97.0	43.0	48.5	45.9	25.4
Asian or Pacific Islander male[5]								
All ages, age adjusted[4]	- - -	- - -	- - -	19.0	17.9	10.6	10.8	10.3
All ages, crude	- - -	- - -	- - -	17.1	15.8	9.8	10.0	9.4
1–14 years	- - -	- - -	- - -	8.2	6.3	2.5	2.5	2.4
15–24 years	- - -	- - -	- - -	27.2	25.7	17.0	20.0	18.3
25–34 years	- - -	- - -	- - -	18.8	17.0	10.4	8.9	8.2
35–44 years	- - -	- - -	- - -	13.1	12.2	6.9	7.8	6.8
45–64 years	- - -	- - -	- - -	13.7	15.1	10.1	8.7	9.7
65 years and over	- - -	- - -	- - -	37.3	33.6	21.1	23.3	20.1
Hispanic or Latino male[5,7]								
All ages, age adjusted[4]	- - -	- - -	- - -	- - -	29.5	21.3	22.2	22.0
All ages, crude	- - -	- - -	- - -	- - -	29.2	20.1	21.3	21.1
1–14 years	- - -	- - -	- - -	- - -	7.2	4.4	5.1	4.9
15–24 years	- - -	- - -	- - -	- - -	48.2	34.7	38.9	37.2
25–34 years	- - -	- - -	- - -	- - -	41.0	24.9	26.4	27.6
35–44 years	- - -	- - -	- - -	- - -	28.0	21.6	22.6	22.1
45–64 years	- - -	- - -	- - -	- - -	28.9	21.7	19.9	20.4
65 years and over	- - -	- - -	- - -	- - -	35.3	28.9	30.7	29.2
White, not Hispanic or Latino male[7]								
All ages, age adjusted[4]	- - -	- - -	- - -	- - -	25.7	21.7	22.2	21.6
All ages, crude	- - -	- - -	- - -	- - -	26.0	21.5	22.3	21.8
1–14 years	- - -	- - -	- - -	- - -	6.4	4.9	4.2	4.6
15–24 years	- - -	- - -	- - -	- - -	52.3	40.3	42.1	39.1
25–34 years	- - -	- - -	- - -	- - -	34.0	24.7	26.1	24.9
35–44 years	- - -	- - -	- - -	- - -	23.1	21.6	22.0	22.4
45–64 years	- - -	- - -	- - -	- - -	19.8	19.3	20.4	20.4
65 years and over	- - -	- - -	- - -	- - -	31.1	29.3	29.6	28.6
White female[5]								
All ages, age adjusted[4]	11.4	11.7	14.9	12.2	11.2	9.8	9.8	9.5
All ages, crude	10.9	11.2	14.8	12.8	11.6	10.0	10.1	9.8
Under 1 year	7.8	7.5	10.2	7.1	4.7	3.5	2.2	3.0
1–14 years	7.2	6.2	7.5	6.2	4.8	3.7	3.2	3.2
15–24 years	12.6	15.6	22.7	23.0	19.5	17.1	17.9	17.2
25–34 years	9.0	9.0	12.7	12.2	11.6	8.9	9.0	8.6
35–44 years	8.1	8.9	12.3	10.6	9.2	8.9	9.4	9.0
45–64 years	12.7	13.1	15.1	10.4	9.9	8.7	8.7	8.5
65 years and over	22.2	20.8	23.7	15.3	17.4	16.2	16.3	15.8

See footnotes at end of table.

This table will be updated on the Web. Go to www.cdc.gov/nchs/hus.htm.

Table 44 (page 3 of 4). Death rates for motor vehicle-related injuries, by sex, race, Hispanic origin, and age: United States, selected years 1950–2003

[Data are based on death certificates]

Sex, race, Hispanic origin, and age	1950[1,2]	1960[1,2]	1970[2]	1980[2]	1990	2000[3]	2002	2003
Black or African American female[5]				Deaths per 100,000 resident population				
All ages, age adjusted[4]	9.3	10.4	14.1	8.5	9.6	8.4	8.2	8.3
All ages, crude	10.2	9.7	13.4	8.3	9.4	8.2	8.0	8.0
Under 1 year	- - -	8.1	11.9	*	7.0	*	*	*
1–14 years[6]	7.2	6.9	10.2	6.3	5.3	3.9	3.5	3.5
15–24 years	11.6	9.9	13.4	8.0	9.9	11.7	11.6	9.6
25–34 years	10.8	9.8	13.3	10.6	11.1	9.4	8.8	8.7
35–44 years	11.1	11.0	16.1	8.3	9.4	8.2	9.4	8.9
45–64 years	11.8	12.7	16.7	9.2	10.7	9.0	8.4	8.9
65 years and over	14.3	13.2	15.7	9.5	13.5	10.4	9.5	12.4
American Indian or Alaska Native female[5]								
All ages, age adjusted[4]	- - -	- - -	- - -	32.0	17.5	19.5	19.3	20.8
All ages, crude	- - -	- - -	- - -	32.0	17.3	18.6	19.1	19.8
1–14 years	- - -	- - -	- - -	15.0	8.1	6.5	6.8	6.3
15–24 years	- - -	- - -	- - -	42.3	31.4	30.3	29.2	27.7
25–34 years	- - -	- - -	- - -	52.5	18.8	22.3	21.1	24.5
35–44 years	- - -	- - -	- - -	38.1	18.2	22.0	24.4	18.7
45–64 years	- - -	- - -	- - -	32.6	17.6	17.8	20.9	22.6
65 years and over	- - -	- - -	- - -	*	*	24.0	*	32.3
Asian or Pacific Islander female[5]								
All ages, age adjusted[4]	- - -	- - -	- - -	9.3	10.4	6.7	6.2	6.8
All ages, crude	- - -	- - -	- - -	8.2	9.0	5.9	5.7	6.4
1–14 years	- - -	- - -	- - -	7.4	3.6	2.3	1.9	1.7
15–24 years	- - -	- - -	- - -	7.4	11.4	6.0	7.3	9.7
25–34 years	- - -	- - -	- - -	7.3	7.3	4.5	4.4	4.5
35–44 years	- - -	- - -	- - -	8.6	7.5	4.9	3.7	4.5
45–64 years	- - -	- - -	- - -	8.5	11.8	6.4	7.3	7.5
65 years and over	- - -	- - -	- - -	18.6	24.3	18.5	15.6	16.2
Hispanic or Latino female[5,7]								
All ages, age adjusted[4]	- - -	- - -	- - -	- - -	9.6	7.9	8.1	8.0
All ages, crude	- - -	- - -	- - -	- - -	8.9	7.2	7.4	7.3
1–14 years	- - -	- - -	- - -	- - -	4.8	3.9	3.2	3.0
15–24 years	- - -	- - -	- - -	- - -	11.6	10.6	12.4	11.9
25–34 years	- - -	- - -	- - -	- - -	9.4	6.5	7.2	6.6
35–44 years	- - -	- - -	- - -	- - -	8.0	7.3	7.3	8.0
45–64 years	- - -	- - -	- - -	- - -	11.4	8.3	8.4	8.4
65 years and over	- - -	- - -	- - -	- - -	14.9	13.4	13.1	13.1

See footnotes at end of table.

This table will be updated on the Web. Go to www.cdc.gov/nchs/hus.htm.

Table 44 (page 4 of 4). Death rates for motor vehicle-related injuries, by sex, race, Hispanic origin, and age: United States, selected years 1950–2003

[Data are based on death certificates]

Sex, race, Hispanic origin, and age	1950[1,2]	1960[1,2]	1970[2]	1980[2]	1990	2000[3]	2002	2003
White, not Hispanic or Latino female[7]				Deaths per 100,000 resident population				
All ages, age adjusted[4]	- - -	- - -	- - -	- - -	11.3	10.0	10.1	9.7
All ages, crude	- - -	- - -	- - -	- - -	11.7	10.3	10.5	10.2
1–14 years	- - -	- - -	- - -	- - -	4.7	3.5	3.2	3.2
15–24 years	- - -	- - -	- - -	- - -	20.4	18.4	19.0	18.3
25–34 years	- - -	- - -	- - -	- - -	11.7	9.3	9.4	9.0
35–44 years	- - -	- - -	- - -	- - -	9.3	9.0	9.7	9.1
45–64 years	- - -	- - -	- - -	- - -	9.7	8.7	8.6	8.5
65 years and over	- - -	- - -	- - -	- - -	17.5	16.3	16.5	15.9

- - - Data not available.

* Rates based on fewer than 20 deaths are considered unreliable and are not shown.

[1]Includes deaths of persons who were not residents of the 50 states and the District of Columbia.

[2]Underlying cause of death was coded according to the Sixth Revision of the International Classification of Diseases (ICD) in 1950, Seventh Revision in 1960, Eighth Revision in 1970, and Ninth Revision in 1980–1998. See Appendix II, Cause of death; tables IV and V.

[3]Starting with 1999 data, cause of death is coded according to ICD–10. See Appendix II, Cause of death; Comparability ratio; tables V and VI.

[4]Age-adjusted rates are calculated using the year 2000 standard population. Prior to 2003, age-adjusted rates were calculated using standard million proportions based on rounded population numbers. Starting with 2003 data, unrounded population numbers are used to calculate age-adjusted rates. See Appendix II, Age adjustment.

[5]The race groups, white, black, Asian or Pacific Islander, and American Indian or Alaska Native, include persons of Hispanic and non-Hispanic origin. Persons of Hispanic origin may be of any race. Death rates for the American Indian or Alaska Native and Asian or Pacific Islander populations are known to be underestimated. See Appendix II, Race, for a discussion of sources of bias in death rates by race and Hispanic origin.

[6]In 1950, rate is for the age group under 15 years.

[7]Prior to 1997, excludes data from states lacking an Hispanic-origin item on the death certificate. See Appendix II, Hispanic origin.

NOTES: Starting with *Health, United States, 2003*, rates for 1991–1999 were revised using intercensal population estimates based on the 2000 census. Rates for 2000 were revised based on 2000 census counts. Rates for 2001 and later years were computed using 2000-based postcensal estimates. See Appendix I, Population Census and Population Estimates. Age groups were selected to minimize the presentation of unstable age-specific death rates based on small numbers of deaths and for consistency among comparison groups. For additional injury-related statistics, see Web-based Injury Statistics Query and Reporting System, available from: www.cdc.gov/ncipc/wisqars. Starting with 2003 data, California, Hawaii, Idaho, Maine, Montana, New York, and Wisconsin reported multiple-race data. The multiple-race data for these states were bridged to the single race categories of the 1977 Office of Management and Budget standards for comparability with other states. Data for additional years are available. See Appendix III.

SOURCES: Centers for Disease Control and Prevention, National Center for Health Statistics, National Vital Statistics System; Grove RD, Hetzel AM. Vital statistics rates in the United States, 1940–1960. Washington, DC: U.S. Government Printing Office. 1968; numerator data from National Vital Statistics System, annual mortality files; denominator data from national population estimates for race groups from Table 1 and unpublished Hispanic population estimates for 1985–1996 prepared by the Housing and Household Economic Statistics Division, U.S. Census Bureau; additional mortality tables are available from: www.cdc.gov/nchs/datawh/statab/unpubd/mortabs.htm; Hoyert DL, Heron M, Murphy SL, Kung HC. Deaths: Final data for 2003. National vital statistics reports. Vol 54 no 13. Hyattsville, MD: National Center for Health Statistics. 2006.

This table will be updated on the Web. Go to www.cdc.gov/nchs/hus.htm.

Table 45 (page 1 of 3). Death rates for homicide, by sex, race, Hispanic origin, and age: United States, selected years 1950–2003

[Data are based on death certificates]

Sex, race, Hispanic origin, and age	1950[1,2]	1960[1,2]	1970[2]	1980[2]	1990	2000[3]	2002	2003
All persons			Deaths per 100,000 resident population					
All ages, age adjusted[4]	5.1	5.0	8.8	10.4	9.4	5.9	6.1	6.0
All ages, crude	5.0	4.6	8.1	10.6	9.9	6.0	6.1	6.1
Under 1 year	4.4	4.8	4.3	5.9	8.4	9.2	7.5	8.5
1–14 years	0.6	0.6	1.1	1.5	1.8	1.3	1.4	1.2
1–4 years	0.6	0.7	1.9	2.5	2.5	2.3	2.7	2.4
5–14 years	0.5	0.5	0.9	1.2	1.5	0.9	0.9	0.8
15–24 years	5.8	5.6	11.3	15.4	19.7	12.6	12.9	13.0
15–19 years	3.9	3.9	7.7	10.5	16.9	9.5	9.3	9.5
20–24 years	8.5	7.7	15.6	20.2	22.2	16.0	16.5	16.5
25–44 years	8.9	8.5	14.9	17.5	14.7	8.7	9.1	9.1
25–34 years	9.3	9.2	16.2	19.3	17.4	10.4	11.2	11.3
35–44 years	8.4	7.8	13.5	14.9	11.6	7.1	7.2	7.0
45–64 years	5.0	5.3	8.7	9.0	6.3	4.0	4.1	4.1
45–54 years	5.9	6.1	10.0	11.0	7.5	4.7	4.8	4.9
55–64 years	3.9	4.1	7.1	7.0	5.0	3.0	3.2	2.8
65 years and over	3.0	2.7	4.6	5.5	4.0	2.4	2.3	2.4
65–74 years	3.2	2.8	4.9	5.7	3.8	2.4	2.3	2.4
75–84 years	2.5	2.3	4.0	5.2	4.3	2.4	2.3	2.5
85 years and over	2.3	2.4	4.2	5.3	4.6	2.4	2.1	2.2
Male								
All ages, age adjusted[4]	7.9	7.5	14.3	16.6	14.8	9.0	9.4	9.4
All ages, crude	7.7	6.8	13.1	17.1	15.9	9.3	9.6	9.7
Under 1 year	4.5	4.7	4.5	6.3	8.8	10.4	7.9	10.0
1–14 years	0.6	0.6	1.2	1.6	2.0	1.5	1.5	1.4
1–4 years	0.5	0.7	1.9	2.7	2.7	2.5	2.9	2.5
5–14 years	0.6	0.5	1.0	1.2	1.7	1.1	0.9	1.0
15–24 years	8.6	8.4	18.2	24.0	32.5	20.9	21.5	21.8
15–19 years	5.5	5.7	12.1	15.9	27.8	15.5	15.3	15.9
20–24 years	13.5	11.8	25.6	32.2	36.9	26.7	27.7	27.6
25–44 years	13.8	12.8	24.4	28.9	23.5	13.3	14.2	14.3
25–34 years	14.4	13.9	26.8	31.9	27.7	16.7	18.2	18.5
35–44 years	13.2	11.7	21.7	24.5	18.6	10.3	10.7	10.4
45–64 years	8.1	8.1	14.8	15.2	10.2	6.0	6.2	6.1
45–54 years	9.5	9.4	16.8	18.4	11.9	6.9	7.1	7.4
55–64 years	6.3	6.4	12.1	11.8	8.0	4.6	4.8	4.2
65 years and over	4.8	4.3	7.7	8.8	5.8	3.3	3.2	3.4
65–74 years	5.2	4.6	8.5	9.2	5.8	3.4	3.3	3.4
75–84 years	3.9	3.7	5.9	8.1	5.7	3.2	3.1	3.3
85 years and over	2.5	3.6	7.4	7.5	6.7	3.3	3.0	3.2
Female								
All ages, age adjusted[4]	2.4	2.6	3.7	4.4	4.0	2.8	2.8	2.6
All ages, crude	2.4	2.4	3.4	4.5	4.2	2.8	2.7	2.6
Under 1 year	4.2	4.9	4.1	5.6	8.0	7.9	7.1	6.9
1–14 years	0.6	0.5	1.0	1.4	1.6	1.1	1.3	1.0
1–4 years	0.7	0.7	1.9	2.2	2.3	2.1	2.5	2.3
5–14 years	0.5	0.4	0.7	1.1	1.2	0.7	0.8	0.5
15–24 years	3.0	2.8	4.6	6.6	6.2	3.9	3.8	3.7
15–19 years	2.4	1.9	3.2	4.9	5.4	3.1	2.9	2.6
20–24 years	3.7	3.8	6.2	8.2	7.0	4.7	4.6	4.8
25–44 years	4.2	4.3	5.8	6.4	6.0	4.0	4.0	3.8
25–34 years	4.5	4.6	6.0	6.9	7.1	4.1	4.2	3.9
35–44 years	3.8	4.0	5.7	5.7	4.8	4.0	3.8	3.6
45–64 years	1.9	2.5	3.1	3.4	2.8	2.1	2.2	2.1
45–54 years	2.3	2.9	3.7	4.1	3.2	2.5	2.6	2.5
55–64 years	1.4	2.0	2.5	2.8	2.3	1.6	1.6	1.5
65 years and over	1.4	1.3	2.3	3.3	2.8	1.8	1.6	1.7
65–74 years	1.3	1.3	2.2	3.0	2.2	1.6	1.4	1.5
75–84 years	1.4	1.3	2.7	3.5	3.4	2.0	1.8	1.9
85 years and over	2.1	1.6	2.5	4.3	3.8	2.0	1.7	1.8
White male[5]								
All ages, age adjusted[4]	3.8	3.9	7.2	10.4	8.3	5.2	5.3	5.3
All ages, crude	3.6	3.6	6.6	10.7	8.8	5.2	5.4	5.4
Under 1 year	4.3	3.8	2.9	4.3	6.4	8.2	6.2	8.1
1–14 years	0.4	0.5	0.7	1.2	1.3	1.2	1.0	0.9
15–24 years	3.2	5.0	7.6	15.1	15.2	9.9	10.6	10.6
25–44 years	5.4	5.5	11.6	17.2	13.0	7.4	7.7	7.7
25–34 years	4.9	5.7	12.5	18.5	14.7	8.4	8.9	9.2
35–44 years	6.1	5.2	10.8	15.2	11.1	6.5	6.8	6.3
45–64 years	4.8	4.6	8.3	9.8	6.9	4.1	4.2	4.2
65 years and over	3.8	3.1	5.4	6.7	4.1	2.5	2.6	2.7

See footnotes at end of table.

This table will be updated on the Web. Go to www.cdc.gov/nchs/hus.htm.

[Data are based on death certificates]

Sex, race, Hispanic origin, and age	1950[1,2]	1960[1,2]	1970[2]	1980[2]	1990	2000[3]	2002	2003
Black or African American male[5]				Deaths per 100,000 resident population				
All ages, age adjusted[4]	47.0	42.3	78.2	69.4	63.1	35.4	36.4	36.7
All ages, crude	44.7	35.0	66.0	65.7	68.5	37.2	38.4	38.9
Under 1 year	- - -	10.3	14.3	18.6	21.4	23.3	16.3	17.8
1–14 years[6]	1.8	1.5	4.4	4.1	5.8	3.1	3.8	4.1
15–24 years	53.8	43.2	98.3	82.6	137.1	85.3	83.1	84.6
25–44 years	92.8	80.5	140.2	130.0	105.4	55.8	60.0	61.0
25–34 years	104.3	86.4	154.5	142.9	123.7	73.9	82.2	82.5
35–44 years	80.0	74.4	124.0	109.3	81.2	38.5	38.8	40.2
45–64 years	46.0	44.6	82.3	70.6	41.4	21.9	22.9	22.2
65 years and over	16.5	17.3	33.3	30.9	25.7	12.8	11.2	10.9
American Indian or Alaska Native male[5]								
All ages, age adjusted[4]	- - -	- - -	- - -	23.3	16.7	10.7	11.6	10.5
All ages, crude	- - -	- - -	- - -	23.1	16.6	10.7	12.0	11.3
15–24 years	- - -	- - -	- - -	35.4	25.1	17.0	18.8	19.7
25–44 years	- - -	- - -	- - -	39.2	25.7	17.0	18.3	14.8
45–64 years	- - -	- - -	- - -	22.1	14.8	*	9.9	9.5
Asian or Pacific Islander male[5]								
All ages, age adjusted[4]	- - -	- - -	- - -	9.1	7.3	4.3	4.2	4.2
All ages, crude	- - -	- - -	- - -	8.3	7.9	4.4	4.5	4.5
15–24 years	- - -	- - -	- - -	9.3	14.9	7.8	9.7	9.8
25–44 years	- - -	- - -	- - -	11.3	9.6	4.6	4.9	4.5
45–64 years	- - -	- - -	- - -	10.4	7.0	6.1	4.1	4.3
Hispanic or Latino male[5,7]								
All ages, age adjusted[4]	- - -	- - -	- - -	- - -	27.4	11.8	11.6	12.1
All ages, crude	- - -	- - -	- - -	- - -	31.0	13.4	13.2	13.6
Under 1 year	- - -	- - -	- - -	- - -	8.7	6.6	6.6	7.9
1–14 years	- - -	- - -	- - -	- - -	3.1	1.7	1.6	1.3
15–24 years	- - -	- - -	- - -	- - -	55.4	28.5	29.6	30.3
25–44 years	- - -	- - -	- - -	- - -	46.4	17.2	16.5	17.6
25–34 years	- - -	- - -	- - -	- - -	50.9	19.9	19.8	21.2
35–44 years	- - -	- - -	- - -	- - -	39.3	13.5	12.1	12.9
45–64 years	- - -	- - -	- - -	- - -	20.5	9.1	8.6	8.7
65 years and over	- - -	- - -	- - -	- - -	9.4	4.4	4.4	6.0
White, not Hispanic or Latino male[7]								
All ages, age adjusted[4]	- - -	- - -	- - -	- - -	5.6	3.6	3.7	3.6
All ages, crude	- - -	- - -	- - -	- - -	5.8	3.6	3.8	3.6
Under 1 year	- - -	- - -	- - -	- - -	5.4	8.3	5.8	8.0
1–14 years	- - -	- - -	- - -	- - -	0.9	1.0	0.8	0.8
15–24 years	- - -	- - -	- - -	- - -	7.5	4.7	5.2	5.0
25–44 years	- - -	- - -	- - -	- - -	8.7	5.2	5.5	5.1
25–34 years	- - -	- - -	- - -	- - -	9.3	5.2	5.3	5.2
35–44 years	- - -	- - -	- - -	- - -	8.0	5.2	5.6	4.9
45–64 years	- - -	- - -	- - -	- - -	5.7	3.6	3.7	3.7
65 years and over	- - -	- - -	- - -	- - -	3.7	2.3	2.4	2.4
White female[5]								
All ages, age adjusted[4]	1.4	1.5	2.3	3.2	2.7	2.1	2.0	2.0
All ages, crude	1.4	1.4	2.1	3.2	2.8	2.1	2.0	2.0
Under 1 year	3.9	3.5	2.9	4.3	5.1	5.0	4.6	5.7
1–14 years	0.4	0.4	0.7	1.1	1.0	0.8	0.9	0.7
15–24 years	1.3	1.5	2.7	4.7	4.0	2.7	2.5	2.5
25–44 years	2.0	2.1	3.3	4.2	3.8	2.9	2.8	2.8
45–64 years	1.5	1.7	2.1	2.6	2.3	1.8	1.9	1.8
65 years and over	1.2	1.2	1.9	2.9	2.2	1.6	1.4	1.5
Black or African American female[5]								
All ages, age adjusted[4]	11.1	11.4	14.7	13.2	12.5	7.1	6.9	6.4
All ages, crude	11.5	10.4	13.2	13.5	13.4	7.2	7.0	6.6
Under 1 year	- - -	13.8	10.7	12.8	22.8	22.2	18.5	14.2
1–14 years[6]	1.8	1.2	3.1	3.3	4.7	2.7	2.6	2.4
15–24 years	16.5	11.9	17.7	18.4	18.9	10.7	10.3	10.1
25–44 years	22.5	22.7	25.3	22.6	21.0	11.0	11.1	9.8
45–64 years	6.8	10.3	13.4	10.8	6.5	4.5	4.5	4.8
65 years and over	3.6	3.0	7.4	8.0	9.4	3.5	3.1	3.3

See footnotes at end of table.

This table will be updated on the Web. Go to www.cdc.gov/nchs/hus.htm.

Table 45 (page 3 of 3). Death rates for homicide, by sex, race, Hispanic origin, and age: United States, selected years 1950–2003

[Data are based on death certificates]

Sex, race, Hispanic origin, and age	1950[1,2]	1960[1,2]	1970[2]	1980[2]	1990	2000[3]	2002	2003
American Indian or Alaska Native female[5]				Deaths per 100,000 resident population				
All ages, age adjusted[4]	- - -	- - -	- - -	8.1	4.6	3.0	5.2	3.9
All ages, crude	- - -	- - -	- - -	7.7	4.8	2.9	5.3	4.0
15–24 years	- - -	- - -	- - -	*	*	*	*	7.2
25–44 years	- - -	- - -	- - -	13.7	6.9	5.9	6.3	5.4
45–64 years	- - -	- - -	- - -	*	*	*	*	*
Asian or Pacific Islander female[5]								
All ages, age adjusted[4]	- - -	- - -	- - -	3.1	2.8	1.7	1.8	1.6
All ages, crude	- - -	- - -	- - -	3.1	2.8	1.7	1.8	1.6
15–24 years	- - -	- - -	- - -	*	*	*	2.1	*
25–44 years	- - -	- - -	- - -	4.6	3.8	2.2	2.4	1.9
45–64 years	- - -	- - -	- - -	*	*	2.0	1.6	1.5
Hispanic or Latino female[5,7]								
All ages, age adjusted[4]	- - -	- - -	- - -	- - -	4.3	2.8	2.5	2.7
All ages, crude	- - -	- - -	- - -	- - -	4.7	2.8	2.6	2.8
Under 1 year	- - -	- - -	- - -	- - -	*	7.4	5.9	5.9
1–14 years	- - -	- - -	- - -	- - -	1.9	1.0	1.2	1.2
15–24 years	- - -	- - -	- - -	- - -	8.1	3.7	3.8	4.5
25–44 years	- - -	- - -	- - -	- - -	6.1	3.7	3.4	3.6
45–64 years	- - -	- - -	- - -	- - -	3.3	2.9	2.3	2.3
65 years and over	- - -	- - -	- - -	- - -	*	2.4	*	1.9
White, not Hispanic or Latino female[7]								
All ages, age adjusted[4]	- - -	- - -	- - -	- - -	2.5	1.9	1.9	1.8
All ages, crude	- - -	- - -	- - -	- - -	2.5	1.9	1.9	1.8
Under 1 year	- - -	- - -	- - -	- - -	4.4	4.1	4.1	5.5
1–14 years	- - -	- - -	- - -	- - -	0.8	0.8	0.9	0.6
15–24 years	- - -	- - -	- - -	- - -	3.3	2.3	2.2	1.9
25–44 years	- - -	- - -	- - -	- - -	3.5	2.7	2.6	2.6
45–64 years	- - -	- - -	- - -	- - -	2.2	1.6	1.8	1.7
65 years and over	- - -	- - -	- - -	- - -	2.2	1.6	1.4	1.4

- - - Data not available.

* Rates based on fewer than 20 deaths are considered unreliable and are not shown.

[1]Includes deaths of persons who were not residents of the 50 states and the District of Columbia.

[2]Underlying cause of death was coded according to the Sixth Revision of the International Classification of Diseases (ICD) in 1950, Seventh Revision in 1960, Eighth Revision in 1970, and Ninth Revision in 1980–1998. See Appendix II, Cause of death; tables IV and V.

[3]Starting with 1999 data, cause of death is coded according to ICD–10. See Appendix II, Cause of death; Comparability ratio; tables V and VI.

[4]Age-adjusted rates are calculated using the year 2000 standard population. Prior to 2003, age-adjusted rates were calculated using standard million proportions based on rounded population numbers. Starting with 2003 data, unrounded population numbers are used to calculate age-adjusted rates. See Appendix II, Age adjustment.

[5]The race groups, white, black, Asian or Pacific Islander, and American Indian or Alaska Native, include persons of Hispanic and non-Hispanic origin. Persons of Hispanic origin may be of any race. Death rates for the American Indian or Alaska Native and Asian or Pacific Islander populations are known to be underestimated. See Appendix II, Race, for a discussion of sources of bias in death rates by race and Hispanic origin.

[6]In 1950, rate is for the age group under 15 years.

[7]Prior to 1997, excludes data from states lacking an Hispanic-origin item on the death certificate. See Appendix II, Hispanic origin.

NOTES: Starting with *Health, United States, 2003*, rates for 1991–1999 were revised using intercensal population estimates based on the 2000 census. Rates for 2000 were revised based on 2000 census counts. Rates for 2001 and later years were computed using 2000-based postcensal estimates. See Appendix I, Population Census and Population Estimates. Figures for 2001 include September 11-related deaths for which death certificates were filed as of October 24, 2002. For the period 1980–1998, homicide was coded using ICD–9 codes that are most nearly comparable with homicide codes in the 113 cause list for ICD–10. See Appendix II, Cause of death; table V for terrorism-related ICD–10 codes. Age groups were selected to minimize the presentation of unstable age-specific death rates based on small numbers of deaths and for consistency among comparison groups. For additional injury-related statistics, see Web-based Injury Statistics Query and Reporting System, available from: www.cdc.gov/ncipc/wisqars. Starting with 2003 data, California, Hawaii, Idaho, Maine, Montana, New York, and Wisconsin reported multiple-race data. The multiple-race data for these states were bridged to the single race categories of the 1977 Office of Management and Budget standards for comparability with other states. Data for additional years are available. See Appendix III.

SOURCES: Centers for Disease Control and Prevention, National Center for Health Statistics, National Vital Statistics System; Grove RD, Hetzel AM. Vital statistics rates in the United States, 1940–1960. Washington, DC: U.S. Government Printing Office. 1968; numerator data from National Vital Statistics System, annual mortality files; denominator data from national population estimates for race groups from Table 1 and unpublished Hispanic population estimates for 1985–1996 prepared by the Housing and Household Economic Statistics Division, U.S. Census Bureau; additional mortality tables are available from: www.cdc.gov/nchs/datawh/statab/unpubd/mortabs.htm; Hoyert DL, Heron M, Murphy SL, Kung HC. Deaths: Final data for 2003. National vital statistics reports. Vol 54 no 13. Hyattsville, MD: National Center for Health Statistics. 2006.

This table will be updated on the Web. Go to www.cdc.gov/nchs/hus.htm.

Table 46 (page 1 of 3). Death rates for suicide, by sex, race, Hispanic origin, and age: United States, selected years 1950–2003

[Data are based on death certificates]

Sex, race, Hispanic origin, and age	1950[1,2]	1960[1,2]	1970[2]	1980[2]	1990	2000[3]	2002	2003
All persons	Deaths per 100,000 resident population							
All ages, age adjusted[4]	13.2	12.5	13.1	12.2	12.5	10.4	10.9	10.8
All ages, crude	11.4	10.6	11.6	11.9	12.4	10.4	11.0	10.8
Under 1 year	. . .	. . .	. . .	. . .	. . .	. . .	. . .	*
1–4 years	. . .	. . .	. . .	. . .	. . .	. . .	. . .	*
5–14 years	0.2	0.3	0.3	0.4	0.8	0.7	0.6	0.6
15–24 years	4.5	5.2	8.8	12.3	13.2	10.2	9.9	9.7
15–19 years	2.7	3.6	5.9	8.5	11.1	8.0	7.4	7.3
20–24 years	6.2	7.1	12.2	16.1	15.1	12.5	12.4	12.1
25–44 years	11.6	12.2	15.4	15.6	15.2	13.4	14.0	13.8
25–34 years	9.1	10.0	14.1	16.0	15.2	12.0	12.6	12.7
35–44 years	14.3	14.2	16.9	15.4	15.3	14.5	15.3	14.9
45–64 years	23.5	22.0	20.6	15.9	15.3	13.5	14.9	15.0
45–54 years	20.9	20.7	20.0	15.9	14.8	14.4	15.7	15.9
55–64 years	26.8	23.7	21.4	15.9	16.0	12.1	13.6	13.8
65 years and over	30.0	24.5	20.8	17.6	20.5	15.2	15.6	14.6
65–74 years	29.6	23.0	20.8	16.9	17.9	12.5	13.5	12.7
75–84 years	31.1	27.9	21.2	19.1	24.9	17.6	17.7	16.4
85 years and over	28.8	26.0	19.0	19.2	22.2	19.6	18.0	16.9
Male								
All ages, age adjusted[4]	21.2	20.0	19.8	19.9	21.5	17.7	18.4	18.0
All ages, crude	17.8	16.5	16.8	18.6	20.4	17.1	17.9	17.6
Under 1 year	. . .	. . .	. . .	. . .	. . .	. . .	. . .	*
1–4 years	. . .	. . .	. . .	. . .	. . .	. . .	. . .	*
5–14 years	0.3	0.4	0.5	0.6	1.1	1.2	0.9	0.9
15–24 years	6.5	8.2	13.5	20.2	22.0	17.1	16.5	16.0
15–19 years	3.5	5.6	8.8	13.8	18.1	13.0	12.2	11.6
20–24 years	9.3	11.5	19.3	26.8	25.7	21.4	20.8	20.2
25–44 years	17.2	17.9	20.9	24.0	24.4	21.3	22.2	21.9
25–34 years	13.4	14.7	19.8	25.0	24.8	19.6	20.5	20.6
35–44 years	21.3	21.0	22.1	22.5	23.9	22.8	23.7	23.2
45–64 years	37.1	34.4	30.0	23.7	24.3	21.3	23.5	23.5
45–54 years	32.0	31.6	27.9	22.9	23.2	22.4	24.4	24.4
55–64 years	43.6	38.1	32.7	24.5	25.7	19.4	22.2	22.3
65 years and over	52.8	44.0	38.4	35.0	41.6	31.1	31.8	29.8
65–74 years	50.5	39.6	36.0	30.4	32.2	22.7	24.7	23.4
75–84 years	58.3	52.5	42.8	42.3	56.1	38.6	38.1	35.1
85 years and over	58.3	57.4	42.4	50.6	65.9	57.5	50.7	47.8
Female								
All ages, age adjusted[4]	5.6	5.6	7.4	5.7	4.8	4.0	4.2	4.2
All ages, crude	5.1	4.9	6.6	5.5	4.8	4.0	4.3	4.3
Under 1 year	. . .	. . .	. . .	. . .	. . .	. . .	. . .	*
1–4 years	. . .	. . .	. . .	. . .	. . .	. . .	. . .	*
5–14 years	0.1	0.1	0.2	0.2	0.4	0.3	0.3	0.3
15–24 years	2.6	2.2	4.2	4.3	3.9	3.0	2.9	3.0
15–19 years	1.8	1.6	2.9	3.0	3.7	2.7	2.4	2.7
20–24 years	3.3	2.9	5.7	5.5	4.1	3.2	3.5	3.4
25–44 years	6.2	6.6	10.2	7.7	6.2	5.4	5.8	5.7
25–34 years	4.9	5.5	8.6	7.1	5.6	4.3	4.6	4.6
35–44 years	7.5	7.7	11.9	8.5	6.8	6.4	6.9	6.6
45–64 years	9.9	10.2	12.0	8.9	7.1	6.2	6.7	7.0
45–54 years	9.9	10.2	12.6	9.4	6.9	6.7	7.4	7.7
55–64 years	9.9	10.2	11.4	8.4	7.3	5.4	5.7	5.9
65 years and over	9.4	8.4	8.1	6.1	6.4	4.0	4.1	3.8
65–74 years	10.1	8.4	9.0	6.5	6.7	4.0	4.1	3.8
75–84 years	8.1	8.9	7.0	5.5	6.3	4.0	4.2	4.0
85 years and over	8.2	6.0	5.9	5.5	5.4	4.2	3.8	3.3
White male[5]								
All ages, age adjusted[4]	22.3	21.1	20.8	20.9	22.8	19.1	20.0	19.6
All ages, crude	19.0	17.6	18.0	19.9	22.0	18.8	19.9	19.5
15–24 years	6.6	8.6	13.9	21.4	23.2	17.9	17.7	16.9
25–44 years	17.9	18.5	21.5	24.6	25.4	22.9	24.0	23.9
45–64 years	39.3	36.5	31.9	25.0	26.0	23.2	25.9	26.1
65 years and over	55.8	46.7	41.1	37.2	44.2	33.3	34.2	32.1
65–74 years	53.2	42.0	38.7	32.5	34.2	24.3	26.8	25.2
75–84 years	61.9	55.7	45.5	45.5	60.2	41.1	40.6	37.5
85 years and over	61.9	61.3	45.8	52.8	70.3	61.6	53.9	51.4

See footnotes at end of table.

This table will be updated on the Web. Go to www.cdc.gov/nchs/hus.htm.

Table 46 (page 2 of 3). Death rates for suicide, by sex, race, Hispanic origin, and age: United States, selected years 1950–2003

[Data are based on death certificates]

Sex, race, Hispanic origin, and age	1950[1,2]	1960[1,2]	1970[2]	1980[2]	1990	2000[3]	2002	2003
Black or African American male[5]				Deaths per 100,000 resident population				
All ages, age adjusted[4]	7.5	8.4	10.0	11.4	12.8	10.0	9.8	9.2
All ages, crude	6.3	6.4	8.0	10.3	12.0	9.4	9.1	8.8
15–24 years	4.9	4.1	10.5	12.3	15.1	14.2	11.3	12.1
25–44 years	9.8	12.6	16.1	19.2	19.6	14.3	15.1	14.3
45–64 years	12.7	13.0	12.4	11.8	13.1	9.9	9.6	9.0
65 years and over	9.0	9.9	8.7	11.4	14.9	11.5	11.7	9.2
65–74 years	10.0	11.3	8.7	11.1	14.7	11.1	9.7	8.3
75–84 years[6]	*	*	*	10.5	14.4	12.1	13.8	11.3
85 years and over	- - -	*	*	*	*	*	*	*
American Indian or Alaska Native male[5]								
All ages, age adjusted[4]	- - -	- - -	- - -	19.3	20.1	16.0	16.4	16.6
All ages, crude	- - -	- - -	- - -	20.9	20.9	15.9	16.8	17.1
15–24 years	- - -	- - -	- - -	45.3	49.1	26.2	27.9	27.2
25–44 years	- - -	- - -	- - -	31.2	27.8	24.5	26.8	30.1
45–64 years	- - -	- - -	- - -	*	*	15.4	14.1	9.5
65 years and over	- - -	- - -	- - -	*	*	*	*	*
Asian or Pacific Islander male[5]								
All ages, age adjusted[4]	- - -	- - -	- - -	10.7	9.6	8.6	8.0	8.5
All ages, crude	- - -	- - -	- - -	8.8	8.7	7.9	7.6	8.0
15–24 years	- - -	- - -	- - -	10.8	13.5	9.1	8.7	9.0
25–44 years	- - -	- - -	- - -	11.0	10.6	9.9	9.3	9.2
45–64 years	- - -	- - -	- - -	13.0	9.7	9.7	9.1	10.0
65 years and over	- - -	- - -	- - -	18.6	16.8	15.4	14.4	17.5
Hispanic or Latino male[5,7]								
All ages, age adjusted[4]	- - -	- - -	- - -	- - -	13.7	10.3	9.9	9.7
All ages, crude	- - -	- - -	- - -	- - -	11.4	8.4	8.3	8.3
15–24 years	- - -	- - -	- - -	- - -	14.7	10.9	10.6	11.2
25–44 years	- - -	- - -	- - -	- - -	16.2	11.2	10.9	10.9
45–64 years	- - -	- - -	- - -	- - -	16.1	12.0	11.9	12.0
65 years and over	- - -	- - -	- - -	- - -	23.4	19.5	17.5	15.6
White, not Hispanic or Latino male[7]								
All ages, age adjusted[4]	- - -	- - -	- - -	- - -	23.5	20.2	21.4	21.0
All ages, crude	- - -	- - -	- - -	- - -	23.1	20.4	21.9	21.6
15–24 years	- - -	- - -	- - -	- - -	24.4	19.5	19.3	18.2
25–44 years	- - -	- - -	- - -	- - -	26.4	25.1	26.9	26.8
45–64 years	- - -	- - -	- - -	- - -	26.8	24.0	27.2	27.4
65 years and over	- - -	- - -	- - -	- - -	45.4	33.9	35.1	33.1
White female[5]								
All ages, age adjusted[4]	6.0	5.9	7.9	6.1	5.2	4.3	4.7	4.6
All ages, crude	5.5	5.3	7.1	5.9	5.3	4.4	4.8	4.7
15–24 years	2.7	2.3	4.2	4.6	4.2	3.1	3.1	3.1
25–44 years	6.6	7.0	11.0	8.1	6.6	6.0	6.6	6.4
45–64 years	10.6	10.9	13.0	9.6	7.7	6.9	7.5	7.8
65 years and over	9.9	8.8	8.5	6.4	6.8	4.3	4.3	4.0
Black or African American female[5]								
All ages, age adjusted[4]	1.8	2.0	2.9	2.4	2.4	1.8	1.6	1.9
All ages, crude	1.5	1.6	2.6	2.2	2.3	1.7	1.5	1.8
15–24 years	1.8	*	3.8	2.3	2.3	2.2	1.7	2.0
25–44 years	2.3	3.0	4.8	4.3	3.8	2.6	2.4	2.8
45–64 years	2.7	3.1	2.9	2.5	2.9	2.1	2.1	2.4
65 years and over	*	*	2.6	*	1.9	1.3	1.1	1.4

See footnotes at end of table.

This table will be updated on the Web. Go to www.cdc.gov/nchs/hus.htm.

[Data are based on death certificates]

Sex, race, Hispanic origin, and age	1950[1,2]	1960[1,2]	1970[2]	1980[2]	1990	2000[3]	2002	2003
American Indian or Alaska Native female[5]			Deaths per 100,000 resident population					
All ages, age adjusted[4]	- - -	- - -	- - -	4.7	3.6	3.8	4.1	3.5
All ages, crude	- - -	- - -	- - -	4.7	3.7	4.0	4.3	3.7
15–24 years	- - -	- - -	- - -	*	*	*	7.4	8.3
25–44 years	- - -	- - -	- - -	10.7	*	7.2	5.6	4.6
45–64 years	- - -	- - -	- - -	*	*	*	*	*
65 years and over	- - -	- - -	- - -	*	*	*	*	*
Asian or Pacific Islander female[5]								
All ages, age adjusted[4]	- - -	- - -	- - -	5.5	4.1	2.8	3.0	3.1
All ages, crude	- - -	- - -	- - -	4.7	3.4	2.7	2.9	3.1
15–24 years	- - -	- - -	- - -	*	3.9	2.7	*	3.4
25–44 years	- - -	- - -	- - -	5.4	3.8	3.3	3.3	3.4
45–64 years	- - -	- - -	- - -	7.9	5.0	3.2	3.8	4.3
65 years and over	- - -	- - -	- - -	*	8.5	5.2	6.8	4.6
Hispanic or Latino female[5,7]								
All ages, age adjusted[4]	- - -	- - -	- - -	- - -	2.3	1.7	1.8	1.7
All ages, crude	- - -	- - -	- - -	- - -	2.2	1.5	1.6	1.5
15–24 years	- - -	- - -	- - -	- - -	3.1	2.0	2.1	2.2
25–44 years	- - -	- - -	- - -	- - -	3.1	2.1	2.0	2.0
45–64 years	- - -	- - -	- - -	- - -	2.5	2.5	2.5	2.4
65 years and over	- - -	- - -	- - -	- - -	*	*	1.9	*
White, not Hispanic or Latino female[7]								
All ages, age adjusted[4]	- - -	- - -	- - -	- - -	5.4	4.7	5.1	5.0
All ages, crude	- - -	- - -	- - -	- - -	5.6	4.9	5.3	5.3
15–24 years	- - -	- - -	- - -	- - -	4.3	3.3	3.4	3.3
25–44 years	- - -	- - -	- - -	- - -	7.0	6.7	7.5	7.2
45–64 years	- - -	- - -	- - -	- - -	8.0	7.3	8.0	8.3
65 years and over	- - -	- - -	- - -	- - -	7.0	4.4	4.5	4.2

. . . Category not applicable.

* Rates based on fewer than 20 deaths are considered unreliable and are not shown.

- - - Data not available.

[1]Includes deaths of persons who were not residents of the 50 states and the District of Columbia.

[2]Underlying cause of death was coded according to the Sixth Revision of the International Classification of Diseases (ICD) in 1950, Seventh Revision in 1960, Eighth Revision in 1970, and Ninth Revision in 1980–1998. See Appendix II, Cause of death; tables IV and V.

[3]Starting with 1999 data, cause of death is coded according to ICD–10. See Appendix II, Cause of death; Comparability ratio; tables V and VI.

[4]Age-adjusted rates are calculated using the year 2000 standard population. Prior to 2003, age-adjusted rates were calculated using standard million proportions based on rounded population numbers. Starting with 2003 data, unrounded population numbers are used to calculate age-adjusted rates. See Appendix II, Age adjustment.

[5]The race groups, white, black, Asian or Pacific Islander, and American Indian or Alaska Native, include persons of Hispanic and non-Hispanic origin. Persons of Hispanic origin may be of any race. Death rates for the American Indian or Alaska Native and Asian or Pacific Islander populations are known to be underestimated. See Appendix II, Race, for a discussion of sources of bias in death rates by race and Hispanic origin.

[6]In 1950, rate is for the age group 75 years and over.

[7]Prior to 1997, excludes data from states lacking an Hispanic-origin item on the death certificate. See Appendix II, Hispanic origin.

NOTES: Starting with *Health, United States, 2003*, rates for 1991–1999 were revised using intercensal population estimates based on the 2000 census. Rates for 2000 were revised based on 2000 census counts. Rates for 2001 and later years were computed using 2000-based postcensal estimates. See Appendix I, Population Census and Population Estimates. Figures for 2001 include September 11-related deaths for which death certificates were filed as of October 24, 2002. See Appendix II, Cause of death; table V for terrorism-related ICD–10 codes. Age groups were selected to minimize the presentation of unstable age-specific death rates based on small numbers of deaths and for consistency among comparison groups. For additional injury-related statistics, see Web-based Injury Statistics Query and Reporting System, available from: www.cdc.gov/ncipc/wisqars. Starting with 2003 data, California, Hawaii, Idaho, Maine, Montana, New York, and Wisconsin reported multiple-race data. The multiple-race data for these states were bridged to the single race categories of the 1977 Office of Management and Budget standards for comparability with other states. Data for additional years are available. See Appendix III.

SOURCES: Centers for Disease Control and Prevention, National Center for Health Statistics, National Vital Statistics System; Grove RD, Hetzel AM. Vital statistics rates in the United States, 1940–1960. Washington, DC: U.S. Government Printing Office. 1968; numerator data from National Vital Statistics System, annual mortality files; denominator data from national population estimates for race groups from Table 1 and unpublished Hispanic population estimates for 1985–1996 prepared by the Housing and Household Economic Statistics Division, U.S. Census Bureau; additional mortality tables are available from: www.cdc.gov/nchs/datawh/statab/unpubd/mortabs.htm; Hoyert DL, Heron M, Murphy SL, Kung HC. Deaths: Final data for 2003. National vital statistics reports. Vol 54 no 13. Hyattsville, MD: National Center for Health Statistics. 2006.

This table will be updated on the Web. Go to www.cdc.gov/nchs/hus.htm.

Table 47 (page 1 of 3). Death rates for firearm-related injuries, by sex, race, Hispanic origin, and age: United States, selected years 1970–2003

[Data are based on death certificates]

Sex, race, Hispanic origin, and age	1970[1]	1980[1]	1990	1995	2000[2]	2001	2002	2003
	Deaths per 100,000 resident population							
All persons								
All ages, age adjusted[3]	14.3	14.8	14.6	13.4	10.2	10.3	10.4	10.3
All ages, crude	13.1	14.9	14.9	13.5	10.2	10.4	10.5	10.4
Under 1 year	*	*	*	*	*	*	*	*
1–14 years	1.6	1.4	1.5	1.6	0.7	0.7	0.7	0.7
1–4 years	1.0	0.7	0.6	0.6	0.3	0.5	0.4	0.3
5–14 years	1.7	1.6	1.9	1.9	0.9	0.8	0.8	0.8
15–24 years	15.5	20.6	25.8	26.7	16.8	16.7	16.7	16.6
15–19 years	11.4	14.7	23.3	24.1	12.9	12.4	12.1	12.1
20–24 years	20.3	26.4	28.1	29.2	20.9	21.2	21.3	21.1
25–44 years	20.9	22.5	19.3	16.9	13.1	13.5	13.7	13.4
25–34 years	22.2	24.3	21.8	19.6	14.5	15.5	15.4	15.5
35–44 years	19.6	20.0	16.3	14.3	11.9	11.7	12.1	11.5
45–64 years	17.6	15.2	13.6	11.7	10.0	10.3	10.6	10.7
45–54 years	18.1	16.4	13.9	12.0	10.5	10.5	10.8	11.2
55–64 years	17.0	13.9	13.3	11.3	9.4	10.1	10.2	10.1
65 years and over	13.8	13.5	16.0	14.1	12.2	12.4	12.4	11.8
65–74 years	14.5	13.8	14.4	12.8	10.6	10.9	10.9	10.4
75–84 years	13.4	13.4	19.4	16.3	13.9	14.3	14.4	13.5
85 years and over	10.2	11.6	14.7	14.4	14.2	12.8	12.5	12.5
Male								
All ages, age adjusted[3]	24.8	25.9	26.1	23.8	18.1	18.5	18.6	18.4
All ages, crude	22.2	25.7	26.2	23.6	17.8	18.2	18.4	18.3
Under 1 year	*	*	*	*	*	*	*	*
1–14 years	2.3	2.0	2.2	2.3	1.1	1.0	1.0	1
1–4 years	1.2	0.9	0.7	0.8	0.4	0.5	0.5	0.3
5–14 years	2.7	2.5	2.9	2.9	1.4	1.2	1.2	1.2
15–24 years	26.4	34.8	44.7	46.5	29.4	29.6	29.3	29.2
15–19 years	19.2	24.5	40.1	41.6	22.4	21.8	21.1	21.2
20–24 years	35.1	45.2	49.1	51.5	37.0	37.7	37.6	37.1
25–44 years	34.1	38.1	32.6	28.4	22.0	22.8	23.1	22.9
25–34 years	36.5	41.4	37.0	33.2	24.9	26.7	26.5	27.1
35–44 years	31.6	33.2	27.4	23.6	19.4	19.2	20.1	19.1
45–64 years	31.0	25.9	23.4	20.0	17.1	17.6	18.1	18.3
45–54 years	30.7	27.3	23.2	20.1	17.6	17.8	18.2	18.8
55–64 years	31.3	24.5	23.7	19.8	16.3	17.4	18.0	17.7
65 years and over	29.7	29.7	35.3	30.7	26.4	26.8	26.9	25.4
65–74 years	29.5	27.8	28.2	25.1	20.3	21.1	21.3	20.3
75–84 years	31.0	33.0	46.9	37.8	32.2	32.8	32.9	30.2
85 years and over	26.2	34.9	49.3	47.1	44.7	40.2	38.9	37.8
Female								
All ages, age adjusted[3]	4.8	4.7	4.2	3.8	2.8	2.8	2.8	2.7
All ages, crude	4.4	4.7	4.3	3.8	2.8	2.8	2.8	2.7
Under 1 year	*	*	*	*	*	*	*	*
1–14 years	0.8	0.7	0.8	0.8	0.3	0.4	0.5	0.3
1–4 years	0.9	0.5	0.5	0.5	*	0.4	0.3	0.3
5–14 years	0.8	0.7	1.0	0.9	0.4	0.4	0.5	0.3
15–24 years	4.8	6.1	6.0	5.9	3.5	3.2	3.5	3.3
15–19 years	3.5	4.6	5.7	5.6	2.9	2.6	2.7	2.4
20–24 years	6.4	7.7	6.3	6.1	4.2	3.8	4.2	4.2
25–44 years	8.3	7.4	6.1	5.5	4.2	4.2	4.1	3.8
25–34 years	8.4	7.5	6.7	5.8	4.0	4.0	4.0	3.6
35–44 years	8.2	7.2	5.4	5.2	4.4	4.3	4.2	4.0
45–64 years	5.4	5.4	4.5	3.9	3.4	3.4	3.4	3.4
45–54 years	6.4	6.2	4.9	4.2	3.6	3.5	3.6	3.8
55–64 years	4.2	4.6	4.0	3.5	3.0	3.3	3.1	2.9
65 years and over	2.4	2.5	3.1	2.8	2.2	2.2	2.0	2.1
65–74 years	2.8	3.1	3.6	3.0	2.5	2.4	2.3	2.2
75–84 years	1.7	1.7	2.9	2.8	2.0	2.2	2.1	2.2
85 years and over	*	1.3	1.3	1.8	1.7	1.3	1.1	1.3
White male[4]								
All ages, age adjusted[3]	19.7	22.1	22.0	20.1	15.9	16.3	16.2	16.0
All ages, crude	17.6	21.8	21.8	19.9	15.6	16.2	16.1	16.0
1–14 years	1.8	1.9	1.9	1.9	1.0	0.9	0.8	0.7
15–24 years	16.9	28.4	29.5	30.8	19.6	19.5	19.4	19.2
25–44 years	24.2	29.5	25.7	23.2	18.0	18.9	18.5	18.1
25–34 years	24.3	31.1	27.8	25.2	18.1	19.9	18.5	18.8
35–44 years	24.1	27.1	23.3	21.2	17.9	18.0	18.5	17.5
45–64 years	27.4	23.3	22.8	19.5	17.4	18.3	18.7	19.0
65 years and over	29.9	30.1	36.8	32.2	28.2	28.6	28.9	27.4

See footnotes at end of table.

This table will be updated on the Web. Go to www.cdc.gov/nchs/hus.htm.

Table 47 (page 2 of 3). Death rates for firearm-related injuries, by sex, race, Hispanic origin, and age: United States, selected years 1970–2003

[Data are based on death certificates]

Sex, race, Hispanic origin, and age	1970[1]	1980[1]	1990	1995	2000[2]	2001	2002	2003
Black or African American male[4]			Deaths per 100,000 resident population					
All ages, age adjusted[3]	70.8	60.1	56.3	49.2	34.2	34.5	36.0	35.6
All ages, crude	60.8	57.7	61.9	52.9	36.1	36.4	37.8	37.8
1–14 years	5.3	3.0	4.4	4.4	1.8	1.6	1.8	2.1
15–24 years	97.3	77.9	138.0	138.7	89.3	90.3	87.1	87.6
25–44 years	126.2	114.1	90.3	70.2	54.1	54.8	60.6	60.5
25–34 years	145.6	128.4	108.6	92.3	74.8	77.7	85.6	87.2
35–44 years	104.2	92.3	66.1	46.3	34.3	33.2	36.9	34.8
45–64 years	71.1	55.6	34.5	28.3	18.4	17.2	18.6	18.1
65 years and over	30.6	29.7	23.9	21.8	13.8	14.9	14.2	12.1
American Indian or Alaska Native male[4]								
All ages, age adjusted[3]	- - -	24.0	19.4	19.4	13.1	13.0	14.8	14.1
All ages, crude	- - -	27.5	20.5	20.9	13.2	12.9	15.3	14.7
15–24 years	- - -	55.3	49.1	40.9	26.9	24.3	30.0	27.6
25–44 years	- - -	43.9	25.4	31.2	16.6	18.8	21.7	21.8
45–64 years	- - -	*	*	14.2	12.2	9.6	12.4	10.5
65 years and over	- - -	*	*	*	*	*	*	*
Asian or Pacific Islander male[4]								
All ages, age adjusted[3]	- - -	7.8	8.8	9.2	6.0	5.2	5.5	5.4
All ages, crude	- - -	8.2	9.4	10.0	6.2	5.4	5.7	5.7
15–24 years	- - -	10.8	21.0	24.3	9.3	9.6	11.7	10.5
25–44 years	- - -	12.8	10.9	10.6	8.1	6.6	6.3	6.9
45–64 years	- - -	10.4	8.1	8.2	7.4	5.7	5.8	5.7
65 years and over	- - -	*	*	*	*	5.3	*	*
Hispanic or Latino male[4,5]								
All ages, age adjusted[3]	- - -	- - -	27.6	23.8	13.6	13.7	13.4	13.6
All ages, crude	- - -	- - -	29.9	26.2	14.2	14.6	14.2	14.6
1–14 years	- - -	- - -	2.6	2.8	1.0	0.7	0.9	0.8
15–24 years	- - -	- - -	55.5	61.7	30.8	31.4	32.1	32.8
25–44 years	- - -	- - -	42.7	31.4	17.3	19.1	17.6	18.6
25–34 years	- - -	- - -	47.3	36.4	20.3	22.7	21.2	22.8
35–44 years	- - -	- - -	35.4	24.2	13.2	14.4	12.9	13.3
45–64 years	- - -	- - -	21.4	17.2	12.0	10.0	9.9	10.3
65 years and over	- - -	- - -	19.1	16.5	12.2	12.0	12.3	10.6
White, not Hispanic or Latino male[5]								
All ages, age adjusted[3]	- - -	- - -	20.6	18.6	15.5	16.0	16.0	15.6
All ages, crude	- - -	- - -	20.4	18.5	15.7	16.3	16.3	16.0
1–14 years	- - -	- - -	1.6	1.6	1.0	1.0	0.7	0.7
15–24 years	- - -	- - -	24.1	23.5	16.2	16.0	15.6	15.2
25–44 years	- - -	- - -	23.3	21.4	17.9	18.6	18.4	17.7
25–34 years	- - -	- - -	24.7	22.5	17.2	18.9	17.4	17.3
35–44 years	- - -	- - -	21.6	20.4	18.4	18.4	19.3	18.1
45–64 years	- - -	- - -	22.7	19.5	17.8	19.0	19.4	19.8
65 years and over	- - -	- - -	37.4	32.5	29.0	29.4	29.8	28.4
White female[4]								
All ages, age adjusted[3]	4.0	4.2	3.8	3.5	2.7	2.7	2.7	2.6
All ages, crude	3.7	4.1	3.8	3.5	2.7	2.7	2.7	2.6
15–24 years	3.4	5.1	4.8	4.5	2.8	2.7	2.6	2.5
25–44 years	6.9	6.2	5.3	4.9	3.9	3.9	3.8	3.6
45–64 years	5.0	5.1	4.5	4.0	3.5	3.7	3.6	3.7
65 years and over	2.2	2.5	3.1	2.8	2.4	2.3	2.2	2.1

See footnotes at end of table.

This table will be updated on the Web. Go to www.cdc.gov/nchs/hus.htm.

Table 47 (page 3 of 3). Death rates for firearm-related injuries, by sex, race, Hispanic origin, and age: United States, selected years 1970–2003

[Data are based on death certificates]

Sex, race, Hispanic origin, and age	1970[1]	1980[1]	1990	1995	2000[2]	2001	2002	2003
Black or African American female[4]			Deaths per 100,000 resident population					
All ages, age adjusted[3]	11.1	8.7	7.3	6.2	3.9	3.8	4.1	3.8
All ages, crude	10.0	8.8	7.8	6.5	4.0	3.8	4.2	3.9
15–24 years	15.2	12.3	13.3	13.2	7.6	6.1	8.1	7.4
25–44 years	19.4	16.1	12.4	9.8	6.5	6.9	6.7	6.1
45–64 years	10.2	8.2	4.8	4.1	3.1	2.6	3.0	2.7
65 years and over	4.3	3.1	3.1	2.6	1.3	1.4	1.2	1.8
American Indian or Alaska Native female[4]								
All ages, age adjusted[3]	- - -	5.8	3.3	3.8	2.9	2.8	3.1	2.4
All ages, crude	- - -	5.8	3.4	4.1	2.9	2.9	3.4	2.6
15–24 years	- - -	*	*	*	*	*	*	*
25–44 years	- - -	10.2	*	7.0	5.5	5.0	*	*
45–64 years	- - -	*	*	*	*	*	*	*
65 years and over	- - -	*	*	*	*	*	*	*
Asian or Pacific Islander female[4]								
All ages, age adjusted[3]	- - -	2.0	1.9	2.0	1.1	1.0	1.1	1.1
All ages, crude	- - -	2.1	2.1	2.1	1.2	1.1	1.2	1.2
15–24 years	- - -	*	*	3.9	*	*	*	2.1
25–44 years	- - -	3.2	2.7	2.7	1.5	1.5	1.7	1.3
45–64 years	- - -	*	*	*	*	*	*	1.5
65 years and over	- - -	*	*	*	*	*	*	*
Hispanic or Latino female[4,5]								
All ages, age adjusted[3]	- - -	- - -	3.3	3.1	1.8	1.7	1.6	1.6
All ages, crude	- - -	- - -	3.6	3.3	1.8	1.7	1.6	1.7
15–24 years	- - -	- - -	6.9	6.1	2.9	3.3	2.8	3.5
25–44 years	- - -	- - -	5.1	4.7	2.5	2.5	2.4	2.2
45–64 years	- - -	- - -	2.4	2.4	2.2	1.6	1.6	1.5
65 years and over	- - -	- - -	*	*	*	*	*	*
White, not Hispanic or Latino female[5]								
All ages, age adjusted[3]	- - -	- - -	3.7	3.4	2.8	2.8	2.8	2.7
All ages, crude	- - -	- - -	3.7	3.5	2.9	2.9	2.8	2.7
15–24 years	- - -	- - -	4.3	4.1	2.7	2.5	2.5	2.2
25–44 years	- - -	- - -	5.1	4.8	4.2	4.1	4.1	3.9
45–64 years	- - -	- - -	4.6	4.1	3.6	3.8	3.8	3.9
65 years and over	- - -	- - -	3.2	2.8	2.4	2.4	2.3	2.2

* Rates based on fewer than 20 deaths are considered unreliable and are not shown.

- - - Data not available.

[1]Underlying cause of death was coded according to the Eighth Revision in 1970 and Ninth Revision in 1980–1998. See Appendix II, Cause of death; tables IV and V.
[2]Starting with 1999 data, cause of death is coded according to ICD–10. See Appendix II, Cause of death; Comparability ratio; tables V and VI.
[3]Age-adjusted rates are calculated using the year 2000 standard population. Prior to 2003, age-adjusted rates were calculated using standard million proportions based on rounded population numbers. Starting with 2003 data, unrounded population numbers are used to calculate age-adjusted rates. See Appendix II, Age adjustment.
[4]The race groups, white, black, Asian or Pacific Islander, and American Indian or Alaska Native, include persons of Hispanic and non-Hispanic origin. Persons of Hispanic origin may be of any race. Death rates for the American Indian or Alaska Native and Asian or Pacific Islander populations are known to be underestimated. See Appendix II, Race, for a discussion of sources of bias in death rates by race and Hispanic origin.
[5]Prior to 1997, excludes data from states lacking an Hispanic-origin item on the death certificate. See Appendix II, Hispanic origin.

NOTES: Starting with *Health, United States, 2003*, rates for 1991–1999 were revised using intercensal population estimates based on the 2000 census. Rates for 2000 were revised based on 2000 census counts. Rates for 2001 and later years were computed using 2000-based postcensal estimates. See Appendix I, Population Census and Population Estimates. Age groups were selected to minimize the presentation of unstable age-specific death rates based on small numbers of deaths and for consistency among comparison groups. For additional injury-related statistics, see Web-based Injury Statistics Query and Reporting System, available from: www.cdc.gov/ncipc/wisqars. Starting with 2003 data, California, Hawaii, Idaho, Maine, Montana, New York, and Wisconsin reported multiple-race data. The multiple-race data for these states were bridged to the single race categories of the 1977 Office of Management and Budget standards for comparability with other states. Data for additional years are available. See Appendix III.

SOURCES: Centers for Disease Control and Prevention, National Center for Health Statistics, National Vital Statistics System; numerator data from annual mortality files; denominator data from national population estimates for race groups from Table 1 and unpublished Hispanic population estimates for 1985–1996 prepared by the Housing and Household Economic Statistics Division, U.S. Census Bureau; additional mortality tables are available from: www.cdc.gov/nchs/datawh/statab/unpubd/mortabs.htm; Hoyert DL, Heron M, Murphy SL, Kung HC. Deaths: Final data for 2003. National vital statistics reports. Vol 54 no 13. Hyattsville, MD: National Center for Health Statistics. 2006.

This table will be updated on the Web. Go to www.cdc.gov/nchs/hus.htm.

Table 48. Deaths from selected occupational diseases among persons 15 years of age and over: United States, selected years 1980–2003

[Data are based on death certificates]

Cause of death[1]	1980[2]	1985	1990	1995	2000[3]	2001	2002	2003
Underlying and nonunderlying cause of death	Number of death certificates with cause of death code(s) mentioned							
Angiosarcoma of liver[4]	- - -	- - -	- - -	- - -	16	25	23	24
Malignant mesothelioma[5]	699	715	874	897	2,531	2,508	2,573	2,625
Pneumoconiosis[6]	4,151	3,783	3,644	3,151	2,859	2,743	2,715	2,635
Coal workers' pneumoconiosis	2,576	2,615	1,990	1,413	949	886	858	772
Asbestosis	339	534	948	1,169	1,486	1,449	1,467	1,464
Silicosis	448	334	308	242	151	163	146	177
Other (including unspecified)	814	321	413	343	290	260	263	236
Underlying cause of death	Number of deaths							
Angiosarcoma of liver[4]	- - -	- - -	- - -	- - -	15	22	20	20
Malignant mesothelioma[5]	531	573	725	780	2,384	2,371	2,429	2,476
Pneumoconiosis	1,581	1,355	1,335	1,117	1,142	1,110	1,094	1,101
Coal workers' pneumoconiosis	982	958	734	533	389	367	354	318
Asbestosis	101	139	302	355	558	550	529	583
Silicosis	207	143	150	114	71	82	89	102
Other (including unspecified)	291	115	149	115	124	111	122	98

- - - Data not available.

[1]Cause-of-death titles for selected occupational diseases and corresponding code numbers according to the *International Classification of Diseases*, Ninth and Tenth Revisions. See Appendix II, Cause of death; table IV.

Cause of death	ICD–9 code	ICD–10 code
Angiosarcoma of liver	- - -	C22.3
Malignant mesothelioma	158.8,158.9,163	C45
Pneumoconiosis	500–505	J60–J66
Coal workers' pneumoconiosis	500	J60
Asbestosis	501	J61
Silicosis	502	J62
Other (including unspecified)	503–505	J63–J66

[2]For the period 1980–1998, underlying cause of death was coded according to the Ninth Revision of the International Classification of Diseases (ICD). See Appendix II, Cause of death; tables IV and V.

[3]Starting with 1999 data, ICD–10 was introduced for coding cause of death. Discontinuities exist between 1998 and 1999 due to ICD–10 coding and classification changes. Caution should be exercised in interpreting trends for the causes of death in this table, especially for those with major ICD–10 changes (e.g., malignant mesothelioma). See Appendix II, *International Classification of Diseases* (ICD).

[4]Prior to 1999, there was no discrete code for this condition.

[5]Prior to 1999, the combined ICD–9 categories of malignant neoplasm of peritoneum and malignant neoplasm of pleura served as a crude surrogate for malignant mesothelioma category under ICD–10.

[6]For underlying and nonunderlying cause of death, counts for pneumoconiosis subgroups may sum to slightly more than total pneumoconiosis due to the reporting of more than one type of pneumoconiosis on some death certificates.

NOTES: See Appendix I, National Vital Statistics System, Multiple Cause of Death File, for information about tabulating cause-of-death data in this table. Selection of occupational diseases is based on definitions in Mullan RJ, Murthy LI. Occupational sentinel health events: An updated list for physician recognition and public health surveillance. 1991; Am J Ind Med 19(6):775–99. For more detailed information about pneumoconiosis deaths, see *Work-Related Lung Disease Surveillance Report 2002*, DHHS (NIOSH) Publication Number 2003–111 available from: www.cdc.gov/niosh/publistd.html. Data for additional years are available. See Appendix III.

SOURCE: Centers for Disease Control and Prevention, National Center for Health Statistics, National Vital Statistics System; annual mortality files for underlying and multiple cause of death.

This table will be updated on the Web. Go to www.cdc.gov/nchs/hus.htm.

Table 49 (page 1 of 2). Occupational injury deaths and rates, by industry, sex, age, race, and Hispanic origin: United States, selected years 1992–2004

[Data are compiled from various federal, state, and local administrative sources]

Characteristic	1992[1]	1995	1998	1999	2000	2001[2]	2002	2003	2004
	Deaths per 100,000 employed workers[3]								
Total work force	5.2	4.9	4.5	4.5	4.3	4.3	4.0	4.0	4.1
Sex									
Male	- - -	8.3	7.7	7.7	7.4	7.4	6.9	7.0	7.2
Female	- - -	0.9	0.8	0.7	0.7	0.7	0.7	0.7	0.6
Age									
16–17 years	- - -	1.6	1.2	1.6	1.6	1.3	1.1	1.2	1.1
18–19 years	- - -	3.3	3.1	2.7	2.7	2.8	2.2	2.3	2.8
20–24 years	- - -	3.8	3.3	3.4	3.3	3.2	3.2	3.4	3.1
25–34 years	- - -	4.3	3.9	3.8	3.8	3.8	3.3	3.4	3.3
35–44 years	- - -	4.6	4.2	4.1	4.0	4.1	4.0	3.8	3.9
45–54 years	- - -	5.2	4.6	4.6	4.4	4.5	4.0	4.1	4.3
55–64 years	- - -	7.2	6.5	6.1	6.1	5.5	5.0	4.8	5.2
65 years and over	- - -	14.0	14.5	14.6	12.0	12.7	11.5	11.3	11.8
Race and Hispanic origin[4]									
White	- - -	4.7	4.5	4.4	- - -	- - -	- - -	- - -	- - -
Black or African American	- - -	5.1	4.0	4.1	- - -	- - -	- - -	- - -	- - -
Hispanic or Latino	- - -	5.5	5.2	5.2	5.6	6.0	5.0	4.5	5.0
Not Hispanic or Latino	- - -	4.9	4.5	4.4	4.2	4.1	3.9	4.0	4.0
White	- - -	- - -	- - -	- - -	4.2	4.2	3.9	4.0	4.1
Black or African American	- - -	- - -	- - -	- - -	3.9	3.8	3.5	3.8	3.8
Asian, Native Hawaiian or Other Pacific Islander	- - -	- - -	- - -	- - -	- - -	- - -	- - -	2.8	3.0
Industry[5]									
Private sector	. . .	. . .	. . .	. . .	. . .	. . .	. . .	4.7	4.8
Goods producing	. . .	. . .	. . .	. . .	. . .	. . .	. . .	9.1	9.6
Natural resources and mining	. . .	. . .	. . .	. . .	. . .	. . .	. . .	55.7	47.9
Construction	. . .	. . .	. . .	. . .	. . .	. . .	. . .	14.3	14.6
Manufacturing	. . .	. . .	. . .	. . .	. . .	. . .	. . .	2.5	2.9
Service providing	. . .	. . .	. . .	. . .	. . .	. . .	. . .	3.2	3.3
Trade, transportation, and utilities	. . .	. . .	. . .	. . .	. . .	. . .	. . .	5.6	6.0
Information	. . .	. . .	. . .	. . .	. . .	. . .	. . .	1.9	1.8
Financial activities	. . .	. . .	. . .	. . .	. . .	. . .	. . .	1.5	1.3
Professional and business services	. . .	. . .	. . .	. . .	. . .	. . .	. . .	3.9	3.8
Educational and health services	. . .	. . .	. . .	. . .	. . .	. . .	. . .	0.8	0.9
Leisure and hospitality	. . .	. . .	. . .	. . .	. . .	. . .	. . .	2.6	2.3
Other services, except public administration	. . .	. . .	. . .	. . .	. . .	. . .	. . .	3.4	3.5
Government[6]	. . .	. . .	. . .	. . .	. . .	. . .	. . .	2.7	2.7
	Number of deaths[7]								
Total work force	6,217	6,275	6,055	6,054	5,920	5,915	5,534	5,575	5,764
Sex									
Male	5,774	5,736	5,569	5,612	5,471	5,442	5,092	5,129	5,349
Female	443	539	486	442	449	473	442	446	415
Age									
Under 16 years	27	26	33	26	29	20	16	25	13
16–17 years	41	42	32	46	44	33	25	28	25
18–19 years	107	130	137	122	127	122	92	84	103
20–24 years	544	486	421	451	446	441	436	462	421
25–34 years	1,556	1,409	1,238	1,175	1,163	1,142	1,023	1,018	996
35–44 years	1,538	1,571	1,525	1,510	1,473	1,478	1,403	1,329	1,342
45–54 years	1,167	1,256	1,279	1,333	1,313	1,368	1,253	1,301	1,384
55–64 years	767	827	836	816	831	775	784	802	907
65 years and over	467	515	541	565	488	530	495	523	569
Unspecified	3	13	13	10	6	6	7	3	4

See footnotes at end of table.

Table 49 (page 2 of 2). Occupational injury deaths and rates, by industry, sex, age, race, and Hispanic origin: United States, selected years 1992–2004

[Data are compiled from various federal, state, and local administrative sources]

Characteristic	1992[1]	1995	1998	1999	2000	2001[2]	2002	2003	2004
Race and Hispanic origin					Number of deaths[8]				
White	5,173	5,120	5,041	4,990	- - -	- - -	- - -	- - -	- - -
Black or African American	624	697	594	626	- - -	- - -	- - -	- - -	- - -
Hispanic or Latino	533	619	707	730	815	895	841	794	902
Not Hispanic or Latino	5,684	5,656	5,348	5,324	5,105	5,020	4,693	4,781	4,862
White	4,712	4,599	4,478	4,410	4,244	4,175	3,926	3,988	4,066
Black or African American	618	684	583	616	575	565	491	543	546
American Indian or Alaska Native	36	27	28	54	33	48	40	42	28
Asian[8]	192	188	164	180	171	173	131	147	168
Native Hawaiian or Other Pacific Islander	- - -	- - -	- - -	- - -	14	9	9	11	12
Multiple races	- - -	- - -	- - -	- - -	- - -	6	4	3	4
Other races or not reported	126	158	95	64	68	44	92	47	38
Industry[5]									
Private sector	- - -	- - -	- - -	- - -	- - -	- - -	- - -	5,043	5,229
Goods producing	- - -	- - -	- - -	- - -	- - -	- - -	- - -	2,401	2,518
Natural resources and mining	- - -	- - -	- - -	- - -	- - -	- - -	- - -	850	821
Construction	- - -	- - -	- - -	- - -	- - -	- - -	- - -	1,131	1,234
Manufacturing	- - -	- - -	- - -	- - -	- - -	- - -	- - -	420	463
Service providing	- - -	- - -	- - -	- - -	- - -	- - -	- - -	2,642	2,711
Trade, transportation, and utilities	- - -	- - -	- - -	- - -	- - -	- - -	- - -	1,375	1,473
Information	- - -	- - -	- - -	- - -	- - -	- - -	- - -	64	55
Financial activities	- - -	- - -	- - -	- - -	- - -	- - -	- - -	129	116
Professional and business services	- - -	- - -	- - -	- - -	- - -	- - -	- - -	453	452
Educational and health services	- - -	- - -	- - -	- - -	- - -	- - -	- - -	143	157
Leisure and hospitality	- - -	- - -	- - -	- - -	- - -	- - -	- - -	275	247
Other services, except public administration	- - -	- - -	- - -	- - -	- - -	- - -	- - -	194	207
Government[6]	- - -	- - -	- - -	- - -	- - -	- - -	- - -	532	535

- - - Data not available.
. . . Data not applicable.

[1]1992 and 1993 employment data by demographic characteristics are not available from the Current Population Survey (CPS) for calculation of rates.

[2]2,871 fatalities due to the September 11 terrorist attacks are not included.

[3]Numerator excludes deaths to workers under the age of 16 years. Starting with 2003 data, employment data in denominators are average annual estimates of employed civilians 16 years of age and over from the CPS; in prior years, it also included resident armed forces figures from the U.S. Census Bureau (1992–1998) and Department of Defense (1999–2002).

[4]Employment data for American Indian or Alaska Native workers and, prior to 2003, Asian or Pacific Islander workers, were not available for the calculation of rates. Employment data for non-Hispanic white and non-Hispanic black workers were not available before the year 2000. In 1999 and earlier years, the race groups white and black included persons of Hispanic and non-Hispanic origin.

[5]Totals for major categories may include subcategories not shown separately. Starting with 2003 data, establishments were classified by industry according to the 2002 North American Industry Classification System (NAICS). Prior to 2003, the Standard Industrial Classification (SIC) system was used. Because of substantial differences between these systems, industry data classified by these two systems are not comparable. Industry data for 1992–2002 classified by SIC are available in *Health, United States, 2004*, Table 49 available from: www.cdc.gov/nchs/hus.htm. See Appendix II, Industry of employment.

[6]Includes fatalities to workers employed by governmental organizations, regardless of industry.

[7]Includes fatalities to all workers, regardless of age.

[8]In 1999 and earlier years, category also included Native Hawaiian or Other Pacific Islander.

NOTES: Fatalities and rates are based on revised data and may differ from originally published data from the Census of Fatal Occupational Injuries (CFOI). See Appendix I, CFOI. CFOI began collecting fatality data in 1992. For data for prior years, see Centers for Disease Control and Prevention. Fatal Occupational Injuries—United States, 1980–1997. MMWR 2001;50(16):317–20, which reports trend data from the National Traumatic Occupational Fatalities (NTOF) surveillance system. NTOF was established at the National Institute of Occupational Safety and Health (NIOSH) to monitor occupational injury deaths through death certificates. Data for additional years are available. See Appendix III.

SOURCE: Department of Labor, Bureau of Labor Statistics, Census of Fatal Occupational Injuries. Revised annual data.

Table 50. Occupational injuries and illnesses with days away from work, job transfer, or restriction, by industry: United States, 2003–2004

[Data are based on employer records from a sample of business establishments]

Industry	Injuries and illnesses with days away from work, job transfer, or restriction			
	Cases per 100 full-time workers[1]		Number of cases in thousands[2]	
	2003	2004	2003	2004
Total private industry[3]	2.6	2.5	2,301.9	2,225.0
Goods producing	3.7	3.5	796.5	776.5
Natural resources and mining[4]	2.8	3.1	40.5	44.5
Agriculture, forestry, fishing, and hunting[4]	3.3	3.7	29.3	31.5
Mining	2.0	2.3	11.2	12.9
Construction	3.6	3.4	218.0	212.2
Manufacturing	3.8	3.6	538.0	519.9
Service providing	2.3	2.2	1,505.4	1,448.5
Trade, transportation, and utilities	3.2	3.1	683.2	673.1
Wholesale trade	2.8	2.7	147.4	146.2
Retail trade	2.7	2.7	319.6	322.8
Transportation and warehousing	5.4	4.9	204.0	190.0
Utilities	2.2	2.5	12.2	14.1
Information	1.1	1.1	30.8	31.1
Financial activities	0.8	0.7	56.9	51.8
Finance and insurance	0.4	0.3	21.3	18.4
Real estate and rental and leasing	2.1	1.9	35.6	33.4
Professional and business services	1.4	1.3	157.7	150.5
Professional, scientific, and technical services	0.6	0.5	36.0	32.2
Management of companies and enterprises	1.6	1.5	25.1	23.4
Administrative and support and waste management and remediation services	2.4	2.2	96.7	94.9
Education and health services	2.9	2.7	355.8	337.3
Educational services	1.2	1.0	17.9	14.5
Health care and social assistance	3.1	2.9	337.9	322.8
Leisure and hospitality	2.1	1.9	169.3	157.7
Arts, entertainment, and recreation	2.9	3.1	34.1	35.2
Accommodation and food services	2.0	1.7	135.2	122.5
Other services	1.7	1.6	51.7	47.0

[1]Incidence rate calculated as (N/EH) x 200,000, where N = total number of injuries and illnesses, EH = total hours worked by all employees during the calendar year, and 200,000 = base for 100 full-time equivalent employees working 40 hours per week, 50 weeks per year.
[2]Because of rounding, components may not add to totals.
[3]Totals include data for industries not shown separately. Excludes self-employed, private households, and employees in federal, state, and local government agencies.
[4]Excludes farms with fewer than 11 employees.

NOTES: Starting with 2003 data, the Survey of Occupational Injuries and Illnesses began using the 2002 North American Industry Classification System (NAICS) to classify establishments by industry. Prior to 2003, the survey used the Standard Industrial Classification (SIC) system. Because of substantial differences between these systems, the data measured by these surveys are not directly comparable. See Appendix II, Industry of employment. Data for previous years are presented in *Health, United States, 2004*, Table 50. Available from: www.cdc.gov/nchs/hus.htm. See Appendix I, Survey of Occupational Injuries and Illnesses.

SOURCE: U.S. Department of Labor, Bureau of Labor Statistics, Survey of Occupational Injuries and Illnesses: Workplace injuries and illnesses, 2004 edition. Summary News Release. 2005. Available from: www.bls.gov/iif/home.htm.

Table 51 (page 1 of 2). Selected notifiable disease rates: United States, selected years 1950–2004

[Data are based on reporting by state health departments]

Disease	1950	1960	1970	1980	1990	2000	2002	2003	2004
					Cases per 100,000 population				
Diphtheria	3.83	0.51	0.21	0.00	0.00	0.00	0.00	0.00	–
Haemophilus influenzae, invasive. . . .	- - -	- - -	- - -	- - -	- - -	0.51	0.62	0.70	0.72
Hepatitis A.	- - -	- - -	27.87	12.84	12.64	4.91	3.13	2.66	1.95
Hepatitis B.	- - -	- - -	4.08	8.39	8.48	2.95	2.84	2.61	2.14
Lyme disease.	- - -	- - -	- - -	- - -	- - -	6.53	8.44	7.39	6.81
Meningococcal disease.	- - -	- - -	1.23	1.25	0.99	0.83	0.64	0.61	0.47
Mumps	- - -	- - -	55.55	3.86	2.17	0.13	0.10	0.08	0.09
Pertussis (whooping cough).	79.82	8.23	2.08	0.76	1.84	2.88	3.47	4.04	8.88
Poliomyelitis, total.	22.02	1.77	0.02	0.00	0.00	–	–	–	–
Paralytic[1].	- - -	1.40	0.02	0.00	0.00	–	–	–	–
Rocky Mountain spotted fever	- - -	- - -	0.19	0.52	0.26	0.18	0.39	0.38	0.59
Rubella (German measles)	- - -	- - -	27.75	1.72	0.45	0.06	0.01	0.00	0.00
Rubeola (measles)	211.01	245.42	23.23	5.96	11.17	0.03	0.02	0.02	0.01
Salmonellosis, excluding typhoid fever	- - -	3.85	10.84	14.88	19.54	14.51	15.73	15.16	14.51
Shigellosis.	15.45	6.94	6.79	8.41	10.89	8.41	8.37	8.19	4.88
Tuberculosis[2].	- - -	30.83	18.28	12.25	10.33	6.01	5.36	5.17	5.03
Sexually transmitted diseases:[3]									
Syphilis[4]	146.02	68.78	45.26	30.51	54.32	11.20	11.41	11.79	11.49
Primary and secondary.	16.73	9.06	10.89	12.06	20.26	2.12	2.38	2.47	2.74
Early latent	39.71	10.11	8.08	9.00	22.19	3.35	2.92	2.88	2.67
Late and late latent[5].	70.22	45.91	24.94	9.30	10.32	5.53	5.95	6.30	5.95
Congenital[6].	8.97	2.48	0.97	0.12	1.55	0.21	0.16	0.15	0.12
Chlamydia[7]	- - -	- - -	- - -	- - -	160.19	251.38	289.41	301.74	319.61
Gonorrhea[8]	192.50	145.40	297.22	445.10	276.43	128.67	122.01	115.23	113.52
Chancroid.	3.34	0.94	0.70	0.30	1.69	0.03	0.02	0.02	0.01
					Number of cases				
Diphtheria	5,796	918	435	3	4	1	1	1	–
Haemophilus influenzae, invasive. . . .	- - -	- - -	- - -	- - -	- - -	1,398	1,743	2,013	2,085
Hepatitis A.	- - -	- - -	56,797	29,087	31,441	13,397	8,795	7,653	5,683
Hepatitis B.	- - -	- - -	8,310	19,015	21,102	8,036	7,996	7,526	6,212
Lyme disease.	- - -	- - -	- - -	- - -	- - -	17,730	23,763	21,273	19,804
Meningococcal disease.	- - -	- - -	2,505	2,840	2,451	2,256	1,814	1,756	1,361
Mumps	- - -	- - -	104,953	8,576	5,292	338	270	231	258
Pertussis (whooping cough).	120,718	14,809	4,249	1,730	4,570	7,867	9,771	11,647	25,827
Poliomyelitis, total.	33,300	3,190	33	9	6	–	–	–	–
Paralytic[1].	- - -	2,525	31	9	6	–	–	–	–
Rocky Mountain spotted fever	- - -	- - -	380	1,163	651	495	1,104	1,091	1,713
Rubella (German measles)	- - -	- - -	56,552	3,904	1,125	176	18	7	10
Rubeola (measles)	319,124	441,703	47,351	13,506	27,786	86	44	56	37
Salmonellosis, excluding typhoid fever.	- - -	6,929	22,096	33,715	48,603	39,574	44,264	43,657	42,197
Shigellosis.	23,367	12,487	13,845	19,041	27,077	22,922	23,541	23,581	14,627
Tuberculosis[2].	- - -	55,494	37,137	27,749	25,701	16,377	15,075	14,874	14,517
Sexually transmitted diseases:[3]									
Syphilis[4]	217,558	122,538	91,382	68,832	135,590	31,616	32,916	34,289	33,401
Primary and secondary.	23,939	16,145	21,982	27,204	50,578	5,979	6,862	7,177	7,980
Early latent	59,256	18,017	16,311	20,297	55,397	9,465	8,429	8,361	7,768
Late and late latent[5].	113,569	81,798	50,348	20,979	25,750	15,594	17,168	18,319	17,300
Congenital[6].	13,377	4,416	1,953	277	3,865	578	457	432	353
Chlamydia[7]	- - -	- - -	- - -	- - -	323,663	709,452	834,555	877,478	929,462
Gonorrhea[8]	286,746	258,933	600,072	1,004,029	690,042	363,136	351,852	335,104	330,132
Chancroid.	4,977	1,680	1,416	788	4,212	78	48	54	30

See footnotes at end of table.

Table 51 (page 2 of 2). Selected notifiable disease rates: United States, selected years 1950–2004

[Data are based on reporting by state health departments]

0.00 Rate greater than zero but less than 0.005.
– Quantity zero.
- - - Data not available.

[1]Data for 1986 and later years may be updated due to retrospective case evaluations or late reports.

[2]Case reporting for tuberculosis began in 1953. Data prior to 1975 are not comparable with subsequent years' data because of changes in reporting criteria effective in 1975. 2004 data were updated through the Division of Tuberculosis Elimination, NCHSTP, as of April 15, 2005.

[3]Reported civilian cases include military cases starting in 1991. Adjustments to the number of cases from state health departments were made for hardcopy forms and for electronic data submissions through April 29, 2005. For 1950, data for Alaska and Hawaii were not included.

[4]Includes stage of syphilis not stated.

[5]Includes cases of unknown duration.

[6]Data reported for 1989 and later years reflect change in case definition introduced in 1988. All cases of congenitally acquired syphilis were reported through 1994; as of 1995, only congenital syphilis for cases less than one year of age were reported. See STD Surveillance Report for congenital syphilis rates per 100,000 live births. In 2004, the rate was 8.8 congenital syphilis cases per 100,000 live births.

[7]Prior to 1994, Chlamydia was not notifiable. In 1994–1999, cases for New York were exclusively reported by New York City. Starting with 2000 data, NY includes both NYC and the entire state.

[8]Data for 1994 do not include cases from Georgia.

NOTES: The total resident population was used to calculate all rates except sexually transmitted diseases (STDs), which used the civilian resident population prior to 1991. For STDs, rates for the period 1990–2002 have been revised and may differ from previous editions of *Health, United States*. Revised rates are due to population estimates revised to incorporate bridged single race estimates. See Appendix I, Population census and Population estimates. Population data from those states where diseases were not notifiable or not available were excluded from the rate calculation. See Appendix I for information on underreporting of notifiable diseases. Data for additional years are available. See Appendix III.

SOURCES: Centers for Disease Control and Prevention. Summary of notifiable diseases, United States, 2004. MMWR 2006;53(53):1–79. National Center for HIV, STD, and TB Prevention, Division of STD Prevention. Sexually transmitted disease surveillance, 2004. Atlanta, GA: U.S. Department of Health and Human Services, Centers for Disease Control and Prevention, September 2005.

Table 52 (page 1 of 2). Acquired immunodeficiency syndrome (AIDS) cases, by year of diagnosis and selected characteristics: United States and outlying U.S. areas, 1999–2004

[Data are based on reporting by state and outlying U.S. area health departments]

Sex, race and Hispanic origin, age at diagnosis, and region of residence	All years[1]	Year of diagnosis					
		1999	2000	2001	2002	2003	2004
		Estimated number of cases[2]					
All persons[3]	944,306	39,551	39,513	39,206	40,267	41,831	42,514
Sex							
Male, 13 years and over	756,399	29,642	28,974	28,743	29,730	30,578	31,024
Female, 13 years and over	178,463	9,718	10,415	10,348	10,429	11,184	11,442
Children, under 13 years	9,443	190	124	115	109	69	48
Not Hispanic or Latino:							
White	375,155	11,901	11,378	11,052	11,604	11,657	12,013
Black or African American	379,278	19,182	19,510	19,473	19,934	20,685	20,965
American Indian or Alaska Native . . .	3,084	158	175	169	186	189	193
Asian or Pacific Islander	7,317	349	350	381	440	478	488
Hispanic or Latino[4]	177,164	7,827	7,957	7,974	7,907	8,632	8,672
Age at diagnosis							
Under 13 years	9,443	190	124	115	109	69	48
13–14 years	959	57	60	79	71	58	60
15–24 years	39,100	1,510	1,620	1,617	1,779	1,965	2,114
25–34 years	310,046	10,850	9,929	9,497	9,290	9,279	9,361
35–44 years	370,163	16,285	16,460	16,151	16,541	17,054	16,778
45–54 years	154,513	7,760	8,207	8,601	9,093	9,774	10,178
55–64 years	45,672	2,170	2,361	2,387	2,648	2,783	3,075
65 years and over	14,410	729	752	759	738	848	901
Region of residence							
Northeast	289,792	11,419	12,105	11,212	10,395	11,149	11,158
Midwest	93,701	3,926	3,968	3,949	4,303	4,495	4,498
South	343,449	16,307	15,841	16,598	17,751	18,612	19,792
West	187,730	6,663	6,443	6,258	6,745	6,474	6,083
U.S. dependencies, possessions, and associated nations[5]	29,634	1,236	1,156	1,190	1,073	1,100	982
		Percent distribution[6]					
All persons[3]	100.0	100.0	100.0	100.0	100.0	100.0	100.0
Sex							
Male, 13 years and over	80.1	74.9	73.3	73.3	73.8	73.1	73.0
Female, 13 years and over	18.9	24.6	26.4	26.4	25.9	26.7	26.9
Children, under 13 years	1.0	0.5	0.3	0.3	0.3	0.2	0.1
Not Hispanic or Latino:							
White	39.7	30.1	28.8	28.2	28.8	27.9	28.3
Black or African American	40.2	48.5	49.4	49.7	49.5	49.4	49.3
American Indian or Alaska Native . . .	0.3	0.4	0.4	0.4	0.5	0.5	0.5
Asian or Pacific Islander	0.8	0.9	0.9	1.0	1.1	1.1	1.1
Hispanic or Latino[4]	18.8	19.8	20.1	20.3	19.6	20.6	20.4

See footnotes at end of table.

Table 52 (page 2 of 2). Acquired immunodeficiency syndrome (AIDS) cases, by year of diagnosis and selected characteristics: United States and outlying U.S. areas, 1999–2004

[Data are based on reporting by State and outlying U.S. area health departments]

Sex, race and Hispanic origin, age at diagnosis, and region of residence	All years[1]	Year of diagnosis					
		1999	2000	2001	2002	2003	2004
Age at diagnosis	Percent distribution[5]						
Under 13 years	1.0	0.5	0.3	0.3	0.3	0.2	0.1
13–14 years.	0.1	0.1	0.2	0.2	0.2	0.1	0.1
15–24 years.	4.1	3.8	4.1	4.1	4.4	4.7	5.0
25–34 years.	32.8	27.4	25.1	24.2	23.1	22.2	22.0
35–44 years.	39.2	41.2	41.7	41.2	41.1	40.8	39.5
45–54 years.	16.4	19.6	20.8	21.9	22.6	23.4	23.9
55–64 years.	4.8	5.5	6.0	6.1	6.6	6.7	7.2
65 years and over	1.5	1.8	1.9	1.9	1.8	2.0	2.1
Region of residence							
Northeast.	30.7	28.9	30.6	28.6	25.8	26.7	26.2
Midwest.	9.9	9.9	10.0	10.1	10.7	10.7	10.6
South	36.4	41.2	40.1	42.3	44.1	44.5	46.6
West	19.9	16.8	16.3	16.0	16.8	15.5	14.3
U.S. dependencies, possessions, and associated nations[5]	3.1	3.1	2.9	3.0	2.7	2.6	2.3

[1]Based on cases reported to the Centers for Disease Control and Prevention from the beginning of the epidemic (1981) through June 30, 2005.

[2]Numbers are point estimates that result from adjustments for reporting delays to AIDS case counts. The estimates do not include adjustments for incomplete reporting. Data are provisional. See Appendix I, AIDS Surveillance.

[3]Total for all years includes 2,308 persons of unknown race or multiple races and two persons of unknown sex. All persons totals were calculated independent of values for subpopulations. Consequently sums of subpopulations may not equal totals for all persons.

[4]Persons of Hispanic origin may be of any race. See Appendix II, Hispanic origin.

[5]Outlying areas include Guam, Puerto Rico, the U.S. Pacific Islands, and the U.S. Virgin Islands.

[6]Percents may not sum to 100% due to rounding and because 0.2% unknown race and Hispanic origin are included in totals.

NOTES: See Appendix II, Acquired immunodeficiency syndrome (AIDS), for discussion of AIDS case reporting definitions and other issues affecting interpretation of trends. This table replaces surveillance data by year of report in previous editions of *Health, United States*.

SOURCES: Centers for Disease Control and Prevention, National Center for HIV, STD, and TB Prevention, Division of HIV/AIDS Prevention—Surveillance and Epidemiology, AIDS Surveillance; CDC HIV/AIDS Surveillance Report, 2004 (vol. 16). Atlanta, GA: US Department of Health and Human Services, Centers for Disease Control and Prevention. 2005. Available from: www.cdc.gov/hiv/stats/hasrlink.htm.

Table 53 (page 1 of 3). Age-adjusted cancer incidence rates for selected cancer sites, by sex, race, and Hispanic origin: Selected geographic areas, selected years 1990–2003

[Data are based on the Surveillance, Epidemiology, and End Results (SEER) Program's 13 population-based cancer registries]

Site, sex, race, and Hispanic origin	1990	1995	1996	1997	1998	1999	2000	2001	2002	2003	1990–2003 APC[1]
All sites	Number of new cases per 100,000 population[2]										
All persons	475.2	469.8	471.2	476.5	477.5	478.3	470.6	471.8	464.6	447.1	−0.5[3]
White	482.6	476.0	478.2	483.9	486.6	487.6	482.0	484.1	474.4	456.0	−0.4[3]
Black or African American	512.1	532.1	529.9	532.3	524.0	528.2	513.2	501.4	509.4	489.0	−0.6[3]
American Indian or Alaska Native[4]	327.9	348.9	335.4	362.1	336.9	365.3	315.6	329.7	298.5	- - -	−0.6
Asian or Pacific Islander	335.4	335.5	331.4	343.2	333.9	336.0	329.7	334.4	331.1	314.7	−0.5[3]
Hispanic or Latino[5]	353.5	354.5	356.1	351.0	365.4	362.4	349.7	348.8	350.8	323.5	−0.5[3]
White, not Hispanic or Latino[5]	490.9	489.8	491.7	499.7	499.7	500.5	497.7	501.3	489.3	471.2	−0.3
Male	583.4	562.6	561.2	563.0	559.8	564.6	559.6	557.4	546.4	525.7	−1.1[3]
White	590.1	561.5	562.9	563.0	561.8	566.5	564.0	563.7	550.0	527.9	−1.1[3]
Black or African American	685.3	730.3	710.8	715.8	704.1	704.5	690.4	668.3	668.7	634.6	−1.2[3]
American Indian or Alaska Native[4]	377.9	401.8	361.4	421.8	359.8	424.2	328.3	373.6	321.0	- - -	−1.3
Asian or Pacific Islander	387.3	393.4	382.6	394.7	378.4	389.0	385.9	380.1	373.1	364.0	−0.8[3]
Hispanic or Latino[5]	415.9	436.0	429.8	424.4	435.9	433.0	421.6	419.1	417.8	384.7	−0.8[3]
White, not Hispanic or Latino[5]	598.5	577.9	577.6	581.2	575.5	579.1	581.7	582.3	566.1	543.9	−1.1[3]
Female	410.8	409.4	412.7	420.1	424.4	421.2	410.4	413.1	409.0	393.3	0.0
White	420.9	422.2	424.5	433.8	439.6	436.6	427.7	430.5	423.7	407.5	0.1
Black or African American	403.2	399.6	411.0	411.4	407.0	411.8	393.7	387.2	402.2	390.5	−0.2
American Indian or Alaska Native[4]	293.9	315.1	319.5	320.7	321.8	327.2	312.9	302.9	281.5	- - -	0.1
Asian or Pacific Islander	294.7	293.1	294.7	306.9	303.9	300.0	291.0	304.2	305.4	283.3	0.1
Hispanic or Latino[5]	320.0	304.4	312.1	306.4	322.0	319.8	307.1	305.3	309.4	285.3	−0.4
White, not Hispanic or Latino[5]	429.9	434.5	437.2	448.0	452.5	449.7	441.4	446.3	437.3	421.8	0.2
Lung and bronchus											
Male	95.0	86.8	84.3	82.5	83.2	80.2	77.4	76.5	74.7	73.0	−2.0[3]
White	94.2	85.0	82.8	80.9	82.1	78.8	76.1	75.7	74.1	72.0	−2.0[3]
Black or African American	133.5	136.5	129.2	124.9	123.4	119.9	109.6	111.9	107.9	107.8	−2.1[3]
Asian or Pacific Islander	64.5	59.9	60.6	61.8	61.0	62.1	62.6	56.1	56.2	56.0	−1.1[3]
Hispanic or Latino[5]	59.5	52.2	48.1	47.9	50.4	43.0	43.7	42.0	46.3	41.3	−2.2[3]
White, not Hispanic or Latino[5]	96.6	88.8	86.4	84.4	84.6	81.2	79.3	79.9	76.5	74.6	−2.0[3]
Female	47.2	49.3	50.0	50.3	50.9	50.3	48.5	48.4	48.7	48.0	0.1
White	48.4	51.7	52.3	52.9	53.1	52.3	50.7	50.6	50.9	50.7	0.2
Black or African American	52.8	49.8	53.8	50.6	56.9	57.9	54.1	53.9	55.0	52.6	0.3
Asian or Pacific Islander	28.3	27.5	27.8	29.6	28.4	28.6	27.0	29.0	28.5	27.2	0.1
Hispanic or Latino[5]	25.7	24.5	25.5	24.8	25.7	24.5	22.1	22.4	22.5	20.8	−1.6[3]
White, not Hispanic or Latino[5]	49.7	53.8	54.6	55.6	55.3	54.4	53.1	53.1	53.8	53.6	0.4[3]
Colon and rectum											
Male	72.2	63.1	64.4	66.2	65.7	63.9	62.4	61.1	59.2	56.8	−1.5[3]
White	72.8	62.5	64.9	66.0	65.5	64.0	62.1	60.6	58.0	55.7	−1.6[3]
Black or African American	72.6	74.1	67.7	74.1	77.2	73.2	72.1	70.5	70.9	73.2	−0.4
Asian or Pacific Islander	61.4	58.1	55.9	59.0	57.4	53.8	56.3	55.4	56.9	50.7	−0.9[3]
Hispanic or Latino[5]	46.9	44.9	49.5	50.0	51.5	48.7	48.6	48.4	43.7	43.8	−0.4
White, not Hispanic or Latino[5]	75.8	64.7	66.5	67.8	67.6	66.3	64.3	62.4	60.5	57.7	−1.6[3]
Female	50.2	45.8	46.0	47.2	48.5	46.9	45.8	45.0	44.5	42.4	−0.9[3]
White	49.7	45.5	45.6	47.0	48.2	46.1	45.4	44.2	43.6	41.9	−0.9[3]
Black or African American	60.9	54.7	53.9	57.7	55.8	58.0	57.0	55.3	54.5	53.0	−0.4
Asian or Pacific Islander	38.2	38.5	38.9	35.6	40.1	39.7	36.5	40.2	40.0	34.8	−0.5
Hispanic or Latino[5]	34.4	31.3	32.8	31.4	33.7	34.1	32.8	30.7	30.6	29.8	−0.7[3]
White, not Hispanic or Latino[5]	51.0	47.0	47.5	48.8	50.5	47.8	47.2	46.3	45.6	43.4	−0.8[3]
Prostate											
Male	166.6	165.6	165.6	170.7	168.2	178.7	176.6	177.2	174.3	160.4	−1.5[3]
White	168.1	160.5	161.1	166.1	162.7	173.6	172.1	174.4	169.9	154.9	−1.7[3]
Black or African American	217.8	272.1	271.2	271.9	277.4	280.5	282.6	261.1	269.9	237.5	−0.9
American Indian or Alaska Native[4]	98.7	83.0	102.5	98.2	72.7	86.7	55.9	71.7	69.9	- - -	−4.4[3]
Asian or Pacific Islander	88.5	102.5	93.7	96.6	91.7	103.7	103.2	104.2	97.8	97.9	−0.9
Hispanic or Latino[5]	118.0	138.5	137.6	140.5	145.7	146.4	144.2	141.2	142.7	127.3	−0.5
White, not Hispanic or Latino[5]	163.1	164.6	164.3	170.6	164.1	174.8	175.4	179.1	173.5	156.7	−1.7[3]
Breast											
Female	129.2	130.5	131.7	135.4	138.4	137.7	133.3	134.2	130.6	121.1	0.1
White	134.2	136.1	136.8	141.2	144.7	144.5	140.4	141.5	136.8	125.7	0.2
Black or African American	116.4	122.0	122.3	123.6	123.0	122.7	119.2	114.2	119.5	119.2	0.1
American Indian or Alaska Native[4]	62.1	86.2	102.4	72.2	76.1	77.9	80.9	76.1	63.7	- - -	−0.6
Asian or Pacific Islander	87.0	85.9	89.5	98.2	98.0	95.9	91.0	97.4	96.6	87.4	1.0[3]
Hispanic or Latino[5]	87.9	86.0	90.9	86.4	90.6	91.1	91.7	86.9	87.7	79.6	−0.2
White, not Hispanic or Latino[5]	139.2	141.8	142.5	146.9	150.8	150.5	145.9	148.3	141.8	131.1	0.2

See footnotes at end of table.

Table 53 (page 2 of 3). **Age-adjusted cancer incidence rates for selected cancer sites, by sex, race, and Hispanic origin: Selected geographic areas, selected years 1990–2003**

[Data are based on the Surveillance, Epidemiology, and End Results (SEER) Program's 13 population-based cancer registries]

Site, sex, race, and Hispanic origin	1990	1995	1996	1997	1998	1999	2000	2001	2002	2003	1990–2003 APC[1]
Cervix uteri					Number of new cases per 100,000 population[2]						
Female	11.9	9.9	10.7	9.8	9.8	9.3	8.8	8.7	8.2	8.0	−2.7[3]
White	11.2	9.1	9.9	9.2	9.3	9.1	8.8	8.4	8.2	7.7	−2.3[3]
Black or African American	16.4	14.6	13.9	13.2	12.4	12.9	10.5	10.4	9.7	10.2	−3.7[3]
Asian or Pacific Islander	12.1	10.9	12.9	11.1	10.7	7.9	7.9	9.5	7.9	7.7	−3.9[3]
Hispanic or Latino[5]	21.6	17.9	18.8	16.5	15.8	17.2	17.1	15.0	14.4	13.8	−3.3[3]
White, not Hispanic or Latino[5]	9.8	7.8	8.6	8.1	8.3	7.8	7.2	7.0	6.9	6.3	−2.5[3]
Corpus uteri[6]											
Female	24.3	24.4	24.0	24.8	24.4	24.1	23.3	24.0	23.3	22.5	−0.3
White	26.0	26.0	25.5	26.5	26.0	25.8	25.1	25.6	24.2	23.9	−0.4
Black or African American	16.2	16.9	18.3	17.3	17.8	17.5	16.3	18.8	20.8	18.1	1.4[3]
Asian or Pacific Islander	12.9	17.0	16.0	16.8	16.7	17.1	15.9	16.9	18.2	15.8	1.4[3]
Hispanic or Latino[5]	17.3	16.2	16.2	16.8	17.6	16.0	14.9	16.3	16.5	15.7	−0.4
White, not Hispanic or Latino[5]	26.5	27.2	26.5	27.8	26.8	27.0	26.8	26.7	25.3	24.8	−0.2
Ovary											
Female	15.5	14.5	13.9	14.2	14.1	14.2	14.0	14.0	13.5	13.0	−1.1[3]
White	16.4	15.4	15.1	14.9	15.0	15.1	15.0	15.2	14.3	13.7	−1.0[3]
Black or African American	11.2	10.8	9.1	10.3	10.5	10.3	10.5	9.2	9.7	10.8	−0.7
Asian or Pacific Islander	11.2	10.4	9.3	11.3	9.9	10.8	9.7	9.4	11.5	9.5	−0.4
Hispanic or Latino[5]	12.4	11.6	11.9	11.2	12.1	10.8	10.5	12.7	13.0	10.3	−0.4
White, not Hispanic or Latino[5]	16.9	15.9	15.1	15.4	15.0	15.4	15.4	15.5	14.1	14.1	−1.0[3]
Oral cavity and pharynx											
Male	18.5	16.4	17.1	16.7	16.4	15.3	15.7	14.9	15.4	14.7	−1.7[3]
White	17.9	16.3	16.7	16.6	16.1	15.2	15.7	15.1	15.5	14.8	−1.4[3]
Black or African American	25.4	22.0	22.5	19.3	21.5	19.0	19.1	18.1	17.8	16.8	−2.7[3]
Asian or Pacific Islander	14.9	11.8	14.0	14.7	12.8	11.1	13.0	9.7	12.4	11.3	−1.7[3]
Hispanic or Latino[5]	10.7	12.1	11.0	10.5	9.9	9.6	8.7	9.1	9.4	8.0	−2.4[3]
White, not Hispanic or Latino[5]	19.0	16.8	17.4	17.3	17.0	16.1	16.8	15.9	16.1	16.0	−1.2[3]
Female	7.3	7.0	6.9	6.9	6.6	6.3	6.1	6.6	6.4	5.7	−1.4[3]
White	7.4	7.1	6.8	6.9	6.7	6.2	6.2	6.6	6.5	5.6	−1.5[3]
Black or African American	6.4	6.7	7.2	7.1	6.6	5.9	5.3	6.4	6.2	6.8	−0.8
Asian or Pacific Islander	6.1	5.2	5.8	6.5	4.4	6.3	6.1	5.6	5.7	4.8	−1.2
Hispanic or Latino[5]	3.8	3.7	3.6	3.9	3.4	4.5	3.6	4.1	3.5	3.4	−1.2
White, not Hispanic or Latino[5]	7.8	7.3	7.3	7.2	6.9	6.5	6.5	7.0	6.9	5.9	−1.2[3]
Stomach											
Male	14.6	13.5	13.7	13.4	12.8	12.8	12.5	11.8	11.9	11.4	−1.9[3]
White	12.8	11.9	11.9	11.3	11.1	11.2	10.6	10.2	10.3	9.9	−2.0[3]
Black or African American	21.5	18.4	22.3	21.9	20.4	17.0	18.4	17.2	15.8	17.7	−2.4[3]
Asian or Pacific Islander	26.9	24.0	23.5	24.7	21.1	22.5	22.2	19.0	20.0	18.0	−3.0[3]
Hispanic or Latino[5]	20.6	19.1	17.3	18.9	19.8	20.4	16.3	15.7	15.8	15.5	−2.2[3]
White, not Hispanic or Latino[5]	12.2	11.2	11.2	10.7	10.1	10.1	10.0	9.4	9.6	9.0	−2.3[3]
Female	6.7	6.2	6.1	6.1	6.4	6.6	6.1	5.7	6.1	5.8	−1.0[3]
White	5.7	5.1	5.0	4.9	5.2	5.5	5.0	4.6	5.0	4.7	−1.3[3]
Black or African American	9.9	9.8	9.1	10.8	10.9	10.4	8.6	8.9	9.6	9.0	−0.7
Asian or Pacific Islander	15.4	13.0	13.6	12.1	12.7	12.0	12.8	11.9	10.8	10.7	−2.8[3]
Hispanic or Latino[5]	11.1	11.3	10.2	9.9	10.7	9.6	10.9	9.8	10.2	9.6	−0.8
White, not Hispanic or Latino[5]	5.2	4.5	4.5	4.4	4.6	5.0	4.3	3.8	4.2	4.0	−2.0[3]
Pancreas											
Male	13.0	12.7	12.5	12.9	12.9	12.5	12.8	12.7	12.6	12.1	−0.3[3]
White	12.7	12.4	12.2	12.5	12.8	12.4	12.6	12.8	12.8	11.9	0.0
Black or African American	19.3	19.1	19.0	18.1	17.3	18.2	18.1	15.0	13.7	16.5	−1.6[3]
Asian or Pacific Islander	11.2	10.4	10.5	12.0	10.5	9.2	10.5	9.7	9.7	9.7	−1.6[3]
Hispanic or Latino[5]	10.8	12.4	11.6	11.9	9.9	9.1	12.0	9.6	10.4	8.9	−0.8
White, not Hispanic or Latino[5]	13.0	12.3	12.3	12.6	13.2	12.6	12.6	13.0	13.2	12.4	0.0
Female	10.0	9.9	10.1	10.1	10.1	9.6	9.8	9.8	10.2	9.9	−0.1
White	9.8	9.6	9.7	9.7	9.9	9.3	9.6	9.5	9.9	9.8	−0.1
Black or African American	12.9	15.5	15.2	16.7	13.7	13.4	12.7	13.4	15.5	13.6	−0.8
Asian or Pacific Islander	9.7	8.0	7.9	8.3	8.5	8.6	9.0	8.9	8.6	7.5	0.2
Hispanic or Latino[5]	10.1	8.9	9.1	10.0	9.8	9.8	9.0	9.6	10.3	7.5	−0.8
White, not Hispanic or Latino[5]	9.3	9.8	9.7	9.6	9.7	9.1	9.5	9.4	9.7	10.2	0.2

See footnotes at end of table.

Table 53 (page 3 of 3). Age-adjusted cancer incidence rates for selected cancer sites, by sex, race, and Hispanic origin: Selected geographic areas, selected years 1990–2003

[Data are based on the Surveillance, Epidemiology, and End Results (SEER) Program's 13 population-based cancer registries]

Site, sex, race, and Hispanic origin	1990	1995	1996	1997	1998	1999	2000	2001	2002	2003	1990–2003 APC[1]
Urinary bladder	Number of new cases per 100,000 population[2]										
Male	37.2	35.3	35.7	35.8	36.6	36.3	36.6	36.3	35.1	35.6	−0.3[3]
White	40.7	38.8	39.3	39.5	40.5	39.9	40.6	40.5	38.6	39.3	−0.2
Black or African American	19.7	19.4	19.0	21.3	20.3	22.0	19.7	18.7	20.3	22.1	0.2
Asian or Pacific Islander	15.6	16.4	15.4	15.1	15.7	16.9	16.3	16.4	18.9	16.8	1.2[3]
Hispanic or Latino[5]	22.4	17.5	17.6	18.1	17.8	18.9	19.6	20.1	19.2	18.1	−0.8
White, not Hispanic or Latino[5]	42.0	40.9	41.4	41.9	42.4	41.9	42.8	42.6	40.3	41.6	−0.1
Female	9.5	9.3	9.0	9.3	9.0	9.3	9.0	9.0	9.1	8.8	−0.4[3]
White	9.9	10.1	9.8	9.9	9.8	10.0	9.8	9.9	10.0	9.6	−0.1
Black or African American	8.6	7.2	7.0	8.1	6.5	8.6	7.8	7.1	8.2	7.2	−0.4
Asian or Pacific Islander	5.3	4.4	3.7	5.2	4.7	3.9	4.1	4.5	3.1	4.6	−0.8
Hispanic or Latino[5]	5.7	5.0	5.6	5.1	4.8	4.4	5.8	5.1	5.7	4.0	−1.1
White, not Hispanic or Latino[5]	10.4	10.6	10.4	10.6	10.4	10.8	10.4	10.5	10.4	10.3	0.0
Non-Hodgkin's lymphoma											
Male	22.6	24.9	24.5	23.8	22.8	24.1	23.3	23.7	23.2	23.1	0.0
White	23.7	26.1	25.8	24.7	24.0	25.1	24.7	24.8	24.4	24.3	0.0
Black or African American	17.4	21.2	18.7	22.5	17.1	18.0	17.4	17.7	17.7	18.3	−0.3
Asian or Pacific Islander	16.5	16.2	16.7	16.2	15.3	18.9	15.7	17.4	15.8	15.3	−0.2
Hispanic or Latino[5]	17.8	20.8	21.0	18.3	19.6	17.9	19.7	18.0	19.4	17.9	−0.2
White, not Hispanic or Latino[5]	24.7	26.7	26.4	25.5	24.7	26.2	25.2	25.4	24.3	24.4	−0.2
Female	14.5	15.1	15.1	15.9	16.1	16.0	15.7	15.8	16.0	16.5	1.0[3]
White	15.4	15.8	15.9	16.7	17.0	17.0	16.6	16.6	17.0	17.2	1.0[3]
Black or African American	10.2	10.0	11.4	11.8	12.7	10.9	11.8	12.0	11.4	12.9	2.1[3]
Asian or Pacific Islander	9.1	11.6	9.4	10.9	10.8	11.1	11.1	12.5	11.6	12.1	1.6[3]
Hispanic or Latino[5]	13.6	12.9	13.2	14.4	14.0	14.1	13.4	14.0	12.6	13.7	0.5
White, not Hispanic or Latino[5]	15.7	16.2	16.4	16.9	17.2	17.4	16.9	16.9	17.6	17.5	1.0[3]
Leukemia											
Male	17.0	17.4	16.6	16.8	16.8	16.3	16.1	16.6	15.6	15.2	−0.7[3]
White	17.8	18.7	17.4	18.0	17.9	17.2	17.1	17.8	16.8	16.0	−0.6[3]
Black or African American	16.0	13.0	14.1	13.8	13.1	13.3	13.2	12.0	11.3	12.5	−1.3[3]
Asian or Pacific Islander	8.5	10.0	10.9	8.8	10.1	10.5	9.9	10.0	8.9	9.4	−0.2
Hispanic or Latino[5]	11.9	14.6	12.1	12.5	12.1	11.5	12.4	10.9	11.3	10.4	−0.6
White, not Hispanic or Latino[5]	18.2	19.0	17.4	17.8	18.5	17.2	17.5	18.2	16.9	16.5	−0.7[3]
Female	9.8	10.0	10.0	9.8	9.8	9.2	9.8	9.8	9.2	8.8	−0.6[3]
White	10.2	10.7	10.4	10.4	10.4	9.7	10.4	10.5	9.8	9.2	−0.5
Black or African American	8.4	8.0	8.5	8.1	7.4	7.5	9.0	8.4	7.1	7.6	−1.2
Asian or Pacific Islander	6.0	6.3	6.3	5.7	6.5	6.2	6.1	4.9	5.9	5.8	−1.0
Hispanic or Latino[5]	8.4	8.2	7.1	8.9	8.9	7.8	7.5	7.0	7.7	5.9	−1.3
White, not Hispanic or Latino[5]	10.4	10.5	10.4	10.4	10.4	9.8	10.3	10.7	9.9	9.4	−0.3

- - - Data not available.

0.0 Annual percent change (APC) is greater than −0.05 but less than 0.05.

[1]Annual percent change (APC) has been calculated by fitting a linear regression model to the natural logarithm of the yearly rates from 1990–2003.

[2]Age adjusted by 5-year age groups to the year 2000 U.S. standard population. Age-adjusted rates are based on at least 25 cases. See Appendix II, Age adjustment.

[3]APC is significantly different from 0 (p < 0.05).

[4]Estimates for American Indian or Alaska Native population include data from Alaska, Atlanta, Connecticut, Detroit, Iowa, New Mexico, Seattle, and Utah. Estimates for American Indian or Alaska Native are not shown for some sites because of the small number of annual cases. Rates for American Indian or Alaska Native are suppressed for diagnosis year 2003 because of on-going research to ensure proper identification of cases among this population. American Indian or Alaska Native APC estimates are based on the time period 1990–2002 rather than 1990–2003.

[5]Hispanic data exclude data from Alaska, Hawaii, and Seattle. The race groups, white, black, Asian or Pacific Islander, and American Indian or Alaska Native, include persons of Hispanic and non-Hispanic origin. Persons of Hispanic origin may be of any race. The NAACCR Hispanic Identification Algorithm was used on a combination of variables to classify cases as Hispanic for analytic purposes. See the report, NAACCR Guideline for Enhancing Hispanic-Latino Identification, for more information; available from: seer.cancer.gov/seerstat/variables/seer/yr1973_2003/race_ethnicity/. See Appendix II, Hispanic origin.

[6]Includes corpus uteri only cases and not uterus, not elsewhere specified cases.

NOTES: See Appendix II, Incidence. Estimates are based on 13 SEER areas November 2005 submission and differ from published estimates based on 9 SEER areas or other submission dates. See Appendix I, SEER. The site variable distinguishes Kaposi Sarcoma and Mesothelioma as individual cancer sites. As a result, Kaposi Sarcoma and Mesothelioma cases do not contribute to other cancer sites. Numbers have been revised and differ from previous editions of *Health, United States*. Data for additional years are available. See Appendix III.

SOURCE: National Institutes of Health, National Cancer Institute, Surveillance, Epidemiology, and End Results (SEER) Program. Available from: www.seer.cancer.gov.

Table 54. Five-year relative cancer survival rates for selected cancer sites, by race and sex: Selected geographic areas, selected years 1975–1977 through 1996–2002

[Data are based on the Surveillance, Epidemiology, and End Results (SEER) Program's 9 population-based cancer registries]

Sex and site	White						Black or African American					
	1975–1977	1981–1983	1987–1989	1990–1992	1993–1995	1996–2002	1975–1977	1981–1983	1987–1989	1990–1992	1993–1995	1996–2002
Both sexes					Percent of patients							
All sites	50.9	52.7	57.7	62.4	64.0	67.5	39.8	39.5	43.7	48.3	53.4	57.2
Oral cavity and pharynx.	54.5	55.0	56.6	58.8	61.4	62.2	36.4	31.6	34.6	33.5	38.7	39.9
Esophagus.	5.7	7.5	11.0	13.5	14.6	17.1	3.1	4.3	6.4	9.4	7.6	11.9
Stomach	14.7	16.9	19.1	19.4	20.9	21.9	16.3	17.2	19.9	24.5	20.0	23.3
Colon	51.6	56.7	61.7	64.0	62.1	66.1	46.3	49.7	53.2	54.4	52.5	54.3
Rectum	49.2	53.7	59.5	61.3	62.4	66.4	45.0	40.9	53.6	52.0	55.4	58.6
Pancreas.	2.5	2.8	3.4	4.6	4.3	4.9	2.3	3.7	5.7	3.6	3.7	4.7
Lung and bronchus.	12.8	13.9	13.8	14.6	15.3	15.8	11.5	11.7	11.2	10.8	13.2	12.8
Urinary bladder.	74.3	79.2	81.4	82.0	83.4	82.9	50.4	60.2	63.4	64.8	62.7	64.5
Non-Hodgkin's lymphoma . . .	48.3	52.7	52.7	52.9	54.8	64.0	48.4	50.4	47.5	42.2	42.1	56.3
Leukemia.	35.8	40.1	45.3	47.8	49.6	50.3	33.4	34.2	37.0	37.2	42.2	38.7
Male												
All sites	43.2	47.5	53.3	61.5	63.5	67.8	32.7	34.2	38.8	47.5	54.7	60.3
Oral cavity and pharynx.	53.9	53.8	54.3	57.2	60.8	62.0	30.2	26.3	30.4	28.6	33.4	35.1
Esophagus.	5.1	6.8	11.4	12.8	14.8	16.9	1.6	3.6	5.0	9.8	8.1	10.8
Stomach	13.7	16.0	16.0	16.4	19.7	20.5	16.4	17.1	17.2	23.7	18.0	21.2
Colon	51.1	57.5	62.5	64.5	62.5	67.6	45.3	46.0	51.6	56.2	52.2	56.3
Rectum	48.3	52.3	59.8	60.6	61.6	66.0	41.6	38.2	49.0	54.2	53.7	57.9
Pancreas.	2.7	2.3	3.2	4.4	4.0	5.3	2.7	4.0	5.1	3.2	3.5	3.2
Lung and bronchus.	11.5	12.3	12.5	13.0	13.3	13.7	10.7	10.5	11.1	9.6	11.7	11.3
Prostate gland	69.6	75.0	85.4	95.8	98.3	99.9	61.3	63.7	72.2	85.9	93.7	98.0
Urinary bladder.	75.5	80.3	83.5	84.4	85.2	84.2	56.4	65.5	68.0	67.9	70.4	68.9
Non-Hodgkin's lymphoma . . .	47.7	52.4	49.2	48.4	51.0	62.5	41.4	49.5	42.6	38.2	35.6	52.9
Leukemia.	34.8	40.0	47.4	48.0	50.5	50.5	30.4	33.7	35.0	31.3	42.0	39.4
Female												
All sites	57.7	57.5	62.0	63.5	64.4	67.1	47.2	45.5	48.9	49.2	51.8	53.9
Colon	52.0	56.0	60.9	63.6	61.7	64.8	46.7	52.4	54.5	53.0	52.6	52.7
Rectum	50.3	55.3	59.2	62.2	63.3	66.9	47.8	43.5	58.0	49.4	57.2	59.2
Pancreas.	2.2	3.3	3.5	4.8	4.5	4.5	2.0	3.2	6.1	4.0	3.8	5.8
Lung and bronchus.	16.0	17.0	15.8	16.7	17.8	18.0	14.0	14.9	11.5	12.9	15.8	14.9
Melanoma of skin	86.5	87.7	91.3	92.1	92.8	93.9	*	*	90.5	*	*	75.0
Breast	75.8	77.7	85.3	86.7	88.0	90.1	62.5	64.0	71.2	71.6	72.9	77.3
Cervix uteri	70.6	68.9	73.6	71.9	74.7	74.6	64.8	61.6	58.4	58.6	64.3	66.3
Corpus uteri[1]	89.0	83.9	85.7	87.2	86.6	87.0	61.8	54.4	59.3	57.1	62.3	62.2
Ovary	36.4	40.2	39.9	42.5	42.6	44.6	43.4	39.3	35.5	36.8	42.6	38.9
Non-Hodgkin's lymphoma . . .	48.9	53.0	57.1	58.6	59.6	65.8	56.1	51.5	53.5	47.8	54.5	60.7

* Data for population groups with fewer than 25 cases are not shown because estimates are considered unreliable.

[1] Includes corpus uteri only cases and not uterus, not elsewhere specified cases.

NOTES: Rates are based on followup of patients through 2003. The rate is the ratio of the observed survival rate for the patient group to the expected survival rate for persons in the general population similar to the patient group with respect to age, sex, race, and calendar year of observation. It estimates the chance of surviving the effects of cancer. The site variable distinguishes Kaposi Sarcoma and Mesothelioma as individual cancer sites. As a result, Kaposi Sarcoma and Mesothelioma cases are excluded from each of the sites shown except all sites combined. The race groups, white and black, include persons of Hispanic and non-Hispanic origin. Due to death certificate race-ethnicity classification and other methodological issues related to developing life tables, survival rates for race-ethnicity groups other than white and black are not calculated. Numbers have been revised and differ from previous editions of *Health, United States*. Data for additional years are available. See Appendix III.

SOURCE: National Institutes of Health, National Cancer Institute, Surveillance, Epidemiology, and End Results (SEER) Program. Available from: www.seer.cancer.gov.

Table 55. Diabetes among adults 20 years of age and over, by sex, age, and race and Hispanic origin: United States, 1988–1994 and 2001–2004

[Data are based on interviews and physical examinations of a sample of the civilian noninstitutionalized population]

Sex, age, and race and Hispanic origin[3]	Physician-diagnosed and undiagnosed diabetes[1,2]		Physician-diagnosed diabetes[1]		Undiagnosed diabetes[2]	
	1988–1994	2001–2004	1988–1994	2001–2004	1988–1994	2001–2004
20 years and over, age adjusted[4]	Percent of population					
All persons[5]	8.4	10.3	5.4	7.3	3.0	3.0
Male	8.8	11.8	5.4	7.6	3.5	4.3
Female.	8.0	8.9	5.4	7.1	2.6	1.8
Not Hispanic or Latino:						
White only.	7.5	8.9	5.0	6.2	2.6	2.8
Black or African American only	12.6	14.3	8.6	11.4	4.2	*3.1
Mexican	14.1	14.9	9.7	11.8	4.7	3.3
20 years and over, crude						
All persons[5]	7.8	10.0	5.1	7.2	2.7	2.9
Male	7.9	11.2	4.8	7.2	3.0	4.0
Female.	7.8	8.9	5.4	7.2	2.4	1.8
Not Hispanic or Latino:						
White only.	7.5	9.4	5.0	6.5	2.5	2.9
Black or African American only	10.4	12.7	6.9	10.1	3.4	*2.6
Mexican	9.0	9.2	5.6	7.0	3.4	*2.1
Age						
20–39 years	1.6	2.3	1.1	1.6	0.6	*
40–59 years	8.9	11.0	5.5	7.9	3.4	3.0
60 years and over	18.9	22.5	12.8	16.2	6.1	6.3

* Estimates are considered unreliable. Data preceded by an asterisk have a relative standard error (RSE) of 20%–30%. Data not shown have an RSE of greater than 30%.

[1]Physician-diagnosed diabetes was obtained by self-report and excludes women who reported having diabetes only during pregnancy.

[2]Undiagnosed diabetes is defined as a fasting blood glucose of at least 126 mg/dL and no reported physician diagnosis.

[3]Persons of Mexican origin may be of any race. Starting with 1999 data, race-specific estimates are tabulated according to the 1997 Revisions to the Standards for the Classification of Federal Data on Race and Ethnicity and are not strictly comparable with estimates for earlier years. The two non-Hispanic race categories shown in the table conform to the 1997 Standards. Starting with 1999 data, race-specific estimates are for persons who reported only one racial group. Prior to data year 1999, estimates were tabulated according to the 1977 Standards. Estimates for single-race categories prior to 1999 included persons who reported one race or, if they reported more than one race, identified one race as best representing their race. See Appendix II, Hispanic origin; Race.

[4]Estimates are age adjusted to the year 2000 standard population using three age groups: 20–39 years, 40–59 years, and 60 years and over. Age-adjusted estimates in this table may differ from other age-adjusted estimates based on the same data and presented elsewhere if different age groups are used in the adjustment procedure. See Appendix II, Age adjustment.

[5]Includes all other races and Hispanic origins not shown separately.

NOTES: Standard errors are available in the spreadsheet version of this table. Available from: www.cdc.gov/nchs/hus.htm. Data have been revised and differ from previous editions of Health, United States. Data for additional years are available. See Appendix III.

SOURCE: Centers for Disease Control and Prevention, National Center for Health Statistics, National Health and Nutrition Examination Survey.

Table 56 (page 1 of 2). Severe headache or migraine, low back pain, and neck pain among adults 18 years of age and over, by selected characteristics: United States, selected years 1997–2004

[Data are based on household interviews of a sample of the civilian noninstitutionalized population]

Characteristic	Severe headache or migraine[1]			Low back pain[1]			Neck pain[1]		
	1997	2003	2004	1997	2003	2004	1997	2003	2004
	Percent of adults with pain during past 3 months								
Total, age-adjusted[2,3]	15.8	15.1	15.3	28.2	27.4	27.1	14.7	14.7	14.6
Total, crude[3]	16.0	15.2	15.3	28.1	27.5	27.2	14.6	14.8	14.8
Age									
18–44 years	18.7	17.8	18.4	26.1	24.2	23.9	13.3	12.5	12.4
18–24 years	18.7	16.8	18.4	21.9	19.6	19.2	9.8	9.1	8.9
25–44 years	18.7	18.1	18.4	27.3	25.8	25.5	14.3	13.7	13.6
45–64 years	15.8	15.1	15.0	31.3	31.5	30.8	17.0	18.2	18.7
45–54 years	17.8	16.5	16.9	31.3	30.2	29.5	17.3	17.9	18.1
55–64 years	12.7	13.1	12.4	31.2	33.4	32.6	16.6	18.5	19.5
65 years and over	7.0	6.9	6.2	29.5	29.9	30.4	15.0	15.1	14.4
65–74 years	8.2	7.9	7.1	30.2	30.8	28.5	15.0	15.6	13.9
75 years and over	5.4	5.7	5.1	28.6	28.9	32.5	15.0	14.5	15.0
Sex[2]									
Male	9.9	9.2	9.7	26.5	25.1	25.0	12.6	12.0	12.1
Female	21.4	20.7	20.7	29.6	29.4	29.0	16.6	17.1	17.0
Sex and age									
Male:									
18–44 years	11.9	10.8	11.0	24.8	22.4	22.0	11.6	10.3	10.0
45–54 years	10.3	9.7	11.2	29.4	29.3	27.4	13.9	14.7	14.6
55–64 years	8.8	8.5	8.8	30.7	30.5	31.2	14.6	15.2	17.0
65–74 years	5.0	5.8	5.6	29.0	25.6	25.7	13.6	12.5	11.8
75 years and over	*2.4	3.2	3.8	22.5	25.1	29.1	12.6	12.6	13.0
Female:									
18–44 years	25.4	24.6	25.6	27.3	26.0	25.8	14.9	14.7	14.9
45–54 years	24.9	22.9	22.3	33.1	31.1	31.6	20.6	21.0	21.4
55–64 years	16.3	17.5	15.7	31.7	36.1	33.9	18.4	21.6	21.7
65–74 years	10.7	9.6	8.2	31.1	35.0	30.9	16.1	18.2	15.6
75 years and over	7.4	7.4	6.0	32.4	31.4	34.6	16.5	15.8	16.3
Race[2,4]									
White only	15.9	15.1	15.5	28.7	27.9	27.8	15.1	15.2	15.4
Black or African American only	16.7	15.2	15.0	26.9	25.0	24.0	13.3	12.1	10.8
American Indian or Alaska Native only	18.9	28.6	19.1	33.3	32.2	35.3	16.2	17.4	18.8
Asian only	11.7	11.9	10.1	21.0	19.7	18.3	9.2	9.1	9.0
Native Hawaiian or Other Pacific Islander only	- - -	*	*	- - -	*	*	- - -	*	*
2 or more races	- - -	23.2	24.8	- - -	34.9	34.4	- - -	20.5	19.0
Hispanic origin and race[2,4]									
Hispanic or Latino	15.5	15.9	15.7	26.4	26.5	23.6	13.9	14.6	13.4
Mexican	14.6	15.3	15.8	25.2	24.6	22.1	12.9	12.5	12.7
Not Hispanic or Latino	15.9	15.2	15.5	28.4	27.6	27.6	14.9	14.9	15.0
White only	16.1	15.3	15.8	29.1	28.4	28.7	15.4	15.6	16.0
Black or African American only	16.8	15.2	15.0	26.9	24.9	23.8	13.3	12.0	10.7
Education[5,6]									
25 years of age and over:									
No high school diploma or GED	19.2	17.7	18.7	33.6	31.6	33.3	16.5	17.0	18.1
High school diploma or GED	16.0	15.3	14.6	30.2	29.6	29.7	15.5	14.8	15.5
Some college or more	13.8	13.8	14.1	26.9	27.3	26.2	14.6	15.3	14.7

See footnotes at end of table.

Table 56 (page 2 of 2). Severe headache or migraine, low back pain, and neck pain among adults 18 years of age and over, by selected characteristics: United States, selected years 1997–2004

[Data are based on household interviews of a sample of the civilian noninstitutionalized population]

Characteristic	Severe headache or migraine[1]			Low back pain[1]			Neck pain[1]		
	1997	2003	2004	1997	2003	2004	1997	2003	2004
Percent of poverty level[2,7]	Percent of adults with pain during the past 3 months								
Below 100%	23.3	21.0	20.8	35.4	33.2	32.9	18.6	17.9	18.6
100%-less than 200%	18.9	18.7	18.8	30.8	30.6	29.8	16.1	16.3	16.0
200% or more	13.8	13.3	13.6	26.3	25.8	25.7	13.8	13.8	13.8
Hispanic origin and race and percent of poverty level[2,4,7]									
Hispanic or Latino:									
Below 100%	18.9	19.8	19.6	29.5	29.7	27.3	16.4	16.1	16.6
100%-less than 200%	15.7	16.4	16.8	26.8	26.6	24.1	12.9	16.9	13.2
200% or more	13.4	13.8	13.3	24.3	25.3	21.9	13.3	12.9	12.1
Not Hispanic or Latino:									
White only:									
Below 100%	26.2	21.7	22.8	38.9	35.9	37.2	20.5	19.7	22.3
100%-less than 200%	20.1	21.0	21.3	33.3	33.0	33.9	18.0	18.0	19.0
200% or more	14.1	13.6	14.1	27.1	26.8	27.0	14.4	14.7	14.9
Black or African American only:									
Below 100%	22.7	21.0	19.4	34.5	31.2	30.9	17.9	16.0	14.3
100%-less than 200%	17.6	15.9	16.5	27.7	27.6	26.3	14.0	12.7	10.7
200% or more	13.4	12.5	12.6	23.1	22.0	20.6	10.9	10.3	9.6
Geographic region[2]									
Northeast	14.5	14.1	13.3	27.1	27.3	27.7	14.0	14.3	14.9
Midwest	15.6	14.9	15.9	28.7	29.0	28.5	15.3	15.2	14.9
South	17.1	15.6	15.8	27.5	25.1	26.0	13.9	13.5	13.6
West	15.3	15.6	15.7	30.0	29.5	27.0	16.1	16.5	15.9
Location of residence[2]									
Within MSA[8]	15.2	14.6	14.6	27.0	26.5	26.2	14.2	14.5	14.1
Outside MSA[8]	18.1	17.4	18.3	32.5	30.7	30.4	16.4	15.2	16.7

* Estimates are considered unreliable. Data preceded by an asterisk have a relative standard error (RSE) of 20%–30%. Data not shown have an RSE greater than 30%.

- - - Data not available.

[1]In three separate questions, respondents were asked, "During the past 3 months, did you have a severe headache or migraine? ...low back pain? ...neck pain?" Respondents were instructed to report pain that had lasted a whole day or more and, conversely, not to report fleeting or minor aches or pains. Persons may be represented in more than one column.

[2]Estimates are age adjusted to the year 2000 standard population using five age groups: 18–44 years, 45–54 years, 55–64 years, 65–74 years, and 75 years and over. Age-adjusted estimates in this table may differ from other age-adjusted estimates based on the same data and presented elsewhere if different age groups are used in the adjustment procedure. See Appendix II, Age adjustment.

[3]Includes all other races not shown separately and unknown education level.

[4]The race groups, white, black, American Indian or Alaska Native, Asian, Native Hawaiian or Other Pacific Islander, and 2 or more races, include persons of Hispanic and non-Hispanic origin. Persons of Hispanic origin may be of any race. Starting with 1999 data, race-specific estimates are tabulated according to the 1997 Revisions to the Standards for the Classification of Federal Data on Race and Ethnicity and are not strictly comparable with estimates for earlier years. The five single race categories plus multiple race categories shown in the table conform to the 1997 Standards. Starting with 1999 data, race-specific estimates are for persons who reported only one racial group; the category 2 or more races includes persons who reported more than one racial group. Prior to 1999, data were tabulated according to the 1977 Standards with four racial groups and the Asian only category included Native Hawaiian or Other Pacific Islander. Estimates for single race categories prior to 1999 included persons who reported one race or, if they reported more than one race, identified one race as best representing their race. Starting with 2003 data, race responses of other race and unspecified multiple race were treated as missing, and then race was imputed if these were the only race responses. Almost all persons with a race response of other race were of Hispanic origin. See Appendix II, Hispanic origin; Race.

[5]Estimates are for persons 25 years of age and over and are age adjusted to the year 2000 standard population using five age groups: 25–44 years, 45–54 years, 55–64 years, 65–74 years, and 75 years and over. See Appendix II, Age adjustment.

[6]GED stands for General Educational Development high school equivalency diploma. See Appendix II, Education.

[7]Percent of poverty level is based on family income and family size and composition using U.S. Census Bureau poverty thresholds. Missing family income data were imputed for 27%–31% of persons 18 years of age and over in 1997–1998 and 33%–36% in 1999–2004. See Appendix II, Family Income; Poverty.

[8]MSA is metropolitan statistical area.

NOTES: Standard errors are available in the spreadsheet version of this table. Available from: www.cdc.gov/nchs/hus.htm. Data for additional years are available. See Appendix III.

SOURCE: Centers for Disease Control and Prevention, National Center for Health Statistics, National Health Interview Survey, sample adult questionnaire.

Table 57 (page 1 of 4). Joint pain among adults 18 years of age and over, by selected characteristics: United States, 2002–2004

[Data are based on household interviews of a sample of the civilian noninstitutionalized population]

Characteristic	Any joint pain[1]			Knee pain[1]			Shoulder pain[1]		
	2002	2003	2004	2002	2003	2004	2002	2003	2004
	Percent of adults reporting joint pain in past 30 days								
Total, age-adjusted[2,3]	29.5	31.6	30.8	16.5	18.8	18.2	8.6	9.7	9.2
Total, crude[3]	29.5	31.8	31.1	16.5	18.9	18.4	8.7	9.7	9.4
Age									
18–44 years	19.3	20.7	19.2	10.5	12.2	11.4	4.9	5.8	5.0
18–24 years	14.2	14.7	12.9	8.3	9.0	8.0	3.4	3.1	2.8
25–44 years	21.0	22.7	21.4	11.2	13.3	12.6	5.4	6.8	5.7
45–64 years	37.5	40.2	39.8	20.4	23.6	22.8	12.3	13.1	13.4
45–54 years	34.3	36.3	36.5	18.4	20.7	20.7	10.5	11.9	12.6
55–64 years	42.3	45.9	44.5	23.4	27.8	25.8	15.1	14.8	14.5
65 years and over	47.2	50.7	51.6	28.6	31.2	31.6	14.1	15.6	15.2
65–74 years	46.0	49.3	49.3	27.6	30.5	30.4	14.0	15.7	14.1
75 years and over	48.7	52.4	54.2	29.7	32.1	32.9	14.1	15.6	16.5
Sex[2]									
Male	28.0	29.2	29.3	15.2	17.1	17.1	8.4	9.4	9.4
Female	30.7	33.7	32.2	17.6	20.3	19.2	8.8	9.8	9.0
Sex and age									
Male:									
18–44 years	20.1	20.6	19.5	10.7	12.4	11.5	5.5	6.4	5.5
45–54 years	31.1	33.4	34.0	16.2	19.0	19.0	9.5	11.3	13.1
55–64 years	37.3	39.3	41.2	20.1	22.3	23.5	13.7	14.4	14.7
65–74 years	41.7	41.9	43.3	24.1	24.3	25.6	13.3	12.9	12.7
75 years and over	43.9	47.3	49.8	25.7	28.0	30.9	11.4	13.8	14.6
Female:									
18–44 years	18.4	20.8	18.9	10.2	12.1	11.3	4.2	5.3	4.4
45–54 years	37.3	39.2	38.9	20.5	22.3	22.3	11.4	12.6	12.1
55–64 years	46.8	51.9	47.6	26.4	32.8	27.9	16.3	15.1	14.3
65–74 years	49.6	55.4	54.4	30.5	35.6	34.5	14.7	17.9	15.3
75 years and over	51.6	55.6	57.0	32.1	34.7	34.2	15.7	16.7	17.8
Race[2,4]									
White only	29.8	32.2	31.6	16.3	18.9	18.6	8.8	9.7	9.5
Black or African American only	30.8	30.2	28.1	20.2	20.3	18.2	8.3	9.8	7.7
American Indian or Alaska Native only	36.7	39.6	38.3	24.5	29.5	23.4	*11.3	*14.4	*14.2
Asian only	18.1	20.1	20.0	8.5	12.2	10.8	3.9	6.8	6.3
Native Hawaiian or Other Pacific Islander only	*	*	*	*	*	*	*	*	*
2 or more races	42.7	39.2	37.7	28.1	23.2	20.3	15.4	12.8	13.1
Hispanic origin and race[2,4]									
Hispanic or Latino	23.4	23.9	23.8	13.6	14.2	14.8	7.6	8.1	7.4
Mexican	24.6	23.4	23.3	14.1	14.3	15.0	8.3	7.5	7.7
Not Hispanic or Latino	30.4	32.8	31.9	17.0	19.6	18.9	8.9	10.0	9.5
White only	30.8	33.8	33.1	16.9	19.9	19.4	9.1	10.2	9.9
Black or African American only	30.8	30.1	28.1	20.1	20.3	18.3	8.3	9.7	7.8
Education[5,6]									
25 years of age and over:									
No high school diploma or GED	33.0	33.4	34.0	19.5	20.9	19.9	10.8	11.2	11.8
High school diploma or GED	32.9	34.4	34.2	18.6	20.4	20.3	10.2	11.2	10.4
Some college or more	31.1	34.4	33.2	16.9	20.0	19.3	8.8	10.1	9.5

See footnotes at end of table.

Table 57 (page 2 of 4). Joint pain among adults 18 years of age and over, by selected characteristics: United States, 2002–2004

[Data are based on household interviews of a sample of the civilian noninstitutionalized population]

Characteristic	Any joint pain[1]			Knee pain[1]			Shoulder pain[1]		
	2002	2003	2004	2002	2003	2004	2002	2003	2004
Percent of poverty level[2,7]	Percent of adults reporting joint pain in past 30 days								
Below 100%	31.7	33.7	35.7	19.9	21.5	22.7	11.2	11.8	11.3
100%–less than 200%	31.7	33.9	33.9	19.0	20.9	20.9	10.4	11.1	12.0
200% or more	28.7	30.8	31.8	15.6	18.0	18.3	8.0	9.1	9.3
Hispanic origin and race and percent of poverty level[2,4,7]									
Hispanic or Latino:									
Below 100%	26.8	24.9	27.5	16.1	15.8	16.1	11.5	8.9	8.4
100%–less than 200%	24.5	24.3	25.1	14.4	13.8	15.5	8.2	8.1	8.8
200% or more	21.4	23.3	24.4	11.7	13.8	15.3	5.4	7.9	7.0
Not Hispanic or Latino:									
White only:									
Below 100%	34.2	37.8	41.2	21.3	23.8	25.8	12.4	12.8	13.2
100%–less than 200%	34.9	39.2	38.9	20.3	24.0	23.8	11.6	12.6	14.0
200% or more	29.8	32.3	33.5	15.9	18.7	19.2	8.4	9.6	9.8
Black or African American only:									
Below 100%	31.6	35.0	33.8	20.8	23.6	24.8	9.1	12.0	9.7
100%–less than 200%	34.0	30.1	31.4	23.2	20.1	21.6	10.9	10.5	9.4
200% or more	29.1	28.2	26.4	18.5	19.0	16.4	7.1	8.4	7.5
Geographic region[2]									
Northeast	27.5	29.4	29.1	15.8	17.4	16.7	7.9	8.7	7.5
Midwest	32.1	35.5	34.7	18.4	21.8	21.2	8.6	10.9	10.2
South	29.3	30.9	30.1	16.7	18.7	18.0	9.1	9.9	9.5
West	28.4	30.2	29.3	14.6	16.8	16.6	8.6	8.7	9.3
Location of residence[2]									
Within MSA[8]	28.3	30.3	29.6	16.0	17.9	17.3	8.1	9.1	8.8
Outside MSA[8]	33.9	36.8	35.9	18.7	22.4	22.1	10.8	11.8	11.0

See footnotes at end of table.

Table 57 (page 3 of 4). Joint pain among adults 18 years of age and over, by selected characteristics: United States, 2002–2004

[Data are based on household interviews of a sample of the civilian noninstitutionalized population]

Characteristic	Finger pain[1]			Hip pain[1]		
	2002	2003	2004	2002	2003	2004
	Percent of adults reporting joint pain in past 30 days					
Total, age-adjusted[2,3]	7.5	7.8	7.6	6.6	7.2	7.5
Total, crude[3]	7.5	7.8	7.7	6.6	7.3	7.6
Age						
18–44 years	3.4	3.5	3.1	3.2	3.3	3.5
18–24 years	2.0	1.5	1.5	1.6	1.7	*1.4
25–44 years	3.9	4.1	3.7	3.8	3.8	4.2
45–64 years	11.0	10.8	11.0	9.1	10.0	10.3
45–54 years	9.1	8.8	8.9	7.8	8.3	8.8
55–64 years	13.9	13.8	14.1	11.0	12.6	12.5
65 years and over	13.9	15.9	15.4	12.9	14.5	15.1
65–74 years	14.4	15.7	14.3	12.6	14.3	13.7
75 years and over	13.3	16.0	16.7	13.3	14.7	16.8
Sex[2]						
Male	5.8	5.6	6.0	5.1	5.3	5.5
Female	8.9	9.6	8.9	8.0	8.9	9.2
Sex and age						
Male:						
18–44 years	3.0	3.0	2.8	2.5	2.5	2.5
45–54 years	6.6	6.1	7.2	5.6	5.8	5.9
55–64 years	10.5	9.4	11.1	8.0	9.0	9.2
65–74 years	11.2	11.0	10.2	10.5	10.4	11.1
75 years and over	10.0	10.6	12.2	10.1	12.0	13.1
Female:						
18–44 years	3.8	3.9	3.4	3.9	4.1	4.4
45–54 years	11.5	11.3	10.6	9.9	10.6	11.6
55–64 years	17.0	18.0	16.8	13.7	15.9	15.5
65–74 years	17.1	19.7	17.7	14.2	17.6	15.9
75 years and over	15.3	19.5	19.5	15.2	16.3	19.1
Race[2,4]						
White only	7.6	8.1	8.0	6.9	7.5	7.8
Black or African American only	6.5	5.5	5.1	5.6	5.7	6.1
American Indian or Alaska Native only	*12.9	*11.4	*9.1	*10.4	*11.2	*7.9
Asian only	*3.2	*5.1	*4.0	*2.3	*2.9	4.0
Native Hawaiian or Other Pacific Islander only	*	*	*	*	*	*
2 or more races	12.8	10.3	9.2	10.0	10.4	7.7
Hispanic origin and race[2,4]						
Hispanic or Latino	6.8	5.8	6.5	3.8	4.5	4.3
Mexican	7.8	5.8	6.5	4.0	4.1	3.9
Not Hispanic or Latino	7.6	8.0	7.7	6.9	7.6	7.9
White only	7.8	8.4	8.2	7.3	8.0	8.3
Black or African American only	6.5	5.4	5.0	5.7	5.8	6.1
Education[5,6]						
25 years of age and over:						
No high school diploma or GED	9.5	8.7	8.8	7.3	7.6	9.1
High school diploma or GED	8.3	9.1	8.9	7.3	8.2	8.5
Some college or more	8.2	8.8	8.1	7.5	8.1	8.2

See footnotes at end of table.

Table 57 (page 4 of 4). Joint pain among adults 18 years of age and over, by selected characteristics: United States, 2002–2004

[Data are based on household interviews of a sample of the civilian noninstitutionalized population]

Characteristic	Finger pain[1] 2002	Finger pain[1] 2003	Finger pain[1] 2004	Hip pain[1] 2002	Hip pain[1] 2003	Hip pain[1] 2004
Percent of poverty level[2,7]	Percent of adults reporting joint pain in past 30 days					
Below 100%	9.8	9.0	9.2	8.5	9.2	9.9
100%–less than 200%	8.9	8.2	8.9	7.5	8.3	9.0
200% or more	6.9	7.5	7.7	6.2	6.7	7.5
Hispanic origin and race and percent of poverty level[2,4,7]						
Hispanic or Latino:						
Below 100%	8.6	6.6	8.2	5.9	4.9	4.7
100%–less than 200%	8.2	5.5	6.6	3.9	5.0	4.4
200% or more	5.5	5.6	7.4	2.5	*3.8	5.3
Not Hispanic or Latino:						
White only:						
Below 100%	10.9	11.2	11.4	9.9	11.0	13.2
100%–less than 200%	9.9	9.8	10.8	9.1	10.0	11.2
200% or more	7.3	8.0	8.1	6.7	7.3	8.1
Black or African American only:						
Below 100%	7.9	6.4	5.9	8.1	9.5	7.4
100%–less than 200%	7.4	5.8	4.8	6.4	6.4	7.1
200% or more	5.6	5.0	5.7	4.5	4.0	4.8
Geographic region[2]						
Northeast	6.6	6.7	6.5	5.7	7.0	6.5
Midwest	7.5	8.2	8.2	6.9	8.0	8.5
South	7.6	8.0	7.8	7.0	7.1	7.9
West	8.0	8.0	7.5	6.4	6.7	6.7
Location of residence[2]						
Within MSA[8]	7.2	7.3	7.3	6.2	6.7	7.0
Outside MSA[8]	8.4	9.5	8.6	8.0	9.0	9.4

* Estimates are considered unreliable. Data preceded by an asterisk have a relative standard error (RSE) of 20%–30%. Data not shown have an RSE of greater than 30%.

[1]Starting with 2002 data, respondents were asked, "During the past 30 days, have you had any symptoms of pain, aching, or stiffness in or around a joint?" Respondents were instructed not to include the back or neck. To facilitate their response, respondents were shown a card illustrating the body joints. Respondents reporting more than one type of joint pain were included in each response category. This table shows the most commonly reported joints.

[2]Estimates are age adjusted to the year 2000 standard population using five age groups: 18–44 years, 45–54 years, 55–64 years, 65–74 years, and 75 years and over. See Appendix II, Age adjustment.

[3]Includes all other races not shown separately and unknown education level.

[4]The race groups, white, black, American Indian or Alaska Native, Asian, Native Hawaiian or Other Pacific Islander, and 2 or more races, include persons of Hispanic and not Hispanic origin. Persons of Hispanic origin may be of any race. The five single race categories plus multiple race categories shown in the table conform to the 1997 Revisions to the Standards for the Classification of Federal Data on Race and Ethnicity. Starting with 2003 data, race responses of other race and unspecified multiple race were treated as missing, and then race was imputed if these were the only race responses. Almost all persons with a race response of other race were of Hispanic origin. See Appendix II, Hispanic origin; Race.

[5]Estimates are for persons 25 years of age and over and are age adjusted to the year 2000 standard population using five age groups: 25–44 years, 45–54 years, 55–64 years, 65–74 years, and 75 years and over. See Appendix II, Age adjustment.

[6]GED stands for General Educational Development high school equivalency diploma. See Appendix II, Education.

[7]Percent of poverty level is based on family income and family size and composition using U.S. Census Bureau poverty thresholds. Missing family income data were imputed for 34%–36% of persons 18 years of age and over in 2002–2004. See Appendix II, Family Income; Poverty.

[8]MSA is metropolitan statistical area.

NOTES: Standard errors are available in the spreadsheet version of this table. Available from: www.cdc.gov/nchs/hus.htm.

SOURCE: Centers for Disease Control and Prevention, National Center for Health Statistics, National Health Interview Survey, sample adult questionnaire.

Table 58 (page 1 of 3). Limitation of activity caused by chronic conditions, by selected characteristics: United States, selected years 1997–2004

[Data are based on household interviews of a sample of the civilian noninstitutionalized population]

Characteristic	1997	2002	2003	2004
All ages	Percent of persons with any activity limitation [1]			
Total [2,3]	13.3	12.3	12.1	11.9
Age				
Under 18 years	6.6	7.1	6.9	7.0
Under 5 years	3.5	3.2	3.6	3.5
5–17 years	7.8	8.5	8.1	8.4
18–44 years	7.0	6.2	6.0	6.0
18–24 years	5.1	4.3	4.1	4.4
25–44 years	7.6	6.8	6.6	6.5
45–54 years	14.2	13.8	13.0	12.5
55–64 years	22.2	21.1	21.1	19.9
65 years and over	38.7	34.5	34.6	34.1
65–74 years	30.0	25.2	26.3	25.5
75 years and over	50.2	45.2	44.0	43.9
Sex [3]				
Male	13.1	12.3	11.9	11.8
Female	13.4	12.3	12.2	11.9
Race [3,4]				
White only	13.1	12.1	11.8	11.6
Black or African American only	17.1	14.9	15.3	15.3
American Indian or Alaska Native only	23.1	19.5	21.2	17.1
Asian only	7.5	6.4	6.4	6.4
Native Hawaiian or Other Pacific Islander only	- - -	*	*	*
2 or more races	- - -	22.0	20.2	18.8
Black or African American; White	- - -	*8.3	*16.8	*15.8
American Indian or Alaska Native; White	- - -	30.0	24.8	21.5
Hispanic origin and race [3,4]				
Hispanic or Latino	12.8	10.7	10.2	10.2
Mexican	12.5	10.8	9.7	10.1
Not Hispanic or Latino	13.5	12.6	12.4	12.3
White only	13.2	12.4	12.2	12.1
Black or African American only	17.0	15.0	15.4	15.3
Percent of poverty level [3,5]				
Below 100%	25.4	22.9	23.1	23.0
100%–less than 200%	17.9	17.4	17.0	16.3
200% or more	10.1	9.5	9.2	9.2
Hispanic origin and race and percent of poverty level [3,4,5]				
Hispanic or Latino:				
Below 100%	19.2	16.3	15.5	15.5
100%–less than 200%	12.7	12.2	9.9	10.5
200% or more	9.2	7.7	8.2	7.7
Not Hispanic or Latino:				
White only:				
Below 100%	27.8	25.4	26.2	26.2
100%–less than 200%	19.2	19.5	19.3	18.7
200% or more	10.4	9.7	9.4	9.5
Black or African American only:				
Below 100%	28.2	25.0	26.1	27.1
100%–less than 200%	19.5	17.9	19.0	16.6
200% or more	10.7	10.0	9.7	10.3
Geographic region [3]				
Northeast	13.0	11.8	11.3	11.0
Midwest	13.1	13.1	13.3	12.7
South	13.9	12.6	12.4	12.3
West	13.0	11.5	11.1	11.4
Location of residence [3]				
Within MSA [6]	12.7	11.4	11.2	11.2
Outside MSA [6]	15.5	15.9	15.7	14.9

See footnotes at end of table.

[Data are based on household interviews of a sample of the civilian noninstitutionalized population]

Characteristic	1997	2002	2003	2004	1997	2002	2003	2004
65 years of age and over	Percent with ADL limitation[7]				Percent with IADL limitation[7]			
All adults 65 years of age and over[2,8]	6.7	6.1	6.4	6.1	13.7	12.2	12.2	11.5
Age								
65–74 years	3.4	2.7	3.1	2.9	6.9	6.0	6.5	5.5
75 years and over	10.4	9.8	9.9	9.5	21.2	19.1	18.4	18.1
Sex[8]								
Male.	5.2	4.7	5.2	4.8	9.1	7.8	8.6	8.4
Female.	7.7	7.0	7.2	6.9	16.9	15.2	14.6	13.6
Race[4,8]								
White only.	6.3	5.6	5.9	5.8	13.1	11.5	11.5	11.0
Black or African American only	11.7	10.0	10.5	8.7	21.3	18.5	19.2	17.0
American Indian or Alaska Native only.	*	*	*	*	*	*	*	*
Asian only.	*	*	*	*8.0	*9.1	*11.2	*11.8	12.3
Native Hawaiian or Other Pacific Islander only	- - -	*	*	*	- - -	*	*	*
2 or more races.	- - -	*	*	*	- - -	*20.8	*20.4	*21.4
Hispanic origin and race[4,8]								
Hispanic or Latino	10.8	9.2	10.3	10.4	16.3	13.1	13.8	14.8
Mexican.	11.4	10.2	9.8	10.7	18.8	14.0	15.1	15.3
Not Hispanic or Latino	6.5	5.9	6.1	5.8	13.6	12.2	12.1	11.3
White only	6.1	5.5	5.7	5.5	13.0	11.5	11.4	10.7
Black or African American only.	11.7	10.1	10.4	8.7	21.2	18.7	19.0	17.1
Percent of poverty level[5,8]								
Below 100%	12.5	9.5	10.4	10.1	25.3	21.1	21.6	20.9
100%–less than 200%	7.4	6.9	7.0	6.7	15.8	14.7	15.0	13.3
200% or more	5.3	5.1	5.5	5.2	10.4	9.5	9.4	9.1
Hispanic origin and race and percent of poverty level[4,5,8]								
Hispanic or Latino:								
Below 100%	16.0	12.5	*15.2	15.9	25.5	17.3	20.1	24.0
100%–less than 200%	11.1	10.0	*8.4	*10.3	15.5	15.6	12.3	14.4
200% or more	*6.6	*6.7	*8.5	*6.6	10.2	8.7	*11.1	*8.9
Not Hispanic or Latino:								
White only:								
Below 100%.	11.8	8.2	8.9	8.2	24.9	20.4	20.7	19.2
100%–less than 200%.	6.6	6.3	6.4	6.2	15.2	14.2	14.8	12.7
200% or more.	5.0	4.8	5.1	4.9	10.3	9.2	9.0	8.8
Black or African American only:								
Below 100%.	13.5	13.8	14.0	13.9	27.8	26.6	28.3	26.0
100%–less than 200%.	12.4	*9.8	10.4	*7.4	22.4	19.3	18.9	17.7
200% or more.	9.8	8.1	8.4	*6.3	15.1	13.4	13.9	10.5

See footnotes at end of table.

Table 58 (page 3 of 3). Limitation of activity caused by chronic conditions, by selected characteristics: United States, selected years 1997–2004

[Data are based on household interviews of a sample of the civilian noninstitutionalized population]

Characteristic	1997	2002	2003	2004	1997	2002	2003	2004
Geographic region[8]	Percent with ADL limitation[7]				Percent with IADL limitation[7]			
Northeast	6.1	6.3	6.6	5.6	12.2	11.0	11.4	9.9
Midwest	5.8	5.2	4.7	5.4	13.1	11.7	11.3	11.9
South...................................	8.2	6.3	7.2	6.8	15.8	13.0	13.1	12.7
West	5.9	6.5	6.5	6.1	12.4	12.7	12.1	11.0
Location of residence[8]								
Within MSA[6]...........................	6.6	6.2	6.3	6.3	13.5	12.1	12.0	11.3
Outside MSA[6]..........................	7.2	5.6	6.7	5.3	14.4	12.6	12.8	12.4

* Estimates are considered unreliable. Data preceded by an asterisk have a relative standard error (RSE) of 20%–30%. Data not shown have an RSE of greater than 30%.

- - - Data not available.

[1]Limitation of activity is assessed by asking respondents a series of questions about limitations in their ability to perform activities usual for their age group because of a physical, mental, or emotional problem. The category limitation of activity includes limitations in personal care (ADL), routine needs (IADL), and other limitations due to a chronic condition. See Appendix II, Limitation of activity; Activities of daily living; Condition; Instrumental activities of daily living.

[2]Includes all other races not shown separately.

[3]Estimates for all persons are age adjusted to the year 2000 standard population using six age groups: Under 18 years, 18–44 years, 45–54 years, 55–64 years, 65–74 years, and 75 years and over. Age-adjusted estimates in this table may differ from other age-adjusted estimates based on the same data and presented elsewhere if different age groups are used in the adjustment procedure. See Appendix II, Age adjustment.

[4]The race groups, white, black, American Indian or Alaska Native, Asian, Native Hawaiian or Other Pacific Islander, and 2 or more races, include persons of Hispanic and non-Hispanic origin. Persons of Hispanic origin may be of any race. Starting with 1999 data, race-specific estimates are tabulated according to 1997 Revisions to the Standards for the Classification of Federal Data on Race and Ethnicity and are not strictly comparable with estimates for earlier years. The five single race categories plus multiple race categories shown in the table conform to the 1997 Standards. Starting with 1999 data, race-specific estimates are for persons who reported only one racial group; the category 2 or more races includes persons who reported more than one racial group. Prior to 1999, data were tabulated according to the 1977 Standards with four racial groups and the Asian only category included Native Hawaiian or Other Pacific Islander. Estimates for single race categories prior to 1999 included persons who reported one race or, if they reported more than one race, identified one race as best representing their race. Starting with 2003 data, race responses of other race and unspecified multiple race were treated as missing, and then race was imputed if these were the only race responses. Almost all persons with a race response of other race were of Hispanic origin. See Appendix II, Hispanic origin; Race.

[5]Percent of poverty level is based on family income and family size and composition using U.S. Census Bureau poverty thresholds. Missing family income data were imputed for 25% of persons in 1997 and 30%–35% in 1999–2004. See Appendix II, Family income; Poverty.

[6]MSA is metropolitan statistical area.

[7]These estimates are for noninstitutionalized older persons. ADL is activities of daily living and IADL is instrumental activities of daily living. Respondents were asked about needing the help of another person with personal care (ADL) and routine needs such as chores and shopping (IADL) because of a physical, mental, or emotional problem. See Appendix II, Activities of daily living; Condition; Instrumental activities of daily living.

[8]Estimates are age adjusted to the year 2000 standard population using two age groups: 65–74 years and 75 years and over. See Appendix II, Age adjustment.

NOTES: Standard errors for selected years are available in the spreadsheet version of this table. Available from: www.cdc.gov/nchs/hus.htm. Data for additional years are available. See Appendix III.

SOURCE: Centers for Disease Control and Prevention, National Center for Health Statistics, National Health Interview Survey, family core questionnaire.

Table 59 (page 1 of 2). Vision and hearing limitations among adults 18 years of age and over, by selected characteristics: United States, selected years 1997–2004

[Data are based on household interviews of a sample of the civilian noninstitutionalized population]

Characteristic	Any trouble seeing, even with glasses or contacts[1]					A lot of trouble hearing or deaf[2]				
	1997	2000	2002	2003	2004	1997	2000	2002	2003	2004
	Percent of adults									
Total, age-adjusted[3,4]	10.0	9.0	9.3	8.8	8.8	3.2	3.2	3.2	3.1	3.1
Total, crude[4]	9.8	8.9	9.3	8.7	8.9	3.1	3.1	3.1	3.0	3.1
Age										
18–44 years	6.2	5.3	5.6	5.2	5.1	1.0	0.9	0.9	0.9	0.8
18–24 years	5.4	4.2	4.4	5.1	4.3	*0.5	*0.7	*	*	*0.4
25–44 years	6.5	5.7	6.0	5.2	5.4	1.2	1.0	1.1	1.0	1.0
45–64 years	12.0	10.7	11.0	10.6	10.9	3.1	3.0	2.8	2.8	2.8
45–54 years	12.2	10.9	11.5	10.5	11.2	2.6	2.3	1.9	1.9	2.0
55–64 years	11.6	10.5	10.3	10.7	10.5	3.9	4.0	4.2	4.1	4.0
65 years and over	18.1	17.4	17.6	16.6	16.8	9.8	10.5	11.1	10.5	10.8
65–74 years	14.2	13.6	14.5	13.1	14.1	6.6	7.4	7.2	6.7	7.3
75 years and over	23.1	21.9	21.1	20.6	19.9	14.1	14.3	15.6	14.9	14.8
Sex[3]										
Male	8.8	7.9	8.1	7.3	7.6	4.2	4.3	4.2	4.0	4.1
Female	11.1	10.1	10.4	10.1	10.0	2.4	2.3	2.4	2.3	2.4
Sex and age										
Male:										
18–44 years	5.3	4.4	4.8	4.1	4.4	1.2	1.1	1.0	1.1	0.8
45–54 years	10.1	8.8	10.1	8.6	9.2	3.6	2.9	2.2	2.7	2.7
55–64 years	10.5	9.5	8.7	8.6	9.1	5.4	6.2	5.8	5.4	5.9
65–74 years	13.2	12.8	13.3	11.8	12.0	9.4	10.8	10.8	10.2	10.7
75 years and over	21.4	20.7	18.6	18.1	17.7	17.7	18.0	19.7	17.8	18.9
Female:										
18–44 years	7.1	6.2	6.5	6.2	5.8	0.9	0.8	0.7	0.7	0.9
45–54 years	14.2	12.8	12.9	12.3	13.1	1.7	1.8	1.5	1.2	1.3
55–64 years	12.6	11.5	11.9	12.5	11.7	2.6	1.9	2.7	2.8	2.3
65–74 years	15.0	14.4	15.5	14.1	15.9	4.4	4.5	4.1	3.8	4.5
75 years and over	24.2	22.7	22.6	22.3	21.4	11.7	12.1	13.0	12.9	12.2
Race[3,5]										
White only	9.7	8.8	9.0	8.5	8.8	3.4	3.4	3.3	3.3	3.4
Black or African American only	12.8	10.6	11.7	10.8	10.3	2.0	1.6	1.6	1.7	1.5
American Indian or Alaska Native only	19.2	16.6	*11.1	18.9	14.8	14.1	*	*10.1	*	*
Asian only	6.2	6.3	7.2	6.1	5.1	*	*2.4	*2.3	*	*
Native Hawaiian or Other Pacific Islander only	- - -	*	*	*	*	- - -	*	*	*	*
2 or more races	- - -	16.2	14.9	11.6	11.0	- - -	*5.7	*6.3	*	*
Hispanic origin and race[3,5]										
Hispanic or Latino	10.0	9.7	9.0	9.1	8.8	1.5	2.3	2.0	2.0	1.8
Mexican	10.2	8.3	8.6	9.0	9.0	1.8	3.0	3.0	2.6	1.8
Not Hispanic or Latino	10.0	9.1	9.4	8.8	8.9	3.3	3.3	3.3	3.2	3.2
White only	9.8	8.9	9.1	8.6	8.9	3.5	3.5	3.5	3.4	3.5
Black or African American only	12.8	10.6	11.8	10.7	10.3	2.0	1.6	1.6	1.8	1.5
Education[6,7]										
25 years of age and over:										
No high school diploma or GED	15.0	12.2	14.4	12.6	13.8	4.8	4.6	4.6	4.9	4.8
High school diploma or GED	10.6	9.5	10.3	9.3	10.3	3.7	3.9	3.9	3.5	3.7
Some college or more	8.9	8.9	8.7	8.1	7.9	2.9	2.8	3.3	2.8	3.0

See footnotes at end of table.

Table 59 (page 2 of 2). Vision and hearing limitations among adults 18 years of age and over, by selected characteristics: United States, selected years 1997–2004

[Data are based on household interviews of a sample of the civilian noninstitutionalized population]

Characteristic	Any trouble seeing, even with glasses or contacts[1]					A lot of trouble hearing or deaf[2]				
	1997	2000	2002	2003	2004	1997	2000	2002	2003	2004
Percent of poverty level[3,8]	Percent of adults									
Below 100%	17.0	12.9	14.5	13.7	14.2	4.5	3.7	4.4	3.9	3.9
100%–less than 200%	12.9	11.6	12.0	11.6	12.0	3.6	4.2	3.6	3.6	3.6
200% or more	8.2	7.8	8.0	7.3	7.4	3.0	2.8	3.0	2.8	2.9
Hispanic origin and race and percent of poverty level[3,5,8]										
Hispanic or Latino:										
Below 100%	12.8	11.0	12.9	12.4	11.2	*1.9	3.3	*2.3	*3.4	*3.0
100%–less than 200%	11.2	9.4	9.4	10.3	10.8	*1.5	*2.3	*1.7	*1.6	*1.2
200% or more	7.8	9.7	7.2	6.7	6.3	*1.2	*1.7	*1.9	*1.4	*1.5
Not Hispanic or Latino:										
White only:										
Below 100%	17.9	13.1	14.7	14.3	15.8	5.8	4.5	5.2	4.7	4.9
100%–less than 200%	13.1	12.0	12.7	11.8	13.1	4.3	5.0	4.5	4.2	4.5
200% or more	8.2	7.8	7.9	7.3	7.5	3.2	3.0	3.1	3.1	3.1
Black or African American only:										
Below 100%	17.9	13.6	16.6	14.2	15.2	3.3	*1.6	*2.3	*2.1	*2.3
100%–less than 200%	16.0	12.9	14.6	13.0	10.6	*2.0	*2.0	*	*2.3	*
200% or more	8.5	8.1	9.1	8.5	8.4	*	*	*1.6	*	*1.3
Geographic region[3]										
Northeast	8.6	7.4	7.8	7.5	7.0	2.2	2.4	2.7	2.9	2.6
Midwest	9.5	9.6	9.3	9.3	10.0	3.5	3.5	3.1	3.3	3.5
South	11.4	9.2	9.9	9.4	9.2	3.5	3.3	3.3	3.0	3.2
West	9.7	9.9	9.7	8.1	8.6	3.4	3.5	3.8	3.2	3.0
Location of residence[3]										
Within MSA[9]	9.5	8.5	8.7	8.2	8.4	2.9	3.0	3.0	2.7	2.8
Outside MSA[9]	12.0	11.1	11.5	10.7	10.6	4.5	3.9	3.8	4.4	4.2

* Estimates are considered unreliable. Data preceded by an asterisk have a relative standard error (RSE) of 20%–30%. Data not shown have an RSE greater than 30%.

- - - Data not available.

[1]Respondents were asked, "Do you have any trouble seeing, even when wearing glasses or contact lenses?" In 2004, 0.3% of adults 18 years of age and over identified themselves as blind.

[2]Respondents were asked, "Which statement best describes your hearing without a hearing aid: good, a little trouble, a lot of trouble, or deaf?" In this analysis, a lot of trouble and deaf are combined into one category. In 2004, 0.2% of adults 18 years of age and over identified themselves as deaf.

[3]Estimates are age adjusted to the year 2000 standard population using five age groups: 18–44 years, 45–54 years, 55–64 years, 65–74 years, and 75 years and over. Age-adjusted estimates in this table may differ from other age-adjusted estimates based on the same data and presented elsewhere if different age groups are used in the adjustment procedure. See Appendix II, Age adjustment.

[4]Includes all other races not shown separately and unknown education level.

[5]The race groups, white, black, American Indian or Alaska Native, Asian, Native Hawaiian or Other Pacific Islander, and 2 or more races, include persons of Hispanic and non-Hispanic origin. Persons of Hispanic origin may be of any race. Starting with 1999 data, race-specific estimates are tabulated according to the 1997 Revisions to the Standards for the Classification of Federal Data on Race and Ethnicity and are not strictly comparable with estimates for earlier years. The five single race categories plus multiple race categories shown in the table conform to the 1997 Standards. Starting with 1999 data, race-specific estimates are for persons who reported only one racial group; the category 2 or more races includes persons who reported more than one racial group. Prior to 1999, data were tabulated according to the 1977 Standards with four racial groups and the Asian only category included Native Hawaiian or Other Pacific Islander. Estimates for single race categories prior to 1999 included persons who reported one race or, if they reported more than one race, identified one race as best representing their race. Starting with 2003 data, race responses of other race and unspecified multiple race were treated as missing, and then race was imputed if these were the only race responses. Almost all persons with a race response of other race were of Hispanic origin. See Appendix II, Hispanic origin; Race.

[6]Estimates are for persons 25 years of age and over and are age adjusted to the year 2000 standard population using five age groups: 25–44 years, 45–54 years, 55–64 years, 65–74 years, and 75 years and over. See Appendix II, Age adjustment.

[7]GED stands for General Educational Development high school equivalency diploma. See Appendix II, Education.

[8]Percent of poverty level is based on family income and family size and composition using U.S. Census Bureau poverty thresholds. Missing family income data were imputed for 27%–31% of persons 18 years of age and over in 1997–1998 and 33%–36% in 1999–2004. See Appendix II, Family Income; Poverty.

[9]MSA is metropolitan statistical area.

NOTES: Standard errors are available in the spreadsheet version of this table. Available from: www.cdc.gov/nchs/hus.htm. Data for additional years are available. See Appendix III.

SOURCE: Centers for Disease Control and Prevention, National Center for Health Statistics, National Health Interview Survey, sample adult questionnaire.

[Data are based on household interviews of a sample of the civilian noninstitutionalized population]

Characteristic	1991[1]	1995[1]	1997	2000	2001	2002	2003	2004
	Percent of persons with fair or poor health[2]							
Total[3,4]	10.4	10.6	9.2	9.0	9.2	9.3	9.2	9.3
Age								
Under 18 years	2.6	2.6	2.1	1.7	1.8	1.9	1.8	1.8
Under 6 years	2.7	2.7	1.9	1.5	1.6	1.6	1.4	1.5
6–17 years	2.6	2.5	2.1	1.8	1.9	2.1	2.0	2.0
18–44 years	6.1	6.6	5.3	5.1	5.4	5.5	5.6	5.7
18–24 years	4.8	4.5	3.4	3.3	3.3	3.6	3.8	3.6
25–44 years	6.4	7.2	5.9	5.7	6.0	6.2	6.3	6.4
45–54 years	13.4	13.4	11.7	11.9	11.8	12.7	12.1	12.3
55–64 years	20.7	21.4	18.2	17.9	19.1	17.9	18.9	17.9
65 years and over	29.0	28.3	26.7	26.9	26.5	26.3	25.5	26.7
65–74 years	26.0	25.6	23.1	22.5	22.9	22.0	22.3	22.4
75 years and over	33.6	32.2	31.5	32.1	30.7	31.3	29.2	31.5
Sex[3]								
Male	10.0	10.1	8.8	8.8	9.0	8.9	8.8	9.0
Female	10.8	11.1	9.7	9.3	9.5	9.6	9.5	9.6
Race[3,5]								
White only	9.6	9.7	8.3	8.2	8.2	8.5	8.5	8.6
Black or African American only	16.8	17.2	15.8	14.6	15.4	14.1	14.7	14.6
American Indian or Alaska Native only	18.3	18.7	17.3	17.2	14.5	13.2	16.3	16.5
Asian only	7.8	9.3	7.8	7.4	8.1	6.7	7.4	8.6
Native Hawaiian or Other Pacific Islander only	- - -	- - -	- - -	*	*	*	*	*
2 or more races	- - -	- - -	- - -	16.2	13.9	12.5	14.7	12.6
Black or African American; White	- - -	- - -	- - -	*14.5	*10.1	13.8	21.4	*10.7
American Indian or Alaska Native; White	- - -	- - -	- - -	18.7	15.0	13.5	18.1	12.3
Hispanic origin and race[3,5]								
Hispanic or Latino	15.6	15.1	13.0	12.8	12.6	13.1	13.9	13.3
Mexican	17.0	16.7	13.1	12.8	12.4	13.3	13.7	13.4
Not Hispanic or Latino	10.0	10.1	8.9	8.7	8.9	8.9	8.7	8.9
White only	9.1	9.1	8.0	7.9	7.9	8.2	7.9	8.0
Black or African American only	16.8	17.3	15.8	14.6	15.5	14.0	14.6	14.6
Percent of poverty level[3,6]								
Below 100%	22.8	23.7	20.8	19.6	20.2	20.3	20.4	21.3
100%–less than 200%	14.7	15.5	13.9	14.1	14.5	14.6	14.4	14.4
200% or more	6.8	6.7	6.1	6.3	6.4	6.4	6.1	6.3
Hispanic origin and race and percent of poverty level[3,5,6]								
Hispanic or Latino:								
Below 100%	23.6	22.7	19.9	18.7	18.6	20.8	20.6	20.2
100%–less than 200%	18.0	16.9	13.5	15.3	14.7	15.4	15.5	15.2
200% or more	9.3	8.7	8.5	8.4	8.7	8.7	9.8	8.8
Not Hispanic or Latino:								
White only:								
Below 100%	21.9	22.8	19.7	18.8	19.1	19.1	19.5	20.8
100%–less than 200%	14.0	14.8	13.3	13.4	13.6	14.3	13.9	13.8
200% or more	6.4	6.2	5.6	5.8	5.9	6.0	5.6	5.7
Black or African American only:								
Below 100%	25.8	27.7	25.3	23.8	24.9	24.5	24.4	25.7
100%–less than 200%	17.0	19.3	19.2	18.2	19.6	17.4	18.6	16.7
200% or more	10.9	9.9	9.7	9.7	9.9	8.8	9.1	9.6

See footnotes at end of table.

Table 60 (page 2 of 2). Respondent-assessed health status, by selected characteristics: United States, selected years 1991–2004

[Data are based on household interviews of a sample of the civilian noninstitutionalized population]

Characteristic	1991[1]	1995[1]	1997	2000	2001	2002	2003	2004
Geographic region[3]	Percent of persons with fair or poor health[2]							
Northeast	8.3	9.1	8.0	7.6	7.4	8.1	8.2	7.6
Midwest	9.1	9.7	8.1	8.0	8.8	8.3	8.3	8.2
South.	13.1	12.3	10.8	10.7	10.8	10.9	10.7	11.2
West	9.7	10.1	8.8	8.8	8.5	8.7	8.4	8.9
Location of residence[3]								
Within MSA[7].	9.9	10.1	8.7	8.5	8.7	8.7	8.6	8.8
Outside MSA[7].	11.9	12.6	11.1	11.1	11.0	11.7	11.5	11.5

* Estimates are considered unreliable. Data preceded by an asterisk have a relative standard error (RSE) of 20%–30%. Data not shown have an RSE greater than 30%.

- - - Data not available.

[1]Data prior to 1997 are not strictly comparable with data for later years due to the 1997 questionnaire redesign. See Appendix I, National Health Interview Survey.
[2]See Appendix II, Health status, respondent-assessed.
[3]Estimates are age adjusted to the year 2000 standard population using six age groups: Under 18 years, 18–44 years, 45–54 years, 55–64 years, 65–74 years, and 75 years and over. See Appendix II, Age adjustment.
[4]Includes all other races not shown separately.
[5]The race groups, white, black, American Indian or Alaska Native, Asian, Native Hawaiian or Other Pacific Islander, and 2 or more races, include persons of Hispanic and non-Hispanic origin. Persons of Hispanic origin may be of any race. Starting with 1999 data, race-specific estimates are tabulated according to the 1997 Revisions to the Standards for the Classification of Federal Data on Race and Ethnicity and are not strictly comparable with estimates for earlier years. The five single race categories plus multiple race categories shown in the table conform to the 1997 Standards. Starting with 1999 data, race-specific estimates are for persons who reported only one racial group; the category 2 or more races includes persons who reported more than one racial group. Prior to 1999, data were tabulated according to the 1977 Standards with four racial groups and the Asian only category included Native Hawaiian or Other Pacific Islander. Estimates for single race categories prior to 1999 included persons who reported one race or, if they reported more than one race, identified one race as best representing their race. Starting with 2003 data, race responses of other race and unspecified multiple race were treated as missing, and then race was imputed if these were the only race responses. Almost all persons with a race response of other race were of Hispanic origin. See Appendix II, Hispanic origin; Race.
[6]Percent of poverty level is based on family income and family size and composition using U.S. Census Bureau poverty thresholds. Missing family income data were imputed for 16%–18% of persons in 1991 and 1995, 25%–29% of persons in 1997–1998, and 32%–35% in 1999–2004. See Appendix II, Family income; Poverty.
[7]MSA is metropolitan statistical area.

NOTES: Standard errors for selected years are available in the spreadsheet version of this table. Available from: www.cdc.gov/nchs/hus.htm. Data for additional years are available. See Appendix III.

SOURCE: Centers for Disease Control and Prevention, National Center for Health Statistics, National Health Interview Survey, family core questionnaire.

Table 61 (page 1 of 2). Serious psychological distress among adults 18 years of age and over, by selected characteristics: United States, average annual 1997–1998, 2000–2001, and 2003–2004

[Data are based on household interviews of a sample of the civilian noninstitutionalized population]

Characteristic	1997–1998	2000–2001	2003–2004
	Percent of persons with serious psychological distress [1]		
Total, age adjusted [2,3].	3.2	3.2	3.1
Total, crude [3].	3.2	3.2	3.1
Age			
18–44 years	2.9	3.1	2.9
18–24 years.	2.7	2.7	2.8
25–44 years.	3.0	3.2	2.9
45–64 years	3.7	3.7	3.9
45–54 years.	3.9	3.7	3.9
55–64 years.	3.4	3.8	3.9
65 years and over	3.1	2.7	2.4
65–74 years.	2.5	2.8	2.3
75 years and over	3.8	2.5	2.5
Sex [2]			
Male.	2.5	2.4	2.3
Female.	3.8	3.9	3.9
Race [2,4]			
White only.	3.1	3.1	3.1
Black or African American only	4.0	3.5	3.4
American Indian or Alaska Native only.	7.8	*9.3	*5.5
Asian only.	2.0	*	*1.8
Native Hawaiian or Other Pacific Islander only	- - -	*	*
2 or more races.	- - -	5.2	9.1
Hispanic origin and race [2,4]			
Hispanic or Latino	5.0	4.2	3.9
Mexican.	5.2	4.0	3.6
Not Hispanic or Latino	3.0	3.1	3.1
White only	2.9	3.1	3.0
Black or African American only.	3.9	3.5	3.2
Percent of poverty level [2,5]			
Below 100%.	9.1	8.3	8.8
100%–less than 200%	5.0	5.3	5.4
200% or more.	1.8	2.0	1.7
Hispanic origin and race and percent of poverty level [2,4,5]			
Hispanic or Latino:			
Below 100%	8.6	7.2	7.4
100%–less than 200%	5.4	4.4	3.8
200% or more	2.9	2.8	2.4
Not Hispanic or Latino:			
White only:			
Below 100%.	9.6	9.4	10.1
100%–less than 200%.	5.2	6.1	6.4
200% or more.	1.8	2.0	1.7
Black or African American only:			
Below 100%.	8.7	7.3	7.3
100%–less than 200%.	4.3	4.9	*4.0
200% or more.	1.6	*1.6	*1.3

See footnotes at end of table.

Table 61 (page 2 of 2). Serious psychological distress among adults 18 years of age and over, by selected characteristics: United States, average annual 1997–1998, 2000–2001, and 2003–2004

[Data are based on household interviews of a sample of the civilian noninstitutionalized population]

Characteristic	1997–1998	2000–2001	2003–2004
	Percent of persons with serious psychological distress [1]		
Northeast	2.7	3.1	2.9
Midwest	2.6	3.0	2.7
South	3.8	3.4	3.5
West	3.3	3.2	3.0
Location of residence [2]			
Within MSA [6]	3.0	3.1	2.9
Outside MSA [6]	3.9	3.5	3.8

* Estimates are considered unreliable. Data preceded by an asterisk have a relative standard error (RSE) of 20%–30%. Data not shown have an RSE greater than 30%.

- - - Data not available.

[1] Serious psychological distress is measured by a six-question scale that asks respondents how often they experience each of six symptoms of psychological distress. See Appendix II, Serious psychological distress.

[2] Estimates are age adjusted to the year 2000 standard population using five age groups: 18–44 years, 45–54 years, 55–64 years, 65–74 years, and 75 years and over. See Appendix II, Age adjustment.

[3] Includes all other races not shown separately.

[4] The race groups, white, black, American Indian or Alaska Native, Asian, Native Hawaiian or Other Pacific Islander, and 2 or more races, include persons of Hispanic and non-Hispanic origin. Persons of Hispanic origin may be of any race. Starting with 1999 data, race-specific estimates are tabulated according to the 1997 Revisions to the Standards for the Classification of Federal Data on Race and Ethnicity and are not strictly comparable with estimates for earlier years. The five single race categories plus multiple race categories shown in the table conform to the 1997 Standards. Starting with 1999 data, race-specific estimates are for persons who reported only one racial group; the category 2 or more races includes persons who reported more than one racial group. Prior to 1999, data were tabulated according to the 1977 Standards with four racial groups and the Asian only category included Native Hawaiian or Other Pacific Islander. Estimates for single race categories prior to 1999 included persons who reported one race or, if they reported more than one race, identified one race as best representing their race. Starting with 2003 data, race responses of other race and unspecified multiple race were treated as missing, and then race was imputed if these were the only race responses. Almost all persons with a race response of other race were of Hispanic origin. See Appendix II, Hispanic origin; Race.

[5] Percent of poverty level is based on family income and family size and composition using U.S. Census Bureau poverty thresholds. Missing family income data were imputed for 27%–31% of persons 18 years of age and over in 1997–1998 and 33%–36% in 1999–2004. See Appendix II, Family Income; Poverty.

[6] MSA is metropolitan statistical area.

NOTES: Standard errors for selected years are available in the spreadsheet version of this table. Available from: www.cdc.gov/nchs/hus.htm.

SOURCE: Centers for Disease Control and Prevention, National Center for Health Statistics, National Health Interview Survey, family core questionnaire.

Table 62 (page 1 of 2). Suicidal ideation, suicide attempts, and injurious suicide attempts among students in grades 9–12, by sex, grade level, race, and Hispanic origin: United States, selected years 1991–2005

[Data are based on a national sample of high school students, grades 9–12]

Sex, grade level, race, and Hispanic origin	1991	1993	1995	1997	1999	2001	2003	2005
	Percent of students who seriously considered suicide[1]							
Total	29.0	24.1	24.1	20.5	19.3	19.0	16.9	16.9
Male								
Total	20.8	18.8	18.3	15.1	13.7	14.2	12.8	12.0
9th grade	17.6	17.7	18.2	16.1	11.9	14.7	11.9	12.2
10th grade	19.5	18.0	16.7	14.5	13.7	13.8	13.2	11.9
11th grade	25.3	20.6	21.7	16.6	13.7	14.1	12.9	11.9
12th grade	20.7	18.3	16.3	13.5	15.6	13.7	13.2	11.6
Not Hispanic or Latino:								
White	21.7	19.1	19.1	14.4	12.5	14.9	12.0	12.4
Black or African American.........	13.3	15.4	16.7	10.6	11.7	9.2	10.3	7.0
Hispanic or Latino	18.0	17.9	15.7	17.1	13.6	12.2	12.9	11.9
Female								
Total	37.2	29.6	30.4	27.1	24.9	23.6	21.3	21.8
9th grade	40.3	30.9	34.4	28.9	24.4	26.2	22.2	23.9
10th grade	39.7	31.6	32.8	30.0	30.1	24.1	23.8	23.0
11th grade	38.4	28.9	31.1	26.2	23.0	23.6	20.0	21.6
12th grade	30.7	27.3	23.9	23.6	21.2	18.9	18.0	18.0
Not Hispanic or Latino:								
White	38.6	29.7	31.6	26.1	23.2	24.2	21.2	21.5
Black or African American.........	29.4	24.5	22.2	22.0	18.8	17.2	14.7	17.1
Hispanic or Latino	34.6	34.1	34.1	30.3	26.1	26.5	23.4	24.2
	Percent of students who attempted suicide[1]							
Total	7.3	8.6	8.7	7.7	8.3	8.8	8.5	8.4
Male								
Total	3.9	5.0	5.6	4.5	5.7	6.2	5.4	6.0
9th grade	4.5	5.8	6.8	6.3	6.1	8.2	5.8	6.8
10th grade	3.3	5.9	5.4	3.8	6.2	6.7	5.5	7.6
11th grade	4.1	3.4	5.8	4.4	4.8	4.9	4.6	4.5
12th grade	3.8	4.5	4.7	3.7	5.4	4.4	5.2	4.3
Not Hispanic or Latino:								
White	3.3	4.4	5.2	3.2	4.5	5.3	3.7	5.2
Black or African American.........	3.3	5.4	7.0	5.6	7.1	7.5	7.7	5.2
Hispanic or Latino	3.7	7.4	5.8	7.2	6.6	8.0	6.1	7.8
Female								
Total	10.7	12.5	11.9	11.6	10.9	11.2	11.5	10.8
9th grade	13.8	14.4	14.9	15.1	14.0	13.2	14.7	14.1
10th grade	12.2	13.1	15.1	14.3	14.8	12.2	12.7	10.8
11th grade	8.7	13.6	11.4	11.3	7.5	11.5	10.0	11.0
12th grade	7.8	9.1	6.6	6.2	5.8	6.5	6.9	6.5
Not Hispanic or Latino:								
White	10.4	11.3	10.4	10.3	9.0	10.3	10.3	9.3
Black or African American.........	9.4	11.2	10.8	9.0	7.5	9.8	9.0	9.8
Hispanic or Latino	11.6	19.7	21.0	14.9	18.9	15.9	15.0	14.9

See footnotes at end of table.

Table 62 (page 2 of 2). Suicidal ideation, suicide attempts, and injurious suicide attempts among students in grades 9–12, by sex, grade level, race, and Hispanic origin: United States, selected years 1991–2005

[Data are based on a national sample of high school students, grades 9–12]

Sex, grade level, race, and Hispanic origin	1991	1993	1995	1997	1999	2001	2003	2005
	Percent of students with an injurious suicide attempt[1,2]							
Total	1.7	2.7	2.8	2.6	2.6	2.6	2.9	2.3
Male								
Total	1.0	1.6	2.2	2.0	2.1	2.1	2.4	1.8
9th grade	1.0	2.1	2.3	3.2	2.6	2.6	3.1	2.1
10th grade	0.5	1.3	2.4	1.4	1.8	2.5	2.1	2.2
11th grade	1.5	1.1	2.0	2.6	2.1	1.6	2.0	1.4
12th grade	0.9	1.5	2.2	1.0	1.7	1.5	1.8	1.0
Not Hispanic or Latino:								
White	1.0	1.4	2.1	1.5	1.6	1.7	1.1	1.5
Black or African American	0.4	2.0	2.8	1.8	3.4	3.6	5.2	1.4
Hispanic or Latino	0.5	2.0	2.9	2.1	1.4	2.5	4.2	2.8
Female								
Total	2.5	3.8	3.4	3.3	3.1	3.1	3.2	2.9
9th grade	2.8	3.5	6.3	5.0	3.8	3.8	3.9	4.0
10th grade	2.6	5.1	3.8	3.7	4.0	3.6	3.2	2.4
11th grade	2.1	3.9	2.9	2.8	2.8	2.8	2.9	2.9
12th grade	2.4	2.9	1.3	2.0	1.3	1.7	2.2	2.2
Not Hispanic or Latino:								
White	2.3	3.6	2.9	2.6	2.3	2.9	2.4	2.7
Black or African American	2.9	4.0	3.6	3.0	2.4	3.1	2.2	2.6
Hispanic or Latino	2.7	5.5	6.6	3.8	4.6	4.2	5.7	3.7

[1]Response is for the 12 months preceding the survey.
[2]A suicide attempt that required medical attention.

NOTES: Only youths attending school participated in the survey. Persons of Hispanic origin may be of any race. See Appendix II, Hispanic origin; Race; Suicidal ideation. Standard errors for selected years are available in the spreadsheet version of this table. Available from: www.cdc.gov/nchs/hus.htm.

SOURCE: Centers for Disease Control and Prevention, National Center for Chronic Disease Prevention and Health Promotion, National Youth Risk Behavior Survey (YRBS).

Table 63 (page 1 of 2). Current cigarette smoking among adults 18 years of age and over, by sex, race, and age: United States, selected years 1965–2004

[Data are based on household interviews of a sample of the civilian noninstitutionalized population]

Sex, race, and age	1965[1]	1974[1]	1979[1]	1985[1]	1990[1]	1995[1]	1999	2000	2001	2002	2003	2004
18 years and over, age adjusted[2]				Percent of persons who are current cigarette smokers[3]								
All persons	41.9	37.0	33.3	29.9	25.3	24.6	23.3	23.1	22.6	22.3	21.5	20.8
Male	51.2	42.8	37.0	32.2	28.0	26.5	25.2	25.2	24.6	24.6	23.7	23.0
Female	33.7	32.2	30.1	27.9	22.9	22.7	21.6	21.1	20.7	20.0	19.4	18.7
White male[4]	50.4	41.7	36.4	31.3	27.6	26.2	25.0	25.4	24.8	24.9	23.8	23.0
Black or African American male[4]	58.8	53.6	43.9	40.2	32.8	29.4	28.4	25.7	27.5	26.6	25.3	23.5
White female[4]	33.9	32.0	30.3	27.9	23.5	23.4	22.5	22.0	22.0	21.0	20.1	19.5
Black or African American female[4]	31.8	35.6	30.5	30.9	20.8	23.5	20.5	20.7	18.0	18.3	17.9	16.9
18 years and over, crude												
All persons	42.4	37.1	33.5	30.1	25.5	24.7	23.5	23.2	22.7	22.4	21.6	20.9
Male	51.9	43.1	37.5	32.6	28.4	27.0	25.7	25.6	25.1	25.1	24.1	23.4
Female	33.9	32.1	29.9	27.9	22.8	22.6	21.5	20.9	20.6	19.8	19.2	18.5
White male[4]	51.1	41.9	36.8	31.7	28.0	26.6	25.3	25.7	25.0	25.0	24.0	23.2
Black or African American male[4]	60.4	54.3	44.1	39.9	32.5	28.5	28.6	26.2	27.6	27.0	25.7	23.9
White female[4]	34.0	31.7	30.1	27.7	23.4	23.1	22.1	21.4	21.5	20.6	19.7	19.1
Black or African American female[4]	33.7	36.4	31.1	31.0	21.2	23.5	20.6	20.8	18.1	18.5	18.1	17.3
All males												
18–24 years	54.1	42.1	35.0	28.0	26.6	27.8	29.5	28.1	30.2	32.1	26.3	25.6
25–34 years	60.7	50.5	43.9	38.2	31.6	29.5	29.1	28.9	26.9	27.2	28.7	26.1
35–44 years	58.2	51.0	41.8	37.6	34.5	31.5	30.0	30.2	27.3	29.7	28.1	26.5
45–64 years	51.9	42.6	39.3	33.4	29.3	27.1	25.8	26.4	26.4	24.5	23.9	25.0
65 years and over	28.5	24.8	20.9	19.6	14.6	14.9	10.5	10.2	11.5	10.1	10.1	9.8
White male[4]												
18–24 years	53.0	40.8	34.3	28.4	27.4	28.4	30.5	30.4	32.3	34.3	27.7	26.7
25–34 years	60.1	49.5	43.6	37.3	31.6	29.9	30.8	29.7	28.7	27.7	28.8	26.3
35–44 years	57.3	50.1	41.3	36.6	33.5	31.2	29.5	30.6	27.8	29.7	28.8	26.6
45–64 years	51.3	41.2	38.3	32.1	28.7	26.3	24.5	25.8	25.1	24.4	23.3	24.4
65 years and over	27.7	24.3	20.5	18.9	13.7	14.1	10.0	9.8	10.7	9.3	9.6	9.4
Black or African American male[4]												
18–24 years	62.8	54.9	40.2	27.2	21.3	*14.6	23.6	20.9	21.6	22.7	18.6	18.0
25–34 years	68.4	58.5	47.5	45.6	33.8	25.1	22.7	23.2	23.8	28.9	31.0	21.2
35–44 years	67.3	61.5	48.6	45.0	42.0	36.3	34.8	30.7	29.9	28.3	23.6	28.4
45–64 years	57.9	57.8	50.0	46.1	36.7	33.9	35.7	32.2	34.3	29.8	30.1	29.2
65 years and over	36.4	29.7	26.2	27.7	21.5	28.5	17.3	14.2	21.1	19.4	18.0	14.1
All females												
18–24 years	38.1	34.1	33.8	30.4	22.5	21.8	26.3	24.9	23.2	24.5	21.5	21.5
25–34 years	43.7	38.8	33.7	32.0	28.2	26.4	23.5	22.3	22.7	21.3	21.3	21.0
35–44 years	43.7	39.8	37.0	31.5	24.8	27.1	26.5	26.2	25.7	23.7	24.2	21.6
45–64 years	32.0	33.4	30.7	29.9	24.8	24.0	21.0	21.7	21.4	21.1	20.2	19.8
65 years and over	9.6	12.0	13.2	13.5	11.5	11.5	10.7	9.3	9.1	8.6	8.3	8.1
White female[4]												
18–24 years	38.4	34.0	34.5	31.8	25.4	24.9	29.6	28.5	27.1	26.7	23.6	22.9
25–34 years	43.4	38.6	34.1	32.0	28.5	27.3	25.5	24.9	25.2	23.8	22.5	22.6
35–44 years	43.9	39.3	37.2	31.0	25.0	27.0	26.9	26.6	26.9	24.4	25.2	22.7
45–64 years	32.7	33.0	30.6	29.7	25.4	24.3	21.2	21.4	21.6	21.5	20.1	20.1
65 years and over	9.8	12.3	13.8	13.3	11.5	11.7	10.5	9.1	9.4	8.5	8.4	8.2
Black or African American female[4]												
18–24 years	37.1	35.6	31.8	23.7	10.0	*8.8	14.8	14.2	10.0	17.1	10.8	15.6
25–34 years	47.8	42.2	35.2	36.2	29.1	26.7	18.2	15.5	16.8	13.9	17.0	18.3
35–44 years	42.8	46.4	37.7	40.2	25.5	31.9	28.8	30.2	24.0	24.0	23.2	18.9
45–64 years	25.7	38.9	34.2	33.4	22.6	27.5	22.3	25.6	22.6	22.2	23.3	20.9
65 years and over	7.1	*8.9	*8.5	14.5	11.1	13.3	13.5	10.2	9.3	9.4	8.0	6.7

See footnotes at end of table.

Table 63 (page 2 of 2). Current cigarette smoking among adults 18 years of age and over, by sex, race, and age: United States, selected years 1965–2004

[Data are based on household interviews of a sample of the civilian noninstitutionalized population]

---

* Estimates are considered unreliable. Data preceded by an asterisk have a relative standard error of 20%–30%.

[1]Data prior to 1997 are not strictly comparable with data for later years due to the 1997 questionnaire redesign. See Appendix I, National Health Interview Survey.

[2]Estimates are age adjusted to the year 2000 standard population using five age groups: 18–24 years, 25–34 years, 35–44 years, 45–64 years, 65 years and over. Age-adjusted estimates in this table may differ from other age-adjusted estimates based on the same data and presented elsewhere if different age groups are used in the adjustment procedure. See Appendix II, Age adjustment.

[3]Starting with 1993 data, current cigarette smokers were defined as ever smoking 100 cigarettes in their lifetime and smoking now on every day or some days. See Appendix II, Cigarette smoking.

[4]The race groups, white and black, include persons of Hispanic and non-Hispanic origin. Starting with 1999 data, race-specific estimates are tabulated according to 1997 Revisions to the Standards for the Classification of Federal Data on Race and Ethnicity and are not strictly comparable with estimates for earlier years. The single race categories shown in the table conform to the 1997 Standards. Starting with 1999 data, race-specific estimates are for persons who reported only one racial group. Prior to 1999, data were tabulated according to the 1977 Standards. Estimates for single race categories prior to 1999 included persons who reported one race or, if they reported more than one race, identified one race as best representing their race. Starting with 2003 data, race responses of other race and unspecified multiple race were treated as missing, and then race was imputed if these were the only race responses. Almost all persons with a race response of other race were of Hispanic origin. See Appendix II, Hispanic origin; Race. For additional data on cigarette smoking by racial groups, see Table 65.

NOTES: Standard errors for selected years are available in the spreadsheet version of this table. Available from: www.cdc.gov/nchs/hus.htm. For more data on cigarette smoking see the Early Release reports on the National Health Interview Survey home page: www.cdc.gov/nchs/nhis.htm. Data for additional years are available. See Appendix III.

SOURCES: Centers for Disease Control and Prevention, National Center for Health Statistics, National Health Interview Survey. Data are from the core questionnaire (1965) and the following questionnaire supplements: hypertension (1974), smoking (1979), alcohol and health practices (1983), health promotion and disease prevention (1985, 1990–1991), cancer control and cancer epidemiology (1992), and year 2000 objectives (1993–1995). Starting with 1997, data are from the family core and sample adult questionnaires.

Table 64. Age-adjusted prevalence of current cigarette smoking among adults 25 years of age and over, by sex, race, and education: United States, selected years 1974–2004

[Data are based on household interviews of a sample of the civilian noninstitutionalized population]

Sex, race, and education	1974[1]	1979[1]	1985[1]	1990[1]	1995[1]	1999	2000	2001	2002	2003	2004
25 years and over, age adjusted[2]	Percent of persons who are current cigarette smokers[3]										
All persons[4]	36.9	33.1	30.0	25.4	24.5	22.7	22.6	22.0	21.4	21.1	20.4
No high school diploma or GED	43.7	40.7	40.8	36.7	35.6	32.2	31.6	30.5	30.5	29.7	29.1
High school diploma or GED	36.2	33.6	32.0	29.1	29.1	28.0	29.2	28.1	27.9	27.8	25.8
Some college, no bachelor's degree	35.9	33.2	29.5	23.4	22.6	23.3	21.7	22.2	21.5	21.1	21.4
Bachelor's degree or higher	27.2	22.6	18.5	13.9	13.6	11.1	10.9	10.8	10.0	10.2	10.0
All males[4]	42.9	37.3	32.8	28.2	26.4	24.5	24.7	23.8	23.5	23.3	22.6
No high school diploma or GED	52.3	47.6	45.7	42.0	39.7	36.2	36.0	34.2	34.0	34.4	33.6
High school diploma or GED	42.4	38.9	35.5	33.1	32.7	30.4	32.1	30.2	31.0	29.9	28.2
Some college, no bachelor's degree	41.8	36.5	32.9	25.9	23.7	24.8	23.3	24.3	23.2	22.7	23.4
Bachelor's degree or higher	28.3	22.7	19.6	14.5	13.8	11.8	11.6	11.2	11.0	11.2	10.8
White males[4,5]	41.9	36.7	31.7	27.6	25.9	24.2	24.7	23.7	23.5	23.2	22.4
No high school diploma or GED	51.5	47.6	45.0	41.8	38.7	36.3	38.2	34.8	35.6	33.6	32.6
High school diploma or GED	42.0	38.5	34.8	32.9	32.9	30.5	32.4	30.3	31.0	29.6	28.9
Some college, no bachelor's degree	41.6	36.4	32.2	25.4	23.3	24.7	23.5	24.5	23.2	23.3	22.9
Bachelor's degree or higher	27.8	22.5	19.1	14.4	13.4	11.8	11.3	11.2	11.1	11.2	10.5
Black or African American males[4,5]	53.4	44.4	42.1	34.5	31.6	29.1	26.4	28.4	27.2	26.3	24.4
No high school diploma or GED	58.1	49.7	50.5	41.6	41.9	43.8	38.2	37.9	37.2	37.4	36.7
High school diploma or GED	*50.7	48.6	41.8	37.4	36.6	32.5	29.0	33.4	31.3	33.4	23.1
Some college, no bachelor's degree	*45.3	39.2	41.8	28.1	26.4	23.4	19.9	24.1	25.6	19.5	24.7
Bachelor's degree or higher	*41.4	*36.8	*32.0	*20.8	*17.3	11.3	14.6	11.3	*10.8	*10.3	11.3
All females[4]	32.0	29.5	27.5	22.9	22.9	20.9	20.5	20.4	19.3	19.1	18.3
No high school diploma or GED	36.6	34.8	36.5	31.8	31.7	28.2	27.1	26.9	26.9	24.9	24.5
High school diploma or GED	32.2	29.8	29.5	26.1	26.4	25.9	26.6	26.4	25.2	25.8	23.7
Some college, no bachelor's degree	30.1	30.0	26.3	21.0	21.6	21.9	20.4	20.4	20.0	19.7	19.7
Bachelor's degree or higher	25.9	22.5	17.1	13.3	13.3	10.4	10.1	10.5	9.0	9.3	9.3
White females[4,5]	31.7	29.7	27.3	23.3	23.1	21.4	21.0	21.3	20.2	19.6	19.0
No high school diploma or GED	36.8	35.8	36.7	33.4	32.4	29.5	28.4	29.2	29.0	25.0	24.4
High school diploma or GED	31.9	29.9	29.4	26.5	26.8	27.2	27.8	28.3	26.8	26.8	24.7
Some college, no bachelor's degree	30.4	30.7	26.7	21.2	22.2	22.3	21.1	21.3	20.5	20.6	21.1
Bachelor's degree or higher	25.5	21.9	16.5	13.4	13.5	10.5	10.2	10.9	9.6	9.4	9.9
Black or African American females[4,5]	35.6	30.3	32.0	22.4	25.7	21.4	21.6	19.1	18.4	18.9	17.1
No high school diploma or GED	36.1	31.6	39.4	26.3	32.3	30.1	31.1	26.3	27.1	26.9	29.2
High school diploma or GED	40.9	32.6	32.1	24.1	27.8	22.4	25.4	21.3	19.5	23.3	21.0
Some college, no bachelor's degree	32.3	*28.9	23.9	22.7	20.8	22.3	20.4	17.4	20.7	17.0	13.9
Bachelor's degree or higher	*36.3	*43.3	26.6	17.0	17.3	13.4	10.8	11.6	*7.7	11.4	*6.9

* Estimates are considered unreliable. Data preceded by an asterisk have a relative standard error of 20%–30%.

[1] Data prior to 1997 are not strictly comparable with data for later years due to the 1997 questionnaire redesign. See Appendix I, National Health Interview Survey.

[2] Estimates are age adjusted to the year 2000 standard population using four age groups: 25–34 years, 35–44 years, 45–64 years, and 65 years and over. See Appendix II, Age adjustment. For age groups where smoking was 0% or 100%, the age-adjustment procedure was modified to substitute the percentage smoking from the next lower education group.

[3] Starting with 1993 data, current cigarette smokers were defined as ever smoking 100 cigarettes in their lifetime and smoking now on every day or some days. See Appendix II, Cigarette smoking.

[4] Includes unknown education. Education categories shown are for 1997 and subsequent years. GED stands for General Educational Development high school equivalency diploma. In 1974–1995 the following categories based on number of years of school completed were used: less than 12 years, 12 years, 13–15 years, 16 years or more. See Appendix II, Education.

[5] The race groups, white and black, include persons of Hispanic and non-Hispanic origin. Starting with 1999 data, race-specific estimates are tabulated according to 1997 Revisions to the Standards for the Classification of Federal Data on Race and Ethnicity and are not strictly comparable with estimates for earlier years. The single race categories shown in the table conform to the 1997 Standards. Starting with 1999 data, race-specific estimates are for persons who reported only one racial group. Prior to 1999, data were tabulated according to the 1977 Standards. Estimates for single race categories prior to 1999 included persons who reported one race or, if they reported more than one race, identified one race as best representing their race. Starting with 2003 data, race responses of other race and unspecified multiple race were treated as missing, and then race was imputed if these were the only race responses. Almost all persons with a race response of other race were of Hispanic origin. See Appendix II, Hispanic origin; Race. For additional data on cigarette smoking by racial groups, see Table 65.

NOTES: Standard errors for selected years are available in the spreadsheet version of this table. Available from: www.cdc.gov/nchs/hus.htm. For more data on cigarette smoking see the Early Release reports on the National Health Interview Survey home page: www.cdc.gov/nchs/nhis.htm. Data for additional years are available. See Appendix III.

SOURCES: Centers for Disease Control and Prevention, National Center for Health Statistics, National Health Interview Survey. Data are from the following questionnaire supplements: hypertension (1974), smoking (1979), alcohol and health practices (1983), health promotion and disease prevention (1985, 1990–1991), cancer control and cancer epidemiology (1992), and year 2000 objectives (1993–1995). Starting with 1997, data are from the family core and sample adult questionnaires.

Table 65 (page 1 of 2). Current cigarette smoking among adults, by sex, race, Hispanic origin, age, and education: United States, average annual 1990–1992, 1995–1998, and 2002–2004

[Data are based on household interviews of a sample of the civilian noninstitutionalized population]

Characteristic	Male			Female		
	1990–1992[1]	1995–1998[1]	2002–2004	1990–1992[1]	1995–1998[1]	2002–2004
18 years of age and over, age adjusted[2]	Percent of persons who are current cigarette smokers[3]					
All persons[4]	27.9	26.5	23.8	23.7	22.1	19.4
Race[5]						
White only.	27.4	26.4	23.8	24.3	22.9	20.2
Black or African American only	33.9	30.7	25.1	23.1	21.8	17.7
American Indian or Alaska Native only	34.2	40.5	34.3	36.7	28.9	28.7
Asian only.	24.8	18.1	17.0	6.3	11.0	6.0
Native Hawaiian or Other Pacific Islander only	- - -	- - -	*	- - -	- - -	*
2 or more races.	- - -	- - -	33.1	- - -	- - -	29.2
American Indian or Alaska Native; White.	- - -	- - -	44.5	- - -	- - -	35.5
Hispanic origin and race[5]						
Hispanic or Latino	25.7	24.4	20.1	15.8	13.7	10.6
Mexican.	26.2	24.5	19.8	14.8	12.0	9.5
Not Hispanic or Latino	28.1	26.9	24.5	24.4	23.1	20.7
White only	27.7	26.9	24.8	25.2	24.1	21.9
Black or African American only.	33.9	30.7	25.1	23.2	21.9	17.8
18 years of age and over, crude						
All persons[4]	28.4	27.0	24.2	23.6	22.0	19.2
Race[5]						
White only.	27.8	26.8	24.1	24.1	22.6	19.8
Black or African American only	33.2	30.6	25.5	23.3	21.8	18.0
American Indian or Alaska Native only	35.5	39.2	36.5	37.3	31.2	30.9
Asian only.	24.9	20.0	18.1	6.3	11.2	6.0
Native Hawaiian or Other Pacific Islander only	- - -	- - -	*	- - -	- - -	*
2 or more races.	- - -	- - -	35.0	- - -	- - -	29.9
American Indian or Alaska Native; White.	- - -	- - -	45.0	- - -	- - -	35.4
Hispanic origin and race[5]						
Hispanic or Latino	26.5	25.5	21.2	16.6	13.8	10.7
Mexican.	27.1	25.2	21.0	15.0	11.6	9.3
Not Hispanic or Latino	28.5	27.2	24.7	24.2	22.9	20.3
White only	28.0	27.0	24.6	24.8	23.5	21.1
Black or African American only.	33.3	30.6	25.5	23.3	21.9	18.1
18–24 years:						
Hispanic or Latino.	19.3	26.5	21.3	12.8	12.0	9.7
Not Hispanic or Latino:						
White only.	28.9	35.5	31.8	28.7	31.6	27.5
Black or African American only	17.7	21.3	19.3	10.8	9.8	14.7
25–34 years:						
Hispanic or Latino.	29.9	25.9	20.8	19.2	12.6	9.4
Not Hispanic or Latino:						
White only.	32.7	30.5	29.7	30.9	28.5	26.3
Black or African American only	34.6	28.5	26.5	29.2	22.0	16.2
35–44 years:						
Hispanic or Latino.	32.1	26.2	24.7	19.9	17.6	12.5
Not Hispanic or Latino:						
White only.	32.3	31.5	29.1	27.3	28.1	26.2
Black or African American only	44.1	34.7	26.7	31.3	30.3	22.2
45–64 years:						
Hispanic or Latino.	26.6	26.8	21.3	17.1	14.7	13.2
Not Hispanic or Latino:						
White only.	28.4	26.8	24.3	26.1	22.3	21.3
Black or African American only	38.0	38.8	30.1	26.1	26.9	22.3
65 years and over:						
Hispanic or Latino.	16.1	14.7	10.2	6.6	9.4	5.4
Not Hispanic or Latino:						
White only.	14.2	10.6	9.4	12.3	11.6	8.5
Black or African American only	25.2	20.9	17.2	10.7	11.2	8.1

See footnotes at end of table.

Table 65 (page 2 of 2). Current cigarette smoking among adults, by sex, race, Hispanic origin, age, and education: United States, average annual 1990–1992, 1995–1998, and 2002–2004

[Data are based on household interviews of a sample of the civilian noninstitutionalized population]

	Male			Female		
Characteristic	1990–1992[1]	1995–1998[1]	2002–2004	1990–1992[1]	1995–1998[1]	2002–2004
Education, Hispanic origin, and race[5,6]	Percent of persons who are current cigarette smokers[3]					
25 years of age and over, age adjusted[7]						
No high school diploma or GED:						
Hispanic or Latino...............	30.2	27.6	22.7	15.8	13.3	9.5
Not Hispanic or Latino:						
White only...................	46.1	43.9	44.0	40.4	40.7	41.3
Black or African American only	45.4	44.6	37.9	31.3	30.0	28.0
High school diploma or GED:						
Hispanic or Latino...............	29.6	26.7	19.4	18.4	16.4	12.6
Not Hispanic or Latino:						
White only...................	32.9	32.8	31.5	28.4	28.8	28.4
Black or African American only	38.2	35.7	29.3	25.4	26.6	21.4
Some college or more:						
Hispanic or Latino...............	20.4	16.6	15.6	14.3	13.5	10.9
Not Hispanic or Latino:						
White only...................	19.3	18.3	16.9	18.1	17.2	15.6
Black or African American only	25.6	23.3	18.5	22.8	18.9	14.1

* Estimates are considered unreliable. Data preceded by an asterisk have a relative standard error (RSE) of 20%–30%. Data not shown have an RSE of greater than 30%.

- - - Data not available.

[1]Data prior to 1997 are not strictly comparable with data for later years due to the 1997 questionnaire redesign. See Appendix I, National Health Interview Survey. Cigarette smoking data were not collected in 1996.

[2]Estimates are age adjusted to the year 2000 standard population using five age groups: 18–24 years, 25–34 years, 35–44 years, 45–64 years, and 65 years and over. See Appendix II, Age adjustment. For age groups where smoking is 0% or 100%, the age-adjustment procedure was modified to substitute the percentage smoking from the previous 3-year period.

[3]Starting with 1993 data, current cigarette smokers were defined as ever smoking 100 cigarettes in their lifetime and smoking now on every day or some days. See Appendix II, Cigarette smoking.

[4]Includes all other races not shown separately and unknown education level.

[5]The race groups, white, black, American Indian or Alaska Native (AI/AN), Asian, Native Hawaiian or Other Pacific Islander, and 2 or more races, include persons of Hispanic and non-Hispanic origin. Persons of Hispanic origin may be of any race. Starting with 1999 data, race-specific estimates are tabulated according to 1997 Revisions to the Standards for the Classification of Federal Data on Race and Ethnicity and are not strictly comparable with estimates for earlier years. The five single race categories plus multiple race categories shown in the table conform to the 1997 Standards. The 2002–2004 race-specific estimates are for persons who reported only one racial group; the category 2 or more races includes persons who reported more than one racial group. Prior to 1999, data were tabulated according to the 1977 Standards with four racial groups and the Asian only category included Native Hawaiian or Other Pacific Islander. Estimates for single race categories prior to 1999 included persons who reported one race or, if they reported more than one race, identified one race as best representing their race. Starting with 2003 data, race responses of other race and unspecified multiple race were treated as missing, and then race was imputed if these were the only race responses. Almost all persons with a race response of other race were of Hispanic origin. See Appendix II, Hispanic origin; Race.

[6]Education categories shown are for 1997 and subsequent years. GED stands for General Educational Development high school equivalency diploma. In years prior to 1997, the following categories based on number of years of school completed were used: less than 12 years, 12 years, 13 years or more. See Appendix II, Education.

[7]Estimates are age adjusted to the year 2000 standard using four age groups: 25–34 years, 35–44 years, 45–64 years, and 65 years and over. See Appendix II, Age adjustment.

NOTES: Standard errors for selected years are available in the spreadsheet version of this table. Available from: www.cdc.gov/nchs/hus.htm. For more data on cigarette smoking see the Early Release reports on the National Health Interview Survey home page available from: www.cdc.gov/nchs/nhis.htm. Data for additional years are available. See Appendix III.

SOURCES: Centers for Disease Control and Prevention, National Center for Health Statistics, National Health Interview Survey. Data are from the following questionnaire supplements: health promotion and disease prevention (1990–1991), cancer control and cancer epidemiology (1992), and year 2000 objectives (1993–1995). Starting with 1997, data are from the family core and sample adult questionnaires.

Table 66 (page 1 of 2). Use of selected substances in the past month among persons 12 years of age and over, by age, sex, race, and Hispanic origin: United States, 2002–2004

[Data are based on household interviews of a sample of the civilian noninstitutionalized population 12 years of age and over]

Age, sex, race, and Hispanic origin	Any illicit drug[1]			Marijuana			Nonmedical use of any psychotherapeutic drug[2]		
	2002	2003	2004	2002	2003	2004	2002	2003	2004
	Percent of population								
12 years and over	8.3	8.2	7.9	6.2	6.2	6.1	2.6	2.7	2.5
Age									
12–13 years	4.2	3.8	3.8	1.4	1.0	1.1	1.7	1.8	1.7
14–15 years	11.2	10.9	10.9	7.6	7.2	7.3	4.0	4.1	4.1
16–17 years	19.8	19.2	17.3	15.7	15.6	14.5	6.2	6.1	5.1
18–25 years	20.2	20.3	19.4	17.3	17.0	16.1	5.4	6.0	6.1
26–34 years	10.5	10.7	11.1	7.7	8.4	8.3	3.6	3.4	3.6
35 years and over	4.6	4.4	4.2	3.1	3.0	3.1	1.6	1.5	1.3
Sex									
Male	10.3	10.0	9.9	8.1	8.1	8.0	2.7	2.7	2.6
Female	6.4	6.5	6.1	4.4	4.4	4.3	2.6	2.6	2.4
Age and sex									
12–17 years	11.6	11.2	10.6	8.2	7.9	7.6	4.0	4.0	3.6
Male	12.3	11.4	10.6	9.1	8.6	8.1	3.6	3.7	3.2
Female	10.9	11.1	10.6	7.2	7.2	7.1	4.3	4.2	4.1
Hispanic origin and race[3]									
Not Hispanic or Latino:									
White only	8.5	8.3	8.1	6.5	6.4	6.2	2.8	2.8	2.7
Black or African American only	9.7	8.7	8.7	7.4	6.7	7.0	2.0	1.8	1.6
American Indian or Alaska Native only	10.1	12.1	12.3	6.7	10.3	9.1	3.2	4.8	3
Native Hawaiian or Other Pacific Islander only	7.9	11.1	*	4.4	7.3	*	3.8	3.2	4.6
Asian only	3.5	3.8	3.1	1.8	1.9	2.0	0.7	1.7	0.9
2 or more races	11.4	12.0	13.3	9.0	9.3	9.6	3.5	2.4	5.7
Hispanic or Latino	7.2	8.0	7.2	4.3	4.9	5.0	2.9	3.0	2.4

Age, sex, race, and Hispanic origin	Alcohol use			Binge alcohol use[4]			Heavy alcohol use[5]		
	2002	2003	2004	2002	2003	2004	2002	2003	2004
	Percent of population								
12 years and over	51.0	50.1	50.3	22.9	22.6	22.8	6.7	6.8	6.9
Age									
12–13 years	4.3	4.5	4.3	1.8	1.6	2.0	0.3	0.1	0.2
14–15 years	16.6	17.0	16.4	9.2	9.4	9.1	1.9	2.2	1.6
16–17 years	32.6	31.8	32.5	21.4	21.2	22.4	5.6	5.5	6.3
18–25 years	60.5	61.4	60.5	40.9	41.6	41.2	14.9	15.1	15.1
26–34 years	61.4	60.2	60.5	33.1	32.9	32.2	9.0	9.4	9.4
35 years and over	52.1	50.7	51.2	18.6	18.1	18.5	5.2	5.1	5.3
Sex									
Male	57.4	57.3	56.9	31.2	30.9	31.1	10.8	10.4	10.6
Female	44.9	43.2	44.0	15.1	14.8	14.9	3.0	3.4	3.5
Age and sex									
12–17 years	17.6	17.7	17.6	10.7	10.6	11.1	2.5	2.6	2.7
Male	17.4	17.1	17.2	11.4	11.1	11.6	3.1	2.9	3.2
Female	17.9	18.3	18.0	9.9	10.1	10.5	1.9	2.3	2.1
Hispanic origin and race[3]									
Not Hispanic or Latino:									
White only	55.0	54.4	55.2	23.4	23.6	23.8	7.5	7.7	7.9
Black or African American only	39.9	37.9	37.1	21.0	19.0	18.3	4.4	4.5	4.4
American Indian or Alaska Native only	44.7	42.0	36.2	27.9	29.6	25.8	8.7	10.0	7.7
Native Hawaiian or Other Pacific Islander only	*	43.3	*	25.2	29.8	*	8.3	10.4	4.9
Asian only	37.1	39.8	37.4	12.4	11.0	12.4	2.6	2.3	2.7
2 or more races	49.9	44.4	52.4	19.8	21.8	23.5	7.5	6.1	6.9
Hispanic or Latino	42.8	41.5	40.2	24.8	24.2	24.0	5.9	5.2	5.3

See footnotes at end of table.

Table 66 (page 2 of 2). Use of selected substances in the past month among persons 12 years of age and over, by age, sex, race, and Hispanic origin: United States, 2002–2004

[Data are based on household interviews of a sample of the civilian noninstitutionalized population 12 years of age and over]

Age, sex, race, and Hispanic origin	Any tobacco[6]			Cigarettes			Cigars		
	2002	2003	2004	2002	2003	2004	2002	2003	2004
	Percent of population								
12 years and over	30.4	29.8	29.2	26.0	25.4	24.9	5.4	5.4	5.7
Age									
12–13 years	3.8	3.2	3.4	3.2	2.5	2.8	0.7	0.8	0.9
14–15 years	13.4	13.3	13.2	11.2	11.0	10.9	3.8	3.9	3.8
16–17 years	29.0	27.0	27.0	24.9	23.2	22.2	9.3	8.8	9.7
18–25 years	45.3	44.8	44.6	40.8	40.2	39.5	11.0	11.4	12.7
26–34 years	38.2	38.8	37.2	32.7	33.4	32.4	6.6	6.9	6.5
35 years and over	27.9	27.0	26.5	23.4	22.6	22.2	4.1	3.9	4.1
Sex									
Male............................	37.0	35.9	35.7	28.7	28.1	27.7	9.4	9.0	9.8
Female..........................	24.3	24.0	23.1	23.4	23.0	22.3	1.7	2.0	1.9
Age and sex									
12–17 years	15.2	14.4	14.4	13.0	12.2	11.9	4.5	4.5	4.8
Male	16.0	15.6	15.3	12.3	11.9	11.3	6.2	6.2	6.6
Female	14.4	13.3	13.5	13.6	12.5	12.5	2.7	2.7	2.8
Hispanic origin and race[3]									
Not Hispanic or Latino:									
White only	32.0	31.6	31.4	26.9	26.6	26.4	5.5	5.4	6.0
Black or African American only........	28.8	30.0	27.3	25.3	25.9	23.5	6.8	7.2	6.0
American Indian or Alaska Native only ..	44.3	41.8	33.8	37.1	36.1	31.0	5.2	8.3	4.9
Native Hawaiian or Other Pacific									
Islander only...................	28.8	37.0	*	*	33.1	*	4.1	8.0	*
Asian only	18.6	13.8	11.7	17.7	12.6	10.3	1.1	1.8	1.8
2 or more races	38.1	34.4	41.3	35.0	30.7	38.3	5.5	6.2	9.1
Hispanic or Latino	25.2	23.7	23.3	23.0	21.4	21.3	5.0	4.9	4.7

* Estimates are considered unreliable if the relative standard error is greater than 17.5% of the log transformation of the proportion, the minimum effective sample size is less than 68, the minimum nominal sample size less than 100, or the prevalence close to 0% or 100%.

[1]Any illicit drug includes marijuana/hashish, cocaine (including crack), heroin, hallucinogens (including LSD and PCP), inhalants, or any prescription-type psychotherapeutic drug used nonmedically.

[2]Psychotherapeutic drugs include prescription-type pain relievers, tranquilizers, stimulants, or sedatives; does not include over-the-counter drugs.

[3]Persons of Hispanic origin may be of any race. Race and Hispanic origin were collected using the 1997 Revisions to the Standards for the Classification of Federal Data on Race and Ethnicity. Single race categories shown include persons who reported only one racial group. The category 2 or more races includes persons who reported more than one racial group. See Appendix II, Hispanic origin; Race.

[4]Binge alcohol use is defined as drinking five or more drinks on the same occasion on at least 1 day in the past 30 days. Occasion is defined as at the same time or within a couple of hours of each other. See Appendix II, Binge drinking.

[5]Heavy alcohol use is defined as drinking five or more drinks on the same occasion on each of 5 or more days in the past 30 days; all heavy alcohol users are also binge alcohol users.

[6]Any tobacco product includes cigarettes, smokeless tobacco (i.e., chewing tobacco or snuff), cigars, or pipe tobacco.

NOTES: The National Survey on Drug Use & Health (NSDUH), formerly called the National Household Survey on Drug Abuse (NHSDA), began a new baseline in 2002 and cannot be compared with previous years. Because of methodological differences among the National Survey on Drug Use & Health, Monitoring the Future Study (MTF), and Youth Risk Behavior Survey (YRBS), rates of substance use measured by these surveys are not directly comparable. See Appendix I, NSDUH, MTF, and YRBS.

SOURCE: Substance Abuse and Mental Health Services Administration, Office of Applied Studies, National Survey on Drug Use & Health. Available from: www.oas.samhsa.gov/nhsda.htm.

Table 67 (page 1 of 3). Use of selected substances among high school seniors, tenth-, and eighth-graders, by sex and race: United States, selected years 1980–2005

[Data are based on a survey of high school seniors, tenth-, and eighth-graders in the coterminous United States]

Substance, grade in school, sex, and race	1980	1990	1991	1995	2000	2002	2003	2004	2005
Cigarettes	Percent using substance in the past month								
All seniors	30.5	29.4	28.3	33.5	31.4	26.7	24.4	25.0	23.2
Male	26.8	29.1	29.0	34.5	32.8	27.4	26.2	25.3	24.8
Female	33.4	29.2	27.5	32.0	29.7	25.5	22.1	24.1	20.7
White	31.0	32.5	31.8	37.3	36.6	30.9	28.2	28.2	27.6
Black or African American	25.2	12.0	9.4	15.0	13.6	11.3	9.0	11.3	10.7
All tenth-graders	- - -	- - -	20.8	27.9	23.9	17.7	16.7	16.0	14.9
Male	- - -	- - -	20.8	27.7	23.8	16.7	16.2	16.2	14.5
Female	- - -	- - -	20.7	27.9	23.6	18.6	17.0	15.7	15.1
White	- - -	- - -	23.9	31.2	27.3	20.8	19.3	18.1	17.6
Black or African American	- - -	- - -	6.4	12.2	11.3	9.1	8.8	9.6	8.7
All eighth-graders	- - -	- - -	14.3	19.1	14.6	10.7	10.2	9.2	9.3
Male	- - -	- - -	15.5	18.8	14.3	11.0	9.6	8.3	8.7
Female	- - -	- - -	13.1	19.0	14.7	10.4	10.6	9.9	9.7
White	- - -	- - -	15.0	21.7	16.4	11.1	10.6	9.4	9.4
Black or African American	- - -	- - -	5.3	8.2	8.4	7.3	6.4	7.5	7.1
Marijuana									
All seniors	33.7	14.0	13.8	21.2	21.6	21.5	21.2	19.9	19.8
Male	37.8	16.1	16.1	24.6	24.7	25.3	24.7	23.0	23.6
Female	29.1	11.5	11.2	17.2	18.3	17.4	17.3	16.6	15.8
White	34.2	15.6	15.0	21.5	22.0	22.8	22.8	21.5	21.6
Black or African American	26.5	5.2	6.5	17.8	17.5	16.4	16.1	14.2	14.6
All tenth-graders	- - -	- - -	8.7	17.2	19.7	17.8	17.0	15.9	15.2
Male	- - -	- - -	10.1	19.2	23.3	19.3	19.0	17.4	16.7
Female	- - -	- - -	7.3	15.0	16.2	16.4	15.0	14.2	13.4
White	- - -	- - -	9.4	17.7	20.1	19.1	17.4	15.8	15.7
Black or African American	- - -	- - -	3.8	15.1	17.0	14.4	15.6	17.2	15.3
All eighth-graders	- - -	- - -	3.2	9.1	9.1	8.3	7.5	6.4	6.6
Male	- - -	- - -	3.8	9.8	10.2	9.5	8.5	6.3	7.6
Female	- - -	- - -	2.6	8.2	7.8	7.1	6.4	6.3	5.7
White	- - -	- - -	3.0	9.0	8.3	7.9	7.0	5.5	5.8
Black or African American	- - -	- - -	2.1	7.0	8.5	7.1	7.4	8.1	8.2
Cocaine									
All seniors	5.2	1.9	1.4	1.8	2.1	2.3	2.1	2.3	2.3
Male	6.0	2.3	1.7	2.2	2.7	2.7	2.6	2.9	2.6
Female	4.3	1.3	0.9	1.3	1.6	1.8	1.4	1.7	1.8
White	5.4	1.8	1.3	1.7	2.2	2.8	2.1	2.5	2.4
Black or African American	2.0	0.5	0.8	0.4	1.0	0.2	1.0	0.9	0.7
All tenth-graders	- - -	- - -	0.7	1.7	1.8	1.6	1.3	1.7	1.5
Male	- - -	- - -	0.7	1.8	2.1	1.8	1.3	1.9	1.9
Female	- - -	- - -	0.6	1.5	1.4	1.4	1.3	1.4	1.2
White	- - -	- - -	0.6	1.7	1.7	1.7	1.4	1.7	1.6
Black or African American	- - -	- - -	0.2	0.4	0.4	0.4	0.5	0.4	0.6
All eighth-graders	- - -	- - -	0.5	1.2	1.2	1.1	0.9	0.9	1.0
Male	- - -	- - -	0.7	1.1	1.3	1.1	1.0	0.8	0.9
Female	- - -	- - -	0.4	1.2	1.1	1.1	0.8	1.0	1.0
White	- - -	- - -	0.4	1.0	1.1	1.0	0.8	0.8	0.8
Black or African American	- - -	- - -	0.4	0.4	0.5	0.5	0.5	0.8	0.5

See footnotes at end of table.

Table 67 (page 2 of 3). Use of selected substances among high school seniors, tenth-, and eighth-graders, by sex and race: United States, selected years 1980–2005

[Data are based on a survey of high school seniors, tenth-, and eighth-graders in the coterminous United States]

Substance, grade in school, sex, and race	1980	1990	1991	1995	2000	2002	2003	2004	2005
Inhalants				Percent using substance in the past month					
All seniors	1.4	2.7	2.4	3.2	2.2	1.5	1.5	1.5	2.0
Male	1.8	3.5	3.3	3.9	2.9	2.2	2.0	1.7	2.4
Female.	1.0	2.0	1.6	2.5	1.7	0.8	1.1	1.3	1.6
White.	1.4	3.0	2.4	3.7	2.1	1.3	1.7	1.6	1.9
Black or African American	1.0	1.5	1.5	1.1	2.1	1.2	0.7	1.0	1.2
All tenth-graders.	- - -	- - -	2.7	3.5	2.6	2.4	2.2	2.4	2.2
Male	- - -	- - -	2.9	3.8	3.0	2.3	2.3	2.4	1.9
Female.	- - -	- - -	2.6	3.2	2.2	2.4	2.2	2.3	2.5
White.	- - -	- - -	2.9	3.9	2.8	2.6	2.6	2.6	2.4
Black or African American	- - -	- - -	2.0	1.2	1.5	1.5	0.5	1.4	1.4
All eighth-graders.	- - -	- - -	4.4	6.1	4.5	3.8	4.1	4.5	4.2
Male	- - -	- - -	4.1	5.6	4.1	3.5	3.4	4.0	3.1
Female.	- - -	- - -	4.7	6.6	4.8	3.9	4.7	5.1	5.3
White.	- - -	- - -	4.5	7.0	4.5	3.9	4.3	4.4	4.2
Black or African American	- - -	- - -	2.3	2.3	2.3	2.7	2.3	3.8	3.3
MDMA (Ecstasy)									
All seniors	- - -	- - -	- - -	- - -	3.6	2.4	1.3	1.2	1.0
Male	- - -	- - -	- - -	- - -	4.1	2.6	1.3	1.6	1.0
Female.	- - -	- - -	- - -	- - -	3.1	2.1	1.2	0.9	1.0
White.	- - -	- - -	- - -	- - -	3.9	2.5	1.3	1.2	1.1
Black or African American	- - -	- - -	- - -	- - -	1.9	0.5	0.6	1.1	1.0
All tenth-graders.	- - -	- - -	- - -	- - -	2.6	1.8	1.1	0.8	1.0
Male	- - -	- - -	- - -	- - -	2.5	1.6	1.2	1.0	1.0
Female.	- - -	- - -	- - -	- - -	2.5	1.8	1.1	0.6	0.9
White.	- - -	- - -	- - -	- - -	2.5	2.3	1.2	0.9	0.9
Black or African American	- - -	- - -	- - -	- - -	1.8	0.5	0.7	0.1	0.2
All eighth-graders.	- - -	- - -	- - -	- - -	1.4	1.4	0.7	0.8	0.6
Male	- - -	- - -	- - -	- - -	1.6	1.5	0.7	0.7	0.8
Female.	- - -	- - -	- - -	- - -	1.2	1.3	0.7	0.9	0.4
White.	- - -	- - -	- - -	- - -	1.4	1.0	0.7	0.6	0.6
Black or African American	- - -	- - -	- - -	- - -	0.8	0.6	0.4	1.2	1.1
Alcohol[1]									
All seniors	72.0	57.1	54.0	51.3	50.0	48.6	47.5	48.0	47.0
Male	77.4	61.3	58.4	55.7	54.0	52.3	51.7	51.1	50.7
Female.	66.8	52.3	49.0	47.0	46.1	45.1	43.8	45.1	43.3
White.	75.8	62.2	57.7	54.8	55.3	52.7	52.0	52.5	52.3
Black or African American	47.7	32.9	34.4	37.4	29.3	30.7	29.2	29.2	29.0
All tenth-graders.	- - -	- - -	42.8	38.8	41.0	35.4	35.4	35.2	33.2
Male	- - -	- - -	45.5	39.7	43.3	35.3	35.3	36.3	32.8
Female.	- - -	- - -	40.3	37.8	38.6	35.7	35.3	34.0	33.6
White.	- - -	- - -	45.7	41.3	44.3	39.0	38.4	37.3	37.0
Black or African American	- - -	- - -	30.2	24.9	24.7	23.2	24.0	25.4	23.0
All eighth-graders.	- - -	- - -	25.1	24.6	22.4	19.6	19.7	18.6	17.1
Male	- - -	- - -	26.3	25.0	22.5	19.1	19.4	17.9	16.2
Female.	- - -	- - -	23.8	24.0	22.0	20.0	19.8	19.0	17.9
White.	- - -	- - -	26.0	25.4	23.9	20.4	19.9	18.6	17.9
Black or African American	- - -	- - -	17.8	17.3	15.1	14.7	16.5	16.0	14.9

See footnotes at end of table.

Table 67 (page 3 of 3). Use of selected substances among high school seniors, tenth-, and eighth-graders, by sex and race: United States, selected years 1980–2005

[Data are based on a survey of high school seniors, tenth-, and eighth-graders in the coterminous United States]

Substance, grade in school, sex, and race	1980	1990	1991	1995	2000	2002	2003	2004	2005
Binge drinking[2]				Percent in last 2 weeks					
All seniors	41.2	32.2	29.8	29.8	30.0	28.6	27.9	29.2	28.1
Male	52.1	39.1	37.8	36.9	36.7	34.2	34.2	34.3	33.4
Female.	30.5	24.4	21.2	23.0	23.5	23.0	22.1	24.2	22.7
White.	44.6	36.2	32.9	32.9	34.4	32.9	31.9	33.1	33.0
Black or African American	17.0	11.6	11.8	15.5	11.0	10.4	11.1	11.7	11.6
All tenth-graders.	- - -	- - -	22.9	24.0	26.2	22.4	22.2	22.0	21.0
Male	- - -	- - -	26.4	26.4	29.8	23.8	23.2	23.8	22.0
Female.	- - -	- - -	19.5	21.5	22.5	21.0	21.2	20.2	19.9
White.	- - -	- - -	24.4	25.7	28.5	24.6	24.3	23.7	23.5
Black or African American	- - -	- - -	14.4	12.3	12.9	12.4	11.7	11.5	11.0
All eighth-graders.	- - -	- - -	12.9	14.5	14.1	12.4	11.9	11.4	10.5
Male	- - -	- - -	14.3	15.1	14.4	12.5	12.2	10.8	10.2
Female.	- - -	- - -	11.4	13.9	13.6	12.1	11.6	11.8	10.6
White.	- - -	- - -	12.6	14.5	14.6	12.3	11.4	11.2	10.8
Black or African American	- - -	- - -	9.9	10.0	9.3	9.9	10.9	8.6	8.2

- - - Data not available.
0.0 Quantity more than zero but less than 0.05.
[1]In 1993, the alcohol question was changed to indicate that a drink meant more than a few sips. Data for 1993, available in the spreadsheet version of this table, are based on a half sample.
See Appendix II, Binge drinking.
[2]Five or more alcoholic drinks in a row at least once in the prior 2-week period.

NOTES: Because of methodological differences among the National Survey on Drug Use & Health (NSDUH), Monitoring the Future Study (MTF), and Youth Risk Behavior Survey (YRBS), rates of substance use measured by these surveys are not directly comparable. See Appendix I, NSDUH, MTF, and YRBS. Data for additional years are available. See Appendix III.

SOURCE: National Institutes of Health, National Institute on Drug Abuse (NIDA), Monitoring the Future Study, Annual surveys.

Table 68 (page 1 of 3). Alcohol consumption by adults 18 years of age and over, by selected characteristics: United States, selected years 1997–2004

[Data are based on household interviews of a sample of the civilian noninstitutionalized population]

Characteristic	Both sexes			Male			Female		
	1997	2003	2004	1997	2003	2004	1997	2003	2004
Drinking status [1]				Percent distribution					
18 years and over, age adjusted [2]									
All	100.0	100.0	100.0	100.0	100.0	100.0	100.0	100.0	100.0
Lifetime abstainer	21.4	24.9	24.6	14.1	17.8	17.8	27.8	31.3	30.6
Former drinker [3]	15.8	14.3	14.5	16.4	15.2	14.9	15.4	13.6	14.4
Infrequent	9.0	7.7	8.0	7.8	7.1	6.9	10.2	8.4	9.0
Regular	6.8	6.5	6.5	8.6	8.0	8.0	5.3	5.2	5.4
Current drinker [3]	62.8	60.8	60.8	69.5	67.1	67.3	56.8	55.2	54.9
Infrequent	13.9	12.9	13.3	10.2	9.8	10.0	17.4	15.9	16.4
Regular	48.5	47.4	47.1	58.7	56.7	56.7	39.2	39.0	38.3
18 years and over, crude									
All	100.0	100.0	100.0	100.0	100.0	100.0	100.0	100.0	100.0
Lifetime abstainer	21.3	24.8	24.6	14.1	17.7	17.8	27.8	31.4	30.7
Former drinker [3]	15.6	14.3	14.6	15.7	14.9	14.5	15.5	13.7	14.6
Infrequent	8.9	7.8	8.0	7.5	7.0	6.8	10.2	8.5	9.2
Regular	6.7	6.5	6.5	8.2	7.9	7.8	5.3	5.2	5.4
Current drinker [3]	63.1	60.9	60.8	70.2	67.4	67.6	56.7	54.9	54.6
Infrequent	14.0	13.0	13.3	10.2	9.8	10.0	17.4	15.9	16.3
Regular	48.8	47.5	47.1	59.4	57.1	57.0	39.1	38.7	38.0
Age				Percent current drinkers among all adults					
All persons:									
18–44 years	68.5	66.4	65.7	73.8	72.3	72.4	63.3	60.7	59.2
18–24 years	61.3	59.5	58.0	65.5	64.6	63.6	57.0	54.5	52.5
25–44 years	70.6	68.7	68.3	76.3	74.9	75.4	65.2	62.8	61.5
45–64 years	62.7	60.4	61.7	69.8	65.7	66.4	55.9	55.4	57.4
45–54 years	66.5	63.8	64.4	73.0	68.0	69.1	60.3	59.9	59.9
55–64 years	56.7	55.5	57.9	64.8	62.4	62.4	49.2	49.0	53.9
65 years and over	42.8	42.4	43.6	52.0	51.1	52.8	36.0	36.0	36.9
65–74 years	47.9	46.5	49.5	56.1	53.7	58.1	41.4	40.6	42.4
75 years and over	36.0	37.8	37.0	45.9	47.6	45.8	29.7	31.4	31.4
Race [2,4]									
White only	65.3	63.3	63.6	71.0	69.1	69.4	60.1	58.0	58.2
Black or African American only	46.7	47.4	46.6	55.5	54.7	55.7	40.0	41.8	39.7
American Indian or Alaska Native only	52.2	46.5	48.8	64.6	47.8	50.2	43.4	45.2	46.7
Asian only	45.7	39.1	43.8	59.8	49.4	56.9	31.6	30.3	30.8
Native Hawaiian or Other Pacific Islander only	- - -	*	*	- - -	*	*	- - -	*	*
2 or more races	- - -	54.5	62.0	- - -	62.4	68.2	- - -	48.4	57.3
Hispanic origin and race [2,4]									
Hispanic or Latino	52.9	49.5	49.6	63.9	61.7	63.7	41.9	37.3	35.7
Mexican	52.7	47.5	47.8	66.3	60.9	62.4	38.7	33.4	32.8
Not Hispanic or Latino	63.3	62.1	62.4	69.3	67.4	67.9	58.0	57.4	57.6
White only	66.7	65.7	66.0	71.7	70.3	70.4	62.2	61.6	62.0
Black or African American only	46.7	47.2	46.3	55.7	54.3	55.4	39.8	41.8	39.3
Geographic region [2]									
Northeast	67.9	67.8	67.7	73.4	73.7	73.8	63.3	62.9	62.2
Midwest	65.7	64.5	66.3	71.6	68.8	71.5	60.3	60.7	61.9
South	55.5	54.3	54.2	63.0	61.7	61.5	48.7	47.6	47.5
West	64.4	60.4	59.9	71.2	67.0	67.2	58.1	54.1	52.9
Location of residence [2]									
Within MSA [5]	63.9	62.3	61.3	70.1	68.2	68.0	58.5	57.0	55.4
Outside MSA [5]	56.5	53.8	58.4	64.6	61.5	64.3	48.8	47.1	51.5

See footnotes at end of table.

Table 68 (page 2 of 3). Alcohol consumption by adults 18 years of age and over, by selected characteristics: United States, selected years 1997–2004

[Data are based on household interviews of a sample of the civilian noninstitutionalized population]

Characteristic	Both sexes			Male			Female		
	1997	2003	2004	1997	2003	2004	1997	2003	2004
Level of alcohol consumption in past year for current drinkers[6]	Percent distribution of current drinkers[7]								
18 years and over, age adjusted[2]									
All drinking levels	100.0	100.0	100.0	100.0	100.0	100.0	100.0	100.0	100.0
Light	69.6	68.4	69.7	59.5	58.9	60.8	81.0	78.9	79.7
Moderate	22.5	23.7	23.1	31.8	32.8	31.5	12.0	13.7	13.6
Heavier	7.9	7.9	7.2	8.7	8.3	7.7	7.0	7.4	6.7
18 years and over, crude									
All drinking levels	100.0	100.0	100.0	100.0	100.0	100.0	100.0	100.0	100.0
Light	69.8	68.6	69.8	59.6	59.1	60.8	81.4	79.2	79.9
Moderate	22.3	23.5	23.0	31.7	32.5	31.5	11.7	13.5	13.4
Heavier	7.9	7.9	7.3	8.8	8.4	7.8	6.9	7.3	6.7
Number of days in the past year with 5 or more drinks	Percent distribution of current drinkers								
18 years and over, crude									
All current drinkers	100.0	100.0	100.0	100.0	100.0	100.0	100.0	100.0	100.0
No days	65.8	68.1	67.9	54.5	58.1	57.8	78.5	79.1	79.1
At least 1 day	34.2	31.9	32.1	45.5	41.9	42.2	21.5	20.9	20.9
1–11 days	18.5	17.0	18.2	22.0	19.5	21.5	14.6	14.2	14.5
12 or more days	15.6	14.9	13.9	23.5	22.4	20.7	6.9	6.7	6.4
Hispanic origin, race, and age[4]	Percent of adults with five or more drinks on at least 1 day in the past year among current drinkers								
All persons:									
18 years and over, age adjusted[2]	32.3	30.5	31.1	43.1	39.9	40.5	20.1	20.1	20.5
18 years and over, crude	34.2	31.9	32.1	45.5	41.9	42.2	21.5	20.9	20.9
18–44 years	42.5	41.1	41.8	54.8	52.1	52.3	28.7	28.7	29.5
18–24 years	51.6	51.2	55.9	61.5	59.3	66.8	40.2	41.9	43.1
25–44 years	40.2	38.2	37.6	53.0	50.0	48.0	25.8	24.9	25.5
45–64 years	25.3	23.9	24.3	36.1	33.5	34.3	12.8	13.2	13.5
45–54 years	28.5	26.3	27.1	40.2	37.0	36.7	15.2	14.9	16.8
55–64 years	19.5	19.8	19.7	28.8	28.0	30.5	8.3	10.2	8.4
65 years and over	11.2	8.4	8.9	17.8	12.5	13.9	4.3	4.2	3.7
65–74 years	13.8	10.8	11.6	21.6	16.1	16.7	5.4	5.0	5.9
75 years and over	6.6	5.2	4.7	10.8	7.3	9.1	*2.5	*3.1	*
Race[2,4]									
White only	33.3	31.9	32.5	44.4	41.3	41.9	20.9	21.4	21.9
Black or African American only	23.9	21.6	23.4	32.0	31.0	33.4	15.0	12.2	12.4
American Indian or Alaska Native only	54.4	34.1	33.2	70.5	43.8	43.7	37.6	*23.1	*19.5
Asian only	25.6	15.3	18.6	30.8	20.3	25.4	16.6	*8.4	*6.1
Native Hawaiian or Other Pacific Islander only	- - -	*	*	- - -	*	*	- - -	*	*
Hispanic origin and race[2,4]									
Hispanic or Latino	37.0	30.2	31.8	46.6	39.1	40.2	22.4	15.4	17.2
Mexican	39.1	34.2	36.6	50.2	43.0	45.3	20.3	18.2	20.1
Not Hispanic or Latino	31.9	30.6	31.1	42.8	40.1	40.8	20.0	20.6	20.8
White only	33.2	32.3	32.8	44.5	41.9	42.5	21.0	22.1	22.5
Black or African American only	23.7	21.2	23.3	32.0	30.5	33.5	14.5	11.9	12.1

See footnotes at end of table.

Table 68 (page 3 of 3). Alcohol consumption by adults 18 years of age and over, by selected characteristics: United States, selected years 1997–2004

[Data are based on household interviews of a sample of the civilian noninstitutionalized population]

Characteristic	Both sexes			Male			Female		
	1997	2003	2004	1997	2003	2004	1997	2003	2004
	Percent of adults with five or more drinks on at least 1 day in the past year among current drinkers								
Geographic region[2]									
Northeast	31.4	29.1	28.6	43.3	37.2	37.8	19.0	21.0	19.1
Midwest	33.7	33.9	35.8	44.6	44.6	46.6	21.6	22.5	24.6
South	30.9	28.2	28.5	40.6	36.9	37.5	19.3	17.9	17.6
West	33.5	31.5	31.4	44.7	41.7	40.3	20.7	19.6	20.7
Location of residence[2]									
Within MSA[5]	31.7	29.9	30.5	42.4	39.0	40.2	19.9	19.8	20.1
Outside MSA[5]	34.9	33.2	36.1	45.7	43.7	43.7	21.2	21.2	24.5

* Estimates are considered unreliable. Data preceded by an asterisk have a relative standard error (RSE) of 20%–30%. Data not shown have an RSE of greater than 30%.

- - - Data not available.

[1]Drinking status categories are based on self-reported responses to questions about alcohol consumption. Lifetime abstainers had fewer than 12 drinks in their lifetime. Former drinkers had at least 12 drinks in their lifetime and none in the past year. Former infrequent drinkers are former drinkers who had fewer than 12 drinks in any one year. Former regular drinkers are former drinkers who had at least 12 drinks in any one year. Current drinkers had at least 12 drinks in their lifetime and at least one drink in the past year. Current infrequent drinkers are current drinkers who had fewer than 12 drinks in the past year. Current regular drinkers are current drinkers who had at least 12 drinks in the past year. See Appendix II, Alcohol consumption.

[2]Estimates are age adjusted to the year 2000 standard population using four age groups: 18–24 years, 25–44 years, 45–64 years, and 65 years and over. Age-adjusted estimates in this table may differ from other age-adjusted estimates based on the same data and presented elsewhere if different age groups are used in the adjustment procedure. See Appendix II, Age adjustment.

[3]The totals for current and former drinkers include a small number of adults who did not provide sufficient information on frequency or amount of drinking; therefore, infrequent or regular drinking status could not be determined for these people.

[4]The race groups, white, black, American Indian or Alaska Native, Asian, Native Hawaiian or Other Pacific Islander, and 2 or more races, include persons of Hispanic and non-Hispanic origin. Persons of Hispanic origin may be of any race. Starting with 1999 data, race-specific estimates are tabulated according to 1997 Revisions to the Standards for the Classification of Federal Data on Race and Ethnicity and are not strictly comparable with estimates for earlier years. The five single race categories plus multiple race categories shown in the table conform to the 1997 Standards. Starting with 1999 data, race-specific estimates are for persons who reported only one racial group; the category 2 or more races includes persons who reported more than one racial group. Prior to 1999, data were tabulated according to the 1977 Standards with four racial groups and the Asian only category included Native Hawaiian or Other Pacific Islander. Estimates for single race categories prior to 1999 included persons who reported one race or, if they reported more than one race, identified one race as best representing their race. Starting with 2003 data, race responses of other race and unspecified multiple race were treated as missing, and then race was imputed if these were the only race responses. Almost all persons with a race response of other race were of Hispanic origin. See Appendix II, Hispanic origin; Race.

[5]MSA is metropolitan statistical area.

[6]Level of alcohol consumption categories are based on self-reported responses to questions about average alcohol consumption and are defined as follows: light drinkers: three drinks or fewer per week; moderate drinkers: more than three drinks and up to 14 drinks per week for men and more than three drinks and up to seven drinks per week for women; heavier drinkers: more than 14 drinks per week for men and more than seven drinks per week for women. (Most drinking guidelines consider more than seven drinks per week to be a heavier level of consumption for women. U.S. Department of Agriculture: Dietary Guidelines for Americans, 2000, 5th edition.)

[7]Percentage based on current drinkers with known frequency and amount of drinking.

NOTES: Standard errors are available in the spreadsheet version of this table. Available from: www.cdc.gov/nchs/hus.htm. For more data on alcohol consumption see the Early Release reports on the National Health Interview Survey home page: www.cdc.gov/nchs/nhis.htm. Data for additional years are available. See Appendix III.

SOURCE: Centers for Disease Control and Prevention, National Center for Health Statistics, National Health Interview Survey, family core and sample adult questionnaires.

Table 69 (page 1 of 2). Hypertension and elevated blood pressure among persons 20 years of age and over, by sex, age, race and Hispanic origin, and poverty level: United States, 1988–1994 and 2001–2004

[Data are based on interviews and physical examinations of a sample of the civilian noninstitutionalized population]

Sex, age, race and Hispanic origin[1], and poverty level	Hypertension[2,3]		Elevated blood pressure[2]	
	1988–1994	2001–2004	1988–1994	2001–2004
20–74 years, age adjusted[4]	Percent of population (standard error)			
Both sexes[5]	21.7	25.3	15.4	16.0
Male	23.4	24.4	18.2	15.8
Female[5]	20.0	26.0	12.6	15.9
Not Hispanic or Latino:				
White only, male	22.6	23.2	17.3	14.6
White only, female	18.4	23.5	11.2	14.2
Black or African American only, male	34.3	38.2	27.9	26.5
Black or African American only, female	35.0	40.5	23.5	25.7
Mexican male	23.4	19.7	19.1	15.3
Mexican female	21.0	22.1	16.5	14.5
Percent of poverty level:[6]				
Below 100%	27.5	29.6	19.0	19.0
100%–less than 200%	22.6	30.3	15.8	19.9
200% or more	20.4	23.5	14.6	14.6
20 years and over, age adjusted[4]				
Both sexes[5]	25.5	29.7	18.5	19.1
Male	26.4	28.1	20.6	18.3
Female	24.4	30.7	16.4	19.4
Not Hispanic or Latino:				
White only, male	25.6	26.8	19.7	17.0
White only, female	23.0	28.5	15.1	18.0
Black or African American only, male	37.5	41.6	30.3	28.8
Black or African American only, female	38.3	44.7	26.4	28.8
Mexican male	26.9	24.1	22.2	18.8
Mexican female	25.0	26.4	20.4	18.3
Percent of poverty level:[6]				
Below 100%	31.7	34.4	22.5	22.2
100%–less than 200%	26.6	34.4	19.3	22.9
200% or more	23.9	27.6	17.5	17.6
20 years and over, crude				
Both sexes[5]	24.1	29.0	17.6	18.5
Male	23.8	26.3	18.7	17.3
Female[5]	24.4	31.5	16.5	19.7
Not Hispanic or Latino:				
White only, male	24.3	26.9	18.7	17.0
White only, female	24.6	31.8	16.4	20.1
Black or African American only, male	31.1	36.7	25.5	25.6
Black or African American only, female	32.5	41.4	22.2	25.7
Mexican male	16.4	13.3	13.9	11.3
Mexican female	15.9	16.4	12.7	11.0
Percent of poverty level:[6]				
Below 100%	25.7	27.9	18.7	18.0
100%–less than 200%	26.7	33.2	19.8	22.0
200% or more	22.2	27.5	16.2	17.2
Male				
20–34 years	7.1	6.4	6.6	5.9
35–44 years	17.1	16.8	15.2	12.5
45–54 years	29.2	30.2	21.9	20.3
55–64 years	40.6	45.8	28.4	26.1
65–74 years	54.4	58.5	39.9	31.7
75 years and over	60.4	68.8	49.7	47.0
Female				
20–34 years	2.9	*	*2.4	*
35–44 years	11.2	14.0	6.4	7.6
45–54 years	23.9	32.6	13.7	19.9
55–64 years	42.6	54.6	27.0	30.4
65–74 years	56.2	74.3	38.2	54.3
75 years and over	73.6	81.7	59.9	57.1

See footnotes at end of table.

Table 69 (page 2 of 2). Hypertension and elevated blood pressure among persons 20 years of age and over, by sex, age, race and Hispanic origin, and poverty level: United States, 1988–1994 and 2001–2004

[Data are based on interviews and physical examinations of a sample of the civilian noninstitutionalized population]

* Estimates are considered unreliable. Data preceded by an asterisk have a relative standard error of 20%–30%.

[1]Persons of Mexican origin may be of any race. Starting with 1999 data, race-specific estimates are tabulated according to the 1997 Revisions to the Standards for the Classification of Federal Data on Race and Ethnicity and are not strictly comparable with estimates for earlier years. The two non-Hispanic race categories shown in the table conform to the 1997 Standards. Starting with 1999 data, race-specific estimates are for persons who reported only one racial group. Prior to data year 1999, estimates were tabulated according to the 1977 Standards. Estimates for single race categories prior to 1999 included persons who reported one race or, if they reported more than one race, identified one race as best representing their race. See Appendix II, Hispanic origin; Race.

[2]Hypertension is defined as having elevated blood pressure and/or taking antihypertensive medication. Elevated blood pressure is defined as having systolic pressure of at least 140 mmHg or diastolic pressure of at least 90 mmHg. Those with elevated blood pressure may be taking prescribed medicine for high blood pressure. See Appendix II, Blood pressure, elevated.

[3]Respondents were asked, "Are you now taking prescribed medicine for your high blood pressure?"

[4]Age adjusted to the 2000 standard population using five age groups: 20–34 years, 35–44 years, 45–54 years, 55–64 years, and 65 years and over (65–74 years for estimates for 20–74 years). Age-adjusted estimates may differ from other age-adjusted estimates based on the same data and presented elsewhere if different age groups are used in the adjustment procedure. See Appendix II, Age adjustment.

[5]Includes persons of all races and Hispanic origins, not just those shown separately.

[6]Poverty level is based on family income and family size. Persons with unknown poverty level are excluded. See Appendix II, Family income; Poverty.

NOTES: Percents are based on the average of blood pressure measurements taken. In 2001–2004, 77% of participants had three blood pressure readings. See *Health, United States, 2003*, Table 66 for a longer trend based on a single blood pressure measurement, which provides comparable data across five time periods (1960–1962 through 1999–2000). Excludes pregnant women. Estimates for persons 20 years and over are used for setting and tracking *Healthy People 2010* objectives. Standard errors are available in the spreadsheet version of this table. Available from: www.cdc.gov/nchs/hus.htm. Data for additional years are available. See Appendix III.

SOURCE: Centers for Disease Control and Prevention, National Center for Health Statistics, National Health and Nutrition Examination Survey.

Table 70 (page 1 of 3). Serum total cholesterol levels among persons 20 years of age and over, by sex, age, race and Hispanic origin, and poverty level: United States, selected years 1960–1962 through 2001–2004

[Data are based on physical examinations of a sample of the civilian noninstitutionalized population]

Sex, age, race and Hispanic origin[1], and poverty level	1960–1962	1971–1974	1976–1980[2]	1988–1994	2001–2004
20–74 years, age adjusted[3]	Percent of population with high serum total cholesterol				
Both sexes[4]	33.3	28.6	27.8	19.7	16.5
Male	30.6	27.9	26.4	18.8	16.6
Female	35.6	29.1	28.8	20.5	16.2
Not Hispanic or Latino:					
White only, male	- - -	- - -	26.4	18.7	16.5
White only, female	- - -	- - -	29.6	20.7	16.7
Black or African American only, male	- - -	- - -	25.5	16.4	14.4
Black or African American only, female	- - -	- - -	26.3	19.9	14.3
Mexican male	- - -	- - -	20.3	18.7	17.0
Mexican female	- - -	- - -	20.5	17.7	12.8
Percent of poverty level:[5]					
Below 100%	- - -	24.4	23.5	19.3	18.9
100%–less than 200%	- - -	28.9	26.5	19.4	17.5
200% or more	- - -	28.9	29.0	19.6	16.0
20 years and over, age adjusted[3]					
Both sexes[4]	- - -	- - -	- - -	20.8	16.7
Male	- - -	- - -	- - -	19.0	16.1
Female	- - -	- - -	- - -	22.0	16.8
Not Hispanic or Latino:					
White only, male	- - -	- - -	- - -	18.8	16.0
White only, female	- - -	- - -	- - -	22.2	17.4
Black or African American only, male	- - -	- - -	- - -	16.9	14.2
Black or African American only, female	- - -	- - -	- - -	21.4	14.8
Mexican male	- - -	- - -	- - -	18.5	16.9
Mexican female	- - -	- - -	- - -	18.7	14.0
Percent of poverty level:[5]					
Below 100%	- - -	- - -	- - -	20.6	19.3
100%–less than 200%	- - -	- - -	- - -	20.6	17.8
200% or more	- - -	- - -	- - -	20.4	15.9
20 years and over, crude					
Both sexes[4]	- - -	- - -	- - -	19.6	16.7
Male	- - -	- - -	- - -	17.7	16.4
Female	- - -	- - -	- - -	21.3	17.0
Not Hispanic or Latino:					
White only, male	- - -	- - -	- - -	18.0	16.5
White only, female	- - -	- - -	- - -	22.5	18.1
Black or African American only, male	- - -	- - -	- - -	14.7	13.8
Black or African American only, female	- - -	- - -	- - -	18.2	13.5
Mexican male	- - -	- - -	- - -	15.4	15.1
Mexican female	- - -	- - -	- - -	14.3	10.8
Percent of poverty level:[5]					
Below 100%	- - -	- - -	- - -	17.6	17.3
100%–less than 200%	- - -	- - -	- - -	19.8	16.4
200% or more	- - -	- - -	- - -	19.5	16.6
Male					
20–34 years	15.1	12.4	11.9	8.2	9.0
35–44 years	33.9	31.8	27.9	19.4	21.2
45–54 years	39.2	37.5	36.9	26.6	23.1
55–64 years	41.6	36.2	36.8	28.0	19.9
65–74 years	38.0	34.7	31.7	21.9	11.0
75 years and over	- - -	- - -	- - -	20.4	9.9
Female					
20–34 years	12.4	10.9	9.8	7.3	9.3
35–44 years	23.1	19.3	20.7	12.3	11.4
45–54 years	46.9	38.7	40.5	26.7	20.0
55–64 years	70.1	53.1	52.9	40.9	27.6
65–74 years	68.5	57.7	51.6	41.3	26.3
75 years and over	- - -	- - -	- - -	38.2	23.8

See footnotes at end of table.

[Data are based on physical examinations of a sample of the civilian noninstitutionalized population]

Sex, age, race and Hispanic origin[1], and poverty level	1960–1962	1971–1974	1976–1980[2]	1988–1994	2001–2004
20–74 years, age adjusted[3]		Mean serum cholesterol level, mg/dL			
Both sexes[4]	222	216	215	205	202
Male	220	216	213	204	201
Female	224	217	216	205	201
Not Hispanic or Latino:					
White only, male	- - -	- - -	213	204	201
White only, female	- - -	- - -	216	206	202
Black or African American only, male	- - -	- - -	211	201	198
Black or African American only, female	- - -	- - -	216	204	198
Mexican male	- - -	- - -	209	206	202
Mexican female	- - -	- - -	209	204	199
Percent of poverty level:[5]					
Below 100%	- - -	211	211	203	202
100%–less than 200%	- - -	217	213	203	202
200% or more	- - -	217	216	206	202
20 years and over, age adjusted[3]					
Both sexes[4]	- - -	- - -	- - -	206	202
Male	- - -	- - -	- - -	204	201
Female	- - -	- - -	- - -	207	202
Not Hispanic or Latino:					
White only, male	- - -	- - -	- - -	205	201
White only, female	- - -	- - -	- - -	208	203
Black or African American only, male	- - -	- - -	- - -	202	198
Black or African American only, female	- - -	- - -	- - -	207	199
Mexican male	- - -	- - -	- - -	206	201
Mexican female	- - -	- - -	- - -	206	200
Percent of poverty level:[5]					
Below 100%	- - -	- - -	- - -	205	203
100%–less than 200%	- - -	- - -	- - -	205	202
200% or more	- - -	- - -	- - -	207	202
20 years and over, crude					
Both sexes[4]	- - -	- - -	- - -	204	202
Male	- - -	- - -	- - -	202	201
Female	- - -	- - -	- - -	206	203
Not Hispanic or Latino:					
White only, male	- - -	- - -	- - -	203	201
White only, female	- - -	- - -	- - -	208	205
Black or African American only, male	- - -	- - -	- - -	198	197
Black or African American only, female	- - -	- - -	- - -	201	196
Mexican male	- - -	- - -	- - -	199	198
Mexican female	- - -	- - -	- - -	198	194
Percent of poverty level:[5]					
Below 100%	- - -	- - -	- - -	200	199
100%–less than 200%	- - -	- - -	- - -	202	200
200% or more	- - -	- - -	- - -	205	203
Male					
20–34 years	198	194	192	186	186
35–44 years	227	221	217	206	210
45–54 years	231	229	227	216	213
55–64 years	233	229	229	216	208
65–74 years	230	226	221	212	194
75 years and over	- - -	- - -	- - -	205	194
Female					
20–34 years	194	191	189	184	186
35–44 years	214	207	207	195	198
45–54 years	237	232	232	217	209
55–64 years	262	245	249	235	219
65–74 years	266	250	246	233	219
75 years and over	- - -	- - -	- - -	229	213

See footnotes at end of table.

Table 70 (page 3 of 3). Serum total cholesterol levels among persons 20 years of age and over, by sex, age, race and Hispanic origin, and poverty level: United States, selected years 1960–1962 through 2001–2004

[Data are based on physical examinations of a sample of the civilian noninstitutionalized population]

* Estimates are considered unreliable. Data preceded by an asterisk have a relative standard error of 20%–30%.
- - - Data not available.
[1]Persons of Mexican origin may be of any race. Starting with 1999 data, race-specific estimates are tabulated according to the 1997 Revisions to the Standards for the Classification of Federal Data on Race and Ethnicity and are not strictly comparable with estimates for earlier years. The two non-Hispanic race categories shown in the table conform to the 1997 Standards. Starting with 1999 data, race-specific estimates are for persons who reported only one racial group. Prior to data year 1999, estimates were tabulated according to the 1977 Standards. Estimates for single race categories prior to 1999 included persons who reported one race or, if they reported more than one race, identified one race as best representing their race. See Appendix II, Hispanic origin; Race.
[2]Data for Mexicans are for 1982–1984. See Appendix I, National Health and Nutrition Examination Survey (NHANES).
[3]Age adjusted to the 2000 standard population using five age groups: 20–34 years, 35–44 years, 45–54 years, 55–64 years, and 65 years and over (65–74 years for estimates for 20–74 years). Age-adjusted estimates may differ from other age-adjusted estimates based on the same data and presented elsewhere if different age groups are used in the adjustment procedure. See Appendix II, Age adjustment.
[4]Includes persons of all races and Hispanic origins, not just those shown separately.
[5]Poverty level is based on family income and family size. Persons with unknown poverty level are excluded. See Appendix II, Family income; Poverty.

NOTES: High serum cholesterol is defined as greater than or equal to 240 mg/dL (6.20 mmol/L). Borderline high serum cholesterol is defined as greater than or equal to 200 mg/dL and less than 240 mg/dL. Risk levels have been defined by the Third Report of the National Cholesterol Education Program Expert Panel on Detection, Evaluation, and Treatment of High Blood Cholesterol in Adults. National Heart, Lung, and Blood Institute, National Institutes of Health. September 2002. (Available from: www.nhlbi.nih.gov/guidelines/cholesterol/index.htm and summarized in JAMA 2001;285(19):2486–97). Individuals who take medicine to lower their serum cholesterol levels and whose measured total serum cholesterol levels are below the cut-offs for high and borderline high cholesterol are not defined as having high or borderline high cholesterol, respectively. Standard errors for selected years are available in the spreadsheet version of this table. Available from: www.cdc.gov/nchs/hus.htm. Data for additional years are available. See Appendix III.

SOURCES: Centers for Disease Control and Prevention, National Center for Health Statistics, National Health and Nutrition Examination Survey, Hispanic Health and Nutrition Examination Survey (1982–1984), and National Health Examination Survey (1960–1962).

Table 71. Mean energy and macronutrient intake among persons 20–74 years of age, by sex and age: United States, 1971–1974 through 1999–2002

[Data are based on dietary recall interviews of a sample of the civilian noninstitutionalized population]

Sex and age	1971–1974	1976–1980	1988–1994	1999–2002
	Energy intake in kcals			
Male, age adjusted[1]	2,450	2,439	2,666	2,634
20–39 years	2,784	2,753	2,965	2,854
40–59 years	2,303	2,315	2,568	2,601
60–74 years	1,918	1,906	2,105	2,124
Female, age adjusted[1]	1,542	1,522	1,798	1,874
20–39 years	1,652	1,643	1,958	2,031
40–59 years	1,510	1,473	1,736	1,823
60–74 years	1,325	1,322	1,522	1,582
	Percent kcals from carbohydrate			
Male, age adjusted[1]	42.4	42.6	48.2	48.9
20–39 years	42.2	43.1	48.1	50.1
40–59 years	41.6	41.5	47.8	47.7
60–74 years	44.8	44.1	49.7	48.9
Female, age adjusted[1]	45.4	46.0	50.6	51.5
20–39 years	45.8	46.0	50.6	52.6
40–59 years	44.4	45.0	50.0	50.4
60–74 years	46.8	48.6	52.5	51.4
	Percent kcals from total fat			
Male, age adjusted[1]	36.9	36.8	33.9	33.0
20–39 years	37.0	36.2	34.0	32.1
40–59 years	36.9	37.3	34.2	33.7
60–74 years	36.4	36.9	32.9	33.8
Female, age adjusted[1]	36.1	36.0	33.4	33.2
20–39 years	36.3	36.0	33.6	32.5
40–59 years	36.3	36.5	34.0	33.9
60–74 years	34.9	34.7	31.6	33.4
	Percent kcals from saturated fat			
Male, age adjusted[1]	13.5	13.2	11.3	10.8
20–39 years	13.6	13.1	11.5	10.7
40–59 years	13.5	13.5	11.3	10.8
60–74 years	13.3	13.1	10.9	10.7
Female, age adjusted[1]	13.0	12.5	11.2	10.8
20–39 years	13.0	12.6	11.4	10.8
40–59 years	13.1	12.7	11.3	10.9
60–74 years	12.4	11.8	10.4	10.5

[1]Age adjusted to the 2000 standard population using three age groups, 20–39 years, 40–59 years, and 60–74 years. Age-adjusted estimates in this table may differ from other age-adjusted estimates based on the same data and presented elsewhere if different age groups are used in the adjustment procedure. See Appendix II, Age adjustment.

NOTES: Estimates of energy intake include kilocalories (kcals) from all foods and beverages, including alcoholic beverages, consumed during the preceding 24 hours. Standard errors are available in the spreadsheet version of this table. Available from: www.cdc.gov/nchs/hus.htm. Data for additional years are available. See Appendix III.

SOURCE: Centers for Disease Control and Prevention, National Center for Health Statistics, National Health and Nutrition Examination Survey. Wright JD, Kennedy-Stephenson J, Wang CY, McDowell MA, Johnson CL. Trends in intake of energy and macronutrients - United States, 1971–2000. MMWR 2004;53(4):80–2.

Table 72 (page 1 of 2). Leisure-time physical activity among adults 18 years of age and over, by selected characteristics: United States, selected years 1998–2004

[Data are based on household interviews of a sample of the civilian noninstitutionalized population]

Characteristic	Inactive[1]			Some leisure-time activity[1]			Regular leisure-time activity[1]		
	1998	2003	2004	1998	2003	2004	1998	2003	2004
	Percent of adults								
Total, age-adjusted[2,3]	40.5	37.6	39.5	30.0	29.5	30.4	29.5	32.8	30.2
Total, crude[3]	40.2	37.6	39.4	30.0	29.6	30.4	29.8	32.8	30.2
Age									
18–44 years	35.2	32.9	35.4	31.4	30.3	31.5	33.5	36.8	33.1
18–24 years	32.8	29.6	33.1	30.1	28.2	30.2	37.1	42.3	36.6
25–44 years	35.9	34.0	36.1	31.8	31.0	31.9	32.4	34.9	31.9
45–64 years	41.2	38.2	39.2	30.6	30.5	31.0	28.2	31.3	29.7
45–54 years	38.9	36.5	37.5	31.4	30.8	32.8	29.8	32.8	29.7
55–64 years	44.9	40.8	41.8	29.3	30.1	28.5	25.8	29.2	29.8
65 years and over	55.4	51.4	52.7	24.7	25.3	25.6	19.9	23.3	21.7
65–74 years	49.1	45.8	44.3	26.5	25.8	29.0	24.4	28.4	26.7
75 years and over	63.3	57.5	62.1	22.4	24.8	21.8	14.3	17.7	16.1
Sex[2]									
Male	37.8	35.4	38.1	28.7	29.2	30.5	33.5	35.4	31.4
Female	42.9	39.5	40.6	31.1	29.9	30.3	26.0	30.6	29.1
Sex and age									
Male:									
18–44 years	32.0	30.9	34.0	30.7	29.5	31.6	37.2	39.6	34.4
45–54 years	37.7	36.4	38.3	29.6	30.5	33.4	32.6	33.2	28.3
55–64 years	44.5	39.5	40.7	26.9	29.7	·26.9	28.6	30.8	32.4
65–74 years	45.3	43.0	41.7	23.6	24.9	29.1	31.1	32.1	29.2
75 years and over	57.4	48.1	56.8	21.6	28.9	23.1	20.9	23.0	20.1
Female:									
18–44 years	38.2	34.9	36.7	32.0	31.1	31.4	29.8	34.0	31.9
45–54 years	39.9	36.5	36.7	33.0	31.1	32.3	27.1	32.4	31.0
55–64 years	45.2	41.9	42.7	31.5	30.4	29.9	23.3	27.6	27.4
65–74 years	52.2	48.0	46.5	28.7	26.6	28.9	19.0	25.4	24.6
75 years and over	67.0	63.7	65.6	22.9	22.0	21.0	10.1	14.3	13.5
Race[2,4]									
White only	38.8	36.3	38.0	30.5	29.8	30.7	30.7	33.9	31.3
Black or African American only	52.2	48.5	50.5	25.2	26.1	26.1	22.6	25.5	23.3
American Indian or Alaska Native only	49.2	54.7	44.4	19.0	20.0	33.7	31.8	25.2	21.9
Asian only	39.4	35.9	39.1	35.2	31.1	33.4	25.4	33.1	27.5
Native Hawaiian or Other Pacific Islander only	- - -	*	*	- - -	*	*	- - -	*	*
2 or more races	- - -	33.3	28.8	- - -	34.1	38.7	- - -	32.6	32.4
Hispanic origin and race[2,4]									
Hispanic or Latino	55.5	51.9	52.8	23.4	23.6	24.8	21.1	24.4	22.3
Mexican	56.7	52.0	52.4	23.9	23.7	25.5	19.4	24.3	22.1
Not Hispanic or Latino	38.8	35.5	37.5	30.7	30.3	31.1	30.5	34.2	31.4
White only	36.7	33.4	35.3	31.3	30.9	31.6	32.0	35.8	33.1
Black or African American only	52.2	48.5	50.7	25.1	26.0	26.0	22.6	25.5	23.2
Education[5,6]									
No high school diploma or GED	64.8	61.2	63.8	19.4	20.6	21.5	15.8	18.1	14.7
High school diploma or GED	47.6	45.5	48.6	28.7	27.5	28.5	23.7	27.0	22.8
Some college or more	30.2	28.1	28.9	34.3	33.8	34.3	35.5	38.2	36.9

See footnotes at end of table.

Table 72 (page 2 of 2). Leisure-time physical activity among adults 18 years of age and over, by selected characteristics: United States, selected years 1998–2004

[Data are based on household interviews of a sample of the civilian noninstitutionalized population]

Characteristic	Inactive[1]			Some leisure-time activity[1]			Regular leisure-time activity[1]		
	1998	2003	2004	1998	2003	2004	1998	2003	2004
Percent of poverty level[2,7]				Percent of adults					
Below 100%	59.4	55.1	56.7	20.5	22.0	22.8	20.1	22.9	20.4
100%–less than 200%	52.2	50.5	52.4	26.2	24.8	26.4	21.6	24.7	21.2
200% or more	34.7	31.4	33.4	32.4	32.0	32.6	33.0	36.7	34.0
Hispanic origin and race and percent of poverty level[2,4,7]									
Hispanic or Latino:									
Below 100%	68.6	64.2	63.7	18.0	19.1	20.9	13.4	16.7	15.5
100%–less than 200%	60.8	58.8	59.2	21.2	21.0	23.8	18.0	20.3	17.0
200% or more	45.6	41.8	43.1	27.6	27.3	27.7	26.8	30.9	29.3
Not Hispanic or Latino:									
White only:									
Below 100%	53.7	49.3	51.8	22.5	22.6	23.4	23.8	28.0	24.8
100%–less than 200%	49.0	45.7	48.4	27.6	27.4	27.3	23.4	27.0	24.3
200% or more	32.7	29.2	31.1	32.9	32.4	33.4	34.4	38.3	35.5
Black or African American only:									
Below 100%	64.3	61.3	61.3	17.4	20.9	21.6	18.3	17.8	17.1
100%–less than 200%	55.6	55.3	59.5	24.4	22.9	22.9	19.9	21.8	17.6
200% or more	46.0	40.7	42.4	28.7	29.1	29.2	25.3	30.2	28.4
Geographic region[2]									
Northeast	39.4	34.4	36.1	31.3	29.2	30.6	29.4	36.4	33.3
Midwest	37.3	34.7	34.7	31.7	32.2	34.1	31.0	33.1	31.2
South	46.9	42.6	46.7	27.1	27.7	27.1	26.0	29.7	26.2
West	33.9	34.9	35.3	31.6	29.9	31.6	34.6	35.2	33.2
Location of residence[2]									
Within MSA[8]	39.3	36.4	38.2	30.6	29.9	30.6	30.0	33.7	31.1
Outside MSA[8]	44.7	42.4	44.6	27.5	28.1	29.2	27.8	29.5	26.2

* Estimates are considered unreliable. Data not shown have a relative standard error of greater than 30%.

- - - Data not available.

[1]All questions related to leisure-time physical activity were phrased in terms of current behavior and lack a specific reference period. Respondents were asked about the frequency and duration of vigorous and light/moderate physical activity during leisure time. Adults classified as inactive reported no sessions of light/moderate or vigorous leisure-time activity of at least 10 minutes duration; adults classified with some leisure-time activity reported at least one session of light/moderate or vigorous physical activity of at least 10 minutes duration but did not meet the definition for regular leisure-time activity; adults classified with regular leisure-time activity reported 3 or more sessions per week of vigorous activity lasting at least 20 minutes or 5 or more sessions per week of light/moderate activity lasting at least 30 minutes in duration. See Appendix II, Physical activity, leisure-time.

[2]Estimates are age adjusted to the year 2000 standard population using five age groups: 18–44 years, 45–54 years, 55–64 years, 65–74 years, and 75 years and over. Age-adjusted estimates in this table may differ from other age-adjusted estimates based on the same data and presented elsewhere if different age groups are used in the adjustment procedure. See Appendix II, Age adjustment.

[3]Includes all other races not shown separately and unknown education level.

[4]The race groups, white, black, American Indian or Alaska Native, Asian, Native Hawaiian or Other Pacific Islander, and 2 or more races, include persons of Hispanic and non-Hispanic origin. Persons of Hispanic origin may be of any race. Starting with 1999 data, race-specific estimates are tabulated according to the 1997 Revisions to the Standards for the Classification of Federal Data on Race and Ethnicity and are not strictly comparable with estimates for earlier years. The five single race categories plus multiple race categories shown in the table conform to the 1997 Standards. Starting with 1999 data, race-specific estimates are for persons who reported only one racial group; the category 2 or more races includes persons who reported more than one racial group. Prior to 1999, data were tabulated according to the 1977 Standards with four racial groups and the Asian only category included Native Hawaiian or Other Pacific Islander. Estimates for single race categories prior to 1999 included persons who reported one race or, if they reported more than one race, identified one race as best representing their race. Starting with 2003 data, race responses of other race and unspecified multiple race were treated as missing, and then race was imputed if these were the only race responses. Almost all persons with a race response of other race were of Hispanic origin. See Appendix II, Hispanic origin; Race.

[5]Estimates are for persons 25 years of age and over and are age adjusted to the year 2000 standard population using five age groups: 25–44 years, 45–54 years, 55–64 years, 65–74 years, and 75 years and over. See Appendix II, Age adjustment.

[6]GED stands for General Educational Development high school equivalency diploma. See Appendix II, Education.

[7]Percent of poverty level is based on family income and family size and composition using U.S. Census Bureau poverty thresholds. Missing family income data were imputed for 31%–36% of adults 18 years of age and over in 1998–2004. See Appendix II, Family Income; Poverty.

[8]MSA is metropolitan statistical area.

NOTES: For more data on leisure-time physical activity, see National Health Interview Survey. Available from: www.cdc.gov/nchs/nhis/htm. Standard errors are available in the spreadsheet version of this table. Available from: www.cdc.gov/nchs/hus.htm. Data for additional years are available. See Appendix III.

SOURCE: Centers for Disease Control and Prevention, National Center for Health Statistics, National Health Interview Survey, family core and sample adult questionnaires.

Table 73 (page 1 of 4). Overweight, obesity, and healthy weight among persons 20 years of age and over, by sex, age, race and Hispanic origin, and poverty level: United States, 1960–1962 through 2001–2004

[Data are based on measured height and weight of a sample of the civilian noninstitutionalized population]

Sex, age, race and Hispanic origin[1], and poverty level	Overweight[2]				
	1960–1962	1971–1974	1976–1980[3]	1988–1994	2001–2004
20–74 years, age adjusted[4]	Percent of population				
Both sexes[5]	44.8	47.7	47.4	56.0	66.0
Male	49.5	54.7	52.9	61.0	70.7
Female	40.2	41.1	42.0	51.2	61.4
Not Hispanic or Latino:					
White only, male	- - -	- - -	53.8	61.6	71.1
White only, female	- - -	- - -	38.7	47.2	57.1
Black or African American only, male	- - -	- - -	51.3	58.2	66.8
Black or African American only, female	- - -	- - -	62.6	68.5	79.5
Mexican male	- - -	- - -	61.6	69.4	75.8
Mexican female	- - -	- - -	61.7	69.6	73.2
Percent of poverty level:[6]					
Below 100%	- - -	49.3	50.0	59.8	63.9
100%–less than 200%	- - -	50.9	49.0	58.2	66.2
200% or more	- - -	46.7	46.6	54.5	66.1
20 years and over, age adjusted[4]					
Both sexes[5]	- - -	- - -	- - -	56.0	66.0
Male	- - -	- - -	- - -	60.9	70.5
Female	- - -	- - -	- - -	51.4	61.6
Not Hispanic or Latino:					
White only, male	- - -	- - -	- - -	61.6	71.0
White only, female	- - -	- - -	- - -	47.5	57.6
Black or African American only, male	- - -	- - -	- - -	57.8	67.0
Black or African American only, female	- - -	- - -	- - -	68.2	79.6
Mexican male	- - -	- - -	- - -	68.9	74.6
Mexican female	- - -	- - -	- - -	68.9	73.0
Percent of poverty level:[6]					
Below 100%	- - -	- - -	- - -	59.6	63.4
100%–less than 200%	- - -	- - -	- - -	58.0	66.2
200% or more	- - -	- - -	- - -	54.8	66.1
20 years and over, crude					
Both sexes[5]	- - -	- - -	- - -	54.9	66.1
Male	- - -	- - -	- - -	59.4	70.4
Female	- - -	- - -	- - -	50.7	61.9
Not Hispanic or Latino:					
White only, male	- - -	- - -	- - -	60.6	71.6
White only, female	- - -	- - -	- - -	47.4	58.7
Black or African American only, male	- - -	- - -	- - -	56.7	66.3
Black or African American only, female	- - -	- - -	- - -	66.0	79.1
Mexican male	- - -	- - -	- - -	63.9	71.8
Mexican female	- - -	- - -	- - -	65.9	71.4
Percent of poverty level:[6]					
Below 100%	- - -	- - -	- - -	56.8	61.4
100%–less than 200%	- - -	- - -	- - -	55.7	65.3
200% or more	- - -	- - -	- - -	54.2	67.1
Male					
20–34 years	42.7	42.8	41.2	47.5	59.0
35–44 years	53.5	63.2	57.2	65.5	72.9
45–54 years	53.9	59.7	60.2	66.1	78.5
55–64 years	52.2	58.5	60.2	70.5	77.3
65–74 years	47.8	54.6	54.2	68.5	76.1
75 years and over	- - -	- - -	- - -	56.5	66.8
Female					
20–34 years	21.2	25.8	27.9	37.0	51.6
35–44 years	37.2	40.5	40.7	49.6	60.1
45–54 years	49.3	49.0	48.7	60.3	67.4
55–64 years	59.9	54.5	53.7	66.3	69.9
65–74 years	60.9	55.9	59.5	60.3	71.5
75 years and over	- - -	- - -	- - -	52.3	63.7

See footnotes at end of table.

Table 73 (page 2 of 4). Overweight, obesity, and healthy weight among persons 20 years of age and over, by sex, age, race and Hispanic origin, and poverty level: United States, 1960–1962 through 2001–2004

[Data are based on measured height and weight of a sample of the civilian noninstitutionalized population]

Sex, age, race and Hispanic origin[1], and poverty level	Obesity[7]				
	1960–1962	1971–1974	1976–1980[3]	1988–1994	2001–2004
20–74 years, age adjusted[4]	Percent of population				
Both sexes[5]	13.3	14.6	15.1	23.3	32.1
Male	10.7	12.2	12.8	20.6	30.2
Female	15.7	16.8	17.1	26.0	34.0
Not Hispanic or Latino:					
White only, male	- - -	- - -	12.4	20.7	31.0
White only, female	- - -	- - -	15.4	23.3	31.5
Black or African American only, male	- - -	- - -	16.5	21.3	31.2
Black or African American only, female	- - -	- - -	31.0	39.1	51.6
Mexican male	- - -	- - -	15.7	24.4	30.5
Mexican female	- - -	- - -	26.6	36.1	40.3
Percent of poverty level:[6]					
Below 100%	- - -	20.7	21.9	29.2	34.9
100%–less than 200%	- - -	18.4	18.7	26.6	34.6
200% or more	- - -	12.4	12.9	21.4	30.6
20 years and over, age adjusted[4]					
Both sexes[5]	- - -	- - -	- - -	22.9	31.4
Male	- - -	- - -	- - -	20.2	29.5
Female	- - -	- - -	- - -	25.5	33.2
Not Hispanic or Latino:					
White only, male	- - -	- - -	- - -	20.3	30.2
White only, female	- - -	- - -	- - -	22.9	30.7
Black or African American only, male	- - -	- - -	- - -	20.9	30.8
Black or African American only, female	- - -	- - -	- - -	38.3	51.1
Mexican male	- - -	- - -	- - -	23.8	29.1
Mexican female	- - -	- - -	- - -	35.2	39.4
Percent of poverty level:[6]					
Below 100%	- - -	- - -	- - -	28.1	33.7
100%–less than 200%	- - -	- - -	- - -	26.1	33.6
200% or more	- - -	- - -	- - -	21.1	30.0
20 years and over, crude					
Both sexes[5]	- - -	- - -	- - -	22.3	31.5
Male	- - -	- - -	- - -	19.5	29.5
Female	- - -	- - -	- - -	25.0	33.3
Not Hispanic or Latino:					
White only, male	- - -	- - -	- - -	19.9	30.5
White only, female	- - -	- - -	- - -	22.7	31.2
Black or African American only, male	- - -	- - -	- - -	20.7	30.7
Black or African American only, female	- - -	- - -	- - -	36.7	51.1
Mexican male	- - -	- - -	- - -	20.6	27.8
Mexican female	- - -	- - -	- - -	33.3	38.5
Percent of poverty level:[6]					
Below 100%	- - -	- - -	- - -	25.9	33.0
100%–less than 200%	- - -	- - -	- - -	24.3	32.6
200% or more	- - -	- - -	- - -	20.9	30.7
Male					
20–34 years	9.2	9.7	8.9	14.1	23.2
35–44 years	12.1	13.5	13.5	21.5	33.8
45–54 years	12.5	13.7	16.7	23.2	31.8
55–64 years	9.2	14.1	14.1	27.2	36.0
65–74 years	10.4	10.9	13.2	24.1	32.1
75 years and over	- - -	- - -	- - -	13.2	19.9
Female					
20–34 years	7.2	9.7	11.0	18.5	28.6
35–44 years	14.7	17.7	17.8	25.5	33.3
45–54 years	20.3	18.9	19.6	32.4	38.0
55–64 years	24.4	24.1	22.9	33.7	39.0
65–74 years	23.2	22.0	21.5	26.9	37.9
75 years and over	- - -	- - -	- - -	19.2	23.2

See footnotes at end of table.

Table 73 (page 3 of 4). Overweight, obesity, and healthy weight among persons 20 years of age and over, by sex, age, race and Hispanic origin, and poverty level: United States, 1960–1962 through 2001–2004

[Data are based on measured height and weight of a sample of the civilian noninstitutionalized population]

Sex, age, race and Hispanic origin[1], and poverty level	Healthy weight[8]				
	1960–1962	1971–1974	1976–1980[3]	1988–1994	2001–2004
20–74 years, age adjusted[4]	Percent of population				
Both sexes[5]	51.2	48.8	49.6	41.7	32.2
Male	48.3	43.0	45.4	37.9	28.1
Female	54.1	54.3	53.7	45.3	36.2
Not Hispanic or Latino:					
White only, male	- - -	- - -	45.3	37.4	27.8
White only, female	- - -	- - -	56.7	49.2	40.2
Black or African American only, male	- - -	- - -	46.6	40.0	31.3
Black or African American only, female	- - -	- - -	35.0	28.9	18.9
Mexican male	- - -	- - -	37.1	29.8	24.2
Mexican female	- - -	- - -	36.4	29.0	26.3
Percent of poverty level:[6]					
Below 100%	- - -	45.8	45.1	37.3	33.7
100%–less than 200%	- - -	45.1	47.6	39.2	31.8
200% or more	- - -	50.2	51.0	43.4	32.4
20 years and over, age adjusted[4]					
Both sexes[5]	- - -	- - -	- - -	41.6	32.3
Male	- - -	- - -	- - -	37.9	28.3
Female	- - -	- - -	- - -	45.0	36.1
Not Hispanic or Latino:					
White only, male	- - -	- - -	- - -	37.3	28.0
White only, female	- - -	- - -	- - -	48.7	39.8
Black or African American only, male	- - -	- - -	- - -	40.1	30.8
Black or African American only, female	- - -	- - -	- - -	29.2	18.9
Mexican male	- - -	- - -	- - -	30.2	25.3
Mexican female	- - -	- - -	- - -	29.7	26.5
Percent of poverty level:[6]					
Below 100%	- - -	- - -	- - -	37.5	34.3
100%–less than 200%	- - -	- - -	- - -	39.3	31.9
200% or more	- - -	- - -	- - -	43.1	32.4
20 years and over, crude					
Both sexes[5]	- - -	- - -	- - -	42.6	32.2
Male	- - -	- - -	- - -	39.4	28.4
Female	- - -	- - -	- - -	45.7	35.8
Not Hispanic or Latino:					
White only, male	- - -	- - -	- - -	38.2	27.4
White only, female	- - -	- - -	- - -	48.8	38.8
Black or African American only, male	- - -	- - -	- - -	41.5	31.5
Black or African American only, female	- - -	- - -	- - -	31.2	19.3
Mexican male	- - -	- - -	- - -	35.2	28.1
Mexican female	- - -	- - -	- - -	32.4	28.0
Percent of poverty level:[6]					
Below 100%	- - -	- - -	- - -	39.8	36.2
100%–less than 200%	- - -	- - -	- - -	41.5	32.6
200% or more	- - -	- - -	- - -	43.6	31.6
Male					
20–34 years	55.3	54.7	57.1	51.1	38.3
35–44 years	45.2	35.2	41.3	33.4	26.5
45–54 years	44.8	38.5	38.7	33.6	21.2
55–64 years	44.9	38.3	38.7	28.6	22.2
65–74 years	46.2	42.1	42.3	30.1	23.1
75 years and over	- - -	- - -	- - -	40.9	32.1
Female					
20–34 years	67.6	65.8	65.0	57.9	44.2
35–44 years	58.4	56.7	55.6	47.1	38.3
45–54 years	47.6	49.3	48.7	37.2	31.0
55–64 years	38.1	41.1	43.5	31.5	29.2
65–74 years	36.4	40.6	37.8	37.0	27.0
75 years and over	- - -	- - -	- - -	43.0	34.6

See footnotes at end of table.

Table 73 (page 4 of 4). Overweight, obesity, and healthy weight among persons 20 years of age and over, by sex, age, race and Hispanic origin, and poverty level: United States, 1960–1962 through 2001–2004

[Data are based on measured height and weight of a sample of the civilian noninstitutionalized population]

- - - Data not available.

[1]Persons of Mexican origin may be of any race. Starting with 1999 data, race-specific estimates are tabulated according to the 1997 Revisions to the Standards for the Classification of Federal Data on Race and Ethnicity and are not strictly comparable with estimates for earlier years. The two non-Hispanic race categories shown in the table conform to the 1997 Standards. Starting with 1999 data, race-specific estimates are for persons who reported only one racial group. Prior to data year 1999, estimates were tabulated according to the 1977 Standards. Estimates for single race categories prior to 1999 included persons who reported one race or, if they reported more than one race, identified one race as best representing their race. See Appendix II, Hispanic origin; Race.

[2]Body mass index (BMI) greater than or equal to 25. See Appendix II, Body mass index.

[3]Data for Mexicans are for 1982–1984. See Appendix I, National Health and Nutrition Examination Survey (NHANES).

[4]Age adjusted to the 2000 standard population using five age groups: 20–34 years, 35–44 years, 45–54 years, 55–64 years, and 65 years and over (65–74 years for estimates for 20–74 years). Age-adjusted estimates in this table may differ from other age-adjusted estimates based on the same data and presented elsewhere if different age groups are used in the adjustment procedure. See Appendix II, Age adjustment.

[5]Includes persons of all races and Hispanic origins, not just those shown separately.

[6]Poverty level is based on family income and family size. Persons with unknown poverty level are excluded. See Appendix II, Family income; Poverty.

[7]Body mass index (BMI) greater than or equal to 30.

[8]BMI of 18.5 to less than 25 kilograms/meter^2.

NOTES: Percents do not sum to 100 because the percent of persons with BMI less than 18.5 is not shown and the percent of persons with obesity is a subset of the percent with overweight. Height was measured without shoes; two pounds were deducted from data for 1960–1962 to allow for weight of clothing. Excludes pregnant women. Standard errors for selected years are available in the spreadsheet version of this table. Available from: www.cdc.gov/nchs/hus.htm. Data for additional years are available. See Appendix III.

SOURCES: Centers for Disease Control and Prevention, National Center for Health Statistics, National Health and Nutrition Examination Survey, Hispanic Health and Nutrition Examination Survey (1982–1984), and National Health Examination Survey (1960–1962).

Table 74. Overweight among children and adolescents 6–19 years of age, by age, sex, race and Hispanic origin, and poverty level: United States, 1963–1965 through 2001–2004

[Data are based on physical examinations of a sample of the civilian noninstitutionalized population]

Sex, age, race and Hispanic origin[1], and poverty level	1963–1965 1966–1970[2]	1971–1974	1976–1980[3]	1988–1994	2001–2004
6–11 years of age			Percent of population		
Both sexes[4]	4.2	4.0	6.5	11.3	17.5
Boys	4.0	*4.3	6.6	11.6	18.7
Not Hispanic or Latino:					
White only	- - -	- - -	6.1	10.7	16.9
Black or African American only	- - -	- - -	6.8	12.3	17.2
Mexican	- - -	- - -	13.3	17.5	25.6
Girls	4.5	*3.6	6.4	11.0	16.3
Not Hispanic or Latino:					
White only	- - -	- - -	5.2	*9.8	15.6
Black or African American only	- - -	- - -	11.2	17.0	24.8
Mexican	- - -	- - -	9.8	15.3	16.6
Percent of poverty level:[5]					
Below 100%	- - -	- - -	- - -	11.4	20.0
100%–less than 200%	- - -	- - -	- - -	11.1	18.4
200% or more	- - -	- - -	- - -	11.1	15.4
12–19 years of age					
Both sexes[4]	4.6	6.1	5.0	10.5	17.0
Boys	4.5	6.1	4.8	11.3	17.9
Not Hispanic or Latino:					
White only	- - -	- - -	3.8	11.6	17.9
Black or African American only	- - -	- - -	6.1	10.7	17.7
Mexican	- - -	- - -	7.7	14.1	20.0
Girls	4.7	6.2	5.3	9.7	16.0
Not Hispanic or Latino:					
White only	- - -	- - -	4.6	8.9	14.6
Black or African American only	- - -	- - -	10.7	16.3	23.8
Mexican	- - -	- - -	8.8	*13.4	17.1
Percent of poverty level:[5]					
Below 100%	- - -	- - -	- - -	15.8	18.2
100%–less than 200%	- - -	- - -	- - -	11.2	17.0
200% or more	- - -	- - -	- - -	7.9	16.3

* Estimates are considered unreliable. Data preceded by an asterisk have a relative standard error of 20%–30%.

- - - Data not available.

[1]Persons of Mexican origin may be of any race. Starting with 1999 data, race-specific estimates are tabulated according to the 1997 Revisions to the Standards for the Classification of Federal Data on Race and Ethnicity and are not strictly comparable with estimates for earlier years. The two non-Hispanic race categories shown in the table conform to the 1997 Standards. Starting with 1999 data, race-specific estimates are for persons who reported only one racial group. Prior to data year 1999, estimates were tabulated according to the 1977 Standards. Estimates for single race categories prior to 1999 included persons who reported one race or, if they reported more than one race, identified one race as best representing their race. See Appendix II, Hispanic origin; Race.

[2]Data for 1963–1965 are for children 6–11 years of age; data for 1966–1970 are for adolescents 12–17 years of age, not 12–19 years.

[3]Data for Mexicans are for 1982–1984. See Appendix I, National Health and Nutrition Examination Survey (NHANES).

[4]Includes persons of all races and Hispanic origins, not just those shown separately.

[5]Poverty level is based on family income and family size. Persons with unknown poverty level are excluded. See Appendix II, Family income; Poverty.

NOTES: Overweight is defined as body mass index (BMI) at or above the sex- and age-specific 95th percentile BMI cutoff points from the 2000 CDC Growth Charts: United States. Advance data from vital and health statistics; no 314. Hyattsville, MD: National Center for Health Statistics. 2000. Age is at time of examination at mobile examination center. Crude rates, not age-adjusted rates, are shown. Excludes pregnant girls starting with 1971–1974. Pregnancy status not available for 1963–1965 and 1966–1970. Standard errors for selected years are available in the spreadsheet version of this table. Available from: www.cdc.gov/nchs/hus.htm. Data for additional years are available. See Appendix III.

SOURCES: Centers for Disease Control and Prevention, National Center for Health Statistics, National Health and Nutrition Examination Survey, Hispanic Health and Nutrition Examination Survey (1982–1984), and National Health Examination Survey (1963–1965 and 1966–1970).

Table 75 (page 1 of 2). Untreated dental caries, by age, sex, race and Hispanic origin, and poverty level: United States, 1971–1974, 1988–1994, and 1999–2002

[Data are based on dental examinations of a sample of the civilian noninstitutionalized population]

Sex, race and Hispanic origin[1], and poverty level	2–5 years			6–17 years		
	1971–1974	1988–1994	1999–2002	1971–1974	1988–1994	1999–2002
	Percent of persons with untreated dental caries					
Total[2]	25.0	19.1	19.3	54.8	23.6	21.5
Sex						
Male.	26.4	19.3	20.3	54.7	22.6	22.4
Female	23.6	18.9	18.4	55.0	24.5	20.5
Race and Hispanic origin						
Not Hispanic or Latino:						
White only	23.7	13.8	16.9	51.9	18.9	17.5
Black or African American only.	29.0	24.7	24.1	70.1	32.8	27.7
Mexican	34.1	34.9	31.4	60.2	36.6	32.0
Percent of poverty level:[3]						
Below 100%.	32.0	30.2	31.7	68.7	38.2	32.1
100%–less than 200%.	29.9	24.3	20.1	60.7	28.2	28.8
200% or more	17.8	9.4	11.0	45.6	14.9	12.7
Race, Hispanic origin, and poverty level[3]						
Not Hispanic or Latino:						
White only:						
Below 100% of poverty level.	32.1	25.7	34.2	68.2	34.4	29.2
100% or more of poverty level	22.0	11.7	12.8	49.9	16.6	15.2
Black or African American only:						
Below 100% of poverty level.	29.1	27.2	28.7	72.7	35.5	35.0
100% or more of poverty level	27.9	22.5	20.1	66.7	30.9	23.8
Mexican:						
Below 100% of poverty level	*	38.8	39.1	57.1	46.1	38.6
100% or more of poverty level	27.4	30.3	25.7	61.2	26.4	24.7

Sex, race and Hispanic origin[1], and poverty level	18–64 years			65–74 years		
	1971–1974	1988–1994	1999–2002	1971–1974	1988–1994	1999–2002
	Percent of persons with untreated dental caries					
Total[2]	48.4	28.2	23.8	29.7	25.4	17.0
Sex						
Male.	50.9	31.2	25.9	32.6	29.8	20.1
Female	46.0	25.3	21.7	27.4	21.5	14.4
Race and Hispanic origin						
Not Hispanic or Latino:						
White only	45.6	23.6	18.7	28.3	22.7	14.3
Black or African American only.	68.2	47.9	41.5	41.5	46.7	35.0
Mexican	62.0	39.9	35.3	*	43.8	33.9
Percent of poverty level:[3]						
Below 100%.	63.6	47.4	40.1	34.3	46.6	27.9
100%–less than 200%.	56.3	42.6	36.1	35.6	40.1	28.1
200% or more	43.1	19.5	16.1	26.2	19.2	12.2
Race, Hispanic origin, and poverty status[3]						
Not Hispanic or Latino:						
White only:						
Below 100% of poverty level.	59.5	42.4	33.9	33.3	*39.0	*
100% or more of poverty level	44.5	21.6	16.8	28.3	22.7	14.0
Black or African American only:						
Below 100% of poverty level.	73.1	59.2	53.1	39.8	49.7	*31.0
100% or more of poverty level	65.8	43.4	37.0	41.1	43.8	39.0
Mexican:						
Below 100% of poverty level	65.4	52.4	43.1	*	55.5	*45.0
100% or more of poverty level	59.1	31.5	32.0	*	35.6	31.1

See footnotes at end of table.

Table 75 (page 2 of 2). Untreated dental caries, by age, sex, race and Hispanic origin, and poverty level: United States, 1971–1974, 1988–1994, and 1999–2002

[Data are based on dental examinations of a sample of the civilian noninstitutionalized population]

Sex, race and Hispanic origin[1], and poverty level	75 years and over		
	1971–1974	1988–1994	1999–2002
	Percent of persons with untreated dental caries		
Total[2]	- - -	30.3	20.3
Sex			
Male	- - -	34.4	24.4
Female	- - -	28.1	17.4
Race and Hispanic origin			
Not Hispanic or Latino:			
White only	- - -	27.8	18.3
Black or African American only	- - -	62.6	46.8
Mexican	- - -	55.6	48.2
Percent of poverty level:[3]			
Below 100%	- - -	47.1	33.0
100%–less than 200%	- - -	34.5	23.0
200% or more	- - -	23.2	15.8
Race, Hispanic origin, and poverty status[3]			
Not Hispanic or Latino:			
White only:			
Below 100% of poverty level	- - -	38.0	*32.2
100% or more of poverty level	- - -	26.1	17.2
Black or African American only:			
Below 100% of poverty level	- - -	68.6	*
100% or more of poverty level	- - -	60.2	43.8
Mexican:			
Below 100% of poverty level	- - -	79.4	*
100% or more of poverty level	- - -	*	49.7

* Estimates are considered unreliable. Data preceded by an asterisk have a relative standard error (RSE) of 20%–30%. Data not shown have an RSE of greater than 30% or fewer than 30 cases.

- - - Data not available.

[1]Persons of Mexican origin may be of any race. Starting with 1999 data, race-specific estimates are tabulated according to the 1997 Revisions to the Standards for the Classification of Federal Data on Race and Ethnicity and are not strictly comparable with estimates for earlier years. The two non-Hispanic race categories shown in the table conform to the 1997 Standards. Starting with 1999 data, race-specific estimates are for persons who reported only one racial group. Prior to data year 1999, estimates were tabulated according to the 1977 Standards. Estimates for single race categories prior to 1999 included persons who reported one race or, if they reported more than one race, identified one race as best representing their race. See Appendix II, Hispanic origin; Race.

[2]Includes persons of all races and Hispanic origins, not just those shown separately and those with unknown poverty level.

[3]Poverty level is based on family income and family size. Persons with unknown poverty level are excluded (4% in 1971–1974, 6% in 1988–1994, and 8% in 1999–2002). See Appendix II, Family income; Poverty.

NOTES: Untreated dental caries refers to untreated coronal caries, that is, caries on the crown or enamel surface of the tooth. Root caries are not included. For children 2–5 years of age, only dental caries in primary teeth was evaluated. Caries in both permanent and primary teeth was evaluated for children 6–11 years of age. For children 12–17 years of age and adults, only dental caries in permanent teeth was evaluated. Excludes edentulous persons (persons without teeth) of all ages. The majority of edentulous persons are 65 years of age and over. Estimates of edentulism among persons 65 years of age and over are 46% in 1971–1974, 33% in 1988–1994, and 27% in 1999–2002. See Appendix II, Dental caries. Standard errors are available in the spreadsheet version of this table. Available from: www.cdc.gov/nchs/hus.htm. Data have been revised and differ from previous editions of *Health, United States*.

SOURCES: Centers for Disease Control and Prevention, National Center for Health Statistics, National Health and Nutrition Examination Survey.

Table 76 (page 1 of 2). No usual source of health care among children under 18 years of age, by selected characteristics: United States, average annual selected years 1993–1994 through 2003–2004

[Data are based on household interviews of a sample of the civilian noninstitutionalized population]

Characteristic	Under 18 years of age			Under 6 years of age			6–17 years of age		
	1993–1994[1]	2001–2002	2003–2004	1993–1994[1]	2001–2002	2003–2004	1993–1994[1]	2001–2002	2003–2004
	Percent of children without a usual source of health care[2]								
All children[3]	7.7	6.0	5.4	5.2	4.4	3.4	9.0	6.8	6.4
Race[4]									
White only.	7.0	5.2	5.1	4.7	4.0	3.2	8.3	5.8	6.1
Black or African American only . .	10.3	6.6	6.2	7.6	3.6	*4.1	11.9	8.0	7.2
American Indian or Alaska Native only	*9.3	*	*7.6	*	*	*	*8.7	*	*9.6
Asian only.	9.7	11.2	7.7	*3.4	*	*	13.5	13.2	9.3
Native Hawaiian or Other Pacific Islander only	- - -	*	*	- - -	*	*	- - -	*	*
2 or more races.	- - -	7.3	*4.3	- - -	*7.0	*	- - -	*7.5	*
Hispanic origin and race[4]									
Hispanic or Latino	14.3	13.5	11.4	9.3	9.2	7.4	17.7	16.0	13.7
Not Hispanic or Latino	6.7	4.4	4.0	4.4	3.2	2.3	7.8	4.9	4.8
White only	5.7	3.4	3.2	3.7	2.7	1.8	6.7	3.7	3.9
Black or African American only.	10.2	6.6	6.2	7.7	3.6	*4.0	11.6	8.0	7.1
Percent of poverty level[5]									
Below 100%	13.9	11.7	10.6	9.4	8.2	6.3	16.8	13.7	13.1
100%–less than 200%	9.8	8.9	7.7	6.7	7.0	4.9	11.6	9.9	9.3
200% or more	3.7	3.3	3.0	1.8	2.1	1.7	4.6	3.8	3.5
Hispanic origin and race and percent of poverty level[4,5]									
Hispanic or Latino:									
Below 100%	19.6	18.5	14.7	12.7	12.1	8.7	24.8	22.4	18.5
100%–less than 200%	15.3	16.0	13.3	9.9	11.2	8.8	18.9	18.7	16.0
200% or more	5.0	7.1	6.5	*2.7	*4.5	*4.6	6.5	8.6	7.5
Not Hispanic or Latino:									
White only:									
Below 100%	10.2	7.5	8.0	6.5	*	*4.5	12.7	8.2	10.0
100%–less than 200%	8.7	5.4	4.7	6.3	*4.8	*3.0	10.1	5.7	5.7
200% or more	3.4	2.4	2.2	1.6	1.5	*1.0	4.2	2.7	2.7
Black or African American only:									
Below 100%	13.7	9.0	8.8	10.9	*4.0	*	15.5	11.5	10.3
100%–less than 200%	9.1	7.3	5.6	*6.0	*5.1	*	10.8	8.4	6.4
200% or more	4.6	4.2	4.5	*	*	*	5.8	5.1	5.3
Health insurance status at the time of interview[6]									
Insured.	5.0	3.3	2.9	3.3	2.2	2.0	5.9	3.8	3.4
Private	3.8	2.5	2.3	1.9	1.4	1.4	4.6	3.0	2.7
Medicaid	8.9	5.5	4.6	6.4	4.0	3.3	11.3	6.5	5.4
Uninsured.	23.5	29.1	28.8	18.0	25.2	19.8	26.0	30.7	32.1
Health insurance status prior to interview[6]									
Insured continuously all 12 months	4.6	3.0	2.7	3.1	2.0	1.9	5.5	3.4	3.2
Uninsured for any period up to 12 months.	15.3	16.7	14.5	10.9	13.8	9.7	18.1	18.4	17.1
Uninsured more than 12 months	27.6	36.5	36.1	21.4	32.1	26.5	30.0	38.1	38.8

See footnotes at end of table.

Table 76 (page 2 of 2). No usual source of health care among children under 18 years of age, by selected characteristics: United States, average annual selected years 1993–1994 through 2003–2004

[Data are based on household interviews of a sample of the civilian noninstitutionalized population]

Characteristic	Under 18 years of age			Under 6 years of age			6–17 years of age		
	1993–1994[1]	2001–2002	2003–2004	1993–1994[1]	2001–2002	2003–2004	1993–1994[1]	2001–2002	2003–2004
Percent of poverty level and health insurance status prior to interview[5,6]	Percent of children without a usual source of health care[2]								
Below 100%:									
Insured continuously all 12 months	8.6	5.0	5.0	5.8	*2.7	*3.7	10.7	6.4	5.8
Uninsured for any period up to 12 months	21.7	21.2	20.6	18.0	18.5	*15.4	23.7	23.0	23.2
Uninsured more than 12 months	31.2	46.2	44.1	25.5	42.5	27.3	33.4	47.6	48.7
100%–less than 200%:									
Insured continuously all 12 months	5.6	4.0	3.5	3.7	3.3	*2.2	6.7	4.4	4.2
Uninsured for any period up to 12 months	14.5	18.7	15.2	*9.7	*15.8	*11.9	18.0	20.2	16.9
Uninsured more than 12 months	27.6	33.8	35.4	21.4	29.9	28.5	30.2	35.3	37.5
200% or more:									
Insured continuously all 12 months	2.8	2.1	1.9	1.4	1.3	1.2	3.5	2.5	2.2
Uninsured for any period up to 12 months	9.1	11.9	10.2	*5.7	*8.4	*	11.4	13.9	13.2
Uninsured more than 12 months	18.3	27.3	27.2	*10.6	*18.8	*22.0	20.9	29.8	28.5
Geographic region									
Northeast	4.1	2.4	1.8	2.9	*2.4	*0.9	4.8	2.4	2.2
Midwest	5.2	4.2	3.4	4.1	3.8	2.6	5.9	4.4	3.8
South	10.9	7.3	6.7	7.3	4.6	4.3	12.7	8.7	7.9
West	8.6	8.8	8.2	5.3	6.3	4.6	10.6	10.1	10.0
Location of residence									
Within MSA[7]	7.7	6.1	5.4	5.0	4.5	3.4	9.2	6.9	6.3
Outside MSA[7]	7.8	5.7	5.6	6.0	3.9	*3.1	8.7	6.5	6.8

* Estimates are considered unreliable. Data preceded by an asterisk have a relative standard error (RSE) of 20%–30%. Data not shown have an RSE of greater than 30%.

- - - Data not available.

[1]Data prior to 1997 are not strictly comparable with data for later years due to the 1997 questionnaire redesign. See Appendix I, National Health Interview Survey.
[2]Persons who report the emergency department as the place of their usual source of care are defined as having no usual source of care. See Appendix II, Usual source of care.
[3]Includes all other races not shown separately and unknown health insurance status.
[4]The race groups, white, black, American Indian or Alaska Native, Asian, Native Hawaiian or Other Pacific Islander, and 2 or more races, include persons of Hispanic and non-Hispanic origin. Persons of Hispanic origin may be of any race. Starting with 1999 data, race-specific estimates are tabulated according to the 1997 Revisions to the Standards for the Classification of Federal Data on Race and Ethnicity and are not strictly comparable with estimates for earlier years. The five single race categories plus multiple race categories shown in the table conform to the 1997 Standards. Starting with 1999 data, race-specific estimates are for persons who reported only one racial group; the category 2 or more races includes persons who reported more than one racial group. Prior to 1999, data were tabulated according to the 1977 Standards with four racial groups and the Asian only category included Native Hawaiian or Other Pacific Islander. Estimates for single race categories prior to 1999 included persons who reported one race or, if they reported more than one race, identified one race as best representing their race. Starting with 2003 data, race responses of other race and unspecified multiple race were treated as missing, and then race was imputed if these were the only race responses. Almost all persons with a race response of other race were of Hispanic origin. See Appendix II, Hispanic origin; Race.
[5]Percent of poverty level is based on family income and family size and composition using U.S. Census Bureau poverty thresholds. Missing family income data were imputed for 14% of children in 1993–1996, 21%–25% in 1997–1998, and 28%–31% in 1999–2004. See Appendix II, Family income; Poverty.
[6]Health insurance categories are mutually exclusive. Persons who reported both Medicaid and private coverage are classified as having private coverage. Medicaid includes other public assistance through 1996. Starting with 1997 data, Medicaid includes state-sponsored health plans and State Children's Health Insurance Program (SCHIP). The category insured also includes military, other government, and Medicare coverage. Health insurance status was unknown for 8%–9% of children in the sample in 1993–1996 and 1% in 1997–2004. See Appendix II, Health insurance coverage.
[7]MSA is metropolitan statistical area.

NOTES: Standard errors are available in the spreadsheet version of this table. Available from: www.cdc.gov/nchs/hus.htm. Data for additional years are available. See Appendix III.

SOURCES: Centers for Disease Control and Prevention, National Center for Health Statistics, National Health Interview Survey, access to care and health insurance supplements (1993–1996). Starting in 1997 data are from the family core and sample child questionnaires.

Table 77 (page 1 of 2). No usual source of health care among adults 18–64 years of age, by selected characteristics: United States, average annual selected years 1993–1994 through 2003–2004

[Data are based on household interviews of a sample of the civilian noninstitutionalized population]

Characteristic	1993–1994[1]	1995–1996[1]	1997–1998	1999–2000	2001–2002	2003–2004
	Percent of adults without a usual source of health care[2]					
All adults 18–64 years of age[3,4]	18.5	16.6	17.5	17.7	16.5	17.6
Age						
18–44 years	21.7	19.6	21.1	21.6	20.6	21.7
18–24 years	26.6	22.6	27.0	27.2	27.2	28.0
25–44 years	20.3	18.8	19.3	19.9	18.5	19.5
45–64 years	12.8	11.3	11.2	10.9	9.2	10.4
45–54 years	14.1	12.2	12.6	12.0	10.3	11.7
55–64 years	11.1	9.8	9.0	9.2	7.6	8.7
Sex[4]						
Male	23.3	21.0	23.2	23.9	21.7	22.8
Female	13.9	12.5	11.9	11.8	11.5	12.6
Race[4,5]						
White only	18.2	16.3	16.9	16.9	15.8	17.5
Black or African American only	19.2	17.6	18.7	18.7	16.6	18.2
American Indian or Alaska Native only	19.1	15.9	20.7	18.8	16.1	20.8
Asian only	24.0	20.7	21.1	21.4	19.7	19.2
Native Hawaiian or Other Pacific Islander only	- - -	- - -	*	*	*	*
2 or more races	- - -	- - -	*	20.4	19.9	17.7
American Indian or Alaska Native; White	- - -	- - -	*	26.6	19.7	18.0
Hispanic origin and race[4,5]						
Hispanic or Latino	28.8	26.2	28.6	30.6	30.5	30.9
Mexican	30.5	28.1	33.4	34.0	33.8	33.4
Not Hispanic or Latino	17.5	15.5	16.1	15.9	14.3	15.3
White only	17.0	15.0	15.4	15.2	13.6	14.6
Black or African American only	18.9	17.4	18.6	18.6	16.5	17.9
Percent of poverty level[4,6]						
Below 100%	28.2	24.9	28.2	28.2	28.0	28.0
100%–less than 200%	24.6	22.3	24.7	26.2	24.8	26.0
200% or more	14.8	13.5	13.9	14.2	12.7	13.7
Hispanic origin and race and percent of poverty level[4,5,6]						
Hispanic or Latino:						
Below 100%	38.0	32.6	40.8	41.3	43.2	39.8
100%–less than 200%	35.7	31.6	33.3	38.2	37.6	37.2
200% or more	18.3	18.2	19.0	21.7	21.3	22.7
Not Hispanic or Latino:						
White only:						
Below 100%	27.1	22.8	24.5	23.4	22.9	22.7
100%–less than 200%	22.7	20.3	21.8	22.5	20.6	22.0
200% or more	14.4	13.0	13.3	13.1	11.4	12.4
Black or African American only:						
Below 100%	23.8	21.1	23.1	23.0	22.2	24.0
100%–less than 200%	21.6	21.2	24.7	23.6	19.7	22.5
200% or more	14.6	13.6	14.4	15.2	13.1	14.1
Health insurance status at the time of interview[4,7]						
Insured	13.3	11.4	11.4	11.0	9.4	9.8
Private	13.1	11.3	11.5	11.2	9.3	9.9
Medicaid	15.2	12.5	10.0	9.5	10.8	9.8
Uninsured	41.5	40.9	45.3	47.5	47.3	49.1
Health insurance status prior to interview[4,7]						
Insured continuously all 12 months	- - -	- - -	10.7	10.4	8.6	9.1
Uninsured for any period up to 12 months	- - -	- - -	29.1	29.4	31.6	30.6
Uninsured more than 12 months	- - -	- - -	50.1	53.2	52.8	54.1

See footnotes at end of table.

Table 77 (page 2 of 2). No usual source of health care among adults 18–64 years of age, by selected characteristics: United States, average annual selected years 1993–1994 through 2003–2004

[Data are based on household interviews of a sample of the civilian noninstitutionalized population]

Characteristic	1993–1994[1]	1995–1996[1]	1997–1998	1999–2000	2001–2002	2003–2004
Percent of poverty level and health insurance status prior to interview[4,6,7]		Percent of adults without a usual source of health care[2]				
Below 100%:						
Insured continuously all 12 months	- - -	- - -	12.8	11.3	11.1	11.0
Uninsured for any period up to 12 months . .	- - -	- - -	33.7	28.6	34.2	34.3
Uninsured more than 12 months	- - -	- - -	53.2	55.0	56.7	56.1
100%–less than 200%:						
Insured continuously all 12 months	- - -	- - -	12.9	12.1	11.0	10.5
Uninsured for any period up to 12 months . .	- - -	- - -	28.5	32.3	32.8	31.5
Uninsured more than 12 months	- - -	- - -	49.6	53.2	52.8	54.0
200% or more:						
Insured continuously all 12 months	- - -	- - -	10.2	10.1	7.9	8.7
Uninsured for any period up to 12 months . .	- - -	- - -	27.7	28.3	30.2	28.6
Uninsured more than 12 months	- - -	- - -	48.0	51.8	49.9	52.6
Geographic region[4]						
Northeast.	14.5	13.3	13.2	13.0	12.2	12.5
Midwest.	15.8	14.5	14.9	16.9	14.2	15.0
South	21.6	18.4	20.5	19.7	18.4	20.0
West	20.5	19.5	19.8	19.9	19.8	20.9
Location of residence[4]						
Within MSA[8]	18.8	16.9	17.6	17.9	16.7	17.8
Outside MSA[8]	17.4	15.4	17.1	17.0	15.9	16.8

* Estimates are considered unreliable. Data preceded by an asterisk have a relative standard error (RSE) of 20%–30%. Data not shown have an RSE of greater than 30%.

- - - Data not available.

[1]Data prior to 1997 are not strictly comparable with data for later years due to the 1997 questionnaire redesign. See Appendix I, National Health Interview Survey.

[2]Persons who report the emergency department as the place of their usual source of care are defined as having no usual source of care. See Appendix II, Usual source of care.

[3]Includes all other races not shown separately, and unknown health insurance status.

[4]Estimates are for persons 18–64 years of age and are age adjusted to the year 2000 standard population using three age groups: 18–44 years, 45–54 years, and 55–64 years of age. See Appendix II, Age adjustment.

[5]The race groups, white, black, American Indian or Alaska Native, Asian, Native Hawaiian or Other Pacific Islander, and 2 or more races, include persons of Hispanic and non-Hispanic origin. Persons of Hispanic origin may be of any race. Starting with 1999 data, race-specific estimates are tabulated according to the 1997 Revisions to the Standards for the Classification of Federal Data on Race and Ethnicity and are not strictly comparable with estimates for earlier years. The five single race categories plus multiple race categories shown in the table conform to the 1997 Standards. Starting with 1999 data, race-specific estimates are for persons who reported only one racial group; the category 2 or more races includes persons who reported more than one racial group. Prior to 1999, data were tabulated according to the 1977 Standards with four racial groups and the Asian only category including Native Hawaiian or Other Pacific Islander. Estimates for single race categories prior to 1999 included persons who reported one race or, if they reported more than one race, identified one race as best representing their race. Starting with 2003 data, race responses of other race and unspecified multiple race were treated as missing, and then race was imputed if these were the only race responses. Almost all persons with a race response of other race were of Hispanic origin. See Appendix II, Hispanic origin; Race.

[6]Percent of poverty level is based on family income and family size and composition using U.S. Census Bureau poverty thresholds. Missing family income data were imputed for 15%–17% of persons 18–64 years of age in 1993–1996, 25%–29% in 1997–1998, and 31%–34% in 1999–2004. See Appendix II, Family income; Poverty.

[7]Health insurance categories are mutually exclusive. Persons who reported both Medicaid and private coverage are classified as having private coverage. Medicaid includes other public assistance through 1996. Starting with 1997 data, Medicaid includes state-sponsored health plans and State Children's Health Insurance Program (SCHIP). The category insured also includes military, other government, and Medicare coverage. In 1993–1996, health insurance status was unknown for 8%–9% of adults in the sample. In 1997–2004, health insurance status was unknown for 1% of adults in the sample. See Appendix II, Health insurance coverage.

[8]MSA is metropolitan statistical area.

NOTES: Standard errors are available in the spreadsheet version of this table. Available from: www.cdc.gov/nchs/hus.htm. For more data on usual source of care, see the National Health Interview Survey home page, available from: www.cdc.gov/nchs/nhis.htm.

SOURCE: Centers for Disease Control and Prevention, National Center for Health Statistics, National Health Interview Survey, access to care and health insurance supplements (1993–1996). Starting in 1997, data are from the family core and sample adult questionnaires.

Table 78 (page 1 of 2). Reduced access to medical care during the past 12 months due to cost, by selected characteristics: United States, 1997, 2003, and 2004

[Data are based on household interviews of a sample of the civilian noninstitutionalized population]

Characteristic	Did not get care due to cost[1]			Delayed care due to cost[2]			Did not get prescription drugs due to cost[3]		
	1997	2003	2004	1997	2003	2004	1997	2003	2004
	Percent								
Total, age-adjusted[4,5]	4.5	5.2	5.4	7.3	7.1	7.7	4.7	6.2	7.1
Total, crude[5]	4.5	5.3	5.5	7.3	7.1	7.8	4.8	6.3	7.1
Age									
Under 18 years	2.2	2.2	2.3	3.7	3.6	3.8	2.2	2.7	2.8
Under 6 years	1.6	1.7	1.7	3.0	3.0	3.3	1.6	2.1	2.2
6–17 years	2.5	2.5	2.6	4.1	3.9	4.0	2.4	3.0	3.1
18–44 years	6.1	7.2	7.3	9.7	9.3	10.1	6.9	8.4	9.4
45–64 years	5.8	6.7	7.2	9.0	9.1	10.0	5.1	7.6	8.8
65 years and over	2.3	2.7	2.6	3.9	3.7	4.1	2.8	4.4	5.4
Sex[4]									
Male	3.8	4.8	5.0	6.4	6.4	7.0	3.9	5.0	5.9
Female	5.2	5.7	5.8	8.1	7.7	8.4	5.6	7.4	8.2
Race[4,6]									
White only	4.4	5.1	5.3	7.5	7.2	7.8	4.4	6.0	6.8
Black or African American only	5.8	6.4	6.6	6.9	6.8	7.9	7.3	8.6	9.7
American Indian or Alaska Native only	7.8	*9.5	7.1	11.0	11.6	8.9	*8.0	*10.7	9.6
Asian only	2.5	2.1	2.9	3.7	3.4	4.2	*2.1	2.7	2.9
Native Hawaiian or Other Pacific Islander only	- - -	*	*	- - -	*	*	- - -	*	*
2 or more races	- - -	10.3	7.9	- - -	11.4	11.0	- - -	10.4	9.6
Hispanic origin and race[4,6]									
Hispanic or Latino	5.9	6.5	6.3	6.9	7.4	7.8	5.7	8.6	8.9
Mexican	6.0	6.4	6.1	6.8	7.2	7.6	6.1	10.1	8.8
Not Hispanic or Latino	4.4	5.1	5.3	7.3	7.1	7.7	4.7	6.0	6.8
White only	4.2	4.9	5.2	7.6	7.3	7.9	4.3	5.6	6.6
Black or African American only	5.8	6.4	6.5	6.9	6.8	7.9	7.3	8.6	9.7
Education[7]									
No high school diploma or GED	9.7	10.4	10.2	12.1	11.5	11.9	10.2	12.1	14.5
High school diploma or GED	5.2	6.7	6.9	8.4	8.5	9.2	5.9	8.6	9.1
Some college or more	3.9	4.9	5.3	7.3	7.3	8.2	3.9	5.6	6.5
Percent of poverty level[4,8]									
Below 100%	11.2	11.0	11.5	13.2	12.0	13.5	11.6	13.8	14.2
100%–less than 200%	8.3	9.8	10.0	12.2	12.0	12.8	8.7	11.5	12.8
200% or more	2.4	3.1	3.3	4.9	5.0	5.5	2.5	3.6	4.5
Age and percent of poverty level[8]									
Under 18 years of age:									
Below 100%	4.5	3.5	3.3	5.5	4.8	5.2	4.6	5.8	4.8
100%–less than 200%	3.0	3.7	3.7	5.9	5.5	6.0	3.4	3.7	4.6
200% or more	1.1	1.3	1.4	2.2	2.6	2.6	0.8	1.3	1.5
18–44 years:									
Below 100%	12.7	13.3	13.5	14.8	14.0	15.3	13.8	15.6	14.6
100%–less than 200%	10.1	12.7	12.6	14.9	14.8	15.8	11.6	13.9	15.4
200% or more	3.5	4.4	4.6	7.1	6.8	7.4	4.0	5.2	6.4
45–64 years:									
Below 100%	18.4	18.8	20.3	22.0	19.7	22.6	17.9	21.8	25.8
100%–less than 200%	14.0	14.3	16.2	18.6	18.1	19.4	12.1	18.7	20.4
200% or more	2.8	4.0	4.3	5.8	6.3	7.2	2.4	4.2	5.2
65 years and over:									
Below 100%	7.3	5.6	6.2	8.6	7.4	8.6	7.5	10.3	11.5
100%–less than 200%	3.3	5.0	4.3	5.8	6.3	6.2	4.4	7.2	8.4
200% or more	0.9	1.2	1.3	2.1	2.0	2.5	1.1	2.2	3.3

See footnotes at end of table.

Table 78 (page 2 of 2). Reduced access to medical care during the past 12 months due to cost, by selected characteristics: United States, 1997, 2003, and 2004

[Data are based on household interviews of a sample of the civilian noninstitutionalized population]

Characteristic	Did not get care due to cost[1]			Delayed care due to cost[2]			Did not get prescription drugs due to cost[3]		
	1997	2003	2004	1997	2003	2004	1997	2003	2004
Percent of poverty level and health insurance status prior to interview for persons under 65 years of age[4,8,9]					Percent				
Insured continuously all 12 months	1.8	2.3	2.3	4.0	3.7	4.1	2.3	3.1	4.0
Below 100%	4.7	5.2	4.9	6.3	5.9	6.4	6.5	6.9	8.5
100%–less than 200%	3.9	4.7	4.7	7.1	6.4	7.0	4.9	6.8	8.6
200% or more	1.2	1.5	1.6	3.2	3.1	3.3	1.3	2.1	2.7
Uninsured for any period up to 12 months . . .	15.4	20.5	20.0	23.7	26.3	27.3	15.0	20.6	21.5
Below 100%	20.9	26.8	25.0	25.7	27.0	30.4	22.8	30.6	29.5
100%–less than 200%	17.9	22.5	24.4	27.5	28.4	31.4	17.5	23.1	26.1
200% or more	11.5	17.4	16.1	20.7	25.1	24.1	10.3	16.1	16.2
Uninsured more than 12 months	18.9	19.5	21.0	23.8	23.7	25.3	16.3	19.6	19.8
Below 100%	23.0	21.7	24.0	25.1	23.5	26.0	19.3	25.5	22.2
100%–less than 200%	18.6	20.0	21.2	23.1	25.0	24.9	16.6	20.2	20.2
200% or more	15.6	17.7	19.1	23.4	23.1	25.5	13.3	14.1	18.0
Geographic region[4]									
Northeast	3.5	3.9	4.4	5.7	5.3	6.0	3.4	5.1	5.6
Midwest	4.0	4.7	4.4	7.3	7.2	7.6	4.4	5.3	6.0
South	5.3	6.3	6.6	8.1	7.8	8.4	5.7	7.2	8.9
West	4.7	5.2	5.5	7.2	7.2	8.1	4.8	6.7	6.6
Within MSA[10]	4.3	5.0	5.2	6.9	6.7	7.4	4.4	5.8	6.8
Outside MSA[10]	5.4	6.1	6.3	8.7	8.8	9.1	6.1	8.0	8.2

* Estimates are considered unreliable. Data preceded by an asterisk have a relative standard error (RSE) of 20%–30%. Data not shown have an RSE of greater than 30%.

- - - Data not available.

[1]Based on persons responding yes to the question, "During the past 12 months was there any time when person needed medical care but did not get it because person couldn't afford it?"

[2]Based on persons responding yes to the question, "During the past 12 months has medical care been delayed because of worry about the cost?"

[3]Based on persons responding yes to the question, "During the past 12 months was there any time when you needed prescription medicine but didn't get it because you couldn't afford it?"

[4]Estimates are age adjusted to the year 2000 standard population using six age groups: 0–17 years, 18–44 years, 45–54 years, 55–64 years, 65–74 years, and 75 years and over. See Appendix II, Age adjustment.

[5]Includes all other races not shown separately and unknown education level.

[6]The race groups, white, black, American Indian or Alaska Native, Asian, Native Hawaiian or Other Pacific Islander, and 2 or more races, include persons of Hispanic and non-Hispanic origin. Persons of Hispanic origin may be of any race. Starting with 1999 data, race-specific estimates are tabulated according to the 1997 Revisions to the Standards for the Classification of Federal Data on Race and Ethnicity and are not strictly comparable with estimates for earlier years. The five single race categories plus multiple race categories shown in the table conform to the 1997 Standards. Starting with 1999 data, race-specific estimates are for persons who reported only one racial group; the category 2 or more races includes persons who reported more than one racial group. Prior to 1999, data were tabulated according to the 1977 Standards with four racial groups and the Asian only category including Native Hawaiian or Other Pacific Islander. Estimates for single race categories prior to 1999 included persons who reported one race or, if they reported more than one race, identified one race as best representing their race. Starting with 2003 data, race responses of other race and unspecified multiple race were treated as missing, and then race was imputed if these were the only race responses. Almost all persons with a race response of other race were of Hispanic origin. See Appendix II, Hispanic origin; Race.

[7]Estimates are for persons 25 years of age and over and are age adjusted to the year 2000 standard population using five age groups: 25–44 years, 45–54 years, 55–64 years, 65–74 years, and 75 years and over. See Appendix II, Age adjustment. GED stands for General Educational Development high school equivalency diploma. See Appendix II, Education.

[8]Percent of poverty level is based on family income and family size and composition using U.S. Census Bureau poverty thresholds. Missing family income data were imputed for 25%–29% of persons in 1997–1998 and 32%–33% in 2003–2004. See Appendix II, Family Income; Poverty.

[9]For information on the health insurance categories see Appendix II, Health Insurance Coverage.

[10]MSA is metropolitan statistical area.

NOTES: Standard errors and additional data years are available in the spreadsheet version of this table. Available from: www.cdc.gov/nchs/hus.htm. Data for additional years are available. See Appendix III.

SOURCE: Centers for Disease Control and Prevention, National Center for Health Statistics, National Health Interview Survey, family core, sample child, and sample adult questionnaires.

Table 79 (page 1 of 2). No health care visits to an office or clinic within the past 12 months among children under 18 years of age, by selected characteristics: United States, average annual 1997–1998, 2001–2002, and 2003–2004

[Data are based on household interviews of a sample of the civilian noninstitutionalized population]

Characteristic	Under 18 years of age			Under 6 years of age			6–17 years of age		
	1997–1998	2001–2002	2003–2004	1997–1998	2001–2002	2003–2004	1997–1998	2001–2002	2003–2004
	Percent of children without a health care visit[1]								
All children[2]	12.8	12.1	12.0	5.7	6.3	6.3	16.3	14.9	14.8
Race[3]									
White only	12.2	11.5	11.8	5.5	6.4	6.4	15.5	13.9	14.4
Black or African American only	14.3	13.3	11.9	6.5	5.9	5.5	18.1	16.8	14.8
American Indian or Alaska Native only	13.8	*18.6	16.3	*	*	*	*17.6	*23.0	19.5
Asian only	16.3	15.6	17.8	*5.6	*6.8	*7.9	22.1	20.5	22.2
Native Hawaiian or Other Pacific Islander only	- - -	*	*	- - -	*	*	- - -	*	*
2 or more races	- - -	8.3	8.9	- - -	*3.3	*	- - -	12.4	11.8
Hispanic origin and race[3]									
Hispanic or Latino	19.3	18.8	19.1	9.7	9.6	10.4	25.3	24.0	24.1
Not Hispanic or Latino	11.6	10.6	10.3	4.8	5.4	5.2	14.9	13.0	12.7
White only	10.7	9.7	9.5	4.3	5.3	4.9	13.7	11.7	11.6
Black or African American only	14.5	13.4	11.9	6.5	6.0	5.4	18.3	16.8	14.9
Percent of poverty level[4]									
Below 100%	17.6	17.3	15.9	8.1	9.1	7.6	23.6	21.8	20.8
100%–less than 200%	16.2	14.8	15.7	7.2	7.4	8.7	20.8	18.7	19.4
200% or more	9.9	9.6	9.4	4.1	4.8	4.7	12.6	11.7	11.5
Hispanic origin and race and percent of poverty level[3,4]									
Hispanic or Latino:									
Below 100%	23.2	22.1	21.8	11.7	10.4	11.4	31.1	29.4	28.3
100%–less than 200%	20.9	21.3	20.9	9.7	12.3	11.2	28.1	26.2	26.6
200% or more	13.4	13.7	14.9	7.2	6.4	8.5	16.8	17.6	18.1
Not Hispanic or Latino:									
White only:									
Below 100%	14.0	13.2	12.3	*5.6	*8.6	*5.3	19.7	15.6	16.2
100%–less than 200%	14.1	11.8	12.4	6.0	*6.0	7.5	18.0	14.8	15.3
200% or more	9.2	8.8	8.3	3.6	4.5	4.1	11.7	10.5	10.2
Black or African American only:									
Below 100%	15.8	16.1	12.9	7.6	*7.8	*5.4	20.5	20.3	17.0
100%–less than 200%	16.4	13.3	13.4	*7.7	*4.4	*6.9	20.4	17.5	15.8
200% or more	11.8	11.2	10.2	*4.1	*5.4	*4.6	14.8	13.6	12.7
Health insurance status at the time of interview[5]									
Insured.	10.4	9.8	9.8	4.5	4.7	5.3	13.4	12.3	12.1
Private	10.4	9.5	9.8	4.3	4.3	5.4	13.1	11.8	11.6
Medicaid	10.1	10.3	9.7	5.0	5.5	4.8	14.4	13.3	13.1
Uninsured.	28.8	31.9	32.5	14.6	21.0	17.9	34.9	36.3	37.8
Health insurance status prior to interview[5]									
Insured continuously all 12 months	10.3	9.5	9.7	4.4	4.6	5.3	13.2	12.0	12.0
Uninsured for any period up to 12 months	15.9	17.7	15.6	7.7	10.3	7.0	20.9	21.9	20.2
Uninsured more than 12 months.	34.9	41.4	41.7	19.9	30.2	26.0	40.2	45.3	46.0

See footnotes at end of table.

Table 79 (page 2 of 2). No health care visits to an office or clinic within the past 12 months among children under 18 years of age, by selected characteristics: United States, average annual 1997–1998, 2001–2002, and 2003–2004

[Data are based on household interviews of a sample of the civilian noninstitutionalized population]

Characteristic	Under 18 years of age			Under 6 years of age			6–17 years of age		
	1997–1998	2001–2002	2003–2004	1997–1998	2001–2002	2003–2004	1997–1998	2001–2002	2003–2004
Percent of poverty level and health insurance status prior to interview[4,5]	Percent of children without a health care visit[1]								
Below 100%:									
Insured continuously all 12 months . .	12.6	11.7	11.7	5.7	6.1	5.5	17.6	14.9	15.6
Uninsured for any period up to									
12 months	19.9	21.8	17.0	*9.9	*14.4	*	26.1	26.6	22.0
Uninsured more than 12 months	39.9	48.2	47.4	24.9	*28.0	35.3	45.2	55.7	50.8
100%–less than 200%:									
Insured continuously all 12 months . .	12.6	10.9	12.1	4.8	4.2	7.1	16.7	14.5	15.0
Uninsured for any period up to									
12 months	15.6	18.9	18.1	*8.7	*10.7	*10.3	20.2	23.2	22.2
Uninsured more than 12 months	33.7	41.3	42.9	21.3	35.4	26.1	37.9	43.6	48.0
200% or more:									
Insured continuously all 12 months . .	8.9	8.6	8.5	3.8	4.2	4.6	11.3	10.6	10.2
Uninsured for any period up to									
12 months	12.4	13.8	12.7	*	*6.9	*	16.7	17.7	17.3
Uninsured more than 12 months	29.7	32.3	32.8	*10.5	*24.8	*	36.7	34.4	37.6
Geographic region									
Northeast	7.0	6.0	5.6	3.1	3.9	3.0	8.9	6.9	6.7
Midwest	12.2	10.3	10.0	5.9	5.1	4.3	15.3	12.8	12.8
South	14.3	14.0	12.4	5.6	7.0	6.4	18.5	17.4	15.3
West	16.3	16.0	18.4	7.9	8.1	10.5	20.7	20.0	22.2
Location of residence									
Within MSA[6]	12.3	11.7	11.8	5.4	6.1	6.4	15.9	14.5	14.5
Outside MSA[6]	14.6	13.5	12.5	6.9	6.9	5.7	17.9	16.3	15.8

* Estimates are considered unreliable. Data preceded by an asterisk have a relative standard error (RSE) of 20%–30%. Data not shown have an RSE of greater than 30%.

- - - Data not available.

[1] Respondents were asked how many times a doctor or other health care professional was seen in the past 12 months at a doctor's office, clinic, or some other place. Excluded are visits to emergency rooms, hospitalizations, home visits, and telephone calls. Starting with 2000 data, dental visits were also excluded. See Appendix II, Health care contact.

[2] Includes all other races not shown separately and unknown health insurance status.

[3] The race groups, white, black, American Indian or Alaska Native, Asian, Native Hawaiian or Other Pacific Islander, and 2 or more races, include persons of Hispanic and non-Hispanic origin. Persons of Hispanic origin may be of any race. Starting with 1999 data, race-specific estimates are tabulated according to the 1997 Revisions to the Standards for the Classification of Federal Data on Race and Ethnicity and are not strictly comparable with estimates for earlier years. The five single race categories plus multiple race categories shown in the table conform to the 1997 Standards. Starting with 1999 data, race-specific estimates are for persons who reported only one racial group; the category 2 or more races includes persons who reported more than one racial group. Prior to 1999, data were tabulated according to the 1977 Standards with four racial groups and the Asian only category included Native Hawaiian or Other Pacific Islander. Estimates for single race categories prior to 1999 included persons who reported one race or, if they reported more than one race, identified one race as best representing their race. Starting with 2003 data, race responses of other race and unspecified multiple race were treated as missing, and then race was imputed if these were the only race responses. Almost all persons with a race response of other race were of Hispanic origin. See Appendix II, Hispanic origin; Race.

[4] Percent of poverty level is based on family income and family size and composition using U.S. Census Bureau poverty thresholds. Missing family income data were imputed for 21%–25% of children under 18 years of age in 1997–1998 and 28%–31% in 1999–2004. See Appendix II, Family income; Poverty.

[5] Health insurance categories are mutually exclusive. Persons who reported both Medicaid and private coverage are classified as having private coverage. Starting with 1997 data, Medicaid includes state-sponsored health plans and State Children's Health Insurance Program (SCHIP). The category insured also includes military, other government, and Medicare coverage. See Appendix II, Health insurance coverage.

[6] MSA is metropolitan statistical area.

NOTES: In 1997 the National Health Interview Survey questionnaire was redesigned. See Appendix I, National Health Interview Survey. Standard errors for selected years are available in the spreadsheet version of this table. Available from: www.cdc.gov/nchs/hus.htm. Data for additional years are available. See Appendix III.

SOURCE: Centers for Disease Control and Prevention, National Center for Health Statistics, National Health Interview Survey, family core and sample child questionnaires.

Table 80 (page 1 of 3). Health care visits to doctor's offices, emergency departments, and home visits within the past 12 months, by selected characteristics: United States, selected years 1997–2004

[Data are based on household interviews of a sample of the civilian noninstitutionalized population]

| Characteristic | Number of health care visits[1] | | | | | | | | | | | |
| | None | | | 1–3 visits | | | 4–9 visits | | | 10 or more visits | | |
	1997	2003	2004	1997	2003	2004	1997	2003	2004	1997	2003	2004
	Percent distribution											
All persons[2,3]	16.5	15.8	16.1	46.2	45.8	45.8	23.6	24.8	24.6	13.7	13.6	13.5
Age												
Under 18 years	11.8	11.3	10.6	54.1	54.5	55.3	25.2	26.7	26.2	8.9	7.5	8.0
Under 6 years	5.0	5.5	5.3	44.9	46.0	47.5	37.0	39.0	36.9	13.0	9.4	10.3
6–17 years	15.3	14.0	13.1	58.7	58.7	59.0	19.3	20.8	21.1	6.8	6.6	6.8
18–44 years	21.7	22.4	23.8	46.7	46.7	45.6	19.0	19.1	19.2	12.6	11.8	11.5
18–24 years	22.0	23.6	25.7	46.8	47.2	45.0	20.0	18.2	19.2	11.2	11.0	10.1
25–44 years	21.6	22.0	23.1	46.7	46.6	45.8	18.7	19.4	19.2	13.0	12.0	12.0
45–64 years	16.9	14.7	15.0	42.9	42.2	43.3	24.7	26.6	25.3	15.5	16.5	16.3
45–54 years	17.9	16.9	16.9	43.9	44.2	45.0	23.4	24.5	22.9	14.8	14.3	15.2
55–64 years	15.3	11.4	12.3	41.3	39.2	40.9	26.7	29.8	28.9	16.7	19.6	18.0
65 years and over	8.9	6.3	5.6	34.7	31.5	31.6	32.5	35.8	36.8	23.8	26.4	26.1
65–74 years	9.8	7.1	6.8	36.9	34.0	36.0	31.6	35.7	34.5	21.6	23.3	22.6
75 years and over	7.7	5.4	4.1	31.8	28.6	26.4	33.8	36.0	39.5	26.6	30.0	30.0
Sex[3]												
Male	21.3	20.6	20.9	47.1	46.8	46.6	20.6	21.9	21.6	11.0	10.7	10.9
Female	11.8	11.1	11.5	45.4	44.9	45.0	26.5	27.7	27.5	16.3	16.3	16.0
Race[3,4]												
White only	16.0	15.7	16.0	46.1	45.6	45.4	23.9	25.1	24.8	14.0	13.6	13.8
Black or African American only	16.8	14.7	15.8	46.1	45.8	47.0	23.2	25.2	24.6	13.9	14.3	12.6
American Indian or Alaska Native only	17.1	23.3	17.7	38.0	41.4	41.7	24.2	20.6	25.0	20.7	14.7	15.5
Asian only	22.8	22.6	20.8	49.1	47.8	51.5	19.7	20.7	19.7	8.3	8.9	8.1
Native Hawaiian or Other Pacific Islander only	- - -	*	*	- - -	*	*	- - -	*	*	- - -	*	*
2 or more races	- - -	11.1	13.6	- - -	44.9	42.9	- - -	23.0	26.2	- - -	21.0	17.3
Hispanic origin and race[3,4]												
Hispanic or Latino	24.9	25.3	26.7	42.3	42.9	41.8	20.3	20.3	20.6	12.5	11.5	10.9
Mexican	28.9	27.8	29.7	40.8	42.5	41.0	18.5	18.8	18.9	11.8	11.0	10.4
Not Hispanic or Latino	15.4	14.1	14.2	46.7	46.3	46.5	24.0	25.6	25.2	13.9	14.0	14.1
White only	14.7	13.5	13.5	46.6	46.2	46.1	24.4	26.1	25.7	14.3	14.2	14.7
Black or African American only	16.9	14.6	15.6	46.1	45.9	47.3	23.1	25.3	24.6	13.8	14.2	12.5
Respondent-assessed health status[3]												
Fair or poor	7.8	8.7	8.1	23.3	23.2	22.0	29.0	28.8	28.0	39.9	39.3	41.9
Good to excellent	17.2	16.4	16.9	48.4	48.1	48.0	23.3	24.5	24.4	11.1	10.9	10.7
Percent of poverty level[3,5]												
Below 100%	20.6	20.9	21.1	37.8	37.8	37.7	22.7	23.7	23.5	18.9	17.6	17.7
100%–less than 200%	20.1	19.8	20.9	43.3	41.5	42.5	21.7	23.6	22.3	14.9	15.1	14.4
200% or more	14.5	13.7	13.8	48.7	48.4	48.1	24.2	25.4	25.3	12.6	12.6	12.8

See footnotes at end of table.

Table 80 (page 2 of 3). Health care visits to doctor's offices, emergency departments, and home visits within the past 12 months, by selected characteristics: United States, selected years 1997–2004

[Data are based on household interviews of a sample of the civilian noninstitutionalized population]

Characteristic	Number of health care visits[1]											
	None			1–3 visits			4–9 visits			10 or more visits		
	1997	2003	2004	1997	2003	2004	1997	2003	2004	1997	2003	2004
Hispanic origin and race and percent of poverty level[3,4,5]	Percent distribution											
Hispanic or Latino:												
Below 100%	30.2	29.9	31.6	34.8	37.0	35.0	19.9	18.5	19.6	15.0	14.6	13.9
100%–less than 200%	28.7	28.6	30.5	39.7	40.2	39.3	20.4	20.6	19.4	11.2	10.5	10.9
200% or more	18.9	20.7	21.5	48.8	47.7	47.0	20.4	21.2	22.2	11.9	10.3	9.2
Not Hispanic or Latino:												
White only:												
Below 100%	17.0	17.0	16.2	38.3	37.5	37.5	23.9	25.9	25.4	20.9	19.5	20.9
100%–less than 200%	17.3	16.6	16.7	44.1	41.0	43.2	22.2	24.9	23.4	16.3	17.4	16.7
200% or more	13.8	12.5	12.7	48.2	48.1	47.4	24.9	26.3	26.1	13.1	13.1	13.8
Black or African American only:												
Below 100%	17.4	15.7	15.9	38.5	38.1	40.9	23.4	26.5	25.7	20.7	19.6	17.5
100%–less than 200%	18.8	15.4	18.1	43.7	44.2	44.5	22.9	25.9	23.8	14.5	14.5	13.7
200% or more	15.6	13.7	14.3	51.7	50.6	51.3	22.7	24.3	24.4	10.0	11.4	10.0
Health insurance status at the time of interview[6,7]												
Under 65 years of age:												
Insured	14.3	12.8	13.4	49.0	49.1	49.1	23.6	25.2	24.6	13.1	12.9	12.8
Private	14.7	13.2	13.6	50.6	51.1	51.4	23.1	24.6	23.9	11.6	11.1	11.2
Medicaid	9.8	9.9	11.8	35.5	35.2	35.1	26.5	28.1	28.2	28.2	26.8	24.9
Uninsured	33.7	38.1	37.8	42.8	42.4	42.5	15.3	13.4	13.6	8.2	6.1	6.1
Health insurance status prior to interview[6,7]												
Under 65 years of age:												
Insured continuously all 12 months	14.1	12.7	13.4	49.2	49.3	49.4	23.6	25.2	24.6	13.0	12.8	12.7
Uninsured for any period up to 12 months	18.9	20.4	20.0	46.0	46.2	45.7	20.8	21.2	21.9	14.4	12.2	12.3
Uninsured more than 12 months	39.0	44.3	43.9	41.4	39.8	41.3	13.2	11.2	10.0	6.4	4.7	4.8
Percent of poverty level and insurance status prior to interview[5,6,7]												
Under 65 years of age:												
Below 100%:												
Insured continuously all 12 months	13.8	12.7	14.3	39.7	40.9	39.6	25.2	25.8	25.7	21.4	20.5	20.4
Uninsured for any period up to 12 months	19.7	18.4	17.6	37.6	43.9	42.0	21.9	21.6	24.6	20.9	16.1	15.7
Uninsured more than 12 months	41.2	47.7	47.1	39.9	35.7	38.6	12.2	11.7	9.4	6.6	4.9	5.0
100%–less than 200%:												
Insured continuously all 12 months	16.0	13.8	15.7	46.4	45.0	45.4	21.9	24.4	23.5	15.8	16.8	15.5
Uninsured for any period up to 12 months	18.8	20.2	21.7	45.1	42.0	45.1	21.0	24.8	22.1	15.0	12.9	11.1
Uninsured more than 12 months	38.7	43.4	45.0	41.0	39.1	39.4	14.0	12.1	9.9	6.3	5.4	5.7
200% or more:												
Insured continuously all 12 months	13.7	12.4	12.6	51.0	51.1	51.3	23.6	25.3	24.7	11.7	11.3	11.5
Uninsured for any period up to 12 months	17.8	20.4	20.3	50.3	49.6	47.5	20.4	19.1	20.4	11.5	10.9	11.9
Uninsured more than 12 months	36.6	41.8	39.7	43.8	44.7	45.4	13.2	9.6	10.9	6.4	4.0	4.1
Geographic region[3]												
Northeast	13.2	10.4	11.6	45.9	47.6	45.5	26.0	27.0	27.5	14.9	15.0	15.4
Midwest	15.9	14.2	13.9	47.7	47.2	47.5	22.8	25.4	25.1	13.6	13.2	13.5
South	17.2	16.5	16.7	46.1	45.1	46.2	23.3	24.8	23.8	13.5	13.6	13.3
West	19.1	21.0	21.3	44.8	44.2	43.8	22.8	22.2	22.7	13.3	12.6	12.2

See footnotes at end of table.

Table 80 (page 3 of 3). Health care visits to doctor's offices, emergency departments, and home visits within the past 12 months, by selected characteristics: United States, selected years 1997–2004

[Data are based on household interviews of a sample of the civilian noninstitutionalized population]

	Number of health care visits[1]											
	None			1–3 visits			4–9 visits			10 or more visits		
Characteristic	1997	2003	2004	1997	2003	2004	1997	2003	2004	1997	2003	2004
Location of residence[3]	Percent distribution											
Within MSA[8]	16.2	16.0	16.3	46.4	45.9	45.9	23.7	24.8	24.4	13.7	13.3	13.4
Outside MSA[8]	17.3	15.0	15.3	45.4	45.6	45.4	23.3	24.9	25.3	13.9	14.5	14.0

* Estimates are considered unreliable. Data preceded by an asterisk have a relative standard error (RSE) of 20%–30%. Data not shown have an RSE greater than 30%.

- - - Data not available.

[1]This table presents a summary measure of health care visits to doctor's offices, emergency departments, and home visits during a 12-month period. See Appendix II, Emergency department visit; Health care contact; Home visit.

[2]Includes all other races not shown separately and unknown health insurance status.

[3]Estimates are age adjusted to the year 2000 standard population using six age groups: Under 18 years, 18–44 years, 45–54 years, 55–64 years, 65–74 years, and 75 years and over. See Appendix II, Age adjustment.

[4]The race groups, white, black, American Indian or Alaska Native, Asian, Native Hawaiian or Other Pacific Islander, and 2 or more races, include persons of Hispanic and non-Hispanic origin. Persons of Hispanic origin may be of any race. Starting with 1999 data, race-specific estimates are tabulated according to the 1997 Revisions to the Standards for the Classification of Federal Data on Race and Ethnicity and are not strictly comparable with estimates for earlier years. The five single race categories plus multiple race categories shown in the table conform to the 1997 Standards. Starting with 1999 data, race-specific estimates are for persons who reported only one racial group; the category 2 or more races includes persons who reported more than one racial group. Prior to 1999, data were tabulated according to the 1977 Standards with four racial groups and the Asian only category included Native Hawaiian or Other Pacific Islander. Estimates for single race categories prior to 1999 included persons who reported one race or, if they reported more than one race, identified one race as best representing their race. Starting with 2003 data, race responses of other race and unspecified multiple race were treated as missing, and then race was imputed if these were the only race responses. Almost all persons with a race response of other race were of Hispanic origin. See Appendix II, Hispanic origin; Race.

[5]Percent of poverty level is based on family income and family size and composition using U.S. Census Bureau poverty thresholds. Missing family income data were imputed for 25%–29% of persons in 1997–1998 and 32%–35% in 1999–2004. See Appendix II, Family income; Poverty.

[6]Estimates for persons under 65 years of age are age adjusted to the year 2000 standard population using four age groups: Under 18 years, 18–44 years, 45–54 years, and 55–64 years of age. See Appendix II, Age adjustment.

[7]Health insurance categories are mutually exclusive. Persons who reported both Medicaid and private coverage are classified as having private coverage. Starting in 1997 Medicaid includes state-sponsored health plans and State Children's Health Insurance Program (SCHIP). See Appendix II, Health insurance coverage.

[8]MSA is metropolitan statistical area.

NOTES: In 1997 the National Health Interview Survey questionnaire was redesigned. See Appendix I, National Health Interview Survey. Standard errors are available in the spreadsheet version of this table. See www.cdc.gov/nchs/hus.htm. Data for additional years are available. See Appendix III.

SOURCE: Centers for Disease Control and Prevention, National Center for Health Statistics, National Health Interview Survey, family core and sample adult questionnaires.

Table 81 (page 1 of 2).

Table 81 (page 1 of 2). Vaccinations of children 19–35 months of age for selected diseases, by race, Hispanic origin, poverty level, and residence in metropolitan statistical area (MSA): United States, selected years 1995–2004

[Data are based on telephone interviews of a sample of the civilian noninstitutionalized population supplemented by a survey of immunization providers for interview participants]

| Vaccination and year | All | Race and Hispanic origin[1] | | | | | | | Poverty level | | Location of residence | | |
| | | Not Hispanic or Latino | | | | | | | | | Inside MSA[2] | | |
		White	Black or African American	American Indian or Alaska Native	Asian[3]	Native Hawaiian or Other Pacific Islander[3]	2 or more races	Hispanic or Latino	Below poverty level	At or above poverty level	Central city	Remaining area	Outside MSA[2]
Combined series (4:3:1:3):[4]													
1995	74	76	70	69	76	- - -	- - -	68	67	77	72	75	75
1999	78	81	74	75	77	- - -	- - -	75	73	81	77	79	80
2000	76	79	71	69	75	- - -	- - -	73	71	78	73	78	79
2001	77	79	71	76	77	- - -	- - -	77	72	79	75	78	79
2002	78	80	71	*	83	*	74	76	72	79	75	80	77
2003	81	84	75	77	81	*	81	79	76	83	80	82	81
2004	83	85	76	75	84	*	82	81	78	85	81	84	82
DTP/DT/DTaP (4 doses or more):[5]													
1995	78	80	74	71	84	- - -	- - -	75	71	81	77	79	78
1999	83	86	79	80	87	- - -	- - -	80	79	85	82	84	83
2000	82	84	76	75	85	- - -	- - -	79	76	84	80	83	83
2001	82	84	76	77	84	- - -	- - -	83	77	84	81	83	82
2002	82	84	76	*	88	*	78	79	75	84	79	84	80
2003	85	88	80	80	89	*	84	82	80	87	84	86	83
2004	86	88	80	77	90	*	86	84	81	87	84	87	85
Polio (3 doses or more):													
1995	88	89	84	86	90	- - -	- - -	87	85	89	87	88	89
1999	90	90	87	88	90	- - -	- - -	89	87	91	89	90	90
2000	90	91	87	90	93	- - -	- - -	88	87	90	88	90	91
2001	89	90	85	88	90	- - -	- - -	91	87	90	88	90	91
2002	90	91	87	*	92	95	87	90	88	91	89	91	90
2003	92	93	89	91	91	90	91	90	89	93	91	92	92
2004	92	92	90	87	93	*	92	91	90	92	91	92	92
Measles, Mumps, Rubella:													
1995	90	91	87	88	95	- - -	- - -	88	86	91	90	90	89
1999	92	92	90	92	93	- - -	- - -	90	90	92	91	92	90
2000	91	92	88	87	90	- - -	- - -	90	89	91	90	91	91
2001	91	92	89	94	90	- - -	- - -	92	89	92	91	92	91
2002	92	93	90	84	95	94	89	91	90	92	90	93	90
2003	93	93	92	92	96	*	94	93	92	93	93	93	92
2004	93	94	91	89	94	*	94	93	91	94	93	94	92
Hib (3 doses or more):[6]													
1995	91	93	88	93	90	- - -	- - -	89	88	93	91	92	92
1999	94	95	92	91	90	- - -	- - -	92	91	95	92	95	93
2000	93	95	93	90	92	- - -	- - -	91	90	95	92	94	95
2001	93	94	90	91	92	- - -	- - -	93	90	94	91	94	93
2002	93	94	92	*	95	93	90	92	90	94	92	94	93
2003	94	95	92	89	91	*	93	93	91	95	94	94	94
2004	94	95	91	90	92	*	96	93	92	94	93	94	94
Hepatitis B (3 doses or more):													
1995	68	68	66	52	80	- - -	- - -	70	65	69	69	71	59
1999	88	89	87	*	88	- - -	- - -	87	87	89	87	89	88
2000	90	91	89	91	91	- - -	- - -	88	87	91	89	90	92
2001	89	90	85	86	90	- - -	- - -	90	87	90	88	90	89
2002	90	91	88	*	94	94	84	90	88	90	89	91	90
2003	92	93	92	90	94	*	93	91	91	93	92	93	93
2004	92	93	91	91	93	*	94	92	91	93	92	93	93
Varicella:[7]													
1998	43	42	42	28	53	- - -	- - -	47	41	44	45	45	34
1999	58	56	58	*	64	- - -	- - -	61	55	58	59	61	47
2000	68	66	67	62	77	- - -	- - -	70	64	69	69	70	60
2001	76	75	75	69	82	- - -	- - -	80	74	77	78	78	68
2002	81	79	83	71	87	*	79	82	79	81	81	83	75
2003	85	84	85	81	91	*	86	86	84	85	86	86	80
2004	88	87	86	84	91	*	89	89	86	88	88	89	85

See footnotes at end of table.

This table will be updated on the Web. Go to www.cdc.gov/nchs/hus.htm.

Table 81 (page 2 of 2). Vaccinations of children 19–35 months of age for selected diseases, by race, Hispanic origin, poverty level, and residence in metropolitan statistical area (MSA): United States, selected years 1995–2004

[Data are based on telephone interviews of a sample of the civilian noninstitutionalized population supplemented by a survey of immunization providers for interview participants]

Vaccination and year		Race and Hispanic origin[1]							Poverty level		Location of residence		
			Not Hispanic or Latino								Inside MSA[2]		
	All	White	Black or African American	American Indian or Alaska Native	Asian[3]	Native Hawaiian or Other Pacific Islander[3]	2 or more races	Hispanic or Latino	Below poverty level	At or above poverty level	Central city	Remaining area	Outside MSA[2]
PCV (3 doses or more):[8]					Percent of children 19–35 months of age								
2002	41	44	34	33	55	*	38	37	33	43	41	45	32
2003	68	71	62	60	71	*	66	66	62	71	68	71	61
2004	73	75	68	75	76	*	78	70	69	75	72	77	68

Vaccination and year	Not Hispanic or Latino				Hispanic or Latino	
	White		Black or African American			
	Below poverty level	At or above poverty level	Below poverty level	At or above poverty level	Below poverty level	At or above poverty level
Combined series (4:3:1:3):[4]			Percent of children 19–35 months of age			
1995	69	78	70	73	63	72
1999	76	82	72	77	73	78
2000	73	80	69	72	70	74
2001	71	80	69	74	73	79
2002	72	81	68	72	75	76
2003	79	85	70	79	78	81
2004	78	86	74	80	80	84

- - - Data not available.

* Estimates are considered unreliable. Percents not shown if the unweighted sample size for the numerator was less than 30 or relative standard error greater than 50% or confidence interval half width greater than 10%.

[1]Persons of Hispanic origin may be of any race. Starting with 2002 data, estimates were tabulated using the 1997 Revisions to the Standards for the Classification of Federal Data on Race and Ethnicity. Estimates for earlier years were tabulated using the 1977 Standards on Race and Ethnicity. See Appendix II, Race; Hispanic origin.

[2]Metropolitan statistical area.

[3]Prior to data year 2002, the category Asian included Native Hawaiian and Other Pacific Islander.

[4]The 4:3:1:3 combined series consists of 4 or more doses of diphtheria and tetanus toxoids and pertussis vaccine (DTP), diphtheria and tetanus toxoids (DT), or diphtheria and tetanus toxoids and acellular pertussis vaccine (DTaP), 3 or more doses of any poliovirus vaccine, 1 or more doses of a measles-containing vaccine (MCV), and 3 or more doses of Haemophilus influenzae type b vaccine (Hib).

[5]Diphtheria and tetanus toxoids and pertussis vaccine, diphtheria and tetanus toxoids, and diphtheria and tetanus toxoids and acellular pertussis vaccine.

[6]Haemophilus influenzae type b vaccine (Hib).

[7]Recommended in 1996. Data collection for varicella began in July 1996.

[8]Pneumococcal conjugate vaccine. Recommended in 2000. Data collection for PCV began in July 2001.

NOTES: Final estimates from the National Immunization Survey include an adjustment for children with missing immunization provider data. Poverty level is based on family income and family size using U.S. Bureau of the Census poverty thresholds. Children missing information about poverty level were omitted from analysis by poverty level. In 2004, 12.0% of all children, 20.0% of Hispanic, 8.4% of non-Hispanic white, and 9.8% of non-Hispanic black children were missing information about poverty level and were omitted. See Appendix II, Poverty. See Appendix I, National Immunization Survey.
Data for additional years are available. See Appendix III.

SOURCE: Centers for Disease Control and Prevention, National Center for Health Statistics and National Immunization Program, National Immunization Survey. Available from: www.cdc.gov/nip/coverage/ and www.cdc.gov/nis/.

This table will be updated on the Web. Go to www.cdc.gov/nchs/hus.htm.

Table 82 (page 1 of 2). Vaccination coverage among children 19–35 months of age, by geographic division, state, and selected urban area: United States, selected years 1995–2004

[Data are based on telephone interviews of a sample of the civilian noninstitutionalized population supplemented by a survey of immunization providers for interview participants]

Geographic division and state	1995	1997	1998	1999	2000	2001	2002	2003	2004
	Percent of children 19–35 months of age with 4:3:1:3 series[1]								
United States	74	76	79	78	76	77	78	81	83
New England:									
Connecticut	86	86	90	86	85	84	86	95	89
Maine	88	87	86	83	83	82	83	82	85
Massachusetts	81	88	87	85	85	81	89	92	91
New Hampshire	89	85	82	85	83	84	87	88	89
Rhode Island	83	82	86	87	82	84	86	87	88
Vermont	87	87	86	91	83	88	87	90	89
Middle Atlantic:									
New Jersey	70	76	82	81	76	76	80	76	83
New York	74	75	85	81	75	81	81	82	83
Pennsylvania	77	79	83	86	78	82	77	87	87
East North Central:									
Illinois	78	74	78	77	75	76	80	85	84
Indiana	74	72	78	74	76	74	78	82	81
Michigan	68	75	78	74	75	74	84	83	81
Ohio	71	72	78	78	72	75	77	84	82
Wisconsin	74	81	78	85	80	83	82	83	85
West North Central:									
Iowa	83	77	82	83	83	79	80	83	86
Kansas	70	84	82	79	76	76	73	78	80
Minnesota	75	78	82	85	86	79	79	84	86
Missouri	75	79	85	75	78	78	77	84	86
Nebraska	71	74	76	82	79	80	79	82	83
North Dakota	79	80	79	80	81	83	79	83	84
South Dakota	79	77	74	82	78	79	81	83	88
South Atlantic:									
Delaware	68	80	79	78	75	79	81	80	86
District of Columbia	69	71	71	78	71	74	72	77	86
Florida	74	74	79	80	74	77	77	83	90
Georgia	77	78	80	82	81	80	82	77	86
Maryland	77	81	77	79	78	78	81	84	81
North Carolina	80	80	83	82	87	85	87	89	82
South Carolina	78	81	88	81	80	81	80	85	82
Virginia	69	72	80	80	74	78	77	85	83
West Virginia	71	81	82	81	76	81	79	77	88
East South Central:									
Alabama	73	87	82	78	81	83	80	82	83
Kentucky	81	78	82	88	81	79	74	81	80
Mississippi	79	80	84	82	81	84	78	84	86
Tennessee	74	79	82	78	81	84	80	81	83
West South Central:									
Arkansas	73	80	73	77	72	74	74	80	85
Louisiana	77	77	78	77	75	69	69	72	76
Oklahoma	74	70	75	73	71	76	67	72	73
Texas	71	74	74	72	69	74	71	77	74
Mountain:									
Arizona	69	71	76	72	72	73	70	79	81
Colorado	75	74	76	76	74	75	64	69	80
Idaho	66	71	76	69	74	74	73	82	83
Montana	71	75	82	83	77	82	71	85	82
Nevada	67	70	76	73	74	72	78	78	71
New Mexico	74	73	71	73	68	71	67	77	85
Utah	65	69	76	80	77	74	79	80	75
Wyoming	71	75	80	83	79	81	77	77	84
Pacific:									
Alaska	74	75	81	80	77	74	78	81	76
California	70	74	76	75	75	75	76	80	83
Hawaii	75	77	79	82	75	73	81	83	83
Oregon	71	72	76	72	79	73	75	79	81
Washington	76	79	81	75	77	76	73	80	81

See footnotes at end of table.

This table will be updated on the Web. Go to www.cdc.gov/nchs/hus.htm.

Table 82 (page 2 of 2). Vaccination coverage among children 19–35 months of age, by geographic division, state, and selected urban area: United States, selected years 1995–2004

[Data are based on telephone interviews of a sample of the civilian noninstitutionalized population supplemented by a survey of immunization providers for interview participants]

Geographic division and urban area	1995	1997	1998	1999	2000	2001	2002	2003	2004
	Percent of children 19–35 months of age with 4:3:1:3 series [1]								
New England:									
Boston, Massachusetts	85	86	89	84	79	85	80	90	86
Middle Atlantic:									
New York City, New York.	72	72	81	78	68	76	81	77	80
Newark, New Jersey.	67	68	64	67	63	64	60	74	75
Philadelphia, Pennsylvania	67	81	80	81	74	74	74	80	80
East North Central:									
Chicago, Illinois	70	66	64	71	65	69	72	77	81
Cuyahoga County (Cleveland), Ohio.	72	70	75	74	73	73	74	75	86
Detroit, Michigan	54	60	70	66	59	63	66	71	68
Franklin County (Columbus), Ohio	75	73	78	78	77	78	84	83	87
Marion County (Indianapolis), Indiana.	77	80	78	79	69	72	75	79	82
Milwaukee County (Milwaukee), Wisconsin	69	72	73	74	69	70	70	81	80
South Atlantic:									
Baltimore, Maryland	*	84	81	72	70	72	75	81	85
Dade County (Miami), Florida	78	75	75	84	78	78	73	83	85
District of Columbia	67	71	71	78	71	74	72	77	86
Duval County (Jacksonville), Florida.	69	69	79	78	79	76	77	81	75
Fulton/DeKalb Counties (Atlanta), Georgia	*	74	71	83	80	75	79	75	86
East South Central:									
Davidson County (Nashville), Tennessee	72	76	80	73	73	82	80	83	90
Shelby County (Memphis), Tennessee	69	70	71	75	77	74	73	77	74
Jefferson County (Birmingham), Alabama	86	83	85	85	79	87	82	83	84
West South Central:									
Bexar County (San Antonio), Texas	76	79	79	70	68	73	76	79	75
Dallas County (Dallas), Texas	70	75	71	72	67	67	76	75	72
El Paso County (El Paso), Texas	72	63	78	73	70	69	77	81	71
Houston, Texas	64	62	61	63	65	69	64	75	68
Orleans Parish (New Orleans), Louisiana	78	69	79	72	70	68	63	74	76
Mountain:									
Maricopa County (Phoenix), Arizona.	67	70	77	71	71	72	73	80	81
Pacific:									
King County (Seattle), Washington.	84	81	86	77	75	72	77	83	85
Los Angeles County (Los Angeles), California . .	68	72	76	76	77	73	77	84	82
San Diego County (San Diego), California	72	76	77	75	76	80	78	81	80
Santa Clara County (Santa Clara), California . .	76	69	84	82	76	77	84	85	88

* Estimates are considered unreliable. Percents not shown if the unweighted sample size for the numerator was less than 30 or relative standard error greater than 50% or confidence interval half width greater than 10 percentage points.

[1] The 4:3:1:3 combined series consists of 4 or more doses of diphtheria and tetanus toxoids and pertussis vaccine (DTP), diphtheria and tetanus toxoids (DT), or diphtheria and tetanus toxoids and acellular pertussis vaccine (DTaP), 3 or more doses of any poliovirus vaccine, 1 or more doses of a measles-containing vaccine (MCV), and 3 or more doses of *Haemophilus influenzae* type b vaccine (Hib).

NOTES: Urban areas were originally selected because they were at risk for undervaccination. Final estimates from the National Immunization Survey include an adjustment for children with missing immunization provider data. Data for additional years are available. See Appendix III.

SOURCE: Centers for Disease Control and Prevention, National Center for Health Statistics and National Immunization Program, National Immunization Survey. Available from: www.cdc.gov/nip/coverage/ and www.cdc.gov/nis/.

This table will be updated on the Web. Go to www.cdc.gov/nchs/hus.htm.

[Data are based on household interviews of a sample of the civilian noninstitutionalized population]

Characteristic	1989	1995	1999	2000	2001	2002	2003	2004
	Percent receiving influenza vaccination during past 12 months [1]							
18 years and over, age-adjusted [2,3]	9.6	23.6	28.4	28.7	26.7	28.3	29.2	29.5
18 years and over, crude [3]	9.1	24.4	27.9	28.4	26.4	28.0	29.0	29.4
Age								
18–49 years	3.4	13.3	16.4	17.1	15.0	16.2	16.8	17.9
50 years and over	19.9	43.0	48.4	47.9	45.7	47.7	48.9	47.9
50–64 years	10.6	26.9	34.1	34.6	32.2	34.0	36.8	35.9
65 years and over	30.4	57.0	65.7	64.4	63.1	65.7	65.5	64.6
65–74 years	28.0	54.0	61.9	61.1	60.7	60.9	60.5	60.1
75 years and over	34.2	61.2	70.4	68.4	65.8	71.3	71.0	69.7
Age 50 years and over								
Sex								
Male	19.2	40.9	45.9	45.9	44.2	45.1	46.8	45.1
Female	20.6	44.4	50.4	49.5	46.9	49.8	50.7	50.2
Race [4]								
White only	21.0	45.1	49.9	49.8	47.7	49.4	50.4	49.8
Black or African American only	12.5	29.8	36.3	33.2	32.7	36.2	35.3	32.8
American Indian or Alaska Native only	26.2	*35.3	45.6	43.6	41.5	*37.6	44.7	51.3
Asian only	*9.2	36.9	44.9	43.3	35.4	39.5	45.9	41.7
Native Hawaiian or Other Pacific Islander only	- - -	- - -	*	*	*	*	*	*
2 or more races	- - -	- - -	53.3	50.7	41.5	47.9	53.7	44.5
Hispanic origin and race [4]								
Hispanic or Latino	13.2	35.1	37.0	34.4	32.5	33.7	33.6	36.9
Mexican	13.0	36.2	38.0	33.0	34.3	33.9	32.8	39.2
Not Hispanic or Latino	20.3	43.8	49.2	48.8	46.6	48.7	50.1	48.8
White only	21.3	46.0	50.7	50.6	48.6	50.3	51.8	50.9
Black or African American only	12.4	30.0	36.4	33.2	32.8	36.5	35.4	32.9
Percent of poverty level [5]								
Below 100%	19.6	41.4	43.6	44.1	38.8	41.9	41.8	42.5
100%–less than 200%	24.0	43.8	51.5	50.7	47.2	49.8	50.9	49.9
200% or more	19.0	43.0	48.1	47.6	46.1	47.9	49.4	48.1
Hispanic origin and race and percent of poverty level [4,5]								
Hispanic or Latino:								
Below 100%	12.7	36.4	37.1	35.8	33.0	36.6	31.9	36.3
100%–less than 200%	20.4	33.0	36.8	35.6	35.2	32.6	29.9	33.1
200% or more	11.9	35.7	37.0	33.1	30.6	33.2	36.6	39.2
Not Hispanic or Latino:								
White only:								
Below 100%	22.3	47.5	49.2	48.6	42.7	42.7	45.9	48.1
100%–less than 200%	26.1	48.1	55.1	54.8	51.0	54.2	55.9	55.0
200% or more	19.9	45.0	49.8	49.8	48.5	50.3	51.5	50.2
Black or African American only:								
Below 100%	14.7	31.3	31.3	35.5	34.7	41.8	37.4	32.0
100%–less than 200%	12.2	30.2	40.7	37.9	35.3	39.4	40.9	36.8
200% or more	12.0	28.7	36.3	29.9	30.6	33.3	32.1	31.6
Geographic region								
Northeast	17.9	41.6	45.4	45.9	45.4	47.2	50.5	47.9
Midwest	20.0	45.1	51.5	49.3	47.9	49.6	50.2	49.9
South	20.2	42.0	46.5	46.8	43.3	46.5	48.4	47.3
West	21.8	43.4	51.2	50.1	47.7	48.1	46.4	46.5
Location of residence								
Within MSA [6]	18.9	42.3	48.0	47.1	45.0	47.1	48.8	47.6
Outside MSA [6]	23.3	45.3	49.6	50.2	47.8	49.7	49.3	48.9

See footnotes at end of table.

Table 83 (page 2 of 3). Influenza and pneumococcal vaccination among adults 18 years of age and over, by selected characteristics: United States, selected years 1989–2004

[Data are based on household interviews of a sample of the civilian noninstitutionalized population]

Characteristic	1989	1995	1999	2000	2001	2002	2003	2004
				Percent ever receiving pneumococcal vaccination[7]				
18 years and over, age-adjusted[2,3]	4.6	11.8	14.7	15.4	16.1	16.4	16.4	16.8
18 years and over, crude[3]	4.4	12.5	14.3	15.1	15.7	16.0	16.0	16.5
Age								
18–49 years	2.1	6.4	5.5	5.4	5.9	5.6	5.6	5.7
50 years and over	9.0	22.4	29.9	31.7	32.2	33.3	33.1	33.6
50–64 years	4.4	10.3	13.6	14.7	15.4	16.3	16.7	17.2
65 years and over	14.1	32.9	49.7	53.1	54.0	56.0	55.6	56.8
65–74 years	13.1	30.3	46.6	48.2	50.3	50.2	49.8	50.4
75 years and over	15.7	36.7	53.5	59.1	58.4	62.8	62.1	64.2
Age 65 years and over								
Sex								
Male	13.9	32.6	50.1	52.1	54.2	55.9	53.7	54.3
Female	14.3	33.1	49.4	53.9	53.8	56.1	57.0	58.7
Race[4]								
White only	14.9	34.7	51.8	55.6	56.7	58.7	57.9	59.1
Black or African American only	6.5	21.2	32.4	30.6	33.9	37.0	36.9	38.6
American Indian or Alaska Native only	31.2	*46.2	*	70.1	*50.7	*	*	*42.0
Asian only	*	*25.5	37.0	40.9	28.1	32.6	35.3	35.1
Native Hawaiian or Other Pacific Islander only	- - -	- - -	*	*	*	*	*	*
2 or more races	- - -	- - -	64.3	55.6	54.0	52.8	*39.3	*48.8
Hispanic origin and race[4]								
Hispanic or Latino	9.8	21.0	27.9	30.4	32.9	27.1	31.0	33.7
Mexican	12.9	*18.0	27.6	32.0	33.8	30.0	33.6	33.3
Not Hispanic or Latino	14.3	33.8	51.0	54.4	55.2	57.7	57.1	58.3
White only	15.1	35.6	53.1	56.8	57.8	60.4	59.6	60.9
Black or African American only	6.2	20.9	32.3	30.6	34.0	37.0	36.9	38.6
Percent of poverty level[5]								
Below 100%	11.2	26.9	40.5	40.6	43.2	42.6	47.7	42.5
100%–less than 200%	15.1	30.8	46.4	51.4	51.0	54.6	56.7	56.1
200% or more	15.0	36.6	52.6	56.2	57.1	59.2	56.5	59.7
Hispanic origin and race and percent of poverty level[4,5]								
Hispanic or Latino:								
Below 100%	*	*13.7	*22.4	23.8	25.0	20.1	23.8	31.8
100%–less than 200%	*11.0	*16.2	29.4	32.3	32.4	25.1	26.8	29.0
200% or more	*10.4	38.3	29.6	32.9	39.4	33.5	39.5	39.1
Not Hispanic or Latino:								
White only:								
Below 100%	13.4	32.3	48.7	47.9	53.4	51.5	57.5	50.6
100%–less than 200%	16.0	34.4	49.9	56.1	56.0	59.9	62.1	61.9
200% or more	15.6	37.2	54.8	58.3	59.0	61.8	58.9	61.9
Black or African American only:								
Below 100%	*5.0	20.6	27.4	28.8	30.5	27.8	35.1	27.0
100%–less than 200%	7.9	18.5	31.9	28.1	31.3	40.7	39.6	36.4
200% or more	*5.2	24.7	35.7	34.4	39.0	39.4	35.7	49.1
Geographic region								
Northeast	10.4	27.2	45.5	51.2	52.5	56.9	54.8	56.0
Midwest	13.7	30.6	52.3	52.6	57.3	55.8	57.1	59.5
South	14.9	34.5	47.5	51.3	52.4	54.2	55.1	57.2
West	17.9	39.8	55.4	59.7	54.6	59.3	55.7	53.7
Location of residence								
Within MSA[6]	13.1	32.7	49.9	52.4	53.3	56.3	56.0	56.7
Outside MSA[6]	17.1	33.9	49.0	55.4	56.4	55.3	54.3	57.3

See footnotes at end of table.

Table 83 (page 3 of 3). Influenza and pneumococcal vaccination among adults 18 years of age and over, by selected characteristics: United States, selected years 1989–2004

[Data are based on household interviews of a sample of the civilian noninstitutionalized population]

* Estimates are considered unreliable. Data preceded by an asterisk have a relative standard error (RSE) of 20%–30%. Data not shown have an RSE of greater than 30%.

- - - Data not available.

[1]Respondents were asked, "During the past 12 months, have you had a flu shot? A flu shot is usually given in the fall and protects against influenza for the flu season." Estimates exclude 1% of respondents who reported receiving Flu Mist.

[2]Estimates are age adjusted to the year 2000 standard population using four age groups: 18–49 years, 50–64 years, 65–74 years, and 75 years and over. See Appendix II, Age adjustment.

[3]Includes all other races not shown separately, unknown education, and, prior to 1990, unknown poverty status.

[4]The race groups, white, black, American Indian or Alaska Native, Asian, Native Hawaiian or Other Pacific Islander, and 2 or more races, include persons of Hispanic and non-Hispanic origin. Persons of Hispanic origin may be of any race. Starting with 1999 data, race-specific estimates are tabulated according to the 1997 Revisions to the Standards for Federal Data on Race and Ethnicity and are not strictly comparable with estimates for earlier years. The five single race categories plus multiple race categories shown in the table conform to the 1997 Standards. Starting with 1999 data, race-specific estimates are for persons who reported only one racial group; the category 2 or more races includes persons who reported more than one racial group. Prior to 1999, data were tabulated according to the 1977 Standards with four racial groups and the Asian only category included Native Hawaiian or Other Pacific Islander. Estimates for single race categories prior to 1999 included persons who reported one race or, if they reported more than one race, identified one race as best representing their race. Starting with 2003 data, race responses of other race and unspecified multiple race were treated as missing, and then race was imputed if these were the only race responses. Almost all persons with a race response of other race were of Hispanic origin. See Appendix II, Hispanic origin; Race.

[5]Percent of poverty level is based on family income and family size and composition using U.S. Census Bureau poverty thresholds. Poverty status was unknown for 11% of persons 18 years of age and over in 1989. Missing family income data were imputed for 16% of persons 18 years of age and over in 1995, 27%–31% in 1997–1998, and 33%–36% in 1999–2004. See Appendix II, Family Income; Poverty.

[6]MSA is metropolitan statistical area.

[7]Respondents were asked, "Have you ever had a pneumonia shot? This shot is usually given only once or twice in a person's lifetime and is different from the flu shot. It is also called the pneumococcal vaccine."

NOTES: In 2000, the Advisory Committee on Immunization Practices (ACIP) of the Centers for Disease Control and Prevention (CDC) recommended universal influenza vaccination for persons 50 years of age and over (CDC. Prevention and control of influenza: Recommendations of the Advisory Committee on Immunization Practices (ACIP). MMWR 2000;49(RR03):1–38.) Standard errors for selected years are available in the spreadsheet version of this table. Available from: www.cdc.gov/nchs/hus.htm. Data for additional years are available. See Appendix III.

SOURCE: Centers for Disease Control and Prevention, National Center for Health Statistics, National Health Interview Survey, sample adult questionnaire.

Table 84 (page 1 of 2). Use of mammography among women 40 years of age and over, by selected characteristics: United States, selected years 1987–2003

[Data are based on household interviews of a sample of the civilian noninstitutionalized population]

Characteristic	1987	1990	1991	1994	1998	1999	2000	2003
	Percent of women having a mammogram within the past 2 years [1]							
40 years and over, age adjusted [2,3]	29.0	51.7	54.7	61.0	67.0	70.3	70.4	69.5
40 years and over, crude [2]	28.7	51.4	54.6	60.9	66.9	70.3	70.4	69.7
Age								
40–49 years	31.9	55.1	55.6	61.3	63.4	67.2	64.3	64.4
50–64 years	31.7	56.0	60.3	66.5	73.7	76.5	78.7	76.2
65 years and over	22.8	43.4	48.1	55.0	63.8	66.8	67.9	67.7
65–74 years	26.6	48.7	55.7	63.0	69.4	73.9	74.0	74.6
75 years and over	17.3	35.8	37.8	44.6	57.2	58.9	61.3	60.6
Race [4]								
40 years and over, crude:								
White only	29.6	52.2	55.6	60.6	67.4	70.6	71.4	70.1
Black or African American only	24.0	46.4	48.0	64.3	66.0	71.0	67.8	70.4
American Indian or Alaska Native only	*	43.2	54.5	65.8	45.2	63.0	47.4	63.1
Asian only	*	46.0	45.9	55.8	60.2	58.3	53.5	57.6
Native Hawaiian or Other Pacific Islander only	- - -	- - -	- - -	- - -	- - -	*	*	*
2 or more races	- - -	- - -	- - -	- - -	- - -	70.2	69.2	65.3
Hispanic origin and race [4]								
40 years and over, crude:								
Hispanic or Latino	18.3	45.2	49.2	51.9	60.2	65.7	61.2	65.0
Not Hispanic or Latino	29.4	51.8	54.9	61.5	67.5	70.7	71.1	70.1
White only	30.3	52.7	56.0	61.3	68.0	71.1	72.2	70.5
Black or African American only	23.8	46.0	47.7	64.4	66.0	71.0	67.9	70.5
Age, Hispanic origin, and race [4]								
40–49 years:								
Hispanic or Latino	*15.3	45.1	44.0	47.5	55.2	61.6	54.1	59.4
Not Hispanic or Latino:								
White only	34.3	57.0	58.1	62.0	64.4	68.3	67.2	65.2
Black or African American only	27.8	48.4	48.0	67.2	65.0	69.2	60.9	68.2
50–64 years:								
Hispanic or Latino	23.0	47.5	61.7	60.1	67.2	69.7	66.5	69.4
Not Hispanic or Latino:								
White only	33.6	58.1	61.5	67.5	75.3	77.9	80.6	77.2
Black or African American only	26.4	48.4	52.4	63.6	71.2	75.0	77.7	76.2
65 years and over:								
Hispanic or Latino	*	41.1	40.9	48.0	59.0	67.2	68.3	69.5
Not Hispanic or Latino:								
White only	24.0	43.8	49.1	54.9	64.3	66.8	68.3	68.1
Black or African American only	14.1	39.7	41.6	61.0	60.6	68.1	65.5	65.4
Age and percent of poverty level [5]								
40 years and over, crude:								
Below 100%	14.6	30.8	35.2	43.9	50.1	57.4	54.8	55.4
100%–less than 200%	20.9	39.1	44.4	49.3	56.1	59.5	58.1	60.8
200% or more	35.2	59.2	62.2	69.6	72.6	75.0	75.9	74.3
40–49 years:								
Below 100%	18.6	32.2	33.0	44.3	44.8	51.3	47.4	50.6
100%–less than 200%	18.4	39.0	43.8	50.9	46.9	52.8	43.6	54.0
200% or more	36.8	60.1	61.2	67.4	68.4	71.6	69.9	68.3
50–64 years:								
Below 100%	14.6	29.9	37.3	44.7	52.7	63.3	61.7	58.3
100%–less than 200%	24.2	39.8	50.2	50.3	61.8	64.9	68.3	64.0
200% or more	37.0	63.3	66.0	75.1	78.7	80.2	82.6	80.9
65 years and over:								
Below 100%	13.1	30.8	35.2	43.2	51.9	57.6	54.8	57.0
100%–less than 200%	19.9	38.6	41.8	47.9	57.8	60.2	60.3	62.8
200% or more	29.7	51.5	57.8	64.9	70.1	72.5	75.0	72.6

See footnotes at end of table.

Table 84 (page 2 of 2). Use of mammography among women 40 years of age and over by selected characteristics: United States, selected years 1987–2003

[Data are based on household interviews of a sample of the civilian noninstitutionalized population]

Characteristic	1987	1990	1991	1994	1998	1999	2000	2003
Health insurance status at the time of interview[6]	Percent of women having a mammogram within the past 2 years[1]							
40–64 years of age:								
Insured..............................	- - -	- - -	- - -	68.3	72.3	75.5	76.0	75.1
Private	- - -	- - -	- - -	69.4	73.4	76.3	77.1	76.3
Medicaid.........................	- - -	- - -	- - -	54.5	59.7	62.5	61.7	63.5
Uninsured........................	- - -	- - -	- - -	34.0	40.1	44.8	40.7	41.5
Health insurance status prior to interview[6]								
40–64 years of age:								
Insured continuously all 12 months	- - -	- - -	- - -	68.6	73.0	76.1	76.8	75.6
Uninsured for any period up to 12 months ..	- - -	- - -	- - -	49.9	47.6	57.1	53.0	56.0
Uninsured more than 12 months	- - -	- - -	- - -	26.6	36.3	38.9	34.0	37.0
Age and education[7]								
40 years and over, crude:								
No high school diploma or GED.........	17.8	36.4	40.0	48.2	54.5	56.7	57.7	58.1
High school diploma or GED	31.3	52.7	55.8	61.0	66.7	69.2	69.7	67.8
Some college or more...............	37.7	62.8	65.2	69.7	72.8	77.3	76.2	75.1
40–49 years of age:								
No high school diploma or GED	15.1	38.5	40.8	50.4	47.3	48.8	46.8	53.3
High school diploma or GED	32.6	53.1	52.0	55.8	59.1	60.8	59.0	60.8
Some college or more	39.2	62.3	63.7	68.7	68.3	74.4	70.6	68.1
50–64 years of age:								
No high school diploma or GED	21.2	41.0	43.6	51.6	58.8	62.3	66.5	63.4
High school diploma or GED	33.8	56.5	60.8	67.8	73.3	77.2	76.6	71.8
Some college or more	40.5	68.0	72.7	74.7	79.8	81.2	84.2	82.7
65 years of age and over:								
No high school diploma or GED	16.5	33.0	37.7	45.6	54.7	56.6	57.4	56.9
High school diploma or GED	25.9	47.5	54.0	59.1	66.8	68.4	71.8	69.7
Some college or more	32.3	56.7	57.9	64.3	71.3	77.1	74.1	75.1

* Estimates are considered unreliable. Data preceded by an asterisk have a relative standard error (RSE) of 20%–30%. Data not shown have an RSE greater than 30%.

- - - Data not available.

[1]Questions concerning use of mammography differed slightly on the National Health Interview Survey across the years for which data are shown. See Appendix II, Mammography.

[2]Includes all other races not shown separately, unknown poverty status in 1987, unknown health insurance status, and unknown education level.

[3]Estimates are age adjusted to the year 2000 standard population using four age groups: 40–49 years, 50–64 years, 65–74 years, and 75 years and over. See Appendix II, Age adjustment.

[4]The race groups, white, black, American Indian or Alaska Native, Asian, Native Hawaiian or Other Pacific Islander, and 2 or more races, include persons of Hispanic and non-Hispanic origin. Persons of Hispanic origin may be of any race. Starting with 1999 data, race-specific estimates are tabulated according to the 1997 Revisions to the Standards for the Classification of Federal Data on Race and Ethnicity and are not strictly comparable with estimates for earlier years. The five single race categories plus multiple race categories shown in the table conform to the 1997 Standards. Starting with 1999 data, race-specific estimates are for persons who reported only one racial group; the category 2 or more races includes persons who reported more than one racial group. Prior to 1999, data were tabulated according to the 1977 Standards with four racial groups and the Asian only category included Native Hawaiian or Other Pacific Islander. Estimates for single race categories prior to 1999 included persons who reported one race or, if they reported more than one race, identified one race as best representing their race. Starting with 2003 data, race responses of other race and unspecified multiple race were treated as missing, and then race was imputed if these were the only race responses. Almost all persons with a race response of other race were of Hispanic origin. See Appendix II, Hispanic origin; Race.

[5]Percent of poverty level is based on family income and family size and composition using U.S. Census Bureau poverty thresholds. Poverty status was unknown for 11% of women 40 years of age and over in 1987. Missing family income data were imputed for 19%–23% of women 40 years of age and over in 1990–1994 and 35%–39% in 1998–2003. See Appendix II, Family income; Poverty.

[6]Health insurance categories are mutually exclusive. Persons who reported both Medicaid and private coverage are classified as having private coverage. Starting in 1997 Medicaid includes state-sponsored health plans and State Children's Health Insurance Program (SCHIP). In addition to private and Medicaid, the category insured also includes military plans, other government-sponsored health plans, and Medicare, not shown separately. See Appendix II, Health insurance coverage.

[7]Education categories shown are for 1998 and subsequent years. GED stands for General Educational Development high school equivalency diploma. In years prior to 1998 the following categories based on number of years of school completed were used: less than 12 years, 12 years, 13 years or more. See Appendix II, Education.

NOTES: Standard errors are available in the spreadsheet version of this table. Available from: www.cdc.gov/nchs/hus.htm. Data starting in 1997 are not strictly comparable with data for earlier years due to the 1997 questionnaire redesign. See Appendix I, National Health Interview Survey. Data for additional years are available. See Appendix III.

SOURCE: Centers for Disease Control and Prevention, National Center for Health Statistics, National Health Interview Survey. Data are from the following supplements: cancer control (1987), health promotion and disease prevention (1990–1991), and year 2000 objectives (1993–1994). Starting in 1998, data are from the family core and sample adult questionnaires.

Table 85 (page 1 of 2). Use of Pap smears among women 18 years of age and over, by selected characteristics: United States, selected years 1987–2003

[Data are based on household interviews of a sample of the civilian noninstitutionalized population]

Characteristic	1987	1993	1994	1998	1999	2000	2003
	Percent of women having a Pap smear within the past 3 years[1]						
18 years and over, age adjusted[2,3]	74.1	77.7	76.8	79.3	80.8	81.3	79.2
18 years and over, crude[2]	74.4	77.7	76.8	79.1	80.8	81.2	79.0
Age							
18–44 years	83.3	84.6	82.8	84.4	86.8	84.9	83.9
18–24 years	74.8	78.8	76.6	73.6	76.8	73.5	75.1
25–44 years	86.3	86.3	84.6	87.6	89.9	88.5	86.8
45–64 years	70.5	77.2	77.4	81.4	81.7	84.6	81.3
45–54 years	75.7	82.1	81.9	83.7	83.8	86.3	83.6
55–64 years	65.2	70.6	71.0	78.0	78.4	82.0	77.8
65 years and over	50.8	57.6	57.3	59.8	61.0	64.5	60.8
65–74 years	57.9	64.7	64.9	67.0	70.0	71.6	70.1
75 years and over	40.4	48.0	47.3	51.2	50.8	56.7	51.1
Race[4]							
18 years and over, crude:							
White only	74.1	77.3	76.2	78.9	80.6	81.3	78.7
Black or African American only	80.7	82.7	83.5	84.2	85.7	85.1	84.0
American Indian or Alaska Native only	85.4	78.1	73.5	74.6	92.2	76.8	84.8
Asian only	51.9	68.8	66.4	68.5	64.4	66.4	68.3
Native Hawaiian or Other Pacific Islander only	- - -	- - -	- - -	- - -	*	*	*
2 or more races	- - -	- - -	- - -	- - -	86.9	80.0	81.6
Hispanic origin and race[4]							
18 years and over, crude:							
Hispanic or Latino	67.6	77.2	74.4	75.2	76.3	77.0	75.4
Not Hispanic or Latino	74.9	77.8	77.0	79.6	81.3	81.7	79.5
White only	74.7	77.3	76.5	79.3	81.0	81.8	79.3
Black or African American only	80.9	82.7	83.8	84.2	86.0	85.1	83.8
Age, Hispanic origin, and race[4]							
18–44 years:							
Hispanic or Latino	73.9	80.9	80.6	76.4	77.0	78.1	75.9
Not Hispanic or Latino:							
White only	84.5	85.3	82.9	85.7	88.7	86.6	85.8
Black or African American only	89.1	88.0	89.1	88.9	90.8	88.5	88.6
45–64 years:							
Hispanic or Latino	57.7	75.8	70.1	78.3	79.5	77.8	77.9
Not Hispanic or Latino:							
White only	71.2	77.2	77.5	81.7	81.9	85.9	81.4
Black or African American only	76.2	80.3	82.2	84.1	84.6	85.7	84.7
65 years and over:							
Hispanic or Latino	41.7	57.1	43.8	59.8	63.7	66.8	64.6
Not Hispanic or Latino:							
White only	51.8	57.1	58.2	59.7	60.5	64.2	60.7
Black or African American only	44.8	61.2	59.5	61.7	64.5	67.2	59.6
Age and percent of poverty level[5]							
18 years and over, crude:							
Below 100%	64.3	70.6	70.5	69.8	73.6	72.0	70.5
100%–less than 200%	68.2	71.9	70.2	70.6	72.5	73.4	71.4
200% or more	80.0	82.8	82.9	83.5	84.3	85.0	83.0
18–44 years:							
Below 100%	77.1	77.2	80.2	77.1	79.7	77.1	77.1
100%–less than 200%	80.4	83.0	79.3	79.2	84.0	79.4	79.5
200% or more	86.4	88.4	86.6	87.6	89.0	88.0	86.9
45–64 years:							
Below 100%	53.6	65.3	65.7	67.6	73.1	73.6	66.0
100%–less than 200%	60.4	64.4	69.1	69.9	70.4	76.1	71.4
200% or more	74.9	81.6	82.8	85.1	84.6	87.4	85.1
65 years and over:							
Below 100%	33.2	46.8	43.8	48.2	51.9	53.7	52.6
100%–less than 200%	50.4	54.7	50.4	55.1	54.7	61.0	55.4
200% or more	60.0	62.6	67.4	65.3	66.4	68.8	65.4

See footnotes at end of table.

Table 85 (page 2 of 2). Use of Pap smears among women 18 years of age and over, by selected characteristics: United States, selected years 1987–2003

[Data are based on household interviews of a sample of the civilian noninstitutionalized population]

Characteristic	1987	1993	1994	1998	1999	2000	2003
Health insurance status at the time of interview[6]	Percent of women having a Pap smear within the past 3 years[1]						
18–64 years of age, crude:							
Insured	- - -	84.7	83.8	86.0	87.2	87.8	86.4
Private	- - -	84.8	83.6	86.5	87.5	88.0	87.0
Medicaid	- - -	82.7	86.2	83.0	84.2	85.8	82.8
Uninsured	- - -	69.4	68.6	69.6	73.3	70.4	66.6
18–64 years of age, crude:							
Insured continuously all 12 months	- - -	84.8	83.7	86.3	87.3	88.0	86.6
Uninsured for any period up to 12 months	- - -	81.8	83.4	81.7	83.5	83.7	81.8
Uninsured more than 12 months	- - -	65.1	63.6	64.0	68.8	65.1	60.2
Age and education[7]							
25 years and over, crude:							
No high school diploma or GED	57.1	61.9	60.9	65.0	66.1	69.9	64.9
High school diploma or GED	76.4	78.2	76.0	77.4	79.3	79.8	75.9
Some college or more	84.0	84.4	85.2	86.9	87.8	88.0	86.2
25–44 years of age:							
No high school diploma or GED	75.1	73.6	73.6	76.8	79.0	79.6	71.7
High school diploma or GED	85.6	85.4	82.4	83.9	87.6	86.2	84.3
Some college or more	90.1	89.8	89.1	91.5	93.0	91.4	90.8
45–64 years of age:							
No high school diploma or GED	58.0	65.6	66.1	69.2	71.6	75.7	71.4
High school diploma or GED	72.3	77.6	75.9	81.0	79.8	81.8	77.6
Some college or more	80.1	83.0	84.7	85.5	85.7	89.1	86.2
65 years of age and over:							
No high school diploma or GED	44.0	50.7	47.7	52.4	51.8	56.6	52.5
High school diploma or GED	55.4	61.6	61.2	60.7	63.7	66.9	61.2
Some college or more	59.4	62.3	66.5	67.9	68.8	69.8	67.8

* Estimates are considered unreliable. Data not shown have a relative standard error greater than 30%.

- - - Data not available.

[1]Questions concerning use of Pap smears differed slightly on the National Health Interview Survey across the years for which data are shown. See Appendix II, Pap smear.

[2]Includes all other races not shown separately, unknown poverty status in 1987, unknown health insurance status, and unknown education level.

[3]Estimates are age adjusted to the year 2000 standard population using five age groups: 18–44 years, 45–54 years, 55–64 years, 65–74 years, and 75 years and over. Age-adjusted estimates in this table may differ from other age-adjusted estimates based on the same data and presented elsewhere if different age groups are used in the adjustment procedure. See Appendix II, Age adjustment.

[4]The race groups, white, black, American Indian or Alaska Native, Asian, Native Hawaiian or Other Pacific Islander, and 2 or more races, include persons of Hispanic and non-Hispanic origin. Persons of Hispanic origin may be of any race. Starting with 1999 data, race-specific estimates are tabulated according to the 1997 Revisions to the Standards for the Classification of Federal Data on Race and Ethnicity and are not strictly comparable with estimates for earlier years. The five single race categories plus multiple race categories shown in the table conform to 1997 Standards. Starting with 1999 data, race-specific estimates are for persons who reported only one racial group; the category 2 or more races includes persons who reported more than one racial group. Prior to 1999, data were tabulated according to the 1977 Standards with four racial groups and the Asian only category included Native Hawaiian or Other Pacific Islander. Estimates for single race categories prior to 1999 included persons who reported one race or, if they reported more than one race, identified one race as best representing their race. Starting with 2003 data, race responses of other race and unspecified multiple race were treated as missing, and then race was imputed if these were the only race responses. Almost all persons with a race response of other race were of Hispanic origin. See Appendix II, Hispanic origin; Race.

[5]Percent of poverty level is based on family income and family size and composition using U.S. Census Bureau poverty thresholds. Poverty status was unknown for 9% of women 18 years of age and over in 1987. Missing family income data were imputed for 17%–20% of women 18 years of age and over in 1990–1994 and 35%–39% in 1998–2003. See Appendix II, Family income; Poverty.

[6]Health insurance categories are mutually exclusive. Persons who reported both Medicaid and private coverage are classified as having private coverage. Starting in 1997 Medicaid includes state-sponsored health plans and State Children's Health Insurance Program (SCHIP). In addition to private and Medicaid, the category insured also includes military plans, other government-sponsored health plans, and Medicare, not shown separately. See Appendix II, Health insurance coverage.

[7]Education categories shown are for 1998 and subsequent years. GED stands for General Educational Development high school equivalency diploma. In years prior to 1998 the following categories based on number of years of school completed were used: less than 12 years, 12 years, 13 years or more. See Appendix II, Education.

NOTES: Standard errors are available in the spreadsheet version of this table. Available from: www.cdc.gov/nchs/hus.htm. Data starting in 1997 are not strictly comparable with data for earlier years due to the 1997 questionnaire redesign. See Appendix I, National Health Interview Survey.

SOURCES: Centers for Disease Control and Prevention, National Center for Health Statistics, National Health Interview Survey. Data are from the following supplements: cancer control (1987), year 2000 objectives (1993–1994). Starting in 1998, data are from the family core and sample adult questionnaires.

Table 86 (page 1 of 3). Emergency department visits within the past 12 months among children under 18 years of age, by selected characteristics: United States, selected years 1997–2004

[Data are based on household interviews of a sample of the civilian noninstitutionalized population]

Characteristic	Under 18 years of age			Under 6 years of age			6–17 years of age		
	1997	2003	2004	1997	2003	2004	1997	2003	2004
	Percent of children with 1 or more emergency department visits [1]								
All children [2]	19.9	20.9	20.9	24.3	26.5	26.2	17.7	18.2	18.4
Race [3]									
White only	19.4	20.3	20.6	22.6	25.2	25.3	17.8	17.9	18.3
Black or African American only	24.0	23.9	23.1	33.1	32.0	31.1	19.4	20.2	19.4
American Indian or Alaska Native only	*24.1	*22.7	*17.7	*24.3	*	*	*24.0	*21.0	*16.7
Asian only	12.6	14.2	15.8	20.8	*20.7	*19.4	8.6	*11.0	14.3
Native Hawaiian or Other Pacific Islander only	- - -	*	*	- - -	*	*	- - -	*	*
2 or more races	- - -	26.1	27.0	- - -	34.0	35.7	- - -	20.3	21.3
Hispanic origin and race [3]									
Hispanic or Latino	21.1	20.3	20.6	25.7	27.9	26.9	18.1	16.0	16.9
Not Hispanic or Latino	19.7	21.0	21.0	24.0	26.1	26.0	17.6	18.7	18.7
White only	19.2	20.4	20.7	22.2	24.6	24.8	17.7	18.5	18.8
Black or African American only	23.6	23.8	22.8	32.7	31.9	30.7	19.2	20.1	19.1
Percent of poverty level [4]									
Below 100%	25.1	26.9	27.6	29.5	34.5	34.3	22.2	22.6	23.6
100%–less than 200%	22.0	22.8	22.3	28.0	28.8	29.5	19.0	19.3	18.6
200% or more	17.3	18.4	18.5	20.5	22.5	21.9	15.8	16.5	16.9
Hispanic origin and race and percent of poverty level [3,4]									
Hispanic or Latino:									
Percent of poverty level:									
Below 100%	21.9	23.3	23.1	25.0	31.5	29.2	19.6	18.4	19.2
100%–less than 200%	20.8	19.6	20.9	28.8	27.0	26.4	15.6	15.0	17.6
200% or more	20.4	18.1	17.9	23.4	25.0	24.8	18.7	14.7	14.4
Not Hispanic or Latino:									
White only:									
Percent of poverty level:									
Below 100%	25.5	28.4	32.3	27.2	33.8	36.6	24.4	25.3	29.9
100%–less than 200%	22.3	23.4	23.8	25.8	27.4	31.3	20.7	21.0	19.6
200% or more	17.2	18.5	18.3	20.1	22.1	20.9	15.9	17.0	17.2
Black or African American only:									
Percent of poverty level:									
Below 100%	29.3	27.2	29.2	39.5	33.5	37.5	23.0	24.2	24.1
100%–less than 200%	22.5	27.0	21.2	31.7	44.1	27.8	18.5	20.7	18.9
200% or more	17.7	19.0	18.9	22.6	24.1	25.8	15.9	16.7	15.9
Health insurance status at the time of interview [5]									
Insured	19.8	21.4	21.0	24.4	26.7	25.9	17.5	18.7	18.5
Private	17.5	18.1	18.5	20.9	21.6	21.1	15.9	16.6	17.3
Medicaid	28.2	28.9	27.2	33.0	35.1	34.3	24.1	24.5	22.3
Uninsured	20.2	17.1	20.7	23.0	23.9	28.7	18.9	14.7	17.6
Health insurance level prior to interview [5]									
Insured continuously all 12 months	19.6	21.2	20.7	24.1	26.7	25.5	17.3	18.4	18.4
Uninsured for any period up to 12 months	24.0	24.1	27.3	27.1	29.7	37.4	21.9	21.0	22.2
Uninsured more than 12 months	18.4	12.6	16.6	19.3	*16.9	21.9	18.1	11.6	15.0
Percent of poverty level and health insurance status prior to interview [4,5]									
Below 100%:									
Insured continuously all 12 months	26.3	29.1	27.4	30.9	36.7	33.2	22.8	24.5	23.7
Uninsured for any period up to 12 months . .	26.5	28.2	35.4	29.7	32.7	47.5	24.4	25.7	29.5
Uninsured more than 12 months	17.5	*10.7	*18.9	*16.0	*	*	18.0	*10.5	*
100%–less than 200%:									
Insured continuously all 12 months	21.8	23.8	22.3	28.0	29.5	28.7	18.6	20.4	18.8
Uninsured for any period up to 12 months . .	24.5	22.1	27.2	29.7	31.7	39.5	21.0	16.7	21.4
Uninsured more than 12 months	19.5	15.5	16.8	*22.5	*22.9	*27.3	18.6	13.3	13.6
200% or more:									
Insured continuously all 12 months	17.1	18.3	18.5	20.3	22.4	21.7	15.6	16.5	17.1
Uninsured for any period up to 12 months . .	20.7	23.1	22.2	21.3	26.1	30.0	20.4	21.5	18.1
Uninsured more than 12 months	17.9	*11.5	*13.6	*19.2	*	*	17.3	*10.9	*12.6

See footnotes at end of table.

Table 86 (page 2 of 3). Emergency department visits within the past 12 months among children under 18 years of age, by selected characteristics: United States, selected years 1997–2004

[Data are based on household interviews of a sample of the civilian noninstitutionalized population]

Characteristic	Under 18 years of age			Under 6 years of age			6–17 years of age		
	1997	2003	2004	1997	2003	2004	1997	2003	2004
Geographic region	Percent of children with 1 or more emergency department visits[1]								
Northeast	18.5	21.8	24.2	20.7	26.3	28.6	17.4	19.7	22.2
Midwest	19.5	21.4	21.0	26.0	27.2	25.7	16.4	18.7	18.6
South	21.8	21.7	21.5	25.6	27.8	26.7	19.9	18.6	19.0
West	18.5	18.3	17.6	23.5	23.6	24.2	15.9	15.8	14.3
Location of residence									
Within MSA[6]	19.7	20.2	20.5	23.9	25.2	26.0	17.4	17.8	17.8
Outside MSA[6]	20.8	23.6	23.0	26.2	31.8	27.4	18.6	19.7	21.0
	Percent of children with 2 or more emergency department visits[1]								
All children[2]	7.1	7.0	8.0	9.6	8.7	9.4	5.8	6.2	7.4
Race[3]									
White only	6.6	6.3	7.8	8.4	7.6	9.2	5.7	5.7	7.0
Black or African American only	9.6	10.4	9.4	14.9	13.9	10.9	6.9	8.8	8.7
American Indian and Alaska Native only	*	*	*	*	*	*	*	*	*
Asian only	*5.7	*6.7	*6.3	*12.9	*	*	*	*	*6.9
Native Hawaiian and Other Pacific Islander only	- - -	*	*	- - -	*	*	- - -	*	*
2 or more races	- - -	8.7	10.1	- - -	*10.1	*11.9	- - -	*7.6	*8.9
Hispanic origin and race[3]									
Hispanic or Latino	8.9	7.4	8.0	11.8	10.8	10.2	7.0	5.5	6.7
Not Hispanic or Latino	6.8	6.9	8.1	9.2	8.2	9.2	5.7	6.4	7.5
White only	6.2	6.0	7.7	7.8	6.6	8.9	5.5	5.8	7.2
Black or African American only	9.3	10.6	9.4	14.6	14.4	10.7	6.8	8.9	8.8
Percent of poverty level[4]									
Below 100%	11.1	11.6	13.0	14.5	12.9	14.6	8.9	10.8	12.0
100%–less than 200%	8.3	8.6	8.7	12.2	10.6	10.8	6.3	7.4	7.7
200% or more	5.3	5.1	6.3	6.5	6.4	6.9	4.7	4.5	6.0
Hispanic origin and race and percent of poverty level[3,4]									
Hispanic or Latino: Percent of poverty level:									
Below 100%	10.4	9.6	9.0	13.9	13.6	10.5	8.0	7.2	8.1
100%–less than 200%	8.2	7.5	7.9	12.0	11.7	9.7	5.7	*4.9	6.8
200% or more	7.6	5.2	7.0	8.4	6.9	10.4	7.1	4.5	5.3
Not Hispanic or Latino: White only: Percent of poverty level:									
Below 100%	10.7	10.5	16.4	12.2	*10.1	*16.7	9.8	*10.7	16.3
100%–less than 200%	8.0	8.5	8.7	11.2	7.7	11.7	6.4	9.0	7.0
200% or more	5.0	4.8	6.3	5.8	5.7	6.8	4.6	4.4	6.1
Black or African American only: Percent of poverty level:									
Below 100%	12.7	14.6	14.3	19.1	14.7	17.4	8.8	14.5	12.4
100%–less than 200%	9.2	11.7	10.4	*13.5	21.6	*11.7	*7.2	*8.1	*10.0
200% or more	5.5	6.7	5.0	*8.2	*10.1	*3.6	*4.5	*5.1	*5.6
Health insurance status at the time of interview[5]									
Insured	7.0	7.1	7.9	9.6	8.7	9.4	5.7	6.3	7.2
Private	5.2	5.1	6.1	6.8	5.4	6.5	4.5	4.9	6.0
Medicaid	13.1	11.7	12.5	16.2	14.0	14.7	10.4	10.1	10.9
Uninsured	7.7	6.6	9.3	9.8	*8.8	9.6	6.8	5.9	9.2
Health insurance status prior to interview[5]									
Insured continuously all 12 months	6.9	7.0	7.7	9.4	8.9	9.0	5.7	6.1	7.1
Uninsured for any period up to 12 months	8.5	9.4	12.3	11.5	*8.2	14.7	6.6	10.1	11.1
Uninsured more than 12 months	6.8	4.0	*7.3	*8.6	*	*8.2	6.2	*3.7	*

See footnotes at end of table.

Table 86 (page 3 of 3). Emergency department visits within the past 12 months among children under 18 years of age, by selected characteristics: United States, selected years 1997–2004

[Data are based on household interviews of a sample of the civilian noninstitutionalized population]

Characteristic	Under 18 years of age			Under 6 years of age			6–17 years of age		
	1997	2003	2004	1997	2003	2004	1997	2003	2004
Geographic region	Percent of children with 2 or more emergency department visits[1]								
Northeast..........................	6.2	7.8	8.5	7.6	8.0	9.0	5.4	7.6	8.2
Midwest............................	6.6	6.3	8.1	10.4	8.5	11.2	4.8	5.3	6.6
South	8.0	8.0	9.1	10.1	9.5	10.0	6.9	7.3	8.6
West	7.1	5.5	6.0	10.0	8.1	6.9	5.6	4.2	5.5
Location of residence									
Within MSA[6]	7.2	6.7	7.7	9.6	8.3	8.7	5.9	6.0	7.1
Outside MSA[6]	6.8	8.2	9.7	9.7	10.3	12.4	5.6	7.2	8.4

* Estimates are considered unreliable. Data preceded by an asterisk have a relative standard error (RSE) of 20%–30%. Data not shown have an RSE of greater than 30%.

- - - Data not available.

[1] See Appendix II, Emergency department visit.

[2] Includes all other races not shown separately and unknown health insurance status.

[3] The race groups, white, black, American Indian or Alaska Native, Asian, Native Hawaiian or Other Pacific Islander, and 2 or more races, include persons of Hispanic and non-Hispanic origin. Persons of Hispanic origin may be of any race. Starting with 1999 data, race-specific estimates are tabulated according to the 1997 Revisions to the Standards for the Classification of Federal Data on Race and Ethnicity and are not strictly comparable with estimates for earlier years. The five single race categories plus multiple race categories shown in the table conform to the 1997 Standards. Starting with 1999 data, race-specific estimates are for persons who reported only one racial group; the category 2 or more races includes persons who reported more than one racial group. Prior to 1999, data were tabulated according to the 1977 Standards with four racial groups and the Asian only category included Native Hawaiian or Other Pacific Islander. Estimates for single race categories prior to 1999 included persons who reported one race or, if they reported more than one race, identified one race as best representing their race. Starting with 2003 data, race responses of other race and unspecified multiple race were treated as missing, and then race was imputed if these were the only race responses. Almost all persons with a race response of other race were of Hispanic origin. See Appendix II, Hispanic origin; Race.

[4] Percent of poverty level is based on family income and family size and composition using U.S. Census Bureau poverty thresholds. Missing family income data were imputed for 21%–25% of children in 1997–1998 and 28%–31% in 1999–2004. See Appendix II, Family income; Poverty.

[5] Health insurance categories are mutually exclusive. Persons who reported both Medicaid and private coverage are classified as having private coverage. Starting in 1997 Medicaid includes state-sponsored health plans and State Children's Health Insurance Program (SCHIP). The category insured also includes military, other government, and Medicare coverage. See Appendix II, Health insurance coverage.

[6] MSA is metropolitan statistical area.

NOTES: Standard errors are available in the spreadsheet version of this table. Available from: www.cdc.gov/nchs/hus.htm. Data for additional years are available. See Appendix III.

SOURCE: Centers for Disease Control and Prevention, National Center for Health Statistics, National Health Interview Survey, family core and sample child questionnaires.

Table 87 (page 1 of 2). Emergency department visits within the past 12 months among adults 18 years of age and over, by selected characteristics: United States, selected years 1997–2004

[Data are based on household interviews of a sample of the civilian noninstitutionalized population]

Characteristic	1 or more emergency department visits				2 or more emergency department visits			
	1997	2000	2003	2004	1997	2000	2003	2004
	Percent of adults with emergency department visit[1]							
All adults 18 years of age and over[2,3]	19.6	20.2	20.0	20.7	6.7	6.9	7.0	7.5
Age								
18–44 years	20.7	20.5	20.0	20.9	6.8	7.0	6.8	7.4
18–24 years.	26.3	25.7	23.9	24.4	9.1	8.8	8.2	8.6
25–44 years.	19.0	18.8	18.6	19.7	6.2	6.4	6.4	7.0
45–64 years	16.2	17.6	18.5	18.1	5.6	5.6	6.4	6.3
45–54 years.	15.7	17.9	17.8	17.9	5.5	5.8	5.9	6.4
55–64 years.	16.9	17.0	19.3	18.4	5.7	5.3	7.0	6.2
65 years and over	22.0	23.7	22.9	24.5	8.1	8.6	8.7	9.5
65–74 years.	20.3	21.6	19.7	20.8	7.1	7.4	7.1	7.5
75 years and over	24.3	26.2	26.6	28.7	9.3	10.0	10.4	11.8
Sex[3]								
Male.	19.1	18.7	18.2	19.3	5.9	5.7	5.6	6.5
Female.	20.2	21.6	21.8	22.1	7.5	7.9	8.4	8.4
Race[3,4]								
White only.	19.0	19.4	19.2	20.0	6.2	6.4	6.4	7.0
Black or African American only	25.9	26.5	27.8	27.0	11.1	10.8	12.4	11.2
American Indian or Alaska Native only	24.8	30.3	22.5	27.8	13.1	*12.6	*9.1	*12.6
Asian only.	11.6	13.6	12.9	12.2	*2.9	*3.8	*3.5	4.1
Native Hawaiian or Other Pacific Islander only	- - -	*	*	*	- - -	*	*	*
2 or more races.	- - -	32.5	25.2	31.5	- - -	11.3	11.1	14.4
American Indian or Alaska Native; White	- - -	33.9	29.7	32.1	- - -	*9.4	*15.1	*15.8
Hispanic origin and race[3,4]								
Hispanic or Latino	19.2	18.3	18.5	19.2	7.4	7.0	7.3	7.0
Mexican.	17.8	17.4	17.0	17.1	6.4	7.1	6.4	5.9
Not Hispanic or Latino	19.7	20.6	20.3	21.1	6.7	6.9	7.0	7.6
White only	19.1	19.8	19.5	20.4	6.2	6.4	6.3	7.0
Black or African American only.	25.9	26.5	27.7	27.2	11.0	10.8	12.3	11.3
Percent of poverty level[3,5]								
Below 100%	28.1	29.0	26.3	29.3	12.8	13.3	12.6	13.8
100%–less than 200%	23.8	23.9	23.2	23.6	9.3	9.6	9.9	9.5
200% or more	17.0	18.0	18.2	18.7	4.9	5.2	5.4	6.0
Hispanic origin and race and percent of poverty level[3,4,5]								
Hispanic or Latino:								
Below 100%	22.1	22.4	21.2	22.6	9.8	9.7	9.6	10.0
100%–less than 200%	19.2	18.1	17.6	20.2	8.1	6.7	7.3	7.1
200% or more	17.6	16.8	17.9	16.9	5.4	6.1	6.4	5.4
Not Hispanic or Latino:								
White only:								
Below 100%	29.5	30.1	27.0	30.2	13.0	13.9	12.7	14.1
100%–less than 200%	24.3	25.5	24.0	25.1	9.1	10.4	10.0	10.0
200% or more	16.8	17.7	17.8	18.6	4.8	5.0	5.0	5.9
Black or African American only:								
Below 100%	34.6	35.4	33.4	38.2	17.5	17.4	18.1	19.2
100%–less than 200%	29.2	28.5	31.2	28.5	12.8	12.2	15.7	12.1
200% or more	19.7	22.6	24.0	22.5	7.2	8.0	8.7	8.1
Health insurance status at the time of interview[6,7]								
18–64 years of age:								
Insured	18.8	19.5	19.7	20.1	6.1	6.4	6.7	6.9
Private	16.9	17.6	17.4	18.0	4.7	5.1	5.0	5.3
Medicaid	37.6	42.2	39.7	36.8	19.7	21.0	21.6	19.8
Uninsured	20.0	19.3	18.1	19.0	7.5	6.9	6.7	7.4
Health insurance status prior to interview[6,7]								
18–64 years of age:								
Insured continuously all 12 months	18.3	19.0	19.2	19.6	5.8	6.1	6.4	6.6
Uninsured for any period up to 12 months	25.5	28.2	25.7	25.3	9.4	10.3	10.0	10.3
Uninsured more than 12 months	18.9	17.3	16.8	17.9	7.1	6.4	6.3	7.2

See footnotes at end of table.

Table 87 (page 2 of 2). Emergency department visits within the past 12 months among adults 18 years of age and over, by selected characteristics: United States, selected years 1997–2004

[Data are based on household interviews of a sample of the civilian noninstitutionalized population]

Characteristic	1 or more emergency department visits				2 or more emergency department visits			
	1997	2000	2003	2004	1997	2000	2003	2004
Percent of poverty level and health insurance status prior to interview[5,6,7]	Percent of adults with emergency department visit[1]							
18–64 years of age:								
Below 100%:								
Insured continuously all 12 months	30.2	31.6	29.4	32.1	14.7	15.4	14.6	15.9
Uninsured for any period up to 12 months . . .	34.1	43.7	30.8	35.1	16.1	18.1	15.0	16.2
Uninsured more than 12 months	20.8	20.5	19.2	20.7	8.1	9.1	8.7	9.4
100%–less than 200%:								
Insured continuously all 12 months	24.5	25.5	24.7	24.7	8.9	10.2	10.9	10.3
Uninsured for any period up to 12 months . . .	28.7	27.7	30.0	27.9	12.3	11.7	11.3	11.9
Uninsured more than 12 months	19.0	17.4	16.7	17.8	8.3	6.4	6.7	6.5
200% or more:								
Insured continuously all 12 months	16.0	17.0	17.2	17.6	4.4	4.7	4.8	5.1
Uninsured for any period up to 12 months . . .	20.2	22.9	22.4	20.9	5.3	7.0	7.7	7.5
Uninsured more than 12 months	17.4	15.6	15.3	16.3	5.3	4.7	4.3	6.2
Geographic region[3]								
Northeast	19.5	20.0	20.3	21.9	6.9	6.2	6.9	7.7
Midwest	19.3	20.1	20.0	20.7	6.2	6.9	6.4	7.0
South	20.9	21.2	20.9	21.4	7.3	7.6	8.1	8.1
West	17.7	18.6	18.2	18.6	6.0	6.3	5.9	6.8
Location of residence[3]								
Within MSA[8]	19.1	19.6	19.5	20.3	6.4	6.6	6.6	7.2
Outside MSA[8]	21.5	22.5	22.3	22.6	7.8	7.8	8.6	8.4

* Estimates are considered unreliable. Data preceded by an asterisk have a relative standard error (RSE) of 20%–30%. Data not shown have an RSE of greater than 30%.

- - - Data not available.

[1] See Appendix II, Emergency department visit.

[2] Includes all other races not shown separately and unknown health insurance status.

[3] Estimates are for persons 18 years of age and over and are age adjusted to the year 2000 standard population using five age groups: 18–44 years, 45–54 years, 55–64 years, 65–74 years, and 75 years and over. See Appendix II, Age adjustment.

[4] The race groups, white, black, American Indian or Alaska Native, Asian, Native Hawaiian or Other Pacific Islander, and 2 or more races, include persons of Hispanic and non-Hispanic origin. Persons of Hispanic origin may be of any race. Starting with 1999 data, race-specific estimates are tabulated according to the 1997 Revisions to the Standards for the Classification of Federal Data on Race and Ethnicity and are not strictly comparable with estimates for earlier years. The five single race categories plus multiple race categories shown in the table conform to the 1997 Standards. Starting with 1999 data, race-specific estimates are for persons who reported only one racial group; the category 2 or more races includes persons who reported more than one racial group. Prior to 1999, data were tabulated according to the 1977 Standards with four racial groups and the Asian only category included Native Hawaiian or Other Pacific Islander. Estimates for single race categories prior to 1999 included persons who reported one race or, if they reported more than one race, identified one race as best representing their race. Starting with 2003 data, race responses of other race and unspecified multiple race were treated as missing, and then race was imputed if these were the only race responses. Almost all persons with a race response of other race were of Hispanic origin. See Appendix II, Hispanic origin; Race.

[5] Percent of poverty level is based on family income and family size and composition using U.S. Census Bureau poverty thresholds. Missing family income data were imputed for 27%–31% of persons 18 years of age and over in 1997–1998 and 33%–36% in 1999–2004. See Appendix II, Family income; Poverty.

[6] Estimates for persons 18–64 years of age are age adjusted to the year 2000 Standard using three age groups: 18–44 years, 45–54 years, and 55–64 years of age. See Appendix II, Age adjustment.

[7] Health insurance categories are mutually exclusive. Persons who reported both Medicaid and private coverage are classified as having private coverage. Starting with 1997 data, Medicaid includes state-sponsored health plans and State Children's Health Insurance Program (SCHIP). In addition to private and Medicaid, the category insured also includes military plans, other government-sponsored health plans, and Medicare, not shown separately. See Appendix II, Health insurance coverage.

[8] MSA is metropolitan statistical area.

NOTES: Standard errors are available in the spreadsheet version of this table. Available from: www.cdc.gov/nchs/hus.htm. Data for additional years are available. See Appendix III.

SOURCE: Centers for Disease Control and Prevention, National Center for Health Statistics, National Health Interview Survey, family core and sample adult questionnaires.

Table 88 (page 1 of 2). Injury-related visits to hospital emergency departments, by sex, age, and intent and mechanism of injury: United States, average annual 1995–1996, 1999–2000, and 2003–2004

[Data are based on reporting by a sample of hospital emergency departments]

Sex, age, and intent and mechanism of injury[1]	1995–1996	1999–2000	2003–2004	1995–1996	1999–2000	2003–2004
Both sexes	Injury-related visits in thousands			Injury-related visits per 10,000 persons		
All ages[2,3]	36,081	39,029	40,792	1,360.9	1,428.1	1,417.4
Male						
All ages[2,3]	20,030	21,286	21,696	1,530.7	1,585.3	1,537.6
Under 18 years[2]	6,238	6,364	6,226	1,720.2	1,722.2	1,668.0
Unintentional injuries[4]	5,478	5,457	5,022	1,510.5	1,476.7	1,345.4
Falls	1,402	1,303	1,362	386.5	352.6	365.0
Struck by or against objects or persons	1,011	1,378	1,143	278.9	372.8	306.2
Motor vehicle traffic	453	432	381	125.0	116.9	102.0
Cut or pierce	493	455	405	136.0	123.2	108.6
Intentional injuries	290	242	224	80.0	65.6	60.1
18–24 years[2]	2,980	3,096	2,881	2,396.9	2,361.6	2,041.6
Unintentional injuries[4]	2,423	2,416	1,992	1,948.7	1,842.7	1,412.0
Falls	299	307	283	240.8	233.9	200.4
Struck by or against objects or persons	387	405	364	311.0	308.6	257.8
Motor vehicle traffic	347	469	407	279.4	357.5	288.7
Cut or pierce	304	394	226	244.8	300.5	160.0
Intentional injuries	335	322	309	269.2	245.9	219.2
25–44 years[2]	7,245	7,251	6,914	1,767.4	1,796.9	1,661.3
Unintentional injuries[4]	5,757	5,528	4,557	1,404.3	1,370.0	1,094.8
Falls	817	850	861	199.4	210.8	206.8
Struck by or against objects or persons	619	781	564	151.0	193.6	135.6
Motor vehicle traffic	912	848	722	222.6	210.1	173.4
Cut or pierce	860	764	615	209.8	189.4	147.7
Intentional injuries	701	511	493	171.0	126.5	118.5
45–64 years[2]	2,240	2,972	3,805	883.4	1,030.9	1,133.2
Unintentional injuries[4]	1,845	2,325	2,403	727.6	806.7	715.9
Falls	445	582	565	175.6	202.0	168.4
Struck by or against objects or persons	186	232	268	73.3	80.6	79.7
Motor vehicle traffic	244	316	375	96.3	109.6	111.7
Cut or pierce	203	294	290	79.9	101.9	86.4
Intentional injuries	86	99	142	33.8	34.3	42.2
65 years and over[2]	1,327	1,603	1,871	1,000.7	1,158.7	1,280.6
Unintentional injuries[4]	1,009	1,207	1,179	760.6	872.1	807.4
Falls	505	579	644	380.9	418.1	440.6
Struck by or against objects or persons	*39	112	74	*29.4	*80.7	50.3
Motor vehicle traffic	99	114	121	74.7	*82.5	83.2
Cut or pierce	*81	102	89	*61.1	74.0	60.9
Intentional injuries	*	10	20	*	*	*13.9

See footnotes at end of table.

Table 88 (page 2 of 2). Injury-related visits to hospital emergency departments, by sex, age, and intent and mechanism of injury: United States, average annual 1995–1996, 1999–2000, and 2003–2004

[Data are based on reporting by a sample of hospital emergency departments]

Sex, age, and intent and mechanism of injury[1]	1995–1996	1999–2000	2003–2004	1995–1996	1999–2000	2003–2004
Female	Injury-related visits in thousands			Injury-related visits per 10,000 persons		
All ages[2,3]	16,051	17,743	19,096	1,186.4	1,267.4	1,295.3
Under 18 years[2]	4,372	4,443	4,609	1,263.9	1,259.0	1,291.8
Unintentional injuries[4]	3,760	3,722	3,492	1,087.0	1,054.7	978.7
Falls	1,040	1,025	1,092	300.7	290.6	306.0
Struck by or against objects or persons	477	728	552	137.9	206.4	154.8
Motor vehicle traffic	447	430	421	129.3	122.0	118.1
Cut or pierce	253	232	219	73.0	65.7	61.3
Intentional injuries	220	149	218	63.6	42.3	61.2
18–24 years[2]	1,900	2,219	2,458	1,523.4	1,688.1	1,757.8
Unintentional injuries[4]	1,430	1,579	1,548	1,146.7	1,200.9	1,106.8
Falls	268	234	286	214.5	178.0	204.3
Struck by or against objects or persons	134	170	203	107.4	129.6	145.2
Motor vehicle traffic	373	469	468	298.8	357.1	334.5
Cut or pierce	131	156	125	105.3	118.3	89.1
Intentional injuries	239	219	251	191.7	166.8	179.5
25–44 years[2]	5,098	5,584	5,636	1,205.8	1,332.7	1,322.5
Unintentional injuries[4]	3,877	3,976	3,588	916.8	948.9	841.9
Falls	817	947	890	193.3	225.9	208.9
Struck by or against objects or persons	380	382	355	89.8	91.3	83.3
Motor vehicle traffic	872	788	818	206.2	188.0	191.9
Cut or pierce	338	434	309	79.8	103.5	72.5
Intentional injuries	422	425	391	99.8	101.5	91.7
45–64 years[2]	2,369	2,933	3,614	873.7	952.9	1,014.3
Unintentional injuries[4]	1,857	2,180	2,375	685.2	708.2	666.6
Falls	600	749	935	221.5	243.5	262.3
Struck by or against objects or persons	160	192	187	58.8	62.3	52.4
Motor vehicle traffic	343	324	399	126.5	105.2	111.9
Cut or pierce	127	175	212	46.9	56.8	59.4
Intentional injuries	*64	125	134	*23.5	40.5	37.6
65 years and over[2]	2,313	2,564	2,779	1,256.1	1,367.8	1,399.3
Unintentional injuries[4]	1,931	2,013	1,964	1,049.0	1,073.8	988.9
Falls	1,230	1,219	1,345	667.9	650.4	677.4
Struck by or against objects or persons	82	103	133	44.8	54.8	66.9
Motor vehicle traffic	169	132	138	91.6	70.6	69.3
Cut or pierce	*42	72	49	*22.7	*38.3	24.6
Intentional injuries	*	20	10	*	*	*

* Estimates are considered unreliable. Data preceded by an asterisk have a relative standard error (RSE) of 20%–30%. Data not shown have an RSE of greater than 30%.

[1]Intent and mechanism of injury are based on the first-listed external cause of injury code (E code). Intentional injuries include suicide attempts and assaults. See Appendix II, External cause of injury and Appendix II, Table VII for a listing of E codes.

[2]Includes all injury-related visits not shown separately in table including those with undetermined intent (0.6% in 2003–2004), insufficient or no information to code cause of injury (4.3% in 2003–2004), and resulting from adverse effects of medical treatment (20.7% in 2003–2004).

[3]Rates are age adjusted to the year 2000 standard population using six age groups: under 18 years, 18–24 years, 25–44 years, 45–64 years, 65–74 years, and 75 years and over. See Appendix II, Age adjustment.

[4]Includes unintentional injury-related visits with mechanism of injury not shown in table.

NOTES: An emergency department visit was considered injury related if the checkbox for injury was indicated, the physician's diagnosis was injury related (ICD–9-CM 800–999), an external cause of injury code was present (ICD–9-CM E800–E999), or the patient's reason for the visit was injury related. Rates for 1995–2000 were computed using 1990-based postcensal estimates of the civilian noninstitutionalized population as of July 1, adjusted for net underenumeration using the 1990 National Population Adjustment Matrix from the U.S. Census Bureau. Starting with 2001 data, rates were computed using 2000-based postcensal estimates of the civilian noninstitutionalized population as of July 1. The difference between rates for 2000 computed using 1990-based postcensal estimates and rates computed using estimates based on 2000 census counts is minimal. Available from: www.cdc.gov/nchs/about/major/ahcd/census2000.htm. Rates will be overestimated to the extent that visits by institutionalized persons are counted in the numerator (for example, hospital emergency department visits by nursing home residents) and institutionalized persons are omitted from the denominator. Data for additional years are available. See Appendix III.

SOURCE: Centers for Disease Control and Prevention, National Center for Health Statistics, National Hospital Ambulatory Medical Care Survey.

[Data are based on reporting by a sample of office-based physicians and hospital outpatient and emergency departments]

Age, sex, and race	All places[1]				Physician offices			
	1995	2002	2003	2004	1995	2002	2003	2004
	Number of visits in thousands							
Total	860,859	1,157,798	1,114,504	1,106,067	697,082	964,304	906,023	910,857
Under 18 years	194,644	238,571	223,724	220,605	150,351	188,933	169,392	171,459
18–44 years	285,184	337,681	331,015	314,993	219,065	263,672	251,853	241,305
45–64 years	188,320	308,627	301,558	307,736	159,531	267,249	257,258	264,103
45–54 years	104,891	169,871	164,431	160,023	88,266	145,767	138,634	135,082
55–64 years	83,429	138,756	137,126	147,712	71,264	121,482	118,624	129,020
65 years and over	192,712	272,919	258,206	262,734	168,135	244,451	227,520	233,991
65–74 years	102,605	132,116	120,655	126,802	90,544	118,971	106,424	113,426
75 years and over	90,106	140,802	137,552	135,931	77,591	125,479	121,096	120,565
	Number of visits per 100 persons							
Total, age adjusted[2]	334	410	391	383	271	342	317	315
Total, crude	329	409	390	384	266	341	317	316
Under 18 years	275	328	307	302	213	260	232	235
18–44 years	264	306	301	285	203	239	229	219
45–64 years	364	466	442	438	309	404	377	376
45–54 years	339	427	406	388	286	367	343	327
55–64 years	401	525	494	511	343	459	428	446
65 years and over	612	804	753	758	534	720	664	675
65–74 years	560	733	667	696	494	660	588	623
75 years and over	683	884	850	827	588	788	748	734
Sex and age								
Male, age adjusted[2]	290	353	338	334	232	293	273	274
Male, crude	277	343	329	326	220	283	264	266
Under 18 years	273	329	317	307	209	262	241	239
18–44 years	190	214	203	187	139	161	147	136
45–54 years	275	351	335	334	229	298	280	280
55–64 years	351	448	422	457	300	393	365	398
65–74 years	508	703	632	672	445	631	558	604
75 years and over	711	850	881	860	616	762	777	771
Female, age adjusted[2]	377	465	442	431	309	388	360	355
Female, crude	378	472	449	439	310	396	368	363
Under 18 years	277	327	297	296	217	258	223	230
18–44 years	336	397	397	382	265	316	309	300
45–54 years	400	500	475	439	339	433	403	373
55–64 years	446	596	561	561	382	521	486	490
65–74 years	603	757	696	717	534	684	613	638
75 years and over	666	905	830	806	571	804	730	710
Race and age[3]								
White, age adjusted[2]	339	421	399	389	282	359	332	327
White, crude	338	426	404	396	281	364	337	334
Under 18 years	295	346	330	320	237	282	260	257
18–44 years	267	317	308	289	211	256	242	228
45–54 years	334	439	409	391	286	385	352	336
55–64 years	397	534	500	514	345	476	439	456
65–74 years	557	734	653	685	496	669	582	619
75 years and over	689	880	844	832	598	790	747	743
Black or African American, age adjusted	309	427	393	420	204	301	261	298
Black or African American, crude	281	392	365	391	178	269	236	271
Under 18 years	193	307	248	267	100	198	131	165
18–44 years	260	316	329	336	158	191	199	213
45–54 years	387	422	445	453	281	306	315	338
55–64 years	414	563	487	596	294	421	349	455
65–74 years	553	842	761	847	429	*687	602	703
75 years and over	534	*1,019	774	833	395	*842	608	666

See footnotes at end of table.

[Data are based on reporting by a sample of office-based physicians and hospital outpatient and emergency departments]

Age, sex, and race	Hospital outpatient departments				Hospital emergency departments			
	1995	2002	2003	2004	1995	2002	2003	2004
	Number of visits in thousands							
Total.	67,232	83,339	94,578	84,994	96,545	110,155	113,903	110,216
Under 18 years	17,636	21,707	25,412	22,003	26,657	27,932	28,920	27,144
18–44 years	24,299	28,216	32,714	27,853	41,820	45,792	46,449	45,835
45–64 years	14,811	21,436	23,307	22,127	13,978	19,943	20,992	21,506
45–54 years.	8,029	12,054	12,937	11,784	8,595	12,050	12,861	13,156
55–64 years.	6,782	9,382	10,370	10,342	5,383	7,892	8,132	8,349
65 years and over	10,486	11,980	13,144	13,011	14,090	16,488	17,542	15,732
65–74 years.	6,004	6,386	7,077	7,157	6,057	6,759	7,153	6,219
75 years and over.	4,482	5,595	6,067	5,854	8,033	9,728	10,389	9,513
	Number of visits per 100 persons							
Total, age adjusted[2]	26	29	33	29	37	39	40	39
Total, crude	26	29	33	30	37	39	40	38
Under 18 years	25	30	35	30	38	38	40	37
18–44 years	22	26	30	25	39	42	42	42
45–64 years	29	32	34	32	27	30	31	31
45–54 years.	26	30	32	29	28	30	32	32
55–64 years.	33	36	37	36	26	30	29	29
65 years and over	33	35	38	38	45	49	51	45
65–74 years.	33	35	39	39	33	38	40	34
75 years and over.	34	35	38	36	61	61	64	58
Sex and age								
Male, age adjusted[2]	21	24	27	24	37	37	39	36
Male, crude.	21	23	26	24	36	37	38	36
Under 18 years.	25	28	34	30	40	39	41	38
18–44 years.	14	16	19	15	37	37	37	36
45–54 years.	20	25	25	23	26	29	30	31
55–64 years.	26	28	29	30	25	28	29	28
65–74 years.	29	34	34	34	34	38	41	34
75 years and over.	34	31	38	34	61	58	67	56
Female, age adjusted[2]	31	35	40	35	37	41	42	41
Female, crude	31	35	40	35	37	41	42	41
Under 18 years.	25	31	36	30	35	38	38	36
18–44 years.	31	35	41	35	40	46	47	47
45–54 years.	32	36	39	34	29	32	33	33
55–64 years.	38	43	45	41	26	32	30	30
65–74 years.	36	36	44	44	32	37	39	34
75 years and over.	34	38	37	37	61	63	63	59
Race and age[3]								
White, age adjusted[2]	23	27	30	27	34	36	38	35
White, crude	23	27	30	27	34	36	37	35
Under 18 years.	23	28	32	28	35	36	38	35
18–44 years.	20	23	27	23	36	38	39	38
45–54 years.	23	27	28	26	25	27	29	28
55–64 years.	28	31	33	31	24	27	28	26
65–74 years.	29	30	35	35	32	35	36	32
75 years and over.	31	31	35	33	60	59	62	56
Black or African American, age adjusted. . .	48	55	61	53	58	71	71	70
Black or African American, crude.	45	53	60	50	58	70	69	69
Under 18 years.	39	46	55	42	53	63	61	60
18–44 years.	38	46	54	44	64	79	77	79
45–54 years.	55	57	65	50	51	59	65	65
55–64 years.	73	78	86	83	47	65	53	58
65–74 years.	*77	87	83	82	47	68	77	62
75 years and over.	66	85	64	*81	73	92	103	86

See footnotes at end of table.

Table 89 (page 3 of 3). Visits to physician offices and hospital outpatient and emergency departments, by selected characteristics: United States, selected years 1995–2004

[Data are based on reporting by a sample of office-based physicians and hospital outpatient and emergency departments]

---

* Estimates are considered unreliable. Data preceded by an asterisk have a relative standard error of 20%–30%.

[1]All places includes visits to physician offices and hospital outpatient and emergency departments.

[2]Estimates are age adjusted to the year 2000 standard population using six age groups: under 18 years, 18–44 years, 45–54 years, 55–64 years, 65–74 years, and 75 years and over. See Appendix II, Age adjustment.

[3]Starting with 1999 data, the instruction for the race item on the Patient Record Form was changed so that more than one race could be recorded. In previous years only one race could be checked. Estimates for race in this table are for visits where only one race was recorded. Because of the small number of responses with more than one racial group checked, estimates for visits with multiple races checked are unreliable and are not presented.

NOTES: Rates for 1995–2000 were computed using 1990-based postcensal estimates of the civilian noninstitutionalized population as of July 1 adjusted for net underenumeration using the 1990 National Population Adjustment Matrix from the U.S. Census Bureau. Starting with 2001 data, rates were computed using 2000-based postcensal estimates of the civilian noninstitutionalized population as of July 1. The difference between rates for 2000 computed using 1990-based postcensal estimates and 2000 census counts is minimal. More information is available from: www.cdc.gov/nchs/about/major/ahcd/census2000.htm. Starting with *Health, United States, 2005*, data for 2001 and later years for physician offices use a revised weighting scheme. See Appendix I, National Ambulatory Medical Care Survey. Rates will be overestimated to the extent that visits by institutionalized persons are counted in the numerator (for example, hospital emergency department visits by nursing home residents) and institutionalized persons are omitted from the denominator. Data for additional years are available. See Appendix III.

SOURCES: Centers for Disease Control and Prevention, National Center for Health Statistics, National Ambulatory Medical Care Survey and National Hospital Ambulatory Medical Care Survey.

Table 90 (page 1 of 2). Visits to primary care generalist and specialist physicians, by selected characteristics and type of physician: United States, selected years 1980–2004

[Data are based on reporting by a sample of office-based physicians]

| | Type of primary care generalist physician[1] | | | | | | | | | | | |
| | All primary care generalists | | | | General and family practice | | | | Internal medicine | | | |
Age, sex, and race	1980	1990	2000	2004	1980	1990	2000	2004	1980	1990	2000	2004
	Percent of all physician office visits											
Total	66.2	63.6	58.9	56.7	33.5	29.9	24.1	22.5	12.1	13.8	15.3	16.1
Under 18 years.	77.8	79.5	79.7	75.8	26.1	26.5	19.9	15.8	2.0	2.9	*	*
18–44 years.	65.3	65.2	62.1	63.2	34.3	31.9	28.2	26.3	8.6	11.8	12.7	15.5
45–64 years.	60.2	55.5	51.2	51.1	36.3	32.1	26.4	25.9	19.5	18.6	20.1	20.8
45–54 years	60.2	55.6	52.3	53.1	37.4	32.0	27.8	28.6	17.1	17.1	18.7	19.4
55–64 years	60.2	55.5	49.9	48.9	35.4	32.1	24.7	23.1	21.8	20.0	21.7	22.3
65 years and over.	61.6	52.6	46.5	42.4	37.5	28.1	20.2	19.6	22.7	23.3	24.5	21.9
65–74 years	61.2	52.7	46.6	41.6	37.4	28.1	19.7	19.0	22.1	23.0	24.5	21.5
75 years and over	62.3	52.4	46.4	43.2	37.6	28.0	20.8	20.2	23.5	23.7	24.5	22.3
Sex and age												
Male:												
Under 18 years	77.3	78.1	77.7	74.6	25.6	24.1	18.3	15.1	2.0	3.0	*	*
18–44 years	50.8	51.8	51.5	51.4	38.0	35.9	34.2	31.8	11.5	15.0	14.4	18.5
45–64 years	55.6	50.6	49.4	49.5	34.4	31.0	28.7	26.2	20.5	19.2	19.8	23.1
65 years and over	58.2	51.2	43.1	37.8	35.6	27.7	19.3	17.5	22.3	23.3	23.8	20.3
Female:												
Under 18 years	78.5	81.1	82.0	77.1	26.6	29.1	21.7	16.4	2.0	2.8	*	*
18–44 years	72.1	71.3	67.2	68.5	32.5	30.0	25.3	23.8	7.3	10.3	11.9	14.2
45–64 years	63.4	58.8	52.5	52.2	37.7	32.8	24.9	25.7	18.9	18.2	20.2	19.2
65 years and over	63.9	53.5	48.9	45.9	38.7	28.3	20.9	21.2	22.9	23.3	25.0	23.1
Race and age[2]												
White:												
Under 18 years	77.6	79.2	78.5	75.0	26.4	27.1	21.2	16.0	2.0	2.3	*	*
18–44 years	64.8	64.4	61.4	60.9	34.5	31.9	29.2	27.5	8.6	10.6	11.0	12.9
45–64 years	59.6	54.2	49.3	49.7	36.0	31.5	27.3	26.1	19.2	17.6	17.1	19.3
65 years and over	61.4	51.9	45.1	41.0	36.6	27.5	20.3	20.0	23.3	23.1	23.0	20.1
Black or African American:												
Under 18 years	79.9	85.5	87.3	77.9	23.7	20.2	*	*16.7	*2.2	9.8	*	*
18–44 years	68.5	68.3	65.0	75.0	31.7	31.9	22.0	22.0	9.0	18.1	20.9	27.0
45–64 years	66.1	61.6	61.7	58.5	38.6	31.2	23.3	24.7	22.6	26.9	35.9	*29.1
65 years and over	64.6	58.6	52.8	54.6	49.0	28.9	*18.5	*18.6	14.2	28.7	33.4	34.8

See footnotes at end of table.

Table 90 (page 2 of 2). Visits to primary care generalist and specialist physicians, by selected characteristics and type of physician: United States, selected years 1980–2004

[Data are based on reporting by a sample of office-based physicians]

Age, sex, and race	Type of primary care generalist physician[1]								Specialty care physicians			
	Obstetrics and gynecology				Pediatrics							
	1980	1990	2000	2004	1980	1990	2000	2004	1980	1990	2000	2004
	Percent of all physician office visits											
Total	9.6	8.7	7.8	7.1	10.9	11.2	11.7	11.1	33.8	36.4	41.1	43.3
Under 18 years.	1.3	1.2	*1.1	*1.0	48.5	48.9	57.3	57.5	22.2	20.5	20.3	24.2
18–44 years.	21.7	20.8	20.4	20.6	0.7	0.7	*0.9	*0.8	34.7	34.8	37.9	36.8
45–64 years.	4.2	4.6	4.5	4.1	*	*	*	*	39.8	44.5	48.8	48.9
45–54 years	5.6	6.3	5.6	4.9	*	*	*	*	39.8	44.4	47.7	46.9
55–64 years	2.9	3.1	3.3	3.3	*	*	*	*	39.8	44.5	50.1	51.1
65 years and over.	1.4	1.1	1.5	*0.9	*	*	*	*	38.4	47.4	53.5	57.6
65–74 years	1.7	1.6	2.0	*1.1	*	*	*	*	38.8	47.3	53.4	58.4
75 years and over	1.0	*0.6	*1.0	*0.7	*	*	*	*	37.7	47.6	53.6	56.8
Sex and age												
Male:												
Under 18 years	. . .	. . .	. . .	. . .	49.4	50.7	58.0	57.7	22.7	21.9	22.3	25.4
18–44 years	. . .	. . .	. . .	. . .	1.0	0.7	*1.7	*	49.2	48.2	48.5	48.6
45–64 years	. . .	. . .	. . .	. . .	*	*	*	*	44.4	49.4	50.6	50.5
65 years and over	. . .	. . .	. . .	. . .	*	*	*	*	41.8	48.8	56.9	62.2
Female:												
Under 18 years	2.5	2.3	2.1	*2.2	47.4	46.9	56.5	57.3	21.5	18.9	18.0	22.9
18–44 years	31.7	30.4	29.6	29.9	0.6	0.7	*	*	27.9	28.7	32.8	31.5
45–64 years	6.7	7.7	7.3	7.1	*	*	*	*	36.6	41.2	47.5	47.8
65 years and over	2.1	1.8	2.6	*1.6	*	*	*	*	36.1	46.5	51.1	54.1
Race and age[2]												
White:												
Under 18 years	1.1	1.0	*1.2	0.8	48.2	48.8	54.7	56.8	22.4	20.8	21.5	25.0
18–44 years	21.0	21.1	20.4	19.6	0.7	0.7	*0.8	*0.8	35.2	35.6	38.6	39.1
45–64 years	4.1	4.8	4.7	4.2	*	*	*	*	40.4	45.8	50.7	50.3
65 years and over	1.4	1.2	1.5	*0.9	*	*	*	*	38.6	48.1	54.9	59.0
Black or African American:												
Under 18 years	2.8	*3.4	*	*	51.2	52.1	75.0	58.4	20.1	14.5	*12.7	*
18–44 years	27.1	17.9	20.7	*25.5	*	*	*	*	31.5	31.7	35.0	25.0
45–64 years	4.8	3.5	*2.4	*	*	*	*	*	33.9	38.4	38.3	41.5
65 years and over	*	*	*	*	*	*	*	0.0	35.4	41.4	47.2	45.4

* Estimates are considered unreliable. Data preceded by an asterisk have a relative standard error (RSE) of 20%–30%. Data not shown have a RSE of greater than 30%.

. . . Category not applicable.

[1]Type of physician is based on physician's self-designated primary area of practice. Primary care generalist physicians are defined as practitioners in the fields of general and family practice, general internal medicine, general obstetrics and gynecology, and general pediatrics and exclude primary care specialists. Primary care generalists in general and family practice exclude primary care specialities, such as sports medicine and geriatrics. Primary care internal medicine physicians exclude internal medicine specialists, such as allergists, cardiologists, and endocrinologists. Primary care obstetrics and gynecology physicians exclude obstetrics and gynecology specialities, such as gynecological oncology, maternal and fetal medicine, general obstetrics and gynecology critical care medicine, and reproductive endocrinology. Primary care pediatricians exclude pediatric specialists, such as adolescent medicine specialists, neonatologists, pediatric allergists, and pediatric cardiologists. See Appendix II, Physician specialty.

[2]Starting with 1999 data, the instruction for the race item on the Patient Record Form was changed so that more than one race could be recorded. In previous years only one racial category could be checked. Estimates for racial groups presented in this table are for visits where only one race was recorded. Because of the small number of responses with more than one racial group checked, estimates for visits with multiple races checked are unreliable and are not presented.

NOTES: This table presents data on visits to physician offices and excludes visits to other sites, such as hospital outpatient and emergency departments. In 1980 the survey excluded Alaska and Hawaii. Data for all other years include all 50 states. Visits with specialty of physician unknown are excluded. Starting with *Health, United States, 2005*, data for 2001 and later years for physician offices use a revised weighting scheme. See Appendix I, National Ambulatory Medical Care Survey. Data for additional years are available. See Appendix III.

SOURCE: Centers for Disease Control and Prevention, National Center for Health Statistics, National Ambulatory Medical Care Survey.

Table 91 (page 1 of 2). Dental visits in the past year, by selected characteristics: United States, selected years 1997–2004

[Data are based on household interviews of a sample of the civilian noninstitutionalized population]

Characteristic	2 years of age and over[1]			2–17 years of age			18–64 years of age			65 years of age and over[2]		
	1997	2003	2004	1997	2003	2004	1997	2003	2004	1997	2003	2004
	Percent of persons with a dental visit in the past year[3]											
Total[4]	64.9	66.3	65.9	72.7	75.0	76.4	64.1	64.8	64.0	54.8	58.0	56.3
Sex												
Male	62.6	63.6	63.4	72.3	74.1	75.1	60.4	60.9	60.5	55.4	58.4	57.1
Female	67.2	68.9	68.3	73.0	75.9	77.7	67.7	68.6	67.4	54.4	57.7	55.8
Race[5]												
White only	66.5	67.5	67.1	74.0	76.0	77.3	65.7	65.9	65.2	56.8	59.8	58.6
Black or African American only	56.5	58.4	57.4	68.8	70.5	72.5	57.0	58.1	56.9	35.4	38.7	33.6
American Indian or Alaska Native only	51.5	59.9	62.8	66.8	69.9	70.3	49.9	58.0	63.4	*	*49.2	*32.2
Asian only	61.8	65.1	65.4	69.9	72.9	73.8	60.3	63.6	64.2	53.9	57.4	58.1
Native Hawaiian or Other Pacific Islander only	- - -	*	*	- - -	*	*	- - -	*	*	- - -	*	*
2 or more races	- - -	61.6	59.1	- - -	74.5	78.0	- - -	59.6	58.4	- - -	51.0	*28.7
Black or African American; White	- - -	63.6	57.6	- - -	71.3	72.6	- - -	60.3	61.0	- - -	*80.7	*
American Indian or Alaska Native; White	- - -	50.0	53.0	- - -	52.8	78.9	- - -	53.7	49.1	- - -	*	*
Hispanic origin and race[5]												
Hispanic or Latino	52.9	52.4	52.7	61.0	64.5	65.3	50.8	48.3	49.6	47.8	46.0	42.5
Not Hispanic or Latino	66.4	68.6	68.1	74.7	77.3	78.9	65.7	67.4	66.3	55.2	58.7	57.2
White only	68.2	70.5	69.9	76.4	79.4	80.9	67.5	69.3	68.1	57.2	60.9	59.8
Black or African American only	56.5	58.5	57.7	68.8	70.6	72.9	56.9	58.3	57.3	35.3	38.3	33.3
Percent of poverty level[6]												
Below 100%	47.7	48.2	47.0	62.0	65.8	65.5	46.9	44.5	44.5	31.5	37.1	30.7
100%–less than 200%	50.6	52.3	51.9	62.5	66.6	69.0	48.3	49.1	47.6	40.8	43.6	43.2
200% or more	72.5	73.4	73.0	80.1	80.8	82.2	71.2	72.0	71.3	65.9	67.8	66.4
Hispanic origin and race and percent of poverty level[5,6]												
Hispanic or Latino:												
Below 100%	42.1	42.0	42.5	55.9	62.1	61.9	39.2	35.5	38.3	33.6	33.2	29.8
100%–less than 200%	46.4	45.5	45.5	53.8	59.1	59.1	43.5	40.8	41.7	47.9	39.4	37.7
200% or more	64.9	62.7	62.8	73.7	71.6	74.2	62.3	59.4	60.4	58.8	60.7	55.4
Not Hispanic or Latino:												
White only:												
Below 100%	50.6	52.8	50.9	64.4	69.1	68.7	50.6	50.4	48.7	32.0	39.9	33.4
100%–less than 200%	52.9	55.8	54.8	66.1	69.6	73.5	50.4	52.8	50.0	42.2	45.9	45.6
200% or more	73.9	75.6	75.0	81.3	83.2	84.3	72.7	74.2	73.2	67.0	69.1	68.5
Black or African American only:												
Below 100%	47.7	45.1	45.1	66.1	66.7	68.2	46.2	40.8	42.3	27.7	27.6	21.5
100%–less than 200%	46.9	52.0	49.8	61.2	69.1	70.5	46.3	50.6	46.4	26.9	29.3	29.4
200% or more	66.0	66.7	66.5	77.1	74.5	77.7	66.1	67.2	67.0	49.8	51.9	45.0

See footnotes at end of table.

Table 91 (page 2 of 2). Dental visits in the past year, by selected characteristics: United States, selected years 1997–2004

[Data are based on household interviews of a sample of the civilian noninstitutionalized population]

Characteristic	2 years of age and over[1]			2–17 years of age			18–64 years of age			65 years of age and over[2]		
	1997	2003	2004	1997	2003	2004	1997	2003	2004	1997	2003	2004
Geographic region	Percent of persons with a dental visit in the past year[3]											
Northeast	69.6	72.4	71.9	77.5	81.5	82.0	69.6	71.4	71.0	55.5	61.1	58.4
Midwest	68.3	68.8	69.3	76.4	77.6	78.8	67.4	67.6	68.4	57.6	58.8	57.1
South	60.0	61.4	60.3	68.0	70.7	72.7	59.4	59.6	57.6	49.0	53.3	51.4
West	64.9	66.7	66.5	71.5	74.1	75.4	62.9	64.7	64.0	61.9	62.8	62.5
Location of residence												
Within MSA[7]	66.5	67.9	67.3	73.6	75.5	76.5	65.7	66.5	65.6	57.6	61.3	59.4
Outside MSA[7]	59.1	60.0	60.3	69.3	72.9	76.0	58.0	57.9	57.4	46.1	46.7	46.0

* Estimates are considered unreliable. Data preceded by an asterisk have a relative standard error (RSE) of 20%–30%. Data not shown have an RSE greater than 30%.

- - - Data not available.

[1] Estimates are age adjusted to the year 2000 standard population using six age groups: 2–17 years, 18–44 years, 45–54 years, 55–64 years, 65–74 years, and 75 years and over. See Appendix II, Age adjustment.

[2] Based on 1997–2004 National Health Interview Surveys, it was estimated that 25%–30% of persons 65 years of age and over were edentulous (having lost all their natural teeth). In 1997–2004 about 68%–70% of older dentate persons compared with 16%–20% of older edentate persons had a dental visit in the past year.

[3] Respondents were asked "About how long has it been since you last saw or talked to a dentist?" See Appendix II, Dental visit.

[4] Includes all other races not shown separately.

[5] The race groups, white, black, American Indian or Alaska Native, Asian, Native Hawaiian or Other Pacific Islander, and 2 or more races, include persons of Hispanic and non-Hispanic origin. Persons of Hispanic origin may be of any race. Starting with 1999 data, race-specific estimates are tabulated according to the 1997 Revisions to the Standards for the Classification of Federal Data on Race and Ethnicity and are not strictly comparable with estimates for earlier years. The five single race categories plus multiple race categories shown in the table conform to the 1997 Standards. Starting with 1999 data, race-specific estimates are for persons who reported only one racial group; the category 2 or more races includes persons who reported more than one racial group. Prior to 1999, data were tabulated according to the 1977 Standards with four racial groups and the Asian only category included Native Hawaiian or Other Pacific Islander. Estimates for single race categories prior to 1999 included persons who reported one race or, if they reported more than one race, identified one race as best representing their race. Starting with 2003 data, race responses of other race and unspecified multiple race were treated as missing, and then race was imputed if these were the only race responses. Almost all persons with a race response of other race were of Hispanic origin. See Appendix II, Hispanic origin; Race.

[6] Percent of poverty level is based on family income and family size and composition using U.S. Census Bureau poverty thresholds. Missing family income data were imputed for 25%–29% of persons in 1997–1998 and 32%–35% in 1999–2004. See Appendix II, Family income; Poverty.

[7] MSA is metropolitan statistical area.

NOTES: In 1997 the National Health Interview Survey questionnaire was redesigned. See Appendix I, National Health Interview Survey. Standard errors for selected years are available in the spreadsheet version of this table. Available from: www.cdc.gov/nchs/hus.htm. Data for additional years are available. See Appendix III.

SOURCE: Centers for Disease Control and Prevention, National Center for Health Statistics, National Health Interview Survey, sample child and sample adult questionnaires.

Table 92 (page 1 of 3). Selected prescription and nonprescription drugs recorded during physician office visits and hospital outpatient department visits, by sex and age: United States, 1995–1996 and 2003–2004

[Data are based on a sample of visit records from physician offices and hospital outpatient departments]

Age group and National Drug Code (NDC) therapeutic class[1] (common reasons for use)	Total		Male		Female	
	1995–1996	2003–2004	1995–1996	2003–2004	1995–1996	2003–2004
All ages	Visits with at least one drug per 100 population[2]					
Drug visits[3]	189.8	226.4	156.5	190.3	221.5	260.9
	Number of drugs per 100 population[4]					
Total number of drugs[5]	400.3	604.3	321.1	502.1	475.6	701.9
Antidepressants (depression and related disorders)	13.8	30.2	9.1	20.0	18.2	40.0
NSAID[6] (pain relief)	19.9	30.1	16.0	25.4	23.7	34.7
Antiasthmatics/bronchodilators (asthma, breathing)	13.0	24.7	11.7	21.4	14.3	27.9
Hyperlipidemia (high cholesterol)	5.4	23.7	5.4	24.0	5.4	23.4
Hypertension control drugs, not otherwise specified (high blood pressure)	6.0	23.6	4.1	20.5	7.8	26.6
Nonnarcotic analgesics (pain relief)	14.4	23.6	13.0	21.9	15.7	25.3
Antihistamines (allergies)	13.7	22.7	10.8	17.3	16.4	27.9
Acid/peptic disorders (gastrointestinal reflux, ulcers)	12.0	21.4	9.8	18.3	14.1	24.3
Blood glucose/sugar regulators (diabetes)	9.5	19.8	8.6	19.1	10.4	20.6
Vitamins/minerals (dietary supplements)	9.2	16.8	3.4	10.3	14.8	23.1
ACE inhibitors (high blood pressure, heart disease)	9.6	16.8	9.0	16.5	10.2	17.0
Narcotic analgesics (pain relief)	11.2	16.7	10.3	13.4	12.2	19.9
Diuretics (high blood pressure, heart disease)	10.2	16.6	7.8	13.4	12.6	19.6
Penicillins (bacterial infections)	16.6	13.1	15.5	12.6	17.7	13.6
Estrogens/progestins (menopause, hot flashes)	...	...	...	...	19.8	14.9
Under 18 years	Visits with at least one drug per 100 population[2]					
Drug visits[3]	153.9	170.4	152.3	175.2	155.6	165.4
	Number of drugs per 100 population[4]					
Total number of drugs[5]	261.3	326.0	255.6	333.9	267.3	317.7
Penicillins (bacterial infections)	37.2	29.2	36.4	29.9	38.0	28.4
Antiasthmatics/bronchodilators (asthma, breathing)	13.4	27.2	14.8	29.5	11.9	24.8
Antihistamines (allergies)	17.5	25.0	16.7	23.3	18.4	26.9
NSAID[6] (pain relief)	7.4	14.6	6.9	15.0	7.9	14.2
Nonnarcotic analgesics (pain relief)	12.1	13.0	10.4	12.5	13.9	13.5
Cephalosporins (bacterial infections)	18.1	12.4	18.8	12.6	17.3	12.2
Erythromycins/lincosamides (infections)	10.2	11.3	11.0	11.0	9.4	11.6
Nasal corticosteroid inhalants (asthma, breathing, allergies)	3.5	10.4	3.5	11.0	3.5	9.8
Antitussives/expectorants (cough and cold, congestion)	11.8	9.5	11.0	8.8	12.7	10.2
Anorexiants/CNS stimulants (attention deficit disorder, hyperactivity)	3.9	8.5	5.6	12.9	2.1	4.0
Nasal decongestants (congestion)	14.0	8.5	12.4	8.1	15.7	8.8
Antidepressants (depression and related disorders)	1.9	8.0	1.9	9.1	1.9	6.8
18–44 years	Visits with at least one drug per 100 population[2]					
Drug visits[3]	136.2	154.0	90.9	102.3	180.4	204.9
	Number of drugs per 100 population[4]					
Total number of drugs[5]	251.0	327.4	168.8	221.6	331.2	431.4
Antidepressants (depression and related disorders)	14.0	26.9	9.3	16.9	18.5	36.8
NSAID[6] (pain relief)	16.7	21.5	14.5	16.7	18.8	26.2
Antihistamines (allergies)	10.8	16.8	7.5	10.9	14.1	22.5
Narcotic analgesics (pain relief)	11.7	15.2	10.8	10.9	12.7	19.5
Antiasthmatics/bronchodilator (asthma, breathing)	6.8	11.9	3.3	7.1	10.2	16.5
Vitamins/minerals (dietary supplements)	11.8	11.2	1.1	2.1	22.2	20.3
Acid/peptic disorders (gastrointestinal reflux, ulcers)	6.6	9.6	5.3	8.3	7.9	11.0
Erythromycins/lincosamides (infections)	7.5	8.4	5.4	5.6	9.5	11.1
Penicillins (bacterial infections)	9.5	7.9	7.0	5.9	11.9	9.9
Nonnarcotic analgesics (pain relief)	6.0	7.9	4.5	5.7	7.4	10.1
Antitussives/expectorants (cough and cold, congestion)	7.7	7.9	5.8	4.9	9.5	10.8
Nasal corticosteroid inhalants (asthma, breathing, allergies)	4.7	7.3	3.3	5.5	6.1	9.0
Contraceptive agents (prevent pregnancy)	...	...	...	...	13.4	19.8

See footnotes at end of table.

Table 92 (page 2 of 3). Selected prescription and nonprescription drugs recorded during physician office visits and hospital outpatient department visits, by sex and age: United States, 1995–1996 and 2003–2004

[Data are based on a sample of visit records from physician offices and hospital outpatient departments]

Age group and National Drug Code (NDC) therapeutic class[1] (common reasons for use)	Total		Male		Female	
	1995–1996	2003–2004	1995–1996	2003–2004	1995–1996	2003–2004
45–64 years	Visits with at least one drug per 100 population[2]					
Drug visits[3]	222.4	274.7	185.0	232.5	257.4	314.5
	Number of drugs per 100 population[4]					
Total number of drugs[5]	505.1	794.6	403.2	662.9	600.4	918.7
Antidepressants (depression and related disorders)	23.5	48.1	14.9	30.8	31.5	64.5
Hyperlipidemia (high cholesterol)	10.4	42.2	12.0	45.5	8.8	39.0
NSAID[6] (pain relief)	30.3	41.7	23.9	36.3	36.4	46.9
Hypertension control drugs, not otherwise specified (high blood pressure)	9.4	39.8	6.9	38.3	11.7	41.1
Blood glucose/sugar regulators (diabetes)	17.7	35.9	16.7	36.6	18.7	35.2
Acid/peptic disorders (gastrointestinal reflux, ulcers)	19.8	33.4	18.3	29.1	21.3	37.4
Antiasthmatics/bronchodilators (asthma, breathing)	14.4	31.1	11.4	23.6	17.1	38.1
Nonnarcotic analgesics (pain relief)	16.3	29.0	15.6	29.5	17.0	28.5
Narcotic analgesics (pain relief)	17.5	27.8	17.0	25.3	18.0	30.2
ACE inhibitors (high blood pressure, heart disease)	16.8	26.6	17.7	26.8	16.0	26.5
Antihistamines (allergies)	13.5	25.9	9.1	17.5	17.7	33.8
Diuretics (high blood pressure, heart disease)	13.5	23.1	11.2	19.2	15.7	26.7
Beta blockers (high blood pressure, heart disease)	10.6	22.2	10.0	20.2	11.2	24.0
Calcium channel blockers (high blood pressure, heart disease)	19.3	18.8	19.9	18.6	18.8	19.0
Estrogens/progestins (menopause, hot flashes)	...	...	...	...	55.7	30.4
65 years and over	Visits with at least one drug per 100 population[2]					
Drug visits[3]	399.4	479.9	378.1	461.7	414.7	493.3
	Number of drugs per 100 population[4]					
Total number of drugs[5]	1,047.4	1,697.5	956.9	1,612.5	1,112.5	1,760.1
Hypertension control drugs, not otherwise specified (high blood pressure)	29.1	100.2	22.7	91.6	33.8	106.4
Hyperlipidemia (high cholesterol)	24.7	99.8	25.1	110.8	24.5	91.7
Nonnarcotic analgesics (pain relief)	44.9	85.5	49.0	89.0	42.0	82.9
Diuretics (high blood pressure, heart disease)	55.2	81.6	48.5	76.9	60.0	85.0
ACE inhibitors (high blood pressure, heart disease)	42.6	74.4	41.2	84.5	43.6	67.0
Blood glucose/sugar regulators (diabetes)	37.5	74.1	38.0	82.0	37.1	68.2
Acid/peptic disorders (gastrointestinal reflux, ulcers)	42.2	72.3	36.0	67.8	46.6	75.6
Beta blockers (high blood pressure, heart disease)	25.5	71.9	23.6	72.9	26.8	71.2
NSAID[6] (pain relief)	41.8	67.4	31.9	59.1	49.0	73.5
Calcium channel blockers (high blood pressure, heart disease)	57.3	57.5	52.2	53.3	60.9	60.6
Vitamins/minerals (dietary supplements)	17.1	54.5	13.1	44.2	20.0	62.1
Antidepressants (depression and related disorders)	23.5	52.1	16.7	35.1	28.5	64.7
Antiasthmatics/bronchodilators (asthma, breathing)	31.3	47.9	37.1	48.6	27.0	47.3
Anticoagulants/thrombolytics (blood thinning, reduce or prevent blood clots)	20.7	45.0	24.0	53.0	18.3	39.2
Estrogens/progestins (menopause, hot flashes)	...	...	...	...	37.1	29.9
65–74 years	Visits with at least one drug per 100 population[2]					
Drug visits[3]	362.8	428.5	323.0	399.3	394.9	452.9
	Number of drugs per 100 population[4]					
Total number of drugs[5]	930.5	1,452.9	804.7	1,370.4	1,032.1	1,522.1
Hyperlipidemia (high cholesterol)	27.3	96.6	27.1	107.4	27.4	87.6
Hypertension control drugs, not otherwise specified (high blood pressure)	24.8	82.5	19.2	69.0	29.3	93.8
Blood glucose/sugar regulators (diabetes)	35.7	73.5	32.4	81.9	38.4	66.4
Nonnarcotic analgesics (pain relief)	38.0	70.9	40.5	75.6	35.9	66.9
NSAID[6] (pain relief)	42.0	65.1	31.2	56.9	50.8	72.0
Acid/peptic disorders (gastrointestinal reflux, ulcers)	38.7	64.0	30.6	60.4	45.2	67.0
ACE inhibitors (high blood pressure, heart disease)	37.1	61.8	35.6	72.1	38.3	53.3
Diuretics (high blood pressure, heart disease)	40.0	59.5	32.3	56.7	46.3	61.8
Beta blockers (high blood pressure, heart disease)	23.7	59.4	20.7	59.4	26.1	59.4
Calcium channel blockers (high blood pressure, heart disease)	48.9	51.3	46.2	43.8	51.2	57.5
Antidepressants (depression and related disorders)	22.7	48.1	14.2	33.6	29.6	60.3
Antiasthmatics/bronchodilators (asthma, breathing)	31.1	46.8	33.0	43.6	29.5	49.5
Vitamins/minerals (dietary supplements)	14.1	41.7	10.1	38.9	17.4	44.1
Antihistamines (allergies)	14.7	35.1	12.3	28.8	16.6	40.3
Estrogens/progestins (menopause, hot flashes)	...	...	...	...	47.5	37.9

See footnotes at end of table.

Table 92 (page 3 of 3). Selected prescription and nonprescription drugs recorded during physician office visits and hospital outpatient department visits, by sex and age: United States, 1995–1996 and 2003–2004

[Data are based on a sample of visit records from physician offices and hospital outpatient departments]

Age group and National Drug Code (NDC) therapeutic class[1] (common reasons for use)	Total		Male		Female	
	1995–1996	2003–2004	1995–1996	2003–2004	1995–1996	2003–2004
75 years and over	Visits with at least one drug per 100 population[2]					
Drug visits[3]	449.2	537.1	466.3	543.2	438.7	533.3
	Number of drugs per 100 population[4]					
Total number of drugs[5]	1,206.8	1,969.8	1,200.9	1,928.8	1,210.4	1,995.8
Hypertension control drugs, not otherwise specified (high blood pressure)	35.1	119.8	28.4	121.1	39.2	119.0
Diuretics (high blood pressure, heart disease)	75.8	106.2	74.5	103.3	76.6	108.1
Hyperlipidemia (high cholesterol)	21.3	103.4	21.8	115.2	21.0	95.9
Nonnarcotic analgesics (pain relief)	54.4	101.8	62.6	106.5	49.4	98.8
ACE inhibitors (high blood pressure, heart disease)	50.2	88.3	50.2	100.6	50.1	80.5
Beta blockers (high blood pressure, heart disease)	27.9	85.8	28.3	90.5	27.6	82.8
Acid/peptic disorders (gastrointestinal reflux, ulcers)	47.0	81.5	44.7	77.4	48.3	84.1
Blood glucose/sugar regulators (diabetes)	39.8	74.7	46.9	82.1	35.5	70.1
NSAID[6] (pain relief)	41.5	69.9	33.1	61.9	46.7	74.9
Vitamins/minerals (dietary supplements)	21.2	68.7	18.0	51.1	23.2	79.9
Calcium channel blockers (high blood pressure, heart disease)	68.6	64.5	61.8	65.8	72.7	63.7
Anticoagulants/thrombolytics (blood thinning, reduce or prevent blood clots)	28.6	62.3	34.9	75.3	24.7	54.1
Antidepressants (depression and related disorders)	24.6	56.6	20.7	37.0	27.0	69.0
Antiasthmatics/bronchodilators (asthma, breathing)	31.5	49.0	43.7	55.1	24.0	45.2
Thyroid/antithyroid (hyper- and hypothyroidism)	27.1	47.1	15.1	30.2	34.4	57.7

. . . Category not applicable.

[1]The National Drug Code (NDC) therapeutic class is a general therapeutic or pharmacological classification scheme for drug products reported to the Food and Drug Administration (FDA) under the provisions of the Drug Listing Act. See Appendix II, National Drug Code (NDC) Directory therapeutic class; table XII.

[2]Estimated number of drug visits during the 2-year period divided by the sum of population estimates for both years times 100.

[3]Drug visits are physician office and hospital outpatient department visits in which at least one prescription or nonprescription drug was recorded on the patient record form.

[4]Estimated number of drugs recorded during visits during the 2-year period divided by the sum of population estimates for both years times 100.

[5]Until 2002, up to six prescription and nonprescription medications were recorded on the patient record form. Starting with 2003 data, up to eight prescription and nonprescription medications are recorded on the patient record form. If 2003–2004 data were restricted to six instead of eight drugs, the 2003–2004 total drug rate for all ages would be 5.5% lower. See Appendix II, Drug.

[6]NSAID is nonsteroidal anti-inflammatory drug. Aspirin was not included as an NSAID in this analysis. See Appendix II, National Drug Classification (NDC) therapeutic class.

NOTE: Drugs recorded on the patient record form are those prescribed, continued, administered, or provided during a physician office or hospital outpatient department visit.

SOURCE: Centers for Disease Control and Prevention, National Center for Health Statistics, National Ambulatory Medical Care Survey and National Hospital Ambulatory Medical Care Survey.

Table 93. Prescription drug use in the past month by sex, age, race and Hispanic origin: United States, 1988–1994 and 1999–2002

[Data are based on a sample of the civilian noninstitutionalized population]

| Sex and age | All persons[1] | | Not Hispanic or Latino | | | | Mexican[2,3] | |
| | | | White only[2] | | Black or African American only[2] | | | |
	1988–94	1999–2002	1988–94	1999–2002	1988–94	1999–2002	1988–94	1999–2002
	Percent of population with at least one prescription drug in past month							
Both sexes, age adjusted[4]	39.1	45.3	41.1	48.9	36.9	40.1	31.7	31.7
Male	32.7	39.9	34.2	43.1	31.1	35.4	27.5	25.8
Female	45.0	50.4	47.6	54.5	41.4	43.8	36.0	37.8
Both sexes, crude	37.8	45.1	41.4	50.9	31.2	36.0	24.0	23.7
Male	30.6	38.7	33.5	43.9	25.5	30.8	20.1	18.8
Female	44.6	51.2	48.9	57.6	36.2	40.6	28.1	28.9
Under 18 years	20.5	24.2	22.9	27.6	14.8	18.6	16.1	15.9
18–44 years	31.3	35.9	34.3	41.3	27.8	28.5	21.1	19.2
45–64 years	54.8	64.1	55.5	66.1	57.5	62.3	48.1	49.3
65 years and over	73.6	84.7	74.0	85.4	74.5	81.1	67.7	72.0
Male:								
Under 18 years	20.4	26.2	22.3	30.6	15.5	19.8	16.3	16.2
18–44 years	21.5	27.1	23.5	31.2	21.1	21.5	14.9	13.0
45–64 years	47.2	55.6	48.1	57.4	48.2	54.0	43.8	36.4
65 years and over	67.2	80.1	67.4	81.0	64.4	78.1	61.3	66.8
Female:								
Under 18 years	20.6	22.0	23.6	24.4	14.2	17.3	16.0	15.6
18–44 years	40.7	44.6	44.7	51.7	33.4	34.2	28.1	26.2
45–64 years	62.0	72.0	62.6	74.7	64.4	69.0	52.2	62.4
65 years and over	78.3	88.1	78.8	88.8	81.3	83.1	73.0	76.3
	Percent of population with three or more prescription drugs in past month							
Both sexes, age adjusted[4]	11.8	17.7	12.4	18.9	12.6	16.5	9.0	11.2
Male	9.4	14.8	9.9	15.9	10.2	14.4	7.0	9.5
Female	13.9	20.4	14.6	21.7	14.3	18.0	11.0	12.9
Both sexes, crude	11.0	17.6	12.5	20.5	9.2	13.4	4.8	6.1
Male	8.3	13.9	9.5	16.4	7.0	10.9	3.4	4.8
Female	13.6	21.1	15.4	24.5	11.1	15.6	6.4	7.5
Under 18 years	2.4	4.1	3.2	4.9	1.5	2.5	*1.2	2.1
18–44 years	5.7	8.4	6.3	10.1	5.4	6.5	3.0	2.7
45–64 years	20.0	30.8	20.9	31.6	21.9	31.1	16.0	20.7
65 years and over	35.3	51.6	35.0	52.5	41.2	50.1	31.3	39.5
Male:								
Under 18 years	2.6	4.3	3.3	5.2	1.7	3.0	*	1.9
18–44 years	3.6	6.7	4.1	8.4	4.2	4.4	*1.8	*1.7
45–64 years	15.1	23.5	15.8	24.0	18.7	26.3	11.6	18.2
65 years and over	31.3	46.0	30.9	47.0	31.7	48.2	27.6	34.2
Female:								
Under 18 years	2.3	3.9	3.0	4.7	*1.2	*2.0	*1.5	2.2
18–44 years	7.6	10.2	8.5	11.9	6.4	8.3	4.3	4.0
45–64 years	24.7	37.4	25.8	39.1	24.3	35.0	20.3	23.3
65 years and over	38.2	55.7	38.0	56.6	47.7	51.3	34.5	44.0

* Estimates are considered unreliable. Data preceded by an asterisk have a relative standard error (RSE) of 20%–30%. Data not shown have an RSE of greater than 30%.

[1]Includes persons of all races and Hispanic origins, not just those shown separately.

[2]Starting with data year 1999 race-specific estimates are tabulated according to the 1997 Revisions to the Standards for the Classification of Federal Data on Race and Ethnicity and are not strictly comparable with estimates for earlier years. The two non-Hispanic race categories shown in the table conform to the 1997 Standards. Starting with 1999 data, race-specific estimates are for persons who reported only one racial group. Prior to data year 1999, estimates were tabulated according to the 1977 Standards. Estimates for single race categories prior to 1999 included persons who reported one race or, if they reported more than one race, identified one race as best representing their race. See Appendix II, Hispanic origin; Race.

[3]Persons of Mexican origin may be of any race.

[4]Age adjusted to the 2000 standard population using four age groups: Under 18 years, 18–44 years, 45–64 years, and 65 years and over. Age-adjusted estimates in this table may differ from other age-adjusted estimates based on the same data and presented elsewhere if different age groups are used in the adjustment procedure. See Appendix II, Age adjustment.

NOTES: Standard errors are available in the spreadsheet version of this table. Available from: www.cdc.gov/nchs/hus.htm.

SOURCE: Centers for Disease Control and Prevention, National Center for Health Statistics, National Health and Nutrition Examination Survey.

Table 94. Admissions to mental health organizations, by type of service and organization: United States, selected years 1986–2002

[Data are based on inventories of mental health organizations]

Service and organization	1986	1990	1994[1]	2000	2002[2]	1986	1990	1994[1]	2000	2002
24-hour hospital and residential treatment[2]	Admissions[3] in thousands					Admissions per 100,000 civilian population[4]				
All organizations	1,819	2,035	2,267	2,029	2,193	759.9	833.7	874.6	719.3	761.6
State and county mental hospitals.	333	276	238	236	239	139.1	113.2	92.0	83.6	82.8
Private psychiatric hospitals	235	407	485	451	477	98.0	166.5	187.1	159.8	165.8
Non-federal general hospital psychiatric services	849	960	1,067	994	1,095	354.8	393.2	411.5	352.3	380.2
Department of Veterans Affairs medical centers[5]	180	198	173	171	182	75.1	81.2	66.9	60.5	63.2
Residential treatment centers for emotionally disturbed children	25	42	47	46	60	10.2	17.0	18.0	16.2	20.7
All other organizations[6]	198	153	257	132	141	82.7	62.6	99.0	46.8	48.8
Less than 24-hour care[7]										
All organizations	2,955	3,298	3,516	4,057	3,575	1,233.4	1,352.4	1,356.8	1,438.1	1,241.5
State and county mental hospitals.	68	48	42	49	53	28.4	19.8	16.1	17.2	18.3
Private psychiatric hospitals	132	163	214	265	426	55.2	66.9	82.4	94.1	147.8
Non-federal general hospital psychiatric services	533	659	498	1,103	546	222.4	270.0	192.0	391.0	189.6
Department of Veterans Affairs medical centers[5]	133	184	132	139	80	55.3	75.3	51.1	49.1	27.7
Residential treatment centers for emotionally disturbed children	67	100	167	199	208	28.1	40.8	64.6	70.6	72.1
All other organizations[6]	2,022	2,145	2,464	2,302	2,263	844.0	879.6	950.7	816.0	785.9

[1]Starting with 1994 data, for supportive residential clients (moderately staffed housing arrangements such as supervised apartments, group homes, and halfway houses) are included in the totals and the category, All other organizations. This change affects the comparability of trend data prior to 1994 with data for 1994 and later years.
[2]These data exclude mental health care provided in nonpsychiatric units of hospitals such as general medical units.
[3]Admissions sometimes are referred to as additions. See Appendix II, Admission.
[4]Civilian population estimates for 2000 and beyond are based on the 2000 census as of July 1; population estimates for 1992–1998 are 1990 postcensal estimates.
[5]Includes Department of Veterans Affairs (VA) neuropsychiatric hospitals, VA general hospital psychiatric services, and VA psychiatric outpatient clinics.
[6]Includes freestanding psychiatric outpatient clinics, partial care organizations, and multiservice mental health organizations. See Appendix I, Survey of Mental Health Organizations.
[7]Formerly reported as partial care and outpatient treatment, the survey format was changed in 1994 and the reporting of these services was combined due to similarities in the care provided. These data exclude office-based mental health care (psychiatrists, psychologists, licensed clinical social workers, and psychiatric nurses).

NOTES: Data for 2000 are revised and differ from the previous edition of *Health, United States*. Data for additional years are available. See Appendix III.

SOURCES: Substance Abuse and Mental Health Services Administration, Center for Mental Health Services (CMHS). Manderscheid RW, Henderson MJ. *Mental Health, United States, 2002*. Washington, DC: U.S. Government Printing Office, 2004; and Survey of Mental Health Organizations, unpublished data.

Table 95 (page 1 of 3). Persons with hospital stays in the past year, by selected characteristics: United States, selected years 1997–2004

[Data are based on household interviews of a sample of the civilian noninstitutionalized population]

Characteristic	1 or more hospital stays[1]				2 or more hospital stays[1]			
	1997	2002	2003	2004	1997	2002	2003	2004
	Percent							
Total, 1 year of age and over[2,3]	7.8	7.8	7.7	7.4	1.8	1.9	1.8	1.8
Age								
1–17 years	2.8	2.6	2.5	2.4	0.5	0.5	0.4	0.4
1–5 years	3.9	3.7	3.7	4.0	0.7	0.7	0.7	0.9
6–17 years	2.3	2.2	2.0	1.7	0.4	0.4	0.3	0.3
18–44 years	7.4	7.1	7.1	7.0	1.2	1.3	1.1	1.2
18–24 years	7.9	6.7	7.2	6.6	1.3	1.1	1.1	0.8
25–44 years	7.3	7.3	7.1	7.1	1.2	1.3	1.1	1.4
45–64 years	8.2	8.2	8.7	8.1	2.2	2.2	2.4	2.2
45–54 years	6.9	7.0	7.4	7.1	1.7	1.8	1.9	1.9
55–64 years	10.2	10.0	10.6	9.4	2.9	2.7	3.2	2.7
65 years and over	18.0	19.1	18.2	17.4	5.4	5.9	5.6	5.7
65–74 years	16.1	16.2	15.2	14.5	4.8	5.1	4.5	4.6
75 years and over	20.4	22.4	21.6	20.7	6.2	6.9	6.9	6.8
1–64 years of age								
Total, 1–64 years of age[2,4]	6.3	6.1	6.2	5.9	1.3	1.3	1.2	1.2
Sex								
Male	4.5	4.3	4.4	4.1	1.0	0.9	1.0	0.9
1–17 years	2.9	2.9	2.5	2.5	0.6	0.5	0.4	0.5
18–44 years	3.6	3.3	3.4	3.3	0.6	0.6	0.6	0.7
45–54 years	6.0	5.9	6.7	6.0	1.4	1.4	1.9	1.5
55–64 years	11.1	10.2	10.9	9.3	3.0	2.7	3.1	2.5
Female	8.0	7.9	7.9	7.7	1.6	1.6	1.5	1.6
1–17 years	2.6	2.4	2.4	2.2	0.5	0.4	0.5	0.4
18–44 years	11.2	10.9	10.8	10.6	1.8	1.9	1.6	1.8
45–54 years	7.6	8.0	8.0	8.1	2.0	2.3	1.8	2.2
55–64 years	9.4	9.9	10.3	9.5	2.9	2.7	3.3	2.9
Race[4,5]								
White only	6.2	6.0	6.1	5.9	1.2	1.2	1.2	1.2
Black or African American only	7.6	7.6	7.4	6.8	1.9	2.0	1.8	1.8
American Indian or Alaska Native only	7.6	7.3	8.2	6.7	*	*	*	*1.6
Asian only	3.9	3.2	3.9	3.8	*0.5	*	*0.4	*0.4
Native Hawaiian or Other Pacific Islander only	- - -	*	*	*	- - -	*	*	*
2 or more races	- - -	8.2	8.2	6.9	- - -	*2.9	*2.4	*1.4
Hispanic origin and race[4,5]								
Hispanic or Latino	6.8	5.8	5.9	5.5	1.3	1.3	1.3	1.1
Not Hispanic or Latino	6.2	6.2	6.2	6.0	1.3	1.3	1.2	1.3
White only	6.1	6.1	6.2	6.0	1.2	1.2	1.2	1.2
Black or African American only	7.5	7.5	7.4	6.8	1.9	2.0	1.8	1.9
Percent of poverty level[4,6]								
Below 100%	10.3	9.0	8.8	9.2	2.8	2.6	2.5	2.9
100%–less than 200%	7.3	7.5	7.4	6.9	1.7	1.9	1.8	1.7
200% or more	5.3	5.4	5.5	5.2	0.9	1.0	0.9	0.9
Hispanic origin and race and percent of poverty level[4,5,6]								
Hispanic or Latino:								
Below 100%	9.1	8.0	7.6	7.2	2.0	1.7	2.1	1.7
100%–less than 200%	5.9	6.2	6.0	5.3	1.0	1.7	1.5	1.1
200% or more	5.8	4.7	5.1	5.0	1.1	1.0	0.8	0.8
Not Hispanic or Latino:								
White only:								
Below 100%	10.7	9.2	8.8	10.1	3.2	2.7	2.4	3.3
100%–less than 200%	7.7	7.8	8.1	7.7	1.8	1.9	1.9	2.0
200% or more	5.3	5.5	5.5	5.3	0.9	0.9	0.9	0.9
Black or African American only:								
Below 100%	11.4	10.5	10.7	11.0	3.3	3.7	3.4	3.8
100%–less than 200%	8.0	8.4	7.7	7.5	2.1	2.1	1.7	2.3
200% or more	5.5	6.2	6.1	5.1	1.2	1.4	1.3	1.0

See footnotes at end of table.

Table 95 (page 2 of 3). **Persons with hospital stays in the past year, by selected characteristics: United States, selected years 1997–2004**

[Data are based on household interviews of a sample of the civilian noninstitutionalized population]

Characteristic	1 or more hospital stays[1]				2 or more hospital stays[1]			
	1997	2002	2003	2004	1997	2002	2003	2004
Health insurance status at the time of interview[4,7]				Percent				
Insured	6.6	6.4	6.6	6.3	1.3	1.4	1.3	1.3
Private	5.6	5.5	5.6	5.4	1.0	1.0	0.9	0.9
Medicaid	16.1	15.1	15.6	14.0	4.9	4.9	4.6	4.8
Uninsured	4.8	4.7	4.4	4.1	1.0	0.9	0.9	0.8
Health insurance status prior to interview[4,7]								
Insured continuously all 12 months	6.5	6.3	6.5	6.2	1.3	1.3	1.3	1.3
Uninsured for any period up to 12 months	8.5	7.6	8.0	7.6	1.8	1.7	1.7	1.6
Uninsured more than 12 months	3.8	3.9	3.5	3.1	0.8	0.8	0.8	0.6
Percent of poverty level and health insurance status prior to interview[4,6,7]								
Below 100%:								
Insured continuously all 12 months	12.4	10.2	10.7	11.5	3.7	3.3	3.2	3.9
Uninsured for any period up to 12 months	13.7	12.3	11.1	11.5	3.4	*3.3	*2.6	*2.8
Uninsured more than 12 months	4.9	5.0	4.3	3.9	1.0	*1.0	1.2	*1.0
100%–less than 200%:								
Insured continuously all 12 months	8.5	8.5	8.7	8.2	2.0	2.2	2.2	2.2
Uninsured for any period up to 12 months	9.3	8.8	9.9	8.5	*1.9	*2.4	*1.9	*1.8
Uninsured more than 12 months	3.8	4.2	3.5	3.0	*0.7	*0.7	*0.7	*0.6
200% or more:								
Insured continuously all 12 months	5.5	5.6	5.7	5.4	0.9	1.0	0.9	0.9
Uninsured for any period up to 12 months	5.9	5.5	5.9	5.9	*1.1	1.0	1.2	*1.1
Uninsured more than 12 months	3.0	2.8	2.9	2.6	*0.6	*	*0.5	*0.5
Geographic region[4]								
Northeast	6.0	5.9	5.6	5.2	1.2	1.2	1.1	1.1
Midwest	6.5	6.6	6.1	5.9	1.5	1.3	1.3	1.3
South	6.8	6.6	7.0	6.7	1.4	1.5	1.5	1.5
West	5.4	5.1	5.3	5.2	0.8	1.0	0.9	1.0
Location of residence[4]								
Within MSA[8]	6.1	5.9	6.0	5.7	1.2	1.2	1.2	1.2
Outside MSA[8]	7.0	7.2	7.1	6.9	1.6	1.5	1.5	1.6
65 years of age and over								
All persons 65 years of age and over[2,9]	18.1	19.1	18.3	17.5	5.4	5.9	5.6	5.7
65–74 years	16.1	16.2	15.2	14.5	4.8	5.1	4.5	4.6
75 years and over	20.4	22.4	21.6	20.7	6.2	6.9	6.9	6.8
Sex[9]								
Male	19.0	20.4	18.6	18.3	5.8	6.7	5.7	5.9
Female	17.5	18.2	18.0	16.9	5.1	5.4	5.6	5.6
Hispanic origin and race[5,9]								
Hispanic or Latino	17.3	17.7	18.2	18.2	6.2	5.0	6.5	5.5
Not Hispanic or Latino	18.2	19.2	18.3	17.4	5.4	6.0	5.6	5.7
White only	18.3	19.5	18.3	17.4	5.4	6.1	5.4	5.7
Black or African American only	18.9	18.9	20.1	18.5	5.5	6.6	7.6	5.7
Percent of poverty level[4,6]								
Below 100%	20.9	23.4	21.1	19.7	6.4	7.3	7.3	7.9
100%–less than 200%	19.6	19.6	19.1	18.1	6.5	6.5	5.9	5.8
200% or more	17.1	18.2	17.5	17.0	4.9	5.5	5.3	5.3
Geographic region[9]								
Northeast	17.2	18.6	17.2	16.2	5.1	5.3	5.3	4.9
Midwest	18.2	20.5	18.2	18.8	5.6	6.5	4.9	6.3
South	19.4	19.9	20.1	18.3	6.1	6.5	6.3	6.5
West	16.5	16.5	15.8	15.5	4.4	4.9	5.5	4.3

See footnotes at end of table.

Table 95 (page 3 of 3). Persons with hospital stays in the past year, by selected characteristics: United States, selected years 1997–2004

[Data are based on household interviews of a sample of the civilian noninstitutionalized population]

Characteristic	1 or more hospital stays[1]				2 or more hospital stays[1]			
	1997	2002	2003	2004	1997	2002	2003	2004
Location of residence[9]	Percent							
Within MSA[8]	17.8	18.7	17.9	17.1	5.2	5.6	5.6	5.6
Outside MSA[8]	19.1	20.4	19.6	18.7	6.3	7.0	5.6	5.8

* Estimates are considered unreliable. Data preceded by an asterisk have a relative standard error (RSE) of 20%–30%. Data not shown have an RSE of greater than 30%.

- - - Data not available.

[1]These estimates exclude hospitalizations for institutionalized persons and those who died while hospitalized. See Appendix II, Hospital utilization.

[2]Includes all other races not shown separately and unknown health insurance status.

[3]Estimates for all persons are age adjusted to the year 2000 standard population using six age groups: 1–17 years, 18–44 years, 45–54 years, 55–64 years, 65–74 years, and 75 years of age and over. See Appendix II, Age adjustment.

[4]Estimates are for persons 1–64 years of age and are age adjusted to the year 2000 standard population using four age groups: 1–17 years, 18–44 years, 45–54 years, and 55–64 years of age. See Appendix II, Age adjustment.

[5]The race groups, white, black, American Indian or Alaska Native, Asian, Native Hawaiian or Other Pacific Islander, and 2 or more races, include persons of Hispanic and non-Hispanic origin. Persons of Hispanic origin may be of any race. Starting with 1999 data, race-specific estimates are tabulated according to the 1997 Revisions to the Standards for Federal Data on Race and Ethnicity and are not strictly comparable with estimates for earlier years. The five single race categories plus multiple race categories shown in the table conform to the 1997 Standards. Starting with 1999 data, race-specific estimates are for persons who reported only one racial group; the category 2 or more races includes persons who reported more than one racial group. Prior to 1999, data were tabulated according to the 1977 Standards with four racial groups and the Asian only category included Native Hawaiian or Other Pacific Islander. Estimates for single race categories prior to 1999 included persons who reported one race or, if they reported more than one race, identified one race as best representing their race. Starting with 2003 data, race responses of other race and unspecified multiple race were treated as missing, and then race was imputed if these were the only race responses. Almost all persons with a race response of other race were of Hispanic origin. See Appendix II, Hispanic origin; Race.

[6]Percent of poverty level is based on family income and family size and composition using U.S. Census Bureau poverty thresholds. Poverty status was unknown for 11% of persons 18 years of age and over in 1989. Missing family income data were imputed for 24%–28% of persons 1–64 years of age in 1997–1998 and 30%–33% in 1999–2004; and 36%–41% of persons 65 years of age and over in 1997–1998 and 43%–47% in 1999–2004. See Appendix II, Family income; Poverty.

[7]Health insurance categories are mutually exclusive. Persons who reported both Medicaid and private coverage are classified as having private coverage. Starting in 1997, Medicaid includes state-sponsored health plans and State Children's Health Insurance Program (SCHIP). See Appendix II, Health insurance coverage.

[8]MSA is metropolitan statistical area.

[9]Estimates are for persons 65 years of age and over and are age adjusted to the year 2000 standard population using two age groups: 65–74 years and 75 years and over. See Appendix II, Age adjustment.

NOTES: Standard errors are available in the spreadsheet version of this table. Available from: www.cdc.gov/nchs/hus.htm. Data for additional years are available. See Appendix III.

SOURCE: Centers for Disease Control and Prevention, National Center for Health Statistics, National Health Interview Survey, family core questionnaire.

Table 96 (page 1 of 2). Discharges, days of care, and average length of stay in non-federal short-stay hospitals, by selected characteristics: United States, selected years 1980–2004

[Data are based on a sample of hospital records]

Characteristic	1980[1]	1985[1]	1990	1995	2000	2001	2002	2003	2004
	Discharges per 1,000 population								
Total, age adjusted[2]	173.4	151.4	125.2	118.0	113.3	115.1	117.3	119.5	118.4
Total, crude	167.7	148.4	122.3	115.7	112.8	114.9	117.5	120.0	119.2
Age									
Under 18 years	75.6	61.4	46.4	42.4	40.3	43.4	43.4	43.6	43.0
18–44 years	155.3	128.0	102.7	91.4	84.9	87.3	90.3	91.3	91.1
45–54 years	174.8	146.8	112.4	98.5	92.1	94.4	95.6	99.5	99.7
55–64 years	215.4	194.8	163.3	148.3	141.5	139.3	146.5	145.7	143.6
65 years and over	383.7	369.8	334.1	347.7	353.4	354.3	357.5	367.9	362.9
65–74 years	315.8	297.2	261.6	260.0	254.6	256.1	254.0	265.1	259.2
75 years and over	489.3	475.6	434.0	459.1	462.0	460.0	466.6	475.2	470.2
Sex[2]									
Male	153.2	137.3	113.0	104.8	99.1	100.0	102.4	104.4	102.6
Female	195.0	167.3	139.0	131.7	127.7	130.6	132.9	135.1	134.9
Geographic region[2]									
Northeast	162.0	142.6	133.2	133.5	127.5	125.2	123.5	127.6	128.8
Midwest	192.1	158.1	128.8	113.3	110.9	113.5	113.6	117.1	114.4
South	179.7	155.5	132.5	125.2	120.9	126.3	126.7	125.8	125.6
West	150.5	145.7	100.7	96.7	89.4	88.8	99.7	103.9	101.2
	Days of care per 1,000 population								
Total, age adjusted[2]	1,297.0	997.5	818.9	638.6	557.7	562.2	570.9	574.6	568.7
Total, crude	1,216.7	957.7	784.0	620.2	554.6	560.9	571.7	577.8	574.1
Age									
Under 18 years	341.4	281.2	226.3	184.7	179.0	192.5	195.2	195.5	193.2
18–44 years	818.6	619.2	467.7	351.7	309.4	322.7	333.9	339.7	334.9
45–54 years	1,314.9	967.8	699.7	516.2	437.4	455.4	456.7	477.2	491.1
55–64 years	1,889.4	1,436.9	1,172.3	867.2	729.1	732.2	752.2	735.9	735.2
65 years and over	4,098.3	3,228.0	2,895.6	2,373.7	2,111.9	2,064.2	2,085.1	2,088.3	2,048.6
65–74 years	3,147.0	2,437.3	2,087.8	1,684.7	1,439.0	1,449.5	1,411.9	1,428.9	1,405.2
75 years and over	5,578.8	4,381.3	4,009.1	3,247.8	2,851.9	2,725.5	2,795.0	2,776.1	2,714.9
Sex[2]									
Male	1,239.7	973.3	805.8	623.9	535.9	534.5	549.5	546.7	541.1
Female	1,365.2	1,033.1	840.5	654.9	581.0	591.9	596.0	605.2	599.6
Geographic region[2]									
Northeast	1,400.6	1,113.0	1,026.7	839.0	718.6	697.7	690.0	694.4	687.6
Midwest	1,484.8	1,078.6	830.6	590.9	500.5	491.6	502.1	507.9	498.7
South	1,262.3	957.7	820.4	666.0	592.5	623.6	618.6	609.8	614.2
West	956.9	824.7	575.5	451.1	408.2	408.3	454.7	476.4	457.5
	Average length of stay in days								
Total, age adjusted[2]	7.5	6.6	6.5	5.4	4.9	4.9	4.9	4.8	4.8
Total, crude	7.3	6.5	6.4	5.4	4.9	4.9	4.9	4.8	4.8
Age									
Under 18 years	4.5	4.6	4.9	4.4	4.4	4.4	4.5	4.5	4.5
18–44 years	5.3	4.8	4.6	3.8	3.6	3.7	3.7	3.7	3.7
45–54 years	7.5	6.6	6.2	5.2	4.8	4.8	4.8	4.8	4.9
55–64 years	8.8	7.4	7.2	5.8	5.2	5.3	5.1	5.1	5.1
65 years and over	10.7	8.7	8.7	6.8	6.0	5.8	5.8	5.7	5.6
65–74 years	10.0	8.2	8.0	6.5	5.7	5.7	5.6	5.4	5.4
75 years and over	11.4	9.2	9.2	7.1	6.2	5.9	6.0	5.8	5.8
Sex[2]									
Male	8.1	7.1	7.1	6.0	5.4	5.3	5.4	5.2	5.3
Female	7.0	6.2	6.0	5.0	4.6	4.5	4.5	4.5	4.4

See footnotes at end of table.

Table 96 (page 2 of 2). Discharges, days of care, and average length of stay in non-federal short-stay hospitals, by selected characteristics: United States, selected years 1980–2004

[Data are based on a sample of hospital records]

Characteristic	1980[1]	1985[1]	1990	1995	2000	2001	2002	2003	2004
Geographic region[2]	Average length of stay in days								
Northeast	8.6	7.8	7.7	6.3	5.6	5.6	5.6	5.4	5.3
Midwest	7.7	6.8	6.5	5.2	4.5	4.3	4.4	4.3	4.4
South	7.0	6.2	6.2	5.3	4.9	4.9	4.9	4.8	4.9
West	6.4	5.7	5.7	4.7	4.6	4.6	4.6	4.6	4.5

[1]Comparisons of data from 1980–1985 with data from later years should be made with caution as estimates of change may reflect improvements in the survey design rather than true changes in hospital use. See Appendix I, National Hospital Discharge Survey.
[2]Estimates are age adjusted to the year 2000 standard population using six age groups: under 18 years, 18–44 years, 45–54 years, 55–64 years, 65–74 years, and 75 years and over. See Appendix II, Age adjustment.

NOTES: Excludes newborn infants. Rates are based on the civilian population as of July 1. Starting with *Health, United States, 2003*, rates for 2000 and beyond are based on the 2000 census. Rates for 1990–1999 use population estimates based on the 1990 census adjusted for net underenumeration using the 1990 National Population Adjustment Matrix from the U.S. Census Bureau. Rates for 1990–1999 are not strictly comparable with rates for 2000 and beyond because population estimates for 1990–1999 have not been revised to reflect the 2000 census. See Appendix I, National Hospital Discharge Survey; Population Census and Population Estimates. Data for additional years are available. See Appendix III.

SOURCE: Centers for Disease Control and Prevention, National Center for Health Statistics, National Hospital Discharge Survey.

Table 97 (page 1 of 3). Discharges and days of care in non-federal short-stay hospitals, by sex, age, and selected first-listed diagnoses: United States, selected years 1990–2004

[Data are based on a sample of hospital records]

Sex, age, and first-listed diagnosis	Discharges			Days of care		
	1990	2000	2004	1990	2000	2004
Both sexes	Number per 1,000 population					
Total, age adjusted[1,2]	125.2	113.3	118.4	818.9	557.7	568.7
Total, crude[2]	122.3	112.8	119.2	784.0	554.6	574.1
Male						
All ages[1,2]	113.0	99.1	102.6	805.8	535.9	541.1
Under 18 years[2]	46.3	40.9	43.6	233.6	195.6	201.5
Pneumonia	3.7	2.6	2.7	16.7	8.5	8.9
Asthma	3.3	3.5	3.4	9.3	7.4	7.3
Injuries and poisoning	6.8	5.0	5.2	30.1	21.4	18.5
Fracture, all sites	2.2	1.8	1.7	9.3	7.2	4.4
18–44 years[2]	57.9	45.0	46.5	351.7	217.5	225.6
HIV infection	*0.3	0.6	0.4	*3.0	*5.4	3.9
Alcohol and drug[3]	3.7	4.0	3.2	33.1	19.1	14.3
Serious mental illness[4]	3.4	*5.3	5.7	47.1	*43.6	43.4
Diseases of heart	3.0	2.7	2.9	16.3	9.4	10.1
Intervertebral disc disorders	2.6	1.5	1.2	10.7	3.2	2.4
Injuries and poisoning	13.1	7.3	8.0	65.7	33.2	40.8
Fracture, all sites	4.0	2.5	2.8	22.7	12.8	15.5
45–64 years[2]	140.3	112.7	118.4	943.4	570.4	612.4
HIV infection	*0.1	*0.5	0.4	*	*	*4.1
Malignant neoplasms	10.6	6.2	6.0	99.1	42.1	38.6
Trachea, bronchus, lung	2.7	0.9	0.8	19.1	5.2	5.4
Diabetes	2.9	3.7	3.1	21.2	22.5	16.6
Alcohol and drug[3]	3.5	3.5	4.4	29.7	15.8	19.6
Serious mental illness[4]	2.5	*4.0	4.7	34.8	*34.6	42.2
Diseases of heart	31.7	26.4	23.9	185.0	101.5	95.7
Ischemic heart disease	22.6	17.7	14.7	128.2	63.8	54.3
Acute myocardial infarction	7.4	5.9	4.6	55.8	27.8	23.7
Heart failure	3.1	3.4	3.9	21.0	17.3	20.7
Cerebrovascular diseases	4.1	3.8	3.4	40.7	19.8	17.6
Pneumonia	3.4	3.4	3.7	27.1	20.3	19.6
Injuries and poisoning	11.6	8.8	10.9	82.6	49.8	68.9
Fracture, all sites	3.3	2.5	3.0	24.2	16.2	19.1
65–74 years[2]	287.8	264.9	268.5	2,251.5	1,489.7	1,442.3
Malignant neoplasms	27.9	17.6	19.1	277.6	121.2	128.7
Large intestine and rectum	3.0	3.0	3.1	34.2	27.3	29.1
Trachea, bronchus, lung	6.4	2.8	3.0	55.7	19.2	19.4
Prostate	5.1	3.7	2.9	33.1	14.0	9.9
Diabetes	4.4	4.7	5.5	39.8	29.0	29.9
Serious mental illness[4]	2.5	*3.4	2.8	43.8	39.9	26.4
Diseases of heart	69.4	70.6	65.0	487.2	331.9	280.9
Ischemic heart disease	42.0	39.7	35.0	285.2	171.2	141.8
Acute myocardial infarction	14.0	12.5	10.8	122.4	66.5	56.7
Heart failure	11.8	13.6	13.9	93.1	77.6	70.9
Cerebrovascular diseases	13.8	13.2	12.5	114.8	59.0	56.9
Pneumonia	11.2	12.7	12.2	106.9	81.5	75.0
Hyperplasia of prostate	14.4	5.4	4.0	65.0	15.0	11.3
Osteoarthritis	5.5	10.3	11.3	48.5	48.8	42.8
Injuries and poisoning	17.6	17.9	17.4	139.0	105.7	109.7
Fracture, all sites	4.5	4.7	4.2	45.9	29.9	34.1
Fracture of neck of femur (hip)	1.5	*2.0	1.7	*18.1	*15.9	10.9

See footnotes at end of table.

[Data are based on a sample of hospital records]

Sex, age, and first-listed diagnosis	Discharges			Days of care		
	1990	2000	2004	1990	2000	2004
Male—Con.	Number per 1,000 population					
75 years and over[2]	478.5	467.4	483.1	4,231.6	2,888.0	2,815.5
Malignant neoplasms	41.0	21.9	21.3	408.3	165.2	149.0
Large intestine and rectum	5.4	4.2	3.9	80.7	44.1	34.0
Trachea, bronchus, lung	5.4	3.0	3.9	53.4	18.3	27.0
Prostate	9.7	3.2	2.4	65.6	*19.4	8.7
Diabetes	4.6	6.5	6.9	51.2	43.2	37.2
Serious mental illness[4]	*2.6	2.9	2.4	*40.5	*32.6	24.5
Diseases of heart	106.2	113.3	113.1	855.7	600.9	579.0
Ischemic heart disease	49.1	53.0	45.1	398.1	276.1	237.9
Acute myocardial infarction	23.1	23.0	21.6	227.5	136.5	152.0
Heart failure	31.8	30.9	36.6	248.6	178.6	193.7
Cerebrovascular diseases	30.2	30.2	24.9	298.3	171.2	129.9
Pneumonia	38.1	36.7	38.8	391.3	228.6	232.5
Hyperplasia of prostate	17.9	6.8	6.0	109.2	21.6	17.6
Osteoarthritis	6.6	7.2	11.8	60.7	28.7	47.1
Injuries and poisoning	31.2	33.6	33.4	341.3	257.7	207.8
Fracture, all sites	13.7	14.4	14.3	145.1	*119.2	91.2
Fracture of neck of femur (hip)	8.5	8.4	8.8	97.8	63.3	60.9
Female						
All ages[1,2]	139.0	127.7	134.9	840.5	581.0	599.6
Under 18 years[2]	46.4	39.6	42.4	218.7	161.5	184.4
Pneumonia	2.9	2.4	2.4	13.7	9.5	7.9
Asthma	2.2	2.4	2.0	6.8	5.5	4.6
Injuries and poisoning	4.3	3.1	3.4	16.7	*12.0	12.6
Fracture, all sites	1.3	0.9	0.8	6.4	2.3	2.7
18–44 years[2]	146.8	124.8	136.2	582.0	401.1	445.5
HIV infection	*	0.3	0.2	*	*2.1	1.6
Delivery	69.9	64.5	71.4	195.0	160.2	186.2
Alcohol and drug[3]	1.6	*2.1	2.0	14.1	*10.8	*9.2
Serious mental illness[4]	3.7	*5.4	5.9	54.3	*41.1	43.1
Diseases of heart	1.3	1.7	1.7	7.2	6.3	8.3
Intervertebral disc disorders	1.5	1.0	1.1	7.3	2.4	2.8
Injuries and poisoning	6.7	4.3	5.3	36.6	18.1	22.4
Fracture, all sites	1.6	1.0	1.1	10.7	4.5	4.8
45–64 years[2]	131.0	110.2	117.3	886.5	533.6	571.8
HIV infection	*	*	*0.3	*	*	*
Malignant neoplasms	12.7	6.1	5.8	107.4	34.7	36.9
Trachea, bronchus, lung	1.7	0.5	0.7	14.8	3.4	5.0
Breast	2.8	1.3	0.8	12.1	2.6	2.8
Diabetes	2.9	2.9	2.8	25.8	15.0	12.4
Alcohol and drug[3]	1.0	1.5	1.6	8.0	*7.1	7.8
Serious mental illness[4]	4.0	4.6	5.5	60.5	42.7	51.8
Diseases of heart	16.6	14.6	13.3	101.1	59.5	57.1
Ischemic heart disease	9.9	7.8	6.6	57.4	29.5	25.6
Acute myocardial infarction	2.8	2.0	2.0	21.6	10.0	11.6
Heart failure	2.2	2.9	2.7	16.3	13.6	15.0
Cerebrovascular diseases	3.0	3.5	2.8	32.1	19.5	16.2
Pneumonia	3.3	3.6	3.3	26.1	20.7	18.8
Injuries and poisoning	9.4	7.7	9.2	63.3	41.2	50.8
Fracture, all sites	3.1	2.7	2.4	25.0	13.3	13.8

See footnotes at end of table.

Table 97 (page 3 of 3). Discharges and days of care in non-federal short-stay hospitals, by sex, age, and selected first-listed diagnoses: United States, selected years 1990–2004

[Data are based on a sample of hospital records]

Sex, age, and first-listed diagnosis	Discharges			Days of care		
	1990	2000	2004	1990	2000	2004
Female—Con.			Number per 1,000 population			
65–74 years[2]	241.1	246.1	251.4	1,959.3	1,397.1	1,374.0
Malignant neoplasms	20.9	14.1	13.8	189.8	101.0	101.3
Large intestine and rectum	2.4	1.7	1.9	34.9	15.2	17.3
Trachea, bronchus, lung	2.6	2.4	2.2	26.9	*17.5	16.5
Breast	3.9	2.8	1.5	17.6	*	2.9
Diabetes	5.8	4.6	5.0	46.8	26.1	27.9
Serious mental illness[4]	3.9	4.0	3.9	62.8	46.3	47.3
Diseases of heart	45.1	52.1	42.6	316.9	256.0	199.7
Ischemic heart disease	24.4	23.3	18.4	153.8	113.9	77.2
Acute myocardial infarction	7.5	8.0	5.8	58.1	52.8	32.2
Heart failure	9.5	12.8	10.4	84.0	69.1	59.7
Cerebrovascular diseases	11.3	12.3	9.1	96.0	59.4	44.4
Pneumonia	8.5	11.3	12.5	79.6	71.4	72.3
Osteoarthritis	7.8	10.0	15.1	74.5	47.2	60.9
Injuries and poisoning	17.8	18.3	19.6	166.2	109.9	114.6
Fracture, all sites	8.4	7.7	8.8	97.3	43.8	47.4
Fracture of neck of femur (hip)	3.6	3.2	3.4	*59.6	21.1	23.6
75 years and over[2]	409.6	458.8	462.4	3,887.1	2,830.8	2,653.9
Malignant neoplasms	22.1	17.6	15.6	257.3	125.7	103.6
Large intestine and rectum	4.6	3.4	2.8	69.8	28.4	28.8
Trachea, bronchus, lung	2.1	1.9	2.2	20.6	14.0	14.3
Breast	3.9	2.5	2.4	22.0	*8.9	5.9
Diabetes	4.6	6.3	6.1	55.3	34.0	31.1
Serious mental illness[4]	4.2	4.7	3.5	78.4	49.2	37.4
Diseases of heart	84.6	99.1	94.6	672.8	523.4	485.2
Ischemic heart disease	33.7	35.5	31.0	253.2	185.5	155.6
Acute myocardial infarction	13.1	16.5	14.8	125.9	110.7	91.0
Heart failure	28.6	32.5	31.9	240.8	183.4	171.9
Cerebrovascular diseases	29.6	27.6	24.5	302.0	156.8	129.2
Pneumonia	23.5	30.1	28.0	255.8	206.5	179.1
Osteoarthritis	6.2	9.9	13.2	62.2	46.3	54.7
Injuries and poisoning	46.3	44.7	45.1	489.2	275.4	284.0
Fracture, all sites	31.5	30.0	28.3	352.7	190.0	168.8
Fracture of neck of femur (hip)	18.8	17.9	16.3	236.3	125.3	101.4

* Estimates are considered unreliable. Data preceded by an asterisk have a relative standard error (RSE) of 20%–30%. Data not shown have an RSE of greater than 30%.

[1] Estimates are age adjusted to the year 2000 standard population using six age groups: under 18 years, 18–44 years, 45–54 years, 55–64 years, 65–74 years, and 75 years and over. See Appendix II, Age adjustment.

[2] Includes discharges with first-listed diagnoses not shown in table.

[3] Includes abuse, dependence, and withdrawal. These estimates are for non-federal short-stay hospitals only and do not include alcohol and drug discharges from other types of facilities or programs such as the Department of Veterans Affairs or day treatment programs.

[4] These estimates are for non-federal short-stay hospitals only and do not include serious mental illness discharges from other types of facilities or programs such as the Department of Veterans Affairs or long-term hospitals.

NOTES: Excludes newborn infants. Diagnostic categories are based on the *International Classification of Diseases, Ninth Revision, Clinical Modification* (ICD–9-CM). See Appendix II, Diagnosis; Human immunodeficiency virus (HIV) infection; *International Classification of Diseases, Ninth Revision, Clinical Modification*; Table X for ICD–9–CM codes. Rates are based on the civilian population as of July 1. Starting with *Health, United States, 2003*, rates for 2000 and beyond are based on the 2000 census. Rates for 1990–1999 use population estimates based on the 1990 census adjusted for net underenumeration using the 1990 National Population Adjustment Matrix from the U.S. Census Bureau. Rates for 1990–1999 are not strictly comparable with rates for 2000 and beyond because population estimates for 1990–1999 have not been revised to reflect the 2000 census. See Appendix I, National Hospital Discharge Survey; Population Census and Population Estimates. Numbers have been revised and differ from previous editions of *Health, United States*. Data for additional years are available. See Appendix III.

SOURCE: Centers for Disease Control and Prevention, National Center for Health Statistics, National Hospital Discharge Survey.

Table 98 (page 1 of 3). Discharges and average length of stay in non-federal short-stay hospitals, by sex, age, and selected first-listed diagnoses: United States, selected years 1990–2004

[Data are based on a sample of hospital records]

Sex, age, and first-listed diagnosis	Discharges			Average length of stay[1]		
	1990	2000	2004	1990	2000	2004
Both sexes	Number in thousands			Number of days		
Total[2]	30,788	31,706	34,864	6.4	4.9	4.8
Male						
All ages[2]	12,280	12,514	13,844	6.9	5.3	5.2
Under 18 years[2]	1,572	1,515	1,637	5.0	4.8	4.6
Pneumonia	124	95	103	4.6	3.3	3.2
Asthma	111	129	127	2.8	2.1	2.1
Injuries and poisoning	232	185	195	4.4	4.3	3.6
Fracture, all sites	76	68	64	4.2	3.9	2.6
18–44 years[2]	3,120	2,498	2,622	6.1	4.8	4.9
HIV infection	*15	32	25	*10.6	*9.4	8.6
Alcohol and drug[3]	201	224	182	8.9	4.7	4.4
Serious mental illness[4]	184	*296	319	13.8	*8.2	7.7
Diseases of heart	163	148	162	5.4	3.5	3.5
Intervertebral disc disorders	138	81	67	4.2	2.2	2.0
Injuries and poisoning	704	408	453	5.0	4.5	5.1
Fracture, all sites	217	141	160	5.6	5.0	5.5
45–64 years[2]	3,115	3,424	4,073	6.7	5.1	5.2
HIV infection	*3	*15	15	*7.1	*	*9.2
Malignant neoplasms	235	188	206	9.4	6.8	6.4
Trachea, bronchus, lung	60	26	28	7.1	6.0	6.6
Diabetes	65	114	107	7.3	6.0	5.3
Alcohol and drug[3]	77	106	150	8.5	4.5	4.5
Serious mental illness[4]	56	*120	162	13.7	*8.8	9.0
Diseases of heart	704	802	821	5.8	3.8	4.0
Ischemic heart disease	502	539	507	5.7	3.6	3.7
Acute myocardial infarction	165	178	158	7.5	4.7	5.2
Heart failure	68	102	136	6.9	5.2	5.3
Cerebrovascular diseases	91	116	117	10.0	5.2	5.2
Pneumonia	75	102	126	8.0	6.0	5.4
Injuries and poisoning	257	266	374	7.2	5.7	6.3
Fracture, all sites	74	77	102	7.2	6.4	6.4
65–74 years[2]	2,268	2,199	2,263	7.8	5.6	5.4
Malignant neoplasms	220	146	161	9.9	6.9	6.7
Large intestine and rectum	24	24	26	11.4	9.2	9.3
Trachea, bronchus, lung	50	23	25	8.7	6.8	6.4
Prostate	40	31	24	6.5	3.8	3.4
Diabetes	34	39	47	9.1	6.2	5.4
Serious mental illness[4]	20	*28	24	17.4	*11.7	9.3
Diseases of heart	547	586	547	7.0	4.7	4.3
Ischemic heart disease	331	329	295	6.8	4.3	4.1
Acute myocardial infarction	110	104	91	8.8	5.3	5.3
Heart failure	93	113	117	7.9	5.7	5.1
Cerebrovascular diseases	108	109	106	8.3	4.5	4.5
Pneumonia	88	105	103	9.5	6.4	6.2
Hyperplasia of prostate	113	45	34	4.5	2.8	2.8
Osteoarthritis	44	86	96	8.8	4.7	3.8
Injuries and poisoning	139	149	146	7.9	5.9	6.3
Fracture, all sites	36	39	35	10.2	6.4	8.1
Fracture of neck of femur (hip)	12	*17	14	*11.8	*7.9	6.5

See footnotes at end of table.

Table 98 (page 2 of 3). **Discharges and average length of stay in non-federal short-stay hospitals, by sex, age, and selected first-listed diagnoses: United States, selected years 1990–2004**

[Data are based on a sample of hospital records]

Sex, age, and first-listed diagnosis	Discharges			Average length of stay[1]		
	1990	2000	2004	1990	2000	2004
Male—Con.	Number in thousands			Number of days		
75 years and over[2]	2,203	2,878	3,250	8.8	6.2	5.8
Malignant neoplasms	189	135	144	10.0	7.6	7.0
Large intestine and rectum	25	26	26	15.0	10.6	8.6
Trachea, bronchus, lung	25	18	26	10.0	6.1	7.0
Prostate	45	20	16	6.8	*6.1	3.7
Diabetes	21	40	47	11.0	6.6	5.4
Serious mental illness[4]	*12	18	16	*15.5	*11.2	10.3
Diseases of heart	489	697	761	8.1	5.3	5.1
Ischemic heart disease	226	326	303	8.1	5.2	5.3
Acute myocardial infarction	106	141	145	9.9	5.9	7.0
Heart failure	147	190	246	7.8	5.8	5.3
Cerebrovascular diseases	139	186	168	9.9	5.7	5.2
Pneumonia	175	226	261	10.3	6.2	6.0
Hyperplasia of prostate	82	42	40	6.1	3.2	2.9
Osteoarthritis	30	44	79	10.3	4.5	4.0
Injuries and poisoning	144	207	225	10.9	7.7	6.2
Fracture, all sites	63	89	96	10.6	*8.3	6.4
Fracture of neck of femur (hip)	39	52	59	11.5	7.5	6.9
Female						
All ages[2]	18,508	19,192	21,020	6.1	4.6	4.5
Under 18 years[2]	1,500	1,397	1,516	4.7	4.1	4.4
Pneumonia	95	86	86	4.7	3.9	3.3
Asthma	71	85	71	3.1	2.3	2.3
Injuries and poisoning	138	111	122	3.9	*3.8	3.7
Fracture, all sites	42	32	30	5.0	2.5	3.2
18–44 years[2]	8,018	6,941	7,597	4.0	3.2	3.3
HIV infection	*	15	13	*	*7.5	7.2
Delivery	3,815	3,588	3,980	2.8	2.5	2.6
Alcohol and drug[3]	85	*116	109	9.1	*5.2	*4.7
Serious mental illness[4]	200	*300	331	14.8	*7.6	7.3
Diseases of heart	73	95	98	5.4	3.7	4.8
Intervertebral disc disorders	84	58	62	4.7	2.3	2.5
Injuries and poisoning	366	237	298	5.5	4.2	4.2
Fracture, all sites	85	57	59	6.9	4.4	4.5
45–64 years[2]	3,129	3,534	4,249	6.8	4.8	4.9
HIV infection	*	*	*11	*	*	*
Malignant neoplasms	303	195	211	8.5	5.7	6.3
Trachea, bronchus, lung	41	17	25	8.6	6.4	7.2
Breast	67	40	30	4.3	2.1	3.4
Diabetes	70	93	101	8.9	5.2	4.4
Alcohol and drug[3]	23	47	58	8.2	*4.8	4.9
Serious mental illness[4]	95	146	201	15.2	9.4	9.4
Diseases of heart	397	470	483	6.1	4.1	4.3
Ischemic heart disease	237	251	239	5.8	3.8	3.9
Acute myocardial infarction	68	64	72	7.6	5.0	5.9
Heart failure	54	94	100	7.3	4.7	5.5
Cerebrovascular diseases	72	113	101	10.7	5.5	5.8
Pneumonia	78	116	118	8.0	5.7	5.8
Injuries and poisoning	225	248	335	6.7	5.3	5.5
Fracture, all sites	75	87	89	7.9	4.9	5.7

See footnotes at end of table.

[Data are based on a sample of hospital records]

Sex, age, and first-listed diagnosis	Discharges			Average length of stay[1]		
	1990	2000	2004	1990	2000	2004
Female—Con.	Number in thousands			Number of days		
65–74 years[2]	2,421	2,479	2,523	8.1	5.7	5.5
Malignant neoplasms	210	142	138	9.1	7.2	7.3
Large intestine and rectum	24	17	19	14.5	9.0	9.1
Trachea, bronchus, lung	26	25	22	10.2	*7.1	7.5
Breast	40	29	15	4.5	*	2.0
Diabetes	59	47	50	8.0	5.6	5.5
Serious mental illness[4]	39	40	39	16.3	11.7	12.3
Diseases of heart	453	525	428	7.0	4.9	4.7
Ischemic heart disease	245	235	185	6.3	4.9	4.2
Acute myocardial infarction	75	81	59	7.8	6.6	5.5
Heart failure	95	128	105	8.8	5.4	5.7
Cerebrovascular diseases	114	124	92	8.5	4.8	4.9
Pneumonia	85	114	125	9.4	6.3	5.8
Osteoarthritis	78	101	152	9.5	4.7	4.0
Injuries and poisoning	179	185	197	9.3	6.0	5.8
Fracture, all sites	85	77	88	11.5	5.7	5.4
Fracture of neck of femur (hip)	36	32	34	*16.7	6.7	6.9
75 years and over[2]	3,440	4,840	5,135	9.5	6.2	5.7
Malignant neoplasms	185	186	174	11.7	7.1	6.6
Large intestine and rectum	39	36	31	15.1	8.4	10.4
Trachea, bronchus, lung	18	20	24	9.9	7.3	6.6
Breast	33	27	27	5.7	*3.5	2.4
Diabetes	39	67	68	11.9	5.4	5.1
Serious mental illness[4]	35	49	39	18.7	10.5	10.8
Diseases of heart	711	1,045	1,051	8.0	5.3	5.1
Ischemic heart disease	283	375	344	7.5	5.2	5.0
Acute myocardial infarction	110	174	165	9.6	6.7	6.1
Heart failure	240	343	354	8.4	5.6	5.4
Cerebrovascular diseases	249	292	272	10.2	5.7	5.3
Pneumonia	198	317	311	10.9	6.9	6.4
Osteoarthritis	52	105	147	10.1	4.7	4.1
Injuries and poisoning	389	472	501	10.6	6.2	6.3
Fracture, all sites	265	316	314	11.2	6.3	6.0
Fracture of neck of femur (hip)	158	189	181	12.5	7.0	6.2

* Estimates are considered unreliable. Data preceded by an asterisk have a relative standard error (RSE) of 20%–30%. Data not shown have an RSE of greater than 30%.

[1]Crude estimates.

[2]Includes discharges with first-listed diagnoses not shown in table.

[3]Includes abuse, dependence, and withdrawal. These estimates are for non-federal short-stay hospitals only and do not include alcohol and drug discharges from other types of facilities or programs such as the Department of Veterans Affairs or day treatment programs.

[4]These estimates are for non-federal short-stay hospitals only and do not include serious mental illness discharges from other types of facilities or programs such as the Department of Veterans Affairs or long-term hospitals.

NOTES: Excludes newborn infants. Diagnostic categories are based on the *International Classification of Diseases, Ninth Revision, Clinical Modification* (ICD–9-CM). See Appendix II, Diagnosis; Human immunodeficiency virus (HIV) infection; International Classification of Diseases, Clinical Modification; Table X for ICD–9-CM codes. Numbers have been revised and differ from previous editions of *Health, United States*. Data for additional years are available. See Appendix III.

SOURCE: Centers for Disease Control and Prevention, National Center for Health Statistics, National Hospital Discharge Survey.

Table 99 (page 1 of 3). Discharges with at least one procedure in non-federal short-stay hospitals, by sex, age, and selected procedures: United States, average annual 1993–1994 and 2003–2004

[Data are based on a sample of hospital records]

Age and procedure (any listed)	Both sexes		Male		Female	
	1993–1994	2003–2004	1993–1994	2003–2004	1993–1994	2003–2004
18 years and over	Number in thousands[1]					
Hospital discharges with at least one procedure[2]	18,353	19,773	6,791	7,211	11,562	12,562
	Number per 10,000 population[3]					
Hospital discharges with at least one procedure, age adjusted[2,4]	964.1	909.0	815.7	728.4	1,124.3	1,099.6
Hospital discharges with at least one procedure, crude[2]	955.7	907.8	738.9	684.9	1,154.8	1,116.2
Cardiac catheterization	52.4	57.9	66.2	72.0	39.6	44.7
Insertion, replacement, removal, and revision of pacemaker leads or device	8.9	9.4	9.1	9.4	8.7	9.5
Angiocardiography using contrast material	44.0	48.4	55.2	58.6	33.7	38.9
Operations on vessels of heart	36.1	42.1	51.6	58.3	21.9	26.9
Removal of coronary artery obstruction and insertion of stent(s)	20.5	30.5	28.3	41.1	13.3	20.5
Insertion of coronary artery stent(s)[5]	...	26.4	...	36.0	...	17.3
Coronary artery bypass graft	16.3	11.8	24.2	17.5	9.0	6.5
Diagnostic procedures on small intestine	43.0	48.7	40.8	44.2	45.1	52.8
Diagnostic procedures on large intestine	26.6	26.9	22.5	22.2	30.3	31.3
Diagnostic radiology	67.3	35.5	65.3	32.7	69.1	38.1
Computerized axial tomography	47.5	29.8	47.5	27.5	47.6	31.9
Diagnostic ultrasound	60.5	33.3	51.4	31.6	68.9	34.9
Magnetic resonance imaging	10.8	10.2	10.6	9.7	10.9	10.6
Joint replacement of lower extremity	23.0	41.1	16.7	31.8	28.7	49.9
Total hip replacement	6.4	10.3	5.4	9.3	7.3	11.3
Partial hip replacement	4.6	7.7	1.9	5.4	7.0	9.9
Total knee replacement	9.7	19.7	7.4	14.4	11.9	24.5
Reduction of fracture and dislocation	26.2	24.8	22.6	22.6	29.6	26.9
Excision or destruction of intervertebral disc and spinal fusion	16.8	15.1	19.2	16.2	14.6	14.0
Excision or destruction of intervertebral disc	16.8	14.5	19.2	15.6	14.6	13.3
Cholecystectomy	24.7	19.5	15.9	13.5	32.8	25.1
Laparoscopic cholecystectomy	16.7	14.6	9.6	9.2	23.3	19.7
Lysis of peritoneal adhesions	17.3	15.0	6.3	6.0	27.3	23.4
18–44 years	Number in thousands[1]					
Hospital discharges with at least one procedure[2]	7,635	7,380	1,798	1,491	5,837	5,890
	Number per 10,000 population[3]					
Hospital discharges with at least one procedure[2]	698.5	658.6	330.6	264.7	1,062.9	1,056.3
Repair of hernia	4.8	4.4	4.9	3.0	4.6	5.9
Cesarean section and removal of fetus[6]	...	...	...	...	156.7	206.8
Forceps, vacuum, and breech delivery[6]	...	...	...	...	77.4	54.7
Other procedures inducing or assisting delivery[6,7]	...	...	...	...	408.2	401.6
Dilation and curettage of uterus[6]	...	...	...	...	16.4	7.2
Total abdominal hysterectomy[6]	...	...	...	...	35.6	34.4
Vaginal hysterectomy[6]	...	...	...	...	19.2	17.9
Cardiac catheterization	8.0	8.9	11.5	11.5	4.6	6.3
Angiocardiography using contrast material	7.2	8.2	10.5	10.3	4.0	6.0
Operations on vessels of heart	3.8	4.2	6.4	6.2	1.2	2.1
Removal of coronary artery obstruction and insertion of stent(s)	2.7	3.4	4.5	5.1	*0.8	1.7
Insertion of coronary artery stent(s)[5]	...	3.0	...	4.6	...	1.3
Coronary artery bypass graft	1.2	0.8	1.9	1.2	*	*
Diagnostic procedures on small intestine	13.2	13.3	14.1	11.6	12.4	15.0
Diagnostic procedures on large intestine	6.4	6.9	6.1	6.4	6.8	7.4
Diagnostic radiology	29.8	15.1	28.8	12.8	30.9	17.5
Computerized axial tomography	18.8	11.6	22.1	11.3	15.5	11.9
Diagnostic ultrasound	27.2	10.7	16.6	8.6	37.7	12.9
Magnetic resonance imaging	4.5	3.9	5.0	3.8	4.1	4.0
Reduction of fracture and dislocation	14.5	13.4	19.0	18.7	10.1	8.1
Excision or destruction of intervertebral disc and spinal fusion	15.1	11.0	18.2	11.7	11.9	10.3
Excision or destruction of intervertebral disc	15.1	10.7	18.2	11.4	11.9	9.9
Cholecystectomy	14.9	12.2	5.8	5.3	23.9	19.2
Laparoscopic cholecystectomy	11.1	10.5	4.0	4.1	18.2	16.9
Lysis of peritoneal adhesions	14.7	12.3	2.2	1.7	27.0	23.0

See footnotes at end of table.

Table 99 (page 2 of 3). Discharges with at least one procedure in non-federal short-stay hospitals, by sex, age, and selected procedures: United States, average annual 1993–1994 and 2003–2004

[Data are based on a sample of hospital records]

Age and procedure (any listed)	Both sexes 1993–1994	Both sexes 2003–2004	Male 1993–1994	Male 2003–2004	Female 1993–1994	Female 2003–2004
45–64 years	Number in thousands[1]					
Hospital discharges with at least one procedure[2]	4,160	5,131	2,080	2,538	2,080	2,593
	Number per 10,000 population[3]					
Hospital discharges with at least one procedure[2]	831.2	736.5	859.0	748.1	805.1	725.6
Transurethral prostatectomy[8]	. . .	. . .	16.9	5.6	. . .	. . .
Repair of hernia	15.2	12.9	16.6	11.4	13.8	14.3
Total abdominal hysterectomy[6]	. . .	. . .	. . .	. . .	47.6	43.1
Vaginal hysterectomy[6]	. . .	. . .	. . .	. . .	19.2	21.1
Cardiac catheterization	85.5	76.9	116.0	104.0	56.9	51.0
Insertion, replacement, removal, and revision of pacemaker leads or device	5.3	4.1	6.0	5.3	4.8	2.9
Angiocardiography using contrast material.	71.3	63.4	95.5	82.8	48.6	44.9
Operations on vessels of heart	60.6	55.9	92.3	84.9	30.9	28.4
Removal of coronary artery obstruction and insertion of stent(s)	36.1	40.4	53.3	60.5	19.9	21.2
Insertion of coronary artery stent(s)[5]	. . .	35.4	. . .	53.5	. . .	18.3
Coronary artery bypass graft.	26.0	15.8	41.1	24.9	11.8	7.3
Diagnostic procedures on small intestine.	41.8	43.5	44.3	44.8	39.5	42.3
Diagnostic procedures on large intestine.	25.5	21.7	24.8	19.3	26.1	24.1
Diagnostic radiology	66.9	32.3	69.9	31.7	64.2	32.8
Computerized axial tomography	44.2	25.5	47.3	26.9	41.2	24.2
Diagnostic ultrasound	56.4	32.0	59.7	35.9	53.2	28.3
Magnetic resonance imaging	12.8	10.6	13.4	11.2	12.3	10.1
Joint replacement of lower extremity.	18.3	42.1	17.4	34.8	19.0	49.0
Total hip replacement.	5.9	11.3	7.2	12.0	4.8	10.5
Partial hip replacement.	1.0	4.9	*	4.1	*1.1	5.7
Total knee replacement	8.9	22.7	7.0	16.4	10.6	28.6
Reduction of fracture and dislocation	20.8	17.7	19.4	19.2	22.2	16.2
Excision or destruction of intervertebral disc and spinal fusion.	23.2	21.1	25.3	22.9	21.1	19.3
Excision or destruction of intervertebral disc.	23.2	20.2	25.3	22.1	21.1	18.4
Cholecystectomy	29.6	19.6	20.0	14.9	38.6	24.1
Laparoscopic cholecystectomy	21.5	14.3	13.7	9.5	28.9	18.8
Lysis of peritoneal adhesions	16.8	14.6	7.3	7.1	25.6	21.7
65–74 years	Number in thousands[1]					
Hospital discharges with at least one procedure[2]	3,111	2,958	1,542	1,440	1,570	1,518
	Number per 10,000 population[3]					
Hospital discharges with at least one procedure[2]	1,681.0	1,607.8	1,877.2	1,716.7	1,524.5	1,516.5
Transurethral prostatectomy[8]	50.3	19.7	113.3	43.2	. . .	. . .
Repair of hernia	30.9	25.1	41.1	27.2	22.7	23.3
Total abdominal hysterectomy[6]	. . .	. . .	. . .	. . .	23.0	18.8
Vaginal hysterectomy[6]	. . .	. . .	. . .	. . .	18.9	13.2
Cardiac catheterization	170.5	171.2	219.4	219.2	131.5	131.0
Insertion, replacement, removal, and revision of pacemaker leads or device	26.1	24.7	30.5	27.1	22.7	22.7
Angiocardiography using contrast material.	142.0	140.6	182.3	178.6	109.9	108.7
Operations on vessels of heart.	126.5	138.7	183.5	197.8	81.0	89.1
Removal of coronary artery obstruction and insertion of stent(s)	67.2	96.7	91.7	133.2	47.6	66.1
Insertion of coronary artery stent(s)[5]	. . .	83.7	. . .	115.1	. . .	57.3
Coronary artery bypass graft.	61.6	43.1	95.7	66.7	34.4	23.3
Diagnostic procedures on small intestine.	98.8	114.1	101.6	118.3	96.5	110.5
Diagnostic procedures on large intestine.	62.2	65.0	56.8	55.8	66.6	72.7
Diagnostic radiology	140.0	71.6	152.7	75.9	129.9	68.0
Computerized axial tomography	103.1	60.0	111.5	61.0	96.4	59.1
Diagnostic ultrasound	136.0	72.7	141.5	79.5	131.6	67.0
Magnetic resonance imaging	26.1	23.5	27.0	23.4	25.3	23.7
Joint replacement of lower extremity.	83.4	139.9	64.7	113.9	98.3	161.7
Total hip replacement.	22.6	34.4	18.7	28.7	25.6	39.2
Partial hip replacement.	9.0	13.8	4.3	10.6	12.7	16.3
Total knee replacement	44.3	78.7	35.1	61.2	51.6	93.4
Reduction of fracture and dislocation	38.9	38.7	27.4	26.6	48.0	48.9
Excision or destruction of intervertebral disc and spinal fusion.	16.5	20.2	13.8	20.8	18.7	19.6
Excision or destruction of intervertebral disc.	16.5	19.2	13.8	20.3	18.7	18.3
Cholecystectomy	49.0	38.4	42.5	36.4	54.2	40.0
Laparoscopic cholecystectomy	28.3	27.3	20.8	24.3	34.2	29.9
Lysis of peritoneal adhesions	24.9	21.0	21.8	15.5	27.4	25.6

See footnotes at end of table.

Table 99 (page 3 of 3). Discharges with at least one procedure in non-federal short-stay hospitals, by sex, age, and selected procedures: United States, average annual 1993–1994 and 2003–2004

[Data are based on a sample of hospital records]

Age and procedure (any listed)	Both sexes		Male		Female	
	1993–1994	2003–2004	1993–1994	2003–2004	1993–1994	2003–2004
75 years and over	Number in thousands [1]					
Hospital discharges with at least one procedure[2]	3,447	4,304	1,372	1,742	2,075	2,562
	Number per 10,000 population[3]					
Hospital discharges with at least one procedure[2]	2,432.9	2,430.8	2,689.5	2,615.2	2,288.6	2,319.5
Transurethral prostatectomy[8]	. . .	. . .	179.3	70.0	. . .	. . .
Repair of hernia	36.8	29.2	51.2	29.9	28.6	28.7
Total abdominal hysterectomy[6]	. . .	. . .	. . .	. . .	12.4	10.9
Vaginal hysterectomy[6]	. . .	. . .	. . .	. . .	11.1	6.4
Cardiac catheterization	123.3	175.0	167.6	234.2	98.4	139.3
Insertion, replacement, removal, and revision of						
pacemaker leads or device	64.9	72.0	82.1	83.5	55.2	65.2
Angiocardiography using contrast material.	103.5	148.7	136.9	191.5	84.7	122.8
Operations on vessels of heart.	81.0	127.0	127.3	186.6	55.0	91.0
Removal of coronary artery obstruction and insertion						
of stent(s)	42.1	94.1	61.7	131.2	31.1	71.7
Insertion of coronary artery stent(s)[5]	. . .	79.2	. . .	113.3	. . .	58.6
Coronary artery bypass graft.	40.0	33.6	67.2	56.2	24.6	20.0
Diagnostic procedures on small intestine.	204.1	224.6	210.0	223.2	200.8	225.5
Diagnostic procedures on large intestine.	139.2	134.4	132.0	128.4	143.2	138.0
Diagnostic radiology	262.2	139.0	291.9	150.5	245.5	132.1
Computerized axial tomography	209.0	130.4	216.9	125.7	204.5	133.2
Diagnostic ultrasound	233.3	140.1	238.2	143.1	230.6	138.2
Magnetic resonance imaging	31.6	34.3	31.7	35.0	31.5	34.0
Joint replacement of lower extremity.	123.0	169.1	94.5	148.0	139.1	181.8
Total hip replacement.	28.4	38.3	22.4	36.3	31.8	39.4
Partial hip replacement.	46.4	50.5	22.3	37.2	60.0	58.5
Total knee replacement	39.0	66.9	39.4	63.7	38.8	68.7
Reduction of fracture and dislocation	118.8	110.3	67.6	67.8	147.6	136.0
Excision or destruction of intervertebral disc and						
spinal fusion.	8.4	11.7	8.9	13.7	8.1	10.5
Excision or destruction of intervertebral disc.	8.4	10.9	8.9	12.7	8.1	9.8
Cholecystectomy.	51.6	45.4	61.7	47.4	45.9	44.2
Laparoscopic cholecystectomy	27.7	29.3	31.3	32.4	25.6	27.4
Lysis of peritoneal adhesions	29.6	27.1	21.0	24.7	34.4	28.6

* Estimates are considered unreliable. Rates for inpatient procedures preceded by an asterisk are based on 5,000–8,999 estimated procedures; those based on fewer than 5,000 are not shown. Estimates that are not shown generally have a relative standard error of greater than 30%.
. . . Category not applicable.
[1]Average number of procedures per year.
[2]Includes discharges for procedures not shown separately.
[3]Average annual rate.
[4]Estimates are age adjusted to the year 2000 standard population using five age groups: 18–44 years, 45–54 years, 55–64 years, 65–74 years, and 75 years and over. See Appendix II, Age adjustment.
[5]The procedure code for insertion of coronary artery stents (36.06) first appears in the 1996 data. A second procedure code for the insertion of drug-eluting stents (36.07) first appears in the 2003 data.
[6]Rate for female population only.
[7]Includes artificial rupture of membranes, surgical and medical induction of labor, and episiotomy.
[8]Rate for male population only.

NOTES: Excludes newborn infants. Up to four procedures were coded for each hospital discharge. If more than one procedure with the same code (e.g., a coronary artery bypass graft) was performed during the hospital stay, it was counted only once (any listed). Procedure categories are based on the *International Classification of Diseases, Ninth Revision, Clinical Modification (ICD–9-CM)*. See Appendix II, International Classification of Diseases, Ninth Revision, Clinical Modification; Procedure; Table XI. Rates are based on the civilian population as of July 1. Starting with *Health, United States, 2003*, rates for 2000 and beyond are based on the 2000 census. Rates for 1990–1999 use population estimates based on the 1990 census adjusted for net underenumeration using the 1990 National Population Adjustment Matrix from the U.S. Census Bureau. Rates for 1990–1999 are not strictly comparable with rates for 2000 and beyond because population estimates for 1990–1999 have not been revised to reflect the 2000 census. See Appendix I, National Hospital Discharge Survey; Population census and Population estimates. Numbers have been revised and differ from previous editions of *Health, United States*.

SOURCE: Centers for Disease Control and Prevention, National Center for Health Statistics, National Hospital Discharge Survey.

Table 100. Hospital admissions, average length of stay, outpatient visits, and outpatient surgery by type of ownership and size of hospital: United States, selected years 1975–2004

[Data are based on reporting by a census of hospitals]

Type of ownership and size of hospital	1975	1980	1990	1995	2000	2002	2003	2004
Admissions				Number in thousands				
All hospitals	36,157	38,892	33,774	33,282	34,891	36,326	36,611	36,942
Federal	1,913	2,044	1,759	1,559	1,034	1,027	973	1,000
Non-federal[1]	34,243	36,848	32,015	31,723	33,946	35,299	35,637	35,942
Community[2]	33,435	36,143	31,181	30,945	33,089	34,478	34,783	35,086
Nonprofit	23,722	25,566	22,878	22,557	24,453	25,425	25,668	25,757
For profit	2,646	3,165	3,066	3,428	4,141	4,365	4,481	4,599
State-local government	7,067	7,413	5,236	4,961	4,496	4,688	4,634	4,730
6–24 beds	174	159	95	124	141	162	162	182
25–49 beds	1,431	1,254	870	944	995	1,062	1,098	1,092
50–99 beds	3,675	3,700	2,474	2,299	2,355	2,471	2,464	2,451
100–199 beds	7,017	7,162	5,833	6,288	6,735	6,826	6,817	6,663
200–299 beds	6,174	6,596	6,333	6,495	6,702	6,800	6,887	6,929
300–399 beds	4,739	5,358	5,091	4,693	5,135	5,607	5,590	5,765
400–499 beds	3,689	4,401	3,644	3,413	3,617	3,593	3,591	3,821
500 beds or more	6,537	7,513	6,840	6,690	7,410	7,958	8,174	8,184
Average length of stay				Number of days				
All hospitals	11.4	9.9	9.1	7.8	6.8	6.6	6.6	6.5
Federal	20.3	16.8	14.9	13.1	12.8	11.7	11.5	11.6
Non-federal[1]	10.9	9.6	8.8	7.5	6.6	6.5	6.4	6.4
Community[2]	7.7	7.6	7.2	6.5	5.8	5.7	5.7	5.6
Nonprofit	7.8	7.7	7.3	6.4	5.7	5.6	5.5	5.5
For profit	6.6	6.5	6.4	5.8	5.4	5.3	5.3	5.4
State-local government	7.6	7.3	7.7	7.4	6.7	6.6	6.6	6.5
6–24 beds	5.6	5.3	5.4	5.5	4.2	4.1	4.0	4.1
25–49 beds	6.0	5.8	6.1	5.7	5.1	5.0	5.0	5.1
50–99 beds	6.8	6.7	7.2	7.0	6.4	6.4	6.3	6.4
100–199 beds	7.1	7.0	7.1	6.4	5.7	5.7	5.6	5.7
200–299 beds	7.5	7.4	6.9	6.2	5.7	5.5	5.4	5.4
300–399 beds	7.8	7.6	7.0	6.1	5.5	5.5	5.4	5.3
400–499 beds	8.1	7.9	7.3	6.3	5.6	5.5	5.5	5.5
500 beds or more	9.1	8.7	8.1	7.1	6.2	6.1	6.1	6.0
Outpatient visits[3]				Number in thousands				
All hospitals	254,844	262,951	368,184	483,195	592,673	640,515	648,560	662,131
Federal	51,957	50,566	58,527	59,934	63,402	75,781	74,240	79,966
Non-federal[1]	202,887	212,385	309,657	423,261	531,972	564,734	574,320	582,165
Community[2]	190,672	202,310	301,329	414,345	521,405	556,404	563,186	571,569
Nonprofit	131,435	142,156	221,073	303,851	393,168	416,910	424,215	430,262
For profit	7,713	9,696	20,110	31,940	43,378	45,215	44,246	44,962
State-local government	51,525	50,459	60,146	78,554	84,858	94,280	94,725	96,345
6–24 beds	915	1,155	1,471	3,644	4,555	5,930	6,512	7,243
25–49 beds	5,855	6,227	10,812	19,465	27,007	29,726	31,261	32,446
50–99 beds	16,303	17,976	27,582	38,597	49,385	53,342	52,959	53,051
100–199 beds	35,156	36,453	58,940	91,312	114,183	117,573	119,856	117,611
200–299 beds	32,772	36,073	60,561	84,080	99,248	102,424	100,095	99,826
300–399 beds	29,169	30,495	43,699	54,277	73,444	79,092	80,938	84,332
400–499 beds	22,127	25,501	33,394	44,284	52,205	57,841	57,203	56,122
500 beds or more	48,375	48,430	64,870	78,685	101,378	110,475	114,362	120,937
Outpatient surgery				Percent of total surgeries[4]				
Community hospitals[2]	- - -	16.3	50.5	58.1	62.7	63.4	63.3	63.3

- - - Data not available.

[1]The category of non-federal hospitals comprises psychiatric, tuberculosis and other respiratory diseases hospitals, and long-term and short-term general and other special hospitals. See Appendix II, Hospital.

[2]Community hospitals are non-federal short-term general and special hospitals whose facilities and services are available to the public. See Appendix II, Hospital.

[3]Outpatient visits include visits to the emergency department, outpatient department, referred visits (pharmacy, EKG, radiology), and outpatient surgery. See Appendix II, Outpatient visit.

[4]Total surgeries is a measure of patients with at least one surgical procedure. Persons with multiple surgical procedures are counted only once. See Appendix II, Outpatient surgery.

NOTE: Data for additional years are available. See Appendix III.

SOURCES: American Hospital Association Annual Survey of Hospitals. Hospital Statistics, 1976, 1981, 1991–2006 Editions. Chicago, IL. (Copyrights 1976, 1981, 1991–2006: Used with the permission of Health Forum LLC, an affiliate of the American Hospital Association.)

Table 101. Nursing home residents 65 years of age and over, by age, sex, and race: United States, selected years 1973–1999

[Data are based on a sample of nursing home residents]

Age, sex, and race	Residents				Residents per 1,000 population			
	1973–1974	1985	1995	1999	1973–1974	1985	1995	1999
Age								
65 years and over, age adjusted[1]	. . .	. . .	. . .	. . .	58.5	54.0	45.9	43.3
65 years and over, crude	961,500	1,318,300	1,422,600	1,469,500	44.7	46.2	42.4	42.9
65–74 years	163,100	212,100	190,200	194,800	12.3	12.5	10.1	10.8
75–84 years	384,900	509,000	511,900	517,600	57.7	57.7	45.9	43.0
85 years and over	413,600	597,300	720,400	757,100	257.3	220.3	198.6	182.5
Male								
65 years and over, age adjusted[1]	. . .	. . .	. . .	. . .	42.5	38.8	32.8	30.6
65 years and over, crude	265,700	334,400	356,800	377,800	30.0	29.0	26.1	26.5
65–74 years	65,100	80,600	79,300	84,100	11.3	10.8	9.5	10.3
75–84 years	102,300	141,300	144,300	149,500	39.9	43.0	33.3	30.8
85 years and over	98,300	112,600	133,100	144,200	182.7	145.7	130.8	116.5
Female								
65 years and over, age adjusted[1]	. . .	. . .	. . .	. . .	67.5	61.5	52.3	49.8
65 years and over, crude	695,800	983,900	1,065,800	1,091,700	54.9	57.9	53.7	54.6
65–74 years	98,000	131,500	110,900	110,700	13.1	13.8	10.6	11.2
75–84 years	282,600	367,700	367,600	368,100	68.9	66.4	53.9	51.2
85 years and over	315,300	484,700	587,300	612,900	294.9	250.1	224.9	210.5
White[2]								
65 years and over, age adjusted[1]	. . .	. . .	. . .	. . .	61.2	55.5	45.4	41.9
65 years and over, crude	920,600	1,227,400	1,271,200	1,279,600	46.9	47.7	42.3	42.1
65–74 years	150,100	187,800	154,400	157,200	12.5	12.3	9.3	10.0
75–84 years	369,700	473,600	453,800	440,600	60.3	59.1	44.9	40.5
85 years and over	400,800	566,000	663,000	681,700	270.8	228.7	200.7	181.8
Black or African American[2]								
65 years and over, age adjusted[1]	. . .	. . .	. . .	. . .	28.2	41.5	50.4	55.6
65 years and over, crude	37,700	82,000	122,900	145,900	22.0	35.0	45.2	51.1
65–74 years	12,200	22,500	29,700	30,300	11.1	15.4	18.4	18.2
75–84 years	13,400	30,600	47,300	58,700	26.7	45.3	57.2	66.5
85 years and over	12,100	29,000	45,800	56,900	105.7	141.5	167.1	183.1

. . . Category not applicable.

[1]Age adjusted to the year 2000 population standard using the following three age groups: 65–74 years, 75–84 years, and 85 years and over.

[2]Starting with 1999 data, the instruction for the race item on the Current Resident Questionnaire was changed so that more than one race could be recorded. In previous years, only one racial category could be checked. Estimates for racial groups presented in this table are for residents for whom only one race was recorded. Estimates for residents where multiple races were checked are unreliable due to small sample sizes and are not shown.

NOTES: Residents are persons on the roster of the nursing home as of the night before the survey. Residents for whom beds are maintained even though they may be away on overnight leave or in a hospital are included. Excludes residents in personal care or domiciliary care homes. See Appendix II, Nursing home. Age refers to age at time of interview. Civilian population estimates used to compute rates for the 1990s are 1990-based postcensal estimates, as of July 1. Starting with 1997 data, population figures are adjusted for net underenumeration using the 1990 National Population Adjustment Matrix from the U.S. Census Bureau. Data for additional years are available. See Appendix III.

SOURCES: Hing E, Sekscenski E, Strahan G. The National Nursing Home Survey: 1985 summary for the United States. National Center for Health Statistics. Vital Health Stat 13(97). 1989; and Centers for Disease Control and Prevention, National Center for Health Statistics, National Nursing Home Survey for other data years.

This table will be updated on the Web. Go to www.cdc.gov/nchs/hus.htm.

Table 102. Nursing home residents 65 years of age and over, by selected functional status and age, sex, and race: United States, 1985, 1995, and 1999

[Data are based on a sample of nursing home residents]

Age, sex, and race	Functional status[1] Dependent mobility 1985	1995	1999	Incontinent 1985	1995	1999	Dependent eating 1985	1995	1999	Dependent mobility, eating, and incontinent 1985	1995	1999
All persons						Percent						
65 years and over, age adjusted[2]	75.7	79.0	80.3	55.0	63.8	65.7	40.9	44.9	47.3	32.5	36.5	36.9
65 years and over, crude	74.8	79.0	80.4	54.5	63.8	65.7	40.5	44.9	47.4	32.1	36.5	37.0
65–74 years	61.2	73.0	73.9	42.9	61.9	58.5	33.5	43.8	43.1	25.7	35.8	31.7
75–84 years	70.5	76.5	77.8	55.1	62.5	64.2	39.4	45.2	46.6	30.6	35.3	35.4
85 years and over	83.3	82.4	83.8	58.1	65.3	68.6	43.9	45.0	49.0	35.6	37.5	39.4
Male												
65 years and over, age adjusted[2]	71.2	76.6	76.6	54.2	63.8	66.6	36.0	42.1	45.2	28.0	34.3	35.0
65 years and over, crude	67.8	75.8	75.9	51.9	63.9	66.0	34.9	42.7	45.1	26.9	34.8	35.0
65–74 years	55.8	70.6	70.5	38.8	63.4	59.6	32.8	44.2	45.0	24.1	36.9	34.8
75–84 years	65.7	76.6	76.9	54.4	64.6	68.9	32.6	44.1	44.7	25.5	35.5	35.2
85 years and over	79.2	78.2	78.1	58.1	63.4	66.8	39.2	40.2	45.7	30.9	32.7	34.9
Female												
65 years and over, age adjusted[2]	77.3	79.7	81.5	55.4	63.6	65.0	42.4	45.6	47.8	33.9	36.9	37.2
65 years and over, crude	77.1	80.1	81.9	55.4	63.8	65.6	42.4	45.6	48.1	33.8	37.0	37.7
65–74 years	64.5	74.8	76.4	45.4	60.9	57.7	34.0	43.6	41.6	26.7	35.0	29.3
75–84 years	72.3	76.5	78.2	55.3	61.7	62.2	42.0	45.7	47.4	32.6	35.2	35.6
85 years and over	84.3	83.3	85.2	58.1	65.7	69.0	45.0	46.0	49.7	36.7	38.6	40.4
White[3]												
65 years and over, age adjusted[2]	75.2	78.5	79.9	54.6	63.2	64.9	40.4	44.2	46.1	32.1	35.7	35.7
65 years and over, crude	74.3	78.7	80.2	54.2	63.3	65.1	40.1	44.2	46.2	31.7	35.7	35.8
65–74 years	60.2	71.4	72.6	42.2	60.2	57.1	32.6	41.9	40.7	24.9	33.8	28.8
75–84 years	69.6	76.4	77.5	54.2	61.8	63.8	38.9	44.9	45.8	30.1	34.7	34.8
85 years and over	83.1	81.9	83.6	58.2	65.0	67.8	43.5	44.3	47.7	35.5	36.9	38.1
Black or African American[3]												
65 years and over, age adjusted[2]	83.4	83.2	82.1	61.0	69.3	71.9	49.2	52.2	55.9	38.2	44.0	46.8
65 years and over, crude	81.1	82.1	81.5	59.9	69.1	70.6	47.9	51.7	54.9	37.7	43.7	45.7
65–74 years	70.9	79.6	78.7	48.6	68.3	64.6	43.1	51.2	53.3	33.8	43.1	42.6
75–84 years	82.5	77.8	80.1	70.1	68.9	67.5	47.9	49.5	49.7	40.6	42.3	41.0
85 years and over	87.4	88.0	84.5	57.9	69.8	77.0	51.7	54.3	61.0	37.6	45.5	52.1

[1]Nursing home residents who are dependent in mobility and eating require the assistance of a person or special equipment. Nursing home residents who are incontinent have difficulty in controlling bowels and/or bladder or have an ostomy or indwelling catheter.

[2]Age adjusted by the direct method to the 1995 National Nursing Home Survey population using the following three age groups: 65–74 years, 75–84 years, and 85 years and over.

[3]Starting with 1999 data, the instruction for the race item on the Current Resident Questionnaire was changed so that more than one race could be recorded. In previous years, only one racial category could be checked. Estimates for racial groups presented in this table are for residents for whom only one race was recorded. Estimates for residents where multiple races were checked are unreliable due to small sample sizes and are not shown.

NOTES: Age refers to age at time of interview. Excludes residents in personal care or domiciliary care homes. Data for additional years are available. See Appendix III.

SOURCES: Hing E, Sekscenski E, Strahan G. The National Nursing Home Survey: 1985 summary for the United States. National Center for Health Statistics. Vital Health Stat 13(97) Washington, DC: U.S. Government Printing Office, 1989; and Centers for Disease Control and Prevention, National Center for Health Statistics, National Nursing Home Survey for other data years.

Table 103. Persons employed in health service sites, by sex: United States, selected years 2000–2005

[Data are based on household interviews of a sample of the civilian noninstitutionalized population]

Site	2000	2001	2002	2003	2004	2005
Both sexes	Number of persons in thousands					
All employed civilians[1]	136,891	136,933	136,485	137,736	139,252	141,730
All health service sites[2]	12,211	12,558	13,069	13,615	13,817	14,052
Offices and clinics of physicians	1,387	1,499	1,533	1,673	1,727	1,801
Offices and clinics of dentists	672	701	734	771	780	792
Offices and clinics of chiropractors	120	111	132	142	156	163
Offices and clinics of optometrists	95	102	113	92	93	98
Offices and clinics of other health practitioners[3]	143	140	149	250	274	275
Outpatient care centers	772	830	850	873	885	901
Home health care services	548	582	636	741	750	795
Other health care services[4]	1,027	1,101	1,188	943	976	1,045
Hospitals	5,202	5,256	5,330	5,652	5,700	5,719
Nursing care facilities	1,593	1,568	1,715	1,877	1,858	1,848
Residential care facilities, without nursing	652	668	689	601	618	615
Men						
All health service sites[2]	2,756	2,778	2,838	2,986	3,067	3,097
Offices and clinics of physicians	354	379	370	414	424	418
Offices and clinics of dentists	158	150	151	163	158	156
Offices and clinics of chiropractors	32	39	47	53	63	68
Offices and clinics of optometrists	26	27	29	29	24	27
Offices and clinics of other health practitioners[3]	38	41	42	63	69	80
Outpatient care centers	186	185	172	200	203	201
Home health care services	45	51	54	56	65	81
Other health care services[4]	304	345	362	297	314	311
Hospitals	1,241	1,187	1,195	1,263	1,333	1,347
Nursing care facilities	195	189	223	267	251	246
Residential care facilities, without nursing	177	185	193	181	164	162
Women						
All health service sites[2]	9,457	9,782	10,232	10,631	10,750	10,958
Offices and clinics of physicians	1,034	1,120	1,164	1,259	1,302	1,383
Offices and clinics of dentists	514	551	584	607	623	637
Offices and clinics of chiropractors	88	72	85	90	93	95
Offices and clinics of optometrists	69	75	84	64	69	71
Offices and clinics of other health practitioners[3]	106	99	106	186	204	195
Outpatient care centers	586	646	678	673	683	700
Home health care services	503	531	582	685	685	713
Other health care services[4]	723	756	826	646	662	734
Hospitals	3,961	4,069	4,135	4,390	4,366	4,372
Nursing care facilities	1,398	1,380	1,492	1,611	1,607	1,602
Residential care facilities, without nursing	475	483	496	420	454	453
Both sexes	Percent of employed civilians					
All health service sites	8.9	9.2	9.6	9.9	9.9	9.9
	Percent distribution					
All health service sites	100.0	100.0	100.0	100.0	100.0	100.0
Offices and clinics of physicians	11.4	11.9	11.7	12.3	12.5	12.8
Offices and clinics of dentists	5.5	5.6	5.6	5.7	5.6	5.6
Offices and clinics of chiropractors	1.0	0.9	1.0	1.0	1.1	1.2
Offices and clinics of optometrists	0.8	0.8	0.9	0.7	0.7	0.7
Offices and clinics of other health practitioners[3]	1.2	1.1	1.1	1.8	2.0	2.0
Outpatient care centers	6.3	6.6	6.5	6.4	6.4	6.4
Home health care services	4.5	4.6	4.9	5.4	5.4	5.7
Other health care services[4]	8.4	8.8	9.1	6.9	7.1	7.4
Hospitals	42.6	41.9	40.8	41.5	41.3	40.7
Nursing care facilities	13.0	12.5	13.1	13.8	13.4	13.2
Residential care facilities, without nursing	5.3	5.3	5.3	4.4	4.5	4.4

[1]Excludes workers under the age of 16 years.
[2]Data for health service sites for men and women may not sum to total for all health service sites for both sexes due to rounding.
[3]Includes health service sites such as psychologists' offices, nutritionists' offices, speech defect clinics, and other offices and clinics. Complete list of clinics under this category is available from: www.census.gov/hhes/www/ioindex/cens_797_847.html, Census Industry Code 808.
[4]Includes health service sites such as clinical laboratory, blood banks, CT-SCAN (computer tomography) centers, and other offices and clinics. Complete list of clinics under this category is available from: www.census.gov/hhes/www/ioindex/cens_797_847.html, Census Industry Code 818.

NOTES: Annual data are based on data collected each month and averaged over the year. Health service sites are based on the 2002 North American Industry Classification System.

SOURCES: U.S. Department of Labor, Bureau of Labor Statistics, Current Population Survey: Employment and Earnings, January 2006, available from: www.bls.gov/cps/home.htm#annual (table 18), and unpublished data.

Table 104 (page 1 of 2). Active physicians and doctors of medicine in patient care, by geographic division and state: United States, selected years 1975–2004

[Data are based on reporting by physicians]

Geographic division and state	Total physicians[1]				Doctors of medicine in patient care[2]			
	1975	1985	1995[3]	2004[4,5]	1975	1985	1995	2004[5]
	Number per 10,000 civilian population							
United States	15.3	20.7	24.2	26.3	13.5	18.0	21.3	23.2
New England	19.1	26.7	32.5	37.2	16.9	22.9	28.8	32.6
Connecticut.	19.8	27.6	32.8	35.0	17.7	24.3	29.5	31.3
Maine.	12.8	18.7	22.3	29.6	10.7	15.6	18.2	24.0
Massachusetts	20.8	30.2	37.5	41.7	18.3	25.4	33.2	37.4
New Hampshire.	14.3	18.1	21.5	26.2	13.1	16.7	19.8	23.6
Rhode Island.	17.8	23.3	30.4	34.6	16.1	20.2	26.7	30.7
Vermont	18.2	23.8	26.9	35.1	15.5	20.3	24.2	31.9
Middle Atlantic.	19.5	26.1	32.4	35.0	17.0	22.2	28.0	29.4
New Jersey.	16.2	23.4	29.3	31.6	14.0	19.8	24.9	26.8
New York	22.7	29.0	35.3	37.1	20.2	25.2	31.6	33.0
Pennsylvania.	16.6	23.6	30.1	31.7	13.9	19.2	24.6	25.6
East North Central.	13.9	19.3	23.3	26.6	12.0	16.4	19.8	22.5
Illinois.	14.5	20.5	24.8	27.2	13.1	18.2	22.1	24.1
Indiana	10.6	14.7	18.4	21.6	9.6	13.2	16.6	19.6
Michigan.	15.4	20.8	24.8	27.1	12.0	16.0	19.0	21.3
Ohio.	14.1	19.9	23.8	27.2	12.2	16.8	20.0	23.0
Wisconsin	12.5	17.7	21.5	25.3	11.4	15.9	19.6	23.1
West North Central	13.3	18.3	21.8	25.8	11.4	15.6	18.9	21.5
Iowa.	11.4	15.6	19.2	21.0	9.4	12.4	15.1	16.6
Kansas.	12.8	17.3	20.8	23.2	11.2	15.1	18.0	20.1
Minnesota.	14.9	20.5	23.4	27.5	13.7	18.5	21.5	25.3
Missouri	15.0	20.5	23.9	25.7	11.6	16.3	19.7	21.4
Nebraska	12.1	15.7	19.8	23.5	10.9	14.4	18.3	21.6
North Dakota.	9.7	15.8	20.5	23.8	9.2	14.9	18.9	22.1
South Dakota	8.2	13.4	16.7	22.1	7.7	12.3	15.7	20.3
South Atlantic	14.0	19.7	23.4	26.4	12.6	17.6	21.0	23.6
Delaware	14.3	19.7	23.4	25.9	12.7	17.1	19.7	22.2
District of Columbia	39.6	55.3	63.6	74.2	34.6	45.6	53.6	64.2
Florida	15.2	20.2	22.9	25.1	13.4	17.8	20.3	22.2
Georgia	11.5	16.2	19.7	22.0	10.6	14.7	18.0	20.0
Maryland.	18.6	30.4	34.1	39.3	16.5	24.9	29.9	33.8
North Carolina.	11.7	16.9	21.1	24.5	10.6	15.0	19.4	22.6
South Carolina.	10.0	14.7	18.9	22.6	9.3	13.6	17.6	21.0
Virginia.	12.9	19.5	22.5	26.5	11.9	17.8	20.8	24.2
West Virginia.	11.0	16.3	21.0	24.6	10.0	14.6	17.9	20.4
East South Central	10.5	15.0	19.2	23.0	9.7	14.0	17.8	20.7
Alabama.	9.2	14.2	18.4	21.1	8.6	13.1	17.0	19.5
Kentucky.	10.9	15.1	19.2	22.7	10.1	13.9	18.0	21.0
Mississippi	8.4	11.8	13.9	18.4	8.0	11.1	13.0	16.8
Tennessee	12.4	17.7	22.5	25.4	11.3	16.2	20.8	23.4
West South Central	11.9	16.4	19.5	21.6	10.5	14.5	17.3	19.2
Arkansas	9.1	13.8	17.3	20.5	8.5	12.8	16.0	18.9
Louisiana.	11.4	17.3	21.7	25.3	10.5	16.1	20.3	23.9
Oklahoma.	11.6	16.1	18.8	20.3	9.4	12.9	14.7	15.6
Texas.	12.5	16.8	19.4	21.2	11.0	14.7	17.3	18.9
Mountain	14.3	17.8	20.2	21.2	12.6	15.7	17.8	19.8
Arizona.	16.7	20.2	21.4	22.2	14.1	17.1	18.2	18.9
Colorado.	17.3	20.7	23.7	26.6	15.0	17.7	20.6	23.3
Idaho	9.5	12.1	13.9	17.7	8.9	11.4	13.1	16.1
Montana	10.6	14.0	18.4	22.7	10.1	13.2	17.1	20.9
Nevada.	11.9	16.0	16.7	19.2	10.9	14.5	14.6	17.2
New Mexico	12.2	17.0	20.2	23.8	10.1	14.7	18.0	21.2
Utah.	14.1	17.2	19.2	21.0	13.0	15.5	17.6	19.0
Wyoming.	9.5	12.9	15.3	19.2	8.9	12.0	13.9	17.7

See footnotes at end of table.

Table 104 (page 2 of 2). Active physicians and doctors of medicine in patient care, by geographic division and state: United States, selected years 1975–2004

[Data are based on reporting by physicians]

Geographic division and state	Total physicians[1]				Doctors of medicine in patient care[2]			
	1975	1985	1995[3]	2004[4,5]	1975	1985	1995	2004[5]
	Number per 10,000 civilian population							
Pacific	17.9	22.5	23.3	26.2	16.3	20.5	21.2	23.1
Alaska	8.4	13.0	15.7	23.2	7.8	12.1	14.2	20.5
California	18.8	23.7	23.7	25.2	17.3	21.5	21.7	22.9
Hawaii	16.2	21.5	24.8	31.0	14.7	19.8	22.8	28.1
Oregon................	15.6	19.7	21.6	26.3	13.8	17.6	19.5	23.6
Washington.............	15.3	20.2	22.5	26.2	13.6	17.9	20.2	23.6

[1]Includes active doctors of medicine and active doctors of osteopathy. See Appendix II, Physician.
[2]Excludes doctors of osteopathy (DOs); states with more than 3,000 active DOs are Florida, Michigan, New York, Ohio, and Pennsylvania. States with fewer than 100 active DOs are North Dakota, South Dakota, Vermont, Wyoming, and the District of Columbia. Excludes doctors of medicine in medical teaching, administration, research, and other nonpatient care activities.
[3]Data for doctors of osteopathy are as of July 1996.
[4]Data for doctors of osteopathy are as of June 2004.
[5]Data for the year 2004 include federal and non-federal physicians. Prior to the year 2003, the data include non-federal physicians only.

NOTES: Data for doctors of medicine are as of December 31. Data for additional years are available. See Appendix III.

SOURCES: American Medical Association (AMA). Physician distribution and medical licensure in the U.S., 1975; Physician characteristics and distribution in the U.S., 1986 edition; 1996–1997 edition; 2006 edition; Department of Physician Practice and Communication Information, Division of Survey and Data Resources, AMA. (Copyrights 1976, 1986, 1997, 2006: Used with the permission of the AMA); American Osteopathic Association: 1975–76 Yearbook and Directory of Osteopathic Physicians, 1985–86 Yearbook and Directory of Osteopathic Physicians; American Association of Colleges of Osteopathic Medicine: 2004 Annual Report on Osteopathic Medical Education, 2004.

Table 105. Doctors of medicine, by activity and place of medical education: United States and outlying U.S. areas, selected years 1975–2004

[Data are based on reporting by physicians]

Activity and place of medical education	1975	1985	1995	2000	2001	2002	2003[1]	2004[1]
	Number of doctors of medicine							
Doctors of medicine	393,742	552,716	720,325	813,770	836,156	853,187	871,535	884,974
Professionally active[2]	340,280	497,140	625,443	692,368	713,375	719,431	736,211	744,143
Place of medical education:								
U.S. medical graduates	- - -	392,007	481,137	525,691	537,529	544,779	558,167	563,118
International medical graduates[3]	- - -	105,133	144,306	164,437	171,639	172,770	178,044	181,025
Activity:								
Non-federal	312,089	475,573	604,364	672,987	693,358	699,249	- - -	- - -
Patient care[4]	287,837	431,527	564,074	631,431	652,328	658,123	691,873	700,287
Office-based practice	213,334	329,041	427,275	490,398	514,016	516,246	529,836	538,538
General and family practice	46,347	53,862	59,932	67,534	70,030	71,696	73,508	73,234
Cardiovascular diseases	5,046	9,054	13,739	16,300	16,991	16,989	17,301	17,252
Dermatology	3,442	5,325	6,959	7,969	8,199	8,282	8,477	8,651
Gastroenterology	1,696	4,135	7,300	8,515	8,905	9,044	9,326	9,430
Internal medicine	28,188	52,712	72,612	88,699	94,674	96,496	99,670	101,776
Pediatrics	12,687	22,392	33,890	42,215	44,824	46,097	47,996	49,356
Pulmonary diseases	1,166	3,035	4,964	6,095	6,596	6,672	6,919	7,072
General surgery	19,710	24,708	24,086	24,475	25,632	24,902	25,284	25,229
Obstetrics and gynecology	15,613	23,525	29,111	31,726	32,582	32,738	33,636	33,811
Ophthalmology	8,795	12,212	14,596	15,598	15,994	16,052	16,240	16,304
Orthopedic surgery	8,148	13,033	17,136	17,367	17,829	18,118	18,423	18,632
Otolaryngology	4,297	5,751	7,139	7,581	7,866	8,001	8,103	8,160
Plastic surgery	1,706	3,299	4,612	5,308	5,545	5,593	5,725	5,845
Urological surgery	5,025	7,081	7,991	8,460	8,636	8,615	8,804	8,793
Anesthesiology	8,970	15,285	23,770	27,624	28,868	28,661	29,254	29,984
Diagnostic radiology	1,978	7,735	12,751	14,622	15,596	15,896	16,403	16,828
Emergency medicine	- - -	- - -	11,700	14,541	15,823	16,907	17,727	18,961
Neurology	1,862	4,691	7,623	8,559	9,156	9,034	9,304	9,632
Pathology, anatomical/clinical	4,195	6,877	9,031	10,267	10,554	10,103	10,209	10,653
Psychiatry	12,173	18,521	23,334	24,955	25,663	25,350	25,656	25,998
Radiology	6,970	7,355	5,994	6,674	6,830	6,916	7,010	6,900
Other specialty	15,320	28,453	29,005	35,314	37,233	34,084	34,861	36,037
Hospital-based practice	74,503	102,486	136,799	141,033	138,312	141,877	162,037	161,749
Residents and interns[5]	53,527	72,159	93,650	95,125	92,935	96,547	100,033	102,563
Full-time hospital staff	20,976	30,327	43,149	45,908	45,377	45,330	62,004	59,186
Other professional activity[6]	24,252	44,046	40,290	41,556	41,030	41,126	44,338	43,856
Federal	28,191	21,567	21,079	19,381	20,017	20,182	- - -	- - -
Patient care	24,100	17,293	18,057	15,999	16,611	16,701	- - -	- - -
Office-based practice	2,095	1,156	. . .	. . .	. . .	. . .	- - -	- - -
Hospital-based practice	22,005	16,137	18,057	15,999	16,611	16,701	- - -	- - -
Residents and interns	4,275	3,252	2,702	600	739	390	- - -	- - -
Full-time hospital staff	17,730	12,885	15,355	15,399	15,872	16,311	- - -	- - -
Other professional activity[6]	4,091	4,274	3,022	3,382	3,406	3,481	- - -	- - -
Inactive	21,449	38,646	72,326	75,168	81,520	84,166	84,360	92,323
Not classified	26,145	13,950	20,579	45,136	38,314	49,067	50,447	48,011
Unknown address	5,868	2,980	1,977	1,098	2,947	523	517	497

- - - Data not available.
. . . Category not applicable.
[1]Starting with 2003 data, activity data include federal and non-federal physicians.
[2]Excludes inactive, not classified, and address unknown. See Appendix II, Physician.
[3]International medical graduates received their medical education in schools outside the United States and Canada.
[4]Specialty information based on the physician's self-designated primary area of practice. Categories include generalists and specialists. See Appendix II, Physician specialty.
[5]Starting with 1990 data, clinical fellows are included in this category. In prior years clinical fellows were included in the other professional activity category.
[6]Includes medical teaching, administration, research, and other. Prior to 1990, this category also included clinical fellows.

NOTES: Data for doctors of medicine are as of December 31, except for 1990–1994 data, which are as of January 1. Outlying areas include Puerto Rico, the U.S. Virgin Islands, and the Pacific islands of Canton, Caroline, Guam, Mariana, Marshall, American Samoa, and Wake. Data for additional years are available. See Appendix III.

SOURCES: American Medical Association (AMA). Distribution of physicians in the United States, 1970; Physician distribution and medical licensure in the U.S., 1975; Physician characteristics and distribution in the U.S., 1981, 1986, 1989, 1990, 1992, 1993, 1994, 1995–1996, 1996–1997, 1997–1998, 1999, 2000–2001, 2001–2002, 2002–2003, 2003–2004, 2004, 2005, 2006 editions, Department of Physician Practice and Communications Information, Division of Survey and Data Resources, AMA. (Copyrights 1971, 1976, 1982, 1986, 1989, 1990, 1992, 1993, 1994, 1996, 1997, 1997, 1999, 2000, 2001, 2002, 2003, 2004, 2005, 2006: Used with the permission of the AMA.)

Table 106. Doctors of medicine in primary care, by specialty: United States and outlying U.S. areas, selected years 1949–2004

[Data are based on reporting by physicians]

Specialty	1949[1]	1960[1]	1970	1980	1990	1995	2000	2002	2003	2004
	Number									
Total doctors of medicine[2]	201,277	260,484	334,028	467,679	615,421	720,325	813,770	853,187	871,535	884,974
Active doctors of medicine[3]	191,577	247,257	310,929	435,545	559,988	646,022	737,504	768,498	786,658	792,154
General primary care specialists	113,222	125,359	134,354	170,705	213,514	241,329	274,653	286,294	293,701	296,495
General practice/family medicine . .	95,980	88,023	57,948	60,049	70,480	75,976	86,312	89,357	91,545	91,164
Internal medicine	12,453	26,209	39,924	58,462	76,295	88,240	101,353	106,499	109,317	111,800
Obstetrics/Gynecology.	- - -	- - -	18,532	24,612	30,220	33,519	35,922	36,810	37,725	37,779
Pediatrics.	4,789	11,127	17,950	27,582	36,519	43,594	51,066	53,628	55,114	55,752
Primary care subspecialists.	- - -	- - -	3,161	16,642	30,911	39,659	52,294	57,929	60,589	62,322
Family medicine	- - -	- - -	- - -	- - -	- - -	236	483	627	691	768
Internal medicine	- - -	- - -	1,948	13,069	22,054	26,928	34,831	38,821	40,598	41,471
Obstetrics/Gynecology.	- - -	- - -	344	1,693	3,477	4,133	4,319	4,228	4,191	4,280
Pediatrics.	- - -	- - -	869	1,880	5,380	8,362	12,661	14,253	15,109	15,803
	Percent of active doctors of medicine									
General primary care specialist	59.1	50.7	43.2	39.2	38.1	37.4	37.2	37.3	37.3	37.4
General practice/family medicine . .	50.1	35.6	18.6	13.8	12.6	11.8	11.7	11.6	11.6	11.5
Internal medicine	6.5	10.6	12.8	13.4	13.6	13.7	13.7	13.9	13.9	14.1
Obstetrics/Gynecology.	- - -	- - -	6.0	5.7	5.4	5.2	4.9	4.8	4.8	4.8
Pediatrics.	2.5	4.5	5.8	6.3	6.5	6.7	6.9	7.0	7.0	7.0
Primary care subspecialists.	- - -	- - -	1.0	3.8	5.5	6.1	7.1	7.5	7.7	7.9
Family medicine	- - -	- - -	- - -	- - -	- - -	0.0	0.1	0.1	0.1	0.1
Internal medicine	- - -	- - -	0.6	3.0	3.9	4.2	4.7	5.1	5.2	5.2
Obstetrics/Gynecology.	- - -	- - -	0.1	0.4	0.6	0.6	0.6	0.6	0.5	0.5
Pediatrics.	- - -	- - -	0.3	0.4	1.0	1.3	1.7	1.9	1.9	2.0

0.0 Percent greater than zero but less than 0.05.

- - - Data not available.

[1]Estimated by the Bureau of Health Professions, Health Resources Administration. Active doctors of medicine (M.D.s) include those with address unknown and primary specialty not classified.

[2]Includes M.D.s engaged in federal and non-federal patient care (office-based or hospital-based) and other professional activities.

[3]Starting with 1970 data, M.D.s who are inactive, have unknown address, or primary specialty not classified are excluded. See Appendix II, Physician.

NOTES: See Appendix II, Physician specialty. Data are as of December 31 except for 1990–1994 data, which are as of January 1, and 1949 data, which are as of midyear. Outlying areas include Puerto Rico, the U.S. Virgin Islands, and the Pacific islands of Canton, Caroline, Guam, Mariana, Marshall, American Samoa, and Wake. Data for additional years are available. See Appendix III.

SOURCES: Health Manpower Source Book: Medical Specialists, USDHEW, 1962; American Medical Association (AMA). Distribution of physicians in the United States, 1970; Physician characteristics and distribution in the U.S., 1981, 1992, 1996–1997, 1997–1998, 1999, 2000–2001, 2001–2002, 2002–2003, 2003–2004, 2004, 2005, 2006 editions, Department of Data Survey and Planning, Division of Survey and Data Resources, AMA. (Copyrights 1971, 1982, 1992, 1996, 1997, 1997, 1999, 2000, 2001, 2002, 2003, 2004, 2005, 2006: Used with the permission of the AMA.)

Table 107. Active health personnel, by occupation: United States, selected years 1980–2001

[Data are compiled by the Bureau of Health Professions]

Occupation	1980	1985[1]	1990	1995	1999	2000[2]	2001
	Number of active health personnel						
Chiropractors	25,600	35,000	42,400	52,100	61,500	64,100	66,800
Dentists[3]	121,900	133,500	147,500	158,600	164,700	168,000	- - -
Nurses, registered[4]	1,272,900	1,538,100	1,789,600	2,115,800	2,201,800	- - -	- - -
Associate and diploma	908,300	1,024,500	1,107,300	1,235,100	1,237,400	- - -	- - -
Baccalaureate	297,300	419,900	549,000	673,200	731,200	- - -	- - -
Masters and doctorate	67,300	93,700	133,300	207,500	229,200	- - -	- - -
Nutritionists/Dieticians	32,000	- - -	57,000	- - -	- - -	90,000	- - -
Occupational therapists	25,000	- - -	42,000	- - -	- - -	72,000	- - -
Optometrists	21,900	24,000	26,000	28,900	31,500	32,200	- - -
Pharmacists	142,400	153,500	168,000	181,000	193,400	196,000	- - -
Physical therapists	50,000	- - -	92,000	- - -	- - -	130,000	- - -
Physicians	427,122	542,653	567,610	672,859	753,176	772,296	793,263
Federal	17,642	23,305	20,784	21,153	17,338	19,228	20,017
Doctors of medicine[5]	16,585	21,938	19,166	19,830	17,224	19,110	20,017
Doctors of osteopathy[6]	1,057	1,367	1,618	1,323	114	118	- - -
Non-Federal	409,480	519,348	546,826	651,706	735,838	753,068	773,246
Doctors of medicine[5]	393,407	497,473	520,450	617,362	693,345	708,463	731,672
Doctors of osteopathy[6]	16,073	21,875	26,376	34,344	42,493	44,605	41,574
Podiatrists[7]	7,780	9,620	10,353	10,304	11,853	12,242	- - -
Speech therapists	50,000	- - -	65,000	- - -	- - -	121,000	- - -
	Number per 100,000 population						
Chiropractors	11.3	14.6	17.0	19.6	22.0	22.8	23.5
Dentists[3]	54.0	56.5	59.1	59.6	59.0	59.5	- - -
Nurses, registered[4]	560.0	641.4	716.9	794.6	789.1	- - -	- - -
Associate and diploma	399.9	425.8	443.6	463.8	443.4	- - -	- - -
Baccalaureate	130.9	175.6	219.9	252.8	262.0	- - -	- - -
Masters and doctorate	29.6	39.9	53.4	77.9	82.1	- - -	- - -
Nutritionists/Dieticians	14.0	- - -	22.8	- - -	- - -	31.9	- - -
Occupational therapists	10.9	- - -	16.8	- - -	- - -	25.5	- - -
Optometrists	9.6	10.1	10.4	10.9	11.3	11.4	- - -
Pharmacists	62.5	66.3	67.3	68.0	69.3	69.5	- - -
Physical therapists	21.8	- - -	36.9	- - -	- - -	46.1	- - -
Physicians	189.8	221.3	223.9	248.9	265.9	269.7	274.3
Federal	7.8	9.5	8.2	7.8	6.1	6.7	6.9
Doctors of medicine[5]	7.4	8.9	7.6	7.3	6.1	6.7	6.9
Doctors of osteopathy[6]	0.5	0.6	0.6	0.5	0.0	0.0	- - -
Non-Federal	182.0	211.8	215.7	241.1	259.8	263.0	267.3
Doctors of medicine[5]	174.9	202.9	205.3	228.4	244.8	247.4	253.0
Doctors of osteopathy[6]	7.1	8.9	10.4	12.7	15.0	15.6	14.4
Podiatrists[7]	3.4	4.0	4.1	3.9	4.3	4.4	- - -
Speech therapists	21.8	- - -	26.0	- - -	- - -	42.9	- - -

- - - Data not available.

[1]Osteopath, podiatric, and chiropractic data are for 1986.

[2]Data for speech therapists are for 1996.

[3]Excludes dentists in military service, U.S. Public Health Service, and Department of Veterans Affairs.

[4]See Appendix II, Nurse Supply Estimates. In 1999, the total number of registered nurses included an estimated 4,000 nurses whose highest nursing-related educational preparation was unknown.

[5]Excludes physicians with unknown addresses and those who do not practice or practice fewer than 20 hours per week. 1990 data for doctors of medicine are as of January 1; in other years these data are as of December 31. See Appendix II, Physician.

[6]Starting with 2001 data, doctors of osteopathy include federal and non-federal doctors of osteopathy.

[7]Podiatrists in patient care.

NOTE: Ratios for all health occupations are based on resident population.

SOURCES: National Center for Health Workforce Analysis, Bureau of Health Professions: United States Health Personnel FACTBOOK. Health Resources and Services Administration. Rockville, MD, June 2003 and unpublished data; American Medical Association. Physician characteristics and distribution in the U.S., 1981, 1986, 1992, 1996–1997, 2001–2002, 2002–2003, and 2003–2004 editions. Chicago, IL, 1982, 1986, 1992, 1997, 2001, 2002, and 2003; American Osteopathic Association. 1980–1981 Yearbook and Directory of Osteopathic Physicians. Chicago, IL, 1980. American Association of Colleges of Osteopathic Medicine. Annual statistical report, 1990, 1997, 1999, 2000, and 2001 editions. Rockville, MD, 1990, 1997, 2000, 2001, and 2002; Bureau of Labor Statistics: unpublished data.

Table 108. Employees and wages, by selected healthcare occupations: United States, selected years 1999–2004

[Data are based on a semi-annual mail survey of nonfarm establishments]

Occupation title	1999	2000	2002	2004	1999–2004	1999	2000	2002	2004	1999–2004
Healthcare practitioner and technical occupations	Number of employees [1]				AAPC [2]	Mean hourly wage [3]				AAPC [2]
Audiologists	12,950	11,530	10,180	9,830	−5.4	$21.96	$22.92	$24.92	$27.51	4.6
Cardiovascular Technologists and Technicians	41,490	40,080	42,870	43,320	0.9	$16.00	$16.81	$18.12	$19.60	4.1
Dental Hygienists	90,050	148,460	148,530	158,130	11.9	$23.15	$24.99	$27.78	$28.74	4.4
Diagnostic Medical Sonographers	29,280	31,760	36,530	42,500	7.7	$21.04	$22.03	$23.90	$26.36	4.6
Dietetic Technicians	29,190	28,010	28,910	24,210	−3.7	$10.09	$10.98	$11.59	$12.21	3.9
Dietitians and Nutritionists	41,320	43,030	45,150	47,820	3.0	$17.96	$18.76	$20.16	$21.87	4.0
Emergency Medical Technicians and Paramedics	172,360	165,530	178,700	191,070	2.1	$11.19	$11.89	$12.78	$13.43	3.7
Licensed Practical and Licensed Vocational Nurse	688,510	679,470	692,290	706,360	0.5	$13.95	$14.65	$15.53	$17.11	4.2
Nuclear Medicine Technologists	17,880	18,030	17,090	18,120	0.3	$20.40	$21.56	$25.13	$29.22	7.5
Occupational Therapists	78,950	75,150	78,580	86,710	1.9	$24.96	$24.10	$25.50	$27.70	2.1
Opticians, Dispensing	58,860	66,580	61,790	66,000	2.3	$12.11	$12.67	$13.38	$14.65	3.9
Pharmacists	226,300	212,660	219,390	226,200	0.0	$30.31	$33.39	$36.13	$41.78	6.6
Pharmacy Technicians	196,430	190,940	207,380	265,190	6.2	$ 9.64	$10.38	$11.15	$12.09	4.6
Physical Therapists	131,050	120,410	130,290	145,210	2.1	$28.05	$27.62	$28.93	$30.62	1.8
Physician Assistants	56,750	55,490	61,910	63,140	2.2	$24.35	$29.17	$30.53	$32.93	6.2
Psychiatric Technicians	54,560	53,350	58,600	62,960	2.9	$11.30	$12.53	$13.49	$13.80	4.1
Radiation Therapists	12,340	13,100	13,510	14,040	2.6	$20.84	$25.59	$28.90	$30.18	7.7
Radiologic Technologists and Technicians	177,850	172,080	173,540	183,960	0.7	$17.07	$17.93	$19.30	$22.07	5.3
Recreational Therapists	30,190	26,940	26,130	23,350	−5.0	$14.08	$14.23	$15.23	$16.72	3.5
Registered Nurses	2,205,430	2,189,670	2,239,530	2,338,530	1.2	$21.38	$22.31	$23.96	$26.77	4.6
Respiratory Therapists	80,230	82,670	85,350	94,500	3.3	$17.72	$18.37	$19.57	$21.79	4.2
Respiratory Therapy Technicians	33,990	28,230	26,220	21,970	−8.4	$16.07	$16.46	$16.79	$18.19	2.5
Speech-Language Pathologists	85,920	82,850	87,030	93,200	1.6	$22.99	$23.31	$24.75	$27.33	3.5
Healthcare support occupations										
Dental Assistants	175,160	250,870	268,220	268,950	9.0	$11.60	$12.86	$13.42	$14.22	4.2
Home Health Aides	577,530	561,120	569,670	625,770	1.6	$ 9.04	$ 8.71	$ 9.16	$ 9.23	0.4
Massage Therapists	21,910	24,620	27,160	34,200	9.3	$13.82	$15.51	$16.21	$17.87	5.3
Medical Assistants	281,480	330,830	361,960	369,430	5.6	$10.89	$11.46	$11.93	$12.44	2.7
Medical Equipment Preparers	29,070	32,760	35,490	40,200	6.7	$10.20	$10.68	$11.50	$12.26	3.7
Medical Transcriptionists	97,260	97,330	99,160	93,670	−0.7	$11.86	$12.37	$13.33	$14.20	3.7
Nursing Aides, Orderlies, and Attendants	1,308,740	1,273,460	1,329,310	1,395,030	1.3	$ 8.59	$ 9.18	$ 9.87	$10.53	4.2
Occupational Therapist Aides	9,250	8,890	8,040	5,390	−10.2	$10.92	$11.21	$11.78	$12.77	3.2
Occupational Therapist Assistants	17,290	15,910	17,970	21,000	4.0	$15.97	$16.76	$17.76	$18.53	3.0
Pharmacy Aides	48,270	59,890	58,020	45,630	−1.1	$ 9.14	$ 9.10	$ 9.47	$ 9.74	1.3
Physical Therapist Aides	44,340	34,620	37,330	41,430	−1.3	$ 9.69	$10.06	$10.63	$11.19	2.9
Physical Therapist Assistants	48,600	44,120	50,430	57,650	3.5	$16.20	$16.52	$17.48	$18.29	2.5
Psychiatric Aides	51,100	57,680	56,260	56,600	2.1	$10.76	$10.79	$11.42	$11.43	1.2

[1]Estimates do not include self-employed workers and were rounded to the nearest 10.
[2]Average Annual Percent Change. See Appendix II, Average Annual Rate of Change (percent change).
[3]The mean hourly wage rate for an occupation is the total wages that all workers in the occupation earn in an hour divided by the total employment of the occupation. More information is available from: www.bls.gov/oes/current/oec_tec.htm.

NOTES: This table excludes occupations such as dentists, physicians, and chiropractors, with a large percentage of workers who are self-employed and/or not employed by establishments. Data for additional years are available. See Appendix III.

SOURCE: U.S. Department of Labor. Bureau of Labor Statistics. Occupational Employment Statistics. Available from: www.bls.gov.oes.

Table 109. First-year enrollment and graduates of health professions schools, and number of schools, by selected profession: United States, selected years 1980–2004

[Data are based on reporting by health professions associations]

Profession	1980	1985	1990	1995	2000	2003	2004
First-year enrollment				Number			
Dentistry	6,132	5,047	3,979	4,121	4,314	4,448	4,618
Medicine (Allopathic)	16,930	16,997	16,756	17,085	16,856	16,953	17,035
Medicine (Osteopathic)	1,426	1,750	1,844	2,217	2,848	3,079	3,308
Nursing:							
Licensed practical	56,316	47,034	52,969	57,906	- - -	- - -	- - -
Registered, total	105,952	118,224	108,580	127,184	- - -	- - -	- - -
Baccalaureate	35,414	39,573	29,858	43,451	- - -	- - -	- - -
Associate degree	53,633	63,776	68,634	76,016	- - -	- - -	- - -
Diploma	16,905	14,875	10,088	7,717	- - -	- - -	- - -
Optometry	1,202	1,187	1,258	1,390	1,410	- - -	1,416
Pharmacy	8,035	6,986	8,267	8,740	8,382	9,909	10,437
Podiatry	695	811	561	630	475	441	519
Public Health[1]	- - -	- - -	4,392	5,332	5,840	6,786	8,340
Graduates							
Dentistry	5,256	5,353	4,233	3,908	4,171	4,443	4,350
Medicine (Allopathic)	15,113	16,318	15,398	15,883	15,718	15,499	15,821
Medicine (Osteopathic)	1,059	1,474	1,529	1,843	2,279	2,607	2,713
Nursing:[2]							
Licensed practical	41,892	36,955	35,417	44,234	- - -	- - -	- - -
Registered, total	75,523	82,075	66,088	97,052	- - -	- - -	- - -
Baccalaureate	24,994	24,975	18,571	31,254	- - -	- - -	- - -
Associate degree	36,034	45,208	42,318	58,749	- - -	- - -	- - -
Diploma	14,495	11,892	5,199	7,049	- - -	- - -	- - -
Occupational therapy	- - -	- - -	2,424	3,473	- - -	- - -	- - -
Optometry	1,073	1,114	1,115	1,219	1,315	1,305	1,289
Pharmacy	7,432	5,735	6,956	7,837	7,260	7,488	8,158
Podiatry	597	582	679	558	583	436	386
Public Health	3,326	3,047	3,549	4,636	5,879	5,906	6,399
Schools							
Dentistry	60	60	58	54	55	56	56
Medicine (Allopathic)	126	127	127	125	125	126	125
Medicine (Osteopathic)	14	15	15	16	19	19	20
Nursing:[3]							
Licensed practical	1,299	1,165	1,154	1,210	- - -	- - -	- - -
Registered, total	1,385	1,473	1,470	1,516	- - -	- - -	- - -
Baccalaureate	377	441	489	521	- - -	- - -	- - -
Associate degree	697	776	829	876	- - -	- - -	- - -
Diploma	311	256	152	119	- - -	- - -	- - -
Occupational therapy	50	61	69	98	142	- - -	- - -
Optometry	16	17	17	17	17	17	17
Pharmacy	72	72	74	75	81	89	89
Podiatry	5	7	7	7	7	7	7
Public Health	21	23	25	27	28	33	36

- - - Data not available.

[1]Number of students entering Schools of Public Health for the first time. Starting with 2003–2004 data, first-year enrollment data for public health schools include Spring, Summer, and Fall enrollment. Prior to 2003–2004, the data are for Fall enrollment only and are not directly comparable to 2003–2004 data.

[2]Data for 2000–2002 exclude American Samoa, Guam, Puerto Rico, and the Virgin Islands.

[3]Some nursing schools offer more than one type of program. Numbers shown for nursing are number of nursing programs.

NOTES: Some numbers in this table have been revised and differ from previous editions of *Health, United States*. Data on the number of schools are reported as of the beginning of the academic year while data on first-year enrollment and number of graduates are reported as of the end of the academic year. Optometry and Podiatry data on first-year enrollment are reported as of the beginning of the academic year. Data for additional years are available. See Appendix III.

SOURCES: Association of American Medical Colleges: AAMC Data Book, Statistical Information Related to Medical Schools and Teaching Hospitals, Washington, DC. 2004, 2005, (Copyright 2005, 2006: Used with the permission of the AAMC) and unpublished data. Bureau of Health Professions: United States Health Personnel FACTBOOK. Health Resources and Services Administration. Rockville, MD. 2003; National League for Nursing: unpublished data; American Dental Association: 2003–2004 Survey of Predoctoral Dental Education, vol. 1, Academic Programs, Enrollments, and Graduates, Chicago, IL. 2005 (Copyright 2006: Used with the permission of the ADA) and unpublished data. Available from: www.adea.org/ADEA.html; American Association of Colleges of Osteopathic Medicine. 2004 Annual Report on Osteopathic Medical Education, Chevy Chase, MD. 2005, available from: www.aacom.org/data/annualreport/index.html; Association of Schools of Public Health: 2004 Annual Data Report. Washington, DC. 2005, available from: www.asph.org/userfiles/ADR2004/pdf; Association of Schools and Colleges of Optometry: Annual Student Data Report Academic Year 2004–2005 and unpublished data; American Association of Colleges of Pharmacy: Academic Pharmacy's Vital Statistics, 2004 and unpublished data; American Association of Colleges of Podiatric Medicine: unpublished data; American Medical Association: Health Professions Career and Education Directory, 29th edition. Chicago, IL. 2001.

Table 110 (page 1 of 2). Total enrollment of minorities in schools for selected health occupations, by race and Hispanic origin: United States, selected academic years 1980–1981 through 2003–2004

[Data are based on reporting by health professions associations]

Occupation, race, and Hispanic origin	1980–1981	1990–1991	2003–2004	1980–1981	1990–1991	2003–2004
Dentistry	Number of students			Percent distribution of students		
All races	22,842	15,951	17,978	100.0	100.0	100.0
Not Hispanic or Latino:						
White[1]	19,947	11,185	11,789	87.3	70.1	65.6
Black or African American	1,022	940	972	4.5	5.9	5.4
Hispanic or Latino[2]	780	1,254	1,058	3.4	7.9	5.9
American Indian or Alaska Native	53	53	77	0.2	0.3	0.4
Asian or Pacific Islander	1,040	2,519	4,082	4.6	15.8	22.7
Medicine (Allopathic)[3]						
All races[1]	65,189	65,163	67,013	100.0	100.0	100.0
Not Hispanic or Latino:						
White	55,434	47,893	42,241	85.0	73.5	63.0
Black or African American	3,708	4,241	4,945	5.7	6.5	7.4
Hispanic or Latino	2,761	3,538	4,508	4.2	5.4	6.7
Mexican	951	1,109	1,619	1.5	1.7	2.4
Mainland Puerto Rican	329	457	- - -	0.5	0.7	0.0
Other Hispanic or Latino[4]	1,481	1,972	2,889	2.3	3.0	4.3
American Indian or Alaska Native[5]	221	277	627	0.3	0.4	0.9
Asian or Pacific Islander	1,924	8,436	13,601	3.0	12.9	20.3
Medicine (Osteopathic)						
All races[1]	4,940	6,792	11,857	100.0	100.0	100.0
Not Hispanic or Latino:						
White	4,688	5,680	8,748	94.9	83.6	73.8
Black or African American	94	217	425	1.9	3.2	3.6
Hispanic or Latino	52	277	420	1.1	4.1	3.5
American Indian or Alaska Native	19	36	81	0.4	0.5	0.7
Asian or Pacific Islander	87	582	1,822	1.8	8.6	15.4
Nursing, registered[6]						
All races	230,966	221,170	- - -	- - -	100.0	- - -
Not Hispanic or Latino:						
White[1]	- - -	183,102	- - -	- - -	82.8	- - -
Black or African American	- - -	23,094	- - -	- - -	10.4	- - -
Hispanic or Latino	- - -	6,580	- - -	- - -	3.0	- - -
American Indian or Alaska Native	- - -	1,803	- - -	- - -	0.8	- - -
Asian or Pacific Islander	- - -	6,591	- - -	- - -	3.0	- - -
Optometry						
All races[1]	4,641	4,760	5,354	100.0	100.0	100.0
Not Hispanic or Latino:						
White	4,221	3,706	3,230	91.0	77.9	60.3
Black or African American	57	134	171	1.2	2.8	3.2
Hispanic or Latino	108	296	302	2.3	6.2	5.6
American Indian or Alaska Native	12	21	35	0.3	0.4	0.7
Asian or Pacific Islander	243	603	1,254	5.2	12.7	23.4
Pharmacy[7]						
All races[1]	21,628	29,797	43,047	100.0	100.0	100.0
Not Hispanic or Latino:						
White	19,153	21,717	25,121	88.6	80.5	58.4
Black or African American	945	2,103	4,183	4.4	5.7	9.7
Hispanic or Latino	459	1,118	1,605	2.1	4.2	3.7
American Indian or Alaska Native	36	85	191	0.2	0.3	0.4
Asian or Pacific Islander	1,035	3,346	8,991	4.8	9.4	20.9

See footnotes at end of table.

Table 110 (page 2 of 2). Total enrollment of minorities in schools for selected health occupations, by race and Hispanic origin: United States, selected academic years 1980–1981 through 2003–2004

[Data are based on reporting by health professions associations]

Occupation, race, and Hispanic origin	1980–1981	1990–1991	2003–2004	1980–1981	1990–1991	2003–2004
Podiatry	Number of students			Percent distribution of students		
All races[1]	2,577	2,221	1,578	100.0	100.0	100.0
Not Hispanic or Latino:						
White.	2,353	1,671	926	91.3	75.2	58.7
Black or African American	110	235	221	4.3	10.6	14.0
Hispanic or Latino	39	149	121	1.5	6.7	7.7
American Indian or Alaska Native	6	7	11	0.2	0.3	0.7
Asian or Pacific Islander	69	159	189	2.7	7.2	12.0

- - - Data not available.

[1]Includes other and unknown races; may also include foreign students.

[2]Includes students from the University of Puerto Rico.

[3]Starting with 2002–2003 data, allopathic medical students had the option of reporting both their race and ethnicity alone or in combination with some other race or ethnicity. Therefore, the data for 2003–2004 and beyond are not directly comparable to earlier years.

[4]Includes the Commonwealth of Puerto Rico students.

[5]Starting with 1997–1998 data, includes American Indian, Alaska Native, and Native Hawaiian; prior to 1997, included only American Indian and Alaska Native.

[6]In 1990, the National League for Nursing developed a new system for analyzing minority data. An evaluation of the former system revealed considerable underreporting. Therefore, race-specific data before 1990 would not be comparable and are not shown. Additional changes in the minority data question were introduced for academic years 2000–2001 and 2001–2002, resulting in a discontinuity in the trend.

[7]Prior to 1992–1993, pharmacy total enrollment data were for students in the final three years of pharmacy education. Starting with 1992–1993 data, pharmacy data are for all students.

NOTES: Total enrollment data are collected at the beginning of the academic year. Data for chiropractic students, occupational and physical therapy students, and public health students were not available for this table. Some numbers have been revised and differ from previous editions of *Health, United States*. Data for additional years are available. See Appendix III.

SOURCES: Bureau of Health Professions: Minorities and Women in the Health Fields, 1990 Edition; Association of American Medical Colleges: AAMC Data Book: Statistical Information Related to Medical Education. Washington, DC. 2005 (Copyright 2006: Used with the permission of the AAMC); American Association of Colleges of Osteopathic Medicine: 2004 Annual Report on Osteopathic Medical Education. Chevy Chase, MD. 2005. Available from: www.aacom.org/data/annualreport/AROME2004.pdf; American Dental Education Association: Dental Education At-A-Glance 2004, available from: www.adea.org/ADEA.html and unpublished data; Association of Schools and Colleges of Optometry: Annual Student Data Report Academic Year 2002–2004, 2005–2006, and unpublished data (Copyright 2005, 2006: Used with the permission of the AAMC); American Association of Colleges of Pharmacy: Profile of Pharmacy Students, Fall 2005, available from: http://www.aacp.org; American Association of Colleges of Podiatric Medicine: unpublished data; National League for Nursing: unpublished data.

Table 111. First-year and total enrollment of women in schools for selected health occupations: United States, selected academic years 1980–1981 through 2003–2004

[Data are based on reporting by health professions associations]

Enrollment and occupation	Both sexes			Women		
	1980–1981	1990–1991	2003–2004[1]	1980–1981	1990–1991[2]	2003–2004[1]
First-year enrollment	Number of students			Percent of students		
Dentistry	6,030	4,001	4,618	19.8	38.0	43.5
Medicine (Allopathic)	17,186	16,876	17,035	28.9	38.8	49.7
Medicine (Osteopathic)	1,496	1,950	3,308	22.0	34.2	50.2
Nurses, registered[3]	110,201	113,526	- - -	92.7	89.3	- - -
Optometry	1,258	1,239	1,416	25.3	50.6	62.7
Pharmacy[4]	7,377	8,267	9,909	48.4	- - -	67.3
Podiatry	695	561	441	- - -	28.0	46.0
Public Health[5]	3,348	4,289	8,340	- - -	62.1	69.2
Total enrollment						
Dentistry	22,842	15,951	17,978	17.0	34.4	43.2
Medicine (Allopathic)[3]	65,189	65,163	67,013	26.5	37.3	47.9
Medicine (Osteopathic)	4,940	6,792	11,857	19.7	32.7	46.9
Nurses, registered[4]	230,966	221,170	- - -	94.3	- - -	- - -
Optometry	4,641	4,760	5,354	- - -	47.3	60.4
Pharmacy	26,617	29,797	43,047	47.4	62.4	66.9
Podiatry	2,577	2,154	1,578	11.9	28.9	44.7
Public Health[5]	8,486	11,386	19,003	55.2	62.5	68.5

- - - Data not available.

[1]Starting with 2003–2004 data, osteophathic medicine data include the Edward Via Virginia College of Osteopathic Medicine's first class of 154 students, including 74 women.
[2]Percentage of women podiatry students is for 1991–1992.
[3]Excludes American Samoa, Guam, Puerto Rico, and the U.S. Virgin Islands.
[4]First-year enrollment data for pharmacy schools are for students in the first year of the final three years of pharmacy education. Prior to 1992–1993, pharmacy total enrollment data were for students in the final three years of pharmacy education. Starting in 1992–1993, pharmacy total enrollment data are for all students.
[5]Starting with 2003–2004 data, first-year enrollment data for public health schools include Spring, Summer, and Fall enrollment.
Prior to 2003–2004, the data are for Fall enrollment only and are not directly comparable to 2003–2004 data.

NOTES: Total enrollment data are collected at the beginning of the academic year while first-year enrollment data are collected during the academic year. Data for chiropractic students and occupational, physical, and speech therapy students were not available for this table. Some numbers in this table have been revised and differ from previous editions of Health, United States. Data for additional years are available. See Appendix III.

SOURCES: Association of American Medical Colleges: AAMC Data Book: Statistical Information Related to Medical Education. Washington, DC. 2004, 2005 (Copyright 2005, 2006: Used with the permission of the AAMC); American Association of Colleges of Osteopathic Medicine: 2004 Annual Report on Osteopathic Medical Education. Chevy Chase, MD. 2005, available from: www.aacom.org/data/annualreport/index.html; Bureau of Health Professions: Minorities and Women in the Health Fields, 1990 edition; American Dental Association: 2003–2004 Survey of Dental Education, vol.1, Academic Programs, Enrollments, and Graduates, Chicago, IL. 2005 (Copyright 2006: Used with the permission of the ADA) and unpublished data; Association of Schools and Colleges of Optometry: Annual Student Data Report Academic Year 2003–04 and unpublished data; American Association of Colleges of Pharmacy: Profile of Pharmacy Students, Fall 2003, available from: www.aacp.org, and unpublished data; American Association of Colleges of Podiatric Medicine: unpublished data; National League for Nursing: Nursing Data Review. New York, NY. 1997; Nursing data book. New York, NY. 1982 and unpublished data; State-Approved Schools of Nursing-RN. New York, NY. 1973; Association of Schools of Public Health: 2004 Annual Data Report. Washington, DC. 2005, available from: www.asph.org/userfiles/ADR2004.pdf.

Table 112. Hospitals, beds, and occupancy rates, by type of ownership and size of hospital: United States, selected years 1975–2004

[Data are based on reporting by a census of hospitals]

Type of ownership and size of hospital	1975	1980	1990	1995	2000	2003	2004
Hospitals				Number			
All hospitals	7,156	6,965	6,649	6,291	5,810	5,764	5,759
Federal	382	359	337	299	245	239	239
Non-federal[1]	6,774	6,606	6,312	5,992	5,565	5,525	5,520
Community[2]	5,875	5,830	5,384	5,194	4,915	4,895	4,919
Nonprofit	3,339	3,322	3,191	3,092	3,003	2,984	2,967
For profit	775	730	749	752	749	790	835
State-local government	1,761	1,778	1,444	1,350	1,163	1,121	1,117
6–24 beds	299	259	226	278	288	327	352
25–49 beds	1,155	1,029	935	922	910	965	988
50–99 beds	1,481	1,462	1,263	1,139	1,055	1,031	1,028
100–199 beds	1,363	1,370	1,306	1,324	1,236	1,168	1,141
200–299 beds	678	715	739	718	656	624	621
300–399 beds	378	412	408	354	341	349	351
400–499 beds	230	266	222	195	182	172	185
500 beds or more	291	317	285	264	247	256	253
Beds							
All hospitals	1,465,828	1,364,516	1,213,327	1,080,601	983,628	965,256	955,768
Federal	131,946	117,328	98,255	77,079	53,067	47,456	47,386
Non-federal[1]	1,333,882	1,247,188	1,115,072	1,003,522	930,561	917,800	908,382
Community[2]	941,844	988,387	927,360	872,736	823,560	813,307	808,127
Nonprofit	658,195	692,459	656,755	609,729	582,988	574,587	567,863
For profit	73,495	87,033	101,377	105,737	109,883	109,671	112,693
State-local government	210,154	208,895	169,228	157,270	130,689	129,049	127,571
6–24 beds	5,615	4,932	4,427	5,085	5,156	5,635	6,030
25–49 beds	41,783	37,478	35,420	34,352	33,333	33,613	33,206
50–99 beds	106,776	105,278	90,394	82,024	75,865	74,025	73,606
100–199 beds	192,438	192,892	183,867	187,381	175,778	167,451	162,914
200–299 beds	164,405	172,390	179,670	175,240	159,807	152,487	151,197
300–399 beds	127,728	139,434	138,938	121,136	117,220	119,903	120,509
400–499 beds	101,278	117,724	98,833	86,459	80,763	76,333	82,071
500 beds or more	201,821	218,259	195,811	181,059	175,638	183,860	178,594
Occupancy rate[3]				Percent			
All hospitals	76.7	77.7	69.5	65.7	66.1	68.1	68.9
Federal	80.7	80.1	72.9	72.6	68.2	64.8	67.2
Non-federal[1]	76.3	77.4	69.2	65.1	65.9	68.3	69.0
Community[2]	75.0	75.6	66.8	62.8	63.9	66.2	67.0
Nonprofit	77.5	78.2	69.3	64.5	65.5	67.7	68.3
For profit	65.9	65.2	52.8	51.8	55.9	59.6	60.5
State-local government	70.4	71.1	65.3	63.7	63.2	65.3	66.4
6–24 beds	48.0	46.8	32.3	36.9	31.7	31.9	33.8
25–49 beds	56.7	52.8	41.3	42.6	41.3	44.6	45.8
50–99 beds	64.7	64.2	53.8	54.1	54.8	57.2	58.0
100–199 beds	71.2	71.4	61.5	58.8	60.0	62.6	63.5
200–299 beds	77.1	77.4	67.1	63.1	65.0	67.0	67.2
300–399 beds	79.7	79.7	70.0	64.8	65.7	68.5	69.7
400–499 beds	81.1	81.2	73.5	68.1	69.1	70.7	70.4
500 beds or more	80.9	82.1	77.3	71.4	72.2	74.2	75.3

[1]The category of non-federal hospitals comprises psychiatric, tuberculosis and other respiratory diseases hospitals, and long-term and short-term general and other special hospitals. See Appendix II, Hospital.
[2]Community hospitals are non-federal short-term general and special hospitals whose facilities and services are available to the public. See Appendix II, Hospital.
[3]Estimated percentage of staffed beds that are occupied. See Appendix II, Occupancy rate.

NOTE: Data for additional years are available. See Appendix III.

SOURCES: American Hospital Association Annual Survey of Hospitals. Hospital Statistics, 1976, 1981, 1991–2005 editions. Chicago, IL. (Copyrights 1976, 1981, 1991–2006: Used with the permission of Health Forum LLC, an affiliate of the American Hospital Association.)

Table 113. Mental health organizations and beds for 24-hour hospital and residential treatment, by type of organization: United States, selected years 1986–2002

[Data are based on inventories of mental health organizations]

Type of organization	1986	1990	1994[1]	1998	2000	2002
	Number of mental health organizations					
All organizations.	4,747	5,284	5,392	5,722	4,541	4,301
State and county mental hospitals	285	273	256	229	223	222
Private psychiatric hospitals.	314	462	430	348	269	253
Non-federal general hospital psychiatric services. . . .	1,351	1,674	1,612	1,707	1,373	1,285
Department of Veterans Affairs medical centers[2]	139	141	161	145	142	140
Residential treatment centers for emotionally disturbed children.	437	501	459	461	475	508
All other organizations[3].	2,221	2,233	2,474	2,832	2,059	1,893
	Number of beds					
All organizations.	267,613	272,253	290,604	267,796	212,621	211,199
State and county mental hospitals	119,033	98,789	81,911	68,872	60,675	57,263
Private psychiatric hospitals.	30,201	44,871	42,399	33,408	26,484	25,095
Non-federal general hospital psychiatric services. . . .	45,808	53,479	52,984	54,434	39,690	40,202
Department of Veterans Affairs medical centers[2]	26,874	21,712	21,146	16,973	9,363	9,672
Residential treatment centers for emotionally disturbed children.	24,547	29,756	32,110	31,965	33,375	39,049
All other organizations[3].	21,150	23,646	60,054	62,144	43,034	39,918
	Beds per 100,000 civilian population[4]					
All organizations.	111.7	111.6	112.1	99.5	75.4	73.3
State and county mental hospitals	49.7	40.5	31.6	25.6	21.5	19.9
Private psychiatric hospitals.	12.6	18.4	16.4	12.4	9.4	8.7
Non-federal general hospital psychiatric services. . . .	19.1	21.9	20.4	20.2	14.1	14.0
Department of Veterans Affairs medical centers[2]	11.2	8.9	8.2	6.3	3.3	3.4
Residential treatment centers for emotionally disturbed children.	10.3	12.2	12.4	11.9	11.8	13.6
All other organizations[3].	8.8	9.7	23.2	23.1	15.3	13.9

[1]Starting with 1994 data, supportive residential clients (moderately staffed housing arrangements such as supervised apartments, group homes, and halfway houses) are included in the totals and all other organizations. This change affects the comparability of trend data prior to 1994 with data for 1994 and later years.
[2]Includes Department of Veterans Affairs (VA) neuropsychiatric hospitals, VA general hospital psychiatric services, and VA psychiatric outpatient clinics.
[3]Includes freestanding psychiatric outpatient clinics, partial care organizations, and multiservice mental health organizations. See Appendix I, Survey of Mental Health Organizations.
[4]Civilian population estimates for 2000 and beyond are based on the 2000 census as of July 1; population estimates for 1992–1998 are 1990 postcensal estimates.

NOTES: Data for 2000 are revised and differ from the previous edition of *Health, United States*. These data exclude mental health care provided in nonpsychiatric units of hospitals such as general medical units. See Appendix II, Mental health organization. Data for additional years are available. See Appendix III.

SOURCES: Substance Abuse and Mental Health Services Administration, Center for Mental Health Services (CMHS). Manderscheid RW and Henderson MJ. *Mental Health, United States, 2002*. Washington, DC: U.S. Government Printing Office, 2004; and Survey of Mental Health Organizations, unpublished data.

Table 114. Community hospital beds and average annual percentage change, by geographic division and state: United States, selected years 1960–2004

[Data are based on reporting by a census of hospitals]

Geographic division and state	1960[1,2]	1970[1]	1980[1]	1990[3]	2000[3]	2004[3]	1960–1970[1,2]	1970–1980[1]	1980–1990[4]	1990–2000[3]	2000–2004[3]
	Beds per 1,000 resident population[5]						Average annual percent change				
United States	3.6	4.3	4.5	3.7	2.9	2.8	1.8	0.5	−1.9	−2.4	−0.9
New England	3.9	4.1	4.1	3.4	2.5	2.4	0.5	0.0	−1.9	−3.0	−1.0
Connecticut	3.4	3.4	3.5	2.9	2.3	2.2	0.0	0.3	−1.9	−2.3	−1.1
Maine	3.4	4.7	4.7	3.7	2.9	2.7	3.3	0.0	−2.4	−2.4	−1.8
Massachusetts	4.2	4.4	4.4	3.6	2.6	2.5	0.5	0.0	−2.0	−3.2	−1.0
New Hampshire	4.4	4.0	3.9	3.1	2.3	2.2	−0.9	−0.3	−2.3	−2.9	−1.1
Rhode Island	3.7	4.0	3.8	3.2	2.3	2.2	0.8	−0.5	−1.7	−3.2	−1.1
Vermont	4.5	4.5	4.4	3.0	2.7	2.4	0.0	−0.2	−3.8	−1.0	−2.9
Middle Atlantic	4.0	4.4	4.6	4.1	3.4	3.1	1.0	0.4	−1.1	−1.9	−2.3
New Jersey	3.1	3.6	4.2	3.7	3.0	2.5	1.5	1.6	−1.3	−2.1	−4.5
New York	4.3	4.6	4.5	4.1	3.5	3.3	0.7	−0.2	−0.9	−1.6	−1.5
Pennsylvania	4.1	4.7	4.8	4.4	3.4	3.2	1.4	0.2	−0.9	−2.5	−1.5
East North Central	3.6	4.4	4.7	3.9	2.9	2.8	2.0	0.7	−1.8	−2.9	−0.9
Illinois	4.0	4.7	5.1	4.0	3.0	2.7	1.6	0.8	−2.4	−2.8	−2.6
Indiana	3.1	4.0	4.5	3.9	3.2	3.0	2.6	1.2	−1.4	−2.0	−1.6
Michigan	3.3	4.3	4.4	3.7	2.6	2.6	2.7	0.2	−1.7	−3.5	0.0
Ohio	3.4	4.2	4.7	4.0	3.0	2.9	2.1	1.1	−1.6	−2.8	−0.8
Wisconsin	4.3	5.2	4.9	3.8	2.9	2.6	1.9	−0.6	−2.5	−2.7	−2.7
West North Central	4.3	5.7	5.8	4.9	3.9	3.7	2.9	0.2	−1.7	−2.3	−1.3
Iowa	3.9	5.6	5.7	5.1	4.0	3.7	3.7	0.2	−1.1	−2.4	−1.9
Kansas	4.2	5.4	5.8	4.8	4.0	3.8	2.5	0.7	−1.9	−1.8	−1.3
Minnesota	4.8	6.1	5.7	4.4	3.4	3.2	2.4	−0.7	−2.6	−2.5	−1.5
Missouri	3.9	5.1	5.7	4.8	3.6	3.3	2.7	1.1	−1.7	−2.8	−2.2
Nebraska	4.4	6.2	6.0	5.5	4.8	4.2	3.5	−0.3	−0.9	−1.4	−3.3
North Dakota	5.2	6.8	7.4	7.0	6.0	5.6	2.7	0.8	−0.6	−1.5	−1.7
South Dakota	4.5	5.6	5.5	6.1	5.7	6.0	2.2	−0.2	1.0	−0.7	1.3
South Atlantic	3.3	4.0	4.5	3.7	2.9	2.7	1.9	1.2	−1.9	−2.4	−1.8
Delaware	3.7	3.7	3.6	3.0	2.3	2.4	0.0	−0.3	−1.8	−2.6	1.1
District of Columbia	5.9	7.4	7.3	7.6	5.8	6.2	2.3	−0.1	0.4	−2.7	1.7
Florida	3.1	4.4	5.1	3.9	3.2	2.9	3.6	1.5	−2.6	−2.0	−2.4
Georgia	2.8	3.8	4.6	4.0	2.9	2.8	3.1	1.9	−1.4	−3.2	−0.9
Maryland	3.3	3.1	3.6	2.8	2.1	2.1	−0.6	1.5	−2.5	−2.8	0.0
North Carolina	3.4	3.8	4.2	3.3	2.9	2.8	1.1	1.0	−2.4	−1.3	−0.9
South Carolina	2.9	3.7	3.9	3.3	2.9	2.7	2.5	0.5	−1.7	−1.3	−1.8
Virginia	3.0	3.7	4.1	3.3	2.4	2.3	2.1	1.0	−2.1	−3.1	−1.1
West Virginia	4.1	5.4	5.5	4.7	4.4	4.1	2.8	0.2	−1.6	−0.7	−1.7
East South Central	3.0	4.4	5.1	4.7	3.8	3.7	3.9	1.5	−0.8	−2.1	−0.7
Alabama	2.8	4.3	5.1	4.6	3.7	3.4	4.4	1.7	−1.0	−2.2	−2.1
Kentucky	3.0	4.0	4.5	4.3	3.7	3.7	2.9	1.2	−0.5	−1.5	0.0
Mississippi	2.9	4.4	5.3	5.0	4.8	4.5	4.3	1.9	−0.6	−0.4	−1.6
Tennessee	3.4	4.7	5.5	4.8	3.6	3.5	3.3	1.6	−1.4	−2.8	−0.7
West South Central	3.3	4.3	4.7	3.8	3.0	2.9	2.7	0.9	−2.1	−2.3	−0.8
Arkansas	2.9	4.2	5.0	4.6	3.7	3.5	3.8	1.8	−0.8	−2.2	−1.4
Louisiana	3.9	4.2	4.8	4.6	3.9	3.8	0.7	1.3	−0.4	−1.6	−0.6
Oklahoma	3.2	4.5	4.6	4.0	3.2	3.1	3.5	0.2	−1.4	−2.2	−0.8
Texas	3.3	4.3	4.7	3.5	2.7	2.6	2.7	0.9	−2.9	−2.6	−0.9
Mountain	3.5	4.3	3.8	3.1	2.3	2.2	2.1	−1.2	−2.0	−2.9	−1.1
Arizona	3.0	4.1	3.6	2.7	2.1	1.9	3.2	−1.3	−2.8	−2.5	−2.5
Colorado	3.8	4.6	4.2	3.2	2.2	2.0	1.9	−0.9	−2.7	−3.7	−2.4
Idaho	3.2	4.0	3.7	3.2	2.7	2.5	2.3	−0.8	−1.4	−1.7	−1.9
Montana	5.1	5.8	5.9	5.8	4.7	4.7	1.3	0.2	−0.2	−2.1	0.0
Nevada	3.9	4.2	4.2	2.8	1.9	2.0	0.7	0.0	−4.0	−3.8	1.3
New Mexico	2.9	3.5	3.1	2.8	1.9	1.9	1.9	−1.2	−1.0	−3.8	0.0
Utah	2.8	3.6	3.1	2.6	1.9	1.9	2.5	−1.5	−1.7	−3.1	0.0
Wyoming	4.6	5.5	3.6	4.8	3.9	4.0	1.8	−4.1	2.9	−2.1	0.6
Pacific	3.1	3.7	3.5	2.7	2.1	2.0	1.8	−0.6	−2.6	−2.5	−1.2
Alaska	2.4	2.3	2.7	2.3	2.3	2.2	−0.4	1.6	−1.6	0.0	−1.1
California	3.0	3.8	3.6	2.7	2.1	2.0	2.4	−0.5	−2.8	−2.5	−1.2
Hawaii	3.7	3.4	3.1	2.7	2.5	2.5	−0.8	−0.9	−1.4	−0.8	0.0
Oregon	3.5	4.0	3.5	2.8	1.9	1.8	1.3	−1.3	−2.2	−3.8	−1.3
Washington	3.3	3.5	3.1	2.5	1.9	1.8	0.6	−1.2	−2.1	−2.7	−1.3

[1]Data exclude facilities for the mentally retarded. See Appendix II, Hospital.   [2]1960 data include hospital units of institutions such as prisons and college infirmaries.
[3]Starting with 1990 data, hospital units of institutions, facilities for the mentally retarded, and alcoholism and chemical dependency hospitals are excluded. See Appendix II, Hospital.
[4]1990 data used in this calculation (not shown in table) exclude only facilities for the mentally retarded, consistent with exclusions from 1980 data.
[5]Civilian population for 1997 and earlier years.

NOTE: Data for additional years are available. See Appendix III.

SOURCES: American Hospital Association (AHA): Hospitals. JAHA 35(15):383–430, 1961 (Copyright 1961: Used with permission of AHA); National Center for Health Statistics, Division of Health Care Statistics and AHA Annual Survey of Hospitals for 1970, 1980; Hospital Statistics 1991–1992, 2001–2006 Editions. Chicago, IL. (Copyrights 1971, 1981, 1991, 2001–2006: Used with permission of Health Forum LLC, an affiliate of the American Hospital Association.)

Table 115. Occupancy rates in community hospitals and average annual percent change, by geographic division and State: United States, selected years 1960–2004

[Data are based on reporting by a census of hospitals]

Geographic division and state	1960[1,2]	1970[1]	1980[1]	1990[3]	2000[3]	2004[3]	1960–1970[1,2]	1970–1980[1]	1980–1990[4]	1990–2000[3]	2000–2004[3]
	Occupancy rate[5]						Average annual percent change				
United States	75	77	75	67	64	67	0.3	−0.3	−1.1	−0.5	1.2
New England	75	80	80	74	70	73	0.6	0.0	−0.8	−0.6	1.1
Connecticut	78	83	80	77	75	79	0.6	−0.4	−0.4	−0.3	1.3
Maine	73	73	75	72	64	63	0.0	0.3	−0.4	−1.2	−0.4
Massachusetts	76	80	82	74	71	75	0.5	0.2	−1.0	−0.4	1.4
New Hampshire	67	73	73	67	59	63	0.9	0.0	−0.9	−1.3	1.7
Rhode Island	76	83	86	79	72	76	0.9	0.4	−0.8	−0.9	1.4
Vermont	69	76	74	67	67	65	1.0	−0.3	−1.0	0.0	−0.8
Middle Atlantic	78	82	83	81	74	75	0.5	0.1	−0.2	−0.9	0.3
New Jersey	78	83	83	80	69	74	0.6	0.0	−0.4	−1.5	1.8
New York	79	83	86	86	79	79	0.5	0.4	0.0	−0.8	0.0
Pennsylvania	76	82	80	73	68	70	0.8	−0.2	−0.9	−0.7	0.7
East North Central	78	80	77	65	61	64	0.3	−0.4	−1.7	−0.6	1.2
Illinois	76	79	75	66	60	66	0.4	−0.5	−1.3	−0.9	2.4
Indiana	80	80	78	61	56	59	0.0	−0.3	−2.4	−0.9	1.3
Michigan	81	81	78	66	65	66	0.0	−0.4	−1.7	−0.2	0.4
Ohio	81	82	79	65	61	63	0.1	−0.4	−1.9	−0.6	0.8
Wisconsin	74	73	74	65	60	63	−0.1	0.1	−1.3	−0.8	1.2
West North Central	72	74	71	62	60	62	0.3	−0.4	−1.3	−0.3	0.8
Iowa	73	72	69	62	58	59	−0.1	−0.4	−1.1	−0.7	0.4
Kansas	69	71	69	56	53	56	0.3	−0.3	−2.1	−0.5	1.4
Minnesota	72	74	74	67	67	68	0.3	0.0	−1.0	0.0	0.4
Missouri	76	79	75	62	58	63	0.4	−0.5	−1.9	−0.7	2.1
Nebraska	66	70	67	58	59	60	0.6	−0.4	−1.4	0.2	0.4
North Dakota	71	67	69	64	60	59	−0.6	0.3	−0.7	−0.6	−0.4
South Dakota	66	66	61	62	65	62	0.0	−0.8	0.2	0.5	−1.2
South Atlantic	75	78	76	67	65	69	0.4	−0.3	−1.3	−0.3	1.5
Delaware	70	79	82	77	75	90	1.2	0.4	−0.6	−0.3	4.7
District of Columbia	81	78	83	75	74	78	−0.4	0.6	−1.0	−0.1	1.3
Florida	74	76	72	62	61	66	0.3	−0.5	−1.5	−0.2	2.0
Georgia	72	77	70	66	63	68	0.7	−0.9	−0.6	−0.5	1.9
Maryland	74	79	84	79	73	76	0.7	0.6	−0.6	−0.8	1.0
North Carolina	74	79	78	73	70	71	0.7	−0.1	−0.7	−0.4	0.4
South Carolina	77	76	77	71	69	71	−0.1	0.1	−0.8	−0.3	0.7
Virginia	78	81	78	67	68	71	0.4	−0.4	−1.5	0.1	1.1
West Virginia	75	79	76	63	61	63	0.5	−0.4	−1.9	−0.3	0.8
East South Central	72	78	75	63	59	62	0.8	−0.4	−1.7	−0.7	1.2
Alabama	71	80	73	63	60	65	1.2	−0.9	−1.5	−0.5	2.0
Kentucky	73	80	77	62	62	61	0.9	−0.4	−2.1	0.0	−0.4
Mississippi	63	74	71	59	59	58	1.6	−0.4	−1.8	0.0	−0.4
Tennessee	76	78	76	64	56	63	0.3	−0.3	−1.7	−1.3	3.0
West South Central	69	73	70	58	58	61	0.6	−0.4	−1.9	0.0	1.3
Arkansas	70	74	70	62	59	59	0.6	−0.6	−1.2	−0.5	0.0
Louisiana	68	74	70	57	56	61	0.8	−0.6	−2.0	−0.2	2.2
Oklahoma	71	73	68	58	56	60	0.3	−0.7	−1.6	−0.4	1.7
Texas	68	73	70	57	59	62	0.7	−0.4	−2.0	0.3	1.2
Mountain	70	71	70	61	61	64	0.1	−0.1	−1.4	0.0	1.2
Arizona	74	73	74	62	63	68	−0.1	0.1	−1.8	0.2	1.9
Colorado	81	74	72	64	58	64	−0.9	−0.3	−1.2	−1.0	2.5
Idaho	56	66	65	56	53	53	1.7	−0.2	−1.5	−0.5	0.0
Montana	60	66	66	61	67	66	1.0	0.0	−0.8	0.9	−0.4
Nevada	71	73	69	60	71	72	0.3	−0.6	−1.4	1.7	0.4
New Mexico	65	70	66	58	58	58	0.7	−0.6	−1.3	0.0	0.0
Utah	70	74	70	59	56	58	0.6	−0.6	−1.7	−0.5	0.9
Wyoming	61	63	57	54	56	53	0.3	−1.0	−0.5	0.4	−1.4
Pacific	71	71	69	64	65	68	0.0	−0.3	−0.7	0.2	1.1
Alaska	54	59	58	50	57	55	0.9	−0.2	−1.5	1.3	−0.9
California	74	71	69	64	66	70	−0.4	−0.3	−0.7	0.3	1.5
Hawaii	62	76	75	85	76	76	2.1	−0.1	1.3	−1.1	0.0
Oregon	66	69	69	57	59	62	0.4	0.0	−1.9	0.3	1.2
Washington	63	70	72	63	60	61	1.1	0.3	−1.3	−0.5	0.4

[1]Data exclude facilities for the mentally retarded. See Appendix II, Hospital.   [2]1960 data include hospital units of institutions such as prisons and college infirmaries.
[3]Starting with 1990 data, hospital units of institutions, facilities for the mentally retarded, and alcoholism and chemical dependency hospitals are excluded. See Appendix II, Hospital.
[4]1990 data used in this calculation (not shown in table) exclude only facilities for the mentally retarded, consistent with exclusions from 1980 data.
[5]Estimated percent of staffed beds that are occupied. See Appendix II, Occupancy rate.

NOTE: Data for additional years are available. See Appendix III.

SOURCES: American Hospital Association (AHA): Hospitals. *JAHA* 35(15):383–430, 1961. (Copyright 1961: Used with permission of AHA); AHA Annual Survey of Hospitals, 1970 and 1980 unpublished; Hospital Statistics 1991–1992, 2001–2006 Editions. Chicago, IL. (Copyrights 1971, 1981, 1991, 2001–2006: Used with permission of Health Forum LLC, an affiliate of the American Hospital Association.)

Table 116 (page 1 of 2). Nursing homes, beds, occupancy, and residents, by geographic division and state: United States, selected years 1995–2004

[Data are based on a census of certified nursing facilities]

Geographic division and state	Nursing homes				Beds			
	1995	1997	2000	2004	1995	1997	2000	2004
United States.	16,389	17,121	16,886	16,117	1,751,302	1,827,615	1,795,388	1,744,258
New England.	1,140	1,183	1,137	1,044	115,488	121,854	118,562	110,212
Connecticut	267	260	259	246	32,827	32,681	32,433	30,645
Maine	132	135	126	117	9,243	9,363	8,248	7,463
Massachusetts	550	563	526	467	54,532	57,774	56,030	51,574
New Hampshire	74	81	83	81	7,412	8,107	7,837	7,775
Rhode Island	94	100	99	92	9,612	10,190	10,271	9,306
Vermont.	23	44	44	41	1,862	3,739	3,743	3,449
Middle Atlantic.	1,650	1,744	1,796	1,745	244,342	255,366	267,772	262,034
New Jersey	300	331	361	357	43,967	49,402	52,195	50,743
New York.	624	621	665	663	107,750	109,538	120,514	121,908
Pennsylvania	726	792	770	725	92,625	96,426	95,063	89,383
East North Central	3,171	3,324	3,301	3,136	367,879	390,907	369,657	356,291
Illinois	827	866	869	817	103,230	108,406	110,766	105,211
Indiana	556	577	564	512	59,538	62,086	56,762	55,670
Michigan	432	444	439	429	49,473	51,287	50,696	48,486
Ohio	943	1,014	1,009	978	106,884	121,330	105,038	106,898
Wisconsin	413	423	420	400	48,754	47,798	46,395	40,026
West North Central.	2,258	2,350	2,281	2,185	200,109	209,055	193,754	184,843
Iowa	419	469	467	458	39,959	45,359	37,034	35,963
Kansas	429	423	392	369	30,016	29,538	27,067	26,675
Minnesota	432	449	433	415	43,865	45,271	42,149	37,899
Missouri	546	570	551	521	52,679	55,472	54,829	54,208
Nebraska.	231	237	236	228	18,169	18,227	17,877	16,353
North Dakota	87	88	88	83	7,125	7,108	6,954	6,529
South Dakota	114	114	114	111	8,296	8,080	7,844	7,216
South Atlantic	2,215	2,348	2,418	2,363	243,069	253,621	264,147	263,873
Delaware	42	43	43	42	4,739	4,890	4,906	4,660
District of Columbia. . . .	19	21	20	20	3,206	3,097	3,078	3,065
Florida.	627	697	732	689	72,656	77,678	83,365	82,626
Georgia	352	354	363	362	38,097	39,016	39,817	40,082
Maryland	218	248	255	241	28,394	30,851	31,495	29,268
North Carolina	391	402	410	420	38,322	39,508	41,376	43,062
South Carolina	166	176	178	177	16,682	17,463	18,102	18,332
Virginia	271	271	278	279	30,070	29,915	30,595	31,669
West Virginia	129	136	139	133	10,903	11,203	11,413	11,109
East South Central.	1,014	1,090	1,071	1,062	99,707	106,104	106,250	108,745
Alabama	221	224	225	228	23,353	24,787	25,248	26,656
Kentucky	288	315	307	295	23,221	25,282	25,341	25,955
Mississippi	183	203	190	205	16,059	17,026	17,068	18,379
Tennessee	322	348	349	334	37,074	39,009	38,593	37,755
West South Central	2,264	2,313	2,199	2,044	224,695	229,469	224,100	217,262
Arkansas	256	261	255	237	29,952	31,088	25,715	24,286
Louisiana	337	339	337	305	37,769	38,043	39,430	38,192
Oklahoma	405	413	392	365	33,918	34,460	33,903	32,691
Texas	1,266	1,300	1,215	1,137	123,056	125,878	125,052	122,093
Mountain.	800	843	827	781	70,134	74,058	75,152	73,292
Arizona	152	165	150	134	16,162	17,761	17,458	16,389
Colorado	219	225	225	215	19,912	20,150	20,240	20,062
Idaho.	76	86	84	80	5,747	6,515	6,181	6,188
Montana	100	103	104	101	7,210	7,521	7,667	7,477
Nevada	42	45	51	43	3,998	4,178	5,547	5,134
New Mexico.	83	85	80	80	6,969	7,245	7,289	7,367
Utah	91	96	93	89	7,101	7,568	7,651	7,614
Wyoming	37	38	40	39	3,035	3,120	3,119	3,061
Pacific.	1,877	1,926	1,856	1,757	185,879	187,181	175,994	167,706
Alaska	15	16	15	14	814	828	821	781
California	1,382	1,419	1,369	1,311	140,203	140,837	131,762	127,337
Hawaii	34	43	45	45	2,513	3,830	4,006	4,081
Oregon	161	163	150	138	13,885	14,030	13,500	12,663
Washington	285	285	277	249	28,464	27,656	25,905	22,844

See footnotes at end of table.

Table 116 (page 2 of 2). Nursing homes, beds, occupancy, and residents, by geographic division and state: United States, selected years 1995–2004

[Data are based on a census of certified nursing facilities]

Geographic division and state	Residents				Occupancy rate[1]				Resident rate[2]			
	1995	1997	2000	2004	1995	1997	2000	2004	1995	1997	2000	2004
United States.	1,479,550	1,503,102	1,480,076	1,442,503	84.5	82.2	82.4	82.7	404.5	388.3	349.1	296.8
New England.	105,792	110,166	106,308	99,247	91.6	90.4	89.7	90.1	474.2	468.4	419.5	327.8
Connecticut	29,948	30,116	29,657	27,887	91.2	92.2	91.4	91.0	541.7	510.4	461.4	339.8
Maine	8,587	8,244	7,298	6,891	92.9	88.0	88.5	92.3	417.9	386.0	313.0	274.6
Massachusetts	49,765	51,524	49,805	45,619	91.3	89.2	88.9	88.5	477.3	470.9	426.8	335.1
New Hampshire	6,877	7,334	7,158	7,110	92.8	90.5	91.3	91.4	434.1	441.8	392.6	327.3
Rhode Island	8,823	9,399	9,041	8,500	91.8	92.2	88.0	91.3	476.9	475.4	432.6	323.3
Vermont.	1,792	3,549	3,349	3,240	96.2	94.9	89.5	93.9	207.0	392.6	335.0	282.3
Middle Atlantic	228,649	236,037	242,674	239,042	93.6	92.4	90.6	91.2	384.0	376.2	354.2	296.0
New Jersey	40,397	45,052	45,837	44,658	91.9	91.2	87.8	88.0	351.6	364.0	337.0	274.3
New York	103,409	103,948	112,957	113,402	96.0	94.9	93.7	93.0	371.8	358.1	362.6	320.5
Pennsylvania	84,843	87,037	83,880	80,982	91.6	90.3	88.2	90.6	419.2	408.0	353.1	278.4
East North Central	294,319	299,607	289,404	276,947	80.0	76.6	78.3	77.7	476.1	463.5	414.3	338.2
Illinois	83,696	85,059	83,604	79,311	81.1	78.5	75.5	75.4	495.3	480.9	435.4	361.5
Indiana	44,328	44,720	42,328	40,553	74.5	72.0	74.6	72.8	548.9	530.1	462.3	386.7
Michigan	43,271	44,057	42,615	41,369	87.5	85.9	84.1	85.3	345.0	332.6	299.1	236.3
Ohio	79,026	83,408	81,946	80,370	73.9	68.7	78.0	75.2	499.5	506.3	463.5	385.6
Wisconsin	43,998	42,363	38,911	35,344	90.2	88.6	83.9	88.3	518.9	481.1	406.9	318.3
West North Central.	164,660	167,170	157,224	146,552	82.3	80.0	81.1	79.3	489.6	483.6	429.8	370.1
Iowa	27,506	30,527	29,204	27,581	68.8	67.3	78.9	76.7	458.0	497.9	448.5	381.1
Kansas	25,140	24,007	22,230	20,662	83.8	81.3	82.1	77.5	528.9	492.9	429.4	375.3
Minnesota	41,163	41,785	38,813	34,834	93.8	92.3	92.1	91.9	537.4	528.0	453.4	354.7
Missouri.	39,891	40,770	38,586	37,274	75.7	73.5	70.4	68.8	432.8	430.0	391.5	371.3
Nebraska.	16,166	15,641	14,989	13,389	89.0	85.8	83.8	81.9	501.4	475.1	441.5	372.8
North Dakota	6,868	6,771	6,343	6,103	96.4	95.3	91.2	93.5	522.0	491.0	430.7	371.8
South Dakota	7,926	7,669	7,059	6,709	95.5	94.9	90.0	93.0	543.3	512.5	438.8	379.9
South Atlantic	217,303	223,277	227,818	232,622	89.4	88.0	86.2	88.2	335.4	321.3	291.9	259.8
Delaware	3,819	3,865	3,900	3,811	80.6	79.0	79.5	81.8	448.7	419.8	369.7	287.4
District of Columbia. . . .	2,576	2,937	2,858	2,779	80.3	94.8	92.9	90.7	297.6	335.1	318.4	299.2
Florida.	61,845	65,131	69,050	72,759	85.1	83.8	82.8	88.1	228.2	222.3	208.4	191.7
Georgia	35,933	35,838	36,559	35,935	94.3	91.9	91.8	89.7	496.0	463.3	416.1	377.2
Maryland	24,716	26,035	25,629	25,222	87.0	84.4	81.4	86.2	432.7	423.6	383.1	304.8
North Carolina	35,511	37,078	36,658	37,926	92.7	93.8	88.6	88.1	401.1	392.9	347.6	314.4
South Carolina	14,568	14,964	15,739	16,352	87.3	85.7	86.9	89.2	366.0	349.2	313.1	275.1
Virginia	28,119	27,087	27,091	27,982	93.5	90.5	88.5	88.4	385.2	348.1	310.4	272.8
West Virginia	10,216	10,342	10,334	9,856	93.7	92.3	90.5	88.7	355.2	344.0	325.2	302.9
East South Central.	91,563	95,835	96,348	95,395	91.8	90.3	90.7	87.7	416.6	415.5	385.5	383.8
Alabama	21,691	22,729	23,089	23,504	92.9	91.7	91.4	88.2	370.1	370.9	343.1	355.2
Kentucky	20,696	22,289	22,730	22,491	89.1	88.2	89.7	86.7	391.9	401.7	390.1	381.0
Mississippi	15,247	15,865	15,815	16,129	94.9	93.2	92.7	87.8	405.3	403.0	368.7	407.0
Tennessee	33,929	34,952	34,714	33,271	91.5	89.6	89.9	88.1	479.6	469.1	426.1	397.4
West South Central	169,047	164,367	159,160	156,401	75.2	71.6	71.0	72.0	486.1	448.6	397.6	382.9
Arkansas	20,823	20,483	19,317	17,730	69.5	65.9	75.1	73.0	508.3	484.0	415.5	370.6
Louisiana	32,493	30,923	30,735	28,587	86.0	81.3	77.9	74.9	639.3	581.6	523.8	473.9
Oklahoma	26,377	25,393	23,833	21,453	77.8	73.7	70.3	65.6	499.1	464.3	416.8	395.0
Texas	89,354	87,568	85,275	88,631	72.6	69.6	68.2	72.6	439.9	405.0	358.4	360.3
Mountain.	58,738	60,163	59,379	58,069	83.8	81.2	79.0	79.2	335.9	313.0	271.2	218.2
Arizona	12,382	302,637	13,253	12,971	76.6	77.8	75.9	79.1	233.3	234.5	193.4	151.0
Colorado	17,055	16,882	17,045	16,326	85.7	83.8	84.2	81.4	420.6	386.2	353.5	293.4
Idaho.	4,697	4,780	4,640	4,746	81.7	73.4	75.1	76.7	321.7	301.5	257.0	211.1
Montana	6,415	6,243	5,973	5,612	89.0	83.0	77.9	75.1	491.4	437.0	389.5	307.8
Nevada	3,645	3,773	3,657	4,294	91.2	90.3	65.9	83.6	312.0	272.1	215.3	178.9
New Mexico	6,051	6,126	6,503	6,311	86.8	84.6	89.2	85.7	332.0	309.4	279.0	235.3
Utah	5,832	5,904	5,703	5,327	82.1	78.0	74.5	70.0	323.5	298.3	262.2	207.3
Wyoming	2,661	2,640	2,605	2,482	87.7	84.6	83.5	81.1	468.2	440.5	386.8	336.6
Pacific.	149,479	146,480	141,761	138,228	80.4	78.3	80.5	82.4	302.4	275.1	241.3	193.1
Alaska	634	619	595	606	77.9	74.8	72.5	77.6	348.0	297.7	225.9	173.0
California	109,805	108,120	106,460	106,020	78.3	76.8	80.8	83.3	302.9	277.9	250.1	206.3
Hawaii	2,413	3,508	3,558	3,780	96.0	91.6	88.8	92.6	178.5	227.4	202.6	149.1
Oregon	11,673	11,304	9,990	8,203	84.1	80.6	74.0	64.8	244.9	221.3	173.9	117.4
Washington	24,954	22,929	21,158	19,619	87.7	82.9	81.7	85.9	362.5	306.1	251.6	190.0

[1]Percentage of beds occupied (number of nursing home residents per 100 nursing home beds).
[2]Number of nursing home residents (all ages) per 1,000 resident population 85 years of age and over. Resident rates for 1995–1999 are based on population estimates projected from the 1990 census. Starting with 2000 data, resident rates are based on the 2000 census.

NOTES: Annual numbers of nursing homes, beds, and residents are based on a 15-month OSCAR reporting cycle. See Appendix I, Online Survey Certification and Reporting Database (OSCAR). Data for additional years are available. See Appendix III.

SOURCES: Cowles CM, 1995–1997 Nursing Home Statistical Yearbook. Anacortes, WA: Cowles Research Group, 1995, 1997, 1998; Cowles CM, 1998–2001 Nursing Home Statistical Yearbook. Washington, DC: American Association of Homes and Services for the Aging, 1999–2002; and Cowles Research Group, unpublished data. Based on data from the Centers for Medicare & Medicaid Services' Online Survey Certification and Reporting (OSCAR) database.

Table 117. Selected characteristics of office-based physician practices: United States, 1999–2004

[Data are based on reporting by a sample of office-based physicians]

Characteristic	Total	Size of practice[1]				Type of practice[2]	
		1 physician	2–4 physicians	5–9 physicians	10 or more physicians	Solo and single specialty	Multi-specialty
		Percent of office-based physicians					
Distribution of physicians:							
1999–2000	100.0	38.0	33.1	20.0	8.9	- - -	- - -
2001–2002	100.0	33.4	33.3	21.1	12.2	74.7	25.3
2003–2004	100.0	35.8	32.0	20.0	12.2	78.9	21.1
Use electronic medical records:[2]							
1999–2000	- - -	- - -	- - -	- - -	- - -	- - -	- - -
2001–2002	18.3	12.8	17.3	17.6	36.2	16.9	22.9
2003–2004	19.2	13.0	19.5	21.0	34.2	17.3	26.6
Submit claims electronically:[3]							
1999–2000	- - -	- - -	- - -	- - -	- - -	- - -	- - -
2001–2002	78.3	67.0	79.1	89.3	89.6	75.9	86.1
2003–2004	80.8	68.7	86.5	88.8	89.1	79.5	85.4
Perform any lab tests in office:							
1999–2000	44.5	31.1	47.1	56.5	65.0	- - -	- - -
2001–2002	42.2	31.8	42.9	46.5	61.2	37.3	57.0
2003–2004	42.1	27.4	46.6	49.5	61.5	37.7	58.7
Not accepting new Medicare patients:							
1999–2000	14.7	16.8	15.2	12.0	9.4	- - -	- - -
2001–2002	16.1	15.4	17.3	16.1	14.6	16.5	15.1
2003–2004	14.3	13.9	14.2	15.2	14.4	14.7	12.8
Not accepting new Medicaid patients:							
1999–2000	26.2	32.5	24.9	20.9	16.2	- - -	- - -
2001–2002	25.4	32.9	27.5	15.6	15.2	27.3	19.9
2003–2004	26.6	32.1	25.9	22.3	18.9	27.5	23.2
Not accepting new noncapitated privately-insured patients:[2,4]							
1999–2000	- - -	- - -	- - -	- - -	- - -	- - -	- - -
2001–2002	13.4	15.5	14.1	9.7	12.1	13.1	14.9
2003–2004	12.2	13.6	12.4	11.0	9.5	11.5	15.0
Not accepting new capitated privately-insured patients:[2,4]							
1999–2000	- - -	- - -	- - -	- - -	- - -	- - -	- - -
2001–2002	39.8	45.9	38.9	34.6	34.2	42.8	31.0
2003–2004	41.1	43.2	41.6	42.9	29.8	42.8	34.4

- - - Data not available.

[1]Records with unknown practice size were excluded. Less than 0.5% of physicians did not report a practice size.
[2]Collection of data item began in 2001.
[3]Collection of data item began in 2002.
[4]In capitated plans, health insurers pay physicians periodically, usually monthly, without regard to the actual number or nature of covered services provided to the member. The physician practice is responsible for delivering or arranging for the delivery of all health care services required by covered plan members under the conditions of their contract with the health insurer. This is in contrast to contracts with health insurers that pay on a per visit or per service basis.

NOTES: Records with unknown response were excluded. There were no unknown responses for type of physician and perform lab tests in office. There were less than 5% unknown responses for use of medical records, accepting new Medicare patients, and accepting new Medicaid patients. Unknown responses for submit claims electronically ranged from 5%–8%. Unknown responses for accepting new capitated and noncapitated privately-insured patients ranged from 10%–12%. Estimates in this table may differ from other estimates based on the same data and presented elsewhere if unknown responses were included in the denominator.

SOURCE: Centers for Disease Control and Prevention, National Center for Health Statistics, National Ambulatory Medical Care Survey, Physician Induction Form.

Table 118. Medicare-certified providers and suppliers: United States, selected years 1980–2004

[Data are compiled from various Centers for Medicare & Medicaid Services data systems]

Providers or suppliers	1980	1985	1990	1996	1997	2000	2002	2003	2004
	Number of providers or suppliers								
Home health agencies	2,924	5,679	5,730	8,437	10,807	7,857	6,813	6,928	7,519
Clinical Lab Improvement Act Facilities	- - -	- - -	- - -	159,907	164,054	171,018	173,807	176,947	189,340
End stage renal disease facilities	999	1,393	1,937	2,876	3,367	3,787	4,113	4,309	4,618
Outpatient physical therapy	419	854	1,195	2,302	2,758	2,867	2,836	2,961	2,971
Portable X-ray	216	308	443	555	656	666	644	641	608
Rural health clinics	391	428	551	2,775	3,673	3,453	3,283	3,306	3,536
Comprehensive outpatient rehabilitation facilities	- - -	72	186	307	531	522	524	587	635
Ambulatory surgical centers	- - -	336	1,197	2,112	2,480	2,894	3,371	3,597	4,136
Hospices	- - -	164	825	1,927	2,344	2,326	2,275	2,323	2,645

- - - Data not available.

NOTES: Provider and supplier data for 1980–1990 are as of July 1. Provider and supplier data for 1996–2004 are as of December. Providers and suppliers certified for Medicare are deemed to meet Medicaid standards. Data for additional years are available. See Appendix III.

SOURCE: Centers for Medicare & Medicaid Services, Office of Research, Development, and Information.

Table 119. Total health expenditures as a percent of gross domestic product and per capita health expenditures in dollars, by selected countries: Selected years 1960–2003

[Data compiled by the Organisation for Economic Cooperation and Development]

Country	1960	1970	1980	1990	1995	1998	1999	2000	2001[1]	2002[1]	2003[1]
Health expenditures as a percent of gross domestic product											
Australia	4.1	- - -	7.0	7.8	8.2	8.6	8.7	9.0	9.1	9.3	- - -
Austria	4.3	5.1	7.4	7.0	8.0	7.6	7.7	7.6	7.5	7.6	- - -
Belgium	- - -	4.0	6.4	7.4	8.4	8.5	8.6	8.7	8.8	9.1	9.6
Canada	5.4	7.0	7.1	9.0	9.2	9.2	9.0	8.9	9.4	9.6	9.9
Czech Republic	- - -	- - -	- - -	4.7	6.9	6.6	6.6	6.6	6.9	7.2	7.5
Denmark	- - -	- - -	9.1	8.5	8.2	8.4	8.5	8.4	8.6	8.8	9.0
Finland	3.8	5.6	6.4	7.8	7.5	6.9	6.9	6.7	6.9	7.2	7.4
France	3.8	5.4	7.1	8.6	9.5	9.3	9.3	9.3	9.4	9.7	10.1
Germany	- - -	6.2	8.7	8.5	10.6	10.6	10.6	10.6	10.8	10.9	11.1
Greece	- - -	6.1	6.6	7.4	9.6	9.4	9.6	9.9	10.2	9.8	9.9
Hungary	- - -	- - -	- - -	- - -	7.5	7.3	7.4	7.1	7.4	7.8	- - -
Iceland	3.0	4.7	6.2	8.0	8.4	8.7	9.4	9.3	9.3	10.0	10.5
Ireland	3.7	5.1	8.4	6.1	6.8	6.2	6.3	6.3	6.9	7.3	- - -
Italy	- - -	- - -	- - -	7.9	7.3	7.7	7.7	8.1	8.2	8.4	8.4
Japan	3.0	4.5	6.5	5.9	6.8	7.2	7.4	7.6	7.8	7.9	- - -
Korea	- - -	- - -	- - -	4.5	4.2	4.5	4.8	4.7	5.4	5.3	5.6
Luxembourg	- - -	3.6	5.9	6.1	6.4	5.8	6.2	5.5	5.9	6.1	- - -
Mexico	- - -	- - -	- - -	4.8	5.6	5.4	5.6	5.6	6.0	6.0	6.2
Netherlands	- - -	- - -	7.5	8.0	8.4	8.2	8.4	8.3	8.7	9.3	9.8
New Zealand	- - -	5.1	5.9	6.9	7.2	7.8	7.7	7.8	7.9	8.2	8.1
Norway	2.9	4.4	7.0	7.7	7.9	8.5	8.5	7.7	8.9	9.9	10.3
Poland	- - -	- - -	- - -	4.9	5.6	6.0	5.9	5.7	6.0	6.0	- - -
Portugal	- - -	2.6	5.6	6.2	8.2	8.4	8.7	9.2	9.4	9.3	9.6
Slovak Republic	- - -	- - -	- - -	- - -	- - -	5.7	5.8	5.5	5.6	5.7	5.9
Spain	1.5	3.6	5.4	6.7	7.6	7.5	7.5	7.4	7.5	7.6	7.7
Sweden	- - -	6.9	9.1	8.4	8.1	8.3	8.4	8.4	8.8	9.2	- - -
Switzerland	4.9	5.5	7.4	8.3	9.7	10.3	10.5	10.4	10.9	11.1	11.5
Turkey	- - -	2.4	3.3	3.6	3.4	4.8	6.4	6.6	- - -	- - -	- - -
United Kingdom	3.9	4.5	5.6	6.0	7.0	6.9	7.2	7.3	7.5	7.7	- - -
United States[2]	5.0	6.9	8.7	11.9	13.3	13.0	13.0	13.1	13.8	14.6	15.0
Per capita health expenditures[3]											
Australia	$ 93	- - -	$ 691	$1,307	$1,745	$2,078	$2,231	$2,220	$2,404	$2,521	$2,699
Austria	77	191	764	1,338	1,870	1,953	2,067	2,184	2,195	2,280	- - -
Belgium	- - -	149	637	1,345	1,820	2,005	2,109	2,279	2,424	2,607	2,827
Canada	123	289	783	1,737	2,051	2,297	2,400	2,503	2,710	2,845	3,003
Czech Republic	- - -	- - -	- - -	555	873	906	920	962	1,063	1,187	1,298
Denmark	- - -	- - -	955	1,567	1,848	2,138	2,297	2,382	2,556	2,655	2,763
Finland	63	192	592	1,422	1,433	1,604	1,637	1,718	1,857	2,013	2,118
France	70	210	711	1,568	2,033	2,235	2,312	2,456	2,617	2,762	2,903
Germany	- - -	270	965	1,748	2,276	2,483	2,557	2,671	2,784	2,916	2,996
Greece	- - -	160	487	840	1,253	1,375	1,468	1,617	1,756	1,854	2,011
Hungary	- - -	- - -	- - -	- - -	676	774	819	857	975	1,115	- - -
Iceland	57	165	708	1,614	1,858	2,280	2,546	2,625	2,742	2,948	3,115
Ireland	43	117	518	793	1,216	1,482	1,621	1,804	2,089	2,386	- - -
Italy	- - -	- - -	- - -	1,391	1,535	1,804	1,860	2,049	2,154	2,248	2,258
Japan	30	149	580	1,115	1,538	1,743	1,829	1,971	2,092	2,139	- - -
Korea	- - -	- - -	- - -	377	538	616	729	771	932	975	1,074
Luxembourg	- - -	163	643	1,547	2,059	2,298	2,740	2,722	2,940	3,190	- - -
Mexico	- - -	- - -	- - -	293	382	427	463	499	545	559	583
Netherlands	- - -	- - -	757	1,438	1,826	2,044	2,134	2,259	2,520	2,775	2,976
New Zealand	- - -	211	506	995	1,247	1,449	1,522	1,605	1,701	1,850	1,886
Norway	49	142	667	1,396	1,897	2,313	2,562	2,784	3,287	3,616	3,807
Poland	- - -	- - -	- - -	296	417	555	566	587	646	677	- - -
Portugal	- - -	51	295	670	1,079	1,297	1,426	1,594	1,693	1,758	1,797
Slovak Republic	- - -	- - -	- - -	- - -	- - -	559	577	597	641	716	777
Spain	16	96	365	875	1,198	1,356	1,453	1,525	1,618	1,728	1,835
Sweden	- - -	309	936	1,579	1,738	1,960	2,118	2,273	2,403	2,594	- - -
Switzerland	166	352	1,033	2,033	2,579	2,980	3,019	3,182	3,362	3,649	3,781
Turkey	- - -	24	75	166	185	312	392	452	- - -	- - -	- - -
United Kingdom	84	164	482	986	1,374	1,577	1,689	1,833	2,032	2,231	- - -
United States[2]	144	347	1,055	2,738	3,654	4,098	4,295	4,539	4,888	5,287	5,635

- - - Data not available.

[1] Preliminary figures.

[2] The Organisation for Economic Cooperation and Development (OECD) estimates for the United States differ from the National Health Expenditures estimates shown in Table 120 because of differences in methodology.

[3] Per capita health expenditures for each country have been adjusted to U.S. dollars using gross domestic product purchasing power parities (PPP) for each year. See Appendix II, Gross domestic product.

NOTE: These data include revisions in health expenditures and differ from previous editions of Health, United States.

SOURCE: The Organisation for Economic Cooperation and Development Health Data File 2005, incorporating revisions to the annual update. Available from: www.oecd.org/els/health.

Table 120. Gross domestic product, federal, and state and local government expenditures, national health expenditures, and average annual percent change: United States, selected years 1960–2004

[Data are compiled from various sources by the Centers for Medicare & Medicaid Services]

Gross domestic product, government expenditures, and national health expenditures	1960	1970	1980	1990	1995	2000	2002	2003	2004
	Amount in billions								
Gross domestic product (GDP)	$ 526	$1,039	$2,790	$ 5,803	$ 7,398	$ 9,817	$ 10,470	$ 10,971	$ 11,734
Federal government expenditures	$ 86.7	$201.1	$585.7	$1,253.5	$1,603.5	$1,864.4	$2,101.1	$2,251.4	$2,381.3
State and local government expenditures . .	40.2	113.0	329.4	730.5	978.2	1,269.5	1,444.3	1,512.4	1,587.5
National health expenditures	$ 27.6	$ 75.1	$254.9	$ 717.3	$1,020.4	$1,358.5	$1,607.9	$1,740.6	$1,877.6
Private.	20.7	46.8	147.6	427.3	553.8	756.3	881.4	957.2	1,030.3
Public	6.8	28.3	107.3	290.0	466.6	602.2	726.5	783.4	847.3
Federal government.	2.9	17.7	71.6	193.9	325.3	418.4	509.5	554.4	600.0
State and local government	4.0	10.6	35.7	96.2	141.4	183.8	217.1	229.0	247.3
	Amount per capita								
National health expenditures	$ 148	$ 357	$1,106	$ 2,821	$ 3,762	$ 4,729	$ 5,485	$ 5,879	$ 6,280
Private.	111	222	640	1,680	2,042	2,633	3,007	3,233	3,446
Public	37	135	466	1,140	1,720	2,096	2,478	2,646	2,834
	Percent								
National health expenditures as percent of GDP	5.2	7.2	9.1	12.4	13.8	13.8	15.4	15.9	16.0
Health expenditures as a percent of total government expenditures									
Federal.	3.3	8.8	12.2	15.5	20.3	22.4	24.2	24.6	25.2
State and local.	9.9	9.4	10.9	13.2	14.5	14.5	15.0	15.1	15.6
	Percent distribution								
National health expenditures	100.0	100.0	100.0	100.0	100.0	100.0	100.0	100.0	100.0
Private.	75.2	62.3	57.9	59.6	54.3	55.7	54.8	55.0	54.9
Public	24.8	37.7	42.1	40.4	45.7	44.3	45.2	45.0	45.1
	Average annual percent change from previous year shown								
Gross domestic product	. . .	7.0	10.4	7.6	5.0	5.9	3.2	4.8	7.0
Federal government expenditures	. . .	8.8	11.3	7.9	5.0	3.1	6.2	7.2	5.8
State and local government expenditures. .	. . .	10.9	11.3	8.3	6.0	5.4	6.7	4.7	5.0
National health expenditures	. . .	10.5	13.0	10.9	7.3	5.9	8.8	8.2	7.9
Private.	. . .	8.5	12.2	11.2	5.3	6.4	8.0	8.6	7.6
Public	. . .	15.3	14.2	10.5	10.0	5.2	9.8	7.8	8.2
Federal government.	. . .	20.0	15.0	10.5	10.9	5.2	10.3	8.8	8.2
State and local government	. . .	10.3	12.9	10.4	8.0	5.4	8.7	5.5	8.0
National health expenditures, per capita. . .	. . .	9.2	12.0	9.8	5.9	4.7	7.7	7.2	6.8
Private.	. . .	7.2	11.2	10.1	4.0	5.2	6.9	7.5	6.6
Public	. . .	13.9	13.2	9.4	8.6	4.0	8.7	6.8	7.1

. . . Category not applicable.

NOTES: These data include revisions in health expenditures and may differ from previous editions of *Health, United States*. They reflect U.S. Census Bureau resident population estimates as of July 2005, less armed forces overseas and the population of outlying areas. Federal and state and local government total expenditures reflect December 2005 revisions from the Bureau of Economic Analysis. See Appendix II, Gross Domestic Product (GDP); Health Expenditures, national. Percents are calculated using unrounded data.

SOURCE: Centers for Medicare & Medicaid Services, Office of the Actuary, National Health Statistics Group, National health accounts, National health expenditures, 2004. Available from: www.cms.hhs.gov/NationalHealthExpendData/. Unpublished data.

Table 121. Consumer Price Index and average annual percent change for all items, selected items, and medical care components: United States, selected years 1960–2005

[Data are based on reporting by samples of providers and other retail outlets]

Items and medical care components	1960	1970	1980	1990	1995	2000	2002	2003	2004	2005
Consumer Price Index (CPI)										
All items	29.6	38.8	82.4	130.7	152.4	172.2	179.9	184.0	188.9	195.3
All items less medical care	30.2	39.2	82.8	128.8	148.6	167.3	174.3	178.1	182.7	188.7
Services	24.1	35.0	77.9	139.2	168.7	195.3	209.8	216.5	222.8	230.1
Food	30.0	39.2	86.8	132.4	148.4	167.8	176.2	180.0	186.2	190.7
Apparel	45.7	59.2	90.9	124.1	132.0	129.6	124.0	120.9	120.4	119.5
Housing	- - -	36.4	81.1	128.5	148.5	169.6	180.3	184.8	189.5	195.7
Energy	22.4	25.5	86.0	102.1	105.2	124.6	121.7	136.5	151.4	177.1
Medical care	22.3	34.0	74.9	162.8	220.5	260.8	285.6	297.1	310.1	323.2
Components of medical care										
Medical care services	19.5	32.3	74.8	162.7	224.2	266.0	292.9	306.0	321.3	336.7
Professional services	- - -	37.0	77.9	156.1	201.0	237.7	253.9	261.2	271.5	281.7
Physicians' services	21.9	34.5	76.5	160.8	208.8	244.7	260.6	267.7	278.3	287.5
Dental services	27.0	39.2	78.9	155.8	206.8	258.5	281.0	292.5	306.9	324.0
Eye glasses and eye care[1]	- - -	- - -	- - -	117.3	137.0	149.7	155.5	155.9	159.3	163.2
Services by other medical professionals[1]	- - -	- - -	- - -	120.2	143.9	161.9	171.8	177.1	181.9	186.8
Hospital and related services	- - -	- - -	69.2	178.0	257.8	317.3	367.8	394.8	417.9	439.9
Hospital services[2]	- - -	- - -	- - -	- - -	- - -	115.9	134.7	144.7	153.4	161.6
Inpatient hospital services[2,3]	- - -	- - -	- - -	- - -	- - -	113.8	131.2	140.1	148.1	156.6
Outpatient hospital services[1,3]	- - -	- - -	- - -	138.7	204.6	263.8	309.8	337.9	356.3	373.0
Hospital rooms	9.3	23.6	68.0	175.4	251.2	- - -	- - -	- - -	- - -	- - -
Other inpatient services[1]	- - -	- - -	- - -	142.7	206.8	- - -	- - -	- - -	- - -	- - -
Nursing homes and adult day care[2]	- - -	- - -	- - -	- - -	- - -	117.0	127.9	135.2	140.4	145.0
Medical care commodities	46.9	46.5	75.4	163.4	204.5	238.1	256.4	262.8	269.3	276.0
Prescription drugs and medical supplies	54.0	47.4	72.5	181.7	235.0	285.4	316.5	326.3	337.1	349.0
Nonprescription drugs and medical supplies[1]	- - -	- - -	- - -	120.6	140.5	149.5	150.4	152.0	152.3	151.7
Internal and respiratory over-the-counter drugs	- - -	42.3	74.9	145.9	167.0	176.9	178.8	181.2	180.9	179.7
Nonprescription medical equipment and supplies	- - -	- - -	79.2	138.0	166.3	178.1	177.5	178.1	179.7	180.6
Average annual percent change from previous year shown										
All items	...	2.7	7.8	4.7	3.1	2.5	2.2	2.3	2.7	3.4
All items excluding medical care	...	2.6	7.8	4.5	2.9	2.4	2.1	2.2	2.6	3.3
All services	...	3.8	8.3	6.0	3.9	3.0	3.6	3.2	2.9	3.3
Food	...	2.7	8.3	4.3	2.3	2.5	2.5	2.2	3.4	2.4
Apparel	...	2.6	4.4	3.2	1.2	–0.4	–2.2	–2.5	–0.4	–0.7
Housing	...	- - -	8.3	4.7	2.9	2.7	3.1	2.5	2.5	3.3
Energy	...	1.3	12.9	1.7	0.6	3.4	–1.2	12.2	10.9	17.0
Medical care	...	4.3	8.2	8.1	6.3	3.4	4.6	4.0	4.4	4.2
Components of medical care										
Medical care services	...	5.2	8.8	8.1	6.6	3.5	4.9	4.5	5.0	4.8
Professional services	...	- - -	7.7	7.2	5.2	3.4	3.4	2.9	3.9	3.8
Physicians' services	...	4.6	8.3	7.7	5.4	3.2	3.2	2.7	4.0	3.3
Dental services	...	3.8	7.2	7.0	5.8	4.6	4.3	4.1	4.9	5.6
Eye glasses and eye care[1]	...	- - -	- - -	- - -	3.2	1.8	1.9	0.3	2.2	2.4
Services by other medical professionals[1]	...	- - -	- - -	- - -	3.7	2.4	3.0	3.1	2.7	2.7
Hospital and related services	...	- - -	- - -	9.9	7.7	4.2	7.7	7.3	5.9	5.3
Hospital services[2]	...	- - -	- - -	- - -	- - -	- - -	7.8	7.4	6.0	5.3
Inpatient hospital services[2,3]	...	- - -	- - -	- - -	- - -	- - -	7.4	6.8	5.7	5.7
Outpatient hospital services[1,3]	...	- - -	- - -	- - -	8.1	5.2	8.4	9.1	5.4	4.7
Hospital rooms	...	9.8	11.2	9.9	7.4	- - -	- - -	- - -	- - -	- - -
Other inpatient services[1]	...	- - -	- - -	- - -	7.7	- - -	- - -	- - -	- - -	- - -
Nursing homes and adult day care[2]	...	- - -	- - -	- - -	- - -	- - -	4.6	5.7	3.8	3.3
Medical care commodities	...	–0.1	5.0	8.0	4.6	3.1	3.8	2.5	2.5	2.5
Prescription drugs and medical supplies	...	–1.3	4.3	9.6	5.3	4.0	5.3	3.1	3.3	3.5
Nonprescription drugs and medical supplies[1]	...	- - -	- - -	- - -	3.1	1.2	0.3	1.1	0.2	–0.4
Internal and respiratory over-the-counter drugs	...	- - -	5.9	6.9	2.7	1.2	0.5	1.3	–0.2	–0.7
Nonprescription medical equipment and supplies	...	- - -	- - -	5.7	3.8	1.4	–0.2	0.3	0.9	0.5

- - - Data not available.
... Category not applicable.
[1]December 1986 = 100.
[2]December 1996 = 100.
[3]Special index based on a substantially smaller sample.

NOTES: Consumer Price Index for all urban consumers (CPI-U) U.S. city average, detailed expenditure categories. See Appendix I, Consumer Price Index. 1982–1984 = 100, except where noted. Data are not seasonally adjusted. See Appendix II, Consumer Price Index.

SOURCE: U.S. Department of Labor, Bureau of Labor Statistics, Consumer Price Index. Various releases. 2005 data available from: www.bls.gov/cpi/cpid05av.pdf.

Table 122. Growth in personal health care expenditures and percent distribution of factors affecting growth: United States, 1960–2004

[Data are compiled from various sources by the Centers for Medicare & Medicaid Services]

Period	Average annual percent increase	Factors affecting growth				
		All factors	Inflation[1]		Population	Intensity[2]
			Economy-wide	Medical		
		Percent distribution[3]				
1960–2004	10.0	100	39	17	11	33
1960–1965	8.3	100	17	10	18	55
1965–1970	12.7	100	34	12	8	46
1970–1975	12.3	100	55	1	8	36
1975–1980	13.8	100	54	12	7	27
1980–1985	11.6	100	47	32	9	12
1980–1981	15.9	100	61	17	7	15
1981–1982	12.0	100	52	37	9	2
1982–1983	10.3	100	40	34	10	16
1983–1984	9.6	100	40	39	10	11
1984–1985	10.2	100	31	41	10	18
1985–1990	10.3	100	32	26	10	31
1985–1986	8.7	100	26	31	11	31
1986–1987	9.4	100	30	23	10	37
1987–1988	11.2	100	32	25	9	34
1988–1989	10.5	100	37	29	10	23
1989–1990	11.7	100	34	24	11	31
1990–1995	7.3	100	34	29	18	18
1990–1991	10.2	100	36	21	14	30
1991–1992	8.5	100	28	35	17	21
1992–1993	6.6	100	36	35	21	8
1993–1994	5.3	100	41	31	24	4
1994–1995	6.1	100	34	25	21	20
1995–2000	5.7	100	30	18	21	32
1995–1996	5.4	100	36	19	21	24
1996–1997	5.4	100	31	9	22	38
1997–1998	5.3	100	21	20	23	36
1998–1999	5.7	100	26	22	21	31
1999–2000	6.7	100	33	17	17	32
2000–2004	8.2	100	28	20	13	39
2000–2001	8.7	100	28	17	12	43
2001–2002	8.3	100	22	25	12	40
2002–2003	7.8	100	27	22	13	38
2003–2004	7.9	100	34	18	13	35

[1]Total inflation is economy-wide and medical inflation is the medical inflation above economy-wide inflation.
[2]Intensity is the residual percent of growth which cannot be attributed to price increases or population growth. It represents changes in use or kinds of services and supplies.
[3]Percents may not sum to 100 due to rounding.

NOTES: These data include revisions in health expenditures for 1960 forward and revisions in population for 1990 forward. The implicit price deflator for Gross Domestic Product (GDP) is used to measure economy-wide inflation for all years 1960–2004. See Appendix II, Expenditures, national health; Gross Domestic Product (GDP). Previous estimates of the factors accounting for growth used GDP chain-type price index. All indexes used to calculate the factors affecting growth were rebased in 2003 with base year 2000.

SOURCE: Centers for Medicare & Medicaid Services, Office of the Actuary, National Health Statistics Group, National health accounts, National health expenditures, 2004. Available from: www.cms.hhs.gov/NationalHealthExpendData/. Unpublished data.

Table 123 (page 1 of 2). National health expenditures, average annual percent change, and percent distribution, by type of expenditure: United States, selected years 1960–2004

[Data are compiled from various sources by the Centers for Medicare & Medicaid Services]

Type of national health expenditure	1960	1970	1980	1990	1995	2000	2002	2003	2004
					Amount in billions				
National health expenditures	$27.6	$75.1	$254.9	$717.3	$1,020.4	$1,358.5	$1,607.9	$1,740.6	$1,877.6
Health services and supplies	24.9	67.1	234.0	666.7	953.0	1,264.5	1,499.2	1,624.5	1,753.0
Personal health care	23.3	62.9	215.3	607.5	863.7	1,139.9	1,341.4	1,445.7	1,560.2
Hospital care	9.2	27.6	101.0	251.6	340.7	417.0	488.6	525.5	570.8
Professional services	8.3	20.6	67.3	216.8	316.5	426.7	503.2	543.3	587.4
Physician and clinical services	5.4	14.0	47.1	157.5	220.5	288.6	337.9	367.0	399.9
Other professional services	0.4	0.7	3.6	18.2	28.5	39.1	45.7	49.1	52.7
Dental services	2.0	4.7	13.3	31.5	44.5	62.0	73.3	76.9	81.5
Other personal health care	0.6	1.2	3.3	9.6	23.0	37.1	46.3	50.4	53.3
Nursing home and home health	0.9	4.3	21.4	65.2	104.6	125.8	140.0	148.6	158.4
Home health care [1]	0.1	0.2	2.4	12.6	30.5	30.6	34.3	38.1	43.2
Nursing home care [1]	0.8	4.0	19.0	52.6	74.1	95.3	105.7	110.4	115.2
Retail outlet sales of medical products	4.9	10.5	25.7	74.0	101.8	170.3	209.5	228.3	243.7
Prescription drugs	2.7	5.5	12.0	40.3	60.9	120.8	157.9	174.1	188.5
Other medical products	2.3	5.0	13.6	33.7	40.9	49.5	51.6	54.2	55.2
Government administration and net cost of private health insurance	1.2	2.8	12.2	39.2	58.4	81.2	106.1	124.9	136.7
Government public health activities [2]	0.4	1.4	6.4	20.0	31.0	43.4	51.7	54.0	56.1
Investment	2.6	8.0	20.9	50.7	67.4	94.0	108.8	116.1	124.6
Research [3]	0.7	2.0	5.4	12.7	18.3	25.6	32.5	35.6	39.0
Structures and equipment	1.9	6.1	15.5	38.0	49.1	68.4	76.2	80.5	85.7
					Average annual percent change from previous year shown				
National health expenditures	...	10.5	13.0	10.9	7.3	5.9	8.8	8.2	7.9
Health services and supplies	...	10.4	13.3	11.0	7.4	5.8	8.9	8.4	7.9
Personal health care	...	10.4	13.1	10.9	7.3	5.7	8.5	7.8	7.9
Hospital care	...	11.6	13.9	9.6	6.3	4.1	8.2	7.5	8.6
Professional services	...	9.5	12.5	12.4	7.9	6.2	8.6	8.0	8.1
Physician and clinical services	...	10.1	12.9	12.8	7.0	5.5	8.2	8.6	9.0
Other professional services	...	6.6	17.1	17.5	9.5	6.5	8.0	7.5	7.4
Dental services	...	9.1	11.1	9.0	7.1	6.9	8.8	4.8	6.1
Other personal health care	...	7.3	10.1	11.4	19.2	10.0	11.8	8.7	5.8
Nursing home and home health	...	17.2	17.5	11.8	9.9	3.8	5.5	6.1	6.6
Home health care [1]	...	14.5	26.9	18.1	19.4	0.0	5.9	11.1	13.3
Nursing home care [1]	...	17.4	16.8	10.7	7.1	5.2	5.3	4.5	4.3
Retail outlet sales of medical products	...	7.8	9.4	11.2	6.6	10.8	10.9	9.0	6.7
Prescription drugs	...	7.5	8.2	12.8	8.6	14.7	14.3	10.2	8.2
Other medical products	...	8.1	10.6	9.5	4.0	3.9	2.1	5.1	1.9
Government administration and net cost of private health insurance	...	8.6	16.0	12.4	8.3	6.8	14.3	17.7	9.4
Government public health activities	...	12.8	16.5	12.0	9.2	7.0	9.2	4.4	4.0
Investment	...	11.7	10.1	9.3	5.9	6.9	7.6	6.7	7.3
Research [3]	...	10.9	10.8	8.9	7.7	6.9	12.8	9.5	9.3
Structures and equipment	...	12.0	9.8	9.4	5.2	6.9	5.6	5.5	6.5

See footnotes at end of table.

Table 123 (page 2 of 2). National health expenditures, average annual percent change, and percent distribution, by type of expenditure: United States, selected years 1960–2004

[Data are compiled from various sources by the Centers for Medicare & Medicaid Services]

Type of national health expenditure	1960	1970	1980	1990	1995	2000	2002	2003	2004
	Percent distribution								
National health expenditures	100.0	100.0	100.0	100.0	100.0	100.0	100.0	100.0	100.0
Health services and supplies.	90.4	89.3	91.8	92.9	93.4	93.1	93.2	93.3	93.4
Personal health care.	84.5	83.8	84.5	84.7	84.6	83.9	83.4	83.1	83.1
Hospital care.	33.3	36.7	39.6	35.1	33.4	30.7	30.4	30.2	30.4
Professional services	30.2	27.5	26.4	30.2	31.0	31.4	31.3	31.2	31.3
Physician and clinical services.	19.4	18.6	18.5	22.0	21.6	21.2	21.0	21.1	21.3
Other professional services	1.4	1.0	1.4	2.5	2.8	2.9	2.8	2.8	2.8
Dental services	7.1	6.2	5.2	4.4	4.4	4.6	4.6	4.4	4.3
Other personal health care	2.2	1.7	1.3	1.3	2.3	2.7	2.9	2.9	2.8
Nursing home and home health	3.1	5.7	8.4	9.1	10.3	9.3	8.7	8.5	8.4
Home health care[1]	0.2	0.3	0.9	1.8	3.0	2.2	2.1	2.2	2.3
Nursing home care[1]	2.9	5.4	7.5	7.3	7.3	7.0	6.6	6.3	6.1
Retail outlet sales of medical products. . .	17.9	13.9	10.1	10.3	10.0	12.5	13.0	13.1	13.0
Prescription drugs	9.7	7.3	4.7	5.6	6.0	8.9	9.8	10.0	10.0
Other medical products	8.2	6.6	5.3	4.7	4.0	3.6	3.2	3.1	2.9
Government administration and net cost of private health insurance.	4.4	3.7	4.8	5.5	5.7	6.0	6.6	7.2	7.3
Government public health activities.	1.5	1.9	2.5	2.8	3.0	3.2	3.2	3.1	3.0
Investment	9.6	10.7	8.2	7.1	6.6	6.9	6.8	6.7	6.6
Research[3]	2.5	2.6	2.1	1.8	1.8	1.9	2.0	2.0	2.1
Structures and equipment	7.1	8.1	6.1	5.3	4.8	5.0	4.7	4.6	4.6

. . . Category not applicable.

[1]Freestanding facilities only. Additional services of this type are provided in hospital-based facilities and counted as hospital care.

[2]Includes personal care services delivered by government public health agencies.

[3]Research and development expenditures of drug companies and other manufacturers and providers of medical equipment and supplies are excluded from the category research expenditures. They are included in the expenditure class in which the product falls because these expenditures are covered by the payment received for that product. See Appendix II, Expenditures, national health.

NOTES: Percents are calculated using unrounded data. These data include revisions in health expenditures for past years and differ from previous editions of *Health, United States.*

SOURCE: Centers for Medicare & Medicaid Services, Office of the Actuary, National Health Statistics Group, National health accounts, National health expenditures, 2004. Available from: www.cms.hhs.gov/NationalHealthExpendData/.

[Data are compiled from various sources by the Centers for Medicare & Medicaid Services]

Type of personal health care expenditures and source of funds	1960	1970	1980	1990	1995	2000	2002	2003	2004
					Amount				
Per capita....................	$ 125	$ 299	$ 935	$2,389	$3,184	$ 3,968	$ 4,576	$ 4,883	$ 5,219
					Amount in billions				
All personal health care expenditures[1]..................	$ 23.3	$ 62.9	$215.3	$607.5	$863.7	$1,139.9	$1,341.4	$1,445.7	$1,560.2
					Percent distribution				
All sources of funds..............	100.0	100.0	100.0	100.0	100.0	100.0	100.0	100.0	100.0
Out-of-pocket payments..........	55.2	39.6	27.2	22.4	16.9	16.9	15.7	15.5	15.1
Private health insurance..........	21.4	22.3	28.4	33.7	33.4	35.3	35.9	36.0	36.1
Other private funds	2.0	2.8	4.3	5.0	5.1	5.0	4.3	4.4	4.4
Government	21.4	35.3	40.0	38.9	44.6	42.8	44.0	44.2	44.4
Federal	8.7	22.9	28.9	28.4	34.0	32.6	33.6	33.9	33.9
State and local	12.7	12.4	11.1	10.4	10.6	10.2	10.5	10.3	10.5
					Amount in billions				
Hospital care expenditures[2].........	$ 9.2	$ 27.6	$101.0	$251.6	$340.7	$ 417.0	$ 488.6	$ 525.5	$ 570.8
					Percent distribution				
All sources of funds..............	100.0	100.0	100.0	100.0	100.0	100.0	100.0	100.0	100.0
Out-of-pocket payments..........	20.7	9.0	5.4	4.5	3.1	3.3	3.2	3.2	3.3
Private health insurance..........	35.8	32.5	36.6	38.9	32.5	34.4	35.1	35.4	35.6
Other private funds	1.2	3.2	5.0	4.1	4.3	5.2	4.4	4.7	4.9
Government[3]..................	42.2	55.2	53.0	52.5	60.2	57.1	57.4	56.6	56.3
Medicaid[4]	...	9.6	9.1	10.6	16.7	17.0	17.3	17.1	17.3
Medicare	...	19.4	26.1	27.0	31.4	30.1	30.0	29.3	28.6
					Amount in billions				
Physician services expenditures	$ 5.4	$ 14.0	$ 47.1	$157.5	$220.5	$ 288.6	$ 337.9	$ 367.0	$ 399.9
					Percent distribution				
All sources of funds..............	100.0	100.0	100.0	100.0	100.0	100.0	100.0	100.0	100.0
Out-of-pocket payments..........	61.7	46.2	30.4	19.2	11.8	11.2	10.4	10.2	10.0
Private health insurance..........	29.8	30.1	35.5	42.7	48.1	47.4	48.2	48.4	48.5
Other private funds	1.4	1.6	3.9	7.2	8.0	7.7	7.2	7.1	6.9
Government[3]..................	7.2	22.1	30.1	30.9	32.1	33.8	34.2	34.3	34.6
Medicaid[4]	...	4.6	5.2	4.5	6.7	6.6	7.0	6.9	6.9
Medicare	...	11.8	17.0	18.6	18.8	20.2	20.0	20.1	20.5
					Amount in billions				
Nursing home expenditures[5]	$ 0.8	$ 4.0	$ 19.0	$ 52.6	$ 74.1	$ 95.3	$ 105.7	$ 110.4	$ 115.2
					Percent distribution				
All sources of funds..............	100.0	100.0	100.0	100.0	100.0	100.0	100.0	100.0	100.0
Out-of-pocket payments..........	77.3	52.0	37.2	36.1	28.1	30.0	27.9	27.6	27.7
Private health insurance..........	0.0	0.2	1.2	5.6	7.9	8.2	8.2	7.9	7.8
Other private funds	6.3	4.8	4.2	7.2	6.7	4.7	3.8	3.6	3.6
Government[3]..................	16.4	43.0	57.5	51.1	57.3	57.0	60.1	60.9	60.8
Medicaid[4]	...	23.3	53.8	45.8	46.0	44.1	44.6	44.9	44.3
Medicare	...	3.5	1.6	3.2	9.1	10.8	13.3	13.5	13.9

See footnotes at end of table.

[Data are compiled from various sources by the Centers for Medicare & Medicaid Services]

Type of personal health care expenditures and source of funds	1960	1970	1980	1990	1995	2000	2002	2003	2004
	Amount in billions								
Prescription drug expenditures	$ 2.7	$ 5.5	$ 12.0	$ 40.3	$ 60.9	$120.8	$157.9	$174.1	$188.5
	Percent distribution								
All sources of funds.	100.0	100.0	100.0	100.0	100.0	100.0	100.0	100.0	100.0
Out-of-pocket payments	96.0	82.4	70.3	55.5	38.4	27.7	25.3	25.1	24.9
Private health insurance	1.3	8.8	14.8	26.4	40.1	49.4	49.8	48.4	47.6
Other private funds	0.0	0.0	0.0	0.0	0.0	0.0	0.0	0.0	0.0
Government[3].	2.7	8.8	14.9	18.1	21.5	22.9	24.8	26.5	27.5
Medicaid[4]	. . .	0.0	0.0	12.6	15.9	16.7	17.6	18.8	19.3
Medicare	. . .	0.0	0.0	0.5	1.1	1.7	1.5	1.4	1.8
	Amount in billions								
All other personal health care expenditures[6]	$ 5.3	$ 11.8	$ 36.2	$105.5	$167.5	$218.2	$251.2	$268.7	$285.9
	Percent distribution								
All sources of funds.	100.0	100.0	100.0	100.0	100.0	100.0	100.0	100.0	100.0
Out-of-pocket payments	84.5	78.9	64.6	50.4	39.3	38.9	36.0	35.3	34.4
Private health insurance	1.6	3.3	15.3	24.6	24.6	25.1	24.1	23.6	23.5
Other private funds	4.2	3.6	4.3	4.7	4.3	3.8	3.3	3.3	3.2
Government[3].	9.8	14.2	15.8	20.2	31.8	32.2	36.6	37.9	38.9
Medicaid[4]	. . .	3.3	3.9	6.5	12.5	15.9	18.9	19.7	20.1
Medicare	. . .	1.1	3.8	7.1	13.2	9.7	10.9	11.5	12.2

. . . Category not applicable.

[1]Includes all expenditures for specified health services and supplies other than expenses for program administration, net cost of private health insurance, and government public health activities.

[2]Includes expenditures for hospital-based nursing home and home health agency care.

[3]Includes other government expenditures for these health care services, for example, Medicaid State Children's Health Insurance Program (SCHIP) expansions and SCHIP, care funded by the Department of Veterans Affairs, and state and locally financed subsidies to hospitals.

[4]Excludes Medicaid SCHIP expansions and SCHIP.

[5]Includes expenditures for care in freestanding nursing homes. Expenditures for care in hospital-based nursing homes are included with hospital care.

[6]Includes expenditures for dental services, other professional services, home health care, nonprescription drugs and other medical nondurables, vision products and other medical durables, and other personal health care, not shown separately. See Appendix II, Health expenditures, national.

NOTES: Percents are calculated using unrounded data. These data include revisions in health expenditure estimates and differ from previous editions of *Health, United States*.

SOURCE: Centers for Medicare & Medicaid Services, Office of the Actuary, National Health Statistics Group, National Health Accounts, National health expenditures, 2004. Available from: www.cms.hhs.gov/NationalHealthExpendData/.

Table 125 (page 1 of 3). Expenses for health care and prescribed medicine, by selected population characteristics: United States, selected years 1987–2003

[Data are based on household interviews of a sample of the noninstitutionalized population and a sample of medical providers]

Characteristic	Population in millions[2]			Total expenses[1]							
				Percent of persons with expense				Mean annual expense per person with expense[3]			
	1997	2000	2003	1987	1997	2000	2003	1987	1997	2000	2003
All ages	271.3	278.4	290.6	84.5	84.1	83.5	85.6	$2,530	$2,779	$2,885	$3,601
Under 65 years:											
Total	237.1	243.6	253.9	83.2	82.5	81.8	84.0	1,970	2,107	2,273	2,837
Under 6 years.	23.8	24.1	23.1	88.9	88.0	86.7	91.3	1,673	984	1,201	1,337
6–17 years	48.1	48.4	49.9	80.2	81.7	80.0	84.1	1,103	1,104	1,194	1,239
18–44 years	108.9	109.0	111.1	81.5	78.3	77.7	79.0	1,731	1,910	2,036	2,598
45–64 years	56.3	62.1	69.8	87.0	89.2	88.5	89.6	3,353	3,698	3,806	4,750
Sex											
Male	118.0	120.9	126.5	78.8	77.6	76.6	78.7	1,858	1,904	2,176	2,819
Female	119.1	122.7	127.4	87.5	87.4	87.0	89.4	2,065	2,286	2,357	2,852
Hispanic origin and race[4]											
Hispanic or Latino	29.4	32.0	38.5	71.0	69.5	69.0	70.4	1,571	1,754	1,548	1,931
Not Hispanic or Latino:											
White	166.2	169.2	166.2	86.9	87.2	86.6	89.0	1,976	2,261	2,377	2,961
Black or African American . .	31.3	32.1	32.2	72.2	72.1	71.3	76.7	2,383	1,690	2,414	2,698
Other	10.2	10.2	17.0	72.8	75.8	76.0	79.9	1,307	1,401	1,937	*3,542
Insurance status[5]											
Any private insurance	174.0	181.6	180.1	86.5	86.5	85.9	88.9	1,889	2,147	2,165	2,917
Public insurance only	29.8	29.7	38.9	82.4	83.3	83.6	85.5	3,168	2,561	3,450	3,258
Uninsured all year	33.3	32.3	34.8	61.8	61.1	57.3	57.4	1,231	1,259	1,603	1,492
65 years and over	34.2	34.8	36.7	93.7	95.2	95.5	96.3	6,249	6,818	6,561	8,209
Sex											
Male	14.6	15.0	15.8	92.0	94.5	93.4	95.6	6,395	7,662	7,035	8,379
Female	19.6	19.8	20.9	94.9	95.7	97.1	96.9	6,147	6,196	6,216	8,084
Hispanic origin and race[4]											
Hispanic or Latino	1.7	1.9	2.2	82.5	94.2	92.5	90.6	5,951	7,134	5,888	6,964
Not Hispanic or Latino:											
White	28.8	28.9	30.1	94.9	95.9	95.9	97.1	6,152	6,852	6,660	8,265
Black or African American . .	2.8	2.9	3.0	88.5	92.2	94.0	95.0	7,532	6,715	6,310	8,874
Other	*	*	1.3	*	*	*	90.9	*	*	*	7,302
Insurance status[6]											
Medicare only	8.8	12.0	10.9	85.9	92.1	94.8	94.5	4,922	6,281	5,633	7,535
Medicare and private insurance	21.7	19.2	20.6	~95.4	97.0	96.0	97.9	6,182	6,649	6,727	8,344
Medicare and other public coverage	3.2	3.2	4.6	94.4	93.2	96.3	96.5	9,602	9,609	9,002	9,466

See footnotes at end of table.

[Data are based on household interviews of a sample of the noninstitutionalized population and a sample of medical providers]

	Prescribed medicine expenses							
	Percent of persons with expense				Mean annual out-of-pocket expense per person with out-of-pocket expense[3,7]			
Characteristic	1987	1997	2000	2003	1987	1997	2000	2003
All ages	57.3	62.1	62.3	64.4	$149	$232	$293	$427
Under 65 years:								
Total	54.0	58.7	58.5	60.5	110	164	213	312
Under 6 years...........	61.8	61.3	56.9	57.9	39	40	40	69
6–17 years............	44.3	48.2	46.2	51.0	73	62	75	121
18–44 years............	51.3	55.9	56.0	56.5	86	140	161	248
45–64 years	65.3	71.8	73.3	74.5	209	305	401	544
Sex								
Male	46.5	51.5	51.3	52.7	102	146	187	291
Female	61.4	65.8	65.6	68.2	117	178	233	327
Hispanic origin and race[4]								
Hispanic or Latino	41.6	47.7	45.0	45.7	79	109	156	218
Not Hispanic or Latino:								
White.................	57.7	63.1	63.8	66.1	115	178	229	333
Black or African American ..	44.1	50.0	47.6	54.1	97	132	175	318
Other.................	41.1	44.8	47.8	51.8	81	142	150	215
Insurance status[5]								
Any private insurance	56.5	61.6	61.6	64.4	113	156	183	283
Public insurance only	56.5	62.0	62.4	63.6	76	162	305	385
Uninsured all year	35.1	40.2	37.6	36.7	121	236	353	428
65 years and over	81.6	86.0	88.3	91.0	343	554	666	955
Sex								
Male	78.0	82.8	83.9	89.1	319	499	499	793
Female	84.0	88.3	91.5	92.5	358	592	781	1,072
Hispanic origin and race[4]								
Hispanic or Latino	74.7	87.5	83.9	84.1	453	452	561	832
Not Hispanic or Latino:								
White.................	82.3	86.7	89.0	92.3	350	572	690	985
Black or African American ..	79.5	85.3	85.3	86.8	269	460	568	803
Other.................	*	*	*	83.2	*	*	*	773
Insurance status[6]								
Medicare only	70.6	82.1	87.7	89.0	379	640	795	1,253
Medicare and private insurance...............	83.4	88.1	89.0	92.7	356	562	615	871
Medicare and other public coverage	88.2	85.0	88.5	92.1	130	310	527	670

See footnotes at end of table.

Table 125 (page 3 of 3). Expenses for health care and prescribed medicine, by selected population characteristics: United States, selected years 1987–2003

[Data are based on household interviews of a sample of the noninstitutionalized population and a sample of medical providers]

---

* Estimates are considered unreliable. Data not shown are based on fewer than 100 sample cases. Data preceded by an asterisk have a relative standard error equal to or greater than 30%.

[1]Includes expenses for inpatient hospital and physician services, ambulatory physician and nonphysician services, prescribed medicines, home health services, dental services, and other medical equipment, supplies, and services that were purchased or rented during the year. Excludes expenses for over-the-counter medications, alternative care services, phone contacts with health providers, and premiums for health insurance.

[2]Includes persons in the civilian noninstitutionalized population for all or part of the year. Expenditures for persons only in this population for part of the year are restricted to those incurred during periods of eligibility (e.g., expenses incurred during periods of institutionalization and military service are not included in estimates).

[3]Estimates of expenses have been updated to 2003 dollars using the Consumer Price Index (all items) and differ from the previous edition of *Health, United States*. See Appendix II, Consumer Price Index (CPI).

[4]Persons of Hispanic origin may be of any race. Starting with 2002 data, MEPS respondents were allowed to report multiple races and these persons are included in the Other category. As a result, there is a slight increase in percentage of persons classified in the Other category in 2002 compared with prior years.

[5]Any private insurance includes individuals with insurance that provided coverage for hospital and physician care at any time during the year, other than Medicare, Medicaid, or other public coverage for hospital or physician services. Public insurance only includes individuals who were not covered by private insurance at any time during the year but were covered by Medicare, Medicaid, other public coverage for hospital or physician services, and/or CHAMPUS/CHAMPVA (TRICARE) at any point during the year. Uninsured includes persons not covered by either private or public insurance throughout the entire year or period of eligibility for the survey.

[6]Populations do not add to total because uninsured persons and persons with unknown insurance status were excluded.

[7]Includes expenses for all prescribed medications that were purchased or refilled during the survey year.

NOTES: 1987 estimates are based on National Medical Expenditure Survey (NMES) while estimates for other years are based on Medical Expenditure Panel Survey (MEPS). Because expenditures in NMES were based primarily on charges while those for MEPS were based on payments, NMES data were adjusted to be more comparable to MEPS using estimated charge to payment ratios for 1987. Overall, this resulted in about an 11% reduction from the unadjusted 1987 NMES expenditure estimates. See Zuvekas S, Cohen S. A guide to comparing health care expenditures in the 1996 MEPS to the 1987 NMES. Inquiry 2002;39(1):76–86. Data for additional years are available. See Appendix III.

SOURCE: Agency for Healthcare Research and Quality, Center for Cost and Financing Studies. 1987 National Medical Expenditure Survey and 1996–2003 Medical Expenditure Panel Surveys.

Table 126 (page 1 of 3). Sources of payment for health care, by selected population characteristics: United States, selected years 1987–2003

[Data are based on household interviews of a sample of the noninstitutionalized population and a sample of medical providers]

Characteristic	All sources	Out of pocket				Private insurance[1]			
		1987	1997	2000	2003	1987	1997	2000	2003
		Percent distribution							
All ages	100.0	24.8	19.4	19.4	19.6	36.6	40.3	40.3	41.6
Under 65 years:									
Total	100.0	26.2	21.1	20.3	20.0	46.6	53.1	52.5	54.0
Under 6 years	100.0	18.5	14.2	10.3	10.1	39.5	49.3	51.2	53.2
6–17 years	100.0	35.7	29.0	27.7	26.2	47.3	53.2	48.8	47.9
18–44 years	100.0	27.4	21.1	19.9	18.8	46.8	52.9	51.2	52.5
45–64 years	100.0	24.0	20.1	20.2	20.8	47.8	53.6	54.5	56.3
Sex									
Male	100.0	24.5	21.3	18.1	18.0	44.6	50.3	52.2	53.6
Female	100.0	27.5	21.0	22.1	21.8	48.1	55.1	52.7	54.3
Hispanic origin and race[2]									
Hispanic or Latino	100.0	22.0	18.8	20.5	17.7	36.1	42.3	45.8	41.8
Not Hispanic or Latino:									
White	100.0	28.2	21.8	21.7	22.1	50.1	55.8	55.1	59.6
Black or African American . .	100.0	15.5	17.1	11.8	14.2	30.0	42.3	40.5	36.8
Other	100.0	27.2	21.2	17.0	*12.0	46.7	45.2	51.2	40.0
Insurance status									
Any private insurance[3]	100.0	29.0	21.6	21.2	19.7	60.0	67.6	70.2	69.9
Public insurance only[4]	100.0	8.9	10.6	9.8	12.8	. . .	. . .	. . .	. . .
Uninsured all year[5]	100.0	40.6	41.3	40.4	51.8	. . .	. . .	. . .	. . .
65 years and over	100.0	22.0	16.3	17.5	18.8	15.8	16.5	14.9	15.8
Sex									
Male	100.0	21.7	14.2	14.2	15.2	17.6	20.1	16.8	17.3
Female	100.0	22.2	18.1	20.2	21.6	14.4	13.2	13.3	14.7
Hispanic origin and race[2]									
Hispanic or Latino	100.0	*13.5	13.6	13.9	14.9	*4.7	5.9	8.4	5.1
Not Hispanic or Latino:									
White	100.0	23.7	17.0	18.3	19.5	16.7	17.9	15.2	17.0
Black or African American . .	100.0	11.2	11.4	13.6	15.8	*11.9	8.8	9.3	10.2
Other	100.0	*	*	*	16.7	*	*	*	*16.0
Insurance status									
Medicare only	100.0	29.8	19.8	22.2	23.4	. . .	. . .	. . .	. . .
Medicare and private insurance	100.0	23.4	17.3	17.0	18.7	18.9	25.7	25.3	26.9
Medicare and other public coverage	100.0	*6.2	5.2	9.1	10.1	. . .	. . .	. . .	. . .

See footnotes at end of table.

Table 126 (page 2 of 3). Sources of payment for health care, by selected population characteristics: United States, selected years 1987–2003

[Data are based on household interviews of a sample of the noninstitutionalized population and a sample of medical providers]

	Source of payment for health care							
	Public coverage[6]				Other[7]			
Characteristic	1987	1997	2000	2003	1987	1997	2000	2003
	Percent distribution							
All ages	34.1	34.4	35.4	33.1	4.5	5.9	5.0	5.7
Under 65 years:								
Total	21.3	18.1	21.3	19.0	6.0	7.7	6.0	7.0
Under 6 years	35.8	25.4	33.6	31.0	6.2	11.2	4.9	5.7
6–17 years	11.8	14.1	20.1	22.4	5.2	3.7	3.4	3.5
18–44 years	19.4	15.7	21.1	17.3	6.4	10.3	7.8	*11.5
45–64 years	22.4	20.3	20.2	18.6	5.8	6.0	5.2	4.3
Sex								
Male	23.9	19.5	23.5	19.0	7.1	8.9	6.3	*9.5
Female	19.2	17.0	19.5	19.0	5.2	6.8	5.7	4.9
Hispanic origin and race[2]								
Hispanic or Latino	35.8	28.9	27.5	31.2	6.0	10.0	6.2	9.3
Not Hispanic or Latino:								
White	15.9	15.3	18.0	14.2	5.8	7.1	5.2	4.1
Black or African American . .	47.2	30.7	38.8	43.9	7.3	9.9	8.8	5.1
Other	21.0	23.7	19.0	*15.0	5.1	9.9	*12.8	*33.0
Insurance status								
Any private insurance[3]	6.2	6.6	5.3	4.7	4.8	4.2	3.3	*5.7
Public insurance only[4]	87.2	80.7	84.4	81.4	3.9	8.7	5.8	5.8
Uninsured all year[5]	28.6	7.5	*21.2	15.1	30.9	51.1	38.4	33.1
65 years and over	60.8	64.8	64.7	62.5	1.5	2.5	2.9	2.9
Sex								
Male	58.8	63.4	66.9	64.8	*1.9	2.3	2.2	2.8
Female	62.3	65.9	63.0	60.7	1.1	2.7	3.5	3.0
Hispanic origin and race[2]								
Hispanic or Latino	80.2	77.8	75.6	78.3	*1.6	*2.7	*2.2	1.6
Not Hispanic or Latino:								
White	58.0	62.6	64.1	60.9	1.6	2.5	2.4	2.6
Black or African American . .	76.3	77.6	68.3	70.4	0.6	2.2	*8.9	*3.7
Other	*	*	*	58.0	*	*	*	*9.3
Insurance status								
Medicare only	68.8	72.4	72.2	68.2	1.4	7.7	5.7	8.4
Medicare and private insurance	56.1	56.3	57.1	54.0	1.6	0.6	*0.6	0.4
Medicare and other public coverage	92.9	92.7	87.3	87.6	1.0	*2.1	*3.6	*1.6

See footnotes at end of table.

Table 126 (page 3 of 3). Sources of payment for health care, by selected population characteristics: United States, selected years 1987–2003

[Data are based on household interviews of a sample of the noninstitutionalized population and a sample of medical providers]

. . . Category not applicable.

* Estimates are considered unreliable. Estimates based on fewer than 100 sample cases or with a relative standard error of 30% or higher are not shown.

[1]Private insurance includes any type of private insurance payments reported for people with private health insurance coverage during the year.

[2]Persons of Hispanic origin may be of any race. Starting with 2002 data, MEPS respondents were allowed to report multiple races and these persons are included in the Other category. As a result, there is a slight increase in the percent of persons classified in the Other category in 2002 compared with prior years.

[3]Includes individuals with insurance that provided coverage for hospital and physician care at any time during the year, other than Medicare, Medicaid, or other public coverage for hospital or physician services.

[4]Includes individuals who were not covered by private insurance at any time during the year but were covered by Medicare, Medicaid, other public coverage for hospital or physician services, and/or CHAMPUS/CHAMPVA (TRICARE) at any point during the year.

[5]Includes individuals not covered by either private or public insurance throughout the entire year or period of eligibility for the survey. However, a portion of expenses for the uninsured was paid by sources that were not defined as health insurance coverage, such as the Department of Veterans Affairs, community and neighborhood clinics, the Indian Health Service, state and local health departments, state programs other than Medicaid, Workers' Compensation, and other unclassified sources (e.g., automobile, homeowner's, liability insurance).

[6]Public coverage includes payments made by Medicare, Medicaid, the Department of Veterans Affairs, other federal sources (e.g., Indian Health Service, military treatment facilities, and other care provided by the federal government), and various state and local sources (e.g., community and neighborhood clinics, state and local health departments, and state programs other than Medicaid).

[7]Other sources includes Workers' Compensation, unclassified sources (automobile, homeowners', or liability insurance, and other miscellaneous or unknown sources), Medicaid payments reported for people who were not enrolled in the program at any time during the year, and any type of private insurance payments reported for people without private health insurance coverage during the year as defined in the survey.

NOTES: 1987 estimates are based on the National Medical Expenditure Survey (NMES); estimates for other years are based on the Medical Expenditure Panel Survey (MEPS). Because expenditures in NMES were based primarily on charges while those for MEPS were based on payments, data for NMES were adjusted to be more comparable to MEPS using estimated charge to payment ratios for 1987. Overall, this resulted in an approximate 11% reduction from the unadjusted 1987 NMES expenditure estimates. For a detailed explanation of this adjustment, see Zuvekas S, Cohen S. A guide to comparing health care estimates in the 1996 Medical Expenditure Panel Survey to the 1987 National Medical Expenditure Survey. Inquiry 2002;39(1):76–86. Data for additional years are available. See Appendix III.

SOURCE: Agency for Healthcare Research and Quality, Center for Cost and Financing Studies. 1987 National Medical Expenditure Survey and 1996–2003 Medical Expenditure Panel Survey.

Table 127. Out-of-pocket health care expenses among persons with medical expenses, by age: United States, selected years 1987–2003

[Data are based on household interviews for a sample of the noninstitutionalized population and a sample of medical providers]

Age and year	Percent of persons with expenses	Amount paid out of pocket among persons with expenses[1]						
		Total	$0	$1–124	$125–249	$250–499	$500–999	$1,000+
All ages		Percent distribution						
1987	84.5	100.0	10.4	29.2	16.6	17.4	13.3	13.1
1999	84.3	100.0	7.4	35.9	15.5	15.6	12.8	12.7
2000	83.5	100.0	6.9	34.8	15.0	16.2	13.0	14.1
2001	85.4	100.0	7.1	31.7	14.7	16.6	13.8	16.2
2002	85.2	100.0	7.8	29.8	14.3	15.7	14.8	17.6
2003	85.6	100.0	7.6	28.0	14.0	15.8	15.2	19.5
Under 6 years								
1987	88.9	100.0	19.2	38.7	18.9	14.7	5.3	3.2
1999	87.9	100.0	17.7	60.5	12.2	5.9	2.6	1.1
2000	86.7	100.0	16.7	61.0	11.1	7.5	2.4	1.3
2001	88.8	100.0	18.5	57.8	12.9	7.6	2.1	1.1
2002	88.8	100.0	21.5	51.7	14.0	7.7	3.9	1.3
2003	91.3	100.0	20.6	51.7	13.3	8.5	4.2	1.6
6–17 years								
1987	80.2	100.0	15.5	37.9	18.2	12.4	8.5	7.6
1999	81.5	100.0	15.0	46.6	15.4	11.2	6.0	5.8
2000	80.0	100.0	14.7	46.5	14.5	11.2	6.5	6.6
2001	83.2	100.0	15.0	45.2	15.0	11.1	6.0	7.7
2002	83.6	100.0	16.6	43.2	14.7	12.0	6.8	6.7
2003	84.1	100.0	16.1	40.6	15.5	12.2	7.9	7.8
18–44 years								
1987	81.5	100.0	10.1	32.3	17.7	18.2	11.9	9.8
1999	78.9	100.0	6.4	40.2	17.6	16.6	11.1	8.1
2000	77.7	100.0	5.8	39.1	17.8	17.1	11.7	8.5
2001	79.3	100.0	6.0	34.8	17.5	18.8	13.3	9.7
2002	78.5	100.0	6.7	34.2	17.4	17.1	13.9	10.8
2003	79.0	100.0	6.4	31.6	17.4	18.3	14.0	12.3
45–64 years								
1987	87.0	100.0	5.7	20.4	15.6	20.7	18.8	18.8
1999	88.9	100.0	2.7	24.0	16.4	19.7	19.0	18.2
2000	88.5	100.0	2.6	22.3	15.6	19.9	18.8	20.9
2001	89.9	100.0	2.4	19.6	13.9	20.4	19.8	23.8
2002	90.0	100.0	2.3	18.8	12.8	19.1	21.3	25.8
2003	89.6	100.0	2.4	17.2	12.3	17.7	21.4	29.1
65–74 years								
1987	92.8	100.0	5.3	15.4	11.6	18.5	22.1	27.1
1999	95.3	100.0	1.4	16.1	11.3	17.9	23.7	29.6
2000	94.7	100.0	1.5	14.4	10.6	20.2	20.1	33.2
2001	95.6	100.0	1.5	14.4	9.9	18.3	21.7	34.2
2002	96.1	100.0	1.8	10.1	9.9	16.4	22.5	39.3
2003	95.3	100.0	1.7	9.0	8.2	15.6	24.5	41.0
75 years or more								
1987	95.1	100.0	5.6	12.9	10.0	17.1	21.2	33.2
1999	95.3	100.0	2.6	14.5	10.2	18.6	20.2	33.8
2000	96.5	100.0	2.6	14.2	8.4	18.2	22.0	34.6
2001	97.0	100.0	1.7	10.1	9.2	14.4	21.1	43.6
2002	96.5	100.0	2.2	9.0	7.7	14.4	20.4	46.2
2003	97.5	100.0	1.9	8.7	7.0	13.4	20.1	48.9

[1]1987 dollars were converted to 1998 dollars using the national Consumer Price Index. Starting with 1998 data, percent distributions are based on actual dollars (nonadjusted).

NOTES: Out-of-pocket expenses include expenditures for inpatient hospital and physician services, ambulatory physician and nonphysician services, prescribed medicines, home health services, dental services, and various other medical equipment, supplies, and services that were purchased or rented during the year. Out-of-pocket expenses for over-the-counter medications, alternative care services, phone contacts with health providers, and premiums for health insurance policies are not included in these estimates. 1987 estimates are based on the National Medical Expenditure Survey (NMES), while estimates for other years are based on the Medical Expenditure Panel Survey (MEPS). Because expenditures in NMES were based primarily on charges while those for MEPS were based on payments, data for the NMES were adjusted to be more comparable to MEPS using estimated charge to payment ratios for 1987. Overall, this resulted in an approximate 11% reduction from the unadjusted 1987 NMES expenditure estimates. For a detailed explanation of this adjustment, see Zuvekas S, Cohen S. A guide to comparing health care expenditures in the 1996 MEPS to the 1987 NMES. Inquiry 2002;39(1):76–86. Data for additional years are available. See Appendix III.

SOURCES: Agency for Healthcare Research and Quality, Center for Cost and Financing Studies. 1987 National Medical Expenditure Survey and 1998–2003 Medical Expenditure Panel Survey.

Table 128 (page 1 of 2). Expenditures for health services and supplies and percent distribution, by type of payer: United States, selected years 1987–2004

[Data are compiled from various sources by the Centers for Medicare & Medicaid Services]

Type of payer	1987	1993	1997	1999	2000	2001	2002	2003	2004
					Amount in billions				
Total[1]	$477.8	$853.5	$1,054.4	$1,180.0	$1,264.5	$1,375.5	$1,499.2	$1,624.5	$1,753.0
Private	333.3	546.9	667.9	766.4	820.5	867.7	928.1	995.3	1,070.3
Private business	122.1	219.7	266.0	312.4	341.9	367.1	391.2	420.8	448.3
Employer contribution to private health insurance premiums	84.2	159.2	191.6	229.2	250.9	271.8	294.1	320.6	342.8
Private employer contribution to Medicare hospital insurance trust fund[2]	24.6	35.8	49.5	57.6	62.3	63.4	62.9	64.3	67.4
Workers compensation and temporary disability insurance	11.6	21.8	21.3	21.7	24.3	27.5	29.5	30.9	32.8
Industrial inplant health services	1.7	2.9	3.6	4.0	4.3	4.5	4.7	4.9	5.3
Household	188.7	291.2	353.3	399.5	425.0	447.6	482.1	514.5	557.2
Employee contribution to private health insurance premiums and individual policy premiums	43.9	90.3	112.4	124.3	133.6	146.8	167.4	183.5	206.4
Employee and self-employment contributions and voluntary premiums paid to Medicare hospital insurance trust fund[2]	29.4	43.7	63.0	75.0	82.5	82.9	84.1	86.0	90.3
Premiums paid by individuals to Medicare supplementary medical insurance trust fund	6.2	11.9	15.5	16.3	16.3	18.1	19.8	21.6	24.8
Out-of-pocket health spending	109.2	145.3	162.4	183.9	192.6	199.8	210.8	223.5	235.7
Other private revenues	22.4	36.1	48.7	54.4	53.6	53.0	54.8	60.1	64.8
Public	144.5	306.5	386.5	413.6	444.0	507.8	571.1	629.2	682.7
Federal government	74.1	174.6	220.1	221.5	236.5	277.8	317.9	356.0	389.0
Employer contributions to private health insurance premiums	4.9	11.5	11.4	13.2	14.3	15.8	17.7	19.7	21.6
Medicaid[3]	28.1	78.1	97.4	110.3	119.7	134.5	149.4	164.8	175.8
Other[4]	41.1	85.0	111.4	98.0	102.5	127.6	150.8	171.4	191.6
State and local government	70.5	131.9	166.3	192.1	207.5	230.0	253.2	273.2	293.7
Employer contributions to private health insurance premiums	16.0	36.0	43.9	51.1	56.0	63.4	73.0	82.4	87.7
Medicaid[3]	22.8	46.5	64.9	77.6	85.3	94.7	103.9	111.0	122.2
Other[5]	31.7	49.4	57.5	63.4	66.1	72.0	76.3	79.8	83.8
					Percent distribution				
Total	100.0	100.0	100.0	100.0	100.0	100.0	100.0	100.0	100.0
Private	69.8	64.1	63.3	64.9	64.9	63.1	61.9	61.3	61.1
Private business	25.6	25.7	25.2	26.5	27.0	26.7	26.1	25.9	25.6
Employer contribution to private health insurance premiums	17.6	18.7	18.2	19.4	19.8	19.8	19.6	19.7	19.6
Private employer contribution to Medicare hospital insurance trust fund[2]	5.1	4.2	4.7	4.9	4.9	4.6	4.2	4.0	3.8
Workers compensation and temporary disability insurance	2.4	2.6	2.0	1.8	1.9	2.0	2.0	1.9	1.9
Industrial inplant health services	0.4	0.3	0.3	0.3	0.3	0.3	0.3	0.3	0.3
Household	39.5	34.1	33.5	33.9	33.6	32.5	32.2	31.7	31.8
Employee contribution to private health insurance premiums and individual policy premiums	9.2	10.6	10.7	10.5	10.6	10.7	11.2	11.3	11.8
Employee and self-employment contributions and voluntary premiums paid to Medicare hospital insurance trust fund[2]	6.2	5.1	6.0	6.4	6.5	6.0	5.6	5.3	5.2
Premiums paid by individuals to Medicare supplementary medical insurance trust fund	1.3	1.4	1.5	1.4	1.3	1.3	1.3	1.3	1.4
Out-of-pocket health spending	22.9	17.0	15.4	15.6	15.2	14.5	14.1	13.8	13.4
Other private revenues	4.7	4.2	4.6	4.6	4.2	3.9	3.7	3.7	3.7

See footnotes at end of table.

Table 128 (page 2 of 2). Expenditures for health services and supplies and percent distribution, by type of payer: United States, selected years 1987–2004

[Data are compiled from various sources by the Centers for Medicare & Medicaid Services]

Type of payer	1987	1993	1997	1999	2000	2001	2002	2003	2004
				Percent distribution					
Public	30.3	35.9	36.7	35.0	35.1	36.9	38.1	38.7	38.9
Federal government	15.5	20.5	20.9	18.8	18.7	20.2	21.2	21.9	22.2
Employer contributions to private health insurance premiums	1.0	1.3	1.1	1.1	1.1	1.1	1.2	1.2	1.2
Medicaid[3]	5.9	9.2	9.2	9.3	9.5	9.8	10.0	10.1	10.0
Other[4]	8.6	10.0	10.6	8.3	8.1	9.3	10.1	10.6	10.9
State and local government	14.8	15.5	15.8	16.3	16.4	16.7	16.9	16.8	16.8
Employer contributions to private health insurance premiums	3.3	4.2	4.2	4.3	4.4	4.6	4.9	5.1	5.0
Medicaid[3]	4.8	5.5	6.2	6.6	6.7	6.9	6.9	6.8	7.0
Other[5]	6.6	5.8	5.5	5.4	5.2	5.2	5.1	4.9	4.8

[1]Excludes research and construction.
[2]Includes one-half of self-employment contribution to Medicare hospital insurance trust fund.
[3]Includes Medicaid buy-in premiums for Medicare.
[4]Includes expenditures for Medicare (with adjustments for contributions by employers and individuals and premiums paid to the Medicare insurance trust fund), maternal and child health, vocational rehabilitation, Substance Abuse and Mental Health Services Administration, Indian Health Service, federal workers' compensation, other miscellaneous general hospital and medical programs, public health activities, Department of Defense, and Department of Veterans Affairs.
[5]Includes other public and general assistance, maternal and child health, vocational rehabilitation, public health activities, hospital subsidies, and employer contributions to Medicare hospital insurance trust fund.

NOTES: This table disaggregates health expenditures according to four classes of payers: businesses, households (individuals), federal government, and state and local governments with a small amount of revenue coming from nonpatient revenue sources such as philanthropy. Where businesses or households pay dedicated funds into government health programs (for example, Medicare) or employers and employees share in the cost of health premiums, these costs are assigned to businesses or households accordingly. This results in a lower share of expenditures being assigned to the federal government than for tabulations of expenditures by source of funds. Estimates of national health expenditure by source of funds aim to track government-sponsored health programs over time and do not delineate the role of business employers in paying for health care. Figures may not sum to totals due to rounding. These data were revised and differ from previous editions of *Health, United States.*

SOURCE: Centers for Medicare & Medicaid Services, Office of the Actuary, National Health Statistics Group. Sponsors of Health Care Costs: Businesses, Households and Governments, 1987–2004. Available from: www.cms.hhs.gov/NationalHealthExpendData/downloads/bhg06.pdf.

Table 129 (page 1 of 2). Employers' costs per employee-hour worked for total compensation, wages and salaries, and health insurance, by selected characteristics: United States, selected years 1991–2006

[Data are based on surveys of a sample of employers]

Characteristic	1991	1994	1996	1998	2000	2002	2003	2004	2005	2006
	Amount per employee-hour worked									
State and local government.......	$22.31	$25.27	$25.73	$27.28	$29.05	$31.29	$32.62	$34.21	$35.50	$36.96
Total private industry............	15.40	17.08	17.49	18.50	19.85	21.71	22.37	23.29	24.17	25.09
Industry:										
Goods producing...........	18.48	20.85	21.27	22.26	23.55	25.44	26.25	27.19	28.48	29.36
Service providing...........	14.31	15.82	16.28	17.31	18.72	20.66	21.30	22.33	23.11	24.05
Occupational group: [1]										
White collar...............	18.15	20.26	21.10	22.38	24.19	26.43	28.85	- - -	- - -	- - -
Blue collar................	15.15	16.92	17.04	17.56	18.73	20.15	21.21	- - -	- - -	- - -
Service..................	7.82	8.38	8.61	9.37	9.72	10.95	13.68	- - -	- - -	- - -
Management, professional, and related	- - -	- - -	- - -	- - -	- - -	- - -	- - -	40.23	42.09	44.32
Sales and office............	- - -	- - -	- - -	- - -	- - -	- - -	- - -	18.42	19.30	19.93
Service..................	- - -	- - -	- - -	- - -	- - -	- - -	- - -	11.66	12.07	12.3
Natural resources, construction, and maintenance	- - -	- - -	- - -	- - -	- - -	- - -	- - -	26.55	27.26	28.07
Production, transportation, and material moving	- - -	- - -	- - -	- - -	- - -	- - -	- - -	20.21	20.82	21.19
Census region:										
Northeast	17.56	20.03	20.57	20.38	22.67	25.00	25.70	26.29	27.09	28.75
Midwest	15.05	16.26	16.30	18.15	19.22	21.25	22.40	23.26	24.23	24.65
South	13.68	15.05	15.62	16.45	17.81	19.49	19.95	20.80	21.36	22.35
West....................	15.97	18.08	18.78	19.94	20.88	22.68	23.07	24.54	25.98	26.56
Union status:										
Union	19.76	23.26	23.31	23.59	25.88	29.42	30.68	31.94	33.17	34.07
Nonunion	14.54	16.04	16.61	17.80	19.07	20.79	21.36	22.28	23.09	24.03
Establishment employment size:										
1–99 employees	13.38	14.58	14.85	15.92	17.16	18.51	18.93	19.47	20.22	20.43
100 or more	17.34	19.45	20.09	21.20	22.81	25.48	26.42	27.81	28.94	30.34
100–499	14.31	15.88	16.61	17.52	19.30	21.99	22.62	23.91	24.44	25.91
500 or more............	20.60	23.35	24.03	25.56	26.93	29.79	30.94	32.54	34.59	35.94
	Wages and salaries as a percent of total compensation									
State and local government.......	69.6	69.5	69.8	70.3	70.8	70.8	70.0	69.2	68.3	67.6
Total private industry............	72.3	71.1	71.9	72.8	73.0	72.8	72.2	71.5	71.0	70.7
Industry:										
Goods producing...........	68.7	66.5	67.6	69.0	69.0	68.7	67.7	66.7	65.5	66.2
Service providing...........	73.9	73.1	73.8	74.4	74.5	74.2	73.7	72.9	72.6	72.0
Occupational group: [1]										
White collar...............	73.8	72.7	73.2	73.9	74.0	73.7	72.9	- - -	- - -	- - -
Blue collar................	68.4	66.8	68.1	69.2	69.4	69.5	68.5	- - -	- - -	- - -
Service..................	76.2	75.5	75.8	77.4	77.9	76.9	72.4	- - -	- - -	- - -
Management, professional, and related	- - -	- - -	- - -	- - -	- - -	- - -	- - -	72.1	71.5	70.9
Sales and office............	- - -	- - -	- - -	- - -	- - -	- - -	- - -	73.0	72.6	72.2
Service..................	- - -	- - -	- - -	- - -	- - -	- - -	- - -	75.8	75.7	75.3
Natural resources, construction, and maintenance	- - -	- - -	- - -	- - -	- - -	- - -	- - -	69.1	68.0	68.0
Production, transportation, and material moving	- - -	- - -	- - -	- - -	- - -	- - -	- - -	66.9	66.2	66.7
Census region:										
Northeast	72.0	70.5	70.9	72.1	72.2	71.9	71.2	70.4	70.4	70.0
Midwest	71.1	69.7	71.1	71.6	72.4	72.0	71.6	71.1	70.1	69.4
South	73.3	72.1	72.7	73.9	73.5	73.6	73.2	72.5	72.1	72.1
West....................	72.8	72.0	73.1	74.0	74.0	73.5	72.6	71.6	70.9	71.0
Union status:										
Union	65.9	63.5	64.0	65.2	65.2	65.7	65.0	63.6	62.6	62.3
Nonunion	74.1	72.9	73.6	74.2	74.4	74.0	73.5	72.8	72.4	72.1
Establishment employment size:										
1–99 employees	74.7	73.5	74.7	75.4	75.5	75.0	74.6	74.3	73.9	73.7
100 or more	70.5	69.3	69.9	70.8	71.0	70.9	70.2	69.1	68.5	68.4
100–499	72.1	71.6	71.6	72.3	72.8	72.2	71.4	70.7	70.2	70.0
500 or more............	69.3	67.6	68.6	69.6	69.4	69.8	69.1	67.7	67.0	66.9

See footnotes at end of table.

Table 129 (page 2 of 2). Employers' costs per employee-hour worked for total compensation, wages and salaries, and health insurance, by selected characteristics: United States, selected years 1991–2006

[Data are based on surveys of a sample of employers]

Characteristic	1991	1994	1996	1998	2000	2002	2003	2004	2005	2006
	Health insurance as a percent of total compensation									
State and local government	6.9	8.2	7.7	7.5	7.8	8.6	9.2	9.8	10.2	10.6
Total private industry	6.0	6.7	5.9	5.4	5.5	5.9	6.3	6.6	6.8	6.9
Industry:										
Goods producing	6.9	8.1	7.2	6.6	6.9	7.2	7.5	7.8	8.0	8.4
Service providing	5.5	6.0	5.4	4.9	4.9	5.5	5.9	6.2	6.4	6.4
Occupational group: [1]										
White collar	5.6	6.2	5.5	5.0	5.0	5.4	6.4	- - -	- - -	- - -
Blue collar	7.0	8.0	7.2	6.7	6.8	7.3	8.0	- - -	- - -	- - -
Service	4.6	5.4	4.8	4.3	4.3	5.1	7.0	- - -	- - -	- - -
Management, professional,										
and related	- - -	- - -	- - -	- - -	- - -	- - -	- - -	5.4	5.5	5.6
Sales and office	- - -	- - -	- - -	- - -	- - -	- - -	- - -	7.3	7.5	7.5
Service	- - -	- - -	- - -	- - -	- - -	- - -	- - -	6.0	6.1	6.2
Natural resources, construction,										
and maintenance	- - -	- - -	- - -	- - -	- - -	- - -	- - -	6.9	7.5	7.7
Production, transportation, and										
material moving	- - -	- - -	- - -	- - -	- - -	- - -	- - -	8.5	8.9	9.0
Census region:										
Northeast	6.2	6.9	6.2	5.6	5.6	5.9	6.3	6.5	6.8	6.7
Midwest	6.3	7.3	6.3	5.7	5.8	6.4	6.6	7.0	7.3	7.6
South	5.5	6.3	5.9	5.3	5.4	5.8	6.2	6.5	6.6	6.7
West	5.8	6.1	5.2	4.9	5.0	5.6	6.0	6.3	6.3	6.4
Union status:										
Union	8.2	9.8	8.8	8.4	8.4	8.7	9.1	9.6	10.3	10.3
Nonunion	5.4	5.9	5.3	4.8	5.0	5.4	5.8	6.1	6.2	6.3
Establishment employment size:										
1–99 employees	5.1	5.7	5.0	4.6	4.8	5.2	5.5	5.8	5.9	6.0
100 or more	6.6	7.3	6.6	6.0	6.0	6.6	7.0	7.2	7.5	7.5
100–499	6.3	6.5	6.3	5.8	5.6	6.4	6.9	7.1	7.5	7.4
500 or more	6.8	7.9	6.9	6.2	6.4	6.7	7.0	7.3	7.6	7.6

- - - Data not available.

[1] Starting with 2004 data, sample establishments were classified by industry categories based on the 2000 North American Industry Classification (NAICS) system, as defined by the U.S. Office of Management and Budget. Within a sample establishment, specific job categories were selected and classified into about 800 occupational classifications according to the 2000 Standard Occupational Classification (SOC) system. Individual occupations were combined to represent one of five higher-level aggregations, such as management, professional, and related occupations. For more detailed information on NAICS and SOC, including background and definitions, see the websites: www.bls.gov/bls/naics.htm and www.bls.gov/soc/home.htm. NAICS and SOC have replaced the 1987 Standard Industrial Classification System (SIC) and the Occupational Classification System (OCS).

NOTES: Costs are calculated annually from March survey data. Total compensation includes wages and salaries and benefits. See Appendix II, Employer costs for employee compensation. Data for additional years are available. See Appendix III.

SOURCES: U.S. Department of Labor, Bureau of Labor Statistics, National Compensation Survey, Employer Costs for Employee Compensation, March release; News pub no 06–1049, June 21, 2006. Washington, DC. Data are available on the Bureau of Labor Statistics Web site at www.bls.gov/ncs/ect/home.htm.

Table 130. Hospital expenses, by type of ownership and size of hospital: United States, selected years 1980–2004

[Data are based on reporting by a census of hospitals]

Type of ownership and size of hospital	1980	1990	1995	2000	2003	2004	1980–1990	1990–1995	1995–2000	2000–2004
Total expenses	\multicolumn{6}{c}{Amount in billions}					Average annual percent change			
All hospitals	$ 91.9	$234.9	$320.3	$395.4	$ 498.1	$ 533.9	9.8	6.4	4.3	7.8
Federal	7.9	15.2	20.2	23.9	30.9	34.8	6.8	5.9	3.4	9.8
Non-federal[1]	84.0	219.6	300.0	371.5	467.2	499.0	10.1	6.4	4.4	7.7
Community[2]	76.9	203.7	285.6	356.6	450.1	481.2	10.2	7.0	4.5	7.8
Nonprofit	55.8	150.7	209.6	267.1	337.7	359.4	10.4	6.8	5.0	7.7
For profit	5.8	18.8	26.7	35.0	44.0	49.0	12.5	7.3	5.6	8.8
State-local government	15.2	34.2	49.3	54.5	68.5	72.9	8.4	7.6	2.0	7.5
6–24 beds	0.2	0.5	1.1	1.5	2.5	2.9	9.6	17.1	6.4	17.9
25–49 beds	1.7	4.0	7.2	10.4	14.0	15.1	8.9	12.5	7.6	9.8
50–99 beds	5.4	12.6	17.8	22.3	28.2	30.2	8.8	7.2	4.6	7.9
100–199 beds	12.5	33.3	50.7	63.4	75.6	79.7	10.3	8.8	4.6	5.9
200–299 beds	13.4	38.7	55.8	67.1	81.0	86.1	11.2	7.6	3.8	6.4
300–399 beds	11.5	33.1	43.3	54.3	70.4	76.0	11.2	5.5	4.6	8.8
400–499 beds	10.5	25.3	33.7	41.3	51.6	57.4	9.2	5.9	4.2	8.6
500 beds or more	21.6	56.2	76.1	96.3	126.9	134.0	10.0	6.3	4.8	8.6
Expenses per inpatient day	\multicolumn{6}{c}{Amount}								
Community[2]	$ 245	$ 687	$ 968	$1,149	$ 1,379	$ 1,450	10.9	7.1	3.5	6.0
Nonprofit	246	692	994	1,182	1,430	1,501	10.9	7.5	3.5	6.2
For profit	257	752	947	1,057	1,265	1,362	11.3	4.7	2.2	6.5
State-local government	239	634	878	1,064	1,238	1,291	10.2	6.7	3.9	5.0
6–24 beds	203	526	678	896	1,111	1,222	10.0	5.2	5.7	8.1
25–49 beds	197	489	696	891	1,032	1,071	9.5	7.3	5.1	4.7
50–99 beds	191	493	647	745	893	916	9.9	5.6	2.9	5.3
100–199 beds	215	585	796	925	1,082	1,153	10.5	6.4	3.0	5.7
200–299 beds	239	665	943	1,122	1,343	1,436	10.8	7.2	3.5	6.4
300–399 beds	248	731	1,070	1,277	1,522	1,602	11.4	7.9	3.6	5.8
400–499 beds	215	756	1,135	1,353	1,714	1,756	13.4	8.5	3.6	6.7
500 beds or more	239	825	1,212	1,468	1,750	1,829	13.2	8.0	3.9	5.7
Expenses per inpatient stay										
Community[2]	$1,851	$4,947	$6,216	$6,649	$ 7,796	$ 8,166	10.3	4.7	1.4	5.3
Nonprofit	1,902	5,001	6,279	6,717	7,905	8,267	10.2	4.7	1.4	5.3
For profit	1,676	4,727	5,425	5,642	6,590	7,139	10.9	2.8	0.8	6.1
State-local government	1,750	4,838	6,445	7,106	8,205	8,473	10.7	5.9	2.0	4.5
6–24 beds	1,072	2,701	3,578	3,652	4,372	4,743	9.7	5.8	0.4	6.8
25–49 beds	1,138	2,967	3,797	4,381	5,005	5,202	10.1	5.1	2.9	4.4
50–99 beds	1,271	3,461	4,427	4,760	5,553	5,792	10.5	5.0	1.5	5.0
100–199 beds	1,512	4,109	5,103	5,305	6,191	6,608	10.5	4.4	0.8	5.6
200–299 beds	1,767	4,618	5,851	6,392	7,317	7,739	10.1	4.8	1.8	4.9
300–399 beds	1,881	5,096	6,512	6,988	8,184	8,496	10.5	5.0	1.4	5.0
400–499 beds	2,090	5,500	7,164	7,629	9,396	9,720	10.2	5.4	1.3	6.2
500 beds or more	2,517	6,667	8,531	9,149	10,640	10,995	10.2	5.1	1.4	4.7

[1]The category of non-federal hospitals includes psychiatric, tuberculosis and other respiratory diseases hospitals, and long-term and short-term general and other special hospitals. See Appendix II, Hospital.
[2]Community hospitals are non-federal short-term general and special hospitals whose facilities and services are available to the public. See Appendix II, Hospital.

NOTES: In 2004, employee payroll and benefit expenses comprised 52% of expenses in community hospitals and 59% in federal hospitals. Data for additional years are available. See Appendix III.

SOURCES: American Hospital Association Annual Survey of Hospitals. Hospital Statistics, 1981, 1991–2006 editions. Chicago, 1981, 1991–2006 (Copyrights 1981, 1991–2006: Used with the permission of the Health Forum LLC, an affiliate of the American Hospital Association); and unpublished data.

Table 131. Nursing home average monthly charges per resident and percent of residents, by source of payment and selected facility characteristics: United States, 1985, 1995, and 1999

[Data are based on reporting by a sample of nursing homes]

Facility characteristic	Source of payment[1]											
	All sources			Own income or family support[2]			Any Medicare			Any Medicaid		
	1985	1995	1999	1985	1995	1999	1985	1995	1999	1985	1995	1999
	Average monthly charge[3]											
All facilities	$1,508	$3,132	$3,531	$1,522	$2,844	$3,260	$2,258	$3,999	$4,302	$1,509	$2,830	$3,269
Ownership												
Proprietary	1,436	3,044	3,266	1,461	2,806	3,161	1,969	4,004	3,539	1,375	2,642	3,073
Nonprofit and government	1,659	3,293	4,013	1,644	2,904	3,410	2,743	4,003	*5,832	1,847	3,221	3,702
Certification												
Both Medicare and Medicaid	1,797	3,314	3,679	1,811	3,041	3,423	2,346	4,059	4,433	1,739	2,978	3,369
Medicare only	1,550	4,189	3,696	1,549	3,269	3,578	*1,554	*5,808	*3,689	. . .	. . .	. . .
Medicaid only	1,267	2,167	2,396	1,276	2,229	2,374	. . .	. . .	. . .	1,236	2,065	2,408
Neither	954	2,324	2,146	1,005	2,238	2,280	. . .	. . .	. . .	. . .	. . .	. . .
Bed size												
Fewer than 50 beds	1,133	*4,953	3,195	1,085	2,716	2,750	*3,903	*	3,621	1,328	3,021	3,279
50–99 beds	1,394	2,688	3,071	1,400	2,609	3,113	1,655	3,415	3,305	1,333	2,386	2,895
100–199 beds.	1,511	3,025	3,647	1,543	2,898	3,308	2,099	3,756	*4,859	1,425	2,726	3,204
200 beds or more	1,785	3,561	3,858	1,798	3,166	3,501	2,730	3,748	4,146	1,923	3,553	3,872
Geographic region												
Northeast.	1,936	3,895	4,256	1,958	3,704	4,104	2,552	4,184	4,612	2,060	3,729	4,085
Midwest	1,425	2,734	3,589	1,424	2,508	2,993	2,482	3,918	*	1,382	2,529	3,055
South.	1,294	2,743	2,902	1,313	2,675	2,985	2,293	3,502	3,206	1,216	2,385	2,782
West	1,496	3,701	3,663	1,505	3,181	3,692	1,636	4,744	3,682	1,504	2,853	3,443
	Percent of residents[4]											
All facilities	100.0	100.0	100.0	83.0	39.0	33.0	3.3	25.0	26.0	56.8	62.3	63.2
Ownership												
Proprietary	100.0	100.0	100.0	81.7	37.1	30.9	3.1	25.7	26.4	60.0	66.1	67.4
Nonprofit and government	100.0	100.0	100.0	86.0	42.7	37.2	3.9	23.7	25.4	50.0	55.6	55.4
Certification												
Both Medicare and Medicaid	100.0	100.0	100.0	82.8	34.7	30.6	6.2	27.3	27.6	62.2	66.1	65.2
Medicare only	100.0	100.0	100.0	95.8	58.1	57.9	*	41.7	25.8	. . .	. . .	. . .
Medicaid only	100.0	100.0	100.0	82.3	49.4	41.3	. . .	. . .	. . .	62.9	65.3	71.8
Neither	100.0	100.0	100.0	84.5	79.0	76.3	. . .	. . .	. . .	. . .	. . .	. . .
Bed size												
Fewer than 50 beds	100.0	100.0	100.0	83.7	42.4	48.5	*	28.2	23.6	46.5	49.7	50.6
50–99 beds	100.0	100.0	100.0	83.3	46.9	35.7	*2.5	20.7	24.8	49.0	58.2	61.2
100–199 beds.	100.0	100.0	100.0	83.0	37.9	32.0	3.7	25.7	26.2	61.4	63.9	65.0
200 beds or more	100.0	100.0	100.0	82.5	31.4	29.5	4.1	27.8	27.5	60.8	66.3	63.1
Geographic region												
Northeast.	100.0	100.0	100.0	84.6	29.6	25.5	*4.4	29.3	26.7	62.1	67.8	67.1
Midwest	100.0	100.0	100.0	85.1	43.5	40.5	2.6	17.6	25.2	50.8	56.5	55.6
South.	100.0	100.0	100.0	81.0	46.4	35.4	*2.4	25.5	25.8	60.3	64.8	67.6
West	100.0	100.0	100.0	80.3	27.3	24.0	*5.4	33.6	27.5	55.4	60.7	62.7

* Estimates are considered unreliable. Data preceded by an asterisk have a relative standard error of 20%–30%. Data not shown have a relative standard error greater than 30%.

. . . Category not applicable.

[1]Includes all charges in which any payment by payment source was reported.

[2]Includes private health insurance.

[3]Includes life-care residents and no-charge residents.

[4]Residents are persons on the roster of the nursing home as of the night before the survey. Residents for whom beds are maintained even though they may be away on overnight leave or in a hospital are included.

NOTES: Numbers have been revised and differ from previous editions of *Health, United States*. Data for additional years are available. See Appendix III.

SOURCE: Centers for Disease Control and Prevention, National Center for Health Statistics, National Nursing Home Survey.

This table will be updated on the Web. Go to www.cdc.gov/nchs/hus.htm.

Table 132. Mental health expenditures, percent distribution, and per capita expenditures, by type of mental health organization: United States, selected years 1975–2002

[Data are based on an inventory of Mental Health Organizations]

Type of organization	1975	1979	1983	1986	1990	1994[1]	1998	2000	2002
	Amount in millions								
All organizations	$6,564	$8,764	$14,432	$18,458	$28,410	$33,136	$38,512	$34,528	$34,302
State and county psychiatric hospitals	3,185	3,757	5,491	6,326	7,774	7,825	7,117	7,485	7,616
Private psychiatric hospitals	467	743	1,712	2,629	6,101	6,468	4,106	3,885	3,929
Non-federal general hospital psychiatric services	621	723	2,176	2,878	4,662	5,344	5,589	5,853	5,179
Department of Veterans Affairs medical centers[2]	699	848	1,316	1,338	1,480	1,386	1,690	976	1,018
Residential treatment centers for emotionally disturbed children	279	436	573	978	1,969	2,360	3,557	3,781	4,496
All other organizations[3]	1,313	2,256	3,164	4,310	6,424	9,753	16,454	12,549	12,063
	Percent distribution								
All organizations	100.0	100.0	100.0	100.0	100.0	100.0	100.0	100.0	100.0
State and county psychiatric hospitals	48.5	42.9	38.0	34.3	27.4	23.6	18.5	21.7	22.2
Private psychiatric hospitals	7.1	8.5	11.9	14.2	21.5	19.5	10.7	11.3	11.5
Non-federal general hospital psychiatric services	9.5	8.2	15.1	15.6	16.4	16.1	14.5	17.0	15.1
Department of Veterans Affairs medical centers[2]	10.6	9.7	9.1	7.2	5.2	4.2	4.4	2.8	3.0
Residential treatment centers for emotionally disturbed children	4.2	5.0	4.0	5.3	6.9	7.1	9.2	11.0	13.1
All other organizations[3]	20.0	25.7	21.9	23.3	22.6	29.4	42.7	36.4	35.2
	Amount per capita[4]								
All organizations	$ 31	$ 40	$ 62	$ 77	$ 116	$ 128	$ 143	$ 122	$ 119
State and county psychiatric hospitals	15	17	24	26	32	30	26	27	26
Private psychiatric hospitals	2	3	7	11	25	25	15	14	14
Non-federal general hospital psychiatric services	3	3	9	12	19	21	21	21	18
Department of Veterans Affairs medical centers[2]	3	4	6	6	6	5	6	3	4
Residential treatment centers for emotionally disturbed children	1	2	2	4	8	9	13	13	16
All other organizations[3]	6	10	14	18	26	38	61	44	42

[1]Starting with 1994 data, information on supportive residential clients (moderately staffed housing arrangements, such as supervised apartments, group homes, and halfway houses) is included in the totals and All Other Organizations category. This change affects the comparability of trend data prior to 1994 with data for 1994 and later years. See Appendix II, Mental Health Organizations.

[2]Includes Department of Veterans Affairs neuropsychiatric hospitals, general hospital psychiatric services, and psychiatric outpatient clinics.

[3]Includes freestanding psychiatric outpatient clinics, partial care organizations, multiservice mental health organizations, residential treatment centers for adults, substance abuse organizations, and, in 1975 and 1979, federally funded community mental health centers.

[4]Civilian population as of January 1 each year through 1998. The rates for 2000 and later years are based on the July 1 decennial census sample civilian population.

NOTES: Changes in reporting procedures and definitions may affect the comparability of data prior to 1980 with those of later years. Mental health expenditures include salaries, other operating expenditures, and capital expenditures. Excludes expenditures for mental health care provided in nonpsychiatric units of hospitals such as general medical units.

SOURCES: Substance Abuse and Mental Health Services Administration, Center for Mental Health Services. Manderscheid RW, Henderson MJ. Mental health, United States, 2002. Washington, DC. U.S. Government Printing Office, 2004.

Table 133 (page 1 of 3). Private health insurance coverage among persons under 65 years of age, by selected characteristics: United States, selected years 1984–2004

[Data are based on household interviews of a sample of the civilian noninstitutionalized population]

Characteristic	1984	1989	1995	1997[1]	1999	2000	2001	2002	2003	2004
					Number in millions					
Total[2]	157.5	162.7	164.2	165.8	174.3	174.0	175.3	172.4	173.6	174.5
					Percent of population					
Total[2]	76.8	75.9	71.3	70.7	72.8	71.5	71.2	69.4	68.9	68.8
Age										
Under 18 years	72.6	71.8	65.2	66.1	68.8	66.6	66.3	63.5	63.0	63.2
Under 6 years	68.1	67.9	59.5	61.3	64.7	62.7	62.9	60.2	58.2	58.1
6–17 years	74.9	74.0	68.3	68.5	70.9	68.5	67.9	65.1	65.3	65.6
18–44 years	76.5	75.5	70.9	69.4	72.0	70.5	70.1	68.7	67.7	67.3
18–24 years	67.4	64.5	60.8	59.3	63.2	60.3	60.3	60.2	58.8	58.2
25–34 years	77.4	75.9	70.1	68.1	71.2	70.1	70.0	68.0	65.6	65.5
35–44 years	83.9	82.7	77.7	76.4	77.9	77.0	76.2	74.6	75.1	74.8
45–64 years	83.3	82.5	80.1	79.0	79.3	78.7	78.6	77.3	77.3	77.1
45–54 years	83.3	83.4	80.9	80.4	80.4	80.0	79.4	77.5	77.9	77.8
55–64 years	83.3	81.6	79.0	76.9	77.7	76.7	77.4	76.9	76.5	76.1
Sex										
Male	77.3	76.1	71.6	70.9	72.9	71.6	71.2	69.0	69.0	68.7
Female	76.2	75.7	70.9	70.5	72.8	71.3	71.2	69.8	68.9	68.9
Race[3]										
White only	79.9	79.1	74.5	74.2	76.9	75.7	75.1	73.4	71.5	71.4
Black or African American only	58.1	57.7	53.0	54.7	57.2	55.9	56.5	55.1	54.9	53.9
American Indian or Alaska Native only	49.1	45.5	45.3	39.4	39.5	43.7	49.0	37.9	45.0	44.7
Asian only	69.9	71.9	68.4	68.0	73.3	72.1	72.3	70.9	71.4	71.6
Native Hawaiian or Other Pacific Islander only	- - -	- - -	- - -	- - -	*	*	*	*	*	*
2 or more races	- - -	- - -	- - -	- - -	62.7	61.4	61.5	57.1	56.3	62.0
Hispanic origin and race[3]										
Hispanic or Latino	55.7	51.5	46.4	46.4	48.9	47.8	46.1	44.4	41.9	41.7
Mexican	53.3	46.8	42.6	42.3	46.0	45.4	43.1	42.1	39.3	39.1
Puerto Rican	48.4	45.6	47.6	47.0	50.4	51.1	50.5	50.0	48.6	47.3
Cuban	72.5	70.3	63.6	71.0	71.3	63.9	66.1	62.0	55.9	57.9
Other Hispanic or Latino	61.6	61.0	51.4	49.9	52.8	50.7	49.9	46.2	45.3	45.1
Not Hispanic or Latino	78.7	78.4	74.4	74.0	76.3	75.2	75.3	73.7	73.7	73.7
White only	82.3	82.4	78.6	78.1	80.4	79.5	79.4	77.9	77.8	77.9
Black or African American only	58.3	57.8	53.4	54.9	57.3	56.0	56.7	55.2	55.5	54.6
Age and percent of poverty level[4]										
All ages:										
Below 100%	32.2	27.0	22.6	23.3	25.5	25.2	25.3	25.2	23.9	21.8
100%–less than 149%	62.2	55.1	47.8	43.6	42.9	41.7	41.7	38.4	37.5	39.0
150%–less than 200%	77.2	71.0	65.1	62.9	59.4	58.5	56.7	56.2	52.2	52.5
200% or more	91.5	90.8	88.3	86.4	87.1	85.7	85.5	83.9	84.6	84.2
Under 18 years:										
Below 100%	28.5	22.3	16.9	18.3	20.4	19.5	18.2	16.9	15.9	14.2
100%–less than 149%	66.2	59.6	48.5	43.5	42.8	39.8	40.7	35.2	33.9	35.9
150%–less than 200%	80.9	75.9	67.4	65.7	61.0	59.7	56.3	55.3	50.9	51.7
200% or more	92.3	92.5	89.5	87.8	89.0	86.7	86.8	84.5	85.1	85.2
Geographic region										
Northeast	80.5	82.0	75.4	74.2	77.1	76.3	76.4	73.9	74.7	74.0
Midwest	80.6	81.5	77.3	77.1	80.1	78.8	78.1	76.4	75.9	76.3
South	74.3	71.4	66.9	67.3	68.0	66.8	66.0	64.6	64.0	64.1
West	71.9	71.2	67.5	65.4	68.6	66.5	67.9	66.1	64.7	64.1
Location of residence										
Within MSA[5]	77.5	76.5	72.1	71.2	74.1	72.3	72.2	70.7	70.2	69.6
Outside MSA[5]	75.2	73.8	67.9	68.4	67.8	67.8	67.0	64.2	63.7	65.5

See footnotes at end of table.

[Data are based on household interviews of a sample of the civilian noninstitutionalized population]

Characteristic	Private insurance obtained through workplace[6]									
	1984	1989	1995	1997[1]	1999	2000	2001	2002	2003	2004
	Number in millions									
Total[2].........................	141.8	146.3	150.7	155.6	162.6	162.5	164.2	161.3	159.3	161.0
	Percent of population									
Total[2].........................	69.1	68.3	65.4	66.3	68.0	66.7	66.7	65.0	63.3	63.5
Age										
Under 18 years..................	66.5	65.8	60.4	62.7	64.6	62.7	62.8	60.1	58.6	59.2
Under 6 years	62.1	62.3	55.1	58.2	60.8	58.8	59.1	57.0	53.9	54.4
6–17 years	68.7	67.7	63.3	64.9	66.5	64.6	64.5	61.7	60.9	61.5
18–44 years	69.6	68.4	65.3	65.5	67.7	66.1	65.9	64.3	62.2	62.1
18–24 years.	58.7	55.3	53.5	54.7	57.8	54.9	55.3	54.3	52.3	51.6
25–34 years.	71.2	69.5	65.0	64.5	67.2	66.1	66.0	63.9	60.3	60.6
35–44 years.	77.4	76.2	72.7	72.6	73.8	72.8	72.1	70.8	70.0	70.2
45–64 years	71.8	71.6	72.2	72.6	72.7	72.5	72.5	71.4	70.0	70.2
45–54 years.	74.6	74.4	74.7	75.4	75.1	75.3	74.5	72.9	71.5	72.0
55–64 years.	69.0	68.3	68.4	68.3	69.2	68.1	69.5	69.1	68.0	67.6
Sex										
Male..........................	69.8	68.7	65.9	66.6	68.0	67.0	66.7	64.7	63.3	63.6
Female........................	68.4	67.9	64.9	66.0	68.0	66.5	66.6	65.2	63.3	63.4
Race[3]										
White only.....................	72.0	71.2	68.4	69.6	71.6	70.6	70.2	68.7	65.6	65.8
Black or African American only	52.4	52.8	49.3	52.5	54.6	53.1	54.2	52.4	51.5	51.0
American Indian or Alaska Native only...	45.8	40.9	40.2	37.1	36.5	41.6	47.0	35.8	40.5	41.9
Asian only.....................	59.0	61.1	59.6	61.4	65.4	65.1	65.9	62.5	62.1	64.9
Native Hawaiian or Other Pacific Islander only	- - -	- - -	- - -	- - -	*	*	*	*	*	*
2 or more races..................	- - -	- - -	- - -	- - -	59.3	59.7	57.9	54.5	53.1	57.9
Hispanic origin and race[3]										
Hispanic or Latino	52.0	47.3	43.4	43.9	46.1	45.0	43.8	41.9	38.9	39.0
Mexican.......................	50.5	44.2	40.9	40.7	43.7	43.2	41.2	40.1	36.7	37.0
Puerto Rican	45.9	42.3	44.5	45.1	47.4	49.3	47.5	48.0	45.0	43.9
Cuban........................	57.4	56.5	54.0	58.1	63.5	53.4	56.6	52.1	51.1	50.7
Other Hispanic or Latino	57.4	54.7	46.7	46.9	49.6	47.0	47.6	43.1	41.6	41.3
Not Hispanic or Latino	70.6	70.4	68.2	69.4	71.2	70.2	70.5	68.8	67.6	67.9
White only.....................	74.0	74.0	72.1	73.1	74.8	74.1	74.1	72.8	71.3	71.6
Black or African American only.......	52.6	53.0	49.8	52.8	54.6	53.3	54.4	52.6	52.0	51.7
Age and percent of poverty level[4]										
All ages:										
Below 100%	24.1	19.9	17.5	19.9	21.8	20.9	21.8	21.4	19.9	18.1
100%–less than 149%	52.4	46.4	42.1	38.8	38.4	37.1	37.0	34.3	31.8	34.6
150%–less than 200%	69.5	63.1	58.8	58.3	53.9	53.4	51.9	50.9	46.8	47.3
200% or more	85.0	83.7	82.3	81.9	82.1	81.0	80.9	79.3	78.6	78.5
Under 18 years:										
Below 100%	23.0	17.5	13.6	16.2	17.5	16.5	16.2	14.8	14.0	12.8
100%–less than 149%	58.3	52.5	43.6	39.6	39.2	36.3	37.0	32.5	30.1	33.5
150%–less than 200%	75.8	70.1	61.8	62.5	56.3	55.6	52.9	50.8	47.0	47.9
200% or more	86.9	86.6	84.4	83.9	84.4	82.5	82.9	80.8	79.9	80.1

See footnotes at end of table.

Table 133 (page 3 of 3). Private health insurance coverage among persons under 65 years of age, by selected characteristics: United States, selected years 1984–2004

[Data are based on household interviews of a sample of the civilian noninstitutionalized population]

Characteristic	Private insurance obtained through workplace[6]									
	1984	1989	1995	1997[1]	1999	2000	2001	2002	2003	2004
Geographic region	Percent of population									
Northeast	74.0	75.0	69.8	70.9	73.5	72.1	72.9	70.5	69.4	69.6
Midwest	72.0	73.3	71.2	72.4	75.3	74.5	73.7	72.2	70.4	71.5
South	66.2	63.6	61.8	62.8	63.6	62.2	61.6	60.3	58.8	59.1
West	64.7	63.9	60.4	60.6	61.7	60.6	62.1	59.9	57.5	57.0
Location of residence										
Within MSA[5]	70.9	69.6	66.6	67.2	69.5	67.8	67.9	66.3	64.6	64.4
Outside MSA[5]	65.3	63.5	60.7	62.7	61.9	62.4	61.7	59.2	58.0	59.6

* Estimates are considered unreliable. Data not shown have a relative standard error of greater than 30%.
- - - Data not available.
[1]Starting with 1997 data, the National Health Interview Survey (NHIS) was redesigned, and changes to the questions on health insurance coverage were made. See Appendix I, National Health Interview Survey and Appendix II, Health insurance coverage.
[2]Includes all other races not shown separately and, in 1984 and 1989, with unknown poverty level.
[3]The race groups, white, black, American Indian or Alaska Native, Asian, Native Hawaiian or Other Pacific Islander, and 2 or more races, include persons of Hispanic and non-Hispanic origin. Persons of Hispanic origin may be of any race. Starting with 1999 data, race-specific estimates are tabulated according to the 1997 Revisions to the Standards for the Classification of Federal Data on Race and Ethnicity and are not strictly comparable with estimates for earlier years. The five single race categories plus multiple race categories shown in the table conform to the 1997 Standards. Starting with 1999 data, race-specific estimates are for persons who reported only one racial group; the category 2 or more races includes persons who reported more than one racial group. Prior to 1999, data were tabulated according to the 1977 Standards with four racial groups and the Asian only category including Native Hawaiian or Other Pacific Islander. Estimates for single race categories prior to 1999 included persons who reported one race or, if they reported more than one race, identified one race as best representing their race. Starting with 2003 data, race responses of other race and unspecified multiple race were treated as missing, and then race was imputed if these were the only race responses. Almost all persons with a race response of other race were of Hispanic origin. See Appendix II, Hispanic origin; Race.
[4]Percent of poverty level is based on family income and family size and composition using U.S. Census Bureau poverty thresholds. Poverty level was unknown for 10%–11% of persons under 65 years of age in 1984 and 1989. Missing family income data were imputed for 15%–16% of persons under 65 years of age in 1994–1996, 24% in 1997, and 28%–31% in 1998–2004. See Appendix II, Family income; Poverty.
[5]MSA is metropolitan statistical area.
[6]Private insurance originally obtained through a present or former employer or union. Starting with 1997 data, also includes private insurance obtained through workplace, self-employment, or professional association.

NOTES: Standard errors are available in the spreadsheet version of this table. Available from: www.cdc.gov/nchs/hus.htm. Data for additional years are available. See Appendix III.

SOURCES: Centers for Disease Control and Prevention, National Center for Health Statistics, National Health Interview Survey, health insurance supplements (1984, 1989, 1994–1996). Starting with 1997 data, data are from the family core questionnaires.

Table 134 (page 1 of 2). Medicaid coverage among persons under 65 years of age, by selected characteristics: United States, selected years 1984–2004

[Data are based on household interviews of a sample of the civilian noninstitutionalized population]

Characteristic	1984	1989	1995	1997[1]	1999	2000	2002	2003	2004(1)[2]	2004(2)[2]
					Number in millions					
Total[3]	14.0	15.4	26.6	22.9	21.9	23.2	29.4	30.9	31.1	31.6
					Percent of population					
Total[3]	6.8	7.2	11.5	9.7	9.1	9.5	11.8	12.3	12.3	12.5
Age										
Under 18 years	11.9	12.6	21.5	18.4	18.1	19.6	24.8	26.0	25.9	26.4
Under 6 years	15.5	15.7	29.3	24.7	23.5	24.7	30.0	32.3	31.8	32.4
6–17 years	10.1	10.9	17.4	15.2	15.5	17.2	22.3	23.0	23.1	23.4
18–44 years	5.1	5.2	7.8	6.6	5.7	5.6	7.1	7.4	7.5	7.7
18–24 years	6.4	6.8	10.4	8.8	8.1	8.1	9.9	9.6	10.3	10.4
25–34 years	5.3	5.2	8.2	6.8	5.7	5.5	6.6	7.8	7.6	7.8
35–44 years	3.5	4.0	5.9	5.2	4.3	4.3	5.9	5.6	5.7	5.8
45–64 years	3.4	4.3	5.6	4.6	4.4	4.5	5.3	5.3	5.4	5.5
45–54 years	3.2	3.8	5.1	4.0	3.9	4.2	5.1	5.0	5.4	5.5
55–64 years	3.6	4.9	6.4	5.6	5.3	4.9	5.8	5.8	5.4	5.5
Sex										
Male	5.4	5.7	9.6	8.4	7.9	8.2	10.6	10.9	10.8	11.0
Female	8.1	8.6	13.4	11.1	10.3	10.8	13.0	13.6	13.7	13.9
Race[4]										
White only	4.6	5.1	8.9	7.4	6.9	7.1	9.3	10.4	10.2	10.4
Black or African American only	20.5	19.0	28.5	22.4	20.1	21.2	23.2	23.7	24.5	24.9
American Indian or Alaska Native only	*28.2	29.7	19.0	19.6	21.4	15.1	21.1	18.5	18.0	18.4
Asian only	*8.7	*8.8	10.5	9.6	7.9	7.5	9.8	8.0	9.6	9.8
Native Hawaiian or Other Pacific Islander only	---	---	---	---	*	*	*	*	*	*
2 or more races	---	---	---	---	19.7	19.1	21.6	23.5	19.0	19.3
Hispanic origin and race[4]										
Hispanic or Latino	13.3	13.5	21.9	17.6	15.7	15.5	20.8	21.8	21.9	22.5
Mexican	12.2	12.4	21.6	17.2	14.5	14.0	20.2	21.7	21.9	22.4
Puerto Rican	31.5	27.3	33.4	31.0	28.6	29.4	29.0	31.0	28.5	29.1
Cuban	*4.8	*7.7	13.4	7.3	7.6	9.2	14.9	13.8	17.9	17.9
Other Hispanic or Latino	7.9	11.1	18.2	15.3	14.7	14.5	19.6	19.3	19.9	20.8
Not Hispanic or Latino	6.2	6.6	10.2	8.7	8.2	8.5	10.3	10.6	10.5	10.7
White only	3.7	4.2	7.1	6.1	5.8	6.1	7.7	8.0	7.8	7.9
Black or African American only	20.7	19.0	28.1	22.1	20.1	21.0	23.2	23.4	24.1	24.6
Age and percent of poverty level[5]										
All ages:										
Below 100%	33.0	37.6	48.4	40.5	38.8	38.4	42.8	43.2	44.2	45.0
100%–less than 149%	7.7	10.9	19.1	17.9	18.8	20.7	27.6	26.9	26.5	27.1
150%–less than 200%	3.2	5.1	8.3	8.3	10.8	11.5	16.1	17.1	16.6	16.9
200% or more	0.6	1.1	1.7	1.8	2.1	2.3	3.1	3.3	3.5	3.5
Under 18 years:										
Below 100%	43.2	47.9	66.0	58.0	57.7	58.5	66.4	67.5	69.2	70.7
100%–less than 149%	9.0	12.3	27.2	28.7	31.4	35.0	47.1	49.1	46.6	47.6
150%–less than 200%	4.4	6.1	13.1	13.0	17.9	21.3	29.1	33.6	31.9	32.4
200% or more	0.8	1.8	3.3	3.1	4.2	5.1	7.2	7.6	8.0	8.0

See footnotes at end of table.

Table 134 (page 2 of 2). Medicaid coverage among persons under 65 years of age, by selected characteristics: United States, selected years 1984–2004

[Data are based on household interviews of a sample of the civilian noninstitutionalized population]

Characteristic	1984	1989	1995	1997[1]	1999	2000	2002	2003	2004(1)[2]	2004(2)[2]
Geographic region				Percent of population						
Northeast	8.6	6.6	11.7	11.3	10.0	10.6	12.5	12.9	12.8	13.0
Midwest	7.4	7.6	10.5	8.4	7.4	8.0	10.3	10.8	10.2	10.4
South	5.1	6.5	11.3	8.7	9.0	9.4	12.0	12.6	12.2	12.4
West	7.0	8.5	12.9	11.7	10.7	10.4	12.7	12.8	14.2	14.4
Location of residence										
Within MSA[6]	7.1	7.0	11.3	9.7	8.5	8.9	11.0	11.5	11.7	11.9
Outside MSA[6]	6.1	7.9	12.3	10.1	11.7	11.9	15.2	15.3	14.8	15.0

* Estimates are considered unreliable. Data preceded by an asterisk have a relative standard error (RSE) of 20%–30%. Data not shown have an RSE of greater than 30%.

- - - Data not available.

[1]Starting with 1997 data, the National Health Interview Survey (NHIS) was redesigned, and changes to the questions on health insurance coverage were made. See Appendix I, National Health Interview Survey and Appendix II, Health insurance coverage.

[2]Beginning in quarter 3 of the 2004 NHIS, persons under 65 years with no reported coverage were asked explicitly about Medicaid coverage. Estimates were calculated without and with the additional information from this question in the columns labeled 2004(1) and 2004(2), respectively.

[3]Includes all other races not shown separately and, in 1984 and 1989, with unknown poverty level.

[4]The race groups, white, black, American Indian or Alaska Native, Asian, Native Hawaiian or Other Pacific Islander, and 2 or more races, include persons of Hispanic and non-Hispanic origin. Persons of Hispanic origin may be of any race. Starting with 1999 data, race-specific estimates are tabulated according to the 1997 Revisions to the Standards for the Classification of Federal Data on Race and Ethnicity and are not strictly comparable with estimates for earlier years. The five single race categories plus multiple race categories shown in the table conform to the 1997 Standards. Starting with 1999 data, race-specific estimates are for persons who reported only one racial group; the category 2 or more races includes persons who reported more than one racial group. Prior to 1999, data were tabulated according to the 1977 Standards with four racial groups and the Asian only category including Native Hawaiian or Other Pacific Islander. Estimates for single race categories prior to 1999 included persons who reported one race or, if they reported more than one race, identified one race as best representing their race. Starting with 2003 data, race responses of other race and unspecified multiple race were treated as missing, and then race was imputed if these were the only race responses. Almost all persons with a race response of other race were of Hispanic origin. See Appendix II, Hispanic origin; Race.

[5]Percent of poverty level is based on family income and family size and composition using U.S. Census Bureau poverty thresholds. Poverty level was unknown for 10%–11% of persons under 65 years of age in 1984 and 1989. Missing family income data were imputed for 15%–16% of persons under 65 years of age in 1994–1996, 24% in 1997, and 28%–31% in 1998–2004. See Appendix II, Family income; Poverty.

[6]MSA is metropolitan statistical area.

NOTES: Medicaid includes other public assistance through 1996. Starting with 1997 data, state-sponsored health plan coverage is included as Medicaid coverage. Starting with 1999 data, coverage by the State Children's Health Insurance Program (SCHIP) is included as Medicaid coverage. In 2004, 9.7% of persons under 65 years of age were covered by Medicaid, 1.3% by state-sponsored health plans, and 1.5% by SCHIP. Standard errors are available in the spreadsheet version of this table. Available from: www.cdc.gov/nchs/hus.htm. Data for additional years are available. See Appendix III.

SOURCES: Centers for Disease Control and Prevention, National Center for Health Statistics, National Health Interview Survey, health insurance supplements (1984, 1989, 1994–1996). Starting with 1997 data, data are from the family core questionnaires.

Table 135 (page 1 of 2). No health insurance coverage among persons under 65 years of age, by selected characteristics: United States, selected years 1984–2004

[Data are based on household interviews of a sample of the civilian noninstitutionalized population]

Characteristic	1984	1989	1995	1997[1]	1999	2000	2002	2003	2004(1)[2]	2004(2)[2]
					Number in millions					
Total[3]	29.8	33.4	37.1	41.0	38.5	41.4	41.7	41.6	42.1	41.6
					Percent of population					
Total[3]	14.5	15.6	16.1	17.5	16.1	17.0	16.8	16.5	16.6	16.4
Age										
Under 18 years	13.9	14.7	13.4	14.0	11.9	12.6	10.9	9.8	9.7	9.2
Under 6 years	14.9	15.1	11.8	12.5	11.0	11.8	9.2	8.2	8.9	8.2
6–17 years	13.4	14.5	14.3	14.7	12.3	13.0	11.7	10.6	10.0	9.7
18–44 years	17.1	18.4	20.4	22.4	21.0	22.4	23.0	23.5	23.6	23.5
18–24 years	25.0	27.1	28.0	30.1	27.4	30.4	28.8	30.1	30.1	30.0
25–34 years	16.2	18.3	21.1	23.8	22.1	23.3	24.6	25.4	25.7	25.5
35–44 years	11.2	12.3	15.1	16.7	16.3	16.9	18.0	17.5	17.6	17.5
45–64 years	9.6	10.5	10.9	12.4	12.2	12.6	13.1	12.5	12.9	12.8
45–54 years	10.5	11.0	11.6	12.8	12.8	12.8	14.1	13.6	13.7	13.6
55–64 years	8.7	10.0	9.9	11.8	11.4	12.4	11.5	10.9	11.7	11.6
Sex										
Male	15.3	16.8	17.4	18.7	17.2	18.1	18.4	17.7	18.1	17.9
Female	13.8	14.4	14.8	16.3	15.0	15.9	15.2	15.3	15.2	14.9
Race[4]										
White only	13.6	14.5	15.5	16.4	14.6	15.4	15.5	16.0	16.3	16.1
Black or African American only	19.9	21.6	18.0	20.1	19.3	19.5	18.8	18.4	18.1	17.6
American Indian or Alaska Native only . . .	22.5	28.4	34.3	38.1	38.2	38.4	39.1	35.0	35.0	34.6
Asian only	18.5	16.9	18.6	19.5	16.8	17.6	17.4	18.2	16.7	16.5
Native Hawaiian or Other Pacific Islander only	- - -	- - -	- - -	- - -	*	*	*	*	*	*
2 or more races	- - -	- - -	- - -	- - -	14.5	16.8	17.6	15.9	12.6	12.3
Hispanic origin and race[4]										
Hispanic or Latino	29.5	33.7	31.4	34.5	34.0	35.6	33.9	34.7	35.1	34.4
Mexican	33.8	39.9	35.6	39.4	38.2	39.9	37.1	37.8	38.1	37.6
Puerto Rican	18.3	24.7	17.6	19.0	19.4	16.4	19.2	17.7	21.0	20.4
Cuban	21.6	20.6	22.3	21.1	20.4	25.4	20.8	29.1	22.8	22.8
Other Hispanic or Latino	27.4	25.8	30.2	33.0	30.7	33.4	33.2	33.4	33.3	32.3
Not Hispanic or Latino	13.2	13.7	14.2	15.2	13.5	14.0	13.9	13.3	13.3	13.2
White only	12.0	12.2	13.0	13.8	12.1	12.5	12.5	11.9	12.1	12.0
Black or African American only	19.6	21.4	17.9	20.0	19.2	19.5	18.7	18.1	17.8	17.3
Age and percent of poverty level[5]										
All ages:										
Below 100%	33.9	35.0	29.6	33.7	33.8	34.2	30.3	31.1	31.8	31.0
100%–less than 150%	27.2	31.1	31.6	35.1	34.1	34.9	32.2	31.9	31.3	30.8
150%–less than 200%	17.3	21.7	24.0	26.3	26.9	27.0	25.2	27.6	27.4	27.2
200% or more	6.0	7.1	8.7	10.1	9.2	10.1	11.1	10.0	10.2	10.2
Under 18 years:										
Below 100%	29.0	31.4	20.0	23.2	22.3	22.0	17.0	16.8	16.5	15.0
100%–less than 150%	22.8	26.1	24.8	26.5	24.2	25.4	19.4	16.2	17.0	16.0
150%–less than 200%	12.7	15.8	18.0	19.9	19.1	17.7	14.3	14.9	14.5	14.1
200% or more	4.2	4.5	6.4	7.1	5.4	6.5	6.7	5.5	5.3	5.2

See footnotes at end of table.

Table 135 (page 2 of 2). No health insurance coverage among persons under 65 years of age, by selected characteristics: United States, selected years 1984–2004

[Data are based on household interviews of a sample of the civilian noninstitutionalized population]

Characteristic	1984	1989	1995	1997[1]	1999	2000	2002	2003	2004(1)[2]	2004(2)[2]
Geographic region					Percent of population					
Northeast	10.2	10.9	13.3	13.5	12.2	12.2	12.8	11.3	11.9	11.8
Midwest	11.3	10.7	12.2	13.2	11.5	12.3	12.5	12.4	12.6	12.4
South	17.7	19.7	19.4	20.9	19.9	20.5	20.3	19.8	20.2	19.9
West	18.2	18.8	17.9	20.6	18.5	20.7	19.1	19.9	19.1	18.9
Location of residence										
Within MSA[6]	13.6	15.2	15.5	16.9	15.4	16.6	16.3	16.0	16.4	16.2
Outside MSA[6]	16.6	17.0	18.6	19.8	18.8	18.6	18.7	18.7	17.4	17.2

* Estimates are considered unreliable. Data not shown have a relative standard error of greater than 30%.
- - - Data not available.
[1]Starting with 1997 data, the National Health Interview Survey (NHIS) was redesigned, and changes to the questions on health insurance coverage were made. See Appendix I, National Health Interview Survey and Appendix II, Health insurance coverage.
[2]Beginning in quarter 3 of the 2004 NHIS, persons under 65 years with no reported coverage were asked explicitly about Medicaid coverage. Estimates were calculated without and with the additional information from this question in the columns labeled 2004(1) and 2004(2), respectively.
[3]Includes all other races not shown separately and, in 1984 and 1989, persons with unknown poverty level.
[4]The race groups, white, black, American Indian or Alaska Native, Asian, Native Hawaiian or Other Pacific Islander, and 2 or more races, include persons of Hispanic and non-Hispanic origin. Persons of Hispanic origin may be of any race. Starting with 1999 data, race-specific estimates are tabulated according to the 1997 Revisions to the Standards for the Classification of Federal Data on Race and Ethnicity and are not strictly comparable with estimates for earlier years. The five single race categories plus multiple race categories shown in the table conform to the 1997 Standards. Starting with 1999 data, race-specific estimates are for persons who reported only one racial group; the category 2 or more races includes persons who reported more than one racial group. Prior to 1999, data were tabulated according to the 1977 Standards with four racial groups and the Asian only category including Native Hawaiian or Other Pacific Islander. Estimates for single race categories prior to 1999 included persons who reported one race or, if they reported more than one race, identified one race as best representing their race. Starting with 2003 data, race responses of other race and unspecified multiple race were treated as missing, and then race was imputed if these were the only race responses. Almost all persons with a race response of other race were of Hispanic origin. See Appendix II, Hispanic origin; Race.
[5]Percent of poverty level is based on family income and family size and composition using U.S. Census Bureau poverty thresholds. Poverty level was unknown for 10%–11% of persons under 65 years of age in 1984 and 1989. Missing family income data were imputed for 15%–16% of persons under 65 years of age in 1994–1996, 24% in 1997, and 28%–31% in 1998–2004. See Appendix II, Family income; Poverty.
[6]MSA is metropolitan statistical area.

NOTES: Persons not covered by private insurance, Medicaid, State Children's Health Insurance Program (SCHIP), public assistance (through 1996), state-sponsored or other government-sponsored health plans (starting in 1997), Medicare, or military plans are considered to have no health insurance coverage and are included in this table. See Appendix II, Health insurance coverage. Standard errors are available in the spreadsheet version of this table. Available from: www.cdc.gov/nchs/hus.htm. Data for additional years are available. See Appendix III.

SOURCES: Centers for Disease Control and Prevention, National Center for Health Statistics, National Health Interview Survey, health insurance supplements (1984, 1989, 1994–1996). Starting with 1997 data, data are from the family core questionnaires.

Table 136 (page 1 of 2). Health insurance coverage for persons 65 years of age and over, by type of coverage and selected characteristics: United States, selected years 1992–2003

[Data are based on household interviews of a sample of the civilian noninstitutionalized population]

Characteristic	Medicare risk Health Maintenance Organization[1]					Medicaid[2]				
	1992	1995	2000	2002	2003	1992	1995	2000	2002	2003
Age	Number in millions									
65 years and over	1.1	2.6	5.9	4.5	4.3	2.7	2.8	2.7	3.0	3.3
	Percent of population									
65 years and over	3.9	8.9	19.3	14.4	13.7	9.4	9.6	9.0	9.7	10.4
65–74 years	4.2	9.5	20.6	14.7	13.0	7.9	8.8	8.5	8.9	10.4
75–84 years	3.7	8.3	18.5	14.3	15.0	10.6	9.6	8.9	10.0	10.3
85 years and over	*	7.3	16.3	13.4	12.5	16.6	13.6	11.2	12.4	11.3
Sex										
Male.	4.6	9.2	19.3	13.8	12.8	6.3	6.2	6.3	6.8	7.3
Female.	3.4	8.6	19.3	14.8	14.4	11.6	12.0	10.9	11.9	12.9
Race and Hispanic origin										
White, not Hispanic or Latino . . .	3.6	8.4	18.4	13.2	12.5	5.6	5.4	5.1	5.6	6.0
Black, not Hispanic or Latino . . .	*	7.9	20.7	15.6	13.7	28.5	30.3	23.6	26.6	30.0
Hispanic.	*	15.5	27.5	24.9	25.2	39.0	40.5	28.7	29.0	28.4
Percent of poverty level[3]										
Below 100%	3.6	7.7	18.4	13.1	- - -	22.3	17.2	15.9	17.4	- - -
100%–less than 200%	3.7	9.5	23.4	17.4	- - -	6.7	6.3	8.4	9.4	- - -
200% or more	4.2	10.1	18.0	14.3	- - -	*	*	*	*	- - -
Marital status										
Married.	4.6	9.5	18.7	13.7	13.2	4.0	4.3	4.3	4.9	5.2
Widowed	2.3	7.7	19.4	15.4	14.3	14.9	15.0	13.6	15.0	15.8
Divorced.	*	9.7	24.4	16.7	16.0	23.4	24.5	20.2	19.4	22.3
Never married	*	*	15.8	*	*	19.2	19.0	17.0	19.3	21.6

Characteristic	Employer-sponsored plan[4]					Medigap[5]				
	1992	1995	2000	2002	2003	1992	1995	2000	2002	2003
Age	Number in millions									
65 years and over	12.5	11.3	10.7	11.0	11.3	9.9	9.5	7.6	8.1	8.2
	Percent of population									
65 years and over	42.8	38.6	35.2	35.5	35.9	33.9	32.5	25.0	25.9	26.2
65–74 years	46.9	41.1	36.6	37.8	38.4	31.4	29.9	21.7	22.9	23.0
75–84 years	38.2	37.1	35.0	34.2	33.8	37.5	35.2	27.8	28.1	28.9
85 years and over	31.6	30.2	29.4	29.0	31.5	38.3	37.6	31.1	32.3	31.5
Sex										
Male.	46.3	42.1	37.7	38.5	39.0	30.6	30.0	23.4	23.1	23.8
Female.	40.4	36.0	33.4	33.2	33.5	36.2	34.4	26.2	28.0	27.9
Race and Hispanic origin										
White, not Hispanic or Latino . . .	45.9	41.3	38.6	38.5	38.9	37.2	36.2	28.3	29.1	29.6
Black, not Hispanic or Latino . . .	25.9	26.7	22.0	23.9	25.8	13.6	10.2	7.5	10.1	9.2
Hispanic.	20.7	16.9	15.8	20.0	18.9	15.8	10.1	11.3	11.6	12.0
Percent of poverty level[3]										
Below 100%	29.0	32.1	28.1	31.1	- - -	30.8	29.8	22.6	22.6	- - -
100%–less than 200%	37.5	32.0	27.0	26.2	- - -	39.3	39.1	28.4	29.5	- - -
200% or more	58.4	52.8	49.0	46.2	- - -	32.8	32.2	26.2	28.0	- - -
Marital status										
Married.	49.9	44.6	41.0	41.7	41.9	33.0	32.6	25.6	25.8	26.9
Widowed	34.1	30.3	28.7	27.9	28.4	37.5	35.2	26.7	28.3	27.5
Divorced.	27.3	26.6	22.4	22.5	23.7	27.9	24.1	16.9	20.5	19.3
Never married	38.0	35.1	28.5	31.5	31.3	29.1	26.2	21.9	20.7	19.4

See footnotes at end of table.

Table 136 (page 2 of 2). Health insurance coverage for persons 65 years of age and over, by type of coverage and selected characteristics: United States, selected years 1992–2003

[Data are based on household interviews of a sample of the civilian noninstitutionalized population]

Characteristic	Medicare fee-for-service only or Other[6]				
	1992	1995	2000	2002	2003
Age	Number in millions				
65 years and over	2.9	3.1	3.5	4.5	4.4
	Percent of population				
65 years and over	9.9	10.5	11.5	14.5	13.9
65–74 years	9.7	10.7	12.6	15.7	15.3
75–84 years	10.1	9.9	9.9	13.4	12.1
85 years and over	10.8	11.3	12.1	13.0	13.3
Sex					
Male.	12.2	12.6	13.3	17.8	17.1
Female.	8.3	8.9	10.2	12.1	11.4
Race and Hispanic origin					
White, not Hispanic or Latino . . .	7.7	8.7	9.6	13.6	13.0
Black, not Hispanic or Latino . . .	26.7	25.0	26.1	23.8	21.4
Hispanic	18.3	17.1	16.7	14.6	15.4
Percent of poverty level[3]					
Below 100%	14.3	13.3	15.1	15.9	- - -
100%–less than 200%	12.9	13.1	12.7	17.5	- - -
200% or more	4.0	4.5	6.3	11.2	- - -
Marital status					
Married.	8.5	9.0	10.5	13.9	12.8
Widowed	11.2	11.9	11.6	13.4	14.0
Divorced	15.7	15.1	16.1	21.0	18.8
Never married	*	13.1	16.8	18.5	18.2

* Sample cell size is 50 or fewer.

- - - Data not available.

[1]Enrollee has Medicare risk Health Maintenance Organization (HMO) regardless of other insurance. See Appendix II, Managed care.

[2]Enrolled in Medicaid and not enrolled in a Medicare risk HMO. See Appendix II, Managed care.

[3]Percent of poverty level is based on family income and family size and composition using U.S. Census Bureau poverty thresholds. See Appendix II, Family income: Poverty.

[4]Private insurance plans purchased through employers (own, current, or former employer, family business, union, or former employer or union of spouse) and not enrolled in a Medicare risk HMO or Medicaid.

[5]Supplemental insurance purchased privately or through organizations such as AARP or professional organizations, and not enrolled in a Medicare risk HMO, Medicaid, or employer-sponsored plan.

[6]Medicare fee-for-service only or other public plans (except Medicaid).

NOTES: Insurance categories are mutually exclusive. Data for additional years are available. See Appendix III.

SOURCES: Centers for Medicare & Medicaid Services, Medicare Current Beneficiary Survey. Data compiled by the National Center for Health Statistics, Trends in Health and Aging. Available from: www.cdc.gov/nchs/agingact.htm.

Table 137 (page 1 of 2). Medicare enrollees and expenditures and percent distribution, by Medicare program and type of service: United States and other areas, selected years 1970–2005

[Data are compiled from various sources by the Centers for Medicare & Medicaid Services]

Medicare program and type of service	1970	1980	1990	1995	1999	2000	2001	2002	2003	2004	2005[1]
Enrollees					Number in millions						
Total[2]	20.4	28.4	34.3	37.6	39.2	39.7	40.1	40.5	41.2	41.9	42.5
Hospital insurance	20.1	28.0	33.7	37.2	38.8	39.3	39.7	40.1	40.7	41.4	42.0
Supplementary medical insurance[3]	19.5	27.3	32.6	35.6	37.0	37.3	37.7	38.0	38.6	40.3	41.4
Part B	19.5	27.3	32.6	35.6	37.0	37.3	37.7	38.0	38.6	39.1	39.6
Part D[4]	- - -	- - -	- - -	- - -	- - -	- - -	- - -	- - -	- - -	1.2	1.8
Expenditures					Amount in billions						
Total Medicare	$ 7.5	$ 36.8	$111.0	$184.2	$213.0	$221.7	$244.8	$265.8	280.8	308.9	336.4
Total hospital insurance (HI)	5.3	25.6	67.0	117.6	130.6	131.0	143.4	152.7	154.6	170.6	182.9
HI payments to managed care organizations[5]	- - -	0.0	2.7	6.7	20.9	21.4	20.8	19.2	19.5	20.8	24.9
HI payments for fee-for-service utilization	5.1	25.0	63.4	109.5	107.1	105.1	117.0	129.3	134.5	146.5	154.7
Inpatient hospital	4.8	24.1	56.9	82.3	86.5	87.1	96.0	104.2	108.7	116.4	121.7
Skilled nursing facility	0.2	0.4	2.5	9.1	10.4	11.1	13.1	15.2	14.7	17.1	18.5
Home health agency	0.1	0.5	3.7	16.2	7.6	4.0	4.1	5.0	4.8	5.4	5.9
Hospice	- - -	- - -	0.3	1.9	2.6	2.9	3.7	4.9	6.2	7.6	8.6
Home health agency transfer[6]	- - -	- - -	- - -	- - -	0.6	1.7	3.1	1.2	-2.2	0.0	0.0
Administrative expenses[7]	0.2	0.5	0.9	1.4	2.0	2.8	2.5	3.0	2.8	3.3	3.3
Total supplementary medical insurance (SMI)[3]	2.2	11.2	44.0	66.6	82.3	90.7	101.4	113.2	126.1	138.3	153.4
Total Part B	2.2	11.2	44.0	66.6	82.3	90.7	101.4	113.2	126.1	137.9	152.4
Part B payments to managed care organizations[5]	0.0	0.2	2.8	6.6	17.7	18.4	17.6	17.5	17.3	18.7	22.1
Part B payments for fee-for-service utilization[8]	1.9	10.4	39.6	58.4	63.6	72.2	85.1	94.5	104.3	116.2	126.9
Physician/supplies[9]	1.8	8.2	29.6	- - -	- - -	- - -	- - -	- - -	- - -	- - -	- - -
Outpatient hospital[10]	0.1	1.9	8.5	- - -	- - -	- - -	- - -	- - -	- - -	- - -	- - -
Independent laboratory[11]	0.0	0.1	1.5	- - -	- - -	- - -	- - -	- - -	- - -	- - -	- - -
Physician fee schedule	- - -	- - -	- - -	31.7	33.4	37.0	42.0	44.8	48.3	54.1	57.8
Durable medical equipment	- - -	- - -	- - -	3.7	4.3	4.7	5.4	6.5	7.5	7.8	8.0
Laboratory[12]	- - -	- - -	- - -	4.3	3.8	4.0	4.4	5.0	5.5	6.0	6.6
Other[13]	- - -	- - -	- - -	9.9	12.2	13.6	16.0	19.6	22.6	25.0	27.4
Hospital[14]	- - -	- - -	- - -	8.7	8.8	8.4	12.8	13.6	15.3	17.4	20.6
Home health agency	0.0	0.2	0.1	0.2	1.2	4.5	4.5	5.0	5.1	5.9	6.6
Home health agency transfer[6]	- - -	- - -	- - -	- - -	-0.6	-1.7	-3.1	-1.2	2.2	0.0	0.0
Administrative expenses[7]	0.2	0.6	1.5	1.6	1.6	1.8	1.8	2.3	2.4	2.8	2.7
Part D Transitional Assistance and Start-up Costs[15]	- - -	- - -	- - -	- - -	- - -	- - -	- - -	- - -	- - -	0.2	0.7
Total Part D[4]	- - -	- - -	- - -	- - -	- - -	- - -	- - -	- - -	- - -	0.4	1.0
Drug card and transitional subsidy	- - -	- - -	- - -	- - -	- - -	- - -	- - -	- - -	- - -	0.4	1.0
					Percent distribution of expenditures						
Total hospital insurance (HI)	100.0	100.0	100.0	100.0	100.0	100.0	100.0	100.0	100.0	100.0	100.0
HI payments to managed care organizations[5]	- - -	0.0	4.0	5.7	16.0	16.3	14.5	12.6	12.6	12.2	13.6
HI payments for fee-for-service utilization	97.0	97.9	94.6	93.1	82.0	80.2	81.6	84.7	87.0	85.9	84.6
Inpatient hospital	91.4	94.3	85.0	70.0	66.2	66.5	67.0	68.3	70.3	68.2	66.6
Skilled nursing facility	4.7	1.5	3.7	7.8	8.0	8.5	9.1	10.0	9.5	10.0	10.1
Home health agency	1.0	2.1	5.5	13.8	5.8	3.1	2.9	3.3	3.1	3.2	3.2
Hospice	- - -	- - -	0.5	1.6	2.0	2.2	2.6	3.2	4.0	4.4	4.7
Home health agency transfer[6]	- - -	- - -	- - -	- - -	0.5	1.3	2.2	0.8	-1.4	0.0	0.0
Administrative expenses[7]	3.0	2.1	1.4	1.2	1.6	2.1	1.7	2.0	1.8	2.0	1.8

See footnotes at end of table.

Table 137 (page 2 of 2). Medicare enrollees and expenditures and percent distribution, by Medicare program and type of service: United States and other areas, selected years 1970–2005

[Data are compiled from various sources by the Centers for Medicare & Medicaid Services]

Medicare program and type of service	1970	1980	1990	1995	1999	2000	2001	2002	2003	2004	2005[1]
				Percent distribution of expenditures							
Total supplementary medical insurance (SMI)[3]	100.0	100.0	100.0	100.0	100.0	100.0	100.0	100.0	100.0	100.0	100.0
Total Part B	100.0	100.0	100.0	100.0	100.0	100.0	100.0	100.0	100.0	100.0	100.0
Part B payments to managed care organizations[4]	1.2	1.8	6.4	9.9	21.5	20.2	17.3	15.5	13.7	13.6	14.5
Part B payments for fee-for-service utilization[8]	88.1	92.8	90.1	87.6	77.2	79.6	84.0	83.5	82.7	84.0	82.7
Physician/supplies[9]	80.9	72.8	67.3	- - -	- - -	- - -	- - -	- - -	- - -	- - -	- - -
Outpatient hospital[10]	5.2	16.9	19.3	- - -	- - -	- - -	- - -	- - -	- - -	- - -	- - -
Independent laboratory[11]	0.5	1.0	3.4	- - -	- - -	- - -	- - -	- - -	- - -	- - -	- - -
Physician fee schedule	- - -	- - -	- - -	47.5	40.5	40.8	41.5	39.6	38.3	39.2	37.9
Durable medical equipment	- - -	- - -	- - -	5.5	5.2	5.2	5.4	5.8	6.0	5.6	5.3
Laboratory[10]	- - -	- - -	- - -	6.4	4.6	4.4	4.3	4.4	4.3	4.4	4.3
Other[11]	- - -	- - -	- - -	14.8	14.8	15.0	15.8	17.3	17.9	18.1	18.0
Hospital[12]	- - -	- - -	- - -	13.0	10.7	9.3	12.6	12.0	12.1	12.6	13.5
Home health agency	1.5	2.1	0.2	0.3	1.4	4.9	4.5	4.5	4.0	4.3	4.3
Home health agency transfer[6]	- - -	- - -	- - -	0.0	-0.7	-1.9	-3.1	-1.0	1.7	0.0	0.0
Administrative expenses[7]	10.7	5.4	3.5	2.4	2.0	2.0	1.8	2.0	1.9	2.0	1.8
Part D Transitional Assistance and Start-up Costs[15]	- - -	- - -	- - -	- - -	- - -	- - -	- - -	- - -	- - -	0.2	0.4
Total Part D[4]	- - -	- - -	- - -	- - -	- - -	- - -	- - -	- - -	- - -	100.0	100.0
Drug card and transitional subsidy	- - -	- - -	- - -	- - -	- - -	- - -	- - -	- - -	- - -	100.0	100.0

- - - Data not available.

0.0 Quantity greater than 0 but less than 0.05.

[1]Preliminary figures.

[2]Average number enrolled in the hospital insurance (HI) and/or supplementary medical insurance (SMI) programs for the period. See Appendix II, Medicare.

[3]Beginning in 2004, the SMI trust fund consists of two separate accounts, Part B (pays for a portion of the costs of physicians' services, outpatient hospital services, and other related medical and health services for voluntarily enrolled aged and disabled individuals) and Part D (Medicare Prescription Drug Account - pays private plans to provide prescription drug coverage).

[4]The Medicare Modernization Act, enacted on December 8, 2003, established within SMI two Part D accounts related to prescription drug benefits: the Medicare Prescription Drug Account and the Transitional Assistance Account.The Medicare Prescription Drug Account is used in conjunction with the broad, voluntary prescription drug benefits that began in 2006.The Transitional Assistance Account was used to provide transitional assistance benefits, beginning in 2004 and extending through 2005, for certain low-income beneficiaries prior to the start of the new prescription drug benefit.

[5]Medicare-approved managed care organizations.

[6]Reflects annual home health HI to SMI transfer amounts for 1999 and later.

[7]Includes research, costs of experiments and demonstration projects, fraud and abuse promotion, and peer review activity (changed to Quality Improvement Organization in 2002).

[8]Type-of-service reporting categories for fee-for-service reimbursement differ before and after 1991.

[9]Includes payment for physicians, practitioners, durable medical equipment, and all suppliers other than independent laboratory through 1990. Beginning in 1991, physician services subject to the physician fee schedule are shown. Payments for laboratory services paid under the laboratory fee schedule and performed in a physician office are included under Laboratory beginning in 1991. Payments for durable medical equipment are shown separately beginning in 1991. The remaining services from the Physician category are included in Other.

[10]Includes payments for hospital outpatient department services, skilled nursing facility outpatient services, Part B services received as an inpatient in a hospital or skilled nursing facility setting, and other types of outpatient facilities. Starting with 1991 data, payments for hospital outpatient department services, except for laboratory services, are listed under Hospital. Hospital outpatient laboratory services are included in the Laboratory line.

[11]Starting with 1991 data, those independent laboratory services that were paid under the laboratory fee schedule (most of the independent lab category) are included in the Laboratory line; the remaining services are included in the Physician fee schedule and Other lines.

[12]Payments for laboratory services paid under the laboratory fee schedule performed in a physician office, independent lab, or in a hospital outpatient department.

[13]Includes payments for physician-administered drugs; free-standing ambulatory surgical center facility services; ambulance services; supplies; free-standing end-stage renal disease (ESRD) dialysis facility services; rural health clinics; outpatient rehabilitation facilities; psychiatric hospitals; and federally qualified health centers.

[14]Includes the hospital facility costs for Medicare Part B services that are predominantly in the outpatient department, with the exception of hospital outpatient laboratory services, which are included on the Laboratory line. Physician reimbursement is included on the Physician fee schedule line.

[15]Part D Administrative and Transitional Start-Up Costs were funded through the SMI Part B account.

NOTES: Percents are calculated using unrounded data. Table includes service disbursements as of February 2005 for Medicare enrollees residing in Puerto Rico, Virgin Islands, Guam, other outlying areas, foreign countries, and unknown residence. Totals do not necessarily equal the sum of rounded components. Some numbers in this table have been revised and differ from previous editions of *Health, United States*.

SOURCE: Centers for Medicare & Medicaid Services, Office of the Actuary, Medicare and Medicaid Cost Estimates Group, Medicare Administrative Data.

Table 138. Medicare enrollees and program payments among fee-for-service Medicare beneficiaries, by sex and age: United States and other areas, 1994–2003

[Data are compiled from administrative data by the Centers for Medicare & Medicaid Services]

Sex and age	1994	1995	1996	1997	1998	1999	2000	2001	2002	2003
	Fee-for-service enrollees in thousands									
Total.	34,076	34,062	33,704	33,009	32,349	32,179	32,740	33,860	34,977	35,815
Sex										
Male.	14,533	14,563	14,440	14,149	13,902	13,872	14,195	14,746	15,314	15,736
Female.	19,543	19,499	19,264	18,860	18,477	18,307	18,545	19,113	19,664	20,079
Age										
Under 65 years	4,031	4,239	4,413	4,498	4,617	4,742	4,907	5,172	5,448	5,732
65–74 years	16,713	16,373	15,810	15,099	14,433	14,072	14,230	14,689	15,107	15,390
75–84 years	9,845	9,911	9,915	9,847	9,722	9,748	9,919	10,211	10,533	10,701
85 years and over	3,486	3,540	3,566	3,565	3,577	3,618	3,684	3,787	3,889	3,991
	Fee-for-service program payments in billions									
Total.	$ 146.6	$ 159.0	$ 167.1	$ 175.4	$ 168.2	$ 166.7	$ 174.3	$ 197.5	$ 215.4	$ 232.8
Sex										
Male.	63.9	68.8	71.0	75.4	72.9	73.2	76.2	86.3	94.3	102.2
Female.	82.6	90.2	95.1	100.1	95.3	93.5	98.0	111.2	121.1	130.6
Age										
Under 65 years	18.8	21.0	24.2	25.8	23.7	24.3	25.8	29.7	33.2	37.3
65–74 years	55.1	58.1	58.7	59.7	57.3	56.0	57.5	64.6	70.0	75.2
75–84 years	50.7	55.3	58.1	61.7	59.7	59.5	62.7	70.9	77.1	82.5
85 years and over	21.8	24.6	26.1	28.2	27.3	26.9	28.3	32.3	35.1	37.8
	Percent distribution of fee-for-service program payments									
Total.	100.0	100.0	100.0	100.0	100.0	100.0	100.0	100.0	100.0	100.0
Sex										
Male.	43.6	43.2	42.5	43.0	43.3	43.9	43.7	43.7	43.8	43.9
Female.	56.4	56.8	56.9	57.0	56.7	56.1	56.3	56.3	56.2	56.1
Age										
Under 65 years	12.9	13.2	14.5	14.7	14.1	14.6	14.8	15.0	15.4	16.0
65–74 years	37.6	36.5	35.2	34.0	34.1	33.6	33.0	32.7	32.5	32.3
75–84 years	34.6	34.8	34.8	35.2	35.5	35.7	36.0	35.9	35.8	35.4
85 years and over	14.9	15.5	15.6	16.1	16.3	16.1	16.2	16.4	16.3	16.2
	Average fee-for-service payment per enrollee									
Total.	$ 4,301	$ 4,667	$ 4,957	$ 5,314	$ 5,198	$ 5,180	$ 5,323	$ 5,833	$ 6,159	$ 6,501
Sex										
Male.	4,397	4,721	4,918	5,326	5,243	5,275	5,370	5,853	6,157	6,496
Female.	4,229	4,627	4,934	5,306	5,165	5,108	5,286	5,818	6,159	6,505
Age										
Under 65 years	4,673	4,960	5,475	5,735	5,143	5,117	5,252	5,746	6,102	6,499
65–74 years	3,300	3,548	3,715	3,953	3,973	3,982	4,040	4,400	4,635	4,887
75–84 years	5,152	5,576	5,856	6,267	6,145	6,106	6,320	6,939	7,317	7,713
85 years and over	6,267	6,950	7,321	7,919	7,641	7,428	7,684	8,529	9,019	9,474

NOTES: Table includes data for Medicare enrollees residing in Puerto Rico, U.S. Virgin Islands, Guam, other outlying areas, foreign countries, and unknown residence. Number of fee-for-service enrollees is based on 5-percent annual Denominator File using the Centers for Medicare & Medicaid Services' (CMS) Enrollment Database and Group Health Plan data. Fee-for-service program payments are based on a 5-percent annual Denominator File and fee-for-service billing reimbursement for a 5-percent sample of Medicare beneficiaries as recorded in CMS' National Claims History using CMS' Enrollment Database, Group Health Plan, and National Claims History data. See Appendix II, Medicare.

SOURCE: Centers for Medicare & Medicaid Services, Office of Research, Development, and Information. Health Care Financing Review: Medicare and Medicaid Statistical Supplements for years 1996 to 2005. Website: www.cms.hhs.gov/review/supp/.

Table 139 (page 1 of 2). Medicare beneficiaries by race and ethnicity, by selected characteristics: United States, 1992, 2001, and 2002

[Data are based on household interviews of a sample of current Medicare beneficiaries and Medicare administrative records]

| | | | | Not Hispanic or Latino | | | | | | | | | |
| | All | | | White | | | Black or African American | | | Hispanic or Latino | | |
Characteristic	1992	2001	2002	1992	2001	2002	1992	2001	2002	1992	2001	2002
					Number of beneficiaries in millions							
All Medicare beneficiaries	36.8	41.2	41.8	30.9	32.7	32.9	3.3	3.8	3.9	1.9	3.0	3.1
					Percent distribution of beneficiaries							
All Medicare beneficiaries	100.0	100.0	100.0	84.2	79.8	79.2	8.9	9.3	9.4	5.2	7.2	7.4
Medical care use					Percent of beneficiaries with at least one service							
All Medicare beneficiaries:												
Long-term care facility stay	7.7	9.1	9.5	8.0	9.8	10.2	6.2	8.1	8.8	4.2	4.8	5.5
Community-only residents:												
Inpatient hospital.	17.9	19.8	20.2	18.1	20.1	20.2	18.4	20.2	23.4	16.6	16.2	16.3
Outpatient hospital	57.9	70.3	77.7	57.8	71.4	72.8	61.1	69.1	70.3	53.1	61.6	67.7
Physician/supplier [1]	92.4	95.3	95.6	93.0	96.3	96.5	89.1	92.1	91.0	87.9	91.8	93.3
Dental	40.4	44.0	43.6	43.1	48.3	47.5	23.5	21.8	22.8	29.1	30.9	33.2
Prescription medicine	85.2	91.6	91.6	85.5	92.1	92.2	83.1	90.3	88.7	84.6	90.2	90.9
Expenditures					Expenditures per beneficiary							
All Medicare beneficiaries:												
Total health care [2]	$6,716	$11,403	$13,010	$6,816	$11,478	$13,010	$7,043	$13,279	$15,260	$5,784	$8,903	$12,303
Long-term care facility [3]	1,581	2,503	2,485	1,674	2,636	2,609	1,255	2,753	2,931	*758	1,486	1,602
Community-only residents:												
Total personal health care	5,054	8,626	10,313	4,988	8,636	10,314	5,530	9,483	*8,403	4,938	7,121	*12,541
Inpatient hospital	2,098	2,771	2,990	2,058	2,739	2,899	2,493	3,411	3,857	1,999	2,835	2,931
Outpatient hospital	504	957	1,060	478	896	1,009	668	1,483	1,583	511	812	100
Physician/supplier [1]	1,524	2,760	2,968	1,525	2,801	2,950	1,398	2,581	2,846	1,587	2,609	3,216
Dental	142	271	258	153	300	285	70	107	131	97	206	174
Prescription medicine	468	1,338	1,504	481	1,369	1,541	417	1,271	1,425	389	1,069	1,282
Long-term care facility residents only:												
Long-term care facility [4]	23,054	35,384	34,330	23,177	33,939	33,260	21,272	33,903	44,696	*25,026	31,788	36,832
Sex					Percent distribution of beneficiaries							
Both sexes	100.0	100.0	100.0	100.0	100.0	100.0	100.0	100.0	100.0	100.0	100.0	100.0
Male	42.9	43.8	43.9	42.7	43.6	44.1	42.0	42.2	42.5	46.7	46.7	46.5
Female.	57.1	56.2	56.1	57.3	56.4	55.9	58.0	57.9	57.5	53.3	54.3	53.4
Eligibility criteria and age												
All Medicare beneficiaries [5]	100.0	100.0	100.0	100.0	100.0	100.0	100.0	100.0	100.0	100.0	100.0	100.0
Disabled.	10.2	13.9	14.1	8.6	11.9	12.0	19.1	25.6	26.1	16.5	19.2	19.6
Under 45 years	3.5	3.8	3.8	2.9	3.2	3.2	7.6	7.9	7.4	6.9	4.6	5.1
45–64 years	6.5	10.1	10.3	5.8	8.7	8.8	11.5	17.8	18.7	9.6	14.6	14.5
Aged	89.8	86.1	85.9	91.4	88.1	88.0	81.0	74.4	73.9	83.5	80.8	80.4
65–74 years	51.5	45.3	44.8	52.0	45.5	44.9	48.0	40.0	40.7	49.4	48.2	46.0
75–84 years	28.8	30.2	30.3	29.5	31.3	31.8	24.0	25.7	24.3	27.1	24.0	24.7
85 years and over	9.7	10.7	10.8	9.9	11.3	11.3	9.0	8.7	8.9	6.9	8.7	9.7
Living arrangement												
All living arrangements	100.0	100.0	100.0	100.0	100.0	100.0	100.0	100.0	100.0	100.0	100.0	100.0
Alone.	27.0	28.9	29.4	27.5	29.3	29.6	27.7	30.7	33.5	20.2	24.9	24.2
With spouse	51.2	49.5	49.3	53.3	51.6	51.8	33.3	30.7	28.1	50.4	49.3	49.3
With children.	9.1	9.3	9.2	7.7	7.3	7.4	16.8	21.0	19.1	16.6	13.5	13.5
With others.	7.6	7.4	7.2	6.2	6.5	5.9	18.1	13.3	14.9	10.8	9.3	9.9
Long-term care facility	5.1	5.0	4.9	5.3	5.3	5.3	4.0	4.4	4.4	*2.0	2.9	3.1

See footnotes at end of table.

Table 139 (page 2 of 2). Medicare beneficiaries by race and ethnicity, by selected characteristics: United States, 1992, 2001, and 2002

[Data are based on household interviews of a sample of current Medicare beneficiaries and Medicare administrative records]

| | | | | Not Hispanic or Latino | | | | | | | | | |
| | All | | | White | | | Black or African American | | | Hispanic or Latino | | |
Characteristic	1992	2001	2002	1992	2001	2002	1992	2001	2002	1992	2001	2002
Age and limitation of activity[6]					Percent distribution of beneficiaries							
Disabled	100.0	100.0	100.0	100.0	100.0	100.0	100.0	100.0	100.0	100.0	100.0	100.0
None	22.7	28.3	25.9	21.8	27.0	24.8	26.2	32.9	33.3	21.2	27.4	21.9
IADL only	39.0	35.3	36.4	38.9	34.5	37.0	35.8	36.0	32.6	46.1	36.6	40.9
1 or 2 ADL	21.2	20.2	21.3	21.5	21.6	20.8	21.2	20.0	21.8	*20.9	14.4	*22.1
3–5 ADL	17.2	16.2	16.4	17.9	16.9	17.4	*16.8	11.2	*12.3	*11.9	21.6	*15.1
65–74 years	100.0	100.0	100.0	100.0	100.0	100.0	100.0	100.0	100.0	100.0	100.0	100.0
None	67.0	70.9	70.1	68.7	27.0	71.3	55.1	64.2	62.5	59.2	69.7	68.9
IADL only	17.8	16.1	16.1	17.0	34.5	15.7	22.9	20.3	20.0	*20.9	16.4	16.1
1 or 2 ADL	10.4	8.4	9.5	9.6	21.6	9.2	14.4	8.5	*9.1	*15.7	8.4	*9.4
3–5 ADL	4.8	4.6	4.3	4.6	4.2	3.8	*7.6	7.0	*8.3	*4.2	5.5	*5.7
75–84 years	100.0	100.0	100.0	100.0	100.0	100.0	100.0	100.0	100.0	100.0	100.0	100.0
None	46.6	52.6	50.7	47.5	53.5	52.2	42.0	45.9	40.7	44.3	49.9	44.3
IADL only	23.9	23.2	24.0	23.6	23.0	23.5	26.7	25.0	24.7	*27.8	23.7	29.1
1 or 2 ADL	16.5	13.0	13.9	16.8	12.8	13.5	15.3	14.0	*19.0	*14.9	15.6	*13.1
3–5 ADL	13.0	11.2	11.4	12.2	10.8	10.8	*15.9	15.1	15.5	*13.0	*10.8	*13.5
85 years and over	100.0	100.0	100.0	100.0	100.0	100.0	100.0	100.0	100.0	100.0	100.0	100.0
None	19.9	25.1	24.8	20.2	25.8	25.7	*19.6	23.0	*22.8	*19.7	*19.1	*14.5
IADL only	20.9	24.8	23.9	20.2	24.6	24.4	*22.1	24.5	*24.1	*24.7	25.0	*18.3
1 or 2 ADL	23.5	20.9	21.8	23.5	20.7	22.0	*24.3	21.7	*15.9	*23.7	*22.2	*25.7
3–5 ADL	35.8	29.3	29.5	36.1	28.9	27.9	*34.0	30.8	37.3	*31.8	33.7	*41.6

* Estimates are considered unreliable. Estimates based on 50 persons or fewer or with a relative standard error of 30% or higher are not shown.
[1]Physician/supplier services include medical and osteopathic doctor and health practitioner visits; diagnostic laboratory and radiology services; medical and surgical services; and durable medical equipment and nondurable medical supplies.
[2]Total health care expenditures by Medicare beneficiaries, including expenses paid by Medicare and all other sources of payment for the following services: inpatient hospital, outpatient hospital, physician/supplier, dental, prescription medicine, home health, and hospice and long-term care facility care. Does not include health insurance premiums.
[3]Expenditures for long-term care in facilities for all beneficiaries include facility room and board expenses for beneficiaries who resided in a facility for the full year, for beneficiaries who resided in a facility for part of the year and in the community for part of the year, and expenditures for short-term facility stays for full-year or part-year community residents. See Appendix II, Long-term care facility.
[4]Expenditures for facility-based long-term care for facility-based beneficiaries include facility room and board expenses for beneficiaries who resided in a facility for the full year and for beneficiaries who resided in a facility for part of the year and in the community for part of the year. It does not include expenditures for short-term facility stays for full-year community residents. See Appendix II, Long-term care facility.
[5]Medicare beneficiaries with end-stage renal disease (ESRD) are included within the subgroups Aged and Disabled.
[6]Includes data for both community and long-term care facility residents. See Appendix II for definitions of Activities of Daily Living (ADL) and Instrumental Activities of Daily Living (IADL).

NOTES: Percents and percent distributions are calculated using unrounded numbers. Data for additional years are available. See Appendix III.

SOURCE: Centers for Medicare & Medicaid Services, Medicare Current Beneficiary Survey, Health and Health Care of the Medicare Population. Available from: www.cms.hhs.gov/apps/mcbs/Publdt.asp. and unpublished data.

Table 140. Medicaid recipients and medical vendor payments, by basis of eligibility, and race and ethnicity: United States, selected fiscal years 1972–2003

[Data are compiled by the Centers for Medicare & Medicaid Services from the Medicaid Data System]

Basis of eligibility and race and ethnicity	1972	1980	1990	1995	1999[1]	2000	2001	2002	2003
Recipients	Number in millions								
All recipients	17.6	21.6	25.3	36.3	40.1	42.8	46.0	49.3	52.0
Basis of eligibility:[2]	Percent of recipients								
Aged (65 years and over)	18.8	15.9	12.7	11.4	9.4	8.7	8.3	7.9	7.8
Blind and disabled	9.8	13.5	14.7	16.1	16.7	16.1	15.4	15.0	14.8
Adults in families with dependent children[3]	17.8	22.6	23.8	21.0	18.7	20.5	21.1	22.6	22.2
Children under age 21[4]	44.5	43.2	44.4	47.3	46.9	46.1	45.7	47.1	47.8
Other Title XIX[5]	9.0	6.9	3.9	1.7	8.4	8.6	9.5	7.4	7.5
Race and ethnicity:[6]									
White	- - -	- - -	42.8	45.5	- - -	- - -	40.2	40.9	41.2
Black or African American	- - -	- - -	25.1	24.7	- - -	- - -	23.1	22.8	22.4
American Indian or Alaska Native	- - -	- - -	1.0	0.8	- - -	- - -	1.3	1.3	1.4
Asian or Pacific Islander	- - -	- - -	2.0	2.2	- - -	- - -	3.0	3.4	3.3
Hispanic or Latino	- - -	- - -	15.2	17.2	- - -	- - -	17.9	19.0	19.3
Unknown	- - -	- - -	14.0	9.6	- - -	- - -	14.6	12.6	12.5
Vendor payments[7]	Amount in billions								
All payments	$ 6.3	$ 23.3	$ 64.9	$120.1	$ 153.5	$ 168.3	$ 186.3	$ 213.5	$ 233.2
	Percent distribution								
Total	100.0	100.0	100.0	100.0	100.0	100.0	100.0	100.0	100.0
Basis of eligibility:									
Aged (65 years and over)	30.6	37.5	33.2	30.4	27.7	26.4	25.9	24.4	23.7
Blind and disabled	22.2	32.7	37.6	41.1	42.9	43.2	43.1	43.3	43.7
Adults in families with dependent children[3]	15.3	13.9	13.2	11.2	10.3	10.6	10.7	10.9	11.4
Children under age 21[4]	18.1	13.4	14.0	15.0	15.7	15.9	16.3	16.8	17.1
Other Title XIX[5]	13.9	2.6	1.6	1.2	3.4	3.9	3.9	4.6	4.1
Race and ethnicity:[6]									
White	- - -	- - -	53.4	54.3	- - -	- - -	54.4	54.1	53.8
Black or African American	- - -	- - -	18.3	19.2	- - -	- - -	19.8	19.6	19.7
American Indian or Alaska Native	- - -	- - -	0.6	0.5	- - -	- - -	1.1	1.1	1.2
Asian or Pacific Islander	- - -	- - -	1.0	1.2	- - -	- - -	2.5	2.8	2.4
Hispanic or Latino	- - -	- - -	5.3	7.3	- - -	- - -	9.4	9.7	10.6
Unknown	- - -	- - -	21.3	17.6	- - -	- - -	12.9	12.6	12.2
Vendor payments per recipient[7]	Amount								
All recipients	$ 358	$1,079	$2,568	$3,311	$ 3,819	$ 3,936	$ 4,053	$ 4,328	$ 4,487
Basis of eligibility:									
Aged (65 years and over)	580	2,540	6,717	8,868	11,268	11,929	12,725	13,370	13,677
Blind and disabled	807	2,618	6,564	8,435	9,832	10,559	11,318	12,470	13,303
Adults in families with dependent children[3]	307	662	1,429	1,777	2,104	2,030	2,059	2,095	2,296
Children under age 21[4]	145	335	811	1,047	1,282	1,358	1,448	1,545	1,606
Other Title XIX[5]	555	398	1,062	2,380	1,532	1,778	1,680	2,692	2,458
Race and ethnicity:[6]									
White	- - -	- - -	3,207	3,953	- - -	- - -	5,489	5,721	5,869
Black or African American	- - -	- - -	1,878	2,568	- - -	- - -	3,480	3,733	3,944
American Indian or Alaska Native	- - -	- - -	1,706	2,142	- - -	- - -	3,452	3,774	4,001
Asian or Pacific Islander	- - -	- - -	1,257	1,713	- - -	- - -	3,283	3,562	3,328
Hispanic or Latino	- - -	- - -	903	1,400	- - -	- - -	2,126	2,215	2,463
Unknown	- - -	- - -	3,909	6,099	- - -	- - -	3,576	4,338	4,395

- - - Data not available.

[1]Prior to 1999, recipient counts exclude those individuals who only received coverage under prepaid health care and for whom no direct vendor payments were made during the year, and vendor payments exclude payments to health maintenance organizations and other prepaid health plans ($19.3 billion in 1998 and $18 billion in 1997). See Appendix II, Medical vendor payments. Starting in 1999, the Medicaid data system was changed. See Appendix I, Medicaid Data System.

[2]In 1980 and 1985, recipients are included in more than one category. In 1990–1996, 0.2%–2.5% of recipients have unknown basis of eligibility. Starting with 1997 data, unknowns are included in Other Title XIX.

[3]Includes adults in the Aid to Families with Dependent Children (AFDC) program. Starting with 1997 data, includes adults in the Temporary Assistance for Needy Families (TANF) program. Starting with 2001 data, includes women in the Breast and Cervical Cancer Prevention and Treatment Program.

[4]Includes children in the AFDC program. Starting with 1997 data, includes children and foster care children in the TANF program.

[5]Includes some participants in the Supplemental Security Income program and other people deemed medically needy in participating states. Starting with 1997 data, excludes foster care children and includes unknown eligibility.

[6]Race and ethnicity are as determined on initial Medicaid application. Categories are mutually exclusive. Starting with 2001 data, the Hispanic category included Hispanic persons, regardless of race. Persons indicating more than one race were included in the unknown category.

[7]Vendor payments exclude disproportionate share hospital payments ($15.5 billion in FY2001).

NOTES: 1972 data are for fiscal year ending June 30. All other years are for fiscal year ending September 30. Data for additional years are available. See Appendix III.

SOURCE: Centers for Medicare & Medicaid Services, Office of Information Services, Enterprise Databases Group, Division of Information Distribution, Medicaid Data System. Before 1999, Medicaid Statistical Report HCFA–2082. From 1999 onward, Medicaid Statistical Information System, MSIS. Available from: msis.cms.hhs.gov.

Table 141 (page 1 of 2). Medicaid recipients and medical vendor payments, by type of service: United States, selected fiscal years 1972–2003

[Data are compiled by the Centers for Medicare & Medicaid Services from the Medicaid Data System]

Type of service	1972	1980	1990	1995	1999[1]	2000	2001	2002	2003
Recipients				Number in millions					
All recipients	17.6	21.6	25.3	36.3	40.2	42.8	46.0	49.3	52.0
				Percent of recipients					
Inpatient hospital	16.1	17.0	18.2	15.3	11.2	11.5	10.6	10.2	10.0
Mental health facility	0.2	0.3	0.4	0.2	0.2	0.2	0.2	0.2	0.2
Mentally retarded intermediate care facility	- - -	0.6	0.6	0.4	0.3	0.3	0.3	0.2	0.2
Nursing facility	- - -	- - -	- - -	4.6	4.0	4.0	3.7	3.6	3.3
Skilled	3.1	2.8	2.4	- - -	- - -	- - -	- - -	- - -	- - -
Intermediate care	- - -	3.7	3.4	- - -	- - -	- - -	- - -	- - -	- - -
Physician	69.8	63.7	67.6	65.6	45.7	44.7	43.5	44.7	44.0
Dental	13.6	21.5	18.0	17.6	14.0	13.8	15.3	16.0	16.4
Other practitioner	9.1	15.0	15.3	15.2	9.9	11.1	11.1	11.3	11.1
Outpatient hospital	29.6	44.9	49.0	46.1	30.9	30.9	29.8	30.1	29.8
Clinic	2.8	7.1	11.1	14.7	16.8	17.9	18.4	19.2	19.6
Laboratory and radiological	20.0	14.9	35.5	36.0	25.4	26.6	26.8	28.5	28.3
Home health	0.6	1.8	2.8	4.5	2.0	2.3	2.2	2.2	2.3
Prescribed drugs	63.3	63.4	68.5	65.4	49.4	48.0	47.6	49.4	50.2
Family planning	. . .	5.2	6.9	6.9	- - -	- - -	- - -	- - -	- - -
Early and periodic screening	. . .	. . .	11.7	18.2	- - -	- - -	- - -	- - -	- - -
Rural health clinic	. . .	. . .	0.9	3.4	- - -	- - -	- - -	- - -	- - -
Capitated payment services	- - -	- - -	- - -	- - -	51.5	49.7	50.5	68.4	71.5
Primary care case management	- - -	- - -	- - -	- - -	9.7	13.0	13.9	14.6	14.5
Personal support	- - -	- - -	- - -	- - -	10.1	10.6	10.8	1.4	1.5
Other care	14.4	11.9	20.3	31.5	21.6	21.4	21.5	37.2	37.7
Vendor payments[2]				Amount in billions					
All payments	$ 6.3	$ 23.3	$ 64.9	$120.1	$153.5	$168.3	$186.3	$213.5	$233.2
				Percent distribution					
Total	100.0	100.0	100.0	100.0	100.0	100.0	100.0	100.0	100.0
Inpatient hospital	40.6	27.5	25.7	21.9	14.5	14.4	13.9	13.6	13.5
Mental health facility	1.8	3.3	2.6	2.1	1.1	1.1	1.1	1.0	0.9
Mentally retarded intermediate care facility	- - -	8.5	11.3	8.6	6.1	5.6	5.2	5.0	4.7
Nursing facility	- - -	- - -	- - -	24.2	21.7	20.5	20.0	18.4	17.3
Skilled	23.3	15.8	12.4	- - -	- - -	- - -	- - -	- - -	- - -
Intermediate care	- - -	18.0	14.9	- - -	- - -	- - -	- - -	- - -	- - -
Physician	12.6	8.0	6.2	6.1	4.3	4.0	4.0	3.9	3.9
Dental	2.7	2.0	0.9	0.8	0.8	0.8	1.0	1.1	1.1
Other practitioner	0.9	0.8	0.6	0.8	0.3	0.4	0.4	0.4	0.4
Outpatient hospital	5.8	4.7	5.1	5.5	4.0	4.2	4.0	4.0	4.0
Clinic	0.7	1.4	2.6	3.6	3.8	3.7	3.0	3.1	3.1
Laboratory and radiological	1.3	0.5	1.1	1.0	0.8	0.8	0.9	1.0	1.0
Home health	0.4	1.4	5.2	7.8	1.9	1.9	1.9	1.8	1.9
Prescribed drugs	8.1	5.7	6.8	8.1	10.8	11.9	12.7	13.3	14.5
Family planning	. . .	0.3	0.4	0.4	- - -	- - -	- - -	- - -	- - -
Early and periodic screening	. . .	. . .	0.3	1.0	- - -	- - -	- - -	- - -	- - -
Rural health clinic	. . .	. . .	0.1	0.2	- - -	- - -	- - -	- - -	- - -
Capitated payment services	- - -	- - -	- - -	- - -	14.0	14.5	15.7	15.8	16.0
Primary care case management	- - -	- - -	- - -	- - -	0.3	0.1	0.1	0.1	0.1
Personal support	- - -	- - -	- - -	- - -	6.9	6.9	7.0	2.8	2.9
Other care	1.8	1.9	3.7	7.7	8.6	8.8	9.2	14.7	14.6

See footnotes at end of table.

Table 141 (page 2 of 2). Medicaid recipients and medical vendor payments, by type of service: United States, selected fiscal years 1972–2003

[Data are compiled by the Centers for Medicare & Medicaid Services from the Medicaid Data System]

Type of service	1972	1980	1990	1995	1999[1]	2000	2001	2002	2003
Vendor payments per recipient[2]					Amount				
Total payment per recipient	$ 358	$ 1,079	$ 2,568	$ 3,311	$ 3,819	$ 3,936	$ 4,053	$ 4,328	$ 4,487
Inpatient hospital	903	1,742	3,630	4,735	4,943	4,919	5,313	5,771	6,047
Mental health facility	2,825	11,742	18,548	29,847	18,094	17,800	21,482	21,350	20,479
Mentally retarded intermediate care facility . .	- - -	16,438	50,048	68,613	76,443	79,330	83,227	91,588	95,287
Nursing facility	- - -	- - -	- - -	17,424	20,568	20,220	21,894	22,326	23,882
Skilled	2,665	6,081	13,356	- - -	- - -	- - -	- - -	- - -	- - -
Intermediate care	- - -	5,326	11,236	- - -	- - -	- - -	- - -	- - -	- - -
Physician.	65	136	235	309	357	356	371	378	403
Dental.	71	99	130	160	214	238	270	293	305
Other practitioner	37	61	96	178	118	139	149	151	154
Outpatient hospital	70	113	269	397	491	533	546	571	596
Clinic.	82	209	602	804	860	805	662	706	720
Laboratory and radiological	23	38	80	90	114	113	131	154	161
Home health	229	847	4,733	5,740	3,571	3,135	3,478	3,689	3,720
Prescribed drugs	46	96	256	413	837	975	1,083	1,165	1,293
Family planning	. . .	72	151	206	- - -	- - -	- - -	- - -	- - -
Early and periodic screening	. . .	. . .	67	177	- - -	- - -	- - -	- - -	- - -
Rural health clinic.	. . .	. . .	154	174	- - -	- - -	- - -	- - -	- - -
Capitated payment services.	- - -	- - -	- - -	- - -	1,040	1,148	1,257	997	1,007
Primary care case management.	- - -	- - -	- - -	- - -	119	30	29	28	28
Personal support	- - -	- - -	- - -	- - -	2,583	2,543	2,639	8,290	8,804
Other care.	44	172	465	807	1,508	1,600	1,734	1,712	1,741

- - - Data not available.
. . . Category not applicable.
[1]Prior to 1999, recipient counts exclude those individuals who only received coverage under prepaid health care and for whom no direct vendor payments were made during the year, and vendor payments exclude payments to health maintenance organizations and other prepaid health plans ($19.3 billion in 1998 and $18 billion in 1997). Starting in 1999, the Medicaid data system was changed. See Appendix I, Medicaid Data System. See Appendix II, Medicaid.
[2]Payments exclude disproportionate share hospital payments ($15.5 billion in FY2001).

NOTES: 1972 data are for fiscal year ending June 30. All other years are for fiscal year ending September 30. Unknown services are included with Other care (0.2% of recipients and 0.7% of payments in 2001). Data for additional years are available. See Appendix III.

SOURCE: Centers for Medicare & Medicaid Services, Office of Information Services, Enterprise Databases Group, Division of Information Distribution, Medicaid Data System. Before 1999 Medicaid Statistical Report HCFA–2082. From 1999 onward, Medicaid Statistical Information System, MSIS. Available from: msis.cms.hhs.gov. Unpublished data.

Table 142. Department of Veterans Affairs health care expenditures and use, and persons treated, by selected characteristics: United States, selected fiscal years 1970–2004

[Data are compiled from patient records, enrollment information, and budgetary data by the Department of Veterans Affairs]

	1970	1980	1990	1995	2000	2001	2002	2003	2004
Health care expenditures					Amount in millions				
All expenditures [1]	$1,689	$ 5,981	$11,500	$16,126	$19,327	$21,316	$23,003	$25,647	$28,346
					Percent distribution				
All services	100.0	100.0	100.0	100.0	100.0	100.0	100.0	100.0	100.0
Inpatient hospital	71.3	64.3	57.5	49.0	37.3	34.7	33.6	32.2	31.1
Outpatient care	14.0	19.1	25.3	30.2	45.7	48.0	48.8	49.5	49.5
Nursing home care	5.5	7.1	9.5	10.0	8.2	8.1	8.0	8.1	7.9
All other [2]	9.1	9.6	7.7	10.8	8.8	9.2	9.6	10.2	11.5
Health care use					Number in thousands				
Inpatient hospital stays [3]	787	1,248	1,029	879	579	584	590	588	599
Outpatient visits	7,312	17,971	22,602	27,527	38,370	42,901	46,058	49,760	53,745
Nursing home stays [4]	47	57	75	79	91	93	87	93	93
Inpatients [5]									
Total	- - -	- - -	598	527	417	426	436	443	457
					Percent distribution				
Total	- - -	- - -	100.0	100.0	100.0	100.0	100.0	100.0	100.0
Veterans with service-connected disability	- - -	- - -	38.9	39.3	34.4	34.6	35.2	36.2	36.5
Veterans without service-connected disability	- - -	- - -	60.3	59.9	64.7	64.5	63.9	62.9	62.6
Low income	- - -	- - -	54.8	56.2	41.7	41.4	40.9	40.8	40.9
Veterans receiving aid and attendance or housebound benefits or who are catastrophically disabled [6]	- - -	- - -	- - -	- - -	16.0	15.7	13.6	13.5	12.9
Veterans receiving medical care subject to copayments [7]	- - -	- - -	2.8	2.8	5.2	6.0	7.7	8.0	8.7
Other and unknown [8]	- - -	- - -	2.7	0.9	1.8	1.4	1.7	0.6	0.0
Nonveterans	- - -	- - -	0.8	0.8	0.9	0.9	0.9	0.8	0.9
Outpatients [5]					Number in thousands				
Total	- - -	- - -	2,564	2,790	3,657	4,072	4,456	4,715	4,894
					Percent distribution				
Total	- - -	- - -	100.0	100.0	100.0	100.0	100.0	100.0	100.0
Veterans with service-connected disability	- - -	- - -	38.3	37.5	30.7	30.0	29.5	30.3	30.8
Veterans without service-connected disability	- - -	- - -	49.8	50.5	60.8	62.5	63.9	63.4	63.1
Low income	- - -	- - -	41.1	42.2	37.6	36.6	34.1	32.7	32.8
Veterans receiving aid and attendance or housebound benefits or who are catastrophically disabled [6]	- - -	- - -	- - -	- - -	3.8	3.7	3.3	3.4	3.4
Veterans receiving medical care subject to copayments [7]	- - -	- - -	3.6	4.2	15.4	19.9	23.6	26.1	26.9
Other and unknown [8]	- - -	- - -	5.1	4.1	4.0	2.3	2.9	1.1	0.0
Nonveterans	- - -	- - -	11.8	12.0	8.5	7.5	6.6	6.3	6.1

- - - Data not available.

[1] Health care expenditures exclude construction, medical administration, and miscellaneous operating expenses at Department of Veterans Affairs headquarters.

[2] Includes miscellaneous benefits and services, contract hospitals, education and training, subsidies to state veterans hospitals, nursing homes and residential rehabilitation treatment programs (formerly domiciliaries), and the Civilian Health and Medical Program of the Department of Veterans Affairs.

[3] One-day dialysis patients were included in 1980. Interfacility transfers were included starting with 1990 data.

[4] Includes Department of Veterans Affairs nursing home and residential rehabilitation treatment programs (formerly domiciliary) stays, and community nursing home care stays.

[5] Individuals. The inpatient and outpatient totals are not additive because most inpatients are also treated as outpatients.

[6] Includes veterans who are receiving aid and attendance or housebound benefit and veterans who have been determined by the Department of Veterans Affairs to be catastrophically disabled.

[7] Includes financial means-tested veterans who receive medical care subject to copayments according to income level.

[8] Includes prisoner of war, exposed to Agent Orange, and other. Prior to fiscal year 1994, veterans who reported exposure to Agent Orange were classified as exempt. Beginning in fiscal year 1994, those veterans reporting Agent Orange exposure but not treated for it were means tested and placed in the low income or other group depending on income.

NOTES: Figures may not add to totals due to rounding. In 1970, the fiscal year (FY) ended June 30; 1980 and later, the FY ended September 30. The veteran population was estimated at 25.2 million at the end of FY 2003, with 38% age 65 or over, compared with 11% in FY 1980. Seventeen percent had served during World War II, 14% during the Korean conflict, 33% during the Vietnam era, 15% during the Persian Gulf War, and 25% during peacetime. These percentages add to more than 100 due to veterans serving during more than one war. Beginning in FY 1995, categories for health care expenditures and health care use were revised. In FY 1999, a new priority system for reporting data was introduced and, starting with 1999 data, estimates reflect the new categories. Data for additional years are available. See Appendix III.

SOURCES: Department of Veterans Affairs (VA), Office of the Assistant Deputy Under Secretary for Health, National Patient Care Database, National Enrollment Database, budgetary data, and unpublished data. Veteran population estimates were provided by the VA's Office of the Actuary.

Table 143 (page 1 of 2). State mental health agency per capita expenditures for mental health services and average annual percent change, by geographic region and state: United States, selected fiscal years 1981–2003

[Data are based on reporting by state mental health agencies]

Geographic region and state[1]	1981	1985	1990	1993	1997	2001	2002	2003	1981–1990	1990–2001	2001–2003
				Amount per capita					Average annual percent change		
United States	$ 27	$35	$ 48	$ 54	$ 64	$ 81	$ 88	$ 92	6.6	4.9	6.6
New England:											
Connecticut	32	44	73	82	99	129	138	151	9.6	5.3	8.2
Maine	25	36	67	70	88	107	118	128	11.6	4.3	9.4
Massachusetts	32	46	84	83	90	107	107	106	11.3	2.2	−0.5
New Hampshire	35	42	63	78	99	112	116	117	6.7	5.4	2.2
Rhode Island	36	35	50	61	63	88	88	89	3.7	5.3	0.6
Vermont	32	44	54	74	92	130	145	152	6.0	8.3	8.1
Mideast:											
Delaware	44	46	55	56	73	93	86	81	2.5	4.9	−6.7
District of Columbia[2]	- - -	28	268	315	337	398	409	414	- - -	3.7	2.0
Maryland	33	40	61	64	76	127	136	147	7.1	6.9	7.6
New Jersey	26	36	57	68	69	90	120	126	9.1	4.2	18.3
New York	67	90	118	131	113	176	184	192	6.5	3.7	4.4
Pennsylvania	41	52	57	68	68	152	166	195	3.7	9.3	13.3
Great Lakes:											
Illinois	18	24	34	36	51	64	69	66	7.3	5.9	1.6
Indiana	19	27	47	39	40	65	69	72	10.6	3.0	5.2
Michigan	33	49	74	75	87	90	91	98	9.4	1.8	4.3
Ohio	25	30	41	47	52	61	61	62	5.7	3.7	0.8
Wisconsin	22	28	37	35	44	72	91	91	5.9	6.2	12.4
Plains:											
Iowa	8	11	17	13	29	73	53	74	8.7	14.2	0.7
Kansas	18	27	35	48	59	60	70	75	7.7	5.0	11.8
Minnesota[3]	17	32	54	69	87	105	115	119	8.8	6.2	6.5
Missouri	24	28	35	41	56	60	69	67	4.3	5.0	5.7
Nebraska	17	21	29	34	39	51	56	58	6.1	5.3	6.6
North Dakota	39	36	40	43	48	79	82	81	0.3	6.4	1.3
South Dakota	17	22	25	47	54	61	65	66	4.4	8.4	4.0
Southeast:											
Alabama	20	28	38	43	47	57	60	61	7.4	3.8	3.4
Arkansas	17	24	26	30	30	28	28	30	4.8	0.7	3.5
Florida	20	26	37	31	44	35	44	38	7.1	−0.5	4.2
Georgia	25	23	51	49	47	46	47	50	8.2	−0.9	4.3
Kentucky	15	19	23	25	35	49	51	51	4.9	7.1	2.0
Louisiana	19	26	28	39	43	45	48	51	4.4	4.4	6.5
Mississippi	14	24	34	41	56	87	89	93	10.4	8.9	3.4
North Carolina	24	38	46	50	62	76	50	50	7.5	4.7	−18.9
South Carolina	31	33	51	56	64	74	70	67	5.7	3.4	−4.8
Tennessee	18	23	29	37	23	69	84	87	5.4	8.2	12.3
Virginia	23	32	45	40	49	65	67	69	7.7	3.4	3.0
West Virginia	20	22	24	22	23	26	47	49	2.0	0.7	37.3
Southwest:											
Arizona	10	12	27	60	68	89	102	126	11.7	11.5	19.0
New Mexico	24	25	23	24	31	33	29	29	−0.5	3.3	−6.3
Oklahoma	22	31	36	38	41	39	41	39	5.6	0.7	0.0
Texas	13	17	23	31	39	38	38	39	6.5	4.7	1.3
Rocky Mountains:											
Colorado	24	28	34	41	57	64	67	66	3.9	5.9	1.6
Idaho	13	15	20	26	29	46	40	34	4.9	7.9	−14.0
Montana	25	29	28	34	93	124	132	123	1.3	14.5	−0.4
Utah	13	17	21	25	28	33	69	71	5.5	4.2	46.7
Wyoming	23	31	35	42	43	61	78	103	4.8	5.2	29.9

See footnotes at end of table.

Table 143 (page 2 of 2). State mental health agency per capita expenditures for mental health services and average annual percent change, by geographic region and state: United States, selected fiscal years 1981–2003

[Data are based on reporting by state mental health agencies]

Geographic region and state[1]	1981	1985	1990	1993	1997	2001	2002	2003	1981–1990	1990–2001	2001–2003
	Amount per capita								Average annual percent change		
Far West:											
Alaska.................	$38	$45	$72	$86	$79	$ 81	$ 88	$ 85	7.4	1.1	2.4
California...............	28	34	42	50	58	92	105	109	4.6	7.4	8.8
Hawaii.................	19	23	38	71	85	175	162	125	8.0	14.9	−15.5
Nevada................	22	26	33	32	45	57	59	63	4.6	5.1	5.1
Oregon	21	25	41	60	68	97	60	56	7.7	8.1	−24.0
Washington	18	30	43	66	79	88	92	91	10.2	6.7	1.7

- - - Data not available.

[1]Data are shown for Bureau of Economic Analysis (BEA) regions that are constructed to show economically interdependent states. These BEA geographic divisions differ from U.S. Census Bureau geographic divisions shown in some *Health, United States* tables. See Appendix II, Geographic region and division.
[2]Transfer of St. Elizabeths Hospital from the National Institute of Mental Health to the District of Columbia Office of Mental Health took place over the years 1985–1993.
[3]Minnesota data for 1981 not comparable with subsequent data. Average annual percent change is for 1983–1990.

NOTES: Expenditures are for mental illness, excluding mental retardation and substance abuse. Starting in 1990, data for Puerto Rico and starting in 1993, data for Guam are included in the U.S. total. States may vary in type of funds included in mental health expenditures. Medicaid revenues for community programs and children's mental health expenditures are not included by some states. Funds for mental health services in jails or prisons are included by some states. State data omissions and inclusions are likely to be consistent across years. Data for additional years are available. See Appendix III.

SOURCES: National Association of State Mental Health Program Directors and the National Association of State Mental Health Program Directors Research Institute, Inc. Lutterman T, Hollen V, Shaw R. Funding sources and expenditures of state mental health agencies: fiscal year 2003. Final report. Dec. 2005; Available from: www.nri-inc.org.

Table 144 (page 1 of 2). Medicare enrollees, enrollees in managed care, payment per enrollee, and short-stay hospital utilization by geographic region and state: United States, 1994 and 2003

[Data are compiled by the Centers for Medicare & Medicaid Services]

Geographic division and state[1]	Enrollment in thousands[2]	Percent of enrollees in managed care[3]		Payment per fee-for-service enrollee		Short-stay hospital utilization			
						Discharges per 1,000 enrollees[4]		Average length of stay in days[4]	
	2003	1994	2003	1994	2003	1994	2003	1994	2003
United States[5]	40,203	7.9	13.1	$4,375	$6,618	345	369	7.5	5.8
New England:									
Connecticut	524	2.6	5.9	4,426	7,274	287	321	8.1	5.9
Maine	227	0.1	0.1	3,464	5,370	322	307	7.6	5.4
Massachusetts	961	6.1	17.5	5,147	7,436	350	362	7.6	5.6
New Hampshire	180	0.2	1.1	3,414	5,756	281	274	7.6	5.8
Rhode Island	171	7.0	32.8	4,148	6,273	312	349	8.1	6.1
Vermont	93	0.1	0.1	3,182	5,356	283	267	7.6	5.4
Mideast:									
Delaware	122	0.2	0.7	4,712	6,786	326	334	8.1	6.6
District of Columbia	74	3.9	6.9	5,655	7,700	376	393	10.1	7.1
Maryland	676	1.4	3.6	4,997	7,699	362	401	7.5	5.4
New Jersey	1,224	2.6	7.8	4,531	8,029	354	381	10.2	7.0
New York	2,735	6.2	17.2	4,855	7,449	334	370	11.2	7.5
Pennsylvania	2,108	3.3	24.0	5,212	6,900	379	405	8.0	5.9
Great Lakes:									
Illinois	1,657	5.5	5.1	4,324	6,639	374	415	7.3	5.6
Indiana	873	2.6	2.1	3,945	5,940	345	355	6.9	5.6
Michigan	1,438	0.7	1.8	4,307	6,923	328	376	7.6	5.7
Ohio	1,734	2.4	13.3	3,982	6,480	350	390	7.1	5.5
Wisconsin	798	2.0	4.3	3,246	5,455	310	327	6.8	5.2
Plains:									
Iowa	479	3.1	3.7	3,080	5,026	322	333	6.6	5.3
Kansas	390	3.3	3.6	3,847	6,199	348	363	6.5	5.3
Minnesota	676	19.6	13.2	3,394	5,487	334	349	5.7	4.8
Missouri	888	3.4	12.5	4,191	6,024	349	402	7.3	5.6
Nebraska	260	2.2	3.7	2,926	5,500	281	291	6.3	5.5
North Dakota	103	0.6	0.5	3,218	5,360	327	286	6.3	5.1
South Dakota	120	0.1	0.3	2,952	5,044	356	320	6.1	5.1
Southeast:									
Alabama	724	0.8	6.4	4,454	6,461	413	448	7.0	5.4
Arkansas	443	0.2	0.5	3,719	5,680	366	403	7.0	5.8
Florida	2,955	13.8	18.4	5,027	7,507	326	371	7.1	5.8
Georgia	984	0.4	3.9	4,402	6,109	378	367	6.9	5.8
Kentucky	647	2.3	2.9	3,862	5,953	396	411	7.2	5.5
Louisiana	621	0.4	11.3	5,468	7,826	399	461	7.2	6.1
Mississippi	438	0.1	0.6	4,189	6,794	423	446	7.4	6.2
North Carolina	1,208	0.5	4.0	3,465	6,053	314	372	8.0	5.8
South Carolina	607	0.1	0.3	3,777	6,183	319	378	8.3	6.2
Tennessee	879	0.3	7.0	4,441	6,450	375	403	7.1	5.8
Virginia	949	1.5	2.0	3,748	5,703	348	354	7.3	5.9
West Virginia	344	8.3	6.8	3,798	5,940	420	434	7.1	5.6
Southwest:									
Arizona	730	24.8	28.1	4,442	5,963	292	313	5.9	5.1
New Mexico	249	13.6	15.6	3,110	4,980	301	279	6.0	5.2
Oklahoma	523	2.5	7.7	4,098	6,606	355	421	7.0	5.5
Texas	2,404	4.1	6.8	4,703	7,295	333	389	7.2	5.8
Rocky Mountains:									
Colorado	499	17.2	27.3	3,935	5,966	302	305	6.0	5.1
Idaho	179	2.5	9.5	3,045	5,195	274	268	5.2	4.7
Montana	144	0.4	0.5	3,114	5,014	306	287	5.9	4.8
Utah	221	9.4	3.1	3,443	5,234	238	267	5.4	4.6
Wyoming	69	3.3	1.5	3,537	5,254	315	289	5.6	4.8

See footnotes at end of table.

Table 144 (page 2 of 2). Medicare enrollees, enrollees in managed care, payment per enrollee, and short-stay hospital utilization by geographic region and state: United States, 1994 and 2003

[Data are compiled by the Centers for Medicare & Medicaid Services]

Geographic division and state[1]	Enrollment in thousands[2]	Percent of enrollees in managed care[3]		Payment per fee-for-service enrollee		Short-stay hospital utilization			
						Discharges per 1,000 enrollees[4]		Average length of stay in days[4]	
	2003	1994	2003	1994	2003	1994	2003	1994	2003
Far West:									
Alaska.	47	0.6	0.6	3,687	6,036	269	270	6.3	5.9
California.	4,066	30.0	33.2	5,219	7,062	366	327	6.1	6.1
Hawaii.	178	29.8	33.5	3,069	4,553	301	223	9.1	7.3
Nevada.	282	19.0	29.6	4,306	6,580	291	289	7.0	6.0
Oregon	524	27.7	33.7	3,285	5,243	305	306	5.2	4.6
Washington	778	12.5	17.0	3,401	5,374	269	267	5.3	5.0

0.0 less than 0.05.

[1]Data are shown for Bureau of Economic Analysis (BEA) regions that are constructed to show economically interdependent states. These BEA geographic regions differ from U.S. Census Bureau geographic divisions shown in some *Health, United States* tables. See Appendix II, Geographic region and division.

[2]Total persons enrolled in hospital insurance, supplementary medical insurance, or both, as of July 1. Includes fee-for-service and managed care enrollees.

[3]Includes enrollees in Medicare-approved managed care organizations. See Appendix II, Managed Care.

[4]Data are for fee-for-service enrollees only.

[5]Includes residents of any of the 50 states and the District of Columbia. Excludes Puerto Rico, Guam, Virgin Islands, residence unknown, foreign countries, and other outlying areas not shown separately.

NOTES: Enrollment and percent of enrollees in managed care are based on a 5% annual Denominator File using the Centers for Medicare & Medicaid Services' (CMS) Enrollment Database and Group Health Plan data. Payments per fee-for-service enrollee are based on fee-for-service billing reimbursement for a 5% sample of Medicare beneficiaries as recorded in CMS' National Claims History. Short-stay hospital utilization is based on the Medicare Provider Analysis and Review (MEDPAR) stay records for a 20% sample of Medicare beneficiaries. Figures may not sum to totals due to rounding. Data for additional years are available. See Appendix III.

SOURCE: Centers for Medicare & Medicaid Services, Office of Research, Development, and Information. Health Care Financing Review: Medicare and Medicaid Statistical Supplements for the years 1996 to 2005. Available from: www.cms.hhs.gov/HealthCareFinancingReview/.

Table 145 (page 1 of 2). Medicaid recipients, recipients in managed care, payments per recipient, and recipients per 100 persons below the poverty level, by geographic region and state: United States, selected fiscal years 1989–2003

[Data are compiled from Medicaid administrative records by the Centers for Medicare & Medicaid Services]

Geographic region and state[1]	Recipients in thousands		Percent of recipients in managed care		Payments per recipient			Recipients per 100 persons below the poverty level	
	1996[2]	2003	1996[2]	2003	1990	1996[2]	2003	1989–1990	2002–2003
United States	36,118	51,971	40	59	$2,568	$3,369	$4,487	75	144
New England:									
Connecticut	329	497	61	73	4,829	6,179	6,764	167	175
Maine	167	307	1	69	3,248	4,321	6,750	88	183
Massachusetts	715	1,042	70	99	4,622	5,285	6,134	103	162
New Hampshire	100	112	16	15	5,423	5,496	7,015	53	148
Rhode Island	130	202	63	67	3,778	5,280	6,629	163	169
Vermont	102	155	–	65	2,530	2,954	4,149	108	273
Mideast:									
Delaware	82	150	78	71	3,004	3,773	5,006	68	238
District of Columbia	143	158	55	67	2,629	4,955	7,585	86	160
Maryland	399	726	64	63	3,300	5,138	6,060	74	163
New Jersey	714	950	43	67	4,054	5,217	6,349	83	134
New York	3,281	4,450	23	53	5,099	6,811	7,912	95	155
Pennsylvania	1,168	1,722	53	80	2,449	3,993	5,489	88	138
Great Lakes:									
Illinois	1,454	1,830	13	9	2,271	3,689	5,131	69	112
Indiana	594	896	31	71	3,859	4,130	4,410	45	150
Michigan	1,172	1,590	73	66	2,094	2,867	4,076	85	133
Ohio	1,478	1,778	32	29	2,566	3,729	5,756	98	148
Wisconsin	434	829	32	47	3,179	4,384	4,729	95	155
Plains:									
Iowa	308	362	41	91	2,589	3,534	5,518	80	136
Kansas	251	316	32	57	2,524	3,425	5,103	71	109
Minnesota	455	668	33	0	3,709	5,342	7,044	70	184
Missouri	636	1,081	35	69	2,002	3,171	4,075	63	184
Nebraska	191	254	27	72	2,595	3,548	5,055	61	146
North Dakota	61	77	55	66	3,955	4,889	5,795	58	110
South Dakota	77	124	65	97	3,368	4,114	4,385	51	134
Southeast:									
Alabama	546	781	11	53	1,731	2,675	4,447	43	119
Arkansas	363	702	39	67	2,267	3,375	3,151	55	127
Florida	1,638	2,743	64	61	2,273	2,851	4,048	55	129
Georgia	1,185	1,732	32	84	3,190	2,604	3,093	64	173
Kentucky	641	848	53	92	2,089	3,014	4,196	81	143
Louisiana	778	995	6	59	2,247	3,154	3,632	58	124
Mississippi	510	717	7	45	1,354	2,633	3,582	67	148
North Carolina	1,130	1,417	37	70	2,531	3,255	4,602	66	113
South Carolina	503	861	1	8	2,343	3,026	4,229	52	154
Tennessee	1,409	1,730	100	100	1,896	2,049	3,156	67	208
Virginia	623	709	68	45	2,596	2,849	4,484	53	95
West Virginia	395	373	30	51	1,443	2,855	4,904	80	122
Southwest:									
Arizona	528	1,015	86	90	- - -	- - -	3,237	- - -	128
New Mexico	318	452	45	65	2,120	2,757	4,498	39	131
Oklahoma	358	626	19	68	2,516	2,852	3,401	56	135
Texas	2,572	3,340	4	42	1,928	2,672	3,750	47	89
Rocky Mountains:									
Colorado	271	459	80	79	2,705	3,815	4,941	45	102
Idaho	119	193	37	65	2,973	3,402	4,486	36	130
Montana	101	110	59	69	2,793	3,478	4,858	47	82
Utah	152	285	82	86	2,279	2,775	4,208	72	127
Wyoming	51	67	1	–	2,036	3,571	4,874	59	137

See footnotes at end of table.

Table 145 (page 2 of 2). Medicaid recipients, recipients in managed care, payments per recipient, and recipients per 100 persons below the poverty level, by geographic region and state: United States, selected fiscal years 1989–2003

[Data are compiled from Medicaid administrative records by the Centers for Medicare & Medicaid Services]

Geographic region and state[1]	Recipients in thousands		Percent of recipients in managed care		Payments per recipient			Recipients per 100 persons below the poverty level	
	1996[2]	2003	1996[2]	2003	1990	1996[2]	2003	1989–1990	2002–2003
Far West:									
Alaska.................	69	116	–	–	3,562	4,027	7,190	70	191
California...............	5,107	9,319	23	52	1,795	2,178	2,770	88	202
Hawaii.................	41	209	80	79	2,252	6,574	3,605	73	160
Nevada................	109	220	41	46	3,161	3,361	3,998	37	98
Oregon	450	598	91	78	2,283	2,915	3,537	74	148
Washington	621	1,077	100	81	2,128	2,242	4,200	98	149

– Quantity zero.

- - - Data not available.

[1]Data are shown for Bureau of Economic Analysis (BEA) regions that are constructed to show economically interdependent states. These BEA geographic regions differ from U.S. Census Bureau geographic divisions shown in some *Health, United States* tables. See Appendix II, Geographic region and division.

[2]Prior to 1999, recipient counts exclude individuals who only received coverage under prepaid health care and for whom no direct vendor payments were made during the year, and vendor payments exclude payments to health maintenance organizations and other prepaid health plans ($15 billion in 1996). (CMS Medicaid Statistics, Program and Financial Statistics FY1996, unpublished.)

NOTES: Payments exclude disproportionate share hospital payments ($15.5 billion in FY2001). Data for additional years are available. See Appendix III.

SOURCES: Centers for Medicare & Medicaid Services, Office of Information Services, Enterprise Databases Group, Division of Information Distribution, Medicaid Data System; Before 1999, Medicaid Statistical Report HCFA–2082. From 1999 onward, Medicaid Statistical Information System, MSIS. Available from: msis.cms.hhs.gov. Poverty populations are available from: Department of Commerce, U.S. Census Bureau, Housing and Household Economic Statistics Division.

Table 146. Persons enrolled in health maintenance organizations (HMOs) by geographic region and state: United States, selected years 1980–2005

[Data are based on a census of health maintenance organizations]

Geographic region and state[1]	2005	1980	1985	1990	1995	1998	2000	2004	2005
	Number in thousands	Percent of population							
United States[2]	69,226	4.0	7.9	13.4	19.4	28.6	30.0	23.4	23.4
New England:									
Connecticut	1,266	2.4	7.1	19.9	21.2	42.9	44.6	39.1	36.1
Maine	341	0.4	0.3	2.6	7.0	19.1	22.3	19.8	25.9
Massachusetts	2,401	2.9	13.7	26.5	39.0	54.2	53.0	37.4	37.4
New Hampshire	284	1.2	5.6	9.6	18.5	33.8	33.7	22.1	21.9
Rhode Island	280	3.7	9.1	20.6	19.6	29.8	38.1	31.6	25.9
Vermont	100	–	–	6.4	12.5	–	4.6	9.6	16.1
Mideast:									
Delaware	84	–	3.9	17.5	18.4	48.1	22.0	14.7	10.1
District of Columbia[3]	233	- - -	- - -	- - -	- - -	33.0	35.2	28.8	42.2
Maryland[4]	1,557	2.0	4.8	14.2	29.5	43.6	43.9	30.8	28.0
New Jersey	2,175	2.0	5.6	12.3	14.7	31.3	30.9	24.7	25.0
New York	4,615	5.5	8.0	15.1	26.6	37.8	35.8	29.9	24.0
Pennsylvania	3,697	1.2	5.0	12.5	21.5	37.1	33.9	31.2	29.8
Great Lakes:									
Illinois	1,994	1.9	7.1	12.6	17.2	20.8	21.0	12.8	15.7
Indiana	1,407	0.5	3.6	6.1	8.3	14.0	12.4	11.3	22.5
Michigan	2,660	2.4	9.9	15.2	20.5	25.3	27.1	27.2	26.3
Ohio	1,881	2.2	6.7	13.3	16.3	23.4	25.1	18.0	16.4
Wisconsin	1,476	8.5	17.8	21.7	24.0	30.8	30.2	28.4	26.8
Plains:									
Iowa	321	0.2	4.8	10.1	4.5	4.9	7.4	10.0	10.9
Kansas	453	–	3.3	7.9	4.7	14.4	17.9	6.4	16.6
Minnesota	1,295	9.9	22.2	16.4	26.5	32.4	29.9	26.4	25.4
Missouri	1,416	2.3	6.0	8.2	18.5	33.7	35.2	27.4	24.6
Nebraska	92	1.1	1.8	5.1	8.6	16.9	11.2	7.5	5.3
North Dakota	3	0.4	2.5	1.7	1.2	2.2	2.5	0.3	0.4
South Dakota	61	–	–	3.3	2.8	5.1	6.7	10.7	7.9
Southeast:									
Alabama	127	0.3	0.9	5.3	7.3	10.8	7.2	2.8	2.8
Arkansas	176	–	0.1	2.2	3.8	10.7	10.4	5.3	6.4
Florida	4,538	1.5	5.6	10.6	18.8	31.5	31.4	24.8	26.1
Georgia	1,452	0.1	2.9	4.8	7.6	15.5	17.4	13.7	16.4
Kentucky	422	0.9	1.6	5.7	16.1	35.1	31.5	28.3	10.2
Louisiana	485	0.6	0.9	5.4	7.2	16.6	17.0	11.7	10.7
Mississippi	3	–	–	–	0.7	3.6	1.1	0.4	0.1
North Carolina	897	0.6	1.6	4.8	8.3	17.1	17.8	9.9	10.5
South Carolina	298	0.2	1.0	1.9	5.5	9.9	9.9	6.1	7.1
Tennessee	853	–	1.8	3.7	12.2	24.1	33.0	12.8	14.4
Virginia[4]	1,660	–	1.1	6.1	7.7	16.9	18.5	18.2	22.2
West Virginia[4]	147	0.7	1.7	3.9	5.8	10.7	10.3	9.9	8.1
Southwest:									
Arizona	944	6.0	10.3	16.2	25.8	30.3	30.9	19.9	16.4
New Mexico	463	1.4	2.0	12.7	15.1	32.3	37.7	30.8	24.3
Oklahoma	251	–	2.1	5.5	7.6	13.8	14.7	7.9	7.1
Texas	2,652	0.6	3.4	6.9	12.0	17.8	18.5	10.6	11.8
Rocky Mountains:									
Colorado	1,178	6.9	10.8	20.0	23.3	36.4	39.5	27.3	25.6
Idaho	41	1.2	–	1.8	1.4	5.7	7.9	2.9	2.9
Montana	75	–	–	1.0	2.4	3.9	7.0	9.3	8.1
Utah	510	0.6	8.8	13.9	25.1	35.6	35.3	25.4	21.3
Wyoming	11	–	–	–	–	0.7	1.4	2.2	2.1
Far West:									
Alaska	–	–	–	–	–	–	–	–	–
California	17,623	16.8	22.5	30.7	36.0	47.1	53.5	48.0	49.1
Hawaii	472	15.3	18.1	21.6	21.0	32.8	30.0	29.7	37.4
Nevada	589	–	5.8	8.5	15.9	26.8	23.5	24.0	25.2
Oregon	581	12.0	14.0	24.7	40.0	45.3	41.1	21.8	16.2
Washington	1,124	9.4	8.7	14.6	18.7	26.3	15.2	12.8	18.1

– Quantity zero.   - - - Data not available.

[1]Data are shown for Bureau of Economic Analysis (BEA) regions that are constructed to show economically interdependent states. These BEA geographic regions differ from the U.S. Census Bureau geographic regions and divisions shown in some *Health, United States* tables. See Appendix II, Geographic region and division.
[2]HMOs in Guam are included starting in 1994; HMOs in Puerto Rico are included starting in 1998. In 2005, HMO enrollment in Guam was 27,000 and in Puerto Rico, 1,626,000.
[3]Data for the District of Columbia (DC) not included for 1980–1996 because data not adjusted for high proportion of enrollees of DC-based HMOs living in Maryland and Virginia.   [4]Includes partial enrollment for five plans serving the District of Columbia.

NOTES: Data for 1980–1990 are for pure HMO enrollment at midyear. Starting with 1994 data, pure and open-ended enrollment as of January 1 are included. In 1990, open-ended enrollment accounted for 3% of HMO enrollment compared with 14.5% in 2005. In 2005, 3,366 thousand enrollees in Cigna's Flexcare product were added to open-ended enrollment. Without this addition total HMO enrollment would have continued slowly decreasing. See Appendix II, Health maintenance organization. Data for additional years are available. See Appendix III.

SOURCE: InterStudy National Health Maintenance Organization Census. The InterStudy Edge, Managed care: A decade in review 1980–1990. The InterStudy Competitive Edge, Part II Managed Care Industry Report, 1995–2005. St. Paul, Minnesota (Copyrights 1991, 1995–2005: Used with the permission of InterStudy).

Table 147. Persons without health insurance coverage by state: United States, average annual 1995–1997 through 2002–2004

[Data are based on household interviews of a sample of the civilian noninstitutionalized population]

Geographic region and state[1]	1995–1997	1998–2000	2001–2003	2002–2004
	Percent of population			
United States..............................	15.7	14.4	15.1	15.5
New England:				
Connecticut	10.6	9.5	10.4	10.9
Maine	13.5	11.5	10.7	10.6
Massachusetts	12.0	9.2	9.6	10.8
New Hampshire	10.4	8.6	9.9	10.6
Rhode Island	11.0	6.9	9.3	10.5
Vermont...............................	11.3	10.3	9.9	10.5
Mideast:				
Delaware..............................	14.1	11.2	10.1	11.8
District of Columbia......................	16.1	14.5	13.3	13.5
Maryland	13.4	11.9	13.2	14.0
New Jersey	15.8	12.9	13.7	14.4
New York..............................	16.6	15.3	15.5	15.0
Pennsylvania	9.8	8.3	10.7	11.5
Great Lakes:				
Illinois	11.6	13.3	14.0	14.2
Indiana	11.5	11.3	12.9	13.7
Michigan	10.1	10.6	11.0	11.4
Ohio	11.6	10.2	11.7	11.8
Wisconsin	7.9	9.3	9.5	10.4
Plains:				
Iowa	11.6	8.2	9.5	10.1
Kansas	11.8	11.0	10.9	10.8
Minnesota	9.1	8.2	8.2	8.5
Missouri...............................	13.5	9.0	10.9	11.7
Nebraska	10.4	9.5	10.3	11.0
North Dakota	11.1	12.1	10.5	11.0
South Dakota..........................	10.2	12.0	11.0	11.9
Southeast:				
Alabama	14.0	14.2	13.3	13.5
Arkansas..............................	21.3	15.3	16.6	16.7
Florida................................	18.9	17.2	17.6	18.5
Georgia...............................	17.8	15.2	16.4	16.6
Kentucky	15.0	13.1	13.3	13.9
Louisiana	18.8	19.5	19.4	18.8
Mississippi	19.4	15.7	17.0	17.2
North Carolina	15.3	13.7	16.1	16.6
South Carolina	16.2	13.8	13.1	13.8
Tennessee	14.5	10.8	11.8	12.7
Virginia	12.9	12.9	12.5	13.6
West Virginia	15.8	15.2	14.8	15.9
Southwest:				
Arizona	23.0	19.5	17.3	17.0
New Mexico............................	23.5	22.6	21.3	21.4
Oklahoma	18.0	17.7	18.7	19.2
Texas	24.4	22.2	24.6	25.1
Rocky Mountains:				
Colorado	15.5	14.1	16.3	16.8
Idaho.................................	16.1	16.5	17.5	17.3
Montana	15.3	18.3	16.1	17.9
Utah	12.4	13.2	13.6	13.4
Wyoming	15.0	15.1	16.5	15.9
Far West:				
Alaska................................	14.7	18.1	17.8	18.2
California..............................	20.7	19.2	18.7	18.4
Hawaii................................	8.3	9.8	9.9	9.9
Nevada	17.3	17.5	18.3	19.1
Oregon	13.7	13.7	14.8	16.1
Washington	12.4	12.8	14.3	14.2

[1]Data are shown for Bureau of Economic Analysis (BEA) regions that are constructed to show economically interdependent states. These BEA geographic regions differ from U.S. Census Bureau geographic divisions shown in some *Health, United States* tables. See Appendix II, Geographic region and division.

NOTES: Starting with 1997 data, people with no coverage other than access to the Indian Health Service are no longer considered covered by health insurance. The effect of this change on the estimate of number uninsured is negligible. Starting with 1999 data, estimates reflect the results of follow-up verification questions which decreased the percent uninsured by 1.2 percentage points. See Appendix I, Current Population Survey.

SOURCES: U.S. Census Bureau, Current Population Survey, Bennefield RL. Health Insurance Coverage: 1997; Mills RJ. Health Insurance Coverage: 2000; DeNavas-Walt C, Proctor BD, Mills RJ. Income, Poverty, and Health Insurance Coverage in the United States: 2003. Income, Poverty, and Health Insurance Coverage in the United States: 2004. DeNavas-Walt C, Proctor BD, Lee CH. Current population reports, series P–60 nos 202; 215; 226; 229. Washington, DC: U.S. Government Printing Office, 2005. Available from: www.census.gov/hhes/www/hlthins/reports.html.

Appendixes

Appendix Contents

Appendix II: Tables

Appendix II: Figures

Appendix I

Data Sources

Health, United States consolidates the most current data on the health of the population of the United States, the availability and use of health resources, and health care expenditures. Information was obtained from data files and published reports of many federal government and private and global agencies and organizations. In each case, the sponsoring agency or organization collected data using its own methods and procedures. Therefore, data in this report vary considerably with respect to source, method of collection, definitions, and reference period.

Although a detailed description and comprehensive evaluation of each data source are beyond the scope of this Appendix, users should be aware of the general strengths and weaknesses of the different data collection systems. For example, population-based surveys obtain socioeconomic data, data on family characteristics, and information on the impact of an illness, such as days lost from work or limitation of activity. These data are limited by the amount of information a respondent remembers or is willing to report. A respondent may not know detailed medical information, such as precise diagnoses or the types of operations performed, and therefore cannot report it. In contrast, record-based surveys, which collect data from physician and hospital records, usually have good diagnostic information but little or no information about the socioeconomic characteristics of individuals or the impact of illnesses on individuals.

The populations covered by different data collection systems may not be the same, and understanding the differences is critical to interpreting the data. Data on vital statistics and national expenditures cover the entire population. Most data on morbidity and utilization of health resources cover only the civilian noninstitutionalized population. Such statistics may not include data for military personnel, who are usually young; for institutionalized people including the prison population, who may be any age; or for nursing home residents, who are usually old.

All data collection systems are subject to error, and records may be incomplete or contain inaccurate information. Respondents may not remember essential information, a question may not mean the same thing to different respondents, and some institutions or individuals may not respond at all. It is not always possible to measure the magnitude of these errors or their effect on the data. Where possible, table notes describe the universe and method of data collection to assist users in evaluating data quality.

Some information is collected in more than one survey, and estimates of the same statistic may vary among surveys because of different survey methodologies, sampling frames, questionnaires, definitions, and tabulation categories. For example, cigarette use is measured by the National Health Interview Survey, the National Survey on Drug Use & Health, the Monitoring the Future Survey, and the Youth Risk Behavior Survey. These surveys use slightly different questions of persons of differing ages and interview in different settings (at school compared with at home), so estimates will differ.

Overall estimates generally have relatively small sampling errors, but estimates for certain population subgroups may be based on a small sample size and have relatively large sampling errors. Numbers of births and deaths from the vital statistics system represent complete counts (except for births in those states where data are based on a 50% sample for certain years). Therefore, they are not subject to sampling error. However, when the figures are used for analytical purposes, such as the comparison of rates over a period, the number of events that actually occurred may be considered as one of a large series of possible results that could have arisen under the same circumstances. When the number of events is small and the probability of such an event is rare, estimates may be unstable and considerable caution must be observed in interpreting the statistics. Estimates that are unreliable because of large sampling errors or small numbers of events are noted with asterisks in selected tables. The criteria used to designate unreliable estimates are indicated in notes to the applicable tables.

Government data sources are listed alphabetically by data set name; private and global sources are listed separately. To the extent possible, government data systems are described using a standard format. The overview is a brief, general statement about the purpose or objectives of the data system. The selected content section lists major data elements that are collected or estimated using interpolation or modeling. The data years section gives the years that the survey or data system has existed or been fielded. The coverage section describes the population that the data system represents; for example, residents of the United States, the noninstitutionalized population, persons in specific population groups, or other entities that comprise the survey. The methodology section presents a short description of methods used to collect data. Sample size and response rates are given for surveys. The issues affecting interpretation section describes major changes in the data collection methodology or other factors that must be considered when analyzing trends—for example, a major survey redesign that may introduce a discontinuity in the trend. For more information about the methodology, data files, and history of a data source, consult the references and websites at the end of each summary.

Government Sources

Abortion Surveillance

Centers for Disease Control and Prevention National Center for Chronic Disease Prevention and Health Promotion

Overview: The abortion surveillance program documents the number and characteristics of women obtaining legal induced abortions, monitors unintended pregnancy, and assists efforts to identify and reduce preventable causes of morbidity and mortality associated with abortions.

Selected Content: Content includes age, race/ethnicity, marital status, previous live births, period of gestation, and previous induced abortions of women obtaining legal induced abortions.

Data Years: Between 1973 and 1997, the number of abortions is based on reporting from 52 reporting areas: 50 states, the District of Columbia, and New York City. In 1998 and 1999, the Centers for Disease Control and Prevention (CDC) compiled abortion data from 48 reporting areas. Alaska, California, New Hampshire, and Oklahoma did not report, and data for these areas were not estimated. Starting with 2000 data, Oklahoma again reported these data, increasing the number of reporting areas to 49.

Coverage: The system includes women of all ages, including adolescents, who obtain legal induced abortions.

Methodology: Starting with 2000 data, the number and characteristics of women who obtain legal induced abortions are provided for 49 reporting areas by central health agencies, such as state health departments and the health departments of New York City and the District of Columbia,

and by hospitals and other medical facilities. In general, the procedures are reported by the state in which the procedure is performed (i.e., state of occurrence). In 2000, three states (Delaware, Maryland, and Wisconsin) reported characteristics only for women who were residents and who obtained abortions in the state. One state (Iowa) provided numbers and characteristics only for state residents. While the total number of legal induced abortions is available for those 49 reporting areas, not all areas collect information on the characteristics of women who obtain abortions. The number of areas reporting each characteristic and the number of areas with complete data for each characteristic vary from year to year. For example, in 2000, the number of areas reporting different women's characteristics ranged from 26 areas reporting Hispanic ethnicity and 37 areas reporting race and marital status, to 47 areas reporting age. Data from reporting areas with more than 15% unknown for a given characteristic are excluded from the analysis of that characteristic.

Issues Affecting Interpretation: Between 1989 and 1997, the total number of abortions reported to CDC was about 10% less than the total estimated independently by the Alan Guttmacher Institute (AGI), a not-for-profit organization for reproductive health research, policy analysis, and public education. Between 1998 and 2002, the total number of abortions reported to CDC was about 34% less than the total estimated by AGI. The four reporting areas (the largest of which was California) that did not report abortions to CDC in 1998 accounted for 18% of all abortions tallied by AGI's 1995–1996 survey. See Appendix I, Alan Guttmacher Institute Abortion Provider Survey.

Reference:

Abortion Surveillance—United States, 2002. Centers for Disease Control and Prevention, CDC MMWR Surveillance Summaries, November 25, 2005. MMWR 2005;54(SS07):1–31. Available from: www.cdc.gov/mmwr/preview/mmwrhtml/ss5407a1.htm.

For More Information: See the NCCDPHP surveillance and research website: www.cdc.gov/reproductivehealth/Data_Stats/index.htm.

AIDS Surveillance

Centers for Disease Control and Prevention
National Center for HIV, STD, and TB Prevention

Overview: Acquired immunodeficiency syndrome (AIDS) surveillance data are used to detect and monitor cases of human immunodeficiency virus (HIV) disease and AIDS in the United States, identify epidemiologic trends, identify unusual cases requiring follow-up, and inform public health efforts to prevent and control the disease.

Selected Content: Data collected on cases diagnosed with AIDS include age, sex, race/ethnicity, mode of exposure, and geographic region.

Data Years: Reports on AIDS cases are available from the beginning of the epidemic that began in 1981.

Coverage: All 50 states, the District of Columbia (DC), U.S. dependencies and possessions, and independent nations in free association with the United States report AIDS cases to CDC using a uniform surveillance case definition and case report form.

Methodology: AIDS surveillance is conducted by health departments in each state or territory and DC. Although surveillance activities range from passive to active, most areas employ multifaceted active surveillance programs, which include four major reporting sources of AIDS information: hospitals and hospital-based physicians, physicians in nonhospital practice, public and private clinics, and medical record systems (death certificates, tumor registries, hospital discharge abstracts, and communicable disease reports). Using a standard confidential case report form, the health departments collect information that is then transmitted electronically without personal identifiers to CDC.

Adjustments of the estimated data on HIV infection (not AIDS) and on AIDS to account for reporting delays are calculated by a maximum likelihood statistical procedure that takes into account the differences in reporting delays among exposure, geographic, racial/ethnic, age, sex, and vital status categories and is based on the assumption that reporting delays in these categories have not changed over time. AIDS surveillance data are provisional and are updated annually.

Issues Affecting Interpretation: Although completeness of reporting of AIDS cases to state and local health departments differs by geographic region and patient population, studies

conducted by state and local health departments indicate that the reporting of AIDS cases in most areas of the United States is more than 85% complete. To assess trends in AIDS cases, deaths, and prevalence, it is preferable to use case data adjusted for reporting delays and presented by year of diagnosis instead of straight counts of cases presented by year of report.

The definition of AIDS was modified in 1985 and 1987. The case definition for adults and adolescents was modified again in 1993. The revisions incorporated a broader range of AIDS-indicator diseases and conditions and used HIV diagnostic tests to improve the sensitivity and specificity of the definition. Laboratory and diagnostic criteria for the 1987 pediatric case definition were updated in 1994. Effective January 2000, the surveillance case definition for HIV infection was revised to reflect advances in laboratory HIV virologic tests. The definition incorporates the reporting criteria for HIV infection and AIDS into a single case definition for adults and children.

Decreases in AIDS incidence and in the number of AIDS deaths, first noted in 1996, have been ascribed to the effect of new treatments, which prevent or delay the onset of AIDS and premature death among HIV-infected persons and result in an increase in the number of persons living with HIV and AIDS. A growing number of states require confidential reporting of persons with HIV infection and participate in CDC's integrated HIV/AIDS surveillance system that compiles information on the population of persons newly diagnosed and living with HIV infection.

Reference:

Centers for Disease Control and Prevention, HIV/AIDS Surveillance Report, published annually, available from: www.cdc.gov/hiv/topics/surveillance/resources/reports/index.htm.

For More Information: See the NCHSTP website: www.cdc.gov/nchstp/od/nchstp.html.

Annual Survey and Census of Jails

Bureau of Justice Statistics

Overview: The number of jail inmates is determined by a periodic census of jails and a survey of jails in the intervening years. The Census of Jails is taken every 5–6 years. In years between the census, the Annual Survey of Jails is conducted. The census and survey provide estimates of the characteristics of U.S. jails and the inmates they house.

Selected Content: Data are supplied on facility characteristics, staffing, inmate deaths, jail programs, admissions and releases, number of inmates held, and inmate characteristics. Inmate characteristics collected include number of adult and juvenile inmates, conviction status, sex, and race and ethnicity.

Data Years: The first census of jails was conducted in 1970; the annual survey has been conducted every year since 1982, except for years in which the Census of Jails is conducted. Data are requested for activities as of June 30 of the reference year.

Coverage: Data are collected on local jails, multi-jurisdiction (regional) jails, and privately contracted jails in all 50 states and the District of Columbia.

Methodology: Local jails are locally-operated correctional facilities that confine persons before or after adjudication. Inmates sentenced to jails usually have a sentence of a year or less. The census is based on a facility list maintained by the U.S. Census Bureau. For the Annual Survey of Jails, there have been minor changes in the sample selection over time. For more recent surveys, all multijurisdictional jails (jails operated jointly by two or more jurisdictions) were included in the sample. Other jurisdictions were included automatically in the sample if their jails held juvenile inmates and had an average daily population of 250 or more inmates, or housed only adults and had an average daily population of 500 or more, based on the most recent census. The remaining jurisdictions were stratified into two groups: jurisdictions with jails holding at least one juvenile at last census, and jurisdictions with jails holding adults only. Using stratified probability sampling, jurisdictions were then selected from 10 strata based on the average daily population in the 1999 census. All surveys prior to the 1994 survey were based on all jails in jurisdictions with 100 or more jail inmates and a stratified random sample of jurisdictions with an average daily population of fewer than 100 inmates.

Sample Size and Response Rate: Data were obtained by mailed and web-based survey questionnaires. After follow-up phone calls, the response rates for most years approach 100% for critical items such as rated capacity, average daily population, and number of inmates confined.

Reference:

Pastore AL, Maguire K, editors. Sourcebook of Criminal Justice Statistics [Online]. Available from: www.albany.edu/sourcebook/app4.html.

For More Information: See the Bureau of Justice Statistics website: www.ojp.usdoj.gov/bjs/correct.htm.

Census of Fatal Occupational Injuries (CFOI)

Bureau of Labor Statistics

Overview: The Census of Fatal Occupational Injuries (CFOI) compiles comprehensive and timely information on fatal work injuries occurring in the 50 states and the District of Columbia (DC) to monitor workplace safety and to inform private and public health efforts to improve workplace safety.

Selected Content: Information is collected about each workplace fatality, including occupation and other worker characteristics, equipment involved, and circumstances of the event.

Data Years: Data have been collected annually since 1992.

Coverage: The data cover all 50 states and DC.

Methodology: CFOI is administered by the Bureau of Labor Statistics (BLS) in conjunction with participating state agencies to compile counts that are as complete as possible to identify, verify, and profile fatal work injuries. Key information about each workplace fatality (occupation and other worker characteristics, equipment or machinery involved, and circumstances of the event) is obtained by cross-referencing source records. For a fatality to be included in the census, the decedent must have been employed (that is, working for pay, compensation, or profit) at the time of the event, engaged in a legal work activity, or present at the site of the incident as a requirement of his or her job. These criteria are generally broader than those used by federal and state agencies administering specific laws and regulations.

Fatalities that occur during a person's commute to or from work are excluded from the census counts.

Data for the CFOI are compiled from various federal, state, and local administrative sources including death certificates, workers' compensation reports and claims, reports to various regulatory agencies, medical examiner reports, police reports, and news reports. Diverse sources are used because studies have shown that no single source captures all job-related fatalities. Source documents are matched so that each fatality is counted only once. To ensure that a fatality occurred while the decedent was at work, information is verified from two or more independent source documents or from a source document and a follow-up questionnaire.

Issues Affecting Interpretation: The number of occupational fatalities and fatality rates are periodically revised. States have up to 1 year to update their initial published state counts. States may identify additional fatal work injuries after data collection has closed for a reference year. Fatalities initially excluded from the published count because of insufficient information to determine work relationship may subsequently be verified as work related and were included. Increases in the published counts based on additional information have averaged less than 100 fatalities per year, or less than 1.5% of the total.

Beginning with 2003 data, CFOI began using the 2002 North American Industry Classification System (NAICS) to classify industries. Prior to 2003, the program used the Standard Industrial Classification (SIC) system and the U.S. Census Bureau occupational classification system. Although some titles in SIC and NAICS are similar, there is limited comparability between the two systems because the industry groupings are defined differently. See Appendix II, Industry of employment.

Reference:

Bureau of Labor Statistics. National Census of Fatal Occupational Injuries in 2004. Washington, DC: U.S. Department of Labor, April 2006.

For More Information: See the CFOI website: www.bls.gov/iif/oshcfoi1.htm.

Consumer Price Index (CPI)

Bureau of Labor Statistics

Overview: The Consumer Price Index (CPI) is designed to produce a monthly measure of the average change in the prices paid by urban consumers for a fixed market basket of goods and services.

Selected Content: Price indexes are available for the United States, the four census regions, size of city, cross-classifications of regions and size-classes, and 26 local areas. Indexes are available for major groups of consumer expenditures (food and beverages, housing, apparel, transportation, medical care, recreation, education and communications, and other goods and services), for items within each group, and for special categories, such as services. Monthly indexes are available for the United States, the four census regions, and some local areas. More detailed item indexes are available for the United States than for regions and local areas. Indexes are available for two population groups: a CPI for All Urban Consumers (CPI-U), which covers approximately 87% of the total population, and a CPI for Urban Wage Earners and Clerical Workers (CPI-W), which covers 32% of the population.

Data Years: The index has been constructed annually since 1978.

Coverage: The all-urban index (CPI-U) introduced in 1978 covers residents of metropolitan areas as well as residents of urban parts of nonmetropolitan areas (about 87% of the U.S. population in 2000).

Methodology: In calculating the index, price changes for the various items in each location were averaged together with weights that represent their importance in the spending of all urban consumers. Local data were then combined to obtain a U.S. city average.

The index measures price changes from a designated reference date, 1982–1984, which equals 100. An increase of 22%, for example, is shown as 122. Change can also be expressed in dollars as follows: the price of a base period market basket of goods and services bought by all urban consumers has risen from $100 in 1982–1984 to $195 in 2005.

The current revision of the CPI, completed in 2000, reflects spending patterns based on the Survey of Consumer

Expenditures from 1993 to 1995, the 1990 Census of Population, and the ongoing Point-of-Purchase Survey. Using an improved sample design, prices for the goods and services required to calculate the index are collected in urban areas throughout the country and from retail and service establishments. Data on rents are collected from tenants of rented housing and residents of owner-occupied housing units. Food, fuels, and other goods and services are priced monthly in urban locations. Price information is obtained through visits or calls by trained BLS field representatives using computer-assisted telephone interviews.

Issues Affecting Interpretation: A 1987 revision changed the treatment of health insurance in the cost-weight definitions for medical care items. This change has no effect on the overall index result but provides a clearer picture of the role of health insurance in the CPI. As part of the revision, three new indexes have been created by separating previously combined items, for example, eye care is separated from other professional services, and inpatient and outpatient treatment is separated from other hospital and medical care services.

Effective January 1997, the hospital index was restructured by combining the three categories—room, inpatient services, and outpatient services—into one category: hospital services. In addition new procedures for hospital data collection identify a payor, diagnosis, and the payor's reimbursement arrangement from selected hospital bills.

References:

Bureau of Labor Statistics. Handbook of Methods. BLS Bulletin 2490. Washington: U.S. Department of Labor. April 1997; Revising the Consumer Price Index, Monthly Labor Review, Dec 1996.

Ford IK, Ginsburg DH. "Medical care in the consumer price index," in Medical Care Output and Productivity Studies in Income and Wealth, vol. 62, Cutler DM, Berndt ER, eds., Chicago, IL: University of Chicago Press, pp. 203–19, 2001.

For More Information: See the BLS/CPI website: www.bls.gov/cpi/home.htm.

Current Population Survey (CPS)

Bureau of Labor Statistics and U.S. Census Bureau

Overview: The Current Population Survey (CPS) provides current estimates and trends in employment, unemployment, and other characteristics of the general labor force, the population as a whole, and various population subgroups.

Selected Content: The CPS interview is divided into three basic parts: (1) household and demographic information, (2) labor force information, and (3) supplement information in months that include supplements. Comprehensive work experience information is gathered on the employment status, occupation, and industry of persons interviewed.

Estimates of poverty and health insurance coverage presented in *Health, United States* from the CPS are derived from the Annual Social and Economic Supplement (ASEC), formerly called the Annual Demographic Supplement (ADS), or simply, the March Supplement. The ASEC collects data on family characteristics, household composition, marital status, migration, income from all sources, information on weeks worked, time spent looking for work or on layoff from a job, occupation and industry classification of the job held longest during the year, health insurance coverage, and receipt of noncash benefits such as food stamps, school lunch program, employer-provided group health insurance plan, employer-provided pension plan, personal health insurance, Medicaid, Medicare, CHAMPUS or military health care, and energy assistance.

Data Years: The basic CPS has been conducted since 1945, although some data were collected prior to that time. The U.S. Census Bureau has collected data in the ASEC or ADS since 1947.

Coverage: The CPS sample is located in 754 sample areas, with coverage in every state and the District of Columbia. The adult universe (i.e., population of marriageable age) is composed of persons 15 years of age and over in the civilian noninstitutionalized population for CPS labor force data. The sample for the March CPS supplement is expanded to include members of the Armed Forces who are living in civilian housing or with their family on a military base, as well as additional Hispanic households that are not included in the monthly labor force estimates.

Methodology: The basic CPS sample is selected from multiple frames using multiple stages of selection. Each unit is selected with a known probability to represent similar units in the universe. The sample design is state-based, with the sample in each state being independent of the others.

One person generally responds for all eligible members of a household. For those who are employed, employment information is collected on the job held in the reference week. The reference week is defined as the 7-day period, Sunday through Saturday, that includes the 12th of the month. In the CPS, a person with two or more jobs is classified according to the job at which he or she worked the greatest number of hours. In general, the BLS publishes labor force data only for persons age 16 and over, since those under 16 are substantially limited in their labor market activities by compulsory schooling and child labor laws. No upper age limit is used, and full-time students are treated the same as nonstudents.

The additional Hispanic sample is from the previous November's basic CPS sample. If a person is identified as being of Hispanic origin from the November interview and is still residing at the same address in March, that housing unit is eligible for the March survey. This amounts to a near doubling of the Hispanic sample because there is no overlap of housing units between the basic CPS samples in November and March.

For all CPS data files, a single weight is prepared and used to compute the monthly labor force status estimates. An additional weight is prepared for the earnings universe that roughly corresponds to wage and salary workers in the two outgoing rotations. The final weight is the product of (1) the basic weight, (2) adjustments for special weighting, (3) noninterview adjustment, (4) first-stage ratio adjustment factor, and (5) second-stage ratio adjustment factor. This final weight should be used when producing estimates from the basic CPS data. Differences in the questionnaire, sample, and data uses for the March CPS supplement result in the need for additional adjustment procedures to produce what is called the March supplement weight.

Sample Size and Response Rate: Beginning with 2001, the State Children's Health Insurance Program (SCHIP) sample expansion was introduced. This included an increase in the basic CPS sample to 60,000 households per month. Prior to 2001, estimates were based on 50,000 households per month. The expansion also included an additional 12,000

households that were allocated differentially across states, based on prior information of the number of uninsured children in each state, to produce statistically reliable current state data on the number of low-income children who do not have health insurance coverage. In an average month, the nonresponse rate for the basic CPS is about 6%–7%.

Issues Affecting Interpretation: Over the years, the number of income questions has expanded, questions on work experience and other characteristics have been added, and the month of interview was moved to March. In 2002, an ASEC sample increase was implemented requiring more time for data collection. Thus, additional ASEC interviews are now taking place in February and April. However, even with this sample increase, most of the data collection still occurs in March.

In 1994 major changes were introduced, which included a complete redesign of the questionnaire including new health insurance questions and the introduction of computer-assisted interviewing for the entire survey. In addition, there were revisions to some of the labor force concepts and definitions. Prior to the redesign, CPS data were primarily collected using a paper-and-pencil form. Beginning in 1994, population controls were based on the 1990 census and adjusted for the estimated population undercount. Starting with *Health, United States, 2003,* poverty estimates for data years 2000 and beyond were recalculated based on the expanded SCHIP sample, and census 2000-based population controls were implemented. Starting with 2002 data, 1997 race standards were implemented in which people could report more than one race.

Reference:

U.S. Census Bureau. Technical Paper 63RV. Current Population Survey: Design and methodology. TP63RV, March 2002 available from: www.census.gov/prod/2002pubs/tp63rv.pdf.

For More Information: See the CPS website: www.bls.census.gov/cps/cpsmain.htm.

Department of Veterans Affairs National Patient Care Database and National Enrollment Database

Department of Veterans Affairs

Overview: The Department of Veterans Affairs (VA) compiles and analyzes multiple data sets on the health and health care of its clients and other veterans to monitor access and quality of care and to conduct program and policy evaluations.

Selected Content: VA maintains the National Patient Care Database (NPCD) and the National Enrollment Database (NED).

The NPCD is a nationwide system that contains a statistical record for each episode of care provided under VA auspices in VA and non-VA hospitals, nursing homes, VA residential rehabilitation treatment programs (formerly called domiciliaries), and VA outpatient clinics. Three major extracts from the NPCD are the patient treatment file (PTF), the patient census file (PCF), and the outpatient clinic file (OPC).

The PTF collects data at the time of the patient's discharge on each episode of inpatient care provided to patients at VA hospitals, VA nursing homes, VA residential rehabilitation treatment programs, community nursing homes, and other non-VA facilities. The PTF record contains the scrambled social security number (SSN), dates of inpatient treatment, date of birth, state and county of residence, type of disposition, place of disposition after discharge, and ICD–9–CM diagnostic and procedure or operative codes for each episode of care.

The PCF collects data on each patient remaining in a VA medical facility at midnight at the end of each quarter of the fiscal year. The census record includes information similar to that reported in the PTF record.

The outpatient clinic file (OPC) collects data on each instance of medical treatment provided to a veteran in an outpatient setting. The OPC record includes the age, scrambled social security number, state and county of residence, VA eligibility code, clinic(s) visited, purpose of visit, and date of visit for each episode of care.

The VA also maintains the National Enrollment Database (NED) as the official repository of enrollment information for each veteran enrolled in the VA health care system.

Coverage: U.S. veterans who receive services within the VA medical system are included. Data are available for some nonveterans who receive care at VA facilities.

Methodology: NPCD is the source data for the Veterans Health Administration (VHA) Medical SAS Datasets. NPCD is the VHA's centralized relational database (a data warehouse) that receives encounter data from VHA clinical information systems. It is updated daily. Data are collected locally at each VA medical center and are transmitted electronically to the VA Austin Automation Center for use in providing nationwide statistics, reports, and comparisons.

In all of the medical data sets each patient has a unique identifier, which is a formula-based encryption of the individual's SSN. The identifier is consistent for a given patient across data sets and fiscal years. An extract containing selected information from the NPCD, the NED, and the cost distribution system is produced by the Austin Automation Center.

Issues Affecting Interpretation: The databases include users of the VA health care system. VA eligibility is a hierarchy based on service-connected disabilities, income, age, and availability of services. Therefore, different VA programs may serve populations with different sociodemographic characteristics than other health care systems.

For More Information: See the VHA Information Systems website: www.virec.research.va.gov/Support/Training-NewUsersToolkit/IntroToVAData.htm.

Employee Benefits Survey—See National Compensation Survey

Medicaid Data System

Centers for Medicare & Medicaid Services

Overview: The Centers for Medicare & Medicaid Services (CMS) works with its state partners to collect data on persons served by the Medicaid program to monitor and evaluate access and quality of care, trends in program eligibility, characteristics of enrollees, changes in payment policy, and other program-related issues.

Selected Content: Data collected include medical vendor payments for Medicaid recipients by type of service and information on the characteristics of Medicaid recipients, including race/ethnicity, age, and basis of eligibility.

Data Years: Selected state data are available starting in 1992 and data for the 50 states and the District of Columbia are available starting in 1999.

Coverage: The data include individuals enrolled in the Medicaid program or receiving Medicaid benefits.

Methodology: The primary data sources for Medicaid statistical data are the Medicaid Statistical Information System (MSIS) and the CMS-64 reports.

MSIS is the basic source of state-reported eligibility and claims data on the Medicaid population, and their characteristics, utilization, and payments. Beginning in FY 1999, as a result of legislation enacted from the Balanced Budget Act of 1997, states are required to submit individual eligibility and claims data tapes to CMS quarterly through MSIS. Prior to FY 1999, states were required to submit an annual HCFA-2082 report, designed to collect aggregated statistical data on eligibles, recipients, services, and expenditures during a federal fiscal year (October 1 through September 30). The data reported for each year represented people on the Medicaid rolls, recipients of Medicaid services, and payments for claims adjudicated during the year. The data reflected bills adjudicated or processed during the year, rather than services used during the year. States summarized and reported the data processed through their own Medicaid claims processing and payment operations, unless they opted to participate in MSIS, in which case the HCFA-2082 report was produced by the Health Care Financing Administration (the predecessor to CMS).

The CMS-64 is a product of the financial budget and grant system. The CMS-64 is a statement of expenditures for the Medicaid program that states submit to CMS 30 days after each quarter. The report is an accounting statement of actual expenditures made by the states for which they are entitled to receive federal reimbursement under Title XIX for that quarter. The amount claimed on the CMS-64 is a summary of expenditures derived from source documents such as invoices, cost reports, and eligibility records.

The CMS-64 shows the disposition of Medicaid grant funds for the quarter being reported and previous years, the recoupments made or refunds received, and income earned on grant funds. The data on the CMS-64 are used to reconcile the monetary advance made on the basis of states'

funding estimates filed prior to the beginning of the quarter on the CMS-37. As such, the CMS-64 is the primary source for making adjustments for any identified overpayments and underpayments to the states. Also incorporated into this process are disallowance actions forwarded from other federal financial adjustments. Finally, the CMS-64 provides information that forms the basis for a series of Medicaid financial reports and budget analyses. Also included are third party liability (TPL) collections tables. TPL refers to the legal obligation of certain health care sources to pay the medical claims of Medicaid recipients before Medicaid pays these claims. Medicaid pays only after the TPL sources have met their legal obligation to pay.

Issues Affecting Interpretation: Health, United States Medicaid tables are based on MSIS data. Users of Medicaid data may note apparent inconsistencies in Medicaid data that are primarily due to the difference in information captured in MSIS compared to CMS-64 reports. The most substantive difference is due to payments made to disproportionate share hospitals. Payments to disproportionate share hospitals do not appear in MSIS because states directly reimburse these hospitals and there is no fee-for-service billing. Other less significant differences between MSIS and CMS-64 occur because adjudicated claims data are used in MSIS versus actual payments reflected in the CMS-64. Differences also may occur because of internal state practices for capturing and reporting these data through two separate systems. Finally, national totals for the CMS-64 are different because they include other jurisdictions, such as the Northern Mariana Islands and American Samoa.

For More Information: See the CMS website: www.cms.hhs.gov/medicaiddatasourcesgeninfo/ 01_overview.asp? or the Research Data Assistance Center (ResDAC): www.resdac.umn.edu/medicaid/data_available.asp. Also see Appendix II, Medicaid.

Medical Expenditure Panel Survey (MEPS)

Agency for Healthcare Research and Quality

Overview: The Medical Expenditure Panel Survey (MEPS) produces nationally representative estimates of health care use, expenditures, sources of payment, insurance coverage, and quality of care for the U.S. civilian noninstitutionalized population.

Selected Content: MEPS data in *Health, United States* include total health care expenses and prescribed medicine expenses, presented by sociodemographic characteristics, type of health insurance, and sources of payment.

Data Years: The 1977 National Medical Care Expenditure Survey and the 1987 National Medical Expenditure Survey (NMES) are earlier versions of this survey. Since 1996, MEPS has been conducted on an annual basis.

Coverage: U.S. civilian noninstitutionalized population is the primary population represented. The 1987 and 1996 surveys also had an institutionalized population component.

Methodology: MEPS is a national probability survey conducted on an annual basis since 1996. The panel design of the survey features several rounds of interviewing covering 2 full calendar years. The MEPS consists of three components: the Household Component (HC), the Medical Provider Component (MPC), and the Insurance Component (IC).

The HC is a nationally representative survey of the civilian noninstitutionalized population drawn from a subsample of households that participated in the prior year's National Health Interview Survey conducted by the National Center for Health Statistics. Missing expenditure data are imputed using data collected in the MPC whenever possible.

The MPC collects data from hospitals, physicians, and home health providers that were reported in the HC as providing care to MEPS sample persons. Data are collected in MPC to improve the accuracy of expenditure estimates derived solely from the HC. The MPC is particularly useful in obtaining expenditure information for persons enrolled in managed care plans and Medicaid recipients. Sample sizes for the MPC vary from year to year depending on the HC sample size and the MPC sampling rates for providers.

The IC consists of two subcomponent samples: a household sample and list sample. The household sample collects detailed information from employers on the health insurance held by and offered to respondents to the MEPS-HC. The list sample collects data on the types and costs of workplace health insurance from a total of about 40,000 business establishments and governments each year.

The MEPS updates the 1987 NMES. The NMES consists of two components: the Household Survey (HS) and the Medical Provider Survey (MPS). The NMES-HS Component was designed to provide nationally representative estimates of health insurance status, health insurance coverage, and health care use for the U.S. civilian noninstitutionalized population for the calendar year 1987. Data from the NMES-MPS component were used in conjunction with HS data to produce estimates of health care expenditures. The NMES-HS consisted of four rounds of household interviews. Income was collected in a special supplement administered early in 1988. Events under the scope of the NMES-MPS included medical services provided by or under the direction of a physician, all hospital events, and home health care. The sample of events included in the NMES-MPS was all events for persons covered by Medicaid and for a 25% sample of NMES-HS respondents. Missing expenditure data were imputed.

Sample Size and Response Rate: For MEPS first core household interview, 17,500 households were selected. The sample sizes for the MEPS-HC are approximately 10,000 families in 1996 and 1998–2000, 13,500 families in 1997 and 2001, and 15,000 families annually beginning in 2002. The full-year household core response rate has generally been about 66%. The 12-month joint core questionnaire/health questionnaire/access supplement response rate for the household component of the NMES was 80%.

Issues Affecting Interpretation: The 1987 estimates are based on the NMES, and 1996 and later years estimates are based on the MEPS. Because expenditures in NMES were based primarily on charges while those for MEPS were based on payments, data for NMES were adjusted to be more comparable to MEPS using estimated charge-to-payment ratios for 1987. For a detailed explanation of this adjustment, see Zuvekas and Cohen, 2002.

References:

Hahn B, Lefkowitz D. Annual expenses and sources of payment for health care services (AHRQ pub no 93–0007). National Medical Expenditure Survey Research Findings 14, Agency for Healthcare Research and Quality pub no 93–0007. Rockville, MD: Public Health Service, November 1992.

Cohen SB. Sample design of the 1997 Medical Expenditure Panel Survey Household Component. MEPS Methodology Report No. 11. AHRQ pub no. 01–0001. Rockville MD: Agency for Healthcare Research and Quality. 2000.

Zuvekas S, Cohen S. A guide to comparing health care estimates in the 1996 Medical Expenditure Panel Survey to the 1987 National Medical Expenditure Survey. Inquiry 2002;39(1):76–86.

For More Information: See the MEPS website: www.meps.ahrq.gov.

Medicare Administrative Data

Centers for Medicare & Medicaid Services

Overview: The Centers for Medicare & Medicaid Services (CMS) collects and synthesizes Medicare enrollment, spending, and claims data to monitor and evaluate access to and quality of care, trends in utilization, changes in payment policy, and other program-related issues.

Selected Content: Data include claims information for services furnished to Medicare beneficiaries and Medicare enrollment data. Claims data include type of service, procedures, diagnoses, dates of service, and claim amount. Enrollment data include date of birth, sex, race/ethnicity, and reason for entitlement.

Data Years: Some data files are available as far back as 1987, but CMS no longer provides technical support for files with data prior to 1996.

Coverage: Enrollment data are for all persons enrolled in the Medicare program. Claims data include data for Medicare beneficiaries who filed claims.

Methodology: The claims and utilization data files contain extensive utilization information at various levels of summarization for a variety of providers and services. There are many types and levels of these files, including the National Claims History (NCH) files, the Standard Analytic Files (SAF), Medicare Provider and Analysis Review (MedPAR) files, Medicare enrollment files, and various other files.

The National Claims History (NCH) 100 Percent Nearline File contains all institutional and noninstitutional claims and provides records of every Medicare claim submitted, including adjustment claims. The Standard Analytical Files (SAFs) contain final action claims data in which all adjustments have been resolved. These files contain information collected by Medicare to pay for health care services provided to a Medicare beneficiary. SAFs are available for each institutional

(inpatient, outpatient, skilled nursing facility, hospice, or home health agency) and noninstitutional (physician and durable medical equipment providers) claim type. The record unit of SAFs is the claim (some episodes of care may have more than one claim). SAF files include the Inpatient SAF, the Skilled Nursing Facility SAF, the Outpatient SAF, the Home Health Agency SAF, the Hospice SAF, the Clinical Laboratory SAF, and the Durable Medical Equipment SAF.

Medicare Provider and Analysis Review (MedPAR) files contain inpatient hospital and skilled nursing facility (SNF) final action stay records. Each MedPAR record represents a stay in an inpatient hospital or SNF. An inpatient stay record summarizes all services rendered to a beneficiary from the time of admission to a facility through discharge. Each MedPAR record may represent one claim or multiple claims, depending on the length of a beneficiary's stay and the amount of inpatient services used throughout the stay.

The Denominator File contains demographic and enrollment information about each beneficiary enrolled in Medicare during a calendar year. The information in the Denominator File is frozen in March of the following calendar year. Some of the information contained in this file includes the beneficiary unique identifier, state and county codes, ZIP code, date of birth, date of death, sex, race, age, monthly entitlement indicators (for Medicare Part A, Medicare Part B, or Part A and Part B), reasons for entitlement, state buy-in indicators, and monthly managed care indicators (yes/no). The Denominator File is used to determine beneficiary demographic characteristics, entitlement, and beneficiary participation in Medicare Managed Care Organizations.

The Vital Status File contains demographic information about each beneficiary ever entitled to Medicare. Some of the information contained in this file includes the beneficiary unique identifier, state and county codes, ZIP code, date of birth, date of death, sex, race, and age. Often the Vital Status File is used to obtain recent death information for a cohort of Medicare beneficiaries.

The Group Health Plan (GHP) Master File contains data on beneficiaries who are currently enrolled or have ever been enrolled in a Managed Care Organization (MCO) under contract with CMS. Each record represents one beneficiary, and each beneficiary has one record. Some of the information contained in this file includes the Beneficiary Unique Identifier number, date of birth, date of death, state and county, and managed care enrollment information such as dates of membership and MCO contract number. The GHP Master File is used to identify the exact MCO in which beneficiaries were enrolled.

Issues Affecting Interpretation: Because Medicare managed care programs may not file claims, files based only on claims data will exclude care for persons enrolled in Medicare managed care programs. In addition, to maintain a manageable file size, some files are based on a sample of enrollees, rather than on all Medicare enrollees. Coding changes and interpretation of Medicare coverage rules have also changed over the life of the Medicare program.

For More Information: See the CMS Research Data Assistance Center (ResDAC) website: www.resdac.umn.edu/medicare/index.asp or the CMS website: www.cms.hhs.gov/medicare/. Also see Appendix II, Medicare.

Medicare Current Beneficiary Survey (MCBS)

Centers for Medicare & Medicaid Services

Overview: The Medicare Current Beneficiary Survey (MCBS) produces nationally representative estimates of health status, health care use and expenditures, health insurance coverage, and socioeconomic and demographic characteristics of Medicare beneficiaries. It is used to estimate expenditures and sources of payment for all services used by Medicare beneficiaries, including co-payments, deductibles, and noncovered services; to ascertain all types of health insurance coverage and relate coverage to sources of payment; and to trace processes over time, such as changes in health status, spending down to Medicaid eligibility, and the effects of program changes.

Selected Content: The survey collects data on utilization of health services, health and functional status, health care expenditures, and health insurance and beneficiary information (such as income, assets, living arrangement, family assistance, and quality of life).

Data Years: The first round of interviewing was conducted from September through December 1991, and the survey has been continuously in the field since then. The data are designed to support both cross-sectional and longitudinal analyses.

Coverage: The MCBS is a continuous survey of a nationally representative sample of aged, institutionalized, and disabled Medicare beneficiaries.

Methodology: The longitudinal design of the survey allows each sample person to be interviewed three times a year for 4 years, whether he or she resides in the community or a facility or moves between the two settings, using the version of the questionnaire appropriate to the setting. Sample persons in the community are interviewed using computer-assisted personal interviewing (CAPI) survey instruments. Because long-term care facility residents often are in poor health, information about institutionalized patients is collected from proxy respondents such as nurses and other primary caregivers affiliated with the facility. The sample is selected from the Medicare enrollment files, with oversampling among disabled persons under age 65 and among persons 80 years of age and over.

MCBS has two components: the Cost and Use file and the Access to Care file. Medicare claims are linked to survey-reported events to produce the Cost and Use file that provides complete expenditure and source of payment data on all health care services, including those not covered by Medicare. The Access to Care file contains information on beneficiaries' access to health care, satisfaction with care, and usual source of care. The sample for this file represents the always enrolled population—those who participated in the Medicare program for the entire year. In contrast, the Cost and Use file represents the ever enrolled population, including those who enter Medicare during the year and those who died.

Sample Size and Response Rate: Each fall, about one-third of the sample is retired and roughly 6,000 new sample persons are included in the survey—the exact number chosen is based on projections of target samples of 12,000 persons with 3 years of cost and use information distributed appropriately across the sample cells. In the community, response rates for initial interviews range in the mid- to high 80s; once respondents have completed the first interview, their participation in subsequent rounds is 95% or more. In recent rounds, data have been collected from approximately 15,000–19,000 beneficiaries, with the peaks occurring in fall rounds because of the annual and HMO samples. Roughly 90% of the sample is made up of persons who live in the community, with the remaining persons living in long-term care facilities. Response rates for facility interviews approach 100%.

Issues Affecting Interpretation: Because only Medicare enrollees are included in the survey, the survey excludes a small proportion of persons age 65 and over who are not enrolled in Medicare, which should be noted when using the MCBS to make estimates of the entire population age 65 and over in the United States.

References:

Adler GS. A profile of the Medicare Current Beneficiary Survey. Health Care Financ Rev 1994;15(4):153–63.

Lo A, Chu A, Apodaca R. Redesign of the Medicare Current Beneficiary Survey sample, Rockville, MD: Westat, Inc., 2003. Available from: www.cms.hhs.gov/apps/mcbs/PubIBIB/Mbibl8.pdf.

For More Information: See the MCBS website: www.cms.hhs.gov/MCBS.

Monitoring the Future Study (MTF)

National Institute on Drug Abuse

Overview: Monitoring the Future (MTF) is an ongoing study of the behaviors, attitudes, and values of American secondary school students, college students, and young adults.

Selected Content: Data collected include lifetime, annual, and 30-day prevalence of use of specific illegal drugs and substances, inhalants, tobacco, and alcohol. Data are also collected on usage levels, frequency of use, perceived risks associated with use, opinions about whether use is approved or disapproved by others, and opinions about availability of the substances.

Data Years: MTF has been conducted annually since 1975, initially with high school seniors; ongoing panel studies of representative samples from each graduating class have been conducted by mail since 1976; annual surveys of 8th and 10th graders were initiated in 1991.

Coverage: MTF surveys a sample of high school seniors, 10th graders, and 8th graders selected to be representative of all seniors, 10th graders, and 8th graders in public and private high schools in the continental United States.

Methodology: The survey design is a multistage random sample with stage one being selection of particular geographic areas, stage two selection of one or more schools in each area, and stage three selection of students within each school. Data are collected using self-administered questionnaires conducted in the classroom by representatives of the Institute for Social Research. Dropouts and students who are absent on the day of the survey are excluded. Recognizing that the dropout population is at higher risk for drug use, this survey was expanded to include similar nationally representative samples of 8th and 10th graders in 1991, who have lower dropout rates than seniors and include future high-risk 12th grade dropouts. Statistics that are published in the *Dropout Rates in the United States: 2001* (published by the National Center for Educational Statistics, Pub. No. NCES 2005–046) stated that among persons 15–16 years of age, 3.9% have dropped out of school, 2.8% for persons 17 years of age, 6.6% for persons 18 years of age, and 8.4% for persons 19 years of age but dropout rates are higher for certain race and ethnic groups, notably Hispanics (most recently available data).

Sample Size and Response Rates: In 2005, approximately 49,300 8th, 10th, and 12th graders in 402 schools were surveyed. The annual senior samples comprised roughly 15,400 seniors in 129 public and private high schools nationwide. The 10th-grade samples involved about 16,700 students in 127 schools, and the 8th-grade samples had approximately 17,300 students in 146 schools. Response rates were 82%, 88%, and 90% for 12th, 10th and 8th graders and have been relatively constant across time. Absentees constitute virtually all of the nonresponding students.

Issues Affecting Interpretation: Estimates of substance use for youth based on the National Survey on Drug Use & Health (NSDUH) are not directly comparable with estimates based on the MTF and the Youth Risk Behavior Surveillance System (YRBSS). In addition to the fact that the MTF excludes dropouts and absentees, rates are not directly comparable across these surveys because of differences in populations covered, sample design, questionnaires, interview setting, and statistical approaches to make the survey estimates generalizable to the entire population. The NSDUH survey collects data in homes, whereas the MTF and YRBSS collect data in school classrooms. The NSDUH estimates are tabulated by age, while the MTF and YRBSS estimates are tabulated by grade, representing different ages as well as different populations.

References:

Johnston LD, O'Malley PM, Bachman JG, Schulenberg JE. Monitoring the Future national results on adolescent drug use: Overview of key findings, 2005. NIH Publication No. 06–5882. Bethesda, MD: National Institute on Drug Abuse. 2006. Available from: www.monitoringthefuture.org/pubs/monographs/overview2005.pdf.

Johnston LD, O'Malley PM, Bachman JG. Monitoring the Future national survey results on drug use, 1975–2002. Vol I: Secondary school students. NIH pub no 03–5375. Bethesda, MD: National Institute on Drug Abuse. 2003. Available from: monitoringthefuture.org/pubs/monographs/vol1_2002.pdf.

Cowan CD. Coverage, sample design, and weighting in three federal surveys. Journal of Drug Issues 2001;31(3):595–614.

For More Information: See the NIDA website: www.nida.nih.gov/Infofax/HSYouthtrends.html and the Monitoring the Future website: www.monitoringthefuture.org/.

National Ambulatory Medical Care Survey (NAMCS)

Centers for Disease Control and Prevention National Center for Health Statistics

Overview: The National Ambulatory Medical Care Survey (NAMCS) is a national survey designed to provide information about the provision and use of medical care services in office-based physician practices in the United States.

Selected Content: Data are collected from medical records on type of providers seen; reason for visit; diagnoses; drugs ordered, provided, or continued; and selected procedures and tests ordered or performed during the visit. Patient data include age, sex, race, and expected source of payment. Data are also collected on selected characteristics of physician practices.

Data Years: The NAMCS, which began in 1973, was conducted annually until 1981, once in 1985, and resumed an annual schedule in 1989.

Coverage: The scope of the survey covers patient encounters in the offices of non-federally employed physicians classified by the American Medical Association or American Osteopathic Association as office-based, patient care physicians. Patient encounters with physicians engaged in prepaid practices—health maintenance organizations (HMOs), independent practice organizations (IPAs), and other prepaid practices—

are included in NAMCS. Excluded are visits to hospital-based physicians, visits to specialists in anesthesiology, pathology, and radiology, and visits to physicians who are principally engaged in teaching, research, or administration. Telephone contacts and nonoffice visits are also excluded.

Methodology: A multistage probability design is employed. The first-stage sample consisted of 84 primary sampling units (PSUs) in 1985, and beginning in 1989, 112 PSUs, which were selected from about 1,900 such units into which the United States had been divided. In each sample PSU, a sample of practicing non-federal office-based physicians is selected from master files maintained by the American Medical Association and the American Osteopathic Association. The final stage involves systematic random samples of office visits during randomly assigned 7-day reporting periods. In 1985 the survey excluded Alaska and Hawaii. Starting in 1989, the survey included all 50 states and the District of Columbia.

The U.S. Census Bureau acts as the data collection agent for the NAMCS. Screening interviews are conducted by Census field representatives to obtain information about physicians' office-based practices and to ensure that the practice is within the scope of the survey. Field representatives visit eligible physicians prior to their participation in the survey to provide them with survey materials and instruct them on how to sample patient visits and complete patient record forms. Participants are asked to complete forms for a systematic random sample of approximately 30 office visits occurring during a randomly assigned 1-week period, but increasingly patient record forms are abstracted by field representatives.

Sample data are weighted to produce national estimates. The estimation procedure used in the NAMCS has three basic components: inflation by the reciprocal of the probability of selection, adjustment for nonresponse, and ratio adjustment to fixed totals.

Sample Size and Response Rate: In the 2002 survey, a sample of 3,150 physicians was selected: 2,095 were in scope and 1,492 participated for a response rate of 71%. Data were provided on 28,738 visits. In 2003, a sample of 3,000 physicians was selected; 2,007 were in scope and 1,407 participated for a response rate of 67%. Data were provided for 25,288 visits. In 2004, a sample of 3,000 physicians was selected; 1,961 were in scope and 1,372 participated for a response rate of 70%. Data were provided for 25,286 visits.

Issues Affecting Interpretation: The NAMCS patient record form is modified approximately every 2–4 years to reflect changes in physician practice characteristics, patterns of care, and technological innovations. Examples of recent changes include increasing the number of drugs recorded on the patient record form, and adding checkboxes for specific tests or procedures performed. Sample sizes vary by survey year. For some years it is suggested that analysts combine 2 or more years of data if they wish to examine relatively rare populations or events. Starting with *Health, United States, 2005,* data for survey years 2001–2002 were revised to be consistent with the weighting scheme introduced in the 2003 NAMCS data. For more information on the new weighting scheme, see National Ambulatory Medical Care Survey: 2003 summary, Advance data from Vital and Health statistics (2005).

Reference:

Hing E, Cherry D, Woodwell, DA. National Ambulatory Medical Care Survey, 2003 summary. Advance data from vital and health statistics 2005; no 365. Hyattsville, MD: National Center for Health Statistics. Available from: www.cdc.gov/nchs/data/ad/ad365.pdf.

For More Information: See the Ambulatory Health Care Data website: www.cdc.gov/nchs/about/major/ahcd/ahcd1.htm.

National Compensation Survey

Bureau of Labor Statistics

Overview: The National Compensation Survey (NCS) provides comprehensive measures of occupational earnings, compensation cost trends, benefit incidence, and detailed plan provisions.

Selected Content: Detailed occupational earnings are collected for metropolitan and nonmetropolitan areas and broad geographic regions, and on a national basis. The Employment Cost Index (ECI) and Employer Costs for Employee Compensation (ECEC) are compensation measures derived from the NCS. ECI measures changes in labor costs. Average hourly employer cost for employee compensation is presented in the ECEC. National benefits data are presented for three broad occupational groupings: professional, technical, and related; clerical and sales; and blue-collar and service employees. Data are also available by goods- and

service-producing occupations, union affiliation, and full- and part-time status.

Data Years: The NCS replaces three existing BLS surveys: Employment Cost Index (ECI), Occupational Compensation Survey Program (OCSP), and Employee Benefits Survey (EBS). The ECI and EBS were fully integrated into the NCS in 1999. Prior to 1999, the EBS was collected for small private establishments (those employing fewer than 100 workers) and from state and local governments (regardless of employment size). In odd-numbered years, data were collected for medium and large private establishments (those employing 100 workers or more). The ECI was created in the mid-1970s. The EBS was added to an existing data collection effort, the National Pay Survey, in the late 1970s. The Employer Cost for Employee Compensation product was developed in 1987.

Coverage: The NCS provides information for the Nation, for 81 metropolitan areas and 73 nonmetropolitan counties representing the United States, and for the 9 census divisions (although not all areas have information for all occupations). It includes both full- and part-time workers who are paid a wage or salary. It excludes agriculture, fishing and forestry industries, private household workers, and the federal government. The NCS only includes establishments with at least 50 workers.

Methodology: Conducted quarterly by the Bureau of Labor Statistics' Office of Compensation and Working Conditions, the sample for the NCS is selected using a three-stage design. The first stage involves the selection of areas. The NCS sample consists of 154 metropolitan and nonmetropolitan areas that represent the nation's 326 metropolitan statistical areas and the remaining portions of the 50 states. In the second stage, establishments are systematically selected with probability of selection proportionate to their relative employment size within the industry. Use of this technique means that the larger an establishment's employment, the greater its chance of selection.

The third stage of sampling is a probability sample of occupations within a sampled establishment. This step is performed by the BLS field economist during an interview with the respondent establishment in which selection of an occupation is based on probability of selection proportionate to employment in the establishment. Each occupation is classified under its corresponding major occupational group using the Occupational Classification System Manual (OCSM) and the Census Occupation Index, which are based on the 1990 U.S. Census.

Data collection is conducted by the BLS field economists. Data are gathered from each establishment on the primary business activity of the establishment, types of occupations, number of employees, wages and salaries and benefits, hours of work, and duties and responsibilities. Wage data obtained by occupation and work level allows NCS to publish occupational wage statistics for localities, census divisions, and the Nation.

Sample Size and Response Rates: The NCS sample consists of 152 metropolitan and nonmetropolitan areas that represent the Nation's 326 metropolitan statistical areas and the remaining portions of the 50 states. The 2004 NCS included 20,414 establishments representing about 81 million workers within the scope of the survey.

Issues Affecting Interpretation: Because the NCS merges separate surveys, trend analyses prior to 2000 should be interpreted with care. The industrial coverage, establishment size coverage, and geographic coverage for the EBS survey changed since 1990. All surveys conducted from 1979–1989 excluded part-time employees and establishments in Alaska and Hawaii. The surveys conducted from 1979–1986 covered only medium and large private establishments and excluded most of the service industries. Establishments that employed at least 50, 100, or 250 workers, depending on the industry, were included. The survey conducted in 1987 consisted of state and local governments with 50 or more employees. The surveys carried out in 1988 and 1989 included all private-sector establishments that employed 100 or more employees.

The Employer Costs for Employee Compensation (ECEC) switched to new industry and occupation classification systems with the release of the March 2004 data. The 2002 North American Industry Classification System (NAICS) is now used to classify industries and the 2000 Standard Occupational Classification (SOC) system is used to classify occupations. ECEC data by the present classification systems—the 1987 Standard Industrial Classification System (SIC) and the 1990 Occupational Classification System (OCS)—will no longer be produced. The ECEC was the first National Compensation Survey product to make this transition. For more information about this transition, see

the National Compensation Survey website: www.bls.gov/ncs/ect/sp/ecsm0001.htm.

References:

U.S. Department of Labor, Bureau of Labor Statistics, Employer Costs for Employee Compensation Summary— December, 2005, released March 14, 2006. Available from: www.bls.gov/news.release/ecec.nr0.htm.

The National Compensation Survey: Compensation Statistics for the 21st Century. Available from: www.bls.gov/opub/cwc/archive/winter2000art1.pdf.

For More Information: See the National Compensation Survey website: www.bls.gov/ncs.

National Health Accounts

Centers for Medicare & Medicaid Services

Overview: National Health Accounts provide estimates of how much money is spent on different types of health care-related services and programs in the United States.

Selected Content: National Health Expenditures measure spending for health care in the United States by type of service delivered (such as hospital care, physician services, nursing home care) and source of funding for those services (such as private health insurance, Medicare, Medicaid, and out-of-pocket spending).

Data Years: Expenditure estimates are available starting from 1960 in data files or in published articles.

Methodology: The American Hospital Association (AHA) data on hospital finances are the primary source for estimates relating to hospital care. The salaries of physicians and dentists on the staffs of hospitals, hospital outpatient clinics, hospital-based home health agencies, and nursing home care provided in the hospital setting are considered to be components of hospital care. Expenditures for home health care and for services of health professionals (for example, doctors, chiropractors, private duty nurses, therapists, and podiatrists) are estimated primarily using a combination of data from the U.S. Census Bureau Services Annual Survey and the quinquennial Census of Service Industries.

The estimates of retail spending for prescription drugs are based on household and industry data on prescription drug transactions. Expenditures for other medical nondurables and for vision products and other medical durables purchased in retail outlets are based on estimates of personal consumption expenditures prepared by the U.S. Department of Commerce's Bureau of Economic Analysis, U.S. Bureau of Labor Statistics/Consumer Expenditure Survey; the 1987 National Medical Expenditure Survey and the 1996 Medical Expenditure Panel Survey conducted by the Agency for Healthcare Research and Quality; and spending by Medicare and Medicaid. Those durable and nondurable products provided to inpatients in hospitals or nursing homes, and those provided by licensed professionals or through home health agencies are excluded here, but they are included with the expenditure estimates of the provider service category.

Nursing home expenditures cover care rendered in establishments providing inpatient nursing and health-related personal care through active treatment programs for medical and health-related conditions. These establishments cover skilled nursing and intermediate care facilities, including those for the mentally retarded. Spending estimates are primarily based on data from the U.S. Census Bureau's Services Annual Survey and the quinquennial Census of Service Industries.

Expenditures for construction include those spent on the erection or renovation of hospitals, nursing homes, medical clinics, and medical research facilities, but not for private office buildings providing office space for private practitioners. Expenditures for noncommercial research (the cost of commercial research by drug companies is assumed to be imbedded in the price charged for the product; to include this item again would result in double counting) are developed from information gathered by the National Institutes of Health and the National Science Foundation.

Source of funding estimates likewise come from a multiplicity of sources. Data on the federal health programs are taken from administrative records maintained by the servicing agencies. Among the sources used to estimate state and local government spending for health are the U.S. Census Bureau's Government Finances and the National Academy of Social Insurance reports on State-operated workers' compensation programs. Federal and state and local expenditures for education and training of medical personnel are excluded from these measures where they are separable. For the private financing of health care, data on the financial experience of health insurance organizations come from special Centers for Medicare & Medicaid Services analyses of private health insurers and from the Bureau of Labor

Statistics' survey on the cost of employer-sponsored health insurance and on consumer expenditures. Information on out-of-pocket spending from the U.S. Bureau of the Census Services Annual Survey; U.S. Bureau of Labor Statistics Consumer Expenditure Survey; the 1987 National Medical Expenditure Survey and the Medical Expenditure Panel Surveys conducted by the Agency for Healthcare Research and Quality; and from private surveys conducted by the American Hospital Association, American Medical Association, American Dental Association, and IMS Health, an organization that collects data from the pharmaceutical industry, is used to develop estimates of direct spending by customers.

References:

Smith C, Cowan C, Heffler S, Catlin A, and the National Health Accounts Team. National health spending in 2004: recent slowdown led by prescription drug spending. Health Aff 2006;25(1):186–96.

Levit K, Smith C, Cowan C, Sensenig A, Catlin A, and the Health Accounts Team. Health spending rebound continues in 2002. Health Aff 2004;23(1):147–159.

For More Information: See the Centers for Medicare & Medicaid Services National Health Accounts website: www.cms.hhs.gov/NationalHealthExpendData/ 01_Overview.asp#TopOfPage.

National Health Care Survey (NHCS)

Centers for Disease Control and Prevention National Center for Health Statistics

Overview: The National Health Care Survey (NHCS) is a family of surveys that collect data from medical records of health care providers and establishments about the utilization of health services and characteristics of providers and their patients.

Selected Content: The components of the NHCS represent the major sectors of the U.S. health care system providing data on ambulatory, inpatient, and long-term care settings. This family of surveys includes the following components:

- National Ambulatory Medical Care Survey (NAMCS)
- National Hospital Ambulatory Medical Care Survey (NHAMCS)
- National Hospital Discharge Survey (NHDS)

- National Survey of Ambulatory Surgery (NSAS)
- National Home and Hospice Care Survey (NHHCS)
- National Nursing Home Survey (NNHS)

Methodology: Each survey in the family is based on a multistage sampling design that includes the health care facilities or providers and their records. Data are collected through abstraction of medical records, completion of encounter forms, compilation of data from state and professional associations, purchase of data from commercial abstraction services, and surveys of providers. Data from all survey components are collected from the establishment, and in no case is information received directly from the person receiving care.

For More Information: See the NHCS website: www.cdc.gov/nchs/nhcs.htm.

National Health and Nutrition Examination Survey (NHANES)

Centers for Disease Control and Prevention National Center for Health Statistics

Overview: The National Health and Nutrition Examination Survey (NHANES) program includes a series of cross-sectional nationally representative health examination surveys conducted in mobile examination units or clinics (MECs). In the first series of surveys, the National Health Examination Survey (NHES), data were collected on the prevalence of certain chronic diseases, the distributions of various physical and psychological measures, and measures of growth and development. In 1971, a nutrition surveillance component was added and the survey name changed to the National Health and Nutrition Examination Survey (NHANES). See Data Years, below, for more information on the survey name and years conducted.

Selected Content: The NHANES surveys have collected data on chronic disease prevalence and conditions (including undiagnosed conditions) and risk factors such as obesity and smoking, serum cholesterol levels, hypertension, diet and nutritional status, immunization status, infectious disease prevalence, health insurance, and measures of environmental exposures. Other topics addressed include hearing, vision, mental health, anemia, diabetes, cardiovascular disease, osteoporosis, oral health, mental health, pharmaceuticals used, and physical fitness.

NHES I data were collected on the prevalence of certain chronic diseases as well as the distributions of various physical and psychological measures, including blood pressure and serum cholesterol levels. NHES II and NHES III focused on factors related to growth and development in children and youth.

In NHANES I data were collected on indicators of the nutritional and health status of the American people through dietary intake data, biochemical tests, physical measurements, and clinical assessments for evidence of nutritional deficiency. Detailed examinations were given by dentists, ophthalmologists, and dermatologists, with an assessment of need for treatment. In addition, data were obtained for a subsample of adults on overall health care needs and behavior, and more detailed examination data were collected on cardiovascular, respiratory, arthritic, and hearing conditions. For NHANES II the nutrition component was expanded. In the medical area primary emphasis was placed on diabetes, kidney and liver functions, allergy, and speech pathology. The third National Health and Nutrition Examination Survey (NHANES III) also included data on antibodies, spirometry, and bone health.

Beginning in 1999 with continuous NHANES, new topics include cardiorespiratory fitness, physical functioning, lower extremity disease, full body scan (DXA) for body fat as well as bone density, and tuberculosis infection.

Data Years: Data have been collected from surveys conducted during 1960–1962 (NHES I), 1963–1965 (NHES II), 1966–1970 (NHES III), 1971–1974 (NHANES I), 1976–1980 (NHANES II), 1982–1984 (HHANES), and 1988–1994 (NHANES III). Beginning in 1999, the survey has been conducted continuously.

Coverage: With the exception of the Hispanic Health and Nutrition Examination Survey (see Methodology, below), the NHES and NHANES provide estimates of the health status of the civilian noninstitutionalized population of the United States. NHES II and NHES III examined probability samples of the nation's noninstitutionalized children ages 6–11 years and 12–17 years, respectively.

The NHANES I target population was the civilian noninstitutionalized population 1–74 years of age residing in the coterminous United States, except for people residing on any of the reservation lands set aside for the use of American Indians.

The NHANES II target population was the civilian noninstitutionalized population 6 months–74 years of age residing in the United States, including Alaska and Hawaii.

In Hispanic Health and Nutrition Examination Survey (HHANES) three geographically and ethnically distinct populations were studied: Mexican Americans living in Texas, New Mexico, Arizona, Colorado, and California; Cuban Americans living in Dade County, Florida; and Puerto Ricans living in parts of New York, New Jersey, and Connecticut.

The NHANES III target population was the civilian noninstitutionalized population 2 months of age and over. The sample design provided for oversampling among children 2–35 months of age, persons 70 years of age and over, black persons, and persons of Mexican origin.

Beginning in 1999, NHANES oversampled low-income persons, adolescents 12–19 years of age, persons 60 years of age and over, African Americans, and persons of Mexican origin. The sample is not designed to give a nationally representative sample for the total population of Hispanics residing in the United States.

Methodology: The NHANES includes clinical examinations, selected medical and laboratory tests, and self-reported data. The NHANES and previous surveys interviewed persons in their homes and conducted medical examinations, including laboratory analysis of blood, urine, and other tissue samples. Medical examinations and laboratory tests follow very specific protocols and are as standard as possible to ensure comparability across sites and providers. From 1999–2002, as a substitute for the MEC examinations, a small number of survey participants received an abbreviated health examination in their homes if they were unable to come to the MEC.

For the first program or cycle of the NHES I, a highly stratified multistage probability sample was selected to represent the 111 million civilian noninstitutionalized adults 18–79 years of age in the United States at that time. The sample areas consisted of 42 primary sampling units (PSUs) from the 1,900 geographic units. NHES II and NHES III were also multistage stratified probability samples of clusters of households in land-based segments. NHES II and III used the same 40 PSUs.

For NHANES I the sample areas consisted of 65 PSUs. A subsample of persons 25–74 years of age was selected to receive the more detailed health examination. Groups at high risk of malnutrition were oversampled.

NHANES II used a multistage probability design that involved selection of PSUs, segments (clusters of households) within PSUs, households, eligible persons, and finally, sample persons. The sample design provided for oversampling among persons 6 months–5 years of age, 60–74 years of age, and those living in poverty areas.

HHANES was similar in content and design to NHANES I and II. The major difference between HHANES and the previous national surveys is that HHANES used a probability sample of three special subgroups of the population living in selected areas of the United States rather than a national probability sample. The three HHANES universes included approximately 84%, 57%, and 59% of the respective 1980 Mexican-, Cuban-, and Puerto Rican-origin populations in the continental United States.

The survey for the NHANES III was conducted from 1988 to 1994 and consisted of two phases of equal length and sample size. Phase 1 and Phase 2 comprised random samples of the civilian U.S. population living in households. About 40,000 persons 2 months of age and over were selected and asked to complete an extensive interview and an examination. Participants were selected from households in 81 counties across the United States. Children age 2 months to 5 years and persons 60 years of age and over were oversampled to provide precise descriptive information on the health status of selected population groups of the United States.

Beginning in 1999, NHANES became a continuous, annual survey, which also allows increased flexibility in survey content. Since April 1999, NHANES collects data every year from a representative sample of the civilian U.S. population, newborns and older, by in-home personal interviews and physical examinations in the MEC. The sample design is a complex, multistage, clustered design using unequal probabilities of selection. The first-stage sample frame for continuous NHANES during 1999–2001 was the list of PSUs selected for the design of the National Health Interview Survey (NHIS). Typically, an NHANES PSU is a county. For 2002, an independent sample of PSUs (based on current Census data) was selected. This independent design will be used for the period 2002–2006. For 1999, because of delay in the start of data collection, 12 distinct PSUs were in the annual sample. For each year in 2000–2004, 15 PSUs were selected. The within-PSU design involves forming secondary sampling units that are nested within census tracts, selecting dwelling units within secondary units, and then selecting sample persons within dwelling units. The final sample person selection involves differential probabilities of selection according to demographic variables sex (male or female), race/ethnicity (Mexican American, black, all others), and age. Because of the differential probabilities of selection, dwelling units are screened for potential sample persons. Sample weights are available and should be used in estimation of descriptive statistics. The complex design features should be used in estimating standard errors for the descriptive estimates.

The estimation procedure used to produce national statistics for all NHANES involved inflation by the reciprocal of the probability of selection, adjustment for nonresponse, and poststratified ratio adjustment to population totals. Sampling errors also were estimated to measure the reliability of the statistics.

Sample Size and Response Rates: NHES I sampled 7,710 adults. The examination response rate was 87%. NHES II sampled 7,417 children and reported a response rate of 96% for the questionnaire sample and 73% for the examination sample. NHES III sampled 7,514 youth and reported a response rate of 90%.

A sample of 28,043 persons was selected for NHANES I. Household interviews were completed for more than 96% of the persons selected, and about 75% (20,749) were examined. A sample of 27,801 persons was selected for NHANES II; 73% (20,322 persons) were examined.

In the HHANES 9,894 persons in the Southwest were selected (75% or 7,462 were examined); in Dade County 2,244 persons were selected (60% or 1,357 were examined); and in the Northeast 3,786 persons were selected (75% or 2,834 were examined). Over the 6-year survey period of NHANES III, 39,695 persons were selected, the household interview response rate was 86%, and the medical examination response rate was 78%.

In the sample selection for NHANES 1999–2000, there were 22,839 dwelling units screened. Of these, 6,005 households had at least one eligible sample person identified for interviewing. A total of 12,160 eligible sample persons were identified. The overall response rate in NHANES 1999–2000 for those interviewed was 82% (9,965 of 12,160), and the response rate for those examined was 76% (9,282 of

12,160). For NHANES 2001–2002 there were 13,156 persons selected in the sample, of which 84% (11,039) were interviewed and 80% (10,480) of the 13,156 selected completed the health examination component of the survey. For NHANES 2003–2004 6,410 households had at least one eligible sample person identified for interviewing. A total of 12,761 eligible sample persons were identified, of which 79% (10,115) were interviewed and 76% (9,653) completed the health examination component of the survey.

Issues Affecting Interpretation: Data elements, lab tests performed, and the technological sophistication of medical examination and laboratory equipment have changed over time. Therefore, trend analyses should carefully examine how specific data elements were collected across the different NHANES and NHES surveys.

References:

Gordon T, Miller HW. Cycle I of the Health Examination Survey: Sample and response, United States, 1960–1962. National Center for Health Statistics. Vital Health Stat Series no 11 (1). 1974. Available from: www.cdc.gov/nchs/data/series/sr_11/sr11_001.pdf.

Plan, operation, and response results of a program of children's examinations. National Center for Health Statistics. Vital Health Stat Series no 1 (5). 1967. Available from: www.cdc.gov/nchs/data/series/sr_01/sr01_005.pdf.

Schaible WL. Quality control in a National Health Examination Survey. National Center for Health Statistics. Vital Health Stat Series no 2 (44). 1972. Available from: www.cdc.gov/nchs/data/series/sr_02/sr02_044.pdf.

Miller HW. Plan and operation of the Health and Nutrition Examination Survey, United States, 1971–73. National Center for Health Statistics. Vital Health Stat Series no 1 (10a) and 1 (10b). 1977 and 1978. Available from: www.cdc.gov/nchs/data/series/sr_01/sr01_010a.pdf and www.cdc.gov/nchs/data/series/sr_01/sr01_010b.pdf.

Engel A, Murphy RS, Maurer K, Collins E. Plan and operation of the NHANES I Augmentation Survey of Adults 25–74 years, United States, 1974–1975. National Center for Health Statistics. Vital Health Stat Series no 1 (14). 1978. Available from: www.cdc.gov/nchs/data/series/sr_01/sr01_014.pdf.

McDowell A, Engel A, Massey JT, Maurer K. Plan and operation of the second National Health and

Nutrition Examination Survey, 1976–1980. National Center for Health Statistics. Vital Health Stat Series no 1 (15), 1981.Available from: www.cdc.gov/nchs/data/series/sr_01/sr01_015.pdf.

Maurer K. Plan and operation of the Hispanic Health and Nutrition Examination Survey, 1982–1984. National Center for Health Statistics. Vital Health Stat Series no 1 (19). 1985. Available from: www.cdc.gov/nchs/data/series/sr_01/sr01_019.pdf.

Ezzati TM, Massey JT, Waksberg J, et al. Sample design: Third National Health and Nutrition Examination Survey. National Center for Health Statistics. Vital Health Stat Series no 2 (113). 1992.

Plan and operation of the Third National Health and Nutrition Examination Survey, 1988–1994. National Center for Health Statistics. Vital Health Stat Series no 1 (32). 1994. Available from: www.cdc.gov/nchs/data/series/sr_01/sr01_032.pdf.

For More Information: See the NHANES website: www.cdc.gov/nchs/about/major/nhanes/nhanes.htm.

National Health Interview Survey (NHIS)

Centers for Disease Control and Prevention National Center for Health Statistics

Overview: The National Health Interview Survey (NHIS) monitors the health of the U.S. population through the collection and analysis of data on a broad range of health topics. A major strength of this survey lies in the ability to analyze health measures by many demographic and socioeconomic characteristics.

Selected Content: The NHIS obtains information during household interviews on illnesses, injuries, activity limitation, chronic conditions, health insurance coverage, utilization of health care, and other health topics. Demographic data include age, sex, education, race/ethnicity (reported by respondent or proxy), place of birth, income, and place of residence. Other data collected include risk factors such as lack of exercise, smoking, alcohol consumption, and use of prevention services such as vaccinations, mammography, and pap smears. Special modules and supplements focus on different issues each year and have included topics such as

HIV/AIDS, aging, cancer screening, prevention, alternative and complementary medicine, and many other topics.

Data Years: The NHIS has been conducted annually since 1957 with a major redesign every 10–15 years.

Coverage: The NHIS covers the civilian noninstitutionalized population of the United States. Excluded are patients in long-term care facilities, persons on active duty with the Armed Forces (although their dependents are included), and U.S. nationals living in foreign countries.

Methodology: The NHIS is a cross-sectional household interview survey. Sampling and interviewing are continuous throughout each year. The sampling plan follows a multistage area probability design that permits the representative sampling of households. The sampling plan was last redesigned in 1995. Information for only the current sampling plan covering the design years of 1995–2004 is presented. The first stage consists of a sample of 358 primary sampling units (PSUs) drawn from approximately 1,900 geographically defined PSUs that cover the 50 states and the District of Columbia. A PSU consists of a county, a small group of contiguous counties, or a metropolitan statistical area.

Within a PSU, two types of second-stage units are used: area segments and permit area segments. Area segments are defined geographically and contain an expected 8 or 12 addresses. Permit area segments cover geographical areas containing housing units built after the 1990 census. The permit area segments are defined using updated lists of building permits issued in the PSU since 1990 and contain an expected four addresses. Within each segment all occupied households at the sample addresses are targeted for interview.

The total NHIS sample of PSUs is subdivided into four separate panels, or subdesigns, such that each panel is a representative sample of the U.S. population. This design feature has a number of advantages, including flexibility for the total sample size. The households selected for interview each week in the NHIS are a probability sample representative of the target population.

The NHIS that was fielded from 1982–1996 consisted of two parts: (1) a set of basic health and demographic items (known as the Core questionnaire), and (2) one or more sets of questions on current health topics (known as Supplements). The Core questionnaire remained the same over that time period whereas the current health topics changed depending on data needs.

The NHIS questionnaire revision first implemented in 1997 has three parts or modules: a Basic module, a Periodic module, and a Topical module. The Basic module corresponds to the core questionnaire before revision. It remains largely unchanged from year to year and allows for trend analysis and for data from more than 1 year to be pooled to increase sample size for analytic purposes. The Basic module contains three components: the Family Core, the Sample Adult Core, and the Sample Child Core. The Family Core component collects information on everyone in the family and allows the NHIS to serve as a sampling frame for additional integrated surveys as needed. Information collected on the Family Core for all family members includes household composition and sociodemographic characteristics, tracking information, information for matches to administrative data bases, health insurance coverage, and basic indicators of health status and utilization of health care services.

From each family in the NHIS, one sample adult and, for families with children under 18 years of age, one sample child are randomly selected to participate in the Sample Adult Core and the Sample Child Core questionnaires. Because some health issues are different for children and adults, these two questionnaires differ in some items but both collect basic information on health status, use of health care services, health conditions, and health behaviors.

Sample Size and Response Rates: Since 1997, the sample numbered about 100,000 persons with about 30,000 persons participating in the sample adult and about 15,000 persons in the sample child questionnaire. In recent years, the total household response rate was about 90%. Response rates for special health topics (supplements) have generally been lower. For example, the response rate was 80% for the 1994 Year 2000 Supplement, which included questions about cigarette smoking and use of such preventive services as mammography. Since 1997 the final response rate for the sample adult supplement was 70%–80% and 78%–84% for the sample child supplement.

Issues Affecting Interpretation: In 1997, the questionnaire was redesigned and some basic concepts were changed and other concepts were measured in different ways. For some questions there was a change in the reference period. Also in 1997, the collection methodology changed from paper and pencil questionnaires to computer-assisted personal

interviewing (CAPI). Because of the major redesigns of the questionnaire in 1997, most trend tables in *Health, United States* begin with 1997 data. Starting with *Health, United States, 2005* estimates for 2000 and later years use weights derived from the 2000 census.

References:

Massey JT, Moore TF, Parsons VL, Tadros W. Design and estimation for the National Health Interview Survey, 1985–1994. National Center for Health Statistics. Vital Health Stat Series no 2 (110). 1989. Available from: www.cdc.gov/nchs/data/series/sr_02/sr02_110.pdf.

National Center for Health Statistics. National Health Interview Survey: Research for the 1995–2004 redesign. National Center for Health Statistics. Vital Health Stat Series no 2 (126). 1999. Available from: www.cdc.gov/nchs/data/series/sr_02/sr02_126.pdf.

Botman SL, Moore TF, Moriarity CL, Parsons VL. Design and estimation for the National Health Interview Survey, 1995–2004. National Center for Health Statistics. Vital Health Stat Series no 2 (130), 2000. Available from: www.cdc.gov/nchs/data/series/sr_02/sr02_130.pdf.

For More Information: See the NHIS website: www.cdc.gov/nchs/nhis.htm.

National Hospital Ambulatory Medical Care Survey (NHAMCS)

Centers for Disease Control and Prevention National Center for Health Statistics

Overview: The National Hospital Ambulatory Medical Care Survey (NHAMCS) collects data on the utilization and provision of medical care services provided in hospital emergency and outpatient departments.

Selected Content: Data are collected from medical records on type of providers seen; reason for visit; diagnoses; drugs ordered, provided, or continued; and selected procedures and tests performed during the visit. Patient data include age, sex, race, and expected source of payment. Data are also collected on selected characteristics of hospitals included in the survey.

Data Years: Annual data collection began in 1992.

Coverage: The survey is a representative sample of visits to emergency departments (EDs) and outpatient departments (OPDs) of non-federal, short-stay, or general hospitals. Telephone contacts are excluded.

Methodology: A four-stage probability sample design is used in NHAMCS, involving samples of primary sampling units (PSUs), hospitals within PSUs, clinics within OPDs, and patient visits within clinics. The first stage sample of the NHAMCS consists of 112 PSUs selected from 1,900 such units comprising the United States. Within PSUs, 600 general and short-stay hospitals were sampled and assigned to one of 16 panels. In any given year, 13 panels are included. Each panel is assigned to a 4-week reporting period during the calendar year.

In the NHAMCS outpatient department survey, a clinic is defined as an administrative unit of the OPD in which ambulatory medical care is provided under the supervision of a physician. Clinics where only ancillary services, such as radiology, laboratory services, physical rehabilitation, renal dialysis, and pharmacy, are provided, or other settings in which physician services are not typically provided, are considered out of scope. If a hospital OPD has five or fewer in-scope clinics, all are included in the sample. For hospital OPDs with more than five clinics, a systematic sample of clinics proportional to size is included in the survey.

The U.S. Census Bureau acts as the data collection agent for the NHAMCS. Census field representatives contact sample hospitals to determine whether they have a 24-hour ED or an OPD that offers physician services. Visits to eligible EDs and OPDs are systematically sampled over the 4-week reporting period such that about 100 ED encounters and about 200 OPD encounters are selected. Hospital staff are asked to complete patient record forms for each sampled visit, but census field representatives typically abstract data for more than one-half of these visits.

Sample data are weighted to produce national estimates. The estimation procedure used in the NHAMCS has three basic components: inflation by the reciprocal of the probability of selection, adjustment for nonresponse, and ratio adjustment to fixed totals.

Sample Size and Response Rates: In any given year, the hospital sample consists of approximately 500 hospitals, of which 80% have EDs and about one-half have eligible OPDs. Typically, about 1,000 clinics are selected from participating hospital OPDs. In 2002, the number of patient record forms

(PRFs) completed for EDs was 37,337 and for OPDs 35,586. In 2003, the number of PRFs completed for EDs was 40,253 and for OPDs 34,492. In 2004, the number of PRFs completed for EDs was 36,589 and for OPDs 31,783. In 2002, the hospital response rate for NHAMCS was 92% for EDs and 75% for OPDs. In 2003, the hospital response rate was 85% for EDs and 73% for OPDs. In 2004, the hospital response rate was 89% for EDs and 75% for OPDs.

Issues Affecting Interpretation: The NHAMCS PRF is modified approximately every 2–4 years to reflect changes in physician practice characteristics, patterns of care, and technological innovations. Examples of recent changes are the number of drugs recorded on the PRF form, and checkboxes of specific tests or procedures performed. For analyses that present visit rates per population, the civilian noninstitutionalized population is used as the denominator. However, visits to hospital EDs can also include persons who reside in institutional settings.

Reference:

McCaig LF, McLemore T. Plan and operation of the National Hospital Ambulatory Medical Care Survey. National Center for Health Statistics. Vital Health Stat Series no 1 (34). 1994. Available from: www.cdc.gov/nchs/data/series/sr_01/sr01_034acc.pdf.

For More Information: See the National Health Care Survey (NHCS) website: www.cdc.gov/nchs/nhcs.htm or the Ambulatory Health Care website: www.cdc.gov/nchs/about/major/ahcd/ahcd1.htm.

National Hospital Discharge Survey (NHDS)

Centers for Disease Control and Prevention
National Center for Health Statistics

Overview: The National Hospital Discharge Survey (NHDS) collects and produces national estimates on characteristics of inpatient stays in non-federal short-stay hospitals in the United States.

Selected Content: Patient information collected includes demographics, length of stay, diagnoses, and procedures. Hospital characteristics collected include region, ownership, and bedsize.

Data Years: The NHDS has been conducted annually since 1965.

Coverage: The survey design covers the 50 states and the District of Columbia. Included in the survey are hospitals with an average length of stay of less than 30 days for all inpatients, general hospitals, and children's general hospitals. Excluded are federal, military, and Department of Veterans Affairs hospitals, as well as hospital units of institutions (such as prison hospitals), and hospitals with fewer than six beds staffed for patient use. All discharged patients from in-scope hospitals are included in the survey; however, newborns are not included in *Health, United States.*

Methodology: The design implemented in 1965 continued through 1987, and a redesign with a new sample of hospitals fielded in 1988 is currently in place. The sample for the 1965 NHDS was selected in 1964 from a frame of short-stay hospitals listed in the National Master Facility Inventory. A two-stage stratified sample design was used, with hospitals stratified according to bedsize and geographic region. Sample hospitals were selected with probabilities ranging from certainty for the largest hospitals to 1 in 40 for the smallest hospitals. Within each participating hospital, a systematic random sample was selected from a daily listing sheet of discharges. Within-hospital sampling rates for discharges varied inversely with the probability of hospital selection, so the overall probability of selecting a discharge was approximately the same across the sample.

Data collection was conducted by means of manual abstraction of patient information from sampled medical records. Sample selection and transcription of information from inpatient medical records to NHDS survey forms were performed by hospital staff, representatives of NCHS, or both. In 1985, a second data collection procedure was introduced. The procedure involved the purchase of computer data tapes from commercial abstracting services that contained automated discharge data for some hospitals participating in the NHDS. This procedure was used in approximately 17% of the sample hospitals for 1985–1987. Discharges on these computer files were subjected to the NHDS sampling specifications as well as the computer edits and estimation procedures. Two data collection methods, manual and automated, continue to be used in the NHDS.

A redesign of the NHDS was implemented for the 1988 survey. Under the redesign hospitals were selected using a modified three-stage stratified design. Units selected at the first stage consisted of either hospitals or geographic areas. The geographic areas were Primary Sample Units (PSUs) used for the 1985–1994 National Health Interview Survey,

which are geographic areas such as counties or townships. Hospitals within PSUs were then selected at the second stage. Strata at this stage were defined by geographic region, PSU size, abstracting service status, and hospital specialty-size groups. Within these strata, hospitals were selected with probabilities proportional to their annual number of discharges. At the third stage, a sample of discharges was selected by a systematic random sampling technique. The sampling rate was determined by the hospital's sampling stratum and the type of data collection system (manual or automated) used. Discharge records from hospitals submitting data via commercial abstracting services and selected state data systems (approximately 41% of sample hospitals) were arrayed by primary diagnoses, patient sex and age group, and date of discharge, before sampling.

The NHDS hospital sample is updated every 3 years by continuing the sampling process among hospitals that become eligible for the survey during the intervening years and by deleting hospitals that were no longer eligible. This process was conducted in 1991, 1994, 1997, 2000, and 2003.

The basic unit of estimation for NHDS is a sampled discharge. The basic estimation procedure involves inflation by the reciprocal of the probability of selection. There are adjustments for nonresponding hospitals and discharges; a postratio adjustment to fixed totals is employed.

Sample Size and Response Rate: In 2004, 501 hospitals were selected: 476 were within scope, 439 participated (92%), and data were collected from medical records for approximately 371,000 discharges.

Issues Affecting Interpretation: In 1988, the NHDS was redesigned. Caution is required in comparing trend data from before and after the redesign. There are also annual modifications to the ICD–9–CM affecting diagnoses and procedure categories. See Appendix II, ICD–9–CM; Tables X and XI.

Hospital utilization rates per 1,000 population were computed using estimates of the civilian population of the United States as of July 1 of each year. Rates for 1990 through 1999 use postcensal estimates of the civilian population based on the 1990 census adjusted for net underenumeration using the 1990 National Population Adjustment Matrix from the U.S. Census Bureau. The estimates for 2000 and beyond that appear in *Health, United States, 2003* and later editions were calculated using estimates of the civilian population based on census 2000, and therefore are not strictly comparable with postcensal rates calculated for the 1990s. See Appendix I, Population Census and Population Estimates.

References:

DeFrances CJ, Hall MJ, Podgornik MN. 2003 National Hospital Discharge Survey. Advance data from vital and health statistics; no 359. Hyattsville, MD: National Center for Health Statistics. 2005. Available from: www.cdc.gov/nchs/data/ad/ad359.pdf.

Dennison C, Pokras R. Design and operation of the National Hospital Discharge Survey: 1988 redesign. National Center for Health Statistics. Vital Health Stat Series no 1 (39). 2000. Available from: www.cdc.gov/nchs/data/series/sr_01/sr01_039.pdf.

Haupt BJ, Kozak LJ. Estimates from two survey designs: National Hospital Discharge Survey. National Center for Health Statistics. Vital Health Stat Series no 13 (111). 1992. Available from: www.cdc.gov/nchs/data/series/sr_13/sr13_111.pdf.

For More Information: See the National Health Care Survey website: www.cdc.gov/nchs.nhcs.htm or the National Hospital Discharge Survey website: www.cdc.gov/nchs/about/major/hdasd/nhds.htm.

National Immunization Survey (NIS)

Centers for Disease Control and Prevention National Center for Health Statistics and National Immunization Program

Overview: The National Immunization Survey (NIS) is a continuing nationwide telephone sample survey to monitor vaccination coverage rates among children 19–35 months of age.

Selected Content: Data collected include vaccination status and timing for Diphtheria, Tetanus toxoids, and Pertussis vaccine (DTP/DT/DTaP); Polio vaccine; Measles, Mumps, and Rubella vaccine (MMR); Haemophilius influenzae type b vaccine (Hib); Hepatitis B vaccine (Hep B); Varicella vaccine; Pneumococcal conjugate vaccine (PCV); and Combined series (4:3:1:3) by race/ethnicity, poverty level, location of residence, geographic division, state, and selected urban areas.

Data Years: Annual data collection was initiated beginning with the data year 1994. Data collection for Varicella began in July 1996; data collection for PCV began in July 2001.

Coverage: Children 19–35 months of age in the civilian noninstitutionalized population are represented in this survey. Estimates of vaccine-specific coverage are available for the nation, states, and 28 urban areas. In 2004, about 83% of the age-eligible children were up-to-date for the 4:3:1:3 series.

Methodology: The NIS is a nationwide telephone sample survey of households with age-eligible children. The NIS uses a two-phase sample design. First, a random-digit dialing (RDD) sample of telephone numbers is drawn. When households with age-eligible children are contacted, the interviewer collects information on the vaccinations received by all age-eligible children and obtains permission to contact the children's immunization providers. In the second phase, immunization providers are sent vaccination history questionnaires by mail. Providers' responses are compared with information obtained from households to provide a more accurate estimate of vaccination coverage levels. Final estimates are adjusted for households without telephones and nonresponse.

Sample Size and Response Rates: In 2004, vaccination data were collected for 30,987 children aged 19–35 months. In 2004, the overall interview response rate was 73%. Vaccination information from providers was obtained for 71% of all children who were eligible for provider follow-up in 2004.

Issues Affecting Interpretation: For data years 1998, 2002, and 2004, slight modifications to the estimation procedure were implemented to obtain vaccination coverage rates from the provider data. Published estimates of vaccination coverage based on the NIS data for years prior to 1998 (e.g., estimates published in MMWR articles) may differ slightly from estimates published in *Health, United States* and on the NIS website for the same NIS data. All released public-use data files include the sampling weight for the revised estimation procedure.

References:

National, state, and urban area vaccination levels among children aged 19–35 months—United States, 2004. MMWR 2005;54(29);717–21. Available from: www.cdc.gov/mmwr/preview/mmwrhtml/mm5429a1.htm.

Smith PJ, Hoaglin DC, Battaglia M, Michael P, Khare M, Barker LE. Statistical methodology of the National Immunization Survey, 1994–2002.

National Center for Health Statistics. Vital Health Stat Series no 2 (138). 2005. Available from: www.cdc.gov/nchs/data/series/sr_02/sr02_138.pdf.

For More Information: See the NIS website: www.cdc.gov/nis.

National Medical Expenditure Survey (NMES)—See Medical Expenditure Panel Survey

National Notifiable Disease Surveillance System (NNDSS)

Centers for Disease Control and Prevention

Overview: This system provides weekly provisional information on the occurrence of diseases defined as notifiable by the Council of State and Territorial Epidemiologists.

Selected Content: Data include incidence of reportable diseases using uniform case definitions.

Data Years: The first annual summary of The Notifiable Diseases in 1912 included reports of 10 diseases from 19 states, the District of Columbia, and Hawaii. By 1928, all states, the District of Columbia, Hawaii, and Puerto Rico were participating in national reporting of 29 specified diseases. At their annual meeting in 1950, the State and Territorial Health Officers authorized a conference of state and territorial epidemiologists whose purpose was to determine which diseases should be reported to Public Health Service. In 1961, CDC assumed responsibility for the collection and publication of data concerning nationally notifiable diseases.

Coverage: Notifiable disease reports are received from health departments in the 50 states, five territories, New York City, and the District of Columbia. Policies for reporting notifiable disease cases can vary by disease or reporting jurisdiction, depending on case status classification (i.e., confirmed, probable, or suspect).

Methodology: CDC, in partnership with the Council of State and Territorial Epidemiologists (CSTE), operates the National Notifiable Diseases Surveillance System (NNDSS). Notifiable disease surveillance is conducted by public health practitioners at local, state, and national levels to support disease prevention and control activities. The system also provides annual summaries of the data. CSTE and CDC annually review the status of national infectious disease surveillance and recommend additions or deletions to the list of nationally notifiable diseases based on the need to respond to emerging priorities. For example, Q fever and tularemia became nationally notifiable in 2000. However, reporting nationally notifiable diseases to CDC is voluntary. Reporting is currently mandated by law or regulation only at the local and state level. Therefore, the list of diseases that are considered notifiable varies slightly by state. For example, reporting of cyclosporiasis to CDC is not done by some states in which this disease is not notifiable to local or state authorities.

State epidemiologists report cases of notifiable diseases to CDC, which tabulates and publishes these data in the *Morbidity and Mortality Weekly Report* (MMWR) and the *Summary of Notifiable Diseases, United States* (titled *Annual Summary* before 1985).

Issues Affecting Interpretation: These data must be interpreted in light of reporting practices. Some diseases that cause severe clinical illness (for example, plague and rabies) are most likely reported accurately if diagnosed by a clinician. However, persons who have diseases that are clinically mild and infrequently associated with serious consequences (for example, salmonellosis) might not seek medical care from a health care provider. Even if these less severe diseases are diagnosed, they are less likely to be reported.

The degree of completeness of data reporting also is influenced by the diagnostic facilities available, the control measures in effect, public awareness of a specific disease, and the interests, resources, and priorities of state and local officials responsible for disease control and public health surveillance. Finally, factors such as changes in case definitions for public health surveillance, introduction of new diagnostic tests, or discovery of new disease entities can cause changes in disease reporting that are independent of the true incidence of disease.

Reference:

Centers for Disease Control and Prevention. Summary of notifiable diseases—United States, 2004. MMWR 2006; 53 (53). Available from: www.cdc.gov/mmwr/summary.html.

For More Information: See the NNDSS website: www.cdc.gov/epo/dphsi/nndsshis.htm.

National Nursing Home Survey (NNHS)

Centers for Disease Control and Prevention
National Center for Health Statistics

Overview: The National Nursing Home Survey (NNHS) provides information on characteristics of nursing homes and their residents and staff.

Selected Content: The NNHS provides information on nursing homes from two perspectives—that of the provider of services and that of the recipient. Data about the facilities include characteristics such as bed size, ownership, affiliation, Medicare/Medicaid certification, specialty units, services offered, number and characteristics of staff, expenses, and charges. Data about the current residents and discharges include demographic characteristics, health status, level of assistance needed with activities of daily living, vision and hearing impairment, continence, services received, sources of payment, and discharge disposition (for discharges). The redesigned NNHS conducted in 2004 included new facility data items on Joint Commission on Accreditation of Healthcare Organization accreditation, electronic information systems, cultural competency, immunization polices and practices, end-of-life practices, special service programs, and new patient-level data items on hospitalizations and emergency department admissions, pain assessment and pain relief, medications, family and caregiver services, end-of-life care and advance directives, pressure ulcers, behavior or mood symptoms, falls, and out-of-pocket charges. In addition to these facility and resident data items, data on nurse staffing and a supplemental survey on nursing assistants working in nursing homes were also collected.

Data Years: NCHS conducted seven National Nursing Home Surveys: the first survey August 1973–April 1974; the second May–December 1977; the third August 1985–January 1986; the fourth July–December 1995; the fifth July–December 1997; the sixth July–December 1999; and the seventh and most recent NNHS, which has undergone a major redesign, was conducted August–January 2004.

Coverage: The initial NNHS, conducted in 1973–1974, included the universe of nursing homes that provided some level of nursing care and excluded homes providing only personal or domiciliary care. The 1977 NNHS encompassed all types of nursing homes, including personal care and domiciliary care homes. The 1985 NNHS was designed to be similar to the 1973–1974 survey in that it excluded personal or domiciliary care homes. However in 1985, an unknown number of residential care facilities were present in the sampling frame. These facilities were identified in the 1986 inventory survey and can be removed from the estimate of facilities and beds for 1985. The 1995, 1997, 1999, and 2004 NNHS also included only nursing homes that provided some level of nursing care and excluded homes providing only personal or domiciliary care, similar to the 1985 and 1973–1974 surveys.

Data were collected from nursing homes in all 50 states and the District of Columbia (DC) in the 1995, 1997, 1999 and 2004 surveys, but in 1973–1974, 1977, and 1985, data were only collected in the 48 contiguous states and DC. Data on current residents were collected in all surveys; data on discharges were collected in 1977, 1985, 1997, and 1999. Expense data were collected in 1977, 1985, and 1995. Data on characteristics of staff were collected in 1973–1974, 1977, 1985, and 2004.

Methodology: The survey uses a stratified two-stage probability design. The first stage is the selection of facilities, and the second stage is the selection of residents and discharges. Prior to the 2004 NNHS up to six current residents and/or six discharges were selected. The 2004 survey was designed to select only 12 current residents from each facility to participate in the survey. Information on the facility is collected through a personal interview with the administrator or staff designated by the administrator. Resident data were provided by staff familiar with the care provided to the resident. Staff relied on the medical record and personal knowledge of the resident. In addition to employee data that were collected during the interview with the administrator, in several years staffing data were collected via a self-administered questionnaire. Discharge data, when collected, were based on information recorded in the medical record.

Current residents are those on the facility's roster as of the night before the survey. Included are all residents for whom beds are maintained even though they may be away on an overnight leave or in the hospital. Discharges are those who are formally discharged from care by the facility during a designated reference period randomly selected for each facility before data collection. Both live and deceased discharges are included. Residents were counted more than once if they were discharged more than once during the reference period.

Statistics for the NNHS are derived by a multistage estimation procedure that has three major components: (a) inflation by the reciprocals of the probabilities of sample selection; (b) adjustment for nonresponse; and (c) ratio adjustment to fixed totals. The surveys are adjusted for four types of nonresponse: (1) when an eligible nursing facility did not respond; (2) when the facility failed to complete the sampling lists; (3) when the facility did not complete the facility questionnaire but did complete the questionnaire for residents in the facility; and (4) when the facility did not provide information to complete the questionnaire for the sample resident or discharge.

Sample Size and Response Rates: In 1973–1974 the sample of 2,118 homes was selected from the 1971 National Master Facility Inventory (NMFI) and from those that opened for business in 1972. For the 1977 NNHS the sample of 1,698 facilities was selected from nursing homes in the sampling frame, which consisted of all homes listed in the 1973 NMFI and those opening for business between 1973 and December 1976. The sample for the 1985 survey consisted of the 1,220 facilities selected from the 1982 NMFI, data for homes identified in the 1982 Complement Survey of the NMFI, data on hospital-based nursing homes obtained from the Health Care Financing Administration (now known as the Centers for Medicare & Medicaid Services), and data on nursing homes open for business between 1982 and June 1, 1984. The 1995 sample of 1,500 homes was selected from a sampling frame consisting of nursing homes from the 1991 National Health Provider Inventory (NHPI) and updated lists from the Agency Reporting System (ARS). The ARS was an ongoing system designed to periodically update the NHPI and consisted primarily of lists or directories of facilities from state agencies, federal agencies, and national voluntary organizations. For the 1997 survey, data were obtained from about 1,488 nursing homes from a sampling frame consisting of nursing homes listed on the 1991 NHPI that was updated with a current listing of nursing facilities supplied by the Health Care Finance Administration and other national organizations. The facility frame for the 1999 NNHS consisted of all nursing homes identified in the 1997 NNHS and updated with current nursing facilities listed by the Centers for Medicare & Medicaid Services and other national organizations. The 1999 sample consisted of 1,496 nursing homes. In 1995, 1997, and 1999, facility-level response rates were over 93%. For the

2004 redesigned and expanded NNHS, 1,500 nursing homes were selected and a facility response rate of 81% was achieved.

Issues Affecting Interpretation: Samples of discharges and residents contain different populations with different characteristics. The resident sample is more likely to contain long-term nursing home residents and, conversely, to underestimate short nursing home stays. Because short-term residents are less likely to be on the nursing home rolls on a given night, they are less likely to be sampled. Estimates of discharges underestimate long nursing home stays. In addition, analysts should ensure that the underlying populations are similar across survey years—for example, whether the survey includes personal or domiciliary care homes.

References:

Meiners MR. Selected operating and financial characteristics of nursing homes, United States, 1973–1974 National Nursing Home Survey. National Center for Health Statistics. Vital Health Stat Series no 13 (22). 1975. Available from: www.cdc.gov/nchs/data/series/sr_13/sr13_022.pdf.

Van Nostrand JF, Zappolo A, Hing E, et al. The National Nursing Home Survey: 1977 summary for the United States. National Center for Health Statistics. Vital Health Stat Series no 13 (43). 1979. Available from: www.cdc.gov/nchs/data/series/sr_13/sr13_043.pdf.

Hing E, Sekscenski E, Strahan G. The National Nursing Home Survey: 1985 summary for the United States. National Center for Health Statistics. Vital Health Stat Series no 13 (97). 1989. Available from: www.cdc.gov/nchs/data/series/sr_13/sr13_097.pdf.

Strahan G. An overview of nursing homes and their current residents: Data from the 1995 National Nursing Home Survey. Advance data from vital and health statistics; no 280. Hyattsville, MD: National Center for Health Statistics. 1997. Available from: www.cdc.gov/nchs/data/ad/ad280.pdf.

The National Nursing Home Survey: 1997 summary. National Center for Health Statistics. Vital Health Stat Series no 13 (147). 2000. Available from: www.cdc.gov/nchs/data/series/sr_13/sr13_147.pdf.

The National Nursing Home Survey: 1999 summary. National Center for Health Statistics. Vital Health Stat Series no 13 (152). 2002. Available from: www.cdc.gov/nchs/data/series/sr_13/sr13_152.pdf.

For More Information: See the National Health Care Survey website: www.cdc.gov/nchs/nhcs.htm and the NNHS website: www.cdc.gov/nchs/nnhs.htm.

National Prisoner Statistics (NPS)

Bureau of Justice Statistics

Overview: National Prisoner Statistics (NPS) produces semiannual national- and state-level data on the numbers of prisoners in state and federal prison facilities. The NPS provides information on prisoners incarcerated in state and federal correctional institutions, including their characteristics, movements, and locations.

Data Years: Since 1926, the federal government has published data annually on the prisoner count in each state and the federal prison system.

Coverage: Data are collected from all 50 states. The prisoner count in the District of Columbia was included until 2001, when the District ceased operating a prison system.

Methodology: NPS obtains prisoner information from a census of prisons in the United States, conducted by the U.S. Census Bureau. The census is based on a facility list maintained by the Census Bureau. Prisons are mailed the NPS forms that may be returned by mail or facsimile. Starting with 2003 data, respondents were provided with an internet reporting option. NPS distinguishes between prisoners in custody from those under jurisdiction. To have custody of a prisoner, a state must hold that person in one of its facilities. To have jurisdiction, a state has legal authority over the prisoner. Prisoners under a state's jurisdiction may be in the custody of a local jail, another state's prison, or other correctional facility such as a privately-operated institution. NPS collects data on both prisoners in custody and under jurisdiction, though some states are unable to provide both custody and jurisdiction counts. NPS counts include all inmates in state-operated facilities in Alaska, Connecticut, Delaware, Hawaii, Rhode Island, and Vermont, which have combined jail-prison systems.

Sample Size and Response Rate: Data were obtained by mailed and web-based survey questionnaires. After follow-up phone calls, the response rates for most years approach 100%.

For More Information: See the Bureau of Justice Statistics website: www.ojp.usdoj.gov/bjs/correct.htm.

National Survey on Drug Use & Health (NSDUH)

Substance Abuse and Mental Health Services Administration

Overview: The National Survey on Drug Use & Health (NSDUH), formerly called the National Household Survey on Drug Abuse (NHSDA), collects data on substance abuse and dependence, mental health problems, and receipt of substance abuse and mental health treatment.

Selected Content: NSDUH reports on the prevalence, patterns, and consequences of drug and alcohol use and abuse in the general U.S. civilian noninstitutionalized population age 12 and over. Data are collected on the use of illicit drugs, the nonmedical use of licit drugs, and use of alcohol and tobacco products. The survey is conducted annually and is designed to produce drug and alcohol use incidence and prevalence estimates. Data are also collected periodically on special topics of interest such as criminal behavior, treatment, mental health, and attitudes about drugs.

Data Years: The NHSDA survey has been conducted since 1971. In 1999 the NHSDA underwent a major redesign affecting the method of data collection, sample design, sample size, and oversampling. In 2002 the survey underwent a name change to NSDUH as well as additional improvements and modifications to the survey.

Coverage: The survey is representative of persons 12 years of age and over in the civilian noninstitutionalized population in the United States. This includes civilians living on military bases and persons living in noninstitutionalized group quarters, such as college dormitories, rooming houses, and shelters. Persons excluded from the survey include homeless people who do not use shelters, active military personnel, and residents of institutional group quarters, such as jails and hospitals.

Methodology: The data collection method is in-person interviews conducted with a sample of individuals at their place of residence. Prior to 1999, the NSDUH used a paper-and-pencil interviewing (PAPI) methodology. Since 1999, the interview has been carried out with computer assisted interviewing (CAI) methodology. The survey uses a combination of computer-assisted personal-interviewing (CAPI), conducted by the interviewer for some basic demographic information, and audio computer-assisted self-interviewing (ACASI) for most of the questions. ACASI provides a highly private and confidential means of responding to questions to increase the level of honest reporting of illicit drug use and other sensitive behavior. The 2004 NSDUH employed a 50-state sample design with an independent, multistage area probability sample for each of the 50 states and the District of Columbia to support the development of both national and state-level estimates. Each state was stratified into regions (48 regions in each of 8 large states, 12 regions in each of 42 small states and the District of Columbia). At the first stage of sampling, 8 area segments were selected in each region, for a total of 7,200 sample units nationally. The design also oversampled youths and young adults, so that each state's sample was approximately equally distributed among three major age groups: 12–17 years, 18–25 years, and 26 years or over.

Sample Size and Response Rate: Nationally, of the 142,612 eligible households sampled, 130,130 addresses were successfully screened for the 2004 survey, and in these screened households, a total of 81,973 sample persons were selected from which 67,760 completed interviews were obtained. The survey was conducted from January to December 2004. Weighted response rates for household screening and for interviewing were 91% and 77%, respectively.

Issues Affecting Interpretation: Several improvements to the survey were implemented in 2002. In addition to the name change, respondents were offered a $30 incentive payment for participation in the survey starting in 2002, and quality control procedures for data collection were enhanced in 2001 and 2002. Because of these improvements and modifications, estimates from the NSDUH completed in 2002 and later should not be compared with estimates from the 2001 or earlier versions of the survey. The data collected in 2002 represent a new baseline for tracking trends in substance use and other measures. Estimates of substance use for youth based on the NSDUH are not directly comparable with

estimates based on Monitoring the Future (MTF) and Youth Risk Behavior Surveillance System (YRBSS). In addition to the fact that the MTF excludes dropouts and absentees, rates are not directly comparable across these surveys because of differences in populations covered, sample design, questionnaires, interview setting, and statistical approaches to make the survey estimates generalizable to the entire population. The NSDUH survey collects data in homes, whereas the MTF and YRBSS collect data in school classrooms. The NSDUH estimates are tabulated by age, while the MTF and YRBSS estimates are tabulated by grade, representing different ages as well as different populations.

References:

Substance Abuse and Mental Health Services Administration. (2005). Results from the 2004 National Survey on Drug Use and Health: National Findings (Office of Applied Studies, NSDUH Series H-28, DHHS Publication No. SMA 05–4062). Rockville, MD. 2005.

Wright D, Sathe N. (2005). State Estimates of Substance Use from the 2002–2003 National Surveys on Drug Use and Health (DHHS Publication No. SMA 05–3989, NSDUH Series H-26). Substance Abuse and Mental Health Services Administration. Rockville, MD: Office of Applied Studies. 2004.

Cowan CD. Coverage, Sample Design, and Weighting in Three Federal Surveys. Journal of Drug Issues 2001; 31(3):595–614.

For More Information: See the NSDUH website: nsduhweb.rti.org/ or the SAMHSA Office of Applied Studies website: oas.samhsa.gov/.

National Survey of Family Growth (NSFG)

Centers for Disease Control and Prevention
National Center for Health Statistics

Overview: The National Survey of Family Growth (NSFG) provides national data on factors affecting birth and pregnancy rates, adoption, and maternal and infant health.

Selected Content: Data elements include sexual activity, marriage, divorce and remarriage, unmarried cohabitation, contraception and sterilization, infertility, breastfeeding, pregnancy loss, low birthweight, and use of medical care for family planning and infertility.

Data Years: Six cycles of the survey have been completed: 1973, 1976, 1982, 1988, 1995, and 2002.

Coverage: The 1973–1995 cycles of the National Survey of Family Growth (NSFG) were based on samples of women ages 15–44 years in the civilian noninstitutionalized population of the United States. The first and second cycles (1973 and 1976) excluded most women who had never been married. The third, fourth, and fifth cycles (1982, 1988, and 1995) included all women ages 15–44 years in the civilian noninstitutional population of the United States. The sixth cycle (2002) included men and women 15–44 years of age in the household population of the United States.

Methodology: Interviews are conducted in person by professional female interviewers using a standardized questionnaire. In all cycles black women were sampled at higher rates than white women so that detailed statistics for black women could be produced. In cycles 5 and 6 (1995 and 2002) Hispanic persons were also oversampled.

In order to make national estimates from the sample for the millions of women ages 15–44 years in the United States, data for the interviewed sample women were (a) inflated by the reciprocal of the probability of selection at each stage of sampling (for example, if there was a 1 in 5,000 chance that a woman would be selected for the sample, her sampling weight was 5,000); (b) adjusted for nonresponse; and (c) poststratified, or forced to agree with benchmark population values based on data from the U.S. Census Bureau.

Sample Size and Response Rates: For cycle 1, from 101 PSUs, 10,879 women 15–44 years of age were selected, 9,797 of these were interviewed. In cycle 2, from 79 PSUs, 10,202 eligible women were identified; of these, 8,611 were interviewed. In cycle 3 household screener interviews were completed in 29,511 households (95%). Of the 9,964 eligible women identified, 7,969 were interviewed. In cycle 4, 10,566 eligible women ages 15–44 years were sampled. Interviews were completed with 8,450 women. The response rate for the 1990 telephone reinterview was 68% of those responding to the 1988 survey and still eligible for the 1990 survey. In cycle 5, of the 13,795 eligible women in the sample, 10,847 were interviewed. In cycle 6, from 120 PSUs, 7,643 (about 80%) interviews were completed with eligible women and 4,928 (78%) interviews were completed with men.

References:

French DK. National Survey of Family Growth, Cycle I: Sample design, estimation procedures, and variance estimation. National Center for Health Statistics. Vital Health Stat Series no 2 (76). 1978. Available from: www.cdc.gov/nchs/data/series/sr_02/sr02_076.pdf.

Grady WR. National Survey of Family Growth, Cycle II: Sample design, estimation procedures, and variance estimation. National Center for Health Statistics. Vital Health Stat Series no 2 (87). 1981. Available from: www.cdc.gov/nchs/data/series/sr_02/sr02_087.pdf.

Bachrach CA, Horn MC, Mosher WD, Shimizu I. National Survey of Family Growth, Cycle III: Sample design, weighting, and variance estimation. National Center for Health Statistics. Vital Health Stat Series no 2 (98). 1985. Available from: www.cdc.gov/nchs/data/series/sr_02/sr02_098.pdf.

Judkins DR, Mosher WD, Botman SL. National Survey of Family Growth: Design, estimation, and inference. National Center for Health Statistics. Vital Health Stat Series no 2 (109). 1991. Available from: www.cdc.gov/nchs/data/series/sr_02/sr02_109.pdf.

Goksel H, Judkins DR, Mosher WD. Nonresponse adjustments for a telephone follow-up to a National In-Person Survey. Journal of Official Statistics 1992;8(4):417–32.

Kelly JE, Mosher WD, Duffer AP, Kinsey SH. Plan and operation of the 1995 National Survey of Family Growth. Vital Health Stat 1(36). 1997. Available from: www.cdc.gov/nchs/data/series/sr_01/sr01_036.pdf.

Potter FJ, Iannacchione VG, Mosher WD, Mason RE, Kavee JD. Sampling weights, imputation, and variance estimation in the 1995 National Survey of Family Growth. Vital Health Stat Series no 2 (124). 1998. Available from: www.cdc.gov/nchs/data/series/sr_02/sr02_124.pdf.

Groves R, Mosher W, Benson G, et al. Plan and operation of Cycle 6 of the National Survey of Family Growth. National Center for Health Statistics. Vital Health Stat Series no 1 (42). 2005. Available from: http://www.cdc.gov/nchs/data/series/sr_01/sr01_042.pdf.

For More Information: See the NSFG website: www.cdc.gov/nchs/nsfg.htm.

National Vital Statistics System (NVSS)

Centers for Disease Control and Prevention
National Center for Health Statistics

Overview: The National Vital Statistics System (NVSS) collects and publishes official national statistics on births, deaths, fetal deaths, and prior to 1996, marriages and divorces occurring in the United States based on U.S. Standard Certificates. Fetal deaths are classified and tabulated separately from other deaths. Detailed descriptions of the five Vital Statistics files (birth file, mortality file, multiple cause of death file, linked birth/infant death data set, and compressed mortality file) are presented separately below.

Data Years: The death registration area for 1900 consisted of 10 states, the District of Columbia, and a number of cities located in nonregistration states; it covered 40% of the continental U.S. population. The birth registration area was established in 1915 with 10 states and the District of Columbia. The birth and death registration areas continued to expand until 1933, when they included all 48 states and the District of Columbia. Alaska and Hawaii were added to both registration areas in 1959 and 1960, the years in which they gained statehood.

Coverage: The NVSS collects and presents U.S. resident data for the aggregate of 50 states, New York City, and the District of Columbia, as well as for each individual state and the District of Columbia. Vital events occurring in the United States to non-U.S. residents and vital events occurring abroad to U.S. residents are excluded.

Methodology: NCHS's Division of Vital Statistics obtains information on births and deaths from the registration offices of each of the 50 states, New York City, the District of Columbia, Puerto Rico, the U.S. Virgin Islands, Guam, American Samoa, and Northern Mariana Islands. Until 1972 microfilm copies of all death certificates and a 50% sample of birth certificates were received from all registration areas and processed by NCHS. In 1972 some states began sending their data to NCHS through the Cooperative Health Statistics System (CHSS). States that participated in the CHSS program processed 100% of their death and birth records and sent the entire data file to NCHS on computer tapes. Currently, data are sent to NCHS through the Vital Statistics Cooperative Program (VSCP), following the same procedures as CHSS. The number of participating states grew from 6 in 1972 to 46 in 1984. Starting in 1985 all 50 states and the District of Columbia participated in VSCP.

U.S. Standard Certificates—U.S. Standard Live Birth and Death Certificates and Fetal Death Reports are revised periodically, allowing evaluation and addition, modification, and deletion of items. Beginning with 1989 revised standard certificates replaced the 1978 versions. The 1989 revision of the birth certificate included items to identify the Hispanic parentage of newborns and to expand information about maternal and infant health characteristics. The 1989 revision of the death certificate included items on educational attainment and Hispanic origin of decedents, as well as changes to improve the medical certification of cause of death. Standard certificates recommended by NCHS are modified in each registration area to serve the area's needs. However, most certificates conform closely in content and arrangement to the standard certificate, and all certificates contain a minimum data set specified by NCHS. Following 1989, the next revisions of vital records went into effect in some states beginning in 2003, but full implementation in all states will be phased in over several years.

Birth File

Overview: Vital statistics natality data are a fundamental source of demographic, geographic, and medical and health information on all births occurring in the United States. This is one of the few sources of comparable health-related data for small geographic areas over an extended time period. The data are used to present the characteristics of babies and their mothers, track trends such as birth rates for teenagers, and compare natality trends with other countries.

Selected Content: The natality file includes characteristics about the baby such as sex, birthweight, weeks of gestation; demographic information about the parents such as age, race, Hispanic origin, parity, educational attainment, marital status, and state of residence; medical and health information such as prenatal care based on hospital records; and behavioral risk factors for the birth such as mother's tobacco use during pregnancy.

Data Years: The birth registration area began in 1915 with 10 states and the District of Columbia.

Methodology: In the United States, state laws require birth certificates to be completed for all births. The registration of births is the responsibility of the professional attendant at birth, generally a physician or midwife. The birth certificate must be filed with the local registrar of the district in which the birth occurs. Each birth must be reported promptly—the reporting requirements vary from state to state, ranging from 24 hours after the birth to as much as 10 days.

Federal law mandates national collection and publication of birth and other vital statistics data. The National Vital Statistics System is the result of cooperation between NCHS and the states to provide access to statistical information from birth certificates. Standard forms for the collection of the data and model procedures for the uniform registration of the events are developed and recommended for state use through cooperative activities of the states and NCHS. NCHS shares the costs incurred by the states in providing vital statistics data for national use.

Issues Affecting Interpretation: In 2003, two states, Pennsylvania and Washington, implemented the 2003 revision of the U.S. Standard Certificate of Live Birth, and in 2004, seven more states, Florida, Idaho, Kentucky, New Hampshire, New York state (excluding New York City), South Carolina, and Tennessee also implemented the 2003 revision. Data on mother's educational attainment, tobacco use during pregnancy, and prenatal care based on the 2003 revision are not comparable with data based on the 1989 revision of the U.S. Standard Certificate of Live Birth, and are excluded from *Health, United States* statistics. Prior to 2003, the number of states reporting information on maternal education, Hispanic origin, marital status, and tobacco use during pregnancy increased over the years. Interpretation of trend data should take into consideration expansion of reporting areas and immigration. For methodological and reporting area changes for the following birth certificate items, see Appendix II: Age (maternal age); Cigarette smoking; Education (maternal education); Hispanic origin; Marital status; Prenatal care; Race.

Reference:

National Center for Health Statistics, Vital Statistics of the United States 2000, Vol. I Natality, Technical Appendix. Available from: www.cdc.gov/nchs/data/techap00.pdf.

For More Information: See the Birth Data website: www.cdc.gov/nchs/births.htm.

Mortality File

Overview: Vital statistics mortality data are a fundamental source of demographic, geographic, and cause-of-death information. This is one of the few sources of comparable health-related data for small geographic areas over an extended time period. The data are used to present the characteristics of those dying in the United States, to determine life expectancy, and to compare mortality trends with other countries.

Selected Content: The mortality file includes demographic information on age, sex, race, Hispanic origin, state of residence, and educational attainment, and medical information on cause of death.

Data Years: The death registration area began in 1900 with 10 states and the District of Columbia.

Methodology: By law, the registration of deaths is the responsibility of the funeral director. The funeral director obtains demographic data for the death certificate from an informant. The physician in attendance at the death is required to certify the cause of death. Where death is from other than natural causes, a coroner or medical examiner may be required to examine the body and certify the cause of death. Data for the entire United States refer to events occurring within the United States; data for geographic areas are by place of residence. For methodological and reporting area changes for the following death certificate items, see Appendix II: Education; Hispanic origin; Race.

Issues Affecting Interpretation: International Classification of Diseases (ICD), by which cause of death is coded and classified, is revised approximately every 10 to 15 years. Revisions of the ICD may cause discontinuities in trend data by cause of death. Comparing death rates by cause of death across ICD revisions should be conducted with caution and with reference to the comparability ratio. (See Appendix II, Comparability ratio.) The death certificate has been revised periodically. A revised U.S. Standard Certificate of Death was recommended for state use beginning on January 1, 1989. Among the changes were the addition of a new item on educational attainment and Hispanic origin of decedent and changes to improve the medical certification of cause of death.

References:

Grove RD, Hetzel AM. Vital statistics rates in the United States, 1940–1960. Washington, DC: Government Printing Office. 1968.

National Center for Health Statistics, Vital Statistics of the United States, Vol II Mortality part A,

Technical Appendix, available from:
www.cdc.gov/nchs/datawh/statab/pubd/ta.htm.

For More Information: See the Mortality Data website:
www.cdc.gov/nchs/about/major/dvs/mortdata.htm.

Multiple Cause-of-Death File

Overview: Multiple cause-of-death data reflect all medical information reported on death certificates and complement traditional underlying cause-of-death data. Multiple cause data give information on diseases that are a factor in death whether or not they are the underlying cause of death; on associations among diseases; and on injuries leading to death.

Selected Content: In addition to the same demographic variables listed for the mortality file, the multiple cause-of-death file includes record axis and entity axis cause-of-death data (see Methodology section).

Data Years: Multiple cause-of-death data files are available for every data year since 1968.

Methodology: NCHS is responsible for compiling and publishing annual national statistics on causes of death. In carrying out this responsibility, NCHS adheres to the World Health Organization Nomenclature Regulations. These regulations require that (1) cause of death be coded in accordance with the applicable revision of the *International Classification of Diseases* (ICD) (see Appendix II, Table IV and ICD); and (2) underlying cause of death be selected in accordance with international rules. Traditionally, national mortality statistics have been based on a count of deaths, with one underlying cause assigned for each death.

Starting with data year 1968, electronic files exist with multiple cause-of-death information. These files contain codes for all diagnostic terms and related codable information recorded on the death certificate. These codes make up the entity axis and are the input for a software program called TRANSAX. The TRANSAX program eliminates redundant entity axis codes and combines other entity axis codes to create the best set of ICD codes for a record. The output of the TRANSAX program is the record axis. Record axis data are generally used for research and analysis of multiple or nonunderlying cause of death. Because the function of the TRANSAX program is not to select a single underlying cause of death, record axis data may or may not include the underlying cause. Tabulations of underlying and nonunderlying

cause of death in Table 48 (selected occupational diseases) are compiled by searching both underlying cause of death and record axis data.

Reference:

Multiple Causes of Death in the United States. Monthly vital statistics report; vol 32 no 10, supp 2. Hyattsville, MD: National Center for Health Statistics. February 17, 1984. Available from: www.cdc.gov/nchs/data/mvsr/supp/mv32_10s2.pdf.

For More Information: See the Mortality Multiple Cause-of-Death Data File website:
www.cdc.gov/nchs/products/elec_prods/subject/mortmcd.htm.

Linked Birth/Infant Death Data Set

Overview: National linked files of live births and infant deaths are used for research on infant mortality.

Selected Content: The linked birth/infant death data set includes all variables on the natality file, including racial and ethnic information, as well as variables on the mortality file, including cause of death and age at death.

Data Years: National linked files of live births and infant deaths were first produced for the 1983 birth cohort. Birth cohort linked file data are available for 1983–1991 and period linked file data starting with 1995. National linked files do not exist for 1992–1994.

Methodology: To create the linked data files, death certificates are linked with corresponding birth certificates for infants who die in the United States before their first birthday. About 97–99% of files can be linked. The linkage makes available extensive information about the pregnancy, maternal risk factors, infant characteristics, and health items at birth that can be used in analyses of infant mortality.

Starting with data year 1995, more timely linked file data are produced in a period data format preceding the release of the corresponding birth cohort format. Other changes to the data set starting with 1995 data include addition of record weights to correct for the 1.0%–1.4% in 2000–2003 (2.1%–2.5% in 1995–1999) of records that could not be linked and for the addition of an imputation for not stated birthweight. The 1995–2003 weighted mortality rates range from less than 1% to 4.1% higher than unweighted rates for the same period. The 1995–2003 weighted mortality rates with imputed birthweights are less than 1%-6.7% higher than unweighted rates with imputed birthweight for the same period.

Issues Affecting Interpretation: Period linked file data starting with 1995 are not strictly comparable with birth cohort data for 1983–1991. While birth cohort linked files have methodological advantages, their production incurs substantial delays in data availability, because it is necessary to wait until the close of a second data year to include all infant deaths to the birth cohort.

Reference:

Mathews TJ, MacDorman MF. Infant mortality statistics from the 2003 period linked birth/infant death data set. National vital statistics report; vol 54 no 16. Hyattsville, MD: National Center for Health Statistics. 2006. Available from: www.cdc.gov/nchs/data/nvsr/nvsr54/nvsr54_16.pdf.

For More Information: See the NCHS Linked Birth and Infant Death Data website: www.cdc.gov/nchs/linked.htm.

Compressed Mortality File

Overview: The Compressed Mortality File (CMF) is a county-level national mortality and population database.

Selected Content: The compressed mortality database contains mortality data derived from the detailed mortality files of the National Vital Statistics System and from the U.S. Census Bureau estimates of U.S. national, state, and county resident populations. Number of deaths, crude death rates, and age-adjusted death rates can be obtained by place of residence (total U.S., state, and county), age group, race (white, black, and other), sex, year of death, and underlying cause of death.

Data Years: The CMF spans the years 1968–2002. On CDC WONDER, data are available starting with 1979.

Methodology: In *Health, United States*, the CMF is used to compute death rates by urbanization level of decedent's county of residence. Counties are categorized according to level of urbanization based on an NCHS-modified version of the 1993 rural-urban continuum codes for metropolitan and nonmetropolitan counties developed by the Economic Research Service, U.S. Department of Agriculture. See Appendix II, Urbanization.

For More Information: See the Compressed Mortality File website: www.cdc.gov/nchs/products/elec_prods/

subject/mcompres.htm; or the CDC Wonder website: wonder.cdc.gov/mortSQL.html.

Occupational Employment Statistics (OES)

Bureau of Labor Statistics

Overview: The Occupational Employment Statistics (OES) program conducts a semi-annual survey designed to produce estimates of employment and wages for specific occupations.

Selected Content: The OES survey produces estimates of occupational employment and wages for most sector, 3-, 4-, and 5-digit industrial groups in these industrial sectors: Forestry and logging; Mining; Utilities; Construction; Manufacturing; Wholesale trade; Retail trade; Transportation and warehousing; Information; Finance and insurance; Real estate and rental and leasing; Professional, scientific, and technical services; Management of companies and enterprises; Administrative and support and waste management and remediation services; Educational services; Health care and social assistance; Arts, entertainment, and recreation; Accommodation and food services; Other services (except public administration); and Government.

Data Years: Prior to 1996, the OES program collected only occupational employment data for selected industries in each year of the three-year survey cycle, and produced only industry-specific estimates of occupational employment. The 1996 survey round was the first year that the OES program began collecting occupational employment and wage data in every state. In addition, the program's 3-year survey cycle was modified to collect data from all covered industries each year. 1997 is the earliest year available for which the OES program produced estimates of cross-industry as well as industry-specific occupational employment and wages.

Coverage: The OES survey covers all full-time and part-time wage and salary workers in nonfarm industries. Surveys collect data for the payroll period including the 12th day of May or November, depending upon the industry surveyed. The survey does not cover the self-employed, owners and partners in unincorporated firms, household workers, or unpaid family workers.

The OES survey produces estimates of occupational employment and wages for most sector, 3-, 4-, and 5-digit industrial groups in these industrial sectors: Forestry and logging; Mining; Utilities; Construction; Manufacturing;

Wholesale trade; Retail trade; Transportation and warehousing; Information; Finance and insurance; Real estate and rental and leasing; Professional, scientific, and technical services; Management of companies and enterprises; Administrative and support and waste management and remediation services; Educational services; Health care and social assistance; Arts, entertainment, and recreation; Accommodation and food services; Other services (except public administration); and Government.

Methodology: The OES survey is a federal-state cooperative program between the Bureau of Labor Statistics (BLS) and State Workforce Agencies (SWAs). The OES program surveys approximately 200,000 establishments per panel (every six months), taking 3 years to fully collect the sample of 1.2 million establishments. Mail surveys collect data for the payroll period including the 12th day of May or November, depending upon the industry surveyed. The estimates for occupations in nonfarm establishments are based on OES data collected for the reference months of May and November. BLS provides the procedures and technical support, draws the sample, and produces the survey materials, while the SWAs collect the data. SWAs from all 50 states, plus the District of Columbia, Puerto Rico, Guam, and the Virgin Islands participate in the survey. Occupational employment and wage rate estimates at the national level are produced by BLS using data from the 50 states and the District of Columbia. Employers who respond to states' requests to participate in the OES survey make these estimates possible. The nationwide response rate for the November 2004 survey was 79% for establishments, covering 73% of employment. The employment data are benchmarked to an average of the May and November employment levels.

Issues Affecting Interpretation: The OES survey began using the North American Industrial Classification System (NAICS) in 2002. Data prior to 2002 are based on the Standard Industrial Classification (SIC) system. In 1999, the OES survey began using the new Office of Management and Budget (OMB) Standard Occupational Classification (SOC) system. The new SOC system, which will be used by all federal statistical agencies for reporting occupational data, consists of 821 detailed occupations, grouped into 449 broad occupations, 96 minor groups, and 23 major groups. The OES program provides occupational employment and wage estimates at the major group and detailed occupation level. Due to the OES survey's transition to the new SOC system, 1999 and 2000 OES estimates are not directly comparable

with previous years' OES estimates, which were based on a classification system having seven major occupational groups and 770 detailed occupations. Approximately one-half of the detailed occupations were unchanged under the new SOC system, with the other half being new SOC occupations or occupations that are slightly different from similar occupations in the old OES classification system.

Reference:

Bureau of Labor Statistics. Occupational Employment and Wages, November 2004. Washington, DC: Department of Labor. November 2005.

For More Information: See the Occupational Statistics website: www.bls.gov/OES/#overview.

Online Survey Certification and Reporting Database (OSCAR)

Centers for Medicare & Medicaid Services

Overview: The Online Survey Certification and Reporting (OSCAR) is an administrative database containing detailed information on all Medicare- and Medicaid- certified institutional health care providers, including all currently and previously certified Medicare and Medicaid nursing homes in the United States and Territories. (Data for the Territories are not shown in *Health, United States.*) The purpose of the nursing home survey certification process is to ensure that nursing facilities meet the current Centers for Medicare & Medicaid Services (CMS) care requirements and thus can be reimbursed for services furnished to Medicare and Medicaid beneficiaries.

Selected Content: OSCAR contains information on facility and patient characteristics and health deficiencies issued by the government during state surveys.

Data Years: OSCAR has been maintained by CMS, formerly the Health Care Financing Administration (HCFA), since 1992. OSCAR is an updated version of the Medicare and Medicaid Automated Certification System that had been in existence since 1972.

Coverage: All nursing homes in the United States that receive Medicare or Medicaid payments are included. Nursing homes that are intermediate care facilities for the mentally retarded and Department of Veterans Affairs nursing homes are excluded.

Methodology: Information on the number of beds and other facility characteristics comes from HCFA form 671, and information on residents and resident characteristics is collected on HCFA form 672. A nursing home representative fills out the forms, and they are submitted to CMS. The information provided on HCFA forms 671 and 672 can be audited at any time.

All certified nursing homes are inspected by representatives of the state survey agency (generally the department of health) at least once every 15 months. Therefore, a complete census must be based on a 15-month reporting cycle rather than a 12-month cycle. Some nursing homes are inspected twice or more often during any given reporting cycle. To avoid overcounting, the data must be edited and duplicates removed. Data editing and compilation were performed by Cowles Research Group and published in the group's *Nursing Home Statistical Yearbook* series.

References:

Cowles CM. 1995; 1996; 1997 Nursing home statistical yearbook. Anacortes, WA: Cowles Research Group (CRG). 1995; 1997; 1998.

Cowles CM. 1998; 1999; 2000; 2001; 2002. Nursing home statistical yearbook. Washington, DC: American Association of Homes and Services for the Aging (AAHSA). 1999; 2000; 2001; 2002; 2003.

Cowles CM. 2003; 2004. Nursing home statistical yearbook. McMinville, OR: Cowles Research Group (CRG). 2006; 2006.

For More Information: See the CRG website: www.longtermcareinfo.com/crg, the AAHSA website: www.aahsa.org, or the CMS website: www.cms.hhs.gov/NonIdentifiableDataFiles/.

Population Census and Population Estimates

U.S. Census Bureau

Decennial Census

The census of population (decennial census) has been held in the United States every 10 years since 1790. The decennial census has enumerated the resident population as of April 1 of the census year ever since 1930. Data on sex, race, age, and marital status are collected from 100% of the enumerated population. More detailed information such as income, education, housing, occupation, and industry are collected from a representative sample of the population.

Race Data on the 1990 Census

The question on race on the 1990 census was based on the Office of Management and Budget's (OMB) 1977 Statistical Policy Directive 15, Race and Ethnicity Standards for Federal Statistics and Administrative Reporting. This document specified rules for the collection, tabulation, and reporting of race and ethnicity data within the federal statistical system. The 1977 standards required federal agencies to report race-specific tabulations using four single-race categories: American Indian or Alaska Native, Asian or Pacific Islander, black, and white. Under the 1977 standards, race and ethnicity were considered to be two separate and distinct concepts. Thus, persons of Hispanic origin may be of any race.

Race Data on the 2000 Census

The question on race on the 2000 census was based on OMBs 1997 Revisions to the Standards for the Classification of Federal Data on Race and Ethnicity (see Appendix II, Race and Revisions to the Standards for the Classification of Federal Data on Race and Ethnicity. Fed Regist 1997 October 30;62:58781–90). The 1997 Standards incorporated two major changes in the collection, tabulation, and presentation of race data. First, the 1997 standards increased from four to five the minimum set of categories to be used by federal agencies for identification of race: American Indian or Alaska Native, Asian, black or African American, Native Hawaiian or Other Pacific Islander, and white. Second, the 1997 standards included the requirement that federal data collection programs allow respondents to select one or more race categories when responding to a query on their racial identity. This provision means that there are potentially 31 race groups, depending on whether an individual selects one, two, three, four, or all five of the race categories. The 1997 standards continue to call for use, when possible, of a separate question on Hispanic or Latino ethnicity and specify that the ethnicity question should appear before the question on race. Thus, under the 1997 standards, as under the 1977 standards, Hispanics may be of any race.

Modified Decennial Census Files

For several decades the U.S. Census Bureau has produced modified decennial census files. These modified files incorporate adjustments to the 100% April 1 count data for: 1) errors in the census data discovered subsequent to publication, 2) misreported age data, and 3) nonspecified race.

For the 1990 census, the U.S. Census Bureau modified the age, race, and sex data on the census and produced the Modified Age Race Sex (MARS) file. The differences between the population counts on the original census file and the MARS file are primarily due to modification of the race data. Of the 248.7 million persons enumerated in 1990, 9.8 million persons did not specify their race (over 95% were of Hispanic origin). For the 1990 MARS file, these persons were assigned the race reported by a nearby person with an identical response to the Hispanic origin question.

For the 2000 census, the U.S. Census Bureau modified the race data on the census and produced the Modified Race Data Summary File. For this file, persons who reported the category, Some other race, as part of their race response were assigned to one of the 31 race groups, which are the single- and multiple-race combinations of the five race categories specified in the 1997 race and ethnicity standards. Persons who did not specify their race were assigned to one of the 31 race groups using imputation. Of the 18.5 million persons who reported the category, Some other race, as part of their race response, or who did not specify their race, 16.8 million (90.4%) were of Hispanic origin.

Bridged-Race Population Estimates for Census 2000

Race data on the 2000 census are not comparable with race data on other data systems that are continuing to collect data using the 1977 standards on race and ethnicity during the transition to full implementation of the 1997 standards. For example, most of the states in the Vital Statistics Cooperative Program will revise their birth and death certificates to conform to the 1997 standards after 2000. Thus, population estimates for 2000 and beyond with race categories comparable to the 1977 categories are needed so that race-specific birth and death rates can be calculated. To meet this need, NCHS, in collaboration with the U.S. Census Bureau, developed methodology to bridge the 31 race groups in census 2000 to the four single-race categories specified under the 1977 standards.

The bridging methodology was developed using information from the 1997–2000 National Health Interview Survey (NHIS). The NHIS provides a unique opportunity to investigate multiple-race groups because since 1982, the NHIS has allowed respondents to choose more than one race but has also asked respondents reporting multiple races to choose a primary race. The bridging methodology developed by NCHS involved the application of regression models relating person-level and county-level covariates to the selection of a particular primary race by the multiple-race respondents. Bridging proportions derived from these models were applied by the U.S. Census Bureau to the Census 2000 Modified Race Data Summary File. This application resulted in bridged counts of the April 1, 2000, resident single-race populations for four racial groups, American Indian or Alaska Native, Asian or Pacific Islander, black, and white. As bridged-race population estimates continue to be needed for the calculation of vital rates, the Census Bureau annually produces postcensal bridged-race estimates of the July 1 resident single-race populations.

For More Information about bridged-race population estimates, see Ingram DD, Parker JD, Schenker N, et al. United States Census 2000 population with bridged race categories. National Center for Health Statistics. Vital Health Stat 2(135). 2003; and the NCHS website for U.S. Census Populations with Bridged Race Categories: www.cdc.gov/nchs/about/major/dvs/popbridge/popbridge.htm.

Postcensal Population Estimates

Postcensal population estimates are estimates made for the years following a census, before the next census has been taken. National postcensal population estimates are derived annually by updating the resident population enumerated in the decennial census using a components of population change approach. Each annual series includes estimates for the current data year and revised estimates for the earlier years in the decade. The following formula is used to derive the estimates for a given year from those for the previous year, starting with the decennial census enumerated resident population as the base:

(1) resident population,
(2) + births to U.S. resident women,
(3) − deaths to U.S. residents,
(4) + net international migration,

(5) + net movement of U.S. Armed Forces and U.S. civilian citizens.

Estimates for the earlier years in a given series are revised to reflect changes in the components of change data sets (for example, births to U.S. resident women from a preliminary natality file are replaced with counts from a final natality file). To help users keep track of which postcensal estimate is being used, each annual series is referred to as a vintage and the last year in the series is used to name the series. For example, the Vintage 2001 postcensal series has estimates for July 1, 2000, and July 1, 2001, and the Vintage 2002 postcensal series has revised estimates for July 1, 2000, and July 1, 2001, as well as estimates for July 1, 2002. The estimates for July 1, 2000, and for July 1, 2001, from the Vintage 2001 and Vintage 2002 postcensal series differ.

State postcensal estimates are based on similar data and on a variety of other data series, including school statistics from state departments of education and parochial school systems. The postcensal estimates are consistent with official decennial census figures and do not reflect estimated decennial census underenumeration.

The Census Bureau has annually produced a postcensal series of estimates of the July 1 resident population of the United States based on census 2000 by applying the components of change methodology to the Modified Race Data Summary File. These series of postcensal estimates have race data for 31 race groups, in accordance with the 1997 race and ethnicity standards. So that the race data for 2000-based postcensal estimates will be comparable with race data on vital records, the Census Bureau has applied the NHIS bridging methodology to each 31-race group postcensal series of population estimates to obtain bridged-race postcensal estimates (estimates for the four single-race categories: American Indian or Alaska Native, Asian or Pacific Islander, black, and white). Bridged-race postcensal population estimates are available from: www.cdc.gov/nchs/about/major/dvs/popbridge/popbridge.htm.

Note that before the bridged-race April 1, 2000, population counts and the bridged-race 2000-based postcensal estimates were available, the Census Bureau extended their postcensal series of estimates based on the 1990 census (with the four single-race categories needed to compute vital rates) to July 1, 2001. NCHS initially calculated vital rates for 2000 using 1990-based July 1, 2000, postcensal population estimates

and vital rates for 2001 using 1990-based July 1, 2001, postcensal estimates. Vital rates for 2000 have been revised using the bridged-race April 1, 2000, population counts, and vital rates for 2001 have been revised using the 2000-based bridged-race July 1, 2001, postcensal population estimates. Vital rates for 2002 have been calculated using the 2000-based bridged-race July 1, 2002, postcensal estimates from the Vintage 2002 series of postcensal estimates. Vital rates for 2003 have been calculated using the 2000-based bridged-race July 1, 2003, postcensal estimates from the Vintage 2003 series of postcensal estimates.

Intercensal Population Estimates

The further from the census year on which the postcensal estimates are based, the less accurate are the postcensal estimates. With the completion of the decennial census at the end of the decade, intercensal estimates for the preceding decade were prepared to replace the less accurate postcensal estimates. Intercensal population estimates take into account the census of population at the beginning and end of the decade. Thus intercensal estimates are more accurate than postcensal estimates as they correct for the error of closure or difference between the estimated population at the end of the decade and the census count for that date. The error of closure at the national level was quite small for the 1960s (379,000). However, for the 1970s it amounted to almost 5 million; for the 1980s, 1.5 million; for the 1990s, about 6 million. The error of closure differentially affects age, race, sex, and Hispanic origin subgroup populations as well as the rates based on these populations. Vital rates that were calculated using postcensal population estimates are routinely revised when intercensal estimates become available because the intercensal estimates correct for the error of closure.

Intercensal estimates for the 1990s with race data comparable to the 1977 standards have been derived so that vital rates for the 1990s could be revised to reflect census 2000. Calculation of the intercensal population estimates for the 1990s was complicated by the incomparability of the race data on the 1990 and 2000 censuses. The Census Bureau, in collaboration with National Cancer Institute and NCHS, derived race-specific intercensal population estimates for the 1990s using the 1990 MARS file as the beginning population base and the bridged-race population estimates for April 1, 2000, as the ending population base. Bridged-race intercensal population estimates are available from: www.cdc.gov/nchs/about/major/dvs/popbridge/popbridge.htm.

Special Population Estimates

Special population estimates are prepared for the education reporting area for mortality statistics because educational attainment of decedent is not reported by all 50 states. The Housing and Household Economics Statistics Division of the U.S. Bureau of the Census currently produces unpublished estimates of populations by age, race, sex, and educational attainment for NCHS. These population estimates are based on the Current Population Survey, adjusted to resident population controls. The control totals used for July 1, 1994–1996 are 1990-based population estimates for 45 reporting states and the District of Columbia (DC); for July 1, 1997–2000, 1990-based postcensal population estimates for 46 reporting states and DC; and for July 1, 2001–2002, 2000-based postcensal population estimates for 47 reporting states and DC. See Appendix II, Education.

For More Information: See the U.S. Census Bureau website: www.census.gov/.

Sexually Transmitted Disease (STD) Surveillance

Centers for Disease Control and Prevention National Center of HIV, STD, and TB Prevention

Overview: Surveillance information on incidence and prevalence of sexually transmitted diseases (STDs) is used to inform public and private health efforts to control these diseases.

Selected Content: Case reporting data are available for nationally notifiable chanchroid, chlamydia, gonorrhea, and syphilis; surveillance of other STDs, such as genital herpes simplex virus (HSV), genital warts or other human papillomavirus infections, and trichomoniasis are based on estimates of office visits in physicians' office practices provided by the National Disease and Therapeutic Index (NDTI).

Data Years: STD national surveillance data have been collected since 1941.

Coverage: Case reports of STDs are reported to CDC by STD surveillance systems operated by state and local STD control programs and health departments in 50 states, the District of Columbia, selected cities, 3,139 U.S. counties, and outlying areas comprised of U.S. dependencies, possessions, and independent nations in free association with the United States. Data from outlying areas are not included in *Health, United States.*

Methodology: Information is obtained from the following sources of data: (1) case reports from STD project areas; (2) prevalence data from the Regional Infertility Prevention Program, the National Job Training Program (formerly the Job Corps), the Jail STD Prevalence Monitoring Projects, the adolescent Women Reproductive Health Monitoring Project, the Men Who Have Sex With Men (MSM) Prevalence Monitoring Project, and the Indian Health Service; (3) sentinel surveillance of gonococcal antimicrobial resistance from the Gonococcal Isolate Surveillance Project (GISP); and (4) national sample surveys implemented by federal and private organizations. STD data are submitted to CDC on a variety of hard-copy summary reporting forms (monthly, quarterly, and annually) and in electronic summary or individual case-specific (line-listed) formats via the National Electronic Telecommunications System for Surveillance (NETSS).

Issues Affecting Interpretation: Because of incomplete diagnosis and reporting, the number of STD cases reported to CDC undercounts the actual number of cases occurring among the U.S. population.

Reference:

> Centers for Disease Control and Prevention. Sexually Transmitted Disease Surveillance, 2004. Atlanta, GA: Department of Health and Human Services. 2005.

For More Information: See the STD Surveillance Report website: www.cdc.gov/std/stats/ or the STD Prevention website: www.cdc.gov/std/default.htm.

Surveillance, Epidemiology, and End Results Program (SEER)

National Cancer Institute

Overview: The Surveillance, Epidemiology, and End Results (SEER) program tracks incidence of persons diagnosed with cancer during the year as well as follow-up information on all previously diagnosed patients until death.

Selected Content: SEER registries routinely collect data on patient demographics, primary tumor site, morphology, stage at diagnosis, first course of treatment, and follow-up for vital status.

Data Years: Case ascertainment for SEER began on January 1, 1973, and has continued for more than 30 years.

Coverage: SEER cancer registries were initiated in 1973 in Connecticut, Iowa, New Mexico, Utah, Hawaii, Detroit, and San Francisco-Oakland. Registries were added as follows: in 1974–1975, Atlanta and Seattle-Puget Sound; in 1978, 10 predominantly black rural counties in Georgia; in 1980, American Indians in Arizona; New Orleans, Louisiana (1974–1977, rejoined 2001); New Jersey (1979–1989, rejoined 2001); and Puerto Rico (1973–1989); in 1992, Alaska Native populations in Alaska and Hispanics in Los Angeles County and San Jose-Monterey; in 2001, Kentucky, Greater California, New Jersey, and Louisiana. The SEER Program currently collects and publishes cancer incidence and survival data from 14 population-based cancer registries and three supplemental registries covering approximately 26% of the U.S. population.

To ensure continuity in reporting areas for trend data, the following combination of SEER registries are commonly used for statistical analyses and are used for analysis of cancer survival rates in *Health, United States*: the SEER 9 registries of Atlanta, Connecticut, Detroit, Hawaii, Iowa, New Mexico, San Francisco-Oakland, Seattle-Puget Sound, and Utah. Analysis of cancer incidence covers residents in the following SEER 12 registries: the SEER 9 registries plus Los Angeles, San Jose-Monterey, and the Alaska Native Tumor Registry.

Methodology: A cancer registry (or tumor registry) collects and stores data on cancers diagnosed in a specific hospital or medical facility (hospital-based registry) or in a defined geographic area (population-based registry). A population-based registry is generally composed of a number of hospital-based registries. In SEER registry areas, trained coders abstract medical records using the International Classification of Diseases for Oncology, Third Edition (ICD-O-3), which provides a coding system for onset and stage of specific cancers. The third edition, implemented in 2001, is the first complete review and revision of the text and guidelines since its original publication in 1988.

Population estimates used to calculate incidence rates are obtained from the U.S. Census Bureau. NCI uses estimation procedures as needed to obtain estimates for years and races not included in data provided by the U.S. Census Bureau. Life tables used to determine normal life expectancy when calculating relative survival rates were obtained from NCHS and in-house calculations. Separate life tables are used for each race-sex-specific group included in the SEER Program.

Issues Affecting Interpretation: Because of the addition of registries over time, analysis of long-term incidence and survival trends is limited to those registries that have been in SEER for similar lengths of time. Analysis of Hispanic, American Indian and Alaska Native data is limited to shorter trends. Rates presented in this report may differ somewhat from previous reports due to revised population estimates and the addition and deletion of small numbers of incidence cases.

Reference:

Ries LAG, Harkins D, Krapcho M, et al. (eds). SEER Cancer Statistics Review, 1975–2003, National Cancer Institute. Bethesda, MD. 2006. Available from: seer.cancer.gov/csr/1975_2003/ based on November 2005 SEER data submission.

For More Information: See the SEER website: www.seer.cancer.gov.

Survey of Mental Health Organizations (SMHO)

Substance Abuse and Mental Health Services Administration (SAMHSA)

Overview: The Survey of Mental Health Organizations and General Hospital Mental Health Services (SMHO/GHMHS) collects data on the number and characteristics of specialty mental health organizations in the United States.

Selected Content: The inventory collects basic information such as types of mental health organizations, ownership, number of additions and residents, and number of beds. The sample survey is a more detailed questionnaire that covers types of services provided, revenues and expenditures, staffing, and many items addressed to managed behavioral health care.

Data Years: The Inventory of Mental Health Organizations (IMHO/GHMHS) was conducted biannually from 1986 until 1994. The SMHO replaced the IMHO/GHMHS in 1998. The

SMHO and the inventory used as its sampling frame have been conducted biannually starting in 1998.

Coverage: Organizations included are state and county mental hospitals, private psychiatric hospitals, non-federal general hospitals with separate psychiatric services, Department of Veterans Affairs medical centers, residential treatment centers for emotionally disturbed children, freestanding outpatient psychiatric clinics, partial care organizations, freestanding day-night organizations, and multiservice mental health organizations not elsewhere classified.

Methodology: The IMHO was an inventory of all mental health organizations. Its core questionnaire included versions designed for specialty mental health organizations and another for non-federal general hospitals with separate psychiatric services. The data system was based on questionnaires mailed every other year to mental health organizations in the United States. In 1998, the IMHO was replaced by the SMHO. The SMHO is made up of two parts. A complete inventory is done by postcard gathering a limited amount of information. The inventory is used as a sampling frame for the SMHO, which contains most of the information from the IMHO core questionnaire as well as new items about managed behavioral health care.

Sample Size and Response Rate: Phase I, all organizations were inventoried by postcard (about 10,000). A complete enumeration was needed to define the sampling frame for the sample survey. In Phase II, general hospitals without separate mental health units, community residential organizations, and managed behavioral health care organizations are dropped from the sampling frame. From this number, approximately 1,600–2,200 organizations are drawn for the sample survey and sent a questionnaire with a response rate of approximately 90%.

Issues Affecting Interpretation: Revisions to definitions of providers include phasing out Community Mental Health Centers as a category after 1981–1982; increasing the number of multiservice mental health organizations from 1981 to 1986; increasing the number of psychiatric outpatient clinics in 1981–1982, but decreasing the number in 1983–1984, 1986, 1990, and 1992; and increasing the number of partial care services in 1983–1984. These changes should be noted when interyear comparisons for the affected organizations and service types are made. The increase in the number of general hospitals with separate psychiatric

services was partially due to a more concerted effort to identify these organizations. Forms had been sent only to those hospitals previously identified as having a separate psychiatric service. Beginning in 1980–1981, a screener form was sent to general hospitals not previously identified as providing a separate psychiatric service to determine whether they had such a service.

Reference:

Center for Mental Health Services. Mental Health, United States, 2002. Manderscheid R, Henderson MJ, eds. DHHS pub no (SMA) SMA04–3938. Washington, DC: Department of Health and Human Services. 2004. Available from: www.mentalhealth.samhsa.gov/ publications/allpubs/SMA04-3938.

For More Information: See the Center for Mental Health Services website: www.samhsa.gov/centers/cmhs/cmhs.html.

Survey of Occupational Injuries and Illnesses (SOII)

Bureau of Labor Statistics

Overview: The Survey of Occupational Injuries and Illnesses (SOII) is a federal/state program that collects statistics used to identify problems with workplace safety and develop programs to improve workplace safety.

Selected Content: Data include the number of injuries and illnesses by industry. The case and demographic data provide additional details on workers injured, the nature of the disabling condition, and the event and source producing that condition for those cases that involve one or more days away from work.

Data Years: The Bureau of Labor Statistics (BLS) has conducted an annual survey since 1971.

Coverage: The data represent persons employed in private industry establishments in the United States. The survey excludes the self-employed, farms with fewer than 11 employees, private households, federal government agencies, and state and local government agencies.

Methodology: Survey estimates of occupational injuries and illnesses are based on a scientifically selected probability sample of establishments, rather than a census of all establishments. An independent sample is selected for each state and the District of Columbia that represents industries in that jurisdiction. BLS includes all the state samples in the national sample.

Establishments included in the survey are instructed in a mailed questionnaire to provide summary totals of all entries for the previous calendar year to its Log and Summary of Occupational Injuries and Illnesses (OSHA No. 200 form). In addition, from the selected establishments, approximately 550,000 injuries and illnesses with days away from work are sampled to obtain demographic and detailed case characteristic information. An occupational injury is any injury such as a cut, fracture, sprain, or amputation that results from a work-related event or from a single instantaneous exposure in the work environment. An occupational illness is any abnormal condition or disorder other than one resulting from an occupational injury, caused by exposure to factors associated with employment. It includes acute and chronic illnesses or diseases that may be caused by inhalation, absorption, ingestion, or direct contact. Prior to 2002, injury and illness cases involved days away from work, days of restricted work activity, or both (lost workday cases). Starting in 2002, injury and illness cases may involve days away from work, job transfer, or restricted work activity. Restriction may involve shortened hours, a temporary job change, or temporary restrictions on certain duties (for example, no heavy lifting) of a worker's regular job.

Sample Size and Response Rates: Employer reports were collected from about 183,700 private industry establishments in 2003. Survey response rates have typically exceeded 90%.

Issues Affecting Interpretation: The number of injuries and illnesses reported in any given year can be influenced by the level of economic activity, working conditions and work practices, worker experience and training, and number of hours worked. Long-term latent illnesses caused by exposure to carcinogens are believed to be understated in the survey's illness measures. In contrast, new illnesses such as contact dermatitis and carpal tunnel syndrome are easier to relate directly to workplace activity.

Effective January 1, 2002, the Occupational Safety and Health Administration (OSHA) revised its requirement for recording occupational injuries and illnesses. Because of the revised recordkeeping rule, the estimates from the 2002 survey are not comparable with those from previous years. See www.osha-slc.gov/recordkeeping/index.html for details about the revised recordkeeping requirements.

Data for the mining industry and for railroad activities are provided by Department of Labor's Mine Safety and Health Administration and Department of Transportation's Federal Railroad Administration. Neither of these agencies adopted the revised OSHA recordkeeping requirements for 2002. Therefore, estimates for these industries for 2002 and beyond are not comparable with estimates for other industries but are comparable with estimates for prior years. Excluded from the survey are self-employed individuals; farmers with fewer than 11 employees; private households; federal government agencies; and employees in state and local government agencies.

Beginning with the 2003 data year, SOII began using the 2002 North American Industry Classification System (NAICS) to classify industries. Prior to 2003, the program used the Standard Industrial Classification (SIC) system and the Bureau of the Census occupational classification system. Although some titles in SIC and NAICS are similar, there is limited compatibility because industry groupings are defined differently between the two systems. See Appendix II, Industry of employment.

Reference:

Bureau of Labor Statistics. Workplace Injuries and Illnesses in 2003. Washington, DC: Department of Labor. December 2004.

For More Information: See the BLS occupational safety and health website: www.bls.gov/iif/home.htm.

Youth Risk Behavior Survey (YRBS)

Centers for Disease Control and Prevention
National Center for Chronic Disease Prevention and
Health Promotion

Overview: The national Youth Risk Behavior Survey (YRBS) monitors health risk behaviors among students in grades 9–12 that contribute to morbidity and mortality in both adolescence and adulthood.

Selected Content: Data are collected on tobacco use, dietary behaviors, physical activity, alcohol and other drug use, sexual behaviors that contribute to unintended pregnancy and sexually transmitted diseases including HIV infection, and behaviors that contribute to unintentional injuries and violence.

Data Years: The national YRBS of high school students was conducted in 1990, 1991, 1993, 1995, 1997, 1999, 2001, 2003, and 2005.

Coverage: Data are representative of high school students in public and private schools in the United States.

Methodology: The national YRBS school-based surveys employ a three-stage cluster sample design to produce a nationally representative sample of students in grades 9–12 attending public and private high schools. The first-stage sampling frame contains primary sampling units (PSUs) consisting of large counties or groups of smaller, adjacent counties. The PSUs are then stratified based on degree of urbanization and relative percentage of black and Hispanic students in the PSU. The PSUs are selected from these strata with probability proportional to school enrollment size. At the second sampling stage, schools are selected with probability proportional to school enrollment size. To enable separate analysis of data for black and Hispanic students, schools with substantial numbers of black and Hispanic students are sampled at higher rates than all other schools. The third stage of sampling consists of randomly selecting one or two intact classes of a required subject from grades 9–12 at each chosen school. All students in the selected classes are eligible to participate in the survey. A weighting factor is applied to each student record to adjust for nonresponse and for the varying probabilities of selection, including those resulting from the oversampling of black and Hispanic students.

Sample Size and Response Rate: The sample size for the 2005 YRBS was 13,953 students in 159 schools. The school response rate was 78% and the student response rate was 86%, for an overall response rate of 67%.

Issues Affecting Interpretation: National YRBS data are subject to at least two limitations. First, these data apply only to adolescents who attend regular high school. These students may not be representative of all persons in this age group because those who have dropped out of high school or attend an alternative high school are not surveyed. Second, the extent of underreporting or overreporting cannot be determined, although the survey questions demonstrate good test-retest reliability.

Estimates of substance use for youth based on the YRBS differ from the National Survey on Drug Use & Health (NSDUH) and Monitoring the Future (MTF). Rates are not directly comparable across these surveys because of

differences in populations covered, sample design, questionnaires, interview setting, and statistical approaches to make the survey estimates generalizable to the entire population. The NSDUH survey collects data in homes, whereas the MTF and YRBS collect data in school classrooms. The NSDUH estimates are tabulated by age, while the MTF and YRBS estimates are tabulated by grade, representing different ages as well as different populations.

References:

Brener ND, Kann L, Kinchen S, et al. Methodology of the Youth Risk Behavior Surveillance System. MMWR 2004;53(RR-12):1–13.

Eaton DK, Kann L, Kinchen S, et al. Youth Risk Behavior Surveillance—United States, 2005. In: *Surveillance Summaries* June 9, 2006. MMWR 2006;55(SS-5):1–108.

Cowan CD. Coverage, Sample Design, and Weighting in Three Federal Surveys. Journal of Drug Issues 2004;1(3):595–614.

For More Information: See the Division of Adolescent and School Health website: www.cdc.gov/HealthyYouth/index.htm.

Private and Global Sources

Alan Guttmacher Institute Abortion Provider Survey

The Alan Guttmacher Institute (AGI), a not-for-profit organization focused on reproductive health research, policy analysis, and public education, conducts periodic surveys of abortion providers to provide nationally representative statistics on abortion incidence.

Number of induced abortions; number, types, and locations of providers; and types of procedures performed, are presented by state and region. *Health, United States* presents the total for each data year. Thirteen provider surveys have been conducted for selected data years 1973 to midyear 2001. Data were collected from clinics, physicians, and hospitals identified as potential providers of abortion services. Mailed questionnaires were sent to all potential providers, with two additional mailings and telephone follow-up for nonresponse. No surveys were conducted in 1983, 1986, 1989, 1990, 1993, 1994, 1997, or 1998. For 1999–2000, a version of the survey questionnaire was created for each of the three major categories of providers, modeled on the survey questionnaire used for AGI's data collection in 1997. All surveys asked the number of induced abortions performed at the provider's location. State health statistics agencies were contacted, requesting all available data reported by providers to each state health agency on the number of abortions performed in the survey year. For states that provided data to AGI, the health agency figures were used for providers who did not respond to the survey. Estimates of the number of abortions performed by some providers were ascertained from knowledgeable sources in the community.

Of the 2,442 potential providers surveyed for 1999–2000, 1,931 performed abortions between January 1999 and June 2001. Of abortions reported for data year 2000, 77% were reported by providers, 10% came from health department data, 11% were estimated by knowledgeable sources, and 2% were projections or other estimates.

To estimate the number of abortions performed in 2001 and 2002, AGI first estimated the change in the number of abortions between 2000 and 2001, beginning with the number of abortions occurring in each state, as reported by the CDC, in each of those two years. The three states without reporting systems were excluded. AGI also eliminated the states with very incomplete or inconsistent reporting (Arizona, Maryland, Nevada, and the District of Columbia). AGI summed the number of abortions that took place in the 44 remaining states for each year. The percentage change between 2000 and 2001 was then applied to AGI's more complete nationwide count of 1,312,990 abortions in 2000 to arrive at the national estimate for 2001. The same procedure was used to estimate the change in the number of abortions between 2001 and 2002, except that the data for both years were collected directly from state health departments because the CDC abortion surveillance report for 2002 was not yet available. For 2002, no data were available for Wyoming (in addition to the states with no reporting systems), and AGI eliminated Arizona, Colorado, the District of Columbia, and Maryland because of inconsistent reporting. AGI used the remaining 43 states for the calculations.

The number of abortions estimated by AGI through the mid- to late-1980s was about 20% higher than the number reported to CDC. Between 1989 and 1997 the AGI estimates were about 12% higher than those reported by CDC. Beginning in 1998, health departments of four states did not report abortion data to CDC. The four reporting areas (the largest of which is California) that did not report abortions to CDC in 1998 accounted for 18% of all abortions tallied by AGI's 1995–1996 survey. FDA approval of Mifepristone (medical abortion) in September of 2000 accounted for a small proportion (approximately 6%) of abortions performed in nonhospital facilities during the first half of 2001.

References:

Finer LB, Henshaw SK. Abortion incidence and services in the United States in 2000. Perspect Sex Reprod Health 2003;35(1):6–15.

Finer LB, Henshaw SK. Estimates of U.S. Abortion Incidence in 2001 and 2002. The Alan Guttmacher Institute. May 2005. Available from: www.guttmacher.org/pubs/2005/05/18/ab_incidence.pdf.

For More Information: See the AGI website: www.guttmacher.org or write to The Alan Guttmacher Institute, 120 Wall Street, New York, NY 10005.

American Association of Colleges of Osteopathic Medicine

The American Association of Colleges of Osteopathic Medicine (AACOM), founded in 1898, compiles data on various aspects of osteopathic medical education for distribution to the profession, the government, and the public. Questionnaires are sent annually to schools of osteopathic medicine requesting information on characteristics of applicants, students, and graduates, faculty, curriculum, contract and grant activity, revenues and expenditures, and clinical facilities. The response rate is 100%.

For more information: See 2004 Annual Report on Osteopathic Medical Education. American Association of Colleges of Osteopathic Medicine: 5550 Friendship Boulevard, Suite 310, Chevy Chase, Maryland 20815; or see the AACOM website. Available from www.aacom.org.

American Association of Colleges of Pharmacy

The American Association of Colleges of Pharmacy (AACP) compiles data on the Colleges of Pharmacy, including information on student enrollment and types of degrees conferred. Data are collected through an annual survey; the response rate is 100%.

For More Information: See Fall 2005 Profile of Pharmacy Students. The American Association of Colleges of Pharmacy, 1426 Prince Street, Alexandria, VA; or the AACP website: www.aacp.org.

American Association of Colleges of Podiatric Medicine

The American Association of Colleges of Podiatric Medicine (AACPM) compiles data on the Colleges of Podiatric Medicine, including information on the schools and enrollment. Data are collected annually through written questionnaires. The response rate is 100%.

For More Information: Write to The American Association of Colleges of Podiatric Medicine, 15850 Crabbs Branch Way, Suite 320, Rockville, MD 20855; or see the AACPM website: www.aacpm.org.

American Dental Association

The Division of Educational Measurement of the American Dental Association (ADA) conducts annual surveys of predoctoral dental educational institutions. The questionnaire, mailed to all dental schools, collects information on student characteristics, financial management, and curricula.

For More Information: See the American Dental Association, *2003–2004 Survey of Dental Education, vol.1, Academic Programs, Enrollments, and Graduates,* Chicago. 2005 or the ADA website: www.ada.org.

American Hospital Association Annual Survey of Hospitals

Data from the American Hospital Association (AHA) annual survey are based on questionnaires sent to all AHA-registered and nonregistered hospitals in the United States and its associated areas. U.S. government hospitals located outside the United States are excluded. Overall, the average response rate over the past 5 years has been approximately 83%. For nonreporting hospitals and for the survey questionnaires of reporting hospitals on which some information was missing, estimates are made for all data except those on beds, bassinets, and facilities. Data for beds and bassinets of nonreporting hospitals are based on the most recent information available from those hospitals. Data for facilities and services are based only on reporting hospitals.

Estimates of other types of missing data are based on data reported the previous year, if available. When unavailable, estimates are based on data furnished by reporting hospitals similar in size, control, major service provided, length of stay, and geographic and demographic characteristics.

For More Information: Write to the AHA Annual Survey of Hospitals, Health Forum, LLC, an American Hospital Association Company, One North Franklin Street, Chicago, IL 60606; or see the AHA website: www.aha.org/aha/index.jsp.

American Medical Association Physician Masterfile

A masterfile of physicians has been maintained by the American Medical Association (AMA) since 1906. The Physician Masterfile contains data on all physicians in the United States, both members and nonmembers of the AMA, and on those graduates of American medical schools temporarily practicing overseas. The file also includes information on international medical graduates (IMGs), who are graduates of foreign medical schools who reside in the United States and who meet education standards for primary recognition as physicians.

A file is initiated on each individual upon entry into medical school or, in the case of IMGs, upon entry into the United States. Between 1965 and 1985, a mail questionnaire survey was conducted every 4 years to update the file information on professional activities, self-designated area of specialization, and present employment status. Since 1985, approximately one-third of all physicians are surveyed each year.

For More Information: See Division of Survey and Data Resources, American Medical Association, Physician Characteristics and Distribution in the U.S., 2006 ed. Chicago, IL. 2005; or the AMA website: www.ama-assn.org/.

Association of American Medical Colleges

The Association of American Medical Colleges (AAMC) collects information on student enrollment in medical schools through the annual Liaison Committee on Medical Education questionnaire, the fall enrollment questionnaire, and the American Medical College Application Service (AMCAS) data system. Other data sources are the institutional profile system, the premedical students questionnaire, the minority student opportunities in medicine questionnaire, the faculty roster system, data from the Medical College Admission Test, and one-time surveys developed for special projects.

For More Information: See the Association of American Medical Colleges, Statistical Information Related to Medical Schools and Teaching Hospitals, Washington, DC. 2005; or the AAMC website: www.aamc.org.

Association of Schools and Colleges of Optometry

The Association of Schools and Colleges of Optometry (ASCO) compiles data on various aspects of optometric education including data on schools and enrollment. Questionnaires are sent annually to all schools and colleges of optometry. The response rate is 100%.

For More Information: Write to the Annual Survey of Optometric Educational Institutions, Association of Schools and Colleges of Optometry, 6110 Executive Blvd., Suite 510, Rockville, MD 20852; or see the ASCO website: www.opted.org.

Association of Schools of Public Health

The Association of Schools of Public Health (ASPH) compiles data on schools of public health in the United States and Puerto Rico. Questionnaires are sent annually to all member schools. The response rate is 100%.

Unlike health professional schools that emphasize specific clinical occupations, schools of public health offer study in specialty areas such as biostatistics, epidemiology, environmental health, occupational health, health administration, health planning, nutrition, maternal and child health, social and behavioral sciences, and other population-based sciences.

For More Information: Write to the Association of Schools of Public Health, 1101 15th Street, NW, Suite 910, Washington, DC 20005; or see the ASPH website: www.asph.org.

European Health for All Database

World Health Organization Regional Office for Europe

The WHO Regional Office for Europe (WHO/Europe) provides country-specific and topic-specific health information via the Internet for people who influence health policy in the WHO European Region and the media.

WHO/Europe collects statistics on health and makes them widely available through

■ European Health for all Database (www.euro.who.int/hfadb) (HFA-DB), which contains data on about 600 health indicators collected from national counterparts in 52 European countries, and data from other WHO technical programs and some international organizations.

■ Highlights on Health (www.euro.who.int/InformationSources/ Evidence/20011015_1) from countries in the WHO European Region that give an overview of the health situation in each country in comparison with other countries. Highlights complement the public health reports produced by a number of member states in the region.

■ Health Status Overview for Countries of Central and Eastern Europe (www.euro.who.int/Document/E76888.pdf) that are candidates for accession to the European Union (Bulgaria, the Czech Republic, Estonia, Hungary, Latvia, Lithuania, Poland, Romania, Slovakia, and Slovenia).

WHO/Europe helps countries strengthen their national health information systems, particularly by supporting

■ development of National Health Indicator Databases (www.euro.who.int/eprise/main/WHO/Progs/HIS/products/ 20020514_2)

■ exchange of experience on national public health reports between countries; a database of public health reports is maintained and available for consultation and networking

■ implementation of International Classifications (www.who.int/whosis/en/) and definitions in countries

■ Regional Networks (www.euro.who.int/main/WHO/Home/ TopPage) of health information professionals

For More Information: See the European health for all database: data.euro.who.int/hfadb/.

InterStudy National Health Maintenance Organization Census

From 1976 to 1980, the Office of Health Maintenance Organizations conducted a census of health maintenance organizations (HMOs). Since 1981, InterStudy has conducted the census. A questionnaire is sent to all HMOs in the United States asking for updated enrollment, profit status, and federal qualification status. New HMOs are also asked to provide information on model type. When necessary, information is obtained, supplemented, or clarified by telephone. For nonresponding HMOs state-supplied information or the most current available data are used.

In 1985, a large increase in the number of HMOs and enrollment was partly attributable to a change in the categories of HMOs included in the census: Medicaid-only and Medicare-only HMOs were added. Component HMOs, which have their own discrete management, could be listed separately, whereas previously the oldest HMO reported for all of its component or expansion sites, even when the components had different operational dates or were different model types.

For More Information: See Waller RL, et al. The HealthLeaders-InterStudy Competitive Edge, September 2005, Part II: Managed Care Industry Report. Nashville, TN. Available from: www.healthleaders.com.

National League for Nursing

The division of research of the National League for Nursing (NLN) conducts The Annual Survey of Schools of Nursing in October of each year. Questionnaires are sent to all graduate nursing programs (master's and doctoral), baccalaureate programs designed exclusively for registered nurses, basic registered nursing programs (baccalaureate, associate degree, and diploma), and licensed practical nursing programs. Data on enrollments, first-time admissions, and graduates are completed for all nursing education programs. Response rates of approximately 80% are achieved for other areas of inquiry.

For More Information: See the NLN website: www.nln.org.

Organisation for Economic Co-operation and Development Health Data

The Organisation for Economic Co-operation and Development (OECD) provides annual data on statistical indicators on health and health systems collected from 30 member countries, with some time series going back to 1960. The international comparability of health expenditure estimates depends on the quality of national health accounts in OECD member countries. In recent years, an increasing number of countries have adopted the standards for health accounting defined by OECD, greatly increasing the comparability of national health expenditure data reporting. Additional limitations in international comparisons include differing boundaries between health care and other social care, particularly for the disabled and elderly, and underestimation of private expenditures on health.

The OECD was established in 1961 with a mandate to promote policies to achieve the highest sustainable economic growth and a rising standard of living among member countries. The Organisation now comprises 30 member countries: Australia, Austria, Belgium, Canada, Czech Republic, Denmark, Finland, France, Germany, Greece, Hungary, Iceland, Ireland, Italy, Japan, Korea, Luxembourg, Mexico, the Netherlands, New Zealand, Norway, Poland, Portugal, Slovak Republic, Spain, Sweden, Switzerland, Turkey, the United Kingdom, and the United States.

As part of its mission, the OECD has developed a number of activities in relation to health and health care systems. The main aim of OECD work on health policy is to conduct cross-national studies of the performance of OECD health systems and to facilitate exchanges between member countries of their experiences of financing, delivering, and managing health services. To support this work, each year the OECD compiles cross-country data in OECD Health Data, one of the most comprehensive sources of comparable health-related statistics. OECD Health Data is an essential tool to carry out comparative analyses and draw lessons from international comparisons of diverse health care systems. This international database now incorporates the first results arising from the implementation of the OECD manual, A System of Health Accounts (2000), which provide a standard framework for producing a set of comprehensive, consistent, and internationally comparable data on health spending. The OECD collaborates with other international organizations such as the WHO.

For More Information: See the OECD website: www.oecd.org/health.

United Nations Demographic Yearbook

The Statistical Office of the United Nations prepares the *Demographic Yearbook*, a comprehensive collection of international demographic statistics.

Questionnaires are sent annually and monthly to more than 220 national statistical services and other appropriate government offices. Data from these questionnaires are supplemented, to the extent possible, by data taken from official national publications and by correspondence with the national statistical services. To ensure comparability, rates, ratios, and percents have been calculated in the statistical office of the United Nations.

Lack of international comparability among estimates arises from differences in concepts, definitions, and time of data collection. The comparability of population data is affected by several factors, including (a) definitions of the total population, (b) definitions used to classify the population into its urban and rural components, (c) difficulties relating to age reporting, (d) extent of over- or underenumeration, and (e) quality of population estimates. The completeness and accuracy of vital statistics data also vary from one country to another.

Differences in statistical definitions of vital events may also influence comparability.

International demographic trend data are available on a CD-ROM entitled United Nations, 2000. Demographic Yearbook—Historical Supplement 1948–1997. CD-ROM Special Issue. United Nations publication sales number E/F.99.XIII.12.

For More Information: See the United Nations, Statistics Division website: unstats.un.org/unsd/demographic/products/dyb/dyb2.htm.

World Health Organization Statistical Information System (WHOSIS)

World Health Organization

WHO Statistical Information System (WHOSIS) is a guide to health and health-related epidemiological and statistical information from the World Health Organization. Statistics are listed by country or region and by topic. WHOSIS contains the following databases: Core Health Indicators for 192 countries; World Health Statistics 2005; Statistics from WHO Regional Offices; Statistics by country or region; Burden of Disease statistics; and Family of International Classifications.

For More Information: See the World Health Organization, *World Health Statistics Annual 2005:* www3.who.int/statistics/; or the WHO website: www.who.int/en/.

Appendix II

Definitions and Methods

Appendix II is an alphabetical listing of terms used in *Health, United States*. It includes cross-references to related terms and synonyms. It also describes the methods used for calculating age-adjusted rates, average annual rates of change, relative standard errors, birth rates, death rates, and years of potential life lost. Appendix II includes standard populations used for age adjustment (Tables I, II, and III); *International Classification of Diseases* (ICD) codes for cause of death from the Sixth through Tenth Revisions and the years when the Revisions were in effect (Tables IV and V); comparability ratios between ICD–9 and ICD–10 for selected causes (Table VI); ICD–9–CM codes for external cause of injury, diagnostic, and procedure categories (Tables VII, X, and XI); classification of generic analgesic drugs (Table XII); and industry codes from the North American Industry Classification System (NAICS) that has replaced the Standard Industrial Classification (SIC) system (Table IX). Standards for presenting federal data on race and ethnicity are described, and sample tabulations of National Health Interview Survey (NHIS) data comparing the 1977 and 1997 Standards for the Classification of Federal Data on Race and Ethnicity are presented in Tables XIII and XIV. New this year is a table on the effects of adding probe questions for Medicare and Medicaid coverage on health insurance rates in the National Health Interview Survey (Table VIII).

Acquired immunodeficiency syndrome (AIDS)—Human immunodeficiency virus (HIV) disease is the pathogen that causes AIDS and encompasses all the condition's stages, from infection to the deterioration of the immune system and the onset of opportunistic diseases. However, AIDS is still the name that most people use to refer to the immune deficiency caused by HIV. An AIDS diagnosis (indicating that the person has reached the late stages of the disease) is given to people with HIV who have counts below 200 CD4+ cells/mm3 (also known as T cells or T4 cells, which are the main target of HIV) or when they become diagnosed with at least one of a set of opportunistic diseases. All 50 states and the District of Columbia report AIDS cases to CDC using a uniform surveillance case definition and case report form. The case reporting definitions were expanded in 1985 (MMWR 1985; 34:373–5); 1987 (MMWR 1987; 36 (No. SS-1):1S–15S); 1993

for adults and adolescents (MMWR 1992; 41 (no. RR-17): 1–19); and 1994 for pediatric cases (MMWR 1994; 43 (no. RR-12):1–19). The revisions incorporated a broader range of AIDS-indicator diseases and conditions and used HIV diagnostic tests to improve the sensitivity and specificity of the definition. The 1993 expansion of the case definition caused a temporary distortion of AIDS incidence trends. In 1995 new treatments (protease inhibitors) for HIV and AIDS were approved. These therapies have prevented or delayed the onset of AIDS and premature death among many HIV-infected persons, which should be considered when interpreting trend data. AIDS surveillance data are published annually by CDC in the HIV/AIDS Surveillance Report. Available from: www.cdc.gov/hiv/topics/surveillance/resources/reports/index.htm. See related Human immunodeficiency virus (HIV) disease.

Active physician—See Physician.

Activities of daily living (ADL)—Activities of daily living are activities related to personal care and include bathing or showering, dressing, getting in or out of bed or a chair, using the toilet, and eating. In the National Health Interview Survey, respondents were asked whether they or family members 3 years of age and over need the help of another person with personal care because of a physical, mental, or emotional problem. Persons are considered to have an ADL limitation if any condition(s) causing the respondent to need help with the specific activities was chronic.

In the Medicare Current Beneficiary Survey, if a sample person had any difficulty performing an activity by him or herself and without special equipment, or did not perform the activity at all because of health problems, the person was categorized as having a limitation in that activity. The limitation may have been temporary or chronic at the time of the interview. Sampled people who were administered a community interview answered health status and functioning questions themselves, if able to do so. A proxy such as a nurse answered questions about the sample person's health status and functioning for those in a long-term care facility. Beginning in 1997, interview questions for people residing in long-term care facilities were changed slightly from those administered to people living in the community to differentiate residents who were independent from those who received supervision or assistance with transferring, locomotion on unit, dressing, eating, toilet use, and bathing. See related Condition; Instrumental activities of daily living (IADL); Limitation of activity.

Table I. United States standard population and age groups used to age adjust data

Data system and age	Number
DVS mortality data	
Total	274,633,642
Under 1 year	3,794,901
1–4 years	15,191,619
5–14 years	39,976,619
15–24 years	38,076,743
25–34 years	37,233,437
35–44 years	44,659,185
45–54 years	37,030,152
55–64 years	23,961,506
65–74 years	18,135,514
75–84 years	12,314,793
85 years and over	4,259,173
NHIS, NAMCS, NHAMCS, NNHS, and NHDS	
All ages	274,633,642
18 years and over	203,852,188
25 years and over	177,593,760
40 years and over	118,180,367
65 years and over	34,709,480
Under 18 years	70,781,454
2–17 years	63,227,991
18–44 years	108,151,050
18–24 years	26,258,428
25–34 years	37,233,437
35–44 years	44,659,185
45–64 years	60,991,658
45–54 years	37,030,152
55–64 years	23,961,506
65–74 years	18,135,514
75 years and over	16,573,966
18–49 years	127,956,843
40–64 years:	
40–49 years	42,285,022
50–64 years	41,185,865
NHES and NHANES	
20 years and over	195,850,985
20–74 years	179,277,019
20–34 years	55,490,662
35–44 years	44,659,185
45–54 years	37,030,152
55–64 years	23,961,506
65–74 years	18,135,514
or	
65 years and over	34,709,480

See footnotes at end of table.

Table I. United States standard population and age groups used to age adjust data—Con.

NHANES (Table 71 only)	
20–39 years	77,670,618
40–59 years	72,816,615
60–74 years	28,789,786
NHANES (Table 93 only)	
Under 18 years	70,781,454
18–44 years	108,151,050
45–64 years	60,991,658
65 years and over	34,709,480

SOURCE: National Institutes of Health, National Cancer Institute, Surveillance, Epidemiology, and End Results (SEER). Standard population - single ages. Available from: seer.cancer.gov/stdpopulations/ stdpop.singleages.html.

Addition—See Admission.

Admission—The American Hospital Association defines admissions as persons, excluding newborns, accepted for inpatient services during the survey reporting period. See related Days of care; Discharge; Inpatient.

An admission (also sometimes referred to as an addition) to a mental health organization is defined by the Substance Abuse and Mental Health Services Administration's Center for Mental Health Services as a new admission, a re-admission, a return from long-term leave, or a transfer from another service of the same organization or another organization. See related Mental health organization; Mental health service type.

Age—Age is reported as age at last birthday, that is, age in completed years, often calculated by subtracting date of birth from the reference date, with the reference date being the date of the examination, interview, or other contact with an individual.

Mother's (maternal) age is reported on the birth certificate by all states. Birth statistics are presented for mothers age 10–49 years through 1996 and 10–54 years starting in 1997, based on mother's date of birth or age as reported on the birth certificate. The age of mother is edited for upper and lower limits. When the age of the mother is computed to be under 10 years or 55 years or over (50 years or over in 1964–1996), it is considered not stated and imputed according to the age of the mother from the previous birth record of the same race and total birth order (total of fetal deaths and live births). Before 1963, not stated ages were distributed in proportion to the known ages for each racial group. Beginning in 1997, the birth rate for the maternal age group 45–49 years includes data for mothers age 50–54 years in the numerator and is based on the population of women 45–49 years in the denominator.

Age adjustment—Age adjustment is used to compare risks of two or more populations at one point in time or one population at two or more points in time. Age-adjusted rates are computed by the direct method by applying age-specific rates in a population of interest to a standardized age distribution, to eliminate differences in observed rates that result from age differences in population composition. Age-adjusted rates should be viewed as relative indexes rather than actual measures of risk.

Age-adjusted rates are calculated by the direct method as follows:

$$\sum_{i=1}^{n} r_i \times (p_i / P)$$

where r_i = rate in age group i in the population of interest

p_i = standard population in age group i

$$P = \sum_{i=1}^{n} p_i$$

n = total number of age groups over the age range of the age-adjusted rate

Age adjustment by the direct method requires use of a standard age distribution. The standard for age adjusting death rates and estimates from surveys in *Health, United States* is the projected year 2000 U.S. resident population. Starting with *Health, United States, 2000*, the year 2000 U.S. standard population replaced the 1970 civilian noninstitutionalized population for age adjusting estimates from most NCHS surveys and starting with *Health, United States, 2001* it was used uniformly and replaced the 1940 U.S. population for age adjusting mortality statistics and the 1980 U.S. resident population, which previously had been used for age adjusting estimates from the NHANES surveys.

Changing the standard population has implications for racial and ethnic differentials in mortality. For example, the mortality ratio for the black to white populations is reduced from 1.6

using the 1940 standard to 1.4 using the 2000 standard, reflecting the greater weight that the 2000 standard gives to the older population where race differentials in mortality are smaller.

Age-adjusted estimates from any data source presented in *Health, United States* may differ from age-adjusted estimates based on the same data presented in other reports if different age groups are used in the adjustment procedure.

For more information on implementing the 2000 population standard for age adjusting death rates, see Anderson RN, Rosenberg HM. Age standardization of death rates: Implementation of the year 2000 standard. National vital statistics reports 1998; 47 (3), Hyattsville, MD: National Center for Health Statistics. For more information on the derivation of age adjustment weights for use with NCHS survey data, see Klein RJ, Schoenborn CA. Age adjustment using the 2000 projected U.S. population. Healthy People Statistical Notes no. 20. Hyattsville, MD: National Center for Health Statistics. 2001. Both reports are available from the NCHS home page: www.cdc.gov/nchs. The year 2000 U.S. standard population is available from the National Cancer Institute, Surveillance, Epidemiology, and End Results, seer.cancer.gov/stdpopulations/stdpop.singleages.html.

Mortality data—Death rates are age adjusted to the year 2000 U.S. standard population (Table I). Prior to 2003 data, age-adjusted rates were calculated using standard million proportions based on rounded population numbers (Table II). Starting with 2003 data, unrounded population numbers are used to age adjust. Adjustment is based on 11 age groups with two exceptions. First, age-adjusted death rates for black males and black females in 1950 are based on nine age groups, with under 1 year and 1–4 years of age combined as one group and 75–84 years and 85 years of age and over combined as one group. Second, age-adjusted death rates by educational attainment for the age group 25–64 years are based on four 10-year age groups (25–34 years, 35–44 years, 45–54 years, and 55–64 years).

Age-adjusted rates for years of potential life lost before age 75 years also use the year 2000 standard population and are based on eight age groups (under 1 year, 1–14 years, 15–24 years, and 10-year age groups through 65–74 years).

Table II. United States standard population and proportion distribution by age, for age adjusting death rates prior to 2003

Age	Population	Proportion distribution (weights)	Standard million
Total.	274,634,000	1.000000	1,000,000
Under 1 year.	3,795,000	0.013818	13,818
1–4 years.	15,192,000	0.055317	55,317
5–14 years	39,977,000	0.145565	145,565
15–24 years	38,077,000	0.138646	138,646
25–34 years	37,233,000	0.135573	135,573
35–44 years	44,659,000	0.162613	162,613
45–54 years	37,030,000	0.134834	134,834
55–64 years	23,961,000	0.087247	87,247
65–74 years	18,136,000	0.066037	66,037
75–84 years	12,315,000	†0.044842	44,842
85 years and over	4,259,000	0.015508	15,508

† Figure is rounded up instead of down to force total to 1.0.

SOURCE: Anderson RN, Rosenberg HM. Age standardization of death rates: Implementation of the year 2000 standard. National vital statistics reports; vol 47 no. 3. Hyattsville, MD: National Center for Health Statistics. 1998.

Maternal mortality rates for pregnancy, childbirth, and the puerperium are calculated as the number of deaths per 100,000 live births. These rates are age adjusted to the 1970 distribution of live births by mother's age in the United States as shown in Table III. See related Rate: Death and related rates; Years of potential life lost.

National Health and Nutrition Examination Survey— Estimates based on the National Health Examination Survey and the National Health and Nutrition Examination Survey are age adjusted to the year 2000 U.S. standard population generally using five age groups: 20–34 years, 35–44 years, 45–54 years, 55–64 years, and 65–74 years or 65 years and over (see Table I). Prior to *Health, United States, 2001*, these estimates were age adjusted to the 1980 U.S. resident population.

National Health Care Surveys—Estimates based on the National Hospital Discharge Survey, the National Ambulatory Medical Care Survey, the National Hospital Ambulatory Medical Care Survey, and the National Nursing Home Survey are age adjusted to the year 2000 U.S. standard population (Table I). Information on the age groups used in the age adjustment procedure is contained in the footnotes to the relevant tables.

National Health Interview Survey—Estimates based on the National Health Interview Survey are age adjusted to

the year 2000 U.S. standard population (Table I). Prior to the 2000 edition of *Health, United States*, National Health Interview Survey estimates were age adjusted to the 1970 civilian noninstitutionalized population. Information on the age groups used in the age adjustment procedure is contained in the footnotes to the relevant tables.

AIDS—See Acquired immunodeficiency syndrome.

Alcohol consumption—Alcohol consumption is measured differently in various data systems. See related Binge drinking.

Monitoring the Future Study—This school-based survey of secondary school students collects information on alcohol use using self-completed questionnaires. Information on consumption of alcoholic beverages, defined as beer, wine, wine coolers, and liquor, is based on the following question: "On how many occasions (if any) have you had alcohol to drink—more than just a few sips—in the last 30 days?" Students responding affirmatively are then asked "How many times have you had five or more drinks in a row in the last 2 weeks?" For this question, a "drink" means a 12-ounce can (or bottle) of beer, a 4-ounce glass of wine, a 12-ounce bottle or can of wine cooler, or a mixed drink or a shot of liquor.

Table III. Number of live births and mother's age group used to adjust maternal mortality rates to live births in the United States in 1970

Mother's age	Number
All ages.	3,731,386
Under 20 years	656,460
20–24 years.	1,418,874
25–29 years.	994,904
30–34 years.	427,806
35 years and over	233,342

SOURCE: Summary report final natality statistics, 1970. Monthly vital statistics report; vol 22 no 12, supp. Hyattsville, MD: National Center for Health Statistics. 1974.

National Health Interview Survey (NHIS)—Starting with the 1997 NHIS, information on alcohol consumption is collected in the sample adult questionnaire. Adult respondents are asked two screening questions about their lifetime alcohol consumption: "In any one year, have you had at least 12 drinks of any type of alcoholic beverage? In your entire life, have you had at least 12 drinks of any type of alcoholic beverage?" Persons who report at least 12 drinks in a lifetime are then asked a series of questions about alcohol consumption in the past year: "In the past year, how often did you drink any type of alcoholic beverage? In the past year, on those days that you drank alcoholic beverages, on the average, how many drinks did you have?"

National Survey on Drug Use and Health (NSDUH)—Starting in 1999, NSDUH information about the frequency of the consumption of alcoholic beverages in the past 30 days has been obtained for all persons surveyed who are 12 years of age and over. An extensive list of examples of the kinds of beverages covered was given to respondents prior to the question administration. A drink is defined as a can or bottle of beer, a glass of wine or a wine cooler, a shot of liquor, or a mixed drink with liquor in it. Those times when the respondent had only a sip or two from a drink are not considered consumption. Alcohol use is based on the following questions: "During the past 30 days, on how many days did you drink one or more drinks of an alcoholic beverage?" "On the days that you drank during the past 30 days, how many drinks did you usually have?" and "During the past 30 days, on how many days did you have five or more drinks on the same occasion?"

Youth Risk Behavior Survey (YRBS)—Starting in 1991, the YRBS has collected information on alcohol use among high school students. Questions on alcohol use have the following introduction: "The next five questions ask about drinking alcohol. This includes drinking beer, wine, wine coolers, and liquor such as rum, gin, vodka, or whiskey. For these questions, drinking alcohol does not include drinking a few sips of wine for religious purposes." Alcohol use is based on the questions that follow, including: "During the past 30 days, on how many days did you have at least one drink of alcohol?"

Any-listed diagnosis—See Diagnosis.

Average annual rate of change (percentage change)—In *Health, United States* average annual rates of change or growth rates are calculated as follows:

$$[(P_n / P_o)^{1/N} - 1] \times 100$$

where P_n = later time period

P_o = earlier time period

N = number of years in interval.

This geometric rate of change assumes that a variable increases or decreases at the same rate during each year between the two time periods.

Average length of stay—In the National Health Interview Survey, average length of stay in a hospital per discharged inpatient is computed by dividing the total number of hospital days for a specified group by the total number of discharges for that group. Similarly, in the National Hospital Discharge Survey, average length of stay is computed by dividing the total number of hospital days of care, counting the date of admission but not the date of discharge, by the number of patients discharged. The American Hospital Association computes average length of stay by dividing the number of inpatient days by the number of admissions. See related Days of care; Discharge; Inpatient.

Bed, health facility—The American Hospital Association defines the bed count as the number of beds, cribs, and pediatric bassinets that are set up and staffed for use by inpatients on the last day of the reporting period. In the Center for Medicare & Medicaid Service's Online Survey Certification and Reporting (OSCAR) database, all beds in certified facilities are counted on the day of certification inspection. The World Health Organization defines a hospital bed as one regularly maintained and staffed for the accommodation and full-time care of a succession of inpatients and situated in a part of the hospital where continuous medical care for inpatients is provided. The Center for Mental Health Services within the Substance Abuse and Mental Health Services Administration counts the number of beds set up and staffed for use in inpatient and residential treatment services on the last day of the survey reporting period. See related Hospital; Mental health organization; Mental health service type; Occupancy rate.

Binge drinking—Binge drinking and binge alcohol use are measured in three different data systems. See related Alcohol consumption.

Monitoring the Future Survey—This school-based survey of secondary school students collects information on alcohol use using self-completed questionnaires. Information on binge drinking is obtained for high school seniors (starting in 1975) and 8th and 10th graders (starting in 1991) based on the following question for the prior two-week period: "How many times have you had five or more drinks in a row?"

National Health Interview Survey—Information about binge alcohol use is defined as "In the past year, on how many days did you have five or more drinks of any alcoholic beverage?"

National Survey on Drug Use and Health (NSDUH)—Information about binge alcohol use, defined as "Five or more drinks on the same occasion (i.e., at the same time or within a couple of hours of each other) at least once in the past 30 days." Heavy alcohol use is defined as "Five or more drinks on the same occasion (binge drinking) on at least 5 different days in the past 30 days."

Birth cohort—A birth cohort consists of all persons born within a given period of time, such as a calendar year.

Birth rate—See Rate: Birth and related rates.

Birthweight—Birthweight is the first weight of the newborn obtained after birth. Low birthweight is defined as less than 2,500 grams or 5 pounds 8 ounces. Very low birthweight is defined as less than 1,500 grams or 3 pounds 4 ounces.

Before 1979, low birthweight was defined as 2,500 grams or less and very low birthweight as 1,500 grams or less.

Blood pressure, elevated—In *Health, United States*, elevated blood pressure or hypertension is defined as having an average systolic blood pressure reading of at least 140 mmHg or diastolic pressure of at least 90 mmHg, which is consistent with the Seventh Report of the Joint National Committee on Prevention, Detection, Evaluation, and Treatment of High Blood Pressure (available from: www.nhlbi.nih.gov/guidelines/hypertension/jnc7full.pdf). People are also considered to have hypertension if they report that they are taking a prescription medicine for high blood pressure, even if their blood pressure readings are within normal range.

Blood pressure is measured by averaging the blood pressure readings taken. Blood pressure readings of 0mmHg are assumed to be in error and are not included in the estimates. The methods to measure the blood pressure of NHANES participants have changed over the different NHANES survey years. Changes include:

- Number of BP measures taken (from 1 to 4);
- Equipment maintenance procedures;
- Training of persons taking readings (physician, nurse, interviewer);
- Proportion zero end digits for systolic and diastolic readings;
- Published diastolic definition;
- Location where the measurements were taken (Mobile Examination Component (MEC) or home).

Blood pressure is measured in 1999 and subsequent years in the MEC of the NHANES. Participants who are 50 years and older or less than one year of age who are unable to travel to the MEC are offered an abbreviated examination in their homes. Blood pressure measurements are taken by one of the MEC examiners. For people age 20 and over, three consecutive blood pressure readings are obtained, using the same arm. If a blood pressure measurement was interrupted or the measurer was unable to get one or more of the readings, a fourth attempt may be made. Both systolic and diastolic measurements are recorded to the nearest even number.

In NHANES III, three sets of blood pressure measurements were taken in the examination center on examinees aged 5 years and over. Blood pressure measurements were also taken by trained interviewers during the household interview, on sample persons age 17 years and over. Systolic and diastolic average blood pressure were computed as the arithmetic mean of six or fewer measurements obtained at the household interview (maximum of three) and the MEC examination (maximum of three). If the examinee did not have blood pressure measurements taken in the examination center, this variable was calculated from measurements taken at the household interview. Both systolic and diastolic measurements were recorded to the nearest even number.

See Burt VL, Cutler JA, Higgings M, Horan MJ, Labarthe D, Whelton P, et al. Trends in the prevalence, awareness, treatment, and control of hypertension in the adult US population. Hypertension 1995;26(1):60–9 for more information on changes in high blood pressure measurement in the NHANES up to 1991.

Body mass index (BMI)—BMI is a measure that adjusts bodyweight for height. It is calculated as weight in kilograms divided by height in meters squared. Overweight for children and adolescents is defined as BMI at or above the sex- and age-specific 95th percentile BMI cut points from the 2000 CDC Growth Charts (www.cdc.gov/growthcharts/). Healthy weight for adults is defined as a BMI of 18.5 to less than 25; overweight, as greater than or equal to a BMI of 25; and obesity, as greater than or equal to a BMI of 30. BMI cut points are defined in the Report of the Dietary Guidelines Advisory Committee on the Dietary Guidelines for Americans, 2000. U.S. Department of Agriculture, Agricultural Research Service, Dietary Guidelines Advisory Committee, p. 23.

Available from: www.health.gov/dietaryguidelines/dgac/; NHLBI Obesity Education Initiative Expert Panel on the Identification, Evaluation, and Treatment of Overweight and Obesity in Adults. Clinical guidelines on the identification, evaluation, and treatment of overweight and obesity in adults—The evidence report. Obes Res 1998. 6:51S-209S. Available from: www.nhlbi.nih.gov/guidelines/obesity/ob_gdlns.htm; and in U.S. Department of Health and Human Services. Tracking Healthy People 2010. Washington, DC: U.S. Government Printing Office, November 2000. Objectives 19.1, 19.2, and 19.3. Available from: www.healthypeople.gov/document/html/volume2/19nutrition.htm.

Cause of death—For the purpose of national mortality statistics, every death is attributed to one underlying condition, based on information reported on the death certificate and using the international rules for selecting the underlying cause of death from the conditions stated on the death certificate. The underlying cause is defined by the World Health Organization (WHO) as the disease or injury that initiated the train of events leading directly to death, or the circumstances of the accident or violence that produced the fatal injury. Generally more medical information is reported on death certificates than is directly reflected in the underlying cause of death. The conditions that are not selected as underlying cause of death constitute the nonunderlying causes of death, also known as multiple cause of death.

Cause of death is coded according to the appropriate revision of the *International Classification of Diseases* (ICD) (see Table IV). Effective with deaths occurring in 1999, the United States began using the Tenth Revision of the ICD (ICD–10);

Table IV. Revision of the International Classification of Diseases (ICD) by year of conference by which adopted and years in use in the United States

Revision of the International Classification of Diseases	Year of conference by which adopted	Years in use in United States
First	1900	1900–1909
Second	1909	1910–1920
Third	1920	1921–1929
Fourth	1929	1930–1938
Fifth	1938	1939–1948
Sixth	1948	1949–1957
Seventh	1955	1958–1967
Eighth	1965	1968–1978
Ninth	1975	1979–1998
Tenth	1990	1999–present

SOURCE: National Center for Health Statistics. Available from: www.cdc.gov/nchs/about/major/dvs/icd9des.htm.

during the period 1979–1998, causes of death were coded and classified according to the Ninth Revision (ICD–9). Table V lists ICD codes for the Sixth through Tenth Revisions for causes of death shown in *Health, United States*.

Each of these revisions has produced discontinuities in cause-of-death trends. These discontinuities are measured using comparability ratios and are essential to the interpretation of mortality trends. For further discussion, see the Mortality Technical Appendix on the NCHS website, available from: www.cdc.gov/nchs/deaths.htm. See related Comparability ratio; *International Classification of Diseases* (ICD); Appendix I, National Vital Statistics System, Multiple Cause-of-Death File.

Cause-of-death ranking—Selected causes of death of public health and medical importance comprise tabulation lists and are ranked according to the number of deaths assigned to these causes. The top-ranking causes determine the leading causes of death. Certain causes on the tabulation lists are not ranked if, for example, the category title represents a group title (such as Major cardiovascular diseases and Symptoms, signs, and abnormal clinical and laboratory findings, not elsewhere classified); or the category title begins with the words Other and All other. In addition when one of the titles that represents a subtotal (such as malignant neoplasms) is ranked, its component parts are not ranked. The tabulation lists used for ranking in the *Tenth Revision of the International Classification of Diseases* (ICD) include the List of 113 Selected Causes of Death, which replaces the ICD–9 List of 72 Selected Causes, HIV infection and Alzheimer's disease; and the ICD–10 List of 130 Selected Causes of Infant Death, which replaces the ICD–9 List of 60 Selected Causes of Infant Death and HIV infection. Causes that are tied receive the same rank; the next cause is assigned the rank it would have received had the lower-ranked causes not been tied, that is, skip a rank. See related *International Classification of Diseases* (ICD).

Cholesterol, serum—Serum cholesterol is a measure of the total blood cholesterol. Elevated total blood cholesterol—a combination of high-density lipoproteins (HDL), low-density lipoproteins (LDL), and very-low density lipoproteins (VLDL)—is a risk factor for cardiovascular disease. According to the National Cholesterol Education Program, high serum cholesterol is defined as greater than or equal to 240 mg/dL (6.20 mmol/L). Borderline high serum cholesterol is defined as greater than or equal to 200 mg/dL and less than 240 mg/dL.

Assessments of the components of total cholesterol or lower thresholds for high total cholesterol may be used for individuals with other risk factors for cardiovascular disease. (For more information on high cholesterol guidelines, see the Third Report of the Expert Panel on Detection, Evaluation, and Treatment of High Blood Cholesterol in Adults (Adult Treatment Panel III) Full Report. Available from: www.nhlbi.nih.gov/guidelines/cholesterol/atp3_rpt.htm.) In *Health, United States*, the conservative threshold of 240 mg/dL is used to define high total serum cholesterol. Individuals who take medication to lower their serum cholesterol levels and whose measured total serum cholesterol levels are below the cut-offs for high and borderline high cholesterol, are not defined as having high or borderline cholesterol, respectively.

Venous blood serum samples that are collected from National Health and Nutrition Examination Survey (NHANES) participants at mobile examination centers are frozen and shipped on dry ice to the laboratory conducting the lipid analyses. Serum total cholesterol was measured on all examined adults regardless of whether they had fasted and data were analyzed regardless of fasting status. Cholesterol measurements are standardized according to the criteria of the CDC and later the CDC-National Heart, Lung, and Blood Institute Cholesterol Standardization Program to ensure comparable and accurate measurements (for more information, see Myers GL, Cooper GR, Winn CL, Smith SJ. The CDC-National, Heart, Lung, and Blood Institute Lipid Standardization Program. Clin Lab Med 1989;9(1):105–35). A detailed summary of the procedures used for measurement of total cholesterol in the earlier NHANES survey years has been published (see Johnson CL, Rifkind BM, Sempos CT, Carroll MD, Bachorik PS, Briefel RR, et al. Declining serum total cholesterol levels among US adults: The National Health and Nutrition Examination Surveys. JAMA 1993;269(23):3002–8.) A description of the laboratory procedures for the total cholesterol measurement for different NHANES survey years is published by NCHS. Available from: www.cdc.gov/nchs/nhanes.htm).

Chronic condition—See Condition.

Table V. Cause-of-death codes, by applicable revision of *International Classification of Diseases* (ICD)

Cause of death (Tenth Revision titles)	Sixth and Seventh Revisions	Eighth Revision	Ninth Revision	Tenth Revision
Communicable diseases	. . .	. . .	001–139, 460–466, 480–487, 771.3	A00–B99, J00–J22
Chronic and noncommunicable diseases	. . .	. . .	140–459, 470–478, 490–799	C00–I99, J30–R99
Injuries[1]	. . .	. . .	E800–E869, E880–E929, E950–E999	*U01–*U03, V01–Y36, Y85–Y87, Y89
Meningococcal Infection	. . .	. . .	036	A39
Septicemia	. . .	. . .	038	A40–A41
Human immunodeficiency virus (HIV) disease[2]	. . .	. . .	*042–*044	B20–B24
Malignant neoplasms	140–205	140–209	140–208	C00–C97
Colon, rectum, and anus	153–154	153–154	153, 154	C18–C21
Trachea, bronchus, and lung	162–163	162	162	C33–C34
Breast	170	174	174–175	C50
Prostate	177	185	185	C61
In situ neoplasms and benign neoplasms	. . .	. . .	210–239	D00–D48
Diabetes mellitus	260	250	250	E10–E14
Anemias	. . .	. . .	280–285	D50–D64
Meningitis	. . .	. . .	320–322	G00, G03
Alzheimer's disease	. . .	. . .	331	G30
Diseases of heart	6th: 410–443 7th: 400–402, 410–443	390–398, 402, 404, 410–429	390–398, 402, 404, 410–429	I00–I09, I11, I13, I20–I51
Ischemic heart disease	. . .	. . .	410–414, 429.2	I20–I25
Cerebrovascular diseases	330–334	430–438	430–434, 436–438	I60–I69
Atherosclerosis	. . .	. . .	440	I70
Influenza and pneumonia	480–483, 490–493	470–474, 480–486	480–487	J10–J18
Chronic lower respiratory diseases	241, 501, 502, 527.1	490–493, 519.3	490–494, 496	J40–J47
Chronic liver disease and cirrhosis	581	571	571	K70, K73–K74
Nephritis, nephrotic syndrome, and nephrosis	. . .	. . .	580–589	N00–N07, N17–N19, N25–N27
Pregnancy, childbirth, and the puerperium	640–689	630–678	630–676	A34, O00–O95, O98–O99
Congenital malformations, deformations, and chromosomal abnormalities	. . .	. . .	740–759	Q00–Q99
Certain conditions originating in the perinatal period	. . .	. . .	760–779	P00–P96
Newborn affected by maternal complications of pregnancy	. . .	. . .	761	P01
Newborn affected by complications of placenta, cord, and membranes	. . .	. . .	762	P02
Disorders related to short gestation and low birthweight, not elsewhere classified	. . .	. . .	765	P07
Birth trauma	. . .	. . .	767	P10–P15
Intrauterine hypoxia and birth asphyxia	. . .	. . .	768	P20–P21
Respiratory distress of newborn	. . .	. . .	769	P22
Sudden infant death syndrome	. . .	. . .	798.0	R95

See footnotes at end of table.

Table V. Cause-of-death codes, by applicable revision of *International Classification of Diseases* (ICD)—Con.

Cause of death (Tenth Revision titles)	Sixth and Seventh Revisions	Eighth Revision	Ninth Revision	Tenth Revision
Unintentional injuries[3]	E800–E936, E960–E965	E800–E929, E940–E946	E800–E869, E880–E929	V01–X59, Y85–Y86
Motor vehicle-related injuries[3]	E810–E835	E810–E823	E810–E825	V02–V04, V09.0, V09.2, V12–V14, V19.0–V19.2, V19.4–V19.6, V20–V79, V80.3–V80.5, V81.0–V81.1,V82.0–V82.1, V83–V86, V87.0–V87.8, V88.0–V88.8, V89.0, V89.2
Suicide[1]	E963, E970–E979	E950–E959	E950–E959	*U03, X60–X84, Y87.0
Homicide[1]	E964, E980–E983	E960–E969	E960–E969	*U01–*U02, X85–Y09, Y87.1
Injury by firearms	...	E922, E955, E965, E970, E985	E922, E955.0–E955.4, E965.0–E965.4, E970, E985.0–E985.4	W32–W34, X72–X74, X93–X95, Y22–Y24, Y35.0

. . . Cause-of-death code numbers are not provided for causes not shown in *Health, United States*.
[1]Starting with 2001 data, NCHS introduced categories *U01–*U03 for classifying and coding deaths due to acts of terrorism. The * indicates codes are not part of the Tenth Revision.
[2]Categories for coding human immunodeficiency virus infection were introduced in 1987. The * indicates codes are not part of the Ninth Revision.
[3]In the public health community, the term "unintentional injuries" is preferred to "accidents" and "motor vehicle-related injuries" to "motor vehicle accidents."
SOURCE: Advance report of final mortality statistics, 1976. Monthly vital statistics report; vol 24 no 11, supp. B110. Hyattsville, MD: National Center for Health Statistics. 1976. Available from: www.cdc.gov/nchs/data/mvsr/supp/mv24_11sacc.pdf. Hoyert DL, Kochanek KD, Murphy SL. Deaths: Final Data for 1997. National vital statistics reports; vol 47 no. 19. Hyattsville, MD: National Center for Health Statistics. 1999. Available from: www.cdc.gov/nchs/data/nvsr/nvsr47/nvs47_19.pdf. Hoyert DL, Heron MP, Murphy SL, Kung H. Deaths: Final Data for 2003. National vital statistics reports; vol 54 no 13. Hyattsville, MD: National Center for Health Statistics. 2006. Available from: www.cdc.gov/nchs/data/nvsr/nvsr54/nvsr54_13.pdf.

Cigarette smoking—Cigarette smoking and related tobacco use are measured in several different data systems.

Birth File—Information on cigarette smoking by the mother during pregnancy is based on Yes/No responses to the birth certificate item "Other risk factors for this pregnancy: Tobacco use during pregnancy" and the average number of cigarettes per day with no specificity on timing during pregnancy. This information became available for the first time in 1989 with revision of the U.S. Standard Certificate of Live Birth. In 1989, 43 states and the District of Columbia collected data on tobacco use. The following states did not require the reporting of tobacco use in the standard format on the birth certificate: California, Indiana, Louisiana, Nebraska, New York, Oklahoma, and South Dakota. In 1990, information on tobacco use became available from Louisiana and Nebraska, increasing the number of reporting states to 45 and the District of Columbia. In 1991–1993, with the addition of Oklahoma to the reporting area, information on tobacco use was available for 46 states and the District of Columbia; in 1994–1998, 46 states, the District

of Columbia, and New York City reported tobacco use; in 1999 information on tobacco use became available from Indiana and New York, increasing the number of reporting states to 48 and the District of Columbia; starting in 2000, with the addition of South Dakota, the reporting area includes 49 states and the District of Columbia. During 1989–2004 California did not require the reporting of tobacco use. The area reporting tobacco use comprised 87% of U.S. births in 1999–2002. Starting in 2003, some states began implementation of the 2003 revision of the U.S. Standard Certificate of Live Birth. The 2003 revision asked for the number of cigarettes smoked at different intervals before and during pregnancy. Tobacco use during pregnancy data from the 2003 revision of the birth certificate are not comparable with data from the 1989 revision. Therefore, data on tobacco use during pregnancy were excluded for states that implemented the 2003 revision of the U.S. Standard Certificate of Live Birth: these reporting areas included Pennsylvania and Washington starting in 2003, and Florida, Idaho, Kentucky, New Hampshire, New York state (excluding New York City), South Carolina, and

Tennessee starting in 2004. The reporting area for mother's tobacco use decreased to 47 states and the District of Columbia in 2003, and 40 states, the District of Columbia, and New York City in 2004.

Monitoring the Future Survey—Information on current cigarette smoking is obtained for high school seniors (starting in 1975) and 8th and 10th graders (starting in 1991) based on the following question: "How frequently have you smoked cigarettes during the past 30 days?"

National Health Interview Survey (NHIS)—Information about cigarette smoking is obtained for adults 18 years of age and over. Starting in 1993, current smokers are identified by asking the following two questions: "Have you smoked at least 100 cigarettes in your entire life?" and "Do you now smoke cigarettes every day, some days, or not at all?" Persons who smoked 100 cigarettes and who now smoke every day or some days are defined as current smokers. Before 1992, current smokers were identified based on positive responses to the following two questions: "Have you smoked 100 cigarettes in your entire life?" and "Do you smoke now?" (traditional definition). In 1992, the definition of current smoker in the NHIS was modified to specifically include persons who smoked on some days (revised definition). In 1992 cigarette smoking data were collected for a half-sample with half the respondents (one-quarter sample) using the traditional smoking questions and the other half of respondents (one-quarter sample) using the revised smoking question ("Do you smoke every day, some days, or not at all?"). An unpublished analysis of the 1992 traditional smoking measure revealed that the crude percentage of current smokers 18 years of age and over remained the same as for 1991. The statistics for 1992 combine data collected using the traditional and the revised questions.

In 1993–1995, estimates of cigarette smoking prevalence were based on a half-sample. Smoking data were not collected in 1996. Starting in 1997, smoking data were collected in the sample adult questionnaire. For further information on survey methodology and sample sizes pertaining to the NHIS cigarette smoking data for data years 1965–1992 and other sources of cigarette smoking data available from the National Center for Health Statistics, see National Center for Health Statistics. Bibliographies and Data Sources, Smoking Data Guide,

no 1, DHHS pub no (PHS) 91-1308-1, Public Health Service. Washington, DC: U.S. Government Printing Office. 1991.

National Survey on Drug Use & Health (NSDUH)— Information on current cigarette smoking is obtained for all persons surveyed who are 12 years of age and over based on the following question: "During the past 30 days, have you smoked part or all of a cigarette?"

Youth Risk Behavior Survey—Information on current cigarette smoking is obtained from high school students (starting in 1991) based on the following question: "During the past 30 days, on how many days did you smoke cigarettes?"

Civilian noninstitutionalized population; Civilian population—See Population.

Community hospital—See Hospital.

Comparability ratio—About every 10–20 years the *International Classification of Diseases* (ICD) is revised to stay abreast of advances in medical science and changes in medical terminology. Each of these revisions produces breaks in the continuity of cause-of-death statistics. Discontinuities across revisions are due to changes in classification and rules for selecting underlying cause of death. Classification and rule changes affect cause-of-death trend data by shifting deaths away from some cause-of-death categories and into others. Comparability ratios measure the effect of changes in classification and coding rules. For causes shown in Table VI, comparability ratios range between 0.6974 and 1.1404. Influenza and pneumonia had the lowest comparability ratio (0.6974), indicating that influenza and pneumonia is about 30% less likely to be selected as the underlying cause of death in ICD–10 than in ICD–9. Pregnancy, childbirth, and the puerperium had the highest comparability ratio (1.1404), indicating that pregnancy is more than 14% more likely to be selected as the underlying cause using ICD–10 coding.

For selected causes of death, the ICD–9 codes used to calculate death rates for 1980 through 1998 differ from the ICD–9 codes most nearly comparable with the corresponding ICD–10 cause-of-death category, which also affects the ability to compare death rates across ICD revisions. Examples of these causes are ischemic heart disease; cerebrovascular diseases; trachea, bronchus and lung cancer; unintentional injuries; and homicide. To address this source of discontinuity, mortality trends for 1980–1998 were recalculated, using ICD–9 codes that are more comparable with codes for corresponding ICD–10 categories. Table V shows the ICD–9 codes used for these causes. Although this modification may lessen the discontinuity between the Ninth and Tenth Revisions, the effect on the discontinuity between the Eighth and Ninth Revisions is not measured.

Comparability ratios shown in Table VI are based on a comparability study in which the same deaths were coded by both the Ninth and Tenth Revisions. The comparability ratio was calculated by dividing the number of deaths classified by ICD–10 by the number of deaths classified by ICD–9. The resulting ratios represent the net effect of the Tenth Revision on cause-of-death statistics and can be used to adjust mortality statistics for causes of death classified by the Ninth Revision to be comparable with cause-specific mortality statistics classified by the Tenth Revision.

The application of comparability ratios to mortality statistics helps make the analysis of change between 1998 and 1999 more accurate and complete. The 1998 comparability-modified death rate is calculated by multiplying the comparability ratio by the 1998 death rate. Comparability-modified rates should be used to estimate mortality change between 1998 and 1999.

Caution should be taken when applying the comparability ratios presented in Table VI to age-, race-, and sex-specific mortality data. Demographic subgroups may sometimes differ with regard to their cause-of-death distribution, and this would result in demographic variation in cause-specific comparability ratios.

For more information, see Anderson RN, Minino AM, Hoyert DL, Rosenberg HM. Comparability of cause of death between ICD–9 and ICD–10: Preliminary estimates; Kochanek KD, Smith BL, Anderson RN. Deaths: Preliminary data for 1999. National vital statistics reports 2001;49(2) and 49(3). Hyattsville, MD: National Center for Health Statistics; and Final ratios for 113 selected causes of death. Available from: ftp://ftp.cdc.gov/pub/Health_Statistics/NCHS/Datasets/Comparability/icd9_icd10/. See related Cause of death; *International Classification of Diseases* (ICD); Tables IV, V, and VI.

Compensation—See Employer costs for employee compensation.

Table VI. Comparability of selected causes of death between the Ninth and Tenth Revisions of the *International Classification of Diseases* (ICD)

Cause of death[1]	Final comparability ratio[2]
Human immunodeficiency virus (HIV) disease . . .	1.0821
Malignant neoplasms	1.0093
Colon, rectum, and anus	0.9988
Trachea, bronchus, and lung	0.9844
Breast	1.0073
Prostate	1.0144
Diabetes mellitus	1.0193
Diseases of heart	0.9852
Ischemic heart diseases	1.0006
Cerebrovascular diseases	1.0502
Influenza and pneumonia	0.6974
Chronic lower respiratory diseases	1.0411
Chronic liver disease and cirrhosis	1.0321
Pregnancy, childbirth, and the puerperium	1.1404
Unintentional injuries	1.0251
Motor vehicle-related injuries	0.9527
Suicide	1.0022
Homicide	1.0020
Injury by firearms	1.0012
Chronic and noncommunicable diseases	1.0100
Injuries	1.0159
Communicable diseases	0.8582
HIV disease	1.0821
Other communicable diseases	0.7997

[1]See Table V for ICD–9 and ICD–10 cause-of-death codes.
[2]Ratio of number of deaths classified by ICD–10 to number of deaths classified by ICD–9.

SOURCE: National Center for Health Statistics. Final comparability ratios for 113 selected causes of death. Available from: ftp://ftp.cdc.gov/pub/Health_Statistics/NCHS/Datasets/Comparability/icd9_icd10/Comparability_Ratio_tables.xls.

Condition—A health condition is a departure from a state of physical or mental well-being. In the National Health Interview Survey, each condition reported as a cause of an individual's activity limitation has been classified as chronic, not chronic, or unknown if chronic, based on the nature and duration of the condition. Conditions that are not cured once acquired (such as heart disease, diabetes, and birth defects in the original response categories, and amputee and old age in the ad hoc categories) are considered chronic, whereas conditions related to pregnancy are always considered not chronic. In addition, other conditions must have been present 3 months or longer to be considered chronic. An exception is made for children less than 1 year of age who have had a condition since birth, as these conditions are always considered chronic. The National Nursing Home Survey uses a specific list of chronic conditions, disregarding time of onset.

Consumer Price Index (CPI)—The CPI is prepared by the U.S. Bureau of Labor Statistics. It is a monthly measure of the average change in the prices paid by urban consumers for a fixed market basket of goods and services. The medical care component of CPI shows trends in medical care prices based on specific indicators of hospital, medical, dental, and drug prices. A revision of the definition of CPI has been in use since January 1988. See related Gross domestic product (GDP); Health expenditures, national; Appendix I, Consumer Price Index.

Contraception—The National Survey of Family Growth collects information on contraceptive use as reported by women 15–44 years of age, during heterosexual vaginal intercourse. For current contraceptive use, women were asked about contraceptive use during the month of interview. Women were classified by whether they reported using each of 19 methods of contraception at any time in the month of interview. Contraceptive methods listed as other methods include the following: for 2002, the female condom, foam, cervical cap, Today Sponge®, suppository or insert, jelly or cream, or other method; for 1995, the female condom or vaginal pouch, foam, cervical cap, Today Sponge®, suppository or insert, jelly or cream, or other method; for 1988, foam, douche, Today Sponge®, suppository or insert, jelly or cream, or other method; and for 1982, foam, douche, suppository or insert, or other method.

Crude birth rate; Crude death rate—See Rate: Birth and related rates; Rate: Death and related rates.

Days of care—Days of care is defined similarly in different data systems. See related Admission; Average length of stay; Discharge; Hospital; Hospital utilization; Inpatient.

American Hospital Association—Days, hospital days, or inpatient days are the number of adult and pediatric days of care rendered during the entire reporting period. Days of care for newborns are excluded.

National Health Interview Survey (NHIS)—Hospital days during the year refer to the total number of hospital days occurring in the 12-month period before the interview week. A hospital day is a night spent in the hospital for

persons admitted as inpatients. Starting in 1997 hospitalization data from NHIS are for all inpatient stays, whereas estimates for prior years published in previous editions of *Health, United States* excluded hospitalizations for deliveries and newborns.

National Hospital Discharge Survey—Days of care refers to the total number of patient days accumulated by inpatients at the time of discharge from non-federal short-stay hospitals during a reporting period. All days from and including the date of admission but not including the date of discharge are counted.

Death rate—See Rate: Death and related rates.

Dental caries—Dental caries is evidence of dental decay on any surface of a tooth. Dental caries was determined by an oral examination conducted by a trained dentist as part of the National Health and Nutrition Examination Survey. In *Health, United States,* dental caries refers to coronal caries, that is, caries on the crown or enamel surface of the tooth. Root caries is not included. Study participants 2 years of age and over were eligible for the examination, as long as they did not meet other exclusion criteria. Both permanent and primary (or baby) teeth were evaluated, depending on the age of the participant. For children 2–5 years of age, only caries in primary teeth was included. For children 6–11 years of age, caries in both primary and permanent teeth were included. For children 12 years of age and over, and for adults, only caries in permanent teeth was included.

Dental visit—Starting in 1997 National Health Interview Survey respondents were asked "About how long has it been since you last saw or talked to a dentist? Include all types of dentists, such as orthodontists, oral surgeons, and all other dental specialists as well as hygienists." Starting in 2001 the question was modified slightly to ask respondents how long it had been since they last saw a dentist. Questions about dental visits were not asked for children under 2 years of age for years 1997–1999 and under 1 year of age for 2000 and beyond. Starting with 1997 data, estimates are presented for people with a dental visit in the past year. Prior to 1997, dental visit estimates were based on a 2-week recall period.

Diagnosis—Diagnosis is the act or process of identifying or determining the nature and cause of a disease or injury through evaluation of patient history, examination, and review of laboratory data. Diagnoses in the National Hospital

Discharge Survey, the National Ambulatory Medical Care Survey, the National Hospital Ambulatory Medical Care Survey, and the National Nursing Home Survey are abstracted from medical records and coded to the *International Classification of Diseases, Ninth Revision, Clinical Modification* (ICD–9–CM). For a given medical care encounter, the first-listed diagnosis can be used to categorize the visit, or if more than one diagnosis is recorded on the survey abstraction form, the visit can be categorized based on all diagnoses recorded. Analyzing first-listed diagnoses avoids double-counting events such as visits or hospitalizations; the first-listed diagnosis is often, but not always, considered the most important or dominant condition among all comorbid conditions. For example, a hospital discharge would be considered a first-listed stroke discharge if the ICD–9–CM diagnosis code for stroke was recorded in the first diagnosis field on the survey form. An any listed stroke discharge would classify all diagnoses of stroke recorded on the survey abstraction form regardless of order. Any-listed diagnoses double count events such as visits or hospitalizations with more than one recorded diagnosis but provide information on the burden a specific diagnosis presents to the health care system. See related External cause of injury; Injury; Injury-related visit.

Diagnostic and other nonsurgical procedure—See Procedure.

Discharge—The National Health Interview Survey defines a hospital discharge as the completion of any continuous period of stay of 1 night or more in a hospital as an inpatient. According to the National Hospital Discharge Survey, a discharge is a completed inpatient hospitalization. A hospitalization may be completed by death or by releasing the patient to the customary place of residence, a nursing home, another hospital, or other locations. See related Admission; Average length of stay; Days of care; Inpatient.

Domiciliary care home—See Long-term care facility; Nursing home.

Drug abuse—See Illicit drug use.

Drug—Drugs are pharmaceutical agents—by any route of administration—for prevention, diagnosis, or treatment of medical conditions or diseases. Data on specific drug use are collected in three NCHS surveys.

National Ambulatory Medical Care Survey (NAMCS) and *National Hospital Ambulatory Medical Care Survey (NHAMCS)*—Data collection in the NAMCS and NHAMCS outpatient and emergency department components is from the medical record of an inperson physician office or hospital outpatient department visit, rather than from the patient. Generic or brand name drugs are abstracted from the medical record, including prescription and over-the-counter drugs, immunizations, allergy shots, and anesthetics that were prescribed, ordered, supplied, administered, or continued during the visit. Prior to 1995, up to five drugs per visit could be reported on the patient record form; in data years 1995 and beyond, up to six drugs could be reported. Starting with data year 2003, up to eight drugs could be reported, as well as a count of the total number of drugs prescribed, ordered, supplied, administered, or continued during the visit.

For more information on drugs collected by the NAMCS and NHAMCS, see the NAMCS drug database, available from: www.cdc.gov/nchs/about/major/ahcd/ambulatory.htm, or ftp://ftp.cdc.gov/pub/Health_Statistics/NCHS/Dataset_Documentation/NAMCS/doc01.pdf.
For more information on how drugs are classified into therapeutic use categories, See National Drug Code (NDC) Directory therapeutic class. See related Appendix I, National Ambulatory Medical Care Survey and National Hospital Ambulatory Medical Care Survey.

National Health and Nutrition Examination Survey (NHANES)—Drug information from NHANES III and 1999–2002 NHANES was collected during an inperson interview conducted in the participant's home. Participants were asked whether they had taken a medication in the past month for which they needed a prescription. Those who answered, Yes, were asked to produce the prescription medication containers for the interviewer. For each medication reported, the interviewer entered the product's complete name from the container. If no container was available, the interviewer asked the participant to verbally report the name of the medication. In addition, participants were asked how long they had been taking the medication and the main reason for use.

All reported medication names were converted to their standard generic ingredient name. For multi-ingredient products, the ingredients were listed in alphabetical order and counted as one drug (e.g., Tylenol #3 was listed as Acetaminophen; Codeine). No trade or proprietary names are provided on the data file.

Drug data from NHANES provide a snapshot of all prescribed drugs reported by a sample of the civilian noninstitutionalized population for a 1-month period. Drugs taken on an irregular basis such as every other day, once per week, or for a 10 day period, etc. were captured in the 1-month recall period. Data shown in *Health, United States* for the percentage of the population reporting three or more prescription drugs during the past month include a range of drug utilization patterns—for example, persons who took three or more drugs on a daily basis during the past month or persons who took a different drug three separate times—as long as at least three different drugs were taken during the past month.

For more information on prescription drug data collection and coding in the NHANES 1999–2002, see: www.cdc.gov/nchs/data/nhanes/frequency/rxq_rxdoc.pdf. For more information on NHANES III prescription drug data collection and coding, see: www.cdc.gov/nchs/data/nhanes/nhanes3/PUPREMED-acc.pdf. See related Appendix I, National Health and Nutrition Examination Survey.

Education—Several approaches to defining educational categories are used in this report. In survey data, educational categories are based on information about educational credentials, such as diplomas and degrees. In vital statistics, educational attainment is based on years of school completed.

Birth File—Information on educational attainment of mother is based on number of years of school completed, as reported by the mother on the birth certificate. Between 1970 and 1992 the reporting area for maternal education expanded.

Mother's education was reported on the birth certificate by 38 states in 1970. Data were not available from Alabama, Arkansas, California, Connecticut, Delaware, the District of Columbia, Georgia, Idaho, Maryland, New Mexico, Pennsylvania, Texas, and Washington. In 1975 these data became available from Connecticut, Delaware, Georgia, Maryland, and the District of Columbia, increasing the number of states reporting

mother's education to 42 and the District of Columbia. Between 1980 and 1988 only three states, California, Texas, and Washington, did not report mother's education. In 1988 mother's education was also missing from New York state outside New York City. In 1989–1991 mother's education was missing only from Washington and New York state outside New York City. During 1992–2002 mother's education was reported by all 50 states and the District of Columbia. Starting in 2003, some states began implementation of the 2003 revision of the U.S. Standard Certificate of Live Birth. The education item on the 2003 revision asks for the highest degree or level of school completed whereas the education item on the 1989 revision asks for highest grade completed. Data from the 1989 and 2003 certificate items on educational attainment are too dissimilar to be reliably combined. Therefore, data on maternal education were excluded for states that implemented the 2003 revision of the U.S. Standard Certificate of Live Birth: these reporting areas included Pennsylvania and Washington starting in 2003, and Florida, Idaho, Kentucky, New Hampshire, New York state (outside New York City), South Carolina, and Tennessee starting in 2004. The reporting area for education decreased to 48 states and the District of Columbia in 2003, and 41 states, the District of Columbia, and New York City in 2004.

Mortality File—Information on educational attainment of decedent became available for the first time in 1989 because of a revision of the U.S. Standard Certificate of Death. Decedent's educational attainment is reported on the death certificate by the funeral director based on information provided by an informant such as next of kin. Mortality data by educational attainment for 1989 were based on data from 20 states and by 1994–1996, increased to 45 states and the District of Columbia (DC). In 1994–1996 either the following states did not report educational attainment on the death certificate or the information was more than 20% incomplete: Georgia, Kentucky, Oklahoma, Rhode Island, and South Dakota. In 1997–2000 information on decedent's education was available from Oklahoma, increasing the reporting area to 46 states and DC. With the addition of Kentucky, the reporting area increased to 47 states and DC in 2001 and 2002. Starting with 2003 data, California, Idaho, Montana, and New York implemented the 2003 revision of the U.S. Standard Certificate of Death. Educational attainment data from the revised death certificate is not comparable with educational attainment data collected using the 1989 revision of the U.S. Standard Certificate of Death. Therefore, these states are excluded from educational attainment mortality data beginning with 2003. Because of different education profiles of the four excluded states compared with the remaining states and the District of Columbia, 2003 data are not directly comparable to earlier years. For more information on the revised educational attainment item, see the technical notes of Hoyert DL, Heron M, Murphy SL, Kung HC. Deaths: Final data for 2003. National vital statistics reports. Vol 54 no 13. Hyattsville, MD: National Center for Health Statistics. 2006. Available from: www.cdc.gov/nchs/data/nvsr/nvsr54/nvsr54_13.pdf.

Calculation of unbiased death rates by educational attainment based on the National Vital Statistics System requires that the reporting of education on the death certificate be complete and consistent with the reporting of education on the Current Population Survey (CPS), the source of population estimates for denominators for death rates. Death records that are missing information about decedent's education are not included in the calculation of rates. Therefore the levels of death rates by educational attainment shown in this report are underestimated by approximately the percentage with not stated education, which ranges from 3%–9%.

The validity of information about the decedent's education was evaluated by comparing self-reported education obtained in the CPS with education on the death certificate for decedents in the National Longitudinal Mortality Survey (NLMS). (Sorlie PD, Johnson NJ. Validity of education information on the death certificate. Epidemiology 1996;7(4):437–9). Another analysis compared self-reported education collected in the first National Health and Nutrition Examination Survey (NHANES I) with education on the death certificate for decedents in the NHANES I Epidemiologic Followup Study. (Makuc DM, Feldman JJ, Mussolino ME. Validity of education and age as reported on death certificates. American Statistical Association. 1996 Proceedings of the Social Statistics Section 102–6.) Results of both studies indicated that there is a tendency for some people who did not graduate from high school to be reported as high school graduates on the death

certificate. This tendency results in overstating the death rate for high school graduates and understating the death rate for the group with less than 12 years of education. The bias was greater among older than younger decedents and somewhat greater among black than white decedents.

In addition, educational gradients in death rates based on the National Vital Statistics System were compared with those based on the NLMS, a prospective study of persons in the CPS. Results of these comparisons indicate that educational gradients in death rates based on the National Vital Statistics System were reasonably similar to those based on NLMS for white persons 25–64 years of age and black persons 25–44 years of age. The number of deaths for persons of Hispanic origin in NLMS was too small to permit comparison for this ethnic group. For further information on measurement of education, see Kominski R, Siegel PM. Measuring education in the Current Population Survey. Monthly Labor Review September 1993;34–8.

National Health Interview Survey (NHIS)—Starting in 1997, the NHIS questionnaire was changed to ask "What is the highest level of school ___ has completed or the highest degree received?" Responses were used to categorize adults according to educational credentials (e.g., no high school diploma or general educational development (GED) high school equivalency diploma; high school diploma or GED; some college, no bachelor's degree; bachelor's degree or higher).

Prior to 1997, the education variable in NHIS was measured by asking, "What is the highest grade or year of regular school ___ has ever attended?" and "Did ___ finish the grade/year?" Responses were used to categorize adults according to years of education completed (e.g., less than 12 years, 12 years, 13–15 years, and 16 or more years).

Data from the 1996 and 1997 NHIS were used to compare distributions of educational attainment for adults 25 years of age and over using categories based on educational credentials (1997) with categories based on years of education completed (1996). A larger percentage of persons reported some college than 13–15 years of education and a correspondingly smaller percentage reported high school diploma or GED than 12 years of education. In 1997, 19% of adults reported no high school diploma, 31% a high school diploma or GED, 26% some college, and 24% a bachelor's degree or higher. In 1996, 18% of adults reported less than 12 years of education, 37% reported 12 years of education, 20% 13–15 years, and 25% 16 or more years of education.

Emergency department—According to the National Hospital Ambulatory Medical Care Survey, an emergency department is a hospital facility that provides unscheduled outpatient services to patients whose conditions require immediate care and is staffed 24 hours a day. Off-site emergency departments open less than 24 hours are included if staffed by the hospital's emergency department. See related Emergency department or emergency room visit; Outpatient department.

Emergency department or emergency room visit—Starting with the 1997 National Health Interview Survey, respondents to the sample adult and sample child questionnaires (generally the parent) were asked about the number of visits to hospital emergency rooms during the past 12 months, including visits that resulted in hospitalization. In the National Hospital Ambulatory Medical Care Survey an emergency department visit is a direct personal exchange between a patient and a physician or other health care providers working under the physician's supervision, for the purpose of seeking care and receiving personal health services. See related Emergency department; Injury-related visit.

Employer costs for employee compensation—This is a measure of the average cost per employee hour worked to employers for wages and salaries and benefits. Wages and salaries are defined as the hourly straight-time wage rate or, for workers not paid on an hourly basis, straight-time earnings divided by the corresponding hours. Straight-time wage and salary rates are total earnings before payroll deductions, excluding premium pay for overtime and for work on weekends and holidays, shift differentials, nonproduction bonuses, and lump-sum payments provided in lieu of wage increases. Production bonuses, incentive earnings, commission payments, and cost-of-living adjustments are included in straight-time wage and salary rates. Benefits covered are paid leave—paid vacations, holidays, sick leave, and other leave; supplemental pay—premium pay for overtime and work on weekends and holidays, shift differentials, nonproduction bonuses, and lump-sum payments provided in lieu of wage increases; insurance benefits—life, health, and

sickness and accident insurance; retirement and savings benefits—pension and other retirement plans and savings and thrift plans; legally required benefits—Social Security, railroad retirement and supplemental retirement, railroad unemployment insurance, federal and state unemployment insurance, workers' compensation, and other benefits required by law, such as state temporary disability insurance; and other benefits—severance pay and supplemental unemployment plans. See related Appendix I, National Compensation Survey.

Ethnicity—See Hispanic origin.

Exercise—See Physical activity, leisure-time.

Expenditures—See Health expenditures, national; Appendix I, National Health Accounts.

External cause of injury—The ICD–9 External Cause Matrix is a two-dimensional array describing both the mechanism or external cause of the injury (e.g., fall, motor vehicle traffic) and the manner or intent of the injury (e.g., self inflicted or assault). Although this matrix was originally developed for mortality, it has been adapted for use with the ICD–9–CM. For more information, see the NCHS website: www.cdc.gov/nchs/about/otheract/injury/tools.htm.

Family income—For purposes of the National Health Interview Survey and the National Health and Nutrition Examination Survey, all people within a household related to each other by blood, marriage, or adoption constitute a family. Each member of a family is classified according to the total income of the family. Unrelated individuals are classified according to their own income.

National Health Interview Survey (NHIS)—In the NHIS (prior to 1997) family income was the total income received by members of a family (or by an unrelated individual) in the 12 months before the interview. Starting in 1997 the NHIS collected family income data for the calendar year prior to the interview (e.g., 2004 family income data were based on calendar year 2003 information). Family income includes wages, salaries, rents from property, interest, dividends, profits and fees from their own businesses, pensions, and help from relatives. Family income data are used in the computation of poverty level. Starting with *Health, United States, 2004* a new methodology for imputing family income data for NHIS data was implemented for data years 1997 and beyond. Multiple imputations were performed for survey years 1997 and beyond with five sets of imputed values created to allow for the assessment of variability caused by imputation. Family income was missing for 24%–29% of persons in 1997–1998 and 31%–33% in 1999–2004. A detailed description of the multiple imputation procedure, as well as data files for 1997 and beyond, are available from: www.cdc.gov/nchs/nhis.htm, via the Imputed Income Files link under that year. For data years 1990–1996, about 16%–18% of persons had missing data for family income. In those years, missing values were imputed for family income using a sequential hot deck within matrix cells imputation approach. A detailed description of the imputation procedure, as well as data files with imputed annual family income for 1990–1996, is available from NCHS on CD-ROM, NHIS Imputed Annual Family Income 1990–1996, series 10, no. 9A.

National Health and Nutrition Examination Survey (NHANES)—In the NHANES 1999 and onward, family income is asked in a series of questions about possible sources of income, including wages, salaries, interest and dividends, federal programs, child support, rents, royalties, and other possible sources of income. After the information about sources of income was obtained in the family interview income section of the questionnaire, the respondent was asked to report total combined family income for themselves and the other members of their family, in dollars. If the respondent did not provide an answer or did not know the total combined family income, they were asked if the total family income was less than $20,000 or $20,000 or more. If the respondent answered, a follow-up question asked the respondent to select an income range from a list on a printed hand card. The midpoint of the income range was then used as the total family income value. Family income values were used to calculate the poverty income ratio. NHANES III did not ask the detailed components of income questions but asked respondents to identify their income based on a set of ranges provided on a flashcard, whereas NHANES II did include questions on components of income. Family income was not imputed for individuals or families with no reported income information in any of the NHANES survey years. See related Poverty.

Federal hospital—See Hospital.

Fee-for-service health insurance—This is private (commercial) health insurance that reimburses health care providers on the basis of a fee for each health service provided to the insured person. It is also known as indemnity health insurance. Medicare Parts A and B are sometimes referred to as Medicare fee-for-service. See related Health insurance coverage; Medicare.

Fertility rate—See Rate: Birth and related rates.

General hospital—See Hospital.

General hospital providing separate psychiatric services—See Mental health organization.

Geographic region and division—The U.S. Census Bureau groups the 50 states and the District of Columbia for statistical purposes into four geographic regions—Northeast, Midwest, South, and West—and nine divisions, based on geographic proximity. See Figure I.

The Department of Commerce's Bureau of Economic Analysis (BEA) groups states into eight regions based on their homogeneity with respect to income characteristics, industrial composition of the employed labor force, and such noneconomic factors as demographic, social, and cultural characteristics. See Figure II.

Three U.S. Census Bureau divisions—West North Central, East North Central, and New England—and three BEA regions—Plains, Great Lakes, and New England—are composed of the same states. The states composing the remaining Census Bureau divisions differ from those composing the corresponding BEA regions.

Gestation—For the National Vital Statistics System and the Centers for Disease Control and Prevention's Abortion Surveillance, the period of gestation is defined as beginning with the first day of the last normal menstrual period and ending with the day of birth or day of termination of pregnancy.

Gross domestic product (GDP)—GDP is the market value of the goods and services produced by labor and property located in the United States. As long as the labor and property are located in the United States, the suppliers (i.e., the workers and, for property, the owners) may be U.S.

Figure I. **Census Bureau**: Four Geographic Regions and 9 Divisions of the United States

residents or residents of other countries. See related Consumer Price Index (CPI); Health expenditures, national.

Group quarters—All people not living in housing units are classified by the U.S. Census Bureau as living in group quarters. Census recognizes two general categories of people in group quarters: the institutionalized population and the noninstitutionalized population. The institutionalized population includes people under formally authorized, supervised care or custody in institutions at the time of enumeration. Such people are classified as patients or inmates of an institution regardless of the availability of nursing or medical care, the length of stay, or the number of people in the institution. Generally, the institutionalized population is restricted to the institutional buildings and grounds (or must have passes or escorts to leave) and thus have limited interaction with the surrounding community. Also, they are generally under the care of trained staff, which has responsibility for their safekeeping and supervision. The type of institution was determined as part of census enumeration activities. For institutions that specialize in only one specific type of service,

all patients or inmates were given the same classification. For institutions that had multiple types of major services (usually general hospitals and Veterans' Administration hospitals), patients were classified according to selected types of wards. For example, in psychiatric wards of hospitals, patients were classified in mental (psychiatric) hospitals; in general hospital wards for people with chronic diseases, patients were classified in other hospitals for the chronically ill. Each patient or inmate was classified in only one type of institution. Institutions include correctional facilities, nursing homes, and mental hospitals.

People living in noninstitutionalized group quarters include staff residing in military and nonmilitary group quarters on institutional grounds that provide formally authorized, supervised care or custody for the institutionalized population. Also included are college dormitories, military bases and ships, hotels, motels, rooming houses, group homes, missions, shelters, and flophouses.

For Census 2000, the definition of the institutionalized population was consistent with the definition used in the 1990

Figure II. **Bureau of Economic Analysis:** Eight Geographic Regions of the United States

census. As in 1990, the definition of care only includes people under organized medical or formally authorized, supervised care or custody. In Census 2000, the 1990 and 1980 rule of classifying 10 or more unrelated people living together as living in noninstitutional group quarters was dropped. In 1970, the criterion was six or more unrelated people. Several changes have occurred in the tabulation of specific types of group quarters. In Census 2000, police lockups were included with local jails and other confinement facilities, and homes for unwed mothers were included in other group homes; in 1990, these categories were shown separately. For the first time, Census 2000 tabulates separately the following types of group quarters: military hospitals or wards for the chronically ill, other hospitals or wards for the chronically ill, hospices or homes for the chronically ill, wards in military hospitals with patients who have no usual home elsewhere, wards in general hospitals with patients who have no usual home elsewhere, and job corps and vocational training facilities. For Census 2000, rooming and boarding houses were classified as housing units rather than group quarters as in 1990. For more

information, see the Census Bureau's website: www.census.gov/prod/cen2000/doc/sf1.pdf.

Health care contact—Starting in 1997, the National Health Interview Survey has been collecting information on health care contacts with doctors and other health care professionals using the following questions: "During the past 12 months, how many times have you gone to a hospital emergency room about your own health?", "During the past 12 months, did you receive care at home from a nurse or other health care professional? What was the total number of home visits received?", and "During the past 12 months, how many times have you seen a doctor or other health care professional about your own health at a doctor's office, a clinic, or some other place? Do not include times you were hospitalized overnight, visits to hospital emergency rooms, home visits, or telephone calls." Starting with 2000 data, this question was amended to exclude dental visits also. For each question respondents were shown a flashcard with response categories of 0, 1, 2–3, 4–9, 10–12, or 13 or more visits in 1997–1999. Starting with 2000 data, response categories were expanded to 0, 1, 2–3, 4–5, 6–7, 8–9, 10–12, 13–15, or 16 or more.

Analyses of the percentage of persons with health care visits were tabulated as follows: For tabulation of the 1997–1999 data, responses of 2–3 were recoded to 2, and responses of 4–9 were recoded to 6. Starting with 2000 data, tabulation of responses of 2–3 were recoded to 2, and other responses were recoded to the midpoint of the range. A summary measure of health care visits was constructed by adding recoded responses for these questions and categorizing the sum as none, 1–3, 4–9, or 10 or more health care visits in the past 12 months.

Analyses of the percentage of children without a health care visit are based upon the following question: "During the past 12 months, how many times has ___ seen a doctor or other health care professional about (his/her) health at a doctor's office, a clinic, or some other place? Do not include times ____ was hospitalized overnight, visits to hospital emergency rooms, home visits, or telephone calls." See related Emergency department or emergency room visit; Home visit.

Health expenditures, national—National Health Expenditures are estimated by the Centers for Medicare & Medicaid Services (CMS) and measure spending for health care in the United States by type of service delivered (e.g., hospital care, physician services, nursing home care) and source of funding for those services (e.g., private health insurance, Medicare, Medicaid, out-of-pocket spending). CMS produces both historical and projected estimates of health expenditures by category. See related Consumer price index (CPI); Gross domestic product (GDP).

Health services and supplies expenditures—These are outlays for goods and services relating directly to patient care plus expenses for administering health insurance programs and government public health activities. This category is equivalent to total national health expenditures minus expenditures for research and construction.

National health expenditures—This measure estimates the amount spent for all health services and supplies and health-related research and construction activities consumed in the United States during the calendar year. Detailed estimates are available by source of expenditures (e.g., out-of-pocket payments, private health insurance, and government programs) and by type of expenditures (e.g., hospital care, physician services, and

drugs) and are in current dollars for the year of report. Data are compiled from a variety of sources.

Nursing home expenditures—These cover care rendered in establishments primarily engaged in providing inpatient nursing and rehabilitative services and continuous personal care services to persons requiring nursing care (skilled nursing and intermediate care facilities, including those for the mentally retarded) and continuing care retirement communities with on-site nursing care facilities. The costs of long-term care provided by hospitals are excluded.

Personal health care expenditures—These are outlays for goods and services relating directly to patient care. The expenditures in this category are total national health expenditures minus expenditures for research and construction, health insurance program administration, and government public health activities.

Private expenditures—These are outlays for services provided or paid for by nongovernmental sources—consumers, insurance companies, private industry, and philanthropic and other nonpatient care sources.

Public expenditures—These are outlays for services provided or paid for by federal, state, and local government agencies or expenditures required by governmental mandate (such as worker's compensation insurance payments).

Health insurance coverage—Health insurance is broadly defined to include both public and private payors who cover medical expenditures incurred by a defined population in a variety of settings.

National Health Interview Survey (NHIS)—For point-in-time health insurance estimates, NHIS respondents were asked about their coverage in the previous month in 1993–1996 and at the time of the interview in other years. Questions on health insurance coverage were expanded starting in 1993 compared with previous years. In 1997 the entire questionnaire was redesigned and data were collected using a computer-assisted personal interview (CAPI).

Respondents are covered by private health insurance if they indicate private health insurance or if they are covered by a single-service hospital plan, except in 1997 and 1998, when no information on single-service plans was obtained. Private health insurance includes managed care such as health maintenance organizations (HMOs).

Until 1996, persons were defined as having Medicaid or other public assistance coverage if they indicated that they had either Medicaid or other public assistance or if they reported receiving Aid to Families with Dependent Children (AFDC) or Supplemental Security Income (SSI). After welfare reform in late 1996, Medicaid was delinked from AFDC and SSI. Starting in 1997, persons are considered to be covered by Medicaid if they report Medicaid or a state-sponsored health program. Starting in 1998, persons are considered covered by Medicaid if they report being covered by the State Children's Health Insurance Program (SCHIP). Medicare or military health plan coverage is also determined in the interview, and starting in 1997 other government-sponsored program coverage is determined as well.

If respondents do not report coverage under one of the above types of plans and they have unknown coverage under either private health insurance or Medicaid, they are considered to have unknown coverage.

The remaining respondents are considered uninsured. The uninsured are persons who do not have coverage under private health insurance, Medicare, Medicaid, public assistance, a state-sponsored health plan, other government-sponsored programs, or a military health plan. Persons with only Indian Health Service coverage are considered uninsured. Estimates of the percentage of persons who are uninsured based on the NHIS may differ slightly from those based on the March Current Population Survey (CPS) because of differences in survey questions, recall period, and other aspects of survey methodology.

In the NHIS less than 2% of people age 65 years and over reported no current health insurance coverage, but the small sample size precludes the presentation of separate estimates for this population. Therefore, the term uninsured refers only to the population under age 65.

Two additional questions were added to the health insurance section of the NHIS beginning with the third quarter of 2004. One question was asked of persons 65 years and over who had not indicated that they had Medicare: "People covered by Medicare have a card

which looks like this. [Are/Is] [person] covered by Medicare?" The other question was asked of persons under age 65 who had not indicated any type of coverage: "There is a program called Medicaid that pays for health care for persons in need. In this state it is also called [state name]. [Are/Is] [person] covered by Medicaid?"

Respondents who originally classified themselves as uninsured, but whose classification was changed to Medicare or Medicaid on the basis of a yes response to either question, subsequently received appropriate follow-up questions concerning periods of noncoverage for insured respondents. Of the 892 people (unweighted) who were eligible to receive the Medicare probe question in the third and fourth quarter of 2004, 55.4% indicated that they were covered by Medicare. Of the 9,146 people (unweighted) who were eligible to receive the Medicaid probe question in the third and fourth quarter of 2004, 3.0% indicated that they were covered by Medicaid. Estimates for this report are calculated using the responses to the two additional probe questions. For a complete discussion of the implications of the addition of these two probe questions on the estimates for insurance coverage see Cohen RA and Martinez ME. Impact of Medicare and Medicaid probe questions on health insurance estimates from the National Health Interview Survey, 2004. Health E-Stat, 2005, available from: www.cdc.gov/nchs/products/pubs/pubd/hestats/impact.htm and Table VIII (p. 504).

Survey respondents may be covered by health insurance at the time of the interview, but may have experienced one or more lapses in coverage during the 12 months prior to the interview. Starting with *Health United States, 2006*, NHIS estimates are presented for the following three exhaustive categories: people with health insurance continuously for the full 12 months prior to the interview, those who had a period of up to 12 months prior to the interview without coverage, and those who were uninsured for more than 12 months prior to interview. This stub variable has been added to selected tables. Two additional NHIS questions were used to determine the appropriate category for the survey respondents: all persons without known comprehensive health insurance plan were asked, "About how long has it been since person last had health care coverage?" and all persons with known health insurance coverage were asked, "In the past 12 months, was there any time when person did NOT have ANY health insurance coverage?" See related Fee-for-service health insurance; Health maintenance organization (HMO); Managed care; Medicaid; Medicare; State Children's Health Insurance Program (SCHIP); Uninsured.

Health maintenance organization (HMO)—An HMO is a health care system that assumes or shares both the financial risks and the delivery risks associated with providing comprehensive medical services to a voluntarily enrolled population in a particular geographic area, usually in return for a fixed, prepaid fee. Pure HMO enrollees use only the prepaid capitated health services of the HMO panel of medical care providers. Open-ended HMO enrollees use the prepaid HMO health services but, in addition, may receive medical care from providers who are not part of the HMO panel. There is usually a substantial deductible, copayment, or coinsurance associated with use of nonpanel providers.

HMO model types are these:

Group model HMO—A group model HMO is an HMO that contracts with a single multispecialty medical group to provide care to the HMO's membership. The group practice may work exclusively with the HMO, or it may provide services to non-HMO patients as well. The HMO pays the medical group a negotiated per capita rate, which the group distributes among its physicians, usually on a salaried basis.

Staff model HMO—A staff model HMO is a closed-panel HMO (where patients can receive services only through a limited number of providers) in which physicians are HMO employees. The providers see members in the HMO's own facilities.

Network model HMO—A network model HMO is an HMO that contracts with multiple physician groups to provide services to HMO members and may include single or multispecialty groups.

Individual practice association (IPA)—An individual practice association is a healthcare provider organization composed of a group of independent practicing physicians who maintain their own offices and band together for the purpose of contracting their services to HMOs, preferred provider organizations (PPOs), and insurance companies. An IPA may contract with and

provide services to both HMO and non-HMO plan participants.

Mixed model HMO—A mixed model HMO combines features of more than one HMO model.

See related Managed care; Preferred provider organization (PPO).

Health services and supplies expenditures—See Health expenditures, national.

Health status, respondent-assessed—Health status was measured in the National Health Interview Survey by asking the family respondent about his or her health or the health of a family member: "Would you say _____'s health is excellent, very good, good, fair, or poor?"

Hispanic origin—Hispanic or Latino origin includes persons of Mexican, Puerto Rican, Cuban, Central and South American, and other or unknown Latin American or Spanish origins. Persons of Hispanic origin may be of any race.

Birth File—The reporting area for an Hispanic-origin item on the birth certificate expanded between 1980 and 1993. Trend data on births of Hispanic and non-Hispanic parentage in this report are affected by expansion of the reporting area and by immigration. These two factors affect numbers of events, composition of the Hispanic population, and maternal and infant health characteristics.

In 1980 and 1981, information on births of Hispanic parentage was reported on the birth certificate by the following 22 states: Arizona, Arkansas, California, Colorado, Florida, Georgia, Hawaii, Illinois, Indiana, Kansas, Maine, Mississippi, Nebraska, Nevada, New Jersey, New Mexico, New York, North Dakota, Ohio, Texas, Utah, and Wyoming. In 1982 Tennessee, and in 1983 the District of Columbia, began reporting this information. Between 1983 and 1987, information on births of Hispanic parentage was available for 23 states and the District of Columbia. In 1988, this information became available for Alabama, Connecticut, Kentucky, Massachusetts, Montana, North Carolina, and Washington, increasing the number of states reporting information on births of Hispanic parentage to 30 states and the District of Columbia. In 1989 this information became available from an additional 17 states, increasing the number of Hispanic-reporting states to 47 and the District of Columbia. In 1989, only Louisiana, New Hampshire, and Oklahoma did not report Hispanic parentage on the birth certificate. With the inclusion of Oklahoma in 1989 and Louisiana in 1990 as Hispanic-reporting states, 99% of birth records included information on mother's origin. Hispanic origin of the mother was reported on the birth certificates of 49 states and the District of Columbia in 1991 and 1992; only New Hampshire did not provide this information. Starting in 1993 Hispanic origin of mother was reported by all 50 states and the District of Columbia.

Mortality File—The reporting area for an Hispanic-origin item on the death certificate expanded between 1985 and 1997. In 1985, mortality data by Hispanic origin of decedent were based on deaths to residents of the following 17 states and the District of Columbia whose data on the death certificate were at least 90% complete on a place-of-occurrence basis and of comparable format: Arizona, Arkansas, California, Colorado, Georgia, Hawaii, Illinois, Indiana, Kansas, Mississippi, Nebraska, New York, North Dakota, Ohio, Texas, Utah, and Wyoming. In 1986 New Jersey began reporting Hispanic origin of decedent, increasing the number of reporting states to 18 and the District of Columbia in 1986 and 1987. In 1988, Alabama, Kentucky, Maine, Montana, North Carolina, Oregon, Rhode Island, and Washington were added to the reporting area, increasing the number of states to 26 and the District of Columbia. In 1989 an additional 18 states were added, increasing the Hispanic reporting area to 44 states and the District of Columbia; only Connecticut, Louisiana, Maryland, New Hampshire, Oklahoma, and Virginia were not included in the reporting area. Starting with 1990 data in this book, the criterion was changed to include states whose data were at least 80% complete. In 1990 Maryland, Virginia, and Connecticut, in 1991 Louisiana, and in 1993 New Hampshire were added, increasing the reporting area for Hispanic origin of decedent to 47 states and the District of Columbia in 1990, 48 states and the District of Columbia in 1991 and 1992, and 49 states and the District of Columbia in 1993–1996. Only Oklahoma did not provide this information in 1993–1996. Starting in 1997, Hispanic origin of decedent was reported by all 50 states and the District of Columbia. Based on data from the U.S. Census Bureau, the 1990 reporting area

encompassed 99.6% of the U.S. Hispanic population. In 1990 more than 96% of death records included information on Hispanic origin of decedent.

National Health Interview Survey (NHIS) and *National Health and Nutrition Examination Survey (NHANES)*—Questions on Hispanic origin are self-reported in the NHANES III and subsequent years and all years of the NHIS and precede questions on race. The NHANES sample was designed to provide estimates specifically for persons of Mexican origin and not for all Hispanic-origin persons in the United States. Persons of Hispanic origin other than Mexicans were entered into the sample with different selection probabilities that are not nationally representative of the total U.S. Hispanic population.

Surveillance, Epidemiology, and End Results (SEER) Program—Data are available from the National Institutes of Health, National Cancer Institute. SEER Hispanic data used in *Health, United States* tables exclude data from Alaska, Hawaii, and Seattle. The North American Association of Central Cancer Registries, Inc. (NAACCR) Hispanic Identification Algorithm was used on a combination of variables to classify incidence cases as Hispanic for analytic purposes. See the report, NAACCR Guideline for Enhancing Hispanic-Latino Identification. Available from: seer.cancer.gov/seerstat/variables/seer/yr1973_2003/race_ethnicity/.

Youth Risk Behavior Survey (YRBS)—Prior to 1999, a single question was asked about race and Hispanic origin with the option of selecting one of the following categories: white (not Hispanic), black (not Hispanic), Hispanic or Latino, Asian or Pacific Islander, American Indian or Alaska Native, or other. Between 1999 and 2003, respondents were asked a single question about race and Hispanic origin with the option of choosing one or more of the following categories: white, black or African American, Hispanic or Latino, Asian, Native Hawaiian or Pacific Islander, or American Indian or Alaska Native. In 2005, respondents were asked a question about Hispanic origin (Are you Hispanic or Latino?) and a second separate question about race that included the option of selecting one or more of the following categories: American Indian or Alaska Native, Asian, black or African American, Native Hawaiian or Other Pacific Islander, or white. Because of the differences between questions, the data about race and

Hispanic ethnicity for the years prior to 1999 are not strictly comparable with estimates for the later years. However, analyses of data collected between 1991 and 2003 have indicated that the data are comparable across years and can be used to study trends. See related Race.

See Brender ND, Kann L, McManus, T. A comparison of two survey questions on race and ethnicity among high school students. Public opinion quarterly 2003;67(2):227–36.

HIV—See Human immunodeficiency virus (HIV) disease.

Home visit—Starting in 1997, the National Health Interview Survey has been collecting information on home visits received during the past 12 months. Respondents are asked "During the past 12 months, did you receive care at home from a nurse or other health care professional? What was the total number of home visits received?" These data are combined with data on visits to doctors' offices, clinics, and emergency departments to provide a summary measure of health care visits. See related Emergency department or emergency room visit; Health care contact.

Hospital—According to the American Hospital Association, hospitals are licensed institutions with at least six beds whose primary function is to provide diagnostic and therapeutic patient services for medical conditions by an organized physician staff and that have continuous nursing services under the supervision of registered nurses. The World Health Organization considers an establishment to be a hospital if it is permanently staffed by at least one physician, can offer inpatient accommodation, and can provide active medical and nursing care. Hospitals may be classified by type of service, ownership, size in terms of number of beds, and length of stay. In the National Hospital Ambulatory Medical Care Survey, hospitals include all those with an average length of stay for all patients of less than 30 days (short-stay) or hospitals whose specialty is general (medical or surgical) or children's general. Federal hospitals and hospital units of institutions and hospitals with fewer than six beds staffed for patient use are excluded. See related Average length of stay; Bed, health facility; Days of care; Emergency department; Inpatient; Outpatient department.

Community hospital—Community hospitals based on the American Hospital Association definition include all non-federal short-term general and special hospitals whose facilities and services are available to the public. Special hospitals include obstetrics and gynecology; eye, ear, nose, and throat; rehabilitation; orthopedic; and other specialty services. Short-term general and special childrens hospitals are also considered to be community hospitals. A hospital may include a nursing-home-type unit and still be classified as short-term, provided that the majority of its patients are admitted to units where the average length of stay is less than 30 days. Hospital units of institutions such as prisons and college infirmaries that are not open to the public and are contained within a nonhospital facility are not included in the category of community hospitals. Traditionally the definition included all non-federal short-stay hospitals except facilities for the mentally retarded. In a revised definition the following additional sites were excluded: hospital units of institutions, and alcoholism and chemical dependency facilities.

Federal hospital—Federal hospitals are operated by the federal government.

For-profit hospitals—For-profit hospitals are operated for profit by individuals, partnerships, or corporations.

General hospital—General hospitals provide diagnostic, treatment, and surgical services for patients with a variety of medical conditions. According to the World Health Organization, these hospitals provide medical and nursing care for more than one category of medical discipline (e.g., general medicine, specialized medicine, general surgery, specialized surgery, and obstetrics). Excluded are hospitals, usually in rural areas, that provide a more limited range of care.

Nonprofit hospital—Nonprofit hospitals are controlled by nonprofit organizations, including religious organizations, fraternal societies, and others.

Psychiatric hospital—Psychiatric hospitals are ones whose major type of service is psychiatric care. See related Mental health organization.

Registered hospital—Registered hospitals are registered with the American Hospital Association. About 98% of hospitals are registered.

Short-stay hospital—Short-stay hospitals in the National Hospital Discharge Survey, are those in which the average length of stay is less than 30 days. The National Health Interview Survey defines short-stay hospitals as any hospital or hospital department in which the type of service provided is general; maternity; eye, ear, nose, and throat; children's; or osteopathic.

Specialty hospital—Specialty hospitals such as psychiatric, tuberculosis, chronic disease, rehabilitation, maternity, and alcoholic or narcotic, provide a particular type of service to the majority of their patients.

Hospital-based physician—See Physician.

Hospital day—See Days of care.

Hospital utilization—Estimates of hospital utilization (such as hospital discharge rate, days of care rate, average length of stay, and percentage of the population with a hospitalization) presented in *Health, United States* are based on data from three different sources—the National Health Interview Survey (NHIS), the National Hospital Discharge Survey (NHDS), and the American Hospital Association. NHIS data are based on household interviews of the civilian noninstitutionalized population and thus exclude hospitalizations for institutionalized persons and those who died while hospitalized. NHDS data are based on hospital discharge records of all persons who have an inpatient stay in a non-federal short-stay hospital. NHDS includes hospital discharge records for all persons discharged alive or deceased and institutionalized persons and tables shown in *Health, United States* exclude data for newborn infants. Estimates for average length of stay between the NHDS and the AHA presented in *Health, United States* also differ because of different methods for counting days of care. See related Average length of stay; Days of care; Discharge; Appendix I, National Health Interview Survey, National Hospital Discharge Survey.

Human immunodeficiency virus (HIV) disease—HIV disease is a serious disease caused by a cytopathic retrovirus that is the cause of Acquired Immunity Syndrome (AIDS). It is also called AIDS-related virus, human T-cell leukemia virus type III, human T-cell lymphotrophic virus type III, and lymphadenopathy-associated virus. Mortality and morbidity coding for HIV disease are similar and have evolved over time.

Mortality coding—Starting with 1999 data, and the introduction of the Tenth Revision of the *International Classification of Diseases* (ICD–10), the title for this cause of death was changed to HIV disease from HIV infection and the ICD codes changed to B20–B24. Starting with 1987 data, NCHS introduced category numbers *042–*044 for classifying and coding HIV infection as a cause of death in ICD–9. The asterisk before the category numbers indicates that these codes were not part of the original ICD–9. HIV infection was formerly referred to as human T-cell lymphotropic virus-III/lymphadenopathy-associated virus (HTLV-III/LAV) infection. Before 1987 deaths involving HIV infection were classified to Deficiency of cell-mediated immunity (ICD–9 279.1) contained in the title All other diseases; to Pneumocystosis (ICD–9 136.3) contained in the title All other infectious and parasitic diseases; to Malignant neoplasms, including neoplasms of lymphatic and hematopoietic tissues; and to a number of other causes. Therefore, before 1987, death statistics for HIV infection are not strictly comparable with data for 1987 and later years and are not shown in this report.

Morbidity coding—The National Hospital Discharge Survey codes diagnosis data using the *International Classification of Diseases, Ninth Revision, Clinical Modification* (ICD–9–CM). During 1984 and 1985 only data for AIDS (ICD–9–CM 279.19) were included. In 1986–1994 discharges with the following diagnoses were included: Acquired immunodeficiency syndrome (AIDS), Human immunodeficiency virus (HIV) infection and associated conditions, and Positive serological or viral culture findings for HIV (ICD–9–CM 042–044, 279.19, and 795.8). Beginning in 1995 discharges with the following diagnoses were included: Human immunodeficiency virus (HIV) disease and Asymptomatic human immunodeficiency virus (HIV) infection status (ICD–9–CM 042 and V08).

See related Acquired immunodeficiency syndrome (AIDS); Cause of death; *International Classification of Diseases* (ICD); *International Classification of Diseases, Ninth Revision, Clinical Modification* (ICD–9–CM).

Hypertension—See Blood pressure, elevated.

ICD; ICD codes—See Cause of death; *International Classification of Diseases (ICD)*.

Illicit drug use—Illicit drug use refers to use and misuse of illegal and controlled drugs.

Monitoring the Future Study—In this school-based survey of secondary school students, information on marijuana use is collected using self-completed questionnaires. The information is based on the following questions: "On how many occasions (if any) have you used marijuana in the last 30 days?" and "On how many occasions (if any) have you used hashish in the last 30 days?" Questions on cocaine use include the following: "On how many occasions (if any) have you taken crack (cocaine in chunk or rock form) during the last 30 days?" and "On how many occasions (if any) have you taken cocaine in any other form during the last 30 days?"

National Survey on Drug Use & Health (NSDUH)—Information on illicit drug use is collected for survey participants 12 years of age and over. Information on any illicit drug use, including marijuana or hashish, cocaine, heroin, hallucinogens, and nonmedical use of prescription drugs is based on the following question: "During the past 30 days, on how many days did you use (specific illicit drug)?" See related Substance use.

Incidence—Incidence is the number of cases of disease having their onset during a prescribed period of time. It is often expressed as a rate (e.g., the incidence of measles per 1,000 children 5–15 years of age during a specified year). Incidence is a measure of morbidity or other events that occur within a specified period of time. Measuring incidence may be complicated because the population at risk for the disease may change during the period of interest, for example, due to births, deaths, or migration. In addition, determining that a case is new—that is, that its onset occurred during the prescribed period of time—may be difficult. Because of these difficulties in measuring incidence, many health statistics are measured using prevalence. See related Prevalence.

Income—See Family income.

Individual practice association (IPA)—See Health maintenance organization (HMO).

Industry of employment—Starting with 2003 data, industries are classified according to the 2002 North American Industry Classification System (NAICS) for the presentation of health data in *Health, United States*. The NAICS classification system groups establishments into industries based on their production or supply function—establishments using similar raw material inputs, capital equipment, and labor are classified in the same industry. This approach creates homogeneous categories well suited for economic analysis. NAICS uses a six-digit hierarchical coding system to classify all economic activity into 20 industry sectors. The first two digits of the six-digit code designate the highest level of aggregation, with 20 such two-digit industry sectors (Table IX). Five sectors are primarily goods-producing sectors, and 15 are entirely services-providing sectors. NAICS allows for the classification of 1,170 industries.

NAICS replaces the Standard Industrial Classification (SIC) system, originally designed in the 1930s and revised and updated periodically to reflect changes in the U.S. economy. The last SIC revision was in 1987. The SIC system focused on the manufacturing sector of the economy and provided significantly less detail for the now dominant service sector, including newly developed industries in information services, health care delivery, and high-tech manufacturing. Although some titles in SIC and NAICS are similar, there is little comparability between the two systems because industry groupings are defined differently. Estimates of deaths, injuries, and illnesses classified by NAICS industry should not be compared with earlier estimates that used the SIC.

Starting with *Health United States, 2005*, health data by industry from the Bureau of Labor Statistics' Census of Fatal Occupational Injuries (CFOI) and Survey of Occupational Injuries and Illnesses (SOII) data systems are classified using the NAICS system and replace trends in occupational health data based on the SIC system in previous editions of *Health, United States*.

Infant death—An infant death is the death of a live-born child before his or her first birthday. Age at death may be further classified according to neonatal and postneonatal. Neonatal deaths are those that occur before the 28th day of life; postneonatal deaths are those that occur between 28 and 365 days of age. See related Rate: Death and related rates.

Injury—The International Classification of External Causes of Injuries (ICECI) Coordination and Maintenance Group defines injury as a (suspected) bodily lesion resulting from acute overexposure to energy (this can be mechanical, thermal, electrical, chemical, or radiant) interacting with the body in amounts or rates that exceed the threshold of physiological tolerance. In some cases an injury results from an insufficiency of any of the vital elements. Acute poisonings and toxic effects, including overdoses of substances and wrong substances given or taken in error are included, as are adverse effects and complications of therapeutic, surgical, and medical care. Psychological harm is excluded. Injuries can be intentional or unintentional (i.e., accidental). External causes of nonfatal injuries in NCHS data systems are coded to the *International Classification of Diseases, Ninth Revision, Clinical Modification* Supplementary Classification of External Causes of Injury and Poisoning, often referred to as E-codes. See Table VII for a list of external causes of injury categories and E-codes used in *Health, United States.* See related Diagnosis; Injury-related visit. See ICECI Coordination and Maintenance Group (2004). International Classification of External Causes of Injuries (ICECI), version 1.2. Consumer Safety Institute, Amsterdam and AIHW National Injury Surveillance Unit, Adelaide. Available from: www.iceci.org.

Injury-related visit—In the National Hospital Ambulatory Medical Care Survey an emergency department visit was considered injury related if, on the patient record form (PRF), the checkbox for injury was indicated. In addition, injury visits were identified if the physician's diagnosis was injury related (ICD–9–CM code of 800–999), an external cause-of-injury code was present (ICD–9–CM E800–E999), or the patient's reason for visit code was injury-related. See related Emergency department or emergency room visit; External cause of injury; Injury.

Inpatient—An inpatient is a person who is formally admitted to the inpatient service of a hospital for observation, care, diagnosis, or treatment. See related Admission; Average length of stay; Days of care; Discharge; Hospital.

Inpatient care—See Hospital utilization; Mental health service type.

Inpatient day—See Days of care.

Instrumental activities of daily living (IADL)—Instrumental activities of daily living are activities related to independent living and include preparing meals, managing money, shopping for groceries or personal items, performing light or heavy housework, and using a telephone. In the National Health Interview Survey (NHIS) respondents are asked whether they or family members 18 years of age and over need the help of another person for handling routine IADL

needs because of a physical, mental, or emotional problem. Persons are considered to have an IADL limitation in the NHIS if any causal condition is chronic.

In the Medicare Current Beneficiary Survey if a sample person had any difficulty performing an activity by him- or herself and without special equipment, or did not perform the activity at all because of health problems, the person was categorized as having a limitation in that activity. The limitation may have been temporary or chronic at the time of the interview. Sample persons in the community answered health status and functioning questions themselves, if able to do so. For sample persons in a long-term care facility, a proxy such as a nurse answered questions about the sample person's health status and functioning. See related Activities of daily living (ADL); Limitation of activity.

Insurance—See Health insurance coverage.

Intermediate care facility—See Nursing home.

International Classification of Diseases (ICD)—The ICD provides the ground rules for coding and classifying cause-of-death data. The ICD is developed collaboratively by the World Health Organization (WHO) and 10 international centers, one of which is housed at NCHS. The purpose of the ICD is to promote international comparability in the collection, classification, processing, and presentation of health statistics. Since 1900, the ICD has been modified about once every 10 years, except for the 20-year interval between ICD–9 and ICD–10 (see Table IV). The purpose of the revisions is to stay abreast with advances in medical science. New revisions usually introduce major disruptions in time series of mortality statistics (see Tables V and VI). For more information, see the NCHS website. Available from:

Table VII. Codes for first-listed external causes of injury from the *International Classification of Diseases, Ninth Revision, Clinical Modification*

External cause of injury category	E-Code numbers
Unintentional	E800–E869, E880–E929
Motor vehicle traffic	E810–E819
Falls	E880–E886, E888
Struck by or against objects or persons	E916–E917
Caused by cutting and piercing instruments or objects	E920
Intentional (suicide and homicide)	E950–E969

Table VIII. Percentage of persons under 65 years of age with Medicaid or who are uninsured, by selected demographic characteristics using Method 1 and Method 2 estimation procedures: United States, 2004

	Medicaid[1]		Uninsured[2]	
Characteristic	Method 2[3]	Method 1[3]	Method 2[3]	Method 1[3]
	Percent (standard error)			
Age				
Under 65 years	12.0 (0.24)	11.8 (0.24)	16.4 (0.23)	16.6 (0.23)
Under 18 years	25.4 (0.49)	24.9 (0.49)	9.2 (0.30)	9.7 (0.29)
18–64 years	6.6 (0.17)	6.5 (0.17)	19.3 (0.26)	19.4 (0.26)
Percent of poverty level[4]				
Below 100%	47.5 (1.03)	46.6 (1.03)	29.6 (0.89)	30.5 (0.92)
100%-less than 200%	22.0 (0.59)	21.5 (0.60)	28.9 (0.66)	29.4 (0.66)
200% or more	2.9 (0.13)	2.8 (0.13)	9.4 (0.23)	9.5 (0.23)
Age and percent of poverty level[4]				
Under 18 years				
Below 100%	71.9 (1.35)	70.2 (1.35)	14.5 (1.15)	16.2 (1.22)
100%-less than 200%	39.2 (1.13)	38.4 (1.14)	15.0 (0.81)	15.8 (0.82)
200% or more	6.2 (0.33)	6.1 (0.33)	4.9 (0.30)	4.9 (0.30)
18–64 years				
Below 100%	31.2 (1.02)	30.8 (1.02)	39.7 (1.09)	40.1 (1.09)
100%-less than 200%	12.0 (0.48)	11.8 (0.48)	37.0 (0.72)	37.2 (0.72)
200% or more	1.7 (0.11)	1.7 (0.10)	11.0 (0.26)	11.1 (0.26)
Hispanic origin and race[5]				
Hispanic or Latino	22.2 (0.55)	21.5 (0.55)	34.4 (0.64)	35.1 (0.65)
Mexican.	22.0 (0.63)	21.5 (0.63)	37.6 (0.82)	38.1 (0.83)
Not Hispanic or Latino	10.2 (0.25)	10.1 (0.25)	13.2 (0.23)	13.3 (0.23)
White only	7.4 (0.26)	7.4 (0.26)	12.0 (0.25)	12.1 (0.25)
Black or African American only.	23.9 (0.80)	23.5 (0.79)	17.3 (0.58)	17.8 (0.58)

[1]The category Medicaid includes persons who do not have private coverage, but who have Medicaid or other state-sponsored health plans, including the State Children's Health Insurance Program (SCHIP).

[2]The category Uninsured includes persons who have not indicated that they are covered at the time of interview under private health insurance, Medicare, Medicaid, SCHIP, a state-sponsored health plan, other government programs, or military health plan (includes VA, TRICARE, and CHAMP-VA). This category includes persons who are only covered by Indian Health Service (IHS) or only have a plan that pays for one type of service, such as accidents or dental care.

[3]Starting with the third quarter of 2004, two additional questions were added to the NHIS insurance section to reduce potential errors in reporting of Medicare and Medicaid status. Persons 65 years of age and over not reporting Medicare coverage were asked explicitly about Medicare coverage, and persons under 65 years of age with no reported coverage were asked explicitly about Medicaid coverage. Estimates calculated without using the additional information from these questions are noted as Method 1. Estimates calculated using the additional information from these questions are noted as Method 2.

[4]Percent of poverty level is based on family income and family size and composition using the U.S. Census Bureau's poverty thresholds. The percentage of respondents with unknown poverty level was 28.2% in 2004. See the NHIS Survey Description Document for 2004 . Available from: www.cdc.gov/nchs/nhis.htm.

[5]Persons of Hispanic origin may be of any race or combination of races. Similarly, the category Not Hispanic or Latino refers to all persons who are not of Hispanic or Latino origin, regardless of race.

SOURCE: Family Core component of the 2004 National Health Interview Survey. Data are based on household interviews of a sample of the civilian noninstitutionalized population. Available from: www.cdc.gov/nchs/products/pubs/pubd/hestats/impact.htm.

www.cdc.gov/nchs/about/major/dvs/icd10des.htm. See related Cause of death; Comparability ratio; *International Classification of Diseases, Ninth Revision, Clinical Modification* (ICD–9–CM).

International Classification of Diseases, Ninth Revision, Clinical Modification (ICD–9–CM)—The ICD–9–CM is based on and is compatible with the World Health Organization's

International Classification of Diseases, Ninth Revision (ICD–9). The United States currently uses ICD–9–CM to code morbidity diagnoses and inpatient procedures. ICD–9–CM consists of three volumes. Volumes 1 and 2 contain the diagnosis tabular list and index. Volume 3 contains the procedure classification (tabular and index combined).

ICD–9–CM is divided into 17 chapters and 2 supplemental classifications. The chapters are arranged primarily by body system. In addition there are chapters for Infectious and parasitic diseases; Neoplasms; Endocrine, nutritional, and metabolic diseases; Mental disorders; Complications of pregnancy, childbirth, and puerperium; Certain conditions originating in the perinatal period; Congenital anomalies; and Symptoms, signs, and ill-defined conditions. The two supplemental classifications are for factors influencing health status and contact with health services (V codes), and external causes of injury and poisoning (E codes).

In *Health, United States* morbidity data are classified using ICD–9–CM. Diagnostic categories and codes for ICD–9–CM are shown in Table X; ICD–9–CM procedure categories and codes are shown in Table XI. For additional information about ICD–9–CM, see the NCHS website. Available from: www.cdc.gov/nchs/icd9.htm. See related *International Classification of Diseases (ICD)*.

Late fetal death rate—See Rate: Death and related rates.

Leading causes of death—See Cause-of-death ranking.

Length of stay—See Average length of stay.

Life expectancy—Life expectancy is the average number of years of life remaining to a person at a particular age and is based on a given set of age-specific death rates, generally the mortality conditions existing in the period mentioned. Life expectancy may be determined by race, sex, or other characteristics using age-specific death rates for the population with that characteristic. See related Rate: Death and related rates.

Limitation of activity—Limitation of activity may be defined different ways, depending on the conceptual framework. In the National Health Interview Survey limitation of activity refers to a long-term reduction in a person's capacity to perform the usual kind or amount of activities associated with his or her age group as a result of a chronic condition. Limitation of activity is assessed by asking persons a series of questions about limitations in their or household members' ability to perform activities usual for their age group because of a physical, mental, or emotional problem. Persons are asked about limitations in activities of daily living, instrumental activities of daily living, play, school, work, difficulty walking or remembering, and any other activity limitations. For reported limitations, the causal health conditions are determined, and

Table IX. Codes for industries, by the 2002 North American Industry Classification System (NAICS)

Industry	Code numbers
Goods producing	
Natural resources and mining:	
Agriculture, forestry, fishing and hunting	11
Mining	21
Construction	23
Manufacturing	31–33
Service providing	
Trade, transportation, and utilities:	
Wholesale trade	42
Retail trade	44–45
Transportation and warehousing.	48–49
Utilities.	22
Information	51
Financial activities:	
Finance and insurance	52
Real estate and rental and leasing	53
Professional and business services:	
Professional, scientific, and technical services . . .	54
Management of companies and enterprises.	55
Administrative and support and waste management and remediation services	56
Education and health services:	
Education services	61
Health care and social assistance	62
Leisure and hospitality:	
Arts, entertainment, and recreation.	71
Accommodation and food services	72
Other services, except public administration	81
Public administration	92

SOURCE: Bureau of Labor Statistics. Available from: www.bls.gov/bls/naics_aggregation.htm.

persons are considered limited if one or more of these conditions is chronic. Children under 18 years of age who receive special education or early intervention services are considered to have a limitation of activity. See related Activities of daily living; Condition; Instrumental activities of daily living.

Long-term care facility—A long-term care facility is a residence that provides a specific level of personal or medical care or supervision to residents. In the Medicare Current Beneficiary Survey, a residence is considered a long-term care facility if it has three or more long-term care beds and provides personal care services to residents, continuous supervision of residents, or long-term care services

Table X. Codes for diagnostic categories from the *International Classification of Diseases, Ninth Revision, Clinical Modification*

Diagnostic category	Code numbers
Females with delivery	V27
Human immunodeficiency virus (HIV) (1984–1985)	279.19
(1986–1994)	042–044, 279.19, 795.8
(Starting in 1995)	042, V08
Malignant neoplasms	140–208
Large intestine and rectum	153–154, 197.5
Trachea, bronchus, and lung	162, 176.4, 197.0, 197.3
Breast	174–175, 198.81
Prostate	185
Diabetes	250
Alcohol and drug	291–292, 303–305
Serious mental illness	295–298
Diseases of the nervous system and sense organs	320–389
Diseases of the circulatory system	390–459
Diseases of heart	391–392.0, 393–398, 402, 404, 410–416, 420–429
Ischemic heart disease	410–414
Acute myocardial infarction	410
Heart failure	428
Cerebrovascular disease	430–438
Diseases of the respiratory system	460–519
Pneumonia	480–486
Asthma	493
Hyperplasia of prostate	600
Decubitus ulcers	707
Diseases of the musculoskeletal system and connective tissue	710–739
Osteoarthritis	715, 721
Intervertebral disc disorders	722
Injuries and poisoning	800–999
Fracture, all sites	800–829
Fracture of neck of femur (hip)	820

throughout the facility or in a separately identifiable unit. Types of long-term care facilities include licensed nursing homes, skilled nursing homes, intermediate care facilities, retirement homes (that provide services), domiciliary or personal care facilities, distinct long-term care units in a hospital complex, mental health facilities and centers, assisted and foster care homes, and institutions for the mentally retarded and developmentally disabled. See related Nursing home.

Low birthweight—See Birthweight.

Mammography—Mammography is an x-ray image of the breast used to detect irregularities in breast tissue. In the National Health Interview Survey questions concerning use of mammography were asked on an intermittent schedule, and question content differed slightly across years. In 1987 and

1990 women were asked to report when they had their last mammogram. In 1991 women were asked whether they had a mammogram in the past 2 years. In 1993 and 1994 women were asked whether they had a mammogram within the past year, between 1 and 2 years ago, or over 2 years ago. In 1998 women were asked whether they had a mammogram a year ago or less, more than 1 year but not more than 2 years, or more than 2 years ago. In 1999 women were asked when they had their most recent mammogram in days, weeks, months, or years. In 1999, 10% of women in the sample responded 2 years ago, and in this analysis these women were coded as within the past 2 years although a response of 2 years ago may include women whose last mammogram was more than 2 but less than 3 years ago. Thus, estimates for 1999 are overestimated to some degree in comparison with estimates in previous years. In 2000 and 2003 women were asked when they had their most recent mammogram (give month and year). Women who did not respond were given a follow-up question that used the 1999 wording, and women who did not answer the follow-up question were asked a second follow-up question that used the 1998 wording. In 2000 and 2003, 2% of women in the sample answered 2 years ago using the 1999 wording, and they were coded as within the past 2 years. Thus, estimates for 2000 and 2003 may be slightly overestimated in comparison with estimates for years prior to 1999.

Managed care—Managed care is a term originally used to refer to the prepaid health care sector (health maintenance organizations or HMOs) where care is provided under a fixed budget and costs are therein capable of being managed. Increasingly, the term is being used to include preferred provider organizations (PPOs) and even forms of indemnity insurance coverage (or fee-for-service insurance) that incorporate preadmission certification and other utilization controls.

Medicare managed care, begun in 1985, has included a combination of risk-based and cost-based plans. Risk-based plans receive a fixed pre-payment per beneficiary per month to cover the cost of all services that a beneficiary would receive. The Centers for Medicare & Medicaid Services (CMS) sets the per-member-per-month rate to reimburse risk-based plans based on the fee-for-service equivalent cost adjusted for certain demographic factors. Cost-based plans are offered by a Health Maintenance Organization (HMO) or a Competitive Medical Plan (CMP) and receive payment on a fee-for-service basis, similar to the traditional Medicare plan. While the payment system under cost-based plans is similar to the traditional Medicare plan, the cost-based plans generally cover more preventative services than the traditional Medicare plan. For current definitions of the various Medicare managed care plans, refer to the Medicare Managed Care Manual, (100–16) Chapter 1, Section 30 – Types of MA Plans. Available from: www.resdac.umn.edu/Tools/TBs/TN-009.asp. Medicare enrollees have the choice to enroll in a managed care program (if available) or receive services on a fee-for-service basis.

The two major Medicaid managed care categories are risk-based plans and primary care case management (PCCM) arrangements. In risk-based plans, managed care organizations (MCO) are paid a fixed monthly fee per enrollee. The MCOs assume some or all of the financial risk for providing care. PCCM providers are usually physicians, physician group practices, or entities employing or having other arrangements with such physicians, but sometimes also including nurse practitioners, nurse midwives, or physician assistants. These PCCM providers, sometimes called gatekeepers, contract directly with the state to locate, coordinate, and monitor covered primary care (and sometimes additional services). PCCM providers are paid a per-patient case management fee and usually do not assume financial risk for the provision of services. Some states allow Medicaid enrollees to voluntarily enroll in managed care plans; other states require that certain categories of Medicaid beneficiaries join managed care plans. Within both risked-based plans and PCCM arrangements there are plans that provide specialized services to certain categories of Medicaid beneficiaries. For more information on state Medicaid managed care plans, see www.cms.hhs.gov/medicaid/stateplans/. See related Health maintenance organization (HMO); Medicare; Medicaid; Preferred provider organization (PPO).

Marital status—Marital status is classified through self-reporting into the categories married and unmarried. The term married encompasses all married people including those separated from their spouses. Unmarried includes those who are single (never married), divorced, or widowed. The abortion surveillance program classified separated people as unmarried before 1978.

Birth File—In 1970, 39 states and the District of Columbia (DC) and in 1975, 38 states and DC included a direct question about mother's marital status on the birth certificate. Since 1980, national estimates of births to unmarried women have been based on two methods for determining marital status, a direct question in the birth registration process and inferential procedures. In 1980–1996 marital status was reported on the birth certificates of 41–45 states and DC; with the addition of California in 1997, 46 states and DC; and in 1998–2001, 48 states and DC. In 1997, all but four states (Connecticut, Michigan, Nevada, and New York), and in 1998, all but two states (Michigan and New York) included a direct question about mother's marital status on their birth certificates. In 1998–2001, marital status was imputed as married on those 0.03–0.05% of birth records with missing information in the 48 states and DC where this information was obtained by a direct question.

For states lacking a direct question, marital status was inferred. Before 1980 the incidence of births to unmarried women in states with no direct question on marital status was assumed to be the same as the incidence in reporting states in the same geographic division. Starting in 1980 for states without a direct question, marital status was inferred by comparing the parents' and child's surnames. Inferential procedures in current use depend on the presence of a paternity acknowledgment or missing information on the father. Changes in reporting procedures by some states in 1995 and 1997 had little effect on national totals, but they did affect trends for age groups and some state trends. Details of the changes in reporting procedures are described in Ventura SJ, Bachrach CA. Nonmarital childbearing in the United States, 1940–1999. National Vital Statistics Reports 2000; 48 (16). Hyattsville, MD: National Center for Health Statistics. Available from: www.cdc.gov/nchs/births.htm.

Maternal age—See Age.

Maternal death—Maternal death is defined by the World Health Organization as the death of a woman while pregnant or within 42 days of termination of pregnancy, irrespective of the duration and site of the pregnancy, from any cause related to or aggravated by the pregnancy or its management, but not from accidental or incidental causes. A maternal death is one for which the certifying physician has designated a maternal condition as the underlying cause of death. Maternal conditions are those assigned to pregnancy, childbirth, and the puerperium, ICD–10 codes A34, O00–O95, O98–O99 (see Table V). Changes have been made in the classification and coding of maternal deaths between ICD–9 and ICD–10, effective with mortality data for 1999. ICD–10 changes pertain to indirect maternal causes and timing of death relative to pregnancy. If only indirect maternal causes of death (i.e., a previously existing disease or a disease that developed during pregnancy that was not due to direct obstetric causes but was aggravated by physiologic effects of pregnancy) are reported in Part I of the death certificate and pregnancy is reported in either Part I or Part II, ICD–10 classifies this as a maternal death. ICD–9 only classified the death as maternal if pregnancy was reported in Part I. Some state death certificates include a separate question regarding pregnancy status. A positive response to the question is interpreted as, pregnant, being reported in Part II of the cause-of-death section of the death certificate. If the medical certifier did not specify when death occurred relative to the pregnancy, it is assumed that the pregnancy terminated 42 days or less prior to death. In 2003, 21 states had a separate question related to pregnancy status of female decedents around the time of their death, and 2 states had a prompt encouraging certifiers to report recent pregnancies on the death certificate; however, there were at least 6 different questions used. The 2003 revision of the U.S. Standard Certificate of Death introduced a standard question format with categories designed to utilize additional codes available in ICD–10 for deaths associated with pregnancy, childbirth, and the puerperium. As states revise their certificates, most states are expected to introduce the standard item or replace pre-existing questions with the standard item, so that there will be wider adoption of a pregnancy status item across the country and greater standardization of the particular item used. Maternal mortality rates tend to be consistently greater in areas with a separate item on the death certificate (7% greater for 1996–1998 and 1999–2001). In 2002–2003, the rates for areas with a separate question are 11% greater than those for areas without a separate question.

Under ICD–10 a new category has been added for deaths from maternal causes that occurred more than 42 days after delivery or termination of pregnancy (O96–O97). In 1999, there were 15 such deaths, and in 2000 there were 8. See related Rate: Death and related rates.

Maternal education—See Education.

Maternal mortality rate—See Rate: Death and related rates.

Medicaid—Medicaid was authorized by Title XIX of the Social Security Act in 1965 as a jointly funded cooperative venture between the federal and state governments to assist states in the provision of adequate medical care to eligible needy persons. Within broad federal guidelines, each of the states establishes its own eligibility standards; determines the type, amount, duration, and scope of services; sets the rate of payment for services; and administers its own program.

Medicaid is the largest program providing medical and health-related services to America's poorest people. However, Medicaid does not provide medical assistance to all poor persons. Under the broadest provisions of the federal statute, Medicaid does not provide health care services even for very poor childless adults under age 65 years unless they are disabled. Except as noted, all states must provide Medicaid coverage to the following:

■ Individuals who meet the requirements for the Aid to Families with Dependent Children (AFDC) program that were in effect in their state on July 16, 1996, or, at state option, more liberal criteria (with some exceptions).

■ Children under age 6 whose family income is at or below 133% of the federal poverty level.

■ Pregnant women whose family income is below 133% of the federal poverty level (services to these women are limited to those related to pregnancy, complications of pregnancy, delivery, and postpartum care).

■ Supplemental Security Income (SSI) recipients in most states (some states use more restrictive Medicaid eligibility requirements that predate SSI).

■ Recipients of adoption or foster care assistance under Title IV of the Social Security Act.

■ Special protected groups (typically individuals who lose their cash assistance because of earnings from work or from increased Social Security benefits but who may keep Medicaid for a period of time).

■ Children age 6–18 years in families with incomes at or below the federal poverty level.

■ Certain Medicare beneficiaries (low income is only one test for Medicaid eligibility for those within these groups; their resources also are tested against threshold levels, as determined by each state within federal guidelines).

States also have the option of providing Medicaid coverage for other groups.

Medicaid operates as a vendor payment program. States may pay health care providers directly on a fee-for-service basis, or states may pay for Medicaid services through various prepayment arrangements, such as health maintenance organizations (HMOs) or other forms of managed care. Within federally imposed upper limits and specific restrictions, each state for the most part has broad discretion in determining the payment methodology and payment rate for services. Thus, the Medicaid program varies considerably from state to state, as well as within each state over time. For more information see www.cms.hhs.gov/MedicaidEligibility/. See related Health expenditures, national; Health insurance coverage; Health maintenance organization (HMO); Managed care; Appendix I, Medicaid Data System.

Medical specialty—See Physician specialty.

Medical vendor payments—Under the Medicaid program, medical vendor payments are payments (expenditures) to medical vendors from the state through a fiscal agent or to a health insurance plan. Adjustments are made for Indian Health Service payments to Medicaid, cost settlements, third party recoupments, refunds, voided checks, and other financial settlements that cannot be related to specific provided claims. Excluded are payments made for medical care under the emergency assistance provisions, payments made from state medical assistance funds that are not federally matchable, disproportionate share hospital payments, cost sharing or enrollment fees collected from recipients or a third party, and administration and training costs.

Medicare—This is a nationwide health insurance program providing health insurance protection to people 65 years of age and over, people entitled to Social Security disability payments for 2 years or more, and people with end-stage renal disease, regardless of income. The program was enacted July 30, 1965, as Title XVIII, Health Insurance for the Aged of the Social Security Act, and became effective on July 1, 1966. From its inception, it has included two separate but coordinated programs: hospital insurance (Part A) and supplementary medical insurance (Part B). In 1999, additional choices were allowed for delivering Medicare Part A and Part B benefits. Medicare Advantage, previously Medicare+Choice, (Part C) is an expanded set of options for the delivery of health care under Medicare, created in the Balanced Budget Act passed by Congress in 1997. The term Medicare Advantage refers to options other than original Medicare. While all Medicare beneficiaries can receive their benefits through the original fee-for-service (FFS) program, most beneficiaries enrolled in both Part A and Part B can choose to participate in a Medicare Advantage plan instead. Organizations that seek to contract as Medicare Advantage plans must meet specific organizational, financial, and other requirements. Most Medicare Advantage plans are coordinated care plans, which include health maintenance organizations (HMOs), provider-sponsored organizations (PSOs), preferred provider organizations (PPOs), and other certified coordinated care plans and entities that meet the standards set forth in the law. The Medicare Advantage program also includes Medical savings account (MSA) plans, which provide benefits after a single high deductible is met, and private, unrestricted FFS plans, which allow beneficiaries to select certain private providers. These programs are available in only a limited number of states. For those providers who agree to accept the plan's payment terms and conditions, this option does not place the providers at risk, nor does it vary payment rates based on utilization. Only the coordinated care plans are considered managed care plans. Except for MSA plans, all Medicare Advantage plans are required to provide at least the current Medicare benefit package, excluding hospice services. Plans may offer additional covered services and are required to do so (or return excess payments) if plan costs are lower than the Medicare payments received by the plan.

The Medicare Prescription Drug, Improvement, and Modernization Act (MMA) was passed on December 8, 2003. The MMA established a voluntary drug benefit for Medicare beneficiaries and created a new Medicare Part D. People eligible for Medicare can choose to enroll in Part D beginning in January of 2006. For more information see www.medicare.gov/publications/pubs/pdf/10050.pdf. See related Fee-for-service health insurance; Health insurance coverage; Health maintenance organization (HMO); Managed care; Appendix I, Medicare Administrative Data.

Mental health organization—The Center for Mental Health Services of the Substance Abuse and Mental Health Services Administration defines a mental health organization as an administratively distinct public or private agency or institution whose primary concern is provision of direct mental health services to the mentally ill or emotionally disturbed. Excluded are private office-based practices of psychiatrists, psychologists, and other mental health providers; psychiatric services of all types of hospitals or outpatient clinics operated by federal agencies other than the Department of Veterans Affairs (e.g., Public Health Service, Indian Health Service, Department of Defense, and Bureau of Prisons); general hospitals that have no separate psychiatric services but admit psychiatric patients to nonpsychiatric units; and psychiatric services of schools, colleges, halfway houses, community residential organizations, local and county jails, state prisons, and other human services providers. The major types of mental health organizations are described below.

Freestanding psychiatric outpatient clinic—These clinics provide only outpatient mental health services on either a regular or emergency basis. A psychiatrist generally assumes the medical responsibility for services.

Psychiatric hospital—These hospitals (public or private) primarily provide 24-hour inpatient care and treatment in a hospital setting to persons with mental illnesses. Psychiatric hospitals may be under state, county, private for profit, or private nonprofit auspices.

General hospital psychiatric service—These are organizations that provide psychiatric services with assigned staff for 24-hour inpatient or residential care and/or less than 24-hour outpatient care in a separate ward, unit, floor, or wing of the hospital.

Department of Veterans Affairs medical center—These are hospitals operated by the Department of Veterans Affairs (formerly Veterans Administration) and include Department of Veterans Affairs general hospital psychiatric services (including large neuropsychiatric units) and Department of Veterans Affairs psychiatric outpatient clinics.

Residential treatment center for emotionally disturbed children—These centers must meet all of the following criteria: (a) provide 24-hour residential services; (b) are not licensed as a psychiatric hospital and have the primary purpose of providing individually planned mental health treatment services in conjunction with residential care; (c) include a clinical program directed by a psychiatrist, psychologist, social worker, or psychiatric nurse with a graduate degree; (d) serve children and youth primarily under the age of 18; and (e) have the primary diagnosis as mental illness, classified as other than mental retardation, developmental disability, or substance-related disorders, according to DSM-II/ICDA-8 or DSM-IIIR/ICD-9–CM codes, for the majority of admissions.

Multiservice mental health organization—These organizations provide services in both 24-hour and less than 24-hour settings and are not classifiable as a psychiatric hospital, general hospital, or residential treatment center for emotionally disturbed children. (The classification of a psychiatric or general hospital or residential treatment center for emotionally disturbed children takes precedence over a multiservice classification, even if two or more services are offered.)

Partial care organization—These organizations provide a program of ambulatory mental health services or rehabilitation, habitation, or education programs.

See related Admission; Mental health service type.

Mental health service type—This term refers to the following types of mental health services:

24-hour mental health care, formerly called inpatient care, provides care in a mental health hospital setting.

Less than 24-hour care, formerly called outpatient or partial care treatment, provides mental health services on an ambulatory basis.

Residential treatment care provides overnight mental health care in conjunction with an intensive treatment program in a setting other than a hospital. Facilities may offer care to emotionally disturbed children or mentally ill adults.

See related Admission; Mental health organization.

Metropolitan statistical area (MSA)—The 2003 Office of Management and Budget (OMB) standards define metropolitan areas according to published standards that are applied to U.S. Census Bureau data. An MSA is a county or group of contiguous counties that contains at least one urbanized area of 50,000 or more population. In addition to the county or counties that contain all or part of the urbanized area, an MSA may contain other counties that are economically and socially integrated with the main city as measured by work commuting. Counties that are not within an MSA are considered to be nonmetropolitan.

For National Health Interview Survey (NHIS) data before 1995, metropolitan population is based on MSAs as defined by OMB in 1983 using the 1980 census. Starting with the 1995 NHIS, metropolitan population is based on MSAs as defined by OMB in 1993 using the 1990 census. The 1993 criteria for designating MSAs differs from the 2003 criteria. For example, under the 1993 standards the metropolitan character of a county could be considered in determining whether to classify a county as metropolitan. For additional information about metropolitan statistical areas see the Census website, available from: www.census.gov/population/www/estimates/metrodef.html. See related Urbanization.

Micropolitan statistical area—The Office of Management and Budget (OMB) defines micropolitan areas based on published standards that are applied to U.S. Census Bureau data. A micropolitan statistical area is a nonmetropolitan county or group of contiguous nonmetropolitan counties that contains an urban cluster of 10,000 to 49,999 persons. A micropolitan statistical area may include surrounding counties if there are strong economic ties between the counties, based on commuting patterns. Nonmetropolitan counties that are not classified as part of a micropolitan statistical area are considered nonmicropolitan. For additional information about micropolitan statistical areas see www.census.gov/population/www/estimates/metrodef.html. See related Urbanization.

Multiservice mental health organization—See Mental health organization.

National Drug Code (NDC) Directory therapeutic class—The NDC system was originally established as an essential part of an out-of-hospital drug reimbursement program under Medicare. The NDC serves as a universal product identifier for human drugs. The current edition of the NDC is limited to prescription drugs and a few selected over-the-counter (OTC) products. The directory consists of prescription and selected OTC insulin, domestic, and foreign drug products that are in commercial distribution in the United States. The products have been listed in accordance with the Drug Listing Act and applicable Code of Federal Regulations for submitting drug product information to the Food and Drug Administation (FDA). NDC therapeutic class codes are used to identify each of 20 major drug classes to which the drug entry may belong, adapted from Standard Drug Classifications in the NDC Directory, 1995. The two-digit categories are general and represent all subcategories (e.g., Antimicrobial agents), and the specific four-digit categories represent the breakouts of the general category (e.g., Penicillin). The general two-digit codes include medications that do not fit into any of the subcategories (four-digit codes). Starting in 1995, the NDC four-digit classes were changed to include more classes than the previous classification in 1985. Therefore, some drugs switched from a general two-digit class into a more specific four-digit class. In addition, drugs may be approved for several different therapeutic classes. Some drugs receive approval for additional therapeutic uses after their initial approval, so the same drug can change classes because of new uses.

Numerous drug products have many uses or indications. In an effort to categorize the vast number of the broad analgesic or pain-relief individual products in the marketplace into manageable and nonoverlapping categories, all four-digit

Table XI. Codes for procedure categories from the *International Classification of Diseases, Ninth Revision, Clinical Modification*

Procedure category	Code numbers
Operations on vessels of heart	36
Removal of coronary artery obstruction and insertion of stent(s)	36.0
Insertion of coronary artery stent(s)[1]	36.06, 36.07
Coronary artery bypass graft	36.1
Cardiac catheterization	37.21–37.23
Insertion, replacement, removal, and revision of pacemaker leads or device	37.7–37.8
Diagnostic procedures on small intestine	45.1
Diagnostic procedures on large intestine	45.2
Cholecystectomy	51.2
Laparoscopic cholecystectomy	51.23
Repair of hernia	53
Lysis of peritoneal adhesions	54.5
Transurethral prostatectomy	60.2
Total abdominal hysterectomy	68.4
Vaginal hysterectomy	68.5, 68.7
Dilation and curettage of uterus	69.0
Forceps, vacuum, and breech delivery	72
Other procedures inducing or assisting delivery	73
Cesarean section and removal of fetus	74
Reduction of fracture and dislocation	79
Excision or destruction of intervertebral disc and spinal fusion	80.5, 81.3
Excision or destruction of intervertebral disc	80.5
Joint replacement of lower extremity	81.5
Total hip replacement	81.51
Partial hip replacement	81.52
Total knee replacement	81.54
Diagnostic radiology	87
Computerized axial tomography	87.03, 87.41, 87.71, 88.01, 88.38
Angiocardiography using contrast material	88.5
Diagnostic ultrasound	88.7
Magnetic resonance imaging	88.91–88.97

[1]The procedure code for insertion of coronary artery stents (36.06) first appears in the 1996 data. A second procedure code for the insertion of drug-eluting stents (36.07) first appears in the 2003 data.

categories within the analgesic two-digit therapeutic class were recoded by staff of the FDA's Center for Drug Center for Drug Evaluation and Research. Thus the codes presented in *Health, United States* do not match the published NDC codes for analgesic therapeutic categories. The NDC contains the following four-digit analgesic therapeutic categories: 1720—general analgesic, 1721—narcotic analgesic, 1722—nonnarcotic analgesic, 1724—antiarthritics, 1723—antimigraine/headache, 1726—central pain syndrome, 1727—nonsteroidal anti-inflammatory drugs (NSAID), 1728—antipyretic, and 1729—menstrual products. These categories were collapsed into broader and mutually exclusive categories of narcotic analgesics, nonnarcotic analgesics, and NSAIDs. Under the NDC system, aspirin is coded as an

NSAID because of its anti-inflammatory properties, but also as an analgesic, an antiarthritic, and an antipyretic. In this report aspirin has been recoded into the nonnarcotic analgesic category. Aspirin was not included as an NSAID because of its common use for cardiac therapy and its many other indications.

Table XII shows how generic analgesic drugs were reclassified for *Health, United States*. Analgesic drugs were reclassified based on the product's main ingredients or indication of use. For example, Robitussin AC contains several ingredients, one of which is codeine, a narcotic. However, its main use is not for pain but for cough suppression, and it is therefore categorized as a cough and cold product as opposed to a narcotic analgesic product. Another example is methotrexate, which is used for treating certain neoplastic diseases and severe psoriasis in some formulations, but it is also used to treat rheumatoid arthritis and therefore appears in the list of nonnarcotic analgesic drugs, which include previously defined antiarthritic drugs in Table XII.

Neonatal mortality rate—See Rate: Death and related rates.

Nonprofit hospital—See Hospital.

North American Industry Classification System (NAICS)—See Industry of employment.

Notifiable disease—A notifiable disease is one that, when diagnosed, health providers are required, usually by law, to report to state or local public health officials. Notifiable diseases are those of public interest by reason of their contagiousness, severity, or frequency.

Nursing home—In the Online Survey Certification and Reporting database, a nursing home is a facility that is certified and meets the Center for Medicare & Medicaid Services' long-term care requirements for Medicare and Medicaid eligibility.

In the National Master Facility Inventory (NMFI), which provided the sampling frame for the 1973–1974, 1977, and 1985 National Nursing Home Surveys, a nursing home was an establishment with three or more beds that provided nursing or personal care services to the aged, infirm, or chronically ill. The 1977 National Nursing Home Survey included personal care homes and domiciliary care homes, whereas the National Nursing Home Surveys of 1973–1974, 1985, 1995, 1997, 1999, and 2004 excluded them. The following definitions of nursing home types applied to facilities listed in the NFMI:

Nursing care home—These homes employ one or more full-time registered or licensed practical nurses and provide nursing care to at least one-half the residents.

Personal care home with nursing—These homes have fewer than one-half the residents receiving nursing care. In addition, such homes employ one or more registered or licensed practical nurses or provided administration of medications and treatments in accordance with physicians' orders, supervision of self-administered medications, or three or more personal services.

Personal care home without nursing—These homes have no residents who receive nursing care. These homes provide administration of medications and treatments in accordance with physicians' orders, supervise self-administered medications, or provide three or more personal services.

Domiciliary care home—These homes primarily provide supervisory care and one or two personal services.

The following definitions of certification levels apply to data collected in the National Nursing Home Surveys of 1973–1974, 1977, and 1985:

Skilled nursing facility—These facilities provide the most intensive nursing care available outside a hospital. Facilities certified by Medicare provide posthospital care to eligible Medicare enrollees. Facilities certified by Medicaid as skilled nursing facilities provide skilled nursing services on a daily basis to individuals eligible for Medicaid benefits.

Intermediate care facility—These facilities are certified by the Medicaid program to provide health-related services on a regular basis to Medicaid eligibles who do not require hospital or skilled nursing facility care but do require institutional care above the level of room and board.

Not certified facility—These facilities are not certified as providers of care by Medicare or Medicaid.

Beginning with the 1995 National Nursing Home Survey, nursing homes have been defined as facilities that routinely provide nursing care services and have three or more beds set up for residents. Facilities may be certified by Medicare or Medicaid or not certified but licensed by the state as a nursing home. The facilities may be freestanding or a distinct unit of a larger facility.

After October 1, 1990, long-term care facilities that met the Omnibus Budget Reconciliation Act of 1987 (OBRA 87) nursing home reform requirements that were formerly certified under the Medicaid program as skilled nursing, nursing home, or intermediate care facilities were reclassified as nursing facilities. The Medicare program continues to certify skilled

Table XII. National Drug Code (NDC) therapeutic class analgesic drug recodes

Narcotic analgesics	Nonnarcotic analgesics	Nonsteroidal anti-inflammatory drugs (NSAIDs)
Alfentanil Hydrochloride	Acetaminophen	Bromfenac Sodium
Alphaprodine	Acetylsalicylic Acid	Celecoxib
Bupernorphine	Aminobenzoic Acid	Diclofenac Potassium
Butorphanol	Aspirin	Diclofenac Sodium
Codeine	Auranofin	Difunisal
Dihydrocodeine	Aurothioglucose	Etodolac
Fentanyl	Butalbital	Fenoprofen
Hydrocodone Bitartrate	Capsaicin	Flurbiprofen Sodium
Hydromorphone	Carbaspirin Calcium	Ibuprofen
Levorphanol	Choline Salicylate	Indomethacin
Meperidine	Etanercept	Ketoprofen
Meperidine HCI	Fluprednisolone	Ketorolac Tromethamine
Methadone	Gold Sodium Thiomalate	Meclofenamate
Morphine	Gold Sodium Thiosulfate	Meclofenamic Acid
Morphine Sulfate	Hyaluronic Acid	Mefenamic Acid
Nalbuphine	Leflunomide	Meloxicam
Opium	Magnesium Salicylate	Nabumetone
Oxycodone	Menthol	Naproxen
Oxycodone HCI	Methotrexate	Oxaprozin
Pentazocine	Methylprednisolone	Piroxicam
Propoxyphene	Methylsulfonylmethane	Rofecoxib
Remifentanyl	Oxyphenbutazone	Sulindac
	Phenyl Salicylate	Suprofen
	Phenylbutazone	Tolmetin
	Prednisolone	Valdecoxib
	Salicylamide	
	Salsalate	
	Sodium Hyaluronate	
	Sodium Salicylate	
	Sodium Thiosalicylate	
	Tramadol	
	Triamcinilone	
	Zomepirac	

NOTE: Drugs originally classified as National Drug Code (NDC) therapeutic category 1720 (general analgesics); 1721 (narcotic analgesics); 1722 (non-narcotic analgesics); 1724 (antiarthritics); 1727 (NSAIDs); 1728 (antipyretics); and 1729 (menstrual products) were recoded into the three mutually exclusive categories shown above. NDC codes for the analgesic categories 1723 (antimigraine) and 1725 (antigout) were not recoded.

nursing facilities, but not intermediate care facilities. State Medicaid programs can certify intermediate care facilities for the mentally retarded or developmentally disabled. Nursing facilities must also be certified to participate in the Medicare program to be certified for participation in Medicaid except those facilities that have obtained waivers. Thus most nursing home care is now provided in skilled care facilities.

See related Long-term care facility; Nursing care; Resident.

Nursing home expenditures—See Health expenditures, national.

Obesity—See Body mass index (BMI).

Occupancy rate—In American Hospital Association statistics, hospital occupancy rate is calculated as the average daily census divided by the number of hospital beds, cribs, and pediatric bassinets set up and staffed on the last day of the reporting period, expressed as a percentage. Average daily census is calculated by dividing the total annual number of inpatients, excluding newborns, by 365 days to derive the number of inpatients receiving care on an average day during the annual reporting period. The occupancy rate for facilities other than hospitals is calculated as the number of residents at the facility reported on the day of the interview divided by the number of reported beds. In the Online Survey Certification and Reporting database, occupancy is determined as of the day of certification inspection as the total number of residents on that day divided by the total number of beds on that day.

Office-based physician—See Physician.

Office visit—In the National Ambulatory Medical Care Survey, a physician's ambulatory practice (office) can be in any location other than in a hospital, nursing home, other extended care facility, patient's home, industrial clinic, college clinic, or family planning clinic. Offices in health maintenance organizations and private offices in hospitals are included. An office visit is any direct personal exchange between an ambulatory patient and a physician or members of his or her staff for the purposes of seeking care and rendering health services. See related Outpatient visit.

Operation—See Procedure.

Outpatient department—According to the National Hospital Ambulatory Medical Care Survey (NHAMCS), an outpatient department (OPD) is a hospital facility where nonurgent ambulatory medical care is provided. The following types of OPDs are excluded from the NHAMCS: ambulatory surgical centers, chemotherapy, employee health services, renal dialysis, methadone maintenance, and radiology. See related Emergency department; Outpatient visit.

Outpatient surgery—According to the American Hospital Association, outpatient surgery is a surgical operation, whether major or minor, performed on patients who do not remain in the hospital overnight. Outpatient surgery may be performed in inpatient operating suites, outpatient surgery suites, or procedure rooms within an outpatient care facility. A surgical operation involving more than one surgical procedure is considered one surgical operation. See related Procedure.

Outpatient visit—The American Hospital Association defines outpatient visits as visits for receipt of medical, dental, or other services at a hospital by patients who are not lodged in the hospital. Each appearance by an outpatient to each unit of the hospital is counted individually as an outpatient visit, including all clinic visits, referred visits, observation services, outpatient surgeries, and emergency department visits. In the National Hospital Ambulatory Medical Care Survey an outpatient department visit is a direct personal exchange between a patient and a physician or other health care provider working under the physician's supervision for the purpose of seeking care and receiving personal health services. See related Emergency department or emergency room visit; Outpatient department.

Overweight—See Body mass index (BMI).

Pap smear—A Pap smear (also known as a Papanicolaou smear or Pap test) is a microscopic examination of cells scraped from the cervix that is used to detect cancerous or precancerous conditions of the cervix or other medical conditions. In the National Health Interview Survey questions concerning Pap smear use were asked on an intermittent schedule, and the question content differed slightly across years. In 1987 women were asked to report when they had their most recent Pap smear in days, weeks, months, or years. Women who did not respond were asked a follow-up question, "Was it 3 years ago or less, between 3 and 5 years, or 5 years or more ago?" Pap smear data in the past 3 years were not available in 1990 and 1991. In 1993 and 1994 women were asked whether they had a Pap smear within the past year, between 1 and 3 years ago, or more than 3 years ago. In 1998 women were asked whether they had a Pap smear 1 year ago or less, more than 1 year but not more than 2 years, more than 2 years but not more than 3 years, more than 3 years but not more than 5 years, or more than 5 years ago. In 1999 women were asked when they had their most recent Pap smear in days, weeks, months, or years. In 1999, 4% of women in the sample responded 3 years ago. In this analysis these women were coded as within the past 3 years, although a response of 3 years ago may include women whose last Pap smear was more than 3 but less than 4 years ago. Thus estimates for 1999 are overestimated to some degree in comparison with estimates for previous years. In 2000 and 2003 women were asked when they had their most recent Pap smear (give month and year). Women who did not respond were given a follow-up question that used the 1999 wording and women who did not answer the follow-up question were asked a second follow-up question that used the 1998 wording. In 2000 and 2003 less than 1% of women in the sample answered 3 years ago using the 1999 wording, and they were coded as within the past 3 years. Thus estimates for 2000 and 2003 may be slightly overestimated in comparison with estimates for years prior to 1999.

Partial care organization—See Mental health organization.

Partial care treatment—See Mental health service type.

Patient—See Inpatient; Office visit; Outpatient visit.

Percent change/percentage change—See Average annual rate of change.

Perinatal mortality rate; ratio—See Rate: Death and related rates.

Personal care home with or without nursing—See Nursing home.

Personal health care expenditures—See Health expenditures, national.

Physical activity, leisure-time—All questions related to leisure-time physical activity were phrased in terms of current behavior and lack a specific reference period. Starting with 1998 data, leisure-time physical activity is assessed in the National Health Interview Survey by asking adults a series of questions about how often they do vigorous or light/moderate physical activity of at least 10 minutes duration and for about how long these sessions generally last. Vigorous physical activity is described as causing heavy sweating or a large increase in breathing or heart rate and light/moderate as causing light sweating or a slight to moderate increase in breathing or heart rate. Adults classified as inactive did not report any sessions of light/moderate or vigorous leisure-time physical activity of at least 10 minutes duration or reported they were unable to perform leisure-time physical activity. Adults classified with some leisure-time activity reported at least one session of light/moderate or vigorous activity of at least 10 minutes duration but did not meet the requirement for regular leisure-time activity. Adults classified with regular leisure-time activity reported at least three sessions per week of vigorous leisure-time physical activity lasting at least 20 minutes in duration or at least five sessions per week of light/moderate physical activity lasting at least 30 minutes in duration.

Physician—Data on physician characteristics are obtained through physician self-report for the American Medical Association's (AMA) Physician Masterfile. The AMA tabulates data only for doctors of medicine (MDs), but some tables in *Health, United States* include data for both MDs and doctors of osteopathy (DOs).

Active (or professionally active) physician—These physicians are currently engaged in patient care or other professional activity for a minimum of 20 hours per week. Other professional activity includes administration, medical teaching, research, and other activities, such as employment with insurance carriers, pharmaceutical companies, corporations, voluntary organizations, medical societies, and the like. Physicians who are retired, semiretired, working part-time, or not practicing are classified as inactive and are excluded. Also excluded are physicians with address unknown and physicians who did not provide information on type of practice or present employment (not classified).

Hospital-based physician—These physicians are employed under contract with hospitals to provide direct patient care and include physicians in residency training (including clinical fellows) and full-time members of the hospital staff.

Office-based physician—These physicians are engaged in seeing patients in solo practice, group practice, two-physician practice, other patient care employment, or inpatient services such as those provided by pathologists and radiologists.

Data for physicians are presented by type of education (doctors of medicine and doctors of osteopathy); place of education (U.S. medical graduates and international medical graduates); activity status (professionally active and inactive); area of specialty; and geographic area. See related Physician specialty.

Physician specialty—A physician specialty is any specific branch of medicine in which a physician may concentrate. Data are based on physician self-reports of their primary area of specialty. Physician data are broadly categorized into two areas of practice: those who provide primary care, and those who provide specialty care.

Primary care generalist—These physicians practice in the general fields of family medicine, general practice, internal medicine, obstetrics and gynecology, and pediatrics. They specifically exclude primary care specialists associated with these generalist fields.

Primary care specialist—These specialists practice in the primary care subspecialties of family medicine, internal medicine, obstetrics and gynecology, and pediatrics. Family medicine subspecialties include geriatric medicine and sports medicine. Internal medicine subspecialties include adolescent medicine, critical care medicine, diabetes, endocrinology, diabetes and metabolism, hematology, hepatology, hematology/oncology, cardiac electrophysiology, infectious diseases, clinical and laboratory immunology, geriatric medicine, sports medicine, nephrology, nutrition, medical oncology, pulmonary critical care medicine, and rheumatology. Obstetrics and gynecology subspecialties include gynecological oncology, gynecology, maternal and fetal medicine, obstetrics, critical care medicine, and reproductive endocrinology. Pediatric subspecialties include adolescent medicine, pediatric critical care medicine, pediatrics/internal medicine, neonatal-perinatal medicine, pediatric allergy, pediatric cardiology, pediatric endocrinology, pediatric infectious disease, pediatric pulmonology, medical toxicology (pediatrics), pediatric emergency medicine, pediatric gastroenterology, pediatric hematology/oncology, clinical and laboratory immunology (pediatrics), pediatric nephrology, pediatric rheumatology, and sports medicine (pediatrics).

Specialty care physician—These physicians are sometimes called specialists, and include primary care specialists listed above in addition to all other physicians not included in the generalist definition. Specialty fields include allergy and immunology, aerospace medicine, anesthesiology, cardiovascular diseases, child and adolescent psychiatry, colon and rectal surgery, dermatology, diagnostic radiology, forensic pathology, gastroenterology, general surgery, medical genetics, neurology, nuclear medicine, neurological surgery, occupational medicine, ophthalmology, orthopedic surgery, otolaryngology, psychiatry, public health and general preventive medicine, physical medicine and rehabilitation, plastic surgery, anatomic and clinical pathology, pulmonary diseases, radiation oncology, thoracic surgery, urology, addiction medicine, critical care medicine, legal medicine, and clinical pharmacology.

See related Physician.

Population—The U.S. Census Bureau collects and publishes data on populations in the United States according to several different definitions. Various statistical systems then use the appropriate population for calculating rates. See also Appendix I, Population Census and Population Estimates.

Total population—This is the population of the United States, including all members of the Armed Forces living in foreign countries, Puerto Rico, Guam, and the U.S. Virgin Islands. Other Americans abroad (e.g., civilian federal employees and dependents of members of the Armed Forces or other federal employees) are not included.

Resident population—This population includes persons whose usual place of residence (i.e., the place where one usually lives and sleeps) is in one of the 50 states or the District of Columbia. It includes members of the Armed Forces stationed in the United States and their families. It excludes international military, naval, and diplomatic personnel and their families located in this country and residing in embassies or similar quarters. Also excluded are international workers and international students in this country and Americans living abroad. The resident population is the denominator for calculating birth and death rates and incidence of disease.

Civilian population—The civilian population is the resident population excluding members of the Armed Forces. However, families of members of the Armed Forces are included. This population is the denominator in rates calculated for the National Hospital Discharge Survey, and the National Nursing Home Survey.

Civilian noninstitutionalized population—This is the civilian population not residing in institutions such as correctional institutions, detention homes, and training schools for juvenile delinquents; homes for aged and dependent persons (e.g., nursing homes and convalescent homes); homes for dependent and neglected children; homes and schools for mentally or physically handicapped persons; homes for unwed mothers; psychiatric, tuberculosis, and chronic disease hospitals; and residential treatment centers. U.S. Census Bureau estimates of the civilian noninstitutionalized population are used to calculate sample weights for the National Health Interview Survey, National Health and Nutrition Examination Survey, and National Survey of Family Growth, and as denominators in rates calculated for the National Ambulatory Medical Care Survey and the National Hospital Ambulatory Medical Care Survey.

Introduction of census 2000 population estimates—Health United States, 2003 marked the transition to the use of year 2000 resident population estimates based on the 2000 census for calculation of rates. Previously, 1991–2000 rates were based on post-1990 population estimates. Birth rates and death rates for 1991–1999 were revised using intercensal population estimates based on the 2000 census. Rates for 2000 were revised using Census 2000 counts. Data systems and surveys that use civilian and civilian noninstitutionalized population estimates as denominators for computation of rates for the period 1991–1999 have not been updated with intercensal estimates based on the 2000 civilian and civilian noninstitutionalized populations. See Appendix I, Population Census and Population Estimates.

Postneonatal mortality rate—See Rate: Death and related rates.

Poverty—Poverty statistics are based on definitions originally developed by the Social Security Administration. These include a set of money income thresholds that vary by family size and composition. Families or individuals with income below their appropriate thresholds are classified as below poverty. These thresholds are updated annually by the U.S. Census Bureau to reflect changes in the Consumer Price Index for all urban consumers (CPI-U). For example, the average poverty threshold for a family of four was $19,307 in 2004, $17,603 in 2000, and $13,359 in 1990. For more information, see Income, poverty and health insurance coverage in the United States: 2004 (P60–229). Series P-60 No 229. Washington, DC. U.S. Government Printing Office. 2004 and the Census website. Available from: www.census.gov/hhes/www/poverty.html.

National Health Interview Survey (NHIS) and *National Health and Nutrition Examination Survey (NHANES)*—Percent of poverty level, for years prior to 1997, was based on family income and family size using U.S. Census Bureau poverty thresholds. Starting with 1997 data, percent of poverty level is based on family income, family size, number of children in the family, and for families with two or fewer adults, the age of the adults in the family. Percent of poverty level in the NHANES is also based on family income and family size and composition. See related Consumer Price Index (CPI); Family income; Appendix I, Current Population Survey;

National Health Interview Survey; National Health and Nutrition Examination Survey.

Preferred provider organization (PPO)—A PPO is a type of medical plan where coverage is provided to participants through a network of selected health care providers (such as hospitals and physicians). The enrollees may go outside the network, but they would pay a greater percentage of the cost of coverage than within the network. See related Health maintenance organization (HMO); Managed care.

Prenatal care—Prenatal care is medical care provided to a pregnant woman to prevent complications and decrease the incidence of maternal and prenatal mortality. Information on when pregnancy care began is recorded on the birth certificate. Between 1970 and 1980, the reporting area for prenatal care expanded. In 1970, 39 states and the District of Columbia reported prenatal care on the birth certificate. Data were not available from Alabama, Alaska, Arkansas, Connecticut, Delaware, Georgia, Idaho, Massachusetts, New Mexico, Pennsylvania, and Virginia. In 1975, these data were available from three additional states—Connecticut, Delaware, and Georgia—increasing the number of states reporting prenatal care to 42 and the District of Columbia. During 1980–2002, prenatal care information was available for the entire United States. Starting in 2003, some states began implementation of the 2003 revision of the U.S. Standard Certificate of Live Birth. While all states collected information on prenatal care, the prenatal care item on the 2003 certificate, Date of first prenatal visit, is not comparable with the prenatal care item on the 1989 revision, Month prenatal care began. In addition, the 2003 revision recommends that information on prenatal care be gathered from prenatal care or medical records whereas the 1989 revision did not recommend a source for these data. Therefore, data on prenatal care were excluded for states that implemented the 2003 revision of the U.S. Standard Certificate of Live Birth: these reporting areas included Pennsylvania and Washington starting in 2003, and Florida, Idaho, Kentucky, New Hampshire, New York state (excluding New York City), South Carolina, and Tennessee starting in 2004. The reporting area for prenatal care decreased to 48 states and the District of Columbia in 2003, and 41 states, the District of Columbia, and New York City in 2004.

Prevalence—Prevalence is the number of cases of a disease, infected persons, or persons with some other attribute present during a particular interval of time. It is often expressed as a rate (e.g., the prevalence of diabetes per 1,000 persons during a year). See related Incidence.

Primary care specialty—See Physician specialty.

Private expenditures—See Health expenditures, national.

Procedure—The National Hospital Discharge Survey (NHDS) used to classify a procedure as a surgical or nonsurgical operation, diagnostic procedure, or therapeutic procedure (such as respiratory therapy); however the distinction between types of procedures has become less meaningful because of the development of minimally invasive and noninvasive surgery. Thus the practice of classifying the type of procedure has been discontinued. Procedures are coded according to the *International Classification of Diseases, Ninth Revision, Clinical Modification* (see Table XI). Up to four different procedures are coded in the NHDS. Procedures per hospital stay can be classified as any-listed—that is, if more than one procedure with the same code is performed it is counted only once—or all-listed where multiple occurrences of the same procedure would be counted the number of times it appears on the medical record up to the maximum of four available codes. For example, a triple coronary artery bypass graft would be counted once as any-listed but three times as all-listed. All-listed procedures double-count the number of procedures of a given type that are performed, thus all listed procedure counts are greater than the number of hospital stays that occurred. Any-listed procedure counts approximate the number of hospital stays where a procedure was performed at any time during the stay. See related Outpatient surgery.

Proprietary hospital—See Hospital.

Psychiatric hospital—See Hospital; Mental health organization.

Public expenditures—See Health expenditures, national.

Race—In 1977, the Office of Management and Budget (OMB) issued Race and Ethnic Standards for Federal Statistics and Administrative Reporting to promote comparability of data among federal data systems. The 1977 Standards called for the federal government's data systems to classify individuals into the following four racial groups: American Indian or Alaska Native, Asian or Pacific Islander, Black, and White. Depending on the data source, the classification by race was based on self-classification or on observation by an interviewer or other person filling out the questionnaire.

In 1997, revisions were announced for classification of individuals by race within the federal government's data systems (Revisions to the Standards for the Classification of Federal Data on Race and Ethnicity. Fed Regist 1997 October 30;62:58781–90). The 1997 Standards have five racial groups: American Indian or Alaska Native, Asian, Black or African American, Native Hawaiian or Other Pacific Islander, and White. These five categories are the minimum set for data on race in federal statistics. The 1997 Standards also offer an opportunity for respondents to select more than one of the five groups, leading to many possible multiple-race categories. As with the single-race groups, data for the multiple-race groups are to be reported when estimates meet agency requirements for reliability and confidentiality. The 1997 Standards allow for observer or proxy identification of race but clearly state a preference for self-classification. The federal government considers race and Hispanic origin to be two separate and distinct concepts. Thus Hispanics may be of any race. Federal data systems were required to comply with the 1997 Standards by 2003.

National Health Interview Survey (NHIS)—Starting with *Health, United States, 2002*, race-specific estimates based on the NHIS were tabulated using the 1997 Standards for data year 1999 and beyond and are not strictly comparable with estimates for earlier years. The 1997 Standards specify five single-race categories plus multiple-race categories. Estimates for specific race groups are shown when they meet requirements for statistical reliability and confidentiality. The race categories White only, Black or African American only, American Indian or Alaska Native only, Asian only, and Native Hawaiian or Other Pacific Islander only include persons who reported only one racial group; the category 2 or more races includes persons who reported more than one of the five racial groups in the 1997 Standards or one of the five racial groups and Some other race. Prior to data year 1999, data were tabulated according to the 1977 Standards with four racial groups, and the Asian only category included Native Hawaiian or Other Pacific Islander. Estimates for single-race categories prior to 1999 included persons who reported one race or, if they reported more than one race, identified one race as best representing their race. Differences between estimates tabulated using the two Standards for data year 1999 are discussed in the footnotes for each NHIS table in the *Health, United States, 2002, 2003,* and *2004* editions.

Tables XIII and XIV illustrate NHIS data tabulated by race and Hispanic origin according to the 1997 and 1977 Standards for two health statistics (cigarette smoking and private health insurance coverage). In these illustrations, three separate tabulations using the 1997 Standards are shown: 1) Race: mutually exclusive race groups, including several multiple-race combinations; 2) Race, any mention: race groups that are not mutually exclusive because each race category includes all persons who mention that race; and 3) Hispanic origin and race: detailed race and Hispanic origin with a multiple-race total category. Where applicable, comparison tabulations by race and Hispanic origin are shown based on the 1977 Standards. Because there are more race groups with the 1997 Standards, the sample size of each race group under the 1997 Standards is slightly smaller than the sample size under the 1977 Standards. Only those few multiple-race groups with sufficient numbers of observations to meet standards of statistical reliability are shown. Tables XIII and XIV also illustrate changes in labels and group categories in the 1997 Standards. The race designation of black was changed to black or African American, and the ethnicity designation of Hispanic was changed to Hispanic or Latino.

Data systems included in *Health, United States,* other than the NHIS, the National Survey of Drug Use & Health (NSDUH), and the National Health and Nutrition Examination Survey (NHANES), generally do not permit tabulation of estimates for the detailed race and ethnicity categories shown in Tables XIII and XIV, either because race data based on the 1997 standard categories are not yet available or because there are insufficient numbers of observations to meet statistical reliability or confidentiality requirements.

In an effort to improve the quality of data on ethnicity and race in the NHIS, hot-deck imputation of selected race and ethnicity variables was done for the first time in the 2000 NHIS and continued to be used for subsequent data years. Starting with 2003 data, records for persons for whom Other race was the only race response were treated as having missing data on race, and were added to the pool of records for which selected race and ethnicity variables were imputed. Prior to the 2000 NHIS,

a crude imputation method that assigned a race to persons with missing values for the variable MAINRACE (the respondent's classification of the race he or she most identified with) was used. Under these procedures, if an observed race was recorded by the interviewer, it was used to code a race value. If there was no observed race value, all persons who had a missing value for MAINRACE and were identified as Hispanic on the Hispanic origin question were coded as white. In all other cases, non-Hispanic persons were coded as Other race. Additional information on the NHIS methodology for imputing race and ethnicity is available from: www.cdc.gov/nchs/data/nhis/srvydesc.pdf and www.cdc.gov/nchs/about/major/nhis/rhoi/rhoi.htm.

National Health and Nutrition Examination Survey (NHANES)—Starting with *Health, United States, 2003* race-specific estimates based on NHANES were tabulated using the 1997 Standards for data years 1999 and beyond. Prior to data year 1999, the 1977 Standards were used. Because of the differences between the two Standards, the race-specific estimates shown in trend tables based on the NHANES for 1999–2004 are not strictly comparable with estimates for earlier years. Race in NHANES I and II was determined primarily by interviewer observation; starting with NHANES III, race was self-reported by survey participants.

The NHANES sample was designed to provide estimates specifically for persons of Mexican origin and not for all Hispanic-origin persons in the United States. Persons of Hispanic origin other than Mexicans were entered into the sample with different selection probabilities that are not nationally representative of the total U.S. Hispanic population. Estimates are shown for non-Hispanic white, non-Hispanic black, and Mexican-origin persons. Although data were collected according to the 1997 Standards, there are insufficient numbers of observations to meet statistical reliability or confidentiality requirements for reporting estimates for additional race categories.

National Survey on Drug Use & Health (NSDUH)—Race-specific estimates based on NSDUH are tabulated using the 1997 Standards. Estimates in the NSDUH trend table begin with the data year 1999. Estimates for specific race groups are shown when they meet requirements for statistical reliability and confidentiality. The race

Table XIII. Current cigarette smoking among persons 18 years of age and over, by race and Hispanic origin under the 1997 and 1977 Standards for federal data on race and ethnicity: United States, average annual 1993–1995

1997 Standards	Sample size	Percent	Standard error	1977 Standards	Sample size	Percent	Standard error
White only	46,228	25.2	0.26	White	46,664	25.3	0.26
Black or African American only	7,208	26.6	0.64	Black	7,334	26.5	0.63
American Indian or Alaska Native only	416	32.9	2.53	American Indian or Alaska Native	480	33.9	2.38
Asian only	1,370	15.0	1.19	Asian or Pacific Islander	1,411	15.5	1.22
2 or more races total	786	34.5	2.00				
Black or African American; White	83	*21.7	6.05				
American Indian or Alaska Native; White	461	40.0	2.58				
			Race, any mention				
White, any mention	46,882	25.3	0.26				
Black or African American, any mention	7,382	26.6	0.63				
American Indian or Alaska Native, any mention	965	36.3	1.71				
Asian, any mention	1,458	15.7	1.20				
Native Hawaiian or Other Pacific Islander, any mention	53	*17.5	5.10				
			Hispanic origin and race				
Not Hispanic or Latino:				Non-Hispanic:			
White only	42,421	25.8	0.27	White	42,976	25.9	0.27
Black or African American only	7,053	26.7	0.65	Black	7,203	26.7	0.64
American Indian or Alaska Native only	358	33.5	2.69	American Indian or Alaska Native	407	35.4	2.53
Asian only	1,320	14.8	1.21	Asian or Pacific Islander	1,397	15.3	1.24
2 or more races total	687	35.6	2.15				
Hispanic or Latino	5,175	17.8	0.65	Hispanic	5,175	17.8	0.65

* Relative standard error is 20%-30%

NOTES: The 1997 Standards for the Classification of Federal Data on Race and Ethnicity specified five race groups (white, black or African American, American Indian or Alaska Native, Asian, and Native Hawaiian or Other Pacific Islander) and allow respondents to report one or more race groups. Estimates for single-race and multiple-race groups not shown above do not meet standards for statistical reliability or confidentiality (relative standard error greater than 30%). Race groups under the 1997 Standards were based on the question, What is the group or groups which represents _____ race? For persons who selected multiple groups, race groups under the 1977 Standards were based on the additional question, Which of those groups would you say best represents ____ race? Race-specific estimates in this table were calculated after excluding respondents of other and unknown race. Other published race-specific estimates are based on files in which such responses have been edited. Estimates are age adjusted to the year 2000 standard using five age groups: 18–24 years, 25–34 years, 35–44 years, 45–64 years, and 65 years and over. See Appendix II, Age adjustment.

SOURCE: Centers for Disease Control and Prevention, National Center for Health Statistics. National Health Interview Survey.

categories White only, Black or African American only, American Indian or Alaska Native only, Asian only, and Native Hawaiian or Other Pacific Islander only include persons who reported only one racial group; and the category 2 or more races includes persons who reported more than one of the five racial groups in the 1997 Standards or one of the five racial groups and Some other race.

National Vital Statistics System—Most of the states in the Vital Statistics Cooperative Program are still revising their birth and death records to conform to the 1997 standards on race and ethnicity. During the transition to full implementation of the 1997 standards, vital statistics data will continue to be presented for the four major race groups—white, black or African American, American Indian or Alaska Native, and Asian or Pacific Islander—in accordance with 1977 standards.

Birth File—Information about the race and Hispanic ethnicity of the mother and father are provided by the mother at the time of birth and recorded on the birth

Table XIV. Private health care coverage among persons under 65 years of age, by race and Hispanic origin under the 1997 and 1977 Standards for federal data on race and ethnicity: United States, average annual 1993–1995

1997 Standards	Sample size	Percent	Standard error	1977 Standards	Sample size	Percent	Standard error
White only	168,256	76.1	0.28	White	170,472	75.9	0.28
Black or African American only	30,048	53.5	0.63	Black	30,690	53.6	0.63
American Indian or Alaska Native only	2,003	44.2	1.97	American Indian or Alaska Native	2,316	43.5	1.85
Asian only	6,896	68.0	1.39	Asian and Pacific Islander	7,146	68.2	1.34
Native Hawaiian or Other Pacific Islander only	173	75.0	7.43				
2 or more races total	4,203	60.9	1.17				
Black or African American; White	686	59.5	3.21				
American Indian or Alaska Native; White	2,022	60.0	1.71				
Asian; White	590	71.9	3.39				
Native Hawaiian or Other Pacific Islander; White	56	59.2	10.65				
			Race, any mention				
White, any mention	171,817	75.8	0.28				
Black or African American, any mention	31,147	53.6	0.62				
American Indian or Alaska Native, any mention	4,365	52.4	1.40				
Asian, any mention	7,639	68.4	1.27				
Native Hawaiian or Other Pacific Islander, any mention	283	68.7	6.23				
			Hispanic origin and race				
Not Hispanic or Latino:				Non-Hispanic:			
White only	146,109	78.9	0.27	White	149,057	78.6	0.27
Black or African American only	29,250	53.9	0.64	Black	29,877	54.0	0.63
American Indian or Alaska Native only	1,620	45.2	2.15	American Indian or Alaska Native	1,859	44.6	2.05
Asian only	6,623	68.2	1.43	Asian and Pacific Islander	6,999	68.4	1.40
Native Hawaiian or Other Pacific Islander only	145	76.4	7.79				
2 or more races total	3,365	62.6	1.18				
Hispanic or Latino	31,040	48.8	0.74	Hispanic	31,040	48.8	0.74

NOTES: The 1997 Standards for the Classification of Federal Data on Race and Ethnicity specified five race groups (white, black or African American, American Indian or Alaska Native, Asian, and Native Hawaiian or Other Pacific Islander) and allow respondents to report one or more race groups. Estimates for single-race and multiple-race groups not shown above do not meet standards for statistical reliability or confidentiality (relative standard error greater than 30%). Race groups under the 1997 Standards were based on the question, What is the group or groups which represents _____ race? For persons who selected multiple groups, race groups under the 1977 Standards were based on the additional question, Which of those groups would you say best represents _____ race? Race-specific estimates in this table were calculated after excluding respondents of other and unknown race. Other published race-specific estimates are based on files in which such responses have been edited. Estimates are age adjusted to the year 2000 standard using three age groups: Under 18 years, 18–44 years, and 45–64 years of age. See Appendix II, Age adjustment.

SOURCE: Centers for Disease Control and Prevention, National Center for Health Statistics. National Health Interview Survey.

certificate and fetal death record. Since 1980, birth rates, birth characteristics, and fetal death rates for live-born infants and fetal deaths are presented in this report according to race of mother. Before 1980 data were tabulated by race of newborn and fetus, taking into account the race of both parents. If the parents were of different races and one parent was white, the child was classified according to the race of the other parent. When neither parent was white, the child was classified according to father's race, with one exception: if either parent was Hawaiian, the child was classified Hawaiian. Before 1964, if race was unknown, the birth was classified as white. Starting in 1964 unknown race was classified according to information on the birth record. Starting with 2000 data, the race and ethnicity data used for denominators (population) to calculate birth rates are collected in accordance with 1997 revised OMB standards for race and ethnicity. However, the numerators (births) will not be compatible with the denominators until all the states revise their birth certificates to reflect the new standards. In order to compute rates, it is necessary to bridge population data for multiple-race persons to single-race categories. See Appendix I, Population Census and Population Estimates, Bridged-Race Population Estimates for Census 2000.

Starting with 2003 data, multiple-race data were reported by both Pennsylvania and Washington, which used the 2003 revision of the U.S. Standard Certificate of Live Birth, as well as California, Hawaii, Ohio (for births occurring in December only), and Utah, which used the 1989 revision of the U.S. Standard Certificate of Live Birth. In 2004 multiple race was reported on the revised birth certificates of Florida, Idaho, Kentucky, New Hampshire, New York state (excluding New York City), Pennsylvania, South Carolina, Tennessee, and Washington, as well as on the unrevised certificates of California, Hawaii, Michigan, Minnesota, Ohio, and Utah (a total of 15 states). These 15 states, which account for 43% of births in the United States in 2004, reported 3% of the mothers as multiracial. Data from the vital records of the remaining 35 states, New York City, and the District of Columbia followed the 1977 OMB standards in which a single race is reported. In order to provide uniformity and comparability of the data during the transition period, before multiple-race data are available for all reporting areas, it is necessary to bridge the responses of those who reported more than one race to a single race. See Martin JA, Hamilton BE, et al. Births: final data for 2003. Natl Vital Stat Rep. 2005 Sep 8;54(2):1–116.

Although the bridging procedure imputes multiple-race of mothers to one of the four minimum races stipulated in the 1977 race and ethnicity standards, mothers of a specified Asian or Pacific Islander (API) subgroup (Chinese, Japanese, Hawaiian, or Filipino) in combination with another race (American Indian or Alaska Native, black, and/or white) or another API subgroup cannot be imputed to a single Asian or Pacific Islander subgroup. In

2003 API mothers were disproportionately represented in the six states reporting multiple-race (44%). Data are not shown for the API subgroups or reported alone or in combination with other races or other API subgroups because the bridging technique cannot be applied in this detail. These data are available in the 2003 Natality public-use data file, which can be found at www.cdc.gov/nchs/births.htm.

Mortality File—Information about the race and Hispanic ethnicity of the decedent is reported by the funeral director as provided by an informant, often the surviving next of kin, or, in the absence of an informant, on the basis of observation. Death rates by race and Hispanic origin are based on information from death certificates (numerators of the rates) and on population estimates from the Census Bureau (denominators). Race and ethnicity information from the census is by self-report. To the extent that race and Hispanic origin are inconsistent between these two data sources, death rates will be biased. Studies have shown that persons self-reported as American Indian, Asian, or Hispanic on census and survey records may sometimes be reported as white or non-Hispanic on the death certificate, resulting in an underestimation of deaths and death rates for the American Indian, Asian, and Hispanic groups. Bias also results from undercounts of some population groups in the census, particularly young black males, young white males, and elderly persons, resulting in an overestimation of death rates. The net effects of misclassification and undercoverage result in overstated death rates for the white population and black population are estimated to be 1% and 5%, respectively; understated death rates for other population groups are estimated as follows: American Indians, 21%; Asian or Pacific Islanders, 11%; and Hispanics, 2%. For more information, see Rosenberg HM, Maurer JD, Sorlie PD, et al. Quality of death rates by race and Hispanic origin: A summary of current research, 1999. National Center for Health Statistics. Vital Health Stat 2 1999 Sep; 2(128):1–13.

Denominators for infant and maternal mortality rates are based on number of live births rather than population estimates. Race information for the denominator is supplied from the birth certificate. Before 1980 race of child for the denominator took into account the races of both parents. Starting in 1980 race information for the denominator was based solely on race of mother. Race information for the numerator is supplied from the death certificate. For the infant mortality rate, race information for the numerator is race of the deceased child; for the maternal mortality rate, it is race of the mother.

Vital event rates for the American Indian or Alaska Native population shown in this book are based on the total U.S. resident population of American Indians and Alaska Natives, as enumerated by the U.S. Census Bureau. In contrast the Indian Health Service calculates vital event rates for this population based on U.S. Census Bureau county data for American Indians and Alaska Natives who reside on or near reservations. Interpretation of trends for the American Indian and Alaska Native population should take into account that population estimates for these groups increased by 45% between 1980 and 1990, partly because of better enumeration techniques in the 1990 decennial census and the increased tendency for people to identify themselves as American Indian in 1990.

Interpretation of trends for the Asian population in the United States should take into account that this population more than doubled between 1980 and 1990, primarily because of immigration. Between 1990 and 2000, the increase in the Asian population was 48% for persons reporting that they were Asian alone, and 72% for persons who reported they were either Asian alone or in combination with another race.

For more information on coding race using vital statistics, see National Center for Health Statistics, Technical Appendix. Vital Statistics of the United States, Vol. I, Natality, and Vol. II, Mortality, Part A. Available from: www.cdc.gov/nchs/nvss.htm.

Youth Risk Behavior Survey (YRBS)—Prior to 1999, the 1977 Standards were used. Respondents could select only one of the following categories: White (not Hispanic), Black (not Hispanic), Hispanic or Latino, Asian or Pacific Islander, American Indian or Alaska Native, or Other. Beginning in 1999, the 1997 standards were used for race-specific estimates and respondents were given the option of selecting more than one category to describe their race and ethnicity. Between 1999 and 2003, students were asked a single question about race and Hispanic origin with the option of choosing more than one of the following responses: White, Black or African American, Hispanic or Latino, Asian, Native

Hawaiian or Other Pacific Islander, or American Indian or Alaska Native. In 2005, students were asked a question about Hispanic origin (Are you Hispanic or Latino?) and a second separate question about race that included the option of selecting more than one of the following categories: American Indian or Alaska Native, Asian, Black or African American, Native Hawaiian or Other Pacific Islander, or White. Because of the differences between questions, the data about race and Hispanic ethnicity for the years prior to 1999 are not strictly comparable with estimates for the later years. However, analyses of data collected between 1991 and 2003 have indicated that the data are comparable across years and can be used to study trends.

See Brender ND, Kann L, McManus, T. A comparison of two survey questions on race and ethnicity among high school students. Public opinion quarterly. 2003;67(2) 227–236.

See related Hispanic origin; Appendix I, Population Census and Population Estimates.

Rate—A rate is a measure of some event, disease, or condition in relation to a unit of population, along with some specification of time. See related Age adjustment; Population.

■ *Birth and related rates*

Birth rate is calculated by dividing the number of live births in a population in a year by the midyear resident population. For census years, rates are based on unrounded census counts of the resident population, as of April 1. For the noncensus years 1981–1989, rates were based on national estimates of the resident population, as of July 1, rounded to 1,000s. Rounded population estimates for 5-year age groups were calculated by summing unrounded population estimates before rounding to 1,000s. Starting in 1991, rates were based on unrounded national population estimates. Beginning in 1997, the birth rate for the maternal age group 45–49 years includes data for mothers age 50–54 years in the numerator and is based on the population of women age 45–49 years in the denominator. Birth rates are expressed as the number of live births per 1,000 population. The rate may be restricted to births to women of specific age, race, marital status, or geographic location (specific rate), or it may be related to the entire population (crude rate).

Fertility rate is the total number of live births, regardless of age of mother, per 1,000 women of reproductive age, 15–44 years.

■ *Death and related rates*

Death rate is calculated by dividing the number of deaths in a population in a year by the midyear resident population. For census years, rates are based on unrounded census counts of the resident population, as of April 1. For the noncensus years 1981–1989, rates were based on national estimates of the resident population, as of July 1, rounded to thousands. Rounded population estimates for 10-year age groups were calculated by summing unrounded population estimates before rounding to 1,000s. Starting in 1991 rates were based on unrounded national population estimates. Rates for the Hispanic and non-Hispanic white populations in each year are based on unrounded state population estimates for states in the Hispanic reporting area. Death rates are expressed as the number of deaths per 100,000 population. The rate may be restricted to deaths in specific age, race, sex, or geographic groups or from specific causes of death (specific rate), or it may be related to the entire population (crude rate).

Fetal death rate is the number of fetal deaths with stated or presumed gestation of 20 weeks or more divided by the sum of live births plus fetal deaths, per 1,000 live births plus fetal deaths. *Late fetal death rate* is the number of fetal deaths with stated or presumed gestation of 28 weeks or more divided by the sum of live births plus late fetal deaths, per 1,000 live births plus late fetal deaths. See related Gestation.

Infant mortality rate based on period files is calculated by dividing the number of infant deaths during a calendar year by the number of live births reported in the same year. It is expressed as the number of infant deaths per 1,000 live births. *Neonatal mortality rate* is the number of deaths of children under 28 days of age, per 1,000 live births. *Postneonatal mortality rate* is the number of deaths of children that occur between 28 days and 365 days after birth, per 1,000 live births. See related Infant death.

Birth cohort infant mortality rates are based on linked birth and infant death files. In contrast to period rates in which the births and infant deaths occur in the same period or calendar year, infant deaths constituting the numerator of a birth cohort rate may have occurred in the same year as, or in the year following, the year of birth. The birth cohort infant mortality rate is expressed as the number of infant deaths per 1,000 live births. See related Birth cohort.

Perinatal relates to the period surrounding the birth event. Rates and ratios are based on events reported in a calendar year. *Perinatal mortality rate* is the sum of late fetal deaths plus infant deaths within 7 days of birth divided by the sum of live births plus late fetal deaths, per 1,000 live births plus late fetal deaths. *Perinatal mortality ratio* is the sum of late fetal deaths plus infant deaths within 7 days of birth divided by the number of live births, per 1,000 live births.

Maternal mortality rate is defined as the number of maternal deaths per 100,000 live births. The maternal mortality rate is a measure of the likelihood that a pregnant woman will die from maternal causes. The number of live births used in the denominator is a proxy for the population of pregnant women who are at risk of a maternal death. See related Maternal death.

Visit rate is a basic measure of service utilization for event-based data. Examples of events include physician office visits with drugs provided or hospital discharges. In the visit rate calculation, the numerator is the number of estimated events, and the denominator is the corresponding U.S. population estimate for those who possibly could have had events during a given period of time. The interpretation is that for every person in the population there were, on average, *x* events. It does not mean that *x* percentage of the population had events, because some persons in the population had no events while others had multiple events. The only exception is when an event can occur just once for a person (e.g., if an appendectomy were performed during a hospital stay). The visit rate is best used to compare utilization across various subgroups of interest such as age or race groups or geographic regions (e.g., the rate of hospital discharges in 2002 was 43.4 per 1,000 population for children under 18 years of age and 466.6 per 1, 000 population for adults 75 years and over).

Region—See Geographic region and division.

Registered hospital—See Hospital.

Registration area—The United States has separate registration areas for birth, death, marriage, and divorce statistics. In general, registration areas correspond to states and include two separate registration areas for the District of Columbia and New York City. The term reporting area may be used interchangeably for the term registration area. All states have adopted laws that require registration of births and deaths and reporting of fetal deaths. It is believed that more than 99% of births and deaths occurring in this country are registered.

The death registration area was established in 1900 with 10 states and the District of Columbia, and the birth registration area was established in 1915, also with 10 states and the District of Columbia. Beginning with 1933, all states were included in the birth and death registration areas. The specific states added year by year are shown in History and Organization of the Vital Statistics System. Reprinted from Vital Statistics of the United States Vol. I, 1950, chapter 1. National Center for Health Statistics, 1978. Currently, Puerto Rico, U.S. Virgin Islands, and Guam each constitutes a separate registration area, although their data are not included in statistical tabulations of U.S. resident data. See related Reporting area.

Relative standard error—The relative standard error (RSE) is a measure of an estimate's reliability. The RSE of an estimate is obtained by dividing the standard error of the estimate (SE(r)) by the estimate itself (r). This quantity is expressed as a percentage of the estimate and is calculated as follows: $RSE = 100 \times (SE(r)/r)$. Estimates with large RSEs are considered unreliable. In *Health, United States* most statistics with large RSEs are preceded by an asterisk or are not presented.

Relative survival rate—The relative survival rate is the ratio of the observed survival rate for the patient group to the expected survival rate for persons in the general population similar to the patient group with respect to age, sex, race, and calendar year of observation. The 5-year relative survival rate is used to estimate the proportion of cancer patients potentially curable. Because over one-half of all cancers occur in persons 65 years of age and over, many of these individuals die of other causes with no evidence of recurrence of their cancer. Thus, because it is obtained by adjusting observed survival for the normal life expectancy of the general population of the same age, the relative survival rate is an estimate of the chance of surviving the effects of cancer.

Reporting area—In the National Vital Statistics System, the reporting area for such basic items on the birth and death certificates as age, race, and sex is based on data from residents of all 50 states in the United States, the District of Columbia (DC), and New York City (NYC). The term reporting area may be used interchangeably for the term registration area. The reporting area for selected items such as Hispanic origin, educational attainment, and marital status is based on data from those states that require the item to be reported, whose data meet a minimum level of completeness (such as 80% or 90%), and are considered to be sufficiently comparable to be used for analysis. In 1993–1996 the reporting area for Hispanic origin of decedent on the death certificate included 49 states and DC. Starting in 1997 the Hispanic reporting area includes all 50 states and DC. See related Registration area; Appendix I, National Vital Statistics System.

Resident, health facility—In the Online Survey Certification and Reporting database, all residents in certified facilities are counted on the day of certification inspection. In the National Nursing Home Survey, a resident is a person on the roster of the nursing home as of the night before the survey. Included are all residents for whom beds are maintained even though they may be on overnight leave or in a hospital. See related Nursing home.

Resident population—See Population.

Residential treatment care—See Mental health service type.

Residential treatment center for emotionally disturbed children—See Mental health organization.

Rural—See Urbanization.

Self-assessment of health—See Health status, respondent-assessed.

Serious psychological distress—The K6 instrument is a measure of psychological distress associated with unspecified but potentially diagnosable mental illness that may result in a higher risk for disability and higher utilization of health services. The K6 was asked of adults 18 years of age and older. The answers were self-reported and no proxies were allowed. The K6 is designed to identify persons with serious psychological distress using as few questions as possible. The six items included in the K6 are as follows: During the past 30 days, how often did you feel . . .

> so sad that nothing could cheer you up?
> nervous?
> restless or fidgety?
> hopeless?
> that everything was an effort?
> worthless?

Possible answers are all of the time (4 points), most of the time (3 points), some of the time (2 points), a little of the time (1 point), and none of the time (0 points).

To score the K6, the points are added together yielding a possible total of 0 to 24 points. A threshold of 13 or more is used to define serious psychological distress. Persons answering some of the time to all six questions would not reach the threshold for serious psychological distress, because to achieve a score of 13 they would need to answer most of the time to at least one item.

For more information, see Kessler RC, Barker PR, Colpe LJ, et al. Screening for serious mental illness in the general population. Arch Gen Psychiatry 2003; 60:184–189.

Short-stay hospital—See Hospital.

Skilled nursing facility—See Nursing home.

Smoker—See Cigarette smoking.

Specialty hospital—See Hospital.

State Children's Health Insurance Program (SCHIP)—Title XXI of the Social Security Act, known as the State Children's Health Insurance Program (SCHIP), is a program initiated by the Balanced Budget Act of 1997 (BBA). SCHIP provides more federal funds for states to provide health care coverage to low-income, uninsured children. SCHIP gives states broad flexibility in program design while protecting beneficiaries through federal standards. Funds from SCHIP may be used to expand Medicaid or to provide medical assistance to children during a presumptive eligibility period for Medicaid. This is one of several options from which states may select to provide health care coverage for more children, as prescribed within the BBA's Title XXI program. See related Health insurance coverage; Medicaid.

State mental health agency—Refers to the agency or department within state government, headed by the state or territorial health official, dealing with mental health issues. Generally, the state mental health agency is responsible for setting statewide mental health priorities, carrying out national and state mandates, responding to mental health hazards, and assuring access to mental health care for underserved state residents.

Substance use—refers to the use of selected substances including alcohol, tobacco products, drugs, inhalants, and other substances that can be consumed, inhaled, injected, or otherwise absorbed into the body with possible detrimental effects.

The Monitoring the Future Study (MTF)—The MTF collects information on use of selected substances using self-completed questionnaires to a school-based survey of secondary school students. MTF has tracked 12th-graders' illicit drug use and attitudes towards drugs since 1975. In 1991, 8th and 10th graders were added to the study. The survey includes questions on abuse of substances including (but not limited to) marijuana, inhalants, illegal drugs, alcohol, cigarettes, and other tobacco products. A standard set of three questions is used to assess use of the substances in the past month. Past month refers to an individual's use of a substance at least once during the month preceding their response to the survey. See related Appendix I, Monitoring the Future Study.

National Survey on Drug Use & Health (NSDUH)—The NSDUH conducts in-person interviews of a sample of individuals 12 years of age and older at their place of residence. For illicit drug use, alcohol use, and tobacco use, information is collected about use in past month. For information on illicit drug use, respondents in the NSDUH are asked about use of marijuana/hashish, cocaine (including crack), inhalants, hallucinogens, heroin, and prescription-type drugs used nonmedically (pain relievers, tranquilizers, stimulants, and sedatives). A series of questions is asked about each substance: "Have you ever, even once, used [e.g., Ecstacy, also known as MDMA/substance]?" "Think specifically about the past 30 days, from [data] up to and including today. During the past 30 days, on how many days did you use [substance]?" Numerous probes and checks are included in the computer-assisted interview system.

Nonprescription medications and legitimate uses under a doctor's supervision are not included in the survey. Summary measures, such as any illicit drug use, are produced. See related Alcohol consumption; Cigarette smoking; Illicit drug use; Appendix I, National Survey on Drug Use & Health.

Suicidal ideation—Suicidal ideation is having thoughts of suicide or of taking action to end one's own life. Suicidal ideation includes all thoughts of suicide, both when the thoughts include a plan to commit suicide and when they do not include a plan. Suicidal ideation is measured in the Youth Risk Behavior Survey by the question "During the past 12 months, did you ever seriously consider attempting suicide?"

Surgery—See Outpatient surgery; Procedure.

Surgical specialty—See Physician specialty.

Tobacco use—See Cigarette smoking.

Uninsured—In the Current Population Survey (CPS) persons are considered uninsured if they do not have coverage through private health insurance, Medicare, Medicaid, State Children's Health Insurance Program, military or Veterans coverage, another government program, a plan of someone outside the household, or other insurance. Persons with only Indian Health Service coverage are considered uninsured. In addition, if the respondent has missing Medicaid information but has income from certain low-income public programs, then Medicaid coverage is imputed. The questions on health insurance are administered in March and refer to the previous calendar year.

In the National Health Interview Survey (NHIS), the uninsured are persons who do not have coverage under private health insurance, Medicare, Medicaid, public assistance, a state-sponsored health plan, other government-sponsored programs, or a military health plan. Persons with only Indian Health Service coverage are considered uninsured. Estimates of the percentage of persons who are uninsured based on the NHIS (Table 135) may differ slightly from those based on the March CPS (Table 147) because of differences in survey questions, recall period, and other aspects of survey methodology. Estimates for the uninsured are shown only for the population under age 65.

Survey respondents may be covered by health insurance at the time of the interview, but may have experienced one or more lapses in coverage during the year prior to the interview. Starting in *Health United States, 2006*, NHIS estimates for people with health insurance coverage for all 12 months prior to the interview, for those who were uninsured for any period up to 12 months, and for those who were uninsured for more than 12 months were added as stub variables to selected tables.

See related Health insurance coverage; Appendix I, Current Population Survey.

Urbanization—Urbanization is the degree of urban (city-like) character or nature of a particular geographic area. In this report death rates are presented according to the urbanization level of the decedent's county of residence. Counties and county equivalents were assigned to one of five urbanization levels using Office of Management and Budget's (OMB) standards for metropolitan statistical areas (MSAs) and micropolitan statistical areas and the Rural-Urban Continuum code system to differentiate among metropolitan areas based on population.

There are three major categories of counties. OMB classifies counties as metropolitan or micropolitan. Counties not categorized by OMB are neither metropolitan nor micropolitan.

OMB's classification of metropolitan counties are further differentiated in *Health, United States* by population size using the Rural-Urban Continuum code system (August 2003 Revision) developed by the Economic Research Service, U.S. Department of Agriculture. Metropolitan counties are classified by the population size of their metropolitan area to one of three metropolitan urbanization levels:

(a) *Large*—counties in MSAs with 1 million or more population.
(b) *Medium*—counties MSAs with 250,000 to 1 million population.
(c) *Small*—counties in MSAs with less than 250,000 population.

See Metropolitan statistical area (MSA) for definitions of metropolitan and nonmetropolitan counties.

Nonmetropolitan counties are categorized using the OMB's classification of nonmetropolitan micropolitan statistical areas (February 2004 Revision). Nonmetropolitan counties are classified into two categories:

(a) *Micropolitan*—counties defined by OMB as micropolitan based on population criteria.

(b) *Nonmicropolitan*—nonmetropolitan counties that do not meet the population criteria for micropolitan.

See Micropolitan statistical area for definitions of micropolitan and nonmicropolitan counties.

Usual source of care—Usual source of care was measured in the National Health Interview Survey (NHIS) in 1993 and 1994 by asking the respondent "Is there a particular person or place that ____ usually goes to when ____ is sick or needs advice about ___ health?" In the 1995 and 1996 NHIS, the respondent was asked "Is there one doctor, person, or place that ____ usually goes to when ____ is sick or needs advice about health?" Starting in 1997 the respondent was asked "Is there a place that ____ usually goes when he/she is sick or you need advice about (his/her) health?" Persons who report the emergency department as their usual source of care are defined as having no usual source of care in this report.

Wages and salaries—See Employer costs for employee compensation.

Years of potential life lost (YPLL)—YPLL is a measure of premature mortality. Starting with *Health, United States, 1996–1997*, YPLL is presented for persons under 75 years of age because the average life expectancy in the United States is over 75 years. YPLL-75 is calculated using the following eight age groups: under 1 year, 1–14 years, 15–24 years, 25–34 years, 35–44 years, 45–54 years, 55–64 years, and 65–74 years. The number of deaths for each age group is multiplied by years of life lost, calculated as the difference between age 75 years and the midpoint of the age group. For the eight age groups, the midpoints are 0.5, 7.5, 19.5, 29.5, 39.5, 49.5, 59.5, and 69.5. For example, the death of a person 15–24 years of age counts as 55.5 years of life lost. Years of potential life lost is derived by summing years of life lost over all age groups. In *Health, United States, 1995* and earlier editions, YPLL was presented for persons under 65 years of age. For more information, see Centers for Disease Control. MMWR 35(2S):suppl. 1986. Available from: www.cdc.gov/mmwr/preview/mmwrhtml/00001773.htm.

Appendix III

Additional Data Years Available

For trend tables spanning long periods, only selected data years are shown to highlight major trends. Additional years of data are available for some of the tables in electronic spreadsheets available through the Internet and on CD-ROM.

To access spreadsheet files on the Internet, go to the *Health, United States* website at www.cdc.gov/nchs/hus.htm, scroll down to "Spreadsheet Files," and click on 2006 Edition.

Downloadable spreadsheet files for trend tables, many of which include more data years than are shown in the printed report, are available in Excel. Standard errors are included in spreadsheet files for trend tables based on the National Health Interview Survey (NHIS), National Health and Nutrition Examination Survey (NHANES), and National Survey of Family Growth (NSFG).

Spreadsheet files in Excel are also available on CD-ROM. A limited supply of CD-ROMs is available from the National Center for Health Statistics upon request, or CD-ROMs may be purchased from the Government Printing Office.

Table number	Table topic	Additional data years available
1	Resident population	2001
3	Poverty	1986–1989, 1991–1994, 1996–1999, 2001
4	Fertility rates and birth rates	1981–1984, 1986–1989, 1991–1994, 1996–1999, 2001
5	Live births	1972–1974, 1976–1979, 1981–1984, 1986–1989, 1991–1994, 1996–1999, 2001–2002
6	Twin births	1972–1974, 1976–1979, 1981–1984, 1986–1989, 1991–1994, 1996, 1998–1999, 2001
7	Prenatal care	1981–1984, 1986–1989, 1991–1994, 1996–1999, 2001
9	Teenage childbearing	1981–1984, 1986–1989, 1991–1994, 1996–1999
10	Nonmarital childbearing	1981–1984, 1986–1989, 1991–1994, 1996–1999
11	Maternal education	1981–1984, 1986–1989, 1991–1994, 1996–1999, 2001
12	Maternal smoking	1991–1994, 1996–1999, 2001
13	Low birthweight	1981–1984, 1986–1989, 1991–1994, 1996–1998, 2001
14	Low birthweight	1991–1994, 1996–1999, 2001
16	Abortions	1981–1984, 1986–1989, 1991–1994, 1996–1997
18	Breastfeeding	1972–1974
19	Infant mortality rates	1996–1998, 2001
20	Infant mortality rates	1984, 1986–1989, 1991, 1996–1998
21	Infant mortality rates	1984, 1986–1989, 1991, 1996–1999
22	Infant mortality rates	1981–1989, 1991–1994, 1996
26	International life expectancy	1999
27	Life expectancy	1975, 1981–1989, 1991–1994
29	Age-adjusted death rates for selected causes	1981–1989, 1991–1999
30	Years of potential life lost	1991–1999; Crude 1999–2002
35	Death rates for all causes	1981–1989, 1991–1999, 2001
36	Diseases of heart	1981–1989, 1991–1999, 2001
37	Cerebrovascular diseases	1981–1989, 1991–1999, 2001
38	Malignant neoplasms	1981–1989, 1991–1999, 2001
39	Malignant neoplasms of trachea, bronchus, and lung	1981–1989, 1991–1999, 2001
40	Malignant neoplasm of breast	1981–1989, 1991–1999, 2001
41	Chronic lower respiratory diseases	1981–1989, 1991–1994, 1996–1999
42	Human immunodeficiency virus (HIV) disease	1988–1989, 1991–1994, 1996–1999
43	Maternal mortality	1981–1989, 1991–1999
44	Motor vehicle-related injuries	1981–1989, 1991–1999, 2001
45	Homicide	1981–1989, 1991–1999, 2001

Table number	Table topic	Additional data years available
46	Suicide	1981–1989, 1991–1999, 2001
47	Firearm-related injuries	1981–1989, 1991–1994, 1996–1999
48	Occupational diseases	1981–1984, 1986–1989, 1991–1994, 1996–1999
49	Occupational injury deaths	1993–1994, 1996–1997
51	Notifiable diseases	1985, 1988–1989, 1991–1999, 2001
53	Cancer incidence rates	1991–1994
54	Five-year relative cancer survival rates	1978–1980, 1984–1986
55	Diabetes	1999–2002
56	Severe headache or migraine, low back pain, and neck pain	1998–2002
58	Limitation of activity	1999–2001
59	Vision and hearing limitations	1998–1999, 2001
60	Respondent-assessed health status	1998–1999
63	Cigarette smoking	1983, 1987–1988, 1991–1994, 1997–1998
64	Cigarette smoking	1983, 1987–1988, 1991–1994, 1997–1998
65	Cigarette smoking	1993–1995, 1994–1997
67	Use of selected substances	1981–1989, 1992–1994, 1996–1999, 2001
68	Alcohol consumption	1998–2002
69	Hypertension (elevated blood pressure)	1999–2002
70	Serum cholesterol levels	1999–2002
71	Mean energy and macronutrient intake	1999–2000
72	Leisure-time physical activity	1999, 2000–2002
73	Overweight, obesity, and healthy weight	1999–2002
74	Overweight among children and adolescents	1999–2002
75	Untreated dental caries	1999–2000
76	No usual source of health care	1995–1996, 1997–1998, 1999–2000
78	Reduced access to medical care	1998–2002
79	No heath care visits	1999–2000
80	Health care visits	1998–2002
81	Vaccinations	1996–1998
82	Vaccination coverage among children	1996
83	Influenza and pneumococcal vaccination	1991, 1993–1994, 1997–1998
84	Mammography	1993
86	Emergency department visits for children	1998–2002
87	Emergency department visits for adults	1998–1999, 2001–2002
88	Injury-related visits	1997–1998, 1998–1999, 2000–2001, 2001–2002, 2002–2003
89	Ambulatory care visits	1997–2001
90	Ambulatory care visits	1997–1999, 2001–2003
91	Dental visits	1998–2002
93	Prescription drug use	1999–2000
94	Additions to mental health organizations	1992, 1998
95	Discharges	1998–2001
96	Discharges	1991–1994, 1996–1999
97	Rates of discharges	1995–1999, 2001–2003
98	Discharges	1995–1999, 2001–2003
99	Inpatient procedures	1991–1992, 1992–1993, 2001–2002, 2002–2003
100	Hospital admissions	1985, 1991–1994, 1996–1999, 2001
101	Nursing home residents	1997
102	Nursing home residents	1997
104	Active physicians and doctors of medicine	2002–2003
105	Physicians	1970, 1980, 1987, 1989–1990, 1992–1994, 1996–1999

Table number	Table topic	Additional data years available
106	Primary care doctors of medicine	1994, 1996–1999, 2001
108	Employees and wages	2001, 2003
109	Health professions schools	1996, 1998–1999, 2001–2002
110	Total enrollment of minorities in schools	2000–2001, 2001–2002, 2002–2003
111	Enrollment of women in schools	2000–2001, 2001–2002, 2002–2003
112	Hospitals	1985, 1991–1994, 1996–1999, 2001–2002
113	Mental health organizations	1992
114	Community hospital beds	1985, 1988–1989, 1995–1999, 2001–2003
115	Occupancy rates	1985, 1988–1989, 1995–1999, 2001–2003
116	Nursing homes	1996, 1998–1999, 2001–2003
118	Medicare-certified providers and suppliers	1975, 1998, 2001
125	Expenditures for health care	1996, 1998–1999, 2001–2002
126	Sources of payment for health care	1996, 1998–1999, 2001–2002
127	Out-of-pocket health care expenses	1998
129	Employers' costs and health insurance	1992–1993, 1995, 1997, 1999, 2001
130	Hospital expenses	1975, 1985, 1991–1994, 1996–1998, 2001–2002
131	Nursing home average monthly charges	1997
132	Mental health expenditures	1992
133	Private health insurance	1994, 1996, 1998
134	Medicaid coverage	1994, 1996, 1998, 2001
135	No health insurance coverage	1994, 1996, 1998, 2001
136	Health care coverage	1993–1994, 1996–1999, 2001
139	Medicare	1993–2000
140	Medicaid	1975, 1985–1989, 1991–1994, 1996–1998
141	Medicaid	1975, 1985–1989, 1991–1994, 1996–1998
142	Department of Veterans Affairs	1985, 1988–1989, 1991–1994, 1996–1999
143	State mental health agency per capita expenditures	1983, 1987
144	Medicare	1995–2002
145	Medicaid	1998, 2000–2001
146	Health maintenance organizations	1994, 1996–1997, 1999, 2001–2003

Index to Trend Tables

(Numbers refer to table numbers)

H—Con.

Table

H—Con.

Table

M—Con.

M—Con.

W—Con.

Y